Australia

a travel survival kit

Australia – a travel survival kit
  5th edition

Published by
  Lonely Planet Publications
  Head Office: PO Box 617, Hawthorn, Victoria 3122, Australia
  US Office: PO Box 2001A, Berkeley, CA 94702, USA

Printed by
  Singapore National Printers Ltd, Singapore

Photographs by
  Sonia Berto (SB)
  David Curl (DC)
  Chris Lee Ack (CLA)
  Richard Nebesky (RN)
  Paul Steel (PS)
  Peter Turner (PT)
  Bernard Wertheim (BW)
  Tony Wheeler (TW)
  New South Wales Government Tourist Bureau (NSWGTB)
  Northern Territory Government Tourist Bureau (NTGTB)
  Tourism Tasmania (TT)
  Front cover: Climbing Ayers Rock (TW)
  Back cover: Heron Island (TW)
            Sydney Opera House (TW)
  Aboriginal painting: Depiction of 'Langabun' Country Dreaming by Willie Gudabi of Ngukurr

First published
  February 1977

This edition
  November 1989

Although the author and publisher have tried to make the information as
accurate as possible, they accept no responsibility for any loss, injury or
inconvenience sustained by any person using this book.

National Library of Australia Cataloguing in Publication Data

Wheeler, Tony
   Australia, a travel survival kit.

   5th ed.
   Includes index.
   ISBN 0 86442 040 4.

   1. Australia – Description and travel – 1976- Guide-books. I. Title.

919.4'0463

Tony Wheeler

Tony was born in England but spent his school years in Pakistan, the West Indies and the USA. He then did an engineering degree in the UK, worked for a short time as an automotive engineer, went back to university and did an MBA, then dropped out on the Asian overland trail with his wife Maureen. They've been travelling, writing and publishing guidebooks ever since, having set up Lonely Planet Publications in the mid-70s.

John Noble & Susan Forsyth

Susan Forsyth and John Noble come from Melbourne (Oz) and Clitheroe (England) respectively. They met in 1986 in Sri Lanka, where John was leaving no stone unturned on LP's behalf and Susan was a volunteer English teacher. They went off to India together, then John co-authored LP's *Mexico – A Travel Survival Kit* and Susan taught English to migrants in Australia. After driving LP's Ozmobile from Melbourne to Darwin, they travelled in Indonesia, before heading off to the USSR.

Richard Nebesky

Born in Prague, Czechoslovakia, Richard left the country after the Soviet-led invasion of 1968 and settled in Australia. He has a BA in politics and history and has travelled and worked in Europe, Asia, North America and North Africa. He began working with LP in 1986 and now helps compile the Stop Press sections of all LP books. For this edition Richard covered southern Western Australia, South Australia and parts of Victoria.

Peter Turner

Peter was born in Melbourne and studied English, politics and Asian studies at university before setting off on the Asian trail. To finance further trips to Asia, the Pacific, North America and Europe, he worked as an immigration officer and taxi driver, before joining LP as an editor. For this edition Peter travelled to Tasmania, Broken Hill and south-west Victoria.

Lonely Planet Credits

Editors	Adrienne Ralph
	Lyn McGaurr
Maps	Ralph Roob
	Chris Lee Ack
Design &	Vicki Beale
illustrations	Glenn Beanland
Typesetting	Gaylene Miller
	Ann Jeffree

Copy editing Lindy Cameron, Katie Cody, Jon Murray and Tom Smallman. Thanks also to Frith Pike for editing and proofing; James Lyon for proofing; Peter Flavelle, Greg Herriman, Graham Imeson and Valerie Tellini for additional mapping; Trudi Canavan for the title page illustration; Sharon Wertheim and Julie Sallows for indexing; and Vicki Beale, Glenn Beanland, Duane MacDonald, Roberto Petroni, Hugh Sibly, Chris Taylor and Tony Wheeler for black & white photographs.

A Warning & a Request

Things change – prices go up, schedules change, good places go bad and bad places go bankrupt – nothing stays the same. So if you find things better or worse, recently opened or long since closed, please write and tell us and help make the next edition better.

Between editions, when it is possible, we'll publish the most interesting letters and important information in a Stop Press section at the back of the book.

All information is greatly appreciated and the best letters will receive a free copy of the next edition, or any other Lonely Planet book of your choice.

This Edition

Australia continues to grow in popularity as a travellers' centre – the proliferation of backpackers hostels all around the country, the numerous long distance bus services, the crowded poste restante counters are all solid evidence. It's hardly surprising, as travellers have always liked Australia and this is a great country to travel around.

Australia covers a huge area and updating this guidebook took a lot of effort from a number of people. To cover all those km with the maximum efficiency in the minimum time and at the same time to get a real feel for travelling in Australia today we decided to buy a car, drive it all around the country and sell it again at the end. You can read the full story on Lonely Planet's 'mighty Falcon' in the Getting Around chapter.

Principal updaters were John Noble and Susan Forsyth who set off from Melbourne and made their way north through Victoria via Canberra to Sydney and up the coast all the way to Cairns and Cooktown. Then they turned inland and went through Mt Isa to the Northern Territory and up to Darwin where they left the car. They then flew back to Byron Bay to write up their part of the book.

Part two of the grand circuit was done by Tony Wheeler who flew up to Darwin with Maureen and their children Tashi and Kieran to collect the car. Tony, Maureen and family had earlier made a circuit trip from Melbourne to central Australia and back to cover Alice Springs, Ayers Rock, Coober Pedy and other points in the centre. From Darwin the Wheelers headed south to Katherine then across to Western Australia, through the Kimberley and down the coast to Perth. When they reached the Exmouth turn-off Tony and Maureen had completed the circuit of Australia they'd begun 15 years earlier when they'd stepped ashore at Exmouth after hitching a yacht ride from Bali.

In Perth the Falcon, after another 10,000 km service, was handed over to Richard Nebesky who made the long trek across the Nullarbor, down to Adelaide and back to Melbourne. Our one quick circuit had covered most of the country, put 30,000 km on the car and included visits to thousands of hotels, motels,

continued on page 878

Contents

Contents

Introduction

It may be cliched to say Australia is a big country but there are few places on earth with as much variety as Australia has to offer. And not just variety in things to see – in things to do, places to eat, entertainment, activities and just general good times.

What to see and do while tripping around our island continent is an open-ended question. There are cities big and small, some of them amazingly beautiful. If you fly in over its magnificent harbour, for example, Sydney is a city which can simply take your breath away. To really get to grips with the country, however, you must get away from the cities. Australian society may be a basically urban one but, myth or not, it's in the outback where you really find Australia – the endless skies, the endless red dirt, the laconic Aussie characters. And when you've seen the outback that still leaves you mountains and coast, superb bushwalks and big surf, the Great Barrier Reef and the Northern Territory's 'top end'.

Best of all Australia can be far from the rough and ready country its image might indicate. In the big cities you'll find some of the prettiest Victorian architecture going; Australian restaurants serve up an astounding variety of national cuisine with the freshest ingredients you could

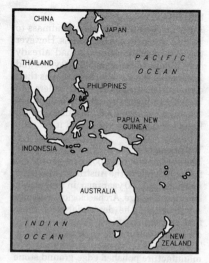

ask for (it's all grown here) and it's no problem at all to fall in love with Australian wines; plus Australia is still one of those lucky countries where you can walk down most streets at any time of day or night without worrying about your safety. It's not just exciting and invigorating, it's also very civilised. There's some fantastic travelling waiting for you around Australia, go for it.

Facts about the Country

HISTORY

Australia was the last great landmass to be 'discovered' by the Europeans. However the continent of Australia had already been inhabited for about 40,000 years and long before the British claimed it as their own, European explorers and traders had been dreaming of the riches to be found in the unknown, some said mythical, South Land – if only they could find it.

The Aborigines

The ancestors of the Aborigines journeyed from Indonesia to the Australian mainland more than 40,000 years ago, in the earliest known sea voyage. Archaeological evidence suggests that the descendants of these first settlers colonised the whole of the continent within a few thousand years. They were the first people in the world to manufacture polished edge-ground stone tools, cremate their dead and engrave and paint representations of themselves and the animals they hunted.

Aborigines were traditionally tribal people living in extended family groups. Wisdom and skills obtained over millennia enabled Aborigines to use their environment to the maximum. An intimate knowledge of the behaviour of animals and the correct time to harvest the many plants they utilised ensured that food shortages were rare. They never hunted an animal species or harvested a plant species to the point where it was threatened with extinction. Like other hunter/gatherer peoples of the world, the Aborigines were true ecologists.

Although Aborigines in northern Australia had been in regular contact with the farming peoples of Indonesia for at least 1000 years, the farming of crops and domestication of livestock held no appeal. The only major modification of the landscape practised by the Aborigines was the selective burning of undergrowth in forests and dead grass on the plains. This encouraged new growth, attracted game animals to the area, and prevented the build-up of combustible material in the forests, making hunting easier and reducing the possibility of major bush fires. Dingoes were domesticated to assist in the hunt and to guard the camp from intruders.

Similar technology – for example the boomerang and spear – was used throughout the continent, but techniques were adapted to the environment and the species being hunted. In the wetlands of northern Australia fish traps hundreds of metres long made of bamboo and cord were built to catch fish at the end of the wet season. In the area now known as Victoria, permanent stone weirs many km long were used to trap migrating eels, while in the tablelands of Queensland finely woven nets were used to snare herds of wallabies and kangaroos. Dwellings ranged from the beehive stone houses of Victoria's windswept western district, to elevated platforms constructed by the peoples of the humid, mosquito infested tropics.

The simplicity of the Aborigines' technology is in contrast with the sophistication of their cultural life. Religion, history, law and art are integrated in complex ceremonies which depict the activities of the ancestral beings who created the landscape and its people, and prescribe codes of behaviour and responsibilities for looking after the land and all living things. Songs explain how the landscape contains these powerful creator ancestors, who can still exert either a benign or a malevolent influence. They also tell of the best places and the best times to hunt, where to find water in drought years, and specify kinship relations and correct marriage partners.

Ceremonies are still performed in many

parts of Australia and the features of the landscape believed to be metamorphosed ancestral beings of the *Dreamtime* are commonly known as 'sacred sites'. Many such sites are believed to be dangerous and entry is prohibited under traditional Aboriginal law.

These restrictions may seem merely the result of superstition, but in many cases they have a pragmatic origin. One site in Northern Australia was believed to cause sores to break out all over the body of anyone visiting the area. Subsequently, the area was found to have a dangerously high level of radiation from naturally occurring radon gas. In another instance, fishing from a certain reef was traditionally prohibited. This restriction was scoffed at by local Europeans until it was discovered that fish from this area had a high incidence of ciguatera, which renders fish poisonous if eaten by humans.

At the time of the settlement of Sydney Cove 200 years ago, there were 300,000 Aborigines in Australia and over 200 regional languages. Many are as distinct from each other as English is from Chinese.

In a society based on family groups with an egalitarian political structure, a co-ordinated response to the European colonisers was not possible. When Governor Phillip raised the flag at Sydney Cove in 1788, the laws of England became the law governing all Aborigines in the Australian continent. All land in Australia was from that moment the property of the English Crown.

If the Aborigines had had a readily recognisable political system and had resisted colonisation by organised force of arms, then the English may have been forced to recognise their prior title to the land and therefore legitimise their colonisation by entering into a treaty with the Aboriginal land owners.

Without any legal right to the lands they once lived on, Aborigines throughout the country became dispossessed; some were driven from their country by force, and thousands more succumbed to exotic diseases. Others voluntarily left their lands to travel to the fringes of settled areas to obtain new commodities such as steel and cloth, and experience hitherto

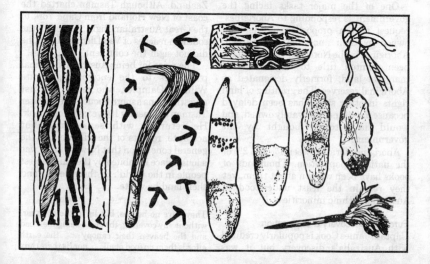

unknown drugs such as tea, tobacco, alcohol and narcotics.

At a local level, individuals resisted the encroachment of settlers. Warriors including Pemulwy, Yagan, Dundalli and Nemarluk were, for a time, feared by the colonists in their areas. But although some settlements had to be abandoned, the effect of such resistance only temporarily postponed the inevitable.

By the early 1900s legislation designed to segregate and 'protect' Aboriginal people was passed in all states. The legislation imposed restrictions on Aborigines' right to own property, to seek employment, and even allowed the state to remove children from Aboriginal mothers if it was suspected that the father was non-Aboriginal. Many Aborigines are still bitter about being separated from their families and being forced to grow up apart from their people.

The process of social change was accelerated by WW II and white Australians became increasingly aware of the inequity of their treatment of Aborigines. In 1967 Australians voted to give the Commonwealth government power to legislate for Aborigines in all states.

One of the major tasks facing the government is responding to Aborigines' request that a proportion of the land owned by their ancestors be returned. Aborigines in the Northern Territory have been granted title to large areas of marginal land, formerly designated as Aboriginal reserves. The granting of land rights in other states has been delayed because most land is privately owned, and would have to be bought by the government.

Aborigines form between 1% and 2% of the nation's population. Thousands of books have been written about them, yet they remain the least understood of Australia's ethnic minorities.

European Discovery & Exploration

Captain James Cook is popularly credited with Australia's discovery but it was probably a Portuguese who first sighted the country, while credit for its earliest coastal exploration must go to a Dutchman.

Portuguese navigators had come within sight of the coast in the first half of the 16th century and in 1606 the Spaniard Torres sailed through the strait between Cape York and New Guinea that still bears his name, though there's no record of his actually sighting the southern continent.

In the early 1600s Dutch sailors, in search of gold and spices, reached the west coast of Cape York and several other places on the west coast. What they found was a dry, harsh, unpleasant country and they rapidly scuttled back to the kinder climes of Batavia in the Dutch East Indies (now Jakarta in Indonesia).

In 1642 the Dutch East India Company, in pursuit of fertile lands and riches of any sort, mounted an expedition to explore the land to the south. Abel Tasman made two voyages from Batavia in the 1640s during which he discovered the region he called *Van Diemens Land* (which was renamed Tasmania some 200 years later), though he was unaware that it was an island, and the west coast of New Zealand. Although Tasman charted the coast of New Holland from Cape York to the Great Australian Bight, as well as the southern reaches of Van Diemens Land, he did not sight the continent's east coast.

The prize for being Australia's original pom goes to the enterprising pirate William Dampier, who made the first investigations ashore about 40 years after Tasman and nearly 100 years before Cook. He returned with sensational, but accurate, reports of the wildlife and the general conclusion that New Holland was a lousy place inhabited by the 'miserablest people in the world'. Of these people and their land he wrote:

They have no houses, but lie in the open air, without any covering, the earth being their bed and the heaven their canopy ... the earth affords them no food at all ... nor (is there) any sort of bird or beast that they can catch, having no instruments wherewithal to do so. I did not perceive that they did worship anything . . .

Dampier's records of New Holland, from visits made to Shark Bay on the west coast in 1688 and 1698, influenced the European idea of a primitive and godless land that remained unchanged until Cook's more informed and well documented voyages of discoveries spawned romantic and erotic notions of the South Seas and the idealised view of the 'noble savage'.

This dismal continent was forgotten until 1768, when the British Admiralty instructed Captain James Cook to lead a scientific expedition to Tahiti, to observe the transit of the planet Venus, and then begin a search for the Great South Land. On board his ship *Endeavour* were also several scientists including an astronomer and a group of naturalists and artists led by Joseph Banks.

After circumnavigating both islands of New Zealand, Cook set sail in search of the Great South Land, planning to head west until he found the unexplored east coast of the land known as New Holland.

On 19 April 1770 the extreme south-eastern tip of the continent was sighted, and named Point Hicks, and when the *Endeavour* was a navigable distance from shore Cook turned north to follow the coast and search for a suitable landfall. It was nine days before an opening in the cliffs was sighted and the ship and crew found sheltered anchorage in a harbour they named Botany Bay.

During their forays ashore the scientists recorded descriptions of plants, animals and birds, the likes of which had never been seen, and attempted to communicate with the few native inhabitants who all but ignored these, the first white men to set foot on the east coast. Cook wrote of the Blacks: 'All they seemed to want was for us to be gone.'

After leaving Botany Bay Cook continued north, charting the coastline and noting that the fertile east coast was a different story from the inhospitable land the earlier explorers had seen to the south and west. When the *Endeavour* was badly damaged on a reef off North Queensland, Cook was forced to make a temporary settlement. It took six weeks to repair the ship, during which time Cook and the scientists investigated their surroundings further, this time making contact with the local Aborigines.

Unlike the unimpressed Dampier, Cook was quite taken with the indigenous people and wrote:

They may appear to some to be the most wretched people on earth but in reality they are far happier than we Europeans . . . They live in a tranquillity which is not disturbed by the inequality of condition . . . they seem to set no value upon anything we gave them, nor would they ever part with anything of their own . . .

After repairing the *Endeavour*, navigating the Great Barrier Reef and rounding Cape York, Cook again put ashore to raise the Union Jack, rename the continent New South Wales and claim it for the British in the name of King George III.

James Cook was resourceful, intelligent, and popularly regarded as one of the greatest and most humane explorers of all time. His incisive reports of his voyages make fascinating reading, even today. By the time he was killed, in the Sandwich Islands (now Hawaii) in 1779, he had led two further expeditions to the South Pacific.

Convicts & Settlement

Following the American Revolution, Britain was no longer able to transport convicts to North America. With jails and prison hulks already overcrowded, it was essential that an alternative be found quickly. In 1779 Joseph Banks suggested New South Wales as a fine site for a colony of thieves and in 1786 Lord Sydney announced that the king had decided upon Botany Bay as a place for convicts under sentence of transportation. The fact that the continent was already inhabited was not considered significant.

Less than two years later, in January 1788, the First Fleet sailed into Botany Bay under the command of Captain Arthur Phillip, who was to be the colony's first governor. Phillip was immediately disappointed with the landscape and sent a small boat north to find a more suitable landfall. The crew soon returned with the news that in Port Jackson they had found the finest harbour in the world and a good sheltered cove.

The fleet, comprised of 11 ships carrying about 750 male and female convicts, 400 sailors, four companies of marines and enough livestock and supplies for two years, weighed anchor again and headed for Sydney Cove to begin settlement.

For the new arrivals New South Wales was a harsh and horrible place. The reasons for transportation were often minor and the sentences, of no less than seven years with hard labour, were tantamount to life sentences as there was little hope of returning home.

Although the colony of soldiers, sailors, pickpockets, prostitutes, sheep stealers and petty thieves managed to survive the first difficult years, the cruel power of the military guards made the settlement a prison hell.

At first, until farming could be developed, the 'settlers' were dependent upon supplies from Europe and a late or, even worse, a wrecked supply ship would have been disastrous. The threat of starvation hung over the colony for at least 16 years.

The Second Fleet arrived in 1790 with more convicts and some supplies, and a year later, following the landing of the Third Fleet, the population increased to around 4000.

As crops began to yield, New South Wales became less dependent on Britain for food. There were still, however, huge social gulfs in the fledgling colony: officers and their families were in control and

clinging desperately to a modicum of civilised British living; soldiers, free settlers and even emancipated convicts were beginning to eke out a living; yet the majority of the population were still in chains, regarded as the dregs of humanity and living in squalid conditions.

Little of the country was explored during those first years; few people ventured further than Sydney Cove and though Governor Phillip had instructed that every attempt should be made to befriend the Blacks, this was not to be.

Phillip believed New South Wales would not progress if the colony continued to rely solely on the labour of convicts, who were already busy constructing government roads and buildings. He believed prosperity depended on attracting free settlers, to whom convicts could be assigned as labourers, and in the granting of land to officers, soldiers and worthy emancipists (convicts who had served their time).

This began to happen when Phillip returned to England and his second in command, Grose, took over. In a classic case of 'jobs for the boys', Grose tipped the balance of power further in favour of the military by granting land to officers of the New South Wales Corps.

With money, land and cheap labour suddenly at their disposal the so-called Rum Corps became exploitative, making huge profits at the expense of the small farmers. They began paying for labour and local products in rum, and were soon able to buy whole shiploads of goods and resell them at two or three times their original value. New South Wales was becoming an important port on trade routes, and whaling and sealing were increasing.

The Rum Corps, meeting little resistance, continued to do virtually as they pleased, all the while getting richer and more arrogant. They – and in particular one John Macarthur – managed to upset, defy, out-manoeuvre and out-last three governors, including William Bligh of the *Bounty* mutiny fame.

Bligh actually faced a second mutiny when the Rum Corps officers rebelled and ordered his arrest. The 'Rum Rebellion' was the final straw for the British government, which dispatched Lieutenant-Colonel Lachlan Macquarie with his own regiment and orders for the return to London of the New South Wales Corps.

John Macarthur, incidentally, was to have far-reaching effects on the colony's first staple industry. It was his understanding of the country's grazing potential that fostered his own profitable sheep breeding concerns and prompted his introduction of the merino in the belief that careful breeding could produce wool of exceptional quality. Though it was his vision, it was his wife, Elizabeth, who did most of the work – Macarthur remained in England for nearly a decade for his part in the Rum Rebellion.

Governor Macquarie, having broken the stranglehold of the Rum Corps, set about laying the groundwork for social reforms. He felt that the convicts who had served their time should be allowed rights as citizens, and began appointing emancipists to public positions.

While this meant the long-term future for convicts didn't appear quite so grim, by the end of Macquarie's term in 1821 New South Wales was still basically a convict society and there were often clashes between those who had never been imprisoned and those who had been freed.

During the 1830s and 1840s the number of free settlers to the colonies of New South Wales, Western Australia, Van Diemens Land and Port Phillip (Victoria) was increasing, although it was the discovery of gold in the 1850s that was truly to change the face of the young country.

By the time transportation was abolished (to the eastern colonies in 1852 and to the west in 1868) more than 168,000 convicts had been shipped to Australia.

Colonial Expansion

Australia never enjoyed the systematic push westward that characterised the European settlement of America. Exploration and expansion basically took place for one of three reasons: to find suitable places of secondary punishment, like the barbaric penal settlements at Port Arthur in Van Diemens Land; to create another colony in order to occupy land before anyone else arrived; or in later years because of the quest for gold.

By 1800 there were only two small settlements on the Australian continent – at Sydney Cove and Norfolk Island. While unknown areas on world maps were becoming few and far between, most of Australia was still one big blank. It was even suspected that it might be two large, separate islands and it was hoped that there might be a vast sea in the centre.

In the ensuing 40 years a great period of discovery started as the vast inland was explored and settlements were established at Hobart, Brisbane, Perth, Adelaide and Melbourne. Some of the early explorers, particularly those who braved the hostile centre, suffered great hardship.

George Bass had charted the coast south of Sydney almost down to the present location of Melbourne during 1797 and 1798 and in the following year, with Matthew Flinders, he sailed around Van Diemens Land, establishing that it was an island. Flinders went on, in 1802 to sail right round Australia.

The first settlement in Van Diemens Land, in 1803, was close to the present site of Hobart; by the 1820s Hobart Town rivalled Sydney in importance. The island was not named Tasmania, after its original European discoverer, until 1856 when, after the end of transportation, the inhabitants requested the name be changed to remove the stigma of what had been vicious penal colonies.

The Blue Mountains at first proved an impenetrable barrier, fencing in Sydney to the sea, but in 1813 a path was finally forced through and the western plains were reached by the explorers Blaxland, Wentworth and Lawson.

Port Phillip Bay in Victoria was originally considered as a site for the second settlement in Australia but was rejected in favour of Hobart, so it was not looked at again until 1835 when settlers from Tasmania, in search of more land, selected the present site of Melbourne.

Perth was first settled in 1829, but as it was isolated from the rest of the country, growth there was very slow.

The first settlement in the Brisbane area was made by a party of convicts sent north from Sydney because the (by then) good citizens of that fair city were getting fed up with having all those crims about the place. By the time the Brisbane penal colony was abandoned, in 1839, free settlers had arrived in force.

Adelaide, established in 1837, was initially an experiment in free enterprise colonisation. It failed due to bad management and the British government had to take over from the bankrupt organisers and bail the settlement out of trouble.

In 1824 the explorers Hume and Hovell, starting from near present day Canberra, made the first overland journey southwards, reaching the western shores of Port Phillip Bay.

Twelve years later the colony's surveyor -general, Major Mitchell, wrote glowing reports of the beautiful and fertile country he had crossed in his expedition across the Murray River and as far south as Portland Bay. He dubbed the region (now called Victoria) *Australia Felix*, or 'Australia Fair'.

In 1840 Edward John Eyre left Adelaide to try to reach the centre of Australia. He gave up at Mt Hopeless and then decided to attempt a crossing to Albany in Western Australia. The formidable task nearly proved too much as both food and water were virtually unobtainable and his companion, Baxter, was killed by two of their Aboriginal guides. Eyre struggled on, encountering a French whaling ship in Rossiter Bay and, reprovisioned, managed to reach Albany. The road across the Nullarbor Plains from South Australia to Western Australia is named the Eyre Highway.

From 1844 to 1845 a German scientist by the name of Leichhardt travelled through northern Queensland, skirting the Gulf of Carpentaria, to Port Essington, near modern-day Darwin. He turned back during an attempt in 1846 and 1847 to cross Australia from east to west, only to disappear on his second attempt. He was never seen again.

In 1848 Edmund Kennedy set out to travel by land up Cape York Peninsula while a ship, *HMS Rattlesnake*, explored the coast and islands. Starting from Rockingham Bay, south of Cairns, the expedition almost immediately struck trouble when their heavy supply carts could not be dragged through the swampy ground around Tully. The rugged land, harsh climate, lack of supplies, hostile Aborigines and missed supply drops, all took their toll and nine of the party of 13 died. Kennedy himself was speared to death in an attack by Aborigines when he was only 30 km from the end of his fearsome trek. His Aboriginal servant, Jacky Jacky, was the only expedition member to finally reach the supply ship.

Leaving Melbourne in 1860, the Burke & Wills expedition's attempt to cross the continent from south to north was destined to be one of the most tragic. After reaching a depot at Coopers Creek in Queensland they intended to make a dash north to the Gulf of Carpentaria with a party of four. Their camels proved far slower than anticipated in the swampy land close to the gulf and on their way back one of the party died of exhaustion.

Burke, Wills and the third survivor, King, eventually struggled back to Coopers Creek, virtually at the end of their strength and nearly two months behind schedule, only to find the depot group had given up hope and left for Melbourne just hours earlier. They remained at Coopers Creek, but missed a returning search party and never found the supplies that had been left for them.

Burke and Wills finally starved to death, literally in the midst of plenty – their companion, King, was able to survive on food provided by local Aborigines until a rescue party arrived.

Departing from Adelaide in 1860, chasing a £2000 reward for the first south-north crossing, John Stuart reached the geographical centre of Australia, Central Mt Stuart, but shortly after was forced to turn back. A second attempt in 1861 got much closer to the top end before he again had to return. Finally, in 1862, he managed to reach the north coast near Darwin. The overland telegraph line, completed in 1872, and the modern Stuart Highway, follow a similar route.

Gold, Stability & Growth

The discovery of gold in the 1850s brought about the most significant changes in the social and economic structure of Australia, particularly in Victoria, where most of the gold was found.

Earlier gold discoveries had been all but ignored, partly because they were only small finds and mining skills were still undeveloped, but mostly because the law stated that all gold discovered belonged to the government.

The discovery of large quantities near Bathurst in 1851, however, caused a rush of hopeful miners from Sydney and forced the government to abandon the law of ownership. Instead, it introduced a compulsory diggers' licence fee of 30 shillings a month, whether the miners found gold or not, to ensure the country earned some revenue from the incredible wealth that was being unearthed. Victorian businessmen at the time, fearing their towns would soon be devoid of able-bodied men, offered a reward for the discovery of gold in their colony.

In 1851 one of the largest gold discoveries in history was made at Ballarat, followed by others at Bendigo and Mt Alexander, starting a rush of unprecedented magnitude.

While the first diggers at the gold fields that soon sprang up all over Victoria came from the other Australian colonies, it wasn't long before they were joined by thousands of migrants. The Irish and English, as well as Europeans and Americans began arriving in droves and within 12 months there were about 1800 hopeful diggers disembarking at Melbourne every week.

Similar discoveries in other colonies, in particular the Western Australian gold rush of the 1890s, further boosted populations and levels of economic activity.

The 19th century development of Australia, however, also had a much more shameful side. The Aborigines, who were looked upon as little more than animals, were ruthlessly pushed off their tribal lands as the white diggers and settlers continued to take up the land for mining and farming. In some places, Tasmania in particular, they were hunted and killed like vermin while those that survived on the fringes of the new white society became a dispossessed and oppressed people.

The gold rushes also brought floods of diligent Chinese miners and market gardeners onto the Australian diggings where violent white opposition led to a series of unpleasant race riots and a morbid fear of Asian immigration which persisted well into this century.

Although few people actually made their fortunes on the gold fields, many stayed to settle the country, as farmers, workers and shop keepers. At the same time the Industrial Revolution in England started to produce a strong demand for raw materials so, with the agricultural and mining potential of such a vast country, Australia's economic base became secure.

Besides the population and economic growth that followed the discovery of gold, the rush also contributed greatly to the development of a distinctive Australian folklore. The music brought by the English and Irish, for instance, was tuned in to life on the diggings, while poets, singers and writers began telling stories of the people, the roaring gold towns and the boisterous hotels, the squatters and their sheep and cattle stations, the swagmen, and the derring-do of the notorious bushrangers, many of whom became folk heroes.

The 20th Century

During the 1890s calls for the separate colonies to federate became increasingly strident. Supporters argued that it would improve the economy and the position of the workers by enabling the abolition of intercolonial tariffs and the protection of workers from competition from foreign labour.

Each colony was determined, however, that its interests should not be overshadowed by those of the other colonies. For this reason, the constitution that was finally adopted gave only very specific powers to the Commonwealth, leaving all residual powers with the states. It also gave each state equal representation in the upper house of parliament (the Senate) regardless of size or population. Today Tasmania, with a population of less than half a million, has as many senators in federal parliament as New South Wales, with a population of more than 5½ million. As the upper house is able to reject legislation passed by the lower house, this legacy of Australia's colonial past has had a profound effect on its politics ever since, entrenching state divisions and ensuring that the smaller states have remained powerful forces in the government of the nation.

With federation, which came on 1 January 1901, Australia became a nation, but its loyalty and many of its legal and cultural ties to Britain remained. The mother country still expected to be able to rely on military support from its Commonwealth allies in any conflict, and Australia fought beside Britain in battles as far from Australia's shores as the Boer War in South Africa. This willingness to follow western powers to war would be demonstrated time and again during the 20th century. Seemingly unquestioning loyalty to Britain and later the USA was only part of the reason. Xenophobia born of isolation, an Asian location and a vulnerable economy was also to blame.

The extent to which Australia regarded itself as a European outpost became evident with the passage of the Immigration Restriction Bill of 1901. The bill, known as the white Australia policy, was designed to prevent the immigration of Asians and Pacific Islanders. Prospective immigrants were required to pass a dictation test in a European language. The language in which the test was given could be as obscure a tongue as the authorities wished. The dictation test was not abolished until 1958.

The desire to protect the jobs and conditions of white Australian workers that had helped bring about the white Australia policy did, however, have some positive results. The labour movement had been a strong political force for many years, and by 1908 the principle of a basic wage sufficient to enable a worker to support himself, a wife and three children had been established. By that time also, old age and invalid pensions were being paid.

When war broke out in Europe, Australian troops were again sent to fight thousands of miles from home. The most infamous of the WW I battles in which diggers took part, from Australia's perspective, was that intended to force a passage through the Dardanelles to Constantinople. Australian and New Zealand troops landed at Gallipoli only to be slaughtered by well equipped and strategically well positioned Turkish soldiers. Ever since, the sacrifices made by all Australian soldiers have been commemorated on Anzac Day, the anniversary of the Gallipoli landing.

Interestingly, while Australians rallied to the aid of Britain during WW I, the majority of voters were only prepared to condone voluntary military service.

Efforts to introduce conscription during the war led to bitter argument both in parliament and in the streets, and in referenda compulsory national service was rejected by a small margin.

Australia was hard hit by the Depression. In 1931 almost a third of breadwinners were unemployed and poverty was widespread. Swagmen became a familiar sight once more, as hundreds of men took to the 'wallaby track' in search of work in the country. By 1932, however, Australia's economy was starting to recover, a result of rises in wool prices and a rapid revival of manufacturing.

In the years before WW II Australia became increasingly fearful of Japan. When war did break out, Australian troops fought beside the British in Europe, but after the Japanese bombed Pearl Harbor Australia's own national security finally began to take priority.

Singapore fell, the northern Australian towns of Darwin and Broome and the New Guinean town of Port Morseby were bombed, the Japanese advanced southward, and still Britain called for more Australian troops. This time the Australian Prime Minister, John Curtin, refused. Australian soldiers were needed to fight the Japanese advancing over the mountainous Kokoda Trail towards Port Moresby. In appalling conditions Australian soldiers confronted and defeated the Japanese at Milne Bay, east of Port Moresby, and began the long struggle to push them from the conquered Pacific territories.

Ultimately it was the USA, not Britain, that helped protect Australia from the Japanese, defeating them in the Battle of the Coral Sea. This event was to mark the beginning of a profound shift in Australia's allegiance away from Britain and towards the USA. Although Australia continued to support Britain in the war in Europe, its appreciation of its own vulnerability had been sharpened immeasurably by the Japanese advance.

One result of this was the post war immigration programme, which offered assisted passage not only to the British but also to refugees from eastern Europe in the hope that the increase in population would strengthen Australia's economy and contribute to its ability to defend itself. 'Populate or Perish' became the catch-cry. Between 1947 and 1968 more

than 800,000 non-British European migrants came to Australia. They have since made an enormous economic and social contribution to the country, enlivening its culture and broadening its vision.

As living conditions improved after the war Australia came to accept the US view that it was not so much Asia but *communism* in Asia that threatened the increasingly Americanised Australian way of life. Accordingly Australia followed the USA into the Korean War and joined it as a signatory to the treaties of ANZUS and the anti-communist South East Asia Treaty Organization (SEATO). Australia also provided aid to south-east Asian nations under the Colombo Plan, a scheme initiated by Australia but subscribed to by many other countries, including the USA, Britain, Canada and Japan.

In the light of Australia's willingness to join SEATO, it is not surprising that its conservative government applauded the USA's entry into the Vietnam War and, in 1965, committed troops to the struggle. Support for involvement was far from absolute, however. The leader of the Australian Labor Party, for example, believed the Vietnam conflict to be a civil war in which Australia had no part. Still more troubling for many young Australian men was the fact that conscription had been introduced during the previous year and those undertaking national service could now be sent overseas. By 1967 as many as 40% of Australians serving in Vietnam were conscripts.

The civil unrest aroused by conscription was one factor that contributed to the rise to power, in 1972, of the Australian Labor Party for the first time in more than 20 years. The Whitlam government withdrew Australian troops from Vietnam, abolished national service and higher-education fees, instituted a scheme of free and universally available health care, and supported land rights for Aborigines.

Labor, however, was hampered by a hostile Senate and talk of mismanagement.

On 11 November 1975 the governor general (the British monarch's representative in Australia) dismissed parliament and installed a caretaker government led by the Leader of the Opposition, Malcolm Fraser. Labor supporters were appalled. Such action was unprecedented in the history of the Commonwealth of Australia and the powers that the governor general had been able to invoke had long been regarded by many as an anachronistic vestige of Australia's now remote British past, the office itself as that of an impotent figurehead.

Nevertheless, it was a conservative coalition of the Liberal and National Country parties that won the ensuing election. A Labor government was not returned until 1983, when a former trade union leader, Bob Hawke, led the party to victory. The current Labor government, pragmatic by comparison to the Whitlam government, has maintained close links with the union movement, which have helped it steer Australia through some economically difficult times.

Socially, Australia is still coming to terms with its Asian environment. While it has accepted large numbers of Vietnamese and other Asian refugees during the past two decades, debate about its immigration policy surfaces periodically, as it did in 1988. It cannot be denied, however, that Asian immigration, together with immigration from other areas, has changed Australia, heightening its understanding of its neighbours and altering the aspect of its cities.

Perhaps Australia's most disturbing contemporary social failure has been its inability to improve significantly the situation of its Aborigines. Land rights remain a contentious issue, but perhaps more controversial recently has been the increasing number of Aboriginal deaths in custody. Scores of Aborigines imprisoned for petty crimes have been found dead in their cells and at the time of writing an inquiry into the reasons for their deaths was in progress. Undeniably, social dislocation and white ignorance, intolerance and insensitivity have been contributing factors.

GEOGRAPHY

Australia is an island continent whose landscape – much of it uncompromisingly bleak and inhospitable – is the result of gradual changes wrought over millions of years. Although there is still seismic activity in the eastern and western highland areas, Australia is one of the most stable land masses, and for about 100 million years has been free of the mountain-building forces that have given rise to huge mountain ranges elsewhere.

From the east coast a narrow, fertile strip merges into the greatly eroded, almost continent-long Great Dividing Range. The mountains are mere reminders of the mighty range that once stood here. Only in the Snowy Mountains section, straddling the New South Wales border with Victoria, and in Tasmania, are they high enough to have winter snow.

West of the range the country becomes increasingly flat and dry until virtually all habitation ceases. The endless flatness is broken only by salt lakes, occasional mysterious protuberances, like Ayers Rock (Uluru) and the Olgas, and some starkly beautiful mountains, like the MacDonnell Range near Alice Springs. In places, the scant vegetation is sufficient to allow some grazing, so long as each animal has a seemingly enormous area of land. However, much of the Australian outback is an eternally barren land of harsh, stone deserts and dry lakes with evocative names like Lake Disappointment.

The extreme north of Australia, the 'top end', is a tropical area within the monsoon belt. Although the annual rainfall there looks adequate on paper, it comes in more or less one short, sharp burst. This has prevented the top end from becoming seriously productive agriculturally.

The west of Australia consists mainly of a broad plateau. In the far west there is a mountain range and fertile coastal strip which heralds the Indian Ocean, but this is only to the south. In the north-central part of Western Australia, the dry country runs right to the sea.

Australia is the world's sixth largest country. Its area is 7,682,300 square km, about the same size as the 48 mainland states of the USA and half as large again as Europe, excluding the USSR. It is approximately 5% of the world's land surface. Lying between the Indian and Pacific Oceans, Australia is about 4000 km from east to west and 3200 km from north to south with a coastline 36,735 km long.

CLIMATE

Australian seasons are the antithesis of those in Europe and North America. It's hot in December and many Australians spend Christmas at the beach, while in July and August it's midwinter. Summer starts in December, autumn in March, winter in June and spring in September.

The climatic extremes aren't too severe in most parts of Australia. Even in Melbourne, the southern-most capital city on the mainland, it's a rare occasion when the mercury hits freezing point, although it's a different story in Ballarat, 112 km north-west of Melbourne, and in Canberra, the national capital. The poor Tasmanians, further to the south, have a good idea of what cold is.

As you head north the seasonal variations become fewer until, in the far north around Darwin, you are in the monsoon belt where there are just two seasons – hot and wet, and hot and dry. When the wet hits Darwin, around November or December, it really does get wet. In the Snowy Mountains of southern New South Wales and the Alps of north-east Victoria there's a snow season with good skiing. The centre is arid – hot and dry during the day, but often bitterly cold at night.

Victoria and Tasmania are probably at their best at the height of summer, although spring and autumn are pretty good too. In the winter months of July and

August, you might head south for the skiing but it's best to avoid Melbourne, which can be rather grey and miserable at this time.

By contrast, in the far north the best season is midwinter. Darwin is just right from July to August, whereas in midsummer it's often unbearably hot and humid; the sea is full of sea wasps (the deadly box jellyfish) and if there are cyclones about this is when they'll arrive. Similarly, in Alice Springs the midsummer temperatures can be far too high for comfort, while in midwinter the nights may be chilly but the days delightful.

Apart from climatic seasons, it's worth bearing the holiday seasons in mind. The Christmas holiday season is part of the long summer school vacation and the time you are most likely to find accommodation booked out and long queues. There are three other, shorter school holiday periods during the year but they vary by a week or two from state to state, falling from mid March to mid April, late June to early July, and late September to early October.

A synopsis of average maximum and minimum temperatures and rainfall follows. (Note that these are *average* maximums – even Melbourne gets a fair number of summer days hotter than 40°C (100°F). Temperatures in Australia are all expressed in degrees Celsius. As a rough rule of thumb, 20°C is about room temperature – 70°F.)

Adelaide Maximum temperatures are from 25°C to 30°C from November to March; minimums can be below 10°C between June and September. Rainfall is heaviest, 50 to 70 mm per month, from May to September.
Alice Springs There are maximums of 30°C and above from October to April; minimums are 10°C and below from May to September. Rainfall is low all year round; from December to February there's an average of 30 mm of rain.
Brisbane Maximums are rarely below 20°C year round, peaking around 30° from November to February; rainfall is fairly heavy all year round,

with more than 130 mm per month falling from December to March.
Canberra Maximums are in the mid to high 20°Cs in the summer and minimums often close to freezing between May and October; rainfall is usually 40 to 70 mm a month, year round.
Cairns Maximums are about 25°C to 33°C year round, with minimums rarely below 20°C; rainfall is below 100 mm a month from May to October (lowest in July and August), but peaks from January to March at 400 to 450 mm.
Darwin Temperatures are even year round, with maximums from 30°C to 34°C and minimums from 20°C to 25°C; rainfall is minimal from May to September, but from December to March there's 250 to 400 mm a month.
Hobart Maximums top 20°C only from December to March, and from April to November minimums are usually below 10°C; rainfall is about 40 to 60 mm a month, year round.
Melbourne Maximums are 20°C and above from October to April, minimums 10°C and below from May to October; rainfall is even year round, at 50 to 60 mm almost every month.
Perth Maximums are around 30°C from December to March, but minimums are rarely below 10°C; rainfall is lightest from November to March (20 mm and below) and heaviest from May to August (120 to 200 mm).
Sydney Usually only in the middle of winter are minimums below 10°C; summer maximums are around 25°C from November to March; rainfall is in the 75 mm to 130 mm range year round.

FLORA & FAUNA
Native Plants
Despite vast tracts of dry and barren land, much of Australia is well-vegetated. Forests cover 5%, or 410,000 square km. Plants can be found even in the arid centre, though many of them grow and flower erratically. Human activities seriously threaten our flora but to date most species have survived.

Origins Australia's distinctive vegetation began to take shape about 55 million years ago when Australia broke from the supercontinent of Gondwanaland, drifting away from Antarctica to warmer climes. At this time, Australia was completely covered by cool-climate rainforest but, due to its geographic isolation and the gradual drying of the continent, rainforests retreated, plants like eucalypts and wattles took over and grasslands expanded. Eucalypts and wattles were able to adapt to warmer temperatures, the increased natural occurrence of fire and the later use of fire for hunting and other purposes by Aborigines. Now many species benefit from fire.

The arrival of Europeans 200 years ago saw the introduction of new flora, fauna and tools. Rainforests were logged, new crops and pasture grasses spread, hooved animals such as cows, sheep and goats damaged the soil, and watercourses were altered by dams. Irrigation, combined with excessive clearing of the land, gradually resulted in a serious increase in the salinity of the soil.

Distinctive Australian Plants The gum tree, or eucalypt, is ubiquitous in Australia except in the deepest rainforests and the most arid regions. Of the 700 species of the genus eucalyptus, 95% occur naturally in Australia, the rest in New Guinea, the Philippines and Indonesia.

Gum trees vary in form and height from the tall, straight hardwoods such as jarrah, karri, mountain ash and red river gum to the stunted, twisted snow gum

with its colourful trunk striations. Other distinctive gums are the spotted variety of New South Wales' coast and the beautiful pink salmon gums of Katherine Gorge and elsewhere. The gum tree features in Australian folklore, art and literature. Many varieties flower, the wood is prized and its oil is used for pharmaceuticals and perfumed products.

Fast growing but short lived acacias or wattles occur in many warm countries but around 600 species are found in Australia, growing in a variety of conditions, from the arid inland to the rainforests of Tasmania. Wattles have deep green leaves and bright yellow to orange flowers. Most species flower during late winter and spring. Then the country is ablaze with wattle and the reason for the choice of green and gold as our national colours is obvious. Wattle is Australia's floral emblem.

Many other species of Australian native plants flower but few are deciduous. Common natives include banksias, grevilleas, hakeas, waratahs, bottlebrushes, paperbarks, tea trees, boronias, and bunya and hoop pines. An interesting book on the topic is *Field Guide to Native Plants of Australia* (Bay Books). You can see our range of flora at the all-native National Botanic Gardens in Canberrra. Brisbane's Mt Coot-tha Botanic Gardens features Australia's arid-zone plants.

Fauna

Among Australia's most distinctive types of fauna are the marsupials and monotremes. Marsupials, such as kangaroos and koalas, give birth to partially developed young which they suckle in a pouch. Monotremes – platypuses and echidnas – lay eggs but also suckle their young on milk.

Since the arrival of Europeans in Australia 17 species of mammal have become extinct and 28 more are currently endangered. Many introduced non-native animals have been allowed to run wild and have caused a great deal of damage to native species and to Australian vegetation. Introduced animals include foxes, cats, pigs, goats, donkeys, water buffalo, horses, starlings, blackbirds, cane toads and, best known of all, the notorious rabbit. Foxes and cats kill small native mammals and birds while rabbits denude vast areas of land, pigs carry disease and the birds take over the habitat of local species.

Kangaroos The extraordinary breeding cycle of the kangaroo is well adapted to Australia's harsh, often unpredictable environment.

The young, just mm long at birth, claws its way unaided to the mother's pouch where it attaches itself to a nipple that expands inside its mouth. A day or two later the mother mates again, but the embryo does not begin to develop until the first joey has left the pouch permanently.

At this point the mother produces two types of milk – one formula to feed the joey at heel, the other for the baby in her pouch. If environmental conditions are right, the mother will then mate again. If

food or water is scarce, however, the breeding cycle will be interrupted until conditions improve.

Although kangaroos generally are not aggressive, males of the larger species, such as reds, can be dangerous when cornered. In the wild boomers, as they are called, will grasp other males with their forearms, rear up on their muscular tales and pound their opponents with their hind feet, sometimes slashing them with their claws. Such behaviour can also be directed against dogs and, very rarely, people. It has also been said that kangaroos being pursued by dogs will sometimes hop into deep water and drown the dogs with their strong forearms.

There are now more kangaroos in Australia than there were when Europeans arrived, a result of the better availability of water and the creation of grasslands for sheep and cattle. Certain species, however, are threatened, as their particular environments are being destroyed. In all there are about 45 species.

About three million kangaroos are culled legally each year, but probably as many more are killed for sport or by those farmers who believe the cull is insufficient

to protect their paddocks from overgrazing by the animals.

Large kangaroos can be a hazard to people driving through the outback – hitting a two metre kangaroo at 110 km an hour can seriously damage vehicles.

Possums There are an enormous range of possums in Australia – they seem to have been able to adapt to all sorts of conditions, including those of the city. Some large species are often found in suburban roofs and will eat cultivated plants and other food scraps.

Certain possums are small and extremely timid, such as the tiny honey possum, which is able to extract nectar from blossoms with its tube-like snout. Others are gliders, able to jump from treetop to treetop by extending flaps of membrane between their legs.

Wombats Wombats are slow, solid, powerfully built marsupials with broad heads and short, stumpy legs. These fairly placid and easily tamed creatures are also legally killed by farmers, who object to the damage done to paddocks by wombats digging large burrows and tunnelling under fences.

Koalas Koalas are distantly related to the wombat and are found along the eastern seaboard. Their cuddly appearance belies an irritable nature, and they will scratch and bite if sufficiently provoked.

Koalas initially carry their babies in pouches but later the larger young cling to their mothers' backs. They feed only on the leaves of certain types of eucalypt and are particularly sensitive to changes to their habitat. Today many koalas suffer from chlamydia, a sexually transmitted disease causing blindness and infertility.

Tasmanian Devils The carnivorous Tasmanian devil is as fierce as it looks. Although it lives in groups, it gives a very good impression of detesting every other devil in sight, including its own offspring.

It's an ugly, smelly little monster found only in Tasmania, where the locals will gleefully torment visitors with morbid tales of its hideous habits. It's ability to chew through bone as easily as if it were cork is at the heart of its fearsome reputation. In fact, it only eats small mammals and birds – so we're told . . .

Tasmanian Tigers The Tasmanian tiger, like the Tasmanian devil, was a carnivorous marsupial. At one time both the tiger and the devil were threatened with extinction. Efforts to avert this disaster ensured the survival of the latter, but the larger, dog-like tiger was unable to recover its numbers. The last known specimen died in Hobart Zoo in 1936.

Platypuses & Echidnas The platypus and echidna are the only living representatives of the most primitive group of mammals, the monotremes. Both lay eggs, as reptiles do, but suckle their young on milk secreted directly through the skin from mammary glands.

The amphibious platypus has a duck-like bill, webbed feet and a beaver-like body. Males have a poisonous spur on their hind feet. Recent research has shown that the platypus is able to sense electric currents in the water and uses this ability to track its prey.

Echidnas are spiny anteaters that hide from predators by digging vertically into the ground and covering themselves with dirt or rolling themselves into a ball and raising their sharp quills.

Dingoes Australia's native dog is the dingo, domesticated by the Aborigines and thought to have arrived with them 40,000 years ago. Dingoes now prey on rabbits and, sometimes, livestock and are considered vermin by many farmers.

Emus & Cassowaries The only bird larger than the emu is the African ostrich, also flightless. It's a shaggy-feathered, often curious bird. After the female lays the eggs the male hatches them and raises the young.

Cassowaries are smaller than emus and more colourful. They are found in the rainforests of north Queensland.

Parrots & Cockatoos There are an amazing variety of these birds throughout Australia. The noisy pink and grey galahs are amongst the most common, although the sulphur crested cockatoos have to be the noisiest. Rosellas have one of the most brilliant colour schemes and in some parks they're not at all backward about taking a free feed from visitors.

Rainbow lorikeets are more extravagantly colourful than you can imagine until you've seen one. They're quite common from northern New South Wales up. Budgerigars are mainly found towards the centre; they often fly in flocks numbering 10,000 more.

Kookaburras A member of the kingfisher family, the kookaburra is heard as much as it is seen – you can't miss its loud, raucous guffaw. Kookaburras can become quite tame and pay regular visits to friendly households, but only if the food is excellent. It's hard to impress a kookaburra with anything less than top class steak.

Bower Birds The bower bird has a unique mating practice. The male builds a bower which he decorates with blue and green objects to attract females. In the wild, flowers or stones are used, but if artificial objects (clothes pegs, plastic pens, bottle tops – anything blue or green) are available, they'll certainly use them. The females are impressed by the males' neatly built bowers and attractively displayed treasures, but once they've mated all the hard work is left to her. He goes back to refurbishing the bower and attracting more females while she hops off to build a nest.

Snakes Australian snakes are generally shy and try to avoid confrontations with humans. A few, however, are deadly. The most dangerous are the taipans and tiger snakes, although death adders, copperheads, brown snakes and red-bellied black snakes should also be avoided. Tiger snakes will actually attack.

Crocodiles There are two types of crocodile in Australia: the extremely dangerous saltwater crocodile, or saltie as it's known, and the less aggressive freshwater crocodile, or freshie.

Salties are not confined to salt water. They inhabit estuaries and following floods may be found many miles from the coast. They may even be found in permanent fresh water more than 100 km inland. It is important to be able to tell the difference between the saltie and its less dangerous relative, as both are prolific in northern Australia.

Freshies are smaller than salties – anything over four metres should be regarded as a saltie. Freshies are also more

Saltwater Crocodile

finely constructed and have much narrower snouts and smaller teeth. Salties, which can grow to seven metres, will attack and kill humans. Freshies, though unlikely to seek human prey, have been known to bite, and children in particular should be kept away from them.

Spiders Two spiders to keep away from are the redback, a relative of the American black widow, and the Sydney funnel-web. The latter is found only in Sydney, while the former is more widespread and has a legendary liking for toilet seats. Both are extremely poisonous and have been lethal. There is an effective antivenin for the redback, but a funnel-web bite can be very serious.

You should also beware of the white-tailed spider, commonly found in fields and gardens. It is about the size of a 2c coin, with a distinct white spot on its grey-black back. Some people have extreme reactions to its bites and gangrene can result.

PARKS
National Parks
Australia has more than 500 national parks – non-urban protected wilderness areas of environmental or natural importance. Each state defines and runs its own national parks, but the principle is the same throughout Australia. National parks include rainforests, vast tracts of empty outback, strips of coastal dune land and long, rugged mountain ranges.

Public access is encouraged if safety and conservation regulations are observed. In all parks you're asked to do nothing to damage or alter the natural environment. Approach roads, campgrounds (often with toilets and showers), walking tracks and information centres are usually provided for visitors.

Some national parks are so isolated, rugged or uninviting that you wouldn't want to do much except look unless you were an experienced, well prepared bushwalker or climber. Others parks, however, are among Australia's major attractions and some of the most beautiful have been included on the the World Heritage List (a United Nations list of natural or cultural places of world significance that would be an irreplaceable loss to the planet if they were altered).

The World Heritage List includes the Taj Mahal, the Pyramids, the Grand Canyon and, at the time of writing, six Australian areas: the Great Barrier Reef; most of Kakadu National Park in the Northern Territory; the Willandra Lakes region of far west New South Wales, where human bones about 40,000 years old have been found; the Lord Howe Island group off New South Wales; the western Tasmanian wilderness national parks (South-West, Franklin – Lower Gordon Wild Rivers, and Cradle Mountain – Lake St Clair); and the east coast temperate and subtropical rainforest parks (15 national parks and reserves, covering 1000 square km in the eastern highlands of New

Freshwater Crocodile

South Wales). A seventh area, the Queensland wet tropics – including nearly all Australia's remaining tropical rainforest – may be added.

Before a site or area is accepted for the World Heritage List it has first to be proposed by its country then must pass a series of tests at the UN culminating, if it is successful, in acceptance by the UN World Heritage Committee which meets late each year. Any country proposing one of its sites or areas for the list must agree to protect the selected area, keeping it for the enjoyment of future generations even if to do so requires help from other countries.

Some political controversy between the federal and state governments surrounded recent proposals for World Heritage listings in Tasmania and Queensland.

While state governments have authority over their own national parks, the federal government is responsible for ensuring that Australia meets its international treaty obligations, and in any dispute arising from a related conflict between a state and the federal government, the latter can override the former.

In this way the federal government can force a state to protect an area with World Heritage listing, as it did when the Tasmanian government attempted, in the early 1980s, to dam the Gordon River in the south-west of the state and thereby flood much of the wild Franklin River.

For National Park authority addresses see the Information section of the Facts for the Visitor chapter.

State Forests

Another form of nature reserve you may discover is the state forest. These are owned by state governments and have fewer regulations than national parks. In theory, the state forests can be logged, but often they are primarily recreational areas with campgrounds, walking trails and signposted forest drives. Some permit horses and dogs.

GOVERNMENT

Australia is a federation of six states and two territories. Under the written constitution, the federal government, called the Commonwealth government, is mainly responsible for the national economy and Reserve Bank, customs and excise, immigration, defence, foreign policy and the post office. The state governments are chiefly responsible for health, education, housing, transport and justice. There are both federal and state police forces.

Australia has a parliamentary system of government based on that of the UK, and the state and federal structures are broadly similar. In federal parliament, the lower house is the House of Representatives, the upper house the Senate. Queensland does not have an upper house: it was abolished in 1922. The party holding the greatest number of lower house seats forms the government. The Commonwealth government is run by a prime minister while the state governments are led by a premier.

Australia is a monarchy but, although Britain's king or queen is also Australia's, Australia is fully autonomous. The British sovereign is represented by a governor general and state governors, whose nominations for their posts by the respective governments are ratified by the monarch of the day.

The federal parliament is based in Canberra, the capital of the nation. Like Washington DC in the USA, Canberra is in its own separate area of land, the Australian Capital Territory (ACT), and is not under the rule of one of the states. Geographically, however, the ACT is completely surrounded by New South Wales. The state parliaments are in each state capital.

Governments are elected for a maximum of three years but elections can be (and often are) called earlier. Voting in Australian elections is compulsory for persons 18 years of age and over. Voting can be somewhat complicated as a preferential system is used whereby each candidate has to be listed in order of preference. This can result, for example, in Senate elections with 50 or more candidates to be ranked!

In federal parliament, the two main political groups are the Australian Labor Party (ALP) and the coalition between the Liberal Party and the National Party. These Parties also dominate state politics but sometimes the Liberal and National Parties are not in coalition. The latter was once known as the National Country Party since it mainly represents country seats. Another important group is the Australian Democrats.

ECONOMY

Australia is a relatively affluent, industrialised nation but much of its wealth still comes from agriculture and mining. It has a small domestic market and a comparatively weak manufacturing sector. Nevertheless, a substantial proportion of the population is employed in manufacturing, and for much of Australia's history it has been argued that these industries need tariff protection from imports to ensure their survival.

Today, however, efforts are being made to increase Australia's international competitiveness. This has become more important as prices of traditional primary exports have become more volatile. The government has sought to restrain real wages with the assistance of the Australian Council of Trade Unions (ACTU), to make Australian products more competitive overseas and to promote employment within Australia.

This policy has seen the creation of many new jobs, but the international trade deficit is still huge, and supported by a growing external debt. There is some development in industries which earn foreign currency, particularly tourism, but the demand for imported goods seems insatiable. The main economic challenge for Australians, as for everyone else, is to earn enough to pay for the standard of living to which they have become accustomed.

POPULATION & PEOPLE

Australia's population is about 16½ million. The most populous states are New South Wales and Victoria, each with capital cities (Sydney and Melbourne) with a population of over three million.

The population is principally found along the east coast strip from Adelaide to Cairns and in the similar but smaller coastal region in Western Australia. The centre of the country is very sparsely populated. There are about 150,000 Aborigines, most heavily concentrated in central Australia and the far north.

Until WW II Australians were predominantly of British and Irish descent but that has changed dramatically since the war. First there was heavy migration from Europe creating major Greek and Italian populations but also adding Yugoslavs, Lebanese, Turks and other groups.

More recently Australia has had large influxes of Asians, particularly Vietnamese after the Vietnam war. In comparison to the country's population Australia probably took more Vietnamese refugees than any other western nation. Although there are always some grumblers, overall these 'new Australians' have been remarkably well accepted and 'multi-culturalism' is a popular concept in Australia. Nevertheless many politicians have recently spent a lot of time talking about immigration policies and limits upon immigration.

If you come to Australia in search of a real Australian you will find one quite easily – they are not known to be a shy breed. He or she may be a Lebanese cafe owner, an English used car salesman, an Aboriginal artist, a Malaysian architect or a Greek greengrocer. And you will find them in pubs, on beaches, at barbecues, mustering yards and art galleries. And yes, you may meet a Mick (Crocodile) Dundee or two but he is strictly a country model – the real Paul Hogan was a Sydney

Harbour Bridge painter, a job apparently where after you finish at one end you just start again at the other end.

FESTIVALS & HOLIDAYS

Some of the most enjoyable Australian festivals are, naturally, the ones which are most typically Australian – like the surf lifesaving competitions on beaches all around the country during summer; or the outback race meetings, which draw together isolated townsfolk, the tiny communities from the huge stations and more than a few eccentric bush characters.

There are happenings and holidays in Australia all year round – the following is just a brief overview; check the relevant state tourist authorities for dates and more details.

January

Sydney to Hobart Yacht Race – Tas. The arrival (29 December to 2 January) in Hobart of the yachts competing in this annual New Year Race is celebrated with a Mardi Gras. The competitors in the Melbourne to Hobart Yacht Race arrive soon after.

Maryborough Highland Gathering – Vic. Highland music, dancing, games and caber tossing are held every New Year's Day.

Australia Day – this national holiday, commemorating the arrival of the First Fleet, in 1788, is observed on the first Monday after 26 January.

Schuetzenfest – SA. The annual 'Shooting Festival', with food, beers and dancing, is held in the old German settlement of Hahndorf.

Cobram Peaches & Cream Festival – Vic. Cobram celebrates its fame for peaches and dairy products every odd-numbered year with a street carnival, canoe regatta and picnic races.

Jabiru Regatta – NT. This is a programme of crazy events and contests at Lake Jabiru.

Montsalvat Jazz Festival – Vic. Australia's biggest jazz festival is held at the beautiful Montsalvat artists' colony at Eltham.

February

Race Meetings – NT. There are race meetings and rodeos at Alice Springs, Tennant Creek and Darwin.

Warrnambool's Wunta Festival – Vic. There's a ball, whale boat races and a seafood and wine carnival.

Daylesford Festival – Vic. This has a programme of health and healing in the natural spa centres of Daylesford and Hepburn Springs.

Clunes Golden Pyramid Festival – Vic. An annual weekend of folk and blues music, dancing and fun.

Royal Hobart Regatta – Tas. This is the largest aquatic carnival in the southern hemisphere with boat races and other activities.

Sydney Gay Mardi Gras – NSW. It's fun – there's a huge procession with extravagant costumes, and an incredible party along Oxford St.

Kangaroo Island Racing Carnival – SA. This great country race meeting is held at Kingscote on lovely Kangaroo Island.

March

Adelaide Arts Festival – SA. Held on even-dated years, this is Australia's biggest festival of the arts – three weeks of music, theatre, opera, ballet, art exhibitions, light relief and plenty of parties.

Hunter Valley Vintage Festival – NSW. Wine enthusiasts flock to the Hunter Valley (north of Sydney) for wine tasting, and grape picking and treading contests.

Moomba – Melbourne. This week long festival culminates in a huge street procession on the Victorian Labour Day holiday.

Port Fairy Folk Festival – Vic. Every Labour Day weekend the small coastal town of Port Fairy comes to life with music, dancing, workshops, story telling, spontaneous entertainment and stalls. Australia's biggest folk music festival attracts all sorts of people and for three days the population swells from 2500 to around 10,000.

Ballarat Begonia Festival – Vic. More than just a flower show, this festival features world famous begonias, theatre, music and a fair.

March to April

Sydney Festival of the Rocks – NSW. In the week before Easter there's a street procession, Rocks pub crawl and a mock court on the green.

Sydney Royal Agricultural Show – NSW. Livestock contests and exhibits, ring events, sideshows and rodeos are features of this Easter show.

Clare Valley Easter Festival – SA. The vineyards are on show with wine tastings, cycle races, music, processions and exhibitions.

Bendigo Easter Fair – Vic. First held in 1871 to aid local charities, this fair features a procession with a Chinese dragon, a lantern parade, a jazz night and heaps more entertainment.

April

Anzac Day – This is a national public holiday, on 25 April, commemorating the landing of Anzac troops at Gallipoli in 1915. Memorial marches by the returned soldiers of both world wars and the veterans of Korea and Vietnam are held all over the country.

Barossa Vintage Festival – SA. This vineyard festival, with all the usual wine-related activities and entertainment, takes place in odd-numbered years.

The Melbourne Comedy Festival – Vic. The comedy capital of Australia puts on a terrific three week festival with local, out-of-town and international comedians, plays and other funny things.

The Australian Motorcycle Grand Prix – Vic. This round of the world championships is held on picturesque Phillip Island.

May

Race Meetings – NT. There is a series of country race meetings at remote Northern Territory stations, and in Alice Springs there's the *The Bangtail Muster* – a colourful float parade and other events; the *Alice Springs Cup* – an annual horse race; and the *Lions Fosters Camel Cup* – camel races, sideshows and fireworks.

May Day – NT. Regarded as the start of the 'no box jellyfish' season in Darwin, this is certainly an occasion for beach parties and rock concerts.

Camel Cup – NT. This is a series of races for camels, held in Alice Springs.

Melrose Mountain Festival – SA. An annual affair with a pioneering theme, held at Melrose in the Flinders Ranges.

June

Queen's Birthday – a public holiday on the second Monday in June.

Darwin Beer Can Regatta – NT. Boat races for boats constructed entirely out of beer cans, of which there are plenty in the world's beer drinking capital.

Sydney Bathtub Regatta – NSW. A bathtub race across the Heads of Sydney Harbour.

Darwin Bougainvillaea Festival – NT. A fortnight of celebrations when the colourful bougainvillaeas are in flower.

Katherine Gorge Canoe Marathon – NT. Organised by the Red Cross this is a 100 km race on the Katherine River.

Melbourne Film Festival – Vic. This is Australia's longest-running international film event, presenting the best in contemporary world cinema.

Rutherglen Winery Walkabout Weekend – Vic. Held on the Queen's birthday weekend, this is a great chance to sample some of the state's finest wines and visit the vineyards of Rutherglen.

July

Willunga Almond Blossom Festival – SA. Willunga is the state's almond producing centre, a fact celebrated annually with entertainment, food, wine and almonds.

Royal Darwin Show – NT.

August

Darwin Mud Crab Tying Competition! – NT.

Darwin Rodeo – NT. This includes international team events between Australia, the USA, Canada and New Zealand.

Alice Springs Rodeo – NT.

Barossa Classic Gourmet Weekend – SA. Spend a self-indulgent weekend in the lovely wineries of the Barossa Valley, with plenty of food and entertainment.

Melbourne Spoleto Fringe Festival – Vic. Three weeks of theatre, dance, comedy, cabaret, writers' readings, exhibitions and other events help Melbourne celebrates the 'alternative' arts.

Sydney City to Surf – NSW. Australia's biggest foot race takes place with up to 25,000 competitors running the 14 km from Hyde Park to Bondi Beach.

September

VFL Grand Final – Vic. Sporting attention turns to Melbourne with the Grand Final of Aussie rules football, when the MCG's 100,000 seats aren't enough to hold the spectators. It's the biggest sporting event in Australia.

The Melbourne Sun Superrun - Vic. Another big fun run with the competitors pounding across the huge West Gate Bridge.

The Royal Melbourne Show - Vic. This attracts agricultural folk for the judging of livestock and produce, and lots of families for the sideshows.

The Royal Perth Show - WA.

Western Australian Folk Festival - WA. Enjoy a weekend of music and dancing in Toodyay.

Tooheys 1000 - NSW. Motor racing enthusiasts flock to Bathurst for the annual 1000 km touring car race on the superb Mt Panorama circuit.

Maryborough Golden Wattle Festival - Vic. An annual event featuring literary events, music, the national gumleaf blowing and bird call championships and street parades.

Melbourne Spoleto Festival - Vic. An annual festival offering the best of opera, theatre, dance and the visual arts from around Australia and the world.

Royal Adelaide Show - SA. One of the oldest royal shows in the country, with major agricultural and horticultural exhibits and entertainment.

October

Oktoberfests Traditional beerfests with food, plenty of beer and live entertainment for all ages are held all over the country including Darwin, Alice Springs and Melbourne.

Henley-on-Todd Regatta - NT. A series of races for leg-powered bottomless boats on the dry Todd River.

McLaren Vale Bushing Festival - SA. New vintage wine releases are celebrated throughout the district.

Royal Shows - Tas. The royal agricultural and horticultural shows of Hobart and Launceston are held this month.

Tallangatta Arts Festival - Vic. This is nine days of arts, crafts, drama, concerts, cultural exchanges, street parades and fetes.

Rich River Festival - Vic. A celebration of the history of Echuca and the part played in the development of the region by the mighty Murray River. There are 10 days of fairs, markets, food and wine, fireworks and the great Paddle-Steamer Race.

Mildura Bottlebrush Festival & Jazz Jamboree - Vic. This features an art exhibition, the Mildura Show and top Australian jazz musicians.

Maldon Spring Folk Festival - Vic. The charming historic town of Maldon provides a great setting for plenty of music and fun.

Mansfield Mountain Country Festival - Vic. A five day celebration (from October to November) of the fine tradition of horsemanship for which Mansfield and the high country men and women are justly famous. It features the Great Mountain Race which pits the country's best brumbies and riders against wild mountain rivers, bush spurs and flats. There are also dances, music and tea parties.

King of the Mountain Festival - Vic. The feature of a weekend's varied entertainment is the running of Australia's toughest foot race, the King of the Mountain, where contestants carry a 63½ kg bag of wheat for a km up the 43 metre high Mt Wycheproof.

November

Melbourne Cup - Vic. On the first Tuesday in November Australia's premier horse race is run at Flemington Race Course. It's a public holiday in Victoria but the whole country shuts down for the three minutes or so when the race is on.

Australian Formula 1 Grand Prix - SA. This premier motor race takes place on a circuit around the streets and parklands of Adelaide. There are also festive events, concerts and street parties.

Castlemaine State Festival - Vic. Held every even-numbered year, this nationally acclaimed festival features local and national concerts, plays, operas, films and exhibitions.

December to January

These are the busiest summer months with Christmas, school holidays, lots of beach activities, rock and jazz festivals, international sporting events including tennis and cricket, a whole host of outdoor activities and lots of parties.

Sydney to Hobart Yacht Race Sydney Harbour is a sight to behold on Boxing Day, 26 December, when boats of all shapes and sizes crowd its waters to farewell the yachts competing in this gruelling race. It's a fantastic sight as the yachts stream out of the harbour and head south. In Hobart there's a Mardi Gras to celebrate the finish of the race.

SPORT

If you're an armchair – or wooden bench – sportsman Australia has plenty to offer. Australians plays at least four types of football, each type being called 'football' by its aficionados. The season runs from about March to September.

Soccer is a bit of a poor cousin; it's widely played on an amateur basis but the national league is only semi-professional and attracts a pathetically small following. It's slowly gaining popularity thanks in part to the surprising success of the national team.

Rugby is the main game in New South Wales and Queensland, and it's rugby league, the 13-a-side working class version, that attracts the crowds. The Winfield Cup competition produces the world's best rugby league – fast, fit and clever. Most of its teams are in Sydney but there are others in Canberra, Wollongong, Newcastle and Brisbane and on the Gold Coast. Rugby union, the 15-a-side game for amateurs, is less popular, usually only making the headlines during international competitions.

Aussie rules is unique – only Gaelic football is anything like it. It's played by teams of 18 on an oval field with an oval ball that can be kicked, caught, hit with the hand and carried and bounced. You get six points for kicking the ball between two central posts (a goal) and one point for kicking it through side posts (a behind). A game lasts for four quarters of 25 minutes each. To take a 'mark' a player must catch a ball on the volley from a kick – in which case the player gets a free kick. A typical final score for one team is between 70 and 110.

Melbourne is the national (and world) centre for Australian Rules and the Victorian Football League (VFL) is the premier competition. Ten of its 14 teams are from Melbourne; the others are from Geelong, Perth, Sydney and Brisbane. Adelaide is also a stronghold of Aussie Rules but it's nowhere near as big-time there as it is in Melbourne, where crowds regularly exceed 30,000 at top regular games and 70,000 at finals.

Australian rules is a great game to get to know. Fast, tactical, skilful, rough and athletic, it can produce gripping finishes when even after 100 minutes of play the outcome hangs on the very last kick. It also inspires fierce spectator loyalties and has made otherwise obscure Melbourne suburbs (Hawthorn, Essendon, Collingwood, etc) national names.

The other (non-football) half of the year there's cricket. The Melbourne Cricket Ground (MCG) is the world's biggest, and international Test and one day matches are played virtually every summer there and in Sydney, Adelaide, Perth and Brisbane. There are also interstate competitions and numerous local grades. Basketball too is growing in popularity as a spectator sport since the recent formation of a national league. And surfing competitions such as that held each year at Bells Beach, Victoria, are of international standard.

Australia loves a gamble, and hardly any town of even minor import is without a horse racing track or a TAB betting office. Melbourne and Adelaide must be amongst the only cities in the world to give public holidays for horse races. The prestigious Melbourne Cup is held on the first Tuesday in November.

There's also yacht racing, some good tennis and golf. The Australian formula 1 Grand Prix is held in Adelaide each November, and in April 1989, for the first time, an international 500cc motorcycle grand prix was held on Phillip Island, near Melbourne.

LANGUAGE

Any visitor from abroad who thinks Australian (that's 'strine') is simply a weird variant of English/American will soon have a few surprises. For a start many Australians don't even speak Australian – they speak Italian, Lebanese, Turkish or Greek (Melbourne is said to be the third largest Greek city in the world). Then those who do speak the native tongue are liable to lose you in a strange collection of unique Australian words – words with completely different meanings in Australia than they have in English-speaking countries north of the equator or commonly used words that have been shortened almost beyond recognition.

There is a slight regional variation in the Australian accent, while the difference between city and country speech is mainly a matter of speed. Some of the most famed Aussie words are hardly heard at all – 'mates' are more common than 'cobbers'. If you want to pass for a native try speaking slightly nasally, shortening any word of more than two syllables and then adding a vowel to the end of it, making anything you can into a diminutive (even the Hell's Angels can become mere 'bikies') and peppering your speech with as many insults as possible. The brief list that follows may help:

abo – Aborigine (usually derogatory)
amber fluid – beer
am I ever – yes I really am
arvo – afternoon
ASIO – Aussie CIA
avagoyermug – traditional rallying call, especially at cricket matches
award wage – minimum pay rate

back o' Bourke – back of beyond, middle of nowhere
bail up – hold up, rob, earbash
banana bender – Queenslander
barbie – barbecue (bbq)
barrack – cheer on team at sporting event
battler – hard trier, struggler
beaut, beauty, bewdie – great, fantastic
beg yours – I beg your pardon
ring, tingle (give someone a) – phone someone up
bible basher – religious fanatic
bikies – motorcyclists
billabong – water hole in dried up riverbed, more correctly an ox bow bend

cut off in the dry season by receding waters
billy – tin container used to boil tea in the bush
bitumen road – surfaced road
black stump – where the 'back o' Bourke' begins
blowies – blow flies
bludger – lazy person, one who won't work
blue (ie have a blue) – to have an argument or fight
bluey – swag
boomer – very big, a particularly large male kangaroo
booze bus – police van used for random breath testing
bonzer – great, ripper
bottle shop – liquor shop
Buckley's – no chance at all
bug (Moreton Bay Bug) – a small yabby
Bulamakanka – place even beyond the back o' Bourke, way beyond the black stump
bull dust – fine dust on outback roads, also bullshit
bunyip – Australia's yeti or bigfoot
bush – country, anywhere away from the city
bush (ie go bush) – go back to the land
bushranger – Australia's equivalent of the outlaws of the American Wild West (some goodies, some baddies).
BYO – Bring Your Own (booze) to a restaurant

caaarn – come on, traditional rallying call, especially at football games, as in 'Caaarn the Blues!'
Captain Cook (ie have a Captain Cook) – look
Chiko roll – vile Australian junk food
chook – chicken
chunder – vomit, technicolour yawn, platform pizza, curbside quiche
cobber – mate
cocky – farmer
come good – turn out all right
compo – compensation such as workers' compensation

TIMOR

SEA

INDIAN

OCEAN

Melville
Island

Bathurst Island

Darwin

Daly River

Kath

Wyndham   Kununurra

Lake Argyle

THE
KIMBERLEY

Derby

Ord R.

Victoria R.

Broome

Fitzroy River

Halls
Creek

Tennant C

Port Hedland

Dampier

Marble Bar

GREAT

SANDY

DESERT

NORTHER

Onslow

THE

Fortescue River

Exmouth

PILBARA

Ashburton R.

Tom
Price

Lake
Disappointment

Lake Mackay

GIBSON

DESERT

Lake
Amadeus

Tropic of Capricorn

WESTERN AUSTRALIA

Ayers
Rock

Carnarvon

Gascoyne River

River

Murchison R.

Shark Bay

Denham

Meekatharra

Lake
Carnegie

SOUTH

Geraldton

Lake Barlee

GREAT

VICTORIA

Coober

DESERT

NULLARBOR   PLAIN

Kalgoorlie

Cocklebiddy

Pen

Swan R.

Perth

Norseman

Fremantle

Esperance

GREAT

Bunbury

AUSTRALIAN

Albany

BIGHT

lp

SOUTHERN   OCE

AUSTRALIA

0   250   500 km

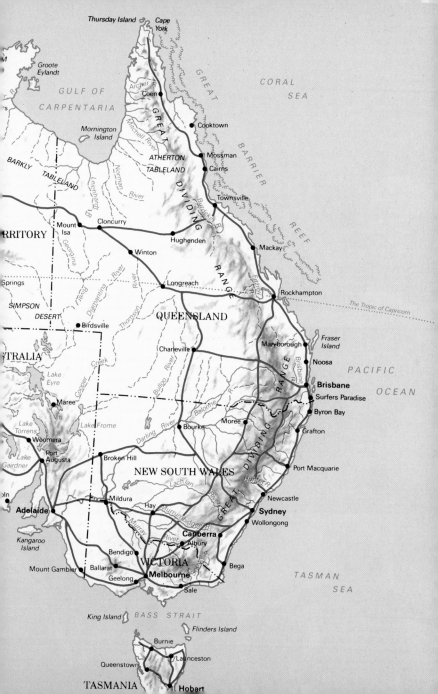

cooee – bush greeting, signal that you are lost

cow cockie – small-scale cattle farmer

crook – ill, badly made, substandard

cut lunch – sandwiches

dag, daggy – dirty lump of wool at back end of a sheep, also a mildly abusive term for a nerd, a square or a socially inept person

daks – trousers

damper – bush loaf made from flour and water

deli – delicatessen, milk bar in South Australia

dill – idiot

dinkum, fair dinkum – honest, genuine

dinky-di – the real thing

divvy van – police divisional van

donk – car engine

don't come the raw prawn – don't try and fool me

drongo – worthless person

duco – car paint

dunny – outhouse

dunny budgies – blowies

earbash – talk nonstop

fair go! – give us a break

fair crack of the whip! – fair go!

fall pregnant – become pregnant

financial (ie to be) – to be OK for $$

fire plug – fire hydrant

FJ – most revered Holden car

flake – shark meat, used in fish & chips

floater – meat pie floating in pea soup – yuk

fossicking – hunting for gems or semiprecious stones

galah – noisy parrot, thus noisy idiot

garbo – person who collects your garbage

gibber – stony desert

give it away – give up

g'day – good day, traditional Australian greeting

good on yer – well done

grazier – large-scale sheep or cattle farmer

hoon – idiot, hooligan

hump – to carry, as in 'hump your bluey'

icy-pole – frozen lolly water or ice cream on a stick

journo – journalist

king hit – knockout blow, especially an unfair one

kiwi – New Zealander

knock – criticise, deride

knocker – one who knocks

lair – layabout, ruffian

lairising – acting like a lair

lamington – square of sponge cake covered in chocolate icing and coconut

larrikin – a bit like a lair

lay-by – put a deposit on an article so the shop will hold it for you

lollies – sweets, candy

lolly water – soft drink

lurk – a scheme

loo – a toilet

manchester – household linen

middy – medium beer glass

milk bar – corner shop

milko – milkman

mozzies – mosquitoes

never-never – remote country in the outback

new Australian – recent immigrant

no hoper – hopeless case, ne'er do well

northern summer – summer in the northern hemisphere

no worries – she'll be right

ocker – an uncultivated or boorish Australian

off-sider – assistant or partner

OS – overseas, as in 'he's gone OS'

outback – remote part of the bush, back o' Bourke

OYO – own your own (flat or apartment)

Oz – Australia

pastoralist – large-scale grazier

pavlova – traditional Australian meringue and cream dessert, named after Anna Pavola

pineapple (rough end of) – stick (sharp end of)

pissed – drunk

pissed off – annoyed

piss turn – boozy party

pom – English person

poofter, poof – derogatory term for a male homosexual

postie – mailman

pot – large mug of beer (Victoria)

push – gang of larrikins

ratbag – friendly term of abuse

ratshit – lousy

rapt – delighted, enraptured

reckon! – you bet!, absolutely!

rego – registration, as in 'car rego'

ripper – good (also 'little ripper')

road train – semi-trailer-trailer-trailer

root – have sexual intercourse

ropable – very bad-tempered or angry

rubbish (ie to rubbish) – deride, tease

salvo – member of the Salvation Army

school – group of drinkers

schooner – large beer glass

scuse I – excuse me

sealed (road) – surfaced road

sea wasp – deadly box jellyfish

semi-trailer – articulated truck

she'll be right – no worries

shoot through – leave in a hurry

shout – buy round of drinks (as in 'it's your shout')

sickie – day off work ill

smoke-o – tea break

spunky – good looking, attractive (as in 'what a spunk')

squatter – pioneer farmer who didn't bother about buying or leasing his land from the government

squattocracy – Australian 'old money' folk, who made it by being first on the scene and grabbing the land

station – large farm

stickybeak – nosy person

strides – daks

strine – Australian slang

sunbake – sunbathe (well, the sun's hot in Australia)

surfies – surfboard riders

swag – gear, possessions

tall poppies – achievers, (knockers like to cut them down)

tea – evening meal

thingo – thing, whatchamacallit, hooza meebob, doo velacki, thingamejig

tinny – can of beer

too right! – absolutely!

true blue – dinkum

tucker – food

two pot screamers – people unable to hold their drink

two-up – traditional heads/tails gambling game

uni – university

ute – utility, pickup truck

wag (ie to wag) – to skip school

walkabout – lengthy walk away from it all

wet (ie the wet) – rainy season in the north

wharfie – docker

whinge – complain, moan

whingeing pom – the worst sort of pom

woolgrower – sheep farmer

wowser – spoilsport, puritan

wobbly – disturbing, unpredictable behaviour (as in throw a wobbly)

yabby – small freshwater crayfish

yahoo – noisy, unruly person

yakka – work

youse – plural of you

yobbo – uncouth, aggressive person

Aboriginal Expressions

boomerang – a curved flat wooden instrument used for hunting

didgeridoo – tube-like musical instrument

Koori – Aborigine

nulla-nulla – wooden club

woomera – stick used for throwing spears

Facts for the Visitor

VISAS & IMMIGRATION

Once upon a time, Australia was fairly free and easy about who was allowed to visit the country, particularly if you were from Britain or Canada. These days, only New Zealanders get any sort of preferential treatment and even they need at least a passport. Everybody else has to have a visa. Visas are issued by Australian consular offices abroad; they are free and valid for a stay of *up to* six months. That is, you can say you want to stay for six months and if they like the look of you the immigration official can give you six months. If they don't you might end up with two weeks.

As well as the visa, visitors are also required to have an onward or return ticket and 'sufficient funds' – the latter is obviously open to interpretation. Like those from any country, Australian visas seem to cause their hassles, although the authorities do seem to be more uniform in their approach these days. Nevertheless if you're kicking around Asia and take a fancy to dropping down to Oz for a spell the travellers' grapevine will doubtless have handy hints about where the best place is to get a visa.

Visa extensions are made through Department of Immigration offices in Australia and there's a $50 application fee. That's a fee simply for applying – if they turn down your application they can still keep your 50 bucks! Some offices, like the one in Sydney, can be very thorough, requiring things like bank statements and interviews. Extending visas has always been a notoriously slow process and Australia's tourist boom has certainly not made it any easier. If you do end up overstaying your visa the fact that you did your damnedest to get the bureaucrats to extend it should stand in your stead.

Young visitors from certain countries – Britain, Ireland, Canada, Holland and Japan – may be eligible for a 'working holiday' visa. Young is fairly loosely interpreted as around 18 to 26 and working holiday means up to 12 months, but the emphasis is supposed to be on casual employment rather than a full-time job.

Officially this visa can only be applied for in your home country but some travellers report the rule can be bent.

Although Australia doesn't have any borders with other countries, we still manage to get plenty of illegal immigrants. Twice since the early '70s the government has granted an amnesty for illegal immigrants; if they had been in the country for at least six months and were otherwise acceptable they could stay. On both occasions the number of illegal immigrants who stepped forward was highly surprising. If you're trying to stay more permanently in Australia the book *Tourist to Permanent Resident in Australia* might be useful.

Embassies

Australian consular offices overseas include:

Canada
   Australian High Commission, Suite 710, 50 O'Connor St, Ottawa K1P 5H6 (tel (613) 236 0841)
   also in Toronto and Vancouver
Denmark
   Australian Embassy, Kristianagade 21, 2100 Copenhagen (tel 26 2244)
Greece
   Australian Embassy, 37 Dimitriou Soutsou St, Ambelokpi, Athens (tel 644 7303)
Hong Kong
   Australian High Commission, Harbour Centre No 27, 24th floor, 25 Harbour Rd, Wanchai, Hong Kong (tel 5 731881)
India
   Australian High Commission, Australian

Compound, No 1/50-G Shantipath, Chanakyapuri, New Delhi (tel 60 1336)

Indonesia
Australian Embassy, Jalan Thamrin 15, Jakarta (tel 323109)
also in Denpasar

Ireland
Australian Embassy, Fitzwilton House, Wilton Terrace, Dublin 2 (tel 76 1517/9)

Italy
Australian Embassy, Via Alessandria 215, Rome 00198 (tel 832 721)
also in Milan and Messina

Japan
Australian Embassy, No 1-12 Shibakoen 1 Chome, Minato-ku, Tokyo (tel 435 0971)
also in Osaka

Malaysia
Australian High Commission, 6 Jalan Yap Kwan Seng, Kuala Lumpur (tel 242 3122)

Netherlands
Australian Embassy, Koninginnegracht 23, 2514 AB The Hague (tel (070) 63 0983)

New Zealand
Australian High Commission, 72-78 Hobson St, Thorndon, Wellington (tel 73 6411/2)
also in Auckland

Papua New Guinea
Australian High Commission, Waigani, Hohola (tel 25 9333)

Philippines
Australian Embassy, China Bank Building, Paseo de Roxas, Makati (tel 81 77911)

Singapore
Australian High Commission, 25 Napier Rd, Singapore 10 (tel 737 9311)

Sweden
Australian Embassy, Sergels Torg 12, Stockholm C, S-101 86 Stockholm (tel 24-46-60)

Switzerland
Australian Embassy, 29 Alpenstrasse, Berne (tel 43 01 43)
also in Geneva

Thailand
Australian Embassy, 37 South Sathorn Rd, Bangkok 12 (tel 287 2680)

UK
Australian High Commission, Australia House, The Strand, London WC2B 4LA (tel (01) 379 4334)
also in Edinburgh and Manchester

USA
Australian Embassy, 1601 Massachusetts Avenue NW, Washington DC, 20036 (tel (202) 797 3000)
also in Los Angeles, Chicago, Honolulu, New York and San Francisco.

West Germany
Australian Embassy, Godesberger Allee 107, 5300 Bonn 2 (tel 02221 376941-7)

Working in Australia

Officially, working in Australia is completely *verboten* on a regular tourist visa, but visitors do sometimes find jobs. There are no social security cards, national insurance cards or the like in Australia *yet*.

The book *Work Your Way Around the World* by Susan Griffiths (Vacation Work, England, or Writers Digest, USA) is a good information source on short-term jobs in many countries. In Australia the newspaper *The Land* is worth checking for jobs on the land. The various backpackers hostels are good information sources – some local employers even advertise on their notice boards.

Fruit picking is one of the best known short-term job prospects. Travellers also sometimes find work at the resorts, particularly along the Barrier Reef. Getting a foot in the door is often difficult and the island resorts tend to work on the NBO (next boat out) principle, sacking excess staff as soon as times go slack, taking more in the school holidays.

CUSTOMS

For visitors from abroad the usual sort of '200 cigarettes, one bottle of whisky' regulations apply to Australia, but there are two areas you should be very careful about. Number one is, of course, dope – Australian customs have a positive mania about the stuff and can be extremely efficient when it comes to finding it. Unless you want to make first-hand investigations of conditions in Australian jails (not very good), don't bring any with you. This particularly applies if you are arriving from Indonesia or South-East Asia. You will be the subject of suspicion!

Problem two is animal and plant quarantine; the authorities are naturally keen to prevent weeds, pests or diseases getting into the country – with all the sheep in Australia, that scruffy Afghani sheepskin coat over your arm is not going to be popular. Fresh food is also unpopular, particularly meat, sausages, fruit, vegetables and flowers. There are also restrictions on taking fruit or vegetables between states.

When it is time to split there are duty free stores at the international airports and their associated cities. Treat them with healthy suspicion. 'Duty Free' is one of the world's most overworked catch phrases and it is often just an excuse to sell things at prices you can easily beat by a little shopping around. Discount film shops in big cities always have film at far cheaper prices than airport duty free shops, for example. City duty free shops are generally cheaper than airport ones.

MONEY

Australia's currency is good, old-fashioned dollars and cents. When they changed over from pounds, shillings and pence there was consideration of calling the new unit the 'royal'; however that foolish idea soon got the chop. There are coins for 1c, 2c, 5c, 10c, 20c, 50c, $1 and $2, and notes for $5, $10, $20, $50 and $100.

US dollars	US$1	= A$1.34
New Zealand dollars	NZ$1	= A$0.76
pounds sterling	£1	= A$2.16
Singapore dollars	S$1	= A$0.68
Hong Kong dollars	HK$1	= A$0.17
Japanese yen	Y100	= A$0.93
Deutsche marks	DM 1	= A$0.69
Dutch guilders	fl 1	= A$0.62
Canadian dollars	C$1	= A$1.12

There are no notable restrictions on importing or exporting currency or travellers' cheques except that you may not take out more than A$5000 in Australian currency except with prior approval.

There is a variety of ways to carry your money around Australia with you. If your stay is limited then travellers' cheques are the most straightforward and they generally enjoy a better exchange rate than foreign cash in Australia. Changing foreign currency or travellers' cheques is no problem at almost any bank. It's done quickly and efficiently and never involves the sort of headaches and grand production that changing foreign currency in the US always entails. American Express, Thomas Cook and other well known international brands of travellers' cheques are all widely used in Australia.

Commissions and fees for changing foreign travellers' cheques seem to vary from bank to bank and year to year. At present Commonwealth banks make no charge, Westpac charge $2, National charge $5 at most (but not all) of their branches, ANZ is the worst place to change travellers' cheques as they charge 1% of the amount converted with a minimum charge of $5. So unless the story has changed the best advice is to change foreign cheques (US dollars, pounds sterling, etc) at Commonwealth or Westpac branches and to avoid National or ANZ branches particularly for very small amounts ($5 on a £10 sterling or US$20 travellers' cheque would really hurt).

If you're planning to stay longer than just a month or so, it's worth considering other ways of handling money that give you more flexibility and are more economical. This applies equally to Australians setting off to travel around the country. With travellers' cheques it is obviously easiest to travel with Australian dollar travellers' cheques as these can be exchanged immediately at the bank cashier's window without having to have them converted from a foreign currency or getting hit for commissions, fees and exchange rate losses.

One of the neatest solutions is to open a passbook savings account. All the banks operate these systems and with your passbook you can withdraw money from any branch of the bank in question in the country. There are limitations as to how much you can pull out in one hit but it's quite reasonable. This way, instead of paying to buy travellers' cheques, you actually get paid for having your money on deposit.

Probably the best bank for the traveller to be with is the Commonwealth Savings Bank. This is a government-owned bank with branches all around the country, as well as in almost every post office. So finding a place to withdraw money is no problem at all and the hours are also longer than normal banking hours. If the branch has 'black light' signature identification facilities you can withdraw any amount of money at any branch.

Credit cards are widely accepted in Australia and are an alternative to carrying large numbers of travellers'

cheques. The most common credit card, however, is the purely Australian Bankcard system. Visa, Mastercard, Diners Club and American Express are widely accepted but mainly in the ritzier places. If you're planning to rent cars while travelling around Australia, a credit card makes life much simpler; they're looked upon with much greater favour by rent-a-car agencies than nasty old cash.

Another possibility for those with an Australian bank account is to use a cash card, with which you can get cash from automatic banking machines now found all over Australia. You put your card in the machine, key in your number and can then withdraw up to $200 a day from your account. Bankcard can also be used to draw cash from a bank but in that case you are charged interest until you pay it back. Westpac, ANZ, National and Commonwealth branches are found nationwide.

COSTS

In comparison to the USA, Canada and European countries, Australia is cheaper in some respects and more expensive in others. Manufactured goods tend to be more expensive because they're either imported and have all the additional costs of transport and duties or, if they're locally manufactured, they suffer from the extra costs entailed in making things in comparatively small quantities. Thus you pay more for clothes, cars and other manufactured items. On the other hand, food is both high quality and low in cost.

In restaurants what you see is what you get – there are no service charges, no sales or value-added taxes.

TIPPING

In Australia tipping isn't a habit the way it is in the US or Europe. It's only customary to tip in more expensive restaurants and only then if you want to. If the service has been especially good and you decide to leave a tip, 10% of the bill is the usual amount. Taxi drivers don't expect tips (of course, they don't hurl it back at you if you decide to leave the change). In contrast, just try getting out of a New York cab, or even a London one, without leaving your 10 to 15%. In fact Australian taxi drivers will often round fares down – if it comes to $8.10 you're quite likely to be told 'make it eight bucks, mate.'

TOURIST INFORMATION

There are a number of information sources for visitors to Australia and, in common with a number of other tourist-conscious western countries, you can easily drown yourself in brochures and booklets, maps and leaflets.

Local Tourist Offices

Within Australia, tourist information is handled by the various state and local offices. Each state and the ACT and Northern Territory have a tourist office of some form and you will find information about these centres in the various state sections. Apart from a main office in the capital cities, they often have regional offices in main tourist centres and also in other states. As well as supplying brochures, price lists, maps and other information, the state tourist offices will often book transport, tours and accommodation for you. Unfortunately, very few of the state tourist offices maintain information desks at the airports and, furthermore, the opening hours of the city offices are very much of the 9 to 5 weekdays and Saturday morning only variety. Addresses of the state tourist offices are:

Australian Capital Territory
    Canberra Tourist Bureau, Jolimont Centre, Northbourne Ave, Canberra City, ACT 2601
New South Wales
    Travel Centre of NSW, corner Pitt and Spring Sts, Sydney, NSW 2000
Northern Territory
    Northern Territory Government Tourist Bureau, 31 Smith St, Darwin, NT 0800
Queensland
    Queensland Government Tourist Bureau, corner Adelaide and Edward Sts, Brisbane, Qld 4000
South Australia
    South Australian Government Travel Centre, 18 King William St, Adelaide, SA 5000
Tasmania
    Tasmanian Travel Centre, 80 Elizabeth St, Hobart, Tas 7000
Victoria
    Victorian Government Travel Centre, 230 Collins St, Melbourne, Vic 3000
Western Australia
    Western Australian Government Travel Centre, 772 Hay St, Perth, WA 6000

A step down from the state tourist offices are the local or regional tourist offices. Almost every town in Australia seems to maintain a tourist office or centre of some type or other and in many cases these are really excellent, with much local information not readily available from the larger, state offices. This particularly applies where there is a strong local tourist trade.

Overseas Reps

The Australian Tourist Commission is the government body intended to inform potential visitors about the country. There's a very definite split between promotion outside Australia and inside it. The ATC is strictly an external operator; they do minimal promotion within the country and have little contact with visitors to Australia. Within the country, tourist promotion is handled by state or local tourist offices.

ATC offices overseas have a useful free booklet that is a good introduction to the country, its geography, flora, fauna, states, transport, accommodation, food and so on. They also have a useful free map of the country. This literature is intended for distribution overseas only; if you want copies, get them before you come to Australia. Addresses of the ATC offices for literature requests are:

Australia
    GPO Box 2721, Sydney, NSW 2001 (tel (02) 360 1111)
Canada
    Suite 1730, 2 Bloor St West, Toronto, Ontario M4W 3E2 (tel (416) 925 9575)
Hong Kong
    Suite 604-605, Sun Plaza, 28 Canton Rd, Tsimshatsui, Kowloon (tel (3) 311 1555)
Japan
    8th floor, Sankaido Building, 9-13, Akasaka 1-chome, Minato-ku, Tokyo 107 (tel (03) 582 2191)
    4th floor, Yuki Building, 3-3-9 Hiranomachi, Chuo-Ku, Osaka 541 (tel (06) 22 3601)
New Zealand
    15th Floor, Quay Tower, 29 Customs St West, Auckland 1 (tel (09) 79 9594)
Singapore
    Suite 1703, United Square, 101 Thomson Rd, Singapore 1130 (tel 255 4555)
UK
    4th Floor, 20 Saville Row, London W1X 1AE (tel (01) 734 1965)
USA
    Suite 2130, 150 North Michigan Ave, Chicago, IL 60601 (tel (312) 781 5150)
    Suite 1200, 2121 Avenue of the Stars, Los Angeles, CA 90067 (tel (213) 552 1988)
    31st floor, 489 Fifth Ave, New York, NY 10017 (tel (212) 687 6300)
West Germany
    Neue Mainzer Strasse 22, D6000 Frankfurt-Main 1 (tel (069) 23 5071)

Foreign Embassies & Consulates

The principal diplomatic representations to Australia are in Canberra and you'll find a list of the addresses of relevant offices in the Canberra section. There are also representatives in various other major cities, particularly from countries with major connections with Australia like the USA, UK or New Zealand; or in cities with important connections, like Darwin which has an Indonesian consulate. Big cities like Sydney and Melbourne have nearly as many consular offices as Canberra. Look up addresses in the yellow pages phone book under 'Consulates & Legations'.

Automobile Associations

Australia has a national automobile association, the Australian Automobile Association, but this exists mainly as an umbrella organisation for the various state associations and to maintain international links. The day-to-day operations are all handled by the state organisations who provide an emergency breakdown service, literature, excellent maps and detailed guides to accommodation and campsites.

The state organisations have reciprocal arrangements amongst the various states in Australia and with the equivalent organisations overseas. So, if you're a member of the NRMA in NSW, you can use RACV facilities in Victoria. Similarly, if you're a member of the AAA in the USA or the RAC or AA in the UK, you can use any of the state organisations' facilities. But bring proof of membership with you. More details about the state automobile organisations can be found in the relevant state sections. Some of the material they produce is of a very high standard, in particular there is a superb set of regional maps to Queensland produced by the RACQ. The most useful state offices are:

New South Wales
  National Roads & Motorists Association (NRMA), 151 Clarence St, Sydney, NSW 2000
Northern Territory
  Automobile Association of the Northern Territory, 79-81 Smith St, Darwin, NT 0800
Queensland
  Royal Automobile Club of Queensland (RACQ), 300 St Pauls Terrace, Fortitude Valley, Qld 4006
South Australia
  Royal Automobile Association of South Australia (RAA), 41 Hindmarsh Square, Adelaide, SA 5000
Tasmania
  Royal Automobile Club of Tasmania (RACT), corner Patrick and Murray Sts, Hobart, Tas 7000
Victoria
  Royal Automobile Club of Victoria (RACV), 422 Little Collins St, Melbourne, Vic 3000
Western Australia
  Royal Automobile Club of Western Australia (RAC), 228 Adelaide Terrace, Perth, WA 6000

English Language Schools

If English isn't your first language and you've come to Australia to learn it, colleges specialising in teaching English include:

Australian College of English, 20th floor, Bondi Junction Plaza Building, 500 Oxford St, Bondi Junction, NSW 2022 (tel (02) 389 0133)

Milner International College of English, 195 Adelaide Terrace, Perth, WA 6000 (tel (09) 325 5708)

The English Teaching Laboratory, 113-115 Oxford St, Sydney, NSW 2010 (tel (02) 331 4589)

The International College of English, 226 Flinders Lane, Melbourne, Vic 3000 (tel (03) 650 1700)

National Park Organisations

Australia has an extensive collection of national parks, in fact, the Royal National Park just outside Sydney is the second oldest national park in the world. Only Yellowstone Park in the USA predates it. The National Park organisations in each state are state operated, not nationally run. They tend to be a little hidden away in their capital city locations, although, if you search them out, they often have excellent literature and maps on the parks. They are much more up front in the actual parks where, in many cases, they have very good guides and leaflets to bushwalking, nature trails and other activities. The state offices are:

Australian Capital Territory
  Parks & Conservation, PO Box 158, Canberra, ACT 2601
  Australian National Parks & Wildlife Service, 3rd floor, Construction House, Turner, ACT 2601 (PO Box 636, Canberra City, ACT 2601)
New South Wales
  National Parks & Wildlife Service, 43 Bridge St, Hurstville, NSW 2220 (PO Box 1967, Hurstville, NSW 2220)
Northern Territory
  Conservation Commission of the Northern Territory, PO Box 1046, Alice Springs, NT 0800
  Australian National Parks & Wildlife Service, Commercial Union Building, Smith St, Darwin, NT 0800 (for Kakadu and Uluru National Parks)
Queensland
  National Parks & Wildlife Service, 160 Ann St, Brisbane, Qld 4000 (PO Box 155, North Quay, Qld 4002)
South Australia
  National Parks & Wildlife Service, Insurance Building, 55 Grenfell St, Adelaide, SA 5061 (GPO Box 667, Adelaide, SA 5001)
Tasmania
  Department of Lands, Parks & Wildlife, 134 Macquarie St, Hobart, Tas 7000 (PO Box 44A, Hobart 7001)
Victoria
  National Parks Service, 240 Victoria Parade, East Melbourne, Vic 3002 (PO Box 41)
Western Australia
  National Parks Authority, Hackett Drive, Crawley, WA 6009

Australian Conservation Foundation

The Australian Conservation Foundation is the largest non-government organisation involved in conservation. Only nine to 10% of its income is from the government; the rest comes from memberships and subscriptions, and from donations (72%, which are mainly from individuals.

The ACF covers a wide range of issues, including the Greenhouse effect and depletion of the ozone layer, the negative effects of logging, preservation of rainforests, the problems of land degradation, and protection of the Antarctic. They frequently work in conjunction with the Wilderness Society and other conservation groups.

With the growing focus on conservation issues and the increasing concern of the Australian public in regard to their environment, the conservation vote has now become increasingly important to all political parties.

The Wilderness Society

The Tasmanian Wilderness Society was formed by conservationists who had been unsuccessful in preventing the damming of Lake Pedder in South West Tasmania but who were determined to prevent the destruction of the Franklin River. The Franklin River campaign was one of Australia's first major conservation confrontations and it caught the attention of the international media. In 1983, after the high court decided against the damming of the Franklin, the group changed its name to the Wilderness Society because of their Australia-wide focus on wilderness issues.

The Wilderness Society is involved in issues concerning protection of the Australian wilderness, including forest management and logging. Like the ACF, government funding is only a small percentage of their income, the rest coming from memberships, donations, the shops and merchandising. There are Wilderness Shops in all states (not in the Northern Territory) where you can buy books, T-shirts, posters, badges, etc.

National Trust

The National Trust is dedicated to preserving historic buildings in all parts of Australia. They actually own a number of buildings throughout the country which are open to the public. Many other buildings are 'classified' by the National Trust to ensure their preservation.

The National Trust also produces some excellent literature, including a fine series of walking-tour guides to many cities around the country, large and small. These guides are often available from local tourist offices or from National Trust offices and are usually free whether you're a member of the National Trust or not. Membership of the trust is well worth considering, however, because it entitles you to free entry to any National Trust property for your year of membership. If you're a dedicated visitor of old buildings this could soon pay for itself. Annual membership costs $33 for individuals, $44 for families and includes the monthly or quarterly magazine put out by the state organisation that you join. Addresses of the various National Trust state offices are:

Australian Capital Territory
  6 Geils Court, Deakin, ACT 2600 (PO Box 3173, Manuka, ACT 2603) 2600
New South Wales
  Observatory Hill, Sydney, NSW 2000
Northern Territory
  14 Knuckey St, Darwin, NT 0800 (GPO Box 3520)
Queensland
  Old Government House, George St, Brisbane, Qld 4000 (GPO Box 1494)
South Australia
  Ayers House, 288 North Terrace, Adelaide, SA 5000
Tasmania
  25 Kirksway Place, Hobart, Tas 7000
Victoria
  Tasma Terrace, Parliament Place, Melbourne, Vic 3002
Western Australia
  Old Perth Boys School, 139 St Georges Terrace, Perth, WA 6000

GENERAL INFORMATION
Post

Australia's postal services are relatively efficient but not too cheap.

It costs 41c to send a standard letter or postcard within Australia, while aerogrammes cost 60c.

Air-mail letters/postcards cost 65/55c to New Zealand, 70/65c to Singapore and Malaysia, 80/70c to Hong Kong and India, $1.00/75c to the USA and Canada, and $1.10/80c to Europe and the UK.

Post offices are open from 9 am to 5 pm Monday to Friday, but you can often get stamps from local post offices operated from newsagencies or shops on Saturday mornings.

All post offices will hold mail for visitors and some city GPOs will have very busy poste restantes. Cairns, for example, can get quite hectic. You can also have mail sent to you at the American Express offices in big cities if you have an Amex card or carry Amex travellers' cheques.

Telephones

The Australian phone system (run by the government-owned Telecom) is really remarkably efficient and, equally important, easy to use. Local phone calls all cost 30c for an unlimited amount of time. You can make local calls from red or gold phones – often found in shops, hotels, bars, etc – and from STD phones.

If you want to make a long-distance (trunk) call from a public phone, look for a grey-green STD (Subscriber Trunk Dialling) phone which allows you to dial direct and only pay for the time actually used – there's no three minute minimum as there is on operator-connected calls. Almost all public phones are STD these days. The trick is to have plenty of 20c, 50c and $1 coins and be prepared to feed them through at a fair old rate. You can insert a handful of coins at the beginning and they just drop down as they're used up. When you're about to be cut off, a red light flashes faster and faster and you can either hurriedly insert more coins or simply speak more quickly! If you complete your call before the money is used up the unused coins are returned to you.

STD calls are cheaper at night, in ascending order of cost:

economy – from 6 pm Saturday to 8 am Monday; 10 pm to 8 am every night
night – from 6 to 10 pm Monday to Friday
day – from 8 am to 6 pm Monday to Saturday

From some STD phones you can also make ISD (International Subscriber Dialling) calls just like making STD calls. Dialling ISD you can get through to overseas numbers almost as quickly as you can locally and if your call is brief it needn't cost very much – 'Hi, I'll be on the flight to London next Tuesday' can cost no more than a postcard.

All you do is dial 0011 for overseas, the country code (44 for Britain, 1 for the USA or Canada, 64 for New Zealand), the city code (1 for London, 212 for New York, etc), and then the telephone number. And have plenty of coins to hand. A call to the USA or Britain costs $1.80 a minute ($1.50 off peak), New Zealand is $1.40 a minute ($1.20 off peak). Off-peak times, if available, vary depending on the destination.

Electricity
Voltage is 220-240 volts and the plugs are three pin, but not the same as British three pin plugs. Users of electric shavers or hairdryers should note that, apart from in fancy hotels, it's difficult to find converters to take either American flat two pin plugs or the European round two pin plugs. You can easily bend the American plugs to a slight angle to make them fit, however.

Time
Australia is divided into three time zones: Western Time is +8 hours from Greenwich Mean Time (WA), Central Time is +9½ hours (NT, SA), and Eastern Time is +10 (Tas, Vic, NSW, Qld). When it's 12 noon in Western Australia it's 1.30 pm in the Northern Territory and South Australia and 2 pm in the rest of the country. During

the summer things get slightly screwed up as daylight saving time (when clocks are put forward an hour) does not operate in Western Australia or Queensland.

Business Hours
Although Australians aren't great believers in long opening hours, they are a long way ahead of the Kiwis, thank you! Most shops close at 5 or 5.30 pm weekdays. Recently shops have started opening all day Saturday but many still close at noon. They are closed all day on Sundays. In most towns there are usually one or two late shopping nights each week, when the doors stay open until 9 or 9.30 pm. Usually it's Thursday and/or Friday night.

Banks are open from 9.30 am to 4 pm Monday to Thursday, and until 5 pm on Friday. Some large city branches are open 8 am to 6 pm Monday to Friday. Some are also open to 9 pm on Fridays. Of course there are some exceptions to Australia's unremarkable opening hours and all sorts of places stay open late and all weekend – particularly milk bars, delis and city bookshops.

Weights & Measures
Australia went metric in the early '70s. We buy petrol and milk by the litre, apples and potatoes by the kg, measure distance by the metre or km, and our speed limits are in km per hour. But there's still a degree of confusion; it's hard to think of a six foot guy as being 183 cm.

For those who need help with metric there's a conversion table at the back of this book.

Emergencies

Each capital city has separate emergency numbers to contact police, fire or ambulance. You'll find them on the inside cover of the phone book. If, however, you don't know the phone number dial 000 and you will be asked which service you require.

MEDIA

Australia has a wide range of media although a few big companies (Rupert Murdoch's corporation being the best known) tend to dominate.

Newspapers

Each major city tends to have at least one important daily, often backed up by a tabloid paper and also by evening papers. The *Sydney Morning Herald* and the Melbourne *Age*, are two of the most important dailies. There's also the *Australian*, a Murdoch-owned nationwide daily paper.

Weekly newspapers and magazines include an Australian edition of *Time* and a combined edition of the Australian news magazine the *Bulletin* and *Newsweek*.

Radio & Television

The national advertising-free television and radio network is the ABC. In most places there are a couple of ABC radio stations and a host of commercial stations, both AM and FM, featuring the whole gamut of radio possibilities, from rock to 'beautiful music'. In Sydney and Melbourne there is the ABC, three commercial television stations and a government-sponsored multi-cultural station. Around the country the number of television stations varies from place to place; there are regional TV stations but in some remote areas the ABC may be all you can receive.

HEALTH

So long as you have not visited an infected country in the past 14 days (aircraft refuelling stops do not count) no vaccinations are required for entry. Naturally, if you're going to be travelling around in outlandish places apart from Australia, a good collection of immunisations is highly advisable.

Medical care in Australia is first-class and only moderately expensive. A typical visit to the doctor costs around $20. Health insurance cover is available in Australia, but there is usually a waiting period after you sign up before any claims can be made. If you have an immediate health problem, contact the casualty section at the nearest public hospital.

Travel Insurance

Even if you normally carry health or hospitalisation insurance or live in a country where health care is provided by the government it's still a good idea to buy some inexpensive travellers' insurance that covers both health and loss of baggage.

Make sure the policy includes health care and medication in the countries you plan to visit and includes a flight home for you and anyone you're travelling with, should your condition warrant it.

Medical Kit

It' always a good idea to travel with a basic medical kit even when your destination is a country like Australia where most first aid supplies are readily available. Some of the items that should be included are: Band-Aids, a sterilised gauze bandage, elastoplast, cotton wool, a thermometer, tweezers, scissors, antibiotic cream and ointment, an antiseptic agent, burn cream, insect repellent and multi vitamins.

Don't forget any medication you're already taking, paracetemol or aspirin (for pain and fever) and contraceptives if necessary.

Health Precautions

Travellers from the Northern Hemisphere need to be aware of the intensity of the sun in Australia. Those ultra violets can have you burnt to a crisp even on an overcast day, so wear protective cream. Australia has a high incidence of skin cancer, a fact directly connected to exposure to the sun. Be careful.

The contraceptive pill is available on prescription only, so a visit to a doctor is necessary. Doctors are listed in the yellow pages phone book or you can visit the outpatients section of a public hospital. Condoms are available from chemists, some all night stores such as 7-eleven, and vending machines in the public toilets of hotels and universities.

DANGERS & ANNOYANCES

In Australia there are a few unique and sometimes dangerous creatures. Although it's unlikely that you'll come across any of them, particularly if you stick to the cities, here's a rundown just in case.

The best known danger in the Australian outback, and the one that captures visitors' imaginations, is snakes. Although there are many venomous snakes there are few that are aggressive and unless you have the bad fortune to stand on one it's unlikely that you'll be bitten. Taipans and tiger snakes, however, will attack if alarmed. Sea snakes can also be dangerous. Snake bite is best treated with the immediate application of a pressure bandage and urgent medical attention.

We've got a couple of nasty spiders too, including the funnel web, the redback and the white tail, so it's best not to play with any spider. Funnel web spiders are found in New South Wales and their bite is treated in the same way as snake bite. For redback bites apply ice and seek medical attention.

Up north the saltwater crocodile can be a real danger and has killed a number of people (travellers and locals). They are found in river estuaries and large rivers, so before diving into that inviting, cool water

find out from the locals whether it's croc-free. (For more information see the Flora & Fauna section of the preceding chapter.)

In the sea, the box jellyfish, or sea wasp as it's known, occurs north of Great Keppel Island (see Queensland chapter) during summer and can be fatal. Douse stings with vinegar, remove tentacles and treat as for snake bite. The blue ringed octopus can also be fatal so don't pick them up. Apply pressure bandage, monitor breathing carefully and conduct mouth to mouth resuscitation if breathing stops.

When reef walking you must always wear shoes to protect your feet against coral. In tropical waters there are stonefish – venomous fish that look like a flat piece of rock on the sea bed. Also, watch out for the scorpion fish which has venomous spines.

On the road, cows and kangaroos can be a real hazard. A collision with one will badly damage your car and probably kill the animal. Unfortunately, other drivers are even more dangerous and particularly those who drink. Australia has an appalling road toll, so don't drink and drive and please take care.

Box Jellyfish

FILM & PHOTOGRAPHY

If you come to Australia via Hong Kong or Singapore it's worth buying film there but otherwise Australian film prices are no longer too far out of line with those of the rest of the western world. Including developing, 36-exposure Kodachrome 64 or Fujichrome 100 slide films cost from around $15, but with with a little shopping around you can find it for less than $12 – even less than $11 if you buy it in quantity.

There are plenty of camera shops in all the big cities and standards of camera service are high. Developing standards are also high, with many places now offering one hour developing of print film. Australia is the main centre for developing Kodachrome slide film in the South-East Asian region. Photography is no problem, but in the outback you have to allow for the exceptional intensity of the light. Best results in the outback regions are obtained early in the morning and late in the afternoon. As the sun gets higher, colours appear washed out. You must also allow for the intensity of reflected light when taking shots on the Barrier Reef or at other coastal locations. In the outback, especially in the summer, allow for temperature extremes and do your best to keep film as cool as possible, particularly after exposure. Other film hazards are dust in the outback and humidity in the tropical regions of the far north.

As in any country politeness goes a long way when taking photographs; ask before taking pictures of people. Note that Aborigines generally do not like to have their photographs taken, even from a distance.

ACCOMMODATION

Australia is very well equipped with youth hostels, backpackers hostels and campsites, the cheapest shelter you can find. Furthermore, there are plenty of motels around the country and in holiday regions like the Queensland coast intense competition tends to keep the prices down.

A typical town of a few thousand people will have a basic motel at around $26/34, an old town centre hotel with rooms (shared bathrooms) at say $20/30, and a caravan park – probably with tent sites for around $7 and on-site vans or cabins for $21 to $25 for two. If the town is on anything like a main road or is bigger, it'll probably have several of each. You'll rarely have much trouble finding *somewhere* to lay your head in Oz, even when there are no hostels. If there's a group of you, the rates for three or four people in a room are always worth checking. Often there are larger 'family' rooms or units with two bedrooms.

The state auto clubs produce accommodation directories listing hotels, motels, holiday flats, campgrounds and even some backpackers hostels, in almost every little town in the country. They're updated every year so the prices will generally be fairly current. They're available from the clubs for a nominal charge if you're a member or a member of an affiliated club enjoying reciprocal rights. Alternatively, the state tourist offices also put out frequently updated guides to local accommodation.

At the time of writing, the federal health department was drafting a new set of health regulations for budget accommodation in Australia. Their new regulations take effect from October 1989 and no doubt will affect many hostels. Hostels will have to meet the standards or close down, so we may see some changes.

Hostels

The number one accommodation choice for backpackers has to be hostels. Australia has a very active youth hostel association and you'll find hostels all over the country with more official hostels and backpackers hostels popping up all the time.

YHA (Youth Hostel Association) hostels provide basic accommodation, usually in small dormitories or bunkrooms although more and more of them are providing twin rooms for couples. The nightly charges are rock bottom – usually just $8 to $12 a night – but in return there are a number of rules and regulations you have to observe. The most important one is that to stay at a youth hostel you must be a YHA member. In Australia this costs $18 a year (there's also a $14 joining fee). You can join at a state office or often at a youth hostel. Youth Hostels are an international organisation, so if you're already a member of the YHA in your own country, your membership entitles you to use the Australian hostels. Hostels are great places for meeting people, great travellers' centres and, in many busier hostels, the visitors will outnumber the Australians.

The rules and regulations for use of the hostels are all fairly simple and are outlined in the annual *YHA Hostels in Australia* booklet which is available from any YHA office in Australia for $1.50 and from some YHA offices overseas. This booklet lists all the YHA hostels around Australia with useful little maps showing how to find them, so it's quite invaluable. YHA members are eligible for discounts at various places and these facilities are also listed in the handbook.

You must have a regulation sheet sleeping bag or bed linen – for hygiene reasons a regular sleeping bag will not do. If you haven't got sheets they can be rented at many hostels (usually for $3), but it's cheaper, after a few nights' stay, to have your own. YHA offices and some larger hostels sell the official YHA sheet bag.

Most hostels have cooking facilities and some place where you can sit and talk. There are usually laundry facilities and often excellent notice boards. Many hostels have a maximum-stay period – because some hostels are permanently full it would hardly be fair for people to stay too long when others are being turned away. Hostels often keep their costs down by getting you to do the work. Before departing each morning there will probably be some chore you must complete.

The YHA defines its hostels as the simpler 'shelter' style and the larger 'standard' hostels. They range from tiny places to big modern buildings with everything from historic convict buildings to a disused railway station in between. Most hostels have a manager who checks you in when you arrive, keeps the peace and assigns the chores. Because you have so much more contact with a hostel manager than the person in charge of other styles of accommodation he or she can really make or break the place. Good managers are often great characters and well worth getting to know.

Accommodation can usually be booked directly with the manager, through the YHA Central Reservations Bureau in Sydney (tel (02) 261 5727) or with the state head office. The YHA handbook tells all.

The Australian head office is in Sydney, at the Australian Youth Hostels Association, 60 Mary St, Surry Hills, NSW 2010. If you can't get a YHA hostel booklist in your own country write to them but otherwise deal with the state offices:

New South Wales
    176 Day St, Sydney, NSW 2000 (tel 267 3044)
Northern Territory
    Darwin Hostel Complex, Beaton Rd via Hidden Valley Rd, Berrimah, NT 0828 (tel 84 3902)
Queensland
    462 Queen St, Brisbane, Qld 4000 (tel 831 2022)
South Australia
    38 Sturt St, Adelaide, SA 5000 (tel 231 5583)
Tasmania
    1st floor, 28 Criterion St, Hobart, Tas 7000 (tel 34 9617)
Victoria
    205 King St, Melbourne, Vic 3000 (tel 670 7991)
Western Australia
    1st floor, 257 Adelaide Terrace, Perth, WA 6000 (tel 325 5844)

Not all of the approximately 150 hostels listed in the handbook are actually owned by the YHA. Some are 'associate hostels', which generally abide by hostel regulations but are owned by other organisations or individuals. Others are 'alternative accommodation' and do not totally fit the hostel blueprint. They might be motels which keep some hostel-style accommodation available for YHA members or campsites with an on-site van or two kept aside, or even a places just like hostels but where the operators don't want to abide by all the hostel regulations.

In addition to the 'official' YHA hostels there are now a great number of unofficial hostels, often called 'backpackers' hostels. They vary greatly in standard, with dormitories, single and double rooms, and varying amounts of common space like TV rooms, kitchens, gardens and so on. Some provide bed linen, others just a bunk and mattress. A few have washing machines for guests' use. Some are new, purpose built, with clean, spacious facilities, pools and bikes or surfboards to lend or rent. Many run or will help you book tours, dive courses, white-water rafting and so on at bargain rates.

Others are scruffy places with low standards. In the worst hostels there will be just one hotplate, no pots, and the fridge will be full of last month's guests' leftover cabbage and yoghurt.

The major difference from YHA hostels is that you don't have to be a YHA member. Independent hostels are in the same price range as YHA hostels. They bill themselves as more relaxed and less restrictive than YHA hostels, but YHA hostels are generally relaxing their rules – if they have a curfew, they'll almost always let you have a key if you want to come in late, and more often than not you can come and go all day. Alcohol is even allowed in a few YHA hostels these days.

Independent hostels sometimes form themselves into loose networks mainly for publicity purposes. Sometimes they offer discount cards. Like some YHAs, some independent hostels have set office hours for checking in or out, usually the couple of hours round 10 am and again around 6 pm. In most of them you're asked to be quiet after 10 or 11 pm. Many hostels have notice boards for rides, deals, messages, etc.

As with YHA hostels a lot depends on the friendliness and willingness of the managers. One practice that many people find objectionable – in independent hostels only, since it *never* happens in YHAs – is the 'vetting' of Australians and sometimes New Zealanders, who may be asked to provide a passport or double ID which they may not carry. Virtually all city hostels ask everyone for some ID – usually a passport – but this can also be used as a way of keeping unwanted customers out.

Some places will actually only admit overseas backpackers. This happens mostly in cities and when it does it's because the hostel in question has had problems with some locals treating the place more as a doss house than a hostel – drinking too much, making too much noise, getting into fights and the like. Hostels which discourage or ban Aussies say it's only a rowdy minority that makes trouble, but they can't take the risk on who'll turn out bad. If you're an Aussie and encounter this kind of reception the best you can do, if you want to overcome it, is persuade the desk people that you're genuinely travelling the country, and aren't just looking for a cheap place to crash for a while.

The Ys

In a number of places in Australia accommodation is provided by the YMCA or YWCA. There are variations from place to place – some are mainly intended for permanent accommodation, some are run like normal commercial guest houses. They're generally excellent value and usually conveniently located. You don't have to be a YMCA or YWCA member to stay at them, although sometimes you get a discount if you are. Accommodation in the Ys is generally in fairly straightforward rooms, usually with shared bathroom facilities. Some Ys also have dormitory-style accommodation. Note, however, that not all YMCA or YWCA organisations around the country offer accommodation; it's mainly in the big cities.

Another organisation that sometimes offers accommodation is the CWA (Country Women's Association), but this is mainly in the country and usually for women only.

Colleges

Although it is students who get first chance at these, non-students can also stay at many university colleges during the uni vacations. These places can be relatively cheap and comfortable and provide an opportunity for you to meet people. Costs are typically from about $15 for bed & breakfast for students, twice that if you're not a student.

This type of accommodation is usually available only during the vacations (from November to February, and in May and August). Additionally, it must almost always be booked ahead; you can't just turn up. Many of Australia's new universities are way out in the suburbs (we call them 'bush unis') and are inconvenient to get to unless you have wheels.

Hotels

For the budget traveller, hotels in Australia are generally older places – new accommodation will usually be motels. To understand why Australia's hotels are the way they are requires delving into the history books a little. At the same time the powers that be decided Australia's drinking should only be at the most inconvenient hours, they also decided that drinking places should also be hotels. So every place which in Britain would be a 'pub' in Australia was a 'hotel', but often in name only.

The original idea of forcing pubs to provide accommodation for weary travellers has long faded into history and this ludicrous law has been rolled back. Every place called a hotel does not necessarily

have rooms to rent, although many still do. A 'private hotel', as opposed to a 'licensed hotel', really is a hotel and does not serve alcohol. A 'guest house' is much the same as a 'private hotel'.

New hotels being built today are mainly of the Hilton variety; smaller establishments will usually be motels. So, if you're staying in a hotel, it will normally mean an older place, often with rooms without private facilities. Unfortunately many older places are on the drab, grey and dreary side. You get a strong feeling that because they've got the rooms they try to turn a dollar on them, but without much enthusiasm. Others, fortunately, are colourful places with some real character. Although the word 'hotel' doesn't always mean they'll have rooms, the places that do have rooms usually make it pretty plain that they are available. If a hotel is listed in an accommodation directory you can be pretty sure it really will offer you a bed. If there's nothing that looks like a reception desk or counter, just ask in the bar.

You'll find hotels all around the town centres in smaller towns while in larger towns the hotels that offer accommodation are often to be found close to the railway stations. In some older towns, or in historic centres like the gold mining towns, the old hotels can be really magnificent. The rooms themselves may be pretty old fashioned and unexciting, but the hotel facade and entrance area will often be quite exotic. In the outback the old hotels are often places of real character. They are often the real 'town centre' and you'll meet all the local eccentrics there. While researching one edition I stayed in a little outback town with a population of about 10, seven of whom were in the bar that night.

A bright word about hotels (guest houses and private hotels, too) is that the breakfasts are usually A1. A substantial breakfast is what this country was built on and if your hotel is still into serving a real breakfast you'll probably feel it could last you until breakfast comes around next morning. In these places, B&B stands for bed & breakfast. Generally, hotels will have rooms for around $20 to $30. When comparing prices, remember to check if it includes breakfast or not.

In airports and bus and railway stations, there are often information boards with direct-dial phones to book accommodation. Sometimes these places offer a discount if you use the direct phone to book. Some hotels around the bus and railway stations also offer discounts to bus-pass travellers. The staff at bus stations are good sources of information on cheap and convenient accommodation.

Motels, Serviced Apartments & Holiday Flats

If you've got wheels and want a more modern place with your own bathroom and other facilities, then you're moving into the motel bracket. Motels cover the earth in Australia, just like in the US, but they're usually located away from the city centres. Prices vary and with motels, unlike hotels, singles are often not much cheaper than doubles. Often there is no difference at all between a single and a double. The reason is quite simple – in the old hotels many of the rooms really are singles, relics from the days when single men travelled the country looking for work. In motels, the rooms are almost always doubles. You'll sometimes find motel rooms for less than $30 and in most places will have no trouble finding something for $45 or less.

Holiday flats and serviced apartments are much the same thing and bear some relationship to motels. Basically, holiday flats are found in holiday areas, serviced apartments in cities. A holiday flat is much like a motel room but usually has a kitchen or kitchen facilities so you can fix your own food. Usually holiday flats are not serviced like motels – you don't get your bed made up every morning and the cups washed out. In some holiday flats you actually have to provide your own

sheets and bedding but others are operated just like motel rooms with a kitchen. Most motels in Australia will provide at least tea and coffee making facilities but a holiday flat will also have cooking utensils, dishes, cutlery and so on.

Holiday flats are often rented on a weekly basis but even in these cases it's worth asking if a daily rate is available. Paying for a week, even if you only stay for a few days, can still be cheaper than having those days at a higher daily rate. If there's more than just two of you, another advantage of holiday flats is that you can often find them with two or more bedrooms. A two bedroom holiday flat is typically priced at about 1½ times the cost of a comparable single bedroom unit.

In holiday areas like the Queensland coast, motels and holiday flats will often be virtually interchangeable terms – there's nothing really to distinguish one from another. In big cities, on the other hand, the serviced apartments are often a little more obscure although they may be advertised in the newspaper's classified ads.

Camping & Caravanning

The camping story in Australia is partly excellent and partly rather annoying! The excellent side is that there are a great number of campsites and you'll almost always find space available. If you want to get around Australia on the cheap then camping is the cheapest way of all with nightly costs for two of around $6 to $9.

One of the drawbacks is that campsites are often intended more for caravanners (house trailers for any Americans out there) than for campers and the tent campers get little thought in these places. The New Zealanders could certainly show Australian campsite operators how it's done. Over there campsites often have a kitchen and a dining area where you can eat. If it's raining you're not stuck with huddling in your car or, even worse, tent. The fact that most of the sites are called 'caravan parks' indicates who gets the most attention.

Equally bad is that in the cities most sites are well away from the centre. This is not inconvenient in smaller towns but, in general, if you're planning to camp around Australia you really need your own transport. Brisbane is the worst city in Australia in this respect because council regulations actually forbid tents within a 22 km radius of the centre. Although there are some sites in Brisbane within that radius, they're strictly for caravans – no campers allowed.

Still, it's not all gloom – in general Australian campsites are well kept, conveniently located and excellent value. Many sites also have on-site vans which you can rent for the night and give you the comforts of caravanning without the necessity of towing a caravan around with you. An on-site van typically costs around $20 to $25 a night. A variant of this is a 'cabin', which has much the same facilities as a caravan but without the pretence that it might be towed away somewhere.

I've made trips around Australia using every sort of accommodation, from youth hostels to motels, but one of the most successful was a trip Maureen and I made on a motorcycle. We had a little tent strapped across the handlebars and managed to camp almost everywhere we went, from Canberra to Cooktown, Airlie Beach to Ayers Rock. On the few occasions when sitting in a tent listening to the rain beat down (one of those times being in Alice Springs, believe it or not!) was too oppressive, we managed to find an on-site van to shelter in. In Alice Springs we were allowed to use a vacant on-site van free during the day.

Other Possibilities

That covers the usual conventional accommodation possibilities but there are lots of less conventional ones. You don't have to camp in campsites, for example. There are plenty of parks where you can camp for free, or roadside shelters where short-term camping is permitted. Australia has lots of bush where nobody is going to complain about you putting up a tent.

In the cities if you want to stay longer, the first place to look for a flat or a room is the classified ad section of the daily paper. Wednesdays and Saturdays are the usual days for these ads. Notice boards in universities, hostel offices, certain popular bookshops and other contact centres are good places to look for flats to share or rooms for rent.

Australia is a land of farms (sorry, stations) and one of the best ways to come to grips with Australian life is to spend a week on a farm. Many farms offer accommodation where you can just sit back and watch how it's done or have a go yourself. The state tourist offices can advise you of what's available; the costs are pretty reasonable. Or how about life on a houseboat (see Victoria or South Australia)?

FOOD

The culinary delights can be one of the real highlights of Australia. Time was – like 25 years ago – when Australia's food (mighty steaks apart) had a reputation for being like England's, only worse. Well, perhaps not quite that bad, but getting on that way. Miracles happen and Australia's miracle was immigration. The Greeks, Yugoslavs, Italians, Lebanese and many others who flooded in to Australia in the '50s and '60s brought, thank God, their food with them.

So in Australia today you can have excellent Greek moussaka (and a good, cheap bottle of retsina to wash it down), delicious Italian saltimbocca and pastas, or good, heavy German dumplings; you can perfume the air with garlic after stumbling out of a French bistro, or try all sorts of Middle Eastern and Arab treats. The Chinese have been sweet & souring since the gold rush days, while more recently Indian, Thai and Malaysian restaurants have been all the rage. And for cheap eats, you can't beat some of our Vietnamese places.

Australian Food

Although there is no real Australian cuisine there is certainly some excellent Australian food to try. And I don't mean witchetty grubs, the huge caterpillars that are an Aboriginal delicacy – you eat 'em live!

Any mention of Australian food has to include a couple of firm favourites, although they are not going to win any competitions. For a start there's the great Australian meat pie – every bit as sacred an institution as the hot dog is to a New Yorker. It is just as frequently slandered as tasteless, unhealthy and not nearly as good as it used to be. The meat pie is an awful concoction of anonymous meat and dark gravy in a soggy pastry container. You'll have to try one though; the number consumed in Australia each year is phenomenal and they're a real part of Australian culture. Of course there are a few places that really do a good job on the classic meat pie.

Even more central to Australian eating habits is Vegemite. This strange, dark-coloured yeast spread is something only an Australian could love. Australians spread Vegemite on bread and become so addicted to it that anywhere in the world you find an Aussie, the jar of Vegemite is bound to be close at hand. Australian embassies the world over have the location of the nearest Vegemite retailer as one of their most-asked-for pieces of information.

The good news about Australian food is the fine ingredients. Nearly everything is grown right here in Australia so you're not eating food that has been shipped halfway around the world. Everybody knows about good Australian steaks ('This is cattle country, so eat beef you bastards', announce the farmers' bumper stickers), but there are lots of other things to try.

Australia has a superb range of seafood: fish like John Dory and the esteemed barramundi, or superb lobsters and other crustaceans like the engagingly named Moreton Bay bugs! Yabbies are freshwater crayfish and very good. Even vegetarians get a fair go in Australia; there are some excellent vegetarian restaurants and, once again, the vegetables are as fresh as you could ask for.

Where to Eat

If you want to feel right at home there are *McDonalds, Kentucky Frieds, Pizza Huts* and all the other familiar names looking no different than they do anywhere from New York to Amsterdam. There are also Chinese restaurants where the script is all in Chinese, little Lebanese places where you'd imagine the local PLO getting together for a meal, and every other national restaurant type you could imagine.

For real value for money there are a couple of dinky-di Australian eating places you should certainly try, though. For a start Australian delis are terrific and they'll put together a superb sandwich. Hunt out the authentic looking ones in any big city and you'll get a sandwich any New York deli would have trouble matching, and I'm willing to bet it'll be half the price.

In the evening the best value is to be found in the pubs. Look for 'counter meals', so called because they used to be eaten at the bar counter. Some places still are just like that, while others are fancier, almost restaurant-like. Good counter meals are hard to beat for value for money and although the food is usually of the simple steak-salad-chips variety, the quality is often excellent and prices are commendably low. The best counter meal places usually have serve-yourself salad tables where you can add as much salad, French bread and so on as you wish.

Counter meals are usually served as counter lunches or counter teas, the latter a hangover from the old northern English terminology where 'tea' meant the evening meal. One catch with pub meals is that they usually operate fairly strict hours. The evening meal time may be just 6 to 7.30 or 8 pm. Pubs doing counter meals often have a blackboard menu outside but some of the best places are quite anonymous – you simply have to know that this is the pub that does great food and furthermore that it's in the bar hidden away at the back. Counter meals vary enormously in price but in general the better class places with good serve-yourself salad tables will be in the $6 to $10 range for all the traditional dishes: steak, veal, chicken, and so on.

For rock-bottom prices the real shoe-stringers can also check out university and college cafeterias, the big department store cafeterias (Woolworths and Coles, for example), or even try sneaking into public service office cafeterias. Australians love their fish & chips just as much as the British and, just like in Britain, their quality can vary enormously – all the way from stodgy and horrible to really superb. Hamburger and fish & chip shops usually serve both these Aussie favourites. We've also got the full range of take-away foods, from Italian to Mexican, Chinese to Lebanese.

DRINKS

In the non-alcoholic department Aust-ralians knock back Coke and flavoured milk like there's no tomorrow and also have some excellent mineral water

brands. Coffee enthusiasts will be relieved to find good Italian cafes serving cappuccino and other coffees, often into the wee small hours and beyond. Beer and wine need their own explanations.

Beer

Australia's beer must be considered alongside the country's drinking habits. Way back in WW I the government of the day decided that all pubs should shut at 6 pm as a wartime austerity measure. Unfortunately when the war ended this wartime emergency move didn't. On one side the wowsers didn't want anybody to drink and if Australia couldn't have prohibition like America, stopping drinking at 6 pm was at least a step in the right direction in their view. The other supporters of this terrible arrangement were, believe it or not, the breweries and pub owners. They discovered that shutting the pubs at 6 pm didn't really cut sales at all and it certainly cut costs. You didn't have to pay staff until late in the evening and you didn't have to worry about making your pub a pleasant place for a drink. People left work, rushed around to the pub and swallowed as much beer as they could before 6 pm. They definitely didn't have time to admire the decor.

This unhappy story didn't even end after WW II. In fact it carried right on into the '50s before common sense finally came into play and the 'six o'clock swill' was consigned to history. Since that time the idea of the Australian pub as a bare and cheerless beer barn has gradually faded and there are now many pleasant pubs where an evening drink is a real pleasure. More recently, drinking hours have been further relaxed and pubs can now open later in the evening and on Sundays.

Enough of the history, now for the beer. To most partakers, it's superb. Fosters is, of course, the best-known international brand with a world wide reputation. Each Australian state has its own beer brand and there'll be someone to sing the praises of everything from XXXX, pronounced fourex, (Queensland) to Swan (Western Australia). Small 'boutique' brewers have also been making a comeback so you'll find one-off brands scattered around the country. A word of warning to visitors: Australian beer has a higher alcohol content than British or American beers; Australian beer sold in the US has to be watered down to meet US regulations. And another warning: people who drive under the influence of alcohol lose their licences (unfortunately, drink driving is a real problem in Australia).

All around Australia beer, the containers it comes in, and the receptacles you drink it from are called by different names. So in the Northern Territory the locals refer to Fosters as the 'blue can', Queenslanders call XXXX 'barbed wire' (because that's what the name looks like), while Victorians' favourite beer is VB or Vic Bitter – properly known as Victorian Bitter. Beer comes in stubbies, tinnies and twisties and you can drink it in a glass, goblet, pony, middy, pot or schooner depending on where you are.

Beer Consumption

Australians are not the world's greatest consumers of beer – that title goes to the West Germans, who knock back nearly 150 litres per capita per year. But Darwin is reckoned to be the number one city for beer drinking. Its peak was the equivalent of 230 litres per man, woman and child in one year; with so much beer disappearing down Darwinites' throats, it's no surprise that they can run a boating regatta solely for boats made out of beer cans. When a party of Darwinites sailed to Singapore in the '70s in a beer-can boat, it was locally mooted that they inspired boatloads of Vietnamese refugees to take their chances in the opposite direction in real boats.

Australians are reckoned to be about the third biggest beer consumers in the world, about five to 10 litres behind the Germans, a litre or so less than the Belgians and neck and neck with the thirsty Czechs. The Poms are about 25 litres back in 10th place. Americans don't even rate. Australia's per capita beer consumption has, however, been on a steady decline for the past decade or so.

Wine

If you're not a beer fancier, then turn to wines. Australia has a great climate for wine producing and some superb wine areas. Best known are the Hunter Valley of New South Wales and the Barossa Valley of South Australia, but there are a great number of other wine-producing areas, each with its own enthusiastic promoters.

Recently, European wine experts have begun to realise just how good Australian wines can be. So good in fact that the French have been getting rather miffed about the number of competitions they've been losing. Furthermore, Australia's wines are cheap and readily available. We pay less for our wine than the Californians do for theirs and the price of a decent bottle in Britain, European Community or not, is positively horrifying.

It takes a little while to become familiar with Australian wineries and their styles but it's an effort worth making. All over Australia, but particularly in Melbourne, you'll find restaurants advertising that they're BYO. The initials stand for 'Bring Your Own' and it means that they're not licensed to serve alcohol but you are permitted to bring your own with you.

This is a real boon to wine-loving but budget-minded travellers because you can bring your own bottle of wine from the local bottle shop or from that winery you visited last week and not pay any mark-up. In fact, most restaurants make no charge at all for you bringing your own booze, even though it's conceivable that without it they might sell you a bottle of mineral water or something.

An even more economical way of drinking Australian wine is to do it free at the wineries. In the wine-growing areas, most wineries have free tastings; you just zip straight in and say what you'd like to try. However, free wine tastings do not mean open slather drinking – the glasses are generally thimble-sized and there is an expectation that you will buy something if, for example, you taste every chardonnay that that vineyard has ever produced.

CINEMA

The Australian film industry began as early as 1896, a year after the Lumière brothers opened the world's first cinema in Paris. Maurice Sestier, one of the Lumières' photographers came to Australia and made the first films in the streets of Sydney and at Flemington Racecourse during the Melbourne Cup.

Cinema historians regard an Australian film, *Soldiers of the Cross*, as the world's first 'real' movie. It was originally screened at the Melbourne Town Hall in 1901, cost £600 to make and was shown throughout America in 1902.

The next significant Australian film, *The Story of the Kelly Gang*, was screened in 1907, and by 1911 the industry was flourishing. Low budget films were being made in such quantities that they could be hired out or sold cheaply. Over 250 silent feature films were made before the 1930s when the *talkies* and Hollywood took over.

In the 1930s, film companies like Cinesound sprang up. Cinesound made 17 feature films between 1931 and 1940, many based on Australian history or literature. *Forty Thousand Horsemen*, directed by Cinesound's great film maker Charles Chauvel, was a highlight of this era of locally made and financed films which ended in 1959, the year of Chauvel's death.

Before the introduction of government subsidies during 1969 and 1970, the Australian film industry found it difficult to compete with American and British interests. The New Wave era of the 1970s, a renaissance of Australian cinema, produced films like *Picnic at Hanging Rock*, *Sunday Too Far Away*, *Caddie*, *The Devil's Playground*, which appealed to large local and international audiences. Since the '70s, Australian actors and directors like Mel Gibson, Judy Davis, Greta Scacchi, Paul Hogan, Peter Weir, Gillian Armstrong and Fred Schepsi have gained international recognition. Films like *Gallipoli*, *The Year of Living Dangerously*, *Mad Max*, *Malcolm* and most recently, *Crocodile Dundee* impressed audiences worldwide.

BOOKS

In almost any bookshop in the country you'll find a section devoted to Australiana with books on every Australian subject you care to mention. If you want a souvenir of Australia, a photographic record, try one of the numerous coffee-table books like *A Day in the Life of Australia*. There are many other Australian books which make good gifts: children's books with very Australian illustrations like Julie Vivar & Mem Fox's *Possum Magic* and Norman Lindsay's *The Magic Pudding* or cartoon books by some of Australia's excellent cartoonists. We've got a lot of bookshops and some of the better-known ones are mentioned in the various city sections.

At the Wilderness Shops in each capital city and the Government Printing Offices in Sydney and Melbourne, you'll find a good range of wildlife posters, calendars and books.

History

For a good introduction to Australian history, read *A Short History of Australia*, a most accessible and informative general history by Manning Clark, the much-loved Aussie historian, or *The Fatal Shore*, Robert Hughes' bestseller account of Australia's story.

Finding Australia, by Russel Ward, traces the story of the early days from the first Aboriginal arrivals up to 1821. It's strong on Aborigines, women and the full story of foreign exploration, not just Captain Cook's role. There's lots of fascinating detail, including information about the appalling crooks who ran the early colony for long periods, and it's intended to be the first of a series.

The Exploration of Australia, by Michael Cannon, is coffee-table book in size, presentation and price, but it's a fascinating reference book about the gradual European uncovering of the continent.

Cooper's Creek, by Alan Moorehead, is a classic account of the ill-starred Burke and Wills expedition which dramatises the horrors and hardships faced by the early explorers.

The Fatal Impact, also by Moorehead, begins with the voyages of James Cook, regarded as one of the greatest and most humane explorers, and tells the tragic story of the European impact on Australia, Tahiti and Antarctica in the years that followed Captain Cook's great voyages of discovery. It details how good intentions and economic necessities of the time led to disaster, corruption and annihilation.

Aborigines

The Australian Aborigines, by Kenneth Maddock, is a good cultural summary.

For a sympathetic historical account of what's happened to the real Australians since whites arrived read *Aboriginal Australians*, by Richard Broome .

A Change of Ownership, by Mildred Kirk, covers similar ground to Broome's book, but does so more concisely, focusing

on the land rights movement and its historical background.

The Other Side of the Frontier, by Henry Reynolds, uses historical records to give a vivid account of an Aboriginal view of the arrival of, and takeover of Australia by, the Europeans.

My Place, Sally Morgan's prize-winning autobiography, traces the discovery of her Aboriginal heritage.

The Fringe Dwellers, by Nene Gare, describes just what it was like to be an Aborigine growing up in a white-dominated society.

Ruby Langford's *Don't Take Your Love to Town* and Kath Walker's *My People* are also recommended reading for people interested in Aborigines' experience.

Fiction

You don't need to worry about bringing a few good novels from home for your trip to Australia; there's plenty of excellent recent Australian literature including the novels and short stories of Helen Garner, Kate Grenville, Elizabeth Jolley, Thomas Kenneally, Peter Carey, Tim Winton and Beverley Farmer.

Some Australian classics (these have also been made into films) include *The Getting of Wisdom* by Henry Handel Richardson, *Picnic at Hanging Rock* by Joan Lindsay, and *My Brilliant Career* by Miles Franklin. *For the Term of his Natural Life*, by Marcus Clarke, was one of the first books to be made into a film, in the late 19th century.

The works of Banjo Paterson (*The Man from Snowy River*, for example), Henry Lawson, Patrick White, Frank Hardy, Alan Marshall (*I Can Jump Puddles*) and Albert Facey (*A Fortunate Life*) make interesting reading. May Gibbs wrote *Snugglepot & Cuddlepie* – the story of two gumnut babies – one of the first bestselling Australian children's books.

Travel Accounts

Accounts of travels in Australia include the marvellous *Tracks*, by Robyn Davidson.

It's the amazing story of a young woman who sets out alone to walk from Alice Springs to the WA coast with her camels – proof that you can do anything if you try hard enough. It almost single handedly inspired the current Australian interest in camel safaris!

Quite another sort of travel is Tony Horwitz's *One for the Road*, an often hilarious account of a high speed hitch-hiking trip around Australia (Oz through a windscreen). In contrast, *The Ribbon & the Ragged Square*, by Linda Christmas, is an intelligent, sober account of a nine month investigatory trip round Oz by a *Guardian* journalist from England. There's lots of background and history as well as first-hand reporting and interviews.

Howard Jacobson also did a circuit of the country, recounted in *In the Land of Oz*. It's amusing at times, but through most of the book you're left wondering when the long-suffering Ros is finally going to thump the twerp!

The late Bruce Chatwin's book *The Songlines* tells of his experiences among central Australian Aborigines and makes more sense of the Dreamtime, sacred sites, sacred songs and the traditional Aboriginal way of life than 10 learned tomes put together. Along the way it also delves into the origins of humankind and throws in some pithy anecdotes about modern Australia.

Guidebooks

Burnum Burnum's Aboriginal Australia is subtitled 'a traveller's guide'. If you want to explore Australia from the Aboriginal point of view, this large and lavish hardback is the book for you.

For trips into the outback in your own car Brian Sheedy's *Outback on a Budget* includes lots of practical advice. There are a number of other books about vehicle preparation and driving in the outback.

Surfing Australia's East Coast by Aussie surf star Nat Young is a slim, cheap, comprehensive guide to the best breaks from Victoria to Fraser Island. He's also written the *Surfing & Sailboard Guide to Australia* which covers the whole country. Surfing enthusiasts can also look for the expensive coffee-table book *Atlas of Australian Surfing*, by Mark Warren.

If you want to really understand the Barrier Reef's natural history, look for *Australia's Great Barrier Reef*. It's colourful, expensive and nearly as big as the Barrier Reef itself. There's also a cheaper abbreviated paperback version.

Australia's Wonderful Wildlife (Australian Women's Weekly) is the shoestringer's equivalent of a coffee-table book – a cheap paperback with lots of great photos of the animals you didn't see or those that didn't stay still when you pointed your camera at them.

LP's *Bushwalking in Australia* describes 23 walks of different lengths and difficulty in various parts of the country, ranging from an easy two day stroll along the coastline of Royal National Park near Sydney, to a strenuous 10 day bushwalk on the exposed peaks of the Western Arthur Range in Tasmania.

There are state by state Reader's Digest guides to coasts and national parks, such as the *Coast of New South Wales*, and Gregory's guides to national parks, such as *National Parks of New South Wales* (a handy reference listing access, facilities, activities and so on for all parks).

Blair's Guide to Victoria is a handy, comprehensive guide including details on accommodation, places to eat and things to do. There's also a guide for New South Wales (incorporating the Australian Capital Territory).

THINGS TO BUY

Australia is not a great place for buying amazing things – there's nothing in particular which you simply 'have' to buy while you're here. There are, however, lots of things definitely not to buy – like plastic boomerangs, Aboriginal ashtrays and all the other terrible souvenirs with which tacky souvenir shops in the big cities are stuffed. Most of them come from Taiwan anyway.

Top of the list for any real Australian purchase, however, would have to be Aboriginal art. It's an amazingly direct and down to earth art which has only recently begun to gain wide appreciation. If you're willing to put in a little effort you can see superb examples of the Aborigines' art in its original form, carved or painted on rocks and caves in many remote parts of Australia. Now, and really just in time, skilled Aboriginal artists are also working on their art in a more portable form. Nobody captures the essence of outback Australia better than the Aborigines, so if you want a real souvenir of Australia this is what to buy.

There are some interesting alternatives, like the sturdy farming gear worn by those bronzed Aussie blokes on outback stations – Akubra hats, Drizabone coats, R M Williams moleskin trousers, or boots and shirts, all made to last. Or there are all sorts of sheepskin products, from car seat covers to ugg boots. Surfing equipment is, of course, a major industry in Australia. You can find some terrific Australian books of the coffee table variety and Australian children's books can be equally attractive.

Recently some amusing Australiana shops have popped up selling delightfully silly examples of Australian kitsch – like lamingtons-in-perspex paperweights or a vegemite jar in an 'in case of emergency break glass' box.

Australia's national gemstone is the opal, most common in South Australia. They're very beautiful but buy wisely; as with all precious and semiprecious stones, there are many tall tales and expert 'salesmen' around.

ACTIVITIES

Apart from the well known spectator sports of football, cricket and tennis, there are plenty of activities that you can take part in while travelling round the country.

Australia has a flourishing skiing industry – a fact that takes a number of travellers by surprise – with snowfields that straddle New South Wales' border with Victoria. There's information on the Victorian snowfields in the Victorian Alps section of the Victoria chapter, and likewise for the Snowy Mountains in the New South Wales chapter. Tasmania's snowfields aren't as developed as those of Victoria and New South Wales, but if you do want to ski while in Tassie you can read all about it in the Activities section of the Tasmania chapter.

If skiing isn't your scene how about bushwalking? Not only is it cheap but you can do it anywhere. There are many fantastic walks in the various national parks around the country and information on how to get there is in LP's *Bushwalking in Australia* as well as in the Activities sections of each state.

If you're interested in surfing you'll find great beaches and surf in most states.

There's great suba diving all around the coast but particularly along the Queensland Great Barrier Reef where there are also many dive schools. Many travellers come to Australia with the goal of getting a scuba certificate during their stay.

In Victoria you can go horse riding in the High Country and follow the route of the Snowy Mountains cattle people, whose lives were the subject of a recent film *The Man from Snowy River*, which in turn was based on the poem by Banjo Paterson. In northern Queensland you can ride horses through rainforests and along sand dunes and swim with them in the sea. You can find horses to hire just about anywhere in the country.

You can cycle all around Australia; for the athletic there are long, challenging routes and for the not so masochistic there are plenty of great day trips. In most states there are excellent roads and helpful bicycle societies with lots of maps and useful tips and advice. See the Getting Around chapter and individual state chapters for more details.

For the more adventurous, camel riding has taken off in the Northern Territory. If you've done it in India or Egypt or you just fancy yourself as the explorer/outdoors type, then here's your chance. (You never know, next it might be croc riding!)

For information on any of these activities see the relevant chapters or contact any of the state tourist bureaus.

Getting There

Basically getting to Australia means flying. Once upon a time the traditional transport between Europe and Australia was by ship but those days have ended. Infrequent and expensive cruise ships apart, there are no regular shipping services to Australia. It is, however, sometimes possible to hitch a ride on a yacht to or from Australia. See the Getting Around chapter for more details.

The basic problem with getting to Australia is that it's a long way from anywhere. Coming from Asia, Europe or North America there are lots of competing airlines and a wide variety of air fares but there's no way you can avoid those great distances. Australia's current international popularity adds another problem - flights are often heavily booked. If you want to fly to Australia at a particularly popular time of year (the middle of summer, ie Christmas time, is notoriously difficult) or on a particularly popular route (like Hong Kong-Sydney) then plan well ahead.

Australia has a large number of international gateways. Sydney and Melbourne are the two busiest international airports with flights from everywhere. Perth also gets many flights from Asia and Europe and has direct flights to New Zealand. Other international airports include Hobart in Tasmania (New Zealand only), Adelaide, Port Hedland (Bali only), Darwin, Cairns, Townsville and Brisbane. One place you can't arrive at directly from overseas is Canberra, the national capital.

Although Sydney is the busiest gateway it makes a lot of sense to avoid arriving or departing there. Sydney's airport is stretched way beyond its capacity and flights are frequently delayed on arrival and departure. Furthermore the customs and immigration facilities are cramped, crowded and too small for the current visitor flow so even after you've finally landed you may face further long delays. If you can organise your flights to avoid Sydney it's a wise idea but unfortunately many flights to or from other cities, Melbourne in particular, still go via Sydney. If you're planning to seriously explore Australia then starting at a quieter entry port like Cairns in far north Queensland or Perth in Western Australia can make a lot of sense.

Discount Tickets

Buying airline tickets these days is like shopping for a car, a stereo or a camera - five different travel agents will quote you five different prices. Rule number one if you're looking for a cheap ticket is to go to an agent, not directly to the airline. The airline can only quote you the absolutely straight-up-and-down, by-the-rule-book regular fare. An agent, on the other hand, can offer all sorts of special deals particularly on competitive routes.

Ideally an airline would like to fly all their flights with every seat in use and every passenger paying the highest fare possible. Fortunately life usually isn't like that and airlines would rather have a half price passenger than an empty seat. Since the airline itself can't very well offer seats at two different prices what they do when faced with the problem of too many seats is let agents sell them at cut prices.

Of course what's available and what it costs depends on what time of year it is, what route you're flying and who you're flying with. If you want to go to Australia at the most popular time of year (ie summer) you'll have to pay more. If you're flying on a popular route (like from Hong Kong) or one where the choice of flights is very limited (like from South America or from Africa) then the fare is likely to be higher or there may be nothing available but the official fare.

Similarly the dirt cheap fares are likely to be less conveniently scheduled, go by a less convenient route or with a less popular airline. Flying London/Sydney, for example, is most convenient with airlines like Qantas, British Airways, Thai International or Singapore Airlines. They have flights every day, they operate the same flight straight through to Australia and they're good reliable, comfortable, safe airlines. At the other extreme you could fly from London to an Eastern European or Middle East city on one flight, switch to another flight from there to Asia, change to another airline from there to Australia. It takes longer, there are delays and changes of aircraft along the way, the airlines may not be so good and furthermore the connection only works once a week and that means leaving London at 1.30 am on a Wednesday morning. The flip side is it's cheaper.

FROM EUROPE

The cheapest tickets in London are from the numerous 'bucket shops' (discount ticket agencies) which advertise in magazines and papers like *Time Out* or *Australasian Express*. Pick up one or two of these publications and ring round a few bucket shops to find the best deal. The magazine *Business Traveller* also has a great deal of good advice on air fare bargains. Most bucket shops are trustworthy and reliable but the occasional sharp operator appears – *Time Out* and *Business Traveller* give some useful advice on precautions to take.

Trailfinders (tel (01) 938-3366) at 46 Earls Court Rd, London W8 and STA Travel (tel (01) 581-1022) at 74 Old Brompton Rd, London SW7 and 117 Euston Rd, London NW1 are good, reliable agents for cheap tickets.

The cheapest London to Sydney or Melbourne bucket shop tickets are about £425 one way or £650 return. Such prices are usually only available if you leave London in the low season – March to June. In September and mid-December fares go up about 30% while the rest of the year they're somewhere in between. Perth is usually about £20 cheaper than Sydney or Melbourne one way, £30 to £50 cheaper return.

Many cheap tickets allow stopovers on the way to or from Australia. Rules regarding how many stopovers you can take, how long you can stay away, how far in advance you have to decide your return date and so on, vary from time to time and ticket to ticket, but recently most return tickets have allowed you to stay away for any period between 14 days and one year, with stopovers permitted anywhere along your route. As usual with heavily discounted tickets the less you pay the less you get. Nice direct flights, leaving at convenient times and flying with popular airlines, are going to be more expensive than flying from London to Singapore or Bangkok with some Eastern European or Middle East airline and then changing to another airline for the last leg.

Regular, by-the-book fares are around £650 one way or from £1000 return but there are all sorts of ticketing variations and rules including advance purchase periods, seasonal variations in fare and so on.

On to New Zealand

Cheap fares to New Zealand from Europe will usually be for flights via the USA. A straightforward London/Auckland one-way ticket will cost from £450, or you could make that London/Auckland/Sydney or Melbourne from £475. Coming via Australia you can continue right around on a Round-The-World ticket which will cost from around £1000 for a ticket with a comprehensive choice of stopovers. Alternatively you can fly to Australia and then tag on a straightforward Australia/New Zealand ticket – count on something from around A$400 one way depending on the season. Regular advance purchase return fares to or from Sydney are around A$450 to A$600, from Melbourne A$525 to A$700. Since British

Airways, Continental and United Airlines compete with Qantas and Air New Zealand on this route there are some good, competitive fares.

FROM NORTH AMERICA

There are a variety of connections across the Pacific from Los Angeles, San Francisco and Vancouver to Australia including direct flights, flights via New Zealand, island hopping routes or more circuitous Pacific rim routes via nations in Asia. Qantas, Air New Zealand, United and Continental all fly USA/Australia, Qantas, Air New Zealand and Canadian Airlines International fly Canada/Australia.

One advantage of flying Qantas or Air New Zealand rather than Continental or United is that if your flight goes via Hawaii the west coast to Hawaii sector is treated as a domestic flight by the US airlines. This means that you have to pay for drinks and headsets; goodies that are free on international sector. Furthermore when coming in through Hawaii from Australasia it's not unknown for passengers who take a long time clearing customs to be left behind by the US airline and have to take the next service!

To find good fares to Australia check the travel ads in the Sunday travel sections of papers like the *Los Angeles Times, San Francisco Chronicle-Examiner, New York Times* or *Toronto Globe & Mail*. The straightforward return excursion fare from the US west coast is around US$1000 to US$1500 depending on the season but plenty of deals are available. You can typically get a one-way ticket from US$500 west coast or US$550 east coast, returns from US$800 west coast or US$900 east coast. At peak seasons – particularly the Australia summer/Christmas time – seats will be harder to get and the price will probably be higher. In the US good agents for discounted tickets are the two student travel operators, Council Travel and STA Travel, both of which have lots of offices around the country. Canadian west coast fares out of Vancouver will be similar to the US west coast. From Toronto fares go from around C$1500 return.

The French airline UTA have an interesting island hopping route between the US west coast and Australia which includes the French colonies of New Caledonia and French Polynesia (Tahiti, etc). The UTA flight is often discounted and its multiple Pacific stopover possibilities makes it very popular with travellers. The UTA ticket typically costs about US$760 Los Angeles/Sydney one way.

If Pacific island hopping is your aim several other airlines offer interesting

opportunities. One is Hawaiian Airlines who fly Honolulu/Sydney via Pago Pago in American Samoa once a week. Qantas can give you Fiji or Tahiti along the way, Air New Zealand can offer both and the Cook Islands as well. See the Circle Pacific section for more details.

FROM NEW ZEALAND

Air New Zealand and Qantas operate a network of trans-Tasman flights linking Auckland, Wellington and Christchurch in New Zealand with most major Australian gateway cities. You can fly directly between a lot of places in New Zealand and a lot of places in Australia.

Fares vary depending on which cities you fly between and when you do it but from New Zealand to Sydney you're looking at NZ$600 to NZ$800 return, to Melbourne NZ$700 to NZ$925. One way fares are not much cheaper than return but there is a lot of competition on this route – with United, Continental and British Airways all flying it as well as Qantas and Air New Zealand, so there is bound to be some good discounting going on.

FROM ASIA

Ticket discounting is widespread in Asia, particularly in Singapore, Hong Kong (currently the discounting capital), Bangkok and Penang. There are a lot of fly by nights in the Asian ticketing scene so a little care is required. Also the Asian routes have been particularly caught up in the capacity shortages on flights to Australia. Flights between Hong Kong and Australia are notoriously heavily booked while flight to or from Bangkok and Singapore are often part of the longer Europe-Australia route so they are also sometimes very full. Plan ahead. For much more information on South-East Asian travel and on to Australia see Lonely Planet's *South-East Asia on a Shoestring*.

Typical one-way fares to Australia from Asia include from Hong Kong for around HK$2750 (US$370) or from Singapore for around S$600 (US$300). These fares are to the east coast capitals. Brisbane, Perth or Darwin are sometimes a bit cheaper.

You can also pick up some interesting tickets in Asia to include Australia on the way across the Pacific. UTA were first in this market but Qantas and Air New Zealand are also offering discounted trans-Pacific tickets. On the UTA ticket you can stop-over in Jakarta, Sydney, Noumea, Auckland and Tahiti.

FROM AFRICA & SOUTH AMERICA

The flight possibilities from these continents are not so varied and you're much more likely to have to pay the full fare. There is only one direct flight between Africa and Australia and that is the Qantas Harare (Zimbabwe)/Perth/Sydney route. An alternative from East Africa is to fly from Nairobi to India and South-East Asia and connect from there to Australia.

Two routes now operate between South America and Australia. The long running Chile connection involves a Lan Chile flight Santiago/Easter Island/Tahiti from where you fly Qantas or another airline to Australia. Alternatively there is a route across the Antarctic, flying Buenos Aires/Auckland/Sydney operated by Aerolineas Argentinas in conjunction with Qantas.

ROUND-THE-WORLD TICKETS

Round-The-World (RTW) tickets have become very popular in the last few years and many of these will take you through Australia. The airline RTW tickets are often real bargains and since Australia is pretty much at the other side of the world from Europe or North America it can work out no more expensive or even cheaper to keep going in the same direction right round the world rather than U-turn when you return.

The official airline RTW tickets are put together, usually by a combination of two airlines, and permit you to fly anywhere you want on their route systems so long as you do not backtrack. Other restrictions are that you (usually) must book the first sector in advance and cancellation penalties then apply. There may be restrictions on how many stops you are permitted and usually the tickets are valid from 90 days up to a year.

Typical prices for these South Pacific RTW tickets are from £1400 to £1700 or US$2500 to US$3000. An alternative type of RTW ticket is one put together by a travel agent using a combination of discounted tickets. A UK agent like Trailfinders can put together interesting London to London RTW combinations including Australia for £850 to £1000.

CIRCLE PACIFIC TICKETS

Circle Pacific fares are a similar idea to RTW tickets which use a combination of airlines to circle the Pacific – combining Australia, New Zealand, North America and Asia. Examples would be Continental-Thai International, Qantas-Northwest Orient, Canadian Airlines International-Cathay Pacific and so on. As with RTW tickets there are advance purchase restrictions and limits to how many stopovers you can take. Typically fares range between US$1500 and US$2000. A possible Circle Pacific route is Los Angeles / Hawaii / Auckland / Sydney / Singapore / Bangkok / Hong Kong / Tokyo / Los Angeles.

ARRIVING & DEPARTING
Arriving in Australia

Australia's dramatic increase in visitor arrivals has caused some severe bottlenecks at the entry points, particularly at Sydney where the airport is often operating at more than full capacity and delays on arrival or departure are frequent. Even when you're on the ground it can take ages to get through immigration and customs. One answer to this problem is to try not to arrive in Australia at Sydney. Sure you'll have to go there sometime but you can save yourself a lot of time and trouble by making Brisbane, Cairns, Melbourne or another gateway city your arrival point.

For information about how to get to the city from the airport when you first arrive in Australia check the Airport Transport section under the relevant city. There is generally an airport bus service at the international airports and there are always taxis available.

Leaving Australia

Australia used to operate a fixed price ticket system but now it's up to airlines, through travel agents of course, to charge whatever they can. As usual a lower fare means a less popular airline, more restricted schedule or less convenient route.

Two good places to look for discounted airline tickets are the STA Travel chain of agencies or Flight Centres International, a chain of agents involved purely in discount tickets. Or scan the travel pages of the major dailies, Saturday is usually the travel section day, for bucket shop ads. Fares usually vary with the time of year but some typical one-way fares from Australia's east coast include:

London and other European capitals from A$850
Los Angeles from $1000
New York from $1150
Singapore from $500
Bangkok from $600
Hong Kong from $625
Kathmandu from $800
Delhi from $760

Departure Tax When you finally go remember to keep $10 aside for the departure tax.

Warning

This chapter is particularly vulnerable to change – prices for international travel are volatile, routes are introduced and cancelled, schedules change, rules are amended, special deals come and go, borders open and close. Airlines and governments seem to take a perverse pleasure in making price structures and regulations as complicated as possible and you should check directly with the airline or travel agent to make sure you understand how a fare (and ticket you may buy) works. In addition, the travel industry is highly competitive and there are many lurks and perks. The upshot of this is that you should get opinions, quotes and advice from as many airlines and travel agents as possible before you part with your hard-earned cash. The details given in this chapter should be regarded as pointers and are not a substitute for careful, up-to-date research.

Getting Around

AIR

Australia is so vast (and at times so empty) that unless your time is unlimited, you will probably have to take to the air sometime. It has been calculated that something like 80% of long distance trips by public transport are made by air. The two major domestic airlines are far from the cheapest per km in the world, although they are among the safest.

The big two are Australian Airlines, which is government owned, and Ansett, which is privately owned with newspaper magnate Rupert Murdoch being one of the principal shareholders. The difference in ownership makes almost no difference to the traveller as both airlines are remarkably similar. They offer a very similar service and absolutely identical prices although that is supposed to change soon when deregulation arrives in Australia.

The 'two airline policy' with its attendant follow-the-leader mentality has changed considerably and their aircraft fleets are now quite different and they don't operate quite such slavishly similar schedules, although there is still a certain degree of similarity on some routes. Still, despite increased competition the fares are identical and, what is worse, they are a lot higher than they used to be. In the last few years air fares have risen with almost clockwork regularity.

There are a number of reasons for the high cost of Australian air travel (although compared to prices in Europe the situation is not at all bad) but a major one is the poor utilisation of the aircraft, since very few flights are made at night. Except for flights between Perth and the east coast – only a couple a night for each airline – most of the fleet sits on the tarmac every night. Stringent regulations about night operations at Sydney are a major reason for this.

Again it's government policy which accounts for another continuing absurdity of Australian air travel; namely the ruling that Qantas shall only fly abroad, Ansett and Australian Airlines only within Australia. There are some overseas sectors (Cairns/Port Moresby, Darwin/Bali and all the flights to New Zealand for example) which would be much more suitable for the domestic carriers. Similarly Sydney/Perth and Melbourne/Perth are domestic sectors so Qantas 747s often fly these long stretches only half full yet domestic passengers aren't allowed to use them. There's now a small crack in these regulations; Ansett has some Pacific connections on behalf of the Pacific island nations and Qantas can carry international visitors to Australia on domestic routes.

Note that all domestic flights in Australia are non-smoking.

Cheap Fares

Standby For travellers the best story on the cheap fares side is the availability of standby fares on some main routes. The air fares chart shows the regular fares and the standby fares in brackets. Basically standby fares save you around 20% of the regular economy fare – Melbourne/Sydney, for example, is $181 economy, only $145 standby.

You have no guarantee of a seat when travelling standby. You buy your ticket at the airport, register at the standby desk and then wait for the flight to board. If at that time there is sufficient room for the standby passengers, on you go. If there's room for 10 additional passengers and 20 are on standby then the first 10 to have registered get on. If you miss the flight you can standby for the next one (you'll be that much further up the line if some standby passengers have got on) or you can try the other airline.

A catch with standby fares is that they

only work on a sector basis. If you want to fly Melbourne/Perth and the flight goes via Adelaide you have to standby on the Melbourne/Adelaide sector and then for the Adelaide/Perth sector. Furthermore the fares will be a combination of the two sectors, not a reduction from the direct Melbourne/Perth fare. Fortunately there are a lot more direct flights these days.

If you intend to standby the most likely flights will be, of course, the ones at the most inconvenient times. Very early in the morning, late at night or in the middle of the day are your best bets. Many inter-

capital flights in Australia are really commuter services – Mr Businessman zipping up from Sydney to Brisbane for a day's dealings – so the flights that fit in with the 9 to 5 life are the most crowded. 'Up for the weekend' flights – leaving Friday evening, coming back Sunday afternoon – also tend to be crowded. At other times you've got a pretty good chance of getting aboard.

I've flown standby to quite a few places around Australia and I've always managed to get there, although once or twice it has not been on the first flight I tried.

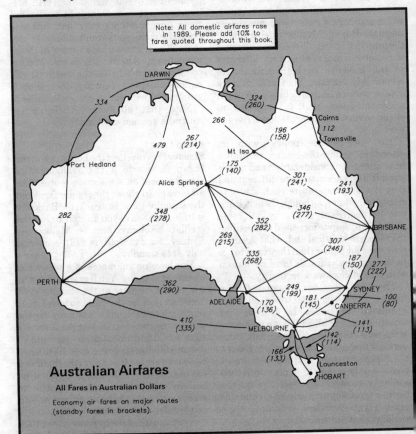

Australian Airfares

All Fares in Australian Dollars

Economy air fares on major routes
(standby fares in brackets).

Incidentally Australia's parallel scheduling can create some scenes of real comedy in the standby game. If you don't get on the Australian Airlines flight you can still try the Ansett one, but that leaves just five minutes later and the Ansett desk is right at the other end of the terminal! Run!

Other Possibilities If you're planning a return trip and you have 30 days up your sleeve then you can save 35% by travelling Apex. You have to book and pay for your tickets 30 days in advance and once you're inside that 30 day period you cannot alter your booking in either direction. If you cancel you lose 50% of the fare.

Excursion fares, called *Excursion 45* by Australian Airlines and *Flexi-Fares* by Ansett, give a 45% reduction on a round-trip ticket, can only be booked between four and 14 days prior to travel and the maximum stay away is 21 days. You book a flight for a nominated day and contact the airline before 12 noon on the day prior to departure to be advised of which flight you will be on. Occasionally to some destinations, you will be on a flight for the following day. Your travel arrangements need to be fairly flexible.

University or other higher education students under the age of 26 can get a 25% discount off the regular economy fare. An airline tertiary concession card is required for Australian students. Overseas students can use their International Student Identity Card, a New Zealand student card or an overseas airline ticket issued at the 25% student reduction. The latter sounds a good bet!

All international travellers can get a 25% discount on internal flights to connect with their arriving or departing international flight – so if you're flying in to Sydney from Los Angeles but intend to go on to the Black Stump you get 25% off the Sydney/Black Stump flight.

Non-Australian travellers coming to Australia on a round trip 'promotional' fare (ie an advance purchase ticket or similar) can get 25% off all regular fares so

long as you travel more than 1000 km, buy the tickets before you arrive or within 30 days of arriving and complete all travel within 60 days of arriving. Whew!

International visitors can also get a good deal on domestic flights with Qantas. Normally Qantas isn't allowed to carry domestic passengers but if you're a visitor to Australia with an international ticket you can fly Qantas at considerable discount. The catch is that these flights are often just the finishing or starting sectors of longer international flights and often operate at less convenient times. Also although domestic passengers are spared a great deal of the international rigmarole the departure and arrival formalities still take rather longer than with a regular domestic flight.

There are also some worthwhile cheaper deals with regional airlines such as East-West. On some lesser routes these operators undercut the big two. Keep your eyes open for special deals at certain times of the year. When the Melbourne Cup horse race is on and when the football grand final happens (also in Melbourne) lots of extra flights are put on. These flights would normally be going in the opposite direction nearly empty so special fares are offered to people wanting to leave Melbourne when everybody else wants to go there. The Australian Grand Prix in Adelaide is a similar one-way-traffic event.

Round Australia Fares

Ansett and Australian Airlines both have special round the country fares – Australian Airlines' is called an *Explorer Airpass*, Ansett's is a *Kangaroo Airpass*. Both have two tickets available – 6000 km for $700 and 10,000 km for $1100. There are a bunch of restrictions applied to these tickets despite which they can be a good deal if you want to see a lot of country in a short period of time. You do not need to start and finish at the same place; you could start in Sydney and end in Darwin for example.

Restrictions include a minimum travel time (10 days) and a maximum (45 days). On the 6000 km pass you must stop at least twice but at most three times. On the 10,000 km pass you must stop at least three times but at most seven. One of the stops must be at a non-capital city destination and be for at least four days. There are requirements about changing reservations although generally there is no charge unless the ticket needs to be rewritten.

On a 6000 km airpass you could, for example, fly Sydney/Alice Springs/Cairns/Brisbane/Sydney. That gives you three stops and two of them are in non-capital cities. The regular fare for that circuit would be $1155 so you save $455. A one-way route might be Adelaide/Melbourne/Sydney/Alice Springs/Perth. There are three stops of which one is a non-capital city. Regular cost for that route would be $1051 so you save $351.

Other Airline Options

There are a number of secondary airlines apart from the two major domestic carriers. In WA there's Ansett WA with an extensive network of flights to the mining towns of the north-west and to Darwin in the Northern Territory. Ansett NT operate from Darwin down to Alice Springs and Ayers Rock and also across to the Queensland and WA coasts. East-West Airlines operate along the east coast, down to Tasmania, across to Ayers Rock and Alice Springs from Sydney and out to Norfolk Island.

There are numerous other smaller operators. Sunstate operate services in Queensland including out to a number of islands. They also have a couple of routes in the south to Mildura and Broken Hill. Skywest have a bunch of services to remote parts of Western Australia. Eastern Airlines operate up and down the NSW coast and also inland from Sydney as far as Bourke and Cobar. Air NSW have services all over NSW, up to Brisbane,

down to Melbourne and in to Alice Springs.

Airport Transport

There are private or public bus services at almost every major town in Australia. In one or two places you may have to depend on taxis but in general you can get between airport and city reasonably economically and conveniently by bus. Quite often a taxi shared between three or more people can be cheaper than the bus.

BUS

Deregulation of the bus system over much of Australia combined with the tourist boom has caused a real bus travel revolution. New companies have come in and the fare wars have been intense. On highly competitive inter-city routes fares have even gone down. Bus travel is generally the cheapest way from A to B, other than hitching of course, but the main problem is to find the best deal.

There are four truly *national* bus networks – Greyhound, Pioneer Express (formerly Ansett Pioneer), Deluxe and the joint network of Bus Australia and (in the east) McCafferty's. Fares are generally very similar, Deluxe is sometimes a dollar or two less and Bus Australia/McCafferty's are often the cheapest of the 'big four' but their services tend to be less frequent in some regions. Greyhound and Pioneer Express also have some 'luxury' services called 5-Star and Silver Service respectively, which are a few dollars more than normal services. Students under 26 years of age can get a discount on some routes, usually it's 10%. Ditto for YHA card holders. YHA travel offices sometimes offer discounts on buses.

There are also many smaller bus companies operating locally or specialising in one or two main inter-city routes. These often offer the best deals – Inter-Capital Express costs $30 for Sydney to Melbourne or Sunliner costs $35. In South Australia Stateliner operate around the state including to the Flinders Ranges. Westrail in Western Australia and V/Line in Victoria operate bus services to places the trains no longer go.

A great many travellers see Australia by bus because it's one of the best ways to come to grips with the country's size and variety of terrain and because the bus companies have such comprehensive route networks – far more comprehensive than the railway system. The buses all look pretty similar. They're similarly equipped with air-conditioning, toilets and quite often videos.

In many locations there is now one bus terminal shared by all the operators. Big city terminals are generally well equipped – they usually have toilets, showers and other facilities.

Routes & Stopovers

The bus companies do not operate identical routes and it's the small print on the tickets which can make the big differences between one company and another when it comes to stopovers and other important considerations. Always check the stopover deals if you want to make stops en route to your final

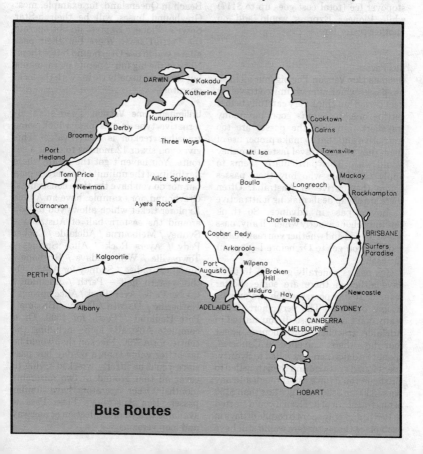

Bus Routes

destination, you can save tens of dollars on supposedly similar fares.

Travelling Alice Springs to Darwin, for example, would cost you $105 with Pioneer Express, $102 with Bus Australia. But if you decided to stop in Katherine on the way Bus Australia would let you stop free while Pioneer Express would then charge you the sector fares, $98 from Alice Springs to Katherine, $30 Katherine to Darwin. The extra cost with Pioneer Express has jumped from $3 more to $26 more. If you wanted to stop at Mataranka as well Bus Australia would add on a $15 stopover fee (total cost goes up to $117) while Pioneer Express would add on another sector fare.

Bus Passes

Unlimited km Version The big four all have bus passes which offer unlimited travel for a set period but think very carefully before getting one. It *sounds* good but many travellers find that the passes are too restrictive and that to make proper use of them they have to travel faster than they would wish. This particularly seems to apply to people who buy their passes before they arrive in Australia. Often there are cheap deals making it attractive to buy a pass in advance. So think carefully about exactly which, if any, pass is best for you and whether you really can't wait till you get to Oz before laying out the cash.

Bus passes generally go from 15 to 60 days although there are some shorter seven or 10 day passes which can only be bought overseas. The very short passes really don't make sense. If you started in Adelaide, travelled to Melbourne, spent four days there, travelled to Canberra, spent two days there, travelled to Sydney, spent four days there and then travelled to Brisbane you'd have run through a 15 day pass ($300 to $330) and got less than $150 of bus travel out of it. Even if you'd started in Perth, and only spent a couple of days in each place the sector fare would still have

cost you only $267 on Greyhound, generally the most expensive bus line.

A 15 day pass typically costs about $300 to $330, a 21 day pass about $450 to $480, a 30 day pass $600 to $630 and a 60 day pass $850 to $880. Greyhound, with the most extensive route network and the most frequent services, is more expensive than Bus Australia or Deluxe. Your bus pass also gives you discounts on local sightseeing tours, accommodation, rental cars and so on. With Greyhound and Pioneer Express you will have to pay extra if you want to travel on their deluxe services. To Airlie Beach in Queensland, for example, most Greyhound buses will be their 5-Star Service. Pioneer Express do not operate the Perth/Darwin route but their pass allows you to use Greyhound buses there. None of the big four operate in Tasmania but there are usually tie ins with the local operators.

Unlimited Time Version There's an alternative type of bus pass which some travellers reckon is better value. This gives you six or 12 months to cover a set route. You haven't got the go-anywhere flexibility of the unlimited travel bus pass but nor do you have the time constraints. Greyhound, for example, have an Aussie Explorer ticket which allows you to loop around the eastern half of Australia – Sydney / Melbourne / Adelaide / Coober Pedy / Ayers Rock / Alice Springs / Townsville / Whitsundays / Brisbane / Surfers Paradise / Sydney for A$430. Or the western half – Perth / Adelaide / Coober Pedy / Ayers Rock / Alice Springs / Katherine / Darwin / Derby / Broome / Port Hedland / Perth for $599. Or a complete Australia loop, including the centre, for A$790. I reckon that would be far better value than a 60-day bus pass since you'd be utterly wrecked trying to cover all that ground in two miserable months! Other operators have similar passes, Bus Australia's Flexi Pass is available in a whole collection of one way and loop versions.

TRAIN

Australia's railway system has never really recovered from the colonial bungling which accompanied its early days over a century ago. Before Australia became an independent country it was governed as six separate colonies, all administered from London. When the colony of Victoria, for example, wanted to build a railway line it checked not with the adjoining colony of New South Wales but with the colonial office in London. When the colonies were federated in 1901 and Australia came into existence, by what

must rate as a sheer masterpiece of misplanning, not one state had railway lines of the same gauge as a neighbouring state!

The immense misfortune of this inept planning has dogged the railway system ever since. The situation between Victoria and New South Wales is a typical example. When NSW started to lay a line from Sydney to Parramatta in 1850 their railway engineer was Irish and convinced the authorities it should be built to wide gauge – five foot three inches. Victoria also started to build to this gauge in order to tie their railways up between Melbourne

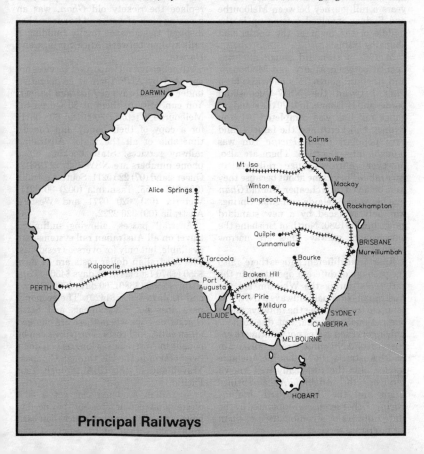

Principal Railways

in with the NSW system if, at some time in the future, a Melbourne-Sydney rail link was completed. Unfortunately NSW then switched railway engineers and their new man was not Irish and not enamoured of wide gauge. NSW railways accordingly switched to standard gauge – four foot eight inches – but Victoria decided their railway construction had gone too far to change now. Thus when the NSW and Victorian railway lines met in Albury in 1883 they, er, didn't meet. The Victorian railway lines were seven inches wider apart than the NSW ones. For the next 79 years a rail journey between Melbourne and Sydney involved getting up in the middle of the night at the border and changing trains!

In 1962 a standard gauge line was opened between Albury and Melbourne and standard gauge lines have also been built between the NSW-Queensland border and Brisbane. In 1970 the standard gauge rail link was completed between Sydney and Perth and the famous, and very popular, *Indian-Pacific* run was brought into operation. There are also, however, narrow gauge railways in Australia. They came about because they were believed to be cheaper. The old *Ghan* line between Adelaide and Alice Springs was only replaced by a new standard gauge line in 1980. North of Brisbane the Queensland railway lines are narrow gauge.

Apart from different gauges there's also the problem of different operators. In the early '70s during the Whitlam era the Australian National Railways (ANR) was set up to try and bring the railways under one national umbrella, but due to non-Labor governed states not wanting to co-operate the ANR only operates railways in South Australia, the Melbourne/Adelaide service plus the two really well known services, the Adelaide/Alice Springs *Ghan* and the Sydney/Perth *Indian-Pacific*. Other services are operated by the state railways or a combination of them for interstate services.

Rail travel in Australia today is basically something you do because you really want to – not because it's cheaper (it isn't) and certainly not because it's fast. Rail travel is generally the slowest way to get from anywhere to anywhere in Australia. On the other hand the trains are comfortable and you certainly see Australia at ground level in a way no other means of travel permits.

Australia is also one of the few places in the world today where new lines are still being laid or are under consideration. The new line from Tarcoola to Alice Springs, to replace the rickety old *Ghan*, was an amazing piece of work and its success has inspired thoughts of finally building a railway line between Alice Springs and Darwin.

Although not all important services are operated by ANR there is co-operation under the Railways of Australia banner. You can write to them at 80 Queen St, Melbourne, Victoria 3000 (tel 608 0811) for a copy of their handy and concise timetable of all the major Australian railway services. State booking office phone numbers are NSW (02) 217 8812, Queensland (07) 225 0211, South Australia (08) 217 4455, Tasmania (002) 30 0211, Victoria (03) 620 0771 and Western Australia (09) 326 2222.

Austrail passes, allowing unlimited travel on all Australian rail systems, are available, but only for overseas residents. The Australian dollar costs are 14 days $350 ($570 1st class), 21 days $450 ($720), 30 days $550 ($880), 60 days $780 ($1230) and 90 days $900 ($1420). The economy pass does not cover meals and berth charges on trips where these are charged for as additional costs. The passes can be bought in Australia (as long as you don't live here) or in the UK through Compass Travel and in the USA through Tour Pacific.

Australian students can get a 50% discount on regular fares but they need to have a railways student concession card from their college or university. Caper fares are an advance purchase deal which gives a saving of up to 30% and on some major routes there are standby tickets. On interstate rail journeys you can usually break your journey at no extra cost provided you complete the trip within two months on a one-way ticket, six months with a return ticket.

On most routes you can take your car with you by train.

CAR

Australia is a big, sprawling country with large cities where public transport is not always very comprehensive or convenient. Like America the car is the accepted means of getting from A to B and many visitors will consider getting wheels to explore the country – either by buying a car or renting one.

Driving in Australia holds few real surprises. We drive on the left hand side of the road just like in England, Japan and most countries in south and east Asia and the Pacific. There are a few local variations from the rules of the road as applied elsewhere in the west. The main one is the 'give way to the right' rule. This means that if you're driving along a main road and somebody appears on a minor road on your right, you must give way to them – unless they are facing a give-way or stop sign. This rule caused so much confusion over the years – with cars zooming out of tiny tracks onto main highways and expecting everything to screech to a stop for them – that most intersections are now signposted to indicate which is the priority road. It's wise to be careful because while almost every intersection will be signposted in southern capitals, when you get up to towns in the north of Queensland, stop signs will still be few and far between and the old give-way rules will apply.

The give-way ruling has a special and very confusing interpretation in Victoria where if two cars travelling in opposite directions both turn into the same street, the vehicle turning right has priority. This rule only seems to apply in Victoria and causes no end of headaches and confusion for non-Victorian drivers.

There's another special hazard in Melbourne – trams. You can only overtake trams from the left lane and must stop behind them when they stop to pick up or drop off passengers. Be aware of trams – they weigh about as much as the *Queen Mary* and do not swerve to avoid foolish drivers. In central Melbourne there are also a number of intersections where a special technique, mastered only by native Melbournians, must be employed when making right hand turns. You must turn from the left hand side of the road.

The general speed limit in built-up areas in Australia is 60 kph (38 mph) and out on the open highway it's usually 100 or 110 kph (60 to 70 mph) depending on where you are. The police have radar speed traps and are very fond of using them in carefully hidden locations in order to raise easy revenue – don't exceed the speed limit in inviting areas where the gentlemen in blue may be waiting for you. On the other hand when you get far from the cities and traffic is light, you'll see a lot of vehicles moving a lot faster than 100 kph.

On the Road

Australia is not criss-crossed by multi-lane highways. There simply is not enough traffic and the distances are too great to justify them. You'll certainly find stretches of divided road, particularly on busy roads like the Sydney to Melbourne Hume Highway or close to the state capital cities – the last stretch into Adelaide from Melbourne, the Pacific Highway from Sydney to Newcastle, the Surfers Paradise-Brisbane road, for example. Elsewhere Australian roads are only two lane but of a good, surfaced standard (though a long way from the billiard table surfaces the poms are used to driving on) on all the main routes. Many roads are rather bumpy and patched.

You don't have to get very far off the

beaten track, however, to find yourself on dirt roads and anybody who sets out to see the country in reasonable detail will have to expect to do some dirt-road travelling. If you really want to explore outlandish places, then you'd better plan on having 4WD (four-wheel drive) and a winch. A few useful spare parts are worth carrying if you're travelling on highways in the Northern Territory or the north of Western Australia. A broken fan belt can be a damn nuisance if the next service station is 200 km away.

Driving standards in Australia aren't exactly the highest in the world but to a large extent the appalling accident rate is due to the habit that suitably boozed country drivers have of flying off the road into the gum trees. Drive carefully, especially on the weekend evenings when the drinking-drivers are about. Note also that the police are doing their best to make drinking and driving a foolish practice, even if you don't hit something. Random breath tests and goodbye licence if you exceed '.05' are the order of the day.

Australia was one of the first countries in the world to make the wearing of seat belts compulsory. All new cars in Australia are required to have seat belts back and front and if your seat has a belt then you're required to wear it. You're liable to be fined if you don't. Small children are only allowed in the front seats if they're belted into an approved safety seat.

Petrol is available from stations sporting the well-known international brand names. Prices vary from place to place and from price war to price war but generally it's in the 50 to 60c a litre range (say around $2.45 to $2.70 an imperial gallon). In the outback the price can soar and some outback service stations are not above exploiting their monopoly position. Distances between fill-ups can be long in the outback and in some remote areas deliveries can be haphazard – it's not unknown to finally arrive at that 'nearest station x hundred km' only to find there's no fuel until next week's delivery!

Although overseas licences are acceptable in Australia for genuine overseas visitors, an International Driving Permit is even more acceptable. Between cities signposting on the main roads is generally quite OK but around cities it's usually abysmal. You can spend a lot of time trying to find street-name signs and as for indicating which way to go to leave the city – until recently you were half way to Sydney from Melbourne before you saw the first sign telling you that you were travelling in the right direction.

Way Outback Travel

Although you can now drive all the way round Australia on Highway 1 or through the middle all the way from Adelaide in the south to Darwin in the north without ever leaving sealed road that hasn't always been so. The Eyre Highway across the Nullarbor Desert in the south was only surfaced in the 1970s, the final stretch of Highway 1 in the Kimberley region of Western Australia was done in the mid-80s and the final section of the Stuart Highway from Port Augusta up to Alice Springs was finished in 1987.

If you really want to see outback Australia there are still lots of roads where the official recommendation is that you report to the police before you leave one

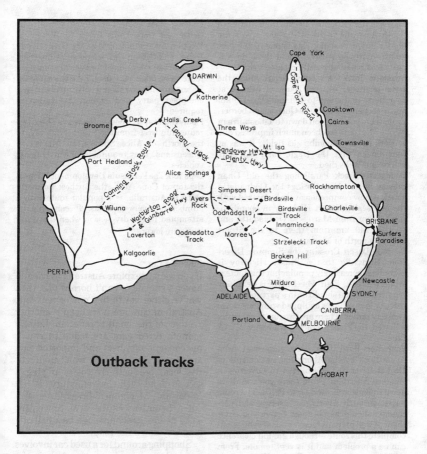

Outback Tracks

end, and again when you arrive at the other. That way if you fail to turn up at the other end they can start the search parties. Nevertheless many of these tracks are now much better kept than in years past and you don't need 4WD or fancy expedition equipment to tackle them. You do need to be carefully prepared and to carry important spare parts, however. Backtracking 500 km to pick up some minor malfunctioning component or, much worse, to arrange a tow, is unlikely to be easy or cheap.

The state automobile associations can advise on preparation and supply maps and track notes. Most tracks have an ideal time of year – in the centre it's not wise to attempt the tough tracks during the heat of summer when the dust can be severe, chances of mechanical trouble are much greater and water will be scarce and hence a breakdown more dangerous. Similarly in the north travelling in the wet season may be impossible due to flooding and mud.

Some of the favourite tracks include:

Birdsville Track Running 499 km from Marree in South Australia to Birdsville just across the border in Queensland, this is one of the best known routes in Australia and these days is quite feasible in any well prepared vehicle.

Strzelecki Track This track covers much the same territory, starting south of Marree at Lyndhurst and going to Innamincka, 473 km north-east and close to the Queensland border. From there you can loop down to Tibooburra in NSW. The route has been much improved due to work on the Moomba gas fields. It was at Innamincka that the tragic early explorers Burke and Wills died.

Oodnadatta Track Paralleling the old Ghan railway line to Alice Springs the Oodnadatta Track is now comprehensively by-passed with the new sealed Stuart Highway in operation. It's 465 km from Marree to Oodnadatta and another 240 km from there to the Stuart Highway north of Marla.

Simpson Desert Crossing the Simpson Desert from Birdsville to the Stuart Highway is becoming increasingly popular but this route is still a real test. Four-wheel drive is definitely required and you should be in a party of at least three or four vehicles equipped with long range two-way radios. There are two routes generally followed, the French Track or the easier WAAA Line.

Warburton Road This route runs west from Ayers Rock by the Aboriginal settlements of Docker River and Warburton to Laverton in Western Australia. From there you can drive down to Kalgoorlie and on to Perth. The route passes through Aboriginal reserves and per-mission should be obtained before you enter them. A well prepared conventional vehicle can complete this route although ground clearance can be a problem and it is very remote. From the Yulara resort at Ayers Rock to Warburton is 567 km, another 568 km from there to Laverton. It's then 361 km on sealed road to Kalgoorlie. For 44 km near the Giles Meteorological Station the Warburton Rd and the Gunbarrel Highway run on the same route, taking the Gunbarrel all the way to Wiluna in Western Australia is a much rougher trip requiring 4WD.

Tanami Track Turning off the Stuart Highway just north of Alice Springs the Tanami Track goes north-west across the Central Desert to Halls Creek in Western Australia. Conventional vehicles with sufficient ground clearance are OK but there are long sandy stretches.

Canning Stock Route This old stock trail runs south-west from Halls Creek to Wiluna in Western Australia. It crosses the Great Sandy Desert and Gibson Desert and since the track has not been maintained for over 30 years it's a route to be taken seriously. Like the Simpson Desert crossing you should only travel in a well equipped party and careful navigation is required.

Plenty Highway & Sandover Highways These two routes run west from the Stuart Highway, to the north of Alice Springs, to Mt Isa in Queensland. They're suitable for conventional vehicles.

Cape York The Peninsula Development Rd up to the top of Cape York, the furthest northerly point in Australia, is a popular route with a number of rivers to cross. It can only be attempted in the dry season when the water levels are lower.

Buying a Car

If you want to explore Australia by car and haven't got one or can't borrow one, then you've either got to buy one or rent one. Australian cars are not cheap – another product of the small population. Locally manufactured cars are made in small, uneconomic numbers and imported cars are heavily taxed so they won't undercut the local products. If you're buying a second-hand vehicle reliability is all important. Mechanical breakdowns way out in the outback can be very inconvenient – the nearest mechanic can be a hell of a long way down the road.

Shopping around for a used car involves much the same rules as anywhere in the western world but with a few local variations. First of all, used car dealers in Australia are just like used car dealers from Los Angeles to London – they'd sell their mother into slavery if it turned a dollar. For any given car you'll probably get it cheaper by buying privately through newspaper small ads rather than through a car dealer. Buying through a dealer does give the the advantage of some sort of guarantee, but a guarantee is not much use if you're buying a car in Sydney and intend setting off for Perth next week.

Used car guarantee requirements vary from state to state – check with the local automotive organisation.

There's much discussion amongst travellers about where is the best place to buy used cars. Popular theories exist that you can buy a car in Sydney or Melbourne, drive it to Darwin and sell it there for a profit. Or was it vice-versa? It's quite possible that car values do vary from place to place but don't count on turning it to your advantage. See the section on buying cars in Sydney for buying cars at that popular starting/finishing point.

What is rather more certain is that the further you get from civilisation, the better it is to be in a Holden or a Falcon. New cars can be a whole different ball game of course, but if you're in an older vehicle, something that's likely to have the odd hiccup from time to time, then life is much simpler if it's a car for which you can get spare parts anywhere from Bourke to Bulamakanka. When your fancy Japanese car goes kaput somewhere back of Bourke it's likely to be a two week wait while the new bit arrives fresh from Fukuoka. On the other hand, when your rusty old Holden goes bang there's probably another old Holden sitting in the ditch with a perfectly good widget waiting to be removed. Every scrap yard in Australia is full of good ole Holdens.

Note that in Australia third party personal injury insurance is always included in the vehicle registration cost. This ensures that every vehicle (as long as it's currently registered) carries at least minimum insurance. You're wise to extend that minimum to at least third party property insurance as well – minor collisions with Rolls-Royces can be surprisingly expensive. When you come to buy or sell a car there are usually some local regulations to be complied with. In Victoria, for example, a car has to have a compulsory safety check (Road Worthiness Certificate – RWC) before it can be registered in the new owner's name – usually the seller will indicate if the car already has a RWC. In NSW, on the other hand, safety checks are compulsory every year when you come to renew the registration. Stamp duty has to be paid when you buy a car and as this is based on the purchase price, it's not unknown for buyer and seller to agree privately to understate the price! It's much easier to sell a car in the same state that it's registered in, otherwise it has to be re-registered in the new state.

Finally, make use of the automotive organisations – see the Information section in the Facts for the Visitor chapter for more details about them. They can advise you on any local regulations you should be aware of, give general guidelines about buying a car and, most importantly, for a fee will check over a used car and report on its condition before you agree to purchase it. They also offer car insurance to their members.

The Lonely Planet Falcon

To update this edition of Australia we decided to buy a car, drive it round Australia and sell it again at the end. Apart from providing the transport we needed to get around it also meant we'd have an idea of what was involved in the buying and selling game. We budgeted $10,000 to get a good set of wheels, a lot more than most travellers probably allow for but with deadlines to meet we couldn't afford any reliability problems.

We quickly found a 1985 Ford Falcon with 111,000 km on the clock. We then forked over $50 to the RACV to have it checked over and having been told it was in fine condition we bought it for $10,150. We had it serviced, paid the state government $417 to transfer the ownership and our insurance company $533 for a year's comprehensive insurance.

John and Susan then jumped aboard and headed off to Darwin where they arrived three months and 14,000 km later. Along the way they'd gone through a couple of radiator hoses and had a 10,000 km service and a new wheel bearing fitted in Cairns. It needed a timing cover oil seal in Darwin where I (Tony speaking here) arrived to pick it up. Maureen and I, with our two children in the back, then set out to drive down to Perth, 6000 km away. The mighty

Falcon, as it was dubbed by all and sundry at LP, performed flawlessly on that long empty route. The only minor problems were a broken headlight and a kinked parking brake cable, both fixed in Broome.

In Perth we handed the keys to Richard who brought it all the way back to Melbourne, adding another 10,000 km to the total. The car was serviced in Perth before he left and nothing went wrong. So we did a six month, 30,500 km circuit of the country with nothing more than minor malfunctions. A nice reliable car.

Along the way we'd put 3576 litres of petrol into it, an average of 11.7 litres per 100 km or 24 miles per gallon. Not bad for a big four litre car, often travelling quite fast and with the air conditioner running. Interestingly our three drivers were about equally economical, I used the most on the Perth-Darwin run. The petrol varied in price enormously, Richard had the cheapest fill (Lyndoch in South Australia where he paid a price war 39.7c a litre) and also the most expensive (Caiguna on the Nullarbor where it cost 78.9c a litre, almost twice as much!). Overall it averaged out to 60.1c a litre.

Back in Melbourne we had to fit two new tyres and a new windscreen (cracked by a stone in WA) plus do some other minor repairs in order to get the RWC (Road Worthiness Certificate) necessary to sell it. Ads in the paper got few enquiries until we knocked the price down to $8000 from where we quickly sold it for $7850. So what had the whole exercise cost us:

depreciation	$2300
RACV test	50
registration transfer	417
10,000 km services plus other repairs & replacements	1603
petrol	2150
six month's insurance	266
car for sale ad	19
Total	$6805

That works out to 22c a km. Could we have done it cheaper? Well we could have searched around a bit more for a better buy to start with, but with an extra 30,000 km on it plus an about to expire registration certificate it obviously had to be worth less when we came to sell it. We didn't scrimp on services or try to fix things ourselves so we could have saved a few dollars there if we'd wanted to.

Calculated over six month's use our total costs except for petrol came out to about $25 a day. For comparison purposes Thrifty or Budget will rent you a medium car (Holden

The Lonely Planet Falcon

Camira or Nissan Pintara size) for about $38 to $44 a day inclusive of insurance or a large car (Ford Falcon or Holden Commodore) for about $42 to $50 a day.

Renting a Car

If you've got the cash there are plenty of car rental companies ready and willing to put you behind the wheel. Competition in the Australian car rental business is pretty fierce so rates tend to be variable and lots of special deals pop up and disappear again. Whatever your mode of travel on the long stretches, it can be very useful to have a car for some local travel. Between a group it can even be reasonably economical. There are some places – like around Alice Springs – where if you haven't got your own wheels you really have to choose between a tour and a rented vehicle since there is no public transport and the distances are too great for walking or even bicycles.

The three major companies are Budget, Hertz and Avis with offices in almost every town that has more than one pub and a general store. The second-string companies which are also represented almost everywhere in the country are Thrifty and National. Then there are a vast number of local firms or firms with outlets in a limited number of locations. You can take it as read that the big operators will generally have higher rates than the local firms but it ain't necessarily so, so don't jump to conclusions.

The big firms have a number of big advantages, however. First of all they're the ones at the airports – Avis, Budget, Hertz and, quite often, Thrifty, are represented at most airports. If you want to pick up a car or leave a car at the airport then they're the best ones to deal with. In some but not all airports other companies will also arrange to pick up or leave their cars there. It tends to depend on how convenient the airport is.

The second advantage of the big companies is if you want to do a one-way rental – pick up a car in Adelaide, leave it in Sydney. There are however, a variety of restrictions on these. Usually it's a minimum hire period rather than re-positioning charges. Only certain cars may be eligible for one-ways. Check the small print on one-way charges before deciding on one company rather than another. One-way rentals are generally not available into or out of the Northern Territory or Western Australia. Special rules may also apply to one-ways into or out of other 'remote areas'.

The major companies all offer unlimited km rates in the city but in country and 'remote' areas it's a flat charge plus so many cents per km. On straightforward off-the-card city rentals they're all pretty much the same price. It's on special deals, odd rentals or longer periods that you find the differences. Weekend specials, usually three days for the price of two, are usually good value. If you just need a car for three days around Sydney make it the weekend rather than midweek. Budget offer 'standby' rates and you may see other special deals available. Picking up a car in Townsville once I saw a sign offering cars free, so long as you got them to Cairns within 24 hours!

Daily metropolitan rates are typically about $50 a day for a small car (Ford Laser, Toyota Corolla, Nissan Pulsar), about $63 a day for a medium car (Holden Camira, Toyota Camry, Nissan Pintara) or about $75 a day for a big car (Holden Commodore, Ford Falcon). Add another $12 a day for insurance. Typically country rates will be metropolitan plus $5 a day plus 25c a km beyond 200 km a day. Remote rates will be metropolitan plus $10 a day plus 25c a km beyond 100 km a day. It soon gets expensive!

There are a whole collection of other factors to bear in mind about this rent-a-car business. For a start if you're going to want it for a week, a month or longer then they all have lower rates. If you're in Tasmania, where competition is very fierce, there are often lower rates especially in the low-season. If you're in the really remote outback (some place like Darwin and Alice Springs are only vaguely remote) then the choice of cars is likely to be limited to the larger, more expensive ones. You usually must be at least 21 to hire from most firms.

OK, that's the big hire companies, what about all the rest of them? Well some of them are still pretty big in terms of numbers of shiny new cars. In Tasmania, for example, the car hire business is really big since many people don't bring their cars with them. There's a plethora of hire companies and lots of competition. In many cases local companies are markedly cheaper than the big boys but in others what looks like a cheaper rate can end up quite the opposite if you're not careful. Quick, what's cheaper: $40 a day, or $20 a day plus 15c a km in excess of 100 km – if you do 200 km? And if you do 300?

Don't forget the 'rent-a-wreck' companies. They specialise in renting older cars – at first they really were old and flat figure like $10 a day and forget the insurance was the usual story. Now many of them have a variety of rates. If you just want to travel around the city, or not too far out, they can be worth considering.

Mokes In lots of popular holiday areas – like on the Gold Coast, around Cairns, on Magnetic Island, around Alice Springs, in Darwin – right at the bottom of the rent-a-car rates will be the ubiquitous Moke. To those not in the know a Moke is a totally open vehicle looking rather like a miniature Jeep. They're based on the Mini so they're FWD (front-wheel drive) not 4WD (four-wheel drive) and they are not suitable for getting way off the beaten track. For general good fun in places with a sunny climate, however, they simply can't be beaten. No vehicle has more air-conditioning than a Moke and as the stickers say 'Moking is not a wealth hazard' – they cover lots of km on a litre of petrol.

If you do hire a Moke there are a few points to watch. Don't have an accident in one, they offer little more protection than a motorcycle. There is absolutely no place to lock things up so don't leave your valuables inside, and the fuel tanks are equally accessible so if you're leaving it somewhere at night beware of petrol thieves – not that there are a great number in Australia, but it does happen.

4WDs Renting a four-wheel drive (4WD) vehicle is within the budget range if a few people get together – often you can get a 4WD for around $60 a day plus fuel (plus a hefty deposit which you get back if you do no damage to it). Four-wheel drive enable you to get right off the beaten track and out to some of the great wilderness and outback places, to see some of the Australian natural wonders that most travellers don't see.

Renting Other Vehicles

There are lots of other vehicles you can rent apart from cars. In remote outback areas you can often rent 4WD vehicles. In many places you can rent camper vans – they're particularly popular in Tasmania. Motorcycles are also available in a number of locations – they are popular on Magnetic Island for example. Best of all, in many places you can rent bicycles.

MOTORCYCLE

Motorcycles are a very popular way of getting around although the accident rate is also rather frightening. The climate is just about ideal for biking most of the year and the long open roads are really made for large capacity highway cruisers. Maureen and I have ridden two-up from Melbourne all the way to Darwin (via Sydney, Brisbane, Cairns, Cooktown, Mt Isa, The Alice and Ayers Rock) on a 250cc trail bike, so doing it on a small bike is not impossible, just more boring.

BICYCLE

Whether you're hiring a bike to ride around a city or wearing out your Bio-Pace chain-wheels on a Melbourne-Darwin marathon, you'll find that Australia is a great place for cycling. There are bike tracks in most cities, and in the country you'll find thousands of km of good roads which carry so little traffic that the biggest hassle is waving back to the drivers. Especially appealing is that in many areas you'll ride a very long way without encountering a hill.

It's possible to plan rides of any duration and through almost any terrain. A day or two cycling around South Australia's wineries is popular, or you could meander along beside the Murrumbidgee for weeks. Tasmania is very popular for touring, and mountain bikes would love Australia's deserts – or its mountains, for that matter.

And from his bike saddle Jon Murray, Lonely Planet editor and bike-tourer, reports:

Cycling has always been popular here, and not only as a sport: some shearers would ride for huge distances between jobs, rather than use less reliable horses. It's rare to find a reasonably-sized town that doesn't have a shop stocking at least basic bike parts.

If you're coming specifically to cycle it makes sense to bring your own bike. Check your airline for costs and the degree of dismantling/packing required. Within Australia you can load your bike onto a bus or train to skip the boring bits. Note that bus companies require you to dismantle your bike, and some don't guarantee that it will travel on the same bus as you. Trains are easier, but supervise the loading and if possible tie your bike upright, otherwise you may find that the guard had stacked crates of Holden spares on you fragile alloy wheels.

You can buy a good steel-framed touring bike here for about $400 (plus panniers). It may be possible to rent touring bikes and equipment from a few of the commercial touring organisations.

Much of eastern Australia seems to have been settled on the principle of not having more than a day's horse-ride between pubs, so it's possible to plan even ultra-long routes and still get a shower at the end of the day. Most people do carry camping equipment, but it's feasible to travel from town to town staying in hotels or on-site vans.

You can get by with standard road maps, but as you'll probably want to avoid both the highways and the low-grade unsealed roads, the Government NatMap series are best. The 1:250,000 scale are the most suitable but you'll need a lot of them if you're covering much territory. The next scale up, 1:1,000,000 is adequate. They are available in capital cities and elsewhere.

Until you get fit you should be careful to eat enough to keep you going – remember that exercise is an appetite suppressant. It's surprisingly easy to be so depleted of energy that you end up camping under a gum tree just 10 km short of a shower and a steak.

No matter how fit you are, water is still vital. Dehydration is no joke and can be life-threatening. I rode my first 200-km-in-a-day on a bowl of cornflakes and a round of sandwiches, but the Queensland sun forced me to drink nearly five litres. Having been involved in a drinking contest with stockmen the night before may have had something to do with it, though.

It can get very hot in summer, and you should take things slowly until you're used to the heat. Cycling in 35°C-plus temperatures isn't too bad if you wear a hat and plenty of sunscreen, and drink *lots* of water. In the eastern states, be aware of the blistering 'hot northerlies', the prevailing winds that make a north-bound cyclist's life uncomfortable in summer. In April, when the south-east's clear autumn weather begins, the Southerly Trades prevail, and you can have (theoretically at least) tailwinds all the way to Darwin.

Of course, you don't have to follow the larger roads and visit towns. It's possible to fill your mountain bike's panniers with muesli, head out into the mulga, and not see anyone for weeks. Or ever again – outback travel is very risky if not properly planned. Water is the main problem in the 'dead heart', and you can't rely on it where there aren't settlements. That tank marked on your map may be dry or unbearably salty, and those station buildings probably blew away years ago. That little creek marked with a dotted blue line? Forget it – the only time it has water is when the country's flooded for hundreds of km.

Always check with locals if you're heading into remote areas, and notify the police if you're about to do something particularly adventurous. That said, you can't rely too much on local knowledge of road conditions – most people have no idea of what a heavily loaded touring bike needs. What they think of as a great road may be pedal-deep in sand or bull-dust, and I've happily ridden along roads that were officially flooded out.

Information

Bicycle Australia, PO Box 1047 Campbelltown, NSW, 2560, is the national touring organisation, with some useful publications about cycling in Australia – send $2 (refunded on first purchase) for their mail-order catalogue. They are researching a 14-stage around Australia route, and can provide route maps of the completed sections, and guides for other tours.

The various state automobile associations publish guides to camping grounds and caravan parks.

In each state there are touring organisations which can help with information and put you in touch with touring clubs:

Australian Capital Territory
    Pedal Power ACT, PO Box 581, Canberra, ACT 2601
New South Wales
    Bicycle Institute of New South Wales, GPO Box 272, Sydney 2001
Queensland
    Brisbane Cycle Touring Association, PO Box 315 Ashgrove 4060
South Australia
    Cyclists' Protection Association, GPO Box 792, Adelaide 5001
Tasmania
    Pedal Power Tasmania, 102 Bathhurst St, Hobart 7000
Victoria
    Bicycle Victoria, GPO Box 1961R, Melbourne 3001 (tel 670 9911)
Western Australia
    Cyclists Action Group, 2 Barsden St, Cottleslowe 6011

There are many organised tours available of varying lengths and if you get tired of talking to sheep as you ride along, it might be a good idea to include one or more in your itinerary. Most provide a support vehicle and take care of accommodation

and cooking, so they can be a nice break from solo chores.

Bicycle Australia has a good range of low-cost tours – they're a non-profit organisation.

HITCHING

Travel by thumb may be frowned upon by the boys in blue in some places but it can be a good way of getting around and it is certainly interesting. Sometimes it can even be fast, but it's usually foolish to try and set yourself deadlines when travelling this way – you need luck. Successful hitching depends on several factors, all of them just plain good sense.

The most important is your numbers – two people are really the ideal, any more makes things very difficult. Ideally those two should comprise one male and one female – two guys hitching together can expect long waits. It is not recommended for women to hitch unaccompanied by a male, and a woman should never hitch solo.

Factor two is position – look for a place where vehicles will be going slowly and where they can stop easily. A junction or freeway slip road are good places if there is stopping room. Position goes beyond just where you stand. The ideal location is on the outskirts of a town – hitching from way out in the country is as hopeless as from the centre of a city. Take a bus out to the edge of town.

Factor three is appearance – the ideal appearance for hitching is a sort of genteel poverty – threadbare but clean. Looking too good can be as much of a bummer as looking too bad! Don't carry too much gear – if it looks like it's going to take half an hour to pack your bags aboard you'll be left on the roadside.

Factor four is knowing when to say no. Saying no to a car load of drunks or your friendly rapist is pretty obvious but it can be time saving to say no to a short ride that might take you from a good hitching point to a lousy one. Wait for the right, long ride to come along. On a long haul, it's pointless to start walking as it's not likely to increase the likelihood of you getting a lift and it's often an awfully long way to the next town.

Trucks are often the best lifts but they will only stop if they are going slowly and can get started easily again. Thus the ideal place is at the top of a hill where they have a downhill run. Truckies often say they are going to the next town and if they don't like you, will drop you anywhere. As they often pick up hitchers for company, the quickest way to create a bad impression is to jump in and fall asleep. It's also worth remembering that while you're in someone else's vehicle, you are their guest and should act accordingly – many drivers no longer pick up people because they have suffered from thought-less hikers in the past. It's the hitcher's duty to provide entertainment!

Hitching in Australia is really very easy, we are supposed to be friendly remember, and if you take care with your rides it is reasonably safe. Of course people do get stuck in outlandish places but that is the name of the game. If you're visiting from abroad a nice prominent flag on your pack will help, and a sign announcing your destination can also be useful. Uni and youth hostel notice boards are good places to look for hitching partners. The main law against hitching is 'thou shalt not stand in the road' – so when you see the law coming, step back.

BOAT

Not really. Once upon a time there was quite a busy coastal shipping service but now it only applies to freight and apart from specialised bulk carriers, even that is declining rapidly. The only regular shipping service is between Victoria and Tasmania and unless you are taking a vehicle with you the very cheapest ticket on that often-choppy route is not all that much cheaper than the air-fare. You can occasionally travel between Australian ports on a liner bound for somewhere but very few people do that.

On the other hand it *is* quite possible to make your way round the coast or even to other countries like NZ, PNG or Indonesia by hitching rides or crewing on yachts. Ask around at harbours, marinas or yacht or sailing clubs. Good places on the east coast include Coffs Harbour, Great Keppel Island, Airlie Beach/Whitsundays, Cairns – anywhere where boats call. Usually you have to chip in something like $10 a day for food.

TOURS

There are all sorts of tours around Australia including some interesting camping tours. Adventure tours include 4WD safaris in the Northern Territory and up into far north Queensland. Some of these go to places you simply couldn't get to on your own without large amounts of expensive equipment. You can also walk, ski, boat, raft, canoe, horse-ride, camel-ride or even fly.

YHA tours are good value – find out about them at YHA Travel offices in capital cities. In major centres like Sydney, Darwin and Cairns there are many tours aimed specially at backpackers – good prices, good destinations, good fun.

STUDENT TRAVEL

STA Travel is the main agent for student travellers in Australia. They have a network of travel offices around the country and apart from selling normal tickets also have special student discounts and tours. STA Travel don't only cater to students, they also act as normal travel agents to the public in general. The STA Travel head office is in Faraday St, Melbourne but there are a number of other offices around the various cities and at the universities. The main offices are:

Australian Capital Territory
    Arts Centre, Australian National University, Canberra 2600 (tel 47 0800)
New South Wales
    1A Lee St, Railway Square, Sydney 2000 (tel 212 1255)

Queensland
Northern Security Building, 40 Creek St, Brisbane 4000 (tel 221 9629)
South Australia
55A O'Connell St, North Adelaide 5006 (tel 267 1855)
Tasmania
Union Building, University of Tasmania, Churchill Avenue, Sandy Bay 7005 (tel 23 3825)
Victoria
220 Faraday St, Carlton 3053 (tel 347 6911)
Western Australia
426 Hay St, Subiaco 6008 (tel 382 3977)

Australian Capital Territory

Area	2366 square km
Population	274,000

When the separate colonies of Australia were federated in 1901 and became states, the decision to build a national capital was part of the constitution. The site was selected in 1908, diplomatically situated between arch rivals Sydney and Melbourne, and an international competition to design the capital was won by the American architect, Walter Burley Griffin. In 1911 the Commonwealth government bought the land of the Australian Capital Territory (ACT), which is 80 km from north to south, and in 1913 decided to call the capital Canberra, believed to be an Aboriginal term for 'meeting place'.

Early development of the site was painfully slow and it was not until 1927 that parliament was first convened in the capital. In the interim, Melbourne acted as the national capital. The Depression virtually halted development again and things really only got under way after WW II. In the '50s, '60s and '70s progress was incredibly rapid and for some time Canberra was Australia's fastest growing city. Satellite cities sprang up at Belconnen and Woden. In 1960 the population topped 50,000, reaching 100,000 by 1967. Today the ACT has more than 250,000 people.

Canberra is unlike other large Australian cities: it's amazingly ordered and neat, and it is an inland, not a coastal, city. Despite its reputation as a boring, soulless place to live, it has a fairly young population and there's a great deal to see and do.

It also has a beautiful setting, surrounded as it is by hills, and is no distance at all from good bushwalking and skiing country.

INFORMATION

The Canberra Tourist Bureau has interstate offices at:

New South Wales
    64 Castlereagh St, Sydney, NSW 2000 (tel 233 3666)
Victoria
    247 Collins St, Melbourne, Vic 3000 (tel 654 5088)
Western Australia
    Allendale Square, 77 St Georges Terrace, Perth, WA 6000 (tel 325 1533)

ACTIVITIES
Bushwalking

The Canberra Bushwalking Club is at The Environment Centre (tel 47 3064), Kingsley St, Acton. Graeme Barrow's *25 Family Bushwalks In & Around Canberra* can be found in most city bookshops. Several of the parks and reserves in the south of the ACT have good bushwalks. Tidbinbilla Fauna Reserve has marked trails. Other good places include the Gudgenby and Mt Kelly areas, the Cotter Reserve, and Mt Franklin – see the Around Canberra section for details.

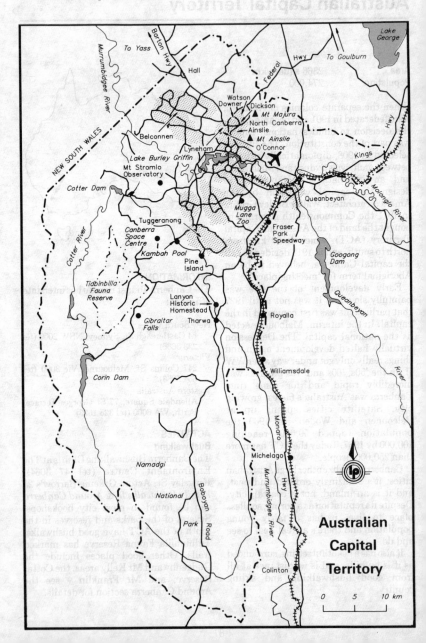

Australian Capital Territory

0   5   10 km

Water Sports

Boating Rowing or paddle boats, canoes, windsurfers and catamarans can be rented from Dobel Boat Hire (tel 49 6861) near the Acton Park Ferry Terminal on Lake Burley Griffin. They're open daily and windsurfers and catamarans are $10 an hour. The Canberra Rowing Club (tel 48 9738) welcomes visitors. A brochure on safety procedure and weather conditions on the lake is available – no power boats are permitted.

Swimming It's a 150 km drive to the nearest surf beaches at Batemans Bay in New South Wales – there's a daily Murrays bus service. Swimming pools around the city include the Canberra Olympic Pool on Allara St, Civic. There's river and lake swimming outside the city – see the Around Canberra section. There's even a nude bathing area along the Murrumbidgee. Swimming in Lake Burley Griffin is not recommended.

Skiing

The New South Wales Snowy Mountains snowfields are within an easy four hour drive of Canberra. The Canberra Tourist Bureau can supply the latest news on conditions, as can the YMCA (tel 49 8733), which has lodges at Guthega and Thredbo. A number of local garages, as well as the conventional ski shops, hire out equipment.

Cycling

Canberra has a great series of bicycle tracks – probably the best and most extensive in Australia. A map of Canberra bicycle tracks is available, as is a brochure called *Canberra: On a Bike Tour*. See the Getting Around section for bike rental information.

One particularly popular track is a circuit of the lake; there are also peaceful stretches of bushland along some of the suburban routes.

Canberra

Population 219,331

The capital is amazingly orderly – there's no gradual disintegration into a jumble of used car lots further from the centre. Canberra is a place of government and public services with few local industries – in fact the popular image of the city is of a boring string of suburbs, a haven for public servants, and an arena for politicians who, if their electorates are elsewhere, can jet away for the weekend.

There's some truth in that, but more importantly, Canberra also has that unique, rarefied, stimulating atmosphere that's only to be found in national capitals. It is also acquiring the furnishings of a true centre of national life – things like the exciting National Gallery, the new and splendid Parliament House and the excellent National Botanic Gardens. There's also a National Museum on the way. What's more, Canberra has quite a young population, including a lot of students, and entertainment there is livelier than we're usually led to expect. Finally, Canberra's the only city in Australia that's really *Australian* – as opposed to South Australian, Victorian, Western Australian or whatever.

Orientation

Canberra is neatly divided in two by the natural looking, but artificial, Lake Burley Griffin. The north side of the lake can be thought of as the residential part and the south side as the working part. Perhaps that's a haphazard description, since Canberra expands in all directions; nevertheless, it's true that most short term accommodation is to the north, while most major government attractions are to the south.

The huge Vernon Circle is the centre point of the north side. Close to the circle are the tourist office, post office, airline and bus terminals, and the shops and

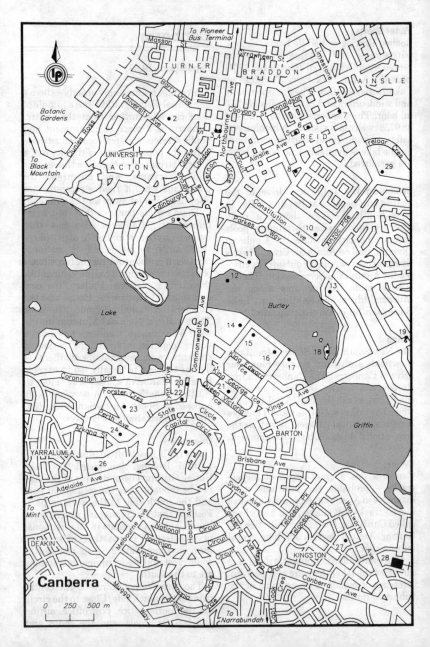

Canberra

0   250   500 m

1	Academy of Science
2	University Students Union
3	GPO
4	Jolimont Centre
5	Gorman House
6	Acacia Motor Lodge
7	Ainslie Hotel
8	Narellan House
9	Ferry Terminal, Bike & Boat Hire
10	Church of St John The Baptist
11	Canberra Planning Exhibition
12	Captain Cook Water Jet
13	Blundell's Farmhouse
14	National Library
15	Australian Science & Technology Centre
16	High Court
17	National Gallery
18	Carillon
19	Australian & American Memorial
20	UK High Commission
21	Old Parliament House
22	PNG High Commission
23	Indonesian Embassy
24	US Embassy
25	Parliament House (on Capital Hill)
26	Thai Embassy
27	Victor Lodge
28	Central Station
29	War Memorial

restaurants of Civic, Canberra's oldest and most established shopping centre. Civic includes Garema Place, City Walk and Petrie Plaza pedestrian malls. There is a fine old fairground merry-go-round where the latter two meet.

From Vernon Circle, Commonwealth Ave runs straight to Capital Circle, which surrounds the new Parliament House on Capital Hill. Capital Circle is the apex of Walter Burley Griffin's parliamentary triangle, formed by Commonwealth Ave, Kings Ave and the lake. Many of the government and other important buildings are concentrated within this triangle, including the National Library, the High Court, the National Gallery and the old parliament house. Kings Ave also crosses the lake on the north-east side. The biggest of Canberra's suburbs and satellite towns are Belconnen to the

north-west and Woden to the south-west. Together with central Canberra they form the rough Y-shape the city planners first envisaged.

Information

The Canberra Tourist Bureau (tel 45 6464) is in the Jolimont Centre on Northbourne Ave, which is also the main long distance bus station. It's open from 8.30 am to 5.15 pm Monday to Friday, from 8.30 am to 5 pm Saturdays and from 8.30 am to 1.30 pm Sundays and holidays. They're helpful and friendly and have a good collection of maps, brochures and information leaflets. The Jolimont Centre is the block bounded by Northbourne Ave, Alinga St, Moore St and Rudd St.

There's another information centre, on Northbourne Ave, Dickson, which you pass as you drive into the city from the north. It's open from 8.30 am to 5 pm daily (7 pm in school holidays). The NRMA (tel 43 3777) has an office at 92 Northbourne Ave where you can get a copy of their excellent map of Canberra.

The YHA has a useful walking tour leaflet. The Petrie Plaza and Monaro Mall shopping complexes both have community notice boards. Canberra is well stocked with overseas information centres and libraries – good places to keep up with foreign magazines, papers and films. For detailed information on Canberra see *The Canberra Handbook* ($3), published by the Australian National University (ANU). There are also books on cycling and bushwalking around Canberra. Canberra has many good bookshops; Dalton's, in the Capital Centre, near Barry Drive, is probably the best.

Have mail addressed to poste restante at the Canberra City Post Office on Alinga St, Civic.

Lookouts

There are fine views of the lake and the city from the surrounding hills. Try 825 metre Black Mountain, rising immediately west

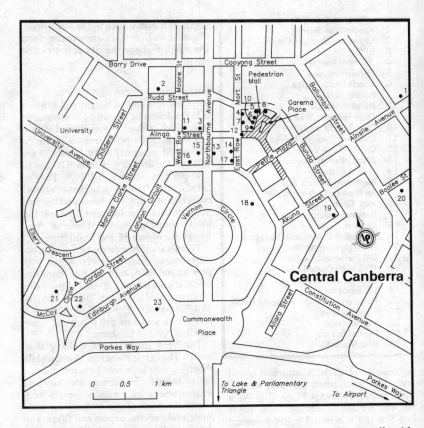

Central Canberra

of Civic and topped by the controversial 195 metre Telecom Telecommunications Tower, complete with a revolving restaurant. The food is the revolving restaurant norm: expensive and inferior to the view. The view alone can be taken in for just $2 from 9 am to 10 pm. There are splendid vistas from nearby lookouts and from the approach road. Bus No 904 runs to the tower from the Jolimont Centre at 12 noon, 1 and 2.45 pm and calls at the Botanic Gardens on the way. Alternatively, you can walk up the mountain, quite a pleasant stroll apart from the mad traffic. There are good bushwalks round the back of the mountain too.

Other mountain lookouts, all with roads to them, are the 722 metre Red Hill, the 840 metre Mt Ainslie and the 665 metre Mt Pleasant. Mt Ainslie is close to the city on the north-east side and has particularly fine views across the city and out over the airport. From the top you'll also appreciate how green and full of parks Canberra is. The view is excellent at night. There are foot trails up Mt Ainslie from behind the War Memorial, and out behind Mt Ainslie to 888 metre Mt Majura four km away. You may see a kangaroo or two on the hike up.

1	Gorman House Restaurant
2	Dalton's Bookshop
3	Tourist Office,
	Australian Airlines Office &
	Bus Station (Jolimont Centre)
4	Ansett Airlines
5	East-West Airlines
6	Angus & Robertson Bookshop &
	Dorettes
7	YWCA
8	Gus's
9	Mama's
10	Pizzeria
11	Post Office
12	Action Information Centre
	(local buses)
13	Private Bin Bistro
14	Sinbad's Restaurant
15	Honeydew Restaurant
16	Malaysian Restaurant
17	Canberra Vietmanese Restaurant
18	Canberra Theatre Centre
19	Bushgear
20	Narellan House
21	National Film & Sound Archive
22	Academy of Science
23	Lakeside International Hotel

Lake Burley Griffin

The lake was named after Canberra's designer, but was not finally created until the Molonglo River, which flows through Canberra, was dammed in 1963. The lake is not recommended for swimming, but you can go boating (beware of strong winds which can blow up suddenly from nowhere) or cycle around it. You can hire boats and bikes from beside the Acton Park Ferry Terminal, on the north side of the lake – see the Canberra Getting Around section and this chapter's introductory Activities section.

There are a number of places of interest around the 35 km shore. The most visible is the Captain Cook Memorial Water Jet which flings six tonnes of water 140 metres into the air and will give you a free shower if the wind is blowing from the right direction. (This is despite an automatic switch-off which is supposed to operate if the wind speed gets too high.) The huge

water jet usually operates from 10 am to 12 noon and 2 to 4 pm daily. It was built in 1970 to commemorate the bicentenary of Captain Cook's visit to Australia. At Regatta Point, nearby on the northern shore, is a skeleton globe, three metres in diameter, with Cook's three great voyages of discovery traced on it.

The Canberra Planning Exhibition, also at Regatta Point, is open daily from 9 am to 5 pm and has models, illustrations and audiovisual displays of the growth of the capital. Further round the lake, to the east, is Blundell's Farmhouse which dates from 1858, long before the selection of the area as the capital and even longer before the lake filled. The simple stone and slab cottage is a reminder of Canberra's early farming history. It's now maintained as a small museum and is open from 2 to 4 pm daily.

A little further around the lake, at the far end of Commonwealth Park which stretches east from the Commonwealth Ave Bridge, is the Carillon, on Aspen Island. The 53-bell tower was a gift from Britain in 1963, Canberra's 50th anniversary. The Carillon was completed in 1970, and the bells weigh from seven kg to six tonnes. There are carillon recitals on Sundays at 2.45 pm, on Wednesdays at 12.45 pm and on public holidays.

West of the bridge, still on the north side of the lake, are Acton and Black Mountain peninsulas. The south-east part of the lake, along which the impressive National Gallery and High Court are situated, forms the base of the parliamentary triangle.

Parliament House

South of the lake, the four legged flagmast on top of Capital Hill marks Parliament House, at the end of Commonwealth Ave. This, the most recent aspect of Walter Burley Griffin's vision to become a reality, sits at the apex of the parliamentary triangle. Opened by the Queen in 1988, it cost $1.1 billion, took eight years to build and replaces the 'temporary' old parliament house lower down the hill on King George Terrace, which served for 11 years longer than its intended 50 year life. The new Parliament was designed by the US based Italian, Romaldo Giurgola, who won a competition entered by more than 300.

It's built into the top of the hill and the roof has been grassed over so that it resembles the original hilltop. Part of the building is subterranean, which has provoked jibes about the MPs being buried in a 'sci-fi mausoleum', but the interior design and decoration is splendid. Eighty new art and craft works were commissioned from Australian artists and a further 3000 bought for the building. A different combination of Australian timbers is used in each of its principal sections.

The main axis of the building runs northeast to south-west, in a direct line from the old parliament, the Australian War Memorial across the lake, and Mt Ainslie. On either side of this axis two high, granite faced walls curve out from the centre to the corners of the site – on a plan they look like back to back boomerangs. The House of Representatives is to the east of these walls, the Senate to the west. They're linked to the centre by covered walkways.

Extensive areas of Parliament House are open to the public from 9 am to 5 pm every day. You enter through the white marble Great Verandah at the north-east end of the main axis, where Nelson Tjakamarra's *Meeting Place* mosaic, within the pool, represents a gathering of Aboriginal tribes. Inside, the grey-green marble columns of the foyer symbolise a forest, while marquetry panels on the walls depict Australian flora. From the 1st floor you look down on the Reception Hall, with its 20 metre long Arthur Boyd tapestry. A public gallery above the Reception Hall has a 16 metre long embroidery, worked on by 1000 embroiderers.

Beyond the Reception Hall you reach the gallery above the Members' Hall, the central 'crossroads' of the building, with the flagmast above it and passages to the debating chambers on each side. Public galleries in the two debating chambers hold about 1000 people in total. South of the Members' Hall are the committee rooms and ministers' offices. The public can view the committee rooms and attend some of their proceedings. Other visitor facilities include a cafeteria, a terrace with views over the city, and a theatrette telling the story of Australian democracy. You can also wander over the grassy top of the building. If you want to make sure of a place in the House of Representatives gallery (much more popular than the Senate), call 77 4889 or write to the Principal Attendant, House of Representatives, Parliament House, Canberra.

Old Parliament House
On King George Terrace, between the new Parliament House and the lake, this was the seat of government from 1927 to 1988. At the time of writing it was anticipated that it would soon be turned into a national political museum. Still, it ended its parliamentary days in style: as the corridors of power echoed to the defence minister's favourite Rolling Stones records, the prime minister and the leader of the opposition sang together arm in arm, and bodies were seen dragging themselves away well after dawn next morning – and that's just what the press was *allowed* to print.

For the present, the building is not open to the public. However, there are fine views from its grounds.

Australian National Gallery
At the bottom of the parliamentary triangle, on Parkes Place, beside the High Court and Lake Burley Griffin, is the art gallery, opened in 1982. It had started buying works back in the '70s when it paid a 'truly fabulous' sum for Jackson Pollock's *Blue Poles*. More gee-whizz purchases from time to time have kept the gallery in the public eye. It's a fine building, with a superb collection of art from Australia and the rest of the world.

The Australian collection ranges from traditional Aboriginal art through to 20th century works by Arthur Boyd, Sidney Nolan and Albert Tucker. Aboriginal works include bark paintings from Arnhem land, burial poles from the Tiwi people of Melville and Bathurst Islands off Darwin, printed fabrics by the women of Utopia and Ernabella in Central Australia, and paintings from Yuendumu, also in Central Australia. There are often temporary exhibitions from the Kimberley and other areas where Aboriginal art is flourishing.

In addition to works from the early decades of European settlement and the 19th century Romantics, there are examples of the early nationalistic statements of Charles Conder, Arthur Streeton and Tom Roberts. The collection is not confined to paintings: sculptures,

prints, drawings, photographs, furniture, ceramics, fashion, textiles and silverware are all on display.

Non-Australian works include pre-Columbian ceramics and textiles from Latin America, works from the ancient Mediterranean and the European Renaissance, 20th century European and North American art, and African and Asian sculptures and textiles.

The delightful Sculpture Garden is landscaped with Australian plants and has a variety of striking sculptures, some incredibly large. The gallery is open from 10 am to 5 pm daily, and tours are given at 11.15 am and 1.15 and 2.15 pm. Admission is $3 (or free if you have a student card). Free lectures are given on Tuesday, Wednesday and Thursday at 12.45 pm and also on Thursday nights. Once a month, on a Thursday night, there's a free three hour session beginning with a guided tour, followed by informal discussion groups, a film and then a guest lecture. There are two gallery restaurants.

High Court

The High Court building, on the lakeside next to the National Gallery, is open from 10 am to 4 pm most days of the year. Opened in 1980, its grandiose magnificence caused it to be dubbed 'Gar's Mahal', a reference to Sir Garfield Barwick, who was Chief Justice of the Australian High Court during the building's construction. To tell the truth, there is a touch of Indian Moghul palace about the ornamental watercourse burbling alongside the entrance path to this grand building.

Australian Science & Technology Centre

This participatory science museum is in the snappy new white building between the High Court and the National Library. It's open daily from 9 am to 5 pm and entry is $3. There are 200 'devices' in the centre's five galleries and outdoor areas where you can get a feeling for a scientific concept by using 'props' and then see its application to an everyday situation. This is an enlarged version of the now defunct Questacon centre north of the lake, where the 'hands-on' approach was trialled for several years.

National Library

Also on Parkes Place, beside the lake, is the National Library, one of the most elegant buildings in Canberra. It has more than three million books, in addition to displays including rare books, paintings, early manuscripts and maps, a cannon from Cook's ship the *Endeavour*, a fine model of the ship itself and varying special exhibitions. The foyer is dominated by three huge tapestries. The exhibition area is open from 9 am to 10 pm Monday to Thursday and from 9 am to 4.45 pm Friday to Sunday and public holidays. There are guided tours Monday to Friday at 11.15 am and 2.15 pm, and sometimes free films.

Royal Australian Mint

The mint, on Denison St, Deakin, south of the lake, produces all Australia's coins. Through a series of plate glass windows (to keep you at arm's length from the ready) you can see the whole process, from raw materials to finished coins. There's a rare-coin collection in the foyer. The mint is open from 9 am to 4 pm Monday to Friday. If you are considering visiting on a Friday, however, ring first (tel 83 3244), as workers have a rostered day off once a month.

Embassies

With Canberra's slow development, embassies were also slow to show up, preferring to stay in the established cities, particularly Sydney and Melbourne, until the capital really existed. The British High Commission was the first diplomatic office to move to Canberra, arriving in 1936. It was followed, in 1940, by the US Embassy. Today there are about 60 high commissions and embassies in Canberra (Commonwealth countries have high commissions instead of embassies).

Enthusiasts of embassy spotting can pick up the tourist office's *Embassies in Canberra* folder or buy *Canberra's Embassies* by Graeme Barrow (Australian National University Press) which is a useful little guide. A few of them are worth looking at, although many operate from nondescript suburban houses. Most are in Yarralumla, the area south of the lake and west and north of Parliament House. Here you'll also find Canberra's mosque, on the corner of Hunter St and Empire Circuit. Three times a year, on a Sunday in January, June and October, there's an embassies open day, when you can visit a number of them for $4.

The US Embassy is a splendid facsimile of a mansion in the style of those in Williamsburg, Virginia, which in turn owe much to the English Georgian style. The Thai Embassy, with its pointed, orange tiled roof, is in a style similar to that of the Thai temples of Bangkok. The Indonesian Embassy is no architectural jewel, but beside the dull embassy building there's a small display centre exhibiting Indonesia's colourful culture. It's open weekdays from 9.30 am to 12.30 pm and from 2 to 5 pm; if you're lucky you might catch an impromptu shadow puppet play put on for a visiting school group. The steps up to the centre are flanked by Balinese temple-guardian statues. Papua New Guinea's High Commission looks like a 'haus tambaran' spirit-house from the Sepik River region of PNG. There's a display room with colour photos and artefacts, open weekdays from 10 am to 12.30 pm and 2.30 to 4.30 pm.

Embassy and High Commission addresses include:

Austria
   107 Endeavour St, Red Hill (tel 95 1533)
Canada
   Commonwealth Ave, Yarralumla (tel 73 3844)
Indonesia
   8 Darwin Ave, Yarralumla (tel 73 3222)
Ireland
   20 Arkana St, Yarralumla (tel 73 3022)
Japan
   112 Empire Circuit, Yarralumla (tel 73 3244)

Top: New Parliament House, Canberra, ACT (PS)
Bottom: High Court building by Lake Burley Griffin, Canberra (TW)

Top: Church with a chimney, Poonindie, Eyre Peninsula, SA (RN)
Left: Rialto building, Melbourne, Vic (TW)
Right: The Rocks, Sydney, NSW (RN)

Malaysia
    7 Perth Ave, Yarralumla (tel 73 1543)
Netherlands
    120 Empire Circuit, Yarralumla (tel 73 3111)
New Zealand
    Commonwealth Ave, Yarralumla (tel 73 3611)
Norway
    17 Hunter St, on the corner of Fitzgerald St,
    Yarralumla (tel 73 3444)
Papua New Guinea
    Forster Crescent, Yarralumla (tel 73 3322)
Singapore
    17 Forster Crescent, Yarralumla (tel 73 3944)
Sweden
    Turrana St, Yarralumla (tel 73 3033)
Switzerland
    7 Melbourne Ave, Forrest (tel 73 3977)
Thailand
    111 Empire Circuit, Yarralumla (tel 73 1149)
UK
    Commonwealth Ave, Yarralumla (tel 70 6666)
USA
    Moonah Place, Yarralumla (tel 70 5000)
West Germany
    119 Empire Circuit, Yarralumla (tel 73 3177)

Australian War Memorial

The massive war memorial, north of the lake and at the foot of Mt Ainslie, looks directly along Anzac Parade to the old parliament house across the lake. The war memorial was conceived in 1925 and finally opened in 1941, not long after WW II entered the Pacific. It houses an amazing collection of pictures, dioramas, relics and exhibitions, including a fine collection of old aircraft.

The exhibition rooms have been modernised and include sections on Gallipoli, Korea and Vietnam which detail the background to each war, its progress, and Australian entry and involvement. They also display maps, equipment and weapons while videos show the role of TV in bringing news of both the Korean and Vietnam Wars. The twisted remains of one of the Japanese miniature submarines that raided Sydney Harbour during WW II – or rather the remains of two, reconstructed to make one – are being restored in the lower gallery.

The shrine is the focus of the memorial.

It features a quite beautiful interior, some superb stained-glass windows and a dome made of six million Italian mosaic pieces. For anyone with a toy soldier interest, the miniature battle scene re-creations are absorbing. The many paintings succeed in bringing history to life. The memorial is open from 9 am to 4.45 pm daily except for Christmas Day and admission is free.

Australian National University

The ANU's spacious and attractive grounds occupy most of the Acton area between Civic and the foot of Black Mountain. It's pleasant to wander around its colleges, lawns, fields, pathways, roads and lakes. The uni was founded in 1946 and the information centre, on Balmain Crescent, open from 9 am to 5 pm Monday to Friday, has free maps and other information. The University Union on University Ave offers a variety of cheap eats and, sometimes, entertainment. On the corner of Kingsley St and Barry Drive is the Drill Hall Gallery, an offshoot of the National Gallery with changing exhibitions of contemporary art. It's open from 12 noon to 5 pm Wednesday to Sunday. Admission is free.

National Film & Sound Archive

The archive is on McCoy Circuit, at the eastern edge of the university area, and is open from 9.30 am to 4 pm daily. Admission is free. Film and sound exhibitions from the archive's collections are shown. Over the road is the Australian Academy of Science – not open to the public – known locally as the Martian Embassy. It does indeed look like a misplaced flying saucer.

National Botanic Gardens

Yes, a botanic garden was part of Walter Burley Griffin's plan too – one dedicated to Australia's unique native flora. Like so much of Canberra it has taken a long time for his vision to become a reality – planting only started in 1950. The garden was officially opened in 1970. On the lower slopes of Black Mountain, behind the ANU, the beautiful 50 hectare gardens have several educational walks. There is a km long walk amongst plants used by Aborigines.

A highlight is the rainforest area, achieved in Canberra's dry climate by a 'misting' system that creates a suitably damp environment in a gully. The eucalypt lawn has 600 species of this ubiquitous Australian plant, while the mallee section consists of four eucalypt-dominated gardens that display the typical vegetation of South Australia and Victoria. The garden's herbarium (collection of pressed and dried plant specimens used for research) and nursery are closed to the public, but if you're a botanist you may be able to talk your way in.

The gardens are reached from Clunies Ross St and are open from 9 am to 6 pm daily. There are guided tours at 10 am and 2 pm on Sunday. The information centre, open from 10 am to 4 pm daily, has an introductory video and there's a theatrette showing films about botany at 11 am and 2 pm. The Botanical Bookshop in the information centre has an excellent range of books, cards and posters. Near where the walks start and finish is a restaurant with good food, reasonable prices and a pleasant outdoor section.

National Museum

This new attraction is supposed to open in 1991 on an impressive site on Lady Denman Drive, beside the north-west shore of Lake Burley Griffin. There's a visitor centre (tel 56 1234) showing items from the museum's collection. One item in the collection is the heart of Phar Lap, Australia's wonder racehorse of the 1930s, who died in suspicious circumstances in California. The rest of him is in another museum in Melbourne. The visitor centre is open from 10 am to 4 pm weekdays and from 1 to 4 pm weekends.

Australian Institute of Sport

Founded in 1981 as part of an effort to improve Australia's performance at events like the Olympics, the AIS is on Leverrier Crescent, in the northern suburb of Bruce, not far from the YHA hostel. It provides training facilities for the country's top sportspeople and includes the National Athletics Stadium, National Indoor Sports Centre, and gymnastics, soccer, basketball and other facilities. The tennis courts and swimming pool are open to visitors (tel 52 1281). Guided tours of the institute ($1) are given at 2 pm Wednesday and Saturday and 11 am holidays (tel 52 1444). Bus Nos 406, 431 and 465 will take you there.

The Museum of Unusual Bicycles

This free exhibition of about 50 bikes of all kinds and ages is good for kids – there is a BMX track next door which hires out bikes. It's in the Canberra Tradesmen's Union Club, Badham St, Dickson, near Dickson Place, and is open daily.

Old Buildings

The Church of St John the Baptist, in Reid, just east of Civic, was built between 1841 and 1845 and thus predates the city of Canberra. The stained-glass windows in the church show pioneering families of the region. There is an adjoining school-house with some early relics, open Wednesday from 10 am to 12 noon, and weekends from 2 to 4 pm.

The Royal Military College, Duntroon, was once a homestead, and parts of it date from the 1830s. Tours of the grounds start at the sign in Starkey Park, Jubilee Ave, on weekdays at 2.30 pm (except from November to March and public holidays).

Other Buildings

You can do no more than drive by and peek in the gates of the Prime Minister's Lodge on Adelaide Ave, Deakin – Australia's 10 Downing St or White House. The same is true of Government House, the residence of the governor general, which is on the south-west corner of Lake Burley Griffin, but there's a lookout beside Scrivener Dam at the end of the lake, giving a good view of the building. The governor general is the representative on earth – sorry, in Australia – of the British monarch, who is still nominally Australia's head of state.

At the east end of Kings Ave the Australian-American Memorial, a 79 metre high pillar topped by an eagle, is a memorial to US support of Australia during WW II. The Serbian Orthodox Church in Forrest has its walls and ceiling painted with a series of biblical murals.

Places to Stay

The tourist bureau in the Jolimont Centre often has a list of discounts, particularly at weekends. You can get a quarter, even half, off normal motel or top end hotel rates.

Hostels The *Canberra YHA Hostel* (tel 48 9759) is on Dryandra St, O'Connor, about six km north-west of Civic. Nightly charges are $13, plus $2 if you need a sleeping sheet. Smaller four to six bed bunkrooms are $15 and there are some twin rooms with attached bathroom for $18 a person. It's a good hostel, recently rebuilt to take over 100 people, and doesn't close during the day except at weekends. Bus Nos 360, 380 and 390 depart every half hour from the city centre for the Scrivener St stop on Miller St, O'Connor. From there, follow the signs. You can hire bicycles at the hostel.

More central than the YHA is *Narellan House* (tel 49 6125), on Boolee St, just off Balumbir St, Reid, less than a km east of Civic. This is an independent hostel charging $17 a person for basic but adequate singles. It's used by students but there's some space for travellers. There are the usual hostel facilities – equipped kitchen, bathrooms and a TV lounge.

Guest Houses & Private Hotels As you enter Canberra from the Hume Highway, there's a clutch of guest houses on the left (east) side of Northbourne Ave, Downer,

just south of where the Barton Highway from Yass and the Federal Highway from Goulburn meet. Standards are similar but prices vary. It's four km or so into town, but buses run along Northbourne Ave.

At 524, The *Blue & White Lodge* (tel 48 0498), which also runs the *Blue Sky* at 528, has shared rooms for two to four people at $14 a person and singles at $24. Prices include cooked breakfast and all rooms have TV, but bathrooms are shared. *Chelsea Lodge* (tel 48 0655), at 526, is $24/31 a single/double including breakfast, or $33 to $42 with private bathroom. At the *Platon Lodge* (tel 47 9139) at 522 you can get a bed in a room shared with two or three others for $11 ($13 with breakfast), or singles/doubles for $18/22 room only or $20/26 with breakfast. Rooms have TV, and bathrooms are communal. All these places are plain and straightforward but clean, quite comfortable and, in true Australian fashion, the breakfast is very filling. They're cheaper by the week.

Closer to the centre, but still a bit of a walk, is *Tall Trees Lodge* (tel 47 9200), a small private hotel on a quiet residential street, at 21 Stephen St, Ainslie. It's a modern, one storey place with central heating and a spacious lawn. Prices are $32/35 – or there's a larger air-con motel section which costs from $51/54.

Within easy walking distance of the city centre is *Gowrie Private Hotel* (tel 49 6033), a large tower block at 210 Northbourne Ave, Braddon, on the corner of Ipima St. It's a former government workers' hostel, still run by the government but now as a hotel, with no less than 570 rooms. Singles/doubles are $26/44 including breakfast (much cheaper by the week). Three course meals are reasonable at $7 and there are other items in the $3 range. The rooms are smallish but clean and many have balconies. You have to wander down the corridor to a bathroom, but the place is well equipped with cafeteria, recreation facilities, TV lounges and laundries.

Macquarie Private Hotel (tel 73 2325), south of the lake, at 18 National Circuit, Barton, on the corner of Bourke St, has 500 rooms and the same setup and prices as the Gowrie. There are a number of other guest houses, but they're mostly not as conveniently situated, or their prices are a lot higher.

Hotels There's not much in this category but the *Kingston Hotel* (tel 95 0123), about 4½ km out of town on the corner of Canberra Ave and Giles St, Manuka, charges $28/39 for singles/doubles.

Motels Most motels in Canberra are quite expensive. *Acacia Motor Lodge* (tel 49 6955), at 65 Ainslie Ave, is $55/61 including light breakfast, and it's only a half km from the centre of Civic. It has barbecues in the courtyard. *Young Town House* (tel 82 1366), a half km north of the centre, on Olympic Way, has some motel rooms at $44/52. Others are a few dollars more. Another possibility is *Tall Trees Lodge Motel* (see the Guest Houses & Private Hotels section).

Cheaper but not so central, *Motel 7* (tel 95 1111), on Cooma Rd, Narrabundah, is about eight km south-east of the centre and is good value. It's got most mod cons, a swimming pool, a restaurant, 63 units and costs $40/44 for a small room. You can get there on bus No 323. There are a few more middle range motels in Narrabundah: try the *Rodeway Crestwood Canberra* (tel 95 0174), at 39 Jerrabomberra Ave, which charges $46/53. *Sundown Village* (tel 49 1932), on the corner of Jerrabomberra Ave and Narrabundah Lane, is quite attractive, with two room self-contained 'villas' costing $44 a single plus $11 for each extra person, and three room villas at $66 plus $11 per extra person.

Victor Lodge (tel 95 7432), at 29 Dawes St, Kingston, a half km from the railway station and a couple of km south-east of Capital Hill, is a simple but decent place with shared facilities from $33/55 including breakfast. *Gunther's Lodge* (tel 81 5499),

at 106 Cotter Road, Curtin, about seven km south-west of the centre, is small but its rooms are well equipped and there's a pool. Singles/doubles are $39/50.

Some caravan parks also have motel type accommodation: the *Canberra Lakes Carotel* (tel 41 1377), just off the Federal Highway at Watson, six km north of the centre, has 'lodges' with their own cooking facilities, TVs and bathrooms at $35/48/53 a single/double/triple. There are 'chalets' without cooking facilities at $35/40/43 a single/double/triple, and up to $64 for eight people. All bedding is provided and there's a pool and a cafeteria. *Red Cedars Accommodation Centre* (tel 41 3222), on the corner of Stirling Ave and Aspinall St, Watson, has two-bedroom lodges with kitchens at $66 for up to six people or $73 for eight. It also has motel rooms from $52 a double. Again, there's a pool and TVs. The *South Side Motor Park* (tel 80 6176), on Canberra Ave, Symonston, about nine km south-east of the centre, charges $34/40 for non air-con rooms with private facilities. There are others with cooking facilities.

Other motels in Canberra can be very expensive, but out in Queanbeyan prices are around $10 cheaper.

Colleges The Australian National University, in Acton, near Civic, has quite a selection of residential places which may have empty rooms during the May, June, August or November to February uni vacations. Charges are around $33/55 for bed & breakfast, but if you can show you're a student, or even if you have a youth hostel card, you can cut 30% or more off those rates. You can get full board at several colleges. The uni campus is a very pleasant place to stay. Try *Ursula College* (tel 48 9055), *Bruce Hall* (tel 49 2828), *Burgmann College* (tel 47 9811), *Toad Hall* (tel 49 4722) or *Burton & Garran Halls* (tel 49 3083).

Camping At the *Canberra Lakes Carotel* (see the Motels section), tent sites cost

$9.50 for two people, and $2 for each extra person. There are on-site vans from $29 for one to $38 for four. There's a standard nightly charge of $50 for a van in peak holiday season. *Canberra Motor Village* (tel 47 5466) three km north-west of the centre, on Kunzea St, O'Connor, has a pleasant bush setting. It charges $12 a double for a tent site, and $33 a double for an on-site van without bedding ($44 plus with bedding). Prices go up a little in the high season. There's a restaurant, guests' kitchen, tennis court and swimming pool.

The *South Side Motor Park* (tel 80 6176) is eight km south of the city on the main road to Queanbeyan and charges $9 for two people with a tent. There are on-site vans from $32, cabins and chalets. More rural camping – cheaper too – can be found out of the city at places like Cotter Dam – see the Around Canberra section.

Places to Eat

Canberra has a reasonable selection of places in Civic and a few further away. *Waffles Restaurant* at the *Private Bin Tavern*, at 50 Northbourne Ave, described eloquently by a local as a 'basic pig-out joint', offers food of the steak, pasta, burger, pizza variety at around $10 for a main meal. Servings are sizeable, it's open daily for breakfast, lunch, dinner and supper. There's also a nightclub upstairs. The *Private Bin* also serves counter lunches and teas for $2.95 with a free drink from Monday to Friday. On the same side of the same block there are Chinese and Indonesian restaurants and a waffle place, all of them medium priced. On the other side of Northbourne Ave the *Honeydew*, at 55, is a 'gourmet wholemeal' place with main courses for lunch from $7.50 and for dinner from $11. It's open Tuesday to Friday for lunch, and Tuesday to Saturday from 6 to 9 pm. There's a Thai place a few doors away.

Mama's, on Garema Place, does good home-made pasta, while *Ali Baba* does a super vegie roll for $3.60, as well as other Lebanese take-aways. On the corner of Bunda St and Garema Place is *Gus's*, which has some outdoor tables. It serves meals like goulash or spaghetti for around $7.50, as well as good sandwiches and cakes. The *Lovely Lady Pancake Parlour*, on Alinga St, is open late and has main courses for around $8.

The *Canberra Vietnamese Restaurant*, upstairs at 21 East Row, Civic, is open daily and offers an all-you-can-eat smorgasbord for $9 at lunch, $11 at dinner, or $7 take-away. There's another Vietnamese place and a French restaurant in the same block. There's also the Greek *Acropolis*, at 35 East Row, which has main courses for around $7. You choose from an appetising display of food, and Greek wines are available for retsina fans. It's open until 9 pm, but closed on Sundays.

At the south end of East Row, on the corner of London Circuit (known as Bailey's Corner) is the *Corner Coffee Shop*, a tiny place doling out what must be Canberra's best coffee.

The *Malaysian Restaurant*, centrally located at 71 London Circuit, is very good but a bit expensive. The *Rasa Sayang*, also Malaysian, at 43 Woolley St, Dickson, is quite good and reasonably priced, but some distance from the centre. There are some Chinese places in Dickson too – fairly convenient if you're staying in one of the guest houses at the top of Northbourne Ave.

The *Zig Zag Cafe*, in the Gorman House Community Arts Centre, on Ainslie Ave, Braddon, a few minutes' walk north-east of Civic, does excellent snacks and light meals at reasonable prices. It's particularly lively on Saturdays when a market is held there.

Cheap food can be found at the union refectory in the university. Late night appetites are catered for by the *Tucker-buses*, known as 'Dog Houses', that appear nightly at strategic spots. They're open till very, very late. *Dolly's*, on the corner of Marcus Clark St and Barry

Drive, is the best of the them. *Jimmy's*, on the corner of Mort and Bunda Sts, is another, with tacos at $2 to $3 and burgers.

North of the centre, and west of Northbourne Ave, the best fish & chips in Canberra are served up at the *Lyneham Fish Shop* in the Lyneham Shopping Centre. The fish is really fresh, and good too. Also in Lyneham, at 96 Wattle St, is *Tilley's*, a women-only cafe, bar and art gallery offering home-made health/ vegetarian food. Men are allowed in on Saturday and Sunday nights if accompanied by women – see the Entertainment section.

South of the lake, not far from Capital Hill, is the Manuka Shopping Village, which services the diplomatic corps and the well-heeled bureaucrats from surrounding neighbourhoods. Amongst the pricey speciality shops you'll find the good and reasonably priced Turkish *Alanya*, on the 2nd floor of the Style Arcade (closed Sundays). Main dishes are around $11, with lamb the speciality. If there are three or more of you, order the banquet (lunch $15, dinner $17). *Grandes*, in the centre of the village, is a small, popular Italian cafe.

West of Capital Hill, the inconspicuous *Gambit* (tel 82 4362), in the Deakin Shopping Centre, has lunch specials which are so popular you have to book. They have sandwiches, salads, omelettes and quiches – like the generous camembert and crab ones for around $6.50. It's open from Monday to Friday until around 5 pm; on Saturdays, which aren't so busy, it closes at 2pm.

Entertainment

Canberra is more lively than its reputation suggests. For one thing, liberal licensing laws allow hotels unlimited opening hours, in contrast to the rest of Australia. The Thursday *Canberra Times* has full entertainment listings, and the excellent Radio 2XX has a 'what's on' slot at 5.15 pm Monday to Friday and 6 pm Saturday.

Probably the best rock pub used to be the atmospheric *Boot & Flogger*, in Green Square, Kingston. It is now two separate venues called the *Oaks* and the *Attic*.

You'll find live music two or three nights a week during term at the ANU union and there's an excellent juke box in the bar too.

The *Ainslie Hotel*, on Limestone Ave, Ainslie, has a piano/jazz bar and a popular, often crowded, beer garden. *Tilley's* often has excellent live music on Friday, Saturday and Sunday nights. The *Southern Cross Club*, in Woden, sometimes has good jazz.

Other places that sometimes have live bands – often top line touring bands – include the central *Canberra Workers' Club*, on Childers St, which has a rock disco, and the *Canberra Labor Club*, on Chandler St, Belconnen. You can usually get cheap meals – and play the pokies – at these and similar clubs.

One of Canberra's most relaxed and comfortable places is *Dorettes*, in the central Garema Place – a semi-Bohemian wine bar with live music nightly, where you can get dinner, although it's not cheap at $20 plus.

The better nightclubs and discos include *New Images*, in Woolley St, Dickson (rock), the *Inner City* and *Pandoras*. *Manhattan* is a bisexual/ alternative nightclub that has ladies' and men's nights, but no live bands. The *Private Bin* restaurant, on Northbourne Ave, Civic, is a nightclub which is open late, but has no live bands. The *Subway*, in Garema Place, is just a pick-up joint and has no bands.

During the summer, the Monaro Folk Group hold a woolshed dance on the last Saturday of the month at the *Woolshed*, Yarralumla (near the governor general's pad). It's a Canberra occasion.

Canberra has a lot of film showings. There are a number of cinemas around the Civic Square and London Circuit area. The *Boulevard Twin Cinema*, on Akuna St, and *The Playhouse*, in the Canberra

Theatre Centre, are collectively known as *Electric Shadows* (tel 47 5060) and all show repertory type films. The *Canberra Theatre Centre*, on Civic Square, has several theatres with a varied range of events from rock bands and drama to ballet, opera and classical concerts. Also check with the foreign cultural organisations like *Maison de France* and the *Goethe Centre* to find out what's on. You have to be a member to get into the ANU film group's showings.

The *National Library* runs free films on Thursday evenings with good, varied programmes, but they're not well advertised. The *National Gallery* has concerts and films on Saturday and Sunday afternoons at around 2.30 pm: this programme is advertised in the weekly TV guide of the *Canberra Times*.

Gorman House Community Arts Centre, on Ainslie Ave, Braddon, close to the centre, sometimes has theatre or dance performances or exhibitions. There's an interesting arts, crafts, books, etc, market there on Saturday from 10 am to 4 pm.

The Canberra Festival takes place over 10 days each March and celebrates the city's birthday with music, food, displays and a big parade. Many of the events are held in Commonwealth Park, which is the site of a carnival.

Getting There & Away

Air Most international flights to and from Canberra fly via Sydney or Melbourne. Canberra is not an international airport.

From Sydney it's normally just half an hour to Canberra; the fare with the two major airlines is $100, or $80 standby – but East-West has daily flights that take 15 minutes more and cost only $78. Air NSW has cheaper flights – $90 to Melbourne and $75 to Sydney. Melbourne is about an hour's flight and costs $141, or $113 standby. You can travel standby on the direct flight to Adelaide for $177 or to Brisbane for $174. Among the smaller airlines that travel to and from Canberra regularly are Air NSW (daily non-stop services to Melbourne and Sydney), Eastern (to Newcastle), Western New South Wales Airlines (Albury) and Hazelton Air Services (Dubbo, Orange).

Airline offices in Canberra include Australian (tel 46 1811) in the Jolimont Centre, Northbourne Ave; Ansett (tel 45 6511), at 4 Mort St; East-West (tel 57 2411), in Shop 3/4, Cinema Centre, Bunda St; and Air NSW (tel 57 3333), at 21-23 London Circuit.

Bus You can travel to Canberra from Sydney daily with the major bus lines. Pioneer has the most frequent service including some direct from Sydney Airport. It takes four to five hours and usually costs $20.

Murrays (tel 95 3677), at the Jolimont Centre, is a smaller company that runs the cheapest Sydney to Canberra service, three times daily for just $17. In Sydney, Murrays leaves from Eddy Ave at Central Station (tel (008) 04 6200 toll free).

Pioneer, Deluxe, Greyhound and Bus Australia also cover the Canberra to Adelaide route (about $80) and Pioneer, Greyhound and Deluxe run between Canberra and Melbourne ($37).

Pioneer has daily services to the New South Wales snowfields (Thredbo $27, Jindabyne $24), Wagga Wagga ($21) and Gundagai ($19). It also travels three times a week to Bega ($25) on the coast. Murrays has daily services from Canberra to Wollongong ($26) and points between, and to other places along the New South Wales south coast including Nowra ($29), Batemans Bay ($17), Moruya ($20) and Narooma ($25). The latter service goes through Bungendore and Braidwood. Capital Coachlines, which can be booked through Pioneer, go to Bathurst ($30), Orange ($30) and Dubbo ($44) two to four times weekly. Other smaller bus lines include MAI (to Griffith and Forbes) and Hunts (to Orange and Bathurst).

Most major bus lines have their booking offices and main stop at the Jolimont Centre. Pioneer (tel 45 6624), however, has its terminal at the Canberra Rex Hotel, on the corner of Northbourne Ave and Ipima Ave, a few blocks north of the centre. It also has a booking office in the Jolimont Centre. Greyhound's telephone number is 57 2658, Deluxe's 47 0588.

Train To/from Sydney there are two or three trains daily. The trip costs $32.60 in 1st class and $23 in economy.

There is no direct train between Melbourne and Canberra. The daily Canberra Link service involves a train between Melbourne and Wodonga and a connecting bus to Canberra. This costs $39 in economy. From Melbourne you depart at 12.10 pm Monday to Friday (a few hours earlier at weekends); from Canberra you leave at 8.05 am Monday to Friday (later at weekends).

The slower, more expensive alternative is to take a Melbourne to Sydney train as far as Yass ($47.80 in economy) and a Transborder bus ($7) for the one hour ride between Yass and Canberra. Although all trains between Melbourne and Sydney go through Yass, only the Intercapital Daylight Expresses connect with the bus. Leaving Melbourne at 8.40 am, you reach Canberra at 6.12 pm. Going the other way, you leave Canberra on the bus at 10.45 am and arrive at Melbourne at 8.20 pm. There's no service on Sunday.

Canberra station (tel 39 0133, 6 am to 6 pm daily) is south of Lake Burley Griffin, on Wentworth Ave, Kingston. You can make bookings for trains and connecting buses at the rail travel centre in the Jolimont Centre.

Getting Around

Airport Transport Canberra's recently expanded airport is just seven km from the city centre. Note all the government cars lined up outside waiting to pick up returning 'pollies'. Hertz, Budget, Avis and Thrifty have airport car rental desks. There's no airport bus service – unless you want to take the Lever's coach (tel 97 3133)

that leaves the city at 6 am on weekdays. The taxi fare is around $7.

Bus Around Canberra there are frequent services on the modern Action buses. The main interchange and the bus information kiosk are on the corner of Alinga St and East Row in Civic. The information kiosk is open Monday to Friday from 7.15 am to 5.30 pm, Saturday from 6 am to 5.30 pm; and Sunday and holidays from 8.30 to 11.15 am and 2.15 to 6.30 pm. You can phone 51 6566 for information from 6 am to 11.30 pm Monday to Saturday and from 8.30 am to 6.30 pm Sunday. A free map of the whole bus system is available, as well as individual timetables for each route.

Normal fares are a flat $1 – there's a 20c inner-city bus service, but it just goes around London Circuit and only during the middle of the day. Some of the Action buses are known as sightseeing specials and for these you need a Day Tripper or Sightseeing ticket ($4, or $8 if you're going further afield to places like Bungendore, Bywong or Tidbinbilla) which enable you to use all Action buses for the day. You get them from main bus interchanges or the tourist bureau – they're not sold on the bus. The bus information kiosk has pamphlets on these services: they include route No 904 which goes to the Botanic Gardens and the tower atop Black Mountain; No 905 to the War Memorial, Parliament House, Regatta Point and Yarralumla; and No 909 to Rehwinkel's Animal Park and Bungendore.

From the tourist bureau you can buy a Canberra Explorer ticket for $9 a day or $14 a week. The Explorer runs hourly every day around a 25 km route with 22 stops at points of interest to visitors. You get a printed guide and can get on and off the bus wherever you like. It starts at the tourist bureau at 15 minutes past each hour from 10.15 am to 4.15 pm, and you can buy the ticket on the bus. If you just want to make one circuit without getting off, you can use a $4.50 ticket. The

Explorer doesn't go up Black Mountain and the ordinary, slightly cheaper Action day pass will get you just about everywhere – if you don't mind an occasional walk and having to sort out the bus routes.

Car One of the cheapest outfits is Discount Rent-a-Car (tel 49 6551), at 16 Mort St, where you'll pay $30 a day for a Toyota Corona, including insurance and 100 km. Rumbles (tel 80 7444), at the corner of Kembla and Wollongong Sts, Fyshwick, has rates a few dollars higher and interesting deals for Friday to Monday rentals.

Tours The Canberra Tourist Bureau has all the latest information on city tours, or half day and longer tours to the surrounding countryside and sheep stations. There is a variety of other day-trips to places like the Snowy Mountains, nature reserves, satellite tracking stations, horse studs and fossicking areas around the ACT. Half day city tours are around $15, while full day tours are around $28; trips further afield vary from about $30 to see the Snowy Mountains to about $55 for a comprehensive tour of Canberra area attractions. A visit to a sheep station, including a barbecue, will be around $35. There are daily cruises on Lake Burley Griffin for $6 an hour, or $9 for two hours.

Bicycle Canberra is a cyclist's paradise, with bike paths making it possible to ride around the city hardly touching a road. Get a copy of the invaluable *Canberra Cycleways* map from the tourist bureau. You can hire bikes from Mr Spokes Bike Hire (tel 57 1188), near the Acton Park Ferry Terminal beside Lake Burley Griffin, for $4 an hour or $16 a day, with a $2 deposit. You can also hire bikes from the youth hostel, or from Canberra Bike Rental (tel 41 2216), which will deliver mountain and touring bikes to your door,

and charges $30 a day from Monday to Friday and $35 at weekends.

Around Canberra

The ACT is 80 km from north to south and about 30 km wide. There's plenty of unspoiled bush just outside the urban area and a network of paved roads into it. Both the NRMA's *Canberra & District* map and the tourist bureau's *Canberra Sightseeing Guide with Tourist Drives* are helpful if you want to explore around the 'Bush Capital'. The plains and isolated hills of the ACT's north, where Canberra lies, rise to rugged ranges in the south and west of the territory. The Murrumbidgee River flows across the territory from south-east to north-west at the foot of the ranges. Namadgi National Park in the south covers 40% of the ACT. You can pick up a variety of leaflets on walking trails, swimming spots and camping sites, put out by the ACT Parks & Conservation Service (tel 46 2308).

PICNIC & WALKING AREAS

There are popular picnic and barbecue spots in and around Canberra. Many of them have gas barbecues. There are good swimming spots along the Murrumbidgee and Cotter rivers. Black Mountain, virtually in the city itself, is a convenient place for picnics. Other riverside areas include Uriarra Crossing (24 km north-west), on the Murrumbidgee near its meeting with the Molonglo River; Casuarina Sands (19 km west), at the meeting of the Cotter and Murrumbidgee; Kambah Pool (21 km), further upstream (south) on the Murrumbidgee; the Cotter Dam (23 km), on the Cotter, which also has a camping site; Pine Island and Point Hut Crossing, on the Murrumbidgee, upstream of Kambah Pool; and Gibraltar Falls, 48 km south-west, which also has a camping site.

There are good walking tracks along the

Murrumbidgee from Kambah Pool to Pine Island (seven km), or to Casuarina Sands (longer).

The spectacular Ginninderra Falls are at Parkwood, north-west of Canberra, and actually just across the New South Wales border. The area they are in is open from 10 am to 5 pm daily and includes a fine nature trail, gorge scenery, canoeing and camping. There's a $2.50 admission charge.

Tidbinbilla Nature Reserve, 40 km south-west of the city, in the hills beyond the Tidbinbilla tracking station, has a series of marked bushwalking tracks, some of them leading to interesting rock formations. There's an animal reserve with kangaroos, koalas and emus. The reserve has an information centre and is open from 9 am to 6 pm; the animal enclosures are open from 11 am to 5 pm.

Other good walking areas include Mt Ainslie, on the north-east side of the city, and Mt Majura behind it (the combined area is called Canberra Nature Park); the Stromlo pine forests out to the west of the city; and Molonglo Gorge, to the east, near Queanbeyan (the Molonglo is the river that is dammed to form Lake Burley Griffin).

Namadgi National Park, occupying the whole south-western part of the ACT and partly bordering New South Wales' mountainous Kosciusko National Park, has seven peaks over 1600 metres and offers more challenging bushwalking. The partly surfaced Boboyan Rd crosses the park, going south from Tharwa in the ACT to Adaminaby on the eastern edge of the Snowy Mountains in New South Wales. There's a park visitor information centre (tel 35 7216) on this road, 24 km from Tharwa, and there are picnic and camping facilities in the park at the Orroral River crossing and Mt Clear.

OBSERVATORIES & TRACKING STATIONS
The Australian National University's Mt Stromlo Observatory is 16 km west of Canberra and has a 188 cm telescope plus a visitors' annexe open from 9.30 am to 4 pm daily. The Canberra Space Centre at Tidbinbilla, 40 km south-west of Canberra, is a joint US-Australian deep space tracking station. It has an information centre with models of spacecraft, open from 9 am to 5 pm daily. It's a popular centre for bushwalks and barbecues.

OLD HOMESTEADS
The beautifully restored Lanyon Homestead is 26 km south of the city, on the Murrumbidgee River near Tharwa. The early stone cottage on the site was built by convicts and the grand homestead was completed in 1859. This National Trust homestead, which now documents the life of the region before Canberra existed, is open from 10 am to 4 pm from Tuesday to Sunday. A major attraction is the collection of 24 Sidney Nolan paintings. Admission to the main homestead is $1.30 – to enter the Nolan gallery costs another 60c. Opposite Lanyon there's a small memorial graveyard to a pioneer of the Australian wheat industry.

Cuppacumbalong, also near Tharwa, is another old homestead, although neither as grand nor of such importance as Lanyon. It now houses a craft studio and gallery and is open from 11 am to 5 pm Wednesday to Sunday.

North of Canberra, on the Barton Highway, is the Old Canberra Inn, built in 1850 and now restored as a restaurant and bistro. Ginninderra Village, also on the Barton Highway, about 14 km out, has a collection of craft workshops and galleries, and a school built in 1883 that has been converted to a store. It's open from 10 am to 5 pm daily and is free. Next door is Cockington Green, a miniature replica of an English village, open from 10 am to 5 pm daily, and to 6 pm in summer. Admission is $4.

QUEANBEYAN (population 24,000)
Just across the New South Wales border, east of Canberra, is Queanbeyan, now virtually a suburb of the capital, although

it predates it. Until 1838 it was known as 'Queen Bean'. There's a history museum in the town and good lookouts on Jerrabomberra Hill five km west and Bungendore Hill four km east.

OTHER ATTRACTIONS

Mugga Lane Zoo, in Red Hill, about seven km south of the city centre, is open from 9 am to 4 pm weekdays, and to 5 pm on weekends. Admission is $3.50. Rehwinkel's Animal Park is on Macks Reef Rd, off the Federal Highway, 24 km north of Canberra and actually across the New South Wales border. It's open daily from 10 am to 5 pm, and admission is $4. There's a selection of Aussie fauna at both places. Australia Park, seven km out on the Federal Highway at Watson, is a funfair with rides and games in an imitation colonial village setting.

DAY-TRIPS

A popular drive is east into New South Wales, past Bungendore, to Braidwood

(an hour or so) with its many antique shops, craft stores and restaurants. There's an old hotel where you can get a pub lunch. Lake George, north of Bungendore, is known for its mysterious, periodic disappearing act. The village square in Bungendore has shops, crafts, foods and an historic re-creation that tells the story of local bushranger William Westwood, who became famous in the mid-1800s.

Another good route takes in Tharwa (see the Old Homesteads section) in fine, hilly grazing lands. There is a coffee shop at the historic site and a grocery store with 'hot pies, cold beer'. From here the route goes north-west to Gibraltar Falls (good walking) and Tidbinbilla Nature Reserve. The Space Tracking Station is on the way back into town along the slow, winding, scenic road.

Lastly, an enjoyable day can be spent slowly riding around Lake Burley Griffin on a bicycle. There's a bike trail all the way around and lots of birds.

New South Wales

Area	802,000 square km
Population	5,500,000

New South Wales is the site of Captain Cook's original landing in Australia, the place where the first permanent settlement was established and today it is both the most populous state and has the country's largest city – Sydney. Of course New South Wales is much more than Sydney with its glistening Opera House and equally well-known (if far less attractive) harbour bridge – but Sydney is certainly a good place to start.

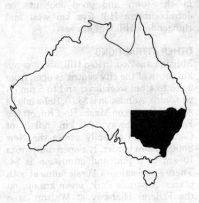

It was down at Sydney Cove, where the ferries run from today, that the first settlement was made in 1788 so it is not surprising that Sydney has an air of history which is missing from most Australian cities. That doesn't stop Sydney from being a far brasher and more lively looking city than its younger rival Melbourne. With a setting like Port Jackson (the harbour) to build around, it would be hard for Sydney to be unattractive.

Sydney has more than the central city going for it; Paddington is without question one of the most attractive inner city residential areas in the world and the Pacific shoreline is dotted with good beaches sporting famous names like Bondi and Manly. Furthermore there are two particularly pleasant national parks marking the southern and northern boundaries of the city – Royal National Park and Ku-ring-gai Chase. Inland, it is only a short drive to the Blue Mountains with some of the most spectacular scenery in Australia.

The Pacific Highway runs north and south from the capital and great beaches, surf and scenery are waiting for you all along the coast. To the north Newcastle is the second city of New South Wales, a major industrial centre (but still with fine beaches), then there are small resorts like Port Macquarie, Nambucca Heads and Coffs Harbour. Close to the Queensland border Byron Bay is one of the best travellers' stops on the whole eastern seaboard, a small, relaxed but lively surfers' favourite with strong links to the 1960s/70s counterculture that has taken root in the nearby hinterland. All the way up there are also long, empty, unspoiled stretches of coast, some protected as national parks. Just inland from the north coast and a short trip from Sydney, the Hunter Valley is one of Australia's premier wine producing areas with a popular annual wine festival. Further north are spectacular, rainforest covered ranges reaching up to the high plateau of the New England region, making for some superb excursions.

South of Sydney, inland, are the Southern Highlands with beautiful scenery and good bushwalks. There is more good coastline on the way down to Victoria, plus Wollongong, the third city of New South Wales and another major industrial centre. In the south of the state the Great Dividing Range climbs up into the heights of the Snowy Mountains, Australia's

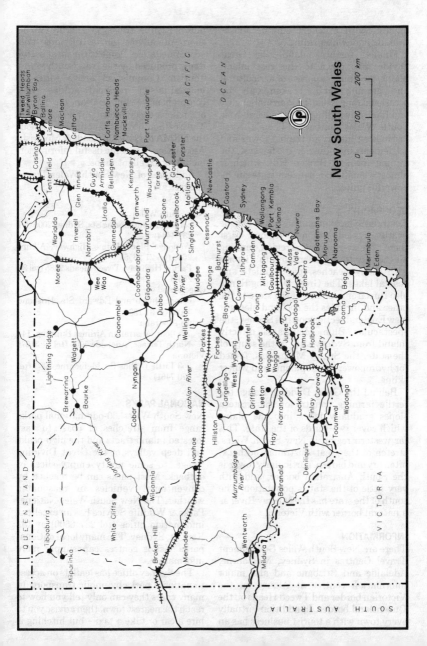

New South Wales

highest, with excellent summer bush-walking and winter skiing.

Finally, further inland, the Great Divide rolls down to the vast inland plains, sweeping expanses of agricultural and grazing land, broken only by occasional ranges like the Warrumbungles, and finally dwindling into the harsh New South Wales outback. There's some fascinating history in the old towns and settlements including, in the far west, the mining town of Broken Hill, which is almost a small, independent state run by powerful unions.

GEOGRAPHY

Australia's most populous state can be neatly divided into four regions. First there's the narrow coastal region, running all the way from Queensland to Victoria with many beaches, parks, inlets and coastal lakes. The Great Dividing Range also runs from one end of the state to the other and includes the cool and pleasant New England section north of Sydney, the spectacular Blue Mountains directly inland from Sydney and, in the south of the state, the Snowy Mountains, famed for hydropower developments and winter skiing.

Behind the Great Dividing Range the fertile farming country of the western slopes gradually fades into the plains which cover two-thirds of the state. This far western region is New South Wales' stretch of the great Australian outback, often dry and barren, particularly towards the South Australian border, and with very little of the state's population. The south of the state has the Murray River as a natural border with Victoria.

INFORMATION

There are New South Wales Government Travel Centres in Sydney, Melbourne, Adelaide and Brisbane and also major information centres at Albury on the Victorian border and Tweed Heads on the Queensland border. In addition virtually every town with a tourist business has an information centre so you'll hardly ever be short of advice on attractions and accommodation. Some of the most useful items produced by the New South Wales Tourism Commission are a series of magazine-size regional guides with comprehensive information on tourist attractions, accommodation and transport. The New South Wales motoring association, the NRMA or National Roads & Motorists Association, has some useful information including excellent maps.

Addresses of New South Wales Travel Centres are:

New South Wales
    corner Pitt and Spring Sts, Sydney 2000 (tel 231 4444)
    Wodonga Place, Hume Highway, Albury 2640 (tel 21 2655)
    Pacific Highway, Tweed Heads 2485 (tel 36 2634)
Queensland
    corner Queen and Edward Sts, Brisbane 4000 (tel 31 1838)
South Australia
    7th floor, Australian Airlines Building, 144 North Terrace, Adelaide 5000 (tel 51 3167)
Victoria
    353 Little Collins St, Melbourne 3000 (tel 670 7461)

NATIONAL PARKS

New South Wales' 60-odd national parks range from stretches of coast to vast forested inland tracts and the high peaks and deep valleys of the Great Dividing Range, to some pretty empty slices of outback. Most parks can be reached by conventional vehicles in reasonable weather. The New South Wales National Parks & Wildlife Service has an excellent information office (tel 237 6500) at 189 Kent St, Sydney. The many local national parks visitor centres can supply more information.

The Sydney office has leaflets on access to national parks by public transport. In many cases they can only tell you how to reach the nearest town, then advise you to hire a car or take a taxi – but hitching is often a reasonable alternative. Parks that you can reach without resorting to walking or private vehicle for more than a short distance include the Blue Mountains, Bouddi, Brisbane Water, Morton, Ku-ring-gai Chase, Royal and Sydney Harbour – all within 150 km of Sydney.

In some national parks there's an entry charge of around $5 per vehicle, but outside busy times there's often no one collecting it. Many parks have drive-in camping grounds with facilities like showers and toilets – usually free, though for the most popular there can be a small charge and a booking procedure – as well as permitting bush camping outside the established camping grounds. It's advisable to check the camping arrangements for a particular park before going there – you may need a permit to bush camp even if you don't have to pay. Only rarely are there other types of accommodation such as cabins or hotels within a park, but you'll usually find these on the fringe of the park.

New South Wales' state forests – owned by the state government and often used for logging – also have a range of drives, camping sites, walking tracks and so on for visitors. The New South Wales Forestry Commission's head office (tel 234 1567) is at 95 York St, Sydney. It's due to move to Oratava Ave, West Pennant Hills, Sydney: check this out. There are many other local offices for information.

ACTIVITIES
Bushwalking
The Federation of Bushwalking Clubs (tel 27 4206), 176 Cumberland St, Sydney, and the National Parks & Wildlife Service (see previous section) have information on bushwalking. A useful book is *100 Walks in New South Wales* by Tyrone Thomas.

Closest to the city are walks like the fine clifftop paths in the Royal National Park or the walks in Ku-ring-gai Chase National Park where you can find gigantic Aboriginal rock carvings. Inland, the Blue Mountains and the adjoining Kanangra

Boyd National Park have fine walks and some spectacular scenery. Morton National Park in the Southern Highlands is also spectacular and within easy reach of the city.

Further south, Kosciusko National Park in the Snowy Mountains has excellent longer walks, camping facilities and vivid wildflowers in summer. It's best to let the snow have plenty of time to thaw and dry up after the winter. Barrington Tops National Park, north of Sydney near the New England tableland, and Warrumbungle National Park, further west near Coonabarabran, are just two of the other national parks offering excellent bushwalking options. Lonely Planet's *Bushwalking in Australia* describes in detail some longer walks in the Royal, Blue Mountains, Morton, Warrumbungle and Kosciusko National Parks.

Running & Cycling
There are tracks and facilities at Narrabeen Lakes north of Sydney. Wollongong is another city with a good bike track network. The Bicycle Institute of New South Wales (tel 212 5628), GPO Box 272, 802 George St, Sydney, is very helpful with information and cycling routes throughout the state.

Sydney joggers do their stuff at Centennial Park which is also popular with cyclists. In August, the City to Surf Fun Run is Australia's biggest foot race.

Swimming & Surfing
This is the true-blue Sydney and New South Wales activity. All the beaches around Sydney – Palm, Whale, Avalon, Colaroy, Manly, Bronte, Maroubra, Cronulla, Bondi, Coogee (need I go on) – have good swimming and/or surfing. The beaches in the Royal National Park are also popular.

Surf carnivals – lifesavers, surf rescue boats, all that stuff – start in December when there are competitions between lifesavers from the various beaches. Phone the Surf Life Saving Association to find out what's on where, or contact the New South Wales Travel Centre.

Officially, Sydney has 34 surf beaches and there are many more along the New South Wales coast. The north coast is more popular during the winter months (warmer of course) at places like Seal Rocks (325 km), Crescent Head (497 km), Scotts Head (538 km), Angourie (744 km) and Lennox Heads (823 km). Byron Bay has been a surfing Mecca for almost as long as Australia has had surfies. South of Sydney there is Stanwell Park (56 km), Wollongong (82 km), Huskisson (187 km) and Mollymook (222 km). Nat Young's *Surfing Australia's East Coast* (Castle Books) details the 'wheres and whens'.

Scuba Diving

Excellent scuba diving and snorkelling can be found at a number of sites along the coast. North of Sydney popular spots include Terrigal (96 km), Port Stephens (235 km), Seal Rocks (325 km) or Byron Bay (850 km). Head south to Jervis Bay in the Royal National Park, to Wattamolia (198 km) or Eden (488 km). You can take diving courses in a number of centres including Sydney and Byron Bay, though most first timers who are heading up to Queensland wait till they can do their learning on the Great Barrier Reef.

Canoeing

With dams, rivers, lakes and coastal lakes there are plenty of opportunities to go canoeing in New South Wales. If you are after white-water then the Richmond and Murray rivers are where you should be heading. The New South Wales Canoe Association (tel 251 3472) has information. For equipment hire try the New South Wales Sport & Recreation Service or B-line Canoe Hire (tel 727 9402) at Lansvale.

White-water Rafting

You can join in this increasingly popular activity on the upper Murray and Snowy Rivers in the south of the state, or the Nymboida and Gwydir in the north.

Jindabyne and Thredbo in the Snowy Mountains are jumping-off points for the southern rivers, Coffs Harbour and Nambucca Heads for the northern. A day-trip usually costs about $65.

Sailing

Sydney Harbour and the Pittwater are both excellent areas for sailing so it is hardly surprising that the sport is so popular. Check with the Australian Yachting Federation about clubs and sailing instructions.

Skiing

See the Snowy Mountains section for information about skiing in New South Wales.

GETTING AROUND

Air

Sydney is connected to Canberra and most major Australian cities by Australian Airlines, Ansett and East-West. Within the state Air NSW and Eastern Airlines operate comprehensive networks, and lesser airlines serve particular regions.

New South Wales Airfares

All Fares in Australian Dollars

Coolangatta

Coffs Harbour *176*

Dubbo

Newcastle *128*

Broken Hill

102

212

60

Sydney

138 *100* *114*

Canberra

Cooma

Albury

The chart details some of the routes and the normal fare costs.

Bus

Buses to or from Brisbane, Melbourne and other interstate centres are no problem – there are so many competing companies that your only poser is to find the best deal. Within New South Wales, bus travel is a little more complicated owing to rules designed to protect the railways. Until recently most bus companies were not allowed to carry passengers on journeys which they could make by rail. You couldn't, for instance, use most Sydney to Brisbane buses just to go from Sydney to Byron Bay. The exceptions were a few local bus lines and routes.

There has been some loosening of these restrictions: you can now travel between Sydney and Canberra on buses which are going on to/from Melbourne, and most companies on the Sydney to Brisbane coastal route can now carry you on intermediate legs provided you go a minimum 160 km. The same applies to the south coast route to Victoria by the Princes Highway. Elsewhere, such as to the New England region, the position at the time of writing remained as before. If you are just making a stopover on an interstate ticket, or are travelling on a bus pass, you can usually escape the restrictions. As in other states, always look into possible cheap stopover deals if you want to make a few stops on the way.

Buses are often a little quicker and cheaper than trains but not always so. Once you've reached your destination, there are often local bus lines, though services may not be very frequent.

Train

The State Rail Authority of New South Wales has the most comprehensive rail service in Australia (see the Bus section for one reason why). State Rail will take you quite quickly to almost any sizeable town in the state, but the frequency and value for money is variable: always compare with bus services.

Some main railway lines, including the ones from Sydney to Grafton (696 km), Armidale (579 km), Dubbo (462 km), Albury (643 km) and Canberra (326 km), are served by high speed XPTs (Express Passenger Trains), which can top 160 kph (100 mph). The other main passenger lines go as far as Wollongong (83 km), Nowra (153 km) and Cooma (432 km) in the south, Broken Hill (1125 km) in the west and Moree (666 km), Tenterfield (774 km), Murwillumbah (935 km) and Kyogle (834 km) in the north. Where there isn't a railway, State Rail usually runs bus services connecting with its trains, and these will take you as far afield as Lightning Ridge (818 km) or Bourke (831 km) in the north, Hay (790 km) or Deniliquin (801 km) in the west, and Tumbarumba (617 km) or Eden (600 km) in the south.

Intrastate services from Sydney include Narooma, 471 km, combined rail/bus service once a week, $35 in economy class; Cooma, six trains a week, seven hours, $31; Bathurst, 240 km, usually three or four trains daily, about 4½ hours, $18; Broken Hill seven trains a week, about 17 hours, $56; Tamworth, 455 km, one or two trains daily, six to nine hours, $35; Bourke combined rail/bus service four times a week, about 12 hours, $47; Coffs Harbour, 608 km, four trains daily, 8½ to 11 hours, $41; Byron Bay, 883 km, one train and three combined rail/bus services daily, 13 to 16 hours, $47.

Other economy fares from Sydney include Armidale $38, Orange (323 km) $23, Dubbo $35, Griffith (637 km) $41, Albury $41.

There are a variety of day tour fares and you can also get a 14 day Nurail Pass for $159 which gives you unlimited 1st class travel throughout the New South Wales rail system, or an economy class Budget Seven Pass, which gives you seven days for $35.

Sydney

Population 3,400,000

As Australia's oldest and largest city it's not surprising that Sydney (Sinney to the locals) has plenty to offer. The harbour, around which the city is built, was named Port Jackson by Captain Cook in 1770 but he actually anchored in Botany Bay, a few km to the south, and only passed by the narrow entrance to the harbour. In 1788 when the convict 'First Fleet' arrived in Sydney it too went first to Botany Bay, but after a few days moved north to Port Jackson. These first settlers established themselves at Sydney Cove, still the centre of harbour shipping to this day.

Down near the waterfront in the area known as The Rocks you can still find some of the earliest buildings in Australia. Because Sydney grew in a somewhat piecemeal fashion, unlike other later Australian cities which were planned from the start, it's a tighter, more congested centre without the wide boulevards you find in other cities, Melbourne in particular. Despite that it's also a dazzlingly modern city, the place with the most energy and style in Australia. In Sydney the buildings soar higher, the colours are brighter, the nightlife's more exciting, the drivers more aggressive and the consumption more conspicuous!

It's also a cosmopolitan city. The Chinese have been here since the 19th century, but since WW II there have been big, new waves of migrants from southern and eastern Europe and Asia. Sydney even has more Maltese than Malta.

It all comes back to that stupendous harbour though. It's more than just the centrepiece for the city, everything in Sydney revolves around the harbour. Would the Opera House, for example, be anything like the place it is were it not perched right beside the harbour?

Orientation

Due to a combination of history and geography Sydney is much less simply laid out than most Australian cities – the streets are narrower, more winding and convoluted. Historically Sydney came into existence before the era of grand plans that was to characterise most later Australian cities. Geographically Sydney's layout is complicated by the harbour with its numerous arms and inlets and by the general hilly nature of the city.

The harbour divides Sydney into north and south. Most places of interest tend to be south of the harbour, including the city centre itself. The centre is connected to the north shore by the huge, but often jammed, harbour bridge. The central city area is relatively long and narrow although only a couple of roads, George and Pitt Sts, run the whole three km south from the waterfront Rocks area down to Central Railway Station at the southern boundary of the city centre – which is where you'll probably arrive if you come by bus or train. Along and near George and Pitt Sts you'll find shops, shopping centres and arcades, airline offices and other central city businesses. The Rocks and the Sydney Cove waterfront mark the northern boundary of the centre, the inlet of Darling Harbour marks the western boundary and a string of pleasant parks border Elizabeth and Macquarie Sts on the eastern edge.

Beyond this park strip are some of the oldest and most interesting inner suburbs of Sydney – Woolloomooloo, Kings Cross and Paddington. Further east again are some of the more exclusive suburbs south of the harbour and then the beachfront suburbs like Bondi. The airport is south of this area, beside Botany Bay.

Sydney's suburbs stretch a good 25 km south, west and north from the centre. To the north and south they're limited by national parks, but to the west even outlying towns like Penrith and Campbelltown are almost part of the urban sprawl.

Information

Excellent places for cheap travel tips and help are the hostel areas where most budget travellers stay – in particular Victoria St in Kings Cross where there are countless posters and notice boards offering everything from flat-shares and backpacks to Blue Mountains tours or unused air tickets.

The Travel Centre of New South Wales (tel 231 4444) is at 16 Spring St, on the corner of Pitt St. It's open Monday to Friday 9 am to 5 pm and has the usual range of brochures, leaflets and accommodation and tour details. They can make bookings. The Sydney Information Booth (tel 235 2424) is in Martin Place, a mall area between George and Macquarie Sts. The office is near the Elizabeth St corner, and is open the same hours as the New South Wales centre. The privately run Tourist Information Service (tel 669 5111) is a telephone information service operating from 8 am to 6 pm daily. Some areas like The Rocks, Manly and Parramatta also have their own tourist offices. There are several free tourist information booklets circulated around Sydney.

The main post office, with its very busy poste restante where you may queue for half an hour or more to pick up mail, is on Martin Place on the corner of Pitt St. Readers have advised against using this poste restante, saying their mail was returned to sender when it shouldn't have been, or suffered unaccountable delays, etc.

The NRMA has its head office at 151 Clarence St (tel 260 9222) and a branch at 324 Pitt St (tel 260 9781).

The New South Wales National Parks & Wildlife Service (tel 237 6500) has its head office at 189 Kent St, and the information section there has hundreds of books and give-away leaflets on the state's national parks, recreation areas, historic sites, wildlife and more.

There's a YHA membership and travel centre (tel 267 3044) at 176 Day St. The YHA Central Reservations Bureau (tel 261 5727), through which you can make telephone bookings for any YHA hostel in Australia, is also in Sydney.

The universities are good information sources and there are university newspapers at Sydney University and the University of New South Wales. The Wayside Chapel (tel 358 6570), up at 29 Hughes St, Kings Cross, is a crisis centre and good for all sorts of local information and problem solving.

If you're heading off to other countries and need vaccinations or health advice, the Traveller's Medical & Vaccination Centre (tel 221 7133) in Suite 3, 2nd Floor, Dymocks Building, 428 George St, is a useful place. It's open from 8.30 am to 6 pm on weekdays, 9 am to 12 noon Saturdays and you don't need an appointment.

Books The best Sydney guide is the widely available *Roland Hughes Wraps Up Sydney*. It's a 368 page paperback, not cheap at $17.95, but very comprehensive if you're planning an extended stay. *Smiths Guide: Sydney City* by Keith & Irene Smith ($12.95) is a good guide to most places of interest. Cheaper at $5.95 is Gregory's *Inside Sydney*.

The Travel Bookshop, with two locations – Shop E8, Circular Quay, and 1 Jamison St on the corner of York St – has lots more books not just on Sydney but also the rest of Australia and the world. Sydney has plenty of other good bookshops including a large Angus & Robertson and two Grahames on Pitt St and Dymocks on George St.

One of the best Sydney maps is the one produced by the NRMA. It shows the city centre including Kings Cross in large scale on one side, and most of greater Sydney on the other to help you locate the various suburbs. A Sydney street directory costs about $18.

The Rocks

Sydney's first settlement was made on the rocky spur of land on the west side of

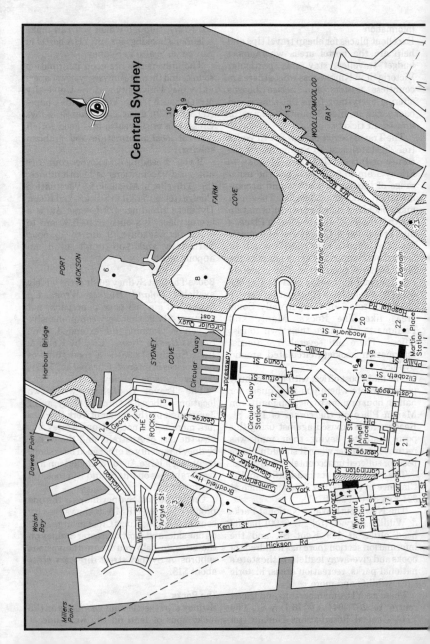

Central Sydney

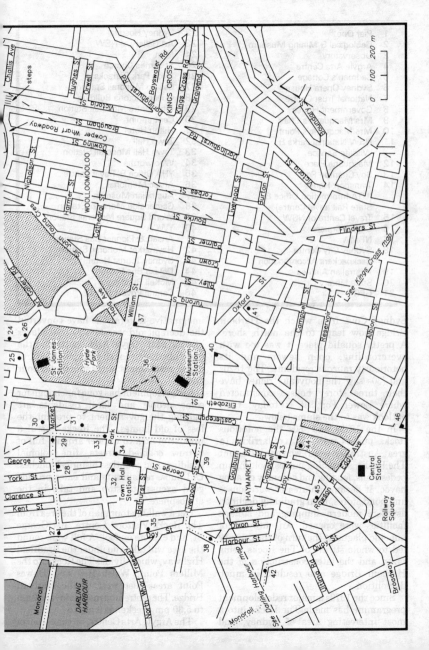

1	Pier One	22	Sydney Hospital
2	Geological & Mining Museum	23	Art Gallery of NSW
3	Observatory	24	Mint
4	Argyle Arts Centre	25	St James Church
5	Cadman's Cottage	26	Hyde Park Barracks
6	Sydney Opera House	27	Casino Monorail Station
7	National Trust Centre	28	Queen Victoria Building
8	Government House	29	City Centre Monorail Station
9	Mrs Macquarie's Chair	30	Centrepoint
10	Mrs Macquarie's Point	31	Hilton Hotel
11	NSW National Parks &	32	Town Hall
	Wildlife Service	33	Town Hall Monorail Station
12	Macquarie Place	34	Woolworths
13	Boy Charlton Pool	35	YHA Office & Travel Centre
14	Transport House	36	Anzac Memorial
	(UTA Information Office &	37	Australian Museum
	State Rail travel Centre)	38	Gardenside Monorail Station
15	Travel Centre of NSW	39	World Square Monorail Station
16	Chifley Square	40	YWCA
17	NRMA	41	Ansett & Pioneer Bus Station
18	Sydney City Centre	42	Haymarket Monorail Station
	Backpackers Accomodation	43	Sydney Tourist Hotel
19	Australian Airlines	44	Deluxe Bus Station
20	State Library	45	McKell Building
21	GPO	46	Central Private Hotel

Sydney Cove from which the Harbour Bridge now leaps to the north shore. A pretty squalid place it was too with overcrowding, open sewers and its notoriously raucous residents. The 1820s and '30s saw the nouveaux riches have their three storey houses constructed where Lower Fort St is today; their outlook was to the slums below.

In the 1870s and '80s the notorious Rocks 'pushes' were gangs of larrikins (a great Australian word) who used to haunt The Rocks, snatching purses, holding up pedestrians, feuding and generally creating havoc. It became an area of warehouses and bond stores, then gradually declined as more modern shipping and storage facilities were opened. An outbreak of bubonic plague at the turn of the century led to whole streets of The Rocks being razed and the later construction of the Harbour Bridge also resulted in much demolition.

Since the 1970s a major redevelopment programme has made The Rocks into a most interesting area of Sydney, and imaginative restorations have converted the decrepit old warehouses into places like the busy Argyle Arts Centre and the tastefully redeveloped Campbell's Warehouse restaurants with superb harbour views.

Redevelopment has gone far enough for some people and local residents are fighting the government to prevent the loss of old homes. The Rocks is still a wonderful area to wander around, full of narrow cobbled streets, fine colonial buildings and countless historical touches. Old pubs, restaurants and cafes provide good excuses to stop and take in the atmosphere.

Get a walking tour map of the area from The Rocks Visitors' Centre, 104 George St, and explore on foot. A full walk round the area will take you under the Bradfield Highway, which divides The Rocks, to the Millers Point, Walsh Bay and Dawes Point areas just west of the Harbour Bridge. The centre is open weekdays 8.30 am to 5.30 pm, weekends 9 am to 5 pm.

The Argyle Arts Centre, on the corner of

Argyle and Playfair Sts, was originally built as bond stores between 1826 and 1881. Today it has a collection of shops, boutiques, studios and eating places. Everything seems geared to rich tourists – Australiana gone mad, but it's still worth a browse. See the Things to Buy section for more information.

Just beyond the arts centre is the Argyle Cut, a tunnel through the hill to the other side of the peninsula. It was begun in 1843 by convict labour but abandoned and not finished until many years later. At the far end of the cut is Millers Point, a delightful district of early colonial homes, some around a real village green, almost in the heart of Sydney.

On George St, close to the visitor centre, you'll come across Cadman's Cottage (1816), the oldest house in Sydney. When the cottage was built this was where the waterfront was, and the arches to the south of it once housed long boats – for this was the home of the last Government Coxswain, John Cadman. The cottage houses a National Parks & Wildlife display and bookshop.

Entry to the large Geological & Mining Museum at 36-64 George St is free and it's open daily, though not on Saturday and Sunday mornings. For wine lovers, the Australian Wine Centre in Campbell's Storehouse at Circular Quay West has wines from all the major growing areas. You can take a tour and get a free tasting and it's open daily from 10 am to 5 pm. You can find the site of the public gallows on Essex St, near the corner of Harrington St up towards St Patrick's Church. On George St from 97 through to 143A, the shops, hotels and restaurants are in historic buildings.

On the Millers Point side of The Rocks there's a colonial museum at 51 Lower Fort St, in one of the elegant Georgian houses. In the pleasant park on Observatory Hill, the Sydney Observatory also has an interesting museum. Close by, the National Trust Centre in the old military hospital houses a museum, art gallery,

bookshop and tearooms. The gallery's interesting exhibitions change every six weeks and admission is $2 (students $1).

Up at Dawes Point just beneath the bridge on this side, Pier One is a tourist, shopping and leisure complex with specialist shops, several expensive restaurants, a tavern, and an amusement centre.

The Rocks has a number of historic old pubs, some with beer on tap, including the *Hero of Waterloo* (believed to be the oldest Sydney pub), the *Lord Nelson*, the *Mercantile Hotel* and the curiously named *Former Young Princess Inn*.

Sydney Harbour Bridge
From the end of The Rocks the 'old coat hanger' rises up on its route to the north shore. It was a far from elegant, but very functional, symbol for the city until the Opera House came along. The bridge was completed in 1932 at a cost of $20 million, quite a bargain in modern terms, but it took until 1988 to pay off!

Crossing the bridge costs $1.50, southbound only, there is no toll in the other direction. There's a cycleway across the bridge and a pedestrian walkway – with stairs up to it from Cumberland St in The Rocks – and you can climb up inside one of the stone pylons (see City Views). The pylons incidentally are purely decorative: they don't help to hold the bridge up in any way. At rush hours the bridge gets very crowded and after years of discussion a harbour tunnel will be built east of the bridge, to ease the congestion. The tunnel will go from about half a km south of the Opera House to meet the bridge road on the north side.

On the north shore, neatly framed beneath the bridge, is the grinning mouthpiece of another Sydney symbol – the Luna Park funfair, a bit shabby these days but still open on Friday nights, Saturdays from 11 am to 11 pm and Sundays from 11 am to 5 pm ($10.50 for over 10s, $6.50 for four to nines).

At the end of Kirribilli Point east of the

bridge stand Admiralty House and Kirribilli House, the Sydney pieds-à-terre of the governor general and prime minister respectively (Admiralty House is the one nearer the bridge). North Sydney has become a smaller replica of the Sydney centre in the past 20 years. Spiralling office rents and central congestion prompted the construction of this second city centre.

Sydney Opera House

From the past symbol to the present one is a short walk around Sydney Cove – to the controversial Sydney Opera House. After countless delays and technical difficulties the Opera House opened in 1973, 14 years after work began. And I was there! During a free Sunday afternoon concert or sitting in the open air restaurant with a carafe of red wine, watching the harbour life, it's a truly memorable place.

There are tours of the building and although the inside is nowhere near as spectacular as the outside, they are worth taking. They cost $3.50 (students $1.80), last an hour and operate every half hour from 9 am to 4 pm. There are also 90 minute tours of the backstage area for $6 on Sundays only.

The Opera House has four auditoriums and puts on plays, concerts and films as well as opera. Popular performances tend to sell out quickly, but there are a limited number of 'restricted view' and standing room only tickets which go on sale for $8 on the day – get there early, the box office opens at 9 am. The best show I've seen at the Opera House? – a Fairport Convention concert recorded live for an LP.

On Sunday afternoons there are free performances on the outer walk of the building. You can also often catch a free lunch time film or organ recital in the concert hall. One free performance to avoid at the Opera House is that given by the notorious band of free-loading seagulls who are expert at collecting meals from outdoor diners – guard your meal carefully.

Before the Opera House was built the site was used as a tram depot. The designer, Jorn Utzon, a Dane, won an international contest with his design but at the height of the cost overruns and construction difficulties and hassles he quit in disgust and the building was completed by a consortium of Australian architects. How were the enormous additional costs covered? – not by the taxpayer but in true-blue Aussie fashion by a series of Opera House lotteries. The Opera House looks fine from any angle, but the view from a ferry coming into Circular Quay is one of the best.

Circular Quay

There's nothing circular about Circular Quay, the departure point for the harbour ferries at the south end of Sydney Cove. There is no finer way of getting around Sydney than these creaky old ships or the sleeker new vessels – take a lunch time trip to get the feel, or zip to Manly on the hydrofoils. Circular Quay was the original landing point for the First Fleet, and the Tank Stream, a creek which provided early Sydney's water supply, ran into the harbour here.

Later this was the shipping centre for Sydney and early photographs show a veritable forest of sailing ship masts crowding the skyline. Across Circular Quay from the Opera House, beside The Rocks, is the overseas passenger terminal where cruise ships and visiting liners moor.

Macquarie Place

Narrow lanes, with some colourful early opening pubs, lead back from Circular Quay towards the real centre of the city which is further south. At the corner of Loftus and Bridge Sts, under the shady Moreton Bay figs in little Macquarie Place, you'll find a cannon and anchor from Phillip's First Fleet flagship HMS Sirius. There are a number of other pieces of colonial memorabilia in this interesting square including gas lamps, a drinking fountain dating from 1857, a National

Trust classified gentlemen's convenience and an obelisk indicating distances to various points in the colony.

City Centre

Central Sydney stretches from Central Railway Station in the south nearly up to Circular Quay in the north. The real business hub is towards the north end of this area and if anywhere is Sydney's real centre it's Martin Place, a pedestrian mall extending from Macquarie St to George St beside the massive GPO. This is a popular lunch time entertainment spot with buskers and more organised acts. The Cenotaph war memorial is here and also the Sydney Information Booth. In December a Christmas tree appears in Martin Place in the summer heat.

Sydney's central area has some attractive and imaginative shopping complexes including the delightful, old Strand Arcade between Pitt and George Sts just south of King St. The Queen Victoria Building on the corner of George and Market Sts, built in the style of a Byzantine palace in 1898 and once a fruit and vegetable market, has recently been restored to house about 200 shops, cafes and restaurants. The MLC Centre, Centrepoint and the Royal Arcade are just three of the other, modern centres off George and Pitt Sts.

In the basement of the Hilton Hotel, under the Royal Arcade between George and Pitt south of Market St, you can find the Marble Bar, a Victorian extravaganza built by George Adams, the fellow with the prescience to foresee Australia's gambling lust and found Tattersall's lotteries (Tattslotto). When the old Adams Hotel (originally O'Brien's Pub) was torn down to build the Hilton, the bar was carefully dismantled and reassembled like some archaeological wonder.

Half a block further south along George St is the 1874 Sydney Town Hall on the corner of Park St. Then the centre begins to fade, becoming rather grotty and ripe for the developers, before you reach Central Railway Station and the inner suburb of Glebe. Just west off George St, before the station, is the colourful Chinatown around Dixon St.

City Views

Sydney is becoming a mini-Manhattan and from up top you can look down on the convoluted streets that are a relic of the unplanned convict past. George St is the main shopping street, once known as High St, while Pitt St was famous for its brothels way back when. Bridge St was the site of the first bridge in Australia, across the Tank Stream, which is now funnelled underground.

Highest in Sydney is the Sydney Tower on top of the Centrepoint complex on the corner of Pitt and Market Sts. This is a tower built purely for the sake of being high – it's nothing more than a gigantic column with a circular viewing gallery and revolving restaurant on the summit, 305 metres above street level. The tower is open from 9.30 am to 9.30 pm daily, except Sundays and holidays when it's open 10.30 am to 6.30 pm. Admission is $3.50 for the observation deck. You can see as far as the Blue Mountains to the west or Wollongong to the south, and there are various audiovisual and other displays. Reservations for either of the restaurants are a good idea, but there's also a snack and coffee bar.

Sydney Harbour Bridge is a good vantage point and a good place for a picture of the Opera House and harbour. You can climb up inside the south-east pylon daily from 9.30 am to 5 pm, entry is free. You enter the pylon from the bridge's pedestrian walkway and at the top of the 200 stairs is a panoramic view of the city. A stone staircase leads up to the bridge and walkway from Cumberland St in The Rocks.

For a view of the Opera House, harbour *and* bridge, from sea level, either take a trip on the harbour waters or go to Mrs Macquarie's Point, one headland east of the Opera House. It has been a lookout

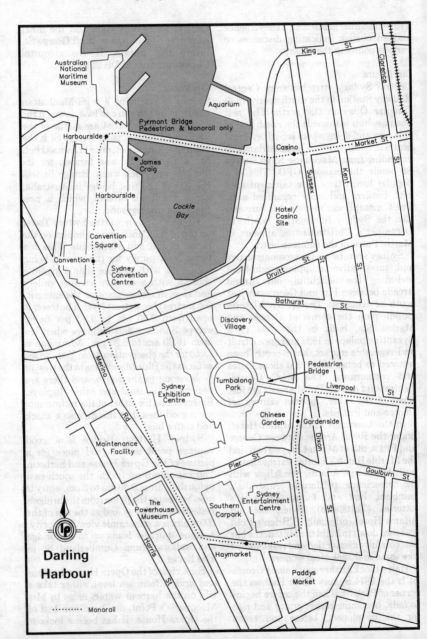

Darling Harbour

.... Monorail

point since at least the 1810s when Elizabeth Macquarie, wife of one of the best early governors of New South Wales, had a stone chair hewn in the rock at the end of the point, where she would watch for ships entering the harbour or keep an eye on hubby's construction projects just across Farm Cove. The seat is still there today.

There are more excellent panoramas of the city centre from the north shore of the harbour. Lastly, there is a good view from the rooftop of the Australian Museum and it too is free.

Darling Harbour

This inlet, half a km west of the city centre, has been turned into a huge waterfront leisure and tourist park. Gardens, walkways, museums, an aquarium, eateries, shops and more have replaced the old wharves and warehouses and Darling Harbour now has some fine buildings and offers a lot to do. The $2 billion transformation started in 1984 and the new Darling Harbour was opened in 1988, despite a series of strikes and political rows over the project's cost.

Also controversial has been the monorail which circles Darling Harbour and links it to the city centre. Traditionalists say its blue steel track, winding round the streets at first floor level, ruins some of Sydney's best vistas, and politicians talk about re-routeing it. It's $1 a ride and there's a train every two minutes. The full circuit takes 12 minutes.

An urban freeway roars along the east side of the harbour (you can cross it on foot bridges) and over the top of the main park area, but you don't really notice it. The two main pedestrian approaches to Darling Harbour are foot bridges from Market St and Liverpool St. The one from Market St leads on to the old Pyrmont Bridge, now a pedestrians and monorail only route right across Darling Harbour.

Sydney Aquarium

The aquarium is beside the east end of Pyrmont Bridge. Its inhabitants include Australian river fish, Barrier Reef fish and coral gardens, and saltwater crocodiles. Two 'oceanarium' tanks, with sharks, rays and other big fish in one, and Sydney Harbour marine life in the other, are moored in the harbour. You walk below water level to view the tanks from underneath. The aquarium's open daily from 9.30 am to 9 pm and admission is $9.

Australian Maritime Museum

Across Pyrmont Bridge from the aquarium the roof of the Maritime Museum billows like sails, echoing the shapes of the Opera House. The museum tells the story of Australia's relationship with the sea from Aboriginal canoes to the America's Cup. Vessels of many different types stand inside or are moored at the wharves. It's intended to be an 'active' museum, with maritime craft demonstrations, entertainments and so on.

Just under the bridge from the museum two more ships are moored at what's called Sydney Seaport – the 1874 sailing ship *James Craig* which traded between Australia and the rest of the world and the *Kanangra*, an old Sydney harbour ferry built in 1912. These two ships are open daily from 10 am to 6 pm and it costs $4 to look round them. There's an audiovisual display of sailing ship life inside the *James Craig*.

Harbourside

This is the shopping and eating centre of Darling Harbour, with over 200 shops and food outlets. Just to the south is a convention centre and a large exhibition centre which continues the maritime theme with its roof suspended from steel masts. Like the aquarium and the maritime museum, the exhibition centre was designed by Australian architect Philip Cox, who has really been the first to take up the adventurous lead given by Jorn Utzon's Opera House. Cox also created the new Sydney Football Stadium, Melbourne's

National Tennis Centre and the resort at Yulara near Ayers Rock.

Powerhouse Museum & Nearby Behind the exhibition centre stands Sydney's most spectacular museum, an outstanding example of the new wave of 'active' museums, housed in a vast new building encompassing the old power station for Sydney's now defunct trams. There are 30 different displays covering the decorative arts, science and technology and social history.

It's a superbly displayed museum with lots to do besides just looking – video and computer activities, experiments, performances and demonstrations, films and so on. Major decorative art sections focus on childhood, Australian crafts, style, and 20th century chairs; the science and technology hall includes working steam engines, the Bugatti that won the 1929 Australian Grand Prix, a Catalina flying boat strung from the ceiling, and space travel exhibits; and the social history areas include a 1930s cinema and a pubs and brewing display.

You can also reach the Powerhouse from Harris and Mary Ann Sts, Ultimo. It's open from 10 am to 5 pm daily and admission is free.

In front of the exhibition centre, Tumbalong Park has playgrounds, an amphitheatre, lawns and trees. Across the park from the exhibition centre, Discovery Village will be a high tech amusement park on Disneyland lines, while in another corner is the Chinese Garden, the biggest outside China, which was planned by landscape architects from New South Wales' sister province, Guangdong. Just south of the Chinese Garden, the old pump house which supplied hydraulic power for many Sydney lifts has been turned into the Pump House Tavern, with its own brewery. A little further south again is the 12,500 capacity Sydney Entertainment Centre, venue for top, touring rock acts.

Early Central Buildings
After the founding governor Phillip left in 1792 the colony was run mainly by officials and soldiers more intent on making a quick fortune through the rum monopoly than anything else, and it was not until Lachlan Macquarie took over as governor in 1810 that order was restored. The narrow streets of parts of central Sydney are a reminder of the chaotic pre-Macquarie period.

Macquarie St Macquarie commissioned Francis Greenway, a convict transported for forgery, to design a series of public buildings, some of which are still among the finest in Sydney. St James Church and the Hyde Park Barracks, two of his early masterpieces, are on Queens Square at the northern end of Hyde Park, facing each other across Macquarie St. The barracks, originally convict quarters, are now an interesting museum of Sydney's social history, complete with a reconstructed convict dormitory where the hammocks are far more comfortable than most Kings Cross hostel beds. The barracks are open daily from 10 am to 5 pm except Tuesday mornings (free).

Next to the barracks on Macquarie St is the Mint Building, originally built as a hospital in 1814 and known as the Rum Hospital because the builders constructed it in return for the lucrative monopoly on the rum trade. It became the mint in 1853 and the northern end of the hospital is now the New South Wales state Parliament House. The Mint, with its collection of decorative arts, stamps and coins, is open from 10 am to 5 pm daily except Wednesday when it opens at 12 noon. Admission is free.

Further up Macquarie St on the botanic gardens side, the State Conservatorium of Music was originally built, by Greenway again, as the stables and servants' quarters of a new government house for Macquarie. Macquarie was replaced as governor before the rest of the house could be finished, partly because of the perceived extravagance of this project. Greenway's life ended in poverty because he could never recoup the money of his own that he had put into the work. Today the building is a musical academy: on Wednesdays during term there are free lunch time concerts.

Parks

Sydney has many parks which, together with the harbour, make it one of the world's most spacious major cities. One string of parks borders the eastern side of the city centre. Stretching back from the harbour front, beside the Opera House, are the Royal Botanic Gardens with a magnificent collection of South Pacific plant life. The gardens were originally established in 1816 and in one corner you can find a stone wall marking the site of the convict colony's first vegetable patch. There is also a big rainforest greenhouse and an Aboriginal plant trail. The gardens are open from 8 am to sunset daily. There's a visitor centre where guided walks start at 10 am every Wednesday and Friday. Just east of the gardens, beside Woolloomooloo Bay, the Boy Charlton Pool is the nearest place to the city centre or Kings Cross where you can get a non-harbour swim. It's saltwater and open daily. The half km from here up to Mrs Macquarie's Point is also parkland (see the City Views section).

The Cahill Expressway separates the botanic gardens from the Domain, another open space to the south. You can cross the expressway on the Art Gallery Rd bridge. In the Domain on Sunday afternoon after 2 pm impassioned soapbox speakers entertain their listeners.

Third of this group of city parks is Hyde Park, between Elizabeth and College Sts, with its delightful fountains and the Anzac Memorial. This is a popular place for a city sandwich lunch on the grass since it's only a few steps from the centre.

Sydney's biggest park, with running, cycling and horse tracks, duck ponds, barbecue sites and lots more, is Centennial Park, five km from the centre and just east of Paddington. Black swans and many other birds nest in the park. You can hire bikes from several places on Clovelly Rd, Randwick, near the southern edge of the park (see Getting Around) – or horses from Centennial Park Horse Hire at the Sydney Showgrounds on Lang Rd, just west of Centennial Park.

Balls Head Reserve, on the north shore of the harbour two headlands west of the Harbour Bridge, is a park with not only great views of the harbour, but also some old Aboriginal rock paintings (in a cave) and carvings.

Apart from parks, Sydney also has wilder areas. Some of these, along the harbour shores, are described in The Harbour section. Another, Davidson Park, is an eight km corridor of bushland in northern Sydney, stretching northwest from Bantry Bay on Middle Harbour up to the border of Ku-ring-gai Chase National Park at St Ives. There's also Lane Cove River recreation area, between the suburbs of Ryde and Chatswood, again north of the harbour. Both areas have extensive walking tracks and Lane Cove River has lots of picnic areas. You may see lyrebirds in Davidson Park – the males make their spectacular mating displays from May to August. You can pick up information sheets on these places at the national parks office.

Art Gallery of New South Wales

Situated in the Domain, only a short walk from the centre, the art gallery has an excellent permanent display of Australian, European, Japanese and tribal art, and from time to time shows really inspired temporary exhibits. It also has a very good cafeteria, ideal for a genteel cup of tea. It's open from 10 am to 5 pm Monday to Saturday, 12 noon to 5 pm Sunday. There's no entry charge to the gallery itself, but fees may apply at certain times for major exhibitions. Free guided tours are available. Sydney is packed with other galleries, particularly in Paddo and Woollahra.

Australian Museum

The Australian Museum, on the corner of College and William Sts, right by Hyde Park, is basically a natural history museum with an excellent Australian wildlife collection, but it also has a good gallery tracing Aboriginal history from the Dreamtime to the present. See the latter before you head off into the country's centre. The mining and Papua New Guinea displays are also good and there are usually temporary exhibitions too. The museum is open from 10 am to 5 pm every day except Monday when it's 12 noon to 5 pm. Admission is free and so are daily guided tours.

Other Museums

On Macquarie St, just north of Parliament House, the State Library of New South Wales has one of the best collections of early records and works on Australia, including Captain Cook's and Joseph Banks' journals and Captain Bligh's log from the *Bounty* (the irascible Bligh recovered from that ordeal to become an early New South Wales governor where he suffered a second mutiny!). Maps, documents, pictures and many other items are displayed in the library galleries, which are open from 10 am to 5 pm Monday to Saturday, 2 to 6 pm on Sunday. Free visiting exhibitions of various kinds are often shown here, too. There's also a general reference library open from 9 am to 9 pm Monday to Saturday, 2 to 6 pm Sunday.

Other good Sydney museums include the Nicholson and Macleay Museums at Sydney University, with Greek, Assyrian, Egyptian and other antiquities at the former, and at the latter a curious collection ranging from stuffed birds and animals to anthropology to early computers and cameras. Both are free and open Monday to Friday, from 8.30 am to 4.15 or

4.30 pm. The university's about a km south-west of Central Railway Station.

Sydney Observatory (tel 241 2478) on Observatory Hill in The Rocks has an interesting museum telling the history of astronomy and timekeeping. The museum is open at various hours most days, but if you want to look through the telescopes in the evenings you must book. Admission is $2, $1 concession. There is also a mining museum at 36 George St in The Rocks.

On the Princes Highway, about a km south of Sutherland, near Royal National Park, there's a tramway museum open on Sundays and holidays – Sydney's last tram rumbled into the history books back in 1961. There's a 600 metre long tram track ($1 a ride). On Underwood Rd in Homebush, a western suburb, there's the Hall of Champions sports museum (tel 763 0111), open erratically. Sydney Cricket Ground has a cricket museum, open on match days.

Paddington

The inner suburb of Paddington, four km east of the city centre, is one of the most attractive inner city residential areas in the world. 'Paddo' is a tightly packed mass of terrace houses, built for aspiring artisans in the later years of the Victorian era. During the lemming-like rush to the dreary outer suburbs after WW II the area became a run-down slum. Then a renewed interest in Victorian architecture (of which Australia has some gems) combined with a sudden recollection of the pleasures of inner city life, led to the quite incredible restoration of Paddo during the '60s.

Today it's a fascinating jumble of often beautifully restored terraces, tumbling up and down the steeply sloping streets. Surprisingly there was an older Paddington of fine gentlemen's residences, a few of which still stand, although the once spacious gardens are now encroached upon by lesser buildings. Paddington is one of the finest examples of totally unplanned urban restoration in the world and is full of trendy shops and restaurants, some fine art galleries and bookshops and interesting people. The best time to visit Paddo is Saturdays when you can catch the 'Paddo Bazaar' at the corner of Newcombe and Oxford Sts with all sorts of eccentric market stalls.

Get a free copy of the 128 page *Paddington Book* (available from shops in the area) to find your way around. If you're in Paddington on a Tuesday morning you can visit the old Victoria Barracks on Oxford St where the impressive changing of the guards takes place at 10 or 11 am. Afterwards you'll get a free tour. The barracks were built between 1841 and 1848: at that time the area was sand dunes and swamps!

You can get to Paddo on bus No 378 from Central Railway Station, or Nos 380 or 389 from Circular Quay along Elizabeth St. The heart of Paddo is along Oxford St past the barracks and in the streets north from there. A couple of blocks past the barracks, you can turn up Underwood St, then follow Heeley St to reach Five Ways, a mass meeting of streets around which are some of Paddington's most interesting shops and places to eat, plus the lovely old Royal pub. Paddington St, further east, has some of the finest looking houses, while many of the antique shops are clustered along Queen St.

Kings Cross

'The Cross' has seedy strip joints, junkie teenage hookers, rambling, leafy old streets, lots of eateries, and it's the main travellers' centre in Sydney, with Australia's greatest concentration of hostels. Darlinghurst Rd is the Cross's main street and a good many of the hostels are on or near Victoria St, which diverges from Darlinghurst Rd just north of William St.

Kings Cross is close to the city centre, with lots of activity, and a great many travellers begin and end their Australian ventures in the Cross. It's a good place to swap information and buy or sell things. Numerous travellers' notice boards line the hostel and shop walls, and an informal car exchange operates here, with travellers and their vehicles for sale lined up along Victoria St. The attractive (when it's working) thistle-like El Alamein Fountain, down in Fitzroy Gardens at the end of Darlinghurst Rd is known locally as the 'elephant douche'! Next door, the Rex Hotel is probably Australia's greatest travellers' gathering place.

From the city you can walk straight up Williams St to the Cross (you can't miss the big Coca-Cola sign which marks the entrance to Darlinghurst Rd), or grab one of a multitude of buses which run there, or take the very quick Eastern Suburbs train service right to the centre of the Cross. There's also a quieter pedestrian route from the city centre which you can find by ducking through Sydney Hospital from Macquarie St, crossing The Domain and descending the hill just on the right of the New South Wales Art Gallery, then going down Palmer St from its junction with Sir John Young Crescent, turning left along Harmer St, and following the paths and backstreets till you reach a flight of steps leading up to Victoria St, just south of its junction with Orwell St.

If you have a vehicle, there are usually empty spaces down at the bottom (north) end of Victoria St where you can leave a vehicle for more than just a couple of hours. Another tip: there are normally several *working* phone boxes in Kings Cross station at the south end of Victoria St.

Between the city and the Cross is Woolloomooloo, the 'loo, one of Sydney's older areas with many narrow streets. This area, extremely run down in the early '70s, has gone through a complete restoration and is now very pleasant. But I bet you can't spell it without looking at it again. Does anywhere else in the world have four double-O's in its name?

Beyond the Cross

The harbour front about half a km north-east of the Cross is called Elizabeth Bay. Here at 7 Onslow St is Elizabeth Bay

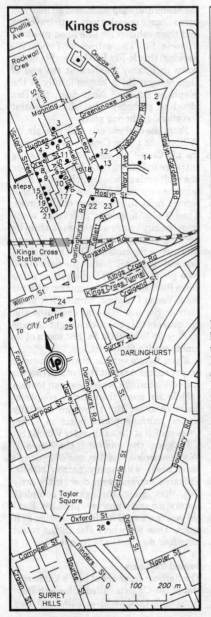

Kings Cross

1	Elizabeth Bay House
2	Young Travellers Hostel
3	Macquarie Hotel
4	The Jolly Swagman Backpackers (Orwell St)
5	Chez Alain (l'Annexe)
6	Downunder Hostel
7	Rex Hotel
8	The Jolly Swagman Backpackers (Victoria St)
9	Cactus Cafe
10	Springfield Lodge
11	The Jolly Swagman Backpackers (Springfield Mall)
12	Kings Cross Library
13	El Alamein Fountain
14	Barncleuth House
15	Travellers Rest
16	Kings Cross Backpackers
17	Bernley Private Hotel
18	Astoria
19	Highfield House
20	International Network Hostel
21	Plane Tree Lodge
22	Geoffrey's Cafe
23	Young Fong's
24	Music Cafe
25	McCafferty's Bus Terminal
26	Balkan Restaurant

House, one of Sydney's finest old homes, built in 1832 in Regency style, overlooking the harbour. It's open daily except Monday from 10 am to 4.30 pm, and admission is $2.50. Bus No 311 from Hunter St passes right by the house. The next bay east – about half a km due east from the Cross – is Rushcutters Bay which has a pleasant harbourside park and lots of boats at anchor. Then there's Darling Point and even trendier Double Bay – swish shops and lots of badly parked Porsches and Benzes.

Next up in this direction is Rose Bay, then Nielsen Park (see Harbour Walks) and Vaucluse where Vaucluse House (open from 10 am to 4.30 pm except Mondays, admission $2.50) on Wentworth Rd is an imposing turreted example of 19th century Australiana in fine grounds. It was built in 1828 for the explorer William Wentworth and you can get there on bus No 325 from Edgecliff station.

At the end of the harbour is Watsons

Top: Sydney Harbour Bridge from the Rocks, Sydney, NSW (RN)
Left: Darling Harbour, Sydney (TW)
Right: Sydney Opera House (PS)

Top: The Three Sisters, Blue Mountains, near Sydney, NSW (TW)
Left: Rolling fields near Byron Bay, north NSW (NSWGTB)
Right: Lighthouse at the most easterly point in Australia, Byron Bay (TW)

Bay with fashionable Doyles restaurant, a couple of Sydney's most 'be seen there' harbour beaches and the magnificent view across the Heads. All along this side of the harbour there are superb views back towards the city.

Other Suburbs

On the other side of the centre from Paddo and the Cross is Balmain, the arty centre of Sydney and in some ways rivalling Paddington in Victorian era Trendiness. Glebe, closer to the centre, has also been going up the social scale but it hasn't yet gone so far and still has a more studenty, Bohemian atmosphere, with lots of good value restaurants.

Hunters Hill on the north shore, west of the centre, is full of elegant Victorian houses. While the eastern suburbs (the harbour to ocean area beyond the Cross) and the north shore (across the harbour) are the wealthy areas of Sydney, the western suburbs are the real suburbs. Heading west you come first to Redfern. Some parts of it are quite interesting, but others are Australia's closest approach to a real slum. Further out it's the red tile roofed, triple front area of the 'slurbs', the dull Bankstowns of Sydney.

The Harbour

Sydney's harbour is best viewed from the ferries. It's extravagantly colourful and always interesting. People have often wondered which great city has the most magnificent harbour – Hong Kong, Rio, San Francisco or Sydney? I've still to get to Rio, but of the others I would have to give Sydney first place. Officially called Port Jackson, the harbour stretches about 20 km inland from the ocean to the mouth of the Parramatta River. The city centre is about eight km inland. The harbour is lined by a maze of headlands and inlets and has several islands. The biggest inlet, which heads off north-west a couple of km from the ocean, is called Middle Harbour.

Apart from the ferries and various harbour cruises (see Getting Around) you can take trips out to some of the islands. One of them, Fort Denison, or Pinchgut as it was uncomfortably named, was the site of a gallows for convicts who misbehaved, before being fortified when Australians were having a bout of Russian fears back in the Tsar's days in the mid-19th century. There are tours there from Jetty 6, Circular Quay at 10.15 am, 12.15 and 2 pm from Tuesday to Sunday. The trip takes 1½ hours and costs $6 including a conducted tour of the island. Tickets are from the Maritime Services Board on the west side of Circular Quay (tel 240 2036 Monday to Friday, tel 27 6606 on weekends).

The same goes for the trips to Goat Island from Jetty 6 at 10.45 am and 12.45 pm, Wednesday to Sunday. They last 2½ hours but cost the same. Early convicts built a gunpowder magazine, a police station and even a canal on Goat Island, for reasons probably best known to their guards. The island also has a stone bench where a convict called Bony Anderson, who kept trying to escape, was finally chained, left in silence and fed his rations on the end of a pole.

You can hire boats (including rowing boats, canoes, yachts of various sizes, motor boats and windsurfers) from Walton's Boatshed (tel 969 6006) at 2 The Esplanade, Balmoral, on Middle Harbour. There are several other harbour boat hire places.

At weekends the harbour is carpeted with the sails of hundreds of yachts and a favourite activity is following the 18 footer yacht races on Sundays from September to March. Spectator ferries, complete with on-board bookies so you can bet on the outcome, follow the exciting races. They usually leave Circular Quay around 1.30 pm, costing about $6 a trip. Eighteen footers are a peculiarly Australian yachting class where virtually anything goes – the end product is boats carrying huge sails, which result in their being fantastically fast and requiring great athletic ability to keep them upright.

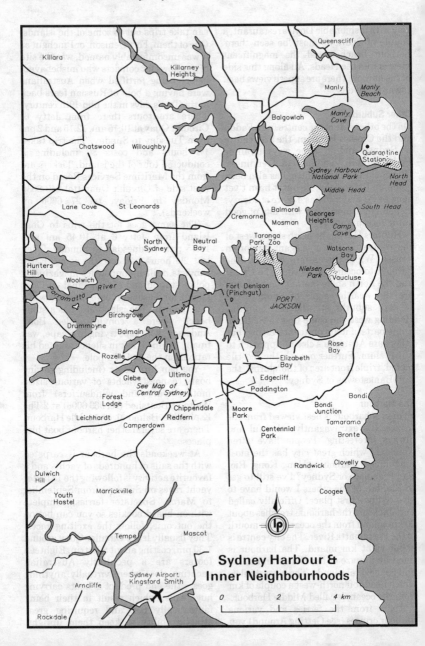

**Sydney Harbour &
Inner Neighbourhoods**

0   2   4 km

Unlike most yachting classes the boats carry advertising on their sails and are heavily sponsored. Ben Lexcen, designer of the America's Cup winning *Australia II*, first made his name as an 18 footer designer and skipper.

Harbour Walks Some of the harbour shore is still quite wild and several undeveloped stretches towards the ocean end have been declared Sydney Harbour National Park. Most of them have walking tracks, beaches, old fortifications and good views. On the south shore is Nielsen Park which covers Vaucluse Point, Shark Bay (very popular in summer, with a shark net) and the Hermitage Walk down round Hermit Bay. The park headquarters (tel 337 5511) is at Greycliffe House in Nielsen Park.

Further out there's a fine short walk round South Head at the harbour entrance from Camp Cove Beach, passing Lady Bay, Inner South Head, The Gap at Watsons Bay which is a popular place for catching the sunrise and sunset, and on to Outer South Head. Bus No 325 from Edgecliff station will take you to Nielsen Park or the South Head area.

On the north shore the fine four km Ashton Park track, round Bradleys Head below Taronga Zoo and up alongside Taylors Bay, is part of the national park. Take the Taronga Zoo ferry from Circular Quay to get to Ashton Park. In the other direction from Taronga you can walk to Cremorne Point by a combination of parks, stairways, streets and bits of bush. Either way you get good views over to the south shore. Georges and Middle Heads and Obelisk Bay a bit further east from Taylors Bay are also parts of the national park. More walks and lookout points are covered in the Manly section.

Taronga Zoo & Koala Park

A short ferry ride across the harbour will deposit you near Taronga Zoo, which has one of the most attractive settings of any zoo in the world. There are over 4000 critters in there including lots of Aussie ones. The ferry ($1.20) goes from Jetty 5, Circular Quay. The zoo is at the top of a hill on the north shore and if you can't be bothered to walk, buses (65c) meet the ferries to carry you up. The zoo is open daily from 9 am to 5 pm. Admission is $9, or $4 for kids.

If koalas are all you're interested in, Koala Park (tel 84 3141) on Castle Hill Rd in West Pennant Hills in north-west Sydney is open daily and costs $5 to enter.

More wildlife parks are covered in Around Sydney.

Manly

It is an excellent, cheap, half hour ferry cruise to Manly at the ocean edge of the harbour. The frequent hydrofoils are a dollar or so more, bumpier, and do the trip in 15 minutes.

Manly is more like a small resort than a city suburb, and all types of people head out here at weekends. It's not a bad place to stay and you can also get there by bus from St Leonards train station on the north shore. It might be an idea to go one way by each method.

Named by New South Wales' first governor, Captain Phillip, after the physique of the local Aborigines, Manly is on a narrow neck of land which points down to North Head at the Sydney Harbour entrance. A short walk across this isthmus from the ferry terminal, which is on Manly Cove (the inner beach), takes you to Manly's fine sandy ocean beach. The main street across the isthmus, The Corso, is a palm lined pedestrian mall with numerous cafes and places to sit. At the ocean end, North and South Steyne – or alternatively just Ocean Beach – are the names of the road running along the beach. There's a tourist information centre (tel 977 1088) on South Steyne, open from 10 am to 4 pm daily.

Manly Museum & Art Gallery on West Esplanade (just to the left when you come off the ferry) has Australian paintings and some intriguing temporary exhibitions on things like the history of surfing or swimming costumes. Manly Underwater World is an interesting oceanarium also on West Esplanade, at the end of the beach. For $9 you can get a close up view of sharks and stingrays, and coral and kelp communities.

Past Underwater World an eight km walking track follows the shoreline all the way back to The Spit bridge over Middle Harbour. Points of interest on the way, from the Manly end, include Fairlight, Forty Baskets and Reef beaches (the latter, a nude beach, involves a slight detour from the main track), great views between Dobroyd Head and Grotto Point, and ancient Aboriginal rock carvings on a sandstone platform between the Cutler Rd Lookout and Grotto Point. Bus Nos 182 and 241 go back from The Spit bridge to the city centre.

South of Manly, it's about three km to spectacular North Head at the Sydney Harbour entrance. Most of the headland is included in Sydney Harbour National Park – including the old quarantine station which housed suspected disease carriers from 1832 until 1984. Bus No 135 runs from Manly to North Head if you're not up to the walk.

North of Manly

A string of oceanfront suburbs stretches north up the coast from Manly, ending in beautiful, wealthy Palm Beach and the spectacular Barranjoey Heads at the mouth of Broken Bay, 30 km from Manly. There are lots of beaches along the way and buses do the route. From Palm Beach you can take cruises on the Pittwater, a fine inlet off Broken Bay, or the Hawkesbury River or get ferries to Ku-ring-gai Chase or across Broken Bay to Patonga.

The latter is part of an interesting alternative route north: from Patonga there are buses four times a day to Gosford, where you can get a bus or train heading up the coast.

Beaches

Sydney's beaches are one of its greatest assets – they're easily accessible and usually very good. However, recently they've been having problems with pollution and in a number of places you're advised not to swim. Measures are being taken to fix this up, so check out the situation when you're there.

There are basically two sorts of beaches in Sydney – harbour beaches and ocean beaches. The harbour beaches are sheltered and calm and generally smaller. The ocean beaches often have quite good surf.

Although they'll get crowded on hot summer weekends Sydney's beaches are never really shoulder to shoulder. Swimming is generally safe – at the ocean beaches you're only allowed to swim within the 'flagged' areas patrolled by the famed voluntary lifeguards. Efforts are made to keep the surfers separate from the swimmers. A high point of Sydney's beach life is the surf-lifesaving competitions with races, rescues and surfboat competitions at various beaches throughout the summer. Shark patrols are operated through the summer months and the ocean beaches are generally netted – Sydney has only had one fatal shark attack since 1937. The shark proof nets do not, incidentally, enclose the beaches – they're installed perpendicular to the beaches, not parallel to them. This dissuades sharks from patrolling along the beaches.

Many of Sydney's beaches are 'topless', but on some beaches this is not approved of so women should observe what other people are doing before forgetting their bikini tops. There are also a couple of nude beaches. Following is a resumé of some of the beaches:

Harbour Beaches On the south side, out near the heads (the harbour entrance), one of the most popular harbour beaches is trendy Camp Cove, a small but pleasant sliver of sand popular with families, and also topless. This was the place where Governor Phillip first landed in Sydney. Just north from Camp Cove and immediately inside the heads, tiny Lady Bay Beach achieved some notoriety in the process of becoming a nude beach. It's mainly a gay scene. There's another nude beach on the north shore of the harbour, Reef Beach (see the earlier Harbour Walks section).

Over on the ocean side from Camp Cove is Watsons Bay with the delightful outdoor seafood restaurant Doyles, where you can gaze back along the harbour towards the city.

Two other popular harbour beaches are Balmoral, with its little 'island', on the north side of the harbour and Nielsen Park on the south side at Vaucluse (see Harbour Walks).

South Ocean Beaches South of the heads there's a string of ocean beaches all the way to the entry to Botany Bay. Bondi, with its crowds, surfies and even fibreglass mermaids is probably the best known beach in Australia. Bondi's beachfront is backed by somewhat run-down Victorian buildings which give it the air of a slightly seedy, antipodean Brighton, but that makes Bondi sound a lot worse than it is. There are good places to eat and it's really quite an enjoyable place. Bondi is rather like Earls Court is (or was) for young Australians in London, only, in this case, Bondi is a favourite with New Zealanders and other young visitors to Sydney. It's a popular gathering place, with a selection of cheap accommodation.

Some of Australia's easiest-reached Aboriginal carvings are a short walk north of the beach – outlines of fish on a flat rock on the golf course.

Tamarama, a little south of Bondi, is another beautiful sweep of sand with strong surf; it's also topless. Take bus No 391 from Bondi Junction station to get there. Then there's Bronte, a wide beach popular with families (bus No 378 from Bondi Junction), and Coogee another wide, sweeping beach where you'll also find the popular Coogee Bay Hotel with its beer garden overlooking the beach. Other beaches towards Botany Bay, which is more for sailing than swimming due to the sharks, include Maroubra.

North Ocean Beaches The 30 km coast up to Barranjoey Heads is dotted with beaches beginning at Manly. Freshwater, first up from Manly, attracts a lot of teenagers, then there's Curl Curl (families and surfers), Dee Why and Collaroy (family beaches), the long sweep of Narrabeen which has some of Sydney's best

surf, and further up the very safe Newport (families again). Up towards Barranjoey Heads three of the best are Avalon, Whale Beach and Palm Beach. Bus Nos 134 and 139 depart from Manly for Freshwater and Curl Curl, while No 190 from York St in the city centre will take you to Newport and north.

Surf Beaches Surfing is a popular pastime in Sydney, and with the large number of good beaches close at hand, it's easy to see why. Apart from Bondi and Tamarama, there's Maroubra south of the heads. Beyond Botany Bay, Cronulla is another serious surf beach. North of the heads there's another dozen or so dotted about 30 km up from Manly , the best being Narrabeen, North Avalon and Palm Beach, the north end of which is a nude beach.

Places to Stay

There's a wide variety of accommodation in Sydney including an excellent selection of very cheap hostels. The information that follows is subdivided by location as well as type so decide where you want to stay first of all. If you want to book a hotel or motel room the New South Wales Travel Centre performs this service. There are cheap places in the 'flats to let' and 'share accommodation' ads in the *Sydney Morning Herald*, particularly on Wednesday and Saturdays. Many travellers also find flat shares through other travellers whom they meet in Kings Cross.

When Maureen and I first set up Lonely Planet we lived in the basement of a Paddington terrace in Sydney and since then we've made lots of trips and visits to the harbour city and tried out all sorts of areas around the city either staying with friends or in a variety of places, more than a few of which feature here. The Cross is the backpacker centre and is great fun if you like a little raucous squalor. Bondi is Sydney's best known beach and like the Cross there's lots of activity and lots of places to eat. If you'd like something quieter the distance to Manly is no big deal because you ride back and forth on the best transport Sydney has to offer – a harbour ferry.

Hostels Sydney has several YHA hostels and an enormous number of privately run backpacker hostels. The backpacker places vary, so you may have to jump around until you find one that best suits you. Some Sydney backpacker hostels – not all – discourage or even ban Australians. See the Facts for the Visitor chapter for the reasons behind this.

Most backpacker hostels have set hours for checking in or out, normally the couple of hours round 9 am and again around 6 pm, but once you're in you usually get a key so you can come and go whenever you like. In most places you're asked to be quiet after 10 or 11 pm. There are often cheap rates if you stay a week, and in winter prices can drop a dollar or so. Many hostels have notice boards for rides, deals, messages, etc. The main concentration of backpacker hostels is in Kings Cross but there are others in the centre, in Surry Hills and Glebe and north of the harbour at St Leonards and Forestville. Others are in the beach suburbs of Coogee, Bondi, Manly and Avalon, and there's one at Rockdale near the airport.

YHA hostels are at Glebe Point (three km west of Central Railway Station), Forest Lodge (2½ km west) and Dulwich Hill (six km south-west). Some of them have twin rooms as well as dormitories. The large YHA hostel at Coogee was due to close about mid-1989 to be replaced, it's hoped, by one in or near the city centre. You can book any YHA hostel in Australia, including the Sydney ones, through the YHA Central Reservations Bureau in Sydney (tel 267 3044).

Hostels – city *Sydney City Centre Backpackers Accommodation* (tel 223 3529, 59 2850) is in a tower block at 7 Elizabeth St, just south of Hunter St. The reception (open from 8.30 to 10.30 am and 4.30 to 6.30 pm) is in unit 63 on floor six. Accommodation is in bunkrooms taking four people at $14 per person, each room with its own bathroom and kitchen, and you have free use of washing machines. If

you call, they'll probably be able to fix transport from the airport.

The nearest backpackers accommodation to Central Railway Station is the *George Private Hotel* (tel 211 1800) at 700A George St. In addition to more expensive hotel rooms, there are six or eight person separate-sex bunkrooms at $14 a night or $78 a week. The rooms are clean and you have use of a kitchen but no pots or plates. The hotel has a cafeteria.

The large and comfortable *YWCA* (tel 264 2451) takes women, married couples or families and is at 5-11 Wentworth Ave, at the corner of Liverpool St across from Hyde Park. Four person bunkrooms go for $17 per person, single rooms for $35 ($60 with private bathroom), twins $58 ($75), triples $75 ($90). Maximum stay is three nights and there is a cheap cafeteria open to all. Sydney's YMCA hostel burnt down but there are plans to rebuild. Call 264 1011 for the latest information.

Hostels – Kings Cross 'The Cross' has several decent hostels but also all of Sydney's dirtiest, noisiest and most crowded ones. The place most people start looking is Victoria St, but despite the ever growing number of backpacker beds the better places are often full. The best time to get there is about 9 or 10 am, when people check out and vacancies come up. To get to Kings Cross, take the quick train ride from Central Railway Station or other city centre stations. Kings Cross station has exits on both Darlinghurst Rd and Victoria St.

Heading down Victoria St from Kings Cross station or from the corner of Darlinghurst Rd, one of the first places you reach is *Plane Tree Lodge* (tel 356 4551) at No 172. Beds here are $12 in a dormitory or a single or double room, and the weekly rate of $60 is good value. The place is quite strictly run, but it's clean with good facilities.

At 170 the *International Network Hostel* (tel 356 3844) is pretty informal and charges $14 for a dormitory bed or $21 each in a double. It also has 12 furnished flats a few streets away in Roslyn St and Barncleuth Square which cost $35 for two plus $12 for each extra person. In the main hostel the common rooms are quite good and there's a good notice board but there aren't many bathrooms.

Highfield House Private Hotel (tel 358 1552) at 166 Victoria St isn't primarily a hostel, but it does have some small dormitories – just two or three beds in each at $18, and it's clean and offers more privacy than normal hostels. Next down the street at 162, *Kings Cross Backpackers* (tel 356 3232) is a large and well established hostel which runs several nearby houses. Prices per person are $12 in a dormitory or a single-sex four person flat, $13 in a double room, with a few dollars discount for a week's stay. The doubles are quite roomy. Kitchens in the main houses are communal: as in most Kings Cross hostels they can get a bit scruffy but at least there's an adequate supply of pots, pans, cutlery, etc. Probably the best building is the main one at 162. There's a good notice board here.

The *Travellers Rest* (tel 358 4606) at 156 Victoria St is one of the cleanest, best run Kings Cross hostels. Dorm beds are $12 in small rooms and there are also singles/doubles at $24/30. Weekly rates are six times the daily cost. All rooms have cooking facilities and TV, most have their own bathrooms. Checkout time here is 9 am, an hour earlier than usual.

Jolly Swagman Backpackers is a relative newcomer to the scene but is one of the biggest operations in three nearby locations – 144 Victoria St (tel 358 6400), 16 Orwell St (tel 358 6600) and 14 Springfield Mall (tel 358 3330). Orwell St is off Victoria St just down from 144, Springfield Mall is a couple of turns off Orwell St. Dorm beds at Jolly Swagman are $13 a night or $80 a week, twin and double rooms are $32 ($170 a week). Each room has its own fridge, stove, sink and cooking gear; bathrooms and toilets are shared.

At 22 Orwell St is one of the entrances to *L'Annexe* or *Chez Alain* (tel 357 2273), a hostel with a friendly French owner. The other entrance is at 19 Hughes St, the next street off Victoria St as you go down the hill. There are dormitory, twin and double rooms from $11 to $15 and bed linen is provided. All rooms have their own TV, fridge and basic cooking facilities, and about half have private bathrooms. Like some other hostels where you can cook in your own room, the common areas are small. The office is open from 8 to 11 am and 5.30 to 8 pm.

Another popular place is at 25 Hughes St – the clean and quite big *Downunder Hostel* (tel 358 1143), where dorm beds are $12 and double rooms $28 a night, cheaper by the week. There are sizeable cooking, dining and TV areas. Bed linen is provided, all bathrooms are shared and the office is open from 8 to 11 am and 5 to 7.30 pm.

Off the bottom end of Victoria St, at 31 Challis Ave, *The Point Inn* has rooms for four or more people at $14 a night per head ($80 a week), triples at $18 per head ($86 a week), and doubles/twins at $21 a head ($105 a week). Also down this end is *Rucksack Rest* (tel 358 2348) at 9 McDonald St with more backpackers accommodation at about $11 a night.

One of the cheapest and most relaxed Kings Cross hostels is *Barncleuth House* (tel 358 1689) which is slightly away from the main drag, in a quieter street at 6 Barncleuth Square, east of Darlinghurst Rd. The house is a rambling Victorian place with a courtyard garden and log fires when it's cold. Dorm beds or small doubles are $9.50 per person ($56 a week), and larger doubles are $11. The hostel's excellent vegetarian dinner costs about $4.

Another sizeable place is the *Young Travellers Hostel* (tel 357 3509) at 15 Roslyn Gardens, reached by following Elizabeth Bay Rd off Darlinghurst Rd then turning right into Roslyn Gardens. It's a fairly typical hostel with a good kitchen/sitting area, in a fine old terraced building. Bus No 316 from Hunter St in the city centre will take you near there.

Hostels - inner suburbs There are a couple of backpacker places on South Dowling St, Surry Hills, opposite Moore Park a block or so north of the Cleveland St corner, and about two km south-east of Central Railway Station. Both are fairly basic, but are friendly and on the cheap side at $11 a night. *Kangaroo Bakpak* has dorm rooms in two houses, No 635 (tel 699 5915) and No 665 (tel 698 3639).

Between the two Kangaroo houses you'll find the *Beethoven Lodge* (tel 698 4203) at No 641. In addition to dorm beds, Beethoven has some twins and doubles all at the same price of $12 per person and good weekly rates. There are the usual shared bathrooms, sitting rooms and kitchens. To get here from Central Railway Station take bus Nos 372, 393 or 395.

The closest YHA hostel to the city centre is *Sydney YHA Hostel* (tel 692 0747) at 28 Ross St, Forest Lodge, 2½ km west of Central Railway Station. Ross St is off the Parramatta Rd, opposite Sydney University. It has only 30 beds and is closed from 10 am to 4 pm. Numerous buses from Railway Square (where George and Pitt Sts meet near Central Railway Station) go to the corner of Parramatta Rd and Ross St, including Nos 412, 438, 461, 480 and 490. From mid-December to mid-February the YHA also operates the summer *St Andrews YHA Hostel* in St Andrew's College at the university, on Carillon Ave. The cost is $12. You can book through the YHA central reservations bureau. When it's operating, this hostel is open from 7 to 10 am and 5 to 10 pm. Buses Nos 422, 423, 426 and 448 will get you there from Pitt St or Railway Square.

In Glebe, the new *Hereford YHA Lodge* (tel 660 5274) at 51 Hereford St has twin and share rooms, at $17 per person for share rooms and $19 for twin. It has a cafeteria, laundry, all the usual facilities plus a swimming pool and sauna. The YHA reckon it's their best Sydney hostel. *Sydney Glebe Point YHA Hostel* (tel 692 8418) is at 262-264 Glebe Point Rd, about three km west of Central Railway Station. This used to be Sydney's best YHA hostel – I guess it's now the second-best. The cost is $15, mostly in twin-bed rooms, and the hostel is open all day until 10 pm.

Next to the YHA Hostel on Glebe Point Rd is *Glebe House* (tel 660 8878), with beds in shared rooms for $12 and doubles from $27. They also have longer term flats. It's run by the same people who operate popular hostels in Melbourne's St Kilda. Also in Glebe, *Wattle House Hostel* (tel 692 0879) is a friendly, well run, little, independent hostel with beds in small shared rooms at $11. It's at 44 Hereford St, about 400 metres off Glebe Point Rd. There's a garden and all the usual facilities. Buses Nos 431 and 433 from Railway Square go along Glebe Point Rd and will drop you outside the YHA.

Dulwich Hill YHA Hostel (tel 569 0272) is at 407 Marrickville Rd, Dulwich Hill, on the corner of Wardell Rd, about six km south-west of the centre. The nightly charge is $13. This hostel is open all day. To get there take the 15 minute train ride from Central Railway Station to Dulwich Hill and walk about 750 metres north to Marrickville Rd. Bus No 426 from Circular Quay or Railway Square, and bus No 490 (daytime only and not Sundays) from behind the Queen Victoria building on York St, will both take you to the corner of Marrickville and Wardell Rds.

Just north of the harbour but not far from the city centre, the *Travellers Rest* people who run one of the best hostels in Kings Cross have a second place at 7 Park Rd, St Leonards (tel 436 3146), 500 metres from St Leonards station, which is about a 10 minute train ride from the centre. For a bed in a three person dormitory you pay $10 a night or $52 a week; for double rooms it's about $128 a week or $24 a night. In Kirribilli, a short ferry ride from Circular Quay, is *Glen Ferrie Guest House* (921 684) at 12A Carabella St. They have singles and twins at $128 a week per person, including two meals a day.

Hostels - beaches For a more relaxing time away from the central city hurly-burly, the beach suburbs are a good bet and the hostels there are generally good. *Coogee Beach Backpackers* (tel 665 7735) at 94 Beach St, close to the beach in Coogee is spacious, clean, bright and comfortable with dorm beds at $12, a garden, two good kitchens, washing machines, a big sitting room with TV and stereo, and good views. You pay $2.50 for sheet hire for your stay. They'll usually arrange transport from the airport if you call. Buses No 373 from Circular Quay, No 372 from Railway Square or No 314 from Bondi Junction all go to the Dolphin St bus stop near the corner of Beach St in Coogee. Walk up the hill (north) on Beach St and look for the '94' sign up on the left.

The more expensive, but very comfortable *Lamrock Hostel* (tel 365 0433) is at 7 Lamrock Ave, just back from the south end of Bondi Beach. It's a bright house, recently and well converted, with rooms taking up to four at $18 each, or twin rooms at $24 a head. You can hire bedding for $6 for your stay. All rooms have a fan and some have private bathrooms. The communal rooms include a kitchen, a dining area and a separate sitting room with its own TV and coffee-making gear. There's a barbecue out the back, Mokes for hire, and even a telex! Bus No 380 goes to Bondi Beach from Bondi Junction station.

Also just back from the beach is *Bondi Beach Travellers' Hostel* (tel 358 1126 or tel 665 0506 after hours) at 124 Curlewis St. It's less comfortable and bigger than the Lamrock but cheaper at $12, and still a decent typical hostel, with a fairly relaxed atmosphere and a garden out the back. You can make inquiries or bookings at The Juice Extractor, 75 Darlinghurst Rd, Kings Cross.

Newly renovated at 63 Fletcher St is the *Bondi Lodge* (tel 305 863). They offer singles and doubles at $128 per week, including two meals a day.

Still in the beach suburbs but north of the harbour, the *Manly Beach Backpackers Hostel* (tel 977 2092) at 68-70 Pittwater Rd, Manly, charges $10 in shared rooms and is close to the beach. Take the Manly ferry from Circular Quay.

At the top end of the northern beach strip and near the Pittwater and some good ocean beaches, the *Avalon Beach Hostel* (tel 918 9709), 59 Avalon Parade, is another good, new place. The nightly cost in shared rooms for two or four is $12. Bus No 190 goes hourly from Wynyard Park on York St in the city centre, or take Manly buses (from Manly at 3.47, 4.55 and 5.10 pm). Some days you can get a train to Brooklyn and then take the Hawkesbury River ferry to Careel Bay at Avalon – call the hostel for details.

Hostels - elsewhere *Sydney Airport Backpackers Accommodation* (tel 59 2850), 46-48 Cameron St, Rockdale, is the nearest hostel to the airport, but it's further from the centre than the airport and not near anywhere else except Botany Bay. A bed is $10 and they'll collect you from the airport if you call.

About seven km inland from Manly and not really near anywhere of interest except perhaps Davidson Park State Recreation Area, there's *Northern Beaches Backpackers Accommodation* (tel 451 1617), 12 Cook St, Forestville. It's a small, straightforward hostel charging $10 in small bunk rooms. To get to the hostel take a train to Chatswood then a Forest Coaches bus to Forestville.

Hotels, Motels, Guest Houses & Flats The main areas are the city, Kings Cross, Bondi Beach and Manly, but there are a few more places about the North Shore and elsewhere. Bed & Breakfast Sydneyside (tel 449 4430), PO Box 555, Turramurra, NSW 2074, will find you accommodation in a private home in Sydney for about $35 to $60 a night single, $55 to $90 double.

The following hotels, motels and guest houses and flats are listed by area.

City There's a clutch of big old hotels in the south of the centre, convenient for Central Railway Station and the bus terminals. The *Sydney Tourist Hotel* (tel 211 5777) at 400 Pitt St, is an old standby (formerly the People's Palace). It's well looked after with singles/doubles for $28/48 and rooms for three to six people at $18 a head. The reception is open 24 hours and there's a small saving if you book in for a week. Most bathrooms are large, modern and communal, but there is also one floor of bathrooms for females only! There is a restaurant serving dinner and buffet breakfast, and a coin laundry.

Across the road, the *CB Private Hotel* (tel 211 5115) at 417 Pitt St is large, clean and very plain - in fact it's a lot like a South-East Asian hotel - open all night and cheap! There are 230 rooms and they keep them full by keeping the tariffs down - daily rates are $25/36 for singles/ doubles, $50 for three. Weekly rates are five times the daily rates. No rooms have private bathrooms, but there is a launderette, TV lounge and phones.

Just a block west, the *George Private Hotel* has had some renovations and offers singles/doubles for $30/46 and rooms for three, four or five at $62, $70 and $80 respectively - all with communal bathrooms. The weekly rate is six times the daily rate. It's clean and there's a guests' kitchen (but no pots, pans, etc) plus a launderette and a cafeteria. There are also dorm beds - see the Hostels section.

Nearest of all to Central Railway Station is the *Central Private Hotel* (tel 212 1068) at 356-358 Elizabeth St - turn right at the top end of Eddy Ave. All rooms have hot and cold water and a refrigerator. Singles/doubles are $30/35, twins a dollar or two more and each additional person about $12 extra. Weekly rates are significantly cheaper - $128/175 a single/ double. You can get breakfast next door and the office is open from 9 am to 5 pm.

Kings Cross This area has almost as many hotels and flats as hostels, and many of them are in the budget range. The places to look are Darlinghurst Rd, Victoria St and the lanes between.

Springfield Lodge (tel 358 3222) is pretty much in the centre of things at 9 Springfield Ave, just off Darlinghurst Rd. It's good in a simple, straightforward manner. The 72 rooms all have fridges, TV and tea-making facilities. Rooms with share bathrooms go for $30 to $35 single, $37 to $42 double. With private bathrooms you pay $48 single, $52 to $56 double. A stay of a week will net you a day's discount.

Close by at 15 Springfield Ave the comfortable *Bernly Private Hotel* (tel 358 3122) is a bit more comfortable and a few dollars more expensive. All have a washbasin, fridge, bedside lights and tea-making facilities and most have a TV. Some have showers, though all toilets are shared. For a single you pay $37 ($46 with private shower), for twins/doubles $49 ($58). There are also rooms with three and four beds for $75. You save the price of about 1½ nights' stay by booking in for a week. It's open 24 hours a day and has a roof terrace with good views over to the harbour and city centre.

The *Highfield House Private Hotel*, with 34 rooms, is clean and has singles/ doubles for $40/50, twins for $55. Bathrooms are shared. There are also dormitories - see the Hostels section.

Off the bottom end of Victoria St at 21-23 Challis Ave, *Challis Lodge* (tel 358 5422) is a 64 room private hotel charging $30 to $34 for singles with shared bathroom, $38 to $40 for doubles with shared bathroom, and $65 for doubles with balcony and private bathroom. Most rooms have TV, fridge and tea/coffee-making facilities.

The *Plaza Hotel* (tel 358 6455) is right in the heart of noisy Kings Cross at 23 Darlinghurst Rd. The entrance is just off the main street, in Llankelly Place. The cost is $20/28 a single/double, per week it's

$98/138. It's a very plain and basic place with one shared bathroom for each floor, but it is quite OK.

Willowbridge Tourist Apartments (tel 331 3178) have three flats for four or five people from $70 to $80 a night. They're at 116-118 Darlinghurst Rd, south of William St, and these modern flats have TV, washing machine, dryer and a fully equipped kitchen.

There are some upper class, budget hotels around Kings Cross, one of the best known being the comfortable *Macquarie Private Hotel* (tel 358 4122) on the corner of Hughes and Tusculum Sts, where the cheapest singles/doubles are $64/70, flats with their own kitchens cost $75 to $105 for three, $80 to $110 for four. There's a surcharge of 10% for smokers! Rooms are well equipped and breakfast in the hotel restaurant costs $4 to $6. Other places in this range include the *Holiday Lodge Private Hotel* (tel 356 3955) at 55 Macleay St charging $48/56, and the *Barclay Hotel* (tel 358 6133) at 18 Bayswater Rd, with singles and doubles both from $52.

North Shore There are a few good possibilities a short way north of the Harbour Bridge – away from the crowds of travellers, but surprisingly close to the city centre with some different views of the city. The *Elite Private Hotel* (tel 929 6365) is just across the bridge at 133 Carabella St, Kirribilli, near Milsons Point station, and has singles/doubles with TV, fridge and tea-making facilities for $35/45.

The next suburb north of Kirribilli is Neutral Bay and the *Neutral Bay Motor Lodge* (tel 90 4199), 45 Kurraba Rd, on the corner of Hayes St, has both motel rooms and cheaper ones which are good if you're planning a longish stay. Motel rooms with their own bathroom cost $58 double ($375 a week). With the other rooms you share bathroom and kitchen – so you can cook your own food – and pay $110/185 a week for a single/double. It's a clean, friendly, well equipped place and a few rooms even have harbour views. It's often full, but worth checking out if you want a place for a few weeks – you can book ahead. You pay two weeks' rent at the beginning and get your last week free.

Another good bet is *Wallaringa Mansions* (tel 953 5231), a couple of short blocks down the hill at 19 Lower Wycombe Rd, Neutral Bay. There are about 100 rooms and flatlets here. For rooms with shared bath and kitchen the weekly rates are about $85 single, $125 or $140 double. Some of these rooms have their own fridge. The nightly rate in them is $23 per person. For longer term stays (a few months or so) there are also self-contained flatlets, many with excellent harbour views, at about $150 to $175 a week for two or three people. You have to pay a deposit for a flatlet.

Inner Suburbs The most central motel with anything approaching a reasonable tariff is the *Crown-Lodge Motel* (tel 331 2433) at 289 Crown St, Surry Hills, between Campbell and Albion Sts. Rooms are $60 to $74 and have private bathroom, TV, phone, fridge, tea/coffee making facilities, toaster, crockery and cutlery.

Another fairly convenient lower priced motel is the *Esron Motel* (tel 398 7022) at the corner of St Pauls and Dudley Sts, Randwick (between Coogee and the city), where well equipped rooms cost from around $46 to $70 and there's a swimming pool. In the same area but a bit nearer the city, the *Thoroughbred Motel* (tel 662 6044) at 11 Alison Rd, Kensington, has singles/doubles from $52/58.

Bondi Beach You can get to Bondi from the city by bus, but it's far quicker to get the Eastern Suburbs train to Bondi Junction and change to a bus, usually No 380, there. There are quite a few places to stay around Bondi apart from the hostels mentioned earlier.

On Consett Ave, a couple of blocks back from the south end of the beach, there are two decent guest houses. The *Bondi*

Beach Guest House (tel 89 8309) at No 11 is neat and clean and has singles/doubles for $30/38. There are fridges and tea-making facilities in all the rooms and a big kitchen, and a few rooms have private bathrooms. Next door at 11A Consett Ave the *Thelellen Lodge* (tel 30 1521) has rates of $30/40 for pleasant rooms with TVs, fridges and tea-making equipment. There are also a TV lounge and a laundry.

A few metres up the hill from the south end of the beach, the *Thelellen Beach Inn* (tel 30 5333), run by the same people as the Thelellen Lodge, is a big, old Bondi hotel at 2 Campbell Parade on the corner of Francis St. Singles/doubles are from $30/35 and there are family rooms at $45 to $52. Bathrooms are shared but each room has a fridge, TV and tea-making facilities. In a similar mould, but a bit more comfortable, is the *Hotel Bondi* (tel 30 3271) at the corner of Campbell Parade and Curlewis St, where rooms with TV, tea-making equipment and shared bathrooms cost $46/58, and rooms with private bathroom and view are $64/69.

The Bondi Beach Motel (tel 30 5344) at 68 Gould St, pretty much in the centre of things, is more modern and has been recommended. Rooms are around $52/64, variable with the season, and they have private bathroom, fridge, TV and tea-making facilities. Breakfast is available and there's a roof with a view of the beach area.

Coogee Down the coast a bit from Bondi, the *Grand Pacific Private Hotel* (tel 665 6301) at the corner of Carr and Beach Sts, costs $23 per person. Weekly rates are quite good value at about $95 to $115 for singles, $150 to $200 for doubles. All rooms have a fridge and TV, there's a shared kitchen and laundry, and it's very close to the beach.

Manly There's a range of places to stay including a backpackers hostel. As at Bondi prices go up and down depending

how busy the place is – December to March is worst.

At 27-29 Victoria Parade, two blocks to the right along the Esplanade from the ferry landing, the *Eversham Private Hotel* (tel 977 2423) is a clean, no frills, 100 room place close to the ocean beach. It usually only takes weekly customers but the rates are good value. There's a big dining room and the weekly tariff – $155/270 a single/double in the low season – includes breakfast or a credit on any other meal. *Manly Lodge* (tel 977 8514) is over the road at 22 Victoria Parade. It's a nice looking place with a Chinese restaurant downstairs and singles/doubles for $25/40, or weekly rates of around $65 to $85 per person.

On The Corso, the main street between the ferry landing and the ocean beach, the *Steyne Hotel* (tel 977 4977) at No 75 has a variety of rooms starting at $27 per person or $30 with breakfast. Most involve communal bathrooms. The hotel has two lounges and a dining room. Over at 61 Pittwater Rd, *Pacific Coast Budget Accommodation* (tel 977 6177) is old, simple and a bit dowdy, but has a certain comfortable character and costs $19/28 a single/double.

Colleges The usual rules apply – vacations only, students for preference. Best bets are the two *International Houses*. The following are at the University of New South Wales in Kensington, about four km south of the city centre. At *New College* (tel 662 6066) non-students pay $35 a night room only, $40 with breakfast and $52 full board. Weekly rates are equal to six separate nights. Students pay less than half these rates – $135 for a week's full board, for instance. *Warrane College* (tel 662 6199) is a Catholic college which offers accommodation with full board to men during the summer vacation. At *International House* (tel 663 0418) full board is $30 a day for students, $45 a day or $288 a week for non-students. You can try the University of New South Wales campus accommodation service (tel 697 3166).

A lot of the colleges at the University of Sydney (tel 692 2222), a couple of km west of the centre along the Parramatta road, tend to be booked out with conferences in the vacations. Ones to try are *Wesley College* (tel 51 2024), *Women's College* (tel 51 1195), *St John's College* (tel 51 1240) which is closed December and January, *Sancta Sophia College* (tel 51 2467) which usually has conferences and otherwise prefers students, *St Andrew's College* (tel 51 1449) and *International House* (tel 692 2040). These all charge around $30 a night.

Camping Sydney's camping sites tend to be a long way out of town. The closest to the city which allows camping is the *Sundowner* at North Ryde, about 14 km out. The sites listed below are within a 30 km radius of the centre, but if you're planning to camp, phone and check first, some may only permit caravans.

Sheralee Tourist Caravan Park (tel 599 7161), 88 Bryant St, Rockdale, 13 km south, sites $14, on-site vans $21 to $46.
Sundowner North Ryde (tel 88 1933), corner Lane Cove and Fontenoy Rds, North Ryde, 14 km north, camping $12 to $16 double, on-site vans $43 to $60 double.
East's Van Park Lane Cove River (tel 88 3649), Plassey Rd, North Ryde, 14 km north, sites $13 double, on-site vans $34 double.
Lakeside Caravan Park (tel 913 7845), Lake Park Rd, Narrabeen, 26 km north, camping $10 to $12 double.
Ramsgate Beach Caravan Park (tel 529 7329), 289 Grand Parade, Ramsgate, 16 km south, sites $14 double, on-site vans $30 to $40 double.

Places to Eat

If you're going to explore seriously Sydney's ethnic variety in restaurants a useful book is *Cheap Eats in Sydney*. There are many places in the city centre from Central Railway Station past Hyde Park to Martin Place, on the western edge of the central area in Chinatown and Darling Harbour, or around The Rocks and Circular Quay, just north of the centre. Away from the centre, Kings Cross, Darlinghurst, Paddington, Balmain, Glebe, Newtown, Redfern and several beach suburbs all offer more good possibilities.

City Centre The Central Railway Station area has some good Asian restaurants and cafes. At the *Central Railway Station Restaurant* itself, open from 5.30 am to 9 pm daily, a good filling breakfast will set you back around $4, lunch or dinner around $7.

A five minute walk from the station at 787 George St, near where George and Pitt Sts meet, the licensed *Malaya* is a long-standing favourite with local students for its reasonably cheap Malay-Chinese food and it's open daily.

Further north at 711 George St the *Mekong* is a must if you like Asian food and you're hungry but not affluent. It's open daily from 11 am to 10 pm. Rice plus three dishes cost $4, tea is free, the food is filling and the service is really fast. The *Vulcano Restaurant* at 707 George St is a BYO pizza place with tables at the rear, delicious Italian dishes and daily specials. Nearby at 201 Hay St, the *Bac Lieu* is a Chinese-Vietnamese place offering a large variety of rice and noodle dishes under $6. This is the eastern fringe of Chinatown which has many more restaurants – see the following Chinatown section.

Just under the railway line from Hay St, at 202 Elizabeth St, the *Roma* is a great place for continental cakes, pastries, coffees and home-made pasta, all at reasonable prices. It's open from 7.30 am to 5.30 pm weekdays and on Saturday mornings.

Moving closer to the centre, on Liverpool St and in the Hyde Park area, there are many more possibilities including several Greek restaurants. On the corner of Liverpool and Kent Sts, three blocks north of Hay St, the *Lantern* offers a good value Chinese buffet for $5.50. It's closed on Sundays. The *Hing Wah* in the Remington Centre, opposite Hyde Park on Liverpool St, offers a take-away Chinese lunch for only $4.50.

Around the corner at 285 Elizabeth St, the Greek *Minerva* looks more expensive than it is. Most dishes are in the $6 to $9 range. On the 5th floor at 251 Elizabeth St, the *Hellenic Club* (tel 264 5883) overlooks Hyde Park and is open from Monday to Friday from 12 noon to 3 pm, and for dinner Monday to Saturday from 5 to 9 pm. Main courses are around $10.

For cheap breakfasts – $3 to $6 – in this part of town, go to the *Selana Coffee Lounge*, north of Liverpool St at 367 Pitt St. In the basement at 336 Pitt St, *Diethnes* is a large and friendly Greek restaurant, but in the more Spartan tradition. Open Monday to Saturday, it has low prices and lots of good food. On Park St between Castlereagh and Elizabeth Sts, *Hakan's* does huge, spicy doner kebabs for around $3. On the corner of George and Park Sts, the cafeteria in *Woolworth's* is good for cheap breakfasts and meals such as lasagna and salad for $6. Over on the other side of the Hilton at 485 George St, one of the city centre's two Lovely Lady Pancake Places is called *Pancakes at the Movies*. The other is at The Rocks. You'll see these restaurants in other cities; they're open long hours and offer a variety of pancake meals from $4 to $8, with breakfast and lunch specials too. This place is open daily from 7 am to midnight or later. On the subject of restaurant chains, the *McDonalds* plague started its march around Australia in Sydney so you'll see plenty of them. There's one on George St done up in art nouveau style – it's worth a hamburger just to look at it. There are also plenty of *Pizza Huts* and *Kentucky Frieds*.

The *Centrepoint Tavern*, downstairs in the Centrepoint shopping complex, at the corner of Pitt and Market Sts, is popular for its large assortment of reasonably priced meals and lower priced children's dishes. Most meals are between $7 and $10.

The next cross street up from Market St is King St and at its eastern end the *Hyde Park Barracks* has a popular three course set menu and other choices if you're less hungry. Open from 10 am to 5 pm daily, it's good value. In the city centre there are a couple of *Sanitarium* health food take-aways, very popular for lunch time sandwiches. One is on King St between George and Pitt Sts, the other in Hunter St, a block north of Martin Place. *El Sano* at shop 2 in the CML Arcade, Martin Place, has interesting vegetarian and South American meals and snacks at moderate prices.

The *Wholemeal* is a long standing health food restaurant on the 1st floor of the Angel Arcade, 121 Pitt St, just north of Martin Place. Everything is really fresh and the prices are reasonable. The menu changes but wholemeal spaghetti, quiches and curries are typical fare and around $6. Nearby at 119 Pitt St, the busy *London Tavern* is similar to the Centrepoint Tavern with meals from around $6 to $12. In Ash St at the end of Angel Arcade, the popular *Fuji Tempura Bar* is a very good place for Japanese food with good main meals under $10. It's open from Monday to Friday for lunches and Wednesday to Friday for dinners.

Chinatown A few minutes' walk north-west from Central Railway Station to the intersection of Hay and Dixon Sts brings you to the heart of Chinatown. Dixon St is a colourful pedestrian mall with trees, benches and lamps with hanging wind chimes. This is one of the best places in Sydney for a good cheap meal.

For a quick introduction try the food centre on the lower floor in the Dixon Centre at the corner of Little Hay and Dixon Sts, halfway between Goulburn and Hay Sts. Stalls offer food from Japan, Vietnam, Thailand, Malaysia, Singapore and other Asian countries. Meals are $4 to $6, with some special deals, such as all you can eat for $5. The food is not only good but authentic – you'll see many Orientals bent over bowls of noodle soup. A similarly priced, perhaps even better, food centre with a comparable range of Asian cuisines is downstairs in the pagoda-style Chinatown Centre on the corner of Dixon and Goulburn Sts.

On the 5th floor of the Chinatown Centre is the *Chinatown Garden Restaurant* with excellent food and particularly good yum cha. A weekend yum cha brunch is popular in Sydney and you may have to queue to get into some of the many places offering it.

The *China Sea* at 94 Hay St is an excellent restaurant with meals under $12. It's very popular with Sydney's Chinese community. The large *Old Tai Yuen* at 110 Hay St above the Covent Garden Hotel, has been around a long time and has a good reputation. Its dishes are in the same price range as the New Tai Yuen ($10 to $12), and the decor is less glamorous but it's still busy.

At the Hay St end of Dixon St, Dixon St becomes Thomas St which doglegs to meet Quay St. On this corner is the *Burlington Centre*, a large Chinese supermarket with lots of snacks to nibble. In the same centre, *Jing May Noodles* is an old-style noodle house fitted out like a modern fast food place, with little on the menu over $10.

Darling Harbour There are lots of good places to eat here, including a food hall with food from everywhere at moderate prices. A couple of cafes of interest include a video cafe and one with a collection of juke boxes with 'swinging '60s' music. There are lots of places to sit outside. Everything at Darling Harbour is open from 10 am to 9 pm weekdays and 10 am to 6 pm on weekends.

The Rocks The Rocks has lots of places but not many in the bargain bracket. At the nearby Circular Quay ferry terminal, the *City Extra* is open 24 hours a day, has outdoor tables, and is really busy during the day. Service can be slow but nearby

buskers will keep you amused. There's lots of variety on the menu from snacks to full meals to desserts. Prices are reasonable.

Over at 101 George St in The Rocks, *Phillip's Foote* has a good barbecue. This is a large place with two courtyards and you cook your own steak or fish for $11; the price includes a glass of wine but salads are extra. At 99 George St, *Rock's Cafe* has low priced cooked breakfasts, sandwiches, burgers, pies, salads and interesting home-made cakes. It's open from 8 am to 7 pm during the week and till late on Friday and Saturday nights.

A string of restaurants, several with outdoor tables, face the waterfront at Circular Quay West, just behind George St and Hickson Rd. The *Italian Village* has reasonably priced soups and pasta dishes though other main meals are around $16. It's worth having a snack at its outside tables to enjoy the stunning view. Close by at 10 Hickson Rd, *Pancakes on the Rocks*, the second of the Lovely Lady chain in central Sydney, is open 24 hours a day, good for odd hour coffees.

The *Gumnut Tea Garden* at 28 Harrington St, the continuation of Playfair St over Argyle St, is a popular daytime eatery. It has tables outside in the garden and specialises in fancy salads, soups, pastas, pies and desserts. Try the carrot cake!

On the other side of the Bradfield Highway which leads onto the Harbour Bridge, there are more places to eat in the glossy *Pier One* centre – expensive but with great views. The *Harbourside Brasserie* here is the exception with its more reasonably priced light meals and cheaper take-away food, from Japanese to Mexican.

Meals with a View If you're visiting the opera house and want to eat, the *Forecourt* is more reasonably priced than either the *Harbour Restaurant* or the exorbitant *Bennelong*. The view's the same – not to be missed – and there's a large outside sitting area. You can eat pasta, a fancy sandwich or a light meal for under $12 or something more exotic for up to $16. The Forecourt is open from 11.30 am to midnight. Between Circular Quay and the opera house, the *Sydney Cove Oyster Bar* at Circular Quay East has another great view, Aussie beers, oysters for $14 a dozen and a mixed seafood plate for $9. It's open from 11.30 am to 8 pm during the week, later on the weekends and in summer. Next door, the *Portobella Cafe*, with outdoor tables, has cheap rolls, croissants, pizzas and cakes.

At Watsons Bay *Doyle's* on Marine Parade has very expensive but very good seafood, and the view and atmosphere are unsurpassed. Doyle's is very popular and doesn't take bookings so get there early. Make sure the sun is shining – you go to Doyle's to eat outside. It also has a cheaper take-away section. Next door to Doyles, *Watsons Bay Hotel* shares the same great view and has cheaper seafood and steaks.

Another place to consider for the setting as much as the food is the *Sydney Tower* (tel 233 3722) atop the Centrepoint Tower, on the corner of Pitt and Market Sts. There are actually three places to eat up here, but the only tolerably priced one is the *Sydney Tower Sky Lounge* on level 3, with light meals, tea, coffee and snacks from $5 to $12. Bookings are essential for the other two restaurants.

East Sydney If you follow the crowds around 12.30 pm into a dull looking little house in Chapel St, East Sydney (close to the Crown and Stanley Sts junction) you will find yourself in *No Names*. It's so called because it has no name, no sign, nothing but dirt cheap and very filling spaghetti and a few other daily dishes. The starter is $4, main course $5 including bread and a glass of cordial. For $7.50, you can have two courses – spaghetti or soup followed by a main course, plus a drink, bread and salad. You may have to queue to get in. It's open daily for lunch and

dinner and is entered through the *Arch Coffee Lounge*, 81 Stanley St. There's another *No Names* in Glebe.

Kings Cross Restaurants and cafes have mushroomed in King's Cross.

The *Rex Hotel* on Darlinghurst Rd, next to the El Alamein fountain, offers a big serve of steak, chips and salad for $7. Other meals are $4 to $5. Just around the corner at 7 Darlinghurst Rd, the *Astoria* is famous for its good value Australian home-style cooking. 'Brilliant' reported one hungry traveller. It's open for lunch and dinner until 8.30 pm except on Sunday.

Several other places with plenty of outdoor tables are near the fountain, all serving coffee, breakfasts, snacks and moderately priced meals. Nearby at 22 Darlinghurst Rd, a take-away Japanese food bar does a roaring trade in tempura at $7 and sushi at $10.

Back on Darlinghurst Rd, towards William St, *Mirrors Continental Restaurant & Coffee House* at No 21 is another busy place with breakfasts and other meals around $5.50, a little more for steaks and fish. At No 87, *Pinnochio's Pizzeria* has pizzas from $7 but its other dishes are more expensive. It's open until 3 am. *Geoffrey's Cafe*, on the corner of Darlinghurst Rd and Roslyn St, has outdoor tables for viewing the street life plus some good large meals at $7 to $9.

The *Cactus Cafe* at 150 Victoria St is a small, slightly expensive place serving French-style food but with some exotic spicing from the Seychelles. It's open Wednesday to Sunday from 6 pm until late and has main courses from $13 to $16. A few doors closer to Orwell St at 142 Victoria St, the *Bandung* is open daily from 6 pm to midnight and has cheap Indonesian food with most main courses around $7. Victoria St also has several quite expensive Japanese restaurants, all good for a splurge.

The *New York* at 23 Bayswater Rd, east off Darlinghurst Rd, is a basic place offering straightforward meals at very low prices. At 57 Bayswater Rd, *Gado-Gado* does spicy Indonesian dishes from $6 to $8, and is open from 6 to 11 pm Monday to Saturday. Kellett St starts from Bayswater Rd near the New York and has several relaxed, vaguely Bohemian eateries in old Victorian terraces, as well as a number of expensive places. *Dean's Cafe* at 1/7 Kellett St is open 24 hours a day on weekends but only for dinner during the week. It's good and reasonably priced. The owners make you feel at home.

The *Music Cafe* at 199 William St, on the south side of the street just down from Darlinghurst Rd near the post office, is an easy-going place with cheap light meals ($6 to $7). It's licensed and has music from 10 pm.

South of William St at 112 Darlinghurst Rd, the Hare Krishnas have *Govinda's Kitchen*, a health food restaurant offering very cheap and delicious Indian-inspired food and drinks, both eat in and take-away. You can have a $6 feast in the upstairs restaurant.

Two km east of Kings Cross at 249 New South Head Rd, Double Bay, the *Golden Sheaf Hotel* is crowded and popular with travellers, particularly on a Sunday night. It's a good meeting place with a huge beer garden and delicious food.

Oxford St Oxford St from Hyde Park through Darlinghurst to Paddington has a huge variety of good value ethnic restaurants and several good cake and pastry shops, plus plenty of interesting shops and faces.

The *Bali Inn* at 80 Oxford St, Darlinghurst is a popular Indonesian place with inexpensive and interesting dishes from $6 to $14, most around $9; the lumpia is great. On the other side of Oxford St, at No 129, *Yolanda's Gourmet Cafe* has a European flavour with healthy breakfasts, a huge range of drinks, and gourmet snacks from $6 to $8. Everything is made on the premises. It's closed on Sundays but open from 8 am to 11 pm other days.

At 130 Oxford St, Darlinghurst, the *Ting Hong* restaurant does very cheap Vietnamese vegetarian food. Nearby, at Taylor Square, 132 Oxford St, the excellent *Eli's Pizza* does pizzas with exotic toppings from around $8 while omelettes, pastas and steaks are from $8 to $10. It's open nightly.

Further up Oxford St towards Paddington at 203, the popular *Thai Silver Spoon* has 'seafood hot pot' with prawns, squid and pieces of fish in a chilli sauce for less than $10. The *Balkan* at 209 Oxford St specialises in those two basic Yugoslavian dishes – raznjici and cevapcici. Ask for a pola pola ($10) and you'll get half of each. It's very filling and definitely for real meat eaters only. The Balkan is closed on Tuesdays. There is a second location open for dinner and specialising in seafood a few doors away at 215 Oxford St. This Balkan is closed on Mondays.

Still in Darlinghurst the *Afrilanka* at 237 Oxford St is run by an African/Sri Lankan couple and the menu combines their cuisines. The place has a great atmosphere with appealing decor though the unusual food is not particularly cheap. At No 263, the *Borobodur* is another good reasonably priced Indonesian place. North of Oxford St at 26 Burton St, Darlinghurst the *Metro Cafe* is a cheap vegetarian place with a changing, imaginative menu. It's very busy and open for dinner from Thursday to Sunday. On the corner of Burton and Victoria Sts, *Laurie's Vegetarian Restaurant* serves good, filling and fairly cheap vegetarian meals.

In Paddington, Oxford St numbers start again just beyond the intersection with Barcom Ave, the first street after Victoria St. There are several good late night cafes including *Cappuccino City* at 12 Oxford St, *Flicks Cafe* over the road, and *Oddy's* at No 116. The *Gajah Mada* at No 86 is yet another low priced Indonesian restaurant.

Some way further along Oxford St another place worth trying, open daily to

6 pm, is *Sloane Rangers* at 312 Oxford St, a vegetarian restaurant with meals at no more than $8. The *New Edition Tea Rooms* at 328A Oxford St is a busy daytime cafe, entered through the attached bookshop.

Paddington's Saturday *Village Bazaar* on the south side of Oxford St at the corner of Newcombe St, has a variety of wholesome food. Finally, not to be missed, if only for a drink, is Paddo's *Royal Hotel* at Five Ways. It has plain 'Aussie' food. From Oxford St, turn left down Henley St, opposite the Town Hall, continue past Underwood St and keep going to the five-way intersection.

Surry Hills This inner suburban area east and south-east of Central Railway Station offers a big range of cuisines, especially Middle Eastern. Try *Abdul's*, right on the corner of Cleveland and Elizabeth Sts, for excellent value meals in unpretentious surroundings, good take-aways and a $12 set-price menu. Across the street is a small cafe that's cheap and good for falafels, kebabs and excellent vine leaves. *Emad's* at 298 Cleveland St, just up from the corner, has good food in slightly posher surroundings.

At 423 Cleveland St you can shift to Turkey at *Erciyes* to try 'pide', a sort of Turkish pizza. If you get to Surry Hills then decide you don't want Middle Eastern after all, there's *L'Aubbergade*, a French place that's been here since the '50s. It's at 353 Cleveland St; main courses range from $6 to $14 and it's open from Monday to Saturday. Another option is *Kakavia*, a Greek place at 458 Elizabeth St. It offers big servings with main dishes around $10, live Greek music on Friday and Saturday nights and Greek wine too.

About five blocks north, still in Surry Hills at 57A Fitzroy St near Crown St, *Johnnie's Fish Cafe* offers great value, both eat in or take-away.

Beaches En route to Bondi Beach at 288

Oxford St at Bondi Junction, *Sennin* is a particularly pleasant place with an imaginative vegetarian menu. It's open for dinner from Monday to Saturday and main meals are $10 to $12. Several blocks further east, at 570 Oxford St, still in Bondi Junction, the *Mekong*, a relative of the one on George St in the city centre, serves the same fantastically cheap Cambodian fare – three dishes plus rice for $4! The *Wei Song* at 96 Bronte Rd, a couple of blocks south of Oxford St, is great for non-smoking vegetarians. *Ya Habibi* at 100 Campbell Parade has good, cheap Middle Eastern fare.

Gelateria Italia at 118 Campbell Parade is popular for inexpensive home-made pasta, and good for breakfast from Thursday to Tuesday. Then there's the *Yum Yum Chinese Smorgasbord* with a serve-yourself deal for $6 to $7. Down the road at 164 *Pancakes at Bondi* is the area's Lovely Lady representative with a 'surfing' twist to its decor. It's open 24 hours a day on the weekend and until 1 am during the week. A couple of blocks back from the beach, on the corner of Hall and O'Brien Sts, you'll find *Positive Vibrations*, open daily from 11 am to 1 am with an eclectic, offbeat menu of low priced meals.

In Coogee Bay Rd there are lots of take-away places, including Lebanese, plus a couple of Chinese restaurants. Two places on Arden St, which faces the sea, are quite good – *Sari Rasa*, closed on Mondays, at No 186 has mixed Asian food with main meals from $8 to $10. *Zesamee's Eatery* at No 190 is small, but combines good value vegetarian meals with speedy service; main dishes are $7. It's open daily from 11 am to 9 or 10 pm.

Manly, on the north shore, has loads of fast food places plus a variety of restaurants and cafes. A good place to start is *Manly Asian Kitchen* (tel 977 1731) at 80 The Corso – on the mall but the door is around the back in the car park. Chinese, Malaysian, Indonesian and vegetarian main dishes are around $8 and the serves are pretty big. At the more expensive *Hammonds* at 38 Pittwater Rd, French vegetarian meals are $12 including salads and tea or coffee. Both restaurants are open nightly for dinner.

North of the harbour, at 334 Pacific Highway, Crows Nest, the *Curry Bazaar* (tel 436 3620) is so popular that it's wise to book. Open for lunch and dinner Tuesday to Saturday, it has good Indian food with spicy vegetable curries at $8, other curries up to $12. Take-aways are cheaper.

Glebe The centre of the action is Glebe Point Rd, where there are over 40 restaurants and cafes, in a one km strip up from the Broadway. Interspersed between restaurant blackboards is an interesting array of small shops and antique stores.

On the Broadway, the *Hot Potato* has excellent vegetarian food with lunch costing around $6. At 37 Glebe Point Rd, on the corner of Francis St, *Badde Manors* is a popular and casual cafe known for its Sunday breakfasts which are on offer until 3.30 pm. The food is wholesome and cheap and they even serve 'chai' (spiced Indian tea). Hours are from 8 am till late. Tucked around in Cowper St, the next one up from Francis St, at No 58 is *No Names 2*, the younger sibling of the one in East Sydney. It's actually in the Friend in Hand Hotel and the surroundings and food are better – a variety of pasta dishes go for $5.50, main meals for $7, salad and bread included. There's jazz on Friday nights.

At 95-97 Glebe Point Rd, *Tien* is one of Sydney's many Vietnamese restaurants. It has a varied menu from $7 to $10 and is open for lunch from Monday to Friday, dinner Monday to Saturday. *Kim Van's* up the road at No 147 is reputedly one of the best Vietnamese places in Sydney. Soups and entrees are around $5, main courses $8 to $13; it's open daily for dinner.

Cafe Troppo (tel 666 7332) at 175 Glebe Point Rd is busy with attractive decor, good food (particularly the desserts) and

an interesting atmosphere. Main meals are from $8.50 to $14.50 including salad. It's open daily and has an outdoor eating area.

North-west of Glebe are the suburbs of Balmain and Birchgrove – and more restaurants! At 37 Cameron St, Birchgrove, the *Salama* is North African with delicious food, and groups can book the 'cushion room'. It's reasonably priced and open for dinner from Tuesday to Saturday. About a km back towards Glebe, at 189 Darling St, Balmain, between Colgate and Waterview Sts, the *Razi Afghan* has good cheap Afghani food. It's open nightly for dinner. In Rozelle, the suburb adjacent to Balmain, *Eve's Harvest* at 71 Evans St is another excellent vegetarian restaurant.

Entertainment

Listen to the What's On service at 6.30 pm on radio 2JJJ or check the listings in the *Daily Telegraph* on Thursdays or the *Sydney Morning Herald*'s Metro section on Fridays.

A lot of Sydney evening entertainment takes place in the Leagues Clubs, where the profits from the assembled ranks of one-armed bandits (poker machines, or 'pokies' as they're called) enable the clubs to put on big name acts at low prices. They may be 'members only' for the locals but as an interstate or, even better, international visitor you're generally welcome to drop in. You can usually get a meal too. Simply ring ahead and ask, then wave your interstate driving licence or your passport at the door. They're a Sydney institution so if you get a chance, visit one. The most glittering and lavish of the lot is the *St George's Leagues Club* on Princes Highway, Kogarah. More centrally there's the *City of Sydney RSL Club* on George St. Acts can vary from Val Doonican or Max Bygraves to good Australian rock, but whatever the show you'll see a good cross-section of Sydneysiders.

Music Sydney doesn't have the same pub music scene that you get in Melbourne, though there are a fair few places where you can count on something going on most nights of the week. What Sydney does have is a number of clubs where you can catch a band and/or a disco, plus some pleasant wine bars/bistros where for a low entry charge (sometimes free) you can catch the music and even get a meal. Friday and Saturday, and to a lesser extent Thursday and Sunday, are the big nights – things can be a bit quiet the rest of the week. Venues which are worth a visit include:

Kardomah Cafe (tel 358 5228), 22 Bayswater Rd, Kings Cross - varied bands and disco nightly, busy and lively, admission usually $5 to $8, dress up a bit, open till very late.

Rex Hotel, Darlinghurst Rd, Kings Cross - rock bands usually Thursday to Saturday till 3 am, free. Open till 1 am other nights. Always packed.

Richie's Caribbean Club (tel 357 3161), 154 Brougham St, Kings Cross - jazz-funk/Caribbean music.

Round Midnight (tel 356 4045), Roslyn St, Kings Cross, late night easy listening jazz, $6 after 10.30 pm.

Golden Sheaf Hotel (tel 327 5877), 429 New South Head Rd, Double Bay, two km east of Kings Cross - pub with free bands several nights. Good food, popular with travellers.

Hip Hop Club (tel 332 2568), 110 Oxford St, Paddington - cabaret/restaurant from 7 to 11 pm, band/disco 11 pm to 3 am, Tuesday to Saturday, cover charge about $6.

Exchange Hotel, Oxford St near Hyde Park end - predominantly but not exclusively gay, dress code relaxed, three bars, two dance floors, low cover charge, pub prices for drinks, best night Friday.

Sydney Brasserie (tel 233 5296), 9A Barrack St, City - good jazz.

Soup Plus Restaurant (tel 29 7728), 383 George St, City, in the basement - good mainstream jazz from 7 to 11 pm daily except Sunday. Good atmosphere.

Orient Hotel (tel 27 2464), corner George and Argyle Sts, The Rocks - mainstream jazz or acoustic music nightly except Sunday plus jazz on Saturday afternoon.

Harbourside Brasserie (tel 27 8222), Pier One, The Rocks - jazz and dancing nightly.

Sydney Trade Union Club, Foveaux St, Surry Hills, live music on three floors most nights, good place to catch up-and-coming Aussie bands, usually $3 to $6.

Hopetoun Hotel (tel 33 5257), 416 Bourke St, Surry Hills - rock pub, bands usually Wednesday to Sunday nights, free. Also good for up-and-coming bands. Wear black!

Graphic Arts Club (tel 211 2916), 26 Regent St, Chippendale - reggae/African, Saturday nights.

Harold Park Hotel, Glebe - rock bands usually Thursday to Saturday nights till 11 pm or midnight, about $6.

Cat & Fiddle Hotel (tel 810 7931), corner Darling and Elliott Sts, Balmain - pub rock usually Friday to Sunday nights, free.

Rose, Shamrock & Thistle Hotel (tel 810 3424) 139 Evans St, Rozelle - rock/folk/jazz some nights. Jazz Saturday afternoons.

Grand Hotel Cock 'n' Bull Tavern (tel 389 3004), corner Bronte & Ebley Sts, Bondi Junction - bands Tuesday and Sunday nights, disco Thursday to Saturday, often free for bands.

Royal Hotel, Bondi Rd at Bondi Beach - bands free.

Selina's (in the Coogee Bay Hotel) (tel 665 0000), Coogee Bay Rd, Coogee Bay - rock, often top Australian bands for which you pay $12 to $18. Main nights Friday and Saturday, but sometimes cheaper bands other nights too.

Hotel Manly (tel 977 0393), opposite Manly Wharf - rock bands or disco nightly, also bands Saturday and Sunday afternoons, often free, otherwise $3 to $7. Open till 3 am.

There are many, many other places. The Paddington Town Hall sometimes has Latin, African or reggae nights. Sunday afternoon is a popular time for jazz in several places round town - for jazz what's-on information phone Jazzlink Australia on 818 5177.

Theatre Sydney has a good selection of mainstream theatres plus fringe and cabaret places. The Halftix booth on Martin Place between Castlereagh and Elizabeth Sts sells half price tickets for all kinds of theatre from 12 noon to 6 pm Monday to Saturday. A list of what's available is posted at the booth each day and you buy tickets in person for performances the same day.

The city's top mainstream company is the Sydney Theatre Company, which puts on many of its shows at the *Opera House*. The Nimrod company has produced much of Sydney's most adventurous and stimulating theatre since the '70s – today it's housed in the three-auditorium *Seymour Centre* (tel 692 0555) at the corner of Cleveland St and City Rd, Chippendale, near Sydney University. The *Belvoir St Theatre* (tel 699 3257) at 25 Belvoir St, Surry Hills, a former home of the Nimrod, now hosts a variety of mainly offbeat shows in its two small theatres. The *Bay St Theatre* (tel 692 0964) could be described as 'Off Broadway' for two reasons: it puts on mostly experimental shows, and it's at 73-79 Bay St in Ultimo, which is off that early stretch of the Parramatta Rd called the Broadway.

Sydney has its own *Comedy Store* (tel 251 1480) on Margaret Lane off Jamison St, City, open Wednesday to Saturday nights and you can get dinner. On the North Shore the *Kirribilli Pub Theatre* at Milsons Point (tel 560 5093) has several different – and usually funny – shows each week. The *Rose, Shamrock & Thistle Hotel* in Rozelle has some cabaret acts as well as music.

Film If mainstream movies are what you want, most films at Hoyts, Village, and Dendy cinemas are half price on Tuesdays. For more unusual fare, you'll find interesting films at the *Mandolin Cinema* at 150 Elizabeth St, between Liverpool and Goulburn Sts – Chinese and repertory style films are regularly featured.

Other offbeat cinemas include the *Academy Twin* at 3A Oxford St, Paddington; the *Valhalla Cinema* at 166 Glebe Point Rd, Glebe, which screens a fair number of rock music movies; and *ABJ's Encore Cinema* at 64 Devonshire St, Surry Hills which specialises in old classics. The *Sydney University Union*

Theatre can always be counted on for something good and at low prices. The Australian Film Institute has many of its screenings at the *Chauvel Cinema* on the corner of Oxford St and Oatley Rd, Paddington. You can also catch interesting films at the Opera House and Paddington Town Hall.

Almost a sight in itself is the *State Movie Theatre* on Market St between Pitt and George Sts. Wow! They don't make them like this anymore. It's the main venue for the Sydney Film Festival in the first half of June.

Odds & Ends On summer weekends there are free music performances in parks. There's music at lunch time in Martin Place and at Darling Harbour. You can sit and listen to the buskers around the Cross and a wander through the Cross at night is always an education! You could never go short of an exhibition to look at in Sydney – the *Sydney Morning Herald*'s Metro section lists about 100 every week.

Try and see something at the Opera House – they have film shows, ballet, theatre, classical music, opera and even rock concerts. The Opera House is the main home of the Sydney Dance Company and the Sydney Symphony Orchestra, which are the top outfits in their fields. The State Conservatorium of Music on Macquarie St is another classical music venue and the students give free lunch time concerts on term time Wednesdays.

Sport Sydney is Australia's rugby league (as opposed to rugby union) capital and home to most of the teams in the Winfield Cup competition, which for years has produced the world's best club teams in this 13 a side, professional version of rugby. They make what can be a dour game into something fast and exciting. The season is April to September and top clubs include Manly-Warringah, Canterbury-Bankstown, Cronulla-Sutherland, Parramatta, Penrith and

Balmain. An average game attracts about 10,000 spectators, so you can usually just turn up at the ground and pay at the turnstiles, but there'll be more for the big clashes. The biggest games, including internationals and the end of season Grand Final are played at the Sydney Cricket Ground (SCG) or the new Sydney Football Stadium, which are side by side in Moore Park, just south of Paddington.

The SCG of course is also the home of interstate and Test cricket in Sydney from about November to March – with most excitement when the West Indies or England are visiting. The liveliest and cheapest section of the ground to watch from is The Hill, a grassy bank beneath the giant electronic scoreboard.

On the second Sunday in August every year about 25,000 athletes or would-be athletes take to their heels from Park St to Bondi Beach in the City to Surf Run.

Festivals The Festival of Sydney is mainly devoted to the arts and lasts for most of January, including open-air opera and music in the parks and the annual Sydney Harbour ferry race. Sydney's Chinese celebrate their new year in suitable style in Chinatown in January or February. A bit later, the highlight of the Gay Mardi Gras festivities is the highly colourful parade which wends its way from the city to the Sydney Showgrounds in Moore Park one night in late February or early March. The showgrounds are also the scene of the Royal Easter Show when agricultural Australia comes to town for two weeks.

In even-numbered years, June sees Sydney's art galleries thronged with the best and most bizarre that modern art can find, for the Sydney Biennale.

Things to Buy

For straightforward shopping there are several complexes in the city including the Centrepoint Mid City Centre, the MLC Centre, the Royal and Strand Arcades and the Queen Victoria Building with 200 shops, cafes and restaurants. Paddington is also an interesting area with its many bookshops, boutiques, art galleries and antique shops. The Rocks, including the Pier One Centre, and Darling Harbour seethe with shops which are open daily. Then there are all the large suburban shopping complexes – Sydney has some good ones.

You can find Aboriginal art in several places. The Dreamtime Aboriginal Art Centre has two locations – one in the Argyle Arts Centre in The Rocks (open daily), the other at 7 Walker Lane, opposite 7A Liverpool St, in Paddington. They have a lot of bark paintings and, as usual, these are attractive but costly. Didgeridoo, also in the Argyle Arts Centre, has a good range of Aboriginal print T-shirts, didgeridoos, boomerangs and baskets.

The Aboriginal Artists Gallery in Civic House, 477 Kent St (behind the Town Hall), has a large range of traditional and contemporary Aborigine and Islander work including bark and canvas paintings, weavings, carvings, weapons, didgeridoos, prints and batik. Quality is high, prices competitive.

At 135 Bathurst St (between Pitt and Castlereagh Sts), the Bush Church Aid Shop sells artefacts made by Aborigines from communities all over Australia. Bark paintings, many types of boomerangs and carrying dishes are among the items displayed. New Guinea Primitive Arts – with two shops, one on the 6th floor at 428 George St, the other at shop 42, Level 2, Queen Victoria Building – has an amazing collection of artefacts from PNG and some Aborigine work. Ethnographics Primitive Art at 46 Oxford St also has both PNG and Aboriginal stuff.

Duncan's Boomerang School has a good shop at 202 William St, up by Kings Cross, and another one just down the hill a bit. They have an excellent array of boomerangs – a good souvenir or present. Every Sunday from 10 am to 12 noon they give free throwing lessons in the park at

Rushcutters Bay. Bennelong Boomerangs at 29-31 Playfair St in The Rocks also has a large collection of boomerangs.

Australian arts and crafts, T-shirts, souvenirs, designer clothing, bushgear and the like are big news these days and available in lots of places. Much of this stuff is high quality, with prices to match, though you can pick up the odd bargain. Places to try include the Argyle Arts Centre in The Rocks, which has a huge variety of Australiana, even studios with the artists at work. One shop here sells genuine Australian road signs – the kangaroo and koala warning variety. For more Australiana possibilities in The Rocks, see the earlier Rocks section. Other places around town specialising in Australiana include Souvenirs of Australia & the Pacific, in shop 606, Royal Arcade, beside the Pitt St entrance to the Hilton, and Everything Australian at shop 311 George St in the Mid City Centre. The Queen Victoria Building has several good craft places including Blue Gum on Level 5 and the Handmade Shop on Level 2.

The Strand Arcade on George St, between Market and King Sts has many places featuring Australia's leading fashion designers and craftspeople. The fabrics from Jenny Kee's Flamingo Park are famous for their bright colours, as are Ken Done's whose Sydney shop is on George St in The Rocks. More reasonably priced are the Australian print T-shirts at Call Us Names, 51 Imperial Arcade, on the Pitt St level.

For 'dinky-di' Aussie bushgear, Morrisons at 105 George St, The Rocks, and Goodwood Saddlery at 237-9 The Broadway, close to Glebe, are specialists. Their stuff includes Akubra hats, moleskin pants, stockman's coats and boots and all. The Repair Centre at 140 Sussex St (between King and Market Sts) is a good place to get your backpack repaired.

The Wilderness Shop at 57 Liverpool St has high quality wilderness posters and books on wilderness issues. At the Gardens Shop in the Royal Botanic Gardens Visitors' Centre there are souvenirs, posters and books with an Australian plant theme.

Sydney has lots of weekend 'flea' markets, the most interesting, Paddo Village Bazaar, is held in the school on the corner of Oxford and Newcombe Sts on Saturdays. It has superb arts and crafts, clothing, general odds and ends and great food, plus lots of buskers. It's quite a scene. Balmain's Saturday market is also interesting with more home-made stuff, including basketware, jewellery and clothing. It's in the church on Darling Rd, opposite Gladstone Park. The food hall here has Asian goodies and home-made jams and chocolates.

Paddington has 30 or so art galleries, most featuring Australian art but there are also Japanese collections, posters and prints. The area has at least five bookshops, some with a heavy emphasis on Australian literature and history, others more general. It's certainly worth wandering around to check out these places. Pamphlets listing all the galleries and bookshops are available.

The Sydney Antique Centre is a conglomeration of 60 antique shops at 531 South Dowling St, Surry Hills. Open every day from 10.30 am to 6 pm, it has items ranging from movie posters to silver, junk to jewellery. There's a cafe too.

If you have money to get rid of, The Rocks has it all laid on for shopping with at least 80 speciality shops selling mainly high quality Australian-made goods. The Argyle Arts Centre is a good place to start or there's the Australian Design Centre at 70 George St which has an interesting variety of original Australian designs and products. The Metcalfe Arcade at 80-84 George St, houses the Society of Arts & Crafts of New South Wales with a gallery and sales, and there's Australian Craftworks at 127 George St in the old police station.

Getting There & Away

Air Sydney's Kingsford Smith Airport,

better known as Mascot because that's where it's situated, is Australia's busiest. It's fairly central which makes getting to or from it a breeze, but it also means that jet flights have to stop at 11 pm due to noise regulations. The main runway stretches out into Botany Bay and these problems of space restrictions and noise hassles have prompted a plan, though as yet little action, to build a new airport out west at Badgerys Creek.

You can fly into Sydney from all the usual international points and from all over Australia. Between Melbourne and Sydney, Australian Airlines and Ansett both have about 17 flights a day Monday to Friday, a few less at weekends, for $181 ($145 standby). Other fares include Adelaide $249 ($199), Alice Springs $352 ($282), Brisbane $187 ($150), Cairns $350 ($281), Canberra $100 ($80), Hobart $231 ($185), Perth $467 ($374).

East-West flies from most other major cities to Sydney, at similar fares to the big two except for the Canberra run which costs only $78. You can also fly direct between Ayers Rock and Sydney with East-West and they have a network of local flights around New South Wales.

Air NSW has daily flights from Melbourne and Brisbane which will save you about $10 on the other airlines' fares and they also fly to places around the state. Other New South Wales airlines include Eastern, Singleton Air Service, Hazelton Air Services and Aeropelican.

Cheap international flights are advertised in the Saturday *Sydney Morning Herald*. The cheapest tickets of all are sold off by travellers around Kings Cross – they're usually advertised on the notice boards there – but there's a risk with these: most tickets are non-transferable, so the person whose name is on the ticket has to check in for the flight, and you then have to trust to luck that no one checks your passport against the ticket. If the ticket involves a change of planes, a stopover, or otherwise checking in more than once, there's a pretty high chance you'll be caught out. If

you're flying out with Qantas see the note under Airport Transport about city check-in.

Bus There's hot competition on the bus routes between Sydney and Brisbane, Melbourne, Adelaide, even Perth, so it pays to shop around. There are also varying stopover deals – McCafferty's for instance will give you three free stopovers between Sydney and Cairns (one must be at Brisbane), while Deluxe and Pioneer Express allow free stopovers in state capitals and on the Queensland Gold Coast. Greyhound says you can't stop over anywhere on a journey starting from Sydney. Dial-A-Coach (tel 231 3815) at Shop 33, Imperial Arcade, Pitt St and Shop 12A (tel 262 2175), Wynyard Station has a bus advice and booking service.

If you want to travel by bus between Sydney and somewhere else in New South Wales, remember New South Wales' bizarre licence laws, which on the coastal routes from Sydney usually mean you must go north of Newcastle or south at least as far as Nowra. Exceptions to this are when the company in question has a special licence to drop off and pick up anywhere along the route, or if you are travelling on a bus pass or interstate ticket. The rules seem to change frequently so check around. Many bus lines make stops in suburbs on the way in or out of the city centres and some have feeder services from the suburbs too.

The Sydney to Brisbane run has more competing bus lines than any other. By the main route, the coastal Pacific Highway, it takes 15 or 16 hours and normally costs $35 to $43. Sometimes special offers cut this to $30, while 'luxury' services cost more. Cheaper lines include Inter-Capital Express, Sunliner, Ambassador/Trans City and Roadranger. You often need to book ahead. Not all buses stop in all the main towns en route.

Some typical fares to/from Sydney are Port Macquarie $25 (seven hours), Coffs Harbour $30 (9½ hours), Byron Bay $36

(13 hours), Surfers Paradise $40 (14½) hours. Companies operating the Pacific Highway route are Ambassador/Trans City, Deluxe, Greyhound, Inter-Capital Express, Intertour, Kirklands, McCafferty's, Pioneer Express, Roadranger Intercity Express, Skennars and Sunliner. There's also Lindsay's which only goes as far as Woolgoolga just north of Coffs Harbour. Deluxe, Greyhound and McCafferty's also go between Sydney and Brisbane by the inland New England Highway which takes an hour or two longer. Skennars and Ambassador have buses between the Queensland Sunshine Coast and Sydney.

Canberra to Sydney takes about four hours and the cheapest service is by Murrays, which depart three times daily for $17. Pioneer Express has the most frequent service on this route, up to nine times daily in each direction for $20, with a few of those operating to/from Sydney Airport (international terminal) ($24) as well as the city centre.

Melbourne to Sydney takes 12 to 13 hours by the most direct route, the Hume Highway. Add another hour or two if your bus detours via Canberra. Price competition is even fiercer than on the Brisbane route with fares ranging from around $25 to $50.

You can also go between Melbourne and Sydney by the coastal Princes Highway for $43 with Greyhound, Pioneer Express and Deluxe, all daily, taking 16½ to 18 hours. A further alternative is Greyhound's four times weekly service via Katoomba, Bathurst, Wagga Wagga and Echuca. This takes 17½ hours.

Adelaide to Sydney takes 18 to 25 hours and costs around $75 to $90, depending on the company and the route. A few of the Pioneer Express services go via Broken Hill which is $69 and 15½ hours from Sydney. Sydney to Perth costs $170 to $180 for the 52 to 56 hour trip. The daily Pioneer Express bus to Alice Springs costs $185 and takes 43 hours. To the Snowy Mountains, Pioneer Express have one or two daily services to Cooma ($33),

Jindabyne ($41) and Thredbo or Perisher ($43).

Sydney doesn't have a central bus station but a number of different terminals for the different companies. Most of these are within a few minutes' walk of Central Railway Station, often on Eddy Ave, immediately outside the station.

Train All interstate and principal regional services operate to and from Sydney's Central Railway Station on Eddy Ave. For information and bookings in Sydney there are Rail Travel Centres at Transport House, 11-31 York St (tel 29 7614); Central Railway Station (tel 219 1808); and Town Hall Station, corner of George and Park Sts (tel 267 1521). For bookings you can also call the Central Reservation Centre (tel 217 8812). Rail fares and journey times to/from major cities in other states are competitive with the buses, and there are cheap offers like standby tickets.

Between Melbourne and Sydney there's the Intercapital Daylight Express which runs daily except Sundays, and a night train which goes every day called the Sydney Express (if you're going from Melbourne) or the Melbourne Express (from Sydney). The trip takes about 13 hours and the fares are $67 in economy, $94 in 1st. On the night trains you can get a sleeping berth, in 1st class only, for an extra $35. Standby tickets are available on the daylight trains for just $30. Caper tickets save about 30% on the Sydney to Melbourne route – you have to buy them at least a week in advance.

There are two or three trains daily to Canberra, the trip takes about 4½ hours and costs $33 in 1st, $23 in economy. To/from Brisbane there's the daily overnight Brisbane Limited Express, which takes 16 hours and costs $69 economy, $97 in 1st class, or $132 in 1st class sleeper. In conjunction with this train there's a connecting bus, run by the railways, from Casino to the New South Wales far north coast and the Queensland Gold Coast. Standby tickets to/from Brisbane are $35 – you buy them four hours or less before departure. There are Caper fares on the Sydney to Brisbane route too. You can also take the train between Sydney and Murwillumbah, just south of the Queensland border, from where Greyhound has a connecting bus to the Gold Coast. This train is called the Pacific Coast Motorail. Sydney to Murwillumbah takes 16½ hours and costs $50 in economy, $70 in 1st. A sleeping berth, available in 1st class only, is an extra $35.

Direct Sydney to Adelaide rail runs are made three times a week by the Indian-Pacific train, which takes about 26 hours and costs $127 in economy, $178 in 1st class. For an extra $71 in 1st class (or $59 in economy on one train a week) you can get a sleeping berth and meals thrown in. The Indian-Pacific route is through the Blue Mountains and Broken Hill. Much cheaper and quicker is the six times weekly 'Speedlink' service which combines a high speed XPT train between Sydney and Albury on the New South Wales-Victoria border, and a bus between Albury and Adelaide. This takes about 20 hours and costs $76 in economy, $79 in 1st class.

Sydney to Perth is on the Indian-Pacific service which runs three times a week – see the Perth section for more details.

On interstate journeys you can generally stop over anywhere for no extra charge as long as you finish the trip within two months.

There's an extensive rail network within New South Wales including frequent commuter-type train services to Sydney from Wollongong ($4.50 in economy), Katoomba ($7), Lithgow ($11) and Newcastle ($12). See the New South Wales introductory Getting Around section for details.

Buying A Car If you want to buy a car to travel round Australia, Sydney's a good place to do it. The Parramatta Rd is lined with used car lots, but there are also two setups geared specially to travellers. One is the informal car exchange outside the hostels along Victoria St in Kings Cross. Travellers with a vehicle to sell simply stick signs on the car and around the notice boards to attract interest, then wait around for as long or as often as it takes to find a buyer. From the buyer's point of view, some of these vehicles have been around a fair bit – one north Queensland backpackers' hostel owner told us he'd seen the same ageing pink Holden three times in two years, under different ownership each time – but you can probably expect to get a more honest account of a vehicle's pros and cons from another traveller than from a professional salesperson.

A second place to look is Mach 1 Autos (tel 569 3374) at 495 New Canterbury Rd, Dulwich Hill, which runs a special 'sell and buy back' deal for budget travellers. They have cars and station wagons from $1000 to $2500 and will guarantee to buy vehicles back when you've finished your travels at previously agreed rates – about half what you bought it for. Registration fees and third party insurance, which normally cost about $400 a year, are included in their prices, and you'll also get the government roadworthiness certificate which is legally required with the sale of any car. To reach Mach 1 take bus No 426 or 448 from Pitt St in central Sydney and get off at Dulwich Hill shopping centre, 150 metres from the car yard – or take a train to Dulwich Hill and call them from the station, they'll pick you up.

If you, or a friend, are a member of the NRMA you can get a vehicle checked over, for a fee, before you buy it. NRMA members can also get good deals on insurance. Every vehicle's registration certificate includes third party insurance, but it's a good idea also to have extended third party insurance, which covers you for damage to other vehicles, or even comprehensive insurance. For more on buying cars and on the motorists' associations, see the introductory Getting Around and Facts for the Visitor chapters.

Getting Around

For information on city trains, buses and ferries, call the Metro Trips service (tel 29 2622) operated by the Urban Transit Authority (UTA), from 7 am to 10 pm any day. Or visit the UTA information office next to the State Rail Travel Centre at 11-31 York St.

Airport Transport The international and domestic terminals at Sydney Airport are just across the runway from each other, about a five km bus trip apart. The yellow Airport Express bus, part of the city bus system, runs every 20 or 30 minutes to/from the city and between the international and domestic terminals. In the city it stops at several places including Central Railway Station, five different places on George St between Eddy Ave and Alfred St, and Circular Quay. From the airport to Central Railway Station takes about 15 minutes, to Circular Quay, 30 minutes. The fare between the airport and the city is $3, between the two terminals it's $2. Buses leave the city from 6 am to 9.30 pm and the international terminal from 6.25 am to 10.45 pm.

A convenient alternative is the privately operated Sydney Airport bus which will take you between either airport terminal and any hotel or hostel in the city centre or Kings Cross for $3.50. It runs half hourly from 6 am to 8 pm. For bookings call 667 3221, 1½ to two hours before you need to be picked up.

For Ansett Airlines passengers only, there's the $3 'Intershuttle' bus between the international and domestic terminals, every 20 minutes from 7 am to 9 pm.

Pioneer Express (tel 268 1881) has a few buses daily direct between the international terminal and Canberra for a one way fare of $24. Watts Coaches (tel (042) 29 5100) runs a six times daily service between Wollongong and both terminals for $11.

If you're willing to walk half an hour

from the international terminal to Arncliffe railway station you can get into the city by train for just $1.40. There are some public bus services from the domestic terminals to the city (Nos 302 and 385 to Circular Quay) or Bondi Junction (No 064), but they operate mainly for airport workers and principally on weekdays.

A taxi between the airport and city will cost you about $15, depending on where you're going. Hertz, Budget, Thrifty and Avis have desks at the airport. Luggage lockers at the airport cost $1 a day.

If you're flying out with Qantas you can check in at their city check-in facility in the Regent Hotel. This way you can get your seat assignment hours early and not have to bother with carrying your bags out to the airport.

Bus There are extensive bus services in Sydney, but they are slow in comparison to the rail services. Some places – including Bondi Beach, Coogee and the north shore east of the Harbour Bridge – are not covered by trains so you do need buses (or ferries) to get there. Most buses are run by the Urban Transit Authority, but some suburban services are run by private operators. For bus information call 20 543 from 7 am to 7 pm daily.

Circular Quay, Wynyard Park on York St, Central Railway Station and Railway Square are the main bus stops in the city centre. You can get 'Metro Ten' tickets, giving you 10 bus rides for the price of eight, at the UTA Travel Centre, or railway stations near bus routes, or some newsagencies or bus depots.

There are two useful free city centre bus services. The No 777, operating every 10 minutes from 9.30 am to 3.30 pm Monday to Friday, goes from York St on to King St, south along Pitt St, east into Park St, around the Domain, back along Market St, up Clarence St and back to its starting point. The No 666 free service goes from Wynyard Park on York St on a loop out to the New South Wales Art Gallery and back, and it runs every half hour from 10.10 am to 4.40 pm Monday to Friday, 12.10 to 4.40 pm Sundays.

The Sydney Explorer is a tourist bus service which operates a continuous loop around the tourist sights of the city at roughly 15 minute intervals from 9.30 am to 5 pm daily. It costs $10 (children $5) for the day, covers 18 km and 20 attractions, and you can hop on and off wherever you like. It would be much cheaper to get around these places by ordinary buses (in fact it's possible to walk around the places visited by the bus), but the Explorer's easy as you don't have to work out routes. Its 20 stops are marked by green and red signs and you can buy the ticket on the bus, from the UTA Travel Centre or the New South Wales Travel Centre. The route is from Circular Quay to the Opera House, down Macquarie St to Hyde Park, up to Mrs Macquarie's Chair, back down to the New South Wales Art Gallery, across to Kings Cross and Elizabeth Bay, through Woolloomooloo, down to Central Railway Station, back up George St and round The Rocks to Circular Quay. The Kings Cross stop is at the railway station on Darlinghurst Rd. You can also use the Explorer ticket on city buses between Central Railway Station and Circular Quay or The Rocks until midnight.

Train Quite a lot of Sydney is covered by the suburban rail service, which has frequent trains and is generally far quicker than the bus network. For city and suburban rail information call 20 942.

If you have to change trains, buy a ticket to your ultimate destination before you board the first train, it's cheaper. Off-peak rail travel – after 9 am Monday to Friday or any time at weekends – is cheaper if you get a return ticket.

The rail system has a central City Circle and a number of lines radiating out from there to the suburbs. Trains round the City Circle go every couple of minutes in both directions and this is often the easiest way of hopping from one part of the

centre to another. The stations on the City Circle, in clockwise order, are Central, Town Hall (on George St near Park St), Wynyard (York St at Wynyard Park), Circular Quay, St James (north end of Hyde Park) and Museum (south end of Hyde Park). A single trip anywhere on the City Circle is 60c.

Suburban trains all stop at Central Railway Station and usually one or more of the other City Circle stations too – most often Town Hall – so it's easy to get from the suburbs on to the City Circle. Trains generally run from around 4 am to about midnight, give or take an hour. You can get a train from Central Railway Station to Kings Cross, or vice versa, up to midnight any day. One way fares from the city centre vary from $1 (Kings Cross, Edgecliff) to $3 (Royal National Park, Liverpool).

Ferries & Cruises Sydney's ferries are one of the nicest ways of getting around in Australia – and they're pretty cheap. Not only are there the fine harbour ferries (Manly $1.60, other places generally $1.20) but also hydrofoils to Manly ($3). All the harbour ferries depart from Circular Quay. The UTA, which runs most of the harbour ferries, puts out a free ferry and hydrofoil timetable. Many ferries have connecting bus services and the timetable lists these too. For instance, from the Taronga ferry you can hop straight onto bus No 238 to Taronga Zoo or Mosman Junction. Cheaper combined ferry/bus tickets are available.

In addition to the ferries there's a whole range of cruises from Circular Quay. Walk along the quay and you'll get leaflets detailing many of them. Best value are the three run by the UTA. Two of these, the 10 am Five Islands Cruise and the 1.30 pm Main and Middle Harbours Cruise, go daily, last 2½ hours and cost $10 each. The UTA also runs a 1½ hour Harbour Lights Cruise in the evening from Monday to Saturday for $7.50. Also interesting are the trips to Goat Island and Fort Denison – see the earlier Harbour section.

The Sydney Harbour Explorer, run by Captain Cook Cruises, is a hop-on, hop-off service around the harbour with stops at Circular Quay, the Opera House, Watsons Bay, Taronga and Pier One at The Rocks. You get a $12 all-day ticket which allows you to get on and off whenever you like. The drawback is that it has a short working day and only makes four circuits, the first starting from Circular Quay at 10.25 am and the last getting back there at 4.30 pm. Captain Cook offers a range of other tours. Other ways of spending time and money on the harbour include disco cruises, gourmet cruises (breakfast, lunch or dinner!) and cabaret cruises.

Combined Deals The UTA has several special deals combining travel on its buses, trains and ferries. If you're planning some serious sightseeing, the $25 SydneyPass gives you five days' unlimited use of blue city buses between Central Railway Station and Circular Quay or The Rocks, Manly ferries except hydrofoils, the Sydney Explorer Bus and UTA Sydney Harbour Cruises. The SydneyPass is on sale at the New South Wales Travel Centre on the corner of Pitt and Spring Sts, or the Rail Travel Centre at 11-31 York St.

For $7 you can get a Day Rover ticket which covers a day's travel on any city bus, train or ferry except the hydrofoils, after 9 am on weekdays or all day on weekends. On similar lines but for longer periods – a week, three months or a year – is the range of Travelpasses, which give you unlimited travel at any time on various combinations of transport in various zones of the city. A Green Travelpass for $16 allows you to use ferries, trains and buses almost anywhere you're likely to want to go in Sydney for a week. You can buy Day Rovers or weekly Travelpasses from suburban railway stations, the UTA Travel Centre at 11-31

York St, or the Circular Quay and Manly ferry terminals.

On the Eastern Suburbs line you can get a combination bus-rail ticket from some stations such as Kings Cross (but not Central Railway Station) so that you can change to a bus for a destination such as Bondi Beach. This works out cheaper than buying the tickets separately.

Car Rental You'll find Avis, Budget, Thrifty and Hertz all on William St up from the city towards Kings Cross, together with a number of local operators. In the Telecom yellow pages there's a long list of agencies, but most of the cheap outfits won't let you take their cars very far afield, and if they do their rates often compare badly with the big operators. One firm that *will* let you take its cars anywhere in New South Wales (except the far west), lower Queensland or Victoria is Bargain Car Rental (tel 648 4844), out at 185 Parramatta Rd, Auburn. It has Holdens, Datsuns and Coronas, but while its rates aren't bad for around the city, if you're going a long way they eventually become more costly than big operators with unlimited km rates. Its cheapest car is a four-door Datsun 120Y, which costs $28.50 a day including insurance and 100 km.

Half Price Rent-A-Car (tel 267 7177) at 29A Oxford St, is a small chain with other offices in Melbourne, Brisbane, Surfers Paradise, Cairns and Adelaide. Its prices are reasonable for a company that doesn't restrict you to the metropolitan area and it has some deals on one way rentals. Rent-a-Bug (tel 428 2322), north of the harbour in Lane Cove, has a fleet of Datsun 120Ys at $16 per day or $99 per week plus insurance and unlimited km but only for use in Sydney. This deal is pretty standard with the cheaper operators. In the Kings Cross area two places worth looking at are Betta Rent-A-Car (tel 331 5333) at 199A Darlinghurst Rd, and Reliable Car Rentals (tel 358 6011) at 18-

36 Palmer St, Woolloomooloo. There are many others around the city.

Usually there are discounts for rentals of three or four days or more. Always check the small print on your rental agreement to see exactly where you can take the car (some firms don't allow dirt road driving) and what your insurance covers.

Bicycle Rental The bike hire places tend to be out in the suburbs. Centennial Park Cycles (tel 398 5027) at 50 Clovelly Rd, Randwick is one of a few places on Clovelly Rd. It charges $4 an hour, $7 for two hours, $10 a half day, and $20 a day, and you have to leave a full deposit. Other relatively central places include Park Rent-a-Bike (tel 357 5663) at 416 Oxford St, Paddington; and Tom's Bike Hire (tel 32 3583) at 43 Jersey Rd, Woollahra. Over towards Manly, north of The Spit Bridge over Middle Harbour, you'll find Seaforth Cycles at 569 Sydney Rd, Seaforth and Health Hire at 52 Balgowlah Rd, Balgowlah. Inner City Cycles (tel 660 6605), 31 Glebe Point Rd rents out good touring bikes for $60 a week and panniers for $30 a week.

Tours Oztrek (tel 360 3444), PO Box 1328, Darlinghurst run popular, good value day-trips and camping tours, designed for people from YHA and backpacker hostels. Twice a week there are $30 day-trips to the Blue Mountains which take you to several of the best lookout points and allow time for walks and a pub visit. Or there's a three day $100 trip on which you camp at the ghost town of Newnes on the edge of the spectacular Wollemi National Park, with camping gear and all meals included. This trip includes stops in the Blue Mountains on the way. They'll pick you up from several hostels in Surry Hills, the city and Kings Cross or the YHAs in Glebe and Forest Lodge.

For trips further afield, Rob King's Outback Tours, based at the Dulwich Hill YHA Hostel, runs 14 days and longer small-group tours over some good-looking outback itineraries for around $30 a day. East Coaster Double Decker Tours (tel 644 9319) of 17 Moss St, Guildford, runs trips up to the Whitsunday Islands in a double-decker bus with beds upstairs, seats and cooking facilities downstairs. Could be fun.

There's a vast array of conventional city and area tours. See the tourist information centre on Pitt St for details, also the giveaway magazines from hotels, etc. Ansett Pioneer, AAT and Clipper are three of the biggies. Half day city or koala-cuddling tours are around $25, a full day city tour is $50 to $60. Longer day tours include the Blue Mountains and koala-cuddling (around $40), Blue Mountains and Jenolan Caves ($45), Hawkesbury River ($50), Old Sydney Town ($38), Southern Highlands ($40 to $50), Canberra ($52).

Around Sydney

Sydney has superb national parks to the north and south of the city and other interesting places within easy reach. In the early days of European settlement small towns were soon established around the major centre and although some of these, like Parramatta, have been engulfed by Sydney's urban sprawl, they're still of great interest today.

ROYAL NATIONAL PARK

Thirty-six km south of the city, this is the second oldest national park in the world – only Yellowstone in the USA predates it. It stretches about 20 km south from Port Hacking and has a fine network of walking tracks through varied country including 22 km along the coast with some spectacular clifftop stretches. There are good surfing and swimming beaches, a number of pleasant, rocky swimming holes, and the Hacking River runs right through the park. The park is carpeted with wildflowers in late winter and early

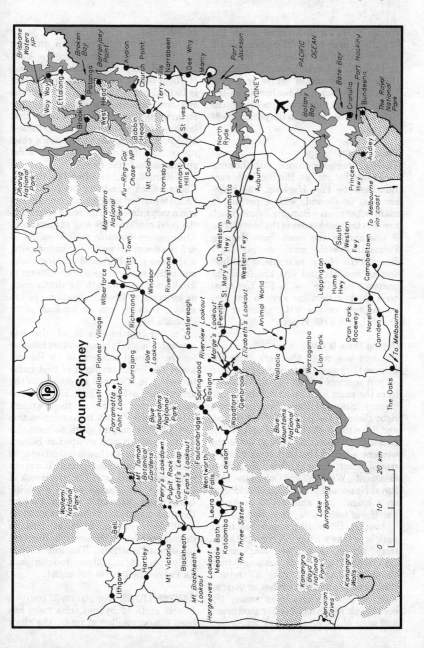

Around Sydney

spring. There's a park visitor centre (tel 521 2230) next to Royal National Park railway station at Audley near the park's northern entrance. Get a camping permit (free) from the visitor centre or from a ranger if you want to bushcamp in the park. You can hire rowing boats on the river at Audley. Entry to the park costs $4 per car.

Places to Stay

There's a camping ground with showers, accessible by car, at Bonnie Vale near Bundeena on Port Hacking, and bushcamping is allowed, with a permit, in many other areas – Burning Palms Beach towards the south is one of the best places. A few km up the coast from Burning Palms there's the small, simple *Garie Beach YHA Hostel* near one of the best surfing beaches and one km from the nearest road. The cost is $5. You must book and collect a key in Sydney beforehand, at the YHA office or the Dulwich Hill YHA Hostel.

Getting There & Away

By road you reach the park from the Princes Highway – from Sydney you turn off just south of Loftus – or alternatively from the coast road up from Wollongong through Stanwell Park. You can drive right through the park from end to end, and down to the coast in a few places. The Sydney to Wollongong railway forms the western edge of the park and walking tracks start from Loftus, Engadine, Heathcote, Waterfall and Otford stations. Royal National Park station at Audley is on a branch line and served by just a handful of trains a day from Sydney.

Another, interesting way to reach the park is to take a train to Cronulla then a ferry across from Port Hacking to Bundeena. The ferries depart hourly from Cronulla wharf and cost $3 return. Bundeena has its own beaches, or you can walk 30 minutes to Jibbon nearer the ocean coast which has another good beach and some old Aboriginal rock art.

BOTANY BAY

It's a common misconception amongst first-time visitors that Sydney is built around Botany Bay. Actually Sydney Harbour is Port Jackson and Botany Bay is 10 to 15 km to the south, although the city now encompasses Botany Bay too. Botany Bay was Captain Cook's first landing point in Australia and was named by Joseph Banks, the expedition's chief naturalist, for the many botanical specimens he found here.

At Kurnell, on the south side of the bay, Captain Cook's landing place (admission $3.50) is marked with various monuments and a very interesting museum relating to the good captain's life and explorations. The museum is open from 10.30 am to 4.30 or 5 pm daily; the rest of the historic site, with some good bushland walking tracks and picnic areas, is open from 7.30 am to 7 or 8 pm. You can reach the site by road, or by train to Cronulla station (10 km away), then by bus or on foot along Cronulla beach.

On the northern side of the bay entrance, beyond the oil tankers heading for the Kurnell refinery, is La Perouse where the French explorer of that name turned up in 1788, just six days after the arrival of the First Fleet. He gave the poms a good scare as they weren't expecting the French to turn up at this part of their empire quite so soon. La Perouse and his men camped at Botany Bay for a few weeks then sailed off into the Pacific and totally disappeared. It was not until many years later that the wreck of their ship was discovered on a Pacific island near Vanuatu. At La Perouse there's a monument to him and a fort on small Bare Island, built in 1885 to discourage a feared Russian (yes Russian) invasion of Australia. The fort is open daily from 9 am to 3.30 pm. You can reach La Perouse by bus No 393 or 394.

CAMPBELLTOWN (population 37,000)

Inland south of Sydney, this town has been almost swallowed up by the city's expansion. Buildings in the town date right back to the 1820s including the 1824 St Peter's Church. Queen St in particular has some early houses.

CAMDEN (population 9000)

On the old Hume Highway and just across the new South-Eastern Freeway from Campbelltown, Camden is virtually an outer suburb of Sydney. This was one of Australia's first European settlements, and has many early buildings with National Trust classification.

Gledswood Cellars at nearby Narellan is a winery built in an 1810 coaching house. It's open daily. Vines were first planted here in 1827 making Camden the first wine producing centre in Australia. Next to the winery, Australiana Park is an all-in-one family entertainment park of the kind that crops up all over Australia. Activities include sheep shearing, water sliding, reptile feeding, horse dancing and koala cuddling.

Camden Aircraft Museum, at Narellan, has 17 old warplanes and is open Sundays and holidays only, admission $3. Green's Motorcade Museum in Leppington, north of Camden, has veteran and vintage cars and motorcycles.

PARRAMATTA (population 128,000)

Sydney today has sprawled out well beyond Parramatta, 24 km from the centre, which was the second European settlement in Australia. Sydney soon proved to be a poor area for farming and in 1788 Parramatta was selected as the first farm settlement. There are a number of places you can visit, which give a glimpse of what life was like then. A good first stop is the tourist information centre (tel 630 3703) at Prince Alfred Park on Market St, open from 10 am to 4 pm weekdays, and shorter hours at weekends and holidays.

Today's Parramatta Park, beside the Parramatta River, is where the first farm started. Elizabeth Farm on Alice St is the oldest home in the country, built in 1793

by John and Elizabeth Macarthur. Their sheep breeding experiments formed the basis for Australia's wool industry. John Macarthur also controlled the lucrative rum trade, and engineered the removal of several governors who tried to control him! You can visit the farmhouse from 10 am to 4.30 pm daily except Monday ($2.50). A couple of blocks away Hambledon Cottage was built for the Macarthurs' daughters' governess. It's open from 11 am to 4 pm Wednesday to Sunday, entry $1.50. Experiment Farm Cottage at 9 Ruse St was built for James Ruse in the early 1800s; it's another fine early homestead, now furnished in 1840s style and open Tuesday to Thursday plus Sunday, from 10 am to 4 pm, admission $3.

The Old Government House, a country retreat for the early rulers, is in Parramatta Park and is a museum today, open the same times as Experiment Farm Cottage, admission $4. Nearby, the Governor's Bath House looks like an overgrown dovecote. Roseneath, in O'Connell St, is a fine example of an 1830s cottage. You can find St Johns Cemetery in Parramatta, the oldest in Australia.

Near Parramatta in Auburn are the Auburn Botanic Gardens which include a billabong, Australian native plants and Japanese ornamental sections. Featherdale Wildlife Park (tel 622 1705) on Kildare Rd, Doonside, about halfway from Parramatta to Penrith, is another 'koala cuddlery'. There are plenty of other native fauna too, in more spacious quarters than a zoo would provide. Featherdale is open daily and costs $5.

PENRITH (population 60,000)

Also on the edge of the capital's urban sprawl, Penrith is on the way to the Blue Mountains. The New South Wales Fire Service Museum on Castlereagh Rd is open Saturday and Sunday only. From Penrith you could reach the drive-through lion park at Warragamba Dam ($8).

KU-RING-GAI CHASE NATIONAL PARK

Ku-ring-gai Chase is to the north, set between Sydney and the Hawkesbury River, 24 km from the city centre. Its east side borders that fine inlet, the Pittwater. There is over 100 km of shoreline, lots of forest and wildlife, many walking tracks and some magnificent Aboriginal rock art. High points in the park offer superb views across deep inlets like Cowan Water and the wide Pittwater, while from West Head at the park's north-east tip there's another fantastic view across the Pittwater to Barranjoey Point at the end of Palm Beach. You may see lyre birds at West Head during their May to July mating period.

The popular Waratah Park (tel 450 2377) on Namba Rd, Terrey Hills, on the edge of the park, is another place where you can hold a koala. The TV series *Skippy the Bush Kangaroo* was filmed here. It has lots of other Aussie wildlife too! It's open daily and admission is $6.50.

Places to Stay

Camping is allowed only at The Basin, on the west side of the Pittwater, which is a walk of about two km from the West Head road, or a ferry ride from Palm Beach. These ferries (tel 918 2747) go about hourly from 9 am to 5 pm. They also operate to Mackerel Beach on the Pittwater. City buses go to Palm Beach. You can make camp bookings for The Basin by phoning 919 4036 from 9.30 to 10.30 am. There's the small, pleasant *Pittwater YHA Hostel* (tel 99 2196) a couple of km south of the camping ground. It costs $10 and you reach it by the ferry from Church Point to Halls Wharf, from where it's a short walk. A variety of bus routes take you from the city centre to Church Point. The hostel is noted for friendly wildlife.

Getting There & Away

There are four road entrances to the park – from Mt Colah (on the Pacific Highway) and Turramurra in the south-west, and Terrey Hills and Church Point in the south-east. The Kalkari visitor centre (tel 457 9853), open from 9 am to 4.30 pm daily, is on Ku-ring-gai Chase Rd about four km into the park from Mt Colah. There's an adjoining nature trail, with some wildlife. This road descends from the visitor centre to Bobbin Head on Cowan Water, where you can hire rowing boats for $12 a day, then goes round to the Turramurra entrance. Deans Buses (tel 888 3022) run about 10 times daily from Turramurra railway station to the nearby park entrance plus about four times on to Bobbin Head.

There's a daily ferry between Palm Beach, the most northerly of Sydney's ocean beaches, and Bobbin Head via Patonga on the north side of the Hawkesbury River – call 918 2747 for Palm Beach ferry information.

At Akuna Bay on Coal and Candle Creek, off Cowan Water, there's a marina with a variety of craft, from rowing boats to cabin cruisers, for hire. This is the starting point for a six hour cruise up the Hawkesbury River to Berowra Creek on the *Bataan* (tel 450 1888) for $25. Roads reach Akuna Bay and West Head from the Terrey Hills or Church Point entrances which are both served by city buses or Forest Coachlines (tel 450 2277). Entry to the park costs $4 per car.

HAWKESBURY RIVER

The Hawkesbury River enters the sea 30 km north of Sydney at Broken Bay. Dotted with coves, beaches, picnic spots and some fine riverside restaurants, it's one of the most attractive rivers in Australia and a popular centre for boating of all types. The Hawkesbury's final 20-odd km before it enters the ocean are fringed by deep inlets like Berowra Creek, Cowan Water and the Pittwater on the south side, and Brisbane Water on the north. The river flows between a succession of national parks – Marramarra and Ku-ring-gai to the south; Dharug, Brisbane Water and Bouddi to the north. About 100 km upstream are the towns of Windsor and Richmond. The main road and railway from Sydney to the north cross the river about 15 km in from the coast.

An excellent way to get a feel for the river is to take the river mail-boat (tel 455 1566) which runs up the river every weekday from Brooklyn on the south bank, about 13 km in from the coast, at 9.30 am and returns at 1.15 pm. There's also an afternoon run Wednesday to Friday. Passengers can come along for $14 and the 8.15 am train from Sydney's Central Railway Station will get you to Brooklyn in time for the morning run.

The same people run other Hawkesbury trips including Brooklyn to Windsor cruises, Broken Bay cruises from Brooklyn and a daily ferry between Brooklyn and Patonga on the north shore ($3 one way). There's a ferry from Brooklyn to Palm Beach and Avalon, on the narrow strip of land separating the Pittwater from the ocean, leaving Brooklyn at 8.30 am on Tuesday, Thursday and Sunday ($3 one way).

Another interesting service is the daily passenger ferry (tel 918 2747) between Palm Beach, Patonga and Bobbin Head in Ku-ring-gai Chase National Park. From Patonga there are buses four times daily to Gosford, where you can pick up buses or trains going north. More Hawkesbury boat trips are covered in the Ku-ring-gai Chase National Park section.

The tiny settlement of Wisemans Ferry is a popular spot up the river. Wisemans Ferry Inn is named after the original ferry operator, and vehicular ferries still cross the river. There are camping/caravan parks nearby but the only one with more than a handful of on-site vans is *Del Rio Riverside Resort* (tel 66 4330), three km south at Webbs Creek. Across the river Dharug National Park is noted for its many Aboriginal rock carvings which date back nearly 10,000 years. The Great Northern Rd which continues north from Wisemans Ferry is an interesting example of early convict road building – it has

scarcely changed since its original construction. The Settlers Arms Inn at St Albans on this road dates from 1836.

WINDSOR AREA

Along with Richmond, Wilberforce, Castlereagh and Pitt Town, Windsor is one of the five 'Macquarie Towns' established by governor Lachlan Macquarie in the early 19th century on rich agricultural land on the upper Hawkesbury River. You can see them on the way to or from the Blue Mountains by the northern route along the Bells Line of Road. The tourist information centre (tel 77 5915) just outside Windsor at McGraths Hill, open daily from 9 am to 5 pm, is the main information office for the whole upper Hawkesbury area. Windsor has its own tourist information centre, which together with the Hawkesbury Museum, is in the 1843 Daniel O'Connell Inn in Thompson Square.

Old buildings include the convict-built St Matthew's Church completed in 1822 and designed, like the courthouse, by the convict architect Francis Greenway. George St has more historic buildings and the 1815 Macquarie Arms Hotel is reckoned to be the oldest pub in Australia. The bushrangers Captain Thunderbolt and Bold Jack Donahue were brought up in Windsor.

The Australiana Pioneer Village at Wilberforce is six km north of Windsor – it includes Rose's Cottage (1798), probably the oldest timber building in the country. The village is open daily except Saturday and Monday, admission $5. At nearby Ebenezer the Presbyterian church, built in 1809, is said to be the oldest in Australia still in regular use.

Richmond, eight km west of Windsor, dates from 1810 and has a few more early buildings. There's a village green-like park in the middle of town. St Peter's Church dates from 1841 and a number of notable pioneers are buried in its cemetery.

Blue Mountains

The Blue Mountains, part of the Great Dividing Range, were once an impenetrable barrier to expansion inland from Sydney. Despite many attempts to find a route through the mountains, and a bizarre belief amongst many convicts that China, and freedom, was just on the other side, it was not until 1813 that a crossing was finally made and the western plains were opened up.

The Blue Mountains National Park has some truly fantastic scenery, excellent bushwalks and all the gorges, gum trees and cliffs you could ask for. The hills rise up just 65 km inland from Sydney and even a century ago this was a popular getaway for affluent Sydneysiders who came to escape the summer heat. Today it also attracts artists, and there are numerous galleries in the mountain towns. The mountains rise as high as 1100 metres and despite the intensive tourist development much of the area is so precipitous that it's still only open for bushwalkers. The blue haze, which gave the mountains their name, is a result of the fine mist of oil given off by eucalyptus trees.

Be prepared for the climatic difference between the Blue Mountains and the coast – you can swelter in Sydney but shiver in Katoomba. A lot of accommodation has heating.

Orientation

The Great Western Highway from Sydney follows a ridge line from east to west through the Blue Mountains. Along this often less-than-beautiful road the Blue Mountains towns, none of them very big, often merge into each other – Glenbrook, Springwood, Woodford, Lawson, Wentworth Falls, Leura, Katoomba (the main accommodation centre), Medlow Bath, Blackheath, Mt Victoria, Hartley. On the western fringe of the mountains is Lithgow – see the later Central West section.

To the south and north of the Blue Mountains highway-ridge the country drops away into the precipitous valleys for which this region is famous, including the Grose Valley to the north, and the Jamison Valley south of Katoomba. Along virtually the whole length of the road through the mountains there's a succession of turn-offs to waterfalls, lookout points or scenic alternative routes.

The old Bells Line of Road, much more scenic than the Great Western Highway, is a more northerly approach from Sydney: from Richmond it goes across north of the Grose Valley to bring you out on the main highway at either Lithgow or Mt Victoria.

Information

If you want to do more than just admire the Katoomba views visit the tourist information centre on the Great Western Highway at Glenbrook (tel (047) 39 6266) or at Echo Point, Katoomba (tel 82 1348). The main national park visitor centre (tel 87 8877) is on Govetts Leap Rd at Blackheath, about three km off the Great Western Highway. It's open daily and while good it's not very conveniently placed if you're coming from Sydney. The second national park visitor centre at Bruce Rd, Glenbrook (tel 39 2950) is usually only open at weekends.

Good books on the Blue Mountains include *Exploring the Blue Mountains* by M E Hungerford and J K Donald (Kangaroo Press) and, for walkers, *Walks in the Blue Mountains* by Neil Paton (Kangaroo Press) and *How to See the Blue Mountains* by Jim Smith (Megalong Books).

National Parks

Large areas to the north and south of the Great Western Highway make up the Blue Mountains National Park. Wollemi National Park, north of Bells Line of Road, is New South Wales' largest

Govetts Leap Falls, Blue Mountains

cliffs or the bottoms of the valleys, are the Jamison Valley immediately south of Katoomba and the Grose Valley area north-east of Katoomba and Blackheath. South of Glenbrook is another good area.

Visit one of the national park visitor centres for information or, for shorter walks, ask at one of the tourist information centres. It's very rugged country and walkers sometimes get lost, so it's highly advisable to seek information from the visitor centres, not to go alone and to tell someone where you're going. Most Blue Mountains watercourses are polluted, so you have to take your own water. And be prepared for rapid weather changes.

Places to Stay

There's plenty of accommodation in the Blue Mountains, but many places charge more at weekends. The places mentioned in the various sections are just a small selection of what's available; Katoomba is the main centre. You usually need a permit to camp and in some parts of the parks camping is banned, so check first.

Getting There & Away

Katoomba is now almost an outer suburb of Sydney, 109 km from the centre, and trains operate frequently. The fare to Katoomba is $7 – it takes about two hours. See the Sydney section for Blue Mountains day tours.

Getting Around

The Katoomba-Leura Bus Service (tel 82 3333) connects those two places (including stops opposite the old Carrington Hotel on Katoomba St, Katoomba, and at Echo Point, site of Katoomba's tourist information centre and one of the best lookouts) about 10 times on weekdays plus a few times on Saturday morning. It also has buses from Katoomba (opposite the Carrington) to Medlow Bath, Blackheath and Mt Victoria along the Great Western Highway. Buses run about five times daily on weekdays from Blackheath

forested wilderness area, stretching almost up to Denman in the Hunter Valley and entered by no paved roads but offering some good rugged bushwalking. It has lots of wildlife and similar landscape to the Blue Mountains. The virtually abandoned town of Newnes is on the western edge of Wollemi.

Kanangra Boyd National Park, west of the southern part of Blue Mountains National Park, has more bushwalking possibilities and grand scenery, and includes the spectacular Kanangra Walls Plateau which is entirely surrounded by sheer cliffs and can be reached by unsealed roads from Oberon or Jenolan Caves.

Walking

There are walks from a few minutes to several days in the Blue Mountains and adjacent areas. The two most popular areas, spectacular from the tops of the

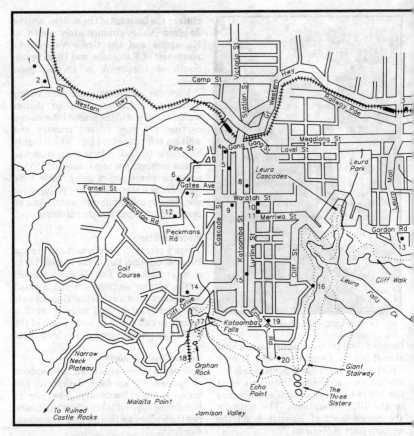

along Hat Hill Rd and Govetts Leap Rd, which lead respectively to Perrys Lookdown and Govetts Leap, two of the most spectacular lookouts over the Grose Valley. The buses don't go all the way to these lookouts: they'll take you within about a km of Govetts Leap but for Perrys Lookdown you'd have to walk several km from the end of the bus route.

On weekends and holidays the Blue Mountains Explorer Bus around Katoomba and Leura is one of those hop on, hop off services for which you buy an all-day ticket (about $9). Contact Golden West Tours (tel 82 1866) of 283 Main St,

Katoomba for information – the same people run Blue Mountains and Jenolan Caves tours starting in Katoomba.

Out And About Bush Experiences (tel 84 2361) at 49 Jersey Ave, Leura, runs mountain bike tours and wilderness walks in the national park for about $100 a person for five days.

GLENBROOK TO KATOOMBA

From Marge's and Elizabeth's Lookouts just north of Glenbrook there are good views back to Sydney. The section of the Blue Mountains National Park south of Glenbrook contains Red Hand Cave, an

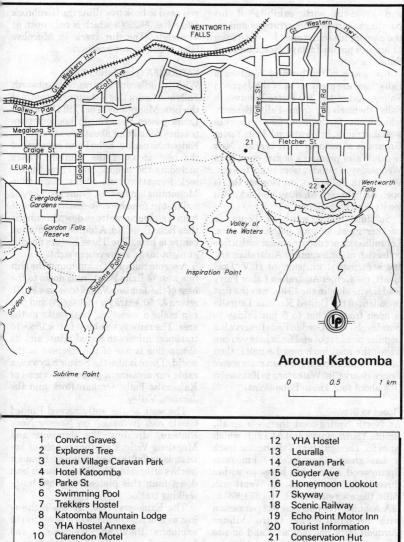

Around Katoomba

| 0 | 0.5 | 1 km |

1	Convict Graves	12	YHA Hostel
2	Explorers Tree	13	Leuralla
3	Leura Village Caravan Park	14	Caravan Park
4	Hotel Katoomba	15	Goyder Ave
5	Parke St	16	Honeymoon Lookout
6	Swimming Pool	17	Skyway
7	Trekkers Hostel	18	Scenic Railway
8	Katoomba Mountain Lodge	19	Echo Point Motor Inn
9	YHA Hostel Annexe	20	Tourist Information
10	Clarendon Motel	21	Conservation Hut
11	RSL Club	22	Kiosk

old Aboriginal shelter with hand stencils on the walls.

The famous (and infamous) artist

Norman Lindsay lived in Springwood from 1912 until he died in 1969. His home at 128 Chapman Parade is now a gallery and museum with exhibits of his paintings, cartoons, illustrations and, in the garden, his sculptures. It's open from 11 am to 5 pm on Fridays, Saturdays and Sundays.

Just south of the town of Wentworth Falls there are great views of the Jamison Valley, and of the 300 metre Wentworth Falls themselves, from Falls Reserve, which is the starting point for a network of walking tracks. In Wentworth Falls Yester Grange is a restored 19th century New South Wales premier's home, open from Wednesday to Sunday from 10 am to 5 pm. Wentworth Falls Zoo, on Horden Rd, is open daily except Monday and is known for its herd of deer.

Sublime Point, south of Leura, is another great lookout point. In Leura, Leuralla is an art deco mansion with a fine collection of 19th century Australian art. It's a memorial museum to H V 'Doc' Evatt, the former Australian Labor Party leader who also, in the 1940s, was the first president of the United Nations. Leuralla is open from 10 am to 5 pm Friday to Sunday. Nearby Gordon Falls Reserve is a popular picnic spot and from here you can follow the road back past Leuralla, then take the Cliff Drive or the even more scenic Prince Henry Cliff Walk along to Katoomba (it's about four km to Echo Point).

Places to Stay

At North Springwood there's a small, simple *Youth Hostel* (tel 54 1213) which costs $6. Though a bit off the beaten track it has great views. It's 10 km from Springwood station but buses go within three km of the hostel. At Wentworth Falls, there's a *guest house* (tel 57 1968) at 18A Asquith Ave charging $23 per person with breakfast. The *Leura Village Caravan Park* has tent sites and on-site vans at the corner of the Great Western Highway and Leura Mall.

There are national park camping areas which can be reached by car at Euroka Clearing near Glenbrook and Murphys Glen near Woodford. For Euroka Clearing you need to book by calling the Glenbrook office (tel 39 2950) which is only open at weekends. The dirt track to Murphys Glen is bad in wet weather.

KATOOMBA (population 7300)

With its adjacent centres of Wentworth Falls and Leura this is the tourist centre of the Blue Mountains. The Cliff Drive from Leura passes Honeymoon Lookout then reaches Echo Point about two km south of Katoomba centre. Echo Point has some of the best views of the Jamison Valley including the magnificent Three Sisters rock formation, one of the main Blue Mountains landmarks. Some good longer walks start from here. To reach Echo Point from Katoomba centre go down Lurline St then Echo Point Rd. A tourist information centre is here. The Three Sisters floodlit at night make an awesome sight.

A scenic railway, 1½ km round the cliff line west of Echo Point, runs down to the base of the Jamison Valley (one way $1.50, return $2.50, extra for rucksacks) and you can make a variety of bushwalks in the area. The railway was built in the 1880s to transport miners to a coal mine, and its 45° incline is one of the steepest in the world. There is also the Scenic Skyway, a cable car crossing a gorge with views of Katoomba Falls, Orphan Rock and the Jamison Valley.

The walk to the aptly named Ruined Castle rock formation on Narrow Neck Plateau, dividing the Jamison and Megalong Valleys another couple of km west, is one of the best, but watch out for leeches after rain. The Golden Stairs lead down from this plateau to more bush-walking tracks.

The Explorers Tree, by the highway just west of Katoomba, was marked by the explorers Blaxland, Wentworth and Lawson who were the first Europeans to find a way across the mountains in 1813.

Places to Stay

Katoomba's *Youth Hostel* (tel 82 1416) at 1 Wellington Rd, on the corner of

Peckmans Rd, has dorm beds at $10. It's in a quiet, woody part of town with an Olympic pool nearby – about a 20 minute walk from the town centre. It has a more central annexe with smaller rooms and central heating on the corner of Katoomba and Waratah Sts – phone the same number for bookings. On Gates Ave near the swimming pool, is *Trekkers*, an independent hostel with accommodation in pleasant new cabins at $9 a head in double or twin rooms. Each cabin has its own sitting room, bathroom and kitchen.

Other cheap accommodation includes the *Katoomba Mountain Lodge* (tel 82 3933), centrally placed at 31 Lurline St, a good clean guest house charging $18 per person, with meals available and various deals for stays of a few days. Bathrooms are shared but log fires, table tennis, TV room and good views are included in the price!

The *Hotel Katoomba* (tel 82 1106) at the corner of Parke and Main Sts, near the railway station, has very plain rooms – shared facilities, just a washbasin in the room – but with tea and coffee-making facilities. Singles/doubles are $30/35. Cheapest of the Katoomba motels is the *Clarendon Motel* (tel 82 1322) at the corner of Lurline and Waratah Sts, with weekday rates of $33/40 for rooms with shared bathrooms, $48/62 with private bathrooms.

At the top of the hotel scale is the *Hydro Majestic Hotel* (tel 88 1002) a few km west of Katoomba at Medlow Bath, a superb relic of an earlier era, at $96 double with breakfast during the week. Another old, equally superb, hotel is *Carrington Hotel* (tel 82 1111) in the middle of Katoomba, which has doubles for around $90 during the week.

If you want to camp, the *Katoomba Holiday Park* (tel 82 1483) is at the corner of the Great Western Highway and Scenic Drive (Cliff Drive), west of the centre. Tent sites cost $7 double and on-site vans cost around $23. The council-run *Katoomba Falls Caravan Park* (tel 82 1835) on

Katoomba Falls Rd has tent sites from $5 a double and on-site vans from $25.

Places to Eat

Most places here shut early in the evening. At guest houses the tariff often includes meals. For cheap pub eats the *Hotel Katoomba* at 15 Parke St, a block over from Katoomba St, has meals from just $5.

Renee's Pizza Bar at 4 Katoomba St, has small pizzas from $5. Close by are a health food place, a Lebanese take-away and a pancake and coffee shop. A little further down Katoomba St the *Paragon Cafe* is worth a look for its superb unspoilt 1920s decor – ask to see the cocktail lounge at the back. At 200 Katoomba St *Tom's Eats* has meals from $5 to $6. It's open later than most, from 11 am to 11 pm during the week and till 1 am on weekends.

Near the top of Katoomba St and close to the station, the *Omelette Parlour* at 287 Main St, is a continental and vegetarian restaurant, open in the evenings and for Sunday lunch. Diagonally opposite the station, *Gang Gang's* at 8 Gang Gang St, is a more expensive licensed cafe/bistro with continental and vegetarian dinners, a log fire and art displays. On weekends it offers take-away lunches but it's closed Monday and Tuesday.

There are two good Indian places on Waratah St, the first cross-street as you go down Katoomba St. At No 54, the *Curry Shop* is open daily, has a three course meal from $10 and take-aways. *Memsahib's Kitchen* at No 94, is BYO but only open for dinner from Friday to Sunday and Sunday lunches. Curries start at $6.50.

There are a few good eateries on the Great Western Highway, still in Katoomba. The *Glasshouse Brasserie* at Level 1 in the Renaissance Centre, 227 Great Western Highway, has main courses from $6.50, cheaper sandwiches, delicious cakes and snacks. The *Singapore Hut* at No 285 specialises in curries, but also does satays, seafood and Malay dishes. A bit further along the highway towards Blackheath, the *Arjuna Cafe & Gallery* has Indian and Asian food, vegetarian meals and home-made cakes. It's a pleasant place with mountain views, open from 12 noon to 10 pm, Friday to Monday.

Getting Around

You can hire bicycles at the Ampol Service Station on the corner of Waratah and Katoomba Sts, the Kedumba Emporium at Echo Point or at Lurline Cottage Tea Room at the corner of Warwick and Lurline Sts. Rates are $5, $6.50 and $8 for one, two and three hours.

There's a bus service (tel 82 4213) linking Katoomba station, the scenic railway and Goyder Ave near Echo Point. It runs roughly hourly till about 4.30 pm on weekdays and a few times on Saturday and Sunday. The Katoomba-Leura Bus Service (tel 82 3333) links central Katoomba with Echo Point.

BLACKHEATH (population 4500)

This little town on the main rail line from Sydney and the Great Western Highway is a good base for visiting – or looking at – the Grose Valley. There are some superb lookouts a few km east of Blackheath, among them Govetts Leap with the adjacent Bridal Veil Falls (the Blue Mountains' highest), Evans Lookout to the south and Pulpit Rock, Perrys Lookdown and Anvil Rock to the north. The last three are all reached from Hat Hill Rd.

A long cliff-edge track leads from Evans Lookout to Pulpit Rock and there are walks down into the Grose Valley itself and on the valley bottom – all involve at least a 300 metre descent and ascent. Get details on walks from the Blue Mountains' main national parks information centre, about three km out of Blackheath on Govetts Leap Rd, shortly before Govetts Leap itself. Perrys Lookdown is one of the few places where national park camping is allowed in this area. It's the beginning of the shortest route to the beautiful Blue

Gum Forest in the valley bottom – about four hours return.

A handful of restaurants, cafes and shops are scattered along the Great Western Highway in Blackheath and along Govetts Leap Rd.

To the west and south-west of Blackheath lie the Kanimbla and Megalong Valleys with yet more spectacular views from places like Hargreaves Lookout.

Places to Stay

The council-run *Blackheath Caravan Park* (tel 87 8101), with tent sites for $5 double and on-site vans at about $25 to $30, is on Prince Edward St, which is off Govetts Leap Rd about 600 metres from the highway. *Gardners Inn* (tel 87 8347) on the highway in Blackheath, just north of the Govetts Leap Rd corner, is the oldest hotel in the Blue Mountains, dating from 1831, and is a clean, pleasant place charging $23 a night per person ($5 extra for breakfast).

On Megalong Rd *Werriberri Lodge Cabins* (tel 87 9127) has comfortable cabins at $50 double during the week, $65 at weekends – you have to stay a minimum of two nights and pay a $58 deposit. *Jemby-Rinjah Lodge* (tel 87 7622) at 336 Evans Lookout Rd, has cabins taking two adults and two children for $52 during the week, $64 at weekends, cheaper out of school holidays.

BEYOND BLACKHEATH

The Mt Victoria Historical Museum, at the railway station, is a small museum in an interesting little National Trust classified town. The museum is open from 2 to 5 pm on weekends and holidays. Off the highway at Mt York there's a memorial to the explorers who first found a way across the Blue Mountains. There is a short stretch of the original road across the mountains here.

Midway between Katoomba and Lithgow is the tiny town of Hartley, with a number of buildings from the 1830s and '40s, open daily except Wednesday.

Off Bells Line of Road, between Lithgow and Bell, is the Zig Zag Railway – see the Central West section later. Between Bell and Richmond on Bells Line of Road, the Mt Tomah Botanic Gardens are the cool climate annexe of the Sydney Royal Botanic Gardens. They're open daily from 10.30 am to 4 or 6 pm.

Places to Stay
At Mt Victoria the *Victoria & Albert Guesthouse* (tel 87 1241) charges $40 per person including breakfast, complete with open fires and billiard tables. Also in Mt Victoria *Cedar Lodge Cabins* (tel 87 1256) on the Great Western Highway, has comfortable cabins from $38 a night for doubles.

JENOLAN CAVES
South-west of Katoomba and on the west edge of Kanangra Boyd National Park are the best known limestone caves in Australia. One cave has been open to the public since 1867 although parts of the system have still not been explored. Three caves are open for independent viewing, and you can visit a further nine by guided tours which go about 10 times a day from 10 am to 4 pm, with an evening tour at 8 pm. Tours last 1½ to two hours and usually cost $4.50 per cave. At holiday time arrive early as the best caves can be 'sold out' by 10 am. There's a network of walking trails outside the caves.

Near Jenolan Caves there are a few cabin setups in the $45 to $55 bracket.

YERRANDERIE
On the opposite (south-east) edge of Kanangra Boyd from Jenolan, Yerranderie is a ghost town slowly being restored. Once a bustling gold and silver mining town of 2000 people, it basically disappeared after the boom at the beginning of this century. The post office, general store and a few other shops and houses still remain.

North to Newcastle

Two main roads follow similar courses for some of the way from Sydney, but diverge as they approach Newcastle. The faster is the excellent Sydney to Newcastle Freeway, but just as scenic are the curves of the Pacific Highway which, once across the Hawkesbury River, runs nearer to the coast and the two large coastal lakes of Tuggerah and Macquarie. There are some interesting spots along the coast itself, off the highways.

GOSFORD (population 38,000)
Less than 100 km north of Sydney this is the centre for visiting the Brisbane Waters National Park. Old Sydney Town is a major Sydney-area attraction near here. Gosford also includes Eric Worrell's Reptile Park, the 1838 cottage of poet Henry Kendall and the Somersby Falls.

Old Sydney Town
On the Pacific Highway nine km south of Gosford, Old Sydney Town is a major reconstruction of early Sydney, including replicas of early ships, plus nonstop street theatre retelling events from the colony's early history. Children love the duels, hangings and floggings!

It's open from 10 am to 5 pm Wednesday to Sunday and every day during school holidays. Admission for adults is around $9. There's a day-trip rail tour here from Sydney for about $30.

National Parks
The Bouddi National Park is an attractive coastal park extending north from the Hawkesbury River mouth, 17 km from Gosford, with excellent bushwalking, camping and swimming. The beautiful Brisbane Water National Park offers similar attractions south-west of Gosford, just in from the mouth of the Hawkesbury. It has many old Aboriginal rock engravings.

GOSFORD TO NEWCASTLE

From Gosford you have the three options of going up the Pacific Highway, the Sydney to Newcastle Freeway or taking a coastal route around the saltwater Tuggerah Lake. All three are scenic but the coastal way – along what's known as the Central Coast – is probably the most interesting if you have time. There are hosts of caravan parks, camping sites and motels along the way. Wyong is on the Pacific Highway while on the coastal route you can visit Terrigal, a popular surfing centre. The Entrance is a very popular resort at the ocean entrance to Tuggerah Lake.

Further north, Macquarie is Australia's biggest saltwater lake, popular for sailing, water-skiing and fishing. The Pacific Highway runs between it and the ocean. Swansea, Belmont and Toronto are the main resorts on the lake. In Wangi Wangi, south of Toronto, you can visit the home of artist William Dobell. There are cruises on the lake in the *Wangi Queen* (tel 58 3211 for bookings) from Toronto and Belmont. There are train services to Toronto, and buses to Belmont and Speers Point.

Newcastle

Population 259,000

New South Wales' second largest city, Newcastle is also one of Australia's largest ports. At the mouth of the Hunter River, 167 km north of Sydney, it's a major industrial and commercial centre, with the massive BHP steelworks and other heavy industries. It's also the export port for the Hunter Valley coalfields: coal exports are still Newcastle's lifeblood. Despite the city's industrial base, its centre has a pleasant feel with wide leafy streets and surf beaches only a few hundred metres away.

Originally named Coal River, the city was founded in 1804 as a place for the worst of Sydney's convicts and was known as the 'hell of New South Wales'. The breakwater out to Nobbys Head with its lighthouse was built by convicts and the Bogey Hole, a swimming pool cut into the rock on the ocean's edge below the pleasant King Edward Park, was built for Major Morriset, a strict disciplinarian. It's still a great place for a dip.

Information & Orientation

The centre of Newcastle is a peninsula bordered by the ocean on one side and the Hunter River on the other. It tapers down to the long sandspit leading to Nobbys Head. Hunter St is the three km long main street. Between Newcomen and Perkins Sts it's a pedestrian mall.

There's a tourist information centre (tel 29 2211) at Queens Wharf on Wharf Rd by the river, open from 9 am to 5 pm Monday to Friday, 9.30 am to 3 pm weekends. The people here have lots of information, sell excellent maps for 50c and are friendly and helpful – as are many other Newcastle folk. The NRMA is at 8 Auckland St.

There are left-luggage lockers at Newcastle's railway station – for one day use only, and they cost 20c. The Scout Outdoor Centre opposite the Civic Hotel in Hunter St is a good place for outdoor gear.

Around the City

The good, modern Newcastle Region Art Gallery is on Laman St next to Civic Park. It's open Monday to Friday from 10 am to 5 pm plus weekend afternoons, and admission is free. In the Lovett Room of the public library next door there are photographic exhibitions which are regularly changed. The nearby Cooks Hill area has several well established private galleries.

The first stage of the new Newcastle Regional Museum at 787 Hunter St, opened in 1988 – admission $3. There are also Maritime and Military Museums (admission free) in Fort Scratchley out towards Nobbys Head, which dates from

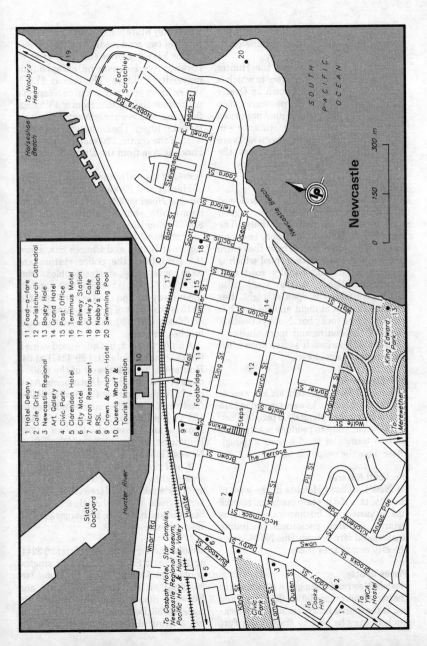

Newcastle

SOUTH PACIFIC OCEAN

To Nobby's Head

Horseshoe Beach

Fort Scratchley

Newcastle Beach

Hunter River

State Dockyard

King Edward Park

To Merewether

0   150   300 m

1   Hotel Delany
2   Cafe Gritz
3   Newcastle Regional
    Art Gallery
4   Civic Park
5   Clarendon Hotel
6   City Motel
7   Alcron Restaurant
8   RSL
9   Crown & Anchor Hotel
10 Queens Wharf &
    Tourist Information
11 Food-a-fare
12 Christchurch Cathedral
13 Bogey Hole
14 Grand Hotel
15 Post Office
16 Terminus Motel
17 Railway Station
18 Curley's Cafe
19 Nobby's Beach
20 Swimming Pool

To Casbah Hotel, Star Complex,
Newcastle Regional Museum,
Pacific Hwy & Hunter Valley

To Cooks Hill

To YWCA Hostel

Wharf Rd

Hunter St

Nobby's Rd

Beach St

Parnell Pl

Stevenson Pl

Bond St

Telford St

Scott St

Pacific St

Ocean St

Watt St

Bolton St

Wolfe St

Church St

Parker St

Ordance St

King St

Mall

Footbridge

Brown St

The Terrace

Perkins

Steps

Pitt St

Tyrell St

McCormack St

Kitchener Pde

Anzac Pde

Swan St

Brooks St

Darby St

Burwood St

Queen St

Laman St

Civic Park

the 1880s. It's open from 12 noon to 4 pm except on Mondays and admission is free.

North of the city across the Hunter River is the Stockton breakwater which is built over a sandbank known as Oyster Bank where many ships were once wrecked. The last to go aground here was a four-masted barque, the *Adolphe*, in 1904. Its hull and various other wrecks are now built into the breakwater; the *Adolphe* is the only one visible today.

Beaches

Newcastle is exceptionally well-endowed with beaches, many of which have good surf. Several are patrolled daily. The main beach, Newcastle Beach, is only a couple of hundred metres from the centre of town and has an ocean pool which is open at night, and usually good surf. Merewether Beach, further south, also has a pool which is open at night. Bar Beach is floodlit at night and the beach is protected by a rocky bar. Nobbys Beach is north of the centre and more sheltered from the southerlies. It's often open when other beaches are closed.

BHP Steelworks

Situated at Port Waratah, six km west of the city, the steelworks were opened in 1915 and today employ about 6000 people. They have the capacity to produce nearly three million tonnes of steel a year although these days the output is far less.

Blackbutt Reserve

At New Lambton Heights in the west of the city, this 166 hectare bushland reserve has a variety of bushwalks as well as aviaries, wildlife enclosures (including koalas) and fern houses. Bus No 363 from the city centre goes there.

Places to Stay

Hostels Newcastle has quite a vacuum in the budget accommodation field, but if you ask at the tourist information centre, backpackers may be able to stay at the Fort Scratchley State Emergency Centre for $6 (and get two good meals for a further $6).

The *YWCA Hostel* (tel 24 031) at 82 Parkway Ave, is usually full except during university holidays. The cost is $12. If you're lucky you may get in to sleep on a mattress on the common room or TV lounge floor. Ask for a key at night as the doors are locked at 10 pm. The hostel is 2½ km southwest of the centre, 250 metres west along Parkway Ave from the Darby St corner.

Hotels At the end of the mall on the corner of Hunter and Perkins Sts, the *Crown & Anchor Hotel* (tel 29 1027) has 22 decent rooms with shared bathrooms for just $14/23 a single/double.

The *Grand Hotel* (tel 29 3489), on the corner of Bolton and Church Sts, across the road from the police station and courthouse, has singles/doubles from $32/49 to $42/65. At 95 Scott St opposite the railway station the *George Hotel* (tel 29 1534) has a lot of permanents. Singles/doubles are $18/30 and they do counter lunches and teas.

A bit further out, but quite good value is the *Clarendon Hotel* (tel 29 4347) at 347 Hunter St, half a km west of the mall. It costs $23/35 with shared bathrooms. A few blocks further along at 471 Hunter St *The Casbah* (29 2904) has singles/doubles for $33/43. The *Cambridge Hotel* (tel 61 2459) about a km beyond the Casbah at 789 Hunter St, on the corner of Wood St in Newcastle West, is noisy but just $18/35.

If you don't mind the rock bands on some nights, the *Beach Hotel* (tel 63 1574) on Frederick St, Merewether, is just across from Merewether Beach, a short bus ride south of town. It charges $21/32 a single/double.

Motels The *Terminus Motel* (tel 26 3244) at 107 Scott St is central with singles/doubles at $44/46. The *City Motel* (tel 29 5855) on the corner of Darby and Burwood Sts, is reasonably central but costs $53/58. Belmont, about 15 km south, has a string of cheaper motels along the

Pacific Highway. *Pelican Palms Motor Inn* (tel 45 4545) at 784 Pacific Highway, is averagely priced at around $37 to $41 single, $41 to $53 double and there's a pool.

Camping Stockton is handy for Newcastle by ferry – it's directly across the Hunter River from the city centre – otherwise it's 19 km by road (there is a bus). *Stockton Beach Caravan Park* (tel 28 1393) is right on the beach in Pitt St. Camping costs $6.50, on-site vans are $29 a night.

Newcastle Caravan Park (tel 68 1394) at 293 Maitland Rd, Mayfield West (the Pacific Highway), is two km from Newcastle centre, but doesn't take tents. On-site vans on this very small site are $23 to $27 double.

There are several sites at Belmont. *Belmont Pines Tourist Park* (tel 45 4750) is on the lake in Ethel St and has tent sites for $7 to $8.50, less by the week. There are a few on-site vans. *Belmont Bay Caravan Park* (tel 45 3653) on Gerald St, has camping ($9 for two) and on-site vans from $21 to $26. There are also sites in Redhead and Swansea.

Places to Eat
Newcastle offers some surprisingly good places to eat apart from the usual *Kentucky Frieds, Pizza Huts, Big Al's* and the like.

Counter Meals At 471 Hunter St about 750 metres west of the mall (on the corner of Union Lane and through to King St), *The Casbah* is a glossy and very popular pub with food from $7 to $9 and 'Healthworks' for good sandwiches. On the corner of Crown St, the *Lucky Country Hotel* has a bistro and the more expensive *Billabong Restaurant*. Two blocks along at the Perkins St end of the mall, the *Crown & Anchor* has food in its pricey upstairs Cannon Room.

Jokers Tavern, upstairs in the Hunter St Mall, has moderately priced pub food. At 23 Watt St, the second last street crossing Hunter St, *Rumours Tavern* has

main courses for $7 to $9. The *Grand Hotel* on the corner of Church and Bolton Sts, a couple of blocks across from the mall, is a popular drinking spot and has light meals and snacks.

The relaxed *Hotel Delany* is at 134 Darby St on the corner of Council St, Cooks Hill, a km or so inland from the town centre. It has the popular *Cravings* restaurant with good food and reasonable prices – starters at $5, main meals up to $13. A couple of blocks west the *Cricketers Arms*, on the corner of Bruce and Bull Sts, is another popular watering hole with pub food available. So too is the *Beach Hotel* in Frederick St, Merewether, a beachside suburb a few km south of town.

Italian Newcastle has some real Italian institutions like the *Centre Italian Restaurant* at 46 Beaumont St in Hamilton, just south of the Pacific Highway as you enter the town. There are more Italian places in this area. Other favourites include *Don Beppino's* at 45 Railway St, Merewether, and *Arrivederci* on the corner of Glebe Rd and Watkins St at The Junction, a little inland from Merewether. Arrivederci is very busy and popular (probably due more to the opening hours than the pizzas) – it's open to 2 or 3 am.

Restaurants The *Food-A-Fare* food hall upstairs in the Hunter St Mall is good value with international food, kebabs, sandwiches and much more. Close by, on the corner of King and Wolfe Sts, the *Thai Courtyard* is recommended by locals. It's open for lunch Monday to Friday and dinner Monday to Saturday. *Smokey Joe's Cafe* in the new Quay 1 complex on Wharf Rd is an American-style restaurant with a '50s flavour.

There are lots of places on Darby St. *Taco Bill's* at No 80 has Mexican food, is BYO and open Wednesday to Sunday until 10 pm. It's popular and usually crowded, but they don't take bookings so you often have to queue to get in. Next door, *Taters* specialises in baked spuds which start at $3. *Emilio's Pizzeria & Trattoria* is at No 127 and a few doors down at No 131, *Cafe Gritz* is a pleasant little place with main courses for $6 to $8, open Tuesday to Saturday.

The *Maharaja* is a licensed north Indian restaurant at 653 Hunter St, Newcastle West. It's open for lunch from Tuesday to Saturday and for dinner every night. Take-aways are available. Also in Newcastle West, at 32 Marketown Shopping Centre, the *Istana Malaysia* is raved about by locals.

Specials *Alcron* at 116 Church St, on a hill overlooking the harbour, has a three course sunset dinner for $14.50. Sunset is 5.30 to 9.30 pm Monday to Thursday, 5.30 to 7.30 pm Friday and Saturday; it's closed on Sundays. The à la carte prices are not cheap.

The *Gallery Cafe* by the rock pool in the Star Complex at 569 Hunter St, has a $7 lunch time special for main course and dessert. In the evening, starters are $7 and main courses $11.50. The atmosphere is pleasant with tables in small private rooms which display paintings by local artists. Other places near here have outdoor tables by the rock pool.

The *Waratah-Mayfield RSL*, a few km north of Hamilton on the Pacific Highway, has a Sunday lunch time smorgasbord which is good value. *Clams* at 87 Frederick St, Merewether, is famous for its seafood. It's next to the Beach Hotel and closed on Sundays.

Entertainment
There's something on most nights; phone the 2NX What's Happening line (11 6889), get Friday's *Newcastle Herald* or the *That's Entertainment* give-away on Wednesdays.

Quay 1 on Wharf Rd is a hub of Newcastle nightlife, with bands (sometimes quite big Aussie touring bands) two or three nights a week. *Fanny's* in the same complex has live music for dancing –

usually a different scene every night. The popular *Newcastle Workers Club* on the corner of Union and King Sts also has regular visiting bands – often quite big names too. There are two auditoria and often an act in each, plus the usual Chinese restaurant and pokies.

Newcastle has lots more leagues and RSL-type clubs although they tend to be fussy about dress and can be quite expensive. Other nightclubs include the *Crazy Horse* and *Palais Royale*. You can catch jazz Wednesday to Saturday at the *Bel-Air Hotel* on Park Ave, Kotara. Plays and concerts are held in the *Civic Theatre* behind the City Hall.

Pubs The *Hotel Delany* is a relaxed little pub on the corner of Council and Darby Sts, Cooks Hill – good music, people and atmosphere most nights and a good restaurant too. The *Cricketers Arms*, on the corner of Bull and Bruce Sts in Cooks Hill, is also popular. The *Grand Hotel* on the corner of Church and Bolton Sts has poetry readings, rock or jazz most nights.

In Newcastle West, at the corner of Hunter and Wood Sts, the *Cambridge Hotel* has live music every night and Sunday afternoons; different music on different nights.

In Merewether the *Beach Hotel* has good music (usually rock) mainly on Wednesday, Saturday and Sunday nights. This is one of the most popular places in the area. The *Prince of Wales*, also in Merewether, is very popular on Friday nights.

Getting There & Away
Air Aeropelican (tel 69 3444) flies several times a day between Sydney and Newcastle. Air NSW (tel 69 3444) and Eastern (tel 69 3055) both fly north to the Gold Coast and Brisbane; Eastern stops at several New South Wales towns en route. Eastern flies direct to/from Canberra and Sydney. The fare from Sydney is

around $55, from Brisbane $150, depending on the airline.

Bus Most Sydney to Brisbane buses stop in Newcastle, but you can't take them between Sydney and Newcastle unless you are using a bus pass or the journey is part of some other longer ticket. Going north from Newcastle, however, buses offer a much better service than trains. Newcastle to Port Macquarie costs about $22, to Byron Bay $37, to Brisbane $37. Jayes Travel (tel 26 2000) at 285 Hunter St, is the main booking office and terminal in Newcastle.

There's a bus to Cessnock, but to anywhere else in the Hunter region you have to go by train, which runs to Maitland and the upper part of the Hunter Valley. See Port Stephens and Forster in the Hunter Valley section.

Train Trains to and from Sydney operate about 20 times daily, and cost $12. A few trains a day are fast 'Flyers', but you must book a seat on these. Heading north, trains are far from frequent.

Getting Around
UTA buses cover all of Newcastle and the eastern side of Lake Macquarie. Services are reasonably frequent but can be slow. The bus information booth at the west end of the mall has timetables. For a spot of sightseeing by local bus, try route No 348 or 358 to Swansea or No 366, 363 or 327 to Speers Point. Newcastle has similar special local transport deals to Sydney.

Trains run to the western side of Lake Macquarie with connecting buses to the south-western shores. A private bus company operates to Stockton – but much quicker is the UTA ferry hop across the river from Wharf Rd, between Merewether St and Queens Wharf. The ferry usually runs every half hour till 11 pm.

The regular car hire firms are here. Bike rental places come and go – the tourist information centre will know if there's one operating currently.

AROUND NEWCASTLE
As well as the Hunter Valley there are several places of interest around Newcastle. Raymond Terrace, just 23 km north of Newcastle, has a number of early buildings from the 1830s and '40s including a courthouse which is still in use. Irrawang is an 1830 homestead.

The Hunter Valley

The Hunter Valley has two curiously diverse products – coal and wine. Steam trains still take coal to Hexham on the Hunter River near Newcastle. Singleton, 77 km inland from Newcastle, and Muswellbrook, a further 47 km, are two wine producing/coal mining areas (see the later New England section for more on these places). The centre of the Hunter Valley vineyards is the Pokolbin area near Cessnock and some of the wineries date back to the 1860s. You'll find many of Australia's best known wine names.

The upper Hunter Valley around Muswellbrook and Denman, less well known than the lower valley, is wilder country but has vineyards and a regular wine festival. The main road through the Hunter Valley is the New England Highway from Tamworth down to Newcastle. The 300 km long Hunter River comes from further west and doesn't meet the highway until Singleton.

Wineries
There are about 30 vineyards in the Lower Hunter, and more in the Upper Hunter around Denman and Muswellbrook, where you can sample and buy wines. Generally they're open for tasting from 9 am to 5 pm (some a little earlier, some a little later) from Monday to Saturday, and slightly reduced hours on Sundays. Many have picnic and barbecue facilities so you can enjoy your lunch while sampling the wine. Several wineries run tours – McWilliams Mt Pleasant is one (at 11 am and 2 pm on

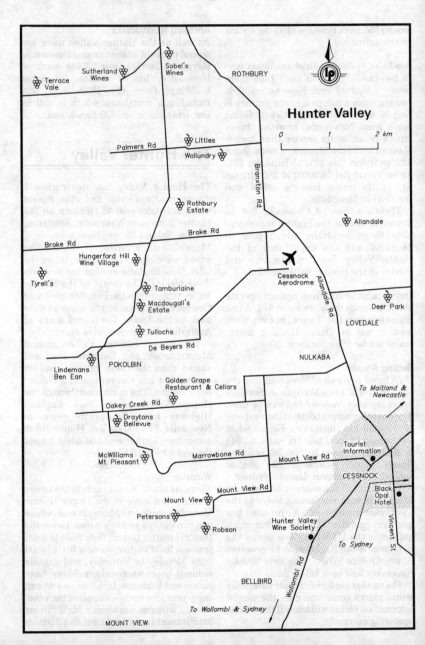

Hunter Valley

0   1   2 km

Terrace Vale
Sutherland Wines
Sobel's Wines
ROTHBURY

Palmers Rd
Littles
Wollundry

Branxton Rd

Rothbury Estate

Broke Rd
Allandale

Broke Rd

Hungerford Hill Wine Village

Tyrell's
Tamburlaine
Macdougall's Estate
Tullochs

De Beyers Rd

Cessnock Aerodrome

Deer Park

LOVEDALE

POKOLBIN

Lindemans Ben Ean

Golden Grape Restaurant & Cellars

Oakey Creek Rd

Draytons Bellevue

McWilliams Mt Pleasant

Marrowbone Rd

NULKABA

To Maitland & Newcastle

Mount View Rd

Tourist Information

CESSNOCK

Mount View Rd

Mount View

Petersons

Robson

Hunter Valley Wine Society

Black Opal Hotel

Vincent St

To Sydney

Wollombi Rd

BELLBIRD

To Wollombi & Sydney

MOUNT VIEW

weekdays) and the Cessnock tourist information centre can tell you of others.

Starting from Cessnock, interesting Lower Hunter wineries include Happy Valley (Saxonvale) with its rather expensive restaurant. Lindeman's Ben Ean is not, surprisingly, the home of Ben Ean Moselle which is blended from a number of grape growing regions. Tulloch's, MacDougalls Estate and Tamburlaine are all side by side.

Hungerford Hill bills itself as a 'wine village'. It has a restaurant, handicrafts shop, 'farmers' market' and wine tours as well as the usual tasting and wine sales facilities – commercial but interesting. Housed in a huge and splendid building the Rothbury Estate sells all its wines direct. Tyrrells is one of the longest established names in the Hunter. Finally Wyndham Estate, again with a restaurant, is several km north of the main vineyard concentration, a little north of the New England Highway.

Getting There & Around

You cannot travel to the Hunter region with the main bus operators, unless you're on a bus pass or travelling from interstate, but there are a number of train services. Maitland is the main train station for the lower Hunter, with services from Newcastle and Sydney.

From Maitland there are buses to Cessnock. Rover Motors (tel 90 1175) at 231 Vincent St in Cessnock (opposite the Black Opal Hotel) has several services a day from Newcastle and Maitland to Cessnock, but fewer on weekends. Singleton Air Service (tel 74 4575 in Singleton) flies at least daily between Sydney, Cessnock and Singleton. Eastern flies daily between Sydney and Maitland.

To explore the vineyards you can join a tour with Hunter Explorer Tours (tel 52 3031 in Newcastle). From Newcastle these cost $50 including lunch, but they'll pick you up from Cessnock for $30 without lunch, $40 with lunch. The tour covers some of the smaller vineyards with plenty of tasting and buying opportunities.

You can hire bicycles from the Trading Post (tel 98 7670) on Broke Rd, Pokolbin, but they're about six km out of Cessnock.

CESSNOCK (population 17,000)

Cessnock is the main town and accommodation centre for the vineyards, a few km from Pokolbin and in the centre of the wineries. There's a useful tourist information centre (tel 90 4477) on the corner of Wollombi and Mount View Rds, open from 9 am to 5 pm daily.

Wollombi, a tiny town 31 km south of Cessnock, has some interesting old buildings and there are good lookouts around the valley.

Places to Stay

There's a basic associate YHA Hostel (tel 90 1070) in the back of the Black Opal Hotel at 216 Vincent St, on the corner of Cessnock St, at the railway station end of Vincent St. Bunks in small dorms are $9 for YHA members, $12 for others. Rooms in the hotel are $17 per person or $23 with breakfast. It's run by a friendly young couple who have done some travelling themselves.

Other cheap hotels include the Royal Oak on the corner of Vincent and Snape Sts at $17 a head, bed only, and the Wentworth (tel 90 1364) at 36 Vincent St, charging $17 per person with breakfast Sunday to Thursday, $20 on Friday and $23 on Saturday. The Cessnock Hotel (tel 90 1002) on Wollombi Rd opposite the post office is $15 per person or $20 with breakfast.

Prices in more expensive places generally rise by 50% to 100% at weekends. The Cessnock Motel (tel 90 2770), 13 Allandale Rd, has singles/doubles for $32/39 from Sunday to Thursday, going up to $50 a double on Friday and $58 on Saturday. The Hunter Valley Motel (tel 90 1849) at 30 Allandale Rd, is $32/39 during the week, but $55 single or double on Friday and Saturday. There are many more places out among the vineyards themselves – *Belford Country Cabins* (tel (065) 74 7100) on Hermitage Rd, Pokolbin has overnight cabins midweek for $46 double plus $12 for each extra person.

Valley View Caravan Park (tel 90 2573) on Mount View Rd, Cessnock has tent sites at $4.50 per person and overnight vans from $18 to $35. *Cessnock Caravan Park* (tel 90 5819) just north of the town at Nulkaba has tent sites for $6.50, and on-site vans and cabins from $20 to $27 double.

Places to Eat

For a good cheap meal try the *Cessnock Workers' Club* bistro (open from 12 noon to 2 pm and 6 to 8 pm) or the *Ex-Services Club*, both on Vincent St. The *Ex-Services Club* snack bar, open lunch time and evenings, will do main meals for $3.50 to $6. It has a restaurant open in the evenings till 9 pm.

The *Hunter Valley Wine Society* (tel 90 6699) at 4 Wollombi Rd on the western edge of Cessnock, has a pleasant bistro with steaks at around $12 and specials for $7 to $9. You can look round the society's display of local wines – and of course buy some if you want! There are more places in town and several around the vineyards – all of the latter are rather expensive, some of them rather indifferent. It's wise to book ahead.

MAITLAND (population 44,000)

Maitland, once a coal mining centre, is 30 km inland from Newcastle. It was settled by convicts in 1818, and at one time Sydney, Parramatta and Maitland were the three main centres in Australia. Today its centre has as great a concentration of historic buildings as anywhere in the country.

Information

The tourist information centre (tel 33 2611) is in King Edward Park on the New England Highway, open daily. *Historical Homes & Buildings* ($1.50) is a good guide to the old buildings in Maitland. The Maitland Lands Office has an excellent *East Maitland Heritage Walk* brochure.

Things to See

The old jail off King St is now a museum with an excellent collection of police and criminal memorabilia – open Friday to Sunday. Other fine old edifices include Brough House, now an art gallery, and Grossman House which is the local history museum (open weekends). There are a number of old homesteads in the area including the 1820, convict-built Windermere Colonial Museum in nearby Lochinvar. Nearby Morpeth village has many reminders of its early history, plus several galleries and craft shops.

Getting There & Away

A regular suburban train runs to Maitland from Newcastle so a visit to this interesting old town is a good excursion for people without their own transport.

Newcastle to Port Macquarie

It's about 250 km up the coast from Newcastle to the popular resort town of Port Macquarie. Most of the way up to the Queensland border there's a narrow coastal band rising into the Great Dividing Range area of New England. The coastal strip has some good resort towns and long, lonely beaches, some with notable surf. In places the main Pacific Highway runs well inland from the coast and rougher roads will take you along quite deserted stretches of beach on the actual coastline. Some superbly scenic roads lead into the New England tableland.

PORT STEPHENS

Port Stephens is a large inlet where Nelson Bay is the main town. It's a popular fishing centre with many fine beaches, a large range of accommodation including a small, remote *YHA Hostel* (tel 97 3075) at Carrington on the north shore, and some minor tourist attractions.

There are cruises on Port Stephens from Nelson Bay. From Tea Gardens, the settlement across the harbour from Nelson Bay, you can drive – or, again, cruise – into Myall Lakes National Park just to the north, one of the most beautiful parks on the whole New South Wales coast.

Port Stephens Buses (tel (049) 81 1207) runs daily buses between Nelson Bay and Sydney ($19), and buses around the Port Stephens townships and to/from Newcastle.

MYALL LAKES NATIONAL PARK

Bulahdelah, with a selection of reasonably priced caravan parks and motels, is on the way to the beautiful beaches and headlands of the coastal Myall Lakes National Park. It's about a 14 km drive from Bulahdelah to Bombah Point where ferries cross one of the lakes to the coastal side of the park. The lakes and the coastline with its sand dunes offer a variety of activities from swimming and boating to surfing, fishing and walking. There are camping grounds, all reachable by car, at Mungo Brush and Bombah Point and at Seal Rocks, a small fishing and surfing village on the north-east edge of the park. There are some excellent bushwalks from Bulahdelah.

FORSTER-TUNCURRY (population 15,500)

Between the top end of Myall Lakes National Park and Taree, on a coastal loop road from Bulahdelah, the twin towns of Forster-Tuncurry are connected by a bridge at the sea entrance to Wallis Lake. Places of interest include the Arts & Crafts Centre in Forster, the Vintage Car Museum a couple of km south and Talabah Park (amusing for children) 20 km north. Tiona Park is an open-air 'cathedral' on the shores of Lake Wallis, 13 km south.

Sid Fogg's (tel (049) 28 1088) runs daily buses between Forster and Newcastle and Sydney ($20.50).

INLAND ROUTES

Another alternative to the Pacific Highway is to travel to Taree along Bucketts Way on the eastern slopes of the Great Dividing Range. It passes through Stroud, which has many buildings from the 1830s, and Gloucester which is at the foot of the hills known as the Bucketts. There are some good lookouts in the hills, particularly at Copeland Tops and Kia Ora. There's a small *YHA Hostel* (tel (049) 97 6639) at Girvan about 15 km from Stroud on the Booral to Bulahdelah road.

Dungog, west of Stroud, is a main access point to the Barrington Tops National Park, which contains two 1600 metre alpine plateaus that fall away steeply to just 400 metres. The park is noted for its wildlife and some unusual local flora, and has a variety of walking trails and picnic areas. Forty-three km from Dungog you reach the park boundary at *Barrington Guest House* (tel (049) 95 3212), which is the nearest accommodation to the park. There's a car-camping site in the park's eastern Gloucester River area, approached from the Stroud to Gloucester road. Outside the park, the Barrington Tops road linking Gloucester with Scone on the Newcastle to Tamworth road is a beautiful drive if the weather is fine.

TAREE (population 16,000)

This is the main town in the Manning River District. There's a clutch of cheap motels – rooms for less than $30 – on the highway a couple of km south of town, plus a few hotels on Victoria St, which is the Pacific Highway as it runs through town. The Manning Valley Tourist Information Centre (tel 52 1900) is four km north of central Taree on the highway.

Just inland from Taree is Wingham where the Brush is a park close to the town, inhabited by countless flying foxes between September and May each year.

As in many other areas along this coast the state forests around Taree provide good forest drives, walks and picnic areas. Other places of interest include the Bulga Plateau, 50 km north, where you can see the 160 metre drop of the Ellenborough Falls.

Crowdy Bay National Park – good for fishing, surfing, walking and viewing spring wildflowers – is 40 km north-east. There's good surfing at Old Bar, 16 km east of Taree.

CAMDEN HAVEN

Fifty km north of Taree at Kew you can turn off the Pacific Highway and take a more scenic coastal route to Port Macquarie. The fishing towns of Laurieton, North Haven and Dunbogan, immediately north of Crowdy Bay National Park, are collectively known as Camden Haven and a bit further north is the small township of Lake Cathie, from where Lighthouse Beach stretches 10 km up to the Port Macquarie Lighthouse. There's excellent fishing along the coast here, plus a range of accommodation and some fine bushwalks around the lakes close to the coast.

Port Macquarie

Population 27,000

One of the bigger resort centres on the New South Wales north coast, Port Macquarie makes a good stopping point on the journey from Sydney (430 km south). It was founded in 1821 making it one of the oldest towns in New South Wales and was a convict settlement until 1840. There is a wide range of accommodation and places to eat, a spot of nightlife, and the competition tends to keep prices down. 'Port' has been blessed with both a river frontage (the Hastings River enters the sea here) and a beautiful series of ocean beaches starting right in the town – good for surfing, snorkelling or just collecting a suntan. It's a small enough place to find everything you need within reasonable walking distance of the centre.

Information

The excellent information centre (tel 83 1077), open till 5 pm Monday to Saturday,

Flynns Beach, Port Macquarie

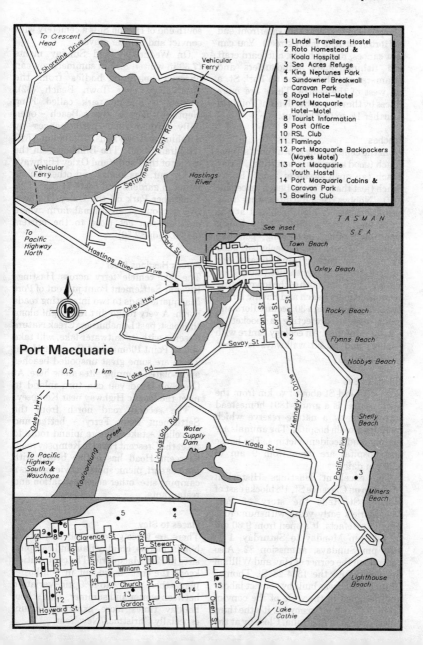

1 Lindel Travellers Hostel
2 Roto Homestead &
   Koala Hospital
3 Sea Acres Refuge
4 King Neptunes Park
5 Sundowner Breakwall
   Caravan Park
6 Royal Hotel–Motel
7 Port Macquarie
   Hotel–Motel
8 Tourist Information
9 Post Office
10 RSL Club
11 Flamingo
12 Port Macquarie Backpackers
   (Mayes Motel)
13 Port Macquarie
   Youth Hostel
14 Port Macquarie Cabins &
   Caravan Park
15 Bowling Club

Port Macquarie

0   0.5   1 km

3.30 pm Sunday, is at the waterfront end of Horton St (the main street). You can rent canoes, rowing boats, outboard craft and fishing boats, windsurfers and catamarans at the marina on Park St, a km west of the centre. There are more places by the river on Settlement Point Rd a further 1½ to two km out.

Beaches

From the centre going south there's Town Beach (good swimming or surfing), Oxley Beach (an open sweep of sand), Rocky Beach (just that), Flynns Beach (excellent surf), Nobbys Beach (interesting rock formations and a high headland at the north end), the popular Shelly Beach (good swimming, interesting, gem-like pebbles), Miners Beach (secluded, good for nude sun bathing) and, finally, the endless stretch of Lighthouse (more good surfing). Five km south of the town centre, between Miners Beach and Pacific Drive, Sea Acres Refuge is a 30 hectare flora and fauna reserve protecting a pocket of coastal rainforest. An ecology centre with displays and raised walkways is being constructed.

Things to See

Roto, off Lord St about two km from the town centre, is a grand 1891 homestead surrounded by a nature reserve which includes a koala hospital. The animals are mainly road accident victims. The house and hospital are open from 9 am to 4.30 pm daily.

The excellent Hastings Historical Museum on Clarence St, 1½ blocks east of Horton St, tells the story of Port Macquarie's early years with numerous convict artefacts. It's open from 9.30 am to 4.30 pm Monday to Saturday, 1 to 4.30 pm Sundays, admission $2. Also central, on the corner of Hay and William Sts you'll find the 1824-28 St Thomas Church which was built by convict labour and designed in the style of the convict architect Francis Greenway. It's the third oldest church in Australia. Close by at the south end of Horton St is a cemetery with convict and pioneer graves.

On Wednesday and Sunday nights (7.30 in winter, 8.15 in summer) you can observe heavenly bodies from the observatory near Town Beach ($2). There's a marine park called King Neptune's Park by Town Beach – open daily with regular performances by dolphins and sea lions, admission $7.50 (children $4.50). The Billabong, on the corner of the Pacific and Oxley Highways 10 km out, has koalas and other Aussie fauna in gardens and costs $4 (kids $2); Kingfisher Park off the Oxley Highway five km out is an animal farm where children can get close to the critters ($4.50, kids $2.50).

Across Hastings River

The 30c vehicle ferry across Hastings River at Settlement Point just out of Port Macquarie leads to two interesting roads north. A very rough dirt road right along the coast, past Limeburners Creek Nature Reserve with its saltwater lake, will take you to Point Plomer and Crescent Head. There are some great unspoiled beaches and isolated camping sites along here. At Crescent Head you can turn inland to meet the Pacific Highway near Kempsey.

The second road north from the Settlement Point Ferry – better and gravelled – takes a more inland route to meet the Crescent Head to Kempsey road. Crescent Head has a fine beach with famous surf, picnic spots and views, plus a camping site, other accommodation and restaurants.

Places to Stay

There are three good hostels and lots of hotels, motels, holiday flats and camping sites in Port Macquarie. The competition keeps the costs down but in non-hostel places there's a 20% to 40% price variation between winter and summer, with school holiday times more expensive again, especially Christmas/New Year.

Hostels The *Port Macquarie Youth Hostel* (tel (065) 83 5512) at 40 Church St, is a good new associate YHA place – you don't have to be a YHA member to stay. The cost is $10 ($2.50 for sleeping sheet hire). Accommodation is mostly in dormitories, but there's one family room. The atmosphere's friendly and the managers provide good breakfasts ($3.50) and dinners ($6). Bicycles are for hire at $2.50 a day.

Even closer to the centre at 135 Horton St, is *Port Macquarie Backpackers* (tel 83 1913) also known as the Mayes Motel. There's a variety of rooms taking two to six people in beds or bunks at $9 each. Each room has a TV and tea/coffee making facilities, and there are shared kitchen areas. There are a few motel-type rooms at around $25 double, plus a TV lounge and free use of bicycles.

Slightly further from the centre, *Lindel Travellers Hostel* (tel 83 1791) is on the rather noisy corner of Gordon St and Hastings River Drive. There are separate male and female dorms and the cost is again $9, with a $1.50 charge for linen hire. It's an interesting old house, recently renovated, and has a big kitchen and a TV room.

Hotels & Motels At the end of Horton St, the main street, the *Royal Hotel-Motel* (tel 83 1896) has pleasant rooms with shower and toilet, some looking out over the river, for $21/29 a single/double – good value for the location. Next door, the *Port Macquarie Hotel-Motel* (tel 83 1011) on the Horton and Clarence St corner has quite spacious singles/doubles for $17/27 with shared bathrooms, a few dollars more with private bathrooms, or $35/40 with private bathrooms in a motel annexe with waterfront views. The main section is noisy at weekends since most of the local nightlife takes place downstairs.

There are scores more places around town, down Pacific Drive and inland along Hastings River Drive, Settlement Point Rd and Oxley Highway. The cheapest motel rooms are around $29 single or double in the low season, rising to around $35/52 at peak. Places in this range include the very central *Port Centre* (tel 83 1566) at 32 Hay St; and, all within two km of the town centre, the *Arrowyn* (tel 83 1633) at 170 Gordon St; the *Burrawan* (tel 83 1799) at 24 Burrawan St; the *John Oxley* (tel 83 1677) at 171 Gordon St; the *Macquarie* (tel 83 1533) on Grant St; and the *Marine* (tel 83 1511) at 239 Hastings River Drive.

The cheapest two-bedroom holiday flats are about $100 a week in winter, $140 in summer, up to $230-plus at Christmas. At non-busy times you'll be able to get nightly rates at about a fifth of the weekly cost.

Camping & Cabins The small *Port Macquarie Cabins & Caravan Park* (tel 83 1115) at 24 Lord St is excellent value. Old-fashioned but spacious and clean cabins with their own bathrooms and kitchens go for around $23 a night or $120 a week for two.

The most central camping/caravan park is the *Sundowner Breakwall* (tel 83 2755) at 1 Munster St, near the river mouth and Town Beach, but it's not cheap at $12 a double to pitch your tent, or $29-plus for an on-site van. You'll find cheaper places down near Flynns Beach or inland along the river or the Oxley highway.

Places to Eat

Towards the south end of Horton St the coffee lounge in the Village Centre arcade offers a 20% discount to backpackers. Also on Horton St but closer to William St, the two Chinese places *Whar Hing* and *Yuen Hing* are popular, the Whar Hing offering a weekend smorgasbord lunch for $7, the Yuen Hing a daily $6 lunch special of two main dishes plus fried rice. At both places main dishes range from $7 to $12 in the evening.

Around the corner on William St, between Horton and Hay Sts, the health food shop next door to the Kywong Coffee

Lounge does very good, cheap and wholesome take-aways.

The *Italian Kitchen* at 16 Hay St, is only open Wednesday to Saturday nights, but has good pastas for $5 and other meals for $7 to $9. Across the road on the corner of Hay and Clarence Sts, *Garrison Charcoal Chicken* is open every day till 8 pm.

On the opposite corner of Clarence and Hay Sts, the *Pancake Palace* has a large range of pancakes and crepes, a full meal around $8.50. It's open for weekday lunches and dinner every night. A few doors down Hay St, closer to the river and opposite the court house, *Sophie's Kitchen* specialises in take-away seafood plus hamburgers and fried chicken; everything is freshly cooked.

For a bit of ethnic variety try the *Shalimar* Indian take-away in shop 3 in the Ritz Centre on the corner of Clarence and Horton Sts, open daily.

For excellent pizza, the *Flamingo* on the corner of Short and William Sts is open until 2 am Friday and Saturday nights, 8 or 9 pm other nights. *Schnitzel Haus*, a BYO on the opposite corner, has schnitzels and seafood at reasonable prices and is open daily.

As always the clubs are a good source of cheap, plain tucker. You'll get an excellent meal at the *Port Macquarie Bowling Club Bistro* on Owen St at the corner of Church St. The *RSL Club*, on Short St, is good value.

Entertainment

The *Lachlan Room* in the Port Macquarie Hotel-Motel near the end of Horton St is the liveliest place in town: it rages till 2 am Wednesday to Saturday, with bands on the first two nights. The *RSL Club* on Short St has a popular disco and sometimes touring acts.

Getting There & Away

Air East-West flies daily from Sydney ($114, standby $91) and Eastern from Brisbane, Gold Coast, Lismore, Coffs Harbour, Taree and Newcastle. Oxley Airlines flies daily to/from Brisbane, Gold Coast, Ballina, Coffs Harbour, Newcastle and Sydney too, and has flights to Lord Howe Island ($230).

Bus Long-distance bus lines include Port Macquarie on their Sydney to Brisbane route, though not every service stops here. From Sydney it costs about $25; from Brisbane $34; from Byron Bay $25. Coffs Harbour is just two hours up the road but can be expensive: with Kirklands you'd pay $22, for instance, so it's worth looking around for a better deal.

Remember the New South Wales rules which decree that you have to travel a minimum 160 km on each journey on a long-distance bus unless you have an interstate ticket or a bus pass, so you can't hop on to Nambucca Heads (119 km) by bus from Port Macquarie. Coffs Harbour however is safely beyond the limit.

Skennars has a service inland three days a week to Armidale ($25) and Tamworth ($35) via Coffs Harbour.

Train The nearest station is Wauchope, 19 km inland, with four services daily northbound to Byron Bay and Murwillumbah, and southbound to Sydney. The Port Macquarie Bus Service (tel 83 2161) runs between Wauchope and Port Macquarie a few times daily and connects with the Holiday Coast XPT train from Sydney. Sydney to Wauchope is $35 in economy class, $49 in 1st.

Getting Around

The Port Macquarie Bus Service (tel 83 2161) runs local buses to and from Wauchope five times on weekdays, twice on Saturdays and Sundays; to Lake Cathie and Kempsey, and a service around the town.

There are several car hire firms in town – the usual big names plus Rag-Top Rentals on the corner of Horton and Hayward Sts. *Port Venture* runs a two hour $9 river cruise, usually daily at 2 pm, from the wharf at the end of Clarence St.

Port Macquarie to Coffs Harbour

WAUCHOPE (population 4200)

Nineteen km inland from Port Macquarie, Wauchope (pronounced 'war hope') is on the Hastings River a few km west of the Pacific Highway. Timbertown is an interesting working replica of an 1880s timber town. It's open from 10 am to 5 pm daily and entry is $8.50 including rides (children $4.50). Lilybank Canoe Hire, on the river one km east of the town, has two-person canoes at $12 for two hours, $30 a day or $70 a week and can advise you on camping spots, etc, up the river. The Big Bull, three km north of Wauchope, houses educational displays, an animal nursery and a restaurant. It's open daily and entry is $4.

Wauchope has a range of accommodation including a small associate *YHA Hostel* (tel 85 6134) at Rainbow Ridge, 11 km west on the Oxley Highway towards Tamworth. The cost in the hostel is $6.50 and you can pitch a tent in the grounds.

About 100 km from Wauchope you can turn north off the Oxley Highway to reach the remote and rugged Werrikimbe National Park on the edge of the New England tableland. The park has diverse wildlife and vegetation, including heathland and rainforest, and there are camping sites and walking tracks at Cobcrofts and Mooraback. Further along the highway, 18 km before Walcha, the spectacular Apsley Falls are about a km off the highway. The falls and the Apsley Gorge downstream from them, are part of the Oxley Wild Rivers National Park and there are basic camping facilities near the falls. This national park is composed of several separate sections covering 300 square km of the upper Apsley and Macleay Rivers and their tributaries. The northern part of the park is close to the Dorrigo to Armidale road.

KEMPSEY AREA

North along the Pacific Highway from Wauchope is Kempsey, which is the home of the Akubra hat and has the Macleay River Historical Museum & Cultural Centre (entry $1) next to the tourist information centre (tel 62 5444) by the highway on the south side of town. There are some cheap on-site vans (around $17) in caravan parks here, but it's worth diverting north-east off the highway to the coast at Hat Head or South West Rocks, both about 32 km from Kempsey.

Hat Head is a village with a caravan park and holiday flats at the foot of Hat Hill Headland. There are good beaches and walks and part of the nearby coast is a national park. South West Rocks is another coastal resort village, near the mouth of the Macleay River, with good beaches and quite a range of accommodation. A big attraction is Trial Bay Gaol on the headland three km east of South West Rocks. This imposing edifice was a civil prison in the late 19th century and housed German POWs in WW I. It's now a museum with wonderful views, open daily from 9 am to 5 pm ($1.50). An attractive camping area surrounds the jail and there's a cafe in the grounds. Trial Bay is named after the brig *The Trial* which was stolen from Sydney by convicts in 1816 and wrecked here. Smoky Cape Lighthouse, a few km down the coast from the jail, can be inspected on Thursdays (and Tuesdays in school holidays) from 10 to 11.45 am and 1 to 2.45 pm. Mercury Roadlines run buses from Kempsey to South West Rocks.

There are great views from the Mt Yarrahapinni Lookout east of the Pacific Highway about 15 km south of Macksville. Macksville is on the Nambucca River and here you can visit the Mary Boulton Pioneer Cottage on River St. In nearby Bowraville there's yet another folk museum – the Joseph & Eliza Newman

Folk Museum. Follow the road 27 km upriver to Taylors Arm and there you'll find the 1903 Cosmopolitan, the hotel immortalised in that sad song *Pub with No Beer*.

NAMBUCCA HEADS (population 4900)

Just in from the mouth of the Nambucca River, this little resort town is one of the best stops on the New South Wales north coast. It's a laid-back place with good coastal scenery – great views from the headland above the river mouth – and you have a choice of salt or fresh water. There are good walks in the immediate area and interesting trips inland to the Bellingen-Dorrigo area. On the river you can take a cruise, swim (at Bellwood) or hire windsurfers, canoes, boats or fishing tackle, while Nambucca Main Beach is one of several good surf spots. You can take white-water rafting trips with Wildwater Adventures (tel 53 4469) – normally $65 for a day, but less for standby if you call after 4 pm the day before. The Nambucca Historical Museum is on Liston St.

Places to Stay

Nambucca Backpackers Hostel (tel 68 6360) at 3 Newman St is a friendly little place charging $9 in four-person dorms or double rooms. The amiable Norwegian-English couple who run it offer a variety of trips ranging from $6 half day outings to Taylors Arm or Bellingen bat colony and winery, to $11 full day visits to Dorrigo National Park. They'll pick you up on arrival and lend bicycles, snorkel gear or boogie boards.

The clean *Max Motel* (tel 68 6138) on Fraser St, the southern half of the town's main street, has rooms with glorious views of the river and ocean for $35, and others for $28. Next door the *Blue Dolphin Motel* (tel 68 6700) is $29/32 and up for a single/double. Or there's the *Golden Sands Hotel-Motel* just up the hill at $30 double.

Nambucca Heads has a clutch of caravan parks, most with tent sites and on-site vans – the *White Albatross* is by the river mouth, and the *Headland Caravan Park* actually overlooks Main Beach. Holiday flats include *Marcel Towers* (tel 68 7041) on Wellington Drive by the river, which has flats from $23 a double.

Places to Eat

A Pizza This A Pizza That at 40 Bowra St, the upper half of the main street, has great pasta dishes at $7, pizzas from $7 to $14. It's BYO and does take-aways. *Nambucca Heads Bowling Club* on Nelson St does main meals of the steak and seafood variety for around $6 to $7. It's open for meals from 12 to 2 pm and 6 to 8 pm daily and sometimes has a good $8.50 smorgasbord offer.

Getting There & Away

Nambucca Heads is on the main rail route from Sydney to the north – but unfortunately the station's three km from town. Most bus companies go into the town on at least some of their Sydney to Brisbane runs – it's about $30 from Sydney or Brisbane, and $27 from Byron Bay.

INLAND FROM NAMBUCCA HEADS

Bellingen is a pleasant, small town on the banks of the Bellingen River, reached by turning off the Pacific Highway near Urunga, a popular fishing spot with a coastal lagoon, about halfway from Nambucca Heads to Coffs Harbour. At Bellingen you can hire two person canoes at the Oasis Cafe.

From here the road climbs steeply up to Dorrigo. The rainforest of Dorrigo National Park is known for its orchids. There are several good walking tracks and it's well worth making the drive through dense forest to the Never Never picnic area, from where you can walk to waterfalls. Camping isn't allowed in the park but there's a range of accommodation, including camping sites, in Dorrigo. The

Dorrigo National Park Visitor Centre (tel 57 2309) is at The Glade picnic area.

Around Ebor, west of Dorrigo, the road to Armidale passes between two national parks on the eastern slopes of the New England plateau – New England with rainforest, heaths, valleys, escarpments and a 30 km walking track network, and Cathedral Rock with spectacular rock formations. In the New England park there is a camping site and two cabins in the Point Lookout area near the park entrance – for information and cabin bookings contact the Dorrigo Visitor Centre. The views back towards the coast from Point Lookout are wonderful if the weather's clear.

North of Ebor and reached from the Grafton to Ebor or Grafton to Newton Boyd roads, Guy Fawkes River National Park is a vast wild area of the New England foothills – great if you like bushwalking for days without seeing anyone. Wildlife is abundant, including platypus in most of the river pools, but facilities are minimal and access difficult.

Coffs Harbour

Population 44,300

With Port Macquarie, Coffs Harbour is the other major central north coast resort. The town centre is busy and nothing to write home about, but there's a harbour and some interesting headlands and a string of good beaches stretch north. Coffs is a base for white-water rafting and river canoeing forays inland, or for visiting the area's national parks. There's a collection of attractions and a bit of nightlife.

Information & Orientation
The Pacific Highway runs through town and it's called Grafton St in the middle. Between Vernon St and Park Ave off Grafton St in the town centre, there's a pedestrian mall encompassing part of High St, where the helpful Tourist Information Centre (tel 52 1522) is. High St runs three km east from the centre, down to the harbour after which the town is named. The harbour end of town is known as The Jetty.

Around Town
Timber used to be the major industry here, but has been overtaken by tourism. Banana growing is also big and Coffs is famed for its Big Banana – 10 metres long in reinforced concrete (you can walk through it) on the Pacific Highway three km north of town. Immortalised in thousands of visitors' photographs, this is part of a banana complex! You can have a look around the banana plantation on the hill behind or sample banana cake, a banana split, a banana shake or even a chocolate covered banana. Open daily from 8.30 am to 5.30 pm, it's free.

In the town, the recently created North Coast Botanic Gardens on Hardacre St off High St, near the town centre, focuses on subtropical coastal flora and is open daily from 10 am to 5 pm. Down at the end of High St the old timber loading jetty still stands in the harbour. There are good views from the lookout above the harbour up at the top of Edinburgh St, or from Corambirra Point on the south side of the harbour. You can walk out along the northern harbour wall to Mutton Bird Island, a nature reserve where mutton birds (more formally called wedge-tailed shearwaters) breed. They lay eggs in underground burrows.

On Orlando St, near the town's Park Beach, there's a Pet Porpoise Pool, with shows twice daily, where you can pat a porpoise, and look at sharks, kangaroos and other beasts. On Park Beach Rd near the corner of the Pacific Highway, the Aquajet is Coffs' water slide. Out of town Kumbaingeri Land is an Australian fauna park 14 km north on the Pacific Highway close to Moonee Beach (open daily). Bruxner Park Flora Reserve with a nature trail, walking tracks and fine views over

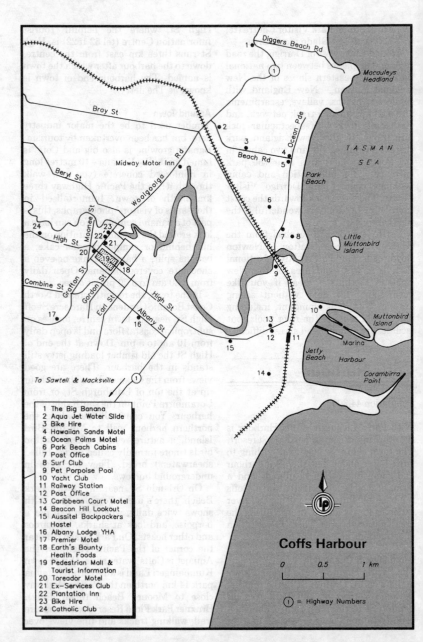

1 The Big Banana
2 Aqua Jet Water Slide
3 Bike Hire
4 Hawaiian Sands Motel
5 Ocean Palms Motel
6 Park Beach Cabins
7 Post Office
8 Surf Club
9 Pet Porpoise Pool
10 Yacht Club
11 Railway Station
12 Post Office
13 Caribbean Court Motel
14 Beacon Hill Lookout
15 Aussitel Backpackers Hostel
16 Albany Lodge YHA
17 Premier Motel
18 Earth's Bounty Health Foods
19 Pedestrian Mall & Tourist Information
20 Toreador Motel
21 Ex–Services Club
22 Plantation Inn
23 Bike Hire
24 Catholic Club

Coffs Harbour

0   0.5   1 km

① = Highway Numbers

the coast, is nine km north-west in Orara East State Forest near Korora. Beyond Bruxner Park you can drive on to another fine lookout point at the top of 900 metre Mt Coramba, about 15 km out of Coffs.

Just eight km south of Coffs Harbour, Sawtell is a popular resort and fishing town.

Beaches

Diggers Beach, protected by two headlands about three km north of the centre and reached by turning opposite the Big Banana, is worth travelling to. It has a nude section. The long beach nearer the town, leading up towards Diggers from the harbour, is called Park Beach. North of Diggers there's another good beach at Korora and then a string of them up to Woolgoolga including Campbells, Sapphire, Moonee, Emerald and Sandys.

The top end of Park Beach, Diggers, the north end of Sapphire, Moonee and Emerald are the places to look for surf.

Activities

Coffs is a centre for 'adventure' activities like white-water rafting on the Nymboida River (medium hard standard, but no experience needed) and canoeing. The season for white-water rafting is November to May and several outfits run day-trips from Coffs – typically you'd pay $60 including two meals. Bushwhacker Expeditions (tel 55 8607) runs $30 Bellingen Valley canoe trips, or for horse trail rides try Valery Trails (tel 53 4301) at Valery, 20 km south-west, where two hours will cost you about $16.

There's interesting scuba diving at the Solitary Islands, a few km up the coast, and Solitary Islands Diver Services (tel 52 2422) are at 396 High St in Coffs. Fishing is popular and it's possible to charter boats at the harbour.

Places to Stay

Except in the hostels, expect prices in school holidays to rise by about 50% in midwinter and about 100% for Easter and Christmas-New Year.

Hostels *Aussitel Backpackers Hostel* (tel 51 1871) at 312 High St, about two km from the town centre, is a lively, busy place with beds at $9 in twin rooms or dormitories. It has bikes to rent and all the usual hostel facilities plus good spacious communal areas. The enthusiastic management will help fix up white-water rafting, canoeing, diving and other trips; and will give a free pick-up on arrival and rides to the beach during the day or the pub at night.

Albany Lodge (tel 52 6462), the YHA hostel at 110 Albany St, a block off High St and only a km from the town centre, is friendly and has a few rooms with double beds. The cost is $9.50 and you can hire bicycles for $5.50 a day. The hostel is open all day and will pick you up if you arrive at a 'reasonable hour' – at night phone in advance to ask. You can fix up trips and activities here and they also run trips including $18 Dorrigo day-trips and a four day $140 expedition to New England.

Motels & Holiday Flats Cheaper motels are around $30/35 a single/double except in holiday seasons when prices can climb very steeply. Motels are strung along the Pacific Highway north and south of the town centre – if you want to be near the ocean, there's a second motel area on Ocean Parade and Park Beach Rd.

Sea Shells Motel at the beach end of Park Beach Rd has doubles at $26. On the corner of Park Beach Rd and Ocean Parade, *Ocean Palms* (tel 52 1264) and the *Hawaiian Sands Motor Inn* (tel 522666) have rooms at $29. The Hawaiian Sands offer a free pick up if you arrive by train or bus.

On the highway is the *Arosa Motel* (tel 52 3826), two km south of the centre, with singles/doubles at $30/32; and the *Premier Motor Inn* (tel 52 2044), a km south, at $28/32. There's the *Caribbean Court Motel* (tel 52 1500) at 353 High St down towards the harbour, with rooms from $30.

The tourist information centre can tell you about holiday flats. These generally cost $35-plus per night and usually demand a seven day minimum booking in the high season.

Camping & Cabins The huge *Park Beach Reserve* (tel 52 3204) on Ocean Parade, one km north of the harbour and just north of the mouth of Coffs Harbour Creek, is right next to the beach and has tent sites at $8.50 a double and on-site vans for a reasonable $17 double. Other places are along the Pacific Highway north or south of town.

Island View Holiday Cabins (tel 53 6753) on Split Solitary Rd, North Sapphire, are pleasant, fully equipped, only 200 metres from the beach and cost $32 a double. *Park Beach Cabins* on Fitzgerald St, 100 metres from Ocean Parade and close to Park Beach, cost from $23 a double.

Places to Eat
As usual in New South Wales, some of the best cheap eats can be found in the various clubs – once you get past the massed ranks of poker machines by which they earn their living! The large Coffs *Ex-Services Club* on the corner of Grafton and Vernon Sts, has cheap lunches and dinners for around $9 in its bistro. For a change of taste, the *Hard Rock Cafe* opposite the Ex-Services Club does good, cheap wholesome lunches and is open at nights from 9.30. The *Catholic Club* on High St, about one km inland from Grafton St, offers even better quality lunches and dinners at reasonable prices and cheap beer.

Cafe Cezanne at 18 Elizabeth St, close to where Grafton St meets the Pacific Highway, has French cooking at its best but it's quite pricey. On Grafton St, near the corner of High St, you have the choice of a Japanese restaurant, the *Ukiyo-Tei*, a Chinese, the *New Red Rose* (with lunch specials) and two pizza places.

There's no shortage of places for a good lunch time feed in and around the mall. Try the *Butternut Pumpkin* at 155 City Centre in the mall, the small food hall upstairs in the Pacific Centre, the busy *Poppie's Coffee Lounge*, or close by, *Coffs Cafe*, halfway between the tourist information centre and Grafton St, for good, plain food for around $7 and cheaper take-aways. The *Tropical Kitchen* on the mall has reasonably priced home-cooked goodies. *Earth's Bounty Health Foods*, on the corner of Gordon and Vernon Sts, has giant-sized burgers for around $2,50 and delicious smoothies.

There's a string of restaurants at the Jetty, the harbour end of High St, a few blocks from the backpackers' hostel, including the *Jade Court*, a Chinese restaurant with lunch time specials for $6 and dinners and take-aways for around $9. In the same block there are Chinese, Mexican, Italian and French restaurants – plus the excellent *Fisherman's Katch* where a slap-up seafood meal will set you back $17 to $23. It's open for Monday to Friday lunches and Monday to Saturday dinners. South of Coffs, the *Sawtell Hotel* has good, cheap seafood meals.

Entertainment
Dukes, a wine bar/restaurant in the block of restaurants at the harbour end of High St often has a singer/guitarist. A couple of km north on Ocean Parade the *Park Beach Hotel Motel*, better known as the Hoey Moey, has bands at weekends, sometimes quite big touring bands. *Crystal's Night Club* in the Ex-Services Club has bands and/or a disco and when top names come to Coffs this is usually where they play.

Getting There & Away
Air Air NSW has direct flights from Sydney ($127), Ballina and Casino; Eastern from Brisbane, the Gold Coast, Lismore, Newcastle, Port Macquarie, Taree and Armidale; and Oxley Airlines from Brisbane and the Gold Coast.

Bus Around 27 buses a day with all the long-distance lines on the Sydney to Brisbane route stop at Coffs. The main stop is in Moonee St just west of the Pacific Highway in the town centre. It's about $30 from Sydney and $28 from Brisbane. Skennars has an inland service to New England (Armidale $13, Tamworth $24).

Train The railway station (tel 52 2312) is down by the harbour at the end of High St. There are four trains a day north and southbound. From Sydney takes nine to 11 hours. Economy fares are $41 from Sydney, $30 from Brisbane.

Boat Coffs is a good place to pick up a ride along the coast on a yacht or cruiser. Ask or put a notice in the yacht club at the harbour – sometimes the hostels know of boat owners who are looking for people to help out.

Getting Around

You can rent motorcycles for $25 a day (plus $50 deposit) from Sports Motorcycles (tel 52 7111) at 70 Grafton St, open daily.

The hostels rent bicycles to people staying with them. You can also rent them at the garage opposite the bowling club on the Pacific Highway, and the Book Exchange (tel 52 4593) on Park Beach Rd opposite the Phillips St corner. A day-trip to the Dorrigo Plateau will cost about $45 in a 4WD, a coach tour to the same area about $30.

Coffs Harbour to Tweed Heads

WOOLGOOLGA (population 2300)

Twenty-six km north of Coffs, Woolgoolga is a pleasant fishing port and small resort with a fine surf beach. It has a sizeable Indian Sikh population who have a gurdwara, the Guru Nanak Temple, on River St, just off the highway at the south end of town. The *Temple View Restaurant* across the road has the best Indian food in the region.

YURAYGIR NATIONAL PARK

Red Rock, off the highway but on the coast 10 km north of Woolgoolga, is on the edge of the southern section of the coastal Yuraygir National Park. Yuraygir covers 60 km of coast in three separate sections, the northern one reaching nearly to Yamba at the mouth of the Clarence River. The park's varied coastal landscape includes quiet beaches, lakes and waterways and there's plenty of scope for activities like fishing, surfing, swimming, canoeing, walking or just lying on beaches. There are several camping sites in the park, plus a range of accommodation in small coastal resorts nearby.

The central section of Yuraygir can be reached from the Wooli Rd off the Pacific Highway 15 km south of Grafton, or from the Maclean to Brooms Head road, north of Grafton. You can reach the northern section through Angourie, south of Yamba, or from the Maclean to Brooms Head road.

GRAFTON (population 16,350)

Grafton, a quiet country town on the Clarence River which flows down from the New England highlands near the Queensland border, is noted for its jacaranda and other tropical trees. There's a Jacaranda Festival in late October to early November. The turn of the century Schaeffer House on Fitzroy St is now a local historical museum. The Lands Department Walking Track west of town offers good views.

Grafton is on the main bus and rail routes north – though now bypassed by the Pacific Highway – and has a range of accommodation, but nothing at the budget level. There's a tourist information centre (tel 42 4677) on Victoria St. You can take cruises on the Clarence River and the tourist information centre can tell you about local farms, breweries and timber mills which run regular tours. There are several interesting national parks in the area and a national parks district office (tel 42 0613) at 50 Victoria St.

The Gwydir Highway, running west up to Glen Innes, crosses Gibraltar Range National Park, with Washpool National Park just to the north, on the rugged eastern slopes of the New England tableland. They feature dramatic mountain, waterfall and rainforest scenery and have camping sites and some walking tracks as well as lots of wilderness.

GRAFTON TO BALLINA
From Grafton the highway follows the Clarence River north-east and the fishing port of Maclean is just off the highway close to the river mouth. Maclean celebrates its Scottish early settlers with a Highland Gathering each Easter.

East of Maclean, off the highway and at the river mouth, Yamba is a fishing town and a small, but busy resort with good beaches and some cheap motels and caravan parks. A ferry links Yamba with Iluka on the north side of the river mouth. There are frequent buses (tel 46 2019) from Grafton and Maclean to Yamba. Just south of Yamba, Angourie is one of the coast's top spots for experienced surfers but beware rip tides. The Blue Pool is a popular picnic spot at Angourie with two very deep pools 50 metres back from the ocean. Angourie is adjacent to the northern section of Yuraygir National Park.

After the Clarence River, Bundjalung National Park lies between the highway and the coast. There are good beaches, canoeing, surfing and fishing in the park, plus lots of wildlife and some old Aboriginal camping sites. The main access points are Iluka and Evans Head at the south and north ends of the park. Both places have camping sites, van parks and motels.

Woodburn is where you turn off the highway for Evans Head, or turn inland for Casino and Lismore. Those with an interest in Papua New Guinea's history may want to see the monument and remains of New Italy, a settlement formed from the tattered remnants of the Marquis de Ray's plan to colonise the New Guinea island of New Ireland.

Evans Head, off the main highway, is a busy prawning centre. You can make a loop off the highway through Evans Head and Broadwater National Park on the coast just north of the town. There are good bushwalks here and superb wildflowers in spring, and Evans Head has some fine surf beaches.

BALLINA (population 12,500)
This busy town, on both the Pacific Highway and an island at the mouth of the Richmond River, is popular for sailing and fishing and has some ocean beaches too. There's often good surf nearby at Black Rock and Speed Reef. Ballina's interesting little Maritime Museum, in the information centre (tel 86 3484) by the river at the south end of Norton St, contains one of the three balsa wood rafts from the La Balsa expedition that drifted across the Pacific from Ecuador to Ballina in 177 days in 1973. This proved whatever one does prove by crossing vast stretches of water in Heath Robinson creations! The museum is open daily.

South Ballina Wildlife Sanctuary, across the Burns Point river ferry on South Ballina Beach Rd, has a collection of Australian fauna and flora. It's open Wednesday to Sunday from 10 am to 5.30 pm.

Ballina has the historic Shaws Bay Hotel in Brighton St, East Ballina, and a busy little shipbuilding yard. Eleven km west on the Bruxner Highway is a Tropical Fruit Research Station open for visits on Monday and Thursday at 10 am.

Places to Stay & Eat
The modern *Ballina Tourist Hostel* (tel 86 6737) at 36-38 Tamar St has single, double and family rooms, a pool and free bikes

and boogie boards for guests. The cost is $9, or $23 for a double room. *Flat Rock Tent Camp* just north of the town is a good tent-only camping ground, next to a surfing beach. There are numerous motels and camping/caravan park too.

Taylor's Restaurant in the town is one of the best seafood places on the north coast, but not cheap at around $16 for a main course. The *RSL Club* has good food and great river views.

LENNOX HEAD (population 2200)

From Ballina the Pacific Highway again runs a little inland but you'll hardly add a km to the journey if you follow the coast road from Ballina to Byron Bay. Lennox Head is the name of both a small coastal town with a fine beach and of the dramatic headland that overlooks it, 11 km out of Ballina and 18 km from Byron Bay. It has some of the best surf on the coast, particularly in winter. Lake Ainsworth just back from the beach is a freshwater lake good for swimming and windsurfing.

Places to Stay & Eat

Lennox Beach House Hostel (tel 87 7636), close to the lake and beach at Lot 2 & 3 Ross St, has small rooms at $9 a head. There's a TV room, a good clean kitchen, and free windsurfers, bicycles and boogie boards for guests. Other accommodation in Lennox Head includes the *Lake Ainsworth Caravan Park* with tent sites over the road from the hostel, and a few motels and holiday flats.

You can get a good meal for $6 to $7 in the *Bowling Club Bistro. Lennox Health & Bulk Foods*, on the main street, has delicious Indonesian meals cooked in banana leaves or, for $3, jumbo chicken, falafel or vegie burgers with salad, cheese and hummus. The *Anglers Arms* pub has bands usually three nights a week.

Getting There & Away

Deluxe, Kirklands and Skennars buses all come through Lennox Head. There are local Blanch's buses to Byron Bay.

BYRON BAY (population 3500)

Byron Bay is one of the most attractive stops on the whole east coast, a relaxed little seaside town with superb beaches and a great climate – warm in winter, hot in summer. Tourism is low key and Byron is a meeting place of alternative cultures: it's a surfing Mecca thanks to the superb surf below Cape Byron just outside the town, and is also close to the 'back to the land' life styles pursued in the beautiful far north coast hinterland. Artists of various kinds also gravitate to the area.

Byron Bay has good music venues, wholefood and vegetarian eateries, offbeat people, distinctive craft and clothes shops, a thriving fashion and surf industry, and numerous opportunities to learn yogic dance, take a massage or naturopathic therapy, have your stars read and so on. The Byron Bay market, in Butler St on the first Sunday of each month, is one of a series around the area at which the counterculture (almost establishment up here!) gets a chance to meet and sell its wares.

Information & Orientation

Byron Bay is six km east of the Pacific Highway. The tourist information centre (tel 85 8050) is in the colourfully painted community centre on Jonson St, about 200 metres south of the roundabout. The best bookshop is the Book Mercer at 6 Byron St. Pick up a copy of the quirky weekly paper *Echo* to get an idea of the unusual way of life around here.

Cape Byron

Cape Byron was named by Captain Cook after the poet Byron's grandfather, who had sailed round the world in the 1760s. One spur of the cape is the most easterly point of the Australian mainland. You can drive right up to the picturesque 1901 lighthouse on top of the cape. The lighthouse is one of the most powerful in the southern hemisphere. There's a fine 3½ km walking track right round the cape

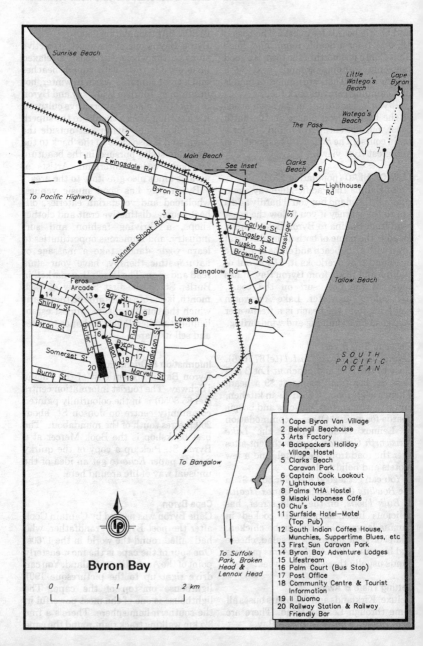

Byron Bay

0   1   2 km

1 Cape Byron Van Village
2 Belongil Beachouse
3 Arts Factory
4 Backpackers Holiday
   Village Hostel
5 Clarks Beach
   Caravan Park
6 Captain Cook Lookout
7 Lighthouse
8 Palms YHA Hostel
9 Misaki Japanese Café
10 Chu's
11 Surfside Hotel–Motel
   (Top Pub)
12 South Indian Coffee House,
   Munchies, Suppertime Blues, etc
13 First Sun Caravan Park
14 Byron Bay Adventure Lodges
15 Lifestream
16 Palm Court (Bus Stop)
17 Post Office
18 Community Centre & Tourist
   Information
19 Il Duomo
20 Railway Station & Railway
   Friendly Bar

from the Captain Cook Lookout on Lighthouse Rd.

Beaches

The Byron area has a glorious collection of beaches, ranging from 10 km stretches of empty sand to secluded little coves, popular sunsoakers' strips to fine surf beaches. Main Beach immediately in front of the town is a good swimming beach and sometimes has decent surf. To the west and north the sand stretches 50 km-plus, all the way to the Gold Coast, interrupted only by river or creek entrances and a few small headlands.

The eastern end of Main Beach, curving away towards Cape Byron, is known as Clarks Beach and can be good for surfers. The headland at the end of Clarks is called The Pass and the best surf is to be found off here and the next beach, Watego's Beach. Little Watego's Beach is a bit further round, almost at the tip of the cape. It's about three km from the town centre to Watego's and a road runs all the way. Dolphins are quite a common sight, particularly in the surf off Watego's and Little Watego's Beaches, and a whale watch is mounted on Cape Byron in June and July each year to count humpback whales migrating from Antarctica to the Great Barrier Reef.

South of Cape Byron, Tallow Beach stretches seven km down to a rockier stretch of shore around Broken Head, where a succession of small beaches (clothes optional) dot the coast before opening on to Seven Mile Beach which goes all the way to Lennox Head, a further 10 km south. You can reach Tallow from various points along the Byron Bay to Lennox Head road, which is parallel to the beach about 750 metres inland. The turning to the small settlement of Suffolk Park (with more good surf, particularly in winter) is five km from Byron Bay.

A further km down the Byron to Lennox road is the turning into the 1¾ km side road leading to the Broken Head Caravan Park at the south end of Tallow Beach.

About 200 metres before the caravan park on this side road, the unsurfaced Seven Mile Beach Rd turns off south and runs along the back of the Broken Head coastal rainforest, a nature reserve. Seven Mile Beach Rd ends after five km (at the north end of Seven Mile Beach), but several tracks lead down from it through the forest to the Broken Head beaches – Kings Beach (for which there's a car park 750 metres down Seven Mile Beach Rd) and Whites Beach (a foot track after about 3¼ km) are just two good ones.

Activities

Julian Rocks, three km offshore, is a meeting point of cold southerly currents and warm northerly ones, with a profusion of marine species from both. You can take diving courses or trips from Byron with Oz Dive (tel 85 6197) on Jonson St near the roundabout or Byron Bay Dive Centre (tel 85 7149) at 9 Lawson St.

Big River Adventures (tel 87 1016) offers $40 canoe day-trips on the gentle Wilson River, where there's a good chance of spotting a platypus. From March to October they run longer and more adventurous trips on the Clarence and Mann Rivers at around $260 for a three day trip. You reach sections of the Mann which are inaccessible by land.

Some hostels will supply surfboards to their guests – or you can hire them from Maddog at 91 Jonson St – $10 for six hours.

Places to Stay

Prices here are higher at holiday times, particularly in summer. Some cafes – especially Suppertime Blues – have notice boards where longer-term places are advertised.

Hostels *Backpackers Holiday Village Hostel* (tel 85 7660), at 116 Jonson St is a clean, friendly, well-equipped place with a small pool. In summer you pay $11 to share a twin room or $25 for a double, and there's one double with bathroom for $30. There are cheaper weekly rates and guests can use the hostel's bicycles, surfboards and boogie boards free.

Three more hostels are varying distances west of the central roundabout – head over the railway crossing. To reach the *Arts Factory Lodge* (tel 85 7709) turn left at the 'Skinners Shoot Rd' sign just past the railway and follow the road (initially called Butler St) for one km. Rooms are around a good-sized pool and you pay $10 a night whether you're in a dorm, a double or a family room. You can camp for $6 a head on a small island in the lodge garden. You can rent bikes too.

Byron Bay Adventure Lodges (tel 85 8231) is at 29 Shirley St, the main road out to the Pacific Highway, about half a km from the town centre. It's another good hostel with a pool, only a couple of minutes walk from Main Beach. Rooms mostly have one double bed and one bunk and you pay $9.50 a head in winter, $10.50 in summer. The hostel is well equipped and clean, with a garden and bicycles for guests.

The third hostel-type place this side of town is *Belongil Beachouse* (tel 85 7868) on Childe St, two km out and just across a quiet road from the beach dunes. Rooms are round a garden and there's a cafe with good, reasonably inexpensive eats and sometimes live music. Rooms take two or three people at $12 sharing or $25 for two. There are bikes for rent and pleasant communal areas. To reach it follow Shirley St west about a km from the centre, then turn right along Kendall St for about a km (Kendall St changes its name to Boronia St then Childe St).

Byron Bay's associate YHA is the *Palms Hostel* (tel 85 6445) about two km south of the centre at 78 Bangalow Rd. This is the cheapest in town at $7 for YHA members or $9 for others (all in dorms) and prices don't rise in summer. The rooms are a bit crowded and it could do with more bathrooms, but it's popular, friendly, open all day, doesn't impose duties and offers free surfboards and bikes. It has a small pool and is about a 10

minutes walk from Tallow Beach. The manager can usually pick you up from the centre on arrival if you ring.

Motels, Flats & Resort Most motels and holiday flats are on Bay St, facing Main Beach, or Lawson St out towards Cape Byron. The small *Beacon Motel* (tel 85 6647) at 6 Bay St, has singles at $29, doubles at $40 to $56 (some with cooking facilities). The even smaller *Hibiscus Court* (tel 85 6195) at 33 Lawson St, is about $32 to $42 single, $37 to $46 double, all with cooking facilities.

For holiday flats you often have to book ahead and commit yourself to several days, but at slack times you'll probably find something on the spot by asking in the tourist information centre or estate agents. Expect to pay at least $55 a night or $250 a week.

The *Byron Bay Beach Resort* (tel 85 8000) out on Bayshore Drive, three km out of town towards the Pacific Highway then 1½ km north, fronts the beach and has tennis, golf and horse riding. Accommodation includes four person cabins with cooking facilities, but shared bathrooms, at $32 a night or $190 a week, and two-bedroom villas with kitchens and bathrooms at $63 a night, $400 a week. Prices go up at holiday times and in the cabins you have to supply your own bedding.

Camping & Caravan Parks *First Sun Caravan Park* (tel 85 6544), council-run, is right by Main Beach, a minute's walk from the town centre and has tent sites at $8.50 to $12 double, on-site vans and cabins at about $23 to $28. Also council-run and with tent sites is *Clarks Beach Caravan Park* (tel 85 3353) a km east of the town centre. Both places levy a charge for day visitors to people staying on the site, and Clarks Beach in particular is not known for its friendliness to suspected 'hippies'.

The other council-run places are the shady *Suffolk Park Caravan Park* (tel 85 3353) beside Tallow Beach, five km south of Byron Bay centre, and *Broken Head Caravan Park* (tel 85 3245), also by Tallow Beach, eight km south. See the earlier Beaches section for directions. Both have kiosks, and tent sites for two cost $8.50 to $12 depending on the season; on-site vans are few in number and cost about $23 and up.

Places with tent sites include *Cape Byron Van Village* (tel 85 7378), one of the cheapest, with on-site vans, cabins, pool and tennis court, two km out of town on the road to the Pacific Highway; the beachside *Byron Bay Beach Resort* (tel 85 8000), more expensive and also with cabins, three km along the same road then 1½ km along Bayshore Drive; and *Glen Villa Mobile Home Park* (tel 85 7382), with on-site vans, on Butler St close to the town centre. The best sites can be full in summer and at Easter.

Places to Eat

Byron Bay has an incredible variety of restaurants, and vegetarians are particularly well catered for.

There are lots of places on Jonson St. Starting from the beach end, the *Waves Bistro* in the fairly seedy Surfside Hotel-Motel (also called the Top Pub) overlooks the beach and offers main meals for around $8 and cheaper hamburgers. The tables outside are a good spot for a beer at sunset. Paul Hogan recently bought the Surfside Hotel-Motel.

Across the street, the very popular *South Indian Coffee House* is open every evening till 10 pm with main courses from around $6 to $10. Just a few doors down, *Cavanbah Coffee Shop* with a few outdoor tables is a busy daytime place with excellent coffee, reasonably priced snacks and breakfast and lunch bargains.

On the same block *Munchies* and the newer *Suppertime Blues* offer similar vegetarian fare, almost side by side. Both are open daily until 6 pm, later in the summer. Munchies has at least 10 'no smoking' signs. Prices are small, servings big. By the roundabout at the corner of

Jonson and Lawson Sts, *Earth & Sea Pizzas* has a large range of pizzas, pasta and salads for reasonable prices. Across the road, the *Oz* and *Thornbirds* cafes are good and cheap for snacks and meals. Oz is popular with travellers, has a notice board and plays good background music. In Feros Arcade, next to Thornbirds, *Annabella's* is a spaghetti bar open to 11 pm in summer, 5 pm on weekdays in winter, later on weekends. The cheap and busy *Indian Curry House* is also in the Feros Arcade.

On Jonson St, between the Earth & Sea and the railway station, you'll find several places in a row, including the more expensive but busy *Katriya*, a Thai place with most main courses over $10. The *Fondue Inn* is next. The idea here is to share main dishes – great value for a group! Another few doors down, *Lifestream* is a large health food eatery with excellent and cheap food, only open from 9.30 am to 5 pm. Nearby in Palm Court, *Panache Creperie* does all manner of pancakes for moderate prices.

The *Railway Friendly Bar*, in what used to be part of the station, is a fine watering hole with outdoor tables and cheap snacks and meals. *Il Duomo* on the corner of Jonson and Marvell Sts has more outdoor tables and is great for a coffee or daytime snack; but evening meals are quite pricey at $12 to $21. Opposite Woolworth's, the long-standing and licensed *Mexican Micks* is still reasonably priced with most main meals less than $12.

In Lawson St, a few metres in the Cape Byron direction from the central roundabout, *Chu's* Chinese restaurant has good cheap food with main meals from $7.50. The *Athena Tavern* over the road is a good, popular Greek restaurant with starters from $4 and main meals from $9.50. It's closed Mondays.

Fletcher St runs the short distance from Lawson St to the beach and here the relaxed *Misaki Japanese Cafe* serves beautifully presented and really delicious food but portions are small. It's open for lunch Wednesday to Sunday and dinner Tuesday to Sunday; main meals start at $6.50. Next door *Coco's* is a licensed French place, upstairs with a spectacular view of the sea in one direction and rolling hills in another. Open from 11 am to 3 am daily, it has a late night supper and cocktail bar and continental cakes and pastries. Further along towards the cape, the *Beach Cafe* just above Clarks Beach has great views, serves breakfast from 7.30 am and does a variety of good snacks.

Entertainment

The *Arts Factory*, also called the Piggery, usually has a band a couple of times a week. There's generally a video dance club on Friday nights. Tickets for such events are often in the $10-plus region but the Arts Factory has a bar and restaurant and usually some food is included in the price. From time to time there are other events like films or fashion shows too. See Places to Stay for how to get there.

The *Railway Friendly Bar* next to Byron's railway station sometimes has bands at weekends, especially after the monthly market. It's a good place for a beer or two in any case, popular with locals and visitors. More regular live music is found at the *Surfside Hotel-Motel*, which has bands several nights a week. The *Services Club* on Jonson St about 750 metres south of the central roundabout, has bands (often touring) once or twice a week (from rock to Kenny Ball) and good free films on Sundays.

Getting There & Away

Bus Numerous buses go through Byron Bay northbound and southbound. To Brisbane it costs $14 to $23 – cheaper with Skennars, Kirklands, Deluxe and Intertour, more expensive with Pioneer Express or McCafferty's. From Sydney costs $35 to $43, with Intertour and McCafferty's among the cheaper lines. From Coffs Harbour costs $15 to $22, from Surfers Paradise it's about $12 to $15.

Kirklands is licensed to avoid the 160 km

limit and take you short distances around Byron Bay – to Murwillumbah, Ballina or Tweed Heads for instance. There are services several times daily to/from Lismore ($5.20), sometimes via Ballina. The local company Swift Express (tel 87 1416) has a weekday service between Brisbane and Ballina through Byron Bay and Lennox Head – but you have to cross the state line on each journey. The main bus stop and booking agent in Byron Bay is Byron Bay Travel (tel 85 6733) in Palm Court, opposite the Great Northern Hotel on Jonson St.

You can get direct buses to Melbourne or Adelaide from Byron Bay – for more details see the Brisbane section.

Train Byron is on the Sydney to Murwillumbah coastal line, but only one train a day comes through in each direction. However there are several coordinated rail-bus services in each direction daily. From Sydney the quickest is the 8 am Holiday Coast XPT, changing to a State Rail bus at Grafton, and reaching Byron at 9 pm. From Byron to Sydney, the 4.45 am bus does the return journey in the same time. The economy fare on these coordinated services is $50. Heading north from Byron, the 8.54 am State Rail bus takes two hours to Surfers Paradise, while the 9.53 am train connects at Murwillumbah with Greyhound buses to the Gold Coast, taking three hours to Surfers Paradise.

Getting Around

Bus Hitching is an accepted part of the scene around the area, but there are a few local bus services, including Kirklands (tel 21 2755) (see Getting There & Away) and Blanch's Bus Service (tel 85 6430). Byron Bus & Coach (tel 85 6554) on Marvell St, has a bus to and from Mullumbimby four times daily Monday to Friday.

Bicycle Hire Most hostels rent or lend bikes to guests, and Backpackers Holiday

Village Hostel on Jonson St will also rent them to non-guests. Maddog (tel 85 6395) at 91 Jonson St, hires them out at $4 an hour or $10 for six hours.

Car Hire Rag Top Rentals (tel 85 8175) at 87 Jonson St, is probably the cheapest with soft-tops at $30 a day including unlimited km. Bigger firms in town include Hertz at 6 Lawson St.

Tours Day-trips in a 4WD to hinterland highlights like Minyon Falls, Mt Warning and the Border Ranges cost around $50 with operators like Damien Wilkinson's Big Scrub Tours. Byron Bus & Coach in Marvell St does some cheaper trips – around $25 – including to the Border Ranges and the Sunday markets at Nimbin and The Channon.

NORTH FROM BYRON BAY

The Pacific Highway continues north from the Byron Bay turn-off to the state border at Tweed Heads. Mullumbimby is a few km north of Byron Bay. Just after the Mullumbimby turn-off is Brunswick Heads, a river-mouth town with a small fishing fleet and several caravan parks and motels.

A few more km up the highway the *New Brighton Hotel*, the old village pub of Billinudgel, is a friendly place for a beer and a counter meal. If you take the next turn to the right off the highway (the sign says South Golden Beach) and work your way through the housing estate to the shore, there's a rough dirt road running north behind the beach, up to Wooyung, and any number of sheltered free camping sites behind the dunes along the way. You can reach the coast by surfaced roads off the highway to Wooyung (from Crabbes Creek) and Pottsville (from Mooball).

A paved road actually runs right up the coast from Wooyung nearly all the way to Tweed Heads and makes an alternative to the Pacific Highway for this stretch. This coast is known as the Tweed Coast, and is much less developed than the Gold Coast

to the north. Bogangar/Cabarita and Kingscliff are two small laid-back resorts where you'll find some fairly cheap accommodation and, in Kingscliff, a pub with the occasional band on weekends.

From Mooball the Pacific Highway continues through Burringbar (close to where busy Lonely Planet writer Geoff Crowther hides out on a banana plantation), over a small range to Murwillumbah.

MURWILLUMBAH (population 7800)

The last sizeable town on the Pacific Highway before you reach the Gold Coast, Murwillumbah is in a banana and sugar cane growing area in the broad Tweed Valley.

There's a tourist information centre (tel 72 1340) over the road from the railway station, on the Pacific Highway, and a range of accommodation including the YHA associate *Riverside Hostel* (tel 72 3763) at 1 Tumbulgum Rd beside the Tweed River. The hostel is open all day and costs $9.50, mainly in separate-sex dorms, though there are also two doubles. They have free canoes and rowing boats for guests, plus evening river trips and a variety of outings of good value to some of the area's many natural highlights, as well as to the weekly Sunday feast at the large Hare Krishna Farm a few km away on Tyalgum Rd, Eungella.

There are several other communes and 'back to the earth' centres in this area and you're within reach of Mt Warning and the spectacular New South Wales-Queensland border ranges. You can cross into Queensland by the Numinbah Rd through the ranges between the Springbrook and Lamington areas (see the Queensland chapter for more details). The excellent Tweed River Gallery is just up the road from the hostel.

From Murwillumbah the main Pacific Highway continues north-east to the coast at Tweed Heads, 31 km away.

Getting There & Away

Murwillumbah is served by nearly all the

buses on the Sydney to Brisbane coastal run (around $38 from Sydney) and is the end of the coastal rail line from Sydney. The overnight Pacific Coast Motorail Express is the only train that makes it this far – $70 for a 1st class seat, $50 in economy. It reaches Murwillumbah at 11 am and connects with Greyhound buses on to the Gold Coast ($4.50 to Coolangatta, and $8 to Surfers Paradise). Going back to Sydney the train leaves at 4.30 pm.

TWEED HEADS (population 44,750)

Tweed Heads, at the mouth of the Tweed River, marks the southern end of the Gold Coast strip and is actually continuous with Coolangatta, the first town in Queensland. The south side of Boundary St, which runs along a short peninsula to Point Danger above the river mouth, is in Tweed Heads and New South Wales while the north side of the same street is in Coolangatta and Queensland. This end of the Gold Coast is a quieter, less commercial place to stay than the resorts closer to Surfers Paradise.

At Point Danger the towering Captain Cook Memorial straddles the state border. The 18 metre high monument was completed in 1970 (the bicentenary of Cook's visit) and is topped by a laser beam lighthouse visible 35 km out to sea. The replica of the *Endeavour*'s capstan is made from ballast dumped by Cook after the *Endeavour* ran aground on the Great Barrier Reef and recovered, along with the ship's cannons, in 1968. Point Danger was named by Cook after he nearly ran aground there too. Three km from Tweed Heads you can get a fine view over the Tweed Valley and the Gold Coast from the Razorback Lookout.

Information

Tweed Heads has a tourist information centre on Wharf St (the Pacific Highway) in the middle of town, open from 9 am to 5 pm daily. Like Albury this is treated as a major entry point to New South Wales for interstate visitors.

Places to Stay

Accommodation in Tweed Heads spills over into Coolangatta and up the Gold Coast. See the Gold Coast section for more details. There's a series of cheapish motels along the last couple of km into Tweed Heads on the Pacific Highway from the south, such as the *City Lights Motel* (tel 54 3004), the *Calico Court Motel* (tel 54 3333), the *Kumul Motor Inn* (tel 54 3405), the *Tweed Fairways Motel* (tel 54 2111) and the *Golden Wanderer* (tel 36 1838). Rates vary with the season, but they usually hang out signs showing prices from around $25 to $40 for a double.

There are several camping/caravan parks between the highway and the river on this side of town. More central is the *Border Caravan Park* by the waterfront on Boundary St, with tent sites and on-site vans. Tweed Heads has a few hotels, and holiday flats like *Panorama* (tel 36 1620) at 16 Boundary St with weekly costs from $115 to $285.

Places to Eat

Fisherman's Cove on Coral St is an excellent and reasonably economical seafood specialist. You can get bistro meals at the *Rowing & Aquatic Club* next door for $6 to $7. Again, see the Coolangatta entries in the Gold Coast section of the Queensland chapter.

Entertainment

The large *Twin Towns Services Club* on the corner of Wharf St and Boundary St, and *Seagulls Rugby Club* on Gollan Drive in West Tweed Heads have regular touring acts.

Getting There & Away

Kirklands buses depart three to five times daily from Tweed Heads to Brisbane for $8.50. Otherwise transport is much the same as for Coolangatta.

Far North Coast Hinterland

The area stretching 60 or so km inland from the Pacific Highway in far north New South Wales is full of interest for the beauty of its green rolling farmland, broken by spectacular forested mountains, and its high population of 'alternative life stylers', 'back to the landers', 'freaks', 'hippies', whatever label you care to apply. These settlers, the first of whom were attracted to the area by the Aquarius Festival at Nimbin in 1973, have become an accepted part of the community now – though there are still occasional run-ins with the drug squad.

Markets & Music

The weekend markets are one place where the colourful alternative community are to be seen in force. The biggest market is at The Channon, 15 km north of Lismore, on the second Sunday of each month. Others are at Uki on the third Sunday of the month, Nimbin on the fourth Sunday, Burringbar on the second Saturday and Mullumbimby on the third Saturday.

There are many accomplished musicians in the area and sometimes they play at the markets or in the village pub after the market (notably at Uki but never at The Channon, which doesn't have a pub). Other places where you can catch good music include the *Chincogan Tavern* at Mullumbimby and the *Kohinur Hall* at Main Arm which has a regular weekly musicians' club. The *Brunswick Byron Echo* newspaper has an informative weekly music column telling who's playing what where.

Getting Around

A web of country roads covers the area and you can nearly always approach a place by one route and leave by another. Nimbin, for instance, can be reached from Lismore, Mullumbimby or Murwillumbah.

If you're planning to explore the area get the New South Wales Forestry Commission's excellent Casino area map ($4) – the tourist information centre in Byron Bay is one place that sells it. There are a few local bus services emanating from Byron Bay, Lismore and Murwillumbah, but hitching is by far the commonest form of public transport.

LISMORE (population 38,250)

Thirty-five km inland from Ballina on the Bruxner Highway to New England, or 48 km in from Byron Bay, Lismore is the interesting 'capital' of New South Wales' far north – the centre of a productive rural district, with a student population from the Northern Rivers College of Advanced Education, and influenced by the alternative community in the country to the north. The rolling landscape between Lismore and the coast was covered in tall subtropical rainforest, known as the Big Scrub, until it was cleared for farming in the late 19th century.

Lismore has a big, new tourist information centre near Wilsons River at the corner of Molesworth and Ballina Sts, and there's a range of accommodation including the central *Currendina Lodge* (tel 21 6118), at 14 Ewing St, which has dormitory bunks at $9.50 plus single and double rooms. There's a TV lounge, a guests' kitchen and breakfast is available. The town has the interesting Richmond River Historical Society Museum, open Tuesday to Friday (50c) and the regional art gallery in the same building.

The Tucki Tucki koala reserve, with an old Aboriginal ceremonial ground nearby, is 16 km south of Lismore on the Woodburn road.

The Channon, a tiny village 15 km north, hosts the biggest of all the region's country markets on the second Sunday of each month and from there it's about 15 km north up Terania Creek Rd into the rainforest of Nightcap National Park. Here a 750 metre walk leads to Protestors' Falls, named after the environmentalists

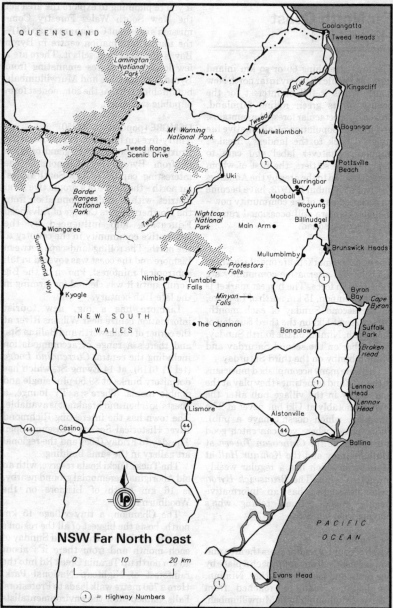

NSW Far North Coast

0   10   20 km

1 = Highway Numbers

whose 1979 campaign to stop logging was a major factor in the creation of the park.

West of Lismore you reach Casino on the main Sydney to Brisbane rail line, with some fine parks and a folk museum. Beyond Casino the Bruxner Highway climbs to Tenterfield in New England.

Getting There & Away

Lismore has daily flights by Eastern from Brisbane, the Gold Coast and some New South Wales coastal towns. By bus, there are several Kirklands services daily from Ballina to Brisbane via various coastal towns for $19. To Byron Bay it's $6. From Sydney costs $40 with Kirklands (change buses at Ballina), or $43 with Pioneer Express. Kirklands runs to Casino, Kyogle and Tenterfield.

The Sydney to Murwillumbah Pacific Coast Motorail train stops at Lismore ($47 in economy). There are three other coordinated rail-bus services daily in each direction, the fastest from Sydney being the 12 hour Holiday Coast XPT which leaves Sydney at 8 am.

NIMBIN (population 1300)

Although Australia's 'back to the land' movement is past its heyday, Nimbin, 30 km north of Lismore, is still a very active alternative centre, with a street of very colourful cafes, murals and shops. This was where the movement to northern New South Wales started with the 1973 Aquarius Festival and there are several communes in the area. Despite a few hassles from the cops and bureaucrats, relations between the old inhabitants and multivaried 'newcomers' are friendly enough now, though you're still quite likely to be asked if you want to buy any ganja as you walk along the street. Nimbin holds a good market on the fourth Sunday of the month and you may catch a good local band playing afterwards.

The country around Nimbin is superb. The 800 metre plus Nightcap Range, originally a flank of the huge Mt Warning volcano, rises north-east of the town and a sealed road leads to one of its highest points, Mt Nardi. The range is part of Nightcap National Park. The Mt Nardi road gives access to a variety of other vehicle and walking tracks along and across the range including the historic Nightcap Track, a packhorse trail which was once the main route between Lismore and Murwillumbah. The views from Pholis Gap on the Googarna road, towards the west end of the range, are particularly spectacular.

The Tuntable Falls commune, one of the biggest with its own shop and school – and some fine houses – is about nine km east of Nimbin and you can reach it by the public Tuntable Falls Rd. You can walk to the 123 metre Tuntable Falls themselves, 13 km from Nimbin. Other good spots include Nimbin Rocks, three km south-west, with an Aboriginal sacred site, and Hanging Rock Creek with a good swimming hole.

Pindari Walkabout (tel 89 1142) at 50A Cullen St (the main street), offers treks and expeditions to the the Nightcap and Border ranges and Bundjalung National Park on the coast – about $30 for the shortest day-trips.

West of Nimbin is Kyogle on the main Sydney to Brisbane railway line.

Places to Stay

Granny's Farm (tel 89 1333), an associate YHA hostel, is a pleasant relaxed place surrounded by farmland, with platypuses in the nearby creek. There are dorms (with beds, not bunks) for $9 and doubles for $22, more for non-members. The friendly managers will sometimes give you rides to local places of interest. To reach the hostel go half a km north down Cullen St from the centre, turn left just before the bridge over the creek, then about a half km along the track.

Freemasons Hotel in the centre is a lively pub with singles/doubles for $16/32. There's a caravan park beside the swimming pool, a couple of hundred metres along the road that runs beside the pub; for two people camping is $8 ($40 a week), on-site vans are $23 ($85 a week).

Places to Eat

The *Rainbow Cafe* in the middle of town has a pleasant shady garden out the back. Wholesome meals cost from $5 to $7, and delicious cakes are around $1.50.

The *Freemasons Hotel* does pizzas, and *Daisy's Cafe* also on Cullen St – less 'hippie' than the Rainbow – is good for food, juices, carrot cake, etc. *The Gallery* is a more expensive restaurant.

Getting There & Away

On weekdays there are five buses daily each way between Lismore and Nimbin, run by: Nimbin Bus Company (tel 89 1220), 4 Thorburn St, Nimbin; Nimbin Bus Service (tel 21 3858), 16 Esmonde St, Lismore; and Fulton's Bus Service (tel 79 5267), 147 Woodlark St, Lismore. On Saturdays there are two buses each way, none on Sundays. There's the daily Fulton's bus to/from Murwillumbah on weekdays (leaving Murwillumbah at 7 am, returning in the afternoon).

The nearest railway station is at Lismore – if you get the overnight train from the south, you can catch the 8.30 am bus out to Nimbin. Hitching is pretty easy in this part of the world.

MULLUMBIMBY (population 2500)

This little town, known simply as Mullum, is in subtropical countryside just four km off the Pacific Highway between Bangalow and Brunswick Heads. Perhaps best known for its marijuana – 'Mullumbimby Madness' – it's a centre for the long-established farming community and for the alternative folk from nearby areas like Main Arm.

There's a tourist information centre (tel 84 1286) at the north end of Dalley St, near the library, and an arts gallery at the corner of Burringbar and Stuart Sts. Cedar House is an old station agent's home in the town, now full of antiques. It's open daily.

West of Mullum in the Whian Whian State Forest, Minyon Falls drop 100 metres into a rainforest gorge. There are good walking tracks around the falls and you can get within a couple of minutes' walk by conventional vehicle, from Repentance Creek on one of the back roads between Mullum and Lismore. The eastern end of the historic Nightcap Track (see Nimbin) emerges at the north of Whian Whian State Forest.

Places to Stay & Eat

The *Mullumbimby Motel* (tel 84 2387) at 121 Dalley St (the south end) has singles/doubles at $30/35.

Mullum has a good collection of health food shops and cafes – including the *Downunder Coffee Shop* on Burringbar St with nothing above $3 – and you'll see some interesting characters in the streets. The *Chincogan Tavern* on Burringbar St does good, imaginative counter meals and has live music a couple of nights a week.

Getting There & Away

There's a four times daily bus service from Byron Bay on weekdays by the Byron Bus & Coach company, and most Kirklands buses go through Mullum on their Lismore, Byron, Brisbane run. Mullum's on the Sydney to Murwillumbah railway, served by one train daily each way.

MT WARNING

The dramatic peak of this 1156 metre mountain is a landmark dominating the whole New South Wales far north region. Mt Warning is solidified volcanic lava – the remains of the central vent of a volcano 20 million years old. Erosion has since carved out the deep Tweed and Oxley Valleys around Mt Warning, but on the far sides of those valleys outer flanks of the volcano remain as the Nightcap Range in the south and parts of the border ranges to the north. Mt Warning was named by Captain Cook as a landmark for avoiding Point Danger off Tweed Heads.

A six km sealed road leads part of the

way up the mountain from the Murwillumbah to Uki to Nimbin road: it's a great four hour walk through rainforest to the summit and back. If you're on the summit at dawn you'll be the first person on the Australian mainland to see the sun's rays that day!

Places to Stay & Eat

Mt Warning is a national park and camping isn't allowed, but *Wollumbin Refuge Caravan Park* (tel 79 5120), four km down the hill on the Mt Warning approach road, has tent sites, cabins and on-site vans. *Mt Warning Forest Hideaway* (tel 79 7139), 12 km south-west of Uki on Byrrill Creek Rd, has motel units with everything supplied including cooking gear, at $30 to $35 single, $35 to $45 double. Meals are available.

The little village of Uki just below the mountain holds a mellow hippie/country market on the third Sunday of the month, and there are counter lunches at Uki's *Mt Warning Hotel*.

Getting There & Away

Fulton's (tel 79 5267 in Lismore) runs a bus on weekdays from Murwillumbah to Uki, Nimbin and Lismore, leaving Murwillumbah at 7 am and returning in the afternoon. It passes the foot of the six km Mt Warning approach road.

BORDER RANGES

The Border Ranges National Park covers the New South Wales side of the McPherson Range along the New South Wales-Queensland border and some of its outlying spurs. The Tweed Range Scenic Drive – gravel but usable in all weathers – loops through the park about 100 km from Lillian Rock (on the Uki to Kyogle road) to Wiangaree (on the Kyogle to Woodenbong road). It's well worth the effort of finding this fine drive which goes through mountain forest most of the way, with some steep hills and really breathtaking lookouts over the Tweed Valley to Mt Warning, and the coast 40 km away. The

adrenalin-charging walk out to the crag called The Pinnacle – about an hour from the road and back – is not for vertigo sufferers! There's a free camping site at the western edge of the park, about 12 km north of Wiangaree.

New England

New England is the area along the Great Dividing Range stretching north from around Newcastle to the Queensland border. It's a vast tableland of valuable sheep and cattle country with many good fishing and bushwalking areas, photogenic scenery and much to recommend it. The New England Highway, running north from Newcastle up to Warwick in Queensland, is an alternative to the coastal Pacific Highway. Scenically the several roads climbing up to New England, particularly on the eastern side, are more spectacular than the tableland itself where too many trees have been cut down. If you're travelling up and down the eastern seaboard, it's worth taking a longer route through an inland area like New England now and then, to get a glimpse of non-coastal Australia – which has a different way of life, is at least as scenic as the coast, and suffers from a great deal less tourist hype.

Places to Stay

Every town has the usual selection of camping/caravan parks, motels and older, central hotels.

Getting There & Away

East-West Airlines and to a lesser extent Eastern Airlines operate flights to New England towns. There are also trains, with XPT expresses going as far north as Armidale.

Bus Several major companies operate through New England on some of their Melbourne to Brisbane or Sydney to

Brisbane services, but the New South Wales bus travel restrictions apply. Regional services – which anyone can use – include Skennars to/from Brisbane and the Coffs Harbour to Port Macquarie strip of the New South Wales coast. Border Coaches (tel 72 5774 in Armidale) runs daily between the New England towns and Brisbane – slightly slower and cheaper than the major operators. Kirklands has a Lismore to Tenterfield service on weekdays only.

NEWCASTLE TO TAMWORTH
Singleton is a coal mining town in the Hunter Valley and one of the oldest towns in New South Wales. At Burdekin Park there's a historical museum in the jail built in 1841. Lake Liddell, north-west of the town, is a water sports centre. You're still in the coal mining area at Muswellbrook. Aberdeen overlooks the Liverpool Plains. Scone is in beautiful country and has a Historical Society Museum. The rural *Scone YHA Hostel* (tel 45 2072) is actually 10 km east at Segenhoe. There's a coal seam at nearby Burning Mountain, Wingen, which has been burning for over 1000 years.

Murrurundi is on the Pages River in lush, green countryside. Quirindi is high in the Liverpool Ranges, slightly off the New England Highway which continues north to Tamworth. It has a big country horse racecourse, with the Quirindi Cup on the last Saturday in February the top event.

TAMWORTH (population 35,000)
Spend much time driving the country roads of Australia and listening to a radio and you'll soon realise that country music has a big following. Tamworth, believe it or not, is the country music centre of the nation: an antipodean Nashville. Each January there's a week-long country music festival here culminating in the Australia Day weekend when the Australasian country music awards are handed out.

At CWA Park there's the Country Music Hands of Fame memorial with the hand imprints of many Australian country and western singers. The tourist information centre (tel 66 3641) is in the park, on the corner of the New England Highway and Kable Ave. Tamworth also has numerous craft workshops and galleries.

The best value of the many motels are on the New England Highway (Newcastle road) on the south side of town. These are several dollars cheaper than any motels in Armidale, the next sizeable place on the highway going north.

Nundle is a historic gold mining town, 63 km south-east, where you can still fossick. Gunnedah is west of Tamworth in the Namoi valley, about halfway to Coonabarabran and the Newell Highway. North of the Tamworth to Gunnedah road, Lake Keepit is a popular water sports centre. Gunnedah has a council caravan park with on-site vans and tent sites at $8, plus six hotels and six motels. All animals at the Waterways Wildlife Park, seven km west of Gunnedah, are reportedly treated like pets – just to make up for all those roadside kangaroo corpses!

The country due north of Tamworth is covered in the New South Wales North-West section.

TAMWORTH TO ARMIDALE
Walcha is off the New England Highway on the eastern slope of the Great Dividing Range, on the winding Oxley Highway route to the coast at Port Macquarie. There's a Tiger Moth, the first aircraft used in Australia for crop dusting, on display at the Pioneer Cottage. East of the town is the Apsley Gorge with magnificent waterfalls.

Back on the highway, Uralla is where the noted bushranger Captain Thunderbolt was buried in 1870. Thunderbolts Rock, by the highway seven km south of town, was one of his hide-outs. Today the graffiti that cover it are almost as unintelligent as the 'Asians Out' scrawls you'll see elsewhere along the New England Highway. In the 1850s this was a gold rush area and some fossicking is still carried on near the Rocky River diggings.

ARMIDALE (population 20,650)

The main centre in the region and site of the New England University, Armidale is a popular halting point. The 1000 metre altitude means it's pleasantly cool in the summer. The town centre is attractive with a pedestrian mall and some well kept old buildings. The tourist information centre and bus station are close by on the corner of Marsh and Dumaresq Sts. Centrally placed on the corner of Rusden and Faulkner Sts, the Armidale Folk Museum is in an 1863 building and is open daily from 1 to 4 pm. The excellent New England Regional Art Museum is on Kentucky St, south of the town centre, and is also open daily. There are a number of other interesting early buildings and fine parks.

Off the Armidale to Kempsey road you can visit Hillgrove, a gold mining ghost town 27 km east of Armidale, on the edge of an impressive gorge area. The Hillgrove Rural Life & Industry Museum is open Wednesday, Saturday and Sunday from 2 to 5 pm, plus 11 am to 1 pm weekends only. The Armidale area is noted for its magnificent waterfalls including the Wollomombi Falls, 39 km east and close to the Armidale to Kempsey road, whose 457 metre drop makes them the highest in Australia. Wollomombi Falls are part of the Oxley Wild Rivers National Park and there are walking trails around and to the bottom of the gorge here. Other falls include the fine Chandler and Dangar Falls. See the Port Macquarie to Coffs Harbour section for more information on national parks east of Armidale.

Places to Stay

Motels are quite expensive – the cheapest are on the New England Highway on the north side of town at the top of the hill and they cost around $37 double. In the town centre there are a few old hotels like *Tattersalls* on Beardy St with rooms around $23/29 a single/double.

ARMIDALE TO TENTERFIELD

Guyra is at an altitude of 1300 metres making it one of the highest towns in the state. There are fine views from Chandlers Peak and, 12 km before Glen Innes, unusual 'balancing rocks' at Stonehenge. You're still at over 1000 metres at Glen Innes which was a good place to meet bushrangers a century ago. The town's old hospital now houses a huge folk museum with the unusual name 'Land of the Beardies'. Glen Innes is still a centre for sapphire mining and you can fossick at Dunvegan Sapphire Reserve on Reddeston Creek. The Gwydir Highway down from Glen Innes to Grafton passes through the Gibraltar Range National Park and close to the Washpool National Park – see the earlier Grafton section.

Tenterfield is the last town of any size before the Queensland border. In the town you can visit Centenary Cottage, dating from 1871, now the centre of a local museum complex, Hillview Doll Museum with more than 1000 dolls on display, and Stannum, a fine old home built in 1888. The Sir Henry Parkes Memorial School of Arts is where Parkes launched the national federation movement in 1889. *Tenterfield Lodge & Caravan Park* (tel (067) 36 1477) at 2 Manners Rd, close to the railway station, is an associate YHA hostel as well, charging $10.

Thunderbolts Hideout, where bushranger Captain Thunderbolt did just that, is 11 km out of town. The rough Mt Lindesay Highway gives access to two small national parks in the spectacular granite boulder country north of Tenterfield. In Boonoo Boonoo (pronounced something like 'bunna b'noo') National Park, entered 22 km from Tenterfield, the Boonoo Boonoo River plunges 210 metres into a gorge at the falls of the same name. In Bald Rock National Park, 35 km from

Tenterfield, 213 metre high Bald Rock is the country's second biggest monolith (after Ayers Rock). It's a relatively easy walk to the top where you'll enjoy superb views over Queensland and New South Wales. You can camp near its base.

South Coast

Though much less well known than the north coast between Sydney and Queensland, New South Wales' south coast from Sydney to the Victorian border has a number of attractive spots including some excellent beaches, of both the secluded and sociable types, good surf and diving in many places, some interesting little fishing towns and lovely national parks. There are a number of small resorts – this is a popular area for Victorian holiday-makers – and, inland, fine mountain national parks like Morton, Deua and Wadbilliga. The Snowy Mountains, Australia's highest, are 150 km in from the southern part of the coast.

The Princes Highway runs right along the south coast from Sydney through Wollongong and on to the Victorian border. Although this is a longer and slower route between Sydney and Melbourne than the Hume Highway, it's infinitely more interesting.

Places to Stay

The towns and small resorts along the coast have camping/caravan parks where you can get an on-site van for around $23 or pitch a tent for $8 or so. There are also the usual motels from the $30/35 a single/double bracket in most places, and in between the settlements some good secluded beach camping spots.

Getting There & Away

Air NSW flies to Merimbula from Sydney, Kendell Airlines from Melbourne. Hazelton Airlines flies to Moruya. The railway from Sydney only goes as far south

as Nowra (160 km). There are rail-coach coordinated services to most towns further south, but they aren't very frequent and involve a circuitous inland route. By bus, Greyhound, Pioneer Express and Deluxe travel the Princes Highway route. Typical fares to Sydney include Bega $27 (eight hours), Narooma $24 (seven hours), Batemans Bay $24 (six hours).

Pioneer Motor Service, runs buses between Eden and Sydney, often a couple of dollars cheaper than the bigger lines. With this line journeys to/from Sydney must be from/to at least as far away as Milton. Murrays' has daily buses between Canberra and the coastal strip from Nowra to Narooma, while Pioneer Express has a three times weekly Canberra to Bega service.

WOLLONGONG (population 209,000)

Only 80 km south of Sydney is New South Wales' third largest city, an industrial centre which includes the biggest steelworks in Australia at Port Kembla. Despite this, Wollongong has some superb surf beaches and the hills soar up behind, giving a fine backdrop, great views over the city and coast, and good walks. And Wollongong is friendly to visitors. The name Illawarra is often applied to Wollongong and its surrounds – it also refers specifically to the hills behind the city (the Illawarra Escarpment) and the coastal Lake Illawarra to the south.

Information & Orientation

The Leisure Coast Tourist Association has an information centre (tel 28 0300) at 87 Crown St which is open from 9 am to 5 pm Monday to Friday, 10 am to 4 pm at weekends. As well as the usual tourist information they organise tours and book accommodation. Just up the hill (inland) from here Crown St becomes a pedestrian mall for two blocks, emerging at the top on Keira St which is another important street, part of the Princes Highway.

Wollongong

1 Hospital
2 Plant Room Restaurant
3 Wollongong Post Office
4 Australian Airlines Office
5 Hotel Illawarra
6 Wollongong Travel Centre
7 Old Lighthouse
8 Wollongong YHA
9 Railway Station
10 Tattersalls Hotel
11 Squirrels
12 Globe Lane
13 Art Gallery
14 Ansett Airlines Office
15 Wollongong East Post Office
16 Tourist Office
17 Historical Museum
18 New Lighthouse
19 NRMA
20 International Centre

Through traffic bypasses the city on the Southern Freeway which runs from near Shellharbour, south of Wollongong, to Royal National Park in the north.

The Wollongong GPO is at 296-98 Crown St near the railway station, but you actually might find the Wollongong East Post Office, lower down Crown St near the tourist centre, more convenient. The NRMA (tel 29 8133) is on the corner of Burelli and Kembla Sts. Wollongong Saddlery & Bushcraft Equipment at 90 Burelli St is interesting; they have bushwalking gear and there are also surplus shops on Crown St.

Things to See

Ask at the tourist information centre about tours of the steelworks – they may be starting again. Wollongong has an interesting harbour, with the fishing fleet based in the southern part called Belmore Basin, which was cut from solid rock in 1868. There's a fish market, a couple of fish restaurants and an 1872 lighthouse beside the harbour. The lighthouse is open weekends from 1 to 5 pm; don't confuse it with the larger, newer lighthouse on the headland. The string of parks along the city shoreline make Wollongong a surprisingly attractive place.

The Illawarra Historical Society's museum is on Market St, open Wednesday from 10 am to 1 pm, Saturday, Sunday and public holidays from 1.30 to 4.30 pm, admission is $1. The museum includes a reconstruction of the 1902 Mt Kembla village mining disaster.

The Wollongong City Gallery on Keira and Burelli Sts is open Tuesday to Sunday from 12 noon to 5 pm. The Sea Treasure Cave Museum in the tourist information centre has an interesting little collection of shells and sea animals.

Wollongong's North Beach, north of the harbour, generally has better surf than the south beach and locals reckon it's better for just relaxing too! The harbour itself has beaches which are good for children. The Wollongong Botanic Garden on Northfields Ave, Keiraville, has both tropical and temperate plants and a lily lake.

Out of Town

The hills rise suddenly and dramatically behind Wollongong and there's a range of walking tracks and lookouts on Mt Kembla and Mt Keira less than 10 km from the city centre, but no buses go up there. You get spectacular views over the town and coast from the Bulli ('bull eye') Pass on the Princes Highway, just north of Wollongong. The country is equally spectacular to the south if you head inland through the Macquarie Pass National Park to Moss Vale or through the Kangaroo Valley. The Fitzroy Falls and other attractions of mountainous Morton National Park can be reached by either route. On the road to Moss Vale you can see a fine local example of Australian kitsch – a huge potato in the middle of town. Yes, this is spud country.

Up the coast there are several excellent beaches. Those with good surf include Sandon Point, Austinmer, Headlands (only for experienced surfers) and Sharkies. On the road to Otford and Royal National Park, the Lawrence Hargraves Lookout at Bald Hill above Stanwell Park is a superb clifftop viewpoint. Hargraves, a pioneer aviator, made his first attempts at flying in the area early this century. Hang gliders hang out there today. If you want to try hang gliding, courses are offered by Aerial Technics (tel 94 2545). Australian wildlife roams free at the Symbio Animal Gardens, Helensburgh.

Just south of Wollongong, Lake Illawarra is popular for water sports and there are also a number of reservoirs and dams in the vicinity. At Jamberoo Recreation Park some 30 km south you can choose from grass skiing, bobsleds, a twin water slide, a mini motor racing track and swimming pools. The Barren Grounds Fauna Reserve on top of Jamberoo Mountain has a bird observatory.

Places to Stay

Hostel The recently opened *Wollongong YHA* (tel 26 2447) is on the top floor of the Piccadilly station arcade at 341 Crown St, near the railway station. There are dorms or family rooms, for $13 or $17 with meals. Many rooms have bathrooms and there are the usual hostel facilities including a kitchen.

Guest Houses Many of Wollongong's guest houses won't take casual visitors, but you could try the *Excelsior Guest House* (tel 28 9320) at 5 Parkinson St, off the top end of Crown St near the hospital. The weekly rate is $85 per person including breakfast and dinner.

Hotels Several hotels offer an alternative to the hostel – nothing luxurious, but straightforward and clean. *Tattersalls Hotel* (tel 29 1952) at 333 Crown St, just down from the station, has decent rooms for $21/35 a single/double, and you can get reasonably priced food. On the corner of Keira and Market Sts the marginally dowdier *Hotel Illawarra* (tel 29 5411) also charges $21/35, $5 more with continental breakfast.

Nearer the sea at 124 Corrimal St, between Crown and Market Sts, the *Harp Hotel* (tel 29 1333) charges $35/50 a single/

double with breakfast and attached bathrooms. Four km south at Figtree, also on the Princes Highway, the *Figtree Hotel* (tel 28 4088) offers attached bathrooms and tea-making facilities for $30/40, plus $6 for breakfast.

Motels Central Wollongong motels are expensive, but south at Figtree, *Sunsets Figtree Village* (tel 71 1122) on the Princes Highway has rooms at $44/52 a single/double. At Fairy Meadow, 3½ km north of Wollongong, the *Cabbage Tree Hotel-Motel* (tel 84 4000) has units for the same prices.

Camping You have to go a little way out before you can camp. The Wollongong City Council have camping areas at Corrimal (at the beach), Bulli (in Farrell Rd, adjacent to the beach) and Windang (in Fern St with beach and lake frontage). Bulli is 11 km north, Corrimal about halfway there and Windang is 15 km south, between Lake Illawarra and the sea. All charge $6 to $8.50 for two people.

There's another camping ground in Windang – the *Oasis Resort* (tel 95 1591) at 142 Windang Rd. It's more expensive to camp ($12 for two) but it does have on-site vans ranging from $30 to $36 and family motel rooms taking up to six people for $90.

Colleges *International House* on the Princes Highway in North Wollongong has accommodation during the vacations.

Places to Eat

The *Plant Room* on Crown St opposite the corner of Gladstone Ave, just up the hill from the railway station, opens seven nights a week. It has a relaxed atmosphere and a tasty, cosmopolitan menu. A main course will set you back about $9 to $12. This is a good place for a late night coffee.

Elsewhere, the pubs offer good value although there are also lots of coffee lounges open during the day. At the *International Centre*, 28 Stewart St, between Kembla and Corrimal Sts, you can enjoy moderately priced Italian food plus steaks and seafood – $7 to $10 for main courses. It's open for lunch and dinner. Vegetarians can head for *Squirrels* in Globe Lane off the top end of Crown St Mall. It has a long, reasonably priced menu.

Good-priced snacks and meals at breakfast and lunch time are available at *Tattersalls Hotel* at 333 Crown St by the railway station. *Hal's Tavern* on the corner of Keira and Burelli Sts does lunch specials for $6.50 to $8.50 and smaller dishes $3.50 to $5. It's a clean, spacious place with a small beer garden.

For seafood down by the harbour there's the good, but expensive *Harbour Front Restaurant* and a reasonably priced cafe with meals at around $5 or $6.

There are a couple of good value Turkish places – the *Topkapi Kebab Restaurant* at 76 Crown St, and the *Istanbul Kebab* next door to the Grand Hotel on Keira St. The *Panorama Hotel* up on Bulli Pass does meals that are almost as good as its fantastic view.

Entertainment

Wollongong activity is mainly in the suburbs – the Friday *Illawarra Mercury* (known as the 'Mockery') has details. The clubs – like the *Illawarra Leagues Club* in Church St, the *Berkeley Sports Club* or the *Dapto Leagues Club* often have weekend bands and non-members can usually get in, except at Corrimal. The *North Wollongong Hotel* has bands, particularly popular on Sunday afternoons. The *Charles Hotel* up at Fairy Meadow and the popular *Cabbage Tree* are others to keep an eye on. Wollongong University Union often has something going on.

South of Wollongong, *Shellharbour Workers Club* often hosts big names. For Sunday afternoon jazz go to the *Panorama Hotel* up on Bulli Pass. Woolshed bushdances are held on Friday and Saturday nights at Albion Park, 20 minutes south near Shellharbour.

Coastline between Sydney and Wollongong

Wollongong's fine new *Performing Arts Centre*, on Burelli St, puts on plays, dance, music and more. There's a Sunday flea market near the railway station. The Wollongong Festival in the first week of the August-September school holidays offers all sorts of activities.

Getting There & Away

Air The local airport at Albion Park, south of town, has some services but generally people use Sydney Airport (Mascot). Watts Coaches (tel 29 5100) operate an Airporter Express bus between Wollongong and Mascot, charging $10.30 for adults. A day return is $16. The main booking and departure point is Wollongong Travel Centre (tel 29 7233) at 193-95 Keira St, between Crown and Market Sts.

You can get to the airport much cheaper, but with a great deal more trouble, by taking a Sydney train to Hurstville, changing there to an Arncliffe train and then making a half hour walk to the international terminal.

Bus Owing to New South Wales bus travel restrictions, the only bus service between Wollongong and Sydney is the Airporter Express. Greyhound, Deluxe, Pioneer Express all have services along the Princes Highway which you can use to get to/from Melbourne ($36) and elsewhere in Victoria, and possibly to places en route on the New South Wales south coast. These companies also have buses from Wollongong to Brisbane via the New South Wales north coast.

Pioneer Motor Service runs buses through Wollongong along the New South Wales south coast: you have to go as far as Milton or beyond to comply with the licensing rules. Murrays has a daily bus to and from Canberra ($26). Wollongong Travel Centre (see Air section) is the chief booking centre and departure point for these services.

Train There are roughly 20 fast electric trains daily to/from Sydney (about 80 minutes, $4 economy), and about 10 a day south along the coast as far as Kiama, Gerringong and Nowra, where the line ends. If you need to catch a second train to get to the part of Sydney you're heading for, you can buy one ticket for the complete journey which is cheaper than buying them separately. There are also a few trains from Wollongong north to Moss Vale, inland near the Hume Highway and Morton National Park.

Getting Around

You can reach a lot of Wollongong from the railway line which has a reasonable service along it. Some of the beaches are accessible by rail and there's a service to Kiama. The main city bus terminal is in Crown St where it meets Marine Drive.

There's a fine 14 km cycleway from Wollongong Harbour north to Bellambi near Corrimal, and there's plenty of scope for other rides including tracks most of the way round Lake Illawarra. Lotap Cycle Hire (tel 84 2796) in Stuart Park, just north of the harbour by North Beach, rents bikes at weekends. You can hire paddleboats, rowing boats, catamarans and power boats at Lake Illawarra, and at Brighton Beach in Wollongong harbour you can hire windsurfers at weekends. Half day tours of Wollongong are available.

WOLLONGONG TO NOWRA

South of Lake Illawarra, Shellharbour is a popular holiday resort. It's one of the oldest towns along the coast and back in 1830 was a thriving port, but it declined after the construction of railway lines. There are good beaches on the Windang Peninsula north of the town.

Kiama is famous for its blowhole: illuminated at night it can spout up to 60 metres high. There is also a Maritime Museum, good beaches and surf, and the scenic Cathedral Rock at Jones Beach. Just south of Kiama is Gerringong with fine beaches and more good surf. Pioneer aviator Charles Kingsford Smith took off from Seven Mile Beach, immediately south of Gerringong and now a national park, to fly to New Zealand in 1933. Take the time to have a look at the excellent Hilltop Gallery on Fern St.

Gerringong has the *Chittick Lodge* hostel (tel 34 1447) on Bridges Rd five minutes' walk back up the hill from Werri Beach. It's a pleasant associate YHA hostel with good facilities and charges $9 whether or not you're a member. The friendly *KA's Coffee Shop* at the top of the hill on Fern St, next to the tourist information centre, does excellent snacks and meals. For other palates the *Gourmet Junk Food* take-away is two doors away.

Berry was an early settlement and has a number of National Trust classified buildings and the almost inevitable Historical Museum. Nearby Coolangatta has a group of buildings now converted for use as a motel which were constructed by convicts in 1822 and are the first buildings in the area.

NOWRA AREA

Inland on Shoalhaven River, Nowra is popular for water sports. The *White House Private Hotel* (tel 21 2084) at 30 Junction St near the centre, is an associate YHA hostel charging $14 a night or $30 for a double (sheet hire extra). You can camp at the riverside Nowra Animal Park. Inland, on the way to Fitzroy Falls, is Kangaroo Valley with old buildings including the Friendly Inn, a pioneer farm museum and a reconstruction of an 1880 dairy farm.

On the coast from Nowra is Culburra-Orient Point, a quiet resort town with a prawning fleet. A bit further south most of the shores of Jervis Bay are untouched bushland. Huskisson is the main settlement on the bay, which is popular with catamaran sailors and windsurfers. The promontory which forms the southern shore of the bay is mostly a nature reserve – though there's also a naval college – and there are some good walks, beaches and beautiful camping grounds, notably Green Patch. Wreck Bay village on the south side of the promontory is an Aborigine settlement. There's also an annexe of Canberra's National Botanic Gardens here for plants which are susceptible to frost.

Ulladulla is an area of beautiful lakes, lagoons and beaches. One traveller recommended the guest house 'halfway up the hill on the main road on the south side of town' run by a woman called Flora. He paid $15 for a single room, could use the fridge and reported that breakfast was available. There's good swimming and surfing in the area or you can make the bushwalk to the top of Pigeon House Mountain (719 metres) in the impressive Budawang Range. It's about a three hour return trip from the end of the road. The mountain is in the south-east of Morton National Park.

BATEMANS BAY (population 5000)

This popular resort is at the mouth of the Clyde River – again there's good bushwalking and swimming. It's also a fishing and diving centre. Along the coast north of Batemans Bay is Murramarang National Park where there's a superb camping site ($3.50 a vehicle) between eucalypt forest and beach at Pebbly Beach. Semi-tame kangaroos hop between the tents, colourful rosellas and kookaburras are among the plentiful bird life. There are some good coast and forest walks in this small national park. You can get to Pebbly Beach, but without your own vehicle you'll have to walk or hitch. It's about nine km off the highway and the turn-off is at East Lynne.

At Batemans Bay you can see Birdland Animal Park or there's a shell museum one km east. It's quite a holiday centre, and river cruises and other tours are available. Prior's (tel 72 4040) run buses between Batemans Bay and Moruya daily except Sunday.

About 80 km inland from Batemans Bay on the route to Canberra is Braidwood with many old sandstone buildings classified by the National Trust and a historical museum. From here there's road access to the superb rugged bushwalking country of the northern Budawang Range. Monolith Valley and The Castle, in the Morton National Park, are a three day or more round trip walk. South of Morton the line of mountain national parks stretches south through Budawang, Deua and Wadbilliga National Parks – all wilderness areas good for rugged bushwalking. The south end of Wadbilliga reaches almost as far south as Bega.

Like other towns along the coast Moruya is a dairy centre but oyster farming is carried on here too. The old Coomerang House is of interest, but south-west is the beautifully situated old gold town of Nerrigundah and the Eurobodalla Historic Museum. There's some fairly unspoiled coast down the side roads south of Moruya, with a good beachside camping ground ($3.50 a vehicle) at Congo, where there are beaches on both sides of a headland.

NAROOMA AREA

Narooma is another oyster town. There are many inlets and lakes nearby. *The Lakes Leathercraft Barn* (tel 76 2824) is an associate YHA hostel about a km inland from from the highway at Narooma, fronting one of the inlets, Forsters Bay. It's a craft farm as well as a hostel and has rowing boats, canoes, fishing and snorkel gear for hire at nominal rates. There's no curfew and it's open all day.

Near Lake Corunna, Mystery Bay has coloured sand and rock formations. Central Tilba, just 15 km south of town, is a little town which has undergone remarkably little change this century. There are now several craft workshops and a cheese factory which gives tastings. Other local attractions include a deer farm, a winery and the landmark of Mt Dromedary which rises behind the village. South of the coastal Wallaga Lake and off the Princes Highway, Bermagui is a fishing centre made famous 50 years ago by American cowboy-novelist Zane Grey.

Inland and on the Princes Highway is Cobargo, another remarkably unspoilt old town. Bega, near the junction of the Princes and Snowy Mountains Highways, is a useful access point to the snow country and it has a small *YHA Hostel* (tel 92 3103) on Kirkland Crescent. Bega also has a couple of good lookout points and the Bega Historical Museum. Mimosa Rocks National Park, on the coast north-east of town, is very picturesque with forests, offshore rock stacks, headlands, islands and beaches. There are some excellent spots to pitch a tent, notably Aragunnu Beach. Candelo, 39 km south-west, is a picturesque little village which, like Tilba, has had a Rip Van Winkle existence.

SOUTH TO THE VICTORIAN BORDER

Continuing south you reach Merimbula – another swimming, fishing and surfing centre. On the main street the Merimbula Old School Museum is just that.

At Eden the road bends away from the coast into Victoria. This old whaling town on Twofold Bay has a whaling museum with a fine killer whale skeleton. The *Australian Hotel* has singles/doubles for around $23/35 and does Chinese take-aways. The bakery over the road is good. To the north and south of Eden is the Ben Boyd National Park – good for walking, camping and swimming.

Boydtown, south of Eden, was founded by Benjamin Boyd – a flamboyant early settler. His grandiose plans aimed at making Boydtown the capital of Australia but his fortune foundered and so did the town – later he did too, disappearing without trace somewhere in the Pacific. Some of his buildings still stand, and the Sea Horse Inn, built by convict labour, is still in use today.

The Snowy Mountains

The first people to ski in Australia were the fur hunters of Tasmania in the 1830s, using three-foot boards. Norwegian miners introduced skiing in Kiandra in the 1860s, and it is the first town in the world where competitive ski races were held. The skis in those days were home-made, crude objects, mainly used for transportation. Early this century the development of the sport began with lodges like the one at Charlotte Pass, and the import of European skis. It slowly developed into the big business and numerous resorts that it is today.

Australia's winter snowfields straddle the New South Wales-Victoria border, but Mt Kosciusko (pronounced 'kozzyosko') in the Snowy Mountains is in New South Wales and at 2228 metres its summit is Australia's highest. Much of the New South Wales Snowies are within the boundaries of the large Kosciusko National Park, an area of year round interest: skiing in winter, bushwalking and vivid wild-flowers in summer. The main ski resorts and the highest country are in the south central part of the park, west of Jindabyne – Thredbo, Perisher Valley, Smiggin Holes, Charlotte Pass, Mt Selwyn, Guthega, Mt Blue Cow and Mt Kosciusko itself are all found here.

The upper waters of the Murray River form the state and national park boundary in the south-west. Another of Australia's best known rivers – the Snowy, made famous by Banjo Paterson's poem *The Man from Snowy River* and the film based on it – rises just below the summit of Mt Kosciusko. The Murrumbidgee also rises in the national park. You can take white-water rafting trips on the Murray and Snowy Rivers in summer when the water is high enough, but the waters are

Alpine vegetation, Snowy Mountains

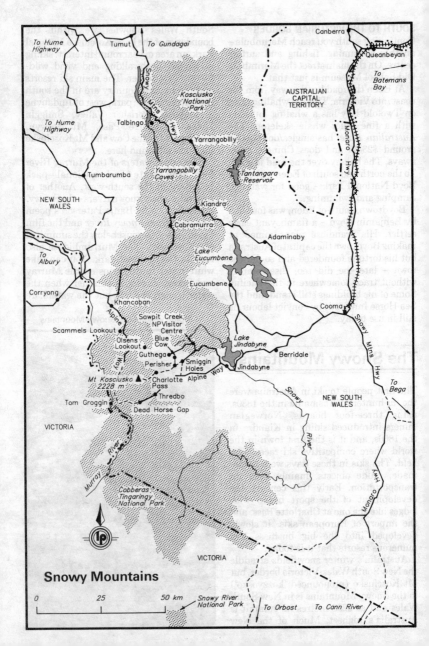

Snowy Mountains

0   25   50 km

Snowy River
National Park

To Orbost   To Cann River

gentler than some you'll find further north in New South Wales and Queensland. In summer, horse trail riding is also popular in the region – there are stables in Cooma, Adaminaby, Jindabyne, Tumut and Tumbarumba.

The Snowy Mountains Scheme is the best known hydroelectric scheme in Australia and irrigates extensive areas of the Murray region west of the mountains. You can visit or view several of the dams and power stations in the mountains.

Getting There & Away

Cooma is the main eastern gateway to the Snowy Mountains. It's at the junction of the Monaro Highway, from Canberra, and the Snowy Mountains Highway, which runs from the Hume Highway and Tumut down to the coast near Bega. The road to Jindabyne and the high Snowies branches off the Snowy Mountains Highway six km west of Cooma. The most spectacular mountain views, however, are from the Alpine Way (sometimes closed in winter) which loops round from Khancoban on the west side of the national park to Jindabyne. Eastern routes up to the high country ascend more gradually and are less dramatic. There are restrictions on car parking in the national park, particularly in the skiing season. Check at Cooma or Jindabyne before you enter the park.

Air NSW flies daily to Cooma from Sydney, Kendell Airlines from Melbourne. Pioneer Express, in conjunction with Snowliner Coaches, has daily buses from Sydney ($33) and Canberra ($16.50), continuing from Cooma up to Jindabyne, Thredbo and Perisher Valley at least twice daily, plus a few buses a week from Bega ($12.50). There are also trains to Cooma from Sydney ($31.50) via Canberra, daily except Sunday. Usually extra transport services are put on in the skiing season. You can rent cars in Cooma.

COOMA (population 8000)

Just 114 km south of Canberra, Cooma

was the construction centre for the Snowy Mountains Scheme. You can walk down Lambie St and see 21 National Trust classified buildings in this interesting town.

A half km west of the town is the Aviation Pioneers Memorial with wreckage of the *Southern Cloud*, an aircraft which crashed in the Snowies in 1931 and was only discovered in 1958. Other attractions include the Avenue of Flags in Centennial Park with flags of the 27 nationalities involved in the Snowy Mountains Scheme. You can see wooden clogs made in Clogs Cabin, while Raglan Gallery, dating from 1854, has painting, pottery and rugs. Eighteen km out on the Adaminaby road is Australia's only llama farm, which you can visit at 10 am or 2 pm Friday to Monday.

Information

The Cooma Visitors' Centre (tel (064) 52 1108), open 8.30 am to 8.30 pm daily, is in the middle of town at 119 Sharp St, beside Centennial Park. For winter snow and road reports ring 52 1108. There's also a Snowy Mountains Scheme Information Centre (tel 53 4218) on Mittagong Rd, Cooma North.

Places to Stay & Eat

Cooma has all types of eateries along Sharp St, its main street, and a large range of accommodation which is generally cheaper than Jindabyne or the ski resorts, so some skiers stay in Cooma and travel up to the mountains daily.

Town centre hotels like the *Alpine, Australian, Royal* and *Dodd's* have singles/doubles for $25/40. Cheaper motels include the *Pine Hill Lodge* at $25/50 a single/double and the *Airport Motel*, $25/40, both on the Snowy Mountains Highway, or, more central, the *Hawaii Motel* at 192 Sharp St charging $42/50. (These are ski-season prices.)

There are also three camping/caravan parks, all with on-site vans.

JINDABYNE (population 1600)

Fifty-six km west of Cooma and a step nearer the mountains, Jindabyne is a new town on the shore of the artificial Lake Jindabyne which covers the old town. In summer you can swim or rent windsurfers or boats on the lake at Jindabyne. The Snowy River Information Centre (tel 56 2444) on Petamin Plaza, just off the main road in Jindabyne, is a helpful tourist information centre.

Places to Stay & Eat

For accommodation inquiries contact the Jindabyne Reservation Centre (tel 56 2457) on Petamin Plaza. Most visitors stay in holiday flats or units of which there are hundreds, ranging from about $17 per person per night, or $230 per flat per week. These apart, there's little in the budget range apart from a handful of camping/caravan parks of which a couple are beside the lake. Motels and lodges are mostly in the $35/45 a single/double range, and up.

There are several eateries around town including the good *Balcony Bistro* on Petamin Plaza, where a grill or seafood dish will cost around $9 or $10 including as much as you can eat from an excellent salad table. A straight plate of salad is $6.

KOSCIUSKO NATIONAL PARK

The 6900 square km of New South Wales' largest national park includes caves, glacial lakes, forest and all of the state's ski resorts as well as the highest mountain in Australia. Although the park is most famous for its snow, it is also popular in summer when there are excellent bushwalks and marvellous alpine wildflowers. Outside the snow season you can drive to within eight km of the top of Mt Kosciusko, up the Kosciusko Rd from Jindabyne past Perisher and Charlotte Valleys. The last section to the summit, from Charlotte Pass, is by footpath. There are other walking trails from Charlotte Pass.

Mt Kosciusko and the main ski resorts are in the south central part of the park. From Jindabyne the Kosciusko Rd leads to the national park headquarters and visitor centre (tel 56 2102, open from 8.30 am to 4.30 pm daily) about 15 km north-west at Sawpit Creek, then on to Smiggin Holes, Perisher Valley (33 km) and Charlotte Pass, with a turn-off before Perisher Valley to Guthega. A shuttle bus operates in winter from the visitor centre to Smiggin Holes and Perisher Valley. In winter you can normally drive as far as Perisher Valley too. There's a privately run camping site (tel 56 2224) at Sawpit Creek close to the visitor centre. Camping is $4.50 a head or there are some chalets at $48 a double, $4.50 for each extra person. Prices go up at holiday and skiing seasons.

The Alpine Way to Thredbo (35 km from Jindabyne) and Khancoban turns off the Kosciusko Rd just outside Jindabyne. The Skitube is a tunnel railway up to Perisher Valley and Blue Cow from Bullocks Flats on the Jindabyne to Thredbo road. A return ticket in 1988 cost $10. Travelling this way means you can avoid the onerous task of having to stop on the sometimes hazardous Kosciusko Rd to fit chains to your car.

SKIING & SKI RESORTS

Snow skiing in Australia can be a marginal activity – the benefits of pushing the mountains up 1000 metres higher or shoving the whole country 1000 km south (but only for the winter!) are frequent topics on ski slopes. The season is short (July, August, September is really all there is) and good snow is by no means a safe bet. Nor, despite claims that Australia offers a larger skiable area than the Swiss Alps, are the mountains ideal – their gently rounded shapes mean most long runs are relatively easy and the hard, fast runs tend to be short and sharp. For a final bummer the short seasons mean the operators have to get their returns quickly and costs can be high.

Having told you the bad, here's the good: when the snow's there (which is less often lately due to warmer conditions) and the sun's shining, the skiing can be just fine. So long as you're not some sort of Jean Claude Killy you will find all the fun (not to mention 'heart in the mouth' fear) you could ask for. Plus, the long open slopes of the Australian Alps are a ski-tourers' paradise – nordic (cross-country or langlauf) skiing is becoming increasingly popular and many resorts now offer lessons and hire equipment.

The cheapest (and by far the most fun) way to get out on the slopes is to gather a bunch of friends and rent a lodge or an apartment. Costs vary enormously but can be within the bounds of reason. Bring as much food and drink as you can, as supplies in some resorts tend to be erratic and they're always expensive.

There's cheaper accommodation in towns like Jindabyne and particularly Cooma, some distance below the ski slopes, than in the resorts like Thredbo and Perisher Valley where the snow's on your doorstep. There are daily buses up from Jindabyne and Cooma to the resorts in the morning and down again in the afternoon. Jindabyne Reservation Centre (tel (008) 02 6331 toll free) can make reservations for all forms of accommodation in Jindabyne, Perisher Valley, Smiggin Holes, Guthega, Charlotte Pass and Thredbo. The Thredbo Resort Centre (tel (064) 57 6360) does much the same just for Thredbo. Cooma Visitors' Centre (tel 52 1108) will also make bookings.

Other costs are ski lifts, lessons and equipment hire. Ski lifts vary depending on the resort, but count on $30 to $40 a day or $190 to $220 a week. Lessons average about $15 to $20 a session. Boots, skis and stocks can be hired for $20 to $30 a weekend or about $60 for a week including both weekends. It's a trade off whether to hire in the city and risk damage and adjustment problems or at the resort and possibly pay more. There are usually hire centres in towns close to the resorts, and many garages hire ski equipment as well as chains. Snow chains must be carried in the mountains during winter even if there

is no snow – there are heavy penalties if you haven't got them.

Australian ski resorts are short of the frenetic nightlife of many European resorts, but compensate with lots of partying between the various lodges. Nor is there a great variety of alternative activities apart from toboggan runs. Australia also doesn't have the range of all-in skiing packages which are the cheapest way to get on the slopes in Europe. Weekends tend to get crowded because the resorts are so convenient, particularly to Canberra.

All the main resorts are connected by bus with Cooma which can be reached by road or air.

Thredbo (1370 metres)

Thredbo has the longest runs (the longest is over three km through 670 metres of vertical drop) and some of the most expensive skiing in Australia. A day ticket costs $38, a five day pass $170 and a five day lift and lesson package costs $225. The new snow-making equipment makes it possible to ski down to the village (just below the snow line) for most of the season. Thredbo hosted World Cup ski races in the giant slalom and slalom competitions in August 1989.

There's a 48 bed *YHA Hostel* (tel 57 6376), but during the ski season it costs $35 on Saturday nights, $25 other nights *if* they allow one night stays. In the summer it's $10. If you want to stay at the hostel in July, August or September, you should apply by April through the main Sydney YHA office. A ballot is held for places.

In summer Thredbo is a popular bushwalking centre with all sorts of excellent and scenic tracks. The chair lift to the top of Mt Crackenback operates right through the summer. From the top of the chair lift it's a two km walk to a good lookout point over Mt Kosciusko, or seven km to the top of the mountain itself.

Perisher Valley (1680 metres)

Rated just one notch below Thredbo (with

a vertical drop of 374 metres) and on a par with the better Victorian resorts Perisher Valley has a wide variety of runs. Together with nearby Smiggin Holes, Perisher has over 100 km of runs and 30 ski lifts. You can reach Perisher Valley either by the Kosciusko Rd or by taking the Skitube. At Perisher/Smiggins a day ticket costs $38, a five day pass costs $180 and, a five day lesson and lift package costs $230.

Charlotte Pass (1780 metres)
At the base of Mt Kosciusko this is the highest and one of the oldest and most isolated resorts in Australia. In winter you have to snowcat the last eight km from Perisher Valley. It has good ski-touring country. There are five lifts at the resort, that service rather short but uncrowded runs.

Smiggin Holes (1680 metres)
Smiggin Holes is just down the road from Perisher and run by the same management so you can get a combined ski-tow ticket for both resorts. A shuttle bus runs between the two resorts and they are also joined by a lift system so it is possible to ski from one resort to the other.

Guthega (1630 metres)
This is mainly a day resort, best suited to intermediate and, to a lesser extent, beginner skiers. *Guthega Lodge* offers the only commercial accommodation. Guthega is relatively smaller, less crowded and serviced by friendlier staff than other places.

Mt Selwyn (1492 metres)
This is the only ski resort in the northern end of the Kosciusko National Park, halfway between Tumut and Cooma. It's another day ski resort – the closest accommodation is at Adaminaby. It has 13 lifts and is an ideal beginners resort.

Mt Blue Cow (1640 metres)
Australia's newest ski resort is between Perisher Valley and Guthega in the Perisher Range. This is a day ski resort (no accommodation at all) accessible by the Skitube. The newest five lifts service a ski area of 4 square km mainly for beginner and intermediate skiers. A day ticket costs $36, a 24 km ticket costs $54 and a 50 km ticket costs $93; tickets are interchangeable.

COOMA TO TUMUT
This 185 km stretch of the Snowy Mountains Highway crosses Kosciusko National Park between Adaminaby and Tumut. Adaminaby is the departure point for Lake Eucumbene. Kiandra, actually in the park, was the site of an 1859 gold rush and the crude ski races organised by miners probably predate the popularity of skiing as a sport in Europe.

KHANCOBAN (population 600)
From Kiandra you can turn south to Cabramurra, Australia's highest town, and continue south to Khancoban, although this road is often closed by snow. From Khancoban the Alpine Way – partly unsealed and also sometimes closed – loops round to the south past some good mountain viewpoints and the Murray 1 power station lookout, to Thredbo and Jindabyne. Two of the best mountain views are from Olsen Lookout, 10 km off the Alpine Way on the Geehi Dam road, and Scammels Spur, just off the Alpine Way.

TUMUT (population 6600)
Tumut is on the Snowy Mountains Highway on the north side of the national park. Australia's largest commercial trout farm is at nearby Blowering Dam. The tourist information centre can tell you about visits to the various centres of the Snowy Hydroelectric Scheme.

Talbingo Dam and the Yarrangobilly limestone caves (60 km east, about midway between Tumut and Kiandra) are other points to visit. The caves are only open at odd times – check at the

Snow gums, Snowy Mountains

tourist information centre. There's also a thermal pool at a constant temperature of 27°C and some beautiful country in the reserve around the caves.

Batlow is south of Tumut in a fruit growing area. There's a 'Big Red Apple' centre if you're collecting notable Australian 'big' tourist attractions. Near Batlow is Hume and Hovell's Lookout where the two explorers did indeed pause for the view in 1824. Paddy's River Dam was built by Chinese gold miners back in the 1850s. Continuing south from Batlow you reach Tumbarumba, site of the early exploits of bushranger Mad Dog Morgan. There's great mountain scenery and good bushwalks in the area and the Paddy's River Falls are only 16 km from the town.

West of Tumut on the Snowy Mountains Highway, before it reaches the Hume Highway, is Adelong, an old gold mining centre with a National Trust classified main street. There's a pleasant picnic

area two km from the town on the Gundagai Rd at the cascade falls.

Along the Hume Highway

The Hume Highway is the main road between Australia's two largest cities. It's the fastest and shortest road and although it's not the most interesting there are places of interest along the route. You can also make some interesting diversions off the Hume. One of the simplest is right at the beginning – when you leave Sydney instead of making the long, weary trek through the outer suburbs towards Camden and Campbelltown you can take the coastal Princes Highway past the Royal National Park to Wollongong. Then just after Wollongong you can cut inland on the Illawarra Highway through the picturesque Macquarie Pass and over beautiful rolling countryside to Moss Vale before rejoining the Hume. Further south you can leave the Hume to visit Canberra or continue beyond Canberra through the Snowy Mountains, rejoining the Hume in Victoria.

Getting There & Away

There are flights to a number of the main towns along the Hume Highway. The Melbourne to Sydney bus services run on the Hume and the train services run close to it. There are several local and area bus services, eg Moss Vale to Nowra or Bundanoon. See the warning in the Victorian Hume Highway section about the dangers of driving on this busy road.

SYDNEY TO GOULBURN

The first 120 or so km out of Sydney can be done on the new South-Western Freeway, avoiding the old Hume. This way bypasses Camden (which with nearby Campbelltown is covered in the Around Sydney section), Picton and Thirlmere.

Picton is an early settlement with a tollkeeper's cottage, an old railway viaduct and the early St Mark's Church of England. The Thirlmere Rail Transport Museum, open weekends and holidays, has about 40 locomotives and other pieces, including an 1864 engine from railway pioneer Robert Stephenson. Wirrimbirra Fauna & Flora Sanctuary is 13 km south.

Mittagong is a local agricultural centre with a tourist information centre on the Hume. Thirty km west of Mittagong, Joadja is now a ghost town. It's on private property but visits can be made at certain times – check in Mittagong. Four km south of Mittagong a winding 65 km road leads west off the highway to the Wombeyan Caves, open from 10 am to 4 pm daily. The drive up is through superb mountain scenery and the caves are in a very attractive bush setting. A little further south on the Hume, Berrima is a tiny town which was founded in 1829 and has changed remarkably little.

Bowral, just south of Mittagong off the highway, is another agricultural centre and from here you can visit the Mt Gibraltar Wildlife Reserve. Bowral was where cricketer Don Bradman, probably Australia's greatest sporting hero, spent his boyhood. In 1926, aged 17, he scored 300 runs for Bowral in a final against Moss Vale, averaging over 100 runs per innings for the season.

Moss Vale is an industrial town just south of Bowral. Throsby Park House, built between 1834 and 1837, is a fine old home built by the area's first settler.

South of Moss Vale are Bundanoon and the large Morton National Park with deep gorges and high sandstone plateaus in the Budawang Range. You can enter the park from several points: two of the easiest are Fitzroy Falls and Bundanoon, both reachable by sealed road from Moss Vale. Bundanoon is also on the main Sydney to Yass railway and has buses from Moss Vale. *Bundanoon YHA* (tel (048) 83 6010) on Railway Ave is a good hostel and you

can hire bicycles in the town. Highlights of the park include the 117 metre Fitzroy Falls on the Moss Vale to Nowra road (where there's camping and a visitor centre), Belmore Falls a few km north, and some good lookout points and walks near Bundanoon. The south of the park offers excellent bushwalks – some for experienced walkers (see the earlier South Coast section).

GOULBURN (population 24,000)
Another Hume centre with a long history, Goulburn was proclaimed a town way back in 1833. It's surrounded by sheep country and as a monument to the source of its wealth there's a three storey high Big Merino beside the Hume Highway in the town, next to where most of the buses stop. It looks truly diabolic with its green eyes glowing at night: in daytime you can climb inside the monster to see displays on wool or watch a 45 minute sheep show, in which examples of Australia's top 20 sheep breeds clamber on to a stage and one of them gets sheared.

Old buildings of interest include the 1840 Riversdale coaching house with its beautiful gardens (open daily except Tuesdays) and Garroorigang, built in 1857, with bushranger, Aboriginal and Victorian displays (also open daily). Other curiosities include the Black Stag Deer Park, a historic brewery and a historic brickworks.

Thirteen km west of Goulburn you can turn south off the Hume along the Federal Highway to Canberra.

YASS (population 4500)
Just east of here, the Barton Highway branches off the Hume for Canberra. Yass is closely connected with the early explorer Hume, for whom the highway is named. On Comur St, next to the tourist information centre, the Hamilton Hume Museum has some exhibits relating to him. Near Yass at Wee Jasper you can visit the limestone Careys Caves on Sunday afternoons from 1 pm. Around

Murrumbateman on the Barton Highway you can visit several wineries.

GUNDAGAI (population 2400)

Though now bypassed by the highway, Gundagai, 386 km from Sydney, is one of the most interesting small towns along the Hume, a good spot to stay overnight. Between Gundagai and South Gundagai the long wooden Prince Alfred Bridge (now closed to traffic, but you can walk it) crosses the flood plain of the Murrumbidgee River, a reminder that in 1852 Gundagai suffered Australia's worst flood disaster when 89 people were drowned. Gold rushes and bushrangers were also part of its colourful early history and the notorious Captain Moonlight was tried in Gundagai's 1859 courthouse. Other places of interest in town include the Gabriel Gallery on the main street (Sheridan St), the Gundagai Historical Museum in Homer St and the information centre, also on Sheridan St, with a 20,000 piece marble cathedral model.

Gundagai is known above all for featuring in a number of famous songs and ballads including *Along the Road to Gundagai*, *My Mabel Waits for Me* and *When a Boy from Alabama Meets a Girl from Gundagai*. Its most famous monument is eight km east of town just off the highway. There, still sitting on his tuckerbox, is a sculpture of the dog who in a 19th century bush ballad (and a more recent, perhaps even better known, poem by Jack Moses) 'sat on the tuckerbox, five miles from Gundagai', and refused to help while its owner's bullock team was bogged in the creek. A popular tale has it that the dog was even less helpful because in the original version there was an 'h' in 'sat'.

The Dog on Tuckerbox memorial is now a popular little tourist centre and roadside stop. Not far away is the Five Mile Pub, an equally popular place to break your journey back in the pioneer days.

Places to Stay & Eat

There are several motels including a number on West St, the northern entry to town from the Hume Highway. At the top of the hill on West St, *Gundagai Auto Cabins & Motel* is one of the cheapest places with cabins and on-site vans from $17/23 a single/double – it's a clean place. The *Garden Motor Inn* (tel 44 1744) over the road, has a small pool and a restaurant, but is much pricier at $40/50.

In the town on Sheridan St, the *Criterion Hotel* (tel 44 1048) is an old-style pub with ordinary rooms at $14/25 a single/double. *Gundagai River Caravan Park* is a pleasant spot, by the river near the south end of the Prince Alfred Bridge, with a few on-site vans and tent sites at $7.

There are several places to eat along Sheridan St or you can get good Chinese or Australian meals for around $7 to $9 in the *RSL Club*.

HOLBROOK (population 1400)

Holbrook, 500 km from Sydney, was known as Germanton until WW I, when it was renamed after a British war hero. In Holbrook Park you can see a replica of the submarine in which he won a Victoria Cross. The local information centre is located in the interesting Woolpack Inn Museum, in an 1860 hotel.

ALBURY (population 41,000)

The New South Wales half of the Albury-Wodonga twin towns is on the north side of the Murray River. It's a busy and expanding industrial centre and is also an access point from Victoria to the New South Wales Snowy Mountains. The town dates from 1840 and has some historic buildings and botanic gardens.

The tourist information centre (tel (060) 21 2655), by the road as you enter Albury, has information on the whole of New South Wales as this is one of the state's major entry points. In summer there's good swimming in the Murray River in Noreuil Park behind the centre and you can take one hour river cruises daily on the paddle-steamer *Cumberoona*. Also in the park is a tree marked by explorer William Hovell where he crossed the Murray on his 1824 expedition with Hamilton Hume from Sydney to Port Phillip (Melbourne wasn't there then). Albury Regional Museum is next to the tourist information centre. Albury Regional Arts Centre, Dean St, is housed in a restored 1907 building and has travelling exhibitions and community activities.

The Ettamogah Wildlife Sanctuary, 11 km north on the highway, has a collection of Aussie fauna, most of which arrived sick or injured, so this is a genuine sanctuary as opposed to the half-baked zoos which many so-called 'sanctuaries' are. It's open daily from 9 am to 5 pm (admission $2). Slightly further out the grotesque Ettamogah Pub looms up near the highway – a real-life recreation of a famous Aussie cartoon pub and proof that life follows art not vice versa. The Jindera Pioneer Museum, which includes several original buildings, is 16 km north-west of Albury, also open daily. The lake behind the Hume Weir dam east of Albury is popular for water sports.

Places to Stay & Eat

The *Tourist Haven Caravan Park* (tel (060) 251 619), four km out of Albury, at 481 Wagga Rd, Lavington, has mobile homes with a double bed, three bunks, TV, air-con, shower and toilet for $46, and on-site vans for $37. *Sodens Hotel Australia* is classified as an historic building and is a pleasant retreat from sterile motel environments. Doubles are $45, including bathroom and continental breakfast.

The *Sailors, Soldiers & Airman Club*

Ettamogah Pub

(SS&A) on the corner of Dean and Olive Sts has a gymnasium, mixed bar with pokies, disco, and a reasonably priced restaurant and bistro. There are several Chinese restaurants and pizza shops on Wagga Rd and Dean St. *Tiffins* in Dean St does good lunches.

South-West & Murray River

A number of roads run through south-western New South Wales – alternative routes from Sydney to Melbourne like the Olympic Way from Cowra to Wagga Wagga and Albury or the Mid Western and Newell Highways to West Wyalong and Narrandera. Or there are routes to Adelaide like the Sturt Highway through Hay and Wentworth. You'll also come through the south-west if travelling between Brisbane and Melbourne. It's wide, rolling, sometimes hypnotic country with some of New South Wales' best farming areas and some interesting history if you have time to seek it out. The Murray River forms the boundary between New South Wales and Victoria and although most of the interesting towns are on the Victorian side New South Wales has some too.

Places to Stay

Every town has a few camping/caravan parks, hotels and motels and there are YHA hostels in Wagga Wagga, Narrandera and Deniliquin.

Getting There & Away

Trains or coordinated rail-bus services reach most towns. The region is also crisscrossed by several major interstate bus routes – from Sydney and Brisbane to Melbourne and Adelaide – but under the New South Wales bus rules you can normally only use these if you have a ticket from or to interstate (a bus pass usually helps you around this problem). Airlines like Air NSW and Kendell fly into the region and Macknight Airlines links Wagga Wagga, Hay, Deniliquin and Tocumwal.

WAGGA WAGGA (population 50,000)

Wagga is a major city on the Murrumbidgee River. The name is pronounced 'wogga' not 'wagga' and is usually abbreviated to one word. It's a busy farming centre with botanic gardens and a zoo. Wallacetown Historical Arms Museum is 20 km south of Wagga. Just north of Wagga is Junee with some historic buildings including the lovely old homestead, Monte Cristo.

WEST WYALONG (population 4000)

This is an old gold mining town at the point where the Mid Western (Sydney to Adelaide) and Newell (Melbourne to Brisbane) Highways meet. The West Wyalong District Museum includes a model of a gold mine and local fossils. When there's water, Lake Cowal, a bird sanctuary 48 km north-east, is the biggest lake in the state. In 1817 John Oxley, the first white explorer in these parts, described the West Wyalong area as 'country that would never again be visited by civilised man'. Lake Cargelligo, north-west of West Wyalong, is a water sports centre and has lots of bird life.

NARRANDERA (population 5000)

Near the junction of the Newell and Sturt Highways, Narrandera is in the Murrumbidgee Irrigation Area (MIA) – there's an information centre on the MIA in the town. You can visit the John Lake Centre which researches Murray/Darling aquatic life. There's a miniature zoo in the town and swimming pools at Lake Talbot. Leeton, 30 km away, was the first of the area's irrigation towns, dating from 1913. On weekdays in Leeton you can tour one of Australia's biggest fruit canneries and other food processing plants.

South of Narrandera on the Newell Highway is Jerilderie, immortalised by the bushranger Ned Kelly who held up the whole town for two days in 1879, locking the local police force in their own jail. Kelly relics can be seen in the Telegraph Office Museum on Powell St.

GRIFFITH (population 13,000)

This busy farming centre, another MIA town, was planned by Canberra's architect, Walter Burley Griffin. Apart from fruit, grain and grapes – it's one of New South Wales' biggest wine producing areas, with around 10 wineries open most days – Griffith also has a reputation for marijuana production and for the unpleasant events that befell people who found out too much about it. You can tour the Griffith Rice Mill at 10.30 am on weekdays. The Pioneer Park Museum is just north of the town (open daily, $4) and bushwalking in the Cocoparra National Park, 30 km north-east. Willandra National Park, 180 km north-west, centres on Willandra Billabong, an oasis in the dry plains. Griffith's tourist information centre is on the corner of Banna and Jondaryan Aves.

HAY (population 3000)

In flat, treeless country at the junction of three highways Hay is a major Merino sheep breeding centre. There are some fine beaches along the Murrumbidgee in this area. The town has some interesting old buildings like the Hay Gaol Museum, a fine old 1883 fountain and a plaque in Lachlan St marking Charles Sturt's journey on the Murrumbidgee and Murray Rivers in 1828-30. There's a mini-zoo in South Hay.

DENILIQUIN (population 7800)

A sheep raising centre where much irrigated farming is also carried out, 'Deni' has the Heritage Centre, an 1879 school being restored as a museum and arts centre. A footbridge from Cressy St runs to the Island Wildlife Sanctuary. There's good swimming at sandy McLean Beach on the river.

ALONG THE MURRAY

Most of the important river towns are on the Victorian side – see the Victoria chapter for more on the river. It's no problem to hop back and forth across the river as in many places roads run along both sides. Albury (see the Hume Highway section) is the main New South Wales town on the Murray and also the first big town on the river down from its source. The Murray was once an important means of communication with paddle-steamers splashing up and down stream like on an antipodean Mississippi.

Corowa is a wine producing centre downstream from Albury. The Lindeman winery has been here since 1860. You can have a meal at the popular services clubs in town or cross the river to visit the wineries in Rutherglen. On the second Sunday of each month and on public holidays there are train rides on the miniature Bangerang Railway.

Tocumwal on the Newell Highway is a quiet Murray town with a giant fibreglass codfish in the town square. The town has a sandy river beach and is a popular gliding centre. The Rocks is a popular picnic spot 11 km from town.

WENTWORTH (population 1250)

Close to the meeting of the Darling and the Murray, Australia's two longest rivers, Wentworth is overshadowed by nearby Mildura on the Victorian side of the Murray. The old paddle-steamer *Ruby* is on display near the Darling River bridge in Fotherby Park. Wentworth has an interesting folk museum and the 1879-81 jail has a display of the sorts of things the authorities used when they wanted to be unpleasant or even sadistic to prisoners. Admission to the jail is $1.50. You can take Darling River cruises on a number of vessels including the 1914 riverboat *Loyalty*.

North of Wentworth on Mungo Station is the Wall of China, a strange 30 km long natural wall. Tours operate there from Mildura in Victoria.

Central West

The central west region starts inland from the Blue Mountains and continues for about 400 km, gradually fading from rolling agricultural land into New South Wales' harsh far west. This region has some of the earliest inland towns in the country. From Sydney, Bathurst is the natural gateway to the region and from here you can turn north-west through Orange and Dubbo or south-west through Cowra and West Wyalong. The Mid Western Highway, running from Bathurst through Cowra and Wagga Wagga to Albury, is an alternative Sydney to Melbourne route. Like the coastal Princes Highway it's longer than the direct Hume route but provides very different scenery.

Central west towns have the usual accommodation choices – motel, hotel, caravan parks, camping – and there are YHA hostels at Dubbo and 10 km from Orange.

Getting There & Away

Air Air NSW flies from Sydney to a number of centres in the central west including Coonabarabran, Coonamble, Dubbo, Mudgee and Walgett. Eastern serves other towns like Bathurst, Cowra, Parkes, Forbes, Young and Cootamundra. There are services from Dubbo to other locations in the central and far west of the state.

Bus The usual New South Wales bus travel complications apply to some extent in the central west region. Major lines including Greyhound, Pioneer Express and Deluxe have services through the region on routes between Sydney and Broken Hill or Adelaide, and from Brisbane to Melbourne or Adelaide. There are also local bus services including Bathurst to Orange (weekdays only).

Train Trains run from Sydney to Lithgow ($10.60), Bathurst ($18), Orange ($23),

Dubbo ($35) and Parkes ($32). From those centres connecting buses operate to most other towns including Cowra ($26), Forbes ($32), Grenfell ($30) and Mudgee ($22).

LITHGOW (population 14,700)

On the western fringe of the Blue Mountains, Lithgow is mainly an industrial town, noted for the famous Zig Zag railway line by which, until 1910, trains descended from the Blue Mountains. The line was built in 1868 and was quite an engineering wonder in its day. Now it's restored and steam trains run for visitors in school holidays and on other Saturdays, Sundays and holidays from 11 am to 4 pm. It's 10 km east of Lithgow. Lithgow also has a frequent rail service from Sydney (155 km, $10.60).

In the city, Eskbank House on Bennet St is a gracious 1841 home housing a pottery gallery and industrial museum. Lithgow tourist information centre (tel 51 2307) is at 285 Main St. There are fine views from Hassan Walls Lookout, five km south of town. The interesting little village of Hartley with its fine courthouse, built by convicts in 1837, is nine km away on the Katoomba side of Lithgow. Newnes, north of Lithgow on the edge of the wild Wollemi National Park, is a ghost town of which virtually only the pub remains – and still functions!

BATHURST (population 25,500)

Bathurst, 208 km from Sydney, is Australia's oldest inland city. It's a fine old town with many early buildings reflecting its long, by Australian standards, history. They include the 1835 Holy Trinity Church and part of the Old Government House of 1817. It has a good historical museum displaying Aboriginal artefacts as well as the usual pioneering exhibits, in the east wing of the 1880 courthouse on Russell St. There is also an art gallery and the Bathurst Museum of Applied Arts & Sciences. You can also visit the old home of the 1940s Labor

Prime Minister Ben Chifley at 10 Busby St. Eight km out of town is Abercrombie House, a huge Gothic mansion of the 1870s.

Close to the town is the Mt Panorama motor racing circuit, a true road circuit and the finest racing track in Australia. Part of the track is closed off and only open during the races but the rest of it is normal public road. One of Australia's best known car races, the Bathurst 1000 km for production cars, takes place here each October. The Easter motorcycle events, traditionally followed by an exciting bikie rampage, no longer take place and there is talk of replacing them with an international sports car race.

Mt Panorama also has a couple of more permanent attractions: the Sir Joseph Banks Nature Park which has koalas, kangaroos and wallabies; and the Bathurst Gold Diggings, a reconstruction of an early gold mining town. Bathurst has a tourist information centre (tel 31 1622) in the Civic Centre on Russell St.

AROUND BATHURST

The Abercrombie Caves are 72 km south of the city. Guided inspections are given several times daily. Between Bathurst and Cowra is Blayney, close to Carcoar, an interesting old place very much like an English village.

North of Bathurst the old mining town of Hill End was the scene for a gold rush from 1871 to 1874 and has many fine buildings from that era. It's an interesting town and worth a visit. It's now administered by the national parks as an historic site. There are camping sites and rooms in the pub, and you can visit old mines or pan for gold in the creek (there's gear for hire). The *Royal Hotel* (tel 37 8261) was opened in 1872 and has been operating ever since. There's an information centre (tel 37 8206) in the old Hill End Hospital. Rockley, 34 km south of Bathurst, is another classified historic village. North-east of Bathurst is Rylstone where there are some interesting Aboriginal

rock paintings just outside the town (ask at the shire council) while 16 km north there are fine tree ferns in Fern Tree Gully.

MUDGEE (population 6000)

Further north, 126 km from Bathurst, Mudgee is a pleasant town with many fine old buildings and a Colonial Inn Museum. Mudgee has many young and enthusiastic small wineries, and people who find the Hunter Valley altogether too commercial report that Mudgee wineries are a delight to visit. Around 18 of them are open six or seven days a week. And they make some nice wine too. Mudgee Tourist Information Centre (tel 72 1944) is at 64 Market St.

Only 30 km north-west is Gulgong, an old gold town which was also the boyhood home of poet Henry Lawson. There's a big collection of 'Lawsonia' in the town's art centre on Main St. Gulgong Pioneers Museum on Bayley St is good, and open daily from 9.30 am to 5 pm, admission $2. Eleven km north at Nagundie there's a rock five metres above the ground which is said always to hold water – it's an old Aboriginal water hole and you can camp there or take a tour from Gulgong – tel 75 9252 for information.

Further east towards New England is Merriwa at the western end of the Hunter with a number of historic buildings including an 1857 historical museum. Nearby Cassilis also has some old stone buildings and between there and Mudgee there are some Aboriginal cave paintings just off the road.

ORANGE (population 29,500)

This important fruit producing centre does not, curiously enough, grow oranges! It was considered as a site for the federal capital before Canberra was eventually selected. This was the home town of pioneer poet Banjo Paterson (he wrote the words of *Waltzing Matilda*) and the foundations of his birthplace are now part of Banjo Paterson Park. There's an art gallery in the civic centre on Byng St while the historical museum on Sale St includes a 300 year old tree carved with Aboriginal designs.

Australia's first real gold rush took place at Ophir, 27 km north of Orange. The area is now a nature reserve and it's still popular with fossickers. You can hire gold pans from Orange Visitors' Centre (tel 62 4155) on Byng St. There are other popular parks and centres around Orange. Lake Canobolas Park, with a camping ground, is eight km south-west while a further six km brings you to the Mt Canobolas Reserve with hills, walking trails and camping. You can hire bicycles to get around the Mini-Bike Tourist Park, 10 km north.

Molong is north-west on the road to Wellington and four km south-east of the town is the grave of Yaranigh, the Aboriginal guide of explorer Sir Thomas Mitchell.

WELLINGTON (population 5300)
Fifty km south-east of Dubbo, Wellington is noted for its limestone caves including the Wellington Cave, nine km from town. In the town there's an historical museum housed in a former bank. Walking trails lead to the lookout at Binjang in the Mt Arthur Reserve. Wellington has several wineries too.

DUBBO (population 32,000)
North of Parkes and Orange and 420 km from Sydney, Dubbo is an agricultural and sheep and cattle raising town with some old buildings and a good museum of colonial life on Macquarie St. You can get tourist information from the museum (tel 82 5359) or at the bus station (tel 874 1422) on the corner of Darling and Erskine Sts. The Old Dubbo Gaol, with the gallows on display, is another attraction, open daily. There is a fair amount of information on the Governor family, whose exploits are related in *The Chant of Jimmy Blacksmith*.

Dubbo, on the Macquarie River and Newell Highway, is a pleasant place with wide streets and some fine old buildings,

including some long verandahed pubs. But its main tourist attraction is five km south-west of town. There, the Western Plains Zoo is the largest open-range zoo in Australia. You can hire bicycles there and ride around the exhibits, which are divided into their continent of origin.

COWRA (population 8400)
On the alternative inland route to Melbourne the pleasant town of Cowra was the site of a Japanese prisoner of war camp during WW II. In 1944 an amazing mass prison break was made by the Japanese, resulting in the death of nearly 250 prisoners, many of them by suicide. Four prison guards were killed, but all the escapees were soon rounded up. The strange tale of this impossible escape attempt was told in the book and film titled *Die Like the Carp*. There's a Japanese war cemetery five km south of the town, and two km south-east of the cemetery a memorial marks the site of the break-out.

The Wyangala dam and recreation area, 40 km east of Cowra, has good water sport facilities. Canowindra, north of Cowra, has a fine curving main street and is a big hot air ballooning centre from April to October. In 1863 bushranger Ben Hall bailed up the whole town!

YOUNG (population 6900)
South-west of Cowra on the Olympic Way towards Wagga Wagga, Young is a fruit growing centre with an earlier gold mining history. This was the site of the anti-Chinese riots at Lambing Flats in 1861 and you can find out more about this unpleasant incident in the Lambing Flats Historic Museum. Between Young and Wagga is Cootamundra.

GRENFELL (population 2000)
This old gold mining town is 56 km west from Cowra towards West Wyalong. It was the birthplace of poet and author, Henry Lawson. There are good walks in the Weddin Mountain National Park, 18 km

south-east, where bushranger Ben Hall reputedly used to hide out.

FORBES (population 8500)

Paired in most travellers' minds with Parkes, 35 km up the Newell Highway, Forbes is actually an oddly atmospheric place to wander round for a couple of hours. It has wide streets and a number of grand, late 19th century buildings reflecting the wealth of its 1860s gold rush. The town hall, with palm trees in front, looks positively tropical! Bushranger Ben Hall is buried in the town's cemetery – he was treacherously killed here in 1865. Forbes has a museum with Hall relics and other memorabilia, open daily from 3 to 5 pm, in Cross St.

A km south of the centre is the Lachlan Vintage Village, a recreation of a 19th century village, which is open daily with working demonstrations most days. There's a tourist information centre at 69 Lachlan St in the centre.

You can get a great Chinese meal – about $16 for two – at the *Hong Kong Chinese Restaurant* next to the central Forbes Inn.

There are good, clean on-site vans for $21 a double at *Forbes River Meadows Caravan Park*, a couple of km south of the centre just off the highway.

Between Forbes and Orange is Eugowra where one of early New South Wales' most spectacular gold-escort robberies took place. The town has a small museum and 15 km east there's rough bushwalking in Nangar National Park.

PARKES (population 9500)

On the Newell Highway, Parkes is another 1860s gold town. It has a motor museum, a pioneer park museum and the pleasant Kelly Reserve on the north side of town.

A huge radio telescope stands 23 km north of the town, six km off the Newell Highway. It's open to the public daily and there's an excellent visitor centre.

North-West

From Dubbo roads radiate out to the north-west. The Newell Highway runs north-east right across the state, an excellent road which provides the quickest route between Melbourne and Brisbane. The Castlereagh Highway, forking off the Newell 66 km from Dubbo at Gilgandra, runs more or less directly north into the rugged opal country towards the Queensland border, its surfaced section ending soon after Lightning Ridge. The Mitchell Highway heads off north-west to Bourke via Nyngan. At Nyngan the Barrier Highway forks off directly west to Broken Hill in New South Wales' far west.

Getting There & Away

Towns on the Newell Highway are served by Brisbane to Melbourne or Adelaide buses, but remember the New South Wales restrictions on intrastate bus travel. Trains run up to Gunnedah ($35 from Sydney), Narrabri ($38) and Moree ($41) and there are coordinated State Rail buses to most other centres including Bourke ($47), Brewarrina ($47), Cobar ($44), Connabarabran ($37), Coonamble ($41), Inverell ($44), Lightning Ridge ($47) and Walgett ($44). Eastern and Air NSW fly to several of the main towns.

ALONG THE NEWELL

Gilgandra has the Gilgandra Observatory & Display Centre with an audiovisual of the moon landing and NASA Gemini flights, plus an historical display. Gilgandra is a junction town where the Newell and Castlereagh divide and a road also cuts across to the Mitchell.

At Coonabarabran you can visit Miniland, eight km west, where there are life-size prehistoric animal models and the almost inevitable historical museum. This is also the main access point for the spectacular mountain domes and spires of the Warrumbungle Range, a national park with superb walks and rock climbing possibilities. There are camping sites in the park and you can get a walks map from the park headquarters at Canyon Camp, in the heart of the park 35 km west of Coonabarabran. The final 10 km of the road once you have entered the park is fairly rough. The largest optical telescope in the southern hemisphere is at Siding Spring, 24 km west of the town at the edge of the park. You can visit it daily. Coonabarabran has a tourist information centre (tel (068) 42 1441) on the Newell Highway at the south end of town. There's an associate YHA hostel ($8 a night) at the *Warrumbungles Mountain Motel* (tel 42 1832) nine km out of town on the road to the national park.

Narrabri is a cotton growing centre with a solar observatory and also a cosmic ray research centre. The Mt Kaputar National Park, good for walking, camping and climbing, is 53 km east of Narrabri by a steep gravel road, while to the west is Wee Waa, a wine and cotton growing centre.

The huge dish of an OTC overseas communications antenna – tours given four times daily on weekdays – marks Moree. The town is on the flood-prone Gwydir River. From Moree the road is fairly dull until you finally reach Boggabilla and cross the border to Goondiwindi in Queensland.

MOREE TO NEW ENGLAND

Between Moree and Glen Innes in New England is Bingara, a gemstone centre with an early gold mining history. The National Trust classified Bingara Historical Society Museum was probably the town's first hotel.

Inverell, further east, is a popular fossicking centre, particularly for sapphires. It's also a base for white-water rafting on the Gwydir River. The town has a National Trust classified courthouse and a pioneer village with buildings collected together which date from the 1830s. Warialda is another gemstone centre in the vicinity. A little south of Inverell is Tingha with the excellent Smith Museum

of Mining & Natural History. Tingha is a tin mining centre and a tin dredge still operates in Copes Creek.

South from here towards Tamworth is Barraba in fine mountain country. The views from the top of Mt Kaputar, which can also be reached from Narrabri, are particularly fine. The Nandewar Mountains and the Horton River Falls are other scenic attractions. South again is Manilla, noted for its production of honey and mead.

ALONG THE CASTLEREAGH

The Castlereagh Highway divides from the Newell at Gilgandra. Gulargambone, 53 km up the road, is another access point for the Warrumbungles. Coonamble is at the edge of the Western Plains and from here you can travel west to the extensive Macquarie Marshes with their prolific bird life. The road continues north to Walgett in harsh, dry country near the Grawin and Glengarry opal fields. This is a popular area for opal fossickers.

A few km off the highway close to the Queensland border, Lightning Ridge is a huge opal field claimed to be the only site in the world where black opals can be found. This remote centre is heavily into tourism with underground opal showrooms, an art gallery, a bottle museum, an opal mine which you can visit and much more. The town centres around the Diggers Rest Hotel. There's an associate YHA hostel in the *Tram-O-Tel* (tel (068) 29 0613) on Morilla St.

ALONG THE MITCHELL

From Dubbo the Mitchell Highway passes through the citrus growing centre of Narromine. Warren, further north and off the Mitchell on the Macquarie Highway, is another jumping off point for the Macquarie marshes, as is Nyngan where the Mitchell and Barrier Highways divide. The huge marshes are breeding grounds for ducks, water hens, swans, pelicans, ibis and herons. Nyngan was the scene of fierce resistance by Aborigines to early white encroachment.

The country north-west of Nyngan, the Western Plains which stretch away on the inland side of the Great Dividing Range, is a vast, tree-dotted plain eventually shelving off into the barren New South Wales outback – the 'back of Bourke'. From Nyngan the highway and the railway both run arrow-straight for 206 km to Bourke and further west really is the 'back of beyond'.

BOURKE (population 3500)

Nearly 800 km north-west of Sydney, Bourke is known for nothing much apart from being the centre of a huge tract of outback. In fact 'back of Bourke' is synonymous with the outer outback, the back of beyond. A glance at the map will show just how outback the area is – there's no town of any size for far around, and the country is flat and featureless as far as the eye can see. Its very remoteness must be what attracts a steady stream of visitors. Bourke is on the Darling River as well as the Mitchell Highway and, believe it or not, used to be a port about 600 km from the ocean. Around the turn of the century paddle steamers and barges plied the Darling regularly.

Look for the Cobb & Co signs on the old Carrier Arms Hotel. The town has a tourist information centre at 14 Richard St. Here you can get a leaflet called *Swagman's Outback Mud Map Tours Bourke* detailing some drives that outback lovers can make to places like Mt Gunderbooka (with Aboriginal cave art and vivid wildflowers in spring), Mt Oxley, or Fort Bourke Stockade, just south of Bourke, where an early explorer tangled with Aborigines. From Bourke the Mitchell Highway heads into Queensland at Cunnamulla.

Brewarrina is 100 km east of Bourke. The name is an Aboriginal word meaning 'good fishing' and there are Aboriginal stone fishing traps, known as the 'rocks' or the 'fisheries', just down from a weir they built in the Barwon River.

The Far West

The far west of New South Wales is rough, rugged and sparsely populated, but it also produces a fair proportion of the state's wealth – particularly from the mines of Broken Hill. The Barrier Highway is the main access route into the region, but Broken Hill is actually closer to Adelaide than Sydney and it's really more closely aligned to the South Australian capital. Although Broken Hill is far from everywhere there are a number of places of great interest in the west of the state.

THE BARRIER HIGHWAY

The Barrier Highway heads west from Nyngan; it's 594 km from there to Broken Hill. This road is an alternative route between Sydney and Adelaide and is also the most direct route between Sydney and Western Australia.

Cobar

Cobar has a modern and highly productive copper mine but it also has an earlier history as evidenced by its old buildings, like the fine Great Western Hotel with its endless stretch of iron lacework ornamenting the verandah. There's a pastoral and mining museum; ask at the tourist information centre in the main street about mine tours.

Near Cobar you can see 'Towser's Huts' – mud and stone huts rented out to miners in the 1890s. Weather balloons are released at 9 am and 3 pm daily from the meteorological station near Cobar. The colourful Mt Grenfell Aboriginal cave paintings are 40 km west of Cobar then 32 km north off the highway.

Wilcannia

Wilcannia is on the Darling River and in the days of paddle-steamers was an important river port. It's a much quieter place today, but you can still see old buildings from that era – including the

Athenaeum Chambers where the tourist information centre is located.

Wilcannia has a couple of motels costing around $45. The local pub may provide meals, but it is best avoided unless you are an experienced bar room brawler.

White Cliffs

About 100 km north-west of Wilcannia is White Cliffs, an old opal mining settlement. For a taste of life in a small outback community, it's worth the drive on a dirt road. You can fossick for opals around the old diggings, and there are a number of opal showrooms and underground homes open for inspection. Jock's Place is worth seeing – he has old relics collected from the area and can tell you about opal mining. Rosavilla is another, and they also offer horse-drawn wagon tours. A tourist pamphlet is available from the general store or the showrooms.

As you enter White Cliffs you pass the high tech dishes of the solar energy research station, where emus often graze out the front. The station is open for inspection daily at 2 pm.

Places to Stay The *White Cliffs Hotel* has basic rooms, but they are air-con and good value at $12 per person. The management is friendly, all meals are available and there is a 4WD for guests' use. Of course the pub is also the centre of the town's social activity and the place to hear a few yarns over a beer. The *Post Office Family Inn* has rooms for $13 per person and there is a caravan park. *Hornby's Underground Motel* is under construction and should be open in late '89.

Getting There & Away The road from Wilcannia is in reasonable condition; traffic is light but regular. Coming from Broken Hill, there is a turn-off before Wilcannia. There is also a back road to Broken Hill via Mootwingee, but traffic on this route is infrequent and outback driving conditions apply. For tours to White Cliffs see the Broken Hill section.

BACK OF BOURKE

Back of Bourke really is just what the name says. There's no sealed road anywhere west of Bourke in New South Wales, and if you cared to drive from Bourke to Broken Hill via Wanaaring and Milparinka it's unsealed for the whole 713 km apart from the final 10 km or so into Broken Hill. Milparinka, once a gold town, now consists of little more than a solitary hotel and some old sandstone buildings.

In 1845 members of Charles Sturt's expedition from Adelaide, searching for an inland sea, were forced to camp near here for six months. The temperatures were high, the conditions terrible and their supplies inadequate. You can see the grave of James Poole, Sturt's second in command, about 14 km north-west of the settlement. Poole died of scurvy. There's a stone cairn built by the expedition members on Mt Poole, 20 km north-west.

Tibooburra, known as the hottest place in New South Wales, is right in the north-west corner and has a number of stone buildings from the 1880s and '90s, including two hotels where you can get rooms. There's also a camping ground. It used to be known as The Granite from the granite outcrops in the area. You can normally reach Tibooburra from Bourke or Broken Hill in a conventional vehicle except after rain (which is pretty rare!). Tibooburra is an entry point for the Sturt National Park in the very corner of the state. The park has 300 km of driveable tracks and more camping areas, even some recommended walks! At Camerons Corner there's a post to mark the place where Queensland, South Australia and New South Wales meet. It's a favourite goal for visitors and a 4WD is not necessary to get there. It is recommended that you inform the park ranger at Tibooburra before venturing into the park, however.

This far western corner of the state is a harsh, dry area of red plains, heat, dust and flies but with interesting physical features and prolific wildlife. The border between New South Wales and Queensland is marked by the dingo proof fence, patrolled every day by boundary riders who each look after a 40 km section. Always seek local advice before setting off to travel in this area, particularly on secondary roads.

Country Race Meets

Some of the country race meetings are real occasions – the one at Louth, about 100 km south-west of Bourke, is particularly revered. The town's population is only about 50 and one year they recorded 29 planes 'flying in for the day'!

MOOTWINGEE NATIONAL PARK

In the Bynguano Range, 131 km north of Broken Hill, there is an Aboriginal tribal ground with rock carvings and cave paintings – a national historic site which has been badly defaced by vandals. The major site is now controlled by the Aboriginal community and is closed to visitors, however the park is teeming with kangaroos and other wildlife and it is a place of quite exceptional beauty. It is well worth the 1½ to two hour drive from Broken Hill, though be warned that it involves travelling on an isolated dirt road.

There are walks through the crumbling sandstone hills to rock pools, which usually have enough water for swimming, and rock paintings can still be seen in the areas that are not off limits. There is a camping ground with toilets and water for washing, but you should bring your own drinking water. The ranger is a good source of information on the park.

MENINDEE LAKES

This water storage development on the Darling River, 112 km south-east of Broken Hill, offers a variety of water sport facilities. Menindee is the town for the area. Bourke and Wills stayed in the

Maiden's Hotel on their unlucky trip north in 1860. The hotel was built in 1854 and has been with the same family for nearly 100 years. The Kinchega National Park is close to the town and the lakes, overflowing from the Darling River, are a haven for bird life.

Broken Hill

Population: 27,000

Out in the far west, Broken Hill is an oasis in the wilderness. It's a fascinating town not only for its comfortable existence in an extremely unwelcoming environment, but also for the fact that it was once a one company town which spawned one equally strong union.

The Broken Hill Proprietary Company (BHP), after which the town was named, was formed in 1885 after a boundary rider, Charles Rasp, discovered a silver lode. Miners working on other finds in the area had failed to notice the real wealth. Other mining claims were staked, but BHP was always the 'big mine' and dominated the town. Charles Rasp went on to amass a personal fortune, and BHP, which later diversified into steel production, became Australia's largest company.

Early conditions in the mine were appalling. Hundreds of miners died and many more suffered from lead poisoning and lung disease. This gave rise to the other great force in Broken Hill, the unions. Many miners were immigrants – from Ireland, Germany, Italy and Malta – but all were united in their efforts to improve mining conditions.

The first 35 years of Broken Hill saw a militancy rarely matched in Australian industrial relations. Many campaigns were fought, police were called in to break strikes, and though there was a gradual improvement in conditions, the miners lost many confrontations. The turning point was the Big Strike of 1919 and 1920

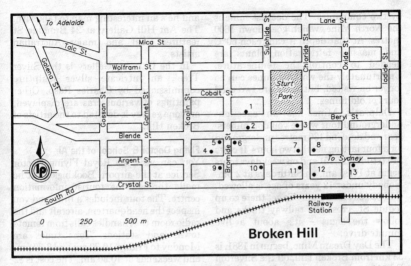

Broken Hill

1 Mario's Motel
2 Railway Museum
3 Entertainment Centre
4 Tourist Lodge
5 Tourist & Travel Centre
6 Black Lion Inn
7 Post Office
8 Royal Exchange Hotel
9 Silver Spade Motel
10 Mario's Palace Hotel
11 Grand Private Hotel
12 RSL Club
13 Papa Joe's Pizza

lasting for over 18 months. The miners won a great victory, achieving a 35 hour week and the end of dry drilling, responsible for the dust that afflicted so many miners.

The concept of 'one big union', which had helped to win the strike, was formalised in 1923 with the formation of the Barrier Industrial Council, which still largely runs the town.

Today the richest silver/lead/zinc deposit in the world is still being worked, but lead and zinc have assumed a greater importance in the Silver City, as Broken Hill is known. There is enough ore left to ensure at least another 20 years of mining, but the new technology has greatly reduced the number of jobs in the mines.

In many ways Broken Hill is closer to South Australia than New South Wales. Broken Hill is 1170 km west of Sydney, but only 509 km from Adelaide and even the clocks are set on Adelaide (central) rather than Sydney (eastern) time.

Information

Broken Hill has a very imposing tourist information centre (tel (080) 6077) on the corner of Bromide and Blende Sts, open every day of the week. This building houses the main bus station, car rental desks and a cafeteria.

The RAA (tel 88 4999) is at 261 Argent St and provides reciprocal service to other autoclub members. The swimming pool is on the corner of Sulphide and Wolfram Sts.

The city is laid out in a straightforward grid pattern, and the central area is easy to get around on foot.

Mines

There are four working mines, controlled

by two companies. The deepest mine is the North Mine, which goes down 1600 metres. At that depth it can reach 60°C and massive refrigeration plants are needed to control the temperature. Unfortunately the working mines can no longer be visited, but there are two good tours of old mines.

Delprat's Mine has an excellent underground tour where you don miners' gear and descend 130 metres underground for a tour lasting nearly two hours. It costs $18 (students $15) and on weekdays tours begin at 10.30 am, on Saturdays at 2 pm. Nobody under 12 years of age is allowed. Call 88 1604 for details. To get there go up Iodide St, cross the railway tracks and follow the signs – it's about a five minute drive.

The Day Dream Mine, begun in 1881, is 33 km from Broken Hill, off the Silverton Rd. A one hour tour costs $9 for adults, $4.50 for children (or $15 and $7.50 including transport from Broken Hill). Sturdy footwear is essential. Contact the tourist information centre for bookings.

The Gladstone Mining Museum in South Broken Hill has life-size working exhibits in an old hotel. It's open from 2 to 5 pm daily and admission is $4.

Artists

Broken Hill seems to inspire artists and there is quite a plethora of galleries in the town. They include the Broken Hill City Art Gallery in the Entertainment Centre, the Pro Hart Gallery at 108 Wyman St, and Jack Absalom's Gallery at 683 Chapple St. Pro Hart, a former miner, is Broken Hill's best known artist and a local personality. Apart from his own work, his gallery displays minor works of major artists (Picasso, Dali, Roualt), but his collection of Australian art is superb. He charges admission ($2), but many others don't.

Some of the artists are friendly characters willing to chat with visitors. I particularly liked Hugh Schulz's Gallery at 51 Morgan St – I liked his naive art style

and he's an interesting man to talk with. The Ant Hill Gallery at 24 Bromide St features local and major Australian artists.

In the City Art Gallery is the 'Silver Tree', an intricate silver sculpture commissioned by Charles Rasp. Other paintings of various eras are displayed, and one gallery is devoted to the artists of Broken Hill.

Flying Doctor & School of the Air

You can visit the Royal Flying Doctor Service at the airport. Bookings must be made through the tourist information centre. The tour includes a film, and you inspect the headquarters, aircraft and the radio room that handles calls from remote towns and stations. Tour times are Monday to Friday, 10.30 am and 3.30 pm, and weekends at 10.30 am. The cost is $2 for adults, $1 for children.

You can sit in on School of the Air broadcasts to kids in isolated homesteads, on weekdays at 8.30 am during school terms. The one hour session costs $1 and must be booked through the information centre.

Afghani Mosque

There's a relic of the Afghani camel trains of the last century in the Afghani Mosque, built in 1891. The Afghani cameleers helped to open up the outback and the mosque was built on the site of a camel camp. It's on the corner of William and Buck Sts in North Broken Hill. Those wishing to visit are welcome on Sunday afternoons at 2.30.

Other Attractions

The Broken Hill Railway, Mineral & Train Museum, housed in the old railway station, is open daily from 9 am to 5 pm, but closed for lunch from 12.30 to 1.30 pm. Admission is $1.

The Bond Store Museum is in a restored building and includes an Aboriginal exhibition. It's open from 10 am to 4 pm daily and admission is $1.

At White's Mineral Art Gallery &

Mining Museum, 1 Allendale St, you can walk into a mining stope and see mining memorabilia and minerals. It has a craft shop and sells crushed mineral collages.

Silverton

Silverton, 25 km to the west, is an old silver mining town with historic buildings and a museum. Mining in the area dates from 1875 and developed further with the establishment of the mine at Umberumberka. Silverton peaked in 1885 when it had a population of 3000 and solid public buildings designed to last for centuries. In 1889 the mines at Silverton were closed and the population (and many of the houses) moved to Broken Hill.

Today it's an interesting little ghost town, used as a setting in the films *Mad Max II*, *A Town Like Alice* and *Razorback*. A number of buildings still stand, including the old jail, now an historical museum (admission $1) and the Silverton Hotel. The hotel displays photographs taken on the film sets. There are also a couple of artists, Peter Brown and Albert Woodroffe, whose galleries are worth viewing.

The road beyond Silverton becomes bleak and lonely almost immediately but the Umberumberka Reservoir, 10 km from Silverton, is a popular picnic spot and Penrose Park has animal and bird life.

A variety of camel tours are operated from Silverton, including a 15 minute tour of the town for $5, a two hour sunset trek for $30 and a two day trek. The camels are often hitched up near the hotel or the School Craft Centre, or contact Bill Canard (tel 91 1682, 91 1652) or Judith or Samantha (tel 88 5372 or 88 5306) at Silverton.

Further Out

Euriowie has interesting rock formations and Aboriginal artefacts. There are more again at Yanco Glen Hotel, just 30 km north of Broken Hill.

Places to Stay

Within a few steps of the information centre/bus station there are a couple of good accommodation possibilities. At 100 Argent St the *Tourist Lodge* (tel 88 2086) is YHA associated and has dorm beds at $9.50 for YHA members and $12 for others. There are also spartan singles/doubles at $18/30. There's a lounge with a TV and pool table and a basic kitchen.

Across the road from the information centre the *Black Lion Inn* (tel 4801) is very good value at $14/20 for singles/doubles. The rooms are old fashioned but well kept with showers and toilets at the end of the corridor.

Along Argent St there is a string of hotels, most of them very grand old places like *Mario's Palace Hotel* (tel 2385) at No 227 with its foyer and stairs painted with garish frescos by local artists. The rooms are nothing special but OK for $23/31 a single/double ($35/50 for better rooms with bathrooms) and breakfast is an extra $6. Further down at 320 Argent St, on the corner of Chloride St, the *Royal Exchange* (tel 2308) is a grand old place with large, comfortable singles/doubles at $28/46. The *Grand Private Hotel* (tel 5305) at No 317 has had a face-lift and costs $33/39 in comfortable rooms with TV. There are lots more hotels around town.

Broken Hill also has plenty of motels, although most of them are expensive. *Mario's Hotel-Motel* (tel 5145) at 172 Beryl St is the cheapest with singles/doubles for $29/44, but it's a bit run down. The *Silver Spade* (tel 7021) at 151 Argent St is a friendly place, conveniently central and the pick of the cheap motels at $40/48 and there's a swimming pool. Most of the motels in Broken Hill are in the $52 to $70 bracket.

Camping The *Broken Hill Caravan Park* (tel 3841) on Rakow St and the *Lake View Caravan Park* (tel 88 2250) at 1 Mann St both have camping sites for around $7. The Lake View has on-site vans at $23 for two or $29 with air-con.

Places to Eat

Broken Hill is a New South Wales club town if ever there was one. They welcome visitors and in most cases you just sign the visitors' book at the front door and walk in. Background music consists of the continuous rattle of one-armed bandits (poker machines), but most have reasonably priced, reasonably good, very filling food. The *Barrier Social Democratic Club*, 218 Argent St, has the best value counter meals, and a $7 breakfast (from 6 am) will keep you going all day. The *Musician's Club* at 267 Crystal St, also has cheap counter meals. The *Broken Hill RSL* is a bit more up-market, but the three course, $18 carvery on Friday and Saturday nights will satisfy the biggest appetite.

There are lots of pubs too – this is a mining town – like the *Royal Exchange Hotel* at the corner of Argent St and Chloride St. The *Pepinella Restaurant* here has a long menu, mostly in the $10 to $14 bracket and a superb serve-yourself salad table. There are others, cheaper too, along Argent St. Otherwise there are snack bars including the popular cafe in the information centre, and greasy spoon places like the *Okeh Cafe* on Argent St, which has good coffee and is open seven days a week.

Papa Joe's on Argent St, has pasta and pizzas and there are some slightly up-market places like the *Black Lion Inn*. Of the Chinese restaurants in town, the *Paragon*, 181 Argent St, is reasonably priced and has good food.

Getting There & Away

Air Adelaide is the usual flight departure point for Broken Hill. The fare is $123 one way or $98 standby with Kendell Airlines. From Sydney it's $212 one way with Air NSW or $276 return with an advance purchase ticket. You can also fly to Mildura, with connections to Melbourne or Adelaide, with Sun State Airlines for $113 one way to Adelaide or $170 to Melbourne.

Bus Greyhound and Murtons have buses daily between Adelaide and Broken Hill for $32. Greyhound have buses to Melbourne for $62 and Mildura for $26. Pioneer Express and Deluxe go to Sydney for $76. All buses depart from the tourist information centre where all the companies have offices, except Deluxe which you can book through the travel agents around town.

Train Broken Hill is on the Sydney to Perth railway line so it can be reached on the Indian Pacific on Tuesday, Wednesday and Saturday for $62.90 in 2nd class or $110.70 including berth and meals. The Comet also goes to Sydney on Tuesday, Thursday and Saturday. To Adelaide the Indian Pacific costs $28 and takes seven hours. It leaves on Monday, Thursday and Saturday at 1.30 pm. The Silver City costs $25 to Adelaide and leaves Monday, Wednesday and Friday at 7.35 am.

Getting Around

There are plenty of taxis around Broken Hill. Avis (tel 7532), Hertz (tel 2719) and Budget (tel 7512) are represented in Broken Hill and at the airport. Their 'remote region' rates can work out to be very expensive as the maximum free km allowance is 100 km per day. Handy Car Rentals (tel 7214) have 1978 Toyota sedans for $39 a day, but you cannot take the car more than 50 km from Broken Hill.

Tours

Walking tours of the city are organised from Monday to Friday at 10.30 am, Sunday at 10.30 am and 2.30 pm. Enquire at the information centre. There are also self-drive tours of the city and a sundown nature trail in the hills north of the city; the information centre has brochures.

Wanderer Tours (tel 6956) is the main operator with tours of the city and mines ($12), art galleries ($12), Royal Flying Doctor Service ($6), Silverton ($17), and further afield to White Cliffs ($82), Mootwingee ($50) and Menindee Lakes

($29), among others. Arnold's Tours (tel 7701) are similar. All tours can be booked through the information centre and they can provide a full list of the many tours that operate from Broken Hill to as far afield as the Flinders Ranges and the Sturt National Park.

A really interesting way to see some of the country beyond Broken Hill is to go along on an outback mail run. Contact Lindon Aviation (tel 88 5257). Their Saturday mail run departs at 7 am and takes you round 30 outback stations and stops in White Cliffs before arriving back at Broken Hill at 5 pm. The cost is $140 including lunch. On Tuesdays they do the mail run to White Cliffs and stop there for six hours. They also do various outback air tours – you can make a day-trip to Milparinka for $170 or to the Bourke and Wills 'dig' tree and Innaminka for $365.

Lord Howe Island

Only 11 km long and 2½ km wide, beautiful Lord Howe Island is a long way out in the Pacific, virtually due east of Port Macquarie and 600 km north-east of Sydney.

Lord Howe is really off the budget track, and apart from the expense of getting there you won't find much by the way of cheap accommodation. Most visitors to Lord Howe are on package tours.

It's heavily forested and has beautiful walks, a wide lagoon sheltered by a coral reef, and some fine beaches. It's small enough to get around on foot or by bicycle. The southern end is dominated by towering Mt Lidgbird (808 metres) and Mt Gower (875 metres). You can climb Mt Gower in around six hours, round trip.

The lagoon has good snorkelling, and you can also inspect the sealife from glass-bottom boats. On the other side of the island there's surf at Blinky Beach. The Lord Howe Island Historical Museum is

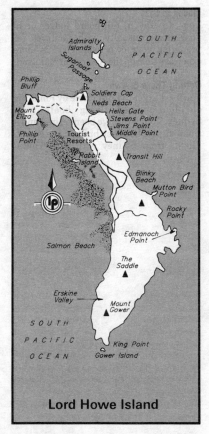

Lord Howe Island

usually open from 8 to 10 pm each evening. There's a shell museum, open Monday to Friday from 10 am to 4 pm and movies are shown in the public hall on Saturdays and Tuesdays.

Information

For more information on Lord Howe Island check with the Lord Howe Island Tourist Centre, 20 Loftus St, Sydney. The phone number is 27 2867 or from elsewhere in the country (008) 22 1713.

Places to Stay

You can stay in full-board lodges or in apartments, usually with facilities for preparing your own food. Food is more expensive than on the Australian mainland.

Getting There & Away

You used to get to Lord Howe by romantic old four-engined flying boats from Sydney. Today they've been retired and a small airport has been built on the island. Flights from Sydney with Lord Howe/ Norfolk Island Airlines are $570 return. You can fly there from Port Macquarie with Oxley Airlines for $460 return.

Getting Around

Getting around the island you can hire bicycles from a number of locations for $2 a day. There are motorcycles and a few rental cars on the island too, but a bike is all you need. There is an overall 25 kph speed limit.

Northern Territory

Area	1,346,000 square km
Population	158,500

The Northern Territory may be the least populated and most barren area of Australia, but it's also one of the most fascinating. Australia is an urban, coastal country, but it is the centre – the *red heart* – where the picture-book, untamed, sometimes almost surreal Australia, exists.

The red centre is not just Ayers Rock, bang in the middle of nowhere. There are meteorite craters, eerie canyons, lost valleys of palms and noisy Alice Springs' festivals. Where else has an annual boat regatta on a river that hardly ever has any water? The red, incidentally, is evident as soon as you arrive – in the soil, the rocks, even Ayers Rock itself.

At the other end of *the track* – the 1500 km of bitumen that connects Alice Springs to the north coast – is Darwin, probably the most cosmopolitan city in Australia, not to mention the heaviest drinking city in the world. There is an annual boat race in Darwin for boats constructed entirely of beer cans – they have to use up the empties somehow.

Even that long, empty road between the two cities isn't dull – there are plenty of interesting places along the way. As you travel up or down that single connecting link you'll notice another of the Territory's real surprises – the contrast between the centre's amazing aridity and the humid, tropical wetness of the top end in the monsoon season. Just two or three hours' drive east of Darwin are the wetlands and escarpments of Kakadu National Park, a treasure house of wildlife and Aboriginal rock paintings.

With a small population and a more fragile economy than other parts of Australia, the Northern Territory isn't classified as a state. Formerly administered by New South Wales then by South

Australia, it has been controlled directly by the federal government since 1911. Since 1978 the Territory has been self-governing, although Canberra still has more say over its internal affairs than over those of the states.

NORTHERN TERRITORY ABORIGINES

Aborigines form a higher proportion of the population in the Northern Territory than in most southern states. About a quarter of the Territory's population is Aboriginal, and in Darwin, Alice Springs and the towns along the track you'll see many of them.

There's hard evidence of Aboriginal presence in the top end 40,000 years ago, and they were probably around a long time before that. The Europeans who arrived in the 19th century had been preceded by Macassans who came from Sulawesi in Indonesia to harvest trepang, a kind of edible sea slug. The Aborigines had mixed relations with the Macassans – sometimes they worked for them, other times they chased them away. Macassans paid these seasonal visits to north Australia for three or four centuries until banned by the Australian government in the early 20th century.

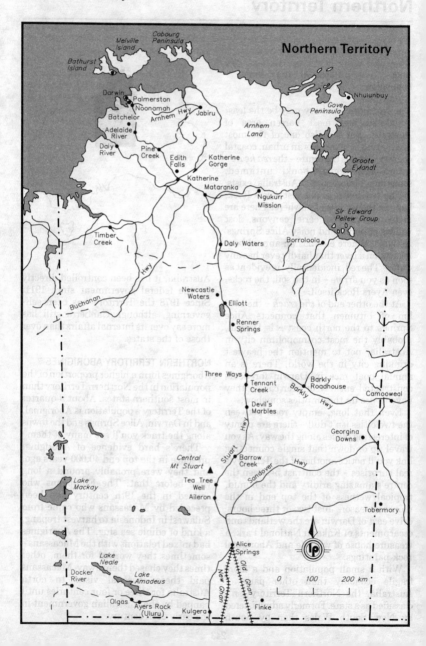

Northern Territory

Melville Island
Cobourg Peninsula
Bathurst Island
Darwin
Palmerston
Noonamah
Batchelor
Adelaide River
Arnhem Hwy
Jabiru
Arnhem Land
Nhulunbuy
Gove Peninsula
Daly River
Pine Creek
Edith Falls
Katherine Gorge
Katherine
Mataranka
Groote Eylandt
Ngukurr Mission
Sir Edward Pellew Group
Timber Creek
Daly Waters
Borroloola
Buchanan Hwy
Newcastle Waters
Elliott
Renner Springs
Three Ways
Tennant Creek
Barkly Roadhouse
Barkly Hwy
Camooweal
Devil's Marbles
Georgina Downs
Stuart Hwy
Barrow Creek
Sandover Hwy
Tobermory
Central Mt Stuart
Tea Tree Well
Aileron
Lake Mackay
Lake Neale
Lake Amadeus
Docker River
Alice Springs
New Ghan
Old Ghan
Olgas
Ayers Rock (Uluru)
Kulgera
Finke

0   100   200 km

The story of white settlement in the Northern Territory was just as troubled and violent as elsewhere in Australia, with Aboriginal groups vainly trying to resist the takeover of lands on which their way of life depended. By the early 20th century, most Aborigines were confined to government-allotted reserves or Christian missions. Others lived on cattle stations where they were employed as skilful and poorly paid stockmen, or were starting a half-life on the edges of towns, attracted there by food and tobacco, sometimes finding low-paid work, too often acquiring an alcohol habit. Only those remote few who hadn't been in contact with Europeans, and some of those on reserves or to a lesser extent cattle stations, maintained much of their traditional way of life.

This situation largely persisted despite a later shift in government policy to 'assimilation' – the belief that Aborigines should become fully integrated into white society. This, among other things, led to the gathering of many bush people, sometimes from different clans, into settlements for education, welfare, etc.

In the 1960s Northern Territory Aborigines began to demand more rights. In 1963 the people of Yirrkala on the Gove Peninsula, part of the Arnhem Land reserve, protested against plans for bauxite mining. In 1966 the Gurindji people on Wave Hill cattle station went on strike and asked for their tribal land, which formed part of the station, to be returned to them. Eventually the Gurindji were given 3238 square km in a government-negotiated deal with the station owners. The Yirrkala people failed to stop the mining, but the way they presented their case, by producing sacred objects and bark paintings that showed their right to the land under Aboriginal custom, was a milestone.

In 1976 the Aboriginal Land (NT) Act was passed in Canberra. It handed over all reserves and mission lands in the Territory to Aboriginal ownership, and allowed Aboriginal groups to claim government land with which they have traditional ties (unless the land is already leased to someone, or in a town, or set aside for some other special purpose). Today, despite one or two tricks by unsympathetic authorities, Aborigines own about one-third of the Northern Territory. This includes Uluru National Park (Uluru is the Aboriginal name for Ayers Rock), which was handed over to its Pitjantjatjara owners in 1985 and immediately leased back to the national government for use as a national park. Minerals on Aboriginal land are still government property – though the landowners' permission for exploration and mining is usually required and has to be paid for.

The NT land rights laws have improved the lot of many Aborigines and encouraged a movement that started in the 1970s, to leave settlements and return to a more traditional, nomadic life style on their own land, called the Outstation Movement. Many, however, still remain in depressing conditions on the fringes of towns. Ironically, equal-pay laws in the 1960s deprived Aborigines of a major source of work, when many cattle station owners reacted by employing white stockmen instead.

While white goodwill is probably on the increase, and more Aborigines are able to deal effectively with whites, there are still many yawning gulfs between the cultures, as the 'dress regulations' posted on many NT doors, and talk of banning camping in the dry bed of the Todd River in Alice Springs, show. Finding a mode of harmonious coexistence remains a serious and long-term problem.

For these and other reasons it's usually hard for short-term visitors to make real contact with Aborigines, who often prefer to be left to themselves. This reticence can extend to other Aboriginal clans who probably speak a different language – there are about 70 separate Aboriginal languages in the Northern Territory. Many Aborigines do not appreciate their photos being taken by strangers, even at a distance.

Aboriginal Art

You'll see lots of Aboriginal art in Alice Springs, Darwin and other towns. Art for sale is a modern development from sacred traditions like body and rock painting, and designs laid out on the earth.

The best known NT Aboriginal artist is Albert Namatjira (1902-59) whose watercolour landscapes rank among the best of all Australian painting. Another important group of Aboriginal painters are the 'dot painters' whose movement started in the early 1970s at Papunya, 258 km west of Alice Springs. Aborigines from several tribes, who were gathered at Papunya often against their will, found a way of keeping traditions alive by depicting Dreamtime stories on canvas.

These works look abstract, but in fact usually show, in a kind of map or code form, events from the journeys of the Dreamtime beings at the beginning of time, who travelled across the land creating its natural features. Aborigines associate themselves and their traditional lands closely with these beings, which are often seen as ancestors whose special places have to be protected.

Paintings from the Papunya 'school' now hang in galleries in Australia and overseas, and Aborigines elsewhere in the Territory have taken up the style. The best examples change hands for five, sometimes six figure sums. Such a success story has its downside – intermediaries usually make most of the profit and a lot of inferior work is flooding onto the market. The best work is far beyond the average traveller's pocket – but you can pick up good poster prints of some paintings, and several reasonably priced books with lots of colour plates and explanatory write-ups are available.

From the centre come some attractive carved wooden animals, with designs burnt into them. Some of these can be picked up for $20 or less in shops and aren't too big for a backpack. More expensive but also attractive, is the batik which has been produced in recent years by women in several places in the Territory – notably Utopia, 250 km northeast of Alice Springs. Some of this work, too, has found its way into major city galleries.

Top end art is, if anything, even more interesting. The rock paintings of Arnhem Land and Kakadu go back in some cases more than 20,000 years, and are among the world's most important ancient art treasures.

Another art form in the north is painting on tree bark – which has a longer tradition in western Arnhem Land than in central and east Arnhem Land, where it was introduced by missionaries this century. Many of the designs from rock painting now appear on bark. In broad terms, western Arnhem Land turns out dominant figures on plain backgrounds either in the famous X-ray style showing animals' bones and internal organs, or in 'Mimi' style developed from ancient 'stick figure' rock art. East and central Arnhem Land produce more detailed, narrative-style pictures. The works differ greatly in quality.

From Arnhem Land, notably the northeast, come some excellent painted wood carvings, mainly of birds – distinguishable from central Australian carvings by their designs and use of softer wood. Some of these aren't too pricey – or too big. Arnhem Land turns out appealing baskets made of pandanus leaf, coloured and patterned with vegetable dyes. Maningrida in north-central Arnhem Land is one of the chief sources of these.

The Tiwi people of Bathurst and Melville islands, north of Darwin, also produce bark paintings and fine, painted wood carvings – pelicans or totem pole-like works showing mythological beings. These poles have developed from *pukamani* burial poles which are erected around graves. The Tiwi also make good pottery, batik and screen printed fabric, some of which is turned into probably the best of the many Aboriginal-design T-shirts on the market.

Aborigine art seems generally cheaper in Alice Springs than in Darwin – though Darwin has a better range of top end stuff.

Permits

You need a permit to enter Aborigine land and in general these aren't granted unless you have friends or relatives working there, or you're on an organised tour. The exception to this rule is travel along public roads through Aboriginal land – though if you want to stop, even for fuel or provisions, you need a permit. If you stick to the main highways, there's no problem. Three land councils deal with all requests for permits: ask the permits officer of the appropriate council for an application form. The Northern Land Council (tel 81 7011) is at 47 Stuart Highway, Stuart Park, Darwin (postal address: PO Box 39843, Winnellie, NT 0820); the Tiwi Land Council (tel 78 3957), for Bathurst and Melville islands, is at Nguiu, Bathurst Island, via Darwin, NT 0800; and the Central Land Council (tel 52 3800) is at 33 Stuart Highway, Alice Springs (postal address: PO Box 3321, Alice Springs, NT 0870).

CLIMATE

Hot, cold, dry and wet – the Northern Territory has it all, but in the top end the climate is either hot and dry or hot and wet. Winter is much more comfortable with daytime temperatures dropping to the high 20°Cs or low 30°Cs. In summer 40°C is the norm and it's sticky and humid. The top end, however, thinks more in terms of 'dry' and 'wet' rather than winter and summer. Roughly, the dry is April to September, and the wet is October to March. April, with the rains tapering off, and October to December, with uncomfortably high humidity and that 'waiting for the rains' feeling, are transition periods. Only about 25 mm of

rain falls from May to October, then from October to May Darwin is deluged with 1500 mm – most of it in January, February and March! The top end is the most thunder-prone part of Australia: Darwin has over 90 'thunderdays' a year, all between September and March.

In the centre the temperatures are much more variable – plummeting below freezing on winter nights (July to August), and soaring into the high 40°Cs on summer days (December to January). Come prepared for both extremes and for the intensity of the sun at any time throughout the year. The annual rainfall is low, but comes in short, sharp bursts at any time of the year. When it comes, dirt roads quickly become a sticky quagmire.

INFORMATION

The NT Government Tourist Bureau has offices in Alice Springs, Tennant Creek, Katherine, Darwin and in most state capitals. Addresses of the NTGTB state offices are:

New South Wales
    Corner Barrack and George Sts, Sydney (tel 345 347)
Queensland
    48 Queen St, Brisbane (tel 229 5799)
South Australia
    9 Hindley St, Adelaide (tel 212 1133)
Victoria and Tasmania
    415 Bourke St, Melbourne (tel 670 6948)
Western Australia
    799 Hay St, Perth (tel 322 4255)

The NTGTB puts out several useful publications including the *Northern Territory Holiday Planner*.

For detailed information on Uluru and Kakadu national parks contact the Australian National Parks & Wildlife Service (tel 81 5299) in Darwin, which administers these two parks. NTGTB offices also have details on them and there are information offices in the parks themselves. Other parks and natural and historic reserves are run by the Conservation Commission of the Northern Territory, which has offices at Alice Springs, Yulara, Katherine and Darwin, plus an information desk in the NTGTB office in Darwin. The NTGTB and Conservation Commission together publish *Northern Territory National Parks & Reserves – a Guide for Visitors*, a useful free pamphlet. The Conservation Commission also puts out leaflets on individual parks – usually available in NTGTB offices.

Money

In 1988 the NT government slapped a 2½% bed tax on hotels and motels. It may be added to quoted prices.

ACTIVITIES

Bushwalking

There are interesting bushwalking trails in the Northern Territory, but take care if you venture off the beaten track. You can climb the ranges surrounding Alice Springs, but wear stout shoes (the spinifex grass and burrs are very sharp). In summer, wear a hat and carry water even for short walks. Walking is best in the dry, although shorter walks are possible in the wet when the patches of monsoon rainforest are at their best. The Darwin Bushwalking Club (tel 85 1484) makes weekend expeditions all year round and welcomes visitors.

Rock Hounding

There are many places in the Northern Territory for the fossicker – check with the NTGTB about where to go and if permission is required. Look around the Harts Range (72 km north-east of Alice Springs) for beryls, garnets and quartz; Eastern MacDonnell Ranges (east of Alice Springs) for beryls and garnets; Tennant Creek for gold and jasper; Anthony Lagoon (215 km east of the Stuart Highway, north of Tennant Creek) for ribbonstone; Pine Creek for gold; Brock's Creek (37 km south-west of Adelaide River, south of Darwin) for topaz, tourmaline, garnet and zircon.

The NT Department of Mines &

Energy publishes *A Guide to Fossicking in the Northern Territory* ($9). One place you can get it is the Arts & Sciences Museum in Darwin.

Gliding

The thermals created by the dry heat of the centre are fantastic for gliding. There are gliding clubs in Darwin and Alice Springs. They operate from Batchelor, 88 km south of Darwin, and from Bond Springs, 25 km north of Alice Springs.

Swimming

Stay out of the sea during the wet because box jellyfish (also known as sea wasps) stings can be fatal. Darwin beaches are popular, however, during the safe months. Beware too, of crocodiles in both salt and fresh waters in the top end – though there are quite a few safe, natural swimming holes.

Fishing

This is good, particularly for barramundi, a perch that often grows over a metre long and is great to eat. Barramundi is found both offshore and inland and there are fishing tours out of Darwin for the express purpose of catching it.

GETTING AROUND

Transport into the Northern Territory by bus, rail, road and air is discussed mainly in the Alice Springs, Darwin and Ayers Rock sections. Within the Territory, there's a fairly good bus network by several of the big national companies. If you're planning a long journey look into the different lines' stopover regulations – some of them allow free stopovers in a number of places on through tickets, others make you buy tickets for each part of your trip, which can work out more costly. Capital cities and major towns are usually free stopovers with the big companies. Bus Australia, for example, allows free stopovers at Katherine, Alice Springs and Ayers Rock, plus Kununurra, Broome, Port Hedland and Carnarvon on

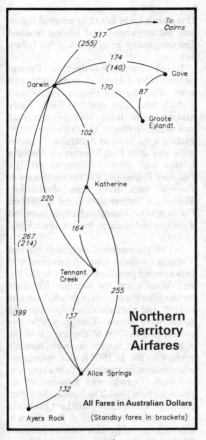

To Cairns
317 (255)
174 (140)
Gove
Darwin
170
87
Groote Eylandt
102
Katherine
220
164
267 (214)
Tennant Creek
255
399
137

Northern Territory Airfares

Alice Springs
132

All Fares in Australian Dollars

Ayers Rock (Standby fares in brackets)

Driving in the Northern Territory

Off the beaten track, 'with care' is the thought to bear in mind. Phone 52 3833 in Alice Springs or 84 4455 in Darwin for information on road conditions. The offices of the NTGTB will advise you on which roads require a 4WD.

It's wise to carry a basic kit of spare parts in case of breakdown. It may not be a matter of life or death, but it can save a lot of time, trouble and expense. Carry spare water and if you do break down off the main roads, remain with the vehicle: you're more likely to be found and you'll have shade and protection from the heat.

Traffic may be fairly light, but a lot of people still manage to run into things, so watch out for the two great NT road hazards – road trains and animals. Road trains are huge trucks, which can only be used on the long outback roads of central and northern Australia – they're not allowed into the southern cities. A road train is very long and very big. If you try to overtake one make sure you have plenty of room to complete the manoeuvre. If you pass one travelling in the opposite direction give it plenty of room – if a road train puts its wheels off the road to pass you, the shower of stones and rocks that result will not do you or your windscreen any good.

At night, dusk and dawn the Territory's wildlife comes out to play. Hitting a kangaroo is all too easy and the damage to your vehicle, not to mention the kangaroo, can be severe. There are also buffaloes, cattle, wild horses and a number of other driving hazards which you are wise to avoid. There's really only one sensible way to deal with these night time road hazards – don't drive!

Hitching

Hitching is possible, but traffic can be scarce outside the towns. Three Ways, where the road to Mt Isa branches off the Darwin to Alice Springs road, is a point notorious for long waits for lifts.

the way to/from Perth in Western Australia, Coober Pedy in South Australia and Mt Isa in Queensland. Of course, on a bus pass you can stop anywhere.

Ansett NT has a denser flight network than Ansett or Australian Airlines and, on a couple of routes, slightly cheaper fares. There are also two small airlines: Air North flying between Darwin, Kakadu, Arnhem Land and between Bathurst and Melville islands; and Tillair which operates between Alice Springs, Tennant Creek, Katherine and Darwin. The chart details regular (and standby) fares.

Darwin

Population 76,500

The 'capital' of northern Australia comes as a surprise to many people. Instead of the hard bitten, rough and ready town you might expect, Darwin's a lively, modern place with a young population, easy-going life style and cosmopolitan atmosphere.

In part this is thanks to Cyclone Tracy, which did a comprehensive job of flattening Darwin on Christmas Day 1974. People there during the reconstruction say a new spirit grew up with the new buildings as Darwinites, showing true top end resilience, took the chance to make their city one of which to be proud. Darwin became a brighter, smarter, sturdier place and development has continued into the 'post-post-cyclone' phase. Darwin's still a frontier town with a fairly transient population and a hard drinking one at that – it's not easy to resist a beer or two after a day in its heat – but these days it has the full trappings of civilisation too. It's also ethnically diverse with anywhere between 45 and 60 ethnic groups represented, depending on who you listen to. Asian and European accents are almost as thick in the air as the Aussie drawl, and Darwin's popular mayor, Alec Fong Lim, is a Chinese-Australian.

A lot of people only live here for a year or two – it's surprising how many people you meet elsewhere who used to live in Darwin. It's reckoned you can consider yourself a 'Territorian' if you've stuck the climate and remoteness for five years. There is a constant flow of travellers coming and going from Asia, or making their way round Australia. Backpacks seem part of the everyday scene and people always appear to be heading somewhere. Darwin's an obvious base for trips to Kakadu or other top end natural attractions. It's a bit of an oasis too – whether you're travelling south to Alice Springs, west to WA or east to Queensland,

there are a lot of km to be covered before you get anywhere, and having reached Darwin, many people rest a bit before leaving.

It took a long time to decide on Darwin as the site for the region's main centre and even after the city became established growth was slow and troubled. Early attempts to settle the top end were mainly due to British fears of the French or Dutch getting a foothold in Australia. Between 1824 and 1829 Fort Dundas on Melville Island and Fort Wellington on the Cobourg Peninsula, 200 km north-east of Darwin, were tried then abandoned. Victoria, a further settlement in 1838 on Cobourg's Port Essington harbour, survived a cyclone and malaria, but was abandoned in 1849.

In 1845 the explorer Leichhardt reached Victoria overland from Queensland and this aroused persistent interest in the top end. What's now the Northern Territory came under the control of South Australia in 1863, and more ambitious development plans were made. Escape Cliffs was established in 1864 at the mouth of the Adelaide River, not too far from Darwin's present locale. In 1866 it was abandoned when its location turned out to be a poor one.

Finally Darwin was founded at its present site in 1869. The harbour had been found back in 1839 by John Lort Stokes in the *Beagle*, who named it Port Darwin after a former shipmate – the evolutionist Charles Darwin. At first the settlement was called Palmerston, but soon became unofficially known as Port Darwin and in 1911 the name was officially changed.

Darwin's growth was accelerated by the discovery of gold at Pine Creek, about 200 km south, in 1871, but once the gold fever had run its course Darwin dropped back to slow and erratic development. The harsh, unpredictable climate – including occasional cyclones – and tenuous connections with the rest of the country held growth back. WW II put Darwin permanently on the map when it became an important base for Allied action against the Japanese. The road south to the railhead at Alice Springs was surfaced, finally putting the city in close contact with the rest of the country. Darwin was attacked 64 times during the war and 243 people lost their lives.

Modern Darwin has an important role as the front door to Australia's northern region and as a centre for administration and mining activities. The port facilities have been expanded – but hopes of a railway line to Alice Springs have receded for the time being. Darwin's population, after rising rapidly, has steadied in the past few years but the place still has a go ahead feel. The tourism industry is growing and, especially in the dry season, Darwin is a good area in which to look for work.

Orientation

Darwin's centre is a fairly compact area at the end of a peninsula. The Stuart Highway does a big loop entering the city and finally heads south until it ends under the name Daly St. The downtown peninsula stretches south-east from here, and the main downtown shopping area, Smith St with its mall, is about a km from Daly St. Long distance buses arrive at the transit centre at 69 Mitchell St, with numerous accommodation possibilities a few minutes' walk away. Most of what you'll want in central Darwin is within two or three blocks of the transit centre or Smith St Mall. The suburbs spread a good 12 to 15 km away to the north and east, but the airport is conveniently central.

Information

The NT Government Tourist Bureau (tel 81 6611) is at 31 Smith St, in the mall. It's open from 8.45 am to 5 pm Monday to Friday, from 9 am to 12 noon on Saturdays. It has free maps of the city and several decent booklets, and arranges a big array of tours. The Conservation Commission of the Northern Territory has a desk in this office. The Australian National Parks & Wildlife Service (tel 81 5299) is in the Commercial Union

building on Smith St between Lindsay and Whitfield Sts. There's a tourist office at the airport.

The NT Government Information Centre (tel 89 7972) at 13 Smith St, open from Monday to Friday from 9 am to 4 pm, is more for locals, but if you're interested in delving into some aspect of the Northern Territory they may be able to help. The city library is in the Paspalis Centrepoint arcade on Smith St Mall and the Northern Territory Reference Library at 25 Cavenagh St (open from Monday to Saturday from 10 am to 6 pm) has stacks of material on the NT, as well as interstate and overseas newspapers. Book World on Smith St Mall is a good bookshop; you'll find all the Lonely Planet guides for travel to Asia here. Also on the mall there's the Darwin Newsagency. Darwin has a daily newspaper, the *NT News*.

There are good notice boards in the mall (a couple of doors from the tourist office) and in the two backpacker hostels on Mitchell St – good for buying and selling things (like vehicles) or looking for rides. The post office is on the corner of Smith and Knuckey Sts. The poste restante, though computerised, is not very efficient, so double check for your mail. The National Trust is just over the road on Knuckey St – pick up a copy of their Darwin walking tour leaflet (or from the tourist office). The Automobile Association of the NT (tel 81 3837) is at 79-81 Smith St.

You can rent camping gear from U-Rent at the corner of Mitchell and Knuckey Sts – a full kit is $18 a day for two people, $15 for one. Cheapa Rent-a-Car has camping gear and boats available at decent rates with some of its vehicles.

Don't swim in Darwin waters from October to May. You only get one sting from a box jellyfish (sea wasp) each lifetime. There are crocodiles along the coast and rivers – but any found in the harbour are removed, and other coasts near the city are patrolled to minimise the risk.

In recent years the Darwin CES office

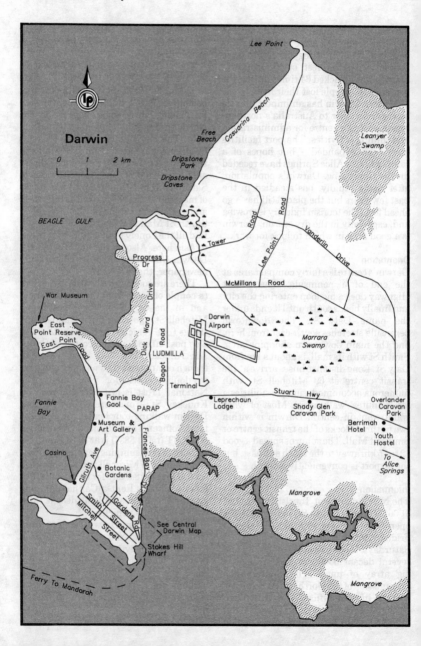

has reportedly had far fewer casual labouring jobs than many other cities. If you go there looking for work they may ask for your work visa.

Remember they're fussy about 'dress rules' here – if you don't meet their 'standards' you don't get in.

Festivals

Aside from the Beer Can Regatta in June, with its sports and contests, there is the Bougainvillea Festival leading up to it, earlier in June. It's a week of concerts, dances, a picnic in the Botanic Gardens and a parade on the final day. Darwin also goes into festive mood for May Day (International Labour Day), regarded as the start of the 'no box jellyfish season' and the occasion of big beach parties, rock concerts the night before, etc. The jellyfish don't always leave on time. Darwinites are as fond of horse races as all other Australians and two big days at the Fannie Bay track are St Patrick's Day (17 March) and the Darwin Cup (October).

Activities

Windsurfers are for hire in front of the casino at Mindil Beach. The Bush Survival School (tel 81 6611, 81 9733) can teach you how to find food and water in the bush and other traditional wilderness skills.

Darwin & Cyclone Tracy

The statistics of Tracy are frightening. The winds built up over Christmas Eve 1974 and by midnight began to reach their full fury. At 3.05 am the airport's anemometer cried 'enough', failing just after it recorded a speed of 217 kph. It's thought the peak wind speeds were as high as 280 kph. Of Darwin's 11,200 houses 50% to 60% were either totally destroyed or so badly damaged that repair was impossible. Only 400 houses survived relatively intact and 66 lives were lost.

Much criticism was levelled at the design and construction of Darwin's houses, but plenty of places a century or more old, and built as solidly as you could ask for, also toppled before the awesome winds. The new and rebuilt houses have been cyclone proofed with strong steel reinforcements and roofs which are firmly pinned down.

Next time a cyclone is forecast, most people say they'll jump straight into their cars and head down the track – and come back afterwards to find out if their houses really were cyclone proof! Those who stay will probably take advantage of the official cyclone shelters.

Town Centre

Despite its shaky beginnings and the destruction of WW II and Cyclone Tracy, Darwin still has a number of historic buildings. The National Trust produces an interesting booklet titled A Walk Through Historical Darwin.

Among the old buildings the Victoria Hotel on Smith St Mall was originally built in 1894 and was badly damaged by Tracy, but has been restored. On the corner of the mall and Bennett St the stone Commercial Bank dates from 1884. The old town hall, a little further down Smith St, was built in 1883 but virtually destroyed by Tracy, despite its solid Victorian construction. Today only its walls remain. Across the road Brown's Mart, a former mining exchange dating from 1885, was badly damaged but has been restored and now houses a theatre. There's a Chinese temple, glossy and new, on the corner of Woods and Bennett Sts.

Christ Church Cathedral, a short distance further towards the harbour, was destroyed by the cyclone. It was originally built in 1902, but all that remained after Tracy was the porch, which was a later addition from 1944. A new cathedral has been built and the old porch retained.

The 1884 police station and old courthouse at the corner of Smith St and the Esplanade were badly damaged, but have been restored and are used as government offices. A little south along the Esplanade, Government House, built in stages from 1870, was known as The Residency until 1911, and has been damaged by just about every cyclone Darwin has been subject to. It is once again in fine condition.

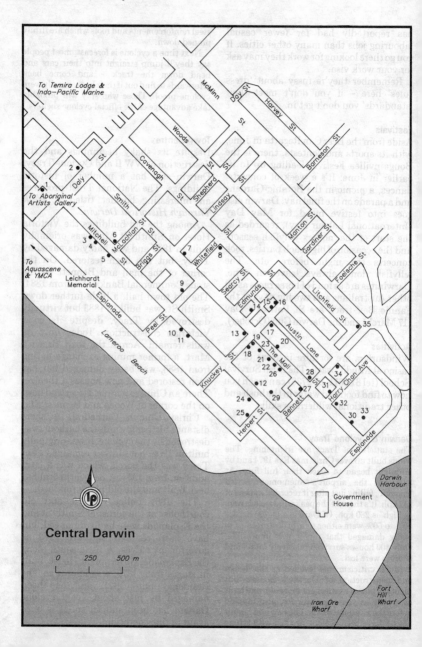

To Temira Lodge &
Indo-Pacific Marine

To Aboriginal
Artists Gallery

To Aquascene
& YMCA

McMinn St

Day St

Harvey St

Barneson St

Manton St

Gardiner St

Faelsche St

Woods St

Cavenagh St

Shepherd St

Lindsay St

Smith St

Doly St

Mitchell St

McLachlan St

Briggs St

Whitfield St

Searcy St

Edmunds St

Litchfield St

Leichhardt
Memorial

Esplanade

Peel St

Lameroo Beach

Knuckey St

Herbert St

Bennett St

The Mall

Austin Lane

Harry Chan Ave

Esplanade

Government
House

Darwin
Harbour

Central Darwin

0   250   500 m

Iron Ore
Wharf

Fort
Hill Wharf

1	YWCA
2	Thai Garden Restaurant
3	International Network Hotel
4	Darwin Motor Inn
5	Backpackers International
6	Performing Arts Centre
7	National Parks &
	Wildlife Service Office
8	Tiwi Lodge
9	Sherwood Lodge
10	Transit Centre & Transit Inn
11	Darwin City YHA Hostel
12	Larrakeyah Lodge
13	GPO
14	Indonesian Food House
15	Simply Foods &
	Maharajah Indian Restaurant
16	Windsor Tourist Lodge Restaurant
17	Pancake Palace
18	Singapore Airlines
19	National Trust
20	Darwin Plaza
21	Paspalis Centrepoint Arcade
22	Ansett
23	Northern Territory
	Government Tourist Bureau
24	Salvation Army Hostel
25	Darwin Hotel
26	Victoria Hotel
27	Book World
28	Qantas
29	Natrabu Travel Agency
30	Government Information Centre
31	City Bus Terminal
32	Brown's Mart
33	Christ Church Cathedral
34	Australian Airlines & Garuda
35	Chinese Temple

Continuing round the Esplanade you reach a memorial marking where the telegraph cable once ran from Darwin into the sea on its crossing to Banyuwangi in Java (just across from Bali). This put Australia into instant communication with Britain for the first time.

Other buildings of interest along the Esplanade include the agreeably tropical Darwin Hotel, and Admiralty House at the corner of Knuckey St, which houses an arts and crafts gallery showing work by professional top end artists, sometimes Aborigine. Underneath is a pleasant cafe.

Across the street at 74 Esplanade, in Lyons Cottage, is the British-Australian Telegraph Residence Museum. It's free and open daily, from 10 am to 12 noon and 12.30 to 5 pm. There are displays on pre-1911 north Australian history, including early exploration, the 18th century Macassan trepang fishermen from south-west Sulawesi in Indonesia, pearling, and the early decades of European settlement. About 500 metres further along the Esplanade is modern Darwin's architectural talking point, the pink and blue Beaufort Darwin Centre, housing a luxury hotel, a couple of up-market cafes, and the Performing Arts Centre.

The Esplanade is fronted by an expanse of grass and trees, and a pleasant pathway runs along near the sea from the Hotel Darwin to Daly St.

Just out of the centre at 28-30 Gardens Hill Crescent, Stuart Park there's an interesting small Aviation Museum with old aircraft and assorted bits and pieces.

Aquascene

This is a tourist attraction actually worth the cost of admission. At Doctor's Gully, near the corner of Daly St and the Esplanade, fish come in for a feed every day at high tide. Half the stale bread in Darwin gets dispensed to a horde of milkfish, mullet, catfish and batfish. Some are quite big – the milkfish grow to over a metre and will demolish a whole slice of bread in one go. It's a great scene and, of course, children love it – the fish will take bread right out of your hand. Feeding times depend on the tides (phone 81 7837 for tide times). Admission is $2.50 for adults, the bread is free.

Botanic Gardens

The gardens' site was used to grow vegetables during the earliest days of Darwin. Tracy severely damaged the gardens, uprooting 75% of the plants. Fortunately vegetation grows fast in Darwin's climate and the Botanic Gardens, with their good collection of tropical flora, were well restored. A coastal section has recently been added over the road, between Gilruth Ave and Fannie Bay. It's an easy bicycle ride out to the gardens from the centre.

Indo-Pacific Marine

This small aquarium is a successful attempt to display living coral and its associated life. Each small tank is a complete ecosystem, with only the occasional fish introduced as food for some of the carnivores such as stonefish or angler fish. It's a friendly place and you're able to ask questions and get a little expert fact and opinion. They sometimes have box jellyfish, as well as more attractive creatures like seahorses, clownfish and butterfly fish. The aquarium is at the corner of Smith St West and Gilruth Ave, about 1½ km from Smith St Mall. Admission is $5 for adults and it's open Wednesdays, Saturdays and Sundays from 12 noon to 4 pm.

Museum of Arts & Sciences

This excellent museum and art gallery is on Conacher St, Fannie Bay, about four km from the city centre. It's bright, spacious, well laid out, not too big and full of interesting displays. A highlight is the Northern Territory Aborigine art collection, with just the right amount of artefacts and explanation to help you start to understand the purpose of this art, its history and regional differences. It's particularly strong on carvings and bark paintings from Bathurst and Melville islands and Arnhem Land.

There's also a good collection on the art of the Pacific and Asian nations closest to Australia, including Indonesian *ikat* and a gamelan instruments; and a sea gypsies' floating home, a *prahu*, from Sabah, Malaysia.

Pride of place among the stuffed NT birds and animals undoubtedly goes to 'Sweetheart', a five metre, 780 kg saltwater crocodile, who became quite a top end personality after numerous encounters with fishing dinghies on the Finnis River south of Darwin. Apparently he had a taste for outboard motors. He died during capture in 1979. You can also see a box jellyfish – safely dead – in a jar.

The non-Aborigine Australian art collection includes works by all the top names like Nolan, Lindsay and Boyd. The museum has a good little bookshop and, outside, an old pearling lugger, a Vietnamese refugee boat and a plant trail explaining the Aborigine uses for over 50 species. Admission is free and it's open from Monday to Friday from 9 am to 5 pm, Saturday and Sunday 10 am to 6 pm. You can get there on bus No 4 or No 6.

Fannie Bay Gaol Museum

Another interesting museum is a little further out of town at the corner of East Point Rd and Ross Smith Ave. This was Darwin's main jail from 1883 to 1979, when a new maximum security lock up opened at Berrimah. You can look round the old cells and see the gallows used in the Territory's last hanging in 1952. There are also good displays on Cyclone Tracy, transport, technology and industrial archaeology. Open daily, from 10 am to 5 pm, admission is free. Take bus No 4 or No 6 from the city centre.

East Point

This spit of undeveloped land north of Fannie Bay is good to visit in the late afternoon when wallabies come out to feed, cool breezes spring up and you can watch the sunset across the bay. There are some walking and riding trails as well as a road to the tip of the point. On the north side of the point is a series of wartime gun emplacements and the Royal Australian Artillery Museum, devoted to Darwin's WW II activity, open daily from 9.30 am to 5 pm. The city was the only place in Australia to suffer continuous attack during the war. Bus No 4 or No 6 will take you five km from downtown to the corner of East Point Rd and Ross Smith Ave;

Top: Climbing Ayers Rock, NT (TW)
Left: Garden of Eden, Kings Canyon, NT (TW)
Right: Ayers Rock, NT (TW)

Top: Lubra's Leap, Katherine Gorge, NT (TW)
Bottom: Corroboree Rock, near Alice Springs, NT (TW)

from there it's three km to the tip of the point.

Beaches

Darwin has plenty of beaches, but you're wise to keep out of the water during the October to May wet season because of deadly box jellyfish ('stingers'). Popular beaches include Mindil and Vestey's on Fannie Bay, and Mandorah, across the bay from the town (see Around Darwin). In north Darwin, there's a stinger net protecting part of Nightcliff beach off Casuarina Drive, and a stretch of the seven km long Casuarina beach further east is an official free beach. Like so many places in tropical Australia, Darwin has a waterslide – it's at Parap Pool on Ross Smith Ave and is open daily.

Places to Stay

Darwin has hostels, guest houses, motels, holiday flats, and a clutch of up-market hotels. Several new places that have opened up in central locations in the last couple of years will ease the former dry season overcrowding. There are also a number of places offering discounts for longer stays – good if you want work. The city's only accommodation shortcoming is that its many caravan parks/camping grounds are all several km out. Darwin is a great meeting place and many travellers convene in Smith St Mall or in various coffee bars and find a place to stay that way.

Hostels & Guest Houses There's a host of choices in this bracket, with several of the cheapest places on or near Mitchell St, conveniently close to the transit centre. Most places have guest kitchens, and the showers and toilets are almost always communal.

The 180-bed *Darwin City YHA Hostel* (tel 81 3995) is at 69A Mitchell St next to the transit centre. Its rooms are all fan cooled twins and cost $10 per person plus $1 for a sleeping sheet. If you're not a YHA member you can take three nights

'introductory membership' for a further $6. The building has new kitchens, bathrooms and an open air sitting area. An office of YHA Travel is planned to open in the hostel or in the transit centre.

Darwin's old youth hostel, 12 km from the city centre at Berrimah, closed down when the Mitchell St hostel opened, but may reopen if there's enough demand. The old hostel is on Beaton Rd, off Hidden Valley Rd, which is off the Stuart Highway.

Backpackers International (tel 81 5385) at 88 Mitchell St has a pool, two kitchens, frequent barbecues, and camping gear for rent. A dormitory bunk or a bed in one of the few twin rooms is $10. It's friendly and informal with air-con dormitories.

Another backpacker hostel, pleasant but sometimes hard to get into, is the small *Darwin Rest House* (tel 81 1638) at 11 Houston St. It has a good pool, and charges $9 whether you're in a dormitory, a double room or a caravan in the back garden. To get there, follow Smith St away from the city centre and turn right opposite the Asti Motel, soon after Daly St. Houston St is the first on the left.

The *Darwin Transit Inn* (tel 81 9733) at 69 Mitchell St has its reception actually in the transit centre. As the Lammeroo Lodge this used to be the grubbiest Darwin hostel, but its new management is planning some much needed improvements, including proper cooking facilities and a dining room. There's a small pool and prices are $17/27/37 for singles/doubles/triples, with a $20 key deposit, or $37 for air-con doubles, some with bathrooms. Singles with fridges are $18, but rates may change as the place is upgraded.

The smaller *Sherwood Lodge* (tel 41 0427) is at 15 Peel St, with a breezy kitchen and sitting area upstairs. The cost is $14 per person, which gets you anything from a single or a decent sized double to a bunk in a cramped dorm. The place is clean, all rooms have fans, and sheets are supplied.

If you can't get into the usual hostels try the *Darwin Motor Inn* (tel 81 1122) at 97 Mitchell St. This is a $50 to $65 range motel, but it often lets out empty rooms, especially out of peak season, to back-packers at $11 a head. It's quite a bargain since $22 will get you an air-con twin with private bathroom, fridge and TV, but no cooker. There's a small pool.

The YWCA, YMCA and the Country Women's Association also have hostels. The big, popular *YWCA* (tel 81 8644) is at 119 Mitchell St. It takes women and men and has no curfew. Rooms have fans and fridges, are clean and well kept, and there are two TV lounges and a kitchen. In the dry season, from 1 April, a dorm bed costs $17, a single $22, a twin room $30 per couple, and a bedsitter with bathroom $25/36 per person/couple, and a few dollars less in the wet season. Weekly rates, which save you two or more nights' cost, are available for some rooms, but there's a three night limit on dorm beds.

The small *CWA Hostel* (tel 41 1536) is nearby, at the corner of Mitchell St and Packard Place, and takes women and men. It has two four-bed units with private bathrooms, fridge, kettle and toaster for $17 per person, plus four twin-share rooms with shared bathrooms for long-stay women only at $14 a head, and a six-bed dormitory at $9. There's a shared kitchen, a big garden and a TV room. You don't have to be a CWA member to stay.

The *YMCA* (tel 81 8377) is at Doctor's Gully, just past the end of the Esplanade. It too takes men and women, but is not so good for solo women. The place could do with some renovations and lacks a kitchen, but it does have a good pool. Rooms are fan cooled. A dorm bed (three nights maximum) costs $14, a single room without fridge is $20, singles with fridge are $22/28 per person/couple, twins with fridge $33/37. Weekly rates are less than the cost of four nights. There's a $15 deposit for key and linen.

Darwin has several small guest houses – good for longer as well as short stays. Among those which aren't too far from the centre is the friendly *Park Lodge* (tel 81 5692) at 42 Coronation Drive, Stuart Park. The house has 20 good, clean, modern rooms and a fine garden on a quiet street. All rooms have fan, air-con and fridge; bathrooms, kitchen, sitting/TV room and laundry are communal. Doubles cost $28 including air-con if you stay just one night. If you stay longer you pay for as much air-con as you use, plus $20 a night or $100 a week, or $90 a week for three or more weeks. Singles cost around 80% of the double rate. To get there, turn right off the Stuart Highway into Kent Court, about two km north of central Darwin. At the end of Kent Court go left along Coronation Drive to Park Lodge – about three minutes' walk from the highway. Numerous city buses, including Nos 5 and 8, run to this part of Darwin along the highway.

Bay Lodge on Mitchell St opposite the YWCA, has eight single rooms for $11 a day or $65 a week. Bathrooms and kitchens are shared. At 144 Mitchell St, about one km from the Daly St junction, is the *Sunset City Lodge* (tel 81 7326), where single or shared rooms with fridges cost from $14. There's a fully equipped kitchen, a laundry and a TV lounge. Another guest house is at 146 Mitchell St.

There's a *Salvation Army Hostel* (tel 81 8188) at 49 Mitchell St. There are quite a few permanents here, but short-stay visitors are welcome. Rooms are decent and there's a kitchen on each floor. Costs are $14 single or $12 each in a shared room. By the week it costs $50 a single or $45 each, shared.

Finally, two holiday flat places in the northern suburbs have cheap dormitory or shared rooms as well as normal flats. *Crocodile Lodge* (tel 85 2566) at 146 Dick Ward Drive, Coconut Grove, about 10 km north of the centre, has a budget guest house with singles for $12 to $19 or shared rooms at $9 to $14 per head. In Nightcliff,

12 km from the centre, *Top Darwin Holiday Units* (tel 85 4166) at 91 Aralia St has beds in an air-con dormitory at $9 a night. There are shared kitchen, bathroom and laundry facilities, plus a swimming pool.

Motels, Hotels & Holiday Flats There are plenty of modern places in Darwin. Prices in this range often differ markedly between the dry season (April to October) and the cheaper wet season, and the NT government's 2½% bed tax is more likely to be charged. Many of them give discounts if you stay a week or more – usually of the 7th-night-free variety. Typically these places have air-con and swimming pools.

Three older and cheaper places in central Darwin lack pools, however. The *Larrakeyah Lodge* (tel 81 7550) at 50 Mitchell St, offers 56 comfortable air-con rooms with fridge and shared facilities for $35 single, $45 or $49 double. There is a TV lounge, laundry and coffee shop.

In the centre at 35 Cavenagh St, the *Air Raid City Lodge* (tel 81 9214) has air-con rooms – all with shower and toilet, fridge and tea/coffee making facilities – at $35/40, room only. At 53 Cavenagh St, on the corner of Whitfield St, the *Tiwi Lodge* (tel 81 6471) is a motel with rooms at $50 and all have the usual motel facilities. Breakfast is available ($6 'tropical', $8 cooked). The newer 12-room *Palms Motel* (tel 81 4188) at 100 McMinn St has a pool, and singles/twins/triples for $42/47/51 in the wet, $50/59/69 in the dry.

Another downtown place worth considering is *Crest Townhouses* (tel 81 1922) at 88 Woods St, which offers 'studios' for three adults or a family for $47 in the wet, $59 in the dry. There are also bigger (two bedroom) 'town houses' for $57 (wet), $79 (dry). *Peninsular Apartments* (tel 81 1922) at 115 Smith St West has studios for three adults or a family at $55 (wet), or $79 (dry).

About two km from the centre *Temira Lodge* (tel 41 1515) is on Kahlin Ave, the continuation of Smith St. Mindil Beach is in easy walking distance. Temira Lodge is a big air-con place, where comfortable singles/doubles with shared bathrooms are $34/45, and family rooms with private bathrooms are $69. Rooms have fridges and tea/coffee making equipment, and there's a good swimming pool, TV lounges and a bistro grill.

There's a good deal to be had sometimes at the *Boulevard Apartment Motel* (tel 81 1544) at 38 Gardens Rd, the continuation of Cavenagh St beyond Daly St. Comfortable modern motel rooms, which normally cost $46 for one, two or three people are let for $33 when the place isn't busy (more likely in the wet). Rooms have private bathroom, fridge and TV and there's a pool, tennis court and restaurant. It's worth checking other motels for similar deals in the off-peak season – or ask in the tourist office.

If you have a vehicle there are places worth considering in the suburbs. In Parap the *Casablanca Motel* (tel 81 2163) at 52 Gregory St is cheap with rooms at $28/33/33 for singles/doubles/triples in the wet or $33/38/44 in the dry. *Parap Village Apartments* (tel 41 0301) at 39 Parap Rd, Fannie Bay, has three-bedroom flats for $95 in the wet, $110 in the dry, and two-bedroom flats for $77 (wet), and $95 (dry). The *Darwin Capricornia Motel* (tel 81 4055) at 3 Kellaway St, Fannie Bay, has singles/twins for $35/39 (wet), $41/46 (dry).

Crocodile Lodge has one bedroom flats from $49 to $77 and two-bedroom flats for $60 to $105. *Top Darwin Holiday Units* has a variety of rooms with the cheapest costing $35/45/50 for one/two/three people. A 20% discount, usually offered for wet season or standby occupancy, makes these reasonable value – even the cheapest rooms are spacious, with fridge, air-con, fan, private bathroom and tea/coffee making facilities.

Directly across from the airport on the Stuart Highway the *Leprechaun Lodge* (tel 84 3400) costs $47/52 for singles/twins. At the *Berrimah Hotel-Motel* (tel 84

3999) also on the Stuart Highway, at Berrimah, 12½ km from town, modern motel-style rooms are $44 to $55.

Other than these places you're generally into the $50 plus bracket. The most expensive are the big modern hotels on Mitchell St and the Esplanade. You'll pay $115 plus for a room at the *Atrium, Sheraton, Beaufort* or *Travelodge*.

Camping Sadly, Darwin takes no advantage of what could be fine camping sites on its many open spaces. East Point, for instance, would be superb. To camp or get an on-site van you must go to one of the privately run caravan parks in the outer city. A second drawback is that a number of the more conveniently situated caravan parks don't take tent campers.

Darwin sites include:

Pandanus Holiday Centre (tel 27 2897), 14 km north of city centre at Lee Point Rd, camping sites and cabins. One of the best. Take a No 2 bus to get there.
Shady Glen Caravan Park (tel 84 3330), 10 km east, at the corner of Stuart Highway and Farrell Crescent, Winnellie, camping sites at $9 for two, on-site vans $30 for two, cabins $36 for two.
Overlander Caravan Park (tel 84 3025), 13 km east at 1064 McMillans Rd, Berrimah, camping sites at $5 to $11 for two, cabins and units from $17, on-site vans $16 to $31 per night, cheaper rates for weekly occupancy, possibly more expensive in the dry.
Sundowner Caravan Park (tel 47 0045), 13 km east at the corner of McMillans Rd and Stuart Highway, Berrimah, camping sites $11 for two, on-site vans $28 for two ($22 in wet), cheaper weekly rates.
Rural Caravan Park (tel 84 3891), 17 km east on Stuart Highway, camping sites.

Also consider camping at Howard Springs, 26 km out, where there are three caravan parks taking campers (see Around Darwin).

Places to Eat

Darwin's closeness to Asia is obvious in its large number of fine Asian eateries, but on the whole it's not cheap to eat out. Take-away places, a growing number of lunch spots in and around Smith St Mall and the excellent Asian-style markets – held two or three times a week at various sites round the city – are the cheapest.

Cafes, Pubs & Take-aways – city Next to the transit centre on Mitchell St there's a new food centre with a variety of reasonably priced stalls and open air tables to sit at. A host of snack bars and cafes in Smith St Mall offers lots of choice during the day – but, except for Thursday, the late shopping night, they're virtually all closed from about 5 pm and on Saturday afternoons and Sundays.

There's a good collection of fast food counters in Darwin Plaza towards the Knuckey St end of the mall – the *Sheik's Tent* for Lebanese, the *Taco House* for Mexican, the *Thai Kitchen* for Thai-Chinese, *Energy Foods* and *La Veg* for health foods, and *Roseland* for yoghurt, fruit salads and ice cream.

Opposite Darwin Plaza in the Paspalis Centrepoint arcade, the *Little Lark* is a popular BYO lunch spot. As well as the usual fast food, it has a Chinese take-away or sit-down menu. Most main dishes are $5 including rice. It's open from 8 am. Next door is the *Lite Bite* for vegetarian food, sandwiches, pitta breads and salads.

Further up the mall the *Central City Cafe* is another very popular place with a few outdoor tables. It's open from 7 am and a full breakfast is around $6. Again further up the mall is Anthony Plaza where the *French Bakehouse* is one of the few places you can get a coffee and snack every day. The *Cosmopolitan Cafe* next door is a busy breakfast and lunch spot – a healthy breakfast of fresh fruit, muesli, juice and toast costs $5.

In Star Village, the last arcade on this side of the mall, the *Danish Connection* offers European open-face sandwiches, stroganoffs, steaks, burgers and moussaka in the $6 to $9 range.

Opposite Anthony Plaza is the Victoria Arcade, where the *Victoria Hotel* has lunch or dinner for as little as $5 in its upstairs Essington Carvery. Downstairs in the bar the barramundi burgers ($7 including chips and salad) are excellent, as are the steaks. In the arcade the *Sate House* has good cheap Indonesian fare. The popular *Brasserie* at the top of the mall is a licensed restaurant with both indoor and outdoor tables. Meals are quite cheap. It's open for breakfast from 9 am.

Simply Foods at 37 Knuckey St is a busy health food place. It's a good spot with appealing decor, music and friendly service. The *Vitality Snack Bar*, opposite the post office on Knuckey St, is a take-away health food shop offering sandwiches with generous fillings from $2.50, plus smoothies, juices and 'health cakes'. *Dusty's Sandwich Bar* on Knuckey St, near Mitchell St, is a good place to escape the heat as it's air-con and has lots of magazines to read.

Round the corner at 17 Cavenagh St, the *Tudor House Antiques & Fine Art Gallery* has a coffee lounge, with delicious home made cakes at $2 a slice and freshly ground coffee. Its double role gives it the most interesting decor of any Darwin cafe! For take-away pizzas, try the *Riviera* on the corner of Cavenagh and Searcy Sts.

In Admiralty House, the open air *Garden Café* provides a welcome breeze in Darwin's heat and humidity. Meals are around $8 and everything is fresh and home made. Open daily.

The *Darwin Hotel*, stretching from the Esplanade to Mitchell St, has a daily barbecue lunch for $10. Evening meals in its *Banjo* restaurant are $13 to $21. *The Pub* in the Sheraton Hotel on Mitchell St has a lunch special from 12 noon to 2 pm, Monday to Friday, offering a carvery sandwich and salad for $6. There's a happy hour (or three), Monday to Friday from 4 to 7 pm.

Restaurants - city The *Maharajah Indian Restaurant*, at 37 Knuckey St, is slightly more expensive - but has a good $7

lunch special including a glass of wine. The menu is extensive with dishes at $7 to $11. The *Pancake Palace* on Cavenagh St near Knuckey St is open daily for lunch and in the evening until 1 am. Conveniently close to many of Darwin's night spots, it has sweet and savoury pancakes from $4. Cheap pasta meals are hard to find in Darwin. There is a $10 midweek pasta feast on Wednesday nights at *Gabby's Bar & Bistro* in the arcade off Cavenagh St, opposite the Pancake Palace. The price includes a carafe of wine and coffee. It opens at 6.30 pm.

Other restaurants include French, steakhouses, seafood specialists, Greek and Italian. The numerous Chinese places are generally rather up-market. The *Jade Garden* on Smith St Mall (upstairs, roughly opposite the Victoria Arcade) offers a nine course meal for $11 a head.

Out of the Centre On Smith St, just beyond Daly St, the *Thai Garden Restaurant* serves not only delicious and reasonably priced Thai food but pizzas too! They have a few outdoor tables. There's *Julia's Pizza* across the road, and a clutch of fast food places nearby, some open 24 hours.

Further out, the *Parap Hotel* on Parap Rd between Gregory and Hingston Sts does counter meals. It also has *Jessie's Bistro* where buffalo and beef steaks are around $10. It's open for lunch and dinner Monday to Saturday, and from 2 pm on Sundays. Locals recommend the food here. There are two other Jessie's Bistro locations - one in the *Casuarina Tavern* and the other in the *Berrimah Hotel* on the Stuart Highway at Berrimah.

At Rapid Creek, the *Beachfront Hotel* on the Esplanade does decent counter meals.

Markets Easily the best all-round eating experience in Darwin is the bustling Asian-style market at Mindil Beach on Thursday nights during the dry season. People begin arriving from 5.30 pm, bringing tables, chairs, rugs, grog and kids to settle under the coconut palms for sunset and decide which of the tantalising foodstall smells has the greatest allure. It's difficult to know whether to choose Thai, Sri Lankan, Indian, Malaysian, Chinese, Greek or Portuguese. You'll even find Indonesian black rice pudding. All prices are reasonable – around $2 to $5 for a meal. There are cake stalls, fruit salad bars, art and craft stalls – and sometimes entertainment in the form of a band or street theatre.

Similar foodstalls can be found at the Parap market on Saturday mornings and the one at Rapid Creek on Sunday mornings, but Mindil Beach is the best for atmosphere and closeness to town. It's about two km from the city centre, off Gilruth Ave. During the wet, it transfers to Rapid Creek. Buses No 4 and No 6 go past Mindil Beach: No 4 goes on to Rapid Creek, No 6 to Parap.

Do-it-Yourself Darwin has plenty of supermarkets, but food is rather more expensive than 'down south'. The difference is not as great as it used to be and the quality difference has also narrowed.

Parap Market

There's even a Northern Territory dairy these days. Fresh vegetables and fruit are cheaper at Darwin's markets.

The Darwin Thirst

Darwin has a reputation as one of the hardest drinking towns in the world. In a dry year an average of 230 litres of the amber fluid disappear down each Darwinian throat. The Darwin thirst is summed up by the famed 'Darwin stubby' – a beer bottle that looks just like any other stubby, except that it contains two litres instead of 375 ml. The record for downing a Darwin stubby is one minute two seconds – but that was the pre-'83 Darwin stubby which was a mite larger at 2.25 litres! That's half an imperial gallon, more than half a US gallon!

The Darwin beer thirst is celebrated at the annual beer can regatta in June. A series of boat races are held for boats constructed entirely of beer cans. Apart from the racing boats some unusual special entries generally turn up – like a beer can Viking longboat or a beer can submarine. Constructed by an Australian navy contingent the submarine actually submerged!

Parap Market

The races also have their controversial elements – on one occasion a boat turned up made entirely of brand new cans, delivered straight from the brewery, sealed but empty. Unfair, cried other competitors, the beer must be drunk!

Entertainment

Darwin is a lively city with bands at several venues and many clubs and discos. More sophisticated tastes are catered for too – there's theatre, film, concerts and a casino.

Live bands play in *Ellie's Balcony Bar* upstairs at the Victoria Hotel, from 9 pm Wednesday to Saturday nights. The *Billabong Bar* in the Atrium Hotel, on the corner of the Esplanade and Peel St, has live bands on Friday and Saturday nights until 1 am. Take a look at the hotel's spectacular seven storey glass-roofed atrium while you're there. The Billabong Bar also has a comedy night on Wednesdays.

The *Darwin Hotel* is pleasant in the evening for a quiet drink. There's a patio section by the pool. It's more lively on Friday nights, when there's a band in the *Green Room*, and on Sunday afternoons at the poolside jazz barbecue – $15 a head. There's also a nightclub in the *Kakadu Bar* here.

Popular clubs and discos, often with live bands, include *Darby's, Fannies, Scandals* and *Beachcombers*. They're open nightly, with cover charges only on Saturdays. Some stay open all night and midweek they offer cheap drinks to early arrivals. Darby's is a dress-up club on Cavenagh St, near Bennett St, open from 9 pm to 6 am. Fannies, in Squires Tavern on Edmunds St, is a little more casual. It's open till very late. Scandals is in the Hot Gossip complex on Cavenagh St, opposite Darby's; there's a $7 cover charge on Saturday nights. Beachcombers is on the corner of Mitchell and Daly Sts.

There's lots of entertainment on Sunday afternoons. Very popular is the *Beachfront Hotel* (formerly Lim's) at Rapid Creek, where you can alternate between two bands – one in the outdoor bar known as the *Cage*, the other in the air-con *Colonial Bar*. The Rage Tours bus (see Getting Around) should take you there. The Beachfront also has bands on Friday and Saturday nights. There are bands on Sundays at the *Humpty Doo Hotel* 10 km along the Arnhem Highway (33 km from Darwin) and at the *Howard Springs Tavern* on Whitewood Rd, Howard Springs.

The *Nightcliff Hotel* at the corner of Bagot and Trower Rds, about 10 km north of the city centre, has live music every night except Monday and Tuesday. It's a wild place with one of the longest bars in the Northern Territory, and on Wednesdays boasts wrestling between women covered in tomato sauce, or is it baked beans? Some say the Nightcliff is part of everyone's Darwin education, others find it bemusing or plain offensive.

More laid back is the *Top End Folk Club* which has regular gatherings and concerts at various places around town, including the Gun Turret at East Point Reserve and more centrally the Esplanade Gallery in Admiralty House. You can take your own guitar to club nights. Ring 85 4521 (27 5899 after hours) for details.

The *Performing Arts Centre* (tel 81 1222) on Mitchell St, opposite McLachlan St, hosts a variety of events from fashion award nights to plays, rock operas, pantomimes and concerts. There are sometimes bands and other shows in the amphitheatre in the Botanic Gardens.

There are several cinemas in town and the Darwin Film Society (tel 81 2215) has regular showings of offbeat/artistic films at the *Museum Theatrette*, Conacher St, Bullocky Point.

Finally, there's the *Diamond Beach Casino* on Mindil Beach off Gilruth Ave. So long as you're 'properly dressed' it's quite good entertainment to watch people cast away large sums of money. Callow youths at the door adjudicate whether the style of your shirt collar and the cut of your trousers is to their master's liking.

Two-up

The Alice and Darwin casinos offer plenty of opportunity to watch the Australian gambling mania in full flight. You can also observe a part of Australia's true cultural heritage, the all-Australian game of two-up.

The essential idea of two-up is to toss two coins and obtain two heads. The players stand around a circular playing area and bet on the coins showing either two heads or two tails when they fall. The 'spinner' uses a 'kip' to toss the coins and the house pays out and takes in as the coins fall – except that nothing happens on 'odd' tosses (one head, one tail) unless they're thrown five times in a row. In this case you lose unless you have also bet on this possibility. The spinner continues tossing until he or she either throws tails, throws five odds or throws three heads. If the spinner manages three heads then he or she also wins at 7½ to one on any bet placed on that possibility, then starts tossing all over again. When the spinner finally loses, the next player in the circle takes over as spinner.

Things to Buy

Aboriginal art is generally cheaper in Alice Springs, but Darwin has greater variety. Easily the best shop is the Aboriginal Artists' Gallery at 153 Mitchell St. It's open from 9 am to 5 pm Monday to Friday, and 10 am to 1 pm on Saturdays during the dry. It has a smaller range in the pharmacy at 46 Smith St Mall.

The gallery has excellent bark paintings from Arnhem Land, and interesting carvings by the Tiwi people of Bathurst and Melville islands, and by the peoples of central Australia. Also for sale are beautiful woven baskets, dilly bags, dot paintings, clothing, Aboriginal literature and postcards. The Raintree Gallery at 29 Knuckey St has a similar collection on a smaller scale.

T-shirts printed with Aboriginal designs are popular but quality and prices vary. Riji Dij-Australian and Original, at 11 Knuckey St, has a large range of T-shirts ($25). They are printed by Tiwi Designs

and Territoriana, both local companies using Aboriginal designs and, to a large extent, Aboriginal labour. It stocks Tiwi printed fabric ($20 a metre) and clothing made from fabric printed by central Australian Aborigines.

Some Darwin boutiques reflect an Asian influence. Balinese and Indian clothing are available at several outlets. The cheapest is Waynes on Smith St, at the corner of Edmunds St. Most of the clothing is direct from Kuta. While the prices are not Indonesian, they're still cheap compared with down south.

You can find Balinese and Indian clothing at Darwin's markets – Mindil Beach (Thursday evening, dry season only), Parap (Saturday morning) and Rapid Creek (Sunday morning, and Thursday evening in the wet season). Local arts and crafts (the market at Parap is said to be the best), jewellery, and bric-a-brac are on sale too. The Esplanade Gallery, upstairs in Admiralty House, has beautiful local jewellery – not cheap, but you may find something special.

Getting There & Away

Air Darwin's becoming increasingly busy as an international as well as domestic gateway to the top of Australia. A popular international route is to/from Indonesia with the Indonesian airlines Merpati or Garuda. You can book Merpati at Natrabu (tel 81 3695), an Indonesian government travel agency, at 16 Westlane Arcade (behind the Victoria Hotel on Smith St Mall). Merpati flies twice a week to/from Kupang in Timor, and from there it has further flights to numerous other places in Indonesia. Kupang is a 'designated entry port' in Indonesia which means you get the normal two-month visit permit on arrival.

Merpati fares are generally quoted in US dollars, so what you pay in Aussie dollars varies with the exchange rate. At the time of writing the costs in Australian dollars of Merpati tickets included Darwin/Kupang one way $164, Darwin/

Kupang return $250, Darwin/Denpasar return $446 and Darwin/Ujung Pandang return $430. Some Merpati fares, but not Darwin/Kupang, rise about 20% to 25% in the 1 December to 15 January peak season.

Garuda has its own office at the corner of Bennett and Cavenagh Sts, and flies twice a week to/from Denpasar and Jakarta – a Darwin/Denpasar return is $591 (subject to US-Australian currency fluctuations). You can get tickets from Darwin to the USA with Garuda – the route is Darwin/Bali/Biak (Irian Jaya)/Los Angeles.

You can buy internal tickets for Indonesia from Garuda and Merpati in Darwin. When you enter Indonesia with Garuda you get a 50% discount on domestic flights – provided you buy the tickets for those flights before entering the country. The discount is off the US dollar price, which is higher than the rupiah price within Indonesia, so how much you save depends on the exchange value of the rupiah. Merpati internal tickets are about 25% more expensive if bought outside Indonesia. There's no point buying one except to ensure a seat on an onward flight from Kupang or Denpasar.

In other Australian cities you can book Merpati flights through Ansett International offices. Natrabu is an agent for Royal Brunei, which flies twice weekly between Darwin and Bandar Seri Begawan, and to Manila and Hong Kong.

Qantas and Singapore Airlines fly to Darwin, and Thai and Continental may join them. Qantas (tel 82 3355) is at the corner of Smith St Mall and Bennett St; Singapore Airlines is in the Paspalis Centrepoint building at the corner of Smith St Mall and Knuckey St. The Royal Brunei office (tel 49 0166) is in Star Village on Smith St Mall.

Within Australia, you can fly to Darwin from other states with Australian Airlines, Ansett, Ansett NT or Ansett WA. There are often stops or transfers at Alice Springs, Mt Isa or Adelaide on longer

flights. Some flights from Queensland stop at Gove or Groote Eylandt. One-way fares include Adelaide $411 ($329 standby), Perth via Alice Springs $467, Perth via Adelaide $581, Port Hedland $334, Kununurra $133, Cairns via Gove $324 ($260 standby), Cairns via Mt Isa $378, Mt Isa $266, Brisbane $433 ($346 standby). In Darwin, Australian Airlines (tel 82 3333) is at 16 Bennett St; Ansett, Ansett NT and Ansett WA (tel 80 3333) are in shop 14, Smith St Mall.

For air travel within the NT see the introductory Getting Around section to this chapter. Air North's office (tel 81 7477) is at Darwin Airport.

Bus You can reach Darwin by bus on three routes – the Western Australia route from Port Hedland, Broome, Derby and Kununurra; the Queensland route through Mt Isa to Three Ways and up the track; or straight up the track from Alice Springs.

Bus Australia, Deluxe, Greyhound and Pioneer Express usually run daily up and down the track to/from Alice Springs. Some buses connect in Alice Springs for Adelaide. All four companies have daily services to/from Townsville via Mt Isa, frequently with connections for Brisbane or Cairns. On Queensland services you often have to change buses at Three Ways or Tennant Creek. Bus Australia doesn't cover Queensland itself, but links up with McCafferty's.

For Western Australia, Greyhound and Deluxe both go daily to/from Perth through Kununurra, Broome and Port Hedland. Bus Australia does this trip two or three times a week, while Pioneer puts its customers (including Aussiepass holders) on the Greyhound bus. With Greyhound you have the option once or twice a week of taking the WA inland route south of Port Hedland, along the Great Northern Highway through Newman. Otherwise WA buses follow the coastal route. All buses stop at Katherine.

Fares only vary by a couple of dollars between the various companies and travel times are very similar, but beware of services that schedule long waits for connections in Tennant Creek or Mt Isa. For example, you pay around $70 one way to Darwin from Tennant Creek (13 hours), $100 from Mt Isa (21 hours), $150 from Townsville (32 hours), $200 from Brisbane (51 hours), $105 from Alice Springs (19 hours), $155 from Port Hedland (32 hours), and $215 from Perth (57 hours). See the introductory Getting Around chapter for notes on stopover rules.

In Darwin all four companies have their arrival and departure points and their booking offices in the transit centre at 69 Mitchell St. Telephone numbers include Pioneer Express 81 6433, Deluxe 81 8788, Greyhound 81 8700. Most bus drivers will let you off on the Stuart Highway as it passes through the Darwin suburbs if you wish.

Getting Around

Airport Transport Darwin's busy airport, only about six km from the centre of town, handles international flights as well as domestic ones. Hertz, Budget, Thrifty and Letz have rent-a-car desks at the airport. The taxi fare into the centre is about $10.

There is an airport shuttle bus for $3, which will pick up or drop off almost anywhere in the centre. When leaving Darwin phone 81 1102, a day before departure to book it. You can also get to the airport on a city bus No 5 or No 8.

Bus Darwin has a fairly good city bus service – Monday to Friday. On Saturdays services cease around lunch time and on Sundays and holidays they shut down completely. The city services start from the small terminal on Harry Chan Ave, near the corner of Smith St. There's a bus information office here – or call 89 7513. Buses enter the city along Mitchell St and leave along Cavenagh St.

Fares are on a zone system – shorter trips are $0.60 or $0.90, the longest $1.30. Bus No 4 (to Fannie Bay, Nightcliff,

Rapid Creek and Casuarina) and No 6 (Fannie Bay, Parap, Stuart Park) are useful for getting to the fish feeding, Botanic Gardens, Mindil beach, the Museum of Arts & Sciences, Fannie Bay Gaol and East Point. Buses No 5 and No 8 go up the Stuart Highway past the airport to Berrimah, from where No 5 goes north to Casuarina and No 8 continues along the highway to Palmerston.

Two buses a day go to Humpty Doo, Monday to Friday only. A privately run Sunday bus service has started up, run by Rage Tours (!). It goes every two hours from 12 noon to 10 pm from the transit centre via Parap, Fannie Bay, Nightcliff and Casuarina to the Royal Darwin Hospital.

Rental Cars Darwin has two 'backpacker special' operators, renting out old cars at bargain rates, as well as several of the national companies.

Rent a Rocket (tel 81 6977) at 9 Daly St, and Rent a Dent (tel 81 1411) at the corner of Smith and McLachlan Sts, offer very similar deals on their mostly 1970s and early 1980s cars. Costs depend on whether you're staying near Darwin, or going further afield to Kakadu, Katherine, Litchfield Park and so on. For local trips, with Rent a Rocket you pay $25 to $35 a day, depending on the vehicle, and must stay within 70 km of Darwin; with Rent a Dent it's $25 and you can't go beyond Humpty Doo or Acacia Store (about 70 km down the track). For more distant trips it's $150 for two days, with longer rentals available. These rates include insurance and there's no km charge. Rent a Rocket has Mokes for $30 a day including insurance, with no km charge.

The bigger companies usually class Darwin as 'remote', which means that cars cost about $10 a day more. Cheapa (tel 81 8400) at 149 Stuart Highway is probably the best value: it has Mokes at $28 a day or Toyota Corollas at $38, both including insurance but every km costs 20c. Thrifty (tel 81 8555) at 131 Stuart

Highway is slightly dearer, with Corollas and Ford Lasers at $59 including insurance, plus 25c for every km beyond 100 daily. Hertz (tel 41 0944) on the corner of Smith and Daly Sts, offers Lasers for $63 per day including insurance, with the same km deal as Thrifty.

Other deals to look for include cheaper rates for four or more days' hire, weekend specials (three days for roughly the price of two), and one-way hires (to Jabiru, Katherine or Alice Springs).

It's not easy to get hold of 4WD vehicles in Darwin: you usually have to book ahead, and fees and deposits can be hefty. The best place to start looking is probably Cheapa, which has several different models - the cheapest, a Suzuki four-seater, costs $73 a day including insurance, plus 20c a km over 100 km.

Rental companies, including the cut price ones, generally operate a free towing or replacement service if the vehicle breaks down. But, especially with the cheaper operators, check the paperwork to see exactly what you're covered for in terms of damage to vehicles and injuries. The usual age and insurance requirements apply in Darwin and there may be restrictions on off-bitumen driving, or on the distance you're allowed to go from the city.

Other firms include Koala (tel 41 1234) at the corner of Bennett and Cavenagh Sts, and Avis (tel 81 9922) at 254 Stuart Highway, Parap. Most rental companies are open every day and have agents in the city centre to save you trekking out to the Stuart Highway. Budget, Hertz, Letz and Thrifty have offices at the airport.

Bicycles, Scooters & Motor Bikes Darwin is surprisingly good for pushbike riding and has a fairly extensive network of bike tracks. It's a pleasant ride out from the city to the Botanical Gardens, Fannie Bay, East Point or even, if you're feeling fit, all the way to Nightcliff and Casuarina.

Bay Lodge, opposite the YWCA on Mitchell St, has good bikes at $3 for two hours, $7 a day or $35 a week. Rent a Rocket has bikes at $9 for 24 hours. Nearer the centre of town, Darwin Bike Rentals in Top End Travel at 57 Mitchell St, has bikes from $8 a day (from 8 am to 5 pm), or $10 for 24 hours - plus tandems and mountain bikes, and hourly, weekly and monthly rates. It's open daily. U Rent (tel 41 1280) at 51 Mitchell St, has bikes at $2 an hour or $12 a day.

For scooters, Rent a Rocket (again) offers a $25 for 24 hours deal. There are similar rates at Kawasaki Darwin, 5 Knuckey St, which also has 200 cc trail bikes at $45 for 24 hours - but you can't take them more than 50 km from the city.

Tours There are innumerable tours in and around Darwin offered by a host of companies. NTGTB offices have a booklet, *Northern Territory Holiday Planner*, which helpfully lists brief details of most of them; this will give you the latest information on tour names and destinations. Many tours go less frequently (if at all) in the wet season. Some of the longer or more adventurous ones have only a few departures a year: enquire beforehand if you're interested.

Among the Darwin city tours, Darwin Day Tours' four hour trip is pretty comprehensive at $32. The same company also does 3 hour, $24 trips to the crocodile farm for feeding time. Coop & Co run dry season horse and carriage city tours from $5 to $20. Wildlife fanatics could try Arura Safaris' twice weekly 4½ hour trip, which includes the crocodile farm, Graeme Gow's Reptile World at Humpty Doo, and Fogg Dam ($25 wet season, $30 dry).

Another local trip is the Billy J harbour cruise ($15 including a stopover at Mandorah). Other more expensive (around $42) harbour cruises by Billy J and Whim-O-Way variously offer meals, a 'corroboree', sunset and night trips, and croc-spotting.

Adelaide River Queen Wildlife River Tours run a $48, six hour trip from Darwin to see Fogg Dam, the Adelaide River jumping crocodiles and Reptile World.

Check with Dial-A-Safari's for tours covering some city sights and some of the outlying 'animal' attractions.

You can take tours from Darwin to almost anywhere of interest in the Northern Territory. With money to burn, you could combine several major destinations or even make it to Kimberley in WA. See Terra Safari Tours for information about a dry season 'Four Ks' trip which takes you to Kakadu, Katherine, Kununurra, Kimberley and numerous other places including a flight over the Bungle Bungles.

The big destination from Darwin is Kakadu, but several tours now go from Darwin to the less known region west of the Stuart Highway south of Darwin. Bushranger Tours does a variety of day-trips to Litchfield Park, Daly River, Douglas Hot Springs and Butterfly Gorge. You can join these tours at Adelaide River township or Batchelor: they cost $70 to $99. Dial-A-Safari has trips for one day ($89 or $99) and two days ($189) to Litchfield Park, while Daly River Safari Tours offers various options for one day ($99) and two days ($230) to Daly River and Litchfield Park. Go Onna Safari Tours does trips for one day ($89) and two days ($150) to Litchfield Park.

Organised canoe trips (dry season only) usually take in this southern region too. With Breakwater Canoe Tours a four day Daly River trip costs $460, while a week on the Katherine and Daly rivers is $805. Pandanus Canoe Safaris has Daly River trips for four or six days at $410 or $560.

For bushwalkers, Willis's Walkabouts have been recommended. Organised by an ex-president of Darwin Bushwalking Club, these are guided hikes in small groups (usually four to eight people). You can join a prearranged walk of 11 to 21 days, or a group can set its own itinerary of two or more days. Some of Willis's Walkabouts are mentioned under Kakadu National Park, but others include Keep River and the Bungle Bungles (16 days, $550), and Mitchell Plateau and Bungle Bungles (21 days, $800). Prices for 'choose your own' bushwalks range from $30 to $50 a day per person depending on the season and length of walk.

Darwin Aircraft Charters offers joy flights over the city or to Kakadu or Katherine. Other interesting – but not cheap – tour destinations from Darwin include Bathurst and Melville Islands, the Cobourg Peninsula, Arnhem Land and Gove. See the sections on those places.

The Top End

There are a number of places of interest close to Darwin, and several remoter and more spectacular top end areas are becoming increasingly accessible. The chief glory among the latter is Kakadu National Park. Litchfield Park, a reserve to the south of Darwin, and Melville and Bathurst Islands to the north are other places that are worth the effort if you have the time and dollars.

A group of people can hire a vehicle in Darwin and get to most of the mainland places quite economically. There are also tours from Darwin to many of these places (see Darwin – Getting Around). For details on where to get information about national parks and reserves in the NT see the Information section at the start of this chapter.

Some additional places that can be reached from Darwin are covered in the Down the Track section.

Crocodiles

The top end has a fair population of crocodiles. After a century of being hunted, wild crocodiles became protected in the Northern Territory in 1971 and their numbers have increased to an estimated 100,000. There are two types of crocodiles in Australia – freshwater and saltwater – and both are present in the Territory.

The smaller freshwater-dwelling crocodile is found in freshwater rivers and billabongs, while the larger saltwater crocodile can be found in or near almost any body of water, fresh or salt. Freshwater crocodiles, which have narrower snouts and rarely exceed three metres long, are harmless to people unless provoked, but saltwater crocodiles can definitely be dangerous.

Ask locally before swimming or even paddling in any rivers or billabongs in the top end – attacks on humans by salties happen more often than you might think. The beasts are apparently partial to dogs and can be attracted by barking some distance away. Since becoming protected, crocodiles are growing less afraid.

Warning signs are posted alongside many dangerous stretches of water, but they're such a curio that a lot get souvenired, although you can buy them from the NT Conservation Commission for $5.

Crocodiles have become a major tourist attraction (eating the odd tourist certainly helps in this respect) and the Northern Territory is very big on crocodile humour. Darwin shops have a plentiful supply of crocodile T-shirts including the Darwin Crocodile Wrestling Club shirt, complete with gory blood stains and a large hole 'bitten' out of one side.

AROUND DARWIN

All the places listed here are within a couple of hours' travel from the city.

Mandorah Resort

It's only 10 km across the harbour by boat to this popular beach resort on the tip of Cox Peninsula – you can reach it by road, but that's nearly 140 km, about half of it on unsealed roads. The return ferry trip is $10, with the first departure from Darwin at 10 am and the last one from Mandorah at 4 pm. The crossing takes about 30 minutes. The *Darwin Duchess* leaves the main Stokes Hill Wharf in Darwin three or four times a day Monday to Friday and on weekends in the tourist season. The *Billy J Express* leaves Fisherman's Wharf three times each Saturday, Sunday or holiday. Billy J Cruises run more elaborate trips: a harbour cruise plus stopover at Mandorah costs $15, while a four hour sunset cruise plus seafood dinner and an Aboriginal corroboree at Mandorah is $45, or $60 if you stay the night at the resort. Normally a unit at the resort costs $45: they each sleep up to four people, and have air-con with private bathrooms and tea/coffee making facilities.

Howard Springs

The springs, with crocodile-free swimming, are 27 km from the city. Turn off 23 km down the Stuart Highway, beyond Palmerston. The forest-surrounded swimming hole can get uncomfortably crowded because it's so convenient to the city. Nevertheless on a quiet day it's a pleasant spot for an excursion and there are short walking tracks and lots of bird life.

Places to Stay There are three nearby caravan parks. The *Coolalinga* (tel 83 1026), on the Stuart Highway four km beyond the Howard Springs turning, has tent sites at $4 to $10; *Howard Springs Caravan Park* (tel 83 1169) at Whitewood Rd, Howard Springs, has tent sites at $8; the *Nook* (tel 83 1048) at 17 Morgan Rd, Howard Springs, has tent sites at $5 per person, on-site vans from $22 a double, and cabins for $32 a double and up.

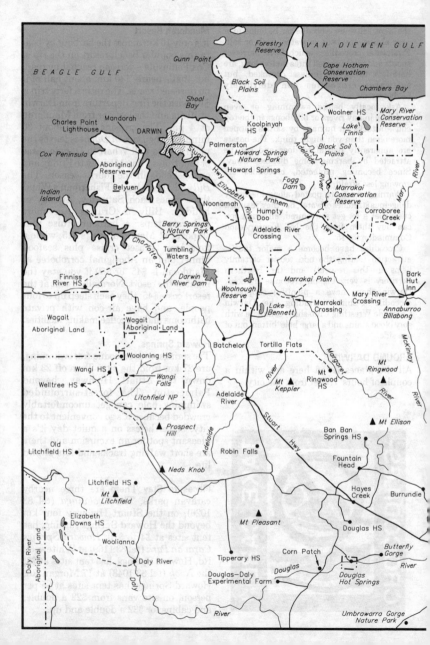

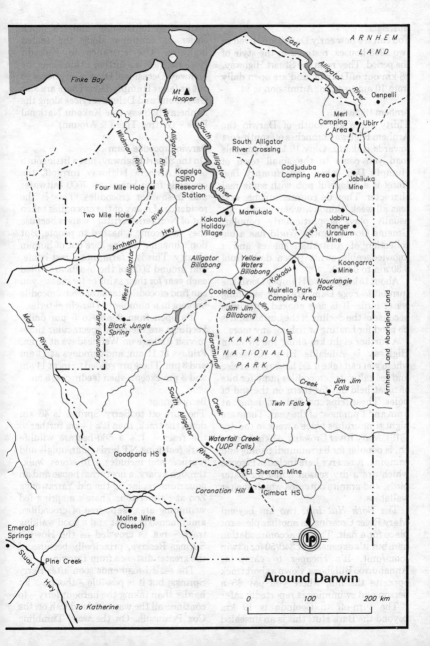

Finke Bay

Mt Hooper ▲

West Alligator River

South Alligator River

East Alligator River

ARNHEM LAND

Oenpelli

Merl Camping Area

Ubirr

Kapalga CSIRO Research Station

Gadjuduba Camping Area

Jabiluka Mine

Four Mile Hole

Wildman River

Arnhem Hwy

Kakadu Holiday Village

Mamukala

Jabiru

Ranger Uranium Mine

Two Mile Hole

Alligator Billabong

Yellow Waters Billabong

Kakadu Hwy

Koongarra Mine

Black Jungle Spring

Cooinda

Jim Jim Billabong

Muirella Park Camping Area

Nourlangie Rock

Mary River

Park Boundary

Baramundi Creek

KAKADU NATIONAL PARK

Jim Jim Creek

Arnhem Land Aboriginal Land

Jim Jim Falls

Twin Falls

South Alligator River

Waterfall Creek (UDP Falls)

Goodparla HS

El Sherana Mine

Coronation Hill ▲

Gimbat HS

Emerald Springs

Pine Creek

Moline Mine (Closed)

Stuart Hwy

To Katherine

Around Darwin

0   100   200 km

Nostalgia

You can see how early Darwinites lived in two 1913 houses, restored in the style of the period. They're on the Stuart Highway, 28 km out of Darwin, and are open daily from 10 am to 4 pm. Admission is $4.

Arnhem Highway

Thirty three km south of Darwin the Arnhem Highway branches off south-east towards Kakadu. Only 10 km along this road you come to the small town of Humpty Doo, where the *Humpty Doo Hotel* is a colourful pub with some real character. They do counter lunches and teas all week. Sunday, when local bands usually play, is particularly popular. Graeme Gow's Reptile World has a big collection of Australian snakes and a knowledgeable owner (open daily from 8.30 am to 6 pm).

About 15 km beyond Humpty Doo is the turn-off to Fogg Dam, great for watching water birds. It is now choked with lilies because of the decline of the buffalo and is no good for boating or fishing any more.

A further eight km along the Arnhem Highway is Adelaide River Crossing, where you can take a 2½ hour river cruise and see saltwater crocodiles jump for bits of meat held out for them on the end of poles. These trips cost $22 and depart at 9 am and 1 pm most of the year. There are night time cruises twice a week in the dry ($19). Mary River Crossing, 47 km further on, is popular for barramundi fishing and camping. A reserve here includes lagoons which are a dry season home for water birds, and granite outcrops which shelter wallabies.

The *Bark Hut Inn*, two km beyond Mary River Crossing, is another pleasant place for a halt. There's accommodation here but it's expensive at $40/50 for a twin room/unit. It's cheaper to camp at Annaburroo Billabong, down a short track opposite the inn, where you pay $5 a person and swimming is reportedly safe.

The turn-off to Cooinda is 19 km beyond the Bark Hut: this is an unsealed road, often impassable, and it's much easier to continue along the sealed highway. The entrance to Kakadu National Park is a further 19 km along the highway. Occasional Darwin city buses go out as far as Humpty Doo. There are also Greyhound and Deluxe services along the Arnhem Highway (see Kakadu National Park - Getting There & Around).

Darwin Crocodile Farm

On the Stuart Highway, just a little south of the Arnhem Highway turn-off, the crocodile farm has about 7000 saltwater and freshwater crocodiles. This is the residence of many of the crocodiles taken out of Northern Territory waters because they've become a hazard to people. But don't imagine they're here out of human charity. This is a farm, not a rest home, and around 2000 of the beasts are killed each year for their skins or for meat - you can find crocodile steaks or even crocodile burgers in a number of Darwin eateries.

It's open from 9 am to 5 pm daily. Feedings are the most spectacular times to visit and are on Wednesdays at 3 pm, Fridays at 11 am, and Sundays at 11 am and 3 pm. There are guided tours at 11 am and 3 pm except when feedings are on.

Berry Springs

The turn-off to Berry Springs is 48 km down the track, then it's 14 km further to the reserve. It's a 560-hectare wildlife park featuring NT birds, marsupials and reptiles, and includes a 10 storey walk-through aviary, a nocturnal house and an aquarium, replacing the old Yarrawonga Zoo at Palmerston. There's a spring-fed swimming area, kept free of crocodiles, amid monsoon forest and a good walking track - not as crowded as the Howard Springs Reserve, principally because of the greater distance from Darwin.

The sealed road ends soon after Berry Springs, but it is possible - though a lot harder than taking the harbour ferry - to continue all the way to Mandorah on the Cox Peninsula. On the way, Tumbling

Waters is reputedly a great swimming spot.

Litchfield Park

This 650 square km area south of Darwin encloses much of the Tabletop Range, a wide sandstone plateau mostly surrounded by cliffs. Four waterfalls which drop off the edge of this plateau and their surrounding rainforest patches are the park's main attractions.

There are two routes to Litchfield Park, both about a two hour drive from Darwin. One, from the north, involves turning south off the Berry Springs to Cox Peninsula road onto a dirt road, which is suitable for conventional vehicles except in the wet season. A second approach is from Batchelor (the road now provides year round access for conventional vehicles) into the east of the park.

The two access roads are linked by an unsealed road (OK for conventional vehicles) through the park. If you enter the park from Batchelor, it is roughly 17 km from the park boundary to Florence Falls on the eastern edge of the plateau, a further 17 km to the top of Tolmer Falls on the western edge, then 13 km north to Wangi Falls. From Wangi it's about 16 km to the ranger station near the park's northern access point.

Wangi Falls has a large swimming hole and a camping site with toilets. Florence Falls has a good swimming hole, surrounded by rainforest. Bush camping is allowed here as well as at Sandy Creek Falls in a rainforest valley in the south of the park (4WD access only) and at Bamboo Creek, reached by a 4WD track in the north. There are several other 4WD tracks in the park, and plenty of great bushwalking possibilities.

As usual in the top end, it's easier to reach and get around the park from May to October.

KAKADU NATIONAL PARK

Kakadu National Park is one of the natural marvels not just of the Northern Territory, but of Australia. The longer you stay, the more rewarding it is.

Kakadu stretches more than 200 km south from the coast and 100 km from east to west, with the main entrance 153 km by road east of Darwin. It encompasses a great variety of superb landscapes, swarms with wildlife and has some of Australia's best Aboriginal rock art.

Kakadu was proclaimed a national park in three stages. Stage one, the east central part of the park including Ubirr, Nourlangie Rock, Jim Jim Falls, Twin Falls and Yellow Water Billabong, was declared in 1979 and is on the World Heritage list for both its natural and its cultural importance – a rare distinction. Stage two, in the north, was declared in 1984 and won World Heritage listing for its natural importance. Stage three, in the south, was added in 1987 bringing virtually the whole South Alligator River system within the park.

The name Kakadu comes from Gagadju, one of the local Aboriginal languages, and part of Kakadu is Aboriginal land, leased to the government for use as a national park. There are several Aboriginal settlements in the park and about half the park rangers are Aborigines. Enclosed by the park, but not part of it, are a few tracts of land designated for other purposes – principally three uranium mining leases in the east.

Geography & Vegetation

A straight line on the map separates Kakadu from the Arnhem Land Aboriginal Land to its east, which you can't enter without a permit. The Arnhem Land escarpment, a dramatic 100 metre to 200 metre sandstone cliffline, which provides the natural boundary of the very rugged Arnhem Land plateau, winds more circuitously some 500 km through east and south-east Kakadu.

Creeks cut across the rocky plateau and tumble off the escarpment as thundering waterfalls in the wet season. They then flow across the lowlands to swamp the vast floodplains of Kakadu's four north-flowing rivers, turning the north of the park into a kind of huge vegetated lake. In west to east order the rivers are the Wildman, the West Alligator, the South Alligator and the East Alligator. Such is the difference between dry and wet seasons that areas on river floodplains, which are perfectly dry underfoot in September, will be standing under three metres of water a few months later. As the waters recede in the dry, some loops of wet season watercourses become cut off, but don't dry up. These are billabongs – and they're often carpeted with water lilies.

The coastline has long stretches of mangrove swamp, important for halting erosion and as a breeding ground for marine and bird species. The southern part of the park is drier, lowland hill country with open grassland and eucalypt woodland. Pockets of monsoon rainforest crop up here as well as in most of the park's other landscapes.

In all, Kakadu has over 1000 plant species, and a number of them are still used by the local Aborigines for food and other practical purposes.

Seasons

The great change between the dry and the November to March wet – when around 1300 mm of rain falls, mostly between January and March – makes a big difference to visitors to Kakadu. Not only is the landscape transformed as the wetlands and waterfalls grow and shrink, but Kakadu's lesser roads become impassable in the wet, cutting off some highlights like Jim Jim Falls or (for shorter periods) Ubirr. In the wet and in the humid October 'build-up', temperatures rise (to 35°C or more) alongside the humidity – and the mosquito population, always thick near water, rises to near plague proportions. The most comfortable time is the late dry, July to September. This is when wildlife, especially birds, congregates in big numbers around the shrinking billabongs and watercourses,

but it's also when most tourists come to the park. May and June is quite a good time to visit – there aren't too many other visitors, the wetlands and waterfalls still have a lot of water and most of the tracks are open.

Wildlife

Kakadu has about 25 species of frog, 50 types of mammals, 55 fish species, 75 types of reptile, 275 bird species (one-third of all Australian bird species), and 4500 kinds of insect. The list is frequently added to, and a few of the rarer species are unique to the park. Kakadu's wetlands are on the UN list of Wetlands of International Importance, principally because of their crucial significance to so many types of water bird.

You'll only see a tiny fraction of these creatures in a visit to the park since many of them are shy, nocturnal or few in numbers. Take advantage of talks and walks led by park rangers – mainly in the dry – to get to know and see more of the wildlife (details from the park information centre). Cruises are run at South Alligator River and Yellow Water Billabong to enable you to see the water life.

Reptiles The park has both types of Australian crocodile: Twin and Jim Jim Falls for instance both have resident freshwater crocodiles, which are considered harmless, and there are about 3500 of the potentially dangerous saltwater variety in the park. This beast ranges widely and is definitely not confined to salt water. Any expanse of water is quite likely to have a 'saltie' or two in it, and you're sure to see a few if you take a South Alligator or Yellow Water cruise. Take note of the plentiful crocodile warning signs: at least two people (a tourist and a fisherman) have been killed by saltwater crocodiles in Kakadu in the last few years. Both ignored warnings.

Kakadu's other reptiles include several types of lizard, like the frilled lizard, and five freshwater turtle species of which the most common is the northern snake-necked turtle. The pig-nosed turtle, found here in 1973, was previously thought to live only in New Guinea. There are many snakes, including three highly poisonous types, but you're unlikely to see any. Oenpelli pythons, probably unique to the Kakadu escarpment, were only discovered in 1977.

Birds Kakadu's abundant water birds, in beautiful wetland settings, make a memorable sight. The park is one of the chief refuges in Australia for several water bird species, among them the magpie goose, green pygmy goose and Burdekin duck. Kakadu is a staging post for birds migrating from the northern hemisphere around the beginning and end of the wet season. In September and October over 100,000 magpie geese gather at Mamukala. Around 80% of the world population of this bird is in Kakadu at this time.

Other fine water birds include the jabiru stork with its distictive red legs and long straight beak, pelicans and darters (also called snake birds for their snakelike movement as they swim for fish underwater).

Herons, egrets, ibis and cormorants are common. You're quite likely to see rainbow bee eaters and kingfishers (of which there are six types in inland Kakadu). Majestic, white-breasted sea eagles are often seen near inland waterways too, and wedge-tailed eagles, whistling kites and black kites are common. At night you may hear barking owls calling – they sound just like dogs. Also spectacular is the red-tailed black cockatoo and there are brolgas and bustards. A few bird species are unique to Kakadu, but they're rarely seen.

Mammals Several types of kangaroo and wallaby inhabit the park, and the shy black wallaroo is more or less unique to Kakadu. You might be lucky enough to see a sugar glider in wooded areas in the daytime. Kakadu is home to 25 bat species and a key refuge for four endangered varieties.

Water buffalo, which ran wild after being introduced to the top end from Timor by European settlers in the first half of the 19th century, are being heavily reduced because they are potential

Magpie geese, Kakadu National Park

carriers of cattle disease and damage the natural environment. By 1980 there were estimated to be well over 200,000 buffalo in the Northern Territory. Many are rounded up for slaughter or domestication by commercial contractors, some are shot humanely by park staff.

Fish You can't miss the silver barramundi, which creates a distinctive swirl near the water surface. It can grow well over a metre long and changes sex from male to female at the age of five or six years!

Rock Art

Kakadu has about 5000 Aboriginal rock painting sites dating from 20,000 or more years ago up to the 1960s. They range from hand prints to paintings of animals, people, mythological beings and European ships, constituting one of the world's most important and fascinating rock art collections. They provide a record of changing environments and Aboriginal life styles over the millennia.

In some places they are concentrated in large galleries, with paintings from different eras sometimes superimposed on one another. Some sites are kept secret – not only to protect them from damage, but also because they are private or sacred to the Aborigines. Some are even believed to be the residences of dangerous beings, who must not be approached by the ignorant. Two of the finest sites, however, have been opened up to visitors with access roads, walkways and explanatory signs. These are Ubirr and Nourlangie Rock. Park rangers conduct free art site tours once or twice a day from May to October.

The dominant colours of all the art are yellow, red and white, obtained by grinding natural minerals to powder and mixing it with water.

Non-Aborigines owe much of their knowledge of the art to George Chaloupka, a Czechoslovakia born Australian who devoted decades to studying it. Keep an eye open for his book on Nourlangie Rock.

Chaloupka identified three main periods in Kakadu art – Pre-Estuarine, Estuarine and Post-Estuarine.

Pre-Estuarine From 20,000 or more years ago until 8000 or 10,000 years ago, Kakadu was probably a lot drier than today, with the coastline about 300 km further north, as much of the world's water was frozen in the larger polar ice caps. Rock paintings of this era show six main styles succeeding each other through time. Following the earliest hand or grass prints came a 'naturalistic' style, with large outline drawings of people or animals filled in with colour. Sticklike humans are shown hunting in this period. Some of the animals depicted, such as the thylacine (Tasmanian tiger) and the long-beaked echidna, have long been extinct in mainland Australia. Other paintings are thought to show large beasts wiped out worldwide millennia ago.

After the naturalistic style came the 'dynamic', in which motion is often cleverly depicted (a dotted line, for example, may show a spear's path through the air). Most humans shown are males with headdresses, necklaces, armlets and so on, carrying weapons or dilly bags. Women are usually naked. In this era the first mythological beings appear – with human bodies and animal heads.

The fourth Pre-Estuarine style mainly shows simple, human silhouettes. They were followed by more 'stick figures' usually carrying fighting picks and wearing head adornments and skirts, and finally by the curious 'yam figures' in which people and animals are drawn in the shape of yams (or yams in the shape of people/animals!), with trailing roots and hairs. Yams must have been an important food source at this time, when the probably increasingly damp climate was becoming suitable for them.

Estuarine With the rising of the oceans about 8000 years ago much of Kakadu was covered with salt marshes. Many fish are depicted in the art – and the X-ray style, showing the bones and internal organs, makes its appearance.

Post-Estuarine By about 1000 years ago, many of the salt marshes had turned into freshwater swamps and billabongs. The birds and plants which provided new food sources in this landscape appear in the art.

From around 400 years ago, Aboriginal artists also depicted the Macassan and European human newcomers to the region – and the things they brought, or their transport such as ships or horses. In the last few decades the rock painting tradition has all but died out following the traumas that European settlement caused in Aboriginal society. Aborigines devote artistic energy instead to painting on eucalyptus bark, often in traditional styles and usually for sale. But they still regard much of the rock art as important and devote care to protecting it.

Mining

The Kakadu region contains nearly 10% of the world's known high grade uranium ore. The national park surrounds three uranium-rich zones which are Aboriginal land, but which outside companies have the right to mine – Ranger, Jabiluka and Koongarra, all near the eastern border of the park. The national government currently maintains a three-mine limit on the number of working uranium mines in Australia, and only Ranger of the Kakadu sites is being worked. (The other two working mines are Nabarlek in Arnhem Land, which has been mined out and is now simply a shrinking stockpile, and Roxby Downs in South Australia.)

You can tour the Ranger mine, opened in 1981. Jabiru town, close by, was built for the mine workers. The highly dubious uses of uranium and its potential damage to the local environment were not the only sources of controversy surrounding the granting of permission for mining here in the 1970s. The NT land rights laws had just been passed, but the Ranger area was excluded from the right which Aborigines were given to say no to mining on their lands. They could, however, still negotiate the terms on which the mine companies would lease the land from them. Under pressure from the national government and mine companies, the Aboriginal negotiators finally signed a deal in 1978, which brought them a decent share of the Ranger profits but, many apparently felt, didn't adequately protect their land or sacred sites.

By 1988 many of the Aboriginal owners of Jabiluka and Koongarra argued in favour of mining there, apparently impressed with the economic benefits brought by Ranger. It was estimated that the Aboriginal owners of the Ranger and Nabarlek mine sites had received about $100 million in royalties from the mine companies in less than a decade.

A large slice of Kakadu's stage three, declared national parkland in 1987, was temporarily set aside as a 'conservation zone', which means that the area is under national park protection except that mineral exploration is allowed. Mining companies were given five years to come to agreement with the Aboriginal land-owners if they want to mine. If no deal is reached by 1992, the land remains national park. The project most likely to go ahead is at Coronation Hill, where BHP, Australia's biggest company, has found gold and platinum. There may be commercially viable uranium there too. Conservationists are strongly opposed to any mining here, partly because of possible pollution to other parts of Kakadu.

Orientation – Along the Arnhem Highway

From where the Arnhem Highway to Kakadu turns east off the Stuart Highway, it's 120 km to the park entrance, and another 103 km east across the park to Jabiru, sealed all the way. The Kakadu Highway to Nourlangie Rock, Cooinda and Pine Creek turns south off the Arnhem Highway shortly before Jabiru.

A turn-off to the north, 18 km into the park along the Arnhem Highway, leads to camping areas at Two Mile Hole (eight km) and Four Mile Hole (42 km) on the Wildman River, popular for fishing. The track's not suitable for conventional vehicles except in the dry, and then only as far as Two Mile Hole. About 35 km further east along the highway, a turn-off to the south, again impassable to conventional vehicles in the wet, leads to Alligator Billabong and the Mary River to Cooinda back road.

South Alligator River Crossing is on the highway 60 km into the park, about two km past Kakadu Holiday Village. The cruises on the tidal river here are the best opportunity for crocodile-spotting in the park. Most days year round there's a two hour ($22) or five hour ($45 including barbecue) cruise leaving at 10 am. There are two-hour early morning and evening trips ($18) most days, April to December. Phone 79 0166 for schedules or ask at Kakadu Holiday Village.

Seven km east of South Alligator, a short side road to the south leads to Mamukala, with a walking trail and birdwatching hides.

Information

The excellent Kakadu Park Information Centre, on the Kakadu Highway a couple of km south of where it turns off the Arnhem Highway, is open daily from 8 am to 5 pm. Here you'll find informative displays, including a special building devoted to birds, and a video room with several interesting films available – also details of ranger led art site and wildlife walks.

There's also an information centre at Jabiru Airport. In Darwin you can get information on Kakadu from the National Parks & Wildlife Service. Top end tourist offices usually have copies of the *Kakadu Visitor Guide* leaflet, which includes a good map. There are some shops in Jabiru and other places in the park, but stock up with provisions before you go – prices are a lot higher in Kakadu.

Kakadu – A World Heritage of Unsurpassed Beauty, published by the Australian National Parks & Wildlife Service, is an informative and finely illustrated (but big) book on the park.

Walking

Kakadu is excellent, but tough bushwalking country. Many people will be satisfied with the range of marked trails from one km to 12 km long. For the more adventurous there are infinite possibilities especially in the drier south and east of the park, but take great care and prepare well. Tell people where you're going and don't go alone. You need a permit from the park information centre to camp outside the established camping sites. The Darwin Bushwalking Club (tel 85 1484) welcomes visitors and may be able to help with information too. It has walks most weekends, often in Kakadu. Or you could join a Willis's Walkabout guided bushwalk (see Tours in the Getting There & Around section).

Ubirr

This spectacular rock art site, also called Obiri Rock, lies 40 km north of the Arnhem Highway. The turn-off is 95 km from the park entrance and the road to Ubirr is dirt most of the way, with several creek crossings, which make it impassable for a conventional vehicle for most of the wet season – sometimes for 4WD too.

Shortly before Ubirr you pass the Border Store, near which are a couple of walking trails close to the East Alligator River, which forms the eastern boundary of the park here. There is a youth hostel and camping site nearby.

An easily followed path from the Ubirr car park takes you through the main galleries and up to a lookout with superb views – a 1½ km round trip. There are paintings on numerous rocks along the path, but the highlight is the main gallery with a large array of well executed and preserved X-ray style wallabies, possums, goannas, tortoises and fish, plus a couple of *balanda* (white men) with hands on hips. Just round the corner from the main gallery, high on a rock face, is a Tasmanian tiger.

The Ubirr paintings are in many different styles and range from probably 20,000 or more years ago up to the 20th century. Allow plenty of time to seek out and study them. The site's usually open from 8.30 am to 4.30 pm and there's plenty of explanatory material.

Jabiru

The township, built to accommodate the Ranger mineworkers, has shops and a public swimming pool. Six km east is Jabiru Airport and, nearby, the Ranger uranium mine which gives free one hour tours several times a day, six or seven days a week, May to October.

Nourlangie Rock

The sight of this looming, mysterious, isolated outlier of the Arnhem Land escarpment makes it easy to understand why it has been important to Aborigines for so long. Its long, red, sandstone bulk – striped in places with orange, white, even black – slopes up from surrounding woodland to finally fall away at one end in sheer, stepped cliffs, at the feet of which is Kakadu's best known collection of rock art.

The name Nourlangie is a corruption of *nawulandja*, an Aboriginal word which referred to an area bigger than the rock itself. The Aboriginal name of the rock is Burrung-gui. You reach it at the end of a 12 km sealed road, which turns east off the Kakadu Highway, 22 km south of the Arnhem Highway. Other interesting spots nearby make it worth spending a whole day in this corner of Kakadu. The last few km of the road are closed from around 5 pm daily.

From the main car park a round-trip walk of about two km takes you first to the Anbangbang shelter, used for 20,000 years as a refuge from heat, rain and the area's

frequent wet season thunderstorms. Namarrgon, the lightning man, appears in the rock art of the area as a skeletal white figure with stone axes attached to his head, elbows and knees. These strike the ground or clouds as he passes to make lightning.

Behind the shelter the path passes a rock painting of Namarrgon on the right before reaching two galleries. The first includes a group of dancing figures. The second is the Anbangbang gallery containing a famous group of paintings done in the 1960s by an artist called Najombolmi or Barramundi Charlie.

From the gallery you can walk onto a lookout where you can see the distant Arnhem Land cliffline, including Lightning Dreaming (Namarrgon Djadjam), which is the home of Namarrgon. There's a 12 km marked walk all the way round the rock, for which the park office has a leaflet.

Heading back towards the highway, you can take three turn-offs to further places of interest. The first, on the left about one km from the main car park, takes you to Anbangbang Billabong, with a dense carpet of lilies and a picnic site. The second, also on the left, leads to a short walk up to the Nawulandja lookout, with good views back over Nourlangie Rock. The well-known Blue Paintings, reached by a short walk from this turn-off, aren't supposed to be visited without a park ranger present.

The third turn-off, a dirt track on the right, takes you to another outstanding – but little visited – rock art gallery, Nangaloar or Nangaluwurr. You turn right off the track after about 1½ km to reach a small car park, from where it's an easily followed walk of about 1½ km to the paintings. There are many different styles and subjects here including a European ship, X-ray style fish, mythical beings and stick figures. Returning from here, if you turn right when you reach the main track (instead of left towards the Nourlangie to Kakadu Highway road) a further 10 km or so, brings you to Baroalba Springs, reputedly a good swimming spot – though you have to walk the last three km.

Jim Jim & Twin Falls

These two most spectacular waterfalls lie down a 4WD-only dry season track that turns south off the Kakadu Highway between the Nourlangie Rock and Cooinda turn-offs. It's about 60 km to Jim Jim Falls, with the last km on foot, and 70 km to Twin Falls, where the last several hundred metres are through the water up a snaking, monsoon forested gorge. Jim Jim – a sheer 215 metre drop – is awesome after the rains, but its waters can shrink to almost nothing at the end of the dry. Twin Falls doesn't dry up.

Yellow Water & Cooinda

The turn-off to the Cooinda accommodation complex and the superb Yellow Water wetlands, with their big water bird population, is 48 km (sealed) down the Kakadu Highway from its junction with the Arnhem Highway. It's then about four km (unsealed, but always passable) to Cooinda, and a couple more to the starting point for the boat trips on Yellow Water Billabong. These go several times daily year-round and cost $15 or $18 for two hours, depending on the time of day. This trip is one of the highlights of most people's visits to Kakadu. Early morning is the best time to go for then the bird life is most active. You're likely to see a saltwater crocodile or two. It's usually advisable to book your cruise the day before at Cooinda – particularly for the early departure. Don't try driving to Yellow Water – it's often very muddy and the cruise people transport you from Cooinda in any case.

Cooinda to Pine Creek

Shortly south of the Yellow Water and Cooinda turn-off the Kakadu Highway ceases to be sealed. It travels south-west out of the park to Pine Creek on the Stuart Highway, about 160 km from Cooinda.

This stretch is often closed to normal traffic in the wet. If you're travelling up the Stuart Highway from the south, ask the police at Pine Creek for information on this route into Kakadu. On the way there are turn-offs to Waterfall Creek (also called Uranium Development Project or UDP Falls) which featured in *Crocodile Dundee*, and to the Arnhem Highway via the dry-season-only back road.

Places to Stay & Eat

Cheap beds are sadly in short supply in Kakadu. There's the 20 bed *Manbiyarra Youth Hostel* a couple of minutes' walk from the Border Store near Ubirr. It costs $7 a night and is closed in the wet season – check with the Darwin Youth Hostel or the Northern Territory YHA office (tel 84 3902) in Darwin for exact opening dates. Inter-Club (formerly International Network) has two backpackers' hostels in Kakadu: the *Jabiru Backpackers Hostel* is at the corner of Buchanan and Lakeside Drives, Jabiru; the *Jim Jim Creek Backpackers' Hostel* is on the old Kakadu Highway at Cooinda. Other than these there's expensive accommodation or camping.

If you're camping, take mosquito repellent and clothes to cover as much of your body as possible. At *Kakadu Holiday Village* (tel 79 0166) near South Alligator River Crossing a tent site costs $5 per adult. There's an expensive dining room and a cheaper cafe, open from 7 am to 8 pm, where meals cost around $9. At *Four Seasons Cooinda* (tel 79 2545) a tent site is $5 for your vehicle plus $2 per person. Good barbecue meals in the bar are $7 to $9. Again there's an expensive dining room. There are swimming pools at both places.

The three main national park camping sites, with showers, flushing toilets and drinking water, are Merl near the Border Store, Muirella Park six km off the Kakadu Highway a few km south of the Nourlangie Rock turn-off, and Mardukal just of the Kakadu Highway 1½ km south of the Cooinda turn-off. The national parks provide about 15 more basic camping sites around the park. To camp away from these you need a permit from the park information centre.

Kakadu Holiday Village has deluxe resort accommodation at \$95/104 for singles/twins in the dry, \$76/84 in the wet. Unfortunately they're phasing out budget units (\$32/42 in the dry). At *Four Seasons Cooinda* rooms cost \$93/109 in the dry, \$70/70 in the wet. The crocodile-shaped hotel at Jabiru is also Four Seasons and a new caravan park may open there.

Getting There & Around

Ideally, take your own vehicle – you can rent for reasonable prices in Darwin. The Arnhem Highway is sealed all the way to Jabiru. The Kakadu Highway is sealed from its junction with the Arnhem Highway, near Jabiru, to just beyond the Cooinda and Mardukal turn-offs. Sealed roads lead from the Kakadu Highway to Nourlangie Rock and the Muirella Park camping area. Other roads are mostly dirt and blocked for varying periods during the wet and early dry.

Greyhound and Deluxe run daily buses from Darwin to Kakadu and back. The Greyhound/Pioneer service leaves Darwin at 7 am, stops at Humpty Doo (one-way fare \$6), the Bark Hut (\$14), Kakadu Holiday Village (\$24), Jabiru (\$29), Nourlangie Rock and Cooinda (\$36). The return service leaves Cooinda at 2.30 pm.

In 1988 Kakadu Parklink started a useful bus shuttle within the park from May to September. The service links all the main visitor destinations, camping sites and accommodation from Kakadu Holiday Village in the west to Ubirr in the north, Jabiru Airport in the east and Mardukal in the south. Sample one-way fares are: Kakadu Holiday Village to Ubirr \$21, Cooinda to Nourlangie Rock \$8, park information centre to Mardukal camping site \$12. You can get one-day passes for \$40, two days for \$75, three days for \$99, extra days for \$33. With two or more day passes, you don't have to use all the days consecutively.

Tours There are hosts of tours to Kakadu from Darwin and a few that start inside the park. Among those aimed at backpackers, the Hunter Safaris and Billy Can Tours camping trips from Darwin are recommended. Hunter Safaris (tel 27 4353) offers a two day trip including Waterfall Creek for \$130 in the wet, or three days including Jim Jim Falls for \$190 in the dry. There are about six in each group and breakfast and evening meal are provided. Billy Can (tel 81 8644) does a two day trip including Ubirr, Nourlangie Rock and a Yellow Water cruise for \$170. Groups are limited to 11 people and all meals and drinks are included.

Other two day tours include Jacana Tours (tel 52 1712) for \$188, Kakadu Dreamtime Safaris (tel 83 1824) for \$180, and Terra Safari Tours (tel 45 0863) for \$195. The Terra trip includes a buffalo station, Barramundi Gorge, Yellow Water cruise and Ubirr. You can get discounts from some Darwin hostels.

A one day tour to Kakadu from Darwin is really too quick – but if you're short of time you could try the Australian Kakadu Tours (tel 81 5144) standby fare of \$88 for a trip to Nourlangie Rock and a Yellow Water cruise. All Terrain Tours (tel 81 2658) or Go Tours (tel 81 1244) do similar trips for \$77. Lunch isn't usually included. Variations on the one day theme include Ubirr and Ranger uranium mine.

Longer tours usually cover most of the main sights plus a couple of extras. Some combine Kakadu with the Katherine Gorge. Among the interesting looking ones are Australian Kakadu Tours' four-day \$400 trip, which includes paddling to Twin Falls (May to October only); Dial-a-Safari's four day camping trips (prices on application) which focus on the south of the park or on Jim Jim and Twin Falls and little visited art sites; and Terra Safari Tours' seven day camping trip for \$395, which includes two nights at Barramundi

Gorge in the south of the park (not January to March).

Some tours offer the option of a scenic flight over Kakadu or one way between Kakadu and Darwin. Air North (tel 81 7477) runs scheduled flights between Darwin, Jabiru and Cooinda daily except Sunday. Darwin to Jabiru one-way costs $80, Darwin to Cooinda $78. Return fares are double. Cheapa Rent-a-Car has an office at Jabiru Airport. Air North does scenic flights from Jabiru. Kakadu Air (tel 79 2031) runs half hour scenic flights from Jabiru for $35 and one hour $60 trips from Jabiru or Cooinda. It also operates day long $198 trips to the Cobourg Peninsula from Jabiru.

You can take 10 hour 4WD tours to Jim Jim and Twin Falls from Cooinda ($90, dry season). Wild Goose Tours start inside Kakadu and are led by a local Aborigine, Mick Alderson, to wetland bird breeding grounds and an old buffalo shooters' camp. It leaves from Cooinda most days July to November, costs $90 and lasts about six hours.

Willis's Walkabouts (tel 85 2134) are bushwalks guided by knowledgeable top end walkers, following your own or pre-set routes of two days or more. Many of the walks are in Kakadu: prices vary, but $400-430 for a two week trip, including evening meals and transport from/to Darwin, is fairly typical. For shorter trips following your own chosen route, you pay $30 to $50 per head depending on the season and the length of the walk.

BATHURST & MELVILLE ISLANDS

These two large flat islands about 80 km north of Darwin are the home of the Tiwi Aborigines. You need a permit to visit them and though you might be given one if you gave tourism or curiosity as your reason, it's virtually impossible to get around the islands on your own. Much better is to go on a tour. Tiwi Tours, a company which employs many Tiwi among its staff, has been recommended by several travellers.

The Tiwi's island homes kept them fairly isolated from mainland developments until this century, and their culture has retained several unique features. Perhaps the best known are the Pukamani burial poles, carved and painted with symbolic and mythological figures, which are erected around graves. More recently the Tiwi have turned their hand to art for sale – bark painting, textile screen printing, batik and pottery, using traditional designs and motifs. The Tiwi had mixed relations with Macassan trepang fisher-people, and a British settlement in the 1820s at Fort Dundas, near Pularumpi on Melville Island, failed partly because of poor relations with the locals. The main settlement on the islands is Nguiu in the south-east of Bathurst Island, which was founded in 1911 as a Catholic mission. Most Tiwi live on Bathurst Island and follow a non-traditional life style. Some go back to their traditional lands on Melville Island for a few weeks each year. Melville Island also has descendants of Japanese pearl fisherpeople who regularly visited here early this century, and 'half castes' (people of mixed Aborigine and European parentage) who were gathered here from around the Territory under government policy half a century ago.

A full day Tiwi Tours trip costs $199 and includes your permit, a flight from Darwin to Nguiu, visits to the early Catholic mission buildings and craft workshops and tea with Tiwi women, a boat crossing of the narrow Apsley Strait to Melville Island, swimming at Turacumbie Falls, a visit to the smaller community of Milikapiti on Melville's north coast, a trip to a Pukamani burial site, and flight back to Darwin from Snake Bay on Melville. This tour is available from April to October. There are day tours to Bathurst Island only ($169, February, March and November only) and half day trips to Nguiu ($135, February to November). Tiwi Tours (tel 81 5115) is at 27 Temira Crescent, in Darwin.

Australian Kakadu Tours runs more

expensive dry season trips from Darwin to Melville Island. You stay in a safari-tent camp at Putjamirra on the north-west tip of the island and join Tiwi in hunting, fishing and foreshore foraging. The cost is $499/699 for two/three day tours.

There's a barramundi fishing lodge at Port Hurd on Bathurst Island. Contact Remote Finz Fishing Tours in Darwin if you're interested.

COBOURG PENINSULA

This remote wilderness, 200 km north-east of Darwin, is Aboriginal land as well as a national park. The ruins of the early British settlement at Victoria can be visited on Port Essington, a superb 30 km long, natural harbour on the north side of the peninsula.

The track to Cobourg is accessible by 4WD vehicles only – and it's closed in the wet season. You pass through part of Arnhem Land and the Aboriginal owners there severely restrict the number of vehicles going through – so you're advised to apply up to a year ahead for the necessary permit (fee $10) from the NT Conservation Commission (tel 22 0211) at PO Box 38496, Palmerston, NT 0830. The drive from Jabiru takes about eight hours and the track's in reasonable condition, the roughest part coming in the hour or so after the turn-off from Murgenella.

There's a shady camping site about 100 metres from the shore at Smith Point, on the north-east corner of Port Essington, with a shower and toilet, and a small store open a couple of hours a day. It costs about $20 a week to stay here.

You can fly to Cobourg from Darwin, but the camping site is some way from the airstrip, which makes things difficult if you're not on a tour. Nimrod Safaris (tel 81 1599) gives you a night in a safari-style camp and a tour of Victoria for $70, plus the return air fare from Darwin. Cobourg Marine (tel 85 6923) does $198 day-trips from Darwin, which include a flight over Melville Island on the way, a 4WD trip, a cruise on Port Essington, visits to

Aboriginal sacred sites, a tour of Victoria and game fishing. If you're already on the peninsula you can take a six hour 4WD and launch tour to Port Essington and Victoria with the same company ($70). From Jabiru, Kakadu Air does a 10 hour, $198 dry season trip which includes a scenic flight, peninsula tour, Port Essington cruise and visit to Victoria.

ARNHEM LAND & GOVE

The entire eastern half of the top end is the Arnhem Land Aboriginal Land which is spectacular, sparsely populated and produces some good Aboriginal art. It's virtually closed to independent travellers apart from Gove, the peninsula at the north-east corner. One Darwin company, Terra Safari Tours, runs a five day Kakadu-Arnhem Land tour, which includes three nights in north-west Arnhem Land, for $673.

At Nhulunbuy on the Gove peninsula there is a bauxite mining centre with a deepwater export port. The Aborigines of nearby Yirrkala made an important early step in the land rights movement in 1963 when they protested at the plans for this mining on their traditional land. They failed to stop it, but forced a government inquiry, won compensation, and their case caught the public eye.

You don't need a permit to visit Nhulunbuy and you can fly there direct from Darwin for $164 ($132 standby) or from Cairns for $230 ($185 standby) with Australian or Ansett. One-way fares are marginally cheaper with Ansett NT. Travelling overland through Arnhem Land is impractical because of the number of different permits you need to get through different parts. The tracks are extremely poor.

You can hire vehicles in Gove to explore the coastline (there are some fine beaches, but beware of crocodiles) and the local area. Get a permit to do this from the Northern Land Council in Gove (a formality). There are a few tours run by Arnhem Land Adventure Safaris, concentrating on bush and coastal scenery. A half day is $60, a full day $95 and a 30 minute joy flight is $50. If you get yourself to the Nabalco bauxite mine and alumina plant on a Thursday morning, there's a free tour.

The *Hideaway Safari Lodge* (tel 87 1833) on Prospect Rd has singles at $45 to $50, doubles at $60 to $70. There's no camping.

Groote Eylandt, a large island off the east Arnhem Land coast, is also Aboriginal land, with a big manganese mining operation.

Down the Track

It's just over 1500 km south from Darwin to Alice Springs and, though at times it can be dreary, there is an amazing variety of things to see or do along the road, or close to it. So you'll find plenty of interest between the boring bits.

Until WW II 'the track' really was just that – a dirt track – connecting the Territory's two main towns, Darwin and 'the Alice'. The need to supply Darwin quickly, which was under attack by Japanese aircraft from Timor, led to a rapid upgrading of the road – thanks in part to US troops. Although it is now sealed and well kept all the way, short, sharp floods during the wet can cut the road and stop all traffic for days at a time.

The Stuart Highway takes its name from John McDouall Stuart, who made the first crossing of Australia from south to north. Twice he turned back due to lack of supplies, ill health and hostile Aborigines, but finally completed his epic trek in 1862.

Only 10 years later the telegraph line to Darwin was laid along the route he had followed, and today the Stuart Highway between Darwin and Alice Springs follows the same path.

DARWIN TO KATHERINE

Some places along the track south of Darwin (Howard Springs, Darwin Crocodile Farm and Litchfield Park) are covered in the Around Darwin section.

Lake Bennett

This is a popular camping, swimming, sailing and windsurfing spot among Darwinites. You can rent canoes. It's 80 km down the track then seven km east.

Batchelor

This small town, 84 km down the track from Darwin, then 13 km west, used to service the now-closed Rum Jungle uranium and copper mine nearby. In recent years it has received a boost from the opening of nearby Litchfield Park. Batchelor is the base of the Top End Gliding Club and has a swimming pool open six days a week and an Aboriginal residential tertiary college. It's about an hour's walk, or a shorter drive, to Rum Jungle Lake where you can canoe or swim.

The *Batchelor Caravillage* (tel 76 0166) on Rum Jungle Rd has on-site vans for $20 a double, or tent sites for $6 a double. The *Rum Jungle Motor Inn* (tel 76 0123) has singles/doubles for $45/55.

Adelaide River

Not to be confused with Adelaide River Crossing on the Arnhem Highway, this small settlement is on the Stuart Highway 111 km south of Darwin. It has a cemetery for those who died in the 1942-43 Japanese air raids. This whole stretch of the highway is dotted with a series of roadside WW II airstrips. Adelaide River has a pub, an Aboriginal art shop, the *Shady River View Caravan Park* (tel 76 7047) with tent sites at $4 for two, and the *Adelaide River Motor Inn* (again tel 76 7047) with singles from $18 to $30, doubles $35 to $55.

You can take tours from here or Batchelor to Litchfield Park, Daly River, Douglas Hot Springs and Butterfly Gorge

– a bit cheaper than visiting the same places from Darwin.

Old Highway

South of Adelaide River a still-sealed section of the old Stuart Highway, makes a loop to the west before rejoining the main road 52 km on. It's a scenic trip and leads to a number of pleasant spots – access to them is often cut in the wet season.

The beautiful 12 metre Robin Falls are a short walk off this road, 17 km along. The falls, set in a monsoon-forested gorge, dwindle to a trickle in the dry season, but are spectacular in the wet. The turning to Daly River is 14 km further, 109 km from the Stuart Highway. There's a Catholic mission (the ruins of an 1886 Jesuit mission) and the Daly River Nature Park where you can camp. Bird life is abundant at some times of the year and quite a few saltwater and freshwater crocodiles inhabit the river. Nearby, *Rainforest Cottage* (tel 75 3410) in Bamboo Creek Rainforest Park on Wooliana Rd, offers accommodation from $14 a person (minimum total $45) in a building with three bedrooms and shared kitchen/living room. You can rent canoes ($15 a day) or trail bikes, or take a crocodile-spotting cruise for $10 an hour (minimum $20).

To reach Douglas Hot Springs, turn south off the old highway just before it rejoins the Stuart Highway and go about 35 km. The nature park here includes a section of the Douglas River and several hot springs – a bit hot for bathing at 40°C. Butterfly Gorge National Park is about 15 km beyond Douglas Hot Springs. A 4WD is advisable to reach it. True to its name butterflies sometimes swarm in the gorge. Although swimming is generally safe from crocodiles in these places, you should still take care. There are camping sites with toilets and barbecues.

Pine Creek

This small town 245 km from Darwin was the scene of a gold rush in the 1870s and some of the old timber and corrugated iron buildings survive. The National Trust publishes a *Pine Creek Heritage Trail* leaflet with details of some of the more interesting ones.

The old railway station has been restored and houses a visitors' information centre and a display on the Darwin to Pine Creek railway, opened in 1889 but now closed. Pine Creek Museum on Railway Parade near the post office has interesting displays on local history. The station and museum are usually open for an hour, each morning and afternoon. Ah Toys general store is a reminder of the gold rush days when Pine Creek's Chinese population heavily outnumbered the Europeans.

Pine Creek's *Youth Hostel* (tel 76 1254), close to the station, was built in the 1880s as quarters for railway workers. It hasn't changed much since. It's one of Australia's most basic hostels, but you get the feel of what NT pioneer life was like – no air-con, no hot water! The cost is $5 a night for YHA members. The town has an unattractive caravan and camping park, and the *Pine Creek Hotel-Motel* (tel 76 1288) with air-con singles/doubles at $20/30 in the hotel section, $50/55 in the motel.

In recent years gold mining has returned to Pine Creek with open cut workings outside the town. Some visitors try panning for the precious stuff themselves. Back o' Beyond Tours (tel 76 1221) in Pine Creek offers trips round the town and old gold rush areas lasting two hours, with the chance to do some panning; or full day tours towards Kakadu.

A dirt road goes north-east from Pine Creek to Kakadu National Park. It reaches the sealed Kakadu Highway after about 150 km, shortly before Cooinda. The dirt road is often closed in the wet – check with Pine Creek police if you have any doubts. Along the way you can take an 80 km round-trip detour to Waterfall Creek (UDP Falls), a popular camping and swimming spot in Kakadu. About three km down the Stuart Highway south of Pine Creek is the turn-off to Umbrawarra Gorge, about 12 km west, where there's a camping site with toilets and barbecues, and you can swim in *normally* crocodile-free pools, one km from the car park.

Edith Falls

At the 293 km mark you can turn off to the beautiful Edith Falls, 19 km east of the road, where there's a free camping site with showers, toilets and barbecues. Swimming is possible in a clear, forest-surrounded pool at the bottom of the series of falls, and you may see freshwater crocodiles, the inoffensive variety, but be careful. There's a good walk up to rapids and more pools above the falls. Edith Falls is part of Katherine Gorge National Park.

KATHERINE (population 6100)

Apart from Tennant Creek this is the only town of any size between Darwin and Alice Springs. It's a bustling little place where the Victoria Highway branches off to the Kimberleys and Western Australia. It's scheduled to grow to about 10,000 people in the 1990s, partly because of a big air force base being built at Tindal just south of town.

Katherine has long been an important stopping point since the river it's built on and named after is the first permanent running water if you're coming north from Alice Springs. The town includes some historic old buildings like the Sportsman's Arms, featured in *We of the Never Never*, Jeannie Gunn's classic novel of turn-of-the-century outback life. The main interest here, however, is the spectacular Katherine Gorge – 30 km to the north-east – a great place to camp, walk, swim, canoe, take a cruise or simply float along on an air mattress.

Information & Orientation

Katherine's main street, Katherine Terrace, is also the Stuart Highway running through the town. Coming from the north, you cross the Katherine River

Bridge just before the town centre. The Victoria Highway to Western Australia branches off a further 300 metres on. After another 300 metres Giles St, the road to Katherine Gorge, branches off in the other direction. At the end of the town centre, is the NTGTB office (tel 72 2650), which is open from Monday to Friday from 9 am to 5 pm and Saturdays from 9 am to 12 noon. The bus station is over the road from the NTGTB. There's an NT Conservation Commission office (tel 72 1799) on Katherine Terrace.

Around Town

The School of the Air, which provides education by radio to children whose homes are too remote for them to get to school, is two km up Giles St from the post office. Conducted tours are given at 11 am on weekdays in the school term. Katherine Museum, devoted to local history, is one km further along Giles St. It's open from 10 am to 4 pm Monday to Friday, from 10 am to 2 pm Saturday and from 2 to 5 pm Sunday. Admission is \$1.50. Katherine's old railway station, owned by the National Trust, houses a display on railway history and is open from Monday to Friday from 11 am to 3 pm. Mimi Arts & Crafts on Pearce St is an Aboriginal-run shop, selling products made over a wide area – from the deserts in the west to the coast in the east.

Springvale Homestead, eight km south-west of town (turn right off the Victoria Highway after 3¾ km) claims to be the oldest cattle station in the Northern Territory. Today it's also a tourist accommodation centre, but free half hour tours around the old homestead are given once or twice daily. From May to October, two hour river cruises (\$13.50 by day or \$23 for the night crocodile-spotting trip) are run from here, and three times a week there are night time Aboriginal corroborees with demonstrations of fire making, traditional dance and spear throwing (\$15.50 including barbecue).

Katherine has a good public swimming

pool, beside the highway on the way out of town, about 750 metres past the bus station. There are also some pleasant thermal pools beside the river, down behind the youth hostel.

Katherine Gorge

Strictly speaking it is 13 gorges, separated from each other by rapids of varying length. The gorge walls aren't high, but Katherine Gorge is a remote, beautiful place and you can have a lot of fun there. It is 12 km long and has been carved out by the Katherine River, which rises in Arnhem Land. Further downstream it becomes the Daly River before flowing into the Timor Sea 80 km south-west of Darwin. During the dry season the gorge waters are calm, but from November to March they can become a raging torrent. The difference in water levels between the wet and dry is staggering.

Swimming in the gorge is safe except when it's in flood. The only crocodiles around are the freshwater-dwelling variety and they're more often seen in the cooler months. The country surrounding the gorge is excellent for walking.

It's 30 km by sealed road from Katherine to the visitors' centre and the camping site, and nearly one km further to the car park where the gorge begins and cruises start. The visitors' centre has displays and information on the national park, which spreads over 1800 square km to include extensive back country and the Edith Falls to the north-west, as well as Katherine Gorge. There are details of marked walking tracks starting here that go through the picturesque country south of the gorge, descending to the river at various points. A feature of the vegetation is the smooth-barked salmon gums. The walks range between a one hour walk to a lookout and a 72 km gorge wilderness trek requiring camping out. Some of them pass Aboriginal rock paintings up to 7000 years old. You can walk to Edith Falls (76 km, five days) or points on the way. For longer

or rugged walks, you need a permit from the visitors' centre.

The camping site, officially *Katherine Gorge Caravan Park* (tel 72 1253), has showers, toilets, barbecues and a store (open from 7 am to 7 pm) which also serves basic hot meals. Wallabies and goannas frequent the camping site and it costs $4.25 per adult to pitch a tent ($3.75 in the wet season). There are on-site tents with beds, cookers and cooking equipment at $21/34 a single/double, up to $54 for six.

At the river you can rent one, two or three person canoes. A one or two person craft costs $5/15 an hour/a half day. For a full day it's $20/25 for a one person/two person canoe. Deposit is $20. You can also be adventurous and take the canoes out overnight. This is a great way of exploring the gorge. You get a map with your canoe showing some of the things of interest along the gorge sides – Aboriginal rock paintings, waterfalls, plant life and so on.

The alternative is a cruise. These depart daily and range from a two hour run which includes a visit to some gorge-side rock paintings for $11, to a nine hour trip to the fifth gorge (the most spectacular) for $49. All involve some walking between gorges (four km on the longest trip). In the wet season there are two hours cruises only. Tour buses will ferry you to/from Katherine for an extra $13 to put you on a cruise.

The twice daily commuter bus costs $15 one way or $20 return between the gorge and any of its stops in Katherine. You can take scenic flights over the gorge from Katherine for $40.

Cutta Cutta Caves

Guided tours of these limestone caverns, 24 km south-east of Katherine along the Stuart Highway, are led by park rangers twice a day in the dry season, and cost $4.50. Orange horseshoe bats, a rare and endangered species, roost in the main cave. The rock formations outside the caves are impressive.

Beswick Aboriginal Land

This is a large area east of the Stuart Highway between Katherine and Mataranka. You normally need a permit to enter, except during the four day festival in June or July at Barunga, 30 km off the highway. Aborigines from all over the territory gather for dancing and sports, and you'll see lots of art and crafts. The Sunday is the highpoint. Take a tent.

Places to Stay

Katherine *Youth Hostel* (tel 72 2942) is two km along the Victoria Highway, on the right. It's a friendly place with 51 beds (no more than three in any room) and charges $6 a night. *Katherine Lodge* (tel 72 1440), 1½ km along Giles St, normally charges $30/44 a single/double and upwards for its air-con rooms with TV, fridge and tea/coffee making facilities, but sometimes offers a 'backpackers special' for $20 a head. Bathrooms are shared.

There are several camping possibilities. One of the nicest is *Springvale Homestead* (tel 72 1355) with shady sites for $4.25 a person. There's a swimming pool, you can rent canoes or rowing boats for $5 an hour on the Katherine River nearby, or take a horse ride. Springvale also has small twin rooms in a bunkhouse for $20/28 a single/double in the dry season, $18/25 in the wet, and motel rooms for $39/49 in the dry, $35/43 in the wet. It has a licensed restaurant and a kiosk which doesn't serve meals. It's eight km out of Katherine: turn right off the Victoria Highway after four km and follow the signs. The 'commuter bus' links Springvale with the town and gorge twice daily.

On the road to Springvale, five km from town, is *Katherine Low Level Caravan Park* (tel 72 3962), a good new place close to the river – but initially a bit short of shade. Tent sites are $8 for two. Nearer town, 2½ km out along the Victoria Highway, the *Riverview Caravan Park* (tel 72 1011) has tent sites at $5 for one, $7 for two people, plus quite comfortable

cabins for $25/32 a single/double and motel units for $39/48. The thermal pools are five minutes' walk away. The *Stuart Caravan Park* is even closer to town, about 1½ km out on the Victoria Highway.

Katherine Frontier Motor Inn (tel 72 1744), four km south of town on the Stuart Highway, has tent sites at $5 a person, plus a pool, barbecue area and restaurant.

Among the motels the *Dreamtime Motor Inn* (tel 72 3998) at the corner of Lindsay and Fourth Sts is probably the cheapest, with singles/doubles for $33/45.

Places to Eat

Basically Katherine has one or two of each of the usual types of Aussie eatery. Over the road from the bus station, which has a 24 hour cafe, there's a *Big Rooster* fast food place with half a chicken for $3.95, plus chips, coleslaw, etc. Behind this, in an alley, is *Leon's*, where you can get fish or chicken and chips for $6 to $8. In the shopping centre next door, the *Terrace Cafe* does breakfasts and snacks for $3.50 to $4.50. The *Katherine Hotel-Motel*, just up the main street, has counter meals as well as a bistro. Over the road there's the *Golden Bowl* Chinese restaurant, and the *Crossways Hotel* a block further up on the corner of Warburton St, does counter meals for around $7. The *John Dory*, open from 7 pm but closed Sunday and Monday, is a seafood and beef restaurant in the back of the Crossways on Warburton St. Opposite the corner of the Victoria Highway, the *Katherine Chinese & Australian Take-Away* has meals for $7 to $10. Several of the motels have restaurants, some of them licensed.

Getting There & Away

All buses between Darwin and Alice Springs, Queensland or Western Australia stop at Katherine, which means two or three daily to/from WA, and usually four to/from Darwin, Alice Springs and Queensland. See Darwin for more details. Typical fares from Katherine are Darwin

Top: Aboriginal painting, Nourlangie Rock, Kakadu National Park, NT (DC)
Bottom: Supermarket mural, Alice Springs, NT (TW)

Top: Devils Pebbles, Stuart Highway, NT (CLA)
Left: Waterhole reflections, Garden of Eden, Kings Canyon, NT (TW)
Right: The road from the Olgas to Ayers Rock, NT (NTGTB)

$30, Alice Springs $98, Mt Isa $80, Townsville $145, Port Hedland $150.

You can fly to Katherine from Darwin daily with Ansett NT (tel 72 1344 in Katherine, the office is on the main street between Giles and Lindsay Sts) or Tillair (tel 72 1711, beside the Woolworths shopping centre) – or three times a week from Alice Springs with Ansett NT. Katherine Airport is eight km south of town, just off the Stuart Highway.

Getting Around

A tourist 'commuter bus' runs three times a day from Springvale Homestead to the youth hostel and Katherine Bus Station. From there it goes twice to the gorge and once to Mataranka Homestead before returning by the same route. Fares from the bus station are $3 to the youth hostel or Springvale, $15 to the gorge ($20 return) or Mataranka.

You can rent bicycles at the youth hostel. Avis, Budget, Hertz and Cheapa all have car rental offices in town.

Tours Tours are available from Katherine taking in various combinations of the town and Springvale Homestead attractions, the gorge, Cutta Cutta Caves, Mataranka and Kakadu. Most accommodation places can book you on these and you'll be picked up from where you're staying – or ask at the NTGTB office or Travel North in the bus station.

You can also join Tillair's outback mail flights three days a week for $135. Air North (tel 81 7188) does fly-and-coach tours between Katherine, Kakadu and Darwin.

KATHERINE TO WESTERN AUSTRALIA

It's 513 km on the Victoria Highway from Katherine to Kununurra in Western Australia. The road is bitumen but very narrow: whenever two vehicles approach they have to edge off the road and inevitably stones shower everywhere. To preserve your windscreen and headlights pull well off and slow down. As you approach the Western Australian border you start to see the boab trees found in much of the north-west of Australia. There's a 1½ hour time change when you cross the border.

The highway is sometimes cut by floods – the wet season here is very wet. In the dry season if you stand on the Victoria River Bridge by the Victoria River Inn it's hard to imagine that the wide river, flowing far below your feet, can actually flow over the top of the bridge!

From April to October, daily boat trips are made on the river from here or from Timber Creek, further west. Max, the boat operator, is a local character and you'll be shown freshwater crocodiles, fish and turtles being fed – try some real billy tea, playing the didgeridoo and lighting a fire using firesticks. Max has a good knowledge of the flora and fauna and local history.

Gregory National Park is a proposed new park of over 10,000 square km. At present access is by 4WD only, but it's good bushwalking and canoeing country although it gets very hot – and wet – in the wet season. Just west of the Victoria River Inn there's a one hour return walk up the escarpment, and more walking trails are being marked out. Gregory's Tree Historical Reserve is west of Timber Creek and you can see a boab marked by the early explorer.

Bordering Western Australia the Keep River National Park is noted for its sandstone landforms and has some excellent walking trails. You can reach the main points in the park by conventional vehicles during the dry season. Aboriginal art can be seen near the car park at the end of the road.

MATARANKA

Mataranka is 103 km south-east of Katherine on the Stuart Highway. The attraction is Mataranka Homestead, seven km off the highway just south of the small town. The crystal-clear thermal pool here, in a pocket of rainforest, is a great place to wind down after a hot day on the road – though it can get crowded. There's no charge.

Just a short walk from the pool is the homestead accommodation area with a youth hostel, camping site and motel rooms – more relaxed than it sounds since you're a long way from anywhere else. A couple of hundred metres away is the Waterhouse River, where you can walk along the banks or rent canoes and rowing boats for $5 an hour. Outside the homestead entrance is a replica of the Elsey Station Homestead which was made for the filming of *We of the Never Never* (whose story is set near Mataranka). There are historical displays inside the replica.

Places to Stay

At Mataranka Homestead (tel 75 4544), the *Youth Hostel* has 18 beds, is quite comfortable and has some twin rooms, though the kitchen is small. It costs $9 per person (YHA members only). Camping is $4.50 per person and air-con motel rooms with private bathroom are $43/56 a single/double. There's a store where you can get basic groceries, a bar with snacks and meals (not cheap), or you can use the camping site barbecues.

Also in Mataranka are the *Old Elsey Inn* (tel 75 4512) with a couple of rooms at $20 a head, and the *Territory Manor* (tel 75 4516), a more luxurious place with a swimming pool, restaurant and motel rooms at $60/75 a single/double ($54/68 in the wet).

Getting There & Around

Long distance buses travelling up and down the Stuart Highway call at Mataranka and the homestead – usually four a day in each direction. The Katherine 'commuter bus' also serves Mataranka and the homestead (see Katherine).

The four hour 'Roper River Adventure Tour' offered from Mataranka Homestead in the dry season for $38 has been recommended by travellers both for its itinerary – a trip to the real Elsey Station (not otherwise open to the public) and a cruise along the Roper River to Red Lily Lagoon, which has spectacular vegetation and bird life – and for the enthusiasm of its leader, Doug Collins.

MATARANKA TO THREE WAYS

Not far south of the Mataranka Homestead turn-off, the Roper Highway branches east off the Stuart Highway. It leads about 200 km to Roper Bar, near the Roper River on the edge of Aboriginal land, where there's a store with a camping site and a few rooms – mainly visited by fishing enthusiasts, though 4WD tours are available (tel 81 9455 in Darwin). All but about 40 km of the road is sealed. Shortly south of the Roper junction the Elsey Cemetery is not far off the highway. Here are the graves of characters like 'the Fizzer' who came to life in *We of the Never Never*.

Continuing south you pass through Larrimah – at one time the railway line from Darwin terminated here, but it was abandoned after Cyclone Tracy. There are three camping sites. The one on the highway at the south end of town, *Green Park* (tel 75 9937), charges $3 per person. There's a swimming pool ($1 if you're not staying) and a few crocodiles in fenced-off ponds – and basic air-con cabins for $20 a double. You can camp free at the *Larrimah Hotel* (tel 75 9931), 100 metres or so off the highway opposite the Green Park, where there are also rooms at $14/28 a single/double, on-site vans and cabins. The hotel does counter meals and sells petrol several cents cheaper than the places on the highway.

Next is Daly Waters, three km off the highway, an important staging post in the early days of aviation – Amy Johnson landed here. The *Daly Waters Pub* (tel 75 9927), with air-con double rooms at $35, is not surprisingly the focus of local life – it also serves as police station, post office, bank, museum and the main source of employment. It's an atmospheric old place, dating from 1893, said to be the oldest in the Territory and good food's available. Daly Waters has a caravan park with tent sites at $2.50 per person – and another WW II airstrip.

Just south of Daly Waters the sealed Carpentaria Highway heads off east to Borroloola (on Aboriginal land, but visited by barramundi fishers) 378 km away near the Gulf of Carpentaria. After 267 km the Carpentaria Highway meets the Tablelands Highway, also sealed, at Cape Crawford Roadhouse. The Tablelands Highway runs 404 km south to meet the Barkly Highway at Barkly Roadhouse and there's no petrol between the two roadhouses.

Back on the Stuart Highway, after Daly Waters there's Newcastle Waters and Elliott, and the land gets drier and drier. Elliott has two caravan parks with tent sites and a hotel-motel. Lake Woods, 14 km west by dirt road, is a great spot for camping, though there are no facilities. Further south, a large rock known as Lubra's Lookout overlooks Renner Springs and this is generally accepted as the dividing line between the seasonally wet top end and the dry centre.

About 50 km from Three Ways is Churchill's Head, a large rock said to look like Britain's wartime prime minister. Soon after, there's a memorial to Stuart at Attack Creek, where the explorer turned back on one of his attempts to cross Australia from south to north, reputedly after his party was attacked by a group of hostile Aborigines. They were running low on supplies and this incident was the final straw.

THREE WAYS

Three Ways, 537 km north of the Alice, 988 km south of Darwin and 643 km west of Mt Isa, is basically a bloody long way from anywhere – apart from Tennant Creek, 26 km down the track. This is a classic 'get stuck' point for hitchhikers – anybody who has hitched around Australia

seems to have a tale about Three Ways. The *Threeways Roadhouse* (tel 62 2744) at the junction has a friendly sign 'Hitchhikers! No Loitering'. If you want to spend the night there you can camp for $5 double, or there are rooms at $30 to $35. The junction is marked by a memorial to John Flynn, the original flying doctor.

TENNANT CREEK (population 3300)

Apart from Katherine, this is the only town of any size between Darwin and Alice Springs. It's 26 km south of Three Ways, 511 km north of Alice Springs. A lot of travellers spend a night here and there are one or two attractions, mainly related to gold mining, to tempt you to stay a bit longer. The NTGTB office (tel 62 3388) is at the corner of the Stuart Highway and Davidson St, in the middle of town.

There's a tale that Tennant Creek was first settled when a wagonload of beer broke down here in the early 1930s and the drivers decided they might as well make themselves comfortable while they consumed the freight. Tennant Creek had a small gold rush around the same time. One of the major workings was Noble's Nob, 16 km east of the town along Peko Rd. Discovered by a one-eyed man called John Noble who formed a surprisingly successful prospecting partnership with the blind William Weaber. This was the biggest open-cut gold mine in the country until mining ceased in 1985. Ore from other local mines is still processed and you can visit the open cut.

Along Peko Rd you can visit the old Tennant Creek Battery, where gold bearing ore was crushed and treated. It's still in working order and guided tours are given one to four times daily from April to October (admission $1). Along the same road are the One Tank Hill lookout and the Argo mine, main operation of the Peko company which used to mine at Warrego, north-west of Tennant Creek.

The National Trust Museum, on Schmidt St near the corner of Windley St, houses six rooms of local memorabilia and reconstructed mining scenes. It's open daily from 10 am to 4 pm from April to October.

Anyinginyi is an interesting small Aboriginal arts and crafts shop on the highway in the centre of town. Most of the stuff sold is made locally and prices are lower than in Alice Springs.

You can swim in the Mary Ann Dam, off the highway six km north of the town. Five km further up the highway, then six km west along a dirt road, are the Pebbles, a group of strange granite formations.

Mulga Track Tours (tel 62 3388) offers trips of up to four hours to see old mineworkings, the nearby McDouall Range and the fault line of the 1988 Tennant Creek earthquakes, which were the biggest series of quakes ever recorded in Australia. Prices are from $20 to $35.

Places to Stay

A basic Youth Hostel (tel 62 2719) at the corner of Leichhardt and Windley Sts has 26 beds. Windley St runs west off the Stuart Highway in the town centre, a block south of the NTGTB office. A bed in the hostel costs $6.

Camping is the only cheap alternative. The Outback Caravan Park (tel 62 2459) is the better located of the two sites, one km along Peko Rd, which runs east off the Stuart Highway opposite Windley St. It

has a swimming pool, tent sites at $8 a double and on-site vans or cabins (some air-con) for $20 to $34 double. The Tennant Creek Caravan Park (tel 62 2325) is on the highway towards the north of town. You can camp for $8/12 a double on an unpowered/powered site; there are rooms for $20/25 a single/double; and on-site vans for $30 single or double.

Motels aren't cheap. The Tennant Creek Hotel-Motel (tel 62 2006) on the highway has singles/doubles in the hotel section for $30/40 and in the motel section for $45/50. Prices include a light breakfast. The Goldfields Hotel-Motel (tel 62 2030), also on the highway, has singles/doubles at similar rates.

Places to Eat

The best food in Tennant Creek is at the Dolly Pot Inn on Davidson St, a block from the highway. It's licensed, open till midnight and quite lively as it has squash courts and is a local social centre. Meals cost around $6 to $11 and range from Mexican, Chinese and Italian to Australian! You can get breakfast from 7 am. Brian's Place on the highway towards the north of town has a range of pub fare. There are also a few take-aways on the highway in town.

TENNANT CREEK TO ALICE SPRINGS

About 90 km south of Tennant Creek are the Devil's Marbles, a haphazard pile of giant spherical boulders scattered on both sides of the road. According to Aboriginal mythology the Rainbow Serpent laid them. The Rainbow Serpent obviously got around because there is a similar collection of boulders on a South Island beach in New Zealand and similar Devil's Pebbles 10 km north-west of Tennant Creek. At Wauchope, just south of the marbles, there's a camping site.

After the Devil's Marbles there are only a few places of interest to pause at on the trip south to the Alice. Near Barrow Creek the Stuart Memorial commemorates John McDouall Stuart. Visible to the east of the highway is Central Mt Stuart, the geographical centre of Australia. At Barrow Creek itself there is an old post office telegraph repeater station. It was attacked by Aborigines in 1874 and the station master and linesman were killed – their graves are by the road. A great number of innocent Aborigines died in the inevitable reprisals.

The road continues through Ti Tree (which has a camping site) and finally Aileron, the last stop before the Alice. Although roadhouses and petrol are fairly plentiful (if expensive) along the track, it is wise to fill up regularly, particularly if you have a limited range – like on a motorcycle.

Alice Springs

Population 23,000

'The Alice', as it's usually known, was originally founded as a staging point for the overland telegraph line in the 1870s. A telegraph station was built near a permanent water hole in the bed of the dry Todd River. The river was named after Charles Todd, Superintendent of Telegraphs back in Adelaide, and a spring near the water hole was named after Alice, his wife.

A town, named Stuart, was first established in 1888, a few km south of the telegraph station, as a railhead for a proposed railway line. Because the railway didn't materialise, the town developed slowly. Not until 1933 did the town come to be known as Alice Springs.

The telegraph line through the centre was built to connect with the undersea line from Darwin to Java which, on its completion, put Australia in direct contact with Europe for the first time. It was a monumental task, but it was achieved in a remarkably short time.

Today Alice Springs is a pleasant, modern town with good shops and restaurants. It acts mainly as a centre for the area and a jumping-off point for the many tourist attractions of central Australia. There is also a major US communications base, Pine Gap, nearby and the American influence is very clear. It's a sobering thought that Alice Springs would be a priority target in the event of a nuclear war. The Alice Springs Peace Group (tel 52 1894) can tell you more about the dangers of Pine Gap.

Alice Springs' growth to its present size has been recent and rapid. When the name was officially changed in 1933 the population had only just reached 200! Even in the 1950s Alice Springs was still a tiny town with a population in the hundreds. Until WW II there was no sealed road leading there and it was only in 1987 that the old road south to Port Augusta and Adelaide was finally replaced by a new, shorter and fully sealed highway.

Recently some people have begun to think that Alice Springs' boom times have been too much of a good thing. When the Marron's Newsagency building on Todd St Mall, the last remaining old verandahed building on Todd St, fell to the wreckers in mid-1988 the reality sunk through that Alice was no longer the outback town it once was. 'Surfer's Paradise in the desert' is a better description according to some locals.

Orientation

The centre of Alice Springs is a conveniently compact area just five streets wide, bounded by the dry Todd River on one side and the Stuart Highway on the other. Anzac Hill forms a northern boundary to the central area while Stuart Terrace is the southern end. Many of the places to stay and virtually all of the places to eat are in this central rectangle. Todd St is the main shopping street of the town. From Wills Terrace to Gregory Terrace there is a pedestrian mall. The bus centre is on Hartley St at the back of

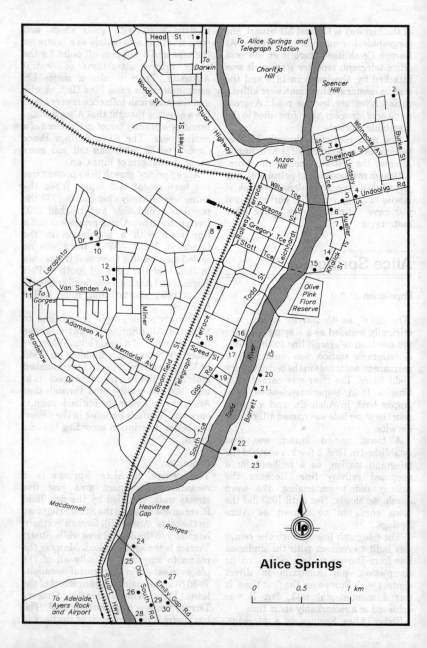

Alice Springs

0   0.5   1 km

N

1	Wintersun Caravan Park
2	Greenleaves Caravan Park
3	Arura Safari Lodge
4	The Fish Shop
5	Golden Inn Chinese Restaurant
6	Casa Nostra Pizza
7	Alice Lodge
8	Pioneer Cemetery
9	Stuart Caravan Park
10	Araluen Art Centre
11	Diarama Village
12	Aviation Museum
13	Lasseter's & Namatjira's Graves
14	Sandrifter Safari Lodge
15	Alice Springs Pacific Resort
16	White Gums Holiday Units
17	Tenpinados Mexican Restaurant
18	Swimming Pool
19	Toddy's Holiday Accommodation
20	Desert Palms Resort
21	Sheraton Hotel
22	Lasseter's Casino
23	Four Seasons Motel
24	Heavitree Gap Caravan Park
25	Pitchi Ritchi Sanctuary
26	Stuart Auto Museum
27	MacDonnell Range Tourist Park
28	Old Timers' Museum
29	Date Garden & Camel Farm
30	G'day Mate Tourist Park

Ford Plaza. If you arrive by bus you can walk through the plaza and come out on Todd St Mall.

Information

The NTGTB office (tel 52 1299) is in the glossy, new Ford Plaza Building on Todd St Mall. It's open from 8.45 am to 5 pm Monday to Friday, and from 9 am to 12.30 pm plus 1 to 4 pm on Saturdays, Sundays and holidays. It's good and has maps and information on just about everything in and about town. *This Month in Alice* is a useful monthly information booklet produced on the Alice Springs area.

The NT Conservation Commission is on Todd St, just south of Stuart Terrace. They have maps, books and those popular

'No Swimming, Beware of Crocodiles' signs. The office is open from Monday to Friday from 8 am to 4.20 pm. They can tell you the dates and time of the guided walks which rangers lead at the Telegraph Station, Finke Gorge and Simpson's Gap.

The Centralian Advocate is Alice Springs' twice weekly newspaper (Wednesday and Friday). There's an Angus & Robertson Bookshop in the Ford Plaza on Todd St Mall, and the Arunta Art Gallery on Todd St has a good selections of books.

Summer days can get very hot, (up to 45°C) and even winter days are pretty warm. However, I've been asked to re-emphasise just how cold winter nights can be. A lot of people get caught off guard as temperatures drop to below zero. In winter (basically June and July), five minutes after the sun goes down you can literally feel the heat disappear. Despite Alice Springs' dry climate and low annual rainfall, the occasional rains can be heavy and the Todd River has been known to flood.

Alice Events

Alice Springs has a string of colourful activities, particularly during the cool tourist months from May to August. The Bangtail Muster takes place in May – it celebrates the old practice of cutting horses' tails when they were rounded up and mustered before being shipped out. Today the Bangtail Muster is a colourful parade, with floats satirising and making fun of local personalities and events.

Also in May there's the Camel Cup, a whole series of races for camels. You'll be surprised at just how many camels they can round up in the centre. All through the cooler months there are a string of country horse races at Alice Springs and surrounding out-stations like Finke, Barrow Creek, Aileron or the Harts Range. They're colourful events and for the out-stations it's the big turn-out of the year.

In August there's the Alice Springs rodeo when, for one week, the whole town seems to be full of cowboys, swaggering around in their stetson hats, Willie Nelson shirts, Levi jeans, and high-heeled boots – and all of them bow-legged.

Finally in early October there's the event

which probably draws the biggest crowds of all – the Henley-on-Todd Regatta. Having a series of boat races in the Todd River is slightly complicated by the fact that there is hardly ever any water in the river. It's as dry and sandy as a desert. Nevertheless a whole series of races are held for sailing boats, doubles, racing eights and every boat race class you could think of. The boats are all bottomless, the crew's legs stick out and they simply run down the course!

A Food & Wine Festival is held early in September, at the end of the regatta. Various restaurants, ethnic groups and local wineries provide a range of food and drink through the day. The Top Half Folk Festival changes location annually, but shows up in Alice every so often.

Telegraph Station

Laying the telegraph line across the dry, harsh centre of Australia was no easy task, as the small museum at the old telegraph station, two km north of the town, shows. The original spring, which the town is named after, is also here. The spring made a good swimming hole in those days and it still does today.

It's easy to walk to the station from Alice – just follow the path on the western (left hand) side of the riverbed. Beside the barbecue place you reach after about 20 minutes, there's a path that branches off the vehicle track. Follow that for a more circuitous route to the station. If you can't find it on the way in, pick it up on the way back, following the path around the emu and kangaroo enclosures. From Burke St on the north-east side of town, you can walk or drive to the station. There's another pleasant circular walk from the station out by the old cemetery and Trig Hill.

The rangers sometimes give guided walking tours of the station: check with the NT Conservation Commission. The station, one of 12 built along the telegraph line in the 1870s, was constructed of local stone in 1871-72 and continued in operation until 1932. The NT Conservation Commission has an interesting pamphlet on the station reserve.

Anzac Hill

At the north end of Todd St you can make the short, sharp ascent to the top of Anzac Hill (or you can drive there). From the top you have a fine view over modern Alice Springs and down to the MacDonnell Range that forms a southern boundary to the town. There are a number of other hills in and around Alice Springs which you can climb, but Anzac Hill is certainly the best known and most convenient.

Todd St

Right at the end of Todd St the picturesque signpost indicating how far Alice Springs is from almost anywhere makes a popular photographic subject.

The *This Month in Alice* booklet has an interesting heritage walk around the historic buildings concentrated in the compact central area. Before you stroll down Todd St Mall note the footbridge over the Todd River from Wills Terrace. The road here crosses by causeway, but until the bridge was built the Todd's infrequent flow could cut off one side of the town from the other.

Todd St is the main shopping street of the town, and most of it is a pleasant pedestrian mall. Along the street you can see Adelaide House, built in the early 1920s and now preserved as the John Flynn Memorial Museum. Originally it was Alice Springs' first hospital. It's open from 10 am to 4 pm Monday to Friday, from 10 am to 12 noon on Saturday. Admission is $1.50 (children 80c) and includes a cup of tea or coffee. Flynn, who was the founding flying doctor, is also commemorated by the John Flynn Memorial Church next door.

Other Old Buildings

There are a number of interesting old buildings along Hartley St including the stone jail built in 1907-08. It's open on Saturday mornings between 9 and 11.30 am.

The courthouse, which was in use until 1980, is on the corner of Hartley St and Parsons St.

Across the road is the Residency which dates from 1926-27. It's now used for historical exhibits and is open from 9 am to 12 noon and from 1 to 4 pm Monday to Friday. Other old buildings include the Hartley St School beyond the post office and Tunk's Store on the corner of Hartley St and Stott Terrace.

Near the corner of Parsons St and Leichhardt Terrace the old Pioneer Theatre, a walk-in (rather than drive-in) cinema dating from 1944, still stands, but is no longer in use. It's nice to think that the tourist boom could revive it, as has happened with walk-in cinemas in some other outback towns. However, Alice Springs is pressing ahead so fast with tearing things down and building shopping centres that it appears unlikely.

Northern Territory Museum

Upstairs in Ford Plaza the Spencer & Gillen Museum of Central Australia has a fascinating collection, including some superb natural history displays. Ever wondered about raining fish or how a crocodile runs? You can find out here. There's an interesting exhibition on meteors and meteorites (Henbury meteorites are on display). There are also fossils, exhibits on Aboriginal culture, some fine Papunya Tula sand paintings and also displays of art of the centre, including Albert Namatjira of course, and temporary exhibits. Admission is $2 and it's open from 9 am to 5 pm daily.

Old Timers' Museum

At the old folks' home, south on the Stuart Highway, this museum concentrates on the pioneering days of the centre and is open daily from 2 to 4 pm. Admission is $1.

Flying Doctor & School of the Air

You can visit both these cornerstones of Australian outback life. The Royal Flying Doctor Base is close to the town centre.

It's open from 9 am to 3.30 pm Monday to Saturday. From Easter to October it's also open from 1 to 4 pm on Sunday. The tours last half an hour and cost $1.50 (children 50c).

The School of the Air, which broadcasts school lessons to children on remote outback stations, is on Head St. It's open from 1.30 to 3.30 pm Monday to Friday but is closed, of course, during school holidays.

Aviation Museum

Alice Springs has an interesting little aviation museum housed in the former Connellan hangar on Memorial Ave, where the town's airport used to be in the early days. The museum includes a couple of poignant exhibits which pinpoint the dangers of outback aviation.

In 1929 pioneer aviator Charles Kingsford-Smith went missing in the north-west in his aircraft Southern Cross. Two other aviators, Anderson and Hitchcock, set off to search for Kingsford-Smith in their tiny aircraft Kookaburra. North of Alice Springs they struck engine trouble and made an emergency landing. Despite their complete lack of tools they managed to fix the fault, but repeated attempts to take off failed due to the sandy, rocky soil. They had foolishly left Alice Springs not only without tools, but with minimal water and food. By the time an aerial search had been organised and their plane located both had died. Their bodies were recovered but the aircraft, intact and completely undamaged, was left. Kingsford-Smith turned up, completely unharmed, a few days later.

The aircraft was accidentally rediscovered, by a mining surveyor, in 1961 and in the '70s it was decided to collect the remains and exhibit them. They proved strangely elusive, however, and it took several years to find them again. They were finally located in 1978 by Sydney electronics whizz Dick Smith. Fifty years of exposure and bushfires had reduced the aircraft to a crumbled wreck, but it's an interesting display only a few steps from where the aircraft took off on its ill-fated mission. A short film tells the sad story of this misadventure.

The museum also displays a Wackett, which went missing in 1961 on a flight from Ceduna in South Australia. The pilot strayed no less than 42° off course and put down when he ran out of fuel. An enormous search failed to find him because he was so far from his expected route. The aircraft was discovered, again completely by accident, in 1965. The museum has a small booklet on this bizarre mishap.

The museum is not all tragedy – there are exhibits on pioneer aviation in the territory and, of course, the famous flying doctor service. The museum is open from Monday to Friday from 9 am to 4 pm, Saturday and Sunday from 10 am to 2 pm. Admission is free.

Old Graves

Just beyond the aviation museum there's a cemetery with a number of interesting graves including those of Albert Namatjira, the renowned Aboriginal artist, and Harold Lasseter who perished while searching for the fabled gold of 'Lasseter's Reef'. Alice Springs has some pioneer graves in the small Stuart Memorial Cemetery on George Crescent, just across the railway lines.

Panorama Guth

Panorama Guth, at 65 Hartley St in the town centre, is a huge circular panorama which you view from an elevated, central observation point. It depicts almost all of the points of interest around the centre with uncanny reality. Painted by a Dutch artist, Henk Guth, it measures about 20 metres in diameter and admission is $2 (children 75c) – whether you think it's worth paying money to see a reproduction of what you may see for real is a different question! It's open from Monday to Saturday from 9 am to 5 pm, Sunday from 2 to 5 pm.

Diorama

On the outskirts of town on Larapinta Drive, the diorama is open from 10 am to 5 pm daily. Admission to this rather hokey collection of three dimensional illustrations of various Aboriginal legends is $2 (children 50c). Children love it.

Olive Pink Flora Reserve

Just across the Todd River from the centre, off Tuncks Rd, the Olive Pink Flora Reserve has a collection of shrubs and trees typical of the 200 km area around Alice Springs. This arid zone botanic garden is open from 10 am to 6 pm. There are some short walks in the reserve including the climb to the top of the Saladeen Range from where there's a fine view over the town.

Pitchi Ritchi

Just south of the Heavitree Gap causeway is Pitchi Ritchi ('gap in the range'), a flower and bird sanctuary and miniature folk museum with a collection of sculptures by Victorian artist William Ricketts – you can see more of his interesting work in the William Ricketts' Sanctuary in the Dandenongs near Melbourne. The pleasant sanctuary is open from 9 am to 5 pm daily and the admission cost is $2 (children 50c).

Date Garden & Camel Farm

On the Old South Rd, just beyond the Heavitree Gap, is Australia's only date garden. It's open daily from 9 am to 4.30 pm but closed in November, December and January. There are tours on the hour.

The camel farm, on Emily Gap Rd, is open from 9 am to 5 pm daily, and here you have the chance to ride a camel. It was these strange 'ships of the desert' and their Afghani masters who really opened up central Australia. There's a museum with displays about camels and early radio communications in the outback – admission is $5 (children $3). Graeme

Gow's Reptile World is here and the Weethalie Angora Goat Farm is adjacent.

Stuart Auto Museum

Just south of Heavitree Gap the motor museum has a number of old cars and some interesting exhibits on pioneer motoring in the Territory. They include the tale of the first car to cross the Northern Territory, way back in 1907. The museum is open from 9 am to 5 pm daily and admission is $2.50 (children $1.50).

Ghan Preservation Society

At the MacDonnell Siding, 10 km south of Alice Springs, a group of local railway enthusiasts are busy restoring a collection of Ghan locomotives and carriages on a stretch of disused siding from the old narrow gauge Ghan railway track. You can wander round the equipment, watch the restoration work and learn more about this extraordinary railway line at the information centre. It's open from 10 am to 4 pm everyday of the week and admission is $1.

Chateau Hornsby

Alice Springs actually has a winery. It's 15 km out of town, five km off the road, before you get to the airport turn-off. The wine they produce here (moselle, riesling-semillon and shiraz) is not bad at all, although most of it gets sold to people intrigued at the novelty of a central Australian wine.

The pleasant restaurant here is open for lunch time barbecues, and is a popular excursion from town. You can pedal out to Chateau Hornsby by bicycle – after tasting a little free wine the distance back seems much shorter.

Places to Stay

Hostels & Guest Houses There are plenty of hostels and guest houses in Alice Springs including a YHA hostel, a YWCA and several private hostels.

The *Alice Springs Youth Hostel* (tel 52 5016) is in the centre of town at the corner of Todd St and Stott Terrace. Although it's still busy, the arrival of other hostels on the scene have eased congestion. Nevertheless, it's still an idea to book at peak times of year. The hostel is open all day, although the office is only open from 7 to 10 am, from 5 to 7.30 pm and at 11 pm for late arrivals. It's a friendly and well run place, and a good source of information on local activities. The nightly cost is $8.

There are a couple of good alternatives across the river from the centre. The *Sandrifter Safari Lodge* (tel 52 4859) at 6 Khalick St, is sometimes still referred to by it's old name, the 'Left Bank Lodge'. To get there, cross the Todd River on Stott Terrace and turn left past the big Alice Springs Pacific Resort. The Sandrifter is a simple, friendly place that's open all day and there's a kitchen, laundry and barbecue facilities. Each room has just two beds and prices are $8 on a share basis, $14/27 for a single/triple. Plus there's a $2 linen charge if you don't have your own sleeping bag or sheets. They sell a few basic groceries and rent bikes for $6 a day.

Just a few minutes away is the *Alice Lodge* (tel 52 7805) at 4 Mueller St, north-east of Khalick St. Located across from the park, the Lodge has a variety of rooms and some facilities for longer term visitors. Nightly rates are $7 or $8 in the dorm, $20 for a single or $10 per person in a double. Sheets are included in these charges. There's a kitchen and laundry and, in the pleasant garden, a pool and barbecue.

The YWCA's *Stuart Lodge* (tel 52 1894), on Stuart Terrace, takes both men and women. It's all air-con with TV lounge, laundry and tea-making equipment, but it's often full as many guests stay on a more-or-less permanent basis. Share rooms (twins) are $17.50, and singles/doubles/triples are $25.50/35/42. Weekly rates are available. At 94 Todd St the *Melanka Lodge* (tel 52 2233) has gone after budget travellers in a big way and is promoted through the 'backpacker' network as the Alice Springs Backpackers

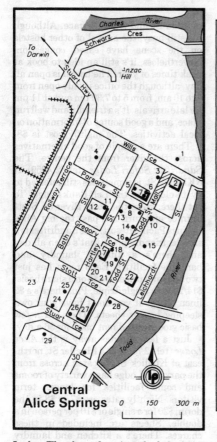

1	Signpost
2	Old Alice Inn
3	Springs Plaza
4	Anglican Hostel (The Lodge)
5	Bus Centre
6	Ford Plaza
7	Northern Territory Government Tourist Bureau
8	The Residency
9	Ansett
10	Australian Airlines
11	Chopsticks Chinese Restaurant
12	Yeperenye Shopping Centre
13	GPO
14	John Flynn Memorial Museum
15	The Jolly Swagman
16	Joanne's Cafe, Sweeties, Red Rock Cafe
17	Diplomat Motel
18	La Casalinga
19	Arunta Art Gallery, Eranova Cafeteria
20	Panorama Guth
21	Centre for Aboriginal Artists & Craftsmen
22	Library & Civic Centre
23	Billy Goat Hill
24	Salvation Army Red Sheild Hostel
25	Oriental Gourmet Chinese Restaurant
26	YWCA Stuart Lodge
27	Melanka Lodge
28	Alice Springs Youth Hostel
29	Royal Flying Doctor Base
30	Conservation Commission

Lodge. They have dormitory beds for $7 in an eight bed dormitory, $9 in a four bed. A 'backpacker' share twin is $12 per person; the same room with bed linen is a 'budget' room and costs $15 per person. Then there are singles at $29 with common bathroom facilities and better rooms at $38 to $45 with attached bathrooms. The lodge has air-con, a swimming pool, a cafeteria and restaurant, and all modern facilities.

The *Anglican Hostel* (tel 52 3108), also known as The Lodge, is on Bath St near Wills Terrace. It's good value with 'backpacker' beds for $7.50 and up. Most

other rates are quoted on a weekly basis. A shared room is $59 per person per week, a single is $76 per week. A room with attached bathroom costs $35 a night or $120 a week. There are also self-contained flats, a communal kitchen and a pool. The whole place is spotless, but it does have an institutional air about it.

The *Salvation Army Red Shield Hostel* (tel 52 1960) on Stuart Terrace on the corner of Hartley St, is cheap at just $5 a night, but caters mainly to long term residents.

Hotels & Motels At 41 Gap Rd, not too far south of the town centre, is *Toddy's*

Holiday Accommodation (tel 52 1322). They have a wide variety of rooms including fully self-contained holiday flats at $50 and $60 or rooms at $35/45 a single/double. The complex has laundry facilities and a communal kitchen for those not in the self-contained units. There's a swimming pool, barbecue and small shop on the site. All in all, it's quite convenient and reasonably priced.

At 67 Gap Rd there's the *Swagman's Rest* (tel 53 1333) with family holiday units at $39/48 a single/double or from $52 to $62 for larger groups. The units are self contained and there's a swimming pool. The *Alice Tourist Apartments* (tel 52 2788) are on the Gap Rd too and have rooms at $40/50 a single/double or larger triple/family rooms at $60/70. Rates are lower in summer or by the week.

There are an awful lot of motels in Alice Springs, at all sorts of prices. Many of them are fairly pricey, but there are often lower prices and special deals during the hot summer months.

On Barrett Drive, next to the Sheraton, the *Desert Palms Resort* (tel 52 5977) is great value with rooms at $48/55 a single/ double or $60 for four. Rates are slightly lower in summer. The rooms are spacious and each has a small kitchen. There's a swimming pool and if you've got a car this is one of the best value motels in the Alice.

Some of the better priced places, virtually all of them with swimming pools, include:

Alice Springs Gap Motor Hotel (tel 52 6611), 115 Gap Rd, rooms at $50/60/70 a single/ double/triple, rates drop sharply in summer.
Alice Sundown Motel (tel 52 8422), 39 Gap Rd, self-contained rooms at $45/55 a single/double, lower rates in summer.
Desert Rose Inn (tel 52 1411), Railway Terrace, budget rooms at $36 to $56, or larger rooms at $62 and $68, deluxe rooms at $56/66 a single/ double or larger rooms at $74.

Camping Alice Springs' camping sites and their high season (winter) rates are:

Alice Travellers Village (tel 52 8955), Lot 6146, North Stuart Highway, north of town, camping from $8, units from $12.
The Camel Farm (tel 52 4498), Emily Gap Rd, south of town, camping from $9, cabins from $85 per week for one or two.
Carmichael Tourist Park (tel 52 1200), Tmara Mara St, three km west on Larapinta Drive, camping from $9, cabins $25 to $35, on-site caravans from $25.
G'Day Mate Tourist Park (tel 52 9589), Palm Circuit, near the date farm and Stuart Auto Museum, camping and cabins.
Greenleaves Tourist Park (tel 52 8645), two km east on Burke St, camping and on-site vans.
Heavitree Gap Caravan Park (tel 56 0973), Emily Gap Rd, camping from $9, on-site caravans from $28 (smaller) or from $33 (larger).
MacDonnell Range Tourist Park (tel 52 6111), Palm Place, camping from $10, on-site caravans from $35.
Stuart Caravan Park (tel 52 2547), two km west on Larapinta Drive, camping from $9, on-site vans from $25.
Wintersun Caravan Park (tel 52 4080), two km north on the Stuart Highway, camping from $10, on-site vans from $25.

Places to Eat

Snacks & Fast Food There are numerous places for a sandwich or light snack along Todd St Mall. Many of them put tables and chairs outside, ideal for a breakfast in the cool morning air.

The *Jolly Swagman* in Todd Plaza off the mall is a pleasant place for sandwiches and light snacks. Off the mall on the other side *Joanne's Cafe* offers similar fare. The *Red Rock Cafe* and *Sweeties* are side by side on the mall and open for breakfast, burgers, sandwiches, etc. Also down this end of the mall there's the good value *Pancake Parlour*, open from 10 am to 11 pm.

At the other end of the mall *Grandad's* has burgers, hot dogs, sandwiches and ice cream. In Springs Plaza *Golly it's Good* offers more sandwiches and snacks. The big Ford Plaza has a big lunch time cafeteria-style eating place called *Hojo's Eatery* with snacks, light meals, sandwiches and a salad bar.

In the Yeperenye Shopping Centre on Hartley St there's *Cassandra's Coffee Shop, The Bakery, Donut King* and a big Woolworths Supermarket.

On Lindsay St, near the corner of Undoolya Rd, across the river, *The Fish Shop* is a good and reasonably cheap ($3) fish & chips shop. There's a *Kentucky Fried Chicken* outlet in the centre, right across from the youth hostel at the corner of Todd St and Stott Terrace.

Pub Meals Upstairs in the Ford Plaza on Todd St Mall the *Stuart Arms Bistro* does pretty good straightforward meals in the $7 to $12 bracket, and you can add a salad plate for $2. Meals are available 12 noon to 2.30 pm and 6 to 10 pm.

Restaurants The *Eranova Cafeteria* at 70 Todd St, is one of the busiest eating spots in town and is a comfortable place with a good selection of excellent food. It's open for breakfast, lunch and dinner Monday to Saturday. Meals range from $6 to $11.

Round the corner at 105 Gregory Terrace, *La Casalinga* is an Italian restaurant that has certainly stood the test of time. It's been serving up pasta and pizza for many years from 5 pm to 1 am every night. Meals cost $8 to $10 It also has a bar.

Just across the river from the centre, on the corner of Undoolya Rd and Sturt Terrace the *Casa Nostra* is another pizza and pasta specialist. You can also get pizzas at the *Mia Pizza Bar* by the diorama.

There are a number of Chinese restaurants around the Alice. The *Oriental Gourmet* is on Hartley St, near the corner of Stott Terrace. *Chopsticks*, on Hartley St at the Yeperenye Shopping Centre, is said by some to be the best, but the bright yellow *Golden Inn* on Undoolya Rd, just over the bridge from the centre is also good. Aside from the usual items you can sample some Malaysian and Szechwan dishes.

Of course the Alice has to have a

steakhouse or two so you can try the *Overlander Steakhouse* at 72 Hartley St or the *Hindquarter Steakhouse* at the Melanka Lodge on Todd St. Both feature buffalo steaks on their menus. At the Old Alice at the top of Todd St Mall there's *Maxim's Restaurant* where you can even get a crocodile steak.

Other possibilities include Mexican food at *Tenpinados* which is, believe it or not, at the ten pin (get it?) bowling centre at 29 Gap Rd. If you can get signed in as a guest, the Memorial Club on Gap Rd has *Romano's Bistro*.

Out of town dining possibilities include the daily barbecue lunches at the *Chateau Hornsby* winery or a late breakfast, lunch or tea at the *White Gums Park* opposite the Simpson's Gap National Park turn-off.

Entertainment
The *Stuart Arms Bistro* in Ford Plaza has music Wednesday, Thursday and Friday nights. At the *Old Alice Inn*, by the river on the corner of Wills and Leichhardt terraces, the rough as guts public bar has entertainment most nights. One wall is embellished with a life size photo of the local rugby team, lined up in typical sports team photo fashion, all stark naked.

More refined entertainment can be found at *Rio's Nite Spot* at Lasseter's Casino or at the *Simpson's Gap Bar* at the Sheraton Alice. *Bojangles* is a restaurant and nightclub on Todd St and the *Alice Junction Tavern* off Ross Highway has a disco on Friday and Saturday nights.

If you want to watch the Australian gambling enthusiasm in a central Australian setting head for *Lasseter's Casino*, but dress up. Outback 'character' Ted Egan puts on a performance of tall tales and outback songs three nights a week at *Chateau Hornsby*.

There are all sorts of events at the glossy *Araluen Art Centre*. They have temporary art exhibits, theatre and music performances and regular films. Bookings can be made at the Araluen booking office or through the NTGTB at Ford Plaza.

Things to Buy

Alice Springs has a number of art galleries and craft centres. If you've got an interest in central Australian art or you're looking for a piece to buy, then visit the Centre for Aboriginal Artists & Craftsmen at 86-88 Todd St. They have a fine display of bark paintings, Papunya sand paintings, carvings, weapons, didgeridoos and much more, plus excellent descriptions of their development and meaning. It's non-profit making and designed both to preserve the crafts and to provide an outlet for quality work. The prices aren't necessarily cheap, but the artefacts are generally good.

The Papunya-Tula Artists Centre is a few doors up on Todd St and has a wide selection of Papunya sand paintings. There are plenty of other, generally more commercial outlets for Aboriginal art including a good one in the Ford Plaza.

Getting There & Away

Air You can fly to Alice Springs with Australian Airlines or Ansett from a variety of places. Ansett (tel 52 4455) and Australian Airlines (tel 50 5222) face each other across Todd St at the Parson St intersection. Ansett NT are with Ansett.

See the chart in the introductory Getting Around section to this chapter for details of air fares to other towns within the Northern Territory. Adelaide to Alice Springs costs $269, Cairns $334, Darwin $267, Melbourne $335, Mt Isa $175, Perth $348 and Sydney $352. You can now fly direct to Ayers Rock from Adelaide, Sydney, Perth and Cairns. So if you're planning to fly to the centre and visit Ayers Rock it would be more economical to fly straight to Ayers Rock, then continue to Alice Springs. See Getting There & Away in the Ayers Rock & The Olgas section for more details.

Buses Pioneer Express, Greyhound, Bus Australia and Deluxe have daily return services from Darwin, Alice Springs and Adelaide to Ayers Rock. It takes about 20 hours from Alice Springs to Darwin (1481 km) or Alice Springs to Adelaide (1543 km). You can connect to other places at various points up and down the track –Three Ways for Mt Isa and the Queensland coast, Katherine for Western Australia, Erldunda for Ayers Rock, Port Augusta for Perth. Fares vary by only a few dollars between the companies. Alice Springs to Darwin, Port Augusta or Adelaide is about $105; to Ayers Rock $40, Coober Pedy $50, Katherine $90, Mt Isa $70.

In Alice Springs the buses all operate from the bus terminus at the Hartley St end of Ford Plaza. Their phone numbers are Bus Australia 53 1022, Deluxe 52 4444, Greyhound 52 3151 and Pioneer Express 53 1222.

Driving & Hitching The basic thing to remember about getting to Alice Springs is that it's a very long way from anywhere. Fortunately in 1987 the last stretch of road from Adelaide to the NT border was sealed so at least that long route is easier. The new road to the border is not only much better, it's also much shorter. Alice Springs to Adelaide is now just 1543 km.

Coming in from Queensland it's 1180 km from Mt Isa to Alice Springs or 529 km from Three Ways, where the Mt Isa road meets the Darwin to Alice Springs road. Darwin to Alice Springs is 1481 km.

These are outback roads, but you're not in the real outer-outback where a breakdown can mean big trouble. Nevertheless, it's wise to have your vehicle well prepared since getting someone to come out to fix it if it breaks down is likely to be very expensive. Similarly, you won't die of thirst waiting for a vehicle to come by if you do break down, but it's still wise to carry water – waiting for help can become a thirsty exercise. Even sealed roads can sometimes be cut by a short, sharp rainfall and in that case the only thing to do is to sit and wait for the water to recede. It usually won't take long on the sealed road, but waiting for dirt roads to dry out can take rather longer.

Petrol is readily available from stops along the road, but the price tends to be high and variable. Some fuel stops are notorious for charging well over the odds, so carrying an extra can of fuel can save a few dollars by allowing you to bypass these places.

Hitching to Alice is not the easiest trip in Australia since traffic is light. Coming south, Three Ways is a notorious bottleneck where hitchers can spend a long time. The notice board in the Alice Springs Youth Hostel is a good place to look for lifts.

Train 'The Ghan' between Adelaide and Alice Springs costs $110 (student or child $71) in coach class (no sleeper and no meals) or $200 ($130) in economy, $285 ($177) in 1st, both including meals and a sleeper.

It departs from Adelaide on Monday (May to October only) and Thursday at 1 pm, arriving in Alice Springs the next morning at 10.30 am. From Alice Springs the departure is on Tuesday (May to October only) and Friday at 5.10 pm arriving in Adelaide the next afternoon at 4 pm.

You can also take it from Port Augusta, the connecting point on the Sydney to Perth route. Fares between Alice Springs and Port Augusta are $112 (student $56) coach, $159 ($103) economy sleeper and $227 ($143) 1st class sleeper.

You can transport cars between Alice Springs and Adelaide for $170 or between Alice Springs and Port Augusta for $160. Double check the times by which you need to have your car at the terminal for loading: they must be there several hours prior to departure for the train to be 'made up'. Unloading at the Adelaide end is slow so be prepared for a long wait.

The Ghan

Australia's great railway adventure would have to be the 'Ghan'. The Ghan went through a major change in 1980 and although it's now a rather more modern and comfortable (dare I say 'safe'?) adventure, it's still a great trip.

The Ghan saga started in 1877 when it was decided to build a railway line from Adelaide to Darwin. It eventually took over 50 years to reach Alice Springs, and they're still thinking about the final 1500 km to Darwin more than a century later. The basic problem was that they made a big mistake right at the start, a mistake that wasn't finally sorted out until 1980. They built the line in the wrong place.

The grand error was a result of concluding that, because all the creek beds north of Marree were bone dry, and because nobody had seen rain, there wasn't going to be rain in the future. In fact they laid the initial stretch of line right across a flood plain and when the rain came, even though it soon dried up, the line was simply washed away. In the century or so that the original Ghan line survived, it was a regular occurrence for the tracks to be washed away.

The wrong route was only part of the Ghan's problems. At first it was built wide gauge to Marree, then extended narrow gauge to Oodnadatta in 1884. And what a jerry-built line it was – the foundations were flimsy, the sleepers were too light, the grading was too steep and it meandered hopelessly. It was hardly surprising that right up to the end the top speed of the old Ghan was a flat out 30 km per hour!

Early rail travellers went from Adelaide to Marree on the broad gauge line, changed there to narrow gauge as far as Oodnadatta, then had to make the final journey to Alice Springs by camel train. The Afghani-led camel trains had pioneered transport through the outback and it was from these Afghanis that the Ghan took its name.

Finally in 1929 the line was extended from Oodnadatta to Alice Springs. Though the Ghan might have been a great adventure, it simply didn't work. At the best of times it was chronically slow and uncomfortable as it bounced and bucked its way down the badly laid line. Worse, it was unreliable and expensive to run. And worst of all, a heavy rainfall could strand it at either end or even in the middle. Parachute drops of supplies to stranded train travellers became part of outback lore and on one occasion the Ghan rolled in 10 days late!

By the early '70s the South Australian state railway system was taken over by the Commonwealth Government and a new line to Alice Springs was planned. The A$145 million line was to be standard gauge, laid from Tarcoola, north-west of Port Augusta on the trans-continental line, to Alice Springs – and it would be laid where rain would not wash it out. In 1980 the line was completed in circumstances that would be unusual for any major project today, let alone an Australian one – it was ahead of time and on budget.

In the late '80s the old Ghan made its last run and the old line was subsequently torn up. One of its last appearances was in the film *Mad Max III*. Whereas the old train took 140 passengers and, under ideal conditions, made the trip in 50 hours, the new train takes twice as many passengers and does it in 24 hours. It's still the Ghan, but it's not the trip it once was.

At present the extension of the line further north from Alice Springs to Darwin is still under consideration. There's really no way the line would make economic sense, but its value as a connection between the top end and the rest of the country plus the smooth construction of the Ghan line has kept the plan a firm possibility.

Getting Around

There is no public transport in Alice Springs apart from taxis. Fortunately the town centre is compact enough to get around on foot. If you want to go further

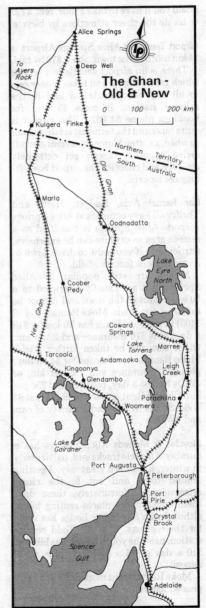

The Ghan -
Old & New

0   100   200 km

afield you'll have to take a tour, rent a car or tackle the closer attractions by bicycle.

Airport Transport Alice Springs Airport is 14 km south of the town, about $16 by taxi.

There is an airport shuttle bus service which meets flights and takes passengers to all city accommodation and to the railway station. It costs $5 and for bookings phone 53 0310. The airport is quite busy and the terminal is fairly small so when, as often happens, several aircraft arrive at once, it can get extremely crowded and chaotic. The airport has left-luggage lockers.

Car Rental Avis, Budget, Hertz and Thrifty all have counters at Alice Springs Airport. Alice Springs is classified as a remote area so car hire can be expensive, particularly if you want to drive down to Ayers Rock or further afield.

Mokes are still popular in Alice Springs, but are usually restricted to a 50 km radius of the town and cannot be taken on dirt roads. Moke Rentals (tel 52 1405) in the Ford Plaza has Mokes for $18 a day, plus $10 insurance and 20c a km. Other cars can be taken further afield. Moke Rentals has Falcons for $42 a day, plus $12 insurance and 25c per km, or 4WDs for $65 a day, plus $12 and 25c per km. Cheapa Rent-a-Car (tel 89 1125) at 94 Todd St has Mokes and a variety of cars and 4WDs.

Bicycles & Mopeds Alice Springs has a number of bicycle tracks and, particularly in winter, a bike is a great way of getting around town and out to the closer attractions. Unfortunately, these days there aren't many places renting bikes, although the Sandrifter Lodge has some for their guests. The BP Todd service station, near the youth hostel, has bikes at $10 a day or $6 a half day, plus a $10 deposit.

Moke Rentals rent mopeds for $15 a day plus $3 insurance.

Tours The NTGTB can tell you about all sorts of organised tours from Alice Springs. There are the usual big name operators and a host of small local operators. There are bus tours, 4WD tours, even balloon tours. Some specialise in animals, some people, others geography and scenery.

Note that many of the tours don't operate everyday, so if you've got some specific trip in mind it's wise to check with a NTGTB office and book ahead. Otherwise you might find you've planned three days in the Alice and there isn't another trip to Kings Canyon until day five.

The youth hostel has a $30 tour of the western ranges, which operates four days a week and stops overnight at Glen Helen. There are beds there for 40 and cooking facilities, so this trip is very good value. You leave at 10 am and return at 10 am the next day (if you come straight back). On the way to Glen Helen you visit the Serpentine and Ormiston gorges.

Rod Steinert operates a variety of tours including his popular $49 Dreamtime Tour. It's a half day trip in which you meet some Aborigines and learn a little of their traditional life. There are demonstrations on weapons and foods and samples of barbecued witchetty grubs.

Other tours include town tours, trips to the nearby gaps or longer day-trips to Palm Valley, Chambers Pillar and other gorges. They start from $25 for the shorter half day tours, and go up to $45 to $70 for longer day-trips. Palm Valley is a popular trip since it requires a 4WD. You can arrange to meet the tour into Palm Valley from Hermannsburg at a cost of $30.

Camel treks are another central Australian attraction. You can have a short ride for a few dollars at the camel farm or at Ross River, or take longer overnight, or two to seven day camel treks costing from $125 to $700. Central Australian Camel Treks (tel 52 9633) is one operator.

Or there are escorted 4WD treks, you

can bring your own 4WD, rent one in Alice Springs, or just get a seat in the escort vehicle. A seven day trip costs $350 for the first adult in your own vehicle ($210 each extra) or $625 for a seat in the escort vehicle. These convoy tours are operated by Centralian.

You can see it from above as well – it's possible to go along on an outback mail run, visiting a string of outback stations to collect and deliver the mails. The trips make seven to 14 calls and cost about $140; phone Chartair on 52 6666 for details. The sunrise balloon trips are operated by Outback Ballooning (tel 52 8723).

You can take a day-trip to Ayers Rock by bus. At a cost of $99 you depart at 7.30 am, get back at 9 pm and have just a few hours at the rock. Is it worth it? For $110 you can make it a more relaxed two day trip, and stay in the dormitory at the Ayers Rock Lodge, $122 in the cabins. Sometimes there are standby fares as well. Flying day tours cost $175 or to Kings Canyon $195.

Around Alice Springs

Outside the town there are a great number of places within day-trip distance or with overnight stops thrown in. Generally they're found by heading east or west along the MacDonnell Range, which is directly south of Alice Springs. Places further south are usually visited on the way to Ayers Rock.

The scenery along the range is quite superb. There are many gorges that cut through the rocky cliffs and their sheer rock walls are extremely spectacular. In the shaded gorges there are rocky water holes and a great deal of wildlife which can be seen if you're quiet and observant. They are often filled with wild flowers in the spring.

You can get out to these gorges on group tours or with your own wheels – some of the closer ones are even accessible by bicycle or on foot. A major advantage of having your own transport around the centre is the immense solitude and quietness you'll experience at many of these places. By yourself the centre's eerie emptiness and peacefulness can get through to you in a way that is completely impossible in a big group.

EASTBOUND

The Ross River road is sealed all the way to Trephina Gorge, about 75 km from Alice Springs. It's in pretty good condition most of the way to Arltunga, about 100 km from Alice Springs. From here the road bends back west and rejoins the Stuart Highway 50 km north of Alice Springs, but this section is a much rougher road and sometimes requires a 4WD.

Emily & Jessie Gaps

Heading south from Alice Springs you're only just through the Heavitree Gap when the sign points to the road east by the Heavitree Gap camping site. Emily Gap, 16 km out of town, is the next gap through the ranges – it's narrow and often has water running through it.

Jessie Gap is only eight km further on and, like the previous gap, is a popular picnic and barbecue spot.

Corroboree Rock

Shortly after Jessie Gap there's the Undoolya Gap, another pass through the range, and the road continues 43 km to Corroboree Rock. There are many strangely shaped outcrops of rocks in the range and this one is said to have been used by Aborigines for their corroborees.

Trephina Gorge

About 75 km out, and a few km north of the road, is Trephina Gorge. It's wider and longer than the other gaps in the range – here you are well north of the main MacDonnell Range and in a new ridge. There's a good walk along the edge of the gorge, somewhat similar to the Kings

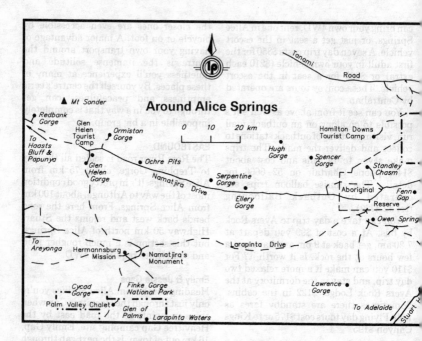

Around Alice Springs

Canyon walk. The trail then drops down to the sandy creek bed and loops back to the starting point. Keen walkers can follow a longer trail, which continues to the John Hayes Rockholes.

John Hayes Rockholes

A few km west of the gorge, reached by a track which can sometimes be unsuitable for conventional vehicles, are the delightful John Hayes Rockholes. A sheltered section of a deep gorge provides a series of water holes which retain their water long after it has dried up in more exposed locations. You can clamber around the rockholes or follow the path to one side up to a lookout above the gorge – perhaps you'll see why it is also called the Valley of the Eagles.

Ross River

Beyond Trephina Gorge it's another 10 km to the *Ross River Homestead*. It's much

favoured by coach tours, but is an equally good place for independent visitors. Rooms cost $53 to $70 in winter, $35 to $50 in summer and there are bunkhouses too. There's a restaurant with good food and a very popular bar. Phone 52 7611 for bookings. It's a friendly sort of place, but the organisation is like an outback version of Fawlty Towers, so don't be surprised if bookings are forgotten or things don't work as planned!

There's lots to do including walks in the spectacular surrounding countryside, excursions to other attractions, short camel rides or safaris and horseback riding. Or simply lazing around with a cold one.

N'Dhala Gorge

The N'Dhala Gorge is about 10 km south of the homestead and has a number of ancient Aboriginal rock carvings, so keep your eyes open for them. You may also see

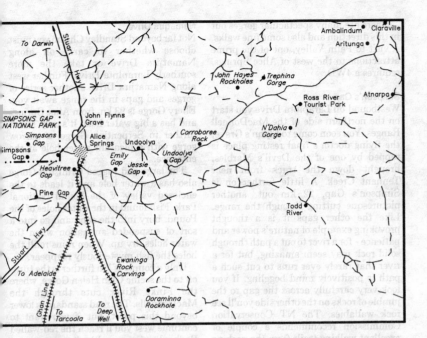

rock wallabies. It's possible to turn off before the gorge and loop around it to return to Alice Springs by the Ringwood Homestead road, but this requires a 4WD.

Arltunga

At the eastern end of the MacDonnell Ranges, 92 km north-east of Alice Springs, Arltunga is an old gold mining ghost town. Gold was discovered here in 1887 and 10 years later reef gold was discovered, but by 1912 the mining activity had petered out. Old buildings, a couple of cemeteries and the many deserted mine sites are all that remain. Alluvial (surface) gold has been completely worked out in the Arltunga Reserve, but there may still be gold further afield in the area. There are plenty of signs to explain things and some old mineshafts you can safely descend and explore a little way.

There's a small camping site and shop at Arltunga if you want to spend longer here. Most of the way to Arltunga is just a graded track, and rain can make the road impassable. You can loop right round and join the Stuart Highway 50 km north of Alice Springs, but this route is just a graded track all the way and can be rough going. With side trips off the road a complete loop from Alice Springs to Arltunga and back would be something over 300 km, a fair drive on outback roads.

WESTBOUND

Heading west the road divides just beyond Standley Chasm. Namatjira Drive continues slightly north of west and is sealed all the way to Glen Helen, 132 km from town. Beyond there the road continues to Haasts Bluff and Papunya, in Aboriginal land. From the split near Standley Chasm the Larapinta Drive continues slightly south of west to Hermannsburg and beyond.

There are many spectacular gorges out in this direction and also some fine walks. A visit to Palm Valley, one of the prime attractions to the west of Alice Springs, requires a 4WD.

Simpson's Gap

Westbound on Larapinta Drive you start on the northern side of the MacDonnell Ranges. You soon come to Flynn's Grave; the flying doctor's final resting place is topped by one of the Devil's Marbles, brought down the track from near Tennant Creek. A little further on is Simpson's Gap, 22 km out, another picturesque cutting through the range. Like the other gaps it is a thought provoking example of nature's power and patience – for a river to cut a path through solid rock may seem amazing, but for a river that rarely ever runs to cut such a path is positively mind boggling. If you look very carefully across the gap to the jumble of rocks on the other side you'll see rock wallabies. The NT Conservation Commission recommends a couple of excellent walking trails from the parking area and visitors' centre. There's a short walk from the road up to Cassia Hill or there are a couple of much longer walks you can make. It's 19½ km to Spring Gap near Mt Lloyd. Along the way you pass through a couple of other interesting gaps in the ranges. Wallaby Gap is 11½ km from the visitors' centre and you can take a different and slightly shorter route on your way back. Pick up a copy of the *Nature Walks* pamphlet.

Standley Chasm

Standley Chasm is 51 km out and is probably the most spectacular gap around Alice Springs. It is incredibly narrow, the near-vertical walls almost seem to close together above you. Only for a brief instant each day does the noonday sun illuminate the bottom of the gorge – at which moment the Instamatics click and a smile must appear on Mr Kodak's face!

Namatjira Drive

Not far beyond Standley Chasm you must choose whether to carry on along Namatjira Drive or take the more southerly Larapinta Drive. Further west along Namatjira Drive another series of gorges and gaps in the range await you. Ellery Gorge is 93 km from Alice Springs and has a big water hole. It's only 13 km further to Serpentine Gorge, a narrow gorge with a pleasant water hole at the entrance.

The large and rugged Ormiston Gorge also has a water hole and it leads to the enclosed valley of the Pound National Park. Fish found in the water holes of the Pound, bury into the sand and go into a sort of suspended animation when the water holes dry up. When rains refill the holes the fish mysteriously reappear.

Only a couple of km further is the turn-off to the scenic Glen Helen Gorge, where the Finke River cuts through the MacDonnells. The road standard is lower beyond this point, but if you want to continue west you'll reach the red-walled Redbanks Gorge with its permanent water, 161 km from Alice Springs. Also out this way is Mt Sonder, at 1340 metres the highest point in the Northern Territory.

At Glen Helen Gorge the *Glen Helen Lodge* has camping sites and a variety of accommodation. Camping costs from $3, rooms are $24/34 a single/double in the lodge section or $50/60 in the more luxurious motel section, plus there's YHA-connected youth hostel with lots of beds at $7. The youth hostel in Alice Springs runs trips out here which are excellent value.

Larapinta Drive

Taking the alternative road from Standley Chasm, Larapinta Drive crosses the Hugh River, and then Ellery Creek before reaching the Namatjira Monument. Today the artistic skills of the central Australian Aborigines are widely known and becoming increasingly appreciated.

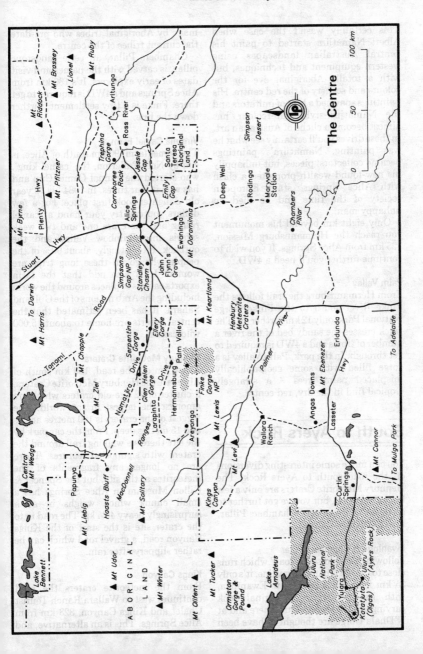

This certainly wasn't the case when Albert Namatjira started to paint his central Australian landscapes using western equipment and techniques, but with a totally Aboriginal eye for the colours and scenery of the red centre. His paintings spawned a host of imitators and the Namatjira-style watercolour has almost become a cliche of Australian art. In these drives you'll certainly see what he was painting. Namatjira's paintings became collectors' pieces, but unhappily his new-found wealth prompted a clash with Alice Springs' staid European society of the time and he died an unhappy man.

Only eight km beyond his monument you reach the Hermannsburg Mission, 125 km from Alice Springs. If you wish to continue further you'll need a 4WD.

Palm Valley

From Hermannsburg the trail follows the Finke River south to the Finke Gorge National Park, only 12 km further on. The track crosses the sandy bed of the river a number of times and a 4WD is required to get through. In the park, Palm Valley is a gorge filled with some geographically misplaced palm trees – a strangely tropical find in the dry, red centre.

South to Ayers Rock

You can make some interesting diversions off the road south to Ayers Rock. The Henbury Meteorite Craters are only a few km off the road, but you've got further to go to get to Ewaninga, Chambers Pillar, Finke or Kings Canyon.

Ewaninga & Chambers Pillar

Following the 'old south road' which runs close to the old Ghan railway line, it's only 35 km from Alice Springs to Ewaninga, with its prehistoric Aboriginal rock carvings. The carvings found here and at N'Dhala Gorge are thought to have been made by Aboriginal tribes who pre-date the current tribes of the centre.

Chambers Pillar, an eerie sandstone pillar, is carved with the names and visit dates of early explorers. It's 130 km from Alice Springs and a 4WD is required to get there. Finke is a tiny settlement, further down the line.

Virginia Camel Farm

The camel farm, 90 km south of Alice, is run by Noel Fullerton, the 'camel king', who started the annual Camel Cup and has won it four times. In 1984 his 12 year old daughter took first place. For a few dollars you can try your hand at camel riding and there are one and two week safaris into Rainbow Valley and the outback. Interestingly, about 90% of the people who go on these long trips are women. It is also odd that the farm exports camels to places around the world including the Arab nations of the Gulf and Sahara. It has been estimated that the central deserts are home to about 15,000 wild camels.

Henbury Meteorite Craters

A few km off the road, 130 km south of Alice, are the Henbury Meteorite Craters, a cluster of 12 age-old craters which are amongst the largest in the world. The biggest of the craters is 180 metres across and 15 metres deep. From the car park by the site there's a walking trail around the craters with signposted features. There are no longer any fragments of the meteorites at the site, but the Spencer & Gillen Museum in Alice Springs has a small chunk which weighs in at a surprisingly heavy 46½ kg. The road in to the crater site is the start of the Kings Canyon road, a gravel road which can be rather slippery after rain.

Kings Canyon

From the meteorite craters the road continues west to Wallara Ranch Tourist Chalet and Kings Canyon, 323 km from Alice Springs. This is an alternative, and rougher, route to Ayers Rock although you have to backtrack the 89 km between Wallara and the canyon.

Dubbed 'Australia's Grand Canyon' it's a spectacular gorge with natural features like the 'Lost City', with its strange building-like outcrops, and the lush palms of the narrow gorge called the 'Garden of Eden'. There are fine views over the canyon from its rim and some superb, and not too difficult, walking trails. The walls of the canyon soar over 200 metres high, and the trail to the Lost City and Garden of Eden offers fine views and even a short crawl through a cave.

There's a daily bus tour to the canyon from Wallara Ranch which departs at 6.30 am and returns at 12.45 pm. The round trip costs $55 (children $35). This is a bit of a rush as you can easily spend several days around the canyon. There's a ranger station with the canyon park.

Places to Stay & Eat There's a bush camping site right at the entrance to the canyon and at the *Kings Creek Station Camping Ground* about 35 km before the canyon. At Kings Creek sites cost $7 and supplies are available.

The other alternative is the *Wallara Ranch* (tel (089) 56 2901) 95 km from the canyon. At the ranch there are camping sites at $7 for two, bunkhouse rooms at $20 for two or regular rooms with attached bathroom and air-con for $60/80 a single/double. The ranch is a real outback roadhouse: at dinner you're seated right next to the last arrival (no chance of 'the quiet table in the corner please') and the bar is definitely the local social centre. Apart from meals you can also get sandwiches from the bar and there's a very limited choice of general supplies available.

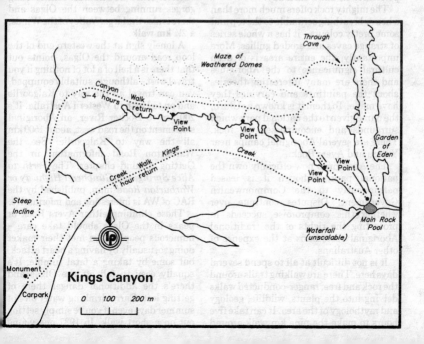

Getting There & Away Tour buses go to Kings Canyon, but not the regular bus services. Diverting to Kings Canyon on your way to or from Ayers Rock adds about 200 km to the Alice Springs to Ayers Rock distance. That means about 350 km on unsealed roads, but they're quite good, you don't need a 4WD or anything fancy.

Ayers Rock & the Olgas

Ayers Rock, the world's best known rock, is 3.6 km long and rises a towering 348 metres from the pancake flat surrounding scrub. It's believed that two-thirds of the rock is beneath the sand. Everybody knows of its colour changes as the setting sun turns it a series of deeper and darker reds before it fades into grey. A repeat in reverse, with far fewer spectators, is performed at dawn each day.

The mighty rock offers much more than a heavy breathing scramble to the top and some pretty colours – it has a whole series of strange caves and eroded gullies. More importantly, the entire area is of deep cultural significance to the Aborigines and there are many interesting theories about the paintings and carvings they have made. To them it is known as Uluru, the name given to the national park which surrounds and encompasses the rock. There are several Aboriginal camps near Yulara and Ayers Rock.

The Aborigines now officially own the national park, although it is leased permanently to the Commonwealth Government. Disputes continue over whether this compromise succeeds in protecting the rights of the traditional Aboriginal custodians at the expense of other Australians.

It is not difficult at all to spend several days here. There are walking trails around the rock and free, ranger-conducted walks delving into the plants, wildlife, geology and mythology of the area. It can take five hours to make the nine km walk around

the base of Ayers Rock looking at caves and paintings. Maggie Springs, at the base, is a permanent water hole, but after rain, water appears in holes all over and around the rock and in countless waterfalls. Note that there are several Aboriginal sacred sites around the base of the rock. They're clearly fenced off and signposted and to enter these areas is a grave offence, not just for travellers but for 'ineligible' Aborigines as well.

The Olgas, a collection of smaller, more rounded rocks, stand 32 km to the west. Though less well known, the Olgas are equally impressive, indeed many people find them more captivating. They are known as Katatjuta to the Aborigines, meaning 'many heads', and are of Dreamtime significance. Mt Olga, at 546 metres, is higher than Ayers Rock and here too, there are many walking trails as well as valleys and quiet, shady pools to explore. There are a number of interesting gorges running between the Olgas and there is also the larger Valley of the Winds, a 2½ km walk.

A lonely sign at the western end of the loop road around the Olgas, points out that there is a hell of a lot of nothing if you travel west – although, suitably equipped, you can travel all the way to Kalgoorlie and on to Perth in Western Australia. It's 200 km to Docker River, an Aboriginal settlement on the road west, about 1500 km all the way to Kalgoorlie. See the Warburton Road information in the Getting Around chapter. The *Perth to Alice Springs via Gunbarrel Highway or Warburton Road* map, published by the RAC of WA is interesting and informative.

Those climbing either Ayers Rock or peaks in the Olgas should take care – numerous people have met their maker doing so, usually by having a heart attack, but some by taking a fatal tumble. It's equally easy to fall off the Olgas and there's the additional danger there of getting lost. Carry drinking water on hot summer days even if you're simply setting out on a short walk. In 1987 one young

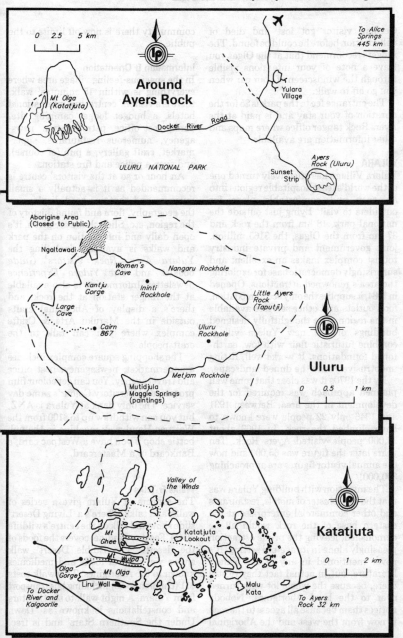

Around Ayers Rock

0   2.5   5 km

Mt Olga (Katatjuta)

To Alice Springs 445 km

Yulara Village

Docker River Road

ULURU NATIONAL PARK

Ayers Rock (Uluru)

Sunset Strip

Uluru

Aborigine Area (Closed to Public)

Ngaltawadi

Women's Cave

Nangaru Rockhole

Kantju Gorge

Ininti Rockhole

Little Ayers Rock (Taputji)

Large Cave

Cairn 867

Uluru Rockhole

Metjam Rockhole

Mutidjula Maggie Springs (paintings)

0   0.5   1 km

Katatjuta

Valley of the Winds

Mt Ghee

Katatjuta Lookout

Mt Wulpa

Olga Gorge

Mt Olga

Liru Wall

Malu Kata

To Docker River and Kalgoorlie

To Ayers Rock 32 km

0   1   2 km

German visitor got lost and died of dehydration before he could be found. The rangers recommend that at the Olgas you leave a note of your intentions visible through the windscreen of your car when you go off to walk.

The entrance fee to the park is $5 for the duration of your stay and is paid at the Ayers Rock ranger office where maps and other information are available.

YULARA

Yulara Village has effectively turned one of the world's least hospitable regions into an easy and comfortable place for outsiders to visit. Lying just outside the national park, 18 km from the rock and 37 km from the Olgas, the $165 million, joint government and private industry tourist complex makes an excellent and surprisingly democratic base for exploring the area's renowned attractions. Opened in 1984, it supplies the only accommodation, food outlets and other services available in the region. The thoughtfully designed buildings of the new Yulara village combine futuristic flair with low, earth-toned foundations. It works well, fitting unobtrusively into the duned landscape.

By the 1970s it was clear that some well planned approach was required for the development of the area. Between 1931 and 1946 only 22 people were known to have climbed the rock. In 1969 about 23,000 people visited Ayers Rock. Ten years later the figure was 65,000 and now the annual visitor figures are approaching 300,000!

The intention with building Yulara was that the ugly cluster of motels, restaurants and other commercial enterprises at the eastern base of the rock would all be demolished, leaving the prime attraction pleasingly alone in its age-old setting. It's never mentioned in any of the Yulara literature, but in actual fact they're still there, because the whole lot were turned over to the local Aborigines. Nobody notices them because all access to the rock is now from the west and the Aboriginal community there is now off limits to the public.

Information & Orientation

In the spacious-feeling village area where everything is within 15 minutes' walk, there is a visitors' centre, two international hotels, a budget lodge, camping site, bank, post office, petrol station, newsagency, numerous restaurants, supermarket, craft gallery, a pub (of course), and even a police and fire station.

An hour or so at the visitors' centre is recommended as it is actually a small museum and contains good displays on the geography, flora and fauna, history of the region, etc. Slide shows are given, it's open daily and information on the park and walks is available including the *Yulara Ayers Rock Visitors' Guide* booklet and *The Yulara Experience* newsletter. Information is also available at the ranger station at the rock, and there's a display of Aboriginal crafts outside in the Maruku Arts & Crafts complex where you can talk to the craftspeople.

The shopping square complex includes a supermarket, newsagency, post office and travel agency. You can get colour film processed at Territory Colour's same day service. The only bank at Yulara is ANZ, but you can withdraw up to $100 from the Westpac Handyway machine in the pub bottle shop if you have a Westpac card, a Bankcard or a Mastercard.

Walks & Talks

The rangers at Yulara give a series of walks and talks. There's a 'Living Desert' slide show and talk on the centre's wildlife while 'Feast or Famine' covers the foods of the desert. 'The Edible Desert' walk shows you natural foods and medicines known to the Aborigines. This walk costs $11 (children $6.50) including bus transport from Yulara. A night walk to see the stars and constellations is known as 'Down Under the Southern Stars' and is free.

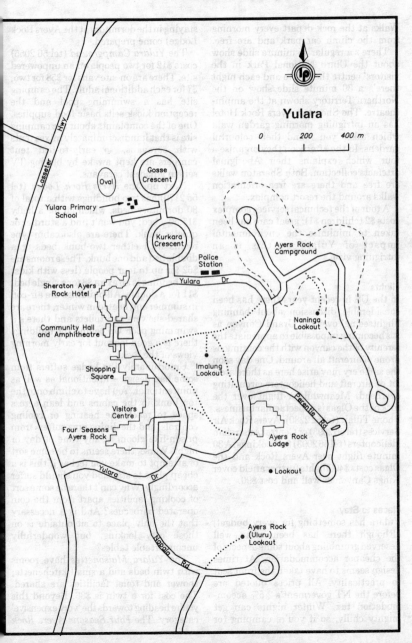

Yulara

0   200   400 m

Oval

Gosse Crescent

Lasseter Hwy

Yulara Primary School

Kurkara Crescent

Police Station

Ayers Rock Campground

Naninga Lookout

Yulara Dr

Sheraton Ayers Rock Hotel

Community Hall and Amphitheatre

Imalung Lookout

Parentie Rd

Shopping Square

Visitors Centre

Four Seasons Ayers Rock

Ayers Rock Lodge

Yulara Dr

Lookout

Napala Rd

Ayers Rock (Uluru) Lookout

Walks at the rock depart every morning from the climb car park and are free.

There's a regular 15 minute slide show about the Uluru National Park in the visitors' centre theatrette and each night there's a 30 minute slide show on the Northern Territory shown at the amphitheatre. The Sheraton Ayers Rock Hotel has an intriguing morning garden walk which takes you round their colourful gardens. In the afternoon they organise a tour which explains their Aboriginal artefacts collection. Both Sheraton walks are free and there are free orientation walks around the resort complex.

A tour of the technical services complex costs $2 (children $1); great care has been taken to minimise the environmental impact of Yulara so this is an intriguing visit.

Flights

In the US in recent years there has been considerable discussion about banning 'flightseeing' over the Grand Canyon as it's becoming impossible to appreciate the serenity of the canyon with the continuous drone of aircraft all around. One day soon the same cry may arise here as there are a lot of aircraft and helicopters circulating overhead. Meanwhile a flight over the rock or the Olgas is a spectacular business. Phone Tillair (tel 52 2280), Ayers Rock Air Services (tel 56 2093) or Central Australian Helicopters (tel 56 2093) for bookings. A 30 minute flight over Ayers Rock and the Olgas costs $40, flights further afield cover Kings Canyon as well and cost $90.

Places to Stay

Yulara has something for every budget, although there has been some well deserved grumbling about some aspects of the cheaper accommodation. At times design seems to have taken the front seat to practicality. All prices quoted are before the NT goverment's 2.5% accommodation tax. Winter nights can get mighty chilly, so if you're camping (or staying in the dormitory at the Ayers Rock Lodge) come prepared.

The *Yulara Campground* (tel 56 2055) costs $12 for two people on an unpowered site. There are on-site vans for $58 for two, $7 for each additional adult. The camping site has a swimming pool and the reception kiosk sells basic food supplies. One of the complaints about the camping site is that it indiscriminately mixes tents with caravans, so early-to-bed tent campers are kept awake by blaring TV sets in adjacent caravans.

Next up, the *Ayers Rock Lodge* (tel 56 2170) has two buildings with a total of 80 dormitory beds, which go for a hefty $15.50 a bed; you won't find a sturdier or quieter bunk. There are also cabin-type rooms with either two-bunk beds or a double bed and one bunk. These rooms are $62 for up to four people (less with kids) and bedding is an extra $8 for a single bed, $11 for a double. All buildings are air-con in summer and heated in winter, there are shared showers and toilets and there's a swimming pool. Up behind the buildings there is a good lookout for early morning views of the rock.

Unfortunately the Lodge suffers from some bad design – intentional as well as unintentional. You have to climb onto the top bunk in the cabins and lean across space to reach the heating or cooling controls, and the dining area suffers from prison-like gloom at any time of day or night. Worse, there seems to be some sort of attempt to make you feel as if this is a cheap place to stay and you should suffer accordingly. Why can't there be some sort of cooking facilities apart from the coin operated barbecues? And is it necessary that the only place to sit outside is on those arty looking, but wonderfully uncomfortable tables?

The *Yulara Maisonettes* have rooms with twin beds and a small kitchenette; shower and toilet facilities are shared. The cost for a twin is $86. Beyond this you're heading towards the 'very expensive' category. The *Four Seasons Ayers Rock* (tel 56 2100) is a nice motel with a pleasant swimming pool and costs $159/185 a single/double, which is definitely the top end of Australian motel prices. Finally the wonderfully designed *Sheraton Ayers Rock Hotel* (tel 56 2200) has 230 rooms costing $200 or $277 depending on whether you have a courtyard view, garden view, desert view or (top price) rock view! If that isn't enough there are some suites as well.

Places to Eat

The Ayers Rock Lodge has a take-away counter offering breakfasts at high prices, lunch time sandwiches from around $2 and cheaper dinners, like stew, for around $8 to $10. There are no kitchen facilities other than fridges and electric barbecues which you must feed with 20c coins. Packs of steak and sausages are $6 or $12 for two. Altogether the food situation is not ideal and the charge for a cup of hot water became instantly infamous on the travellers circuit from the moment the Lodge opened for business!

The camping site kiosk sells canned goods, drinks, tea, coffee, breakfast cereals and the like. Over at the shopping square there is a fairly big supermarket which sells frozen pizzas and other fast foods – you can try to heat them up on the Lodge's barbecues!

Also at the shopping square, the *Ernest Giles Bistro* in the tavern does reasonable counter meals like steak or fish for about $9 to $14. The portions are not bad and this is a good place for a proper sit down meal. Beer and wine are reasonably priced and the place is certainly busy at night, when there is also music. Across the square, *The Old Oak Tree* is a coffee shop with burgers, sandwiches, and pizzas for $6 to $10. There are also more expensive restaurants in the hotels.

Getting There & Away

Air Connellan Airport, about five km from Yulara, was part of the development scheme and takes Fokker F28s. This airport has made longer range flights into Ayers Rock possible – you can now fly directly to Ayers Rock from various major centres as well as from Alice Springs, which remains the popular starting point for the rock. Ansett NT (tel 56 2155) has at least two flights daily for the 45 minute, $132 hop from Alice to the rock.

The numerous flights direct to the rock can be money-savers. If, for example, you were intending to fly to the centre from Adelaide it makes a lot more sense to go Adelaide/Ayers Rock/Alice Springs rather than Adelaide/Alice Springs/Ayers Rock/Alice Springs. You can fly direct between Ayers Rock and Perth ($336), Cairns ($403) with Ansett NT, Sydney ($399) with East-West, and Coober Pedy ($152) with Kendell, Adelaide ($401) and Darwin ($352) with Ansett NT. Day-trips to Ayers Rock by air from Alice Springs cost from about $175.

Bus & Tours Apart from hitching, the cheapest way to get to the rock would probably be to take a bus or a tour. The big operators all have regular services between Alice Springs and Ayers Rock for about $40. The 441 km trip takes about 6½ hours. There are also direct services between Adelaide and Ayers Rock, although this actually means connecting with another bus at Erldunda, the turn-off from the Stuart Highway. Adelaide to Ayers Rock takes about 22 hours for the 1720 km trip and costs about $135.

Tours from Alice Springs start at about $100 for a one day trip to the rock, but that's a lot of driving for not much time at the rock. Even a two day visit is better and, if you stay in the dormitory at the Lodge, only costs about $110. A variety of other more luxurious tours are available although they all tend to be rather rushed. Going yourself and having several days at the rock is really a better proposition.

Basic two day bus tours generally include the trip there and back, guided walks of sections of Ayers Rock, a trip to the Olgas and a stop at the sunset viewing area known as Sunset Strip. Some include accommodation, but on others it's extra. There are also trips for three days, some including Kings Canyon. You have to shop around a bit because different tours run on different days and you may not want to wait for a particular one. Other things to check for include: the time it gets to the rock and the Olgas, whether the return is done early or late in the day and how fast the bus is. Prices can vary with the season and demand, and sometimes there may be cheaper 'standby' fares available. It's also possible to go with one tour, stay longer on your own and return with another, at extra cost. Drive there/fly back tours are another possibility.

Bus pass travellers should note that the bus service to the rock is often booked up – if your schedule is tight it's best to plan ahead.

Car If you haven't got your own wheels, renting a car in Alice Springs to go down to the rock and back can be expensive. You're looking at $65 to $85 a day for a car from the big operators since they usually load on $10 a day as a 'remote rate' surcharge, which only includes 100 km a day, extra kms cost 25c. So if you spent four days and covered 1000 km (the bare minimum) you're up for, say, $450 to $500 including insurance and petrol costs. Still, between four people that's not much worse than taking a bus there and back. Cheaper deals are available from the smaller Alice Springs rent-a-car operators.

The road from Alice to Yulara is sealed and there are regular food and petrol stops along the way. Yulara is 441 km from Alice, 241 km west of Erldunda on the Stuart Highway, and the whole journey takes about six to seven hours. Mt Connor, which is seen on the left shortly before Curtin Springs, is often mistaken for the rock itself. Along the way you may see kangaroos and dingoes or, at night, cows sleeping on the warm bitumen. Note the many old windmill water pumps.

Getting Around

Airport Transport There's an airport bus service connecting with Ansett NT, Ansett WA and East-West flights. The fare is $6 (children $4).

Around Yulara The village may sprawl a bit, but it's not too large to get around on foot. Walking trails lead across the dunes to little lookouts overlooking the village and surrounding terrain. Bicycles can be rented from the Mobil service station for $5 for the first hour, $3 each hour thereafter or $20 a day. Expensive!

Around Uluru National Park To go further afield from the Yulara resort to Ayers Rock or the Olgas in the Uluru National Park several options are available. There's a daily shuttle bus to the rock which costs $13 (children $7) or with a tour of the base of the rock and the rock climb it's $17 ($9). A bus tour to the Olgas and back costs $22 ($11). You can get a three day 'Rock Pass' for unlimited bus and tour travel for $43 ($22).

There are taxis at Yulara which operate on a multiple hire basis. Costs include Yulara to the airport for $7 per person or Yulara to Ayers Rock for $10 per person.

Or you can hire a car – Avis, Budget, Thrifty and Hertz are all represented at Yulara. Their regular 'remote area' rates apply. The Mobil service station hires out mopeds which are fine for scooting between Yulara and the rock. You can't take them to the Olgas, however. They cost $20 for four hours, $25 for eight, $30 for 24.

It's worth noting that the road to the Olgas is terrible. It's just a typical graded dirt outback road, but it gets a hell of a lot more traffic than 99% of typical outback roads. As a result it's corrugated beyond belief and shakes your fillings all the way there and back. This is one bit of central Australian road which definitely has not improved with the tourist boom!

Queensland

Area	1,727,000 square km
Population	2,600,000

Queensland is Australia's holiday state. You're certain to find something to suit whether you prefer glossy, neon lit Surfers Paradise, or long deserted beaches, or the island resorts and excellent diving of the Great Barrier Reef, or wild, remote national parks.

Brisbane, the state capital, is an increasingly lively city and the third biggest in Australia. In the north, Cairns is a busy travellers' centre and base for a whole range of side trips and activities. Between Brisbane and Cairns are scattered a string of towns and islands offering virtually every pastime you can imagine connected with the sea. Inland, several spectacular national parks are scattered over the ranges and between the isolated towns and cattle stations. In the far south-west corner of the state you'll find one of the most isolated towns of all, Birdsville with its famous track.

North of Cairns the Cape York Peninsula remains a wilderness against which people still test themselves. You can get an easy taste of this frontier in Cooktown, Australia's first British settlement and once a riotous gold rush town. Just inland from Cairns is the lush Atherton Tableland with countless beautiful waterfalls and scenic spots. Further inland, on the main route across Queensland to the Northern Territory, is the outback mining town of Mt Isa.

Queensland started as yet another penal colony in 1824. As usual the free settlers soon followed and Queensland became a separate colony independent of New South Wales in 1859. Queensland's early white settlers indulged in one of the greatest land grabs of all time and they encountered fiercer Aboriginal opposition than in other states. For much of the 19th

century what amounted to a guerrilla war went on along the frontiers of the white advance. A good, widely available book on the incredible adventures of the Queensland pioneers is *Queensland Frontier* by Glenville Pike (Pinevale Publications, Mareeba, 1982).

Traditionally, agriculture and mining have been the backbone of the Queensland economy: the state contains a substantial chunk of Australia's mineral wealth. More recently much money has been invested in tourism, which is becoming the state's leading money earner.

Queensland has also long had Australia's most controversial state government. The right wing National Party was led for years by Sir Johannes Bjelke-Petersen (universally known as Joh) until 1987 when even Joh's own party decided he was a liability and replaced him. Whether it is views on rainforests, on Aboriginal land rights, or even on whether condom machines should be allowed in universities, you can count on the Queensland government to take an opposite stand to just about everybody else. Under the Nationals the state has also had more than its fair share of corruption scandals.

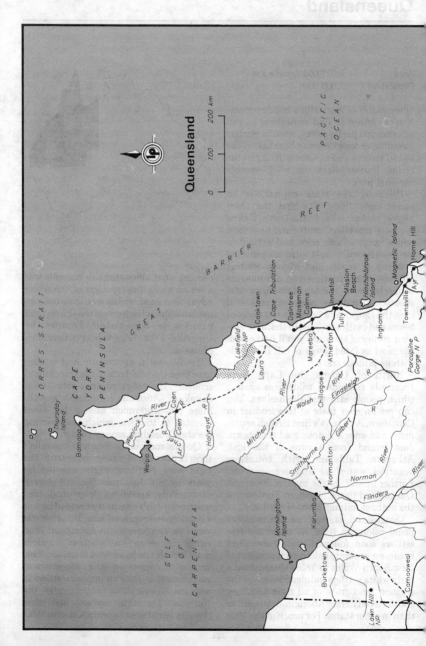

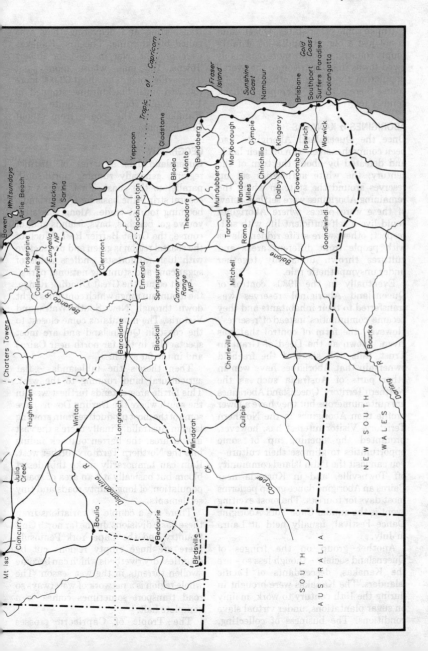

Unlike some other states, Queensland is not just a big city and a lot of fairly empty country; there are more reasonably sized towns in comparison to the overall population than in any other state. Of course there is plenty of empty, outback country too.

ABORIGINES & KANAKAS

Once the Queensland Aborigines had been comprehensively run off their lands and defeated by about the turn of the century, the white authorities set up reserves around the state in which the remaining Aborigines were settled. A few of these were places where Aborigines could live a self-sufficient life with self-respect; others were strife ridden places with people from different areas and cultures thrown unhappily together under unsympathetic rule.

Eventually in the 1980s control of Queensland Aboriginal reserves was transferred to their inhabitants and they became 'communities' instead of 'reserves'. However, the form of control that was given, known as the Deed of Grant in Trust, falls well short of the freehold ownership that Aborigines have won in other parts of Australia such as the Northern Territory. Queensland Aborigines are quite numerous but they have a lower profile than Aborigines in the Northern Territory. Visitor interest has, however, prompted the opening up of some opportunities to glimpse their culture – you can visit the Palm Island community off Townsville, and in Kuranda near Cairns an Aborigine dance group performs most days for tourists. The most exciting event is the annual Cape York Aborigine Dance Festival, usually held at Laura in July.

Another group on the fringes of Queensland society – though less so – are the Kanakas, descendants of Pacific Islanders. The Kanakas were brought in during the 19th century to work, mainly on sugar plantations, under virtual slave conditions. The business of collecting, transporting and delivering them was called blackbirding. The first Kanakas were brought over in 1863 for Robert Towns, the man whose money got Townsville going, and about 60,000 more followed until blackbirding stopped in 1905. You'll come across quite a few Kanakas up the coast from about Rockhampton north.

GEOGRAPHY

Queensland has a series of distinct regions, generally running north-south parallel to the coast. First there's the coastal strip – the basis for Queensland's booming tourist trade. Along this strip you've got beaches, bays, islands and, of course, the Great Barrier Reef. Much of the coastal region is green and productive with lush rainforests, endless fields of sugar cane and stunning national parks.

Next comes the Great Dividing Range, the mountain range which continues right down through New South Wales and Victoria. The mountains come closest to the coast in Queensland and are most spectacular in the far north near Cairns and in the far south.

Then there's the tablelands – flat agricultural land running to the west. This fertile area extends furthest west in the south where the Darling Downs have some of the most productive grain growing land in Australia. Finally there's the vast inland area, the barren outback fading into the Northern Territory further west. Rain can temporarily make this desert bloom but basically it's an area of sparse population, of long empty roads and tiny settlements.

There are a couple of variations from these basic divisions. In the far north Gulf Country and the Cape York Peninsula there are huge empty regions cut by countless dry riverbeds which can become swollen torrents in the wet season. The whole region is a network of waterways so road transport sometimes comes to a complete halt.

The Tropic of Capricorn crosses

Queensland about a quarter of the way up –
it runs right through two major towns,
Rockhampton and Longreach.

CLIMATE

The Queensland seasons are more a case
of hotter and wetter or cooler and drier
than of summer and winter. November/
December to April/May is the wetter,
hotter half of the year and the real wet,
particularly affecting northern coastal
areas, is January to March. Cairns
usually gets about 1300 mm of rain in
these three months, with daily temperatures
regularly reaching the 30°Cs. This is the
time for cyclones too and if one hits, even
the main road north, the Bruce Highway,
can be blocked by the ensuing floods.

In the south, Brisbane and Rockhampton both get about 450 mm of rain
from January to March. Temperatures in
Brisbane peak somewhere in the 20°Cs
just about every day of the year.
Queensland rarely gets anything like cold
weather except at night inland or upland
from about May to September. Inland, of
course, there's also a lot less rain than near
the coast.

INFORMATION

Queensland has none of the state run
tourist information offices that you find in
other states. Instead there are tourism
offices, often privately run, which act as
booking agents for the various hotels, tour
companies and so on that sponsor them.
You may not always get a full or
straightforward answer to your question.

The Queensland Government Travel
Centres around the state and in other
states are primarily booking offices, not
information centres, but they may prove
useful. It's a good idea to check with these
offices when planning a trip to Queensland
as the cost of food and accommodation
can vary greatly with the season, and high
and low seasons often differ from one part
of the coast to another. The interstate
offices are:

Australian Capital Territory
  Garema Place, Canberra City, 2601 (tel 48
  8411)
New South Wales
  516 Hunter St, Newcastle, 2300 (tel 26
  2800)
  75 Castlereagh St, Sydney, 2000 (tel 232
  1788)
South Australia
  10 Grenfell St, Adelaide, 5000 (tel 212
  2399)
Victoria
  257 Collins St, Melbourne, 3000 (tel 654
  3866)
Western Australia
  55 St George's Terrace, Perth (tel 325
  1600)

The RACQ has a series of excellent road
maps covering the whole state, region by
region, available from RACQ offices.
They're very detailed and packed with
information. RACQ offices anywhere are
a very helpful source of information about
road and weather conditions. Also good is
the Sunmap series of area maps,
published by the state government. There
are Sunmap shops in most big towns.

NATIONAL PARKS

Queensland has more than 200 national
parks and while some just cover a single
hill or lake, others are major wilderness
areas. Many islands and stretches of coast
are national parks: inland three of the
most spectacular are Lamington on the
forested rim of an ancient volcano on the
New South Wales border; Carnarvon with
its 30 km gorge south-west of Rockhampton;
and rainforested Eungella, in from
Mackay, swarming with wildlife. Many
parks have camping grounds with water,
toilets and showers and there are also
often privately run camping grounds, or
motel or lodge accommodation, on the
park fringes. There's usually a network of
walking tracks within sizeable parks.

The Queensland National Parks &
Wildlife Service operates four main
information centres, at Gold Coast
Highway, Burleigh Heads, on the Gold
Coast (tel 35 3032); 55 Priors Pocket Rd,

Moggill, in west Brisbane (tel 202 0200); Bruce Highway, Monkland, Gympie (tel 82 4189); and Bruce Highway, Cardwell (tel 66 8601). It's well worth calling at one of these to find out what's where and to get the rundown on camping in the national parks. You can also get info from the national parks offices in most major towns and from the ranger stations at the parks themselves. In central Brisbane you can visit the office at 160 Ann St (tel 227 4111). Pick up a copy of *Ringtail* – the useful quarterly national parks newspaper.

To camp in a national park – whether on a fixed camping ground or in the bush – you need a permit which you can either get in advance by writing or calling in at the appropriate national parks office, or from the rangers at the park itself. Camping in national parks used to be free but charges were introduced in 1988 – up to $7 a night for a site for up to six people. Some camping grounds fill up at holiday times and you can book sites usually six to 12 weeks ahead by writing to the appropriate office. Parks offices can supply lists for each park and *Ringtail* contains the info too.

State Forests

There are also camping areas, walking trails and scenic drives in some state forests which can be just as scenic and wild as national parks. You can get info on state forest camping sites and facilities from tourist offices or from state forestry offices – the head office (tel 224 6018) is in Mineral House, 41 George St, Brisbane. Some others are at Fraser Rd, Two Mile, near Gympie; 11 Lannercost St, Ingham; Gregory St, Cardwell; and at Atherton.

ACTIVITIES
Bushwalking

This is a popular activity in Queensland year round. There are bushwalking clubs in the state and several guidebooks about bushwalks. LP's *Bushwalking in Australia* includes three walks in Queensland, which range between two

and five days in length. National parks and state forests are some of the best places for walking, often with marked trails. You can get full info on walking in the parks and state forests from their own offices.

There are excellent bushwalking possibilities in many parts of the state, including on several of the larger coastal islands such as Fraser and Hinchinbrook. Favourite bushwalkers' national parks on the mainland include Lamington in the southern Border Ranges, Main Range in the Great Divide, Cooloola just north of the Sunshine Coast, and Bellenden Ker south of Cairns which contains Queensland's highest peak, Mt Bartle Frere (1657 metres).

Water Sports

Diving & Snorkelling The Great Barrier Reef provides some of the world's best diving and there's ample opportunity to learn and pursue this activity. The Queensland coast is probably the world's cheapest place to learn to scuba dive – a five day course leading to a recognised open water certificate usually costs somewhere between $240 and $290 and you almost always do a good part of your learning out on the Barrier Reef itself. These courses are now very popular and almost every town up the coast has one or more dive schools. The three most popular places are Airlie Beach, Townsville and above all Cairns.

Important factors to consider when choosing a course include the school's reputation, the relative amounts of time spent on pool/classroom training and out in the ocean, and whether your open water time is spent on the outer reef as opposed to reefs around islands or even just off the mainland. The outer reef is usually more spectacular. Normally you have to show you can tread water for 10 minutes, and swim 200 metres, before you can start a course. Some schools also require a medical which will usually cost extra.

For already certified divers, trips

and equipment hire are available just about everywhere. You usually have to show evidence of qualifications. You can snorkel just about everywhere too. There are coral reefs off some mainland beaches and round several of the islands, and many day-trips out to the Barrier Reef provide snorkel gear free.

During the wet season, usually January to March, floods can wash a lot of mud out into the ocean and visibility for divers and snorkellers is sometimes affected.

White-water Rafting & Canoeing The Tully and North Johnstone rivers between Townsville and Cairns are the big ones for white-water rafting. You can do day-trips for about $65 to $85, or longer expeditions.

Coastal Queensland is full of waterways and lakes so there's no shortage of canoeing territory and you can rent canoes or join canoe tours in several places – among them Noosa and again Townsville and Cairns.

Swimming & Surfing There are plenty of swimming beaches close to Brisbane on sheltered Moreton Bay. Popular surfing beaches are south of the capital on the Gold Coast and north on the Sunshine Coast. North of Fraser Island the beaches are sheltered by the Great Barrier Reef so they're great for swimming but no good for surf. The clear, sheltered waters of the reef hardly need to be mentioned. There are also innumerable, good, freshwater swimming spots around the state.

Other Water Sports Sailing enthusiasts will also find plenty of opportunities and many places which hire boats, both along the coast and inland. Airlie Beach and the Whitsunday Islands are probably the biggest centres and you can find almost any type of boating or sailing you want there. Fishing is probably Queensland's biggest participant sport and you can rent gear or boats for this in many places. Windsurfers too can be hired in several places along the coast.

Warning From around November to April avoid swimming on unprotected northern beaches where deadly box jellyfish may lurk. If in any doubt check with a local. If you're still in doubt, don't swim – you only get stung once in a lifetime. Great Keppel Island is usually the most northerly safe place in the box jellyfish season. Also in northern waters, saltwater crocodiles are a hazard. They may be found in the open sea or near creeks and rivers – especially tidal ones – sometimes surprising distances inland.

Fossicking
There are lots of good fossicking areas in Queensland – see if the Queensland Government Travel Centres are still publishing the *Gem Field* brochure. It tells you the places where you have a fair chance of finding gems and the types you'll find. You'll need a 'miners right' before you set out.

GETTING AROUND
The peak tourist seasons are mid-December to late January, 10 days either side of Easter, and mid-June to mid-October. The low season is February and March.

Air
Ansett and Australian Airlines both fly to the major cities of Queensland, connecting them to the southern states and across to the Northern Territory. East-West flies to Brisbane, the Gold and Sunshine coasts and Cairns. There's also a multitude of smaller airlines operating up and down the coast and the Cape York Peninsula and into the outback. During the wet season such flights are often the only means of getting around the Gulf of Carpentaria or the Cape York Peninsula. These smaller airlines include Sunstate, Australian Regional (both closely linked to Australian Airlines), Sunbird and Flight West.

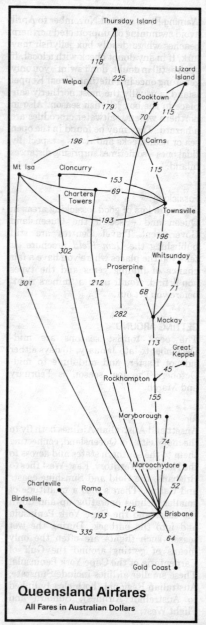

Thursday Island

118

225

Weipa

Lizard
Island

179

Cooktown

70   115

Cairns

196

115

Mt Isa   Cloncurry

153

69

Charters
Towers

193

Townsville

302

196

Whitsunday

Proserpine

301

212

68   71

282

Mackay

113

Great
Keppel

Rockhampton

45

155

Maryborough

74

Maroochydore

Charleville   Roma

52

Birdsville

193   145

Brisbane

335

64

Gold Coast

Queensland Airfares

All Fares in Australian Dollars

Bus

There are numerous bus services up the coast to Cairns and inland from Townsville through Mt Isa to the Northern Territory. The main companies on these routes are Greyhound, Deluxe, Pioneer and McCafferty's. Prices are fairly similar though McCafferty's tends to be a dollar or two cheaper. On the coastal route there's also Sunliner which often undercuts all the others.

There's also a range of stopover deals. Generally you can get a free stopover at Brisbane with most companies, while Deluxe and McCafferty's/Bus Australia also allow one at Mt Isa, and Pioneer Express and Deluxe at the Gold Coast. Of course if you have a bus pass you can stop wherever you want.

You can catch the bus inland from Brisbane to Roma, Charleville, Longreach and up to Mt Isa, or from Rockhampton to Longreach. There are also many local services like Cairns to Cooktown or Brisbane to the Gold Coast.

Train

There are four major rail routes in Queensland. The main one is Brisbane to Cairns with a local extension on the scenic route into the Atherton Tableland. Inland from Brisbane a service runs to Roma, Charleville and Quilpie while from Rockhampton you can go to Emerald, Longreach and Winton, and from Townsville there is a service to Mt Isa. There are other local and outback lines too. The 'Sunshine Rail Pass' provides unlimited travel on all services in Queensland. Fares in economy (1st class) are: 14 days for $211 ($306), 21 days for $244 ($377), and one month for $306 ($461).

Queensland trains are slower than buses but they're similarly priced if you travel in economy class. They're almost all air-con and you can get sleeping berths on most trains for $17 a night in economy, $29 in 1st class. You can break your journey on most services for no extra cost provided you complete the trip within five days (on a journey of up to 500 km), 10 days (501 to 1000 km) or 14 days (over 1000 km). The only interstate rail connection from Queensland is from Brisbane to Sydney.

Hitching

This is perfectly practicable and common, but take care: the police sometimes jump on hitchhikers for little reason, and there are long, lonely stretches of road where strange people are said to pick up unwary hitchers.

Sailing

It's possible to make your way along the coast or even over to Papua New Guinea or Darwin by crewing on the numerous yachts and cruisers that sail the Queensland waters. Ask at harbours, marinas, yacht or sailing clubs. Great Keppel Island, Airlie Beach, Townsville and Cairns are good places to try. Sometimes you'll get a free ride in exchange for your help, but it's not unusual for owners to ask $7 to $10 a day for food, etc.

Brisbane

Population 1,171,340

When Sydney and the colony of New South Wales needed a better place to store its more recalcitrant 'cons' the tropical country further north seemed a good place to drop them. Accordingly, in 1824, a penal settlement was established at Redcliffe on Moreton Bay, but was soon abandoned due to lack of water and hostile Aborigines. The settlement was moved south and inland to Brisbane, a town grew up and though the penal settlement was abandoned in 1839, Brisbane's future was assured when the area was thrown open to free settlers in 1842. As Queensland's huge agricultural potential, and then its mineral riches, was developed, Brisbane grew to be a city

and today it is the third largest in Australia.

For a long time Brisbane kept the air of a large country town rather than a true metropolis but in the past decade it has taken serious steps towards joining the big league. Skyscrapers have rocketed up all over the city centre, the transport system has improved, the Brisbane River waterfront has been tarted up, and in 1988 the city hosted Expo 88, a six month world fair which pulled in 14 million visitors.

Brisbane is now a lively place which is making a lot more use of the Brisbane River as a source of recreation and pleasure, and has come on by leaps and bounds in the entertainment and eating out fields. It's also a scenic city, surrounded by hills and fine lookouts, and with some impressive bridges and squares. The terraced house architecture of the southern capitals only pops up in odd, isolated pockets in Brisbane, but you'll find the tropical Queensland stilt houses with their wide verandahs all over the place.

Several of Queensland's major attractions are within day-trip distance of Brisbane. The Gold and Sunshine coasts and their mountainous hinterlands are easy drives from the city, and you can also visit the islands of Moreton Bay or head inland towards the Great Dividing Range and the Darling Downs.

Orientation

Brisbane is built along and between the looping meanders of the Brisbane River. The city centre occupies the V-shaped piece of land enclosed by one of these loops, about 25 km upstream from the river mouth. Brisbane transit centre, where you'll arrive if you're coming by bus or train, is on Roma St about half a km west of the centre. Walk left out of the transit centre main entrance to reach the city centre – you'll reach King George Square, the large open square in front of City Hall, a popular place to sit and watch the world pass by.

About one km west of the centre is the

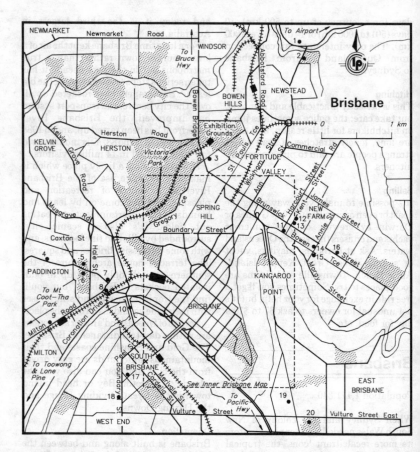

suburb of Paddington with some cheap accommodation and several restaurants. South-west of the centre, across the river, is the Expo site in South Brisbane, and the suburb of West End. North-east up Ann St from the city, you arrive in Fortitude Valley with a large ethnic population and lots more restaurants. A right turn down Brunswick St from Fortitude Valley will take you into another river-looped part of the city at New Farm, with the greatest concentration of hostels, about three km from the centre.

Information

The RACQ (tel 253 2444) is at 190 Edward St. The National Parks & Wildlife Service (tel 227 4111), open from Monday to Friday, is at 160 Ann St. The Queensland Conservation Commission Environment Centre (tel 221 0188), with a library and

1	Breakfast Creek Hotel	12	Backpackers Down Under (Kent St)
2	Newstead House	13	Brunswick Hotel
3	Tourist Private Hotel	14	Pink Galah Hostel
4	Backpackers Paddington	15	Backpackers Down Under
5	Brisbane Underground		(Bowen Tce)
6	Lang Park	16	Brisbane International Backpackers
7	Paddington Barracks Hostel	17	Squirrels
8	Brisbane City YHA	18	Qen Heng's
9	XXXX Brewery	19	Carmel Lodge Holiday Flats
10	William Jolly Bridge	20	Brisbane Cricket Ground
11	Backpackers Bridge Inn		(The Gabba)

information desk open to the public on weekdays from 9 am to 5 pm, is on the 2nd floor of the School of Arts building on Ann St. The YHA state office (tel 221 0961) is at 462 Queen St in the centre and is open from 8.30 am to 5 pm Monday to Friday.

The main post office is on Queen St. There are a number of give away information guides circulated in Brisbane including the useful entertainment guide *Time Off*. Another, *This Week in Brisbane*, contains a list of foreign consulates in the city.

Tourist Office The Tourism Brisbane information desk (tel 221 8411) is in the City Hall. It's open Monday to Friday from 8.30 am to 5 pm. There's also the Brisbane Information Centre (tel 229 5918) in the Queen St mall, between Albert and Edward Sts, open Monday to Thursday from 8.30 am to 5 pm, Friday from 8.30 am to 8.30 pm, and Saturday from 8.30 to 11.30 am. In the transit centre on level two the Greater Brisbane Tourist Association has a helpful info office (tel 221 1562) covering not just the city but the surrounding area too. The Queensland Government Travel Centre (tel 833 5337) on the corner of Adelaide and Edward Sts is more of a booking office than an info

centre but may be able to answer some queries. It's open Monday to Friday from 9 am to 5 pm, Saturday from 9 to 11 am.

Bookshops Queensland Book Depot, on Adelaide St opposite the City Hall, is the city's biggest traditional bookshop. Other good ones include the Book Nook in the Metro Arts building at 109 Edward St, the Mansions Bookshop on George St, the Billabong Bookshop immediately east of Victoria Bridge, Angus & Robertson on Edward St, Folio Books on Elizabeth St and the American Bookstore also on Elizabeth St. Jim the Backpacker at 76 Wickham St, Fortitude Valley, sells backpacking books and outdoor equipment.

City Hall
Brisbane's City Hall on the corner of Adelaide and Albert Sts has gradually been surrounded by skyscrapers but the observation platform still provides one of the best views across the city. The City Hall also houses a museum and art gallery on the ground floor, open Monday to Friday from 10 am to 4 pm, admission free. The large open King George Square fronts the City Hall and makes the building look even more grandiose and

impressive. Built in 1930 the building is one of the biggest city halls in Australia.

Queen St Mall

Running two blocks from Edward St to George St, this is the shopping hub of the city and as malls go it's attractive. Latest additions are an underground bus interchange, a Hilton Hotel and the Myer Centre with 250-plus shops, eight cinemas and even an indoor fun fair. The mall is bustling and alive – this is where Brisbanites try to look their best, particularly on Friday nights.

The Old Windmill

The Old Observatory and Windmill on Wickham Terrace, just north of the city centre, is one of Brisbane's earliest buildings, dating from 1829. It was intended to grind grain for the early convict colony but due to a fundamental design error it did not work properly. In 1837 it was made to work as it was originally intended but the building was then converted to a signal post and later a meteorological observatory. In 1864 a disastrous fire swept Brisbane and the windmill was one of the few early buildings to survive. It stands on a hill, overlooking the city.

Early City Centre Buildings

The National Trust's *Historic Walks* brochure will guide you round the city's most interesting early buildings. The National Trust has its headquarters in Old Government House, the former state governor's residence built in 1862, at the south end of George St. The state Parliament House is nearby at the corner of George and Alice Sts, overlooking the Botanic Gardens. It dates from 1868, is in French Renaissance style and has a roof of Mt Isa copper. There is also a new Legislative Assembly annexe. Tours are given seven times a day Monday to Friday when Parliament isn't sitting. More of Brisbane's best old buildings line George St – notably the Victorian townhouses of The Mansions and Harris Terrace on the Margaret St corner.

On Elizabeth St, the Gothic-style Old St Stephen's (1850) is the oldest church in Brisbane. The GPO is an impressive neoclassical edifice dating from the 1870s. Across Queen St and on the corner of Creek St, the National Bank building (1885) is reckoned to be one of the finest examples of Italian Renaissance style in Australia! Its front doors were made from a single Queensland cedar log.

St John's Cathedral is still under construction – work started in 1901. You can take a guided tour at 11 am on Wednesday or Friday. Queensland's first Government House, built in 1853, is now the Deanery for the Cathedral. The declaration of Queensland's separation from the colony of New South Wales was read here.

Queensland Cultural Centre

This superb new complex spans a block either side of Melbourne St in South Brisbane, just across Victoria Bridge from the city centre. It houses the Queensland Art Gallery, the Queensland Museum and the State Library, all on the north side of Melbourne St, and, to the south, a Performing Arts Complex with two theatres, a concert hall and an auditorium which seats 4700 people. There are also cafeterias, restaurants and shops.

The Queensland Museum is intended to be a 'hands-on' place. Among highlights of its big and well displayed collection, which focuses on the state's natural and human heritage, are a dinosaur garden and biplanes strung from the ceiling – including the 'Avian Cirrus' in which Queensland's Bert Hinkler made the first England to Australia solo flight in 1928. Except for Good Friday, Christmas and Anzac days the museum is open daily from 9 am to 5 pm. It also stays open till 8 pm on Wednesdays. Admission is free.

The Queensland Art Gallery shows

visiting exhibitions as well as its impressive permanent collection which includes many Australian and international big names. It's open daily from 10 am to 5 pm and on Wednesdays till 8 pm, again except for Good Friday and Christmas and Anzac days. Admission's free except for some special exhibitions, and 50 minute guided tours, also free, are given at 11 am, 1 and 2 pm Monday to Friday, 2 and 3 pm on Saturday and Sunday.

You can usually tour the auditoriums of the Performing Arts Complex (tel 840 7483), on the south side of Melbourne St, hourly from 10 am to 4 pm Monday to Saturday. The tours last 50 minutes and cost $2.50. Sometimes there are backstage tours (75 minutes, $5). For info about what's on at the Cultural Centre, call 840 7350.

Expo Site

Immediately south of the Queensland Cultural Centre on the river bank in South Brisbane, this once derelict wharf area was transformed into a fine sight in 1988 with its huge sail-roofed canopies, stages and pavilions circled by a two km monorail. One section – the World Expo Park funfair with its roller coasters, space-age ghost trains, etc – has been retained.

The future of the rest of the site was the subject of wrangling even before Expo started. A casino, a world trade centre and a space/science centre have all been canvassed, but as this edition went to print the only near certainty was that the site would echo to the sound of pneumatic drills and clanging girders well into the '90s.

Museums

On Stanley St in South Brisbane the Queensland Maritime Museum displays include an 1881 dry dock, working models and the WW II frigate HMAS *Diamantina*. It's open Wednesdays, Saturdays and Sundays from 10 am to 3.30 or 4.30 pm (admission $2). Postal enthusiasts could

try the GPO Museum at 261-285 Queen St. It's open Tuesday to Thursday from 10 am to 3 pm, free. Out in St Lucia, the Queensland University on Sir Fred Schonell Drive has anthropology, antiquities and art museums. Brisbane's trams no longer operate but you can ride some early examples at the Tramway Museum at 2 McGinn Rd, Ferny Grove, 11 km from the centre, open from 1.30 to 4 pm Sundays and most public holidays.

Parks & Gardens

Brisbane has a number of parks and gardens including the original Botanic Gardens, established in 1855 on a loop of the Brisbane River, almost in the centre of the city. The park occupies 18 hectares, is open from sunrise to sunset and is a good spot for bike riding.

There are good views from Wickham and Albert parks on the hill just north of the city centre. New Farm Park, by the river at the south end of Brunswick St, is noted for its rose displays, jacaranda trees and Devonshire teas. Captain John Burke Park is a nice little place underneath the towering Story Bridge at the top of Kangaroo Point.

Mt Coot-tha and Brisbane Forest Park west of the city provide the best scenery of all.

Pools

The Spring Hill Baths in Torrington St are probably the oldest in the southern hemisphere! Built in 1886 for £2400, the pool is 23.43 metres long, and surrounded by colourfully painted, old style changing cubicles. It's open from 6 am to 7 pm Monday to Friday and from 8 am to 6 pm on weekends. Admission is $1.

The most central Olympic pool is Centenary Pool (tel 831 8259), on Gregory Terrace. It's open daily from 6 am to 6 or 8.30 pm, September to April, admission $1. The Valley Pool (tel 852 1231) at 432 Wickham St is heated and open all year

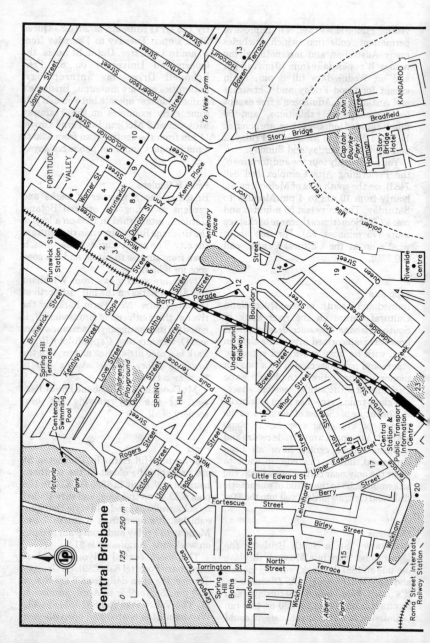

Central Brisbane

0   125   250 m

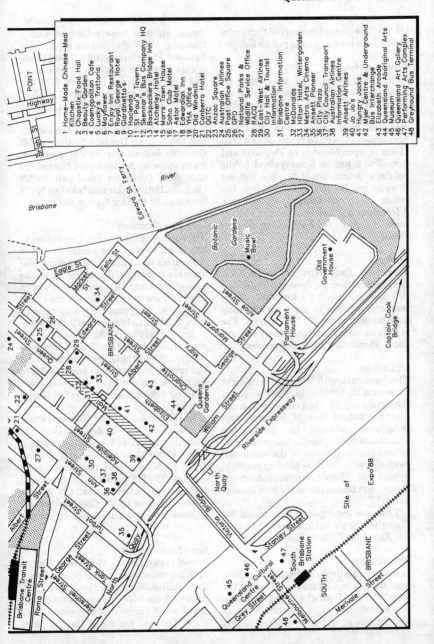

1 Home-Made Chinese-Meal Kitchen
2 Chopstix Food Hall
3 Beauty Garden
4 Cosmopolitan Cafe
5 Macky's Trattoria
6 Enjoy Inn Restaurant
7 Royal George Hotel
8 Giardinetto's
9 Hacienda
10 St Paul's Tavern
11 Skennar's Bus Company HQ
12 Backpackers Bridge Inn
13 Atcherley Hotel
14 Marrs Town House
15 Soho Club Motel
16 Astor Motel
17 Edwardian Inn
18 OHA Office
19 Old Windmill
20 Canberra Hotel
21 QGTC
22 Anzac Square
23 Australian Airlines
24 Post Office Square
25 GPO
26 National Parks & Wildlife Service Office
27 RACQ
28 East—West Airlines
29 City Hall & Tourist Information
30 Brisbane Information
31 McDonalds
32 Hilton Hotel, Wintergarden
33 Metro Arts Cinema
34 Ansett Pioneer
35 City Plaza
36 City Council Transport Information Centre
37 Ansett Airlines
38 Australian Airlines
39 Jo Jo's
40 Hungry Jacks
41 Myer Centre & Underground Bus Interchange
42 Elizabeth Arcade
43 Queensland Aboriginal Arts
44 Museum
45 Queensland Art Gallery
46 Performing Arts Complex
47 Greyhound Bus Terminal

($1.10). The pool at Queensland University in St Lucia is open to the public too.

Newstead House

Four km north-east of the centre on Breakfast Creek Rd, Newstead, this is the oldest surviving home in Brisbane, built in 1846, overlooking the river. It's a stately mansion fully fitted with Victorian furnishings. Newstead House is open from 11 am to 3 pm Monday to Thursday and from 2 to 5 pm on Sundays and public holidays. Admission is $1. You can get there by bus No 160, 180 or 190 from the yellow stop on Edward St between Adelaide and Queen Sts. You can also get there on the Brisbane City Ferries Cruise.

Brewery

There are free tours of the XXXX (pronounced fourex) brewery on Milton Rd, Milton, about 1½ km west of the centre. You need to get a small group together and phone 369 7737 to book. The tour lasts about an hour, then you get about 40 minutes worth of free beer.

Mt Coot-tha

This large park with lookouts is just eight km west of the city centre. The views from the top are superb. On a clear day you can see the distant line of Moreton and Stradbroke islands, the Glasshouse Mountains to the north, the mountains behind the Gold Coast to the south and Brisbane, with the river winding through, at your feet. There's a restaurant serving Devonshire teas at one of the best lookout points.

There are some good walks around Mt Coot-tha and its foothills, like the one to J C Slaughter Falls on Simpsons Rd.

Botanic Gardens

Brisbane's excellent new Botanic Gardens, open daily from 8.30 am to 5 pm, are at the foot of Mt Coot-tha. The gardens concentrate on native Australian plants and include an enclosed tropical display dome, an arid zone collection and a teahouse. You'll also find the Sir Thomas Brisbane Planetarium (tel 377 8896) here; it's the largest in Australia. Admission is $5.40 and there are shows at 3.30 and 7.30 pm Wednesday to Friday; 1.30, 3.30 and 7.30 pm Saturday; 1.30 and 3.30 pm Sunday.

You can reach the Mt Coot-tha lookout and the Botanic Gardens by bus. To Mt Coot-tha lookout bus No 10C goes from green stops on Adelaide and George Sts once daily (twice on Sundays). To Mt Coot-tha Botanic Gardens take bus No 39 from Ann St at King George Square.

Lone Pine Sanctuary

The koala sanctuary at Fig Tree Pocket 11 km south-west of the centre is one of Australia's best known and most popular animal sanctuaries. It has over 100 koalas plus other Australian animals. It's open from 9.30 am to 5 pm daily but not cheap at $7. The platypuses are only on view from 11.30 am to 12 noon and 2.45 to 4 pm.

You can get to the sanctuary by bus, river cruise or bus tour. Take Cityxpress bus No 518 from the Queen St underground bus station hourly to 5.35 pm Monday to Friday, or bus No 84 or 84A from green stops on Adelaide and George Sts four or five times daily.

Koala Cruises (tel 229 7055) runs a tour to the sanctuary. It departs from the Riverside Centre at 1 pm daily and from North Quay 25 minutes later and takes about 1½ hours. There's an extra trip on Sunday. The $19 fare includes entrance to the sanctuary, and for an extra $6 you can take a bus tour to Mt Coot-tha botanic gardens and lookout instead of coming back by boat.

More Fauna & Flora

Bunya Park on Bunya Park Drive, Eatons Hill, has more koalas to cuddle and plenty more native fauna and flora, open daily from 9.30 am to 5 pm (admission $8.50). It's about 16 km north of the centre. Alma Park Zoo at Kallangur has a large collection of palms and Australian and overseas wildlife. It's 28 km north of the city centre, open daily.

Travellers have written to recommend the Australian Woolshed at 148 Samford Rd, Ferny Hills, about 15 km north of the centre. You can watch sheep shearing and roundups, wool spinning and even performing rams. There are yet more koalas. Shows ($5) are at 10.45 am and 2 pm daily.

Other Old Houses

There are a number of interesting old houses and period recreations around Brisbane. Earlystreet Historical Village is on McIlwraith Ave, off Bennetts Rd in Norman Park, four km east of the centre and south of the river. It's a re-creation of early Queensland colonial life with genuine old buildings in a garden setting. Entry is $6 and it's open from 9.30 am to 4.30 pm Monday to Friday, 10.30 am to 4.30 pm on weekends. Get there on a

Carina to Seven Hills bus No 8A, 8B, 8C, 8D or 8E, from Ann St by King George Square, or by train to Norman Park.

At 31 Jordan Terrace, Bowen Hills, just north of Fortitude Valley, the Miegunyah Folk Museum is housed in an 1884 building, a fine example of early Brisbane architecture. It has been furnished and decorated in period style as a memorial to the pioneer women of Queensland and is open from 10.30 am to 3 pm Tuesday and Wednesday, to 4 pm on weekends. Admission is $1. Get there on an airport bus No 160 or Toombul bus No 170, 171 or 190.

Wolston House at Grindle Rd, Wacol, 18 km west of the centre, is an early colonial country residence, built in 1852 of local materials. It's open from 10 am to 4.30 pm from Wednesday to Sunday and on holidays.

Brisbane Forest Park

Musgrave, Waterworks and Mt Nebo Rds

Brisbane house

lead out through the suburbs to the 750 metre high D'Aguilar Range, 20-odd km north-west of the city centre. The drive is well worthwhile for its great views, forest and hill scenery, bird life and away-from-it-all feeling. Some 250 square km of the range is protected in the Brisbane Forest Park. There are several walking tracks and lookouts and there's an information centre (tel 300 4855), open Monday to Friday from 8.30 am to 4.30 pm, a few km after the suburb of The Gap. There's a national park camping area at Manorina between Mts Nebo and Glorious. Buses to The Gap go as close as you can get to Brisbane Forest Park by public transport.

Festivals

The Warana Festival in mid-September is a cultural, theatrical, educational and children's festival with many outdoor events in the City Botanic Gardens, King George Square and Albert Park. Mid-August sees the Royal National Exhibition at the Gregory Terrace exhibition grounds. It's developed from an old style agricultural show. Spring Hill, an old residential area just north of the city centre, hosts a two day street fair in early to mid-September.

Activities

Brisbane Bushwalkers Club (tel 205 3878) is at 43 Coronet Drive, Bray Park. Scuba World (tel 870 9030) at 538 Milton Rd, Toowong, and Coral Cay Diving (tel 357 8293) at Lutwyche both run day diving trips for $100 plus – it's cheaper further north on the Great Barrier Reef.

Places to Stay

Brisbane has plenty of hostels and there are also several well priced hotels, guest houses and motels within easy reach of the centre.

Hostels The two areas to head for are Petrie Terrace/Paddington and New Farm – about three km east of the transit centre. Many hostels will send someone to meet you at the transit centre if you call.

Some even have touts hanging around. Most hostels offer cheaper weekly rates.

New Farm is a residential inner suburb, traditionally with a big Italian population. You can get there by the Golden Mile ferry from the city centre as well as by bus. The hostels are all on or near Brunswick St, the main road heading down the New Farm peninsula from Fortitude Valley. Most are within a km of the valley. Nearest is *Backpackers Bridge Inn* (tel 358 5000) at 196 Bowen Terrace, with views over Story Bridge. This is a relaxed, spacious place occupying two houses, with dorm beds at $9 a night and double rooms at $25.

Backpackers Down Under has two hostels – one at 71 Kent St (tel 358 4504) and the other, more spacious and with a friendlier atmosphere, at 365 Bowen Terrace (tel 358 1488). Prices in both are $9 in dorms or $22 for a double room.

Also on Barker St, at No 29, the *Pink Galah* (tel 358 5155) is a good hostel with space for 48 in dorms and double rooms. It's $9 a night (plus $1.50 for linen). The kitchen and eating areas are big and there's a snooker room as well as a comfortable lounge. On weekends an outing is usually organised for around $10 to Lamington National Park and Tamborine Mountain or Moreton Island.

About three blocks further down Brunswick St at No 836 *Brisbane International Backpackers* (tel 368 1047) is a renovated old-style Brisbane house with dorms at $10 a night. Over towards Paddington, the *Brisbane City YHA* (tel 221 0961) is just 500 metres from the transit centre at 390 Upper Roma St. It's a bit of a dingy place, can be noisy from the road and has rather ageing equipment – but at least it's clean, is open all day and is convenient. The dorms hold six people each and have their own kitchen and bathroom. Everyone gets a front door key to come and go at night. Nightly charge is $11 plus $1.50 for a sleeping sheet.

Paddington Barracks Hostel (tel 369 4128) is above a pub on the corner of Petrie Terrace and Caxton St. The bunks are packed in like sardines and the hostel's on the corner of two noisy streets, but it still brings rave reviews – probably thanks to the free breakfast at 7 am.

The most appealing of the Paddington hostels is *Backpackers Paddington* (tel 368 1047) at 175 Given Terrace. At $8 a night, it accommodates 37 people in a variety of clean rooms. There are two small outdoor sitting areas.

There's a second *YHA Hostel* (tel 857 1245) at 15 Mitchell St, Kedron, on the Bruce Highway eight km north of the city centre. Get there on a Chermside bus No 172 from the town hall side of Adelaide St. Get off at stop 27A, then walk down Broughton Rd to Mitchell St. It's open all day. There's room for 80 people and the nightly cost is $10.

Hotels & Motels – central Some guest houses and holiday flats are included in this category. Prices may be cheaper on a weekly basis.

Probably the best known cheap hotel among international travellers is the *Edwardian Inn* (formerly the Yale Budget Hotel) (tel 832 1663), at 413 Upper Edward St. It's a 10 minute uphill walk from the city centre. Singles/doubles are $40/50 including breakfast. There are laundry facilities and a TV room, the rooms have fans and tea/coffee making equipment. There are some rooms with private bathrooms.

Annie's Shandon Inn (tel 831 8684), just down the street at 405, is similar to the Edwardian, with shared bathrooms and a TV room, but slightly more comfortable. Singles/doubles are $30/40. Or there's the *Dorchester Holiday Units* (tel 831 2967) a little up the road at 484. Singles/doubles are $35/45. There are cooking facilities and utensils, and private bathrooms.

Just down the hill, there's a string of motels, some decently priced. At the *Astor* (tel 831 9522) at 193 Wickham Terrace, air-con singles/doubles are $32/40 with shared bathrooms or $56/64 with private bathrooms. Rooms have tea/

coffee making facilities and breakfast is available. A little further along at 333 the *Soho Club Motel* (tel 831 7722) is $38/46 for singles/doubles. At 391 Wickham Terrace the *Marrs Town House* (tel 831 5388) is a little more expensive, with singles/doubles at $35/50 and up. The management's helpful and there are good views – but those facing the road can be noisy.

Over on the eastern edge of the central area, the *Atcherley Hotel* (tel 832 2591), also called *Pacific Coast Budget Accommodation*, is at 513 Queen St. It's old, faded and basic – but friendly and busy – with singles/doubles at $25/35. Bathrooms are shared and some rooms overlook the river.

About 1½ km from the central King George Square, at 260 Water St, Spring Hill *Spring Hill Terraces* (tel 854 1048) is an attractive place built in 1986. It offers self-contained two bedroom terraced houses at $60 single or double, $66 triple, or $72 for four people. There are also budget rooms at $34 single or double, motel type units with private bathrooms at $42/46. You can have breakfast or dinner in the dining room.

The *Tourist Private Hotel-Motel* (tel 252 4171) at 555 Gregory Terrace, has hotel rooms with shared bathrooms at $22/41, and motel rooms with private bathrooms at $29/50. The prices include breakfast and it's a clean, comfortable place.

Hotels & Motels – suburbs In New Farm the *Elizabeth Private Hotel* (tel 358 1866) at 14 Harcourt St has singles/doubles with shared bathrooms for $25/32 including light breakfast. Just past Breakfast Creek on the way to the airport, the *Kingsford Hall Private Hotel* (tel 262 5414) at 144 Kingsford Smith Drive, Hamilton (corner of Cooksley St) charges $25/32 with shared bathrooms. It has a guest kitchen. In Highgate Hill, south of the Expo site at 180 Gladstone Rd, the *Ambassador Motel* (tel 844 5661) is $49/52 with private bathrooms.

There are several motels and holiday flats in Kangaroo Point, such as *Carmel Lodge Holiday Flats* (tel 391 6855) at 819 Main St with nightly costs of $45 double. *Cliffside Apartments* (tel 345 5534) at 25 Ellis St, at the south end of Kangaroo Point, has two bedroom flats from $240 a week.

In Toowong the *Regatta Hotel* (tel 870 7063), a popular pub near the river on the corner of Coronation Drive and Sylvan St, has rooms at $40/60 including breakfast.

North of the centre on the Bruce Highway, there are a couple of places in Aspley, 13 km out, like the *Aspley Motor Inn* (tel 263 5400) at 1159 Gympie Rd (the Bruce Highway) with singles/doubles from $35/40, and the *Alpha Motel* (tel 263 4442) at 1434 Gympie Rd, charging $32/38.

Colleges *International House* (tel 870 9593) at 5 Rock St, St Lucia offers bed and breakfast for $29/48 single/double. If you want to try your luck, the following colleges at the University of Queensland offer individual accommodation: *Union College* (tel 371 1300), *St John's College* (men only, tel 370 8171), *St Leo's College* (men only, tel 371 1534), *Grace College* (women only, tel 371 3898), *Duchesne College* (women only, tel 371 1534), *King's College* (men only, tel 370 1125), *Cromwell College* (tel 370 1151) and *Women's College* (tel 370 1177). At Griffith University in Nathan in the south of Brisbane, try the *Nathan Housing Company* (tel 275 7575).

Camping Curious Brisbane Council regulations forbid tent camping within a 22 km radius of the centre, and there are no caravan sites very close in. In any case many caravan parks are full up with permanent residents. All in all the camping picture around Brisbane is miserable. It's a much better story south on the Gold Coast or north on the

Sunshine Coast. You could try the following if you wish:

Aspley Acres Caravan Park, 1420 Gympie Rd, Aspley, 13 km north, no camping but on-site Camp-O-Tel 'capsules' (rather like big tents with beds provided) at $7 to $9 a head; also on-site vans from $22.50 (tel 263 2668)
Riviera Caravan Park, 213 Brisbane Terrace, Goodna, 25 km south-west, sites $8 double, on-site vans from $25 (tel 288 3644)
Pines Cara-Park, 27 Goodfellows Rd, Kallangur, 28 km north, sites $10, on-site vans $25 (tel 204 6895)
Springtime Gardens Caravan Park, corner Pacific Highway and Old Chatswood Rd, Springwood, 24 km south, camping $8 double, on-site vans from $16 (tel 208 8184)
Seven Trees Caravan Park, corner Turton and Station Rds, Sunnybank, 13 km south, no camping, on-site vans available (tel 345 1430)
Nestle-In Caravan Park, 905 Manly Rd, Tingalpa, 11 km east, no camping, on-site vans from $20 (tel 390 4404)

Places to Eat

Although Brisbane hasn't got the reputation of Sydney or Melbourne there's a fast growing number of good places, many of them experimenting with local seafood and tropical fruits. Many more cafes and restaurants stay open past 9 pm, some even 24 hours (but don't expect to eat after 8.30 pm in most pubs), and some places are beginning to take advantage of the balmy climate by providing outdoor eating areas.

City You'll find a bit of everything around the central area. Four of the best central areas are Queen St Mall, Edward St, the streets south and north of the mall between Charlotte and Adelaide Sts, and over at the east end of Queen and Elizabeth Sts.

Queen St Mall teems with possibilities. *Jo Jo's*, a large food centre upstairs in the Pavilion Shopping Centre at 130 Queen St is very popular. It has a collection of fast food counters – Greek/Mediterranean, Chinese, European and Middle Eastern.

Tables are scattered about and prices are from $3. It's open till midnight daily.

There are more possibilities in the ritzy *Myer Centre*, bounded by Queen St Mall, Albert, Elizabeth and George Sts. The lower level has fast food outlets with everything from pizza to seafood, at moderate prices.

Jimmy's on the Mall has two excellent open air 24 hour licensed cafes – one at the Edward St end of the mall, the other near the Albert St corner. Coffee is expensive but there are plenty of reasonably priced snacks, meals and desserts.

About halfway between the two Jimmy's, on the 2nd level of the Wintergarden shopping complex, the *New Orleans Food Centre* is open from 10 am until 2 am, and until 10.30 pm on Sundays. You can choose from various cuisines. Most meals are $8 to $10 and often there's live music. On the ground floor of the Wintergarden, near the Elizabeth St entrance, there's another busy food centre with meals for $5 to $8. Downstairs on Edward St, a couple of doors north of the mall, the *Capri Cafe* is another good lunch spot, open from 9.30 am to 4 pm, Monday to Friday. It has a good selection of home-made healthy meals.

There are a few Chinese places south down Edward St, near the corner of Elizabeth St. At 109 Edward St is the busy *Food for Arts*, downstairs in the Metro Arts building. It's open for lunch and dinner on weekdays, offering cheap, wholesome food.

A great place for lunch is the *Port Office Hotel* at 38 Edward St, beyond Metro Arts near the corner of Margaret St. Dishes start from $7. It's open from 10 am to 11 pm Monday to Friday, closes at 6 pm on Saturdays and has Sunday lunches to 4 pm. There's often live jazz on Sunday afternoons.

On the corner of Albert and Charlotte Sts is the *Munich Steak House* which serves steaks and schnitzel. Dinners are $13 but the portions are large. It closes at 9 pm most nights, and 10 pm on Friday

and Saturday. The *Pancake Manor* is in an old church at 18 Charlotte St, and is open 24 hours daily.

The City Plaza, on the corner of George and Adelaide Sts, has a handful of restaurants, some with tables outside by the fountain. Also here, *Tracks* has pub/bistro lunches for $10 from Monday to Friday, and specials for $7 or so.

Michael's Bistro, at the east end of Elizabeth St in the Riverside Centre, has two parts, one offering French food and seafood, the other – the *Waterfront Cafe* – with Italian food. The food is expensive but the river view is terrific. There is a pub and cafes at the Riverside Centre.

Spring Hill The *Spring Hill Hotel*, on the corner of Upper Edward and Leichhardt Sts, has good, cheap pub food and a backyard barbecue. The *Federal Hotel*, close to the same corner at 100 Leichhardt St, and the *Sportsmans*, a little east along Leichhardt St, do simple and cheap pub food. On the corner of Leichhardt and Wharf Sts, *St Paul's Tavern* has good food and an outdoor beer garden. Where Leichhardt St meets Boundary St, it becomes St Paul's Terrace and here the *Commercial Hotel* has counter food and an outside sitting area.

Two blocks west, near the corner of Boundary and Fortescue Sts, the *Main Roads Department Cafeteria* welcomes the public. It serves a hot lunch for $4 from 12 noon to 1.30 pm weekdays.

There are two good restaurants in Spring Hill. The popular *Primavera* (tel 831 3132) at 500 Boundary St has probably the best Italian food in town as well as Lebanese food. Pasta and Lebanese dishes are reasonably priced, while other main meals are more expensive from $12. You usually need to book and it's closed on Sundays. In the same block *Harold's Posh Cafe* at 466 Boundary St has a good gourmet take-away section – open from 10 am to 10 pm Monday to Saturday. In the sit-down section, meals are $12.

Fortitude Valley To the east and up the hill from the city centre lies Fortitude Valley, with lots of interesting eating spots around Brunswick, Ann and Wickham Sts. The many Chinese restaurants on little Duncan St include the excellent *Enjoy Inn* on the corner of Wickham St, open daily until midnight. It's not cheap but its banquet (around $18) is a bargain. Opposite Duncan St at 194 Wickham St, the *Vietnamese Restaurant* serves main meals at $7.

Chopstix is a food hall in an arcade between Brunswick and Wickham Sts. The food is mainly Asian. Most main courses are $6 to $8 but there are lots of cheaper snacks. The deservedly popular *Home-Made Chinese Meal Kitchen* at 257 Wickham St is a small Chinese place. The food is excellent and the prices moderate with main meals from $10. It's open for lunch and dinner until 10 pm Monday to Saturday but only for dinner on Sundays. Opposite, at shop 56 Valley Plaza Centre, Wickham St, the *Sala Thai* is a good reasonably priced Thai restaurant with a four course lunch for $10 from Monday to Friday. It's open nightly for dinner.

Brunswick St itself has more of an Italian flavour. The *Cosmopolitan Cafe* at 332 is a very good place for a coffee and/or breakfast. You can watch the coffee being roasted and ground and hear Italian spoken by the locals. The popular *Giardinetto's* at 366 Brunswick St, a small, pleasant Italian place, does pasta dishes from $10. Small pizzas are $7. You can eat indoors or outside and it's open for lunch Tuesday to Friday and dinner Tuesday to Sunday. Round the corner at 683 Ann St the atmosphere is equally pleasant in *Lucky's Trattoria*, a fine Italian restaurant where two people can eat for around $25. It's open only in the evenings.

New Farm Continuing down Brunswick St from Fortitude Valley you hit New Farm with good eating possibilities near the backpackers hostels. The *Brunswick Hotel* on the corner of Brunswick and Kent Sts has good, cheap counter meals. This pub has special backpacker entertainment nights.

A bit further down Brunswick St at 630, the *Baan Thai* is a reasonably priced Thai restaurant. Main meals are $10 – less to take away. It's open from Tuesday to Sunday from 6 to 10 pm. *Jonny's Pizza Parlour* at 669 Brunswick St is a cheerful place, open nightly, with cheap pizzas and pasta. *Possums Australian Food*, at 681 Brunswick St, is a cheap restaurant with traditional Aussie tucker, billy tea and Aussie music. It's open from 9 am to 10 pm Monday to Saturday. The popular *Cafe Le Mer* at 878 Brunswick St offers 'gourmet' fish, chips and salad for around $12.

Breakfast Creek The pub here is a real Brisbane institution. Breakfast Creek is about four km north-east of the city centre, just past Newstead House. To get there continue along Ann St from Fortitude Valley then along Breakfast Creek Rd. Catch a bus No 160, 180 or 190.

Breakfast Creek Wharf is right beside the creek at 190 Breakfast Creek Rd. The wharf building has an expensive but very good seafood restaurant plus an excellent cheaper take-away section. The nearby *Breakfast Creek Hotel* is a great rambling building dating from 1899, at 2 Kingsford Smith Drive. It's long been a Labor Party and trade union hang-out. In the public bar the beer is still drawn from a wooden keg. The pub's *Spanish Garden Steak House* is renowned for its steaks which are in the $11 bracket.

Paddington West of the city centre, this is becoming a trendy area with lots of places to eat! The *Kookaburra Cafe* at 280 Given Terrace, the far end of Paddington, is open for lunch and dinner daily and pizzas are the go with 22 different combinations on offer. Three people can share a large pizza, garlic bread and salad for $18. There are pasta dishes for $8 and up, and delicious crepes for dessert.

Puzzles at 262 Given Terrace does a fine range of snacks and light meals, from nachos and burgers at $5 to pastas, kebabs, satays or stir-fried vegies at $10. It's well known for its desserts and liqueur coffees and is open 24 hours on Fridays and Saturdays, closing at 1 am other nights.

Still on Given Terrace, you can't miss the *Paddington Tavern*. It's a large pub with indoor and outdoor eating areas. Bistro-style meals, steaks and seafood at $12 are served daily, except on Sundays. *Masakan Indonesia* is an excellent, reasonably priced Indonesian restaurant, just a couple of doors up Given Terrace from the Gun Wah. Rice and noodle dishes are from $6, and seafood and meat are $11. The trendy *Caxton St Brasserie* at 111 Caxton St, is a very popular night spot. Open nightly from 6 pm until late, the Brasserie has reasonably priced international-style snacks and meals.

On the corner of Caxton St and Petrie Terrace, *Paddington Barracks* has cheap meals for $5 or so.

West End A couple of km south-west of the city centre, across the river, there are a number of restaurants in West End. At 93 Hardgrave Rd, *Kim Thanh* is a popular Chinese/Vietnamese place. The menu is long and varied with main meals between $7 and $9. It's open daily. *Qan Heng's*, 151 Boundary St, parallel to Hardgrave St, has similar food and prices and is very busy.

Enzo's Place at 70 Boundary St is a good Italian spot with reasonably priced pasta, pizza, meat and seafood. It's open nightly for dinner and from Tuesday to Friday for lunches. The *Lounge Lizard Cafe* at 69 Boundary St is an offbeat place in the West End markets, open daily from 10 am until 11 or 12 at night, except for Sundays when it's only open in the evening. The menu is international with main dishes between $7 and $12, and on weekends there's cabaret.

Back towards the city centre, on the corner of Melbourne and Edmondstone Sts, South Brisbane, *Squirrels* is a good vegetarian restaurant open daily for lunch and dinner. From the buffet a small plateful is $9, a large one $11 – or you can order from the menu with main dishes $11.

Toowong/St Lucia There are lots of possibilities in these suburbs near the university. *Mama's Down Under* at 217 Hawken Drive, St Lucia, a student hangout, has pizzas from $8. It's only open in the evenings. *Pasta Pasta* at 242 Hawken Drive offers what its name suggests, and is cheap. A small serve is $5, a large $8. This is another popular place with students, open daily from 8 am to midnight.

Toowong has Brisbane's two best Indian restaurants, opposite each other at 524 and 533 Milton Rd. *Scherhazade* is slightly more expensive with main course curries at $11. It's closed on Mondays. The *Sultan's Kitchen* (tel 371 1083) has lots of excellent curries, main meals $11, and there's a Sunday smorgasbord. It's open for lunch and dinner daily except for Saturday lunch time but it's pretty popular so book on weekends.

Entertainment

Brisbane pubs generally stay open until 11 pm or midnight, particularly on Friday nights. Many pubs feature live music and there are several nightclubs. You'll find the rundown on what's on and where in the weekend papers or in the give away entertainment paper *Time Off*.

Pubs & Live Music In the city centre, there's the *Metro* in the Treasury Hotel on the corner of George and Elizabeth Sts, Friday and Saturday nights until late. *Tracks* in the City Plaza Tavern on the corner of George and Adelaide Sts has a couple of bars with live bands as well as its very popular disco/nightclub. It's open until late nightly and there's a $3 to $6 cover charge. For live rock, the *Brisbane Tavern* on the corner of Ann and Wharf

Sts is good on Wednesday, Friday and Sunday nights. Or try *Alice's Rock Cafe* in Adelaide St on a Friday or Saturday night. The *Port Office Hotel*, on the corner of Edward and Margaret Sts, has bands on Wednesday and Friday nights, jazz and blues on Saturday and Sunday.

A short walk from the city centre, the *Jubilee Hotel* on St Paul's Terrace, Spring Hill, has musicians on Friday nights, Saturday and Sunday afternoons, and rock bands on Sunday nights. It has a 'dance bar' from Wednesday to Saturday nights, open until late. Also in Spring Hill, *St Paul's Tavern*, on the corner of Leichhardt and Wharf Sts, has live rock on Friday night, Saturday afternoon and Sunday night.

In Fortitude Valley, *Bonaparte's Hotel* on the corner of Gipps St and St Paul's Terrace has rock bands from Thursday to Saturday, 8 pm until 1 am. The *Outpost* on the corner of Ann and Warner Sts calls itself an alternative spot and hosts several bands nightly. You can get discounted drinks here. The *Beat Nightclub* is a punky, trendy place with live bands, near the Outpost.

Further down Brunswick St in New Farm, the *Brunswick Hotel* has weekly backpacker nights with competitions and prizes, and live music some nights. On the far edge of Fortitude Valley, at the corner of Ann and Commercial Sts, the *Waterloo Hotel* brews its own beer and often offers free transport to backpackers staying in the area.

Over at Kangaroo Point, the *Story Bridge Hotel* (tel 391 2266) at 200 Main Ave is very popular with live music most nights and jazz on Sunday afternoons. On Sunday nights there are informal gatherings with perhaps a jam session or poetry readings.

In Paddington the *Caxton Hotel* on Caxton St has free jazz on Saturday afternoons and more live music at other times. The *Paddington Tavern* on Given Terrace is good for live music on a Thursday night.

Two popular places for a beer in Toowong near the University of Queensland are the *Regatta*, on the corner of Coronation Drive and Sylvan Rd, and the *Royal Exchange*.

Discos & Nightclubs Brisbane's most popular nightclub, the *Brisbane Underground*, is over in Paddington, on the corner of Caxton and Hale Sts. Others are mainly in the city centre. *The Move* in the Majestic Hotel at 382 George St is a dance spot with recorded music and a $3 to $4 cover charge, open Friday and Saturday nights until 3 am. Most other nightclubs are open similar hours (Wednesday to Saturday nights until late, Sunday night until midnight). They include the *Court Jester* in the Criterion Tavern, which is in the MLC building on the corner of George and Adelaide Sts; *Reflections* in the Sheraton Hotel at 249 Turbot St; and the *City Gardens Point Club* at the Queensland Institute of Technology on George St. The latter has live bands on Wednesday nights, entry $4.

Culture Saturday's *Courier Mail* is good for info about what's on where.

The *Performing Arts Complex* in the Queensland Cultural Centre in South Brisbane, has a constant flow of events in its three venues, including concerts, plays, old movies, and lots more. Concerts featuring classical music, ethnic music and jazz are held on Sunday afternoons, entry $2. The *Brisbane Arts Theatre* at 210 Petrie Terrace has some interesting productions.

For alternative/offbeat cinema, you have three choices – the *Schonell* (tel 371 1879) at the University of Queensland in St Lucia, the *Classic* (tel 393 1066) at 963 Stanley St, East Brisbane and the *Metro Arts Cinema* (tel 221 8361) at 109 Edward St. Metro Arts has an 'alternative' theatre/dance centre and a South American art and craft gallery. It's a good spot for information on what's on around the city in the way of poetry readings, art exhibitions, Indian dance performances, belly dancing lessons and even more esoteric stuff.

Sport You can see interstate and test cricket at the Gabba ground in Woolloongabba just south of Kangaroo Point. The season is October to March. The other half of the year, rugby league is the big spectator sport. Local heroes Brisbane Broncos play their home games at Lang Park. Brisbane also has an Australian rules football club, the Brisbane Bears. Like every other town and city in Australia Brisbane has horse racing: the major tracks are at Doomben and Eagle Farm.

Things to Buy

Queensland Aboriginal Creations at 135 George St has a good collection of Aboriginal and Torres Strait Islander artefacts. The Artefact Shop in Queensland University's Anthropology Museum also has a good range.

You'll find the usual collection of Australiana/Ken Done and whoever-else shops dotted around the city. If you're feeling wickedly decadent or you simply need a new pair of shoes, the Mr Christian shoe shop in the mall near Edward St has a fantastic range of shoes and boots, mainly for women and definitely not for paupers.

The Caxton St Market is held Saturday morning in Paddington, about two km west of the city centre. Also on Saturday, from 10 am to 3 pm, the Spring Hill Village Market is just a few minutes from the city centre. Both markets are popular meeting places. Paddy's Markets on the corner of Florence and Commercial Rds, New Farm, are open daily from 9 am to 3 pm, with a huge variety of goods. At weekends, there's an extra Flea Market here.

On Sundays the Riverside Centre market has 150 stalls including glass blowers, weavers, leather workers and children's activities. Also on Sunday the Closeburn Country Market, 26 km out of town, is a similar arty-crafty affair and makes a good day's outing.

Getting There & Away

Arriving in and leaving Brisbane has been simplified by the transit centre on Roma St, about half a km west of the central King George Square. The transit centre is the main terminus and booking point for all long-distance buses and trains, and the airport bus comes here too. It has shops, banks, post office, and plenty of places to eat and drink. There's a foreign exchange counter, open from 6 am to 9 pm daily, at the Skennars bus desk on level 3, and a tourist information office on level 2. Left-luggage lockers are on level 3: they cost $1 but you have to remove your stuff by 9 pm each day.

Radio 4ZZZ FM (102.1 MHz) broadcasts messages about available lifts, air tickets for sale, etc. Call 371 5111 to get a message on the air.

Air There are numerous Ansett and Australian Airlines flights from the southern capitals and north to the main Queensland centres like Rockhampton, Mackay, Townsville and Cairns. East-West flies from Hobart, Devonport, Sydney and Cairns. Air NSW flies daily from Sydney. Both Ansett and Australian have some direct flights every week to Mt Isa and Darwin.

One-way fares include Sydney $187 ($150 standby), Melbourne $277 ($222 standby), Adelaide $307 direct (more expensive via Sydney or Melbourne, standby $246). Air NSW flies from Sydney for about $10 less.

There are numerous connections by smaller airlines with smaller centres. East-West, Air NSW and Oxley Airlines link Brisbane with a string of places on the New South Wales north coast and New England. Sunstate, Sungold and Lloyd Air between them serve south-east Queensland as far north as Townsville and inland as far as Toowoomba and Emerald.

The little outback airline Flight West goes to Roma, Charleville, Quilpie, Blackall, Barcaldine, Longreach, Winton, Cloncurry, Mt Isa, and to Windorah and Birdsville.

Brisbane is also a busy international arrival and departure point with frequent flights by numerous airlines to Asia, Europe, the Pacific Islands, North America, New Zealand and Papua New Guinea.

Airline offices include: Australian and Eastern (tel 260 3311); Ansett, Sungold and Air NSW (tel 854 2828); Qantas (tel 833 3747); East-West (tel 221 8444); Sunstate (tel 268 5466); and Flight West (tel 252 1152).

Bus Numerous bus companies run between Sydney and Brisbane and up the Queensland coast to Cairns. Sydney to Brisbane via the Pacific Highway takes 15 or 16 hours and normally costs $35 to $43. Cheaper lines are Inter-Capital Express, Sunliner, Ambassador/Trans City, and Roadranger. Deluxe has the most frequent service. Companies operating the Pacific Highway route, with their Brisbane telephone numbers, are: Ambassador/Trans City (tel 221 9555/221 3777); Deluxe (tel 844 2466); Greyhound (tel 844 3300); Inter-Capital Express (tel 221 2194); Intertour (tel 236 1033); Kirklands (tel 831 2227); McCafferty's (tel 221 8555); Pioneer (tel 840 9350); Roadranger Intercity Express (tel 236 1030); Skennars (tel 832 1148); and Sunliner (tel 229 6155). All the lines have booking offices at the Brisbane transit centre. You can book Kirklands buses at the Skennars desk.

Deluxe, Greyhound and McCafferty's also run between Sydney and Brisbane by the inland New England Highway which takes an hour or two longer. Cheaper buses between New England and Brisbane are by Border Coaches (tel 221 9555). Between Brisbane and Melbourne the most direct route is the Newell Highway which takes 20 to 23 hours. Trans City, McCafferty's, Intertour, Greyhound,

Pioneer and Deluxe all follow this route daily. Intertour also takes a combination of the New England and Newell Highways (24 hours, daily) while Greyhound, Pioneer and Deluxe have extra services via various combinations of the Gold Coast, northern New South Wales coast and New England which make the trip 28 to 31 hours. The fare between Brisbane and Melbourne is $80 to $85.

From Adelaide to Brisbane the quickest services are by Trans City (26 hours) and Deluxe (29 hours, daily). Deluxe and Greyhound also have 32 hour daily services through the Gold Coast and New England, and Pioneer goes three times weekly via Broken Hill, New England and the Gold Coast (33 hours). Adelaide to Brisbane is $120 except for Trans City which is cheaper.

North to Cairns about 15 buses daily are operated by Greyhound, Pioneer, Deluxe, McCafferty's and Sunliner.

Greyhound and Skennars are the main companies serving inland Queensland from Brisbane and Skennars runs the major service to the Sunshine Coast. Its HQ is at 22-34 Barry Parade, but it also has a desk at the transit centre and most of its buses stop there as well.

To get to Mt Isa and the Northern Territory you normally have to go to Townsville then across. Greyhound, however, goes to/from Mt Isa ($129, 26 to 28 hours).

Train You can reach Brisbane by rail from Sydney and continue north to Cairns or inland to Roma and Charleville. The daily Brisbane Limited Express takes 16 hours between Sydney and Brisbane. Fares are $111 in 1st class ($151 with a sleeping berth), $79 in economy. A Caper ticket (Customer Advance Purchase Excursion Rail) which you have to buy at least seven days in advance cuts about 30% off the price. You can, as on all major interstate trains, break the journey anywhere provided you arrange it in advance and complete the journey within two months (with a one-way ticket) or six months (return ticket).

North from Brisbane the Spirit of Capricorn goes daily except Sunday to Rockhampton (639 km, 13 hours). The Capricornian travels a slightly different route to Rockhampton on Thursday, Friday and Saturday. The Sunlander goes four days a week to Cairns (1681 km, 36 hours). Brisbane to Proserpine takes about 21 hours, Brisbane to Townsville 26 hours. One-way fares are Mackay $144 in 1st, $77 in economy; Proserpine $150 in 1st, $81 economy; Townsville $166 in 1st, $91 economy; Cairns $179 in 1st, $100 economy.

On Sundays only, the Queenslander is a motorail train to Cairns with a special bar for 1st class passengers, who also get sleeping berths and all meals included in their fare, which is nearly twice the usual 1st class fare. You can travel economy on the Queenslander but there are no economy class sleepers. Sleepers on other trains cost $17 economy, $29 1st class.

Inland to Roma, Charleville and Cunnamulla the Westlander runs twice a week. There are more trains inland from Brisbane, Rockhampton and Townsville. To/from the Gold Coast there's a combined rail-bus service.

Main line departures in Brisbane are from the Brisbane transit centre. You can also get info and tickets from the railways office (tel 225 0211) at 208 Adelaide St next to Anzac Square.

Getting Around

The best place for bus information is the City Council Transport Information Centre (tel 225 4444) in the Brisbane Administration Centre at 69 Ann St, open Monday to Friday from 8.15 am to 5.45 pm. The Public Transport Information Centre (tel 225 0211) in Central Station, covers local trains, ferries and buses. It's open Monday to Friday from 8.15 am to 5 pm. For ferry information call 399 4768.

Airport Transport Brisbane's Eagle Farm

Airport is north-east of the centre, near the coast. The international terminal is about nine km by road from the domestic terminal. Skennars runs a shuttle bus from the transit centre to both terminals and back, every half hour from 6.15 am to 6.45 pm. The buses will also stop at various points in the city centre and Fortitude Valley. Between the international terminal and the city costs $3; between the domestic terminal and the city costs $4.50; between the two terminals costs $3. The last departure from the domestic terminal to the international terminal and the city is at 7.45 pm. There are a few daily direct buses between the airport and the Gold and Sunshine coasts.

A taxi to the centre costs about $9.50 from the international terminal, $13 from the domestic. Avis, Budget, Hertz and Thrifty have car rental desks at the airport.

Bus In addition to the normal city buses, there are Cityxpress services which run between the suburbs and centre, and 'Rockets' which are fast peak hour commuter buses. From the transit centre, you need to walk into the city centre to pick up some buses. Most above-ground city-centre bus stops are colour coded to help you find the right one. The underground bus station beneath the Myer Centre is used mainly by Cityxpresses and buses to/from the south of the city.

Within the area between Wharf St and the Queensland Cultural Centre, buses cost just 35c a trip. Other fares are on a zone system costing 70c, $1.10, $1.50 or $1.70. Special deals include the unlimited travel Day Rover ($4.50 from a bus driver, $4 from newsagents or shops with a yellow 'fare deal' sign in their window).

Buses run every 10 to 20 minutes Monday to Friday till about 6 pm and on Saturday mornings. Services are less frequent on weekday evenings, Saturday afternoons and evenings, and Sundays. On Sundays the buses finish at 7 pm on other days at 11 pm. The City Circle bus No 333 does a clockwise loop round the area along George, Adelaide, Wharf, Eagle and Mary Sts till 5.45 pm Monday to Friday.

Useful buses from the city centre include to Fortitude Valley and New Farm on New Farm bus No 177 or 178 (brown stops) from Adelaide St between King George Square and Edward St. To Paddington, Bardon bus No 144 goes from opposite the transit centre or from Coles on Adelaide St (red stops).

To Fortitude Valley, Newstead House and Breakfast Creek bus No 160, 180 or 190 goes from the yellow stop on Edward St between Adelaide and Queen Sts. To West End bus No 177 goes from Edward St opposite Anzac Square (brown stop). This bus starts from the corner of Ann and Brunswick Sts in Fortitude Valley.

Bayside Buslines (tel 893 1047) runs between Brisbane and the southern Bayside (Capalaba Park, Wellington Point, Cleveland, Koala Park and Redland Bay). Hornibrook Bus Lines (tel 284 1622) runs between Brisbane and the northern Bayside (Sandgate, Clontarf, Redcliffe and Scarborough).

Train The fast Citytrain network has seven lines out to Ipswich, Beenleigh and Cleveland in the south and Pinkenba, Shorncliffe, Caboolture and Ferny Grove in the north. You can buy Day Rover tickets – a day ahead, from any station – for $8 which give unlimited train travel for one day (after 9 am on weekdays).

All trains go through Roma St, Central and Brunswick St stations.

Boat Brisbane makes good use of its river and there are cruises as well as the regular ferries. The latest innovation is jet propelled trimaran water buses between the Riverside Centre, at the junction of Eagle and Elizabeth Sts, and Queensland University at St Lucia with a stop at North Quay. The full one-way trip takes just 10 to 15 minutes and costs $1.

There's also the Golden Mile ferry between the Riverside Centre and Oxford St in Bulimba with a few stops including Sydney St in New Farm. It goes every 20 to 30 minutes and return fare is $1.60.

Cross-river ferries cost 60c one way and generally run every 15 minutes till after 11 pm Monday to Saturday, plus shorter hours on Sunday. The most central ones are the Customs House ferry between the Customs House and the top end of Kangaroo Point (closed Sundays), and the Edward St ferry between the corner of Edward and Alice Sts and Thornton St on Kangaroo Point. Others include the New Farm zigzag service which travels from Commercial Rd, Teneriffe, to Oxford St, Bulimba, then on to Merthyr Rd, New Farm, and Scott Rd, Hawthorne, then to Brunswick St, New Farm, and Ferry St, Norman Park, and back again. This is a half hourly service from each stop, operating seven days a week.

One interesting trip is the Brisbane City Ferries Cruise from Edward St (corner of the Botanic Gardens), to Newstead House and the university. It lasts 3½ hours and costs $5, but only goes on Saturdays and Sundays and in school holidays. The ferry stops to let you look round the cultural centre on some days, Newstead House other days. It's advisable to book (tel 399 4768). The MV *Speranza di Capri* (tel 357 6970) runs a three hour cruise to Newstead House from the Riverside Centre Monday to Thursday. The $10 fare includes a visit to the house.

Golden Mile Ferry Services (tel 832 4795) runs a three hour $8 cruise on Sundays and holidays out to Moreton Bay from Edward St, the Riverside Centre and Sydney St, New Farm. Other cruises go out to islands in Moreton Bay.

There is a variety of more expensive trips on the *Kookaburra Queen* and *Kookaburra Queen II* paddle-steamers from Petrie Bight Marina on Howard St, or with Brisbane Paddlewheeler Cruises (jazz and disco cruises), or Adai Cruises ('Rage on the River' night cruises from Breakfast Creek).

You can rent your own small motor boat

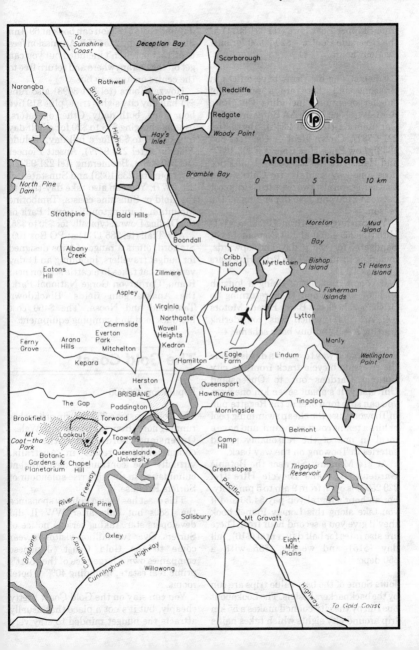

Around Brisbane

from Skipper Boat Hire (tel 391 5971) at the Riverside Centre – $20/30/50 for one/two/four hours.

Car Rental The big firms have offices in Brisbane and there are a number of smaller operators, including Cut Rate Rentals (tel 350 2081), AA Bargain Inedell Car Rentals (tel 350 2353), Betta (tel 221 7787), Crown Rent A Car (tel 854 1848), Low Price Hire Cars (tel 393 1657) and Half-Price (tel 229 3544). Half-Price does one-way rentals to Cairns and southern capitals: two days to Cairns cost between $160 and $240 depending on the season.

You can hire 4WDs from Brisbane 4WD Hire (tel 269 4869) at 139 Connaught St, Sandgate, for $55 a day and upwards, including insurance. Low Price Hire Cars also has 4WDs.

If you're thinking of doing a longish spell of driving and then returning to Brisbane, check out Barry Parade Motors (tel 252 9741) which was considering starting a sell and buy back scheme.

Bicycle A good way to spend a day is to ride the riverside bicycle track from the city Botanic Gardens out to Queensland University. It's about seven km one way: you can stop for a beer at the Regatta pub in Toowong, use the cheap swimming pool or hire a tennis court at the uni, and have a meal in one of the reasonably priced eateries in Toowong on the way back.

At 214 Margaret St, near the Botanic Gardens, Brisbane Bicycle Hire (tel 229 2592) is open from 9 am to 5 pm daily. For an hour's rental you pay $4.50 and if you take along this Lonely Planet book they'll give you a second hour free. There are also rates for half day rental ($10), full day ($15) and weekly ($35 with a $50 deposit).

Tours Some of the best value trips are run by the backpackers hostels. The Lookabout bus run by the city council makes a 55 km trip around city sights which takes half a

day and costs $12. You can book at 69 Ann St or by phoning 225 5555. Admission fees to attractions aren't included but you can get off the bus anywhere and return free to the centre on any city bus.

Howzat Tours (tel 341 3093) also runs $11 half day city sights trips, plus $19 five hour tours, both daily. Other operators, usually charging $18 to $20 for a half day tour or $30 to $35 for a full day, include Aladdin's (tel 229 9477), Ansett Pioneer (tel 240 9391), Boomerang (tel 221 9922), Intertour (tel 236 1033) and Sunstate (tel 229 2577). You can also take day-trips to the Gold or Sunshine coasts, Tamborine Mountain, Lamington National Park or the Darling Downs, typically for $30 to $35.

Aus-Trail (tel 285 1711) at PO Box 109, Stafford, offers a range of trips designed for budget travellers, including an 11 day venture that takes in a cattle station near Roma, Carnarvon Gorge National Park, the Anakie gem fields, Blackdown Tableland and Noosa. The $460 cost includes food and camping equipment.

The Gold Coast

Population 235,000

The Gold Coast is a 35 km strip of beaches running north from the New South Wales-Queensland border. It's the most commercialised resort in Australia, virtually one continuous development culminating in the high rise splendour of Surfers Paradise.

This coast has been a holiday spot since the 1880s but only after WW II did developers start taking serious notice of Surfers. Over two million visitors a year come to the Gold Coast. Japanese companies own a large slice of the coast's prime real estate, including 40% of hotel rooms.

You can stay on the Gold Coast pretty cheaply, but it's not a place that usually attracts the budget minded to stay very

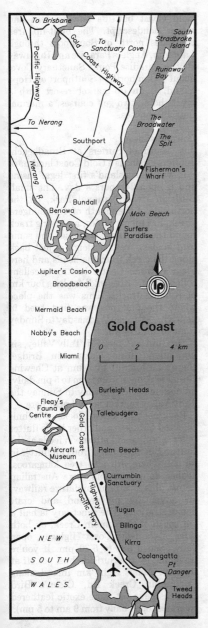

long – unless to earn money. The beaches all along the coast really are excellent but the tourist attractions are mainly artificial creations.

Orientation

The whole coast from Tweed Heads in New South Wales up to Main Beach, north of Surfers Paradise, is developed but most of the real action is around Surfers itself. Tweed Heads and Coolangatta at the south end are older, quieter, cheaper resorts. Moving north from there you pass through Kirra, Bilinga, Tugun, Currumbin, Palm Beach, Tallebudgera, Burleigh Heads, Miami, Nobby's Beach, Mermaid Beach and Broadbeach – all lower key resorts. Southport, the oldest town in the area, is north and just inland from Surfers, behind the sheltered expanse of the Broadwater which is fed by the Nerang and Coomera rivers. The Gold Coast Highway runs right along the coastal strip, leaving the Pacific Highway at Coolangatta and rejoining it inland from Southport.

Gold Coast airport is at Coolangatta. Most buses to the Gold Coast travel the full length of the strip.

Information

The Gold Coast Visitors Bureau (tel 38 4419), on Cavill Ave Mall, in the heart of Surfers Paradise, is open from 8 am to 4 pm Monday to Friday, 9 am to 3 pm Saturday and Sunday. The other big tourist info centre (tel 36 2634) on the Gold Coast, at Tweed Heads, deals with the whole of New South Wales as well as the Gold Coast. There's a smaller info centre (tel 36 7765) in Coolangatta in the Beach House on the corner of Marine Parade and McLean St.

At Burleigh Heads, on the Gold Coast Highway, there's a Queensland National Parks information centre (tel 35 3032), a useful place to call in if you're planning to visit some of the state's national parks. It's open daily.

Surfers Paradise

The centre of the Gold Coast is a real high rise jungle; in fact there is such a skyscraper conglomeration that in the afternoon much of the beach is in shadow! Still, people pack in for the lights, activities, nightlife, shopping, restaurants, attractions and that strip of ocean sand.

Surfers has come a long way since 1936 when there was just the brand new Surfers Paradise Hotel, a little hideaway nine km south of Southport. The hotel has now been swallowed up by a shopping/eating complex called the Paradise Centre. Cavill Ave has a pedestrian mall at its beach end and is the heart of Surfers. Despite all the changes and growth, at most times of year you don't usually have to go very far north or south to find a relatively open, quiet, sunny beach.

The Gold Coast Highway runs right through Surfers, only a block back from the beach. Another block back is the looping Nerang River. The Surfers rich live around the surrounding canals.

Main Beach & The Spit

North from Surfers is Main Beach and beyond that The Spit is a narrow three km long tongue of sand dividing the ocean from the Broadwater.

On the Broadwater side of The Spit, Fisherman's Wharf is the departure point for most pleasure cruises, with a pub, a restaurant, entertainment, swimming pool and shops. Across on the ocean front is the new Sheraton Mirage, while up from Fisherman's Wharf is Sea World, a huge aquatic amusement centre. Sea World has dolphin shows, sea lion shows, water ski shows, a monorail, an *Endeavour* replica, roller coasters and so on. It's open daily from 10 am to 5 pm and admission is $25 for adults and $16 for kids. The north end of The Spit is not developed and it's popular for relatively secluded sunbathing.

Southport & North

Sheltered from the ocean by The Spit, Southport was the original town on the Gold Coast but it's now modern and rather nondescript. The built-up area continues north of Southport through Labrador, Anglers Paradise and Runaway Bay to Paradise Point. Sanctuary Cove, about 10 km north of Southport on Hope Island, is an up-market resort with a Hyatt hotel, two golf courses, a marina, flats and houses.

Down the Coast

Just south of Surfers at Broadbeach, Jupiters Casino is a Gold Coast landmark – it was Queensland's first legal casino and is open 24 hours a day. The small Burleigh Head National Park, on the north side of the mouth of Tallebudgera Creek, has picnic tables, a walking track round the headland, wallabies and some *wild* koalas. West Burleigh is just back along the creek from the heads and here Fleay's Fauna Centre has an excellent collection of native wildlife along four km of walking tracks. This was the place where the platypus was first bred in captivity. It's open Wednesday to Sunday from 10 am to 4 pm.

On Guineas Creek Rd, Tally Valley, six km inland from Currumbin Bridge, there's an aircraft museum at Chewing Gum Field, open from 9 am to 5 pm daily, admission $3. Wednesday to Sunday the Tally Valley market is held near here.

Back near the coast, flocks of techni-coloured lorikeets and other birds flutter in for morning and afternoon feeds at the Currumbin Sanctuary. You can flutter in for $9. There are also tree kangaroos, koalas, emus and lots more Australian fauna, plus a two km miniature railway, an adventure playground and craft demonstrations. The sanctuary is half a km south of Currumbin Creek, on both sides of the Gold Coast Highway, open daily from 8 am to 5.30 pm. If you're travelling by the Surfside bus, get off at stop 20. About eight km inland along Currumbin Creek Rd, Olson's Bird Gardens have yet more exotic feathered creatures (open daily from 9 am to 5 pm).

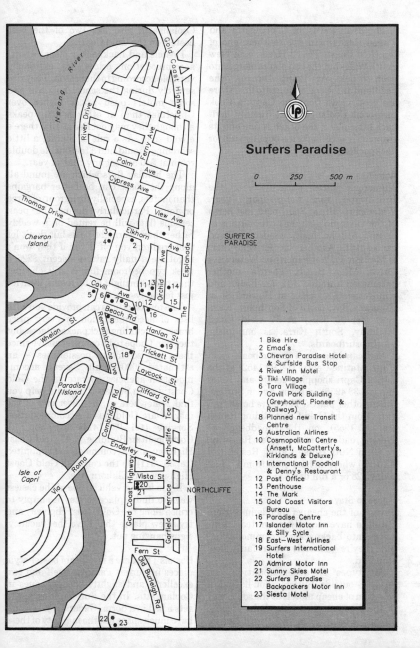

Surfers Paradise

0   250   500 m

SURFERS
PARADISE

NORTHCLIFFE

1 Bike Hire
2 Emad's
3 Chevron Paradise Hotel
   & Surfside Bus Stop
4 River Inn Motel
5 Tiki Village
6 Tara Village
7 Cavill Park Building
   (Greyhound, Pioneer &
   Railways)
8 Planned new Transit
   Centre
9 Australian Airlines
10 Cosmopolitan Centre
   (Ansett, McCafferty's,
   Kirklands & Deluxe)
11 International Foodhall
   & Denny's Restaurant
12 Post Office
13 Penthouse
14 The Mark
15 Gold Coast Visitors
   Bureau
16 Paradise Centre
17 Islander Motor Inn
   & Silly Sycle
18 East-West Airlines
19 Surfers International
   Hotel
20 Admiral Motor Inn
21 Sunny Skies Motel
22 Surfers Paradise
   Backpackers Motor Inn
23 Siesta Motel

The 'twin towns' of Coolangatta and Tweed Heads mark the southern end of the Gold Coast. Tweed Heads is in New South Wales but the two places merge into each other. At Point Danger, the headland at the end of the state line, there are good views from the Captain Cook memorial. Coolangatta is a friendly, laid-back little place, the beach is fine and its two good hostels make it a popular stop for backpackers.

Activities

Numerous places, particularly on the Broadwater, rent water sports gear. Watersport-Hire at Southport, just north of the Olympic pool, has catamarans at around $12 an hour, windsurfers and canoes at $12. Another place for windsurfers is Max Brown Watersports on Waterways Drive, Main Beach. There's another catamaran (around $12 an hour) and windsurfer ($10) place at Howard St in Runaway Bay, north of Southport. Kirra Surf (tel 36 3922) at 57 Gold Coast Highway, South Kirra, is one place renting surfboards.

You can hire small motor boats from Capri Marine Centre (tel 92 1452) at the Isle of Capri shopping centre and River Inn (tel 38 4955) on Ferny Ave in Surfers, among other places. There are horse trail rides from the Gold Coast Riding Ranch (tel 96 1255), on the Broadbeach to Nerang road next to the Surfers Raceway, or Gum Nuts Horse Riding Resort (tel 43 0191) where an hour costs from $7, half a day $28 or a full day $45.

Places to Stay

Several of the cheaper motels in Surfers Paradise have recently converted themselves into backpacker accommodation, but they're generally of a fairly low standard.

All types of accommodation are cheaper outside Surfers. You'll find a selection of cheap motels at the south end of the coast at places like Palm Beach, Bilinga, Coolangatta, and Tweed Heads.

Coolangatta also has two of the best hostels on the Gold Coast.

Hostels and backpacker places apart, accommodation prices are extremely variable according to the season. They rise severely during the school holidays and some motels push prices higher over Christmas than at other holiday peaks although they may not rise at all if there's a cold snap. As a rule of thumb, a little searching should find a reasonable double room at $40 almost any time of year.

The holiday flats which are found all along the coast can be better bargains than motels, especially for a group of three or four. Particularly during the peak seasons flats will be rented on a weekly rather than overnight basis but don't let that frighten you off. Even if they won't negotiate a daily rate, a decent $225 a week two bedroom flat is still cheaper than two $30 a night motel rooms, even for just four days.

The tourist offices can provide you with lists of accommodation in every price bracket, including backpacker places, but they can't hope to be comprehensive since there are so many possibilities – an estimated 3000 in all. Several accommodation agencies operate on the Gold Coast: two in Surfers that could help you find somewhere at the lower end of the market are Gold Coast Accommodation Service (tel 92 1414) in shop 10, Cosmopolitan Building, 3142 Gold Coast Highway, and Accommodation Unlimited (tel 38 3311) on the corner of Gold Coast Highway and Elkhorn Ave.

If you have a vehicle, one of the easiest ways to find a place to stay is simply to cruise along the Gold Coast Highway and try a few places that have the 'vacancy' signs hanging out.

Hostels There are a number of hostel-style places in Surfers Paradise itself and two excellent, and slightly cheaper, ones in Coolangatta. In the Surfers hostels, $12 gets a bed in a dorm. Generally you won't have much space but the majority of these

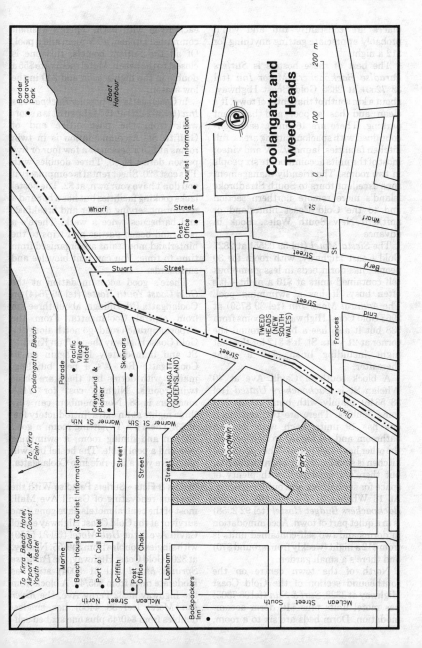

Coolangatta and Tweed Heads

200 m

100

0

Border Caravan Park

Boat Harbour

Tourist Information

Wharf Street

Post Office

Wharf St

Beray Street

Street

Stuart Street

Enid Street

Frances Street

Coolangatta Beach

Pacific Village Hotel

Greyhound & Pioneer

Skennars

COOLANGATTA (QUEENSLAND)

TWEED HEADS (NEW SOUTH WALES)

Dixon Street

To Kirra Point

Parade

Warner St Nth

Warner St Sth

Street

Street

Street

Goodwin Park

To Kirra Beach Hotel, Airport & Gold Coast Youth Hostel

Beach House & Tourist Information

Port o' Call Hotel

Marine Parade

Griffith Street

Chalk Street

Post Office

Lanham Street

Street

Backpackers Inn

McLean Street North

McLean Street South

places are constantly full and you'll probably appreciate getting anything for $12 a night.

The best of these hostels is *Surfers Paradise Backpackers Motor Inn* (tel 38 7250) at 2835 Gold Coast Highway, about a km south of the centre of town. It's clean and has a pool and basement parking. There are 16 units, each self-contained with spacious sitting areas, full kitchen facilities, laundry, TV and video; most of the units accommodate six people in two rooms. The friendly management runs excellent tours to South Stradbroke Island's more remote northern section and to the Gold Coast hinterland or northern New South Wales. Book in advance.

The *Siesta Motel* (tel 39 0355) at 2827 Gold Coast Highway, with room for 30 people, has dorm beds in less glamorous self-contained units at $10 a night – it's often busy. It has a swimming pool. The *Admiral Motor Inn* (tel 39 8759) at 2965 Gold Coast Highway has rooms from $38 but it also has a hostel around the corner at 21 Vista St. It's $12 for the first night including linen, $10 a night thereafter.

A block south of Cavill Ave at 40 Whelan St is *Backpackers United* (tel 38 5346) mainly with bunk rooms but some doubles. There are two sections – one has 19 units, each with its own bathroom and taking up to four people; the other has larger dorms. The communal kitchen is small and only open until 8 pm, but there's a good pool with plenty of space for sunbathing and outdoor eating. At 18 Whelan St the friendly *Surfers Backpackers Budget Hostel* (tel 92 2958) is in a quiet part of town. Accommodation in dorms and two self-contained units is from $12 a night (weekly from around $70) and there's a small garden.

North of the town centre on the southbound section of the Gold Coast Highway at 3323, *Surf & Sun* (tel 38 7305) has motel units plus $10 dorm accommodation. Dorm beds are six to a room,

each room with bath. There's a small communal kitchen, a TV room and a pool. Of all the Surfers hostels, this one is closest to the beach. Motel rooms are $55 a double in the high season and $40 in the low season.

In Coolangatta the popular *Backpackers Inn* (tel 36 2422) at 45 McLean St is a short walk from the post office end of Griffith St. Accommodation is in twin rooms at $10 a person or a few four or five person dorms at $9. Three doubles with TVs cost $20. Sheet rental is compulsory if you don't have your own, at $2. The hostel lacks cooking facilities but has a bar and a restaurant serving dinner and breakfast, and barbecues twice a week. There's a pool, and beach parties and trips to the hinterland mountains are organised from time to time. You can rent bicycles and surfboards.

There's good accommodation at the *Gold Coast Youth Hostel* (tel 36 7644) on Coolangatta Rd, Bilinga, about three km from central Coolangatta. From the airport approach road, go north along the Gold Coast Highway then left on Kirribin St and immediately left again on to Coolangatta Rd. It's a new building, mainly with dorms but there are three twin rooms. Nightly cost for YHA members is $8. Non members can stay three nights at an extra 'introductory fee' of $3. There's a TV/sitting room, a good kitchen and dining room, a swimming pool and a pool table. The hostel bus will often give you a free ride into Coolangatta.

Motels & Flats – Surfers Paradise With the vigorous renovating of Cavill Ave Mall, most of the central motels have gone. One survivor at the Gold Coast Highway end of Cavill Ave is the *Hub Motel* (tel 31 5559) with singles/doubles from $40/55. Nearby, at 3204 Gold Coast Highway, the *Paradise Springs Motel* (tel 31 5004) still has moderate rates from $35/45. A block from the highway at 32 Ferny Ave, the *River Inn Motel* (tel 38 4466) has singles/doubles from $40/45 plus one six bed self-contained room for backpackers. One traveller complained of poor ventilation in the rooms here.

At 2985 Gold Coast Highway, the *Silver Sands Motel* (tel 38 6041) has singles/doubles from $37/40, with cooking facilities. Close by, *Sunny Skies Motel* at 2963 Gold Coast Highway, is good for groups as it has two bedroom self-contained units, taking at least four people, for $45 a night out of school holidays.

Keep your eyes open for specials at some of the resorts. *Surfspray Court* (tel 31 5502) at 21 Old Burleigh Rd charges $280/345 a week for singles/doubles and $70 a week for each extra person. All bedding is included.

Motels & Flats - down the coast A few randomly selected places to consider, moving down the coast from Surfers: in Broadbeach, the *Motel Casa Blanca* (tel 50 3511) at 2649 Gold Coast Highway has rooms from $40 or flats for a few dollars more. At Mermaid Beach the *Red Emu Motel* (tel 55 2748) at the corner of the Gold Coast Highway and Peerless Ave has doubles from $35 in the low season, $120 in the peak season. The *Gold Coast Motor Inn* (tel 55 2016) at 41 Montana Rd, Mermaid Beach, has holiday flats from $35 a night. In Miami the *Blackjack Motel* (tel 52 8435) at 2056 Gold Coast Highway has some singles and doubles at $35.

Burleigh Heads is a bit more expensive, but further south at Palm Beach there's a string of reasonably priced places. The *Moana Motel* (tel 35 1131), a small place on the beach at 1461 Gold Coast Highway, has rooms with fridges and colour TVs for just $25/35. There's another string of low priced motels along the Gold Coast Highway at Bilinga, all on the beachfront with doubles $35. You could try the *Surfside* at 351 or the *Sundowner* at 329.

Coolangatta has another cluster of accommodation. The old *Port O'Call Hotel* (tel 36 3066) in the centre of town at the corner of Griffith and McLean Sts has rooms from $20 and meals are available downstairs. There's a big balcony. Over at Rainbow Bay in Coolangatta, there are holiday flats like *Cooloola* (tel 36 4184) at 239 Boundary St and *Tondio Terrace* (tel 36 6488) at 239 Boundary St charging $200 to $400 a week for two people.

Camping There are dozens of caravan and camping sites along the Gold Coast strip. The Gold Coast city council operates six sites from Kirra to Southport, all with tent sites at $6 to $7 double. Their Main Beach Parade site (tel 31 4225) is very convenient, just north of Surfers. Just south, the *Broadbeach Island Caravan Village* is beside the Gold Coast Highway. There are further clusters of sites at Miami, Burleigh Heads and Palm Beach. Many places have on-site vans, usually from $20 a night. Tourist offices can supply you with lists.

Places to Eat
There are plenty of fast food places along the Gold Coast. A sensible and pleasant development has been the growing number of restaurants and cafes with outdoor eating areas. In the off season many Gold Coast restaurants close early - outside Surfers Paradise, it's often a case of eat early or starve.

Surfers Paradise There's plenty of choice in and around the Cavill Ave Mall. *Charlie's* at the beach end with outdoor tables under umbrellas is reasonably priced and open 24 hours a day. There are others also around the mall's busy giant chess set, like the *Tamari Bistro* and *Confetti*, both more expensive than Charlie's. Both do Italian food. Tamari's pasta dishes and specials are $8, other main meals are $12 to $14.

Along the mall, away from the beach, the busy *Shell Bar* on the corner of Orchid Ave offers good value snacks and meals. Breakfasts for $6 include juice, one of five hot dishes, toast and a bottomless cup of tea or coffee. Opposite, *Surfers Tavern Beergarden* has good cheap pub lunches for $5. On the corner of Cavill Ave and the inland side of the Gold Coast Highway, the very popular *Bavarian Steakhouse* has straightforward steak & chips style food from $10.

A few doors up the highway and on the other side from the Bavarian Steakhouse, in the Dolphin Arcade, is the *International Foodhall* with small moderately priced food bars. *Denny's Restaurant* on the corner of Dolphin Arcade and the highway, charges $5 for breakfast and $11 for a main meal with a choice of grills, fish or chicken.

A block north, Elkhorn Ave has several places to eat. Near its beach end the small *Boonchu* Thai restaurant offers some of the best value food in town. It has mixed Asian dishes for $6 to $7. Next door the *Beachhouse Cafe* is open 24 hours with hamburgers for $3 and pastas for $6. Right on the corner of Elkhorn Ave and the Esplanade *Fitzies Kitchen* is good for breakfasts and lunches. On the inland half of Elkhorn Ave don't miss *Emad's*, a Lebanese place. It has shish kebabs for $4, meals up to $14, with many dishes for $7.

Orchid Ave is another good place to look. *Jenny's Coffee Shop* in the Monte Carlo Arcade is a good daytime place with wholesome meals. Just along Orchid Ave in The Mark complex, the *Curry Pot* is a BYO Indian place open from 6.30 pm with meat and seafood dishes for $10 and vegetarian from $8. Also in The Mark, the excellent and popular *Sweethearts* offers a huge array of health foods. It's open daily from 8.30 am to 8.30 pm.

Just south of Cavill Ave on the Gold Coast Highway, the *Garden Bar & Bistro* has a piano bar and meals from $5. Over at the corner of Ferny and Cavill Aves, *Tara Village* has an $8 barbecue on Saturday afternoons. There are more places on Trickett St, two blocks south of Cavill Ave. For a real feast, *The Carvery* in the Surfers International does a nightly $16 banquet. On the corner of the highway

and Clifford St *Pandas* offers reasonably priced snacks and meals – there's a $5 cooked breakfast special from 6 am. Fisherman's Wharf, on The Spit, has a wonderful view and quite a few eating options. At the southern end, a food hall sells snacks and meals.

Down the Coast There are heaps of places along the highway between Surfers and Burleigh Heads. You can have a good night out at *La Cucaracha*, a licensed restaurant at 2518 Gold Coast Highway in Mermaid Beach. It has Mexican meals for $12, and there's a live band nightly.

The *Pizza Hut* on the highway at Miami Beach has a Tuesday night $5 feast. The *Seaview Room* of the Miami Hotel-Motel on the beachfront at Miami has a daily lunch and dinner seafood platter special for $9.

In Burleigh Heads, the *Masakan Indonesia*, at 1837 Gold Coast Highway, has reasonably priced Indonesian dishes. Around the corner, facing the beach, the Burleigh Hotel has the *Four Seasons Bistro* with good pub fare.

Coolangatta A walk along Griffith St will turn up plenty of places for a meal. There are a few more places in McLean St between Griffith St and Marine Parade, including a creperie and, next door, pub bistro meals up to $7 in the *Port O' Call Hotel*.

On the corner of McLean St and Marine Parade the Beach House shopping complex has a number of eateries and a couple tucked in the arcade running between Griffith St and Marine Parade. *Farley's Coffee Lounge* is good for breakfasts. In the arcade, the *Natural Food Bar* is a busy lunch spot with cheap and filling wholesome food. If you follow Griffith St south to Boundary St towards Point Danger, you'll find the *Patch Hotel* on the corner of Boundary and Hill Sts. On Thursday nights, it has a garden grill for $9.

Entertainment

This is what it's all about on the Gold Coast. There are around 30 nightclubs around Surfers alone. In addition there's Jupiter's Casino, plus live music venues, plenty of cinemas – and even a cultural centre. Most places have fairly strict dress codes. Lots of the nightclubs give away free entry passes, both at their doors and on the streets. Also available are $8 passes which allow entry to four nightclubs – Penthouse, Benson's, Player's and Rumours. Ask in The Mark on Orchid Ave or at the cruise terminal on the corner of Cavill and Ferny Aves.

Benson's Nite Club at 22 Orchid Ave has all sorts of deals which can help you avoid the cover charge and/or get cheap drinks. *Penthouse*, also on Orchid Ave, has four floors of nightlife with a piano bar, an over 25s disco and more. The lively *Player's* in the *Surfers International Hotel* at 7 Trickett St is open from 8 pm till 5 am. The *Tok H* at 19A Cavill Ave has a disco, plus live entertainment some nights – and happy hours from 6 pm to midnight Monday to Wednesday, 6 to 9 pm Thursday to Saturday. *Rumours*, with a casual atmosphere and great music, is on level one in The Mark on Orchid Ave, open Tuesday to Sunday until late.

Jupiter's Casino in Broadbeach has a restaurant and a good disco called *Fortunes*, with mixed music and age groups. Similar 'classy' night spots include *Twains International* in The Mark on Orchid Ave, and *Traders* in the Gold Coast International Hotel.

The *Benowa Tavern* on Ashmore Rd, Benowa, has reasonable bands and a casual atmosphere, and on some nights entry is free. *Tara Village*, on the corner of Cavill and Ferny Aves, has live rock bands. *Surfers Beergarden* on Cavill Ave has live rock Sunday nights and sometimes during the week. There's also live music at Fisherman's Wharf most days.

Quite a few restaurants give you music or entertainment with your meal. *La Cucaracha* Mexican restaurant is one of

the best. A popular cabaret restaurant is *Dracula's* at 1 Sunshine Bouvelard, Miami Keys. Dracula's offers a four course meal served by waiters and waitresses who throw themselves into the Dracula theme. The night climaxes in a disco.

In Coolangatta, *Gossip* is a nightclub open most nights with a variety of entertainment. *Penthouse* is another disco/nightclub in Coolangatta. Live music can be heard several nights a week at the *Port O' Call Hotel*, while the *Patch Hotel* features some of the big name Aussie rock bands. You can expect to hear decent live bands here from Thursday to Sunday nights. Much of the entertainment on the southern Gold Coast revolves around the clubs and pokies in Tweed Heads.

After all this, it may be a relief to know that there is *The Centre*, the Gold Coast's arts complex, beside the Nerang River at Bundall. It houses theatres, galleries, a restaurant and bar. Shows include musicals, concerts, plays and dance, and exhibitions are listed under Entertainment in some Gold Coast tourist publications.

Getting There & Away

Air The Gold Coast is only a couple of hours by road from the centre of Brisbane but it also has its own busy airport at Coolangatta.

Ansett and Australian airlines fly direct from the southern capitals. Fares include Sydney $176 ($141 standby), Melbourne $271 ($217), Adelaide $305 ($244) and Perth $530. East-West also flies daily direct from Albury, Brisbane, Cairns, Hobart and Sydney ($176, standby $123), while Eastern flies daily direct from Brisbane and several New South Wales coastal towns. Air NSW has daily direct flights from Newcastle ($140).

If you need to contact airlines while on the Gold Coast their telephone numbers are Ansett (tel 31 8100), Air NSW (tel 31 8100), Australian (tel 38 1066), Eastern (tel 38 1188) and East-West (tel 50 3800).

Bus All Sydney to Brisbane services along the Pacific Highway route detour along the full length of the Gold Coast. Deluxe has the most frequent service, with six buses daily each way. From Sydney to the Gold Coast costs between $35 and $43, with Sunliner, Ambassador and Road-ranger among the cheaper lines. Some companies including Deluxe and Pioneer will allow you a free stopover on the Gold Coast if you have a through ticket. Nearly all buses between Brisbane and Melbourne or Adelaide also start from or continue on to the Gold Coast. Pioneer runs a twice daily feeder service between Brisbane and the Gold Coast.

Cheapest transport between Brisbane and the Gold Coast is the 'Metro-Link' service which combines a train journey between Brisbane and Beenleigh and a McCafferty's bus between Beenleigh and the Gold Coast. This service runs four to six times in each direction Monday to Friday, slightly less often at weekends. About 20 minutes faster is Greyhound's local bus service between Brisbane and Coolangatta. This runs, via the whole Gold Coast, about 17 times daily Monday to Friday, a few times less often at weekends. The fare between Brisbane and anywhere on the Gold Coast is $9.70.

Coast service leaving Brisbane hourly from 7.30 am, plus a direct service three to five times daily between Brisbane airport and the Gold Coast.

Telephone numbers for the main bus terminals in Surfers Paradise are McCafferty's and Kirklands (tel 38 2700); Deluxe (tel 38 8622); Intertour (tel 38 0000); Pioneer (tel 92 1041); Greyhound (tel 38 8344); Skennars, Trans City Express, and Sunliner (tel 38 9944). Inter-Capital bookings are through Jetset Tours (tel 38 4600).

In Coolangatta the telephone numbers for the main bus terminals are: Greyhound (tel 36 2366); Pioneer (tel 36 6422); Skennars, Deluxe and Sunliner (tel 36 2484); and McCafferty's (tel 36 1700).

Train There's no railway station on the Gold Coast but there are connecting bus services for two trains a day between northern New South Wales and Sydney. There's a railways booking office (tel 39 9280) in the Cavill Park Building on the corner of Beach Rd and the Gold Coast Highway in Surfers Paradise.

Getting Around

Airport Transport Coolangatta Airport is the seventh busiest in Australia. Several different bus companies run airport shuttle buses. Kenny's Coaches (tel 34 4554) goes to Coolangatta and Tweed Heads for $2 one way. Gold Coast Airport Transit (tel 36 6841) from Surfers Paradise meets every Australian Airlines arrival and departure. It costs $5 between the airport and Surfers and will pick up or drop you off from your accommodation. Ansett Pioneer (tel 50 2966) meets all

Ansett arrivals and departures, leaving Surfers 75 minutes before take off. Intertour (tel 38 0000) operates an airport transfer bus to/from Surfers and Coolangatta for Australian and East-West flights.

Bus There's a frequent bus service by the Surfside line (tel 36 7666) up and down the Gold Coast Highway between Southport and Tweed Heads. Last buses leave Tweed Heads at 11.45 pm and Southport at 12.50 am (on Sundays 8.45 pm from Tweed Heads, 9.45 from Southport). You can get a day rover ticket for $5, or a week rover for $18.40. Smekels Buses (tel 32 6211) runs a service around Southport, and to Surfers and to Nerang on the Pacific Highway.

There's a Water Bus (tel 92 0335) running along the canals and river from the Pacific Fair shopping centre in Broadbeach to Sea World on The Spit.

Car & Moped Rental There are stacks of rent-a-car firms along the Gold Coast, particularly in Surfers – pick up any of the give away Gold Coast guides or scan the yellow pages. All the big companies are represented, plus a host of local operators in the Moke and small car field and in the rent-a-wreck category. Rent-A-Bomb (tel 38 8007) in the Chevron Hotel Arcade, Surfers, is one of the cheapest and has cars, Mokes and mopeds. Others you could try are Bargain Wheels (tel 34 4281) or Red Rocket (tel 38 9074) at Shop 28, The Forum, Orchid Ave, Surfers.

For mopeds go to Gold Coast Moped Hire (tel 38 0111) at 3 Beach Rd in Surfers, or Vespa Moped Hire (tel 38 3483) in Shop 3, Surfers International Arcade.

Bicycle Rental In Surfers try Repossessed Office Equipment at 25 Elkhorn Ave or Silly Sycle (tel 38 6991) in the Islander Building on Beach Rd. There is another bicycle and moped rental shop at the other end of the strip at 159 Griffith St, Coolangatta.

Tours Tours run by some of the hostels are probably the best value. Otherwise bus trips up into the mountains behind the coast cost $20 to Tamborine Mountain, $25 to $30 further afield. There are also 4WD mountain tours for $50. If you're into artificial attractions, the Greyhound Fun Bus leaves Coolangatta at 9 am and Surfers 40 minutes later and offers return travel and admission to Dreamworld ($30), Koala Town ($20) or Sea World ($25).

River or canal cruises may include just refreshments, or lunch plus a floating floor show. In the evening you'll probably get music, dancing and dinner. A straight couple of hours along the inland waterways costs $18, while an evening dinner cruise will be $25 to $30. Cruises to South Stradbroke Island usually include lunch and some form of entertainment for around $37.

Cruises leave from Fisherman's Wharf, or the river end of Cavill Ave, or the wharf at the Chevron Hotel on Ferny Ave.

Behind the Gold Coast

The mountains of the McPherson Range, which are about 20 km inland from Coolangatta and stretch about 60 km back along the New South Wales border to meet the Great Dividing Range, are probably the nicest thing about the Gold Coast area. They're a paradise for walkers, and lots of great views and natural features are easily accessible if you just fancy driving round for a day or two. Expect a lot of rain in the mountains from December to March, and in winter the nights can be cold.

PACIFIC HIGHWAY
This, the main road from Coolangatta to Brisbane, runs up inland behind the Gold Coast. Nerang, on this road and nine km inland from Southport, has almost become a suburb of the coastal strip. From Nerang and from Mudgeeraba, a bit

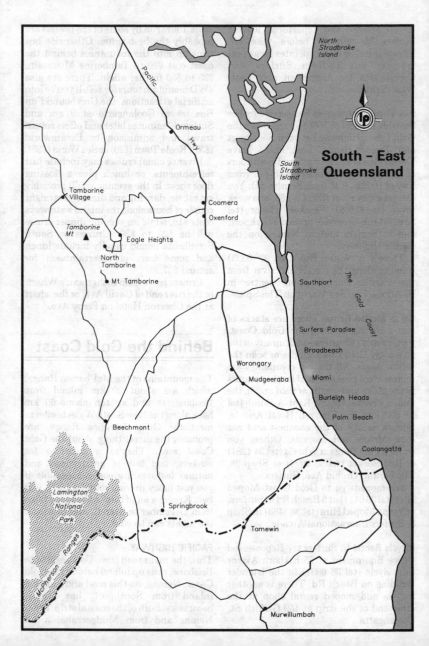

South – East
Queensland

further south on the Pacific Highway, roads lead south-west up to the fine national parks in the McPherson Range.

Several of the artificial Gold Coast 'attractions' are on the Pacific Highway. North of Nerang at Oxenford and Coomera you'll find the Wet 'n Wild water fun park with one metre artificial surf, Koala Town and, virtually over the road from Koala Town, Dreamworld which is a Disneyland-style creation with a $15 admission price. Dreamworld runs its own bus (tel 35 6888) for $8 return from the Gold Coast or you can get there by Greyhound, McCafferty's or Skennars or by countless tours.

Beenleigh is about halfway from the Gold Coast to Brisbane. The rum distillery here dates from 1884 and is open for tours ($3.50) from 10.30 am to 3.30 pm.

TAMBORINE MOUNTAIN

Just 45 km north-west of the Gold Coast, this 600 metre high plateau is on a northern spur of the McPherson Range. Patches of the area's original forests remain in nine small national parks. There are gorges, spectacular waterfalls like Witches Falls and Cedar Creek Falls, great views inland or over the coast, and walking tracks. There's a visitor info centre at Doughty Park, North Tamborine, open daily.

The main turn-off to the mountain is at Oxenford on the Pacific Highway. Some of the best lookouts are in Witches Falls National Park, south-west of North Tamborine, and at Cameron Falls, north-west of North Tamborine. Macrozamia Grove National Park, near Mt Tamborine township, has some extremely old macrozamia palms. Other places of interest on the mountain or on the way up include Jasper Farm, a commercial fossicking site at Upper Coomera; Thunderbird World where you can ride horses or fossick for thunder eggs; and huge trees in MacDonald National Park.

There's a handful of reasonably priced motels and guest houses in Mt Tamborine township and Eagle Heights and a camping site with on-site vans at *Thunderbird Mountain Resort* (tel 45 1468) in Mt Tamborine. Skennars runs buses between Brisbane, Tamborine Mountain and the Gold Coast.

SPRINGBROOK PLATEAU

Reached by paved roads from Nerang or Mudgeeraba or from Murwillumbah in New South Wales, all about 30 to 40 km away, this forested 900 metre high plateau, like the rest of the McPherson Range, is a remnant of the huge volcano which used to be centred on Mt Warning in New South Wales. There are five small national parks in the Springbrook area, with gorges, cliffs, forests, waterfalls, walking tracks and several picnic areas. In Gwongorella National Park, just off the Mudgeeraba to Springbrook road, the Purling Brook Falls drop 109 metres into rainforest. Downstream, Waringa pool is a beautiful summer swimming hole. There's a national park camping area beside the Gwongorella picnic area, a short walk from the falls.

Natural Arch National Park, in the valley to the west of Springbrook Plateau, is just off the Nerang to Murwillumbah road. A one km walking circuit takes you to a rock arch spanning a water formed cave which is home to a huge colony of glow-worms.

There are ranger stations and information centres at Natural Arch and Springbrook. Pick up a copy of their walking tracks leaflet. Camping permits for Gwongorella are available from the ranger at Springbrook (tel 33 5147). Springbrook village itself has a number of restored pioneer buildings and memorabilia including Nerang's original 1889 railway station.

LAMINGTON NATIONAL PARK

West of Springbrook, this large (200 square km) park covers more of the McPherson Range and adjoins the Border Ranges National Park in New South Wales. It includes thickly wooded valleys, ranges rising above 1100 metres, plus most of the Lamington Plateau. Much of the vegetation is subtropical rainforest. There are beautiful gorges, caves, superb views, a great many waterfalls and pools, and lots of wildlife. Bower birds are quite common and pademelons, a type of small wallaby, can be seen on the grassy forest verges in late afternoon.

The park has 160 km of walking tracks ranging from a 'senses trail' for the blind at Binna Burra, to the Border Track which leads from Binna Burra to O'Reillys via the crest of the range.

Places to Stay

Visitors to Lamington usually head first for either Binna Burra, or Green Mountains (also called O'Reillys). Many of the walking tracks start at these two places.

Binna Burra, 35 km from Nerang by paved road, has the *Binna Burra Mountain Lodge* (tel (075) 33 3622) with a small camping ground where a tent site is $5 per person. It's advisable to book (tel 33 3536) if you want to camp. Accommodation in the lodge is normally about $73 per person per night, but that includes all meals, free hiking and climbing gear, and activities like guided walks, bus trips and abseiling. There's a kiosk selling basic supplies.

Green Mountains is 32 km south of Canungra by a mostly paved road. *O'Reilly's Mountain Resort* (tel 45 1611) at Green Mountains has similar fully inclusive prices to those at Binna Burra. There's also a kiosk, and a national parks camping ground about 600 metres away.

It's quite possible to camp in Lamington, but there are restrictions. You can get information from the national parks offices at Burleigh Heads or Brisbane but camping permits must be obtained from the ranger stations at Binna Burra (tel 33 3584) or Green Mountains (tel 45 1734).

Getting There & Away

The Mountain Coach Company (tel 229 9477 in Brisbane) runs a daily bus service from Brisbane transit centre to Binna Burra. It leaves Brisbane in the afternoon and stops at the Commercial Hotel in Nerang on the way. From the Gold Coast you can get a Smekels bus to Nerang. Brisbane to Binna Burra costs $15 and takes about 1¾ hours. Nerang to Binna Burra is $8. Departures from Binna Burra are at 7.15 am daily, except for Sundays (3 pm). On Sundays the same company runs a bus between Coolangatta airport and Binna Burra, also via Nerang, leaving Binna Burra at 9 am and the airport at 12 noon or 1 pm. This takes 1½ hours and costs $12.

Scenic Tours (tel Brisbane 857 5610, 357 9214) runs a bus service four times a week between Brisbane transit centre and Green Mountains/O'Reillys. The one-way trip takes about three hours. Book at the Skennars desk in the Brisbane transit centre.

MT LINDESAY HIGHWAY

This road runs south from Brisbane, across the Great Dividing Range west of Lamington, and into New South Wales at Woodenbong. Beaudesert, in cattle country 66 km from Brisbane, is just 20 km south-west of Tamborine Mountain. It has a pioneer museum and tourist info centre on Jane St.

West of Beaudesert is the stretch of the Great Dividing Range known as the Scenic Rim (see Darling Downs section). Further south, Mt Barney National Park is undeveloped but popular with bushwalkers and climbers. It's in the Great Dividing Range just north of the state border. You reach it from the Rathdowney to Boonah road. There's a tourist info office (tel 44 1222) on the highway at Rathdowney.

Moreton Bay

Moreton Bay, at the mouth of the Brisbane River, is said to have 365 islands. The larger islands shelter a long stretch of

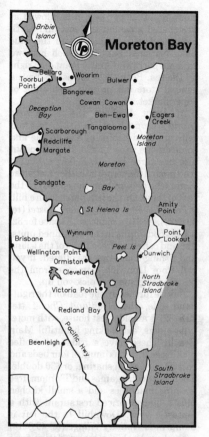

coast: South Stradbroke Island is only just north of the Gold Coast, while Bribie Island is only just south of the Sunshine Coast. In between are North Stradbroke and Moreton islands.

THE BAYSIDE – NORTH
Redcliffe, 35 km north of Brisbane, was the first white settlement in Queensland. The Aborigines called the place Humpybong or 'dead houses' and the name is still applied to the peninsula. Redcliffe is now an outer suburb of Brisbane and a popular place to retire to.

South of Redcliffe, Sandgate is another long running seaside resort, now more of an outer suburb.

THE BAYSIDE – SOUTH
Coastal towns south of the Brisbane River mouth include Wynnum, Ormiston, Cleveland and Redland Bay. Cleveland is the main access point for North Stradbroke Island. The Redland Bay area is a fertile market garden for Brisbane and a strawberry festival is held on the first weekend in September. There's an 1864 lighthouse at Cleveland Point and the 1853 Cleveland Court House is now a restaurant.

Ormiston House in Wellington St, Ormiston, is a very fine home built in 1862 and open for inspection Sunday afternoons between March and November. The first commercially grown sugar cane in Queensland came from this site. Whepstead on Main Rd, Wellington Point, is another early home, built in 1874. It's now also a restaurant.

NORTH & SOUTH STRADBROKE ISLANDS
Until 1896 the two Stradbroke islands were one but in that year a storm cut the sand spit joining the two at Jumpinpin. Today South Stradbroke is virtually uninhabited but it's a popular day-trip from the Gold Coast.

North Stradbroke is a larger island with a permanent population and it's a deservedly popular escape from Brisbane, despite which it is relatively unspoilt. Straddie is a sand island but there's plenty of vegetation as well as three budget priced hostels and several camping grounds.

In 1828 Dunwich was established on the west coast of the island as a quarantine station for immigrants but in 1850 a ship brought cholera and the cemetery tells the sad story of the 28 victims of the outbreak that followed. Dunwich, Amity Point and Point Lookout, the three small centres on the island, are all in the north and connected by paved roads. The southern part of the island is more remote and swampier.

Straddie has plenty of lovely beaches, good surfing, some bays and inlets around Point Lookout, lots of wildlife and good bushwalking around Blue Lake, Brown Lake and Eighteen Mile Swamp. On the ocean side you may even spot a humpback whale or two on their northward migration to the Great Barrier Reef where they breed during the winter months. Dolphins and porpoises are common.

Activities

Apart from beach activities there's the island to explore. Sealed roads only run between the three centres in the north and across the island from Dunwich to Blue Lake; in any case you have to walk the last 2.7 km to the lake. You can swim in the freshwater Blue Lake or nearby Tortoise Lagoon, or walk along the track and watch for snakes, goannas, golden wallabies and birds.

If you're staying at one of the Point Lookout hostels, you may be able to join a tour to investigate some of the island. Otherwise, you could walk from Point Lookout down the beach then 2½ km inland to Blue Lake – 11 km one way in all. If this sounds too much, catch the local bus to Dunwich and then hitch or walk the eight km to Blue Lake. Brown Lake, about three km along the Blue Lake road from Dunwich, offering deep freshwater swimming, is more accessible.

If you want to hike the 15 to 20 km across the island from Dunwich to Point Lookout, a number of dirt track loops break the monotony of the bitumen road. A pleasant diversion is to Myora Springs, surrounded by lush vegetation and walking tracks, near the coast about four km north of Dunwich.

Places to Stay

Dunwich, Amity Point and Point Lookout have caravan parks all with tent sites costing $7 for two people. Foreshore camping at $2 per person is allowed at designated areas on the east and north coasts but you can't camp in the Blue Lake National Park. Dunwich has two caravan parks and Amity Point one, right by the sea. Both these townships have a general store but no pub, restaurant or supermarket.

At Point Lookout the *Stradbroke Island Carapark* (tel 49 8127), has four self-contained cabins at $35 double and some on-site vans for $25. Point Lookout also has three hostels. Follow the main road around the corner from the Stradbroke Hotel (the only pub on the island) to the first of these. On the left, perched on a hill, is *Point Lookout Backpackers Hostel* (tel 49 8279). At $10 a night, with space for 32, it has good dorms in self-contained units. Tea and coffee are free. Tours of the island and fishing/boat trips are offered. If you call from Dunwich, someone from the hostel may come and pick you up.

A little further up the road on the right-hand side, the *Headland Chalet* (tel 49 8252) is an old guest house, with motel type rooms, overlooking beautiful Main Beach. These have a fridge, tea/coffee making gear, a maximum of four beds and cost $9 per person sharing, or $30 double. There is a pool, a games and TV room, free washing machines and a small kitchen plus a budget priced restaurant with a fantastic view. Downhill to the left is *Samarinda Holiday Village* (tel 49 8213) with shared cabin accommodation from $7.50 per night, singles/doubles at $30. There's a licensed restaurant, TV room and laundry. Some of the cabins are self-contained and all have tea making facilities.

Places to Eat

At Point Lookout, the *Stradbroke Hotel* has meals and a $6 Sunday roast lunch smorgasbord. It has a great beer garden with an ocean outlook and a two metre pet carpet snake. *Samarinda Holiday Village* has cheap meals and on Thursday nights a party night – live music and a three course meal for \$15. *Headland Chalet* specialises in local seafood at budget prices.

The general stores in each of the three centres have some supplies and a few take-aways. If you're fixing your own meals bring basic supplies and alcohol as the mark-up on the island is significant.

Getting There & Around

Cleveland, on the southern Bayside, is the departure point from the mainland and there are numerous ways of getting from Brisbane to the island – train/water taxi, bus/water taxi, train/ferry, bus/ferry, through-bus, your own vehicle or a hostel tour from Brisbane.

Cheapest is the Southern Cross Bus Company (tel 376 3791) which runs a bus a day, two on Fridays, direct from Brisbane to the island and return. Buses leave from stop 1 outside the Transit Centre, calling at 190 Ann St about 10 minutes later. The return fare is \$14, including the ferry, and it stops at all three centres on North Stradbroke. Though the ferry trip takes an hour, the advantage of this service is that you don't have to get off the bus from start to finish. It takes about 2½ hours from the city to Point Lookout.

If you're going independently, allow time to catch the last water taxis and ferries which most days leave Cleveland at 6 pm. Trains leave Brisbane for Cleveland (\$2.40 one way) about every half hour from 5 am. The journey takes about an hour. Bayside Buslines (tel 893 1048) runs a weekday and Saturday morning 45 minute service between Brisbane and Cleveland on the Bayside Bullet (routes 621 and 622), plus all stops buses (Nos 600, 611, 615, 625) every day which take about an hour. Both depart about every half hour (less frequently at weekends) from Elizabeth St in central Brisbane.

In Cleveland the buses stop at the railway station, a km or so from the water taxi and ferry terminals. About 15 minutes before water taxis are due to leave for Straddie, free buses pick up travellers at the station. Two water taxi companies operate between Cleveland and Dunwich – the *Spirit of Stradbroke* (tel 286 2666) and the *Stradbroke Flyer* (tel 286 1964). The *Spirit* charges \$6 one way while the *Flyer* costs \$2 more but includes a local bus to your destination on the island. The water taxi trip takes 20 minutes and, with both companies, you get a dollar or so discount on a return ticket. Water taxis depart about hourly from 6 am to 6 pm daily with a break from 12 noon to 2 pm.

Stradbroke Ferries (tel 286 2666) run the vehicle ferry from Cleveland to Dunwich about 12 times a day, less often on Saturdays. It costs \$44 return for a vehicle plus one adult, and it also takes passengers for \$4 return. Last departures from Cleveland are normally at 6 pm but there are late ferries at 7 pm on Sundays and 7.15 and 8 pm on Fridays.

Green's Bus Service (tel 49 9228) plies between the three centres on the island and meets most water taxis and ferries. If you get stuck at Dunwich, you can hitch or call Stradbroke Taxi Service (tel 49 9124). It's roughly 20 km from Dunwich to Point Lookout. It's possible to rent a 4WD vehicle on the island for \$50 per day. Ask at the hostels.

MORETON ISLAND (Population 200)

North of North Stradbroke, Moreton Island is less visited and still almost a wilderness. Apart from a few rocky headlands it's all sand with Mt Tempest, towering to 280 metres, probably the highest sand hill in the world. It's a strange landscape alternating between bare sand, forest, lakes and swamps, with a 30 km surf beach along the east side. The island has prolific bird life and at its northern tip there's a lighthouse built in 1857. Some sand mining has been going on but it's being phased out and 89% of the island is a national park. There are several wrecks off the west coast.

Moreton Island has no paved roads but 4WD vehicles can travel along beaches –

seek local advice about tides and creek crossings – and a few cross-island tracks. Tangalooma, halfway down the western side of the island, is a popular tourist resort sited at an old whaling station. The only other settlements, all on the west coast, are Bulwer near the north-west tip, Cowan Cowan between Bulwer and Tangalooma, and Kooringal near the southern tip. There are shops at Kooringal and Bulwer but they're expensive so bring what you can from the mainland. For a bit of shark spotting, go to the Tangalooma Resort about 5 pm when they dump all the garbage off the end of the jetty.

Walking is the only way to get around without your own vehicle and you need several days to explore the island. There are some trails around the resort area and it's about 14 km from Tangalooma or the Ben-Ewa camping site on the west side to Eagers Creek campsite on the east, then seven km up the beach to Blue Lagoon and a further six to Cape Moreton at the north-east tip.

Mt Tempest is about three km inland from Eagers Creek. A similar distance south and inland from Tangalooma is an area of bare sand known as The Desert, while the Big Sandhills and the Little Sandhills are towards the narrow southern end of the island. The biggest lakes and some swamps are in the north-east, and the west coast from Cowan Cowan past Bulwer is also swampy.

Places to Stay

A twin room at the *Tangalooma Resort* (tel (07) 268 6333) costs from $105 for one night and from $190 for two nights. The $30 return fare to the island is not included.

National park camping sites, with water, toilets and cold showers are at Ben-Ewa and False Patch Wrecks, both between Cowan Cowan and Tangalooma, and at Eagers Creek and Blue Lagoon on the northern half of the ocean coast. Camping is allowed behind foredunes in many places. For information and

camping bookings and permits, contact the National Parks Service (tel (07) 202 0200) at 55 Priors Pocket Rd, Moggill in western Brisbane, or on the island at False Patch Wrecks (tel (075) 48 2710). It's also possible to pitch a tent under the trees by the beach at Reeders Point. There are a few holiday flats or houses for rent at Kooringal, Cowan Cowan or Bulwer.

Getting There & Away

Boat The *Tangalooma Flyer*, a fast catamaran operated by the resort, goes from Brisbane usually daily except Thursday. You can use it for a day-trip to the island ($28 including lunch) or as a ferry if you're going to camp ($20 one way). In Brisbane the dock is at Holt St, off Kingsford Smith Drive in Eagle Farm. Phone 221 8555 or (075) 48 2666 for timetable information and bookings – it's advisable to book a day in advance. Nomad Safaris (tel 277 5043) runs 4WD camping tours to Moreton Island from Brisbane.

Vehicle Ferries The *Moreton Venture* (tel 895 1000) goes four days a week to Tangalooma or to Reeders Point from Whyte Island, which is joined to the mainland by road.

Other ferries include the *Combie Trader II* (tel 203 6399) between Scarborough and Bulwer, normally daily except Tuesday, $35 one way or $65 return for an average vehicle with driver and three passengers, $10 one way or $15 return for pedestrians.

Bribie-Moreton Ferry Services (tel 888 2209) go daily to Bulwer and Cowan Cowan from near Spinnaker Sound, Bribie Island. Bribie Island Barge Services (tel (075) 48 1499) go to Bulwer from Toorbul Point, Bribie Island. Ferry crossings take 1½ to two hours and it's advisable to book.

ST HELENA ISLAND

Just six km out from the mouth of the Brisbane River, little St Helena Island used to be a high security prison from 1867 to 1932. There are remains of several prison buildings on the island, plus the first passenger tramway in Brisbane which, when built in 1884, had cars pulled by horses. Sandy beaches and mangroves alternate around the island's coast.

Several outfits run day-trips to St Helena including guided tours on the island. Adai Cruises (tel 262 6978) leaves from the BP Marina on Kingsford Smith Drive, Breakfast Creek, at 9 am on Saturdays and Sundays, returning at 5 pm. The $20 price includes lunch, but it costs an extra $3 to get onto the island. St Helena Ferries (tel 393 3726) goes for $12 most days from Manly harbour, opposite Cardigan Parade, on the south Bayside. You can reach Manly from central Brisbane in about 35 minutes by train. Koala Cruises started running Thursday and Saturday trips to St Helena in 1988.

OTHER ISLANDS
Bishop Island

Tiny Bishop Island, almost in the river mouth, is artificial, with a series of hulks along its beaches to combat erosion. It has a tavern, swimming pool, picnic/barbecue areas and some cabin accommodation. There's a small mangrove swamp with some bird life. Yulara Marine Tours (tel 283 4334) runs a ferry service to Bishop Island from the Brisbane Riverside Centre on Wednesdays, Fridays and Sundays. Fare is $10, or $19.50 including lunch.

Coochie Island

Coochie Island is a 10 minute ferry ride from Victoria Point on the southern Bayside. It's a popular outing from the mainland, with good beaches, but more built-up than most other Moreton Bay islands you can visit. You can rent bicycles, boats, catamarans and surf skis on the island. The ferry runs continuously from 8 am to 5.30 or 6 pm on weekends and holidays, less often on other days.

Russell Island

Russell Island, between the south end of North Stradbroke and the mainland, is also inhabited. It's about seven km long. The interesting Green Dragon Museum is in the north-west of the island. St Helena Ferries (tel 393 3726) runs cruises there from Manly harbour on the southern Bayside. There's a three or four times daily ferry service (tel 286 2666) from the Banana St ramp in Redland Bay, which does a loop round Russell and nearby Lamb, Macleay and Karragarra islands.

Bribie Island

Bribie Island at the north end of Moreton Bay, is 31 km long but apart from the southern end where there are a couple of small towns, little of the island has been touched. There's a bridge across Pumicestone Passage from the mainland to Bellara on the south-west coast. Bongaree, just south of Bellara, is the main town. Buses run there from Caboolture and Brisbane. There's good surfing on the ocean side and a calm channel towards the mainland. Bongaree and Bellara, and Woorim on the south-east coast, have a few motels and holiday flats in the $30 to $40 double range and there are some restaurants too.

The Sunshine Coast

The stretch of coast from the top of Bribie Island to Noosa is known as the Sunshine Coast. It's much less neon lit and commercial than the Gold Coast and renowned for fine beaches and surfing. The northern half of the Sunshine Coast, from Maroochydore, is less built-up than the southern half.

North of Noosa is the Cooloola wilderness region and Rainbow Beach, an access point for Fraser Island. Inland from the Sunshine Coast the towns along the Bruce Highway, the main road north, have a series of artificial tourist attractions.

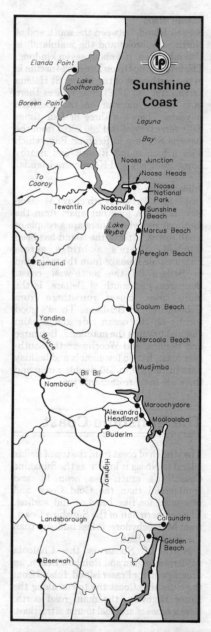

Getting There & Away

Air The Sunshine Coast has airports at Maroochydore and Noosa. Sunstate and Sungold fly from Brisbane ($46), Air NSW and East-West from Sydney ($207 with East-West, standby $166, cheaper with Air NSW). Air NSW and Australian also fly from Melbourne.

Bus Skennars runs about 30 buses daily connecting Brisbane with the Sunshine Coast and its hinterland towns. It's about two hours from Brisbane to Maroochydore, three hours to Noosa. In Brisbane the buses leave from the transit centre except for two daily services from the airport.

To head north up the Bruce Highway from the Sunshine Coast, you first take a bus to Nambour or Cooroy on the highway. Skennars' last bus from Noosa to Cooroy leaves in the early afternoon. From Cooroy to Noosa their last departure is 8.15 pm. There's also the local Noosa District Bus Lines which links Noosa with towns on the Bruce Highway.

You can call Skennars in Maroochydore (tel 43 1011) or Noosa (tel 47 3434). In conjunction with an interstate journey on Deluxe you can use their twice daily free buses between Brisbane and the Sunshine Coast. Ambassador Coachlines (Brisbane, tel 221 9555) and Skennars operate daily services between the Sunshine Coast and Sydney.

Train The most convenient stations for the Sunshine Coast are Nambour and Cooroy. There are services daily to these places from Brisbane and from the north.

CABOOLTURE (Population 6451)

This region, 49 km north of Brisbane, once had a large Aboriginal population. Nowadays it is a prosperous dairy centre famous for its yoghurt. It also has two of the most interesting of the numerous attractions which line the Bruce Highway heading north.

The Abbey Museum on Old Toorbul Point Rd is a world social history museum, looked after by a monastic movement and open on Tuesdays, Thursdays and Saturdays. Its 4500 item collection had been housed in London, Cyprus, Egypt and Sri Lanka before finding its home in Australia. Admission is $3.

Caboolture Historical Village on Beerburrum Rd, open daily from 10 am to 3 pm, has about 30 early Australian buildings in a bush setting. Admission is again $3.

GLASSHOUSE MOUNTAINS

Shortly after Caboolture, the Glasshouse Mountains are a dramatic visual starting point for the Sunshine Coast. They're a bizarre series of volcanic crags rising abruptly out of the plain to 300 metres or more. They were named by Captain Cook. Depending on whose story you believe, he either noted the reflections of the glass-smooth rock sides of the mountains, or he thought they looked like glass furnaces in his native Yorkshire. The mountains are popular with rock climbers although you can walk up some of them, with some steep scrambling.

The Bruce Highway today veers away from the Glasshouse Mountains after Caboolture, but you can take the slightly longer Old Bruce Highway loop through Beerburrum, Glasshouse Mountains village, Beerwah and Landsborough. From Glasshouse Mountains village a road leads 10 km west to a good lookout point.

There are a few caravan/camping parks, hotels and motels in the area.

CALOUNDRA (Population 16,758)

At the southern end of the beach strip, Caloundra has some decent beaches but by comparison with places further north on the Sunshine Coast it's a bit faded these days. Bulcock Beach, good for windsurfing, is just down from the main street, overlooking the north end of Bribie Island.

Points of interest include the Queensland Air Museum at Caloundra Aerodrome,

open Wednesday, Saturday and Sunday from 10 am to 4 pm. There's a two-thirds scale replica of Captain Cook's ship the *Endeavour*, on display from 9 am to 4.45 pm daily at 3 Landsborough Parade, Seafarer's Wharf. You can take cruises around the channels and Bribie Island from Caloundra.

Information

There's a tourist information office (tel 91 3744) on Caloundra Rd. The Skennars bus station (tel 91 2555) is on Minchinton St.

Places to Stay & Eat

Between Bulcock St and the beach, at 27-29 Leeding Terrace, there's a good hostel, *Back Packers United* (tel 91 6278). Cheapest motel is the *Caloundra Motel* (tel 91 1411) at 30 Bowman Rd with air-con singles/doubles for $20/22. Caloundra's main street, Bulcock St, has lots of restaurants.

MAROOCHYDORE AREA

North from Caloundra the coast is built up most of the way to the triple towns of Mooloolaba, Alexandra Headland and Maroochydore. Mooloolaba, has the brightest atmosphere with a beach, a couple of lively seafront pubs and eateries, the odd nightspot (live bands at weekends in the Mooloolaba Hotel) and a smattering of Bali boutiques. Alexandra Headland has a long sandy beach, and Maroochydore is the main centre with both an ocean beach and the Maroochy River with lots of pelicans and a few islands. There's decent surf in several spots.

Information

Tourist information is available at the Sunshine Coast Tourism & Development Board (tel 43 2411) on Alexandra Parade, the main road passing through Alexandra Headland. You can also get info and free maps from the Cotton Tree Tourist Centre (tel 43 1629) at 22 King St, Cotton Tree, Maroochydore.

Places to Stay

Maroochydore has both a YHA and a backpackers hostel. The modern YHA *Holiday Hostel* (tel 43 3151) is on Schirrmann Drive, a couple of turns off Bradman Ave. Nightly cost is $8 and the hostel's open all day and has a pool.

Zord's Inn for Travellers & Backpackers (tel 43 1755) is at 15 The Esplanade, opposite the river. The *Maroochy River Motel* (tel 43 3142) at 361 Bradman Ave has backpacker accommodation for $10 as well as normal motel doubles for $30.

Otherwise there's the usual selection of caravan/camping parks and motels. Most of the caravan parks are in Maroochydore. One of the most popular with travellers is the *Cotton Tree Caravan Park & Camping Area* (tel 43 1253) on Cotton Tree Parade beside the river. In Mooloolaba there's the *Parkyn Parade Caravan Park* (tel 44 1201). Tent sites in both places are $6.50 for two but there are no on-site vans. For on-site vans at $16 or $17 try the *Maroochy River Caravan Park* (tel 43 3078) on Diura St, Maroochydore.

Motels are generally rather expensive. Apart from the Maroochy River Motel, you could try the *Kyamba Court Motel* (tel 44 2439) at 94 Brisbane Rd, Mooloolaba, or the *Headland International Motel* (tel 44 1087) on Buderim Ave, Mooloolaba. Both usually have some rooms in the $25/30 region.

Getting Around

The *Sandpiper* water taxi (tel 48 5821) crosses the Maroochy River to the north shore, where there's a recreation reserve, three times daily. You can hire boats at several places in Maroochydore and Mooloolaba, or take river cruises at Maroochydore. Mokes can be hired from The Moke Bloke (tel 43 5777) on the corner of Third Ave and Aerodrome Rd in Maroochydore. Trusty Car Hire (tel 43 6100) at 24 Aerodrome Rd has Mokes, 4WDs and cars.

MAROOCHYDORE TO NOOSA

West of Maroochydore you can go on to Nambour or turn across the Maroochy River at Bli Bli to follow the coast road up to Noosa. The 45 km stretch from Maroochydore to Noosa is much less developed than south of Maroochydore. There are usually enough quiet little spots in between civilisation to allow you to find your own private beach.

Bli Bli, 10 km from Maroochydore, has Fairyland Castle – open daily from 9 am to 5 pm. A scattering of accommodation places dots the coast north from here. In Marcoola for instance the *Marcoola Motel* has rooms at $24/28 while the *Pacific Palms Motel* has doubles for $28. Yaroomba has a big Hyatt Hotel development going on, while Coolum is a favourite with surfers. *Lorikeet Lodge* north of Coolum has doubles for $25.

NOOSA (Population 17,071)

A surfers' Mecca since the early 1960s, Noosa has now become a resort for the fashionable – with beaches, a spot of nightlife, the fine coastal Noosa National Park and, just to the north, the walks, waterways and beaches of the Cooloola area. Noosa remains a far cry from the hype of the Gold Coast and with more character than the rest of the Sunshine Coast.

Orientation

Noosa is actually a string of small linked centres – with confusingly similar names – stretching back from the mouth of the Noosa River and along its maze of tributary creeks and lakes. The slickest resort area, with a distinct Mediterranean feel, is Noosa Heads, on the coast between the river mouth and rocky Noosa Head. From Noosa Heads two roads lead back to Noosaville, about three km away. One goes across an island known as Noosa Sound, the other circles round to the south through Noosa Junction with most of the area's shops and cheaper restaurants.

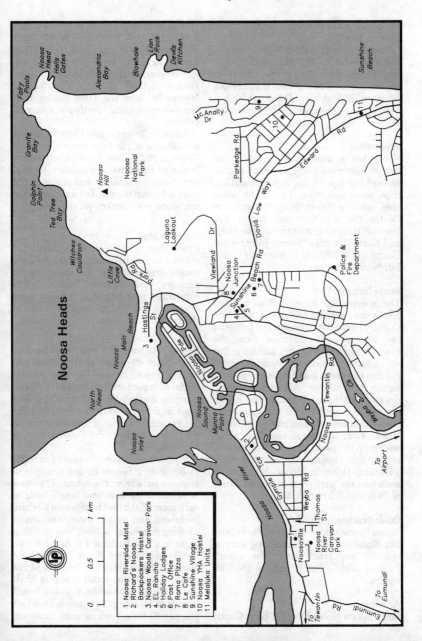

Noosa Heads

1 Noosa Riverside Motel
2 Richard's Noosa
3 Backpackers Hostel
4 Noosa Woods Caravan Park
5 EL Rancho
6 Holiday Lodges
7 Post Office
8 Roma Pizza
9 Le Cafe
10 Sunshine Village
11 Noosa YHA Hostel
   Melaluka Units

0   0.5   1 km

Noosaville is the departure point for most river cruises.

Further inland beyond Noosaville you reach Tewantin, six km from Noosa Heads. Another centre, on the coast three km south-east of Noosa Heads and Noosa Junction, is Sunshine Beach, which has two of the cheapest accommodation places.

Information
Noosa has a number of privately run tourist information offices which double as booking agents for accommodation, trips, tours and so on. Two of the better ones are the Seven Flags Information Centre (tel 49 7344) on Weyba Rd, Noosaville, open from 9 am to 5 pm daily, and Noosa Junction Tourist Information Centre (tel 47 3798) at 15 Sunshine Beach Rd, Noosa Junction.

Noosa National Park
The spectacular cape at Noosa Head marks the northern end of the Sunshine Coast. The coast and hinterland for about two km in each direction from the headland is a national park and it has fine walks, great coastal scenery and a string of bays on the north side whose waves draw surfers from all over. Alexandria Bay on the east side is the best sandy beach. The main vehicle access to the national park is from the corner of Hastings St in Noosa Heads, from where you can drive about one km to the park. You can also drive up to Laguna Lookout in the park from Viewland Drive in Noosa Junction, or walk into the park from McAnally Drive or Parkedge Rd in Sunshine Beach.

Other Beaches
Noosa Heads main beach tends to be busy but Sunshine Beach has a long strip of sparsely populated sand. The water's rougher here – but it can be good for surfing.

Activities
Water Sports Noosa Dive & Sports Centre

at the end of Hastings St in Noosa Heads offers dive trips for $25, more with gear included. Dive courses here cost $300 to $390. They also rent out windsurfers, snorkel gear, surf mats and so on. Jacques' Diving School in The Cockleshell, Noosaville, and the Dive Boatique at Noosa Junction also run dive courses and/ or trips.

Noosa Sailboards (tel 47 5890) rents out windsurfers at the river mouth. Seawind Charters (tel 47 3042) at 10 Cooloosa St, Sunshine Beach has windsurfers, jet skis, and yachts for hire. Several places on the river in Noosaville and Tewantin also rent out boats, windsurfers, jet skis, etc.

Places to Stay
Other than in hostels, accommodation prices can rise as much as 50% in busy times, even 100% in the December to January peak season. Estate agents sometimes rent homes at bargain rates during the low season – look on Sunshine Beach Rd.

Hostels *Richard's Noosa Backpackers Hostel* (tel 49 8151) at 9 William St, Munna Point, Noosaville, is a popular hostel with good cooking and sitting areas, a garden and a pool. Nightly cost is $6 a head in dorms or double rooms and the owners will help you fix up cheap trips on the river or north to the Cooloola area or Fraser Island.

In Sunshine Beach *Melaluka Units* (tel 47 3663) at 7 Selene St are a couple of minutes walk from the beach. The three bedroom units have two single beds in each room. Each unit has its own kitchen, bathroom and sitting room, and use of washing machines is free. You pay $8 a night in a unit without TV, $9 with TV.

Also in Sunshine Beach, *Noosa YHA Hostel* (tel 47 4739) at 35 Douglas St is a small, fairly basic hostel charging $8. It has overflow space in the pleasant, bright *Sunshine Village* at 26 Stevens St, where you pay $9 for a bunk in units for seven, each with kitchen, bathroom and sitting room.

Motels & Holiday Units The best area for cheaper motels is along Gympie Terrace and Hilton Terrace, the main road through Noosaville. *Noosa Riverside Motel*, on Gympie Terrace, is about as cheap as you'll get. In the low season singles/doubles are $22/25; rooms have their own well equipped kitchens. The only drawback is the 9 am check out time. The *Blue River Lodge*, two doors along, has similar prices. In Noosa Junction, *El Rancho Holiday Lodges* on Noosa Rd, just up the hill from the post office, has doubles off season for $25 and family rooms from $35.

Holiday units to try in Noosaville, all charging between $25 and $40 double, include *Noosa River Beach* (tel 49 7873), 281 Gympie Terrace; *Noosa Villa* (tel 49 7131), 86 Hilton Terrace; and *River Breeze* (tel 49 7922), 100 Hilton Terrace.

In Noosa Heads what little cheaper accommodation there is gets snapped up pretty quickly. There are a few rooms upstairs from *Annabelle's Restaurant* on Hastings St which cost $40 for three off season. *Seabreeze Beachfront Holiday Flats* (tel 47 4011) on the Hastings St beachfront has doubles at $30 to $55. At 16 Noosa Drive, *Oasis Palms* (tel 47 5277) has doubles from $25 to $70 and *Mendoza's Noosa Motel* (tel 47 3238) has singles/doubles from $25/28 to $45/50.

Camping & Caravan Parks *Noosa Woods Caravan Park* is close to the centre of things at the end of Hastings St in Noosa Heads and charges $9 double for camping, $20 for an on-site van. Tent sites at *Noosa River Caravan Park* (tel 49 8950) on Robert St, Noosaville, are $6 to $8 double. There are also on-site vans for $18 to $25 double.

Right on the beach at the south end of Sunshine Beach, *Sunrise Beachfront Holiday Village* has on-site vans for $18

double and 'Fijian hutels' (basically cabins) at $23.

Places to Eat
Most of the cheaper places are on Sunshine Beach Rd, the main street in Noosa Junction. *Roma Pizza*, at the south end of the street, is a sit-down restaurant which does good pizzas from $4, as well as other dishes.

Near the north (roundabout) end of the street, on the east side, *Noosa Pizza Pasta Cafe* has pizza from $6 and pasta from $3.50. *Le Cafe* in Suntop Plaza on the same side of the street is good for breakfast or light meals. There are also Greek, Mexican and Chinese places on this street.

Hastings St in Noosa Heads has smart, expensive restaurants plus some cheaper cafes in a couple of arcades. *Le Scoops* in the Bay Village Arcade, with outdoor tables, has lunch specials and also breakfasts.

In Noosaville there are several places, mainly take-aways, along Gympie Terrace.

Entertainment
The *Underground*, opposite Coles supermarket on Lanyana Way, Noosa Junction, is the most popular disco. It's half price Wednesday, Thursday and Friday nights but at all times there's a ban on 'faded jeans, shorts, T-shirts, thongs and soiled sandshoes'! Noosa Cine Centre on Sunshine Beach Rd, Noosa Junction, shows mainstream general release movies.

Getting Around
Bus Noosa District Bus Lines (tel 42 8649) runs a local service between Noosa, Cooroy, Eumundi and Nambour. Monday to Friday there are about 11 services in each direction between Sunshine Beach, Noosa Junction, Hastings St in Noosa Heads, Noosa Sound, Thomas St in Noosaville, and Tewantin. Some also go to Noosa National Park and about four a day in each direction add Cooroy, Eumundi and Nambour and the Big Pineapple to

their route. On Saturdays and Sundays there are fewer services. Last runs start about 5 pm Monday to Saturday and 3.50 pm on Sunday.

Car Hire Mokes are available from the tourist information centre on Sunshine Beach Rd, the main street in Noosa Junction, or from Noosa Harbour Resort (tel 47 5322) in Quamby Place, Noosa Sound, or Noosaville Hire (tel 49 7627) or Konomy Kar Rentals (tel 47 3368). Generally they cost $16 a day plus insurance and km charge. You can't take Mokes north of the Noosa River. Trusty Car Hire (tel 47 4777) has Mokes, 4WDs and cars. Or try Rent-A-Bomb (tel 47 3374). Sunshine 4WD Hire (tel 47 3702) at 42 Hastings St, Noosa Heads is another place renting 4WDs – or try phoning 28 2981. You can also try Budget, Avis, Hertz and Thrifty.

Bicycle & Moped Hire Noosa Dive & Sports Centre at the end of Hastings St rents out mopeds for $8 an hour, $16 a half day and $22 a full day. You can rent bicycles from a shop in the small Noosa Sound shopping centre for $2.50 an hour, $6 a half day, or $12 a day.

Tours & Cruises Most cruises up the Noosa River to Lakes Cooroibah and Cootharaba leave from the river beside Gympie Terrace in Noosaville. Half day or full day trips including a visit to the Kinaba national parks centre are between $28 and $40. With a 4WD trip to the coloured sands, the *Cherry Venture* wreck and maybe a rainforest walk added on, you pay about $50.

A straight 4WD tour north to the coloured sands and Rainbow Beach will cost you about $35 to $40 for five or six hours. You can also take 4WD tours to Fraser Island from Noosa – a day tour is $60, which is $15 to $20 more than from Rainbow Beach or Hervey Bay.

TEWANTIN & COOLOOLA

A couple of km upstream from Noosaville, the Noosa River takes a northward bend at Tewantin and widens out into Lake Cooroibah then Lake Cootharaba, which is at the south end of Cooloola National Park. The park stretches about 50 km north to Rainbow Beach. It's a varied wilderness area of mangrove-lined waterways, forest, heathland, and lakes which has plentiful bird life and lots of wildflowers in spring. Over on the coast here are the Teewah coloured sands.

Tewantin

The House of Bottles at 19 Myles St includes among its exhibits of bottles the 'Big Bottle', constructed out of 17,000 beer bottles. Tewantin also has the Big Shell on Gympie St. Both are open daily.

Lake Cooroibah Holiday Park (tel 47 1225), over the Noosa River ferry from Tewantin, has tent sites at $2 per person per night, lodge accommodation at $5 a head (minimum three people), and cabins for $25 (four berth) or $30 (six berth). There are also tennis courts, trail rides and an aviary.

Cooloola Coast

A vehicle ferry (6 am to 9 pm daily) crosses the river at Tewantin, giving access to the beach north of Noosa which stretches more than 50 km north to Double Island Point. In a 4WD you can go right up this beach, then across the back of Double Island Point and along a further 10 km or so of beach to the small town of Rainbow Beach, one of the access points for Fraser Island. On the way up to Double Island Point along the beach you pass high sand dunes and the Teewah coloured sand cliffs.

Lake Cootharaba

This 90 square km lake is about 20 km upstream from Tewantin. You can reach it by river from Noosaville or Tewantin. By land there's a 20 km direct road (eight km of it unsealed) from Tewantin to Boreen

Point on the west shore of the lake, or a longer paved route via Cooroy on the Bruce Highway and Pomona. Boreen Point has two caravan parks both with tent sites and at least one with on-site vans, plus a couple of motels and holiday units. You can rent windsurfers, canoes, sail cats and motor dinghies from Fred's Fleet Hire.

From Boreen Point the road continues five km north to Elanda Point, where there's a lovely lakeside camping ground ($5 per person for the first night, $2.50 thereafter) but beware of the mosquitoes. At the campground you can rent canoes, windsurfers or sail cats. The Cooloola National Park HQ (tel 85 3245) is also here.

Southern Cooloola

From Elanda Point the Cooloola Wilderness Trail, a 4WD track, heads 46 km north to meet the Gympie to Rainbow Beach road. There's also a seven km walking trail to the Cooloola National Park visitor centre at Kinaba Island (tel 49 7364) near the north end of Lake Cootharaba. This is the only land route to the visitor centre – most people reach it by boat. You can explore a long way further north up the Noosa River beyond Lake Cootharaba by walking trail or canoe and it's OK to camp in some places. There are also some trails over towards the ocean beach from the inland waterways.

Northern Cooloola

This part of the national park is easiest reached from the Rainbow Beach area. It includes camping grounds between Freshwater Lake and the eastern beach, and near Double Island Point on the north facing beach (both 4WD or foot access only). There are several walking tracks and the main vehicle access is from the Gympie to Rainbow Beach road, four km south of Rainbow Beach. The beach between Rainbow Beach and Double Island Point is part of the park. You can get information and camping permits for northern Cooloola from the national parks

information centre in Rainbow Beach (tel 86 3160).

BUDERIM AREA

This fruit growing centre is inland, just off the Bruce Highway on the road to Alexandra Headland. At Tanawha, where the road turns off the highway, Buderim Zoo & Koala Park is open daily from 9 am to 4.30 pm. Just up the highway from the turn-off there's the Super Bee complex, where you can watch beekeeping demos, taste honey and let your kids be entertained at the Three Bears Cottage, Model City, or on pony rides from The House That Jack Built. In Buderim itself is the Pioneer Cottage and Museum on Ballinger Crescent, open daily from 10 am to 4 pm, and a few art galleries. There are good walks nearby in the Footes Sanctuary.

Forest Glen, about four km up the Bruce Highway from the Buderim turn-off, has a drive-through deer sanctuary and a nocturnal house, both open from 9 am to 4 pm daily, plus the Moonshine Valley tropical fruit winery, where you can indulge in free tastings and tours daily except Monday.

NAMBOUR (Population 9579)

You often see sugar cane trains crossing the main street of this sugar growing town. Pineapples and other tropical fruit are also grown in the area and the 'Big Pineapple' is one of Nambour's two superbly kitsch 'big' creations. It looms by the highway at Woombye, about six km south of the town, and you can climb up inside this 15 metre fibreglass wonder to see the full story of pineapple cultivation. There's a whole tourist centre behind it including an animal nursery, a macadamia nut factory, and train rides around the plantation. The latest addition is boat rides through a greenhouse which displays latest agricultural technology and the 'superstar crops of the future'. Also at Woombye is Teddy Bear Land with more than 1400 of the cuddly wonders.

As if all that wasn't enough, six km

north of Nambour at Yandina is the 'Big Cow'. Yandina has lots more to try to stop anyone ever getting out of south-east Queensland – Australia's only Ginger Factory on Pioneer Rd which includes Ginger Town with a cottage of dolls, Partington's Historic Motor Garage also on Pioneer Rd, and Fairhill Native Plants on Fairhill Rd.

Wappa Dam, near Nambour, is a good picnic spot. Further up the highway at Eumundi, you can fossick for thunder eggs at Thunder Egg Farm.

WEST OF THE BRUCE HIGHWAY
Blackall Range

The mountains rise fairly close behind the coast and west of Nambour or Landsborough you can take the scenic Mapleton to Maleny road right along the ridge line of the Blackall Range. Mapleton Falls National Park is four km west of Mapleton and Kondalilla National Park is three km off the Mapleton to Montville stretch of the road. Both have rainforest and the Kondalilla Falls drop 80 metres into a rainforest valley, while at Mapleton Falls Pencil Creek plunges 120 metres. This is a great area for exploring – there's lots of bird life and several walking tracks in the parks. The *Mapleton Hotel* is a good place for a counter meal and/or a cold beer.

The small town of Flaxton, five km south of Mapleton, has a miniature English village and the Flaxton Inn in Tudor style. A little south, Montville has a whole series of tourist attractions including an art gallery, a comprehensive model train collection in The Dome on Main St (daily except Wednesday) and a variety of museums. If you continue north to Imbil, which has an unusual little museum, you come to the Borumba irrigation dam.

There's an alternative accommodation place, *Dealbata Host Farm* (tel 46 0936) on Booloumba Creek Rd, 40 km from Landsborough. It costs from $5 a night. Call for transportation assistance.

South Burnett

Further inland the South Burnett region includes Australia's most important peanut growing area. Kingaroy almost means 'peanuts' in Australia, not least because the big peanut himself, Joh Bjelke-Petersen, hails from here. There's a tourist office (tel 62 3199) at 128 Haly St, Kingaroy, open from Monday to Friday. You can inspect the peanut storage silos over the street, Monday to Friday at 10.30 am and 1.30 pm.

South-east of Kingaroy, Nanango is another peanut town but with an earlier history of gold mining. You can fossick for gold at Seven Mile Diggings, 11 km from Nanango. Murgon is the main town of the region north of Kingaroy. It has the Queensland Dairy Industry Museum, on Gayndah Rd. Six km south of Murgon the Cherbourg Aboriginal community runs a pottery and craft shop, open from Monday to Friday.

The Bunya Mountains, isolated outliers of the Great Dividing Range, rise abruptly to over 1000 metres, about 50 km south-west of Kingaroy by sealed road. The mountains are a national park with a variety of vegetation from rainforest to heathland. There are two camping grounds in the park, plus a network of walking tracks to numerous waterfalls and lookouts. The ranger office (tel 68 3127) is at Dandabah.

There's motel, hotel and caravan/camping accommodation in most of the South Burnett towns. Brisbane Bus Lines (tel 355 0034 in Brisbane) runs a daily service between Brisbane and Murgon ($26.50) through Nanango and Kingaroy ($22.50). Four times a week it goes on from Murgon to Mundubbera and Biloela. Once a week it goes on to Bundaberg.

Hervey Bay Area

North of the Sunshine and Cooloola coasts is 120 km long Fraser Island. The two mainland departure points for the island are Rainbow Beach in the south and Hervey Bay opposite Fraser's west coast. Inland on the Bruce Highway are Gympie, where you turn off for Rainbow Beach, and Maryborough, where you turn off for Hervey Bay.

GYMPIE (Population 10,800)

Gympie came into existence with an 1867 gold rush and gold continued to be mined here right up to 1920. For a week each October there's a big Gold Rush Festival in Gympie.

One of the four main national parks information centres in Queensland (tel 82 4189) is on the Bruce Highway as you enter Gympie from the south. It's open Monday to Friday from 9 am to 5 pm. In the same building there's a tourist information office (tel 82 5444), open from 8.30 am to 3.30 pm daily, and nearby is the interesting Gympie Gold Mining & Historical Museum (admission $2.50, open daily from 9 am to 5 pm).

A few km north of the town on Fraser Rd, Two Mile, a second museum is devoted to another source of Queensland's early wealth, the timber industry. The Woodworks Forestry & Timber Museum is open Monday to Friday from 10 am to 4 pm, Sundays 1 to 4 pm. Admission is $2. You can get info on camping in nearby state forests here.

Gympie has several motels and caravan/camping parks and it's on the main bus and rail routes north from Brisbane. The bus fare from Brisbane is $22 and the trip takes about 2½ hours. There are three or four trains daily from Brisbane: one-way fare is $17.60 and it takes about 3½ hours. From Gympie a good paved road leads through pine plantations to the coast at Tin Can Bay and Rainbow Beach, a gateway to Fraser Island. If you're not going to the coast here you could turn inland at Gympie and link up with the Burnett Highway, an inland route to Rockhampton (see the North to Rockhampton section).

Off the highway between Gympie and Maryborough you can camp on the *Miva Cattle Station* (tel 84 8132), founded in 1861, for $3 a head. Horse riding's available at $7 an hour.

RAINBOW BEACH (Population 726)

This little town, on the coast 70 km from Gympie, is an access point for Fraser Island and a base for visiting the northern part of Cooloola National Park.

From Rainbow Beach it's a 13 km drive north along the beach to Inskip Point where the Fraser Island ferries go from. South-east of the town the beach curves away 13 km to Double Island Point at the top of the Cooloola coast. One km along this beach is the 120 metre high Carlo sandblow and beyond it the coloured sand cliffs after which the town is named. You can walk behind or along the beach all the way from the town and up to the lighthouse on Double Island Point. The privately run Rainbow Beach Tourist Information Centre (tel 86 3227) has a list of other walks in the area. In a 4WD it's possible to drive to Noosa, 70 km south, along the beach most of the way.

The national parks office (tel 86 3160), for Fraser Island vehicle and camping permits and northern Cooloola National Park camping permits, is beside the main road as you enter Rainbow Beach.

Places to Stay & Eat

Rainbow Beach Backpackers (tel 86 3200) is on Cypress Ave, just off the road as you enter Rainbow Beach. It charges $9 per person per night in units with their own kitchen, bathroom, sitting room and TV.

The *Rainbow Beach Hotel-Motel* (tel 86 3125) near the beachfront has rooms from $35 a double during the week and there are two other slightly more expensive motels. *Rainbow Beach Caravan Park* (tel 86 3222) by the main road in the town has tent sites at $8 and on-site vans for $20 to $25 double. *Rainbow Waters Holiday Park* (tel 86 3200) is along Carlo Rd, a block back from Cypress Ave. Tent sites are $7, on-site vans $18, and there are bicycles to rent and a courtesy bus to and from the town.

There's a handful of take-aways and a couple of cafe/restaurants in the shopping centre near the beach.

Getting There & Away

A school bus leaves Polley's Depot in Gympie at 6 am and 3 pm for Rainbow Beach, and heads back from Rainbow Beach at 7.20 am and 4.45 pm. It's open to all comers and runs Monday to Friday, usually in the school holidays too.

Another way to Rainbow Beach is to hitchhike along the beaches up from Noosa or on to Fraser Island. If you have a 4WD vehicle you can drive this way too.

Getting Around

You can rent 4WD vehicles in Rainbow Beach. There are also tours to Fraser Island, plus half day trips for $20 to combinations of places like Carlo sandblow, the coloured sands, Double Island Point, Lake Freshwater, Cooloola rainforest and the 3000 tonne *Cherry Venture* wreck.

MARYBOROUGH (Population 20,111)

Today timber and sugar are Maryborough's major industries but its earlier importance as an industrial centre and port on the Mary River led to construction of a series of imposing Victorian buildings. Maryborough dates from 1847. You can pick up the *Walk & Drive Maryborough Heritage City* booklet detailing walking and driving routes around the town.

Tourist information is available from beside the 'Welcome to Timber City' sign on the highway, just after the bridge as you go north, or from the Maryborough & District Development Board on the corner of Wharf and Bazaar Sts in the centre. The greatest concentration of old buildings is on Wharf St. The imposing post office is just one of the buildings which reflect Maryborough's early prosperity – it was built in 1869. Some of the old hotels are also fine examples of Victoriana. A street market is held every Thursday in the town centre. Maryborough also has a railway museum in the old station on Lennox St.

There are several motels and caravan/camping parks in the town, plus budget accommodation too in some of the old hotels, including the *Criterion* in Wharf St. By bus Maryborough's about 3½ hours from Brisbane and costs $24. Sunstate and Sungold both fly to Maryborough from Brisbane. One-way fare is $74 (standby $60).

HERVEY BAY (Population 13,600)

The five small settlements which make up the town of Hervey Bay, on the bay of the same name, are popular family holiday spots in their own right, with no surf and a huge number of caravan parks, but of more interest is Fraser Island, for which Hervey Bay is a main stepping off point. Hervey Bay's best beach is at Torquay.

Orientation

The five little towns are strung along a 10 km long north facing stretch of coast. From west to east they are Point Vernon, Pialba, Scarness, Torquay and Urangan. Pialba is the main centre and the stopping point for long-distance buses. Fraser Island is 12 km across the Great Sandy Strait from Urangan, with Woody Island in between. Mary River Heads, departure point for one of the Fraser Island ferries, is 15 km south of Urangan.

Things to See

Hervey Bay Wildlife Park, open daily on the corner of Maryborough Rd and Fairway Drive, Pialba, has native Australian fauna from wedge-tailed eagles to koalas as well as introduced species like camels and water buffaloes. Crocodiles are fed at 11.30 am and lorikeets at 3 pm.

Vic Hislop, a locally based shark hunter, has some of his biggest catches, including great white sharks, on display in

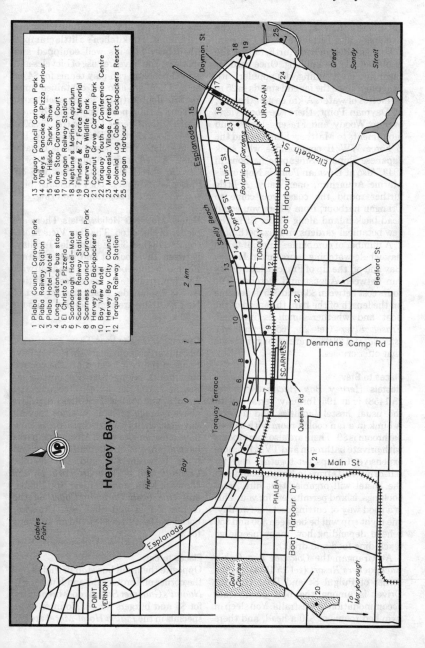

Hervey Bay

1 Pialba Council Caravan Park
2 Pialba Railway Station
3 Pialba Hotel–Motel
4 Long-distance bus stop
5 El Christo's Pizzeria
6 Scarborough Hotel–Motel
7 Scarness Railway Station
8 Scarness Council Caravan Park
9 Hervey Bay Backpackers
10 Bay View Motel
11 Hervey Bay City Council
12 Torquay Railway Station

13 Torquay Council Caravan Park
14 O'Rileys Pancake & Pizza Parlour
15 Vic Hislop Shark Show
16 One Stop Caravan Court
17 Urangan Railway Station
18 Neptune's Marine Aquarium
19 Flinders & Z Force Memorial
20 Hervey Bay Wildlife Park
21 Coconut Grove Caravan Park
22 Torquay Youth & Conference Centre
23 Melanesia Village (resort)
24 Colonial Log Cabin Backpackers Resort
25 Urangan Harbour

his Shark Show at the corner of the Esplanade and Elizabeth St in Urangan.

Urangan Pier, a little further along the Esplanade, is 1.4 km long. Once used for sugar and oil handling, it's popular with fishermen since the far end stands in 25 to 30 metres of water. A km east of the pier, at Dayman Point, there are good views over to Woody and Fraser islands, and monuments to Matthew Flinders and the Z Force WW II commandos who sank Japanese ships in Singapore harbour in 1943. Also at Dayman Point is Neptune's Marine Aquarium, open daily. A little further round the coast you come to Urangan harbour, from where you could head back inland along Miller St to the new botanical gardens on Elizabeth St.

A number of companies run half to full day whale watching tours out of Hervey Bay and off the tip of Fraser Island. They run between August and October. The tours cost between $35 and $45 depending on the length of the trip, the speed of the boat and whether lunch is included. *Fraser Flyer* (tel 25 1655), and MV *Islander* (tel 28 9370) are among the boats that offer cruises.

Places to Stay

Hostels *Hervey Bay Backpackers* (tel 28 1458) is at 195 Torquay Terrace, with the usual hostel facilities and a pool. A bunk in a fan cooled room with shared bathroom is $9. There are also some rooms with private bathroom and TV, a bit more expensive. Groups get together here for self-drive 4WD trips to Fraser Island and the hostel will organise tent hire, ferry bookings, island permits, etc for you. This is a good way of cutting costs: a two day, one night trip will be between $30 and $50 a head depending how many people go (excluding food and drink).

At Urangan the *Colonial Log Cabin Backpackers Resort* (tel 25 1844), on the corner of Pulgul St and Boat Harbour Drive, is among the best backpacker accommodation in Australia. You sleep in twin bed rooms at $10 a head, and there

are big sitting, TV and eating areas and bathrooms. The kitchen's a little cramped when busy but it's well equipped and spotless. You have free use of bicycles and a good pool and can play tennis for $4 an hour. There are also self-contained units for $30 double (plus $5 for each extra person). A third possibility is the *Torquay Youth & Conference Centre* (tel 25 2506) at 449 Boat Harbour Drive, Torquay. It's an associate YHA hostel and is usually quiet. A bed is $8.50 plus $1.50 for a sleeping sheet. The hostel offers 10% off Fraser Island tours. They'll usually pick you up from the bus stop if you ring.

Hotels, Motels & Holiday Flats There are plenty of these too. The *Bay View Motel* (tel 28 1134) at 399 Esplanade, Torquay, between Tavistock St and Dennis Camp Rd, has doubles between $25 and $40 with TV, fan, fridge and tea/coffee facilities. At 533 Esplanade, Urangan, just east of New St, there are some holiday units for $130 a week.

Camping & On-site Vans There are at least 19 caravan/camping parks in Hervey Bay. Some of the best located are the council run parks along the Esplanade at Scarness (tel 28 1274), Torquay (tel 25 1578) and Pialba. Tent sites are a little above average price at $9 since they all have electricity – and these parks only have a few on-site vans. Most other parks have a range of on-site vans, cabins and units between $20 and $40 double. *Coconut Grove Caravan Park* on the corner of Main and McLiver Sts, Pialba, and *One Stop Caravan Court* on the corner of Pier and Shell Sts, Urangan, both have tent sites at $7 and on-site vans for $20.

Places to Eat

Opposite the main bus stop in Pialba, on the corner of Torquay Rd and Hunter St, *Naomi's Gourmet Snacks* does breakfasts for $5 and burgers for $4. Counter meal specials in the *Pialba Hotel-Motel* are $5.

There's also *Scarlets* steakhouse and a piano bar here. The *Scarborough Hotel-Motel* at 24 Esplanade, Scarness, has good counter meals, take-aways and pizzas.

Several more places are scattered along the Esplanade, including *El Cristo's Pizzeria* on the corner of Zephyr St at Scarness. *O'Riley's Pancake & Pizza Parlour* is at 446 Esplanade, Torquay, and a little further along is *Gringo's Mexican Cantina*. The *Seven Seas* at 573 Esplanade, Urangan, is said to be the best seafood restaurant in Hervey Bay. It's open from 6 pm daily. In Urangan the *Melanesia Village* resort on Elizabeth St does Thursday two course lunch specials for $7 in its garden lounge.

The main food shopping centre in Hervey Bay is at Pialba, around the corner of Main St and Torquay Rd. There are smaller shopping centres on Queens Rd, Scarness; Bideford St, Torquay; and King St, Urangan. There's a health food shop on the Esplanade near the corner of Fraser Rd, Torquay.

Getting There & Away
Air Sunstate and Sungold both fly to and from Brisbane six or seven days a week. One-way fare is $74 (standby $60). Hervey Bay airport is off Booral Rd, Urangan.

Bus Around eight buses northbound and southbound – by McCafferty's, Deluxe, Greyhound and Pioneer – pass through Hervey Bay daily. It's about 4½ hours from Brisbane (typical fare $24), 6½ hours from Rockhampton ($40) and 16 hours from Townsville ($75). Hervey Bay's main bus stop is a shelter by a church on the corner of Bryant St and Torquay Rd in Pialba. You can make bus bookings and get info in Pialba through travel agents like Geldard's (tel 28 3355) at 5 Torquay Rd or Bezant's (tel 28 1900) at 15 Torquay Rd.

Getting Around
Bus Maryborough-Hervey Bay Coaches (tel 21 3719) runs a service between the two places several times daily Monday to Friday. In addition there are a few buses along the Esplanade on Saturday mornings.

Rental Vehicles See under Fraser Island for 4WD hire. Wide Bay Rent-A-Centre (tel 25 1766) at 2 Fraser St, Torquay, rents out Mokes, cars, scooters and bicycles. There's also Hervey Bay Rent-A-Car (tel 24 1300) at 363 Esplanade, Torquay, with VW soft tops and scooters. Avis (tel 28 3711) is at 21 Main St and Budget (tel 28 4866) is at 5 Torquay Rd, both in Pialba.

Fraser Island

The world's largest sand island, off Hervey and Tin Can bays, is 120 km long by about 15 km wide. Fraser Island rises to 200 metres above sea level in places and apart from three or four small rock outcrops, it's all sand – mostly covered in vegetation. Here and there the cover is broken by 'sandblows' – dunes that grow, shrink or move as the wind pushes them. The island also has about 200 lakes. Nearly all its northern third forms the Great Sandy National Park.

Fraser Island is a delight for fishing, walking, 4WD drivers and trail bikers and for lovers of nature. There are superb beaches (though swimming in the ocean can be dangerous due to severe undertows), towering dunes, thick forests, walking tracks, interesting wildlife and clear freshwater lakes and streams. You can camp or stay in accommodation. The island is sparsely populated and though more than 20,000 vehicles a year pile on to it, it remains wild. A network of sandy tracks crisscrosses the island and you can drive along great stretches of beach – but it's 4WD or trail bike only. There are no paved roads.

The island takes its name from Eliza Fraser, the wife of the captain of a ship which was wrecked further north in 1836.

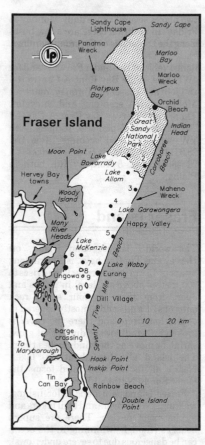

Fraser Island

1	Wathumba
2	Dundubara
3	Cathedral Beach
4	Yidney Scrub
5	Poyungan Rocks
6	Wanggoolba Creek
7	Central Station
8	Lake Birrabeen
9	Lake Benaroon
10	Lake Boomanjin

Making their way south to look for help, a group from the ship fell among Aborigines

on Fraser Island. Some of the group died during their two month wait for rescue, but others including Eliza Fraser survived with Aboriginal help.

The Butchulla Aborigines who used Fraser Island as a seasonal home were driven out onto missions when timber cutters moved on to the island from the 1860s. The Suez Canal was lined with satinay, a rainforest tree almost unique to Fraser Island which is highly resistant to marine borer. Today only limited logging takes place on the island. In the mid-1970s Fraser Island was the subject of one of Australia's bitterest struggles between conservationists and industry – in this case a sand mining company. The decision went to the conservationists.

Information
Ask on the mainland about island driving conditions before renting a 4WD vehicle. Sometimes rain and storms can make beaches or tracks difficult or impossible. The best sources of such information are probably the offices issuing the vehicle permits that you need to drive on the island. These permits cost $15 and can be obtained from the national parks office in Rainbow Beach or from the Hervey Bay city council (tel 25 1855) in Bideford St, Torquay, open Monday to Friday from 9 am to 5 pm; or from the national parks offices in Maryborough, Brisbane or Gympie; or the Forestry Department offices in Maryborough, Bundaberg, Brisbane or Gympie.

If you want to camp in the forestry department or national park areas on Fraser Island, you'll need a second permit ($7.50 a night per site for up to six people) which you get from the same places as the vehicle permits, or from the ranger station/information centres at Central Station, Eurong or Dundubara on the island.

Around the Island
Driving a 4WD is easy enough but on the island watch out for tides, which can

Top: Brisbane city from the Brisbane River, Qld (PS)
Left: Brisbane Town Hall (TW)
Right: Ramsay Bay, Hinchinbrook Island, Qld (TW)

Top: Sunset at Great Keppel Island, Qld (TW)
Left: Black boys growing on South Molle Island, Whitsundays, Qld (TW)
Right: Arthur Bay, Magnetic Island, Qld (CLA)

obliterate long stretches of beach, for creeks running over the beach, and for ridges on the beach that are difficult to see but can have you airborne if you come upon them too quickly. If you don't want to drive yourself, you can walk, hitch lifts, or split a tour into two halves by staying a night or more on the island.

One of the busiest routes is along the east coast whose whole length you can travel on the beach, with occasional detours. Starting from the south at Hook Point, you cross Fourth, then Third, Second and First creeks, all of which drain the southern heathland. Dilli Village, the former sand mining HQ, is between Third and Second. After the settlements of Eurong and Happy Valley, you cross Eli Creek, the largest on the east coast, then about 65 km from Hook Point is the wreck of the *Maheno*, a former passenger liner which was wrecked here in 1935 as it was being towed to a Japanese scrap yard.

Two marked vehicle tracks lead inland from Happy Valley: one goes to Lake Garawongera then south to the beach again at Poyungan Rocks (15 km), the other heads to Yidney Scrub and Lake Bowarrady before returning to the ocean beach north of the *Maheno* (45 km). The latter route will take you to some fine lakes and good lookout points among the highest dunes on the island.

Not far north of the *Maheno* you enter the national park and pass The Cathedrals, 25 km of coloured sand cliffs. Then, past the rock outcrops at Waddy Rock, Middle Rocks and Indian Head are Orchid Beach with its resort and a further 30 km of beach up to Sandy Cape, the northern tip, with its lighthouse a few km to the west. The west coast is less welcoming to drivers, being often swampy in the south, while north of Moon Point there's a creek which is notorious for catching people who try to cross it when the tide isn't well out.

A popular inland area for visitors is the south central lake and rainforest country around Central Station and lakes McKenzie, Wabby, Birrabeen and Boomanjin. Lake Wabby, near the east coast, is being slowly filled by a massive sandblow that advances about three metres a year. The main cross-island tracks between Eurong on the east and Ungowa or Wanggoolba Creek on the west pass through Central Station.

Walking Tracks There are a number of 'walkers only' tracks ranging from the one km Wungul Sandblow Track at Dundubara to the 13 km trail between lakes Wabby and McKenzie. The useful free *Fraser Island Guide* put out by the national parks and forestry people lists several more.

Places to Stay & Eat
Come well equipped since supplies on the island are limited and only available in a few places. And be prepared for mosquitoes and horseflies.

Camping This is the cheapest way to stay on the island and gives you the chance to get into closer touch with Fraser Island's unique nature. The national parks service and the forestry department operate several camping areas on the island. Those in the north at Dundubara, Waddy Point and Wathumba and in the south at Central Station, Lake Boomanjin and Lake McKenzie all have toilets and showers. You can also camp on some

Wreck of the *Maheno*, Fraser Island

stretches of beach. To camp in any of these public areas you need a permit.

There are also two privately owned camping grounds on the east coast, at *Eurong Beach Resort* (tel 28 3411) 35 km north of Hook Point, and *Cathedral Beach Resort & Camping Park* (tel 28 4988) 34 km north of Eurong. A site at Cathedral Beach, which has a store, is $12. At Eurong camping is free if you've come across on the *Fraser Venture* or *Rainbow Venture* ferries, otherwise it's $1. The Eurong resort has a store, bar and restaurant which campers can use.

Other Accommodation *Dilli Village Recreation Camp* is 200 metres from the east coast, 24 km from Hook Point and nine km from Eurong. A cabin for four people with its own shower and equipped kitchen costs $33 a night. There are also 17 twin or double rooms with shared bathrooms for $8 per person per night. If you're in these standard rooms you have to eat at the camp catering service where breakfast and lunch are $5 each, dinner $7. For bookings and info contact the Queensland Recreation Council in Brisbane (tel 221 4905).

Eurong Beach Resort (tel 27 9122), 35 km north of Hook Point on the east coast, has rooms and flats from $55 in addition to its camping ground.

At Happy Valley, 12 km north of Eurong, there are several flats to let mostly with weekly rates from $210, though some will also rent by the night for $35 upwards. There's a store at Happy Valley. It's wise to ask in Hervey Bay or Rainbow Beach first if you're interested in this kind of accommodation, which can be fully booked at busy times.

Orchid Beach Resort (tel 27 9185), about 100 km up the east coast from Hook Point, is the most luxurious place on Fraser Island with doubles at $125 per person for full board. There is also a restaurant, bar and store here.

Getting There & Away
You reach Fraser Island from Rainbow Beach or Hervey Bay.

4WD Hire You can rent 4WDs in Rainbow Beach or Hervey Bay. Rates are high in both places. Usually you pay $85 a day including insurance for a four seat vehicle, $75 for a two seater, or $95 for six seater. You also pay a bond of $300 which you get back if you don't damage the vehicle. In some places you have to be over 21. An obvious way of cutting costs is to get together with other travellers and share a vehicle.

In Rainbow Beach the two rental places are the Tourist Information Centre (tel 86 3227) at 8 Rainbow Beach Rd and Jeep City (tel 86 3223) at 10 Karounda Court, both on the main road. In Hervey Bay there's Fraser Island 4WD Hire (tel 28 3032) at 3A Nissen St, Pialba; Bay 4WD Centre (tel 28 2981) on Islander Rd, Pialba; and Wide Bay Rent-A-Centre (tel 25 1766) at 2 Fraser St, Torquay.

On the island you can get fuel at Eurong, Happy Valley and Cathedral Beach.

Vehicle Ferries These operate to the south end of Fraser Island from Inskip Point near Rainbow Beach, and to the west coast of the island from Urangan at Hervey Bay and Mary River Heads south of Urangan.

The two ferries operating the 10 minute crossing from Inskip Point to Hook Point on Fraser Island are *Eliza Fraser II* and *Rainbow Venture*. Both barges make this crossing every few minutes from about 7 am to about 4.30 pm daily. The price is anybody's guess – it has ranged between $5 and $35 return in the past couple of years. You can get tickets either in Rainbow Beach or on board the ferries.

The *Fraser Venture* runs daily from Mary River Heads to Wanggoolba Creek (also called Woongoolbver Creek) on the west coast of Fraser Island. Departures from Mary River Heads are from 9 am to

3.30 pm; from the island they're between 9.30 am and 4 pm. This crossing takes 30 minutes: the barge takes 22 vehicles but it's still advisable to book, through Bezants Travel (tel 28 1900) in Hervey Bay. Return fare for vehicle and driver is $25, plus $1 for each extra passenger. Use of the *Fraser Venture* or the *Rainbow Venture* entitles you to use the return half of your ticket on either vessel, and to free camping at Eurong Beach Resort.

The ferry from Urangan harbour is the *Fraser II* (tel 28 2777). Its schedules depend on tides but it goes to Moon Point most days, and to Urang Creek, between Moon Point and Wanggoolba Creek, less often. Return fare is $30 for a vehicle and driver, $5 for each extra passenger.

Tours Most day tours to Fraser Island allow you to split the trip and stay a few days on the island before coming back. There are several 4WD bus tour operators in Rainbow Beach and Hervey Bay. Prices for day tours range upwards from $35. Each outfit follows a different route but a typical tour might take in a trip up the east coast to the *Maheno* wreck and coloured sands, plus Central Station and a couple of the lakes in the centre of the island. Fraser Island Top Tours, based in Scarness, concentrates on the northern part of the island. Wendy and Rob's Surf Sand Safaris at Rainbow Beach offer camping trips with some canoeing thrown in. A two day and one night expedition costs $140 including all meals and gear.

Walking & Hitching It's quite possible to make your own way around the island, and hitching along the main tracks and beaches is pretty normal. If you hitch to the ferry departure points on the mainland you can usually go across as a passenger in the car that has given you a lift, at a cost of $1 or less. You can go across from Mary River Heads to Wanggoolba Creek on the Fraser Venture Day Tours boat for $3 but must make your own way to Mary River Heads.

North to Rockhampton

BUNDABERG (Population 55,000)
At the north end of Hervey Bay, Bundaberg is a major sugar growing, processing and exporting centre near the mouth of the Burnett River. Some of the sugar ends up in the famous Bundaberg Rum. The town is 50 km off the Bruce Highway and is the departure point for Lady Elliot and Lady Musgrave islands.

Information & Orientation
A good tourist information centre (tel 72 2406) is on the corner of Isis Highway, the main road as you enter the town from the south, and Bourbong St. It's open daily from 9 am to 5 pm. The town centre and post office are about a km east along Bourbong St from the tourist office.

Things to See
For $1 you can tour the rum distillery (tel 72 1333) on Avenue St in East Bundaberg at 10 am, 12.30 pm and 2.30 pm Monday

to Friday. It's not far off the east end of Bourbong St. Tours of the bulk sugar terminal at Burnett Heads at the river mouth are given at 3.15 pm weekdays.

Aviator Bert Hinkler, who in 1928 made the first solo flight between England and Australia, was born and raised in Bundaberg. The house in Southampton, England, which he lived in for his last years has been dismantled and shipped brick by brick to the corner of Young St and Perry Rd in North Bundaberg. It's an aviation museum, open daily from 10 am to 4 pm.

Bundaberg's Historical Museum, open from 10 am to 3 pm Monday to Friday, is in the School of Arts Building on Bourbong St. Paradise Bird Park is on Paradise Lane off Childers Road (Isis Highway) near the airport. Nearby is the Dreamtime Reptile Reserve. Alexandra Park on the south bank of the river, just north of Bourbong St, has a zoo.

On the Bruce Highway near Bundaberg, Gin Gin is an old pastoral town. The strange Mystery Craters – 35 small craters in a big sandstone slab said to be at least 25 million years old – are 17 km along the Bundaberg road from Gin Gin.

Beaches

There's good surf at Moore Park and Bargara while turtles nest at another good beach, Mon Repos. Local buses go to Bargara and Moore Park a few times on weekdays from Bundaberg post office. Four types of turtle – loggerhead, green, flatback and leatherback – lay their eggs in the sand at Mon Repos from late November to January. It's unusual since turtles generally prefer sandy islands off the coast. The young emerge and quickly make their way to the sea from mid-January to March. You're most likely to see the turtles laying their eggs around midnight when the tide is high.

Places to Stay

Bundaberg and the beaches have hosts of motels and caravan/camping parks. The

Grand Hotel (tel 71 2441) at 89 Bourbong St has singles/doubles at $12/22 and the *Lyelta Lodge* (tel 71 3344) at 8 Maryborough St charges $26/30. At Mon Repos Beach there's the *Turtle Sands Caravan Park* (tel 79 2340) with tent sites at $8, and on-site vans at $20 to $25.

Getting There & Away

There are about 11 buses northbound and southbound daily through Bundaberg with Deluxe, McCafferty's, Greyhound and Pioneer. The main stop is Stewart's Coach Terminal (tel 72 9700) at 66 Targo St. Bundaberg is also a stop for trains between Brisbane and Rockhampton or Cairns. Air services are by Sunstate (from Brisbane, Gladstone, Rockhampton, Mackay and Townsville daily) and Lloyd Air (daily from Brisbane and Gladstone).

AGNES WATERS & 1770

Turning east off the Bruce Highway at Miriam Vale, there's a rough road running 60 km out to the coast at Agnes Waters and 1770, which used to be known as Round Hill but was renamed in 1970 to commemorate Captain Cook's landing. Agnes Waters has a motel and there's a caravan park and camping ground at 1770, six km away, with terrific scenery, on a large secluded bay. It's an area that's hardly developed and, due to a gap in the reef, has one of the most northerly surf beaches on the east coast.

GLADSTONE (Population 22,083)

Twenty km off the highway, Gladstone is one of the busiest ports in Australia, handling agricultural and coal exports from this area of Queensland, plus alumina which is processed in Gladstone from bauxite ore shipped from Weipa on the Cape York Peninsula.

Gladstone is the main departure point for boat services to Heron, Masthead and Wilson islands on the Barrier Reef. It has plenty of motels and caravan/camping parks. There's a visitor information office (tel 72 4000) in Shop 6, City Centre Plaza,

Goondoon St. Most buses going up and down the coast stop at Gladstone and it's also on the Brisbane to Rockhampton rail route. Air services include Sunstate's daily coastal hop and daily flights by Lloyd Air from Bundaberg and Brisbane. Ansett flies from Brisbane once a week.

Near Mt Larcom, 34 km north along the highway from the Gladstone turn-off, the *Lazy G Horse Ranch* (tel 75 1166) offers free accommodation and mountain trail riding at $7 an hour, or $20 for the first day, $15 a day thereafter. The ranch, 11 km towards the coast from the highway, has a self-sufficient lifestyle. The owners will meet trains or buses at Mt Larcom for a small fee if you call.

BURNETT HIGHWAY ROUTE

As an alternative to the less than thrilling Bruce Highway you can travel north on the Burnett Highway, further inland. Along the inland roads there are several motels and camping/caravan parks, and tourist information centres at Gayndah and Mundubberah.

If you turn inland from Gympie you soon reach Gayndah, one of the oldest towns in the state and the citrus growing centre of Queensland. The Historical Museum on Simon St contains part of an old station homestead and is open from Tuesday to Saturday.

On the way to Gayndah you pass by, or can detour to, Kilkivan, a popular fossicking area, the Kinbombi Falls and the Ban Ban Springs. You can also reach Gayndah from Gympie or Maryborough via Biggenden, passing the volcanic crater lakes of the Coalstoun Lakes National Park on the way. North of Gayndah is Mundubbera, another citrus growing centre, from where you can reach the Auburn River National Park, with a gorge and camping area. Eidsvold was a prosperous gold town for 12 years from 1888. Its Historical Complex in Mt Rose St includes an 1859 homestead.

Monto is a dairy cattle centre. The spectacular Cania Gorge National Park is 25 km from the town. There are 70 metre sandstone cliffs, caves, forests, walking tracks and some impressive rock formations in the park. You can't camp in the national park but the *Cania Gorge Caravan Park* (tel 67 8188), beyond the park, is still in the gorge. It has tent sites at $6 and on-site vans for $18 double.

Just 142 km from Rockhampton is Biloela, a busy irrigated agricultural centre. Mt Scoria, 14 km from the town, is a solidified volcano core. From here you continue through Mt Morgan to Rockhampton.

Getting There & Away

McCafferty's has one bus a week from Rockhampton through Gladstone to Biloela, Monto, Eidsvold and Mundubbera, and vice versa. Brisbane Bus Lines (Brisbane, tel 355 0034) has a four times weekly service between Brisbane and Thangool, near Biloela, through Kingaroy, Murgon, Ban Ban Springs, Gayndah, Mundubbera, Eidsvold and Monto. You can fly to Thangool from Brisbane with Sunstate or Sungold.

The Great Barrier Reef

Facts & Figures

The Great Barrier Reef is 2000 km in length. It starts slightly south of the Tropic of Capricorn, somewhere out from Bundaberg or Gladstone, and it ends in the Torres Strait, just south of Papua New Guinea. This huge length makes it not only the most extensive reef system in the world but also the biggest structure made by living organisms. At its southern end the reef is up to 300 km from the mainland, but at the northern end it runs nearer to the coast, has a much more continuous nature and can be up to 80 km from one side to the other. In the 'lagoon' between the outer reef and the coast the waters are dotted with smaller reefs, cays and islands. Drilling on the reef has indicated that the coral can be over 500 metres thick. The reef is mostly about two million years old but the most ancient parts, in the north, go back 18 million years.

What is It?

Coral is formed by a small, primitive animal, a marine polyp of the family *Coelenterata*. Some polyps, known as hard corals, form a hard surface by excreting lime. When they die the hard 'skeletons' remain and these gradually build up the reef. New polyps grow on their dead predecessors and continually add to the reef. The skeletons of hard corals are white and the colours of reefs come from living polyps.

Coral needs a number of preconditions for healthy growth. First the water temperature must not drop below 17.5°C – thus the Barrier Reef does not continue further south into cooler waters. The water must be clear to allow sunlight to penetrate and it must be salty. Coral will not grow below 30 metres depth because the sunlight does not penetrate sufficiently and it will not grow around river mouths. The Barrier Reef ends around Papua New Guinea because the Fly River's enormous water flow is both fresh and muddy.

One of the most spectacular sights of the Barrier Reef occurs for a few nights after a full moon in late spring or early summer each year, when vast numbers of corals all spawn at the same time. The tiny bundles of sperm and eggs are visible to the naked eye and the event has been likened to a gigantic underwater snowstorm.

Reef Types

What's known as the Great Barrier Reef is not one reef but about 2600 separate ones. Basically, reefs are either fringing or barrier. You will find fringing reefs off sloping sides of islands or the mainland coast. Barrier reefs are further out to sea: the 'real' Great Barrier Reef, or outer reef, is at the edge of the Australian continental shelf and the channel between the reef

and the coast can be 60 metres deep. At places the reef rises straight up from that depth. This raises the question of how the reef built up from that depth when coral cannot survive below 30 metres? One theory is that the reef gradually grew as the sea bed subsided, and that the reef was able to keep pace with the rate of sinkage. The alternative is that the sea level gradually rose, and again the coral growth was able to keep pace.

Reef Inhabitants

There are about 400 different types of coral on the Great Barrier Reef. Equally colourful are the many clams which appear to be embedded in the coral. Each seems to have a different colour fleshy area.

Other reef inhabitants include about 1500 species of fish, 4000 types of mollusc (clams, snails, etc), 350 echinoderms (sea urchins, starfish, sea cucumbers and so on, all with a five arm body plan), and countless thousands of species of crustaceans (crabs, shrimps and their relatives), sponges and worms.

Reef waters are also home to dugong (the sea cows which gave rise to the mermaid myth) and breeding grounds for humpback whales, which migrate every winter from Antarctica. The reef's islands form important nesting colonies for many types of seabird, and six of the world's seven species of sea turtle lay eggs on their sandy beaches in spring or summer.

Crown-of-thorns Starfish One reef inhabitant which has enjoyed enormous publicity is the notorious crown-of-thorns starfish that tried to eat the Great Barrier Reef! It's thought that crown-of-thorns starfish develop their taste for coral when the reef ecology is upset – as, for example, when the bivalves (oysters, clams) which comprise their normal diet are over collected.

Nasties Hungry sharks are the usual idea of an aquatic nasty but the Barrier Reef's most unpleasant creatures are generally less dramatic. For a start there are scorpion fish with highly venomous spines. The butterfly cod is a very beautiful scorpion fish and it relies on its colourful, slow moving appearance to warn off possible enemies. In contrast, the stonefish lies hidden on the bottom, looking just like a stone, and is very dangerous to step on. Although they're rather rare it's a good idea to wear shoes when walking on the reef.

Stinging jellyfish are a danger only in coastal waters and only in certain seasons. The deadly 'sea wasp' is in fact a box jellyfish. As for sharks, there has been no recorded case of a visitor to the reef islands meeting a hungry one.

Viewing the Reef
Incomparably the best way of seeing the reef is diving, followed by snorkelling. Otherwise you can walk on it, view it through the floor of glass-bottomed boats or the windows of semisubmersibles, or descend below the ocean surface inside 'underwater observatories'. You can also see a living coral reef and its accompanying life forms without leaving dry land, at the Great Barrier Reef Wonderland aquarium in Townsville.

Innumerable tour operators do day-trips to the outer reef and to coral fringed islands from towns on the Queensland coast. The cost depends on how much reef viewing paraphernalia is used, how far the reef is from the coast, how luxurious the vessel that takes you there, and whether lunch is included. Usually free use of snorkel gear is part of the package. Some islands have good reefs too: they're usually cheaper to reach and you can stay on quite a few of them.

The Great Barrier Reef Marine Park Authority is the body looking after the welfare of most of the reef. Its address is PO Box 1379, Townsville, Queensland 4810 (tel 81 8811). It has an office in Great Barrier Reef Wonderland in Townsville.

Islands
There are three types of island off the Queensland coast. In the south, before you reach the Barrier Reef, are several large vegetated islands made of sand like North Stradbroke, Moreton and Fraser islands. These are interesting to visit for a variety of reasons but not for coral. Strung along the whole coast, mostly close inshore, are continental islands like Great Keppel, most of the Whitsundays, Hinchinbrook and Dunk. At one time these would have been parts of ranges running along the coast, but rising sea levels submerged them. They have vegetation like the adjacent mainland.

The true coral islands, or cays, may be on the outer reef, or may be isolated between it and the mainland. Green Island near Cairns, the Low Isles near Port Douglas and Heron Island off Gladstone are all cays. Cays are formed when a reef is above sea level even at high tide. Dead coral is ground down by water action to form sand and in some cases eventually vegetation takes root. Coral cays are low lying, unlike the often hilly islands closer to the coast. There are about 300 cays on the reef, 69 of them vegetated.

The Queensland islands are extremely variable so don't let the catchword 'reef island' suck you in. Most of the popular resort islands are actually continental islands and some are well south of the Great Barrier Reef. It's not necessarily important since many of them will still have fringing reefs and in any case a bigger continental island will have other attractions that a tiny dot-on-the-map coral cay is simply too small for – like hills to climb, bushwalks, and secluded beaches where you can get away from other island lovers.

The islands also vary considerably in their accessibility – Lady Elliot for instance is a $120 return flight, others are just a few dollars by ferry. If you want to stay on an island rather than just day-trip from the mainland that too can vary widely in cost. Accommodation is generally in the form of expensive resorts where most visitors will be staying on all-inclusive package deals. But there are a few exceptions to this rule, plus on some islands it's possible to camp. A few islands have proper camping sites with toilets and fresh water on tap while, at the other extreme, on some you'll even have to bring drinking water with you.

Southern Reef Islands

The southernmost part of the Great Barrier Reef, known as the Capricornia section, begins north-east of Bundaberg. From Lady Elliot Island, 80 km off Bundaberg, this string of coral reefs and cays dots the ocean for about 140 km up to Tryon Island east of Rockhampton.

Several cays in this part of the reef are excellent for reef walking, snorkelling, diving and just getting back to nature – though reaching them is generally more expensive than reaching islands nearer the coast. Access is from Bundaberg, Gladstone or Rosslyn Bay near Rockhampton.

Several of the islands are important breeding grounds for turtles and sea birds. Turtles arrive at night from late October to early February to lay their eggs, and the young emerge from mid-January to April.

On the four national park islands where camping is allowed (Lady Musgrave, Masthead, Tryon and North West)

campers must be totally self-sufficient. Numbers of campers are limited so it's advisable to apply well ahead for a camping permit. You can book six months ahead for these islands instead of the usual six to 12 weeks for other Queensland national parks. Contact the Queensland National Parks & Wildlife Service (tel 76 1621) on Roseberry St in Gladstone. If you get a permit you'll also receive info on any rules such as restrictions on the use of generators, and on how not to harm the wildlife.

Apart from the regular transport services, there is the Keppel Barge Service (tel 33 6721) at Rosslyn Bay. Barges from Gladstone which will carry around 40 people cost $2200.

LADY ELLIOT ISLAND

Eighty km north-east of Bundaberg, this 0.4 square km resort island is not a national park. You can day-trip from Bundaberg by plane only – for $170 – and the only place you can stay overnight is at the resort (tel 71 6077), which charges $220 per person for the first night, including meals and airfares, and $120 per night thereafter. The resort has good diving facilities and you can take certificate courses there. For information contact Sunstate Airlines (tel 72 2322) at 188 Bourbong St, Bundaberg.

LADY MUSGRAVE ISLAND

This 0.2 square km cay in the Bunker Group is an uninhabited national park about 100 km north-east of Bundaberg. You can day-trip to Lady Musgrave by fast catamaran or seaplane from Bundaberg and you can also camp there with a national parks permit. Campers are limited to 50 and must be totally self-sufficient.

Lady Musgrave Cruises (tel 72 9011) at 1 Quay St in Bundaberg operates the *Lady Musgrave* fast cat. The day-trip costs $75, including lunch, snorkel gear and a glass-bottomed boat ride. You get five hours on the island. The boat leaves from Burnett Heads near Bundaberg. You can use it as a camping drop off service for $150 return.

HERON ISLAND

Only a km long and 0.17 square km in area, Heron Island is 72 km east of Gladstone. A resort (tel 78 1488) owned by P&O covers the north-eastern third of the island: the rest is national park, but you can't camp there. The resort has room for more than 250 people, with normal nightly costs in the cheapest rooms of $90 per person including meals – though there are cheaper standby rates. Getting there, in the new *Reef Adventurer* fast catamaran from Gladstone, is extra. You can also day-trip to nearby Wistari Reef on the *Reef Adventurer*.

Large sections of coral have been killed by silt as a result of dredging for a new longer jetty at the island but Heron is still something of a Mecca for divers. The resort offers lots of dive facilities and trips and has its own dive school – $220 for a certificate course if you're staying there.

WILSON ISLAND

North of Heron Island, Wilson is a national park. You can day-trip there from Gladstone on the *Reef Adventurer* fast cat via Heron Island, and there's talk of P&O setting up a resort on the island. If they do, let's hope they take more care than when they set up their picnic area – in 1986-87 the island's 300 nesting pairs of the endangered roseate tern reportedly abandoned their nests because of the disturbance.

NORTH WEST ISLAND

At 0.9 square km, North West Island is the biggest cay on the Barrier Reef. It's all national park and you can camp there independently with a permit (total self-sufficiency, limit 150 people), but there are also day-trips from Rosslyn Bay near Rockhampton and four commercial enterprises plan to set up camping ventures on the island.

Day-trips are on the *Capricorn Reefseeker* fast catamaran from Rosslyn Bay and Great Keppel Island usually four days a week. The $70 fare includes lunch, a ride in a glass-bottomed boat, snorkelling and transport to/from accommodation in Rockhampton or on the coast. For info contact Great Keppel Island Tourist Services (tel 27 2948, 33 6744) at 168 Denison St, Rockhampton, or at Rosslyn Bay harbour. You may also be able to use the *Capricorn Reefseeker* for camping drop offs. Alternatively the Keppel Barge Service (tel 33 6721) from Rosslyn Bay does North West drop offs three Saturdays a month for about $150 a head return (minimum 10 people).

One of the commercial camping ventures, due to open by mid-1988, is run by Yeppoon Backpackers Hostel (tel 39 2122). The idea is that you'll be supplied with all camping gear and food, etc for $54 a day. Transport will be extra. Diving courses on the island should also be available. There'll be a maximum 15 people at the site and it will be open to the public only outside school holidays.

TRYON ISLAND

There's a limit of 30 campers on this minute national park island (six hectares) north of North West Island. Again, you must be totally self-sufficient. There doesn't appear to be any regular access to the island.

Rockhampton

Population 50,146

Australia's 'beef capital' sits astride the Tropic of Capricorn. First settled by Europeans in 1855, Rockhampton had a relatively small, early gold rush but cattle soon became the big industry.

Rockhampton's an access point for Great Keppel and other islands. The boats leave from Rosslyn Bay on the coast

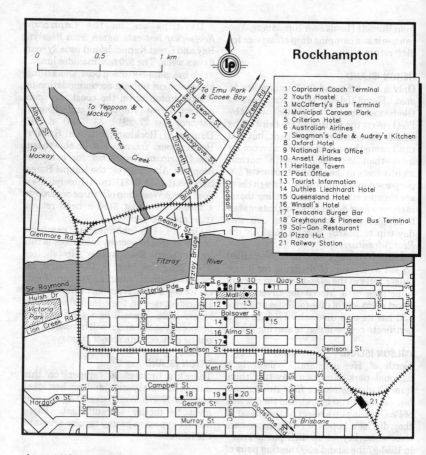

Rockhampton

0   0.5   1 km

To Emu Park
& Cooee Bay

To Yeppoon &
Mackay

To Mackay

Moores Creek

Fitzroy River

Glenmore Rd

Sir Raymond

Huish Dr

Victoria Park

Lion Creek Rd

To Brisbane

1 Capricorn Coach Terminal
2 Youth Hostel
3 McCafferty's Bus Terminal
4 Municipal Caravan Park
5 Criterion Hotel
6 Australian Airlines
7 Swagman's Cafe & Audrey's Kitchen
8 Oxford Hotel
9 National Parks Office
10 Ansett Airlines
11 Heritage Tavern
12 Post Office
13 Tourist Information
14 Duthies Liechhardt Hotel
15 Queensland Hotel
16 Winsall's Hotel
17 Texacana Burger Bar
18 Greyhound & Pioneer Bus Terminal
19 Sai-Gon Restaurant
20 Pizza Hut
21 Railway Station

about 50 km away but transport from Rocky is easy. There's also plenty of accommodation on the coast itself.

Orientation

Rockhampton is about 40 km from the coast, straddling the Fitzroy River. The long Fitzroy Bridge connects the old central part of Rockhampton with the newer suburbs to the north.

The Bruce Highway skirts the town centre and crosses the river upstream from the Fitzroy Bridge. Coming from the south, turn right up Denham or Fitzroy Sts to reach the centre of town.

Information

The Capricorn Information Centre (tel 27 2055) is on the highway as you enter Rocky from the south, beside the Tropic of Capricorn marker and three km from the town centre. It's open from 8.30 am to 5 pm Monday to Friday, 9 am to 1 pm Saturday and 9 am to 4 pm Sunday. There's a more central but smaller tourist information office on the East St mall between Denham and William Sts. The

RACQ (tel 27 2255) is at 134 William St. The national parks regional office (tel 27 6511) is at 194 Quay St.

Things to See

There are many fine buildings in the town, particularly on Quay St, where you'll find one of the best Victorian street frontages in Australia. You can pick up tourist leaflets and magazines which map out town walking trails.

The Botanic Gardens at the end of Spencer St, in the south of the city not far from the airport, were established in 1869 and have an excellent tropical collection, a walk through aviary and a recently created Japanese section.

Places to Stay

Hostels The *Rockhampton Youth Hostel* (tel 27 5288) at 60 MacFarlane St costs $9. It's a spacious YHA hostel with good facilities about a 20 minute walk north of the centre. Except on weekends, you can get there on a High St bus. The hostel has no curfew and you can arrive at any hour so long as you ring and book first. You can book the Great Keppel hostel – which also tends to be heavily booked – through the Rocky hostel. The Rocky hostel can also fix you up with transport to Great Keppel and often has the best deals in town. Discounts on tours to the Koorana Crocodile Farm and Cammoo Caves are available too.

Hotels & Motels There are plenty of old-fashioned hotels around the centre but nothing of great value in the motel line. On Quay St the *Criterion Hotel* (tel 22 1225) is one of Rockhampton's most magnificent old buildings. There are hotel rooms at $17/22 single/double (with communal shower) or $20/26 (private shower), hotel suites at $30/35 ($39 for three people) and motel rooms at $33/38 ($42 for three).

On the mall at the corner of East and Denham Sts the *Oxford Hotel* (tel 21 2837) is a straightforward central hotel with rooms at $14/20. Breakfast costs $5. The *Grand Hotel* isn't special but it's sort of funky with its old pioneer look. It's on the corner of Archer and Bolsover, $15 a head. The *Savoy*, on the corner of Alma and William Sts, is air-con and has rooms for $14/28.

North of the river, if you can't get into the youth hostel, try the *Railway Hotel* on Musgrave St, a block south of MacFarlane St, with singles/doubles at $15/26. Or there are some motel rooms with private bathrooms and cooking facilities at the *Ramblers Caravan Park* (tel 28 2084) on the Bruce Highway. The rooms, are $40 double, plus $4 for each extra person (up to a maximum of six).

You'll find lots of motels on the Bruce Highway into Rockhampton from the north and south. On the south side the *Lodge Motel* (tel 27 3130) at 100 Gladstone Rd, about three quarters of a km north of the Tropic of Capricorn, has singles/doubles at $28/32. The *Saleyards Hotel-Motel* a little further towards the town centre charges $28/30. On the north side of town there's the *Kalka Hotel-Motel* (tel 28 5666) on the corner of Water St and Lakes Creek Rd, with rooms at $20/25.

Camping There are half a dozen camping sites in Rocky including the *Municipal Riverside Caravan Park* (tel 22 3779), just across the river from the centre and beside the bridge. Camping here costs $6 for one or two people. Most of the other sites also have on-site vans and cabins as well as camping facilities. *Southside Caravan Village* (tel 27 3013), across the Bruce Highway from the tourist office, on the southern approach to Rocky, is a well kept place with a pool. Tent sites are $7 double and there are various cabins and on-site vans from $18 double. There's a shop and buses to the town centre.

More places are on the Bruce Highway north of the town. The *Ramblers Caravan Park* (tel 28 2084), three km from the town centre, has five tent sites at $8.50 for two people, on-site vans and cabins from $22.50/25.50 for two/three people and a great pool.

Places to Eat

Places in Rockhampton close early. Steak is a speciality – this is cattle country after all.

Pubs Several of the pubs have sit-down bistro-type sections as well as bar meals. The *Criterion Hotel* does counter meals from $4, and also has a seafood and steak restaurant where main meals are from $8.50. There's a smorgasbord lunch from Wednesday to Friday for $8.

There are similar set ups at the *Heritage Tavern* on the corner of Quay and Denham Sts, *Winsall's Hotel* on the corner of Denham and Alma Sts, and the *Savoy Hotel*. The Winsall's bistro does lunch time specials from $4.50.

The *Union Tavern*, on the corner of East and William Sts, has some of the cheapest feeding in town. It's open at lunch time and till 7.30 pm. There are specials for $4 and bigger counter meals from $6.

Restaurants, Cafes & Take-aways *Pacino's* (tel 22 5833), on the corner of Fitzroy and George Sts, about a km south of the Fitzroy Bridge, is a good Italian restaurant if you're in the mood for a minor splash out. The *Swagman's Cafe* at 8 Denham St is good for cooked breakfasts at $5 to $7. Next door *Audrey's Kitchen* has good salads and healthy take-aways.

The *Tropical Fruit & Juice Bar*, on the mall across from the post office, has fantastic fruit salads from $2 and smoothies. There's a clutch of burger, juice and hot dog places open late at night at the Fitzroy St end of the mall.

A scattering of more substantial eateries, all open quite late, is along Denham St. Near the corner of Alma St there's *Vijay's Curry House*, open till 9 pm Monday to Saturday. The *Texacana Burger Bar* is also near this corner, and it

stays open till 9 or 10 pm. Further along are three Chinese restaurants where you can sit down or take away.

At 61 William St, BYO *My Old Dutch* offers pancakes and crepes. It's closed Sunday and Monday. If you're staying at the youth hostel, there are several restaurants along Musgrave St.

Entertainment

The Criterion Hotel has a busy but relaxed scene in its little *Newsroom Bar* where local musicians and groups play on Wednesday, Thursday and Friday nights. Sounds range through blues, folk, jazz and bush and there's no cover charge. There's also live rock in the beer garden on Sunday afternoons.

On Sundays, from 4 to 8 pm, there's live jazz at the *Savoy Hotel*. Rockhampton has a small collection of clubs. The *Flamingo*, on Quay St between William and Derby Sts, has touring bands and dress rules. *Tricks* nightspot in the *Union Tavern* on the corner of the mall and William St sometimes has live bands.

Getting There & Away

Air You can fly to Rocky from all the usual places along the coast with Ansett or Australian Airlines. Sunstate includes Rockhampton on its daily coastal hop from Brisbane to Townsville and back. Australian Regional Airlines also has flights between Rockhampton, Mackay and Proserpine. Regular fares include Brisbane $155, Mackay $113, Townsville $165, and Cairns direct $277. Australian, Sunstate and Australian Regional (tel 31 0555) are at 75 East St and Ansett (tel 31 0711) is at 137 East St.

Bus The normal 14 or so daily buses up and down the coast all call at Rockhampton. Sunliner is a little cheaper than the other lines between Rockhampton and some points north, but otherwise fares are pretty similar. From Cairns to Rockhampton it's usually 15 hours and $66, and from Brisbane eight to 11 hours and

$46. Inland, Greyhound goes three times a week to/from Longreach (nine hours, $49). McCafferty's has buses to Emerald, Clermont, Moranbah and Mundubberah, and to Brisbane.

There are several different main bus stops in Rockhampton. McCafferty's terminal (tel 27 2844) is north of the river at the corner of Brown and Linnett Sts off Queen Elizabeth Drive. South of the river McCafferty's stops at the Shell Capricorn garage on request. Greyhound (tel 22 5811), Pioneer (tel 22 5753), Deluxe and Sunliner all stop both north of the river at the Capricorn Coach Terminal at the corner of Musgrave and Painswick Sts, and south of the river at Duthies Travel or Duthies Leichhardt Hotel, which face each other across Denham St at the corner of Bolsover St. Greyhound and Pioneer also stop at their own terminal at 91-101 George St near the corner of Archer St.

You can buy tickets for any of the bus lines at the Capricorn Coach Terminal. Duthies Travel (tel 27 6288) handles most tickets too.

Train The four times weekly Sunlander and the once weekly Queenslander between Brisbane and Cairns both stop at Rockhampton. There's also the three times weekly overnight Capricornian and the six times weekly Spirit of Capricorn. Brisbane to Rockhampton takes about 13 hours and costs $51.40 in economy, $110.80 in 1st. Twice weekly the Midlander runs between Rockhampton, Emerald, Longreach and Winton. Phone 31 0211 for railway information.

Getting Around

Rocky's airport is five km south of the centre. Rocky has a fairly modern railway station with luggage lockers – it's about 1½ km from the town centre.

There's a reasonably comprehensive city bus network. Young's Bus Service runs day tours to Mt Morgan and Rotherys Coaches (tel 22 4320) does trips

to Koorana Crocodile Farm and the Capricorn Coast, the town sights and the northern caves.

Around Rockhampton

NORTH OF THE CITY

The rugged Berserker Range starts 26 km north of Rocky, and here you'll find several spectacular limestone caves and passages. Several tours a day are taken through Olsen's Capricorn Caverns and Cammoo Caves, near The Caves township just east off the Bruce Highway. Off the highway back down towards Rocky you can visit the old Glenmore Homestead.

MT MORGAN (Population 3700)

The 325 metre deep open-cut gold and copper mine at Mt Morgan, 38 km south-west of Rockhampton on the Burnett Highway, was worked off and on from the 1880s until 1981. You can still visit the mine – conducted tours by Evan's Coaches (tel 38 1124) leave the mine car park at 9.30 am and 1.30 pm daily – and some of the town buildings are reminders of its more exciting past. There's quite a good museum on the corner of Morgan and East Sts (open daily but limited hours) and a tourist information centre in the library on Morgan St.

Young's Bus Service (tel 22 3813) operates a regular bus from Rockhampton to Mt Morgan four times daily on weekdays, twice on Saturdays. The fare is about $5. In Rockhampton the buses leave from the corner of East and William Sts, except for the 10 am on weekdays which goes from outside Duthies Leichhardt Hotel. Young's also runs day tours to Mt Morgan from Rockhampton.

Capricorn Coast

The 20 odd km long stretch of coast about

40 km east of Rockhampton is known as the Capricorn Coast. This is where you come for boats to Great Keppel, the other islands in Keppel Bay, and North West Island – they all leave from Rosslyn Bay. There are some good beaches on the coast and a few small towns, most of them minor resorts with a variety of accommodation.

Getting There & Away

There are two roads from Rockhampton to the Capricorn Coast. One, from Lakes Creek Rd from just north of the Fitzroy Bridge, brings you out at Emu Park at the southern end of the coast. The other road turns off the Bruce Highway about seven km north of central Rockhampton and reaches the northern part of the coast at Yeppoon.

Most of the cruise and ferry operators will transport you – often free – between your accommodation (in Rockhampton or on the coast) and Rosslyn Bay harbour. Young's Bus Service (tel 22 3813) also runs several buses a day between Rockhampton, Yeppoon and the rest of the Capricorn Coast. One-way fare to the coast is $4.40. Departures in Rockhampton are from Denham St near the corner of Bolsover St. For times, check with Duthies travel agent. Young's are planning a new Rockhampton terminal at 274 George St.

If you're driving to Rosslyn Bay you can leave your vehicle for 80c a day at the harbour, or there's the Kempsea lock up car park on the main road just north of the harbour turn-off. The Kempsea park charges $5 a day ($2 for motor bikes) and runs a free bus to and from the harbour.

YEPPOON (Population 9000)

This small seaside resort is much cooler than Rockhampton in summer.

Places to Stay

Yeppoon Backpackers Hostel (tel 39 2122) is on the seafront at 12 Anzac Parade. It's a quite pleasant place charging $10 per person. Accommodation is in eight person units with their own bathroom, sitting room, balcony and kitchen. The hostel also has a sun deck and pool. A $7 barbecue is held on Sunday nights and they can fix up fishing/diving/ snorkelling trips or island drop offs for you – or an outing to Koorana Crocodile Farm. You may also be able to get bargains on scuba diving courses through the hostel. When there's music in the pub next door, late night revellers hoon noisily up and down the road in their cars.

Normanby St is the first street running back from the seafront if you go north from the hostel. Here you'll find the pleasant *Tidewater Motel* (tel 39 1632) about 100 metres along. It's probably the cheapest motel in town. Normally singles/doubles are $30/35, though like everywhere in Yeppoon they can go up by about one-third in the peak holiday seasons. There's a pool and a laundry, and breakfast is available.

Places to Eat

Most places are on Normanby and James Sts, but *Tony's BYO* next to the Backpackers Hostel on the seafront is one of the better places in town. Main meals range from excellent vegetarian lasagna at $6 to fish or steak dishes at $10.

On Normanby St near the seafront end the *Hong Kong Cafe* at the bottom of the arcade does a $6 meal including starters, main dish, rice and tea or coffee. *Sandy's Cafe*, open from 7.30 am to 9 pm, has wide ranging cafe fare for $8. Over the road *Studio One* is a smarter bistro/coffee lounge doing lunch and dinner. Main meals are from $5.

Along James St the *Sunflower Patch* near the corner of Mary St serves health foods. Nearby at 26 James St, *Pizza Pizzazz* does tasty pizzas from $6.40. It's open daily till 8 or 8.30 pm. A bit further up at 34 James St the *Happy Sun* is a more expensive restaurant, described by one reader as 'one of the finest Chinese eateries anywhere'.

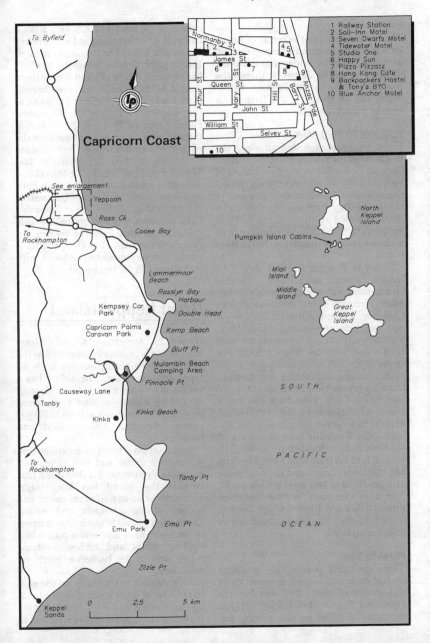

1 Railway Station
2 Sail-Inn Motel
3 Seven Dwarfs Motel
4 Tidewater Motel
5 Studio One
6 Happy Sun
7 Pizza Pizzazz
8 Hong Kong Cafe
9 Backpackers Hostel
  & Tony's BYO
10 Blue Anchor Motel

Normanby St

James St

Queen St

Mary St

Hill St

Barry St

John St

Anzac Pde

Arthur St

William St

Selvey St

Capricorn Coast

To Byfield

See enlargement

Yeppoon

Ross Ck

Cooee Bay

To Rockhampton

Lammermoor Beach

Rosslyn Bay Harbour

Kempsey Car Park

Capricorn Palms Caravan Park

Double Head

Kemp Beach

Bluff Pt

Mulambin Beach Camping Area

Causeway Lane

Pinnacle Pt

Tanby

Kinka

Kinka Beach

To Rockhampton

Tanby Pt

Emu Park

Emu Pt

Zilzie Pt

Keppel Sands

North Keppel Island

Pumpkin Island Cabins

Miall Island

Middle Island

Great Keppel Island

S O U T H

P A C I F I C

O C E A N

0   2.5   5 km

Entertainment

The *Strand Hotel* on the corner of Anzac Parade and Normanby St is a popular pub with live bands on Friday and Saturday nights. Back along James St there's the *Nightowl* disco in the Railway Hotel-Motel and on Hill St is the flashier *La Bamba* disco/nightspot.

YEPPOON TO EMU PARK

There are beaches dotted all along the 19 km coast from Yeppoon south to Emu Park. At Cooee Bay, a couple of km out of Yeppoon, the annual Australian 'cooee' championships are held each August.

Rosslyn Bay harbour, reached by a short side road about seven km south of Yeppoon, is the departure point for trips to the Keppel Bay islands and North West Island.

South of Rosslyn Bay are three fine headlands with good views – Double Head, Bluff Point and Pinnacle Point. After Pinnacle Point the road crosses Causeway Lake, a saltwater inlet where you can rent canoes and windsurfers. Further south at Emu Park there are more good views and the 'Singing Ship' – a series of drilled tubes and pipes which emit whistling or moaning sounds when there's a breeze blowing. It's a memorial to Captain Cook. Emu Park also has a museum (admission $1, open daily) which doubles as a tourist information centre.

Koorana Crocodile Farm is five km off the Emu Park to Rockhampton road. The turn off is 15 km from Emu Park. The farm has hundreds of crocs and tours are given at 1 pm three or four days a week for $7. North of Yeppoon is the Japanese financed Iwasaki Resort, which became something of a white elephant even before it was completed.

Places to Stay

There are many possibilities, including several caravan/camping grounds, along this stretch of coast. At Cooee Bay the *Poinciana Tourist Park* (tel 39 1601) has tent sites at $6.50 for two people, and cabins at $20 double or $25 with private bathroom. Further along, at Lammermoor Beach just before the turning to Rosslyn Bay harbour, *Golden Sands* (tel 33 6193) has pleasant holiday flats at $35 single or double, $40 for three. It's just over the road from the beach. A couple of km south of the Rosslyn Bay turn off, *Capricorn Palms Caravan Park* (tel 33 6144) is a modern, well kept place set back from the road at Mulambin Beach. Tent sites are $7 double, or there are cabins at $25. There's a pool and laundry facilities ($1).

Further south *Lakeside Caravan Park* and the slightly dearer *Coolwaters Holiday Village*, either side of Causeway Lake, both have tent sites and on-site vans.

Finally at Emu Park the council run *Bell Park Caravan Park* (tel 39 6202) is shady and very close to the beach with tent sites at $6 for two people.

Great Keppel Island

Owned by Australian Airlines, Great Keppel has been heavily promoted as the young people's resort, but you'll see all types and ages here. The airline has a variety of package tours to Great Keppel: depending where you start from, seven days there will cost you at least $1125 per person including airfare, food and facilities.

Great Keppel is heavy on entertainment – live rock music and lots of planned activities if you want. But the biggest plus is that the island has low budget accommodation as well as the resort, and is one of the cheapest and easiest Queensland islands to reach. Day-trippers to the resort have access to a pool, a bar, outdoor tables and umbrellas, horse riding and a $6 barbecue lunch on weekends.

Although it's not actually on the reef, Great Keppel is the equal of most islands up the coast. It's 13 km offshore and it's big enough that you won't see all of it in an

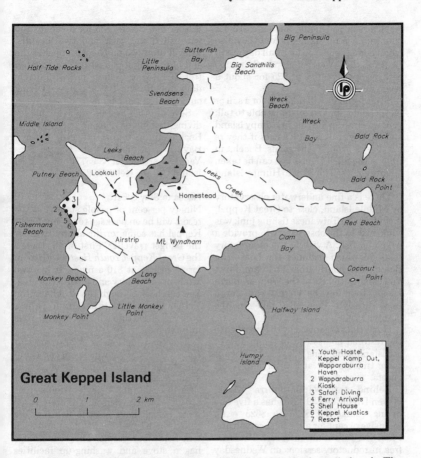

Great Keppel Island

0   1   2 km

1 Youth Hostel,
  Keppel Kamp Out,
  Wapparaburra
  Haven
2 Wapparaburra
  Kiosk
3 Safari Diving
4 Ferry Arrivals
5 Shell House
6 Keppel Kuatics
7 Resort

afternoon but small enough to explore over a few days. It covers 14 square km and boasts 18 km of very fine beach.

It only takes a short stroll from the main resort area to find your own deserted stretch of white sand beach. The water's clear, warm and beautiful. There is good coral at many points around the island, especially between Great Keppel and Humpy Island to the south. About a 20 minute walk around the headland south of the resort brings you to Monkey Beach where there's good snorkelling. There are a number of bushwalking tracks from

Fishermans Beach, the main beach. The longest, and one of the more difficult, goes across to the lighthouse near Bald Rock Point on the far side of the island, taking 2½ hours one way. Some beaches like Red Beach, near the lighthouse, are only accessible by boat.

Activities

The Beach Shed on Putney Beach and Keppel Kuatics on Fishermans Beach both hire out jet skis, windsurfers, catamarans, motor boats, fuel, tackle and bait. The Beach Shed is slightly cheaper.

Keppel Kuatics' motor boats are $12 per hour and $35 for six hours and they also have snorkel gear at $6 for a half day or $10 for a full day. You can go paraflying too with Keppel Kuatics at $25 for about a seven minute ride.

Several outfits will take you for a sail or motor boat trip. You might be able to talk your way into an $18 ride to Humpy Island and back with Keppel Kuatics if they're not busy. From Fishermans Beach, in front of the Shell House, you can be taken for an hour's sail for $6 or to Humpy Island for $20.

There is a fine underwater observatory by Middle Island, close to Great Keppel. A confiscated Taiwanese fishing junk was sunk next to the observatory to provide a haven for fish. A visit to the observatory costs $6 which includes the boat trip. Boats leave hourly from 11.15 am daily. You can buy tickets at the Wapparaburra Kiosk. Tours on the *Victory* catamaran from Rosslyn Bay also take in the observatory.

Horse rides organised by the resort go to the restored homestead in the middle of the island. Hour long rides head off two or three times a day at $15 for non resort guests.

Behind the Wapparaburra Kiosk, Haven Diving (tel 39 4217) has a five day diving course for $225 to $325 – all inclusive except for a medical certificate. Final dives are at the outer reef. There are free introductory sessions on Wednesday afternoons and organised diving trips, $65 (including equipment) for a day on the *Genesis*. Certified divers are catered for on the 26 foot catamaran *Saracen* which does daily dive trips from Rosslyn Bay, picking up at Great Keppel Island on the way. You can do an introductory dive from the *Saracen* if you're not already qualified.

Diving, Fishing & Sailing The *Tropic Diva* (tel 39 4431) runs snorkelling, fishing and diving trips from Rosslyn Bay to various locations around the islands. A day costs $25 for non divers, $35 for divers or $55 with all diving gear and two air fills. They'll drop you on Great Keppel at the end of the day if you wish. The *Saracen* (tel 39 1646) or *Genesis* picks up divers daily from Rosslyn Bay and Haven Diving on Great Keppel Island.

Several other vessels are available for diving, fishing or cruising trips – ask at Rockhampton tourist office or Rosslyn Bay. Two possibilities are Keppel Isles Yacht Charters (tel 33 6577) and Keppel Island Cruises (tel 39 1825).

Places to Stay & Eat
Ninety per cent of people staying at the resort will be on package tours, but Great Keppel has some terrific alternatives for the budget traveller. First of all, there's the *Great Keppel Youth Hostel* with room for 55 people at $10 a night. It has two kitchens, a laundry and a barbecue area. You can book through the Rockhampton YHA but if you want to be certain of a bed, book well ahead through YHA headquarters in Brisbane.

A second option is *Wapparaburra Haven* (tel 39 1907) where you can camp close to the beach for $7 per person, or rent a mattress for $12 in a pre-erected tent, or sleep in a cabin at $50 single or double plus $10 for each extra person. The pre-erected tents, which have electric lighting, are called the Keppel Tent Village and each tent holds four people. The Tent Village has a stove and washing-up facilities under cover but no fridge or kitchen gear. The Wapparaburra cabins sleep six and have full kitchen facilities, laundry and linen.

Next door to Wapparaburra Haven is *Keppel Kamp Out*. It's almost identical in appearance to Keppel Tent Village, but the concept and price are different. It's geared to the 18 to 35 age bracket with organised activities. The cost – $55 per person – includes twin share tent accommodation, three meals and activities like water sports, parties and video nights.

If you want to cook your own food on the

island it's best to bring a few basic supplies from the mainland. You can get some fruit, vegetables, groceries and dairy foods at the Wapparaburra kiosk, but it's pricey. The kiosk also does evening meals from $8 in a small dining room. Sometimes there are pasta and salad nights at $8 for all you can eat.

Over at the resort there are the day-trippers' facilities plus the *Keppel Kafe* with burgers from $2.60, meat pies, etc. There's a daily lunch smorgasbord at $17 for non guests, and a $7 barbecue on weekends only.

Halfway along the path between the resort and the kiosk, the *Shell House* not only has a shell or two, but also sells excellent home-made scones, rock cakes and Devonshire teas. The owner has lived on Keppel for many years and is happy to chat about the island's story. His tropical garden offers a pleasant break from the sun.

Getting There & Away

Air Sunstate Airlines flies at least twice daily between Rockhampton and Great Keppel. One-way fare is $50. Book through Australian.

Boat Ferries for Great Keppel leave from Rosslyn Bay on the Capricorn Coast. At least four make the crossing daily, and some do more than one trip. You can book the ferries through your accommodation or agents in Rockhampton or the Capricorn Coast. The youth hostel in Rockhampton often has special bargain deals.

Cheapest are the slow *Seafari* (tel 27 2948) at $15 and *Denison Star* (tel 27 6996) at $7, both taking about 45 minutes. Both vessels leave around 9 am and return from the island between 3.30 and 5 pm. The *Denison Star* also makes one or two other return trips in between these times, with the last departure from Rosslyn Bay usually at 4 pm.

Two more expensive options are the *Aquajet* and the *Victory*. The *Victory* leaves daily about 9 am and takes 20 minutes: for $25 you get the ride to Great Keppel and back and an optional free cruise from the island, with boom-netting. For a further $6 you can visit the Middle Island observatory. You then have three hours on Great Keppel. Lunch is available for $8. The *Aquajet* is a fast launch which makes two or three return trips daily, taking 15 minutes one way. The $20 return fare entitles you to a cruise on the *Victory* as well. There are free pick ups from Rockhampton and the Capricorn Coast to catch *Victory* departures.

The *Saracen* dive boat (tel 39 1646) also acts as a ferry between Rosslyn Bay harbour and Great Keppel. It costs $15 return and leaves Rosslyn Bay at 8 am, Great Keppel at 4 pm daily. The *Golden Phoenix* catamaran (tel 39 1154) does a $35 day cruise four times a week which takes in Great Keppel and the Middle Island observatory. You get lunch and you can snorkel, windsurf and jet ski for free.

Water taxis (tel 33 6350) from Rosslyn Bay harbour cost $18 a head one way to any of the Keppel Bay islands, minimum two people.

OTHER KEPPEL BAY ISLANDS

Great Keppel is only the biggest of the 18 continental islands dotted around Keppel Bay all within 20 km of the coast. You may get to visit Middle Island, with its underwater observatory, or Halfway or Humpy islands if you're staying on Great Keppel. Most of the islands have clean white beaches and several, notably Halfway, have excellent fringing coral reefs. Some are national parks where you can maroon yourself for a few days' self-sufficient camping.

To camp on a national park island you need to take all your own supplies including water. Numbers of campers on each island are restricted. You can get info and permits from the national parks office at 194 Quay St in Rockhampton (tel 27 6511) or the ranger base at Rosslyn Bay harbour (tel 33 6608).

North Keppel Island

The second largest of the group and one of the most northerly, six square km North Keppel is a national park. The most popular camping spot is Considine Beach on the north-west coast, where there are toilets and well water for washing. Take insect repellent.

Pumpkin Island

Just south of North Keppel, tiny Pumpkin Island has three cabins which accommodate five people each at a cost of $60 per cabin. There's water and solar electricity. Each cabin has a stove, fridge, and a bathroom with shower. Bedding is provided. Phone 39 2431 for info and bookings.

Miall & Middle Islands

These two small islands just north-west of Great Keppel are national parks with no facilities and tight limits on the numbers of people who can camp there at one time – eight on Middle, six on Miall.

Halfway Island

Just south of Great Keppel, little Halfway Island is a national park with a good reef, no facilities and a camping limit of six.

Humpy Island

A short way south of Halfway Island, Humpy has little shade as it bears the brunt of the south-east winds. Like Halfway, it's a national park and a popular snorkelling ground. There's a camping limit of 30, toilets and water for washing.

Capricornia

The country stretching inland from Rockhampton takes its name from its position straddling the Tropic of Capricorn. The Capricorn Highway runs inland, virtually along the tropic, across the central Queensland highlands to Bar-

caldine, from where you can continue west and north-west along the Landsborough Highway to meet the Townsville to Mt Isa road. The area was first opened up by miners chasing gold and copper around Emerald, and sapphires around Anakie, but cattle, grain crops and coal provide its main living today. Carnarvon National Park, south of Emerald, is one of Australia's most spectacular and interesting.

Places to Stay

Most towns in the region have motels plus caravan parks with on-site vans, tent sites and sometimes cabins. The national parks have some camping grounds and there are hostels in Sapphire, Rubyvale and Longreach.

Getting There & Away

Air Sunstate and Sungold link Brisbane with Blackwater and Emerald and Sunstate also flies to Clermont. Flight West has regular flights linking Brisbane, Townsville and Mt Isa with Blackall, Longreach, Winton and Barcaldine.

Bus Greyhound has a three times weekly service between Rockhampton and Longreach. Greyhound also has services daily from Brisbane to Longreach and vice versa, and from Brisbane to Mt Isa and vice versa five times a week. McCafferty's has a daily service both ways between Rockhampton and Mackay, plus services six days a week between Rockhampton and Emerald and Rockhampton and Clermont. It also runs twice weekly between Emerald and Springsure.

Train The twice weekly Midlander runs between Rockhampton and Winton.

ROCKHAMPTON TO EMERALD

On the way to Emerald from Rocky you pass through the coal mining centre of Blackwater. About 30 km before Blackwater and 11 km west of Dingo is the turn-off for Blackdown Tableland National Park, around 800 metres high with spectacular sandstone scenery plus some unique wildlife and plant species. A 20 km gravel road, leads on to the tableland. The road is passable to conventional vehicles but can be unsafe in wet weather.

In the park, you can bushwalk to waterfalls and lookout points, study Aboriginal rock art, and swim. There's a camping area at South Mimosa Creek, about 10 km into the park. There's also a caravan park at Dingo. Camping permits for the park are available from the ranger at Blackdown (tel 86 1964). Wood is in short supply – it's requested that you use gas stoves.

COAL MINES
Several of the massive open-cut Queensland coal mines, about 200 km inland from Rockhampton and Mackay, give free tours lasting about 1½ hours. It's advisable to phone ahead and book. The tour of the Blackwater mine (tel 82 5166), off the Rockhampton to Emerald road, leaves the main mine office on Wednesdays at 10 am. For the Goonyella (tel 42 3224) and Peak Downs (tel 41 6233) mines near Moranbah, buses depart Moranbah Town Square at 10 am Tuesday and Thursday respectively. Tours of Blair Athol mine (tel 83 1866) near Clermont start on Tuesdays at 9 am.

EMERALD (Population 4628)
About 270 km inland from Rockhampton, Emerald is an attractive town with streets lined with Moreton Bay Figs and a 1901 railway station. The surrounding area is picturesque with a backdrop of blue mountains.

GEM FIELDS
West of Emerald, the gem fields round Anakie, Sapphire, Rubyvale and Willows Gemfield are known for producing sapphires, zircons, amethysts, rubies, topaz, jasper, even diamonds and gold. To go fossicking, you need a Fossicking Licence, available at the Emerald Court House or on the gem field for $4.30.

Anakie, 42 km west of Emerald on the Capricorn Highway, has the Gemfields Information Centre where you can find out how to go fossicking and pick up maps of the fossicking areas. Anakie's historic pub dates from 1902.

Sapphire is 10 km north of Anakie on a sealed road. There's large scale open-cut mining between here and Rubyvale, seven km further north, but plenty of room for fossickers as well. Sapphire has an associate YHA hostel and camping at *Sunrise Cabins* (tel (079) 854281), about a km out of town on the Rubyvale road. It costs $7 a night for dorm accommodation. At the hostel you can get information, licences and maps, hire fossicking gear or arrange a gem field tour. There's also the little *Rubyvale Backpackers Hostel* (tel 82 1972) with dorm beds and doubles from $8 a night. Its postal address is PO Rubyvale, Qld 4702.

Sapphires can be found close to the surface at Willows Gemfield, 38 km west of Anakie.

CLERMONT (Population 1659)
North of Emerald is Clermont with the huge Blair Athol open-cut coal mine. Clermont is Queensland's oldest tropical inland town, founded on copper, gold, sheep and cattle. It was the scene of gold field race riots in the 1880s and a military take over of the town in 1891 after a confrontation between striking sheep shearers and non union labour.

SPRINGSURE (Population 774)
Springsure, south of Emerald, has two historical museums and some attractive surrounding countryside – granite mountains and fields of sunflowers, used to produce oil and seed. Nearby is the Old Rainworth Fort at Burnside, built following the Wills Massacre of 1861 when Aborigines killed 19 whites on Cullin-La-Ringo station north-west of Springsure.

CARNARVON NATIONAL PARK

Rugged Carnarvon National Park, in the middle of the Great Dividing Range, has dramatic gorge scenery and many Aboriginal rock paintings and carvings. It's reached from Rolleston, south-east of Springsure, or from Injune, north of Roma. The impressive Carnarvon Gorge is all that most people see of the park as much of the rest is pretty inaccessible.

From Rolleston to Carnarvon Gorge, the road is bitumen for eight km and unsealed for 92 km. From Roma via Injune and Wyseby, the road's good bitumen for 170 km then unsealed and fairly rough for 80 km. After rain both roads become impassable.

Carnarvon Gorge is stunning partly because it's an oasis surrounded by drier plains. Its scenic variety includes sandstone cliffs, moss gardens, deep pools, and rare palms and ferns. There's also lots of wildlife. Though you can drive to the nearby main national park camping site, all the features in the gorge itself are only accessible on foot. There are some great walks to impressive outlooks, and Aboriginal art can be viewed at three main sites – Baloon Cave, the Art Gallery, and Cathedral Cave. It's believed Aborigines were present in the area as many as 19,000 years ago.

To get into the more westerly and rugged Mt Moffatt section of Carnarvon National Park, there are two unsealed roads (passable by conventional vehicle) from Injune, one through Womblebank Station, the other via Westgrove Station, both impassable after heavy rain. There are no through roads from Mt Moffatt to Carnarvon Gorge or to the third and fourth remote sections of the park – Salvator Rosa and Ka Ka Mundi. Mt Moffatt has some beautiful scenery, diverse vegetation and wildlife, and Kenniff Cave, an important Aboriginal archaeological site.

Places to Stay

Oasis Lodge (tel 84 4503), near the entrance to the Carnarvon Gorge section of the park, offers cabins or 'safari tents' from $90 a night per person, including full board and organised activities. There's a general store with fuel.

The national park camping ground is about three km into the Carnarvon Gorge section of the park and has a visitor information centre, showers and toilets. Wood for cooking is not plentiful and you should provide your own gas cooking equipment. You need a permit to camp and it's usually advisable to book (tel 84 4505) ahead. You can also camp at Big Ben camping area 500 metres upstream of Cathedral Cave; this enables the side gorges to be explored unhurriedly.

In the Mt Moffatt section, camping with a permit (tel 82 2246) is allowed at six sites but you need to be completely self-sufficient.

AROUND BARCALDINE

Barcaldine, between Emerald and Longreach and with an historical museum, is another cattle centre. It was the scene of a major step towards the 1902 formation of the Australian Labor Party when in 1891 striking shearers met under a ghost gum tree, before marching to Clermont to continue their struggle. At the same time dock workers in Sydney rioted, refusing to handle bales of wool sheared by non union labour.

South of Barcaldine is Blackall, near which is Black's Palace, an Aboriginal site with burial caves and impressive rock paintings. It's on private property but can be visited with the permission of the warden (tel 57 4455 or 57 4663).

LONGREACH (Population 2971)

This prosperous outback town is home to the Australian Stockman's Hall of Fame & Outback Heritage Centre. It's well worth a visit – entry is $8, or $6 with a student card. Displays are divided into periods from the first white settlement through to today; there are also some

Aboriginal displays, plus audiovisuals and electronics. Developments which helped people 'tame' the outback are also featured, including exploitation of the Great Artesian Basin as a water source, development of the Overland Telegraph and radio, and the Flying Doctor Service. Demonstrations of bush skills and crafts are held in the grounds.

Longreach's human population is vastly outnumbered by the sheep population which is close to a million; there are a fair few cattle too. It was here that the Queensland & Northern Territory Aerial Service, better known as Qantas, was based in its early days in the 1920s. The original Qantas hangar, which still stands at Longreach airport, was also the first aircraft 'factory' in Australia – six DH-50 biplanes were assembled there in 1926.

Longreach was the starting point for one of Queensland's most colourful early crimes when in 1870 a bushranger sporting the title 'Captain Starlight' stole 1000 head of cattle and trotted them 2400 km south to South Australia where he sold them. He then made his way back to Queensland, was arrested and unbelievably acquitted.

Longreach's *Youth Hostel* (tel 58 1529) at 120 Galah St, two blocks south of the railway station on the corner of Swan St, has dorms at $6.50 a night plus some family rooms. You can get tourist information from the travel agent in Eagle St. Greyhound (tel 58 1776) is at 115A Eagle St. You can visit several cattle stations in the area – one reader recommended Longway Ranch, 17 km out, where a day costs $25 (including pick up from Longreach).

WINTON (Population 1259)
Winton is a sheep raising centre and also the railhead from which cattle are transported after being brought from the Channel Country by road train. The road north to Cloncurry has been notoriously bad in the wet with trucks banked up in Winton waiting for it to dry out, but it should soon be fully paved.

Back in 1895 at Combo Waterhole on Dagworth Station, between Winton and Kynuna, Australia's most famous poet/songwriter, Banjo Paterson, is said to have written *Waltzing Matilda*. Later Qantas was founded at Winton in 1920. These two diverse influences are united in Winton's Qantilda pioneer museum!

The country round Winton is rough and rugged with much wildlife, notably brolgas. There are also Aboriginal sites with paintings, carvings and artefacts. At Lark Quarry Environmental Park 120 km south-west of Winton, dinosaur footprints 100 million years old have been perfectly preserved in limestone. It takes around two hours to drive from Winton to Lark Quarry in a conventional vehicle but the dirt road is impassable in wet weather. Winton Shire Council Offices (tel 305) at 78 Vindex St can give directions. There is no water at the site or along the road from Winton.

Lorraine Station Outback Resort (tel 57 1693), a sheep station 54 km south of Winton, has rooms with full board for $60 single or $50 per person twin share – or you can camp for $5 per person a night. A tour of the 310 square km station costs $5.

Rockhampton to Mackay

The 343 km from Rockhampton to Mackay is one of the most boring stretches of the entire east coast Highway 1. After the Berserker Range caverns not far north of Rocky, there's virtually nothing for over 250 km apart from the small town of Marlborough, a handful of roadhouses and a camping site at Lotus Creek. Much of the coast here is a military training area.

About 50 km before Mackay, the coastal Cape Palmerston National Park has fine scenery, beaches, mangroves and freshwater lagoons but the access road, from Ilbilbie, is 4WD only. The highway then drops down over a range to the lusher country around Sarina.

Sarina (Population 2815)

On the Bruce Highway, just 37 km south of Mackay, Sarina is the start of the sugar producing area around Mackay and there are also some fine beaches. There are four motels and two caravan/camping parks. Between Sarina and Mackay is the huge Hay Point bulk loading export terminal for the coal produced inland.

Mackay

Population 48,725

Mackay is surrounded by sugar cane and processes a third of the total Australian sugar crop, which is loaded at the world's largest bulk sugar loading terminal at Port Mackay. Sugar has been grown here since 1865. Mackay is nothing special, though its town centre is attractively planted, and there are some good beaches a bus ride away. But it's an access point for the national parks at Cape Hillsborough and Eungella, and the Barrier Reef and some interesting islands are just an hour or two away.

Orientation

Mackay is on the Pioneer River and its main streets are laid out in a simple grid on the south side of the river. The main intersecting streets are Wood and Victoria. The railway and bus stations are only a few blocks from the centre and the airport is also fairly close. The newer suburbs are north of the river.

Information

Mackay's tourist info centre (tel 52 2677) is about three km south of the centre on Nebo Rd, which is the Bruce Highway. It's open from 9 am to 5 pm Monday to Friday and 9 am to 4 pm Saturday and Sunday.

Next to it stands a Taiwanese fishing junk which was seized in 1976 when it was caught poaching giant clams within Australian waters. The RACQ (tel 57 2198) is at 214 Victoria St and the National Parks district office (tel 57 6292) is at 64 Victoria St.

Things to See

There are Botanic Gardens and an orchid house in Queen's Park, towards the east end of Gordon St. The Museum of Memories at 136 Wood St houses local bric-a-brac from the 1860s to 1930s, open from 10 am to 4 pm Monday to Friday, 9 am to 12 noon Saturday (admission \$3). At the harbour in Port Mackay, six km north of the town centre, the small Mackay Maritime Museum is open daily Thursday to Monday from 10 am to 3 pm. Admission is \$1. Good views over the harbour can be had from Mt Basset or at Rotary Lookout on Mt Oscar in North Mackay.

There's a town beach at the east end of Shakespeare St, two km from the centre, and also Far Beach, six km south of the river mouth, Harbour Beach just south of the harbour wall, and Lamberts Beach north of the harbour. But the best beaches are about 16 km north of Mackay at Blacks Beach, Eimeo and Bucasia. You turn right at the 'Northern Beaches' sign four km north of town on the Bruce Highway to reach them.

In the July to December crushing season you can visit the Racecourse Sugar Mill at 2 pm on weekdays for a \$6 tour. Polstone Sugar Farm gives tours for about \$10 twice a week. In the crushing season you can tour the Mackay Harbour sugar bulk terminals at 9 am on weekdays for \$2 or so. You can also reach the Goonyella, Peak Downs, Blackwater and Blair Athol coal mines from Mackay.

The 19th century home of Mackay's founder, John Mackay, is at Greenmount Homestead, 20 km out shortly after Walkerston on the Peak Downs Highway towards Clermont. It's open to visitors from 9.30 am to 12.30 pm Monday to

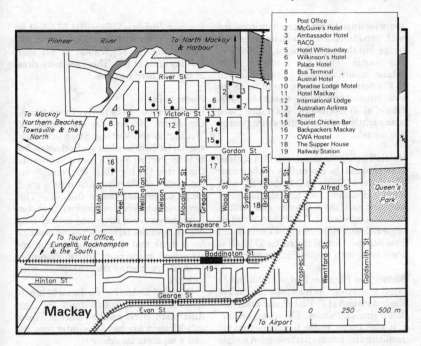

1	Post Office
2	McGuire's Hotel
3	Ambassador Hotel
4	RACQ
5	Hotel Whitsunday
6	Wilkinson's Hotel
7	Palace Hotel
8	Bus Terminal
9	Austral Hotel
10	Paradise Lodge Motel
11	Hotel Mackay
12	International Lodge
13	Australian Airlines
14	Ansett
15	Tourist Chicken Bar
16	Backpackers Mackay
17	CWA Hostel
18	The Supper House
19	Railway Station

Friday and from 10 am to 4 pm on Sundays.

Activities

Brumby Bob's Trail Rides at 10 Jansen St, Slade Point, are only 10 minutes from town and offer three hour trail rides across sand dunes, along the beach and through Melaleuca forests. The $25 cost includes a drink at the local pub, billy tea and damper and transport there and back.

Places to Stay

Backpacker Accommodation *Backpackers Mackay* (tel 51 3728) at 32 Peel St, is an associate YHA hostel with 18 bunk beds and a swimming pool. The charge is $8 a night plus 50c for linen and towel hire. The hostel offers various excursions including a $15 day-trip to Finch Hatton Gorge.

The best value budget accommodation is the bunkhouse at *Kohuna Village*

Resort (tel 54 8555), 16 km north of Mackay at Bucasia. The bunkhouse is large and airy, with its own bathrooms and kitchen/dining room. For $12 a night you also get use of three pools and you can buy meals and drinks at the resort or hire canoes, windsurfers or play tennis. If you're driving, turn right at the 'Northern Beaches' sign on the Bruce Highway and follow signs to Bucasia and Eimeo, then turn right after the Bucasia turn-off. The Northern Beaches bus comes to Kohuna two or three times a day Monday to Friday.

Back in the town centre, the *Palace Hotel* (tel 57 2455) on the corner of Victoria and Sydney Sts has some uncrowded bunk rooms at $9 a head plus $1 for sheets and pillow. Another fairly central option is *Central Lodge* (tel 57 3654) at 231 Alfred St with good clean singles/doubles at $15/20 and motel-type rooms at $20/25.

Tropical Caravan Park (tel 52 1211), about six km from the town centre, has space for up to 12 YHA members in cabins with private cooking facilities, fans and fridge, but shared bathrooms, at $9 single, $15 double. There's a range of other cabins, on-site vans and units here for $20 to $35 double, or you can camp for $8 for two. Women only might check the *CWA Hostel* at 43 Gordon St. It's a nice place with nightly costs of $9 in a share twin or $40 a week.

Hotels There's the usual selection of older hotels around the centre. The *Ambassador Hotel* (tel 57 2368) at 2 Sydney St, with singles/doubles for $20/30, is quite pleasant and has a balcony and rooftop bar. *McGuire's* (tel 57 2419) on Wood St costs $30/40. On the corner of Victoria and Peel Sts the *Austral Hotel* (tel 57 2639) is more basic with singles/doubles at $23/28.

Motels The *Paradise Lodge Motel* (tel 51 3644) is just over the road from the back of the bus station at 19 Peel St and costs $35/45 for singles/doubles. The rooms are air-con with fridge, radio, tea/coffee making facilities and private bathrooms. A couple of blocks over at 40 Macalister St the *International Lodge* (tel 51 1022) is similar but not air-con at $30/40. Breakfast is available.

There's a whole string of motels south along Nebo Rd, the Bruce Highway. *Cool Palms* (tel 57 5477) at 4 Nebo Rd, fairly close to the centre, charges $35/37 with light breakfast.

Camping The *Beach Caravan Park* (tel 57 4021) on Petrie St at Illawong Beach has tent sites at $8/10 single/double, Camp-O-Tel capsules at $9 to $11 a head, and on-site vans, cabins and villas from $25 to $40 double. It's next to the Illawong Tourist Park which has a pool, kiosk and grill bar.

Central Caravan Park (tel 57 6141) is at 15 Malcomson St, just across the river in North Mackay. Camping costs $8 and there are cabins for $20 double. At 152 Nebo Rd on the way out of town the *Premier Holiday Village* (tel 57 6976) is well equipped with camping sites at $8, on-site vans at $18, cabins at $27 and holiday units at $35. There are more sites at the northern beaches.

Places to Eat

Hotels Monday to Saturday lunch times, the *Hotel Mackay* on the corner of Wellington and Victoria Sts, has a daily special for $3 or steak or seafood meals for $7 to $8. Further along Victoria St towards the centre, the big *Hotel Whitsunday* on the corner of Macalister St does a good range of counter meals from $5. The *Ambassador Hotel*, overlooking the river from the corner of River and Sydney Sts, has an upstairs terrace which is popular for a drink and the hotel does counter-style food every night in the $7 range. Downstairs there are cheap counter lunches.

On Wood St *McGuire's* does a $4 lunch special, or other meals from $6. The *Australian Hotel* on the corner of Wood and Victoria Sts has $4 counter lunches and a separate steakhouse.

Snack Bars, Take-aways & Coffee Shops There are pretty slim pickings in this department on weekends but you can get a good bite during the week. For fast food, the *Tourist Chicken Bar* at 94 Wood St between Victoria and Gordon Sts is open daily to 8 pm. *Penny's Pantry* at 7 Wood St, between Victoria and River Sts, is a very cheap sandwich bar/coffee shop. Also on Wood St back towards Victoria St, the *Gourmet Deli* is a really popular lunch spot offering a large range of healthy sandwiches for $2.

On the other side of Wood St at 73, in Jamor House, *Susanne's Coffee House* does good home-made European-style meals ($6) and cakes ($3). It's a pity this place is so tucked away.

Behind the *Plaza Coffee Shop* on Wood St south of Gordon St, a health food shop serves Asian-style vegetarian lunches from 11 am to 2 pm. Opposite the town hall at 68 Sydney St, *Tastes Great Cafe* in the Coolabah Walk arcade has full breakfasts from $4. There's a fruit market, open weekdays from 8 am to 5 pm and weekends from 6 am to 1 pm, on the corner of Gordon and Wood Sts.

Restaurants The *Supper House* is a restaurant and coffee house in an inconspicuous white bungalow at 109A Sydney St near Shakespeare St. Most meals are $9 to $11; it has Mexican and vegetarian food, is BYO and open nightly from 7 pm until late. A little closer to the central area, on the corner of Alfred and Sydney Sts, *Al Pappas* is a pleasant little place with really good, reasonably priced pizzas and other Italian food. The *Creperie* in the Centrepoint Shopping Place, entered from Gordon St, serves lunches and dinners from $7. *Pee Bees* at 27 Sydney St, a licensed Mexican place, is open nightly.

For Chinese, the *Lychee Gardens* on the corner of Victoria and Wellington Sts has a bargain lunch smorgasbord from Monday to Friday for $7 and a Sunday night dinner special for $9.

Entertainment

The *Oriental Hotel* has varied live entertainment Thursdays to Sundays and cabaret some nights. The *Prince of Wales* on River St has bands Friday and Saturday and a disco other nights. *Wilkinson's Hotel* has live bands on Thursday night and Saturday afternoon, and a disco Friday and Saturday nights. In the *Austral Hotel* you'll catch Saturday afternoon jazz about every two weeks, also guitar nights on Wednesdays and Saturdays.

Nightclubs, often with live bands as well as discos, include *Illusions* at 45 River St, *Valentino's* at 99 Victoria St and *Paradise Nights* in Toucan's Arcade, 85 Victoria St.

Getting There & Away

Air Ansett has direct flights most days to/ from Brisbane, Cairns, Hamilton Island, Rockhampton and Sydney and less often to Proserpine. Australian flies daily direct to/from Brisbane and Rockhampton. Fares include Cairns nonstop $218, Proserpine $68, Hamilton Island $82, Rockhampton $107 and Brisbane $195. Sungold goes once or twice daily to and from Townsville ($106 one way, book through Ansett).

Australian Regional Airlines flies to/ from Rockhampton, Proserpine and Brampton Island; Sea Air Pacific to/from Lindeman Island ($65) and Whitsunday airport ($71); Sunstate to/from Townsville, Mackay, Rockhampton, Gladstone, Bundaberg and Brisbane. In Mackay, Ansett and Sungold (tel 57 1571) are at 97 Victoria St; Australian, Sunstate and Australian Regional (tel 57 1411) are at 105-109 Victoria St.

Bus All buses going up and down the coast stop at Mackay. The bus station is on Milton St, about six blocks west of the town centre. Average journey times and typical fares are Cairns 10½ hours ($49), Townsville five hours ($34), Proserpine two hours ($16), Rockhampton four hours ($28), Brisbane 12 to 16 hours ($64).

Train The Brisbane to Cairns Sunlander and Queenslander stop at Mackay. Economy fare from Brisbane is $76.90, in 1st it's $144.40 on the Sunlander, $211.15 on the Queenslander. The station (tel 57 2551) is on Boddington St.

Getting Around

Airport Transport Count on about $5 for a taxi to the city. Avis, Budget and Hertz have counters at the airport but rental cars in Mackay are neither cheap nor plentiful.

Bus The Mackay Northern Beaches Bus Service (tel 54 6088) leaves the RSL Club on Sydney St, between Victoria and Gordon Sts, at 8.45 am and 1.10 pm Monday to Friday for the northern beaches. There's also a 3 pm departure in school terms from the corner of Gregory and River Sts. It's about an hour from Mackay to most of the northern beaches. Returning buses start from Shoal Point at 7.30 am, 9.20 am and 1.45 pm.

Sea & Air Tours Roylen Cruises (tel 55 3066) runs fast catamaran day-trips from Mackay harbour to Brampton Island, Credlin Reef on the Barrier Reef, and Hamilton Island in the Whitsundays. Brampton is $20 return, daily, Hamilton $30 return three days a week. The Credlin trip, four days a week for $60 including lunch, takes you to a pontoon on the reef with an underwater observatory. You also get a semisub ride and you can hire snorkelling or diving gear. Funway Whitsunday Tours (tel 55 2733) runs shuttle buses from the town to the harbour for these cruises – $6 return.

The tourist office has details of other trips including Air Pioneer's flights out to the Barrier Reef for snorkelling and reef walking – $120.

Land Tours Day-trips by a handful of operators cover various combinations of town sights, the sugar terminal, Cape Hillsborough, Greenmount Homestead, Eungella National Park, the southern beaches and Hay Point coal terminal. Prices are $25 to $30 for a full day, $15 to $20 for a half day.

Around Mackay

EUNGELLA NATIONAL PARK

Most days of the year you can be pretty sure to see platypuses close to the Broken River camping ground in this large national park 74 km west of Mackay. Eungella covers nearly 500 square km of the Clarke Range, climbing to 1280 metres at Mt Dalrymple. Much of the park is subtropical rainforest. Apart from platypuses, lots of other spectacular

creatures, such as gliders and many colourful birds, live here.

Eungella has been cut off from other rainforest areas for probably 30,000 years and has at least six life forms which exist nowhere else – the Eungella honeyeater (a bird), the orange-sided skink (a lizard), the Mackay tulip oak (a tall buttressed rainforest tree) and three species of frog of which the Eungella gastric brooding frog is unusual for incubating its eggs in its stomach and giving birth by spitting out the tadpoles!

The road to Eungella heads west from the Bruce Highway just south of Mackay and passes along the sugar growing Pioneer Valley. One km before Finch Hatton, about 60 km from Mackay, the side road to Finch Hatton Gorge heads off to the north. About 10 km further on, the main road zigzags up to the head of the valley, with Eungella village at the top. Here you turn left for Broken River, five km south.

Finch Hatton Gorge

Two walking tracks lead to spectacular waterfalls and swimming holes from the national park camping ground. The Wheel of Fire Falls track, two km one way, mostly follows Finch Hatton Creek and passes three falls. At Araluen Falls the Eungella day frog, one of the species unique to this area, is quite common. The other track leads 3½ km to 60 metre Dooloomai Falls. The last two or three km of the 10 km drive from the main road to the camping ground involve several creek crossings and non 4WD vehicles will have difficulties if it has rained much.

Broken River

The national park ranger station and camping ground, a picnic area and a kiosk are all near the bridge over Broken River, five km from Eungella village. The first three km of the road from Eungella to Broken River run close to the edge of the range and there are six lookouts, all a short walk from the road. An off road walking track takes in all six.

Platypuses are usually seen in pools near the Broken River bridge and upstream. The best times are the hours immediately after dawn and before dark and you must remain patiently still and silent. What you'll probably see in the end is a small creature, up to 50 cm long, paddling on the water surface for 10, maybe 15 seconds, as it chews its food before diving again to find more.

Several walking tracks start from Broken River bridge, and a short walk downstream there's a good swimming hole. Near the bridge colourful birds are prolific – kingfishers, parrots, cockatoos, brush turkeys, rosellas, lorikeets and plenty of kookaburras. At night the rufous bettong, a small kangaroo, is quite common, and there are two types of brushtail possum and two species of glider. Park rangers sometimes lead wildlife watching sessions or night spotlighting trips to pick out nocturnal animals.

Places to Stay & Eat

There are three national park camping grounds. The one at Broken River has showers, toilets, barbecues and sites beside the bridge on the upstream side or a short way down a track on the downstream side. Finch Hatton Gorge has toilets but the third site, Crediton Creek, has no facilities. Get camping permits from the ranger station (tel 58 4552) at Broken River. At holiday times it's advisable to check in advance whether there's room.

The kiosk at Broken River has superb home-made cakes. Also beside the bridge here are the *Broken River Holiday Cabins* (tel 58 4528), with fully equipped two bedroom units sleeping up to six for $50 double and $15 for each extra person.

In Eungella village there's the *Valley View Caravan Park* with tent sites at $8 double and a few on-site vans. Also in the village the *Chalet Hotel-Motel* (tel 58 4509), with a pool and fine views, has

rooms from $17 single, $25 double off season, $25 in busier times. There's a public bar and a restaurant here – most meals are $11. The village has a general store.

Getting There & Away

There are no buses to Eungella but hitching is quite possible. Some day tours go from Mackay but they're a waste of time if you want to see platypuses.

CAPE HILLSBOROUGH NATIONAL PARK

This coastal park 54 km north of Mackay takes in the rocky Cape Hillsborough, 300 metres high, and nearby Andrews Point and Wedge Island which are joined by a causeway at low tide. There are beaches and several walking tracks and the scenery ranges from cliffs, rocky coast, dunes and scrub to rainforest and woodland. Kangaroos, wallabies, sugar gliders and turtles are quite common.

Places to Stay

There's a council camping ground with tent sites at $5 double, close to the beach between Cape Hillsborough and Andrews Point. A couple of hundred metres along the beach is *Cape Hillsborough Resort* (tel 59 0152) with a pool, kiosk and a range of accommodation from tent sites at $6 for two people to 'beach houses' at $55 double or $60 for four. Tame kangaroos hang around both these sites. Near Seaforth is the *Halliday Bay Resort* (tel 59 0322) with a shop, pool, tennis, water sports, tent sites at $6.50 and rooms from $45 double, including meals.

Getting There & Away

Turn right off the Bruce Highway about 24 km north of Mackay, towards Seaforth. After 20 more km turn right. The park is 10 km down this road. A school bus, which anyone can take, leaves Mackay post office at 2.45 pm Monday to Friday in term time. It only goes to Seaforth but if you're staying at Cape Hillsborough Resort they'll probably pick you up.

BRAMPTON & CARLISLE ISLANDS

These two mountainous national park islands in the Cumberland Group, both about five square km in area, are 32 km north-east of Mackay. They're joined by a sandbank which you can walk across at low tides. Carlisle's highest point is 389 metre Skiddaw Peak, Brampton's is 219 metre Brampton Peak. Both have forested slopes, sandy beaches, good walks and fringing coral reefs with good snorkelling.

Brampton has an Australian Airlines owned resort (tel 51 4499) on its north-east coast, opposite Carlisle Island. It's in the luxury class at $220 double or more with tennis, golf, water sports and so on. Carlisle Island is uninhabited: you can camp but there are no facilities and you must even bring water.

The *Spirit of Roylen* fast catamaran leaves Mackay harbour daily for Brampton Island. Return fare is $20 and you can use it for a day-trip. You can also fly daily from Mackay ($46 one way with Australian Regional).

Most other islands in the Cumberland Group and the Sir James Smith Group to the north are also national parks: if you fancy a spot of Robinson Crusoeing and can afford to charter a boat or seaplane, Goldsmith and Scawfell are good bets. Contact the national parks offices in Mackay or Seaforth for all camping permits and info.

NEWRY & RABBIT ISLANDS

These small, little known tropical islands are just off the coast about 40 km up from Mackay. Newry Island, one km long, has a small resort (tel 59 0214) where camping is $3 per person, a bunk is $10 and cabins, sleeping up to five with their own bathrooms and cooking facilities, cost $45 double plus $10 for each extra person. You can also use the resort restaurant.

Rabbit Island, the largest of the group – three km long and 1½ km wide – has a national park camping site with toilets and a rainwater tank which can be empty in dry times. It also has the only sandy beaches in the group. From November to January sea turtles nest here. Contact the Mackay or Seaforth national parks offices for permits and info.

A boat leaves Victor Creek, four km west of Seaforth, twice a week (the days and times seem to vary) for Newry Island. The Newry resort says it'll pick you up from Victor Creek any day, tides permitting, if you phone. Return fare is $10. They can probably also drop you on Rabbit Island – though you can usually walk across from Newry to Rabbit at low tide. To reach Seaforth and Victor Creek, turn off the Bruce Highway 24 km north of Mackay. A school bus leaves Mackay post office for Seaforth at 2.45 pm on weekdays in term time.

Sugar Growing

Sugar is easily the most visible crop from Mackay north, past Cairns, up the Queensland coast. Sugar was a success almost from the day it was introduced in the region back in 1865 but its early days have a distinctly unsavoury air as the plantations were worked by Pacific Islanders who were often forced from their homes to come and work on Australian cane fields. 'Blackbirding', as this virtual slave trading was known, took a long time to be stamped out.

Today cane growing is a highly mechanised business and visitors are welcome to inspect the crushing plants during the harvesting season from about August to December. The most spectacular part of the operation is the firing of the cane fields in which rubbish is burnt off by night fires. Mechanical harvesters cut and gather the cane which is then transported to the sugar mills, often on narrow gauge railway lines laid through the cane fields. These lines are a familiar sight throughout the cane country. The cane is then shredded and passed through a series of crushers. The extracted juice is heated and cleaned of impurities and then evaporated to form a syrup. The next process reduces the syrup to molasses and low grade sugar. Further refining stages end with the sugar loaded into bulk containers for export.

Sugar production is a remarkably efficient process. The crushed fibres, known as bagasse, are burnt as fuel; impurities separated off from the juice are used as fertilisers; and the molasses are used either to produce ethanol or as stock feed.

Proserpine

Population 10,210

A sugar growing centre on the Bruce Highway, 125 km north of Mackay, Proserpine is where you turn off the Bruce Highway to reach Airlie Beach and the Whitsunday Islands. It has an airport and railway station. At 10.30 am and 1.30 pm in the cane harvest season you can take a $5 guided tour of Proserpine Sugar Mill.

Places to Stay & Eat
If you're stuck in Proserpine you could try the *Avalon Motor Inn* (tel 45 1200) at 32 Herbert St which has backpacker accommodation for $10, or $14 with your own bathroom, also motel rooms for $28 single, $35 double. The *Grand Central Hotel* at 69 Main St has rooms at $13 a head, $17 with breakfast, also counter meals. Cheaper motels on the Bruce Highway include the *Solaris Motel* (tel 45 1288) at $32/38 and the *Motel Astro* (tel 45 1288) at $33/40.

You can get a pizza at *Angels Restaurant* on Chapman St just off Main St. The *Midtown Cafe* has standard cafe meals and take-aways.

Getting There & Away
Air Proserpine airport is 15 km south of town. Ansett has direct flights five days a week from Brisbane ($213) and from Mackay ($68) and Sydney ($313) weekly. Australian flies nonstop to/from Brisbane four times weekly.

Australian Regional Airlines has flights to Proserpine from Mackay and Rockhampton, and Reef World Airlines flies to and from Lindeman Island ($50).

Bus All Rockhampton/Mackay/Townsville buses stop at Proserpine. About half of

them go on to Airlie Beach and Shute Harbour, and Greyhound and Pioneer run a connecting shuttle service for a few of the others.

Train Proserpine is on the Brisbane/Cairns Sunlander and Queenslander services. Economy fare from Brisbane is $81. In 1st it's $150.50 on the Sunlander, $217.25 on the Queenslander.

Getting Around
See under Airlie Beach.

Airlie Beach & Shute Harbour

It's 25 km from the Bruce Highway at Proserpine to Airlie Beach, which is the main accommodation centre opposite the Whitsunday Islands. From Airlie Beach it's another eight km to Shute Harbour, where most of the boats to the islands go from. If you want to see the islands by day-tripping, a stream of buses carries people between Airlie Beach and Shute Harbour daily.

Airlie Beach has grown phenomenally over the past 10 years and is now a bustling place. The area is one of the pleasure boating capitals of Australia. Apart from Shute Harbour itself which is packed with craft, lots of boats anchor in Airlie Bay and at least two marinas are being built. Airlie Beach is also a growing centre for learning to scuba dive but despite all this it's still a small place maintaining a relaxed air.

The road between Airlie Beach and Shute Harbour passes through Conway National Park which stretches away north and south along the coast. The southern end of the park separates the Whitsunday Passage from Repulse Bay, named by Captain Cook who strayed into it thinking it was the main passage. Most of the park is rugged ranges and valleys covered in

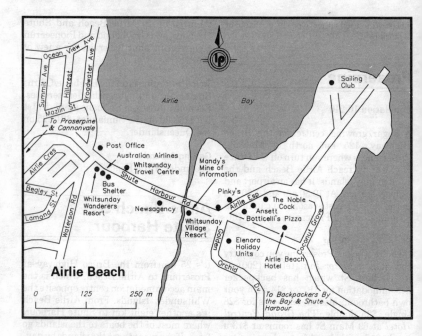

Airlie Beach

0   125   250 m

rainforest, but there is a camping ground and ranger station near the road and a few walking tracks in the surrounding area. The two km walk up to Mt Rooper lookout, north of the road, gives good views of the Whitsunday Passage and islands.

Another pleasant walk is along Mandalay Rd, about three km east of Airlie Beach, up to Mandalay Point. At Jubilee Pocket, off the Shute Harbour road two km east of Airlie Beach, the Whitsunday Aquarium is open daily from 10.30 am to 4.30 pm with feeding at 11 am. Admission is $5. About five km out of Airlie Beach towards Shute Harbour there's a bird sanctuary at Flame Tree Grove.

To reach the beautiful Cedar Creek Falls, turn south off the Proserpine to Airlie Beach road on to Conway Rd, eight km from Proserpine. It's then about 15 km to the falls, with a couple more signposted

turn-offs before you reach them. Down at the end of Conway Rd, 27 km from the Proserpine to Airlie Beach road, is the small settlement of Conway with a beach, the *Black Stump Caravan Park* (camping $4 double) and a pleasant pub.

Beware of stingers in the waters from October to April.

Information

Nearly everything of importance in Airlie Beach is on the main road, Shute Harbour Rd. There's no proper tourist info place but there are hosts of agencies and ticket offices. The notice board outside the newsagent on the main street lists rides, rooms to rent and so on. Many people come to Airlie Beach looking for casual work in hotels, restaurants or on the boats.

The national parks office (tel 46 9430) is down towards Shute Harbour, across the road from the Conway National Park main campsite. It's open from 8 am to 5 pm

Top: Boats on the beach, Brampton Island, Qld (PS)
Left: Keogh's run, Mt Hotham, Vic (RN)
Right: Bridal Veil Falls, Blue Mountains, NSW (CLA)

Top: Hot springs, Mataranka, NT (BW)
Left: Opal miner, Coober Pedy, SA (PS)
Right: Surfers Paradise, Gold Coast, Qld (PS)

Monday to Friday and at varying weekend hours. This office deals with camping bookings and permits for Conway and the island national parks.

Activities

Diving At least six outfits in and around Airlie Beach offer learn to dive certificate courses of five to six days. Standard costs vary from $230 to $290 but sometimes discounts are available. Most involve three days' tuition on the mainland and two days' diving on the Great Barrier Reef. All the firms also offer diving trips for certified divers.

Auscanz Divers (tel 46 7339), on the corner of Shute Harbour Rd and Golden Orchid Drive in Airlie Beach, has a good reputation; their $260 certificate course has the usual three days' theory and pool plus two days' and two nights' diving on the reef. You must provide a medical certificate. They have all sorts of packages for certified divers, prices varying considerably.

Oceania Dive (tel 46 6032), based at Reef Oceania Village, Cannonvale, has at $230 one of the cheapest deals, with tuition at the Reef Oceania resort pool. You get two days and a night on the reef. For experienced divers, they offer two days and one night on the reef for $140, all inclusive with a minimum of five dives.

Down Under Dive (tel 46 6869) is on The Esplanade, Airlie Beach; its five day course is normally $290 but discounts up to $90 are available during the low season. It involves four days' instruction on the mainland and only one day out at sea, on a sailing boat.

Airlie Beach Dive Centre (tel 46 6508) of Shop 1, Shute Harbour Rd, Airlie Beach, has a six day course for $255. The first three days involve classroom tuition and pool training. On the fourth day you take a day-trip out to sea and the fifth and sixth days are spent out on the reef. You do a minimum of seven dives, including a night dive. For qualified divers they offer two days and one night on the reef for $135

all-inclusive or a $70 day-trip to Langford Reef.

Two other outfits to consider are Barrier Reef Diving Services (tel 46 6204), The Esplanade, Airlie Beach; and Shute Harbour Diving Services (tel 46 6865), Shute Harbour Rd, Jubilee Pocket, about two km out of Airlie Beach towards Shute Harbour.

For the experienced, diving and snorkelling are possible on many of the one day and overnight cruises around the Whitsundays and to the Great Barrier Reef. The *Tri Tingira* is one vessel which will take you out. Fantasea Cruises has a certified divers' Barrier Reef day dive package for $55 (gear extra). Whitsunday Dive Charters offers a $60 dive or snorkel trip to the reef (gear extra); you spend four hours on the reef and do two dives. Meet the Reef Snorkelling Safaris advertises a reef trip for $12 which you book on the *Capricorn* at Shute Harbour.

Other Activities The 25 metre freshwater pool at the Coral Sea Resort on Ocean View Ave is open to the public daily from 8 am to 6 pm. You can take horseback trail rides at $18 for a half day with Brandy Creek Trail Rides (tel 46 6848), 12 km from Airlie Beach back towards Proserpine. They can pick you up from your accommodation. Tanlana Stud (tel 47 1005) also offers three hour trail rides and horses for hire ($10 an hour).

Places to Stay

There's a variety of places in Airlie Beach itself, in Cannonvale and along towards Shute Harbour. The cheap accommodation scene has improved greatly with the opening of four hostels in the last few years. In other places prices vary with the season.

Hostels There are four hostels. Some send vehicles to meet buses arriving at Airlie Beach and they'll all offer you deals on island trips, dive courses, etc. Nearest to the centre of things is *Backpackers By*

The Bay (tel 46 7267) at Lot 5, Hermitage Drive. Nightly cost is $12 in smallish fan cooled two bunk rooms, and there are quite spacious cooking and sitting areas, plus a pool, billiard table, garden and good views.

Club Walkabout (tel (008) 075 151 toll free) is on the roadside between Airlie Beach and Cannonvale, 1½ km from Airlie Beach. It has three buildings, one with 10 self-contained units each with six beds, kitchen, bathroom and TV. Cost is $12 a night. Up the hill, two houses full of bunks hold about another 40 people. For $8 a night, the facilities here are adequate and the view is great. Guests also have access to the pool and other facilities at the Club Crocodile resort, about a km back down the road towards Cannonvale. You can rent bicycles and scooters. Further along towards Cannonvale, 2.2 km from Airlie Beach, turn left along St Martin's Lane to reach *Bush Village* (tel 46 6177), with self-contained four person units at $10 a head. Each unit has cooking facilities, fridge, bathroom and TV, and usually two single beds and one bunk. There's a pool too. The units are a bit old-fashioned but clean and the owners are very helpful.

Reef Oceania Village (tel 46 6137), in Cannonvale three km from Airlie Beach, is a larger resort with a section of quite good backpacker bunk rooms. For $8 you get a place in an eight person dorm, for $9 you can share a four person room with its own fridge, and for $10 you share a four person room with fan, fridge and its own bathroom. There's a good big pool, with a restaurant and bar beside it. In the main resort part four people can share a two bedroom unit with TV for $17 each.

Hotels, Motels, Resorts & Holiday Flats In the non peak seasons, some of the resorts like *Whitsunday Wanderers* and *Whitsunday Village*, both on Shute Harbour Rd in Airlie Beach, offer standby twin share accommodation for $17 a night or $23 including breakfast. Whitsunday Wanderers for instance has four pools, tennis, landscaped gardens, bar, restaurant and nightly live entertainment. You might have to stay a few nights to qualify for these offers. Normally a double in these places is $80 or more.

The *Airlie Beach Hotel* (tel 46 6233) near the corner of Coconut Grove has air-con rooms with TV and private bathroom for $30 single, $40 double. There's a pool. Motels are pretty expensive: about the cheapest is the *Airlie Beach Motor Lodge* (tel 46 6418) on Lamond St which has some rooms from $38/45. Generally you'll find better value in some of the holiday flats. Four people sharing a flat will pay $17 each or less in these places and all bed linen and cooking equipment, etc, is supplied. *Sunlit Waters* (tel 46 6352) at the corner of Begley St and Airlie Crescent in Airlie Beach has a pool and charges $33 to $40 for two people, $8 to $10 for each extra person. *Malihini* (tel 46 6459) at 36 Coral Esplanade in Cannonvale also has a pool and charges $30 to $40 double, plus $6 for each extra person.

Camping & On-site Vans There are quite a few camping sites/caravan parks strung along the main road from Cannonvale nearly down to Shute Harbour. They're often packed out. A tent site at the Conway National Park main camping ground, almost down at Shute Harbour, is $8 a night for up to six people, but there's a maximum stay of four nights. There are a couple more sites at Swamp Bay, reached by a 4½ km walking track. The ranger station (tel 46 9430), for info, camping permits and bookings, is over the road from the main Conway camping ground.

Privately run van parks typically have pools and will rent you bed linen. They also usually have tent sites as well as a choice of two or three types of on-site van or units. Three or four people can share one of these quite economically.

Heading back from the national park towards Airlie Beach, *Flame Tree Caravan Village* (tel 46 9388) has tent sites for $10 double and vans from $25. *Airlie Cove Resort Van Park* (tel 46 6727), 2.8 km this same side of Airlie Beach, has good large modern cabins for $27 double, others at $40 for four people, some with their own bathrooms. There's a pool and a tennis court. A couple of hundred metres closer to Airlie Beach, *Shute Harbour Gardens* (tel 46 6483) has the cheapest on-site vans – $17 a double – but they're older and smaller than others. You can camp here for $8 double. Next along, *Island Trader Cabins* are $25 double; then there's *Island Gateway Village* (tel 46 6228) on the corner of Jubilee Pocket, with vans and cabins from $25 and camping at $10 double. This place has cooking facilities for campers plus bicycles for hire.

At Cannonvale there's a cheap council van and camping park near the seafront – turn down opposite St Martin's Lane. *Seabreeze Tourist Park* a bit further along the main road has camping, on-site vans and 'de luxe' cottages. Finally the popular *Pioneer Caravan Park* (tel 46 5266), also with camping, is 5½ km out of Airlie Beach.

Places to Eat
Coconut Grove has a health food shop serving inexpensive lunches. The *Palms Plaza Pizza Bar* has reasonably priced take-away pizzas and pasta and next door the *Airlie Beach Hotel* has a bistro with meals from $8. *La Perouse* is tucked away in an arcade between Coconut Grove and Airlie Esplanade. It's expensive with steaks at $14 but there's a dinner special – three courses for $17.

On Airlie Esplanade, *Noble Cock* and *Annie's Place* are two budget priced eateries almost side by side, both open daily from breakfast to early dinner.

On the corner of Airlie Esplanade and Shute Harbour Rd, *Botticelli's* does good pizzas from $7. It's open from 11.30 am to 9.30 pm. Don't miss *Pinky's*, a popular, moderately priced little place opposite Botticelli's. Its varied menu starts with sandwiches from $3 and meals from $7.

Across Shute Harbour Rd from Botticelli's, the *Spice Island Bistro* specialises in Malaysian, Indonesian and Indian seafood dishes.

On the same side of the main drag, next to the creek, the *Whitsunday Holiday Village* has the very busy *Gallery Reef* restaurant with lunches for $5. It's a popular Saturday afternoon hang-out. Beyond the creek and over the road, *Cafe Le Mignon* is a popular, reasonably priced place open from 8 am to 5 pm, closing earlier on weekends.

If you fancy Italian there are two places either side of Shute Harbour Rd near the post office. *Romeo's* on the post office side, open daily from 7 am to midnight, has two sections – one a gourmet take-away, the other a more expensive restaurant with a sea view. *Chianti's*, over the road, has less in the budget range though you get garlic bread, salad and a glass of wine or a soft drink with a meal which makes it worth considering. It's open from 6 to 10 pm Monday to Saturday.

Entertainment
Airlie Beach is the centre of activities during the annual Whitsunday Village Fun Race (for cruising yachts) each September. The festivities include a Miss Figurehead competition where the contestants traditionally compete topless. A more regular event is the Tuesday and Thursday night toad races at the *Airlie Beach Hotel* (7.30 pm). You can rent a steed if you haven't got your own. This pub is also the place for live rock music or a disco most nights, plus Saturday and Sunday afternoons.

The *Whitsunday Village* and *Whitsunday Wanderers* resorts also have entertainment most nights, ranging from discos and bands to toad or even crab racing and floor shows.

Getting There & Away
Air Sea Air Pacific (tel 46 9133) has some scheduled services to/from the Whitsunday

airstrip down towards Shute Harbour. There are flights to/from Lindeman Island ($52) and Mackay ($71). Australian Airlines and Ansett only fly to Proserpine or, in the case of Ansett, Hamilton Island, but have offices in Airlie Beach. Australian (tel 46 6273) are in the Whitsunday Wanderers resort, Ansett (tel 46 6255) is in Airlie Beach Travel on the Esplanade.

Bus Roughly half the buses with each of the five main companies up and down the coast detour off the Bruce Highway down to Airlie Beach. Most of these services go to Shute Harbour too. Greyhound and Pioneer also run connecting services to/from Proserpine for other north-south buses. From Brisbane it's about 18 hours to Airlie Beach and costs $73. Mackay is about two hours from Airlie Beach, Rockhampton about six hours. To Townsville it's four hours and to Cairns it's nine hours.

Unless you're on a bus pass, to go just between Proserpine and Airlie Beach or Shute Harbour you must take Sampsons Buses (tel 45 2377) which run several times daily between Proserpine Airport, Mill St in Proserpine, Airlie Beach and Shute Harbour. Buses leave Proserpine Airport 25 minutes after each plane arrival. It's $5 one way from Proserpine to Airlie Beach, $2.20 from Airlie Beach to Shute Harbour. Last bus back from Airlie Beach to Proserpine is about 5 pm.

Whitsunday Travel Centre, up towards the post office on the main street, is the main bus stop in Airlie Beach. You can buy tickets here but they charge for making bookings or confirmations on tickets that they haven't sold you.

Boat The Sailing Club at the end of Airlie Beach Esplanade has a notice board with rides/crewing sometimes available. Or ask around Airlie Beach or Shute Harbour. Sometimes you'll be able to work a free passage, but it's not uncommon for boat or yacht owners to charge you $7 to $10 a day.

Getting Around

There are a few land based tours although the real interest lies out on the water. Club Walkabout hostel has bicycles and scooters for hire to guests, and Reef Oceania Village has motor bikes. Several rent-a-car agencies operate locally, with Avis and National opposite each other on Shute Harbour Rd in Airlie Beach. Avis has Mokes for $30 a day including insurance, but there may be a distance charge on top. National and Budget (opposite Airlie Beach post office) rent soft top cars. Auscanz in Airlie Beach also advertises VW soft tops – $35 for eight hours, $48 for 24 hours. Fun Parlour in the arcade on Airlie Esplanade has mopeds for hire.

Whitsunday Islands

The 74 Whitsunday Islands are probably the best known Queensland islands. The group was named by Captain Cook who sailed through here on 3 July 1770. They're scattered on both sides of the Whitsunday Passage and are all within 50 km of Shute Harbour. The Whitsundays are mostly continental islands, the tips of underwater mountains, but many of them have fringing coral reefs. The actual barrier reef is at least 60 km out from Shute Harbour; Hook Reef is the nearest part of it.

The islands – mostly hilly and wooded – and the passages between them are certainly beautiful and while a few are developed with tourist resorts, most are uninhabited and several offer the chance of some back-to-nature beach side camping and bushwalking. All but five of the Whitsundays are predominantly or completely national park. The exceptions include Dent, which has a grazing lease, and Hamilton, Daydream and Hayman with resorts. The other main resorts are on South Molle and Lindeman Islands and at Happy Bay on Long Island.

Camping on the Islands

Although accommodation in the island resorts is mostly expensive it's possible to camp on several islands. Two – Long and Hook – have privately run camping sites and on several other islands you can camp cheaply at locations designated by the national parks people. Self-sufficiency is the key to camping on the national park sites. Some sites have toilets but only a few have drinking water, and then not always year round. You're advised to take five litres of water per person per day, plus three days' extra supply in case you get stuck. You should also have a fuel stove – wood fires are banned on some islands and unwelcome on the others. The national parks service publishes a leaflet describing the various sites and can give you detailed info on what to take and do. Their local office (tel 46 9430) is opposite Conway National Park camping ground, on the Airlie Beach to Shute Harbour road.

The national parks people, it seems, can't tell you which boats will drop you on which islands or how much they'll cost. Booking agencies in Airlie Beach are better sources for this kind of information. A water taxi (tel 46 9202) from Shute Harbour costs $100 one way to most camping islands. Or, for $35 to $45 return per person, several of the day-trip boats will drop you off at the end of a cruise and pick you up again on an agreed date. Generally the sail around boats such as the *Tri Tingira*, *Bacchus D*, *Trinity* or *Nari* are better for this than the island resort boats.

To get your national park camping permit, first you have to book your site, dates and number of people at the national parks office. Numbers at each camping area are limited. Once you have ensured a site, you can then arrange your transport and, having fixed that, you return to the national parks office to get your camping permit which usually costs $2 a night per person, up to a maximum of $5 for a site, which can take six people.

The following is a summary of national park camping possibilities in the Whitsundays:

island	location	No of sites	drinking water
Shute	north end	2	no
North Molle	Hannah Point	5	seasonal
	Cockatoo Beach	10	seasonal
Whitsunday	Whitehaven Beach, south end	20	no
	Scrub Hen Beach	10	no
	Dugong Beach	15	yes, maybe seasonal
	Sawmill Beach	5	seasonal
	Joe's Beach	4	no
Hook	Curlew Beach	10	no
Thomas	Sea Eagle Beach	10	no
Shaw	Neck Bay Beach	3	no
South Repulse	western beach	3	no
Gloucester*	Bona Bay	10	no
Armit*	western beach	5	no
Saddleback*	western side	5	no
Grassy	south-west point	2	no

* northern islands like Armit, Gloucester and Saddleback are harder to reach since the water taxi and cruises from Shute Harbour don't usually go there. Gloucester and Saddleback are best reached from Earlando, Dingo Beach or Bowen.

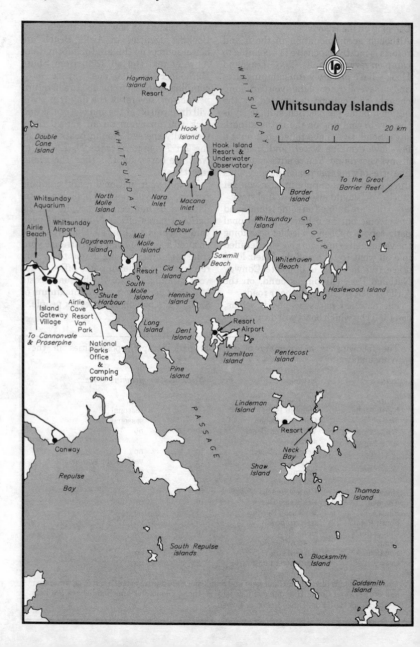

LONG ISLAND

One of the closer in and less commercial of the resort islands, Long Island is about 11 km long but no more than 1½ km wide, and nearly all national park. It has lots of rainforest, 13 km of walking tracks and some fine lookouts. There are three accommodation places. *Happy Bay*, where the cruise boats come to, has a long expanse of proper tropical island beach. The resort here is run by the Contiki package holiday people, with two pools, tennis, archery, water sports and so on as well as the obligatory disco. There's a wreck in the bay that's supposed to be a Spanish galleon!

Palm Bay (tel 46 9233), about a km south of Happy Bay, is one of the two cheapest island resorts with nine simple cabins with cooking facilities and fridges. You can get some supplies here or bring them over from the mainland. A place in a six person cabin costs $17 a night, or you can take the whole thing for $80. Or you can sleep in Camp-O-Tel units – a cross between cabins and tents with beds – for $16 per person twin share or $12 per person four share. There's good snorkelling, a glass-bottomed boat, and dinghies, catamarans and windsurfers for hire. It's wise to book well ahead. The return launch fare from Shute Harbour is $20.

At *Paradise Bay* (tel 45 2838/46 7536 after hours) in the south of the island there's a fishing and camping village, with shared accommodation in self-contained four person units for $14 per person per night – or a whole unit for $45. You can also camp for $7. There's a small shop but take your own supplies. Launch return from Shute Harbour is $25.

HOOK ISLAND

Second largest of the Whitsundays, Hook Island is 53 square km and rises to 450 metres at Hook Peak. There are a number of beaches dotted around the island. It's mainly national park, with a camping area at Curlew Beach in the southern Macona Inlet, but there's also the budget *Hook Island Resort* facing Whitsunday Island in the south.

Accommodation in the resort is in a few eight bunk rooms with communal showers and toilets. You pay $17 a night, with bedding included. There's a kitchen but you have to take your own utensils, or you can eat in the bar/bistro (barbecue lunch or dinner $11, salad $6). You can also camp here for $8 per person but the camping site is small and the ground hard. The booking office (tel 46 6900) is at Shop 1, 283 Shute Harbour Rd in Airlie Beach. The resort is also visited by day-trips so if you're really wanting to escape from civilisation this probably isn't your place.

Near the resort is the Hook Island underwater observatory ($9). You can also see the underwater world in a semisub for $12 or hire snorkel gear for the length of your stay for $3. The return launch trip to the resort is $40.

The beautiful, fjord-like Nara Inlet on Hook Island is a very popular deep water anchorage for visiting yachties.

DAYDREAM ISLAND

This small, two km long island is only a couple of hundred metres across at its widest point. It's the nearest resort island to Shute Harbour and has one of the best swimming pools. The resort aims for a party atmosphere. Accommodation per person is normally from $110 a day including meals, water activities and tennis, but there's a standby rate of $70 including the return trip from Shute Harbour. You can also spend a day on Daydream for $25 including boat transfers, lunch and water sport facilities.

SOUTH MOLLE ISLAND

Largest of the Molle group of islands (four square km) South Molle is virtually joined to Mid Molle and North Molle islands. It has long stretches of beach and is crisscrossed by walking tracks. Highest point is 198 metre Mt Jeffreys but the climb up Spion Kop is also worthwhile.

You can spend a day walking on the island for just the cost of the $20 return ferry trip.

Most of South Molle is national park but there's an Ansett operated resort in the north, where the boats come in, with nightly costs from $135-plus per person including all meals. You may be able to get a much cheaper standby rate. The resort has a big pool, a small golf course and tennis, squash, archery, snorkelling, windsurfing and a gym, all included in the price. Daily at 3 pm hundreds of rainbow lorikeets fly in to feed.

HAMILTON ISLAND

The most flamboyant resort island in the Whitsundays, privately owned Hamilton Island has its own jet airport, a 200 boat marina and accommodation for more than 1000, including one tower block. The range of entertainment possibilities, not surprisingly, is extensive (and expensive): helicopter joy rides, game fishing, parasailing, cruising, scuba diving, about seven restaurants, shops, squash courts, even a dolphin pool and a hilltop fauna reserve with wombats, crocodiles and koalas. The cheapest double room costs $190 (though there are four person suites for $235) but standby rates cut about one-third off these prices. Hamilton is more like a small town than a resort so there are a variety of restaurants, take-aways, even a small supermarket.

Hamilton is more than five square km in area and rises to 200 metres at Passage Peak. It can make an interesting day-trip ($25 from Shute Harbour for the launch return only). You can also reach it from Mackay ($30 return).

The airport is used mainly by people jetting in for holidays on this and the other resort islands, with launches and helicopters laid on to whisk them off to their chosen spots. Ansett flies nonstop to Hamilton from Brisbane ($219 one way), Cairns ($162), Mackay ($82), Melbourne ($384), Mt Isa (Ansett NT, $250) and Sydney ($305). Standby is available on some routes. But there's little point flying to

Hamilton if you're on a budget since you'll probably be staying at Airlie Beach or on one of the non mainstream islands which are easily – and more cheaply – reached from Shute Harbour.

HAYMAN ISLAND

Owned by Ansett, Hayman has been remodelled into such an exclusive resort that day-trips don't even call there. The nearest you'll probably get is some of the reefs or small islands nearby such as Black Island (also called Bali Hai) or Arkhurst, Langford or Bird Islands. Hayman is the most northerly of the main Whitsunday group, with an area of four square km, rising to 250 metres above sea level. It has forested hills, valleys and beaches. The resort, in the south, is fronted by a wide, shallow reef which emerges from the water at low tide. Rooms start above $200 a night and food is equally expensive.

LINDEMAN ISLAND

One of the most southerly of the Whitsundays, Lindeman covers eight square km, mostly national park. It has 20 km of walking trails and the highest point is 210 metre Mt Oldfield. The resort, in the south, has a golf course, tennis and lots of water activities. The resort was completely remodelled and renovated in 1987-88. Double rooms are around $90 excluding meals which add $50 per person. Return launch fare from Shute Harbour is $60. Lindeman also has its own airstrip: Sea Air Pacific flies from Mackay ($65) and the Whitsunday airport near Shute Harbour ($52) and Proserpine ($50).

With plenty of little beaches and secluded bays on Lindeman it's no hassle at all to find one all to yourself. There are also a lot of small islands dotted around, some of which are easy to get across to. Lindeman is pleasant because it's somewhat smaller than the big, crowded resorts and also far enough from the centre of the Whitsundays to avoid the day-trippers.

WHITSUNDAY ISLAND

The largest of the Whitsunday islands, Whitsunday covers 109 square km and rises to 438 metres at Whitsunday Peak. There's no resort but six km Whitehaven Beach on the south-east coast is probably the longest and finest in the group, with good snorkelling off its south end. There are national park camping areas at Whitehaven Beach, Scrub Hen Beach in the north-west, Dugong and Sawmill Beaches on the west, and Joe's Beach.

CID HARBOUR

Between Hook and Whitsunday islands, Cid Harbour was the anchorage for part of the US Navy before the Battle of the Coral Sea, turning point in the Pacific theatre of WW II. Today, visiting ocean cruise liners anchor here.

OTHER ISLANDS

There's a lighthouse on Dent Island, guiding ships through the passage. Near Lindeman Island, Pentecost Island was named by Captain Cook and has a 208 metre high cliff face shaped remarkably like an Indian head.

GETTING AROUND
Sea

There's a bamboozling array of boat trips. Mandy's Mine of Information, on Shute Harbour Rd in Airlie Beach, prints a useful list dividing the trips into manageable categories. You can make bookings at Mandy's or any of the other agents in Airlie Beach.

Most boats depart from Shute Harbour, the end of the road from Airlie Beach. You can bus there from Airlie Beach – some of the cruise operators do coach pick ups from Airlie Beach – or leave your car in the Shute Harbour car park for $2 for 24 hours. There's a lock up car park a few hundred metres back along the road by the Shell service station, costing $4 from 8 am to 5 pm or $8 for 24 hours. To avoid busy Shute Harbour, a few boats now leave from Airlie Beach.

One type of cruise revolves around the resort islands. If you want to spend the whole day on one island, the return fare to South Molle is $20, to Hamilton $25. The popular $25 day-trip to Daydream Island includes lunch and use of resort water sports facilities.

You can also combine two or three islands in one day. You go to island A, have an hour or two to sample the beach, pool and bar then carry on to do the same at island B. South Molle Island Cruises operates a three island cruise (Daydream, Hook and South Molle) for $38 with a semisub ride and the underwater observatory thrown in, but no lunch. Such cruises are worthwhile if you have limited time.

Some cruises take in one or two of the resorts plus an uninhabited beach or island. They range from $20 to $45 depending on where they go and whether lunch is provided. You can usually fit in some snorkelling and try boom-netting which is lots of fun: you jump into a net alongside the boat and get soaked as you're pulled along. This type of trip is offered by Hamilton Island Cruises and the motor launches *Island Wanderer* and *Seafari*. Hamilton's $30 cruise includes Hamilton Island of course but also stops at beautiful Whitehaven Beach on Whitsunday Island. The *Island Wanderer* ventures to Palm Bay on Long Island, Nara inlet on Hook Island, plus Daydream and South Molle Islands, all for $20 – no lunch but this is a popular, good value trip. The *Seafari's* $28 trip (three days a week) cruises past Hamilton and visits Dent and Henning Islands, with a barbecue lunch. Other days, the *Seafari* goes to Daydream and South Molle resorts and an uninhabited island – for $20, without lunch.

A more active day can be spent on the 'nowhere in particular' trips, usually in yachts. You stay away from the resort islands, perhaps try a beach here, a bit of snorkelling there, some fishing elsewhere. You might windsurf or fly a kite and boom-net in between. Usually there's a good lunch too. Some of these boats leave from Airlie Beach and they'll often pick you up from where you're staying. The cheaper ones include the popular *Jade* and the *Trinity*, each $27 for the day. Also popular are the *Tri Tingira* and *Apollo* on which you are invited to help with the sailing. The *Nari* and *Bacchus D* operate this type of trip for around $35. A day on the former America's Cup contender, *Gretel*, is yours for $42. The *La-Ma-Tai* does half day sailing trips from Airlie Beach for $14.

There are also outer reef trips where you power out to the reef for a spot of walking on the reef itself, a bit of snorkelling, a ride in a glass-bottomed boat and/or diving. Getting out to the reef is an other worldly experience that, if you can afford it, should not be missed. Fantasea Cruises and the *Triton II*, both charging $49, are at the cheaper end of the range for reef trips. South Molle Cruises, the fast catamaran *2001* and Hamilton Island Cruises go to the reef for $65.

If you're experienced at sea, you can hire your own yacht or motor cruiser. Prices are high but they look better if shared among a group of people. The Bare Boat Charter Company for instance charges $145 to $380 a day for a yacht in the low season and $190 to $524 in the high season. Their motor cruisers cost $250 in the low season and $340 in the high season. Fuel is extra – for motor cruisers it's $14 per motor hour, for a yacht $6 a day.

Smaller craft can be rented from Harbourside Boat Hire or Royal Mandalay Water Sports. For a 3.6 metre motor dinghy holding four people, Royal Mandalay is slightly cheaper at $25 for a half day or $40 for a full day including fuel. For a 5.2 metre cabin cruiser carrying six people, you pay about $50 for a half day, $80 for a full day, plus a $50 to $100 bond. Fuel is extra.

Then there are overnight cruises. Makaira Reef Adventure offers two days and two nights cruising the islands and the reef for a standby rate of $65 a day. This includes all meals, fishing, snorkelling, diving and even an island pub crawl. Three days and two nights on the schooner *Emma Peel* will cost $150 including meals and accommodation on board, fishing and snorkelling gear. This boat departs three times a week with each cruise mooring overnight at Hook and Hamilton Islands.

Air

Sea Air Pacific (tel 46 9133), based at the Whitsunday airstrip near Shute Harbour, makes scenic flights over the islands and/or reef (minimum two adults) from $30 for 10 minutes to $85 for an hour. Or for $100-plus their seaplanes will 'land' you on the reef for semisub rides, glass-bottomed boating, reef walking or snorkelling. Alternatively you can make a joy flight in an open cockpit Tiger Moth biplane for $35. They also run air taxi flights.

Whitsundays to Townsville

BOWEN (Population 7663)

This agreeable town, founded in 1861, was the first coastal settlement north of Rockhampton.

Though overshadowed before long by Mackay to the south and Townsville to the north, Bowen survived and today is a thriving fruit and vegetable growing centre which attracts hundreds of people for seasonal picking work.

There's a good museum at 22 Gordon St relating to the town's early history. It's open weekdays and Sunday mornings. Just north of Bowen a string of sandy beaches, some of them quite secluded, dot the coast round the cape to the north. In order going from the town they are Kings Beach, Rose Bay, Murrays Bay, Horseshoe Bay (where there's coral just offshore), Greys Bay then the long Queens Beach.

Places to Stay

Bowen Backpackers (tel 86 3433) is at 56 Herbert St, on the main street. Cooking, eating and sitting areas and some bedrooms are in a renovated old style Queensland house, there's more accommodation in a newer section. The nightly cost is $9, plus $2 for bed linen. The hostel is a pleasant place to take a breather from the more hectic scene elsewhere on the coast.

Bowen has a long list of motels, holiday flats and caravan/camping grounds either on the Bruce Highway or in the town or up near Queens and Horseshoe Bay beaches. Cheaper motels on the highway include the *Big Mango* and the *Ocean View* at $30/35.

Places to Eat

The *Club Hotel* and the *Central Hotel*, a block or two down Herbert St from the backpackers, both do counter meals. Near the Central, the *Bowen Tuckerbox* does a range of decently priced snacks and meals for under $7, plus pizzas. You can also get pizzas at *Francos* on Herbert St. The *Denison Hotel* on Powell St has a char grill from 6 to 8 pm.

Getting There & Away

Buses between Rockhampton and Townsville stop at Bowen. Typical fares and travelling times are Rockhampton $47, 6½ hours; Airlie Beach $16, two hours; Townsville $20, 2½ hours. The Sunlander and Queenslander trains also stop at Bowen. Economy fare from Brisbane is $84.20. There's also a Rail Motor service between Bowen and Townsville.

AYR (Population 8787)

This sugar town is on the delta of one of the biggest rivers in Queensland, the Burdekin. Rice is also grown in the area. On Wilmington St the House of Australian Nature has displays of orchids, shells and butterflies, open from 8 am to 5 pm daily.

Across the Burdekin River is Home Hill with an historical museum. Between Ayr and Townsville you pass the Australian Institute of Marine Science on Cape Ferguson. You can visit it from 8 am to 4 pm Monday to Friday, with guided tours given on Fridays.

Townsville

Population 86,112

The third largest city in Queensland and the main centre in the north of the state, Townsville is the port city for the agricultural and mining production of the vast inland region of northern Queensland. Founded in 1864 by the efforts of a Scot, John Melton Black, and the money of Robert Towns, a Sydney based sea captain and financier, Townsville developed mainly on the back of Chinese and Kanaka labour.

Today Townsville is a working city, a major armed forces base, and the site of James Cook University. It's the start of the main road from Queensland to the Northern Territory and the only departure point for Magnetic Island. The Barrier Reef is about 1¾ hours away.

In recent years millions of dollars have been spent in an effort to attract more visitors to stay for a time in Townsville rather than go straight through to Cairns. A Sheraton hotel-casino and a marina have been built on Townsville's ocean front, and the Flinders East area fronting Ross Creek is being redeveloped but managing to keep many of its 19th century buildings. The centrepiece here is the Great Barrier Reef Wonderland complex. Along with these big money efforts, there's been a boom in budget accommodation and in the eating and entertainment scene.

Offshore, what's claimed to be the world's first floating hotel arrived on the Barrier Reef 72 km from Townsville in early 1988. By the end of the year, this

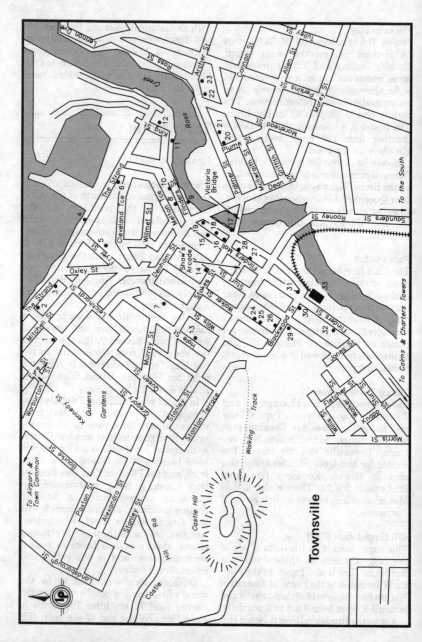

Townsville

1	Hotel Allen
2	Seaview Hotel
3	Strand Motel
4	Tobruk Swimming Pool
5	Yongala Lodge
6	Waterfall
7	Wills Street Hostel
8	Backpackers International
9	Waterfront Quaterdeck Restaurant
10	Exchange Hotel
11	Great Barrier Reef Wonderland & Westmark Ferry Terminal
12	Coachman's Inn Motel
13	Coral House
14	Townsville Museum
15	Tourist Information
16	Townsville International Hotel
17	Food Fair
18	Australian Airlines
19	GPO
20	Transit Centre
21	Globetrotters Hostel
22	Crown Tavern
23	Adventurers Resort
24	Mike Ball Watersports
25	Civic House
26	Pacific Coast Budget Accomodation
27	Coco's
28	Ansett
29	Sunseeker Private Hotel
30	Cafe Nova
31	Great Northern Hotel
32	Barrier Reef Hostel
33	Railway Station

seven storey, 200 room, 6000 tonne creation was in deep financial trouble.

Orientation

Townsville centres on Ross Creek and is dominated by 290 metre Castle Hill with a lookout perched on top. Townsville sprawls a long way but the centre's a fairly compact area that you can easily get around on foot. Most of the accommodation is in the centre. The new transit centre, arrival and departure point for long-distance buses, is on Palmer St, just south of Ross Creek. The city centre is immediately to the north of the creek, over the Dean St bridge. Flinders Mall stretches to the left from the north side of

the bridge, towards the railway station. To the right of the bridge is the Flinders East area, with many of the oldest buildings, several cafes and restaurants, the Great Barrier Reef Wonderland and the ferry departure points.

Information

The Magnetic North tourist information centre (tel 71 2724) is in the middle of Flinders St Mall, between Stokes and Dean Sts. It's open Monday to Friday from 9 am to 5 pm, Saturdays and Sundays from 9 am to 12 noon. Travellers have recommended a free programme run by the centre to introduce overseas visitors to Australians in their homes – you're invited along for a drink or meal and conversation. The RACQ (tel 71 2168) is at 711-717 Flinders St.

Townsville holds an interesting Sunday morning crafts and food market in the Flinders St Mall. Mary Who, on Stanley St, is an excellent bookshop.

Around Town

Pick up a *Townsville Tourist Trails* leaflet from the museum on the corner of Sturt and Stokes Sts if you're interested in a walking tour round Townsville's old buildings.

The Flinders St Mall is bright, breezy and full of interest. Giant games of chess, backgammon and snakes & ladders are part of the mall activities. Just down from the mall, the old Victoria swing bridge has been turned into shops and eateries.

East of the mall you can stroll along Flinders St East beside the creek, past Great Barrier Reef Wonderland. Many of the best 19th century buildings are in this part of town. Out past here on a breakwater at the mouth of Ross Creek is the casino, but a more pleasant walk is north along The Strand, a long beachfront drive with a marina, gardens, some awesome banyan trees, the Tobruk swimming pool and a big artificial waterfall.

Behind The Strand, Queen's Gardens

on Gregory St, a km from the town centre, are the original botanic gardens in Townsville, dating from 1878.

There's a road up to the top of Castle Hill and you can also walk up from Stanton Terrace.

Great Barrier Reef Wonderland

Townsville's top attraction is at the end of Flinders St East beside Ross Creek. While its impressive aquarium is the highlight, there are several other sections including shops, a good National Parks information office, and the Westmark and Reef Link ferry and cruise terminals.

Aquarium The huge main tank has a living coral reef and hundreds of reef fish and other life. To maintain the natural conditions needed to keep this community alive, 'tides' are imitated by raising and lowering the water level, a wave machine simulates the ebb and flow of the ocean and marine algae are used in the purification system. The aquarium also has several smaller tanks, extensive displays on the history and life of the reef, and a theatrette where films on the reef are shown. It's open daily from 9.30 am to 5 pm and admission is $6.

Omnimax Theatre This is a cinema with angled seating and a dome shaped screen for a 3-D effect. Hour long films on the reef and outer space alternate through the day from 9.30 am till 5.30 pm. There are also some evening sessions. Admission to one film is $8.

Queensland Museum This museum has displays focusing on north Queensland, including wetland birds and other wildlife, rainforest, ocean wrecks and Aboriginal artefacts. The museum is open daily from 9 am to 5 pm (Fridays until 8 pm) and admission is $1.

Wonderland Show Half hour slide shows on north Queensland are presented here for $3. Open from 9 am to 5 pm daily.

Galleries & Other Museums

The Townsville Museum on the corner of Sturt and Stokes Sts has a permanent display on early Townsville and the North Queensland independence campaigns, as well as temporary exhibitions. It's open daily from 10 am to 1 or 3 pm.

The Jezzine Military Museum is just off the north end of The Strand. It's open Monday to Friday from 9 am to 3 pm, Saturdays, Sundays and holidays from 2 to 4 pm. There's also a Maritime Museum on Benwell Rd, in South Townsville, open from 10 am to 4 pm (11 am to 4 pm on weekends).

The Perc Tucker Regional Gallery on the mall at the corner of Denham St is one of the best regional art galleries in Australia. It's closed on Monday. There's also the Martin Gallery at 475 Flinders St. The Australian Collection, in Barrier Reef Wonderland, is a gallery selling Aboriginal art and crafts.

Further Out

The new botanic gardens, Anderson Park, are six km out from the centre on Gulliver St, Mundingburra. For a chance to see some wildlife, make your way out to Townsville Town Common, five km north of the centre, just off Cape Pallarenda Rd. This 32 square km area ranges from mangrove swamps and salt marsh to dry grassland and pockets of woodland and forest. The common is best known for water birds such as the magpie geese which herald the start of the wet season, and stately brolgas which gather in the dry. Early morning is the best time to see them.

The Billabong Sanctuary, 17 km south on the Bruce Highway, is a zoo of Australian animals, open daily with shows (including crocodile or giant eel feeding) at 11.30 am, plus 2.30 pm on weekends and holidays. Admission is $7 for adults.

A 30 to 40 minute drive north from Townsville will take you to Balgal Beach near Rollingstone. There's camping and a food stall.

There are a lot of rodeos in Queensland, a number of them in the small towns inland from Townsville. The season is May to October and the tourist office should have details.

National Parks

Twenty-eight km south of Townsville along the Bruce Highway, then six km south by paved road, there's a good camping site by Alligator Creek in the big Bowling Green Bay National Park. Swimming holes in the creek are good during the wet season and some walking tracks start from the camping site. Alligator Creek tumbles down between two rugged ranges which rise steeply from the coastal plains. The taller range peaks in Mt Elliott (1342 metres), whose higher slopes harbour some of Queensland's most southerly tropical rainforest. There's no public transport to the park.

There's more tropical rainforest in Mt Spec National Park which straddles the 1000 metre plus Paluma Range, to the west of the Bruce Highway – 65 km north of Townsville. A paved turn-off from the highway winds up along the south edge of the park, passing Little Crystal Creek and McClelland's Lookout on the way to the small village of Paluma. Pioneer runs $30 day tours up here from Townsville. Also in the park at Big Crystal Creek, four km along a dirt road that turns off the Bruce Highway two km north of the Paluma turn-off, there's a camping site (permits from Townsville, Ingham or on site) and more good swimming. Bower birds are relatively common in the park.

Jourama National Park is nine unpaved km off the highway, 89 km north of Townsville. There are more good swimming holes here, along with waterfalls, a short walking track, a camping ground (permits as for Big Crystal Creek) and a lookout.

For camping permits there are ranger stations in Paluma (tel 70 8526) and near the Alligator Creek camping site (tel 78 8203), or ask at the parks office in Barrier Reef Wonderland in Townsville. For Jourama permits phone 77 3112.

Activities

Townsville has one of Australia's best diving schools – Mike Ball Watersports (tel 72 3022) at 252 Walker St. A training pool, a deep dive tank, and a 'transit tube' to prepare you for diving in narrow spaces, are all on the premises. Five day certificate courses start twice a week and cost $260 to $285 with five trips to the reef – plus two nights there on the more expensive option. You have to take a $30 medical before you start the course. There are free introductory sessions on Tuesdays, with no obligation to continue.

Pro-Dive, another well regarded dive school, also runs courses in Townsville. Its office (tel 21 1760) is in Great Barrier Reef Wonderland. Pro-Dive's five day certificate course costs $245, starts twice a week, and includes one night and two days on the reef. Pro-Dive doesn't require you to see a doctor before starting the course.

You can get cheap or free accommodation at some hostels if you take a dive course.

For experienced divers, the wreck of the *Yongala*, a passenger liner which sank off Cape Bowling Green in 1911 with 122 lives lost, is more of an attraction than the John Brewer Reef to which many day-trips go. The *Yongala* has huge numbers of fish and large marine life like turtles and rays. John Brewer Reef has been damaged by the crown-of-thorns starfish and cyclones, and parts of it have little live coral. Mike Ball and Pro-Dive both run trips out to the *Yongala* – with Pro-Dive you pay $90 for a day-trip or $110 overnight, plus $30 for equipment hire if you need it.

North Queensland Sailboards (tel 72 6399) at 41 Ingham Rd rents canoes and sailboards. You can do white-water rafting trips from Townsville but the same trips are significantly cheaper if you start from Tully, Mission Beach or Cairns.

Beware of box jellyfish off the beaches from October to May.

Places to Stay

Hostels & Backpacker Accommodation

A 240 bed backpacker and budget accommodation section has been built into the *Transit Centre* on Palmer St. It is air conditioned. A few doors along Palmer St at 45, *Globetrotters* (tel 71 3242) is one of Townsville's best hostels. It has a pool and a few twin rooms ($25) as well as bunks in dorms ($10).

Melton Apartments – 'Backpackers On The Hill' are at 16 Willmett Street, a four minute walk from the central post office. The normal rate per person is $12 for share accommodation and $24 for a single room. There is also a standby rate of $10 a night for share accommodation. Facilities include modern kitchens, televisions, videos and a barbecue and entertainment area.

The *Adventurers Resort* (tel 21 1522), is at 79 Palmer St, and has 300 beds, a budget licensed restaurant and a pool where dive classes are held. Accommodation is in rooms taking two, four or 10 people, and there's a kitchen, dining and sitting area, a garden and a take-away kiosk.

Several more places are north of Ross Creek. The busy *Backpackers International* (tel 72 4340) is at 205 Flinders St East. There are about 140 beds in a rambling collection of rooms behind a fine balconied Victorian front. It's a clean place, most of the dorms are spacious and airy, and you get free tea and coffee for your money ($10). The managers also get groups together for cut-price restaurant meals and nights out. But there seems a bit of a shortage of bathroom and kitchen space, and there's little privacy. The doors are locked at 1 am.

Reef Lodge (tel 21 1112) at 4 Wickham St has backpacker beds in addition to its more expensive rooms. You pay $8.50 in a dorm, $10 in a three or four person room, $14 twin share.

Over at 262 Walker St, *Civic House* (tel 71 5381) is popular with a TV room and adequate kitchen, bathroom and sitting space. You can share small four bunk rooms for $9 a head or pay $19 for a single, $24 or $26 for a double.

The *Wills Street Hostel* (tel 72 2820) at 23 Wills St is a cosy place with 18 dorm beds at the top of a long flight of steps opposite the law courts. It's $9 a night.

Some backpackers use *Coral House* (tel 71 5512), a small private hotel-cum-hostel at 32 Hale St. You can share a three bed room for $8 each, or there's a twin room for $18. More comfortable singles/doubles are $18/22. There's a TV lounge, a barbecue area and tea/coffee making facilities, but no kitchen.

The *Barrier Reef Hostel* (tel 21 1691) is at 537 Flinders St, just beyond the railway station. It's cheap ($8) and cheerful, with bunks in two large dorms. Sheets cost $1, and there's no curfew.

Hotels & Guest Houses

Reef Lodge (tel 21 1112) at 4 Wickham St, has 27 smart fan cooled rooms at $20 single or $32 double ($34 with private bathroom). There's a guests' kitchen and laundromat.

At 10 Blackwood St, near Sturt St, the *Sunseeker Private Hotel* (tel 71 3409) has share rooms at $7 each, singles at $20, twins at $28 and triples at $30. There's a pool.

Across the road at 287 Sturt St, *Pacific Coast Budget Accommodation* (tel 71 6874) has 90 rooms at $20 single, $34 double. In an older annexe at the back there are doubles for $19. Light breakfast is included in the prices. Watch your belongings in the ground floor annex as thieves have entered through windows. The hotel has a reasonably priced cafe downstairs.

Finally there are a number of the traditional old hotels like the *Great Northern* (tel 71 6191) at 500 Flinders St down by the railway station. Nightly cost is $18/30. Some doubles have attached bathrooms for an extra $5. The *Seaview Hotel* (tel 71 5005) at 56 The Strand has singles/doubles at $14/24.

Motels

Expect air-con in this bracket. The modern *Coachman's Inn* (tel 72 3140) is conveniently placed, just past the Barrier Reef Wonderland at the corner of Flinders East and King Sts. Singles/doubles are $38/45.

Other cheaper motels include the central *Rex City Motel* (tel 71 6048) at 143 Wills St with rooms at $39/45, and the *Strand Motel* (tel 72 1977) at 51 The Strand with rooms at $37/41.

The *Downtown Motel* (tel 72 5022) at 121 Flinders St East charges $42/47. North of the centre but still reasonably close to town is the recently renovated *Motel Rowes Bay* (tel 71 3494), at 74 Esplanade in Belgian Gardens. It has singles/doubles for $27/33 and self-contained flats at $27 double, $33 triple.

For a few dollars more, *Yongala Lodge* (tel 72 4633) is at 11 Fryer St. For $46 single, $50 double or $60 triple you get a suite with fully equipped kitchenette, sitting area and balcony. There is also a pool and some two bedroom suites for up to four people at $80. Next door, in a lovely 19th century building, is a Greek restaurant, displays of period furniture and memorabilia, and finds from the *Yongala* wreck.

There are numerous motels you could try on the two roads leading into Townsville from the Bruce Highway to the south.

Some holiday flats offer similar prices to the cheaper motels. *Seagren Holiday Apartments* (tel 72 2011) at 94 The Strand charges $33 to $50 for two people. In North Ward, behind The Strand, *Bundock Court* (tel 71 4887) at 2 Bundock St has units for two people at $37.

Camping & On-site Vans There are two caravan parks which are only about two km from town. *Rowes Bay Caravan Park* (tel 71 3576) is just over the road from the beach on Heatley Parade, Rowes Bay and has tent sites for $8 for two and on-site vans for $25 double. The *Showgrounds Caravan Park* (tel 72 1487) on Ingham Rd, West End has tent sites at $9 for two and on-site vans at $22.

Places to Eat

Pubs The *Exchange Hotel* on Flinders St has a courtyard restaurant with steaks from $10. Also on Flinders St East, the *James Cook Tavern* has counter meals in the $5 range and there's live music Friday and Saturday nights. Over on the corner of Palmer and Morehead Sts, just south of Ross Creek, the *Crown Tavern* has very good counter lunches and dinners – large servings for $7 to $9.

On the Strand, the *Seaview Hotel* has *CoCo's Kitchen* with steaks, seafood and other meals from $5. In the evening from Wednesday to Saturday there's live music. The *Criterion Tavern* on the corner of the Strand and King St also has counter meals and a steakhouse/bistro.

Others Twenty-four hour food service is part of the plan for the new *Transit Centre* on Palmer St. The Flinders St Mall has a variety of eateries which can provide anything from breakfast to dinner. At the Dean St end of the mall, the *Crystal Creek Kiosk* offers juices and fruit salads at very reasonable prices. On the other side of the mall at 287, *The Balcony* is a pleasant, partly open air restaurant with main courses in the $10 range.

You can get fairly cheap meals at the *Greenhouse Bistro* on the first floor of the Townsville International hotel halfway along the Mall. It's open daily and has lunch and dinner from $6.50. *Coco's* is downstairs at 350 Flinders St. Open Monday to Friday from 9 am to 5 pm, it's an excellent place for a healthy light meal. On the other side of this section of the mall in the Cat & Fiddle Arcade are the *Fruit & Nut Shop*, good for snacks and lunches, and a pie shop offering tasty vegie pies for just under $1.

Two more good places are in Blackwood St just up from the railway station. At *Golden House*, a take-away Chinese-Vietnamese restaurant, the satay prawns at $10 are delicious. *Cafe Nova*, a few doors back towards Flinders St, is open from 7 pm till late every night except

Monday: it has snacks and light meals from $7 and is BYO.

Beside Ross Creek, near the bottom of Stokes St and just down from the Mall, there's an inviting collection of food stalls and open air tables at the north end of Victoria Bridge. The fare includes Italian, seafood, Mexican, health food and more, all at reasonable prices.

Flinders St East offers a cosmopolitan variety of restaurants. *Fanny's Pancake Parlour* at 145 does all manner of stuffed pancakes for $10. Next door at 146 *South of the Border*, Mexican in food and decor, has main meals for $9. *Higgins* at 144 has a restaurant section and a cheaper cafe which opens at 5 am for breakfast. Lunches are from $4. *Luvit*, underneath Backpackers International, is open daily from 6 am to 9 pm with breakfasts $5 and savoury pancakes $6 to $7.

On the river side of Flinders St East the Paluma Pavilion has a courtyard and a few cafes. The *Waterfront Quarterdeck Restaurant* is here too, with backpacker specials of spaghetti for $6 to $7. Tucked just around the corner on Wickham St is a cafe which is open all night on Friday and Saturdays and till late on Sunday nights. It opens early for breakfast during the week and offers some bargains.

On The Strand opposite the marina the *Ozone Cafe* is a popular take-away including cheap Chinese food. There's a collection of restaurants on the corner of Gregory St and The Strand down by the water. The *Rasa Pinang* offers cheap Malaysian fare. *El Charro* is a very busy Mexican spot with main meals not more than $9. Most of these places are open on Sundays.

Entertainment

Townsville's nightlife is just as lively as Cairns' and ranges from pub bands to flashy clubs and of course the casino. Much of the action is on Flinders St. The *James Cook Tavern* at 273 Flinders St East has live music on Friday and Saturday nights. There's a blues club on Friday nights from 7 pm until late.

Nearby is *Tattersall's Hotel* with live bands on Friday and Saturday nights and Sunday afternoons, entry $4. *The Bank* at 169 Flinders St East is a flashy, busy nightclub, with a cover charge of $5, but sometimes free if you say you're from the backpacker place. The *Terrace Club* at 108 is similar, and also has an over 25s piano bar. Dress regulations apply at both clubs. Further along Flinders St past the mall are two more disco/nightclubs – *Opus 1* at 450 and *Miner's Right* at 575.

The *Criterion Tavern* at 10 The Strand has live bands and entertainment in its outdoor section and in the *Speakeasy* and *Heaven* nightspots. Moving along the Strand, the popular *Seaview Hotel* has rock music on Wednesday to Saturday nights and Sunday afternoons. For a change of pace, the *Hotel Allen* on Gregory St has a guitarist in its beer garden on Friday nights and Sunday afternoons. The *Crown Tavern* on Palmer St, just south of Ross Creek, offers jazz and toad racing on Sunday afternoons. It overlooks the creek and also houses *Eliza's* nightclub which claims to have the best sound system in Townsville.

The *Civic Theatre* (tel 72 2677), on Boundary St in South Townsville, is the regional centre for performing arts and varied cultural pursuits. If you have the right clothes and fancy trying your luck on the spin of the wheel, the *Sheraton Breakwater Casino* is down at the end of Sir Leslie Thiess Drive, beyond Flinders St East.

Cafe Nova has music and good cheap food from Tuesday to Saturday nights until late. Out at 310 Bayswater Rd, Garbutt, the *Dalrymple Hotel* often has big name rock bands. James Cook University is some distance out of town in Douglas but if you feel like venturing out there, it has a beer garden with bands on Friday afternoon during term, and *The Club* where the Friday night action happens.

Getting There & Away

Air You can fly to Townsville from Cairns, Brisbane, Sydney or Melbourne several times a day with Ansett or Australian Airlines – and from other big cities usually once or twice a day. You can also get to/from Mt Isa, Darwin or Alice Springs with either airline. Australian Regional Airlines has services to Cairns and Dunk Island; Sunstate flies to Mackay, Rockhampton, Gladstone and Bundaberg, and Sungold to Mackay.

Some typical one-way fares are Brisbane $241 (standby $193), Rockhampton $165 (standby $138), Mackay ($106), Cairns ($112), Mt Isa $193, Alice Springs $287 (standby $230). Ansett and Sungold (tel 81 6611) are at 350 Flinders St Mall; Australian, Australian Regional and Sunstate (tel 81 6222) are at 320 Flinders St Mall, near the corner of Stokes St.

Sea Air Pacific (tel (077) 25 1470) flies most days between Townsville and Hinchinbrook Island ($109), Orpheus Island ($99), Lindeman and Hayman islands. Flight West (tel 25 1622) goes at least once daily to and from Mt Isa, often with stops at small places on the way. Qantas (tel 71 5097), 280 Flinders St Mall also flies to and from Townsville.

Bus Greyhound, Pioneer, Deluxe, McCafferty's and Sunliner all run up and down the coast at least twice daily between Brisbane and Cairns, stopping in Townsville on the way. It's 18 to 21 hours from Brisbane, 10 to 11 hours from Rockhampton, about six hours from Mackay, 3½ hours from Airlie Beach and 4½ hours from Cairns. Regular one-way fares are Brisbane $86, Rockhampton $52, Mackay $34, Airlie Beach $26, Cairns $27. Greyhound, Pioneer, Deluxe and McCafferty's also run daily both ways between Townsville and Mt Isa, and on to Alice Springs or Darwin. Typical fares are Mt Isa $75, Darwin $150, Alice Springs $125.

All the bus companies are at the new Townsville transit centre on Palmer St.

The Backpackers International hostel on Flinders St East plans to start a bus service between Townsville and Cairns on which you would get a stop on the way, and a night's accommodation on arrival, all for $25.

Train The four times weekly Brisbane to Cairns Sunlander operates through Townsville. It takes about 26 hours from Brisbane to Townsville at $91.10 in economy, $165.60 in 1st. From Proserpine to Townsville it's 5 hours, from Rockhampton 14½ hours. On from Townsville to Cairns is seven hours. The Queenslander does the same Brisbane to Cairns run once a week (leaving Brisbane on Sunday mornings and Cairns on Tuesday mornings). It's a bit faster than the Sunlander and has a special bar for 1st class passengers where movies are shown. Economy fares are the same as on the Sunlander: 1st class from Brisbane to Townsville is $251.10 which includes all meals and a sleeping compartment.

The Inlander operates twice weekly from Townsville to Mt Isa. To Charters Towers it's three hours and $14.50, economy only; to Mt Isa 18 hours and $76.90 in economy or $144.40 in 1st.

Getting Around

Airport Transport Townsville airport is out in the north-west of the city at Garbutt, about five km from the centre. A taxi is $8. The Brolga Airport Shuttle Bus services all main arrivals and departures. It costs $3.50 one way, $6 return and will drop you or pick you up almost anywhere fairly central. Phone 79 7799 to book when you're leaving. Avis, Hertz, Thrifty and Budget have car hire desks at the airport.

Bus The City Explorer bus (tel 71 5024) is one of those hop off hop on services. A day ticket costs $8 and the bus does a 32 km loop with stops near main attractions. Services are usually hourly and the bus normally runs Tuesday to Saturday in the main tourist season, less frequently the rest of the year. There's also a variety of local bus services around Townsville.

Rental Vehicles The regular rent-a-car operators are all represented, plus smaller firms like Brolga Mini-Vehicle Hire (tel 71 4261) at the corner of Hanran and Ogden Sts. From Brolga a Moke for a day is $18 plus 11 cents a km, while a small car is $22 plus 12 cents a km, a 4WD $32 plus 15c a km. There are various other possibilities including shorter or longer rentals and free km deals. Brolga also rents out scooters.

Sun City Rent-a-Moke (tel 72 2702) at 27 Eyre St, North Ward, Rent-a-Rocket (tel 72 6880) at 14 Dean St, south of Ross Creek, Rent-a-Relic (tel 75 4488) at 1 Duckworth St, Garbutt and Rent-a-Wreck on Flinders St East are other places to try. Cars are advertised from $24 a day but check whether that includes insurance and km charge. Some firms limit how far out of the city you can go.

Davo's (tel 72 6418) at 115 Flinders St East charges $3 an hour or $15 for 24 hours for mopeds. Rent-a-Wreck also hires out mopeds. For motorscooters and motorbikes try Rising Sun Honda (tel 79 0211) at 21 Ross River Rd. You can rent bicycles from Downtown Travel at 121 Flinders St East.

Tours There's a growing number of tours around the city, out to other places of interest, and reef and island trips. Several tour agents around town take bookings. The Reef Travel Centre (tel 72 4688) at 181 Flinders St East is open Monday to Friday plus Saturday and Sunday mornings.

Brolga Tours does a three hour city tour for $16 most days. Other trips include to the Stuart refinery south of Townsville where Mt Isa's copper is processed (2½ hours, $12), Mt Spec and Crystal Creek (day tour, $29.50), Charters Towers (day tour, $27.50), Ravenswood and the Burdekin Dam (day tour, $45), and the Marine Science Institute, Ayr and the Burdekin Valley (day tour, $29.50).

Pure Pleasure Cruises does daily $70 cruises to Orpheus Island where you can visit the giant clam research station, take a glass-bottomed boat trip, snorkel or dive. A good lunch is provided. Departures are from the Breakwater Marina.

An interesting looking day cruise is the one by Westmark to Palm Island, an Aboriginal community just south of Orpheus Island. On the way you can swim or snorkel, and on arrival you're welcomed with a feast and Aboriginal dancing. The trip operates intermittently and costs $65.

Helilink (tel 71 3000) does helicopter trips over Magnetic Island ($80).

Magnetic Island

Population 2500

Magnetic is one of the most popular islands for travellers because it's so cheap and convenient to get to. It's big enough to offer plenty of things to do and see, including some fine bushwalks.

Only 13 km offshore from Townsville, Magnetic Island was named by Captain Cook, who thought his ship's compass went funny when he sailed by in 1770. The island has some fine beaches, lots of bird life, bushwalking tracks, a koala sanctuary and an aquarium. It's dominated by 500 metre Mt Cook.

There are several small towns along the coast and the island has quite a different atmosphere to the purely resort islands along the reef. This is one of the larger islands (52 square km) and about 70% national park.

Information & Orientation

Magnetic Island is roughly triangular in shape with Picnic Bay, the main town where the ferries arrive, at the bottom (southern) corner. There's a road up the

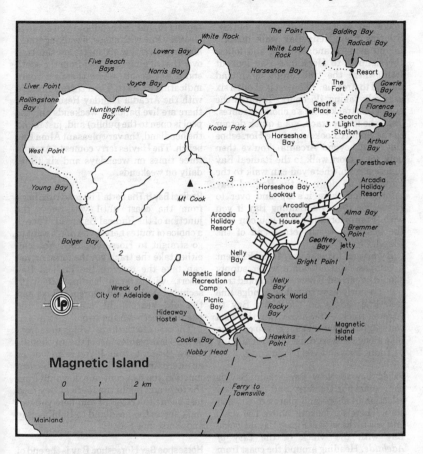

Magnetic Island

White Rock
The Point
Balding Bay
Radical Bay
Lovers Bay
White Lady Rock
Resort
Five Beach Bays
Horseshoe Bay
The Fort
Gowrie Bay
Norris Bay
Geoff's Place
Joyce Bay
Liver Point
Florence Bay
Rollingstone Bay
Huntingfield Bay
Koala Park
Horseshoe Bay
Search Light Station
West Point
Arthur Bay
Foresthaven
Young Bay
Horseshoe Bay Lookout
Arcadia Holiday Resort
Mt Cook
Arcadia Centaur House
Alma Bay
Bolger Bay
Arcadia Holiday Resort
Bremmer Point
Nelly Bay
Geoffrey Bay
jetty
Magnetic Island Recreation Camp
Bright Point
Wreck of City of Adelaide
Picnic Bay
Nelly Bay
Shark World
Rocky Bay
Hideaway Hostel
Magnetic Island Hotel
Cockle Bay
Hawkins Point
Nobby Head
0 1 2 km
Ferry to Townsville
Mainland

eastern side of the island to Horseshoe Bay and a rough track along the west coast. Along the north coast it's walking only. The best place on the island for information is Magnetic Travel & Accommodation (tel 78 5099) at 4 The Esplanade, Picnic Bay. Among other things it rents out bicycles and books tours (with some special backpacker rates), flats and flights.

Bushwalks

The National Parks produce a walks leaflet for Magnetic Island's excellent

bushwalking tracks. Possible walks include:

1 Nelly Bay to Arcadia
2 Picnic Bay to West Point
3 Horseshoe Bay road to Arthur Bay
  Arthur Bay to Florence Bay
  Horseshoe Bay road to The Forts
4 Horseshoe Bay to Balding Bay
  Horseshoe Bay to Radical Bay
5 Mt Cook ascent

Except for the long Mt Cook ascent none of the walks require special preparation.

You can string several walks together to

make an excellent full day's outing. Starting from Nelly Bay walk directly inland along Mandalay Ave and follow the signpost to Horseshoe Bay lookout from where the trail drops down and around to Arcadia. This part is about a six km walk taking 1½ hours. Towards the end of this track there's a choice of routes. Take the longer track, via a quick detour to the Sphinx Lookout, to the Horseshoe Bay road beyond Arcadia. You've then only got a short walk to the Radical Bay junction from where you can walk to the Forts and on down to the Radical Bay resort. From here it's up and over to Horseshoe Bay, via Balding Bay if you wish. From Horseshoe Bay you can take the bus back to the other end of the island.

If you want to make the Mt Cook ascent a compass and adequate water supply should be carried. There is no marked trail but it's fairly easy to follow a ridge line from the saddle on the Nelly Bay to Arcadia track. After heavy rain there's a waterfall on Petersen Creek. You can also hike along the west coast from Picnic Bay to Young Bay and West Point.

Picnic Bay to Nelly Bay Picnic Bay is convenient for the ferry and has a good selection of shops and places to eat and stay. There's a lookout above the town and just to the west of Picnic Bay is Cockle Bay with the wreck of the *City of Adelaide*. Heading around the coast from Picnic Bay you soon come to Rocky Bay where it's a short, steep walk down to a beautiful beach.

Next round the coast is Nelly Bay with the Shark World aquarium and resort complex, which has coral displays, aquarium tanks with tropical fish and tortoises and a group of sharks. The sharks get their daily feed at 2 pm. There's also a snack bar and a licensed restaurant, open from 9 am to 9 pm. Nelly Bay has a good beach with shade and a reef at low tide. At the far end of the bay there are some pioneer graves.

Arcadia Round the headland you come to Geoffrey Bay with shops, a walking track, and an interesting 400 metre low tide trail over the fringing coral reef from the south end of the beach, where there's a board indicating its start. Then there's Arcadia with the Arcadia Holiday Resort (where there are live bands at weekends and the pool is open to the public) and, just round the headland, the very pleasant Alma Bay beach. The Hayles ferry comes to Arcadia three times on weekdays and six times daily on weekends.

Radical Bay & The Forts The road runs back from the coast until you reach the junction of the Radical Bay road. There's a choice of routes here if you don't want to go straight to Horseshoe Bay. You can either take the track via the forts, or you can take the road to the Radical Bay resort, with tracks leading off it to secluded Arthur and Florence Bays and the old searchlight station on the headland between the two.

The track to the forts (which date from WW II) is drivable most of the way but it's also a pleasant stroll. If you're on foot, as an alternative to backtracking to the road junction you can continue downhill from the forts and rejoin the Radical Bay road just before the resort. From here you can walk across the headland to Balding Bay and Horseshoe Bay.

Horseshoe Bay Horseshoe Bay is the end of the road. It has more shops and accommodation and a long stretch of beach. There's a lagoon bird sanctuary a few hundred metres from the beach and a koala park a long drive off the main road. At the beach there are boats, windsurfers and canoes for hire and you can also parasail. You can also walk from here to Maud Bay, round to the west, or over to Radical Bay.

Places to Stay
Hostels There are no fewer than 10 hostel-like places on the island and it's a

competitive scene with some hostels sending representatives and vehicles to meet each ferry at Picnic Bay.

Only a minute's walk from the Picnic Bay ferry pier in Picnic St, the *Hideaway Hostel* (tel 78 5110) has dorm beds at $7 a night, $8 with bedding. Twin or double rooms are $20. It's a clean, friendly place with a small basic kitchen, a TV room and laundry facilities. Also in Picnic Bay, at 80 Picnic St, is the *Magnetic Island Hostel* (tel 78 5759). This is a very pleasant hostel on a quiet street, consisting of two flats, each with a fully equipped kitchen. Rooms have three beds at $8 per person, $1 extra for bedding.

Two more cheap accommodation possibilities are on Picnic Bay Esplanade itself. One is the new *South Pacific – Magnetic Island Backpackers' Hostel* (tel 78 5077). It's $8 per night, clean and comfortable. Right by the pier is the *Magnetic Hotel-Motor Inn* (tel 78 5166) which offers deals called Catpacks for $28 which include return ferry fare and three days' and two nights' accommodation. The rooms have no more than seven bunks, attached bathrooms, fans, fridges and TVs. There's a $3 charge for linen. There are also four 'budget' rooms, each containing a double bed and a bunk plus similar facilities, at $33 for two people and $5 for each extra person, linen included. There are tea/coffee facilities but you can't cook.

A little further out from the centre of Picnic Bay, about a 15 minute walk from the pier, is the *Magnetic Island Recreation Camp* (tel 78 5280) with space for 36. It's an associate YHA hostel, popular with young Australians despite a ban on alcohol! The price for members is $6. For non members, it's $9 on the first night and $6 thereafter. The hostel is open all day but the office is closed from 10 am to 5 pm. To get there, walk along the Esplanade away from town to Granite St, then straight up to the top and turn right. The local bus will take you there free. There's a tennis court and bicycles and snorkelling gear for hire. The manager organises fishing trips, four to five hours for $15 to $20.

North of Picnic Bay, as you round the corner into Nelly Bay, you'll notice blue and white striped 'Camp-O-Tel' accommodation (a cross between a cabin and a tent with beds or bunks) at *Shark World* (tel 78 5187). Costs are $8 to $10 per head. Another possibility in Nelly Bay is *Camp Magnetic* (tel 78 5151), the Uniting Church Camp. They can take 36 in dorms and charge $6. There are cooking facilities and a pool which is also open to the public. It's pretty basic accommodation but among the cheapest on the island and close to some good bushwalks. It's on Mango Parkway, a few blocks from the coastal road. The local bus stops out front.

Up at Arcadia the very popular *Centaur House* (tel 78 5668) is at 27 Marine Parade, opposite the beach. The atmosphere is relaxed, there's a lovely garden and a bed in the clean spacious dorms costs $9. Guests have free use of snorkelling gear and windsurfers and can hire scooters for $18 a day; there's a Moke too at $20 a day. Also in Arcadia at 11 Cook Rd *Foresthaven* (tel 78 5153) has a lovely bush setting with dorms and units. Costs are $8 a night for a dorm bed and $9 in units with self-contained kitchens. Excellent barbecues are held most nights in the large courtyard – $6. There are also free bicycles. Koalas, wallabies and many tropical birds are often seen just a short walk away.

Last but not least, over at Horseshoe Bay is *Geoff's Place* (tel 78 5577), which is one of the island's most popular places for young travellers, although we've had a few less favourable comments from backpackers recently. There are extensive grounds in which you can camp for $5 per person, take a bunk in a marquee for $6 or share a cabin for $8. There are also A-frame cedar cabins each with a double bed and a bunk. In these you pay $8 to share, or $17/20 for singles/doubles.

There's a kitchen, plus a bar and a

restaurant offering breakfast and dinner, where you get a good meal for $5. You can hire bikes for $8 a day, or ride horses at a nearby ranch. There are even Geoff Packs for $20 which will give you a return ferry ticket, free bus to and from the ferry and two nights' accommodation. The beach is about one km from Geoff's but do watch out for stingers during the wet season.

Hotels & Holiday Flats There are hotels and several resorts and motels on the island, plus more than a dozen holiday flat places. At certain times they can be rather packed so it's wise to phone ahead and book if necessary. The *Magnetic Hotel-Motor Inn* mentioned in the hostel section has motel-style accommodation in addition to its hostel and budget rooms. Rooms are $45 double, $5 for each extra person. The *Arcadia Holiday Resort* (tel 78 5177) has rooms holding up to three people for $50.

Holiday flats mostly quote weekly rates. Prices vary with demand – even in the season you may find bargains if there happens to be a flat vacant. Single bedroom flats are mostly $170 to $270 per week, two bedroom flats $250 to $350. You can get further details from the estate agent on The Esplanade in Picnic Bay or from the accommodation leaflet put out by the Magnetic Island Tourist Association. Magnetic Travel & Accommodation at Picnic Bay quotes $30 a day for one bedroom flats and $35 for two bedroom flats, most of the year.

Among the cheapest holiday flats are *Ti-Tree Lodge Flats* at 20 Barbara St in Picnic Bay. One bedroom flats are $160, two bedrooms $230. Other moderately priced units are at *Foresthaven* on Cook Rd in Arcadia. Rates here are $200 and up for two bedroom flats.

Places to Eat
Picnic Bay The *Magnetic Hotel* has Jonah's Bistro with tables outside and counter meals from $6. A snack bar does a budget breakfast for $5. On the Esplanade *Crusoes* is a restaurant with a high reputation where evening meals (from 6 pm) start at $10. For cheap lunches there's *Joan's Coffee Lounge* on the corner of the Mall and one of the arcades.

The popular *Maggie's* at the far end of the Mall has breakfasts from 7 to 10 am, with a full breakfast for $7. It also offers a backpacker lunch special for $5.

Nelly Bay Toward Nelly Bay near the post office the *Tea Gallery* has reasonably priced homely food. There's also a take-away *Possum's Coffee Shop* and a supermarket close by. On Mandalay Rd there's a small group of shops including the *Simply Yummy Sandwich Bar* selling health foods and fresh juices.

Arcadia The *Bosun's Grill* at the Arcadia Holiday Resort has lunches and dinners from $10. There is also a cheap take-away counter in the resort called *Pandora's Hut* with sandwiches, cakes, tea and coffee, open till 4 pm. *A La Capri* on Hayles Ave is a good Italian restaurant offering pasta from $7 and steaks at $10.50. Every evening it has a backpacker dinner for $6 to $7. The Sunday night barbecues here are highly recommended. It's fully licensed and is good for a late night drink.

The *Tea Garden* restaurant in the Arcadia shopping centre on Bright St off Marine Parade is open for lunch and dinner. Sandwiches and burgers are $4, dinners $9. In the same shopping centre the *South Pacific Bakery* opens early and is good for a coffee and croissant. Next door is *Bannister's Fish & Chips*. Locals rave about its seafood.

Horseshoe Bay The *Bounty Snack Bar* has take-aways. *Dooley's Reef* has fish & chips and burgers for $3. Next door is a proper licensed restaurant with seafood specials at $12. A new group of shops should include a chicken bar and a supermarket which will cater for those who stay at Geoff's Place and want to cook their own food. Of course there's also the restaurant at Geoff's Place.

Getting There & Away

Two companies, Hayles and Westmark, both run 10 or 11 ferries a day to and from Townsville for $8 return ($5 with a student card).

All ferries go to Picnic Bay and some of Hayles' go to Arcadia too. In Townsville Hayles (tel 72 7277) departs from Sir Leslie Thiess Drive, near the Sheraton Casino. Westmark (tel 21 1913) goes from Great Barrier Reef Wonderland. Last ferries leave Townsville between 5.45 and 6.45 pm except for Westmark's late services on Friday at 9.30 pm and Saturdays at 10.30 pm and midnight.

Westmark can sell you a $12.50 day ticket which combines the return ferry trip with unlimited bus travel on the island including a scenic tour. Both companies have other deals for $15 to $25 which include combinations of ferry, bus travel, lunch at a resort, tour boats around the island and so on.

Hayles also runs a vehicle ferry to Picnic Bay from the south side of Ross Creek three times a day during the week and twice a day on weekends. It's $36 each way for a car so you'll probably find it cheaper to hire a Moke on the island, use the bus service or hitch.

Rundle Air Service (tel 79 6933) will take four adults from Townsville to the island for $110 one way.

Getting Around

Bus The Magnetic Island Bus Service operates between Picnic Bay and Horseshoe Bay six to 10 times a day. Some bus trips include Radical Bay, others the Koala Park. You can either get tickets from place to place or a $5 full day pass.

Bicycle Hire Magnetic Island would be ideal for biking around if only the bikes available were a bit better. In Picnic Bay you can rent bicycles for $7 a day from Magnetic Travel & Accommodation at 4

The Esplanade. Magnetic Sports (tel 78 5407) at 2/8 The Esplanade has bicycles for $6 per day and tandems for $10 per day. (They also hire out golf clubs, snorkelling gear, fishing gear and handle tour bookings.) In Arcadia you can rent bicycles at the resort, and for $7 per day in the shopping centre on Bright St.

Motorscooter Hire The main place for 50cc machines is Roadrunner Scooter Hire (tel 78 5222) at Shop 2, Picnic Bay Arcade. Roadrunner also has agents at Kate's Video Supermarket Complex (tel 78 5808) in Sooning St, Nelly Bay; Pandora's Hut (tel 78 5491) in Arcadia Holiday Resort; and Geoff's Place (tel 78 5577), Horseshoe Bay. Day hire if you're 25 or over is $16 plus $3 insurance; for 21 to 25 year olds it's $18 plus $4 insurance, for under 21s it's $20 plus $5 insurance. There's a $50 deposit and a $2 helmet charge. The rates include unlimited km and a free tank of petrol. There's also a small charge to cover Queensland government stamp duty. To hire a scooter you don't need a motorbike licence, just a car licence that you have held for six months.

Moke Hire You soon get the impression that 90% of the vehicles on Magnetic Island are Mokes. There seems to be nothing else. Two companies rent Mokes in Picnic Bay and they have depots at other places on the island. Slightly the cheaper is Holiday Moke Hire (tel 78 5703) which operates from the TAB betting shop in the Mall on The Esplanade. Rates for 24 hour hire are $21 for 25 years and over and $23 for 21 to 25 years; you can't rent a Moke if you're under 21. There's a 20c per km charge which includes petrol. Rates also include insurance. Holiday Moke has an agent at Pandora's Hut at the Arcadia resort.

Moke Magnetic (tel 78 5377) is behind the Mall in Picnic St and has a depot at the Arcadia Store (tel 78 5387). Their rates for 24 hour hire are $23 over 25 years and $25 for 21 to 25 years. Other charges are the same as the rival company's. Both companies will deliver a Moke to where you're staying and both offer cheaper rates for longer rental periods.

Tours Three places in Picnic Bay handle tour bookings – Magnetic Sports (tel 78 5407) at 2/8 The Esplanade, Magnetic Travel & Accommodation (tel 78 5099) at 4 The Esplanade and Picnic Bay Reef Centre (tel 78 5374) next to Magnetic Sports. Tours include $25 half day trips around the island, the $75 Reef Link reef trip and the $65 Pure Pleasure Cruise to Orpheus Island. There's also an information office with the usual collection of brochures, some related to tours, to your right as you leave the pier at Picnic Bay.

Townsville to Cairns

It's 374 km from Townsville to Cairns and there's plenty of interest along the way.

INGHAM (Population 6100)
There's a lot of Spanish and Italian influence in this sugar producing town. Lucinda, 24 km from Ingham, is the port from which the sugar is shipped and it has a jetty nearly six km long!

In Ingham most of the accommodation is on Lannercost St. The *Belvedere Hotel* (tel 76 2025) on the corner of Lannercost and Hawkins Sts offers beds to backpackers at $6 each, or there are doubles with private bathroom for $20. The national parks district office (tel 76 1700) at 2 Herbert St deals with camping permits for Mt Spec, Wallaman and Jourama Falls, Orpheus Island and one of the Hinchinbrook Island sites.

There are a number of places to visit around Ingham including the Wallaman Falls, 48 km inland, where a tributary of the Herbert River falls 305 metres, the longest single drop in Australia. The falls are much more spectacular in the wet season. You can normally reach the falls by conventional vehicle along an unpaved road and there's a national parks camping area with a swimming hole nearby.

Only seven km off the highway is the Victoria Mill, the largest sugar mill in the southern hemisphere. Free tours are given in the crushing season.

ORPHEUS ISLAND
North of Townsville and a little south of Hinchinbrook, Orpheus is a narrow 14 square km granite island surrounded by coral reefs. One of the Palm Group, it's mostly national park, heavily forested with lots of bird life. Turtles also nest here. Orpheus is quiet, secluded, and good for camping, snorkelling and diving. Camping's allowed in two places (permits from Ingham) but take your own water. Also on the island are a giant clam research station and a small resort with rooms at over $200.

If you want to camp, you can get there by charter boat from Taylor's Beach, 25 km from Ingham, or from Lucinda – or get the Pure Pleasure Cruises people in Townsville to drop you off on one of their day-trips. You can fly to Orpheus from Townsville ($91) or Hinchinbrook Island ($99) with Sea Air Pacific.

CARDWELL (Population 1249)
South of Cardwell the Bruce Highway climbs high above the coast with tremendous views down across the winding mangrove lined waterways known as the Everglades, which separate Hinchinbrook Island from the coast.

Cardwell is one of north Queensland's very earliest towns, dating from 1864, and is the only town on the highway between Brisbane and Cairns which is actually on the coast. It's more or less a one street place and is the departure point for Hinchinbrook and other continental islands. It also has one of Queensland's four main National Parks Information Centres (tel 66 8601) on the highway in the middle of town, open daily. This office also deals with camping permits for nearby national parks.

There are several good places for freshwater swimming within a short drive from the town. Most of the coastal forest north of Cardwell is protected as the Edmund Kennedy National Park. At the south end of the park is a camping site close to the beach and some walking tracks – turn down Clifts Rd four km north of Cardwell to reach them.

The Murray Falls with fine rock pools for swimming, and a free camping ground, are 22 km west of the highway – turn off at the 'Murray Upper Road' sign about 27 km north of Cardwell.

Places to Stay & Eat

Cardwell Backpackers Hostel (tel 66 8922) is at 178 Bowen St, towards the north end of town. It has a sizeable dorm and a couple of smaller rooms plus the usual kitchen and bathroom facilities. Cost is $8 a night. Bed linen is provided, there are bicycles for rent and breakfast is available at $3.

There are several motel, camping and on-site van possibilities. *Kookaburra Park* (tel 66 8648) on the highway roughly in the middle of town has grassy tent sites for $7 single, $9 double, on-site vans for $20 double or $22 treble, good modern cabins for $25/28 double/treble, and units with their own bathrooms for $30/35. There's a swimming pool. The *Lyndoch Motor Inn* on the highway near the backpackers is one of the cheaper motels with some doubles at $33. At the south end of town the *Marine Hotel-Motel* has singles/doubles for $28/33, and the *Island Lure* has self-contained flats for $30 a night.

You can get good fish & chips from the *Pacific Palms Caravan Park*, on the highway just south of the Lyndoch Motor Inn.

Getting There & Away

All buses between Townsville and Cairns stop at Cardwell. The fare is around $17 from either place. Cardwell's also on the main Brisbane to Cairns rail line.

HINCHINBROOK ISLAND

The entire large island of Hinchinbrook is national park. There's a low key resort on Hinchinbrook's northern peninsula, Cape Richards, and also three national park camping sites. Hinchinbrook is popular with bushwalkers and has several good tracks.

The terrain of the island is varied – lush tropical forest on the mainland side, towering mountains in the middle and long sandy beaches and secluded bays on the eastern side. Hinchinbrook covers 635 square km and the rugged highest peak, Mt Bowen, is 1142 metres. There's plenty of wildlife, especially pretty-faced wallabies and the iridescent blue Ulysses butterfly.

The resort has rooms for just 30 people but it's not cheap at a standby rate of $90 a day per person, including excellent meals and transfer from Cardwell.

There's a five km walking trail from the resort to Macushla via Shepherd Bay, and a fairly hard 12 km track down the east coast from Ramsay Bay to Zoe Bay which, with its beautiful waterfall, is one of the most scenic spots on the island.

Recently a new wilderness trail has been opened from Zoe Bay to George Point on the south-east tip of the island.

The camping sites are at The Haven opposite Cardwell (water available from Pages Creek), Macushla on Missionary Bay in the north (bring drinking water with you), and Zoe Bay on the east coast (water available). Numbers are limited to 30 or 35 at the three camping sites. For camping permits for Macushla Bay, The Haven and bush camping elsewhere, apply to the national parks in Cardwell (tel 66 8601). For Zoe Bay, apply to the Ingham office (tel 76 1700).

Getting There & Away

You can book for the Hinchinbrook resort and various island trips at the Hinchinbrook Booking Office (tel 66 8539) at 91 Bruce

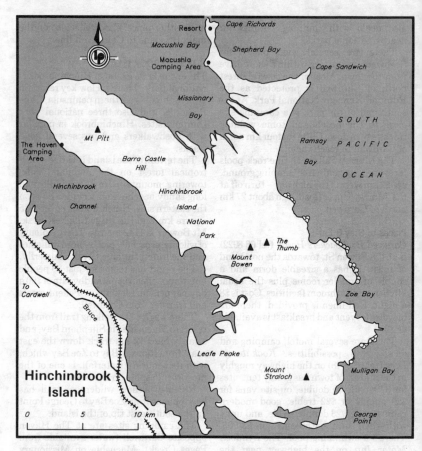

Highway, Cardwell. The resort boat *Reef Venture* leaves Cardwell for Hinchinbrook daily except Monday at 9 am, returning at 4.35 pm. Return fare is $28. It'll drop you at Macushla if you like. The *Hinchinbrook Explorer* does a trip daily except Thursday at 10 am to the Everglades, Macushla and the resort. You can use either of these boats for camping drop offs. Standard return fare with other boats for a camping drop off is $35.

The *Tekin III* (tel 66 8661) does a variety of cruises from Cardwell taking in Hinchinbrook Island, the Palm Islands to the south and Dunk Island to the north. The *Hinchiker II* can take you cruising for a day, on a snorkelling trip or drop you for camping. You can fly to Hinchinbrook with Sea Air Pacific from Orpheus Island ($99) or Townsville ($109).

TULLY (Population 2800)
The wettest place in Australia gets a drenching average of 440 cm a year. There are a couple of caravan parks and a motel and Tully is the cheapest place to start from if you're doing a white-water rafting trip on the Tully River. Tully is a regular

stop for buses and trains between Townsville and Cairns. Nearby Mission Beach however is a much more appealing place to stay, and the Raging Thunder white-water people will pick you up there too.

MISSION BEACH (Population 640)

This name covers a string of small settlements dotted along a 14 km beach east of Tully. Rainforest comes right down to the coast in places. In south to north order, the Mission Beach settlements are South Mission Beach, Wongaling Beach, Mission Beach proper, Clump Point, Bingil Bay and Garners Beach. Mission Beach is named after an Aboriginal mission which was founded here in 1914 but destroyed by a cyclone in 1918.

Tam O'Shanter Point, shortly south of South Mission Beach, was the starting point for the ill-fated 1848 overland expedition to Cape York led by 30 year old Edmund Kennedy. All but three of the party's 13 members, including Kennedy, died. There's a memorial to the expedition at Tam O'Shanter Point today.

Activities & Boat Trips

The rainforest around Mission Beach is a haunt of cassowaries but unfortunately the population has been depleted by road accidents and the destruction of rainforest by logging and cyclones. A four km rainforest walking track goes from the Tully road, about two km west of the South Mission Beach turn-off, to the El Arish road, crossing Luff Hill with fine views on the way. Another rainforest track leads up to Bicton Hill from the Bingil Bay car park. It's a four km circuit with several good lookouts.

The Raging Thunder white-water rafting company (tel 51 4911 in Mission Beach) charges $85 from Mission Beach for its trips on the Tully River. It also offers three day sea kayak expeditions to the Family Islands for $235 including meals. Floating Wilderness Canoe Tours (tel 68 6286) does $45 canoe and fishing trips on the Tully.

From Clump Point you can take boat trips out to Beaver Cay on the Barrier Reef. These usually include snorkelling and a glass-bottomed boat ride for $70 to $80. The trips run by Perry Harvey have been recommended and can be a little cheaper. Services can be reduced during the wet season (roughly January to March). Edmund Kennedy Adventure Cruises (tel 68 7250) runs trips along the Hull River from South Mission Beach, about three times weekly. You may see saltwater crocodiles. Cost is $22 by day, $30 for a four hour night cruise including dinner. There are windsurfers for hire at Wongaling Beach.

Places to Stay

The *Mission Beach Hostel* (tel 68 8317) is at 28 Wongaling Beach Rd, 650 metres from the beach. It's a modern, well equipped, spacious place with a pool and garden. You sleep in spacious dorms for $10.

Treetops (tel 68 7137), an associate YHA hostel, is a wood stilt house with good views over rainforest and the coast, off Bingil Bay Rd – signposted from the El Arish to Mission Beach road. The kitchen and the rooms, which house four or six bunks, are on the small side but the views make up for that. Cost is $8 for YHA members, $10 for others. The hostel runs a free pick up service from the bus stop in Mission Beach proper at certain hours.

Scotty's Beach House (tel 688 676) at 167 Reid Road has 50 beds with a dorm bed for $10 and doubles for $11/12. They have a pool and every second day there's a barbecue on the beach.

The *Hideaway Caravan Park* on Porter Promenade has tent sites at $8 double and on-site vans from $30. On the corner of Mission Beach Rd and Wongaling Beach Rd the *Tropical Hibiscus Caravan Park* has tent sites at $9 double and on-site vans for $28. *Dunk Island View Caravan Park*, 175 Reid Rd, Wongaling Beach, has tent sites for $6 double. In South Mission

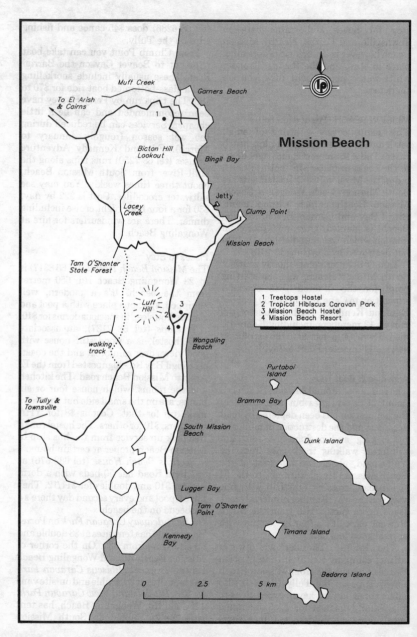

Mission Beach

To El Arish & Cairns

Muff Creek

Garners Beach

Bicton Hill
Lookout

Bingil Bay

Lacey
Creek

Jetty

Clump Point

Mission Beach

Tam O'Shanter
State Forest

Luff Hill

1 Treetops Hostel
2 Tropical Hibiscus Caravan Park
3 Mission Beach Hostel
4 Mission Beach Resort

walking
track

Wongaling
Beach

*To Tully &
Townsville*

Purtaboi
Island

Brammo Bay

South Mission
Beach

Dunk Island

Lugger Bay

Tam O'Shanter
Point

Timana Island

Kennedy
Bay

0   2.5   5 km

Bedarra Island

Beach there's the *Beachcomber Tourist Park* with camping at $8, on-site vans at $28, and cabins at $30.

Otherwise there's a scattering of motels, holiday units and three fairly low key resorts. The cheapest appears to be *Mission Beach Village Motel* (tel 68 7212) at 7 Porter Promenade in Mission Beach proper, with rooms from $35 single, $38 double.

Places to Eat

For a full meal you'd probably have to go to one of the resorts. Otherwise there are a couple of Chinese places in Mission Beach proper. There's a small shopping centre, including a supermarket, open seven days a week, at Mission Beach proper and another supermarket in the resort on Wongaling Beach Rd.

Getting There & Away

Seven or eight buses a day in each direction between Townsville and Cairns make the detour off the Bruce Highway down to Mission Beach. There are two main bus stops in Mission Beach: one in Mission Beach proper, the other five km south at the Mission Beach Resort on the corner of Wongaling Beach Rd, opposite the Mission Beach Hostel. Some buses call at both places, some at one or the other only. Pioneer, Deluxe, and Greyhound charge $14 from Cairns, $24 from Townsville. Sunliner is only $14 from Townsville, $12 from Cairns. McCafferty's is just $8 from Cairns, $24 from Townsville.

DUNK ISLAND & THE FAMILY ISLANDS

One of the more interesting Barrier Reef resorts is 4½ km off Mission Beach at Brammo Bay on the north end of heavily wooded, 10 square km Dunk Island. There's also a national park camping ground close to the resort (get permits from Cardwell or ring 68 7183 in Mission Beach). A couple of places in Mission Beach rent camping gear.

From 1897 to 1923 E J Banfield lived on Dunk and wrote his book *The Confessions of a Beachcomber*; the island is remarkably little changed from his early description. Today it has a small artist colony centred around Bruce Arthur, a tapestry maker and former Olympic wrestler. Dunk is noted for prolific bird life (nearly 150 species) and many butterflies. There are superb views over the entrances to the Hinchinbrook Channel from the top of 271 metre Mt Kootaloo. Thirteen km of walking tracks lead from the camping ground area to headlands and beaches.

South of Dunk are the seven tiny Family Islands. One of them, Bedarra, has a very exclusive resort with costs at around $400 a day for one person! Five of the other Family Islands are national parks and you can bush camp on three of them – Wheeler, Combe and Bowden (permits from Cardwell, take your own water).

Getting There & Away

From Clump Point at Mission Beach, two or three boats run day-trips to Dunk Island. Fare is $12 or $14 return if you just use the service as a ferry, or $18 including a meal. Water taxis operate to Dunk (15 minutes, $7 one way) from Wongaling Beach (tel 68 8310) and from South Mission Beach (tel 68 8333). One of the boats which does day-trips to Beaver Cay picks up people at Dunk on the way. All services can be reduced in the wet season.

You can fly to Dunk with Australian Regional Airlines from Townsville ($83) or Cairns ($75).

TULLY TO CAIRNS

At Mourilyan, seven km before Innisfail, there's the Australian Sugar Museum, open from 9 am to 4.30 pm daily. An export terminal on the coast east of Mourilyan handles the sugar produced in Innisfail, Tully and Mourilyan.

Innisfail has been a sugar city for over a century. It's a busy place with a large Italian population – although on Owen St you can also find a Chinese temple (open daily from 7 am to 5 pm). The Italians first arrived early this century to work the cane fields: some became plantation owners themselves and in the 1930s there was even a local 'mafia' called the Black Hand!

Innisfail is at the junction of the North and South Johnstone rivers. The North Johnstone, flowing down from the Atherton Tableland, is good for white-water rafting and canoeing. There are a few reasonably priced motels in Innisfail and a handful of caravan/camping parks. Flying Fish Point, on the north side of the Johnstone River mouth, is reportedly a good camping spot.

From Innisfail you can visit one of Australia's few tea plantations and factories (tel 64 5177) at Nerada, 28 km north-west, off the Palmerston Highway. It's open daily from 10 am to 4 pm. The Palmerston Highway winds up to the Atherton Tableland, passing through the rainforest of the Palmerston National Park, which has a number of creeks, waterfalls, scenic walking tracks and a camping ground at Henrietta Creek just off the road. The park ranger station (tel 64 5115) is at the eastern entrance to the park, 33 km from Innisfail.

Babinda is the next place on the Bruce Highway north of Innisfail, but before you reach it there's a turning to Josephine Falls, a popular picnic spot at the end of a short rainforest walk eight km inland from the highway. The falls are at the foot of the Bellenden Ker range which includes Queensland's highest peak, Mt Bartle Frere (1657 metres). A trail leads to the Bartle Frere summit from the ranger station near Josephine Falls. The ascent is for fit and experienced walkers – it's a 15 km, two day return trip and rain and cloud can close in suddenly.

Babinda Boulders, where a creek rushes between enormous rocks, is another good picnic place, seven km inland from Babinda. From the boulders you can walk the Goldfield Track – first opened up in the 1930s when there was a minor gold

rush. It leads 10 km to the Goldsborough Valley, across a saddle in the Bellenden Ker range. The track ends at a causeway on the Mulgrave River, from where a forestry road leads eight km to a camping ground in the Goldsborough Valley State Forest Park. From there it's 15 km on to the Gillies Highway between Gordonvale and Atherton.

Back on the Bruce Highway, Gordonvale is almost at Cairns. It has two Sikh *gurdwaras*. The winding Gillies Highway leads from here up on to the Atherton Tableland.

Cairns

Population 68,000

The 'capital' of the far north and the best known city up the Queensland coast, Cairns has become one of Australia's top travellers' destinations in recent years.

Cairns is a centre for a whole host of activities – not just scuba diving but also white-water rafting, canoeing and riding. On the debit side Cairns' rapid tourist growth has destroyed much of its laid-back tropical atmosphere. It also lacks a beach, but there are some good ones not far north.

Cairns is the northern end of the Bruce Highway and the railway line from Brisbane. It came into existence in 1876, a beachhead in the mangroves intended as a port for the Hodgkinson River gold field 100 km inland. Initially it struggled under rivalry from Smithfield 12 km north, a rowdy frontier town that was washed away by a flood in 1879 (now it's an outer Cairns suburb), then from Port Douglas, founded in 1877 after Christie Palmerston discovered an easier route from there to the gold field. What saved Cairns was the Atherton Tableland 'tin rush' from 1880. Cairns became the starting point of the railway to the tableland, built a few years later.

Cairns is at its climatic best – and busiest – from May to October; it gets rather sticky in the summer.

Orientation

The centre of Cairns is a relatively compact area running back from the waterfront Esplanade. Off the southern continuation of The Esplanade, which is Wharf St, you'll find Marlin Jetty and Great Adventures Wharf, the two main boat departure points, flanking the Hilton Hotel. Further round is Trinity Wharf, a new cruise liner dock with shops, cafes, and the transit centre where long-distance buses arrive and depart.

Back from the waterfront, Cairns' most central streets around City Place at the meeting of Shields and Lake Sts are a pedestrian mall.

Cairns is surrounded to the south and north by mangrove swamps and the sea right in front of the town is shallow and at low tide becomes a long sweep of mud – lots of interesting water birds though.

Information

The Far North Queensland Promotion Bureau (tel 51 3588) on the corner of Sheridan and Aplin Sts is helpful and open from 9 am to 5 pm Monday to Friday and from 9 am to 4 pm Saturday. Some travel agents like YHA Travel at 85 The Esplanade, Tropical Paradise at 25 Spence St and Going Places at 26 Abbott St are also pretty helpful. The Community Information Service (tel 51 4953) in Tropical Arcade off Shields St, half a block back from The Esplanade, is good for some tourist info plus more offbeat things like where you can play croquet or do tai chi. It has details on foreign consulates in Cairns and health services and is open from 9 am to 5 pm Monday to Thursday, from 9 am to 9 pm Friday and from 9 am to 12 noon Saturday.

The RACQ Cairns office (tel 51 4788) is at 112 Sheridan St, talk to them for information on road conditions, especially if you're driving up to Cooktown or the Cape York Peninsula or across to the Gulf of Carpentaria. The National Parks & Wildlife Service (tel 51 8911) is at 41 The Esplanade. This office deals with camping permits for Davies Creek, the Frankland Islands, Lizard Island and Jardine River.

Walker's at 96 Lake St between Shields and Aplin Sts, a few doors from the centre of the mall, is the best bookshop in town. The Green Possum Environmental Bookshop, in an arcade off Grafton St right by Rusty's Bazaar, is also interesting. Absell's Newsagency, on Lake St a few doors the other way from the mall centre, has charts and survey maps of the far north.

Around Town

The *Cairns Heritage Walk/Drive Guide* tells about various places of mainly historical interest around the city. The earliest part of town – the old port area around Wharf St and the ends of Abbott and Lake Sts – is being redeveloped. There are some imposing neoclassical buildings from the 1920s on Abbott St and the frontages around the corner of Spence and Lake Sts date from 1909 to 1926.

A walk along the Esplanade, with views over to rainforested mountains across the estuary and cool evening breezes, is pleasant. Shortly before The Esplanade bends at the corner with Minnie St, look for the colourful posters illustrating all the birds you might spot here. Further along is the rather sad Catalina memorial to the aircrew who operated from Cairns during WW II. Marlin are caught off Cairns from September to December and major catches are weighed at the game fishing wharf on The Esplanade.

Right in the centre of town on the corner of Lake and Shields Sts, the Cairns Museum is housed in the old School of Arts building of 1907, an example of fine early Cairns architecture. It has Aboriginal artefacts, a display on the construction of the Cairns to Kuranda railway, the contents of a now demolished Grafton St

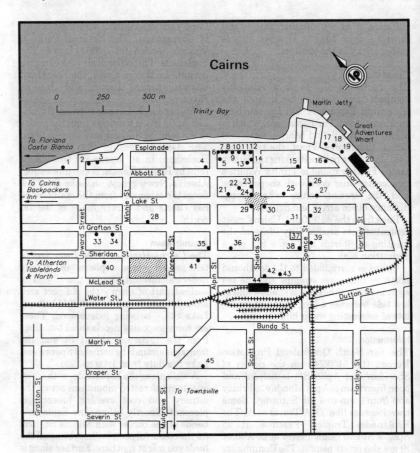

Cairns

Trinity Bay

To Floriana
Costa Blanca

To Cairns
Backpackers Inn

To Atherton
Tablelands
& North

To Townsville

Marlin Jetty

Great
Adventures
Wharf

Esplanade
Abbott St
Lake St
Grafton St
Sheridan St
McLeod St
Water St
Martyn St
Draper St
Severin St
Bunda St
Dutton St

0   250   500 m

joss house, exhibits on the old Palmer
River and Hodgkinson gold fields, and
material on the early timber industry. It's
open daily from 10 am to 3 pm and costs $1.

A colourful part of town is the Rusty's
Bazaar area bounded by Grafton, Spence,
Sheridan and Shields Sts. It's full of cafes,
restaurants and interesting shops and on
Saturday mornings holds a very busy
market with lots of art and crafts and food
on sale. This part of Grafton St used to be
the Cairns Chinatown and also a red light
district.

Up in Edge Hill in the north of town are
the Flecker Botanic Gardens on Collins
Ave. Over the road from the gardens a
boardwalk leads through a patch of
rainforest to Saltwater Creek and the two
small Centenary Lakes. Collins Ave turns
west off Sheridan St (the Cook Highway)
three km from the centre of Cairns. The
gardens are 700 metres from the turning.
Just before you reach the Botanic
Gardens is the entrance to the Whitfield
Range Environmental Park, with walking
tracks which give good views over the city
and coast. You can get there on the
Northland Bus Service or the Red

1	Catalina Memorial
2	Silver Palm
3	Caravella's 149 Hostel
4	Central House & Wintersun Motel
5	Gourmet Seafood Take-away
6	Action Backpackers
7	Hostel 89
8	Bellview YHA Hostel
9	Jimmy's on The Esplanade
10	Caravella's Hostel 77
11	Siesta Motel
12	International Hostel
13	Community Information Service
14	Air Niugini
15	GPO
16	National Parks Information Office
17	Hilton Hotel
18	Yacht Club
19	Great Adventures Office
20	Trinity Wharf & Bus Station
21	Walker's Bookshop
22	Budget Bistro
23	Backpacker's Restaurant
24	Australian Airlines
25	Ansett
26	Qantas
27	Creme de la Creme
28	Parkview Tourist Hostel
29	Cairns Museum
30	Hides Hotel
31	Aussie II Hostel
32	Tropical Paradise Travel
33	Sunshine Villa
34	Tracks Hostel
35	East-West Airlines & Far North Queensland Promotion Bureau
36	Pacific Coast Budget Accommodation
37	Rusty's Bazaar
38	Rusty's Pub
39	Mexican Pete's
40	Inn The Tropics
41	RACQ
42	Grand Hotel
43	McLeod St YHA Hostel
44	Railway Station
45	Gone Walkabout Hostel

Explorer bus. The Tobruk Olympic pool is 400 metres back down Sheridan St towards the centre of town from Collins Ave. Also in Edge Hill the Royal Flying Doctor Service regional HQ at 1 Junction St is open to visitors from 10 am to 12 noon and from 2 to 4 pm Monday to Friday.

Further Out

Kamerunga Rd, off the Cook Highway just north of the International Airport turning, leads inland to the Freshwater Connection, a railway museum complex where you can also catch the commentary train to Kuranda. It's 10 km from the centre of town. Just beyond Freshwater is the turning south along Redlynch Intake Rd to Crystal Cascades, a popular outing with waterfalls and swimming holes 22 km from Cairns.

North along the Cook Highway are the Cairns northern beaches, in reality a string of suburbs though most do also have beaches. In order going north, they're Machans Beach, Holloways Beach, Yorkeys Knob, Trinity Beach, Kewarra Beach, Clifton Beach and Palm Cove. Holloways and Trinity are the best for a short beach trip from Cairns. At Palm Cove, 22 km from Cairns, is Wild World, with lots of crocodiles and snakes, tame kangaroos and Australian birds, and shows daily.

Round the headland past Palm Cove and Double Island, Ellis Beach is a lovely spot and its southern end is an unofficial nude bathing beach. The central part of the beach has a good camping site which has been bought by a Japanese company and won't be a camping site much longer.

Soon after Ellis Beach, Hartleys Creek Zoo, 40 km from Cairns, has a collection of far north Australian wildlife. Most of the enclosures are a bit shoddy and dull but showmanship makes it one of the most interesting 'animal places' in Australia. When they feed Charlie the crocodile in the 'Crocodile Attack Show' you know for certain why it's not wise to get bitten by one! And you've never seen anything eat apples until you've seen a cassowary knock back a dozen of them. The park is open daily (at least during the winter season) but it's best to go at crocodile feeding time which is 3 pm. Tropical Paradise Travel at 25 Spence St in Cairns runs a $14 all in trip to Hartleys Creek for the crocodile show.

Activities

Most of the courses and trips mentioned here can be booked through your accommodation or through a variety of agents, as well as from the operators themselves. Going Places (tel 51 4055) at 26 Abbott St is one agency that specialises in adventure trips like canoeing, white-water rafting and game or reef fishing.

Diving & Snorkelling Cairns is the scuba diving capital of the Barrier Reef and the reef is closer to the coast here than it is further south.

Most people look for a course which takes them to the outer Barrier Reef rather than the reefs around Green or Fitzroy Islands. Some places give you more time on the reef than others – but you may prefer an extra day in the pool and classroom before venturing out. A chat with people who have already done a course can tell you some of the pros and cons. A good teacher can make all the difference to your confidence and the amount of fun you have. Another factor is how big the groups are – the smaller the better if you want personal attention.

Two schools with good reputations are Deep Sea Divers Den (tel 51 2223) at 319 Draper St, and Pro-Dive (tel 51 9915) at Marlin Jetty. But that's not to dismiss the others, which are: South Pacific Dive Centre (tel 51 7933) at 77B Lake St near the centre of the mall, Down Under Dive (tel 31 1288) on the corner of The Esplanade and Aplin St, Peter Tibbs Scuba School (tel 52 1266/51 2604) at Trinity Wharf, Ausdive (tel 31 1255) at 5 Digger St, and Peter Boundy's Fitzroy Island Dive Centre (tel 51 0294).

The most common and popular courses last five days and lead to a recognised open water certificate – check exactly what certificate you'll get and whether the school has a record of actually sending the certificates out to you. These five day courses usually involve two days' pool and classroom tuition, followed by three days on the reef, with one or two overnight stays on board out there. Normally you have to swim 200 metres and tread water for 10 minutes before you start a course.

Prices differ little between schools but usually one or other of them has a discount going. In the winter season, from about April to October, roughly $30 extra goes on the price but the rest of the year expect to pay around $300 for two days in the pool and classroom, one day-trip to the reef and back, and two more days on the reef with an overnight stay on board.

For your money you can expect transport to and from the training sites, use of all equipment, and meals while you're out on the reef. The only hidden extra is a medical, which most schools arrange for you, seems pretty superficial and costs $10. Hostels usually give you a night or two's free accommodation if you book a course through them, and may even give you a discount on the normal course price.

For snorkellers and experienced divers, most of the schools as well as several other operators offer diving trips of varying lengths. An outer reef day-trip costs between $60 and $110 (less if you're just snorkelling) depending how fast and luxurious the boat is, how much gear you need to hire, and how many dives you want. Two days and a night generally comes to about $180 all in. The most renowned diving spot off Cairns is the Cod Hole, inhabited by a colony of potato cod weighing 50 to 60 kg each.

White-water Rafting & Canoeing Three of the rivers flowing down from the Atherton Tableland make for some excellent white-water rafting. Most popular is a day in the rainforested gorges of the Tully River, 150 km south of Cairns. So many people do this trip that there can be 20 or more craft on the river at once, meaning you may have to queue up to shoot each section of rapids – but few people are other than exhilarated at the end of the day. The Tully trips go virtually daily year round and the two companies running them from Cairns are Raging Thunder (tel 51 4911) at 67 Grafton St, and R 'n R (tel 51 7777) at 49 Abbott St. For a Tully day-trip, including transport to and from the river and two meals, you pay about $94 from Cairns, $89 from Innisfail or Mission Beach, $85 from Tully, $92 from Ingham or $99 from Townsville.

Cheaper at about $45 are half day trips on the Barron River, not far inland from Cairns. Or you can make longer expeditions on the North Johnstone River which rises near Malanda and enters the sea at Innisfail. The North Johnstone has some tougher stretches of water than the Tully and you have to be helicoptered in to the start of your run.

For a quieter time, Butlers Canoe Nature Tours offers day canoeing trips on the Mulgrave River, which has some gentle rapids and good wildlife, for $60 including transport from Cairns. Book through the Going Places agency. In the Wild Canoe Tours (tel 51 7777) at 105 Lake St will give you a day canoeing on the North Johnstone for $72.

Riding The day-trip to Springmount Station (tel 93 4445), on tablelands off the Mareeba to Chillagoe road, has received good reports. For $60 you get transport from and back to your Cairns hostel, morning and afternoon rides and a big lunch.

Other Activities Goanna Tour (tel 55 3914) takes small bird-watching groups to the Mt Bartle Frere or Kuranda areas or the Atherton Tableland. The $60 cost includes pick-up from your accommodation and the outings last about eight hours. Cairns Bushwalking Club (tel 55 2445) organises regular bushwalks and can probably

arrange transport if you want to go along.

Places to Stay

Cairns has hostels and cheap guest houses galore and plenty of reasonably priced motels and holiday flats. The accommodation business is extremely competitive and, except usually in hostels, prices go up and down. Lower weekly rates are par for the course. Prices given here for the more expensive places can rise 30 or 40% in the peak season.

Hostels The Cairns hostel scene is a rapidly changing one as new places open up, old ones change hands and others rise and fall in quality and popularity with alarming speed. The type of accommodation is pretty standard – fan cooled bunk rooms with shared kitchen and bathrooms, usually also washing machines and a smallish swimming pool. The dorms are often pretty tightly packed, though many places have spacious sitting areas. Many of the kitchens are small and tatty – but since Cairns has a good range of cheap places to eat out, that's not too much of a problem. Unfortunately you have to beware of theft in some places – use lock up rooms and safes if they're available.

The Esplanade has the biggest hostel concentration, and it's a lively place, though some of the better hostels are in quieter streets elsewhere.

Starting from the corner of Shields St and heading along The Esplanade, the *International Hostel* (tel 31 1424) at 67 is a big, well run place with room for about 200 in bunk rooms which take two to six people. There are also a few double rooms. The hostel has a kiosk with diving equipment for hire and a good notice board. Downstairs is a 140 seat food hall with a bar. Nightly rates are $9 in a six bunk room, $10 in a four bunk room, $11 in a two bunk room and $12 in a double room. Next along at 75 the *Siesta Motel* (tel 51 2866) charges $7 per person in eight bunk rooms with their own bathroom ($8).

There are also motel rooms at $28 for three people. The kitchen's small and there's no pool.

Caravella's Hostel 77 (tel 51 2159) at 77 The Esplanade is a rambling place taking about 150, one of the longest established Cairns hostels and kept pretty clean. Rooms range from four to 10 person fan cooled dorms at $8 a head to air-con four or five person rooms with their own TV and bathroom for $10 a head, or doubles at $20. *Jimmy's on The Esplanade* (tel 51 5670) at 83 has a variety of rooms at $9 or $10 a head. There are four person rooms with private bathroom and TV for $10, and bigger ones with their own small cooking areas.

The *Bellview YHA* hostel (tel 51 9385) at 85 is pretty good. There are dorms at $11 a head or twin rooms at $14 a head. Some are air-con. Non YHA members pay an extra $1 and sheets are $1. The kitchen facilities are good. There are also air-con motel rooms with fridge, TV and private bathroom at $40/48/55/63 for one/two/three/four people. The hostel has a buffet breakfast bar.

Hostel 89 (tel 31 2237) at 89 is one of the best kept hostels on The Esplanade. It's smallish, with room for about 50 in dorms of various sizes, some with attached bathrooms, and charges $8 to $10. There's a security patrol at night. On the corner of Aplin St at 93 The Esplanade, *Action Backpackers* (tel 31 1919) is a lively, friendly place. Doubles are $22 and there are several six to 12 person dorms at $9 a head.

Three blocks further along The Esplanade at 149 is another bigger hostel, *Caravella's 149* (tel 51 2431). Its popularity means that even the big cooking/sitting/TV/pool/games area at the back can get pretty busy. You pay $8 in a dorm, $9 or $10 in smaller rooms. A few six bunk rooms have air-con and their own bathroom. The doubles at the back behind the pool are probably the most spacious rooms.

Over at 255 Lake St, *Cairns Backpackers*

Inn (tel 51 9166) occupies three houses, with entrances on both Lake and Digger Sts. The hostel runs a free bus to and from the town centre several times a day. Beds and bunks are squeezed pretty tightly into the rooms but there's plenty of space in the other areas. You pay $8 in a dorm or there are singles/doubles for $12/22. Meals are served three or four nights a week. You can hire bicycles for $9 a day.

CAIRNS BACKPACKERS INN

Closer to the centre, *Parkview Tourist Hostel* (tel 51 3700) is at 174 Grafton St, three blocks back from The Esplanade. Cost is $9 a night in dorms, $10 per person in double or twin rooms. The hostel is clean and spacious with a large garden. It has a restaurant with cheap breakfasts and dinners as well as a couple of small kitchens. The office is open from 7.30 am to 12 noon and from 5 to 8.30 pm. Free trips to Crystal Cascades and the Kuranda market are offered.

At 72 Grafton St the *Aussie II* hostel (tel 51 7620) is clean and roomy with space for about 80 people. You pay $8 for a dorm bed, with a maximum of six people in each room. There are also twin and double rooms at $10 per person. The hostel has two kitchens and a TV room. There's no pool but you can use the pools at the two Caravella hostels.

Two blocks back from the station at 274 Draper St, *Gone Walkabout Hostel* (tel 51 6160) is one of the best in Cairns but it's small and at times hard to get into. The rooms aren't big and there's no pool but it's a comfortable, clean and friendly place. You pay $8 whether you're in a dorm or one of the little doubles, and use of washing machines is free. It's not a place for late partying however.

Tracks (tel 31 1474) at 151 Grafton St has dorm beds at $8 and double rooms at $20. It seems very popular. *McLeod St YHA Hostel* (tel 51 0772) at 20-24 McLeod St has dorm beds for $8, twin and double rooms for $10 a person and singles for $15. Non members pay $1 extra.

Guest Houses & Hotels A couple of places in this bracket are almost in the hostel price range, the difference being that their emphasis is on rooms rather than dorms.

On The Esplanade the *Silver Palm* (tel 51 2059) at 153, between Upward and Minnie Sts, is a clean guest house with singles/doubles at $19/28 including use of a kitchen, laundry and TV room. *Floriana* at 183 simply looks terrific and has doubles at $25 to $40 and self contained flats at $45 or $50.

Central House (tel 51 2869) at 85 Abbott St, near the corner of Aplin St, is a pleasant place costing $22/26. It has hostel-type facilities like shared bathrooms, kitchen and laundry, plus a large sitting room. There are also some semi-self-contained flats which can fit up to six people for $145 a week double, $11 for each extra person.

Wintersun Motel Holiday Apartments (tel 51 2933), next door at 84 Abbott St, is popular with backpackers. There's an array of rooms starting with fan cooled budget twin shares at $12.50 per person or singles at $22 with shared kitchens and bathrooms. Better rooms with air-con, private bathroom, colour TV, tea/coffee equipment, fridge and toaster are $38 to $60.

Inn The Tropics (tel 31 1088) at 141 Sheridan St, between Minnie and Upward Sts, is a new place with a good pool, a small guests' kitchen and an open air courtyard with tables. For $33 you get a double or twin room with fridge, sink and dollar in the slot air-con. There are family rooms for $39. Bathrooms are communal but the place is kept very clean. In similar style is the *Uptop Downunder Holiday Lodge* (tel 51 3636) at 164-170 Spence St, 1½ km from the town centre. There's a free bus to and from the centre or the airport. It has a good kitchen, two TV lounges and a pool and singles/doubles are $22/33. There are bicycles for hire too.

Tropicana Lodge (tel 51 1729) at 158C Martyn St, about two km from the centre, has singles/doubles at $20/30 including breakfast. It has a good pool and a TV lounge, plus more expensive motel rooms at $33/50 with breakfast. Closer to the centre again, *Pacific Coast Budget Accommodation* (tel 51 1264) is at 100 Sheridan St. Clean fan cooled rooms are $22/35 including continental breakfast. Bathrooms are shared and there's a smallish kitchen. You can also get very cheap dinners in the dining room. There are laundry facilities and a car park.

Motels & Holiday Flats Holiday flats are well worth considering, especially for a group of three or four people who are staying a few days or more. Expect pools, air-con and laundry facilities in this category. Holiday flats generally supply all bedding, cooking and eating equipment, etc.

The somewhat grotty *Cairns Motel* (tel 51 2771) at 48 Spence St is about as central as you could ask for. The 15 fan cooled rooms cost $30/35 for singles/doubles. Eight newer air-con rooms are $45/50. It will be very noisy here when there's music at the nearby Rusty's Pub. Also fairly central, at 169 Lake St, the well kept *Poinsettia Motel* (tel 51 2144) has rooms from \$37/39. There are also several holiday flat places along Lake St.

At 237 *Costa Blanca* has a big pool and large, bright, clean flats at \$40 double. At 161 Grafton St *Sunshine Villa* (tel 51 5288) has excellent fully equipped flats. For brief stays the prices aren't worthwhile, but for five or more nights they start to look more reasonable. In the low season, three people sharing a one bedroom flat for a week would pay \$150 each, while five people in a two-bedroom flat pay \$105 each.

Sheridan St has numerous motels. *Captain Cook Endeavour Inns* (tel 51 6811) is at 204, with singles/doubles from \$40/55 and backpacker accommodation too. *Hollywood Inn* (tel 51 3458) at 239 Sheridan St is another of the cheaper ones. *Tropic Sunrise* holiday flats (tel 51 3537) at 338 charges a nightly rate of \$44 to \$55 for two people.

Camping There are about a dozen camping sites in and close to Cairns, though none central. Almost without exception they take campers as well as caravans. The more conveniently located include:

Cairns Coconut Caravan Village, Bruce Highway, camping \$10 for two, Camp-O-Tel units \$8 to \$10 per person, on-site vans \$30 (tel 54 6644)
City Caravan Park, corner of Little & James Sts, camping \$9, on-site vans \$25 (tel 51 1467)
Cool Waters Caravan Park, Brinsmead Rd, Brinsmead, camping \$10, on-site vans \$20 to \$24 (tel 53 3949)

Places to Eat

For a town of its size Cairns has quite an amazing number and variety of restaurants. Opening hours have been lengthened and more places are taking advantage of the climate by providing open air dining. Most newer places are on The Esplanade or around City Place at the centre of the mall – but there's a big collection of eateries in the streets near Rusty's Bazaar three or four blocks back from the seafront.

Snacks & Take-aways The Esplanade has a growing collection of fast food and take-away joints – and the *International Hostel* at number 67 has opened a 'food hall' with a bar plus good value Indian, Mexican, Chinese, Italian and Filipino food. Between here and the corner of Aplin St you'll find more places doing Italian, Chinese, burgers, seafood and ice cream. The *Siesta Motel* at 75 has a Chinese take-away section with an evening buffet for \$5. Further along near the corner of Aplin St *La Pizza* makes pizzas from \$3, also pasta from \$5.

Just back from The Esplanade on Aplin St the *Gourmet Seafood Take-Away* will do you coral trout with chips and salad for \$9. Nearby *La Mamma's* does great pastas and other Italian dishes. Right by the centre of the mall, *Sidney's Place* is a coffee shop doing full breakfasts at \$5 and light meals at \$6. At Trinity Wharf there's another food hall and a pub.

Rusty's Bazaar at 61-69 Grafton St is a small market-like complex which has many good cheap places. There's *Goodings*, open early if you fancy croissants for breakfast, *Tiny's* with inexpensive seafood salads, and *Sweethearts*, open daily except Sundays until 7 pm with good, cheap vegetarian food. *Flunches* is a busy lunch spot on Grafton St right near Rusty's Bazaar. Other good daytime spots in this area include *Mozart's* on the corner of Grafton and Spence Sts, which has continental cakes and German newspapers. Similar is *Gerald's Paris Croissants & Humble Pies* at 93A Grafton St, open daily to 5.30 pm (Saturdays to 1 pm).

On Sheridan St between Spence and Shields Sts, the *Mouth Trap*, closer to Spence St, serves breakfasts all day for \$5, while *John & Diana's Breakfast & Burger House* at 35 Sheridan St has virtually every combination of cooked breakfast imaginable for \$5 or less. In the Andrejic

Arcade from 55 Lake St through to Grafton St are two good lunch places. *Nibbles* has sandwiches, rolls and pitta breads. The *Hibiscus Coffee Lounge* has a Chinese smorgasbord for $5.

Pub Meals One of the best bargains is the dining room of *Rusty's Pub* on the corner of Spence and Sheridan Sts. Big cooked breakfasts from 6 to 9 am are $4.50 with unlimited tea and coffee. For lunch there are steaks and seafood meals from $5. On McLeod St opposite the railway station the *Grand Hotel* and the *Railway Hotel* offer good $3 to $4 roast lunches. The Grand also has a fancier section with food in the $8 range and evening meals are served until 8.30 pm at both these pubs.

Right in the town centre on City Place *Hides Hotel* has a bistro with some of the best counter food in Cairns. It's open for both lunch (about $7) and dinner for $9 or more from 6 to 9 pm. The *Barrier Reef Hotel* on the corner of Abbott and Wharf Sts does good and inexpensive counter meals too.

Restaurants The extremely popular *Backpackers Restaurant* is close to the centre of the mall, upstairs at 24 Shields St. It has a bar, is open from lunch time until late and offers a buffet-style selection of hot meals and salads for $5 for as much as you can get on your plate. There's better food at the *Budget Bistro* at 96 Lake St, in the small arcade near Australian Airlines, serving an excellent array of hot dishes, salads and fruits. A full plate is $6. It's open from 11.30 am for lunch and dinner. Steaks, grills, fish and salads at semi-budget prices can be found at the *Red Ox* restaurant on the corner of Abbot and Aplin Sts.

Also very good value is *Gopal's*, the Hare Krishna vegetarian restaurant in Rusty's Bazaar. It's open Monday to Friday from 12 noon to 2.30 pm and Saturday from 8.30 am to 2.30 pm. It offers a good $4 fill-your-plate special

including a glass of lassi, the yoghurt drink.

The nearby Grafton St area again offers lots more possibilities. *Riccardo's Italian Restaurant* on Grafton St next to the Rusty's Bazaar newsagent does tasty, imaginative meals; pastas from $10. Two similarly priced restaurants on the terrace in Rusty's Bazaar are the *Ring of Fire Curry House* and the *French Bistro*. The curry place has vegie curries for $7.50 but others are $10 to $15. It's open nightly to 10 pm except Wednesday. Main meals at the French place are $12.50; it's closed on Tuesdays, otherwise open nightly until late.

On Grafton St near Spence St the *Schwarzwald Inn* has German and international food at reasonable prices, from $8 upwards. At 95 Grafton St close to Shields St is *Der Feinschmecker* where goulash or beef curry is $6 to $7. Around the corner at 44 Spence St the *Wilhelm Tell*, open from 9 am to midnight Monday to Saturday, specialises in sausages and schnitzels. It also has lunch specials.

At 61 Spence St, near the corner of Sheridan, the popular *Mexican Pete's* is open from 6 pm until late, Tuesday to Saturday. If you fancy Lebanese food there's the BYO *Omar Khayam* at 82A Sheridan St but at $20 per person for a mixed plate meal it's not good value. There are cheaper take-aways from $7. The *Toko Baru* at 42 Spence St is a very good, slightly expensive Indonesian restaurant. The food is authentically spicy; it's open nightly and is BYO.

Over at 42B Aplin St is the *Bangkok Room* Thai restaurant. Next door but one is *Dundee's*, with a 'Crocktail Bar' – it had to come. The very popular *Swagman's Restaurant/Cafe*, right in the centre of the mall, is open daily from 8 am until 9 pm. There's seafood at $7 to $9, lighter meals at $4 to $5.

Cairns seafood restaurants are mostly not cheap. *Surf & Turf* (open nightly) is at 74 Shields St down towards the station. Its fish of the day is only $7 but other dishes are from $10. *Rio's* at 141 Grafton St does 'Mexican seafood' from $10. *Damari's*, at 64 Shields St, is a pleasantly atmospheric Italian restaurant with pastas at $6 to $9 as starters, $12 to $13 as main courses. It's open Monday to Sunday from 6 pm.

Entertainment

The *Backpackers Restaurant* is licensed and heaving with travellers every night. It's a good meeting place where you're almost bound to run into someone you've met elsewhere. Cairns doesn't have as big a pub rock scene as you might expect but things have improved in recent years. Radio 4CA (846 KHz) has the rundown on who is playing where, or get the Friday *Cairns Post*.

The *Crown Hotel* at 35 Shields St has live bands several nights a week. *Hideaways*, a nightspot in the Great Northern Hotel, is popular with a live band every night except Sunday from 9 pm until 2 am.

Another popular place is *Oscar's Bar* in the Great Northern Hotel with live rock nightly except Sunday. Trinity Wharf is good for live music on Saturday and Sunday afternoons and the *Trinity Wharf Tavern* is popular on a Friday night. The rough and ready *Rusty's Pub* (corner of Spence and Sheridan) has live bands on Saturday and Sunday afternoons.

Then there are several nightclubs and discos. *Scandals* at Tradewinds Sunlodge Motel, corner of Grafton and Florence Sts, has live entertainment nightly from 7 pm. There's no cover charge and it's open until 4 am during the week, 5 am Friday and Saturday nights. Dress regulations apply. *The Nest* at 82 McLeod St bills itself as a Piano Bar/Nightclub, with video clips and dance music. Again dress regulations apply. *Cleo's* is a nightclub with live entertainment; it's at 53 Spence St, open nightly from 8 pm until 3 am. *Playpen International* at 3 Lake St often has big name bands and is open until late.

Things to Buy

Many artists live in the Cairns region so there's a wide range of local handicrafts available – pottery, clothing, stained glass, jewellery, leather work and so on. Aboriginal art is also for sale in a few places. The bustling Saturday morning market behind Rusty's Bazaar on Grafton St is a good place to start looking. Rusty's Bazaar itself has shops selling Asian and local crafts. Several places including El Cheepos and Bagus Batik have Kuta clothing straight from Bali. The two Asian Connection outlets have interesting items from all over Asia and there are several places with Papua New Guinea art and artefacts; Gallery Primitive at 26 Abbott St is the best and they also have Aboriginal art. The Big Boomerang and Koala Kraft's two shops also have Aboriginal art including, at Koala, Yarrabah pottery from near Cairns. Anuaka Arts & Crafts on the corner of Palmer and Toohey Sts in Portsmith is Aborigine staffed and managed.

For local arts and crafts and Australiana try Koala Kraft, Gum Nut Creations, Accent Arts & Crafts and Laser Craft. Crocodiliacs have interesting T-shirt designs in their half dozen shops. Crocodile-eats-tourist T-shirts are definitely a major craze in Cairns.

Getting There & Away

Air Ansett and Australian both fly to Cairns from all the regular places, and East-West too now flies from Ayers Rock (once a week nonstop), Brisbane and Sydney. There are as many as eight to 10 flights daily coming up the east coast from Brisbane and the southern capitals. Australian Airlines flies to/from Dunk Island and Townsville.

Typical fares include Melbourne $385 (standby $309), Sydney $350 ($281), Brisbane $282 ($227), Townsville $106, Mt Isa $196 ($158), Darwin $324 ($260) and Alice Springs $290 ($233). In Cairns, Australian and Australian Regional (tel 50 3777) are on the corner of Shield and

Lake Sts, Ansett (tel 50 2211) is at 84 Lake St, and East-West (tel 51 9400) is at the corner of Aplin and Sheridan Sts.

Flights inland and up the Cape York Peninsula from Cairns are shared amongst three airlines. Australian Regional flies to Bamaga, Lizard Island ($114), Weipa ($179) and Thursday Island ($225). Sunbird Airlines (tel 53 4899 at the airport or book through Australian) covers a big network of places on the Cape York Peninsula, Torres Strait Islands and the Gulf country. Its flights include Cooktown ($84). It also makes interesting flights to/from Mt Isa ($196) via various stops on the Gulf. Flight West (tel 53 5511 or through Ansett) operates a similar Gulf and Mt Isa service.

Cairns is also an international airport with regular flights to and from North America, Papua New Guinea and Asia. Air Niugini (tel 51 4177) is at 4 Shields St: the Port Moresby flight costs $280 one way and goes five times a week. Qantas, at 13 Spence St (tel 51 0100), also flies to Port Moresby.

Bus Greyhound, Pioneer, Deluxe, McCafferty's and Sunliner all run two or three buses a day up the coast from Brisbane and Townsville to Cairns. From Brisbane it's 23 to 27 hours and costs $90 to $100. From Rockhampton it's 14 to 16 hours ($66), Mackay 10 to 12 hours ($49), Townsville 4½ hours ($27). Greyhound (tel 51 3388), Deluxe (tel 31 2600) and Sunliner (tel 51 3444) and the other companies operate from the new Transit Centre at Trinity Wharf.

If you have a YHA card, YHA Travel (tel 51 9385) at 85 The Esplanade in Cairns can get you a 10% discount on most long-distance buses.

Train The Sunlander between Brisbane and Cairns runs four days a week, and the Queenslander motorail train goes once a week (leaving Brisbane on Sunday and Cairns on Tuesday). The 1681 km trip from Brisbane takes about 38 hours. The economy fare from Brisbane is $100.10. In 1st it's $179.10 on the Sunlander, $287.60 including sleeping berth and all meals on the Queenslander. For railway information in Cairns call 51 1111.

Getting Around

Airport Transport Cairns airport is in two parts, both off the Captain Cook Highway in the north of the town. The three main domestic airlines and international flights use the new section, officially called Cairns International Airport. This is reached by an approach road that turns off the highway about 3½ km from central Cairns. The other part of the airport, which some people still call 'Cairns Airport', is reached from a second turning off the highway, 1½ km north of the main one. Sunbird is one of the lines using this old section.

The shuttle bus from the main terminal costs $3.50 and will drop you almost anywhere central in Cairns. Ring 53 4722 to book when you're leaving. A taxi is about $8. Avis, Budget, Hertz and Thrifty have car hire desks at the airport.

Bus There are a number of local bus services in and around Cairns. Schedules for most of them are posted at the centre of the mall where Shields and Lake Sts meet, which is the main city stop. Buses on most routes go roughly once an hour, 7 am to 5 pm, Monday to Friday. On weekends services are less frequent and some routes close down from Saturday lunch time to Monday morning. Bus No 208, run by Marlin Coast Bus Lines (tel 55 3709), goes up to Trinity and Clifton Beaches, Wild World, Palm Cove and Ellis Beach. The last bus back to Cairns leaves Ellis Beach at 4.40 pm Monday to Friday, 3 pm Saturday and 4 pm Sunday.

The Yorkeys Knob-Holloways Beach Bus Service (tel 51 9979) has last buses back from Yorkeys Knob at 5 pm Monday to Friday and 12.40 pm on Saturday. From Holloways Beach they're at 5.40 pm on weekdays, 12.25 pm on Saturdays. There are no services on Sundays. Southern Cross Bus Services (tel 55 1240) goes to Machans Beach. Last buses to Cairns are 4.45 pm Monday to Friday, 10 am Saturday, no service on Sunday.

For the Flecker Botanic Gardens and Whitfield Range walking tracks, take the Northland Bus Service to Edgehill, from Anzac Park opposite the Hilton. This service closes for the weekend around 12 noon on Saturday.

The Red Explorer (tel 55 1240) is one of those bus services that lets you get on and off all day at various stops on a circular route. It runs roughly on the hour from 9 am to 5 pm daily except Sunday and a day ticket is $8. The bus starts from the National Australia Bank on Shields St near City Place and includes Freshwater Creek swimming hole, Lake Placid, Freshwater Connection, the botanic gardens and Centenary Lakes on its route.

Car Rental It's well worth considering renting a car. There is plenty to see and do on land around Cairns whether it's making the beach crawl up to Port Douglas or exploring the Atherton Tableland. Mokes are about the cheapest cars to rent and ideal for relaxed, open air sightseeing. Most of the car rental firms in Cairns have Mokes. Most of the major firms are along Lake St but local firms have mushroomed all over Cairns – some of them offer good deals, particularly for weekly rentals, but don't be taken in by $10 per day advertising. Once you add in all the hidden costs, prices are fairly similar everywhere.

The inclusive rates (with up to 200 or 300 km free but not petrol) for Mokes and VW convertibles are usually $40 and $49 a day respectively. Places which rent Mokes include Cairns Rent-A-Car (tel 51 6077) at 147C Lake St, AMAX (tel 31 1788) at 141 Lake St and Cairns Leisure Wheels (tel 51 8988) at 230 Sheridan St. For VW convertibles try Cairns Rent-A-

Car, AMAX, or Topless Car Rentals (tel 52 1188) at 134 Sheridan St.

Rates for newish small cars are a little more variable. One of the cheapest offers is $36 a day, including insurance and unlimited km at Sheridan Rent-A-Car (tel 51 3942), 196A Sheridan St. Half-Price Rent-A-Car (tel 31 2322) at 3 Aplin St, on the corner of The Esplanade, has a similar deal and it will rent to 19 year olds and up. Other places to try are Mini-Car Rental (tel 51 6288) at 142 Sheridan St and Sam's Cheaper Car Rentals (tel 51 9871) at 51 Sheridan St. At Cairns Rent-A-Car you pay $44 per day, including insurance and up to 300 km, plus 14c for each extra km. Half-Price does one-way rentals south to Brisbane and other state capitals. Two days to Brisbane would cost between $160 and $240 depending on the season.

For 4WD vehicles, Cairns Rent-A-Car seems to offer the best deal – $65 a day, including insurance and 200 km free.

Note that most Cairns rental firms specifically prohibit you from taking most of their cars up the Cape Tribulation road, on the road to Cooktown, or on the Chillagoe caves road. A sign in the car will usually announce this prohibition and the contract will threaten dire unhappiness if you do so. Of course lots of people ignore these prohibitions but if you get stuck in the mud halfway up to Cape Tribulation it could be a little embarrassing. Be warned that these roads are fairly rough and sometimes impassable in conventional vehicles. Also note that a sizeable deposit is generally required for car rental, anything from $100 to $250 in Cairns.

Bicycle & Motorcycle Rental Several hostels rent out bicycles to people who are staying there: at Gone Walkabout or Cairns Backpackers Inn it's $9 a day, at Caravella's 149 it's $7. This last place organises its bikes through Bakpak Bike Hire (tel 51 2431).

You can hire five speed mountain bikes for $8 a day from Campbell's Cycles (tel

51 6853) at 150 Sheridan St. You have to leave a $50 deposit and show ID. North Queensland Rent-A-Car at 82-84A Sheridan St has bikes for rent at $10 per day. There's also the Bicycle Barn at 61 and 150A Sheridan St ($8 a day).

You'll notice mopeds for hire out the front of some hotels. Either enquire there or ring Skeeter Skooter Hire (tel 55 3221). For motor bikes head for Cairns Yamaha at 55 McLeod St. They'll let you take their bikes anywhere. Trail bikes cost $59 a day all up; 250cc road bikes are $59 per day and 1100ccs are $89 per day. Deposits are $150 to $200. You need a current motorcycle licence.

Tours As you'd expect there are hundreds of tours available from Cairns. Some are specially aimed at backpackers and many of these are pretty good value. You can make bookings through the place you're staying or at smaller travel agents which specialise in this type of trip such as YHA Travel (tel 51 9385) at 85 The Esplanade, Tropical Paradise (tel 51 9533) at 25 Spence St or Going Places (tel 51 4055) at 26 Abbott St.

Cairns Hostel Tours (book through hostels) runs some of the most popular trips at very low prices, including to Kuranda. For Cape Tribulation trips, $45 will get transport to and from Crocodylus Village near the cape and two nights' accommodation there, plus visits to Mossman Gorge and Port Douglas. For $49 you can stay at Jungle Lodge instead, or have a night in each place.

The Jimmy's and Caravella's 77 hostels on The Esplanade also run Kuranda and Atherton Tableland trips. Typically for $35 you'd see the Kuranda market, then visit a couple of Tableland lakes and waterfalls for swimming, plus one or two other sights. Trips with these two hostels to Crystal Cascades cost about $9. The Cairns Tour Centre, next to the Siesta Motel on The Esplanade, offers trips to the Behana Gorge for $25, with a guided rainforest walk to the falls, pools and rock jumps and lunch. Cairns Backpackers Inn on Lake St offers a three day 4WD trip with Mike's Safaris to Cape Tribulation for $90. Wait-A-While Rainforest Tours (tel 55 2392) runs day-trips usually led by former national park rangers to places like Mossman Gorge, the Mt Carbine Tableland, Mulgrave River, Barron Gorge and Lake Placid. The trips last about 10½ hours, are limited to 10 people and cost $60 including meals.

Nerada tea plantation combined with Atherton Tableland waterfalls and lakes is offered by several 'conventional' tour companies. It costs $35. With these companies a trip to Mossman Gorge, Port Douglas and back will cost $30 without meals. A day tour to Cape Tribulation and back is $50 to $80 depending on how small the group is and how comfortable the vehicle. You get stops at a few places on the way and often a guided bushwalk thrown in.

Cairns Hinterland Tours does trips to Josephine Falls and Babinda Boulders with a river cruise thrown in for $40 in the summer, and a Gulf and Cape York Peninsula three day tour for $350. Ansett Trailways, Australian Pacific and AAT King's both do Palmer River, Quinkan rock art and Cooktown trips. For three days these cost around $270. From March to May Raging Thunder offers five day camping safaris taking in Lakefield National Park, the Quinkan galleries and Cooktown for around $350.

Half a day round Cairns city sights, or a two hour cruise from Marlin Jetty up along Trinity Inlet and round Admiralty Island, costs $15.

There are several options on day-trips to the reef. Great Adventures (tel 51 0455) does a nine hour $95 outer reef trip which includes a two hour stop on Green Island. You get three hours on the reef itself, with lunch, snorkel gear and semisub and glass-bottomed boat rides thrown in. They also do day-trips to Michaelmas Cay, again including two hours on Green Island, for $76. Cheaper is their nine hour 'no frills' cruise to Fitzroy Island and Moore Reef for $66 with free use of snorkel gear. Departures are from the Great Adventures wharf.

The motor vessel *Seastar II* (tel 53 2066) at Marlin Jetty will take you straight to Michaelmas Cay and Hastings Reef on the outer reef, where you can feed fish and snorkel for $40. Divers can hire full scuba gear for $40. Hastings Reef has excellent coral.

MV *Teal* (tel 31 1116) does $70 day-trips to the reef including lunch, glass-bottomed boat and snorkelling. If you get down to Marlin Jetty early enough in the morning, there are often standby places on offer an hour before departure for $44.

The Frankland Islands are a group of small, undeveloped national parks, with reefs and rainforest, off the coast about 40 km south of Cairns. Bandanyah Marine Tours (tel 55 4966) at 125 Bruce Highway, Edmonton, does day-trips there from Deeral Landing on the Mulgrave River. You get about five hours on the islands for $79. Book through Qintour at 21 Spence St in Cairns. Bandanyah will also drop you off for camping on High or Russell Islands in the group and they can organise camping gear and supplies. You need a national parks permit too.

Yet another possibility is scenic flights. Reef Air Tours (tel 53 7936) can give you 35 minutes over Green Island, Michaelmas Cay and the Cairns area for $55 or, for $150, three hours over Green Island, the Barrier Reef, Cape Tribulation with a landing and rainforest walk at Cow Bay, and the Low Isles. There is also a three hour flight to Fitzroy Island for $80.

Islands off Cairns

Green and Fitzroy are wooded islands off Cairns which attract lots of day-trippers and some overnighters too. North of Green Island and 40 km from Cairns, tiny Michaelmas Cay is a national park and home to thousands of sea birds. In the summer peak nesting season 30,000 or more of them cram on to it. Some day-trips from Cairns to Green Island or the Barrier Reef call at Michaelmas Cay.

Getting There & Away

Great Adventures and others run ferries from Cairns to Fitzroy and Green. Great Adventures (tel 51 0455), at their wharf between the Hilton and Trinity Wharf in Cairns, have a wide choice of services from a 'budget launch' which takes about 90 minutes to Green Island to their high speed catamarans which take about 45 minutes to either island. The budget service to Green Island costs $20 return and gives you six hours on the island. The high speed cats are $28 return to Fitzroy or $33 return to Green. You can visit both for $42.

There are various other operators to the islands including the Big Cat (tel 51 0444) which also does a budget $20 return trip to Green Island.

GREEN ISLAND

Green Island, 27 km north-east of Cairns, is a true coral cay 660 metres long by 260 metres wide. The beautiful island and its surrounding reef are all national park but marred by shonky development. Nevertheless, a 10 minute stroll to the far end of the island will remind you that the beach is beautiful, the water fine, the snorkelling good and the fish prolific.

The artificial attractions start at the end of the pier with the underwater observatory. Glass-bottomed boats go from the pier too while on the island there's the Barrier Reef Theatre and Marineland Melanesia with fish and corals in tanks plus larger creatures (sharks, turtles, crocodiles) in pools or enclosures, and a display of PNG art. The more expensive day-trips to Green Island include entry to all these *wonders*. You can hire windsurfers or canoes.

Places to Stay & Eat

The *Green Island Reef Resort* (tel 51 4644) isn't in the budget range – regular nightly costs are $99 per person or more, though that includes all meals and use of snorkelling and other beach equipment. The whole resort is soon to have a multi-million dollar overhaul including an all new underwater observatory to replace the current ancient looking installation.

FITZROY ISLAND

Six km off the coast and 26 km south-east of Cairns, Fitzroy is a larger continental island with beaches which are covered in coral so they are not ideal for swimming and sunbaking. For snorkellers, there's good coral only 50 metres off the beach in the resort area and the island has its own dive school. There are some fine walks including to the island's high point.

Places to Stay

Unlike Green Island, Fitzroy (tel 51 9588) has a variety of accommodation, starting with a camping ground ($10 for two – book at the Great Adventures Wharf office). There are also hostel-style units accommodating four people in bunks at $24 each ($85 for the whole thing), with shared kitchen and bathrooms. The 'villa units' cost $210 for two people including breakfast and dinner. There are a pool, snack bar with fish & chips and pizza, a bar, shops and a laundromat.

Atherton Tableland

Inland from the coast between Innisfail and Cairns the land rises sharply then rolls gently across the lush Atherton Tableland towards the Great Dividing Range. The tableland's altitude, over 900 metres in places, tempers the tropical heat and the abundant rainfall and rich volcanic soil combine to make this one of the greenest places in Queensland. In the south are Queensland's two highest mountains – Mts Bartle Frere (1657 metres) and Bellenden Ker (1591 metres).

Little more than a century ago this peaceful, pastoral region was still wild jungle. The first pioneers came in 1874 to '76, looking for a repeat of the Palmer River gold rush, further north. As elsewhere in Queensland, the Aboriginal population was violently opposed to this intrusion but was soon overrun. Some gold was found and rather more tin but though mining spurred the development of roads and railways through the rugged, difficult land of the plateau, farming and timber soon became the chief activities. Recently the timber workers have hit the headlines with their heated opposition to rainforest preservation plans.

Getting There & Around

The train ride from Cairns to Kuranda is a major tableland attraction – but without a car the rest of the tableland can be hard to reach. In south to north order the four good roads from the coast are the Palmerston Highway from Innisfail to Millaa Millaa and Ravenshoe; the Gillies Highway from Gordonvale up past Lakes Tinaroo, Barrine and Eacham to Yungaburra and Atherton; the Kennedy Highway from Cairns to Kuranda and Mareeba; and the Peninsula Development Road from Mossman through Mt Molloy to Mareeba.

Train The most popular route is the incredibly scenic railway that winds 34 km from Cairns to Kuranda. This line, which took five years to build, was opened in 1891 and goes through 15 tunnels, climbing over 300 metres in the last 21 km. Kuranda's railway station, decked out in tropical flowers and ferns, is justly famous.

In ascending order of cost there are the local trains (the silver or milk train), the tourist train (the travel train), and the commentary train. The local is $4.40 return – but it doesn't run on Sunday, the main Kuranda market day. It runs twice daily Monday to Saturday and takes 1½ hours. Local trains continue to Mareeba after Kuranda: the Monday to Friday morning run also goes on to Atherton, Herberton and Ravenshoe.

The tourist train ($10.60 one way, $18 return) operates once or twice daily. For your money you get a booklet on the line's history and a photo stop at the 260 metre Barron Falls. The commentary train operates daily and costs $14 one way, $25 return. There are uniformed hostesses, free orange juice, and a commentary. At Cairns station it has its own ticket office (tel 55 2222) – or you can board at the Freshwater Connection 10 km out of Cairns.

Bus White Car Coaches (tel 51 9533) has a bus daily except Saturday from Cairns, except Saturday, which goes just to Kuranda (40 minutes one way, $4.50 return) some days, and on to Mareeba and Atherton (1¼ hours, $18.70 return) other days. White Car also has an afternoon bus to Kuranda, Mareeba, Atherton, Yungaburra, Malanda (3¼ hours, $23.50 return) and Herberton, and a morning run in the opposite direction. The Cairns terminus is Tropical Paradise Travel at 25 Spence St.

KURANDA (Population 300)

This is a beautiful town with tropical vegetation, surrounded by spectacular scenery and walks, with plenty of interest and one of Queensland's most attractive hostels. There is no bank in Kuranda.

Things to See

The very busy Sunday morning market has produce and arts and crafts (including Aboriginal and imported goods) on sale. The Heritage Homestead, in the market area, is a small but fairly well laid out pioneer history museum and the entrance fee of $3.50 includes refreshments.

Another, somewhat smaller market operates on Wednesday mornings but on other days Kuranda reverts to its normal sleepy character.

Near the market area, where the main road meets Coondoo St, the Australian Butterfly Sanctuary has guided tours hourly from 10 am to 3 pm, for $8, and the cheaper Kuranda Wildlife Noctarium ($4.50) where you can see nocturnal rainforest animals like gliders, fruit bats and echidnas (open daily).

On the corner of Coondoo St and the highway is an auditorium where the Tjapukai Aboriginal Dance Theatre goes through its paces daily except Saturday. The hour long performance tells you a few basic things about Aboriginal culture with song, dance and humour and features didgeridoo playing and dancing. Cost is $9 for daytime shows, $12 in the evening.

On Coondoo St the Aborigine run Jilli Binna museum has Aboriginal crafts on sale and a small display (admission free) on Aboriginal culture and the old Mona Mona mission near Kuranda, many of whose people and their descendants live on in the area.

Over the bridge behind the railway station you can hire canoes on the Barron River for $10 an hour, $6 a half hour, or take a one hour *Kuranda Queen* cruise for $6.50.

There are several picturesque walks starting with short signed tracks down through the market. Jumrum Creek Environmental Park off the Barron Falls road, 700 metres from the bottom of Thongon St, has a short walking track and a big population of fruit bats. You can also enter it from the corner of Barang St and the highway. Further down the Barron Falls road, it divides – to the left you soon reach a lookout over the falls, to the right a further 1.4 km brings you to Wrights Lookout where you can see back down the Barron Gorge to Cairns.

Davies Creek Falls are about 30 km from Kuranda down a dirt road off the Mareeba road. A one km circuit walk leads to views over the 75 metre falls and good swimming spots in the creek.

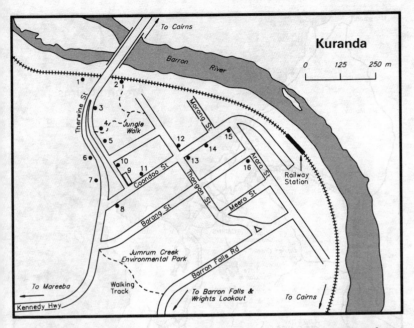

Kuranda

0   125   250 m

To Cairns

Barron River

To Cairns

Therwine St

Jungle Walk

Morong St

Arara St

Railway Station

Coondoo St

Thongon St

Meero St

Barang St

Jumrum Creek Environmental Park

To Mareeba

Walking Track

Barron Falls Rd

To Barron Falls & Wrights Lookout

Kennedy Hwy

1   Pioneer Cemetery
2   Lookout
3   Monkey's Restaurant
4   Market Area
5   Honey House Motel
6   Heritage Homestead & Market Area
7   Australian Butterfly Sanctuary
8   Noctarium
9   Tjapukai Dance Theatre,
     Mandomoni Cafe & Down to
     Earth Foods
10   Kuranda Village Bakery
11   Frogs Restaurant
12   Post Office
13   Top Pub (Fitzpatrick Tavern)
14   Jilli Binna Museum
15   Bottom Pub (Kuranda Hotel)
16   Kuranda Hostel &
     Rainforest Restaurant

Places to Stay

The *Kuranda Hostel* (tel 93 7355) is at 6 Arara St, near the railway station. It's a rambling old place with a huge garden, a fine pool, a restaurant/sitting/video room and a separate TV room. Accommodation is in separate sex dorms for $8.50 (plus $1 for a sheet) or $10 per person in double rooms (sheets provided). Hostel guests can get worthwhile discounts on most Kuranda attractions.

The small *Honey House Motel* (tel 93 7261) right by the market costs $30/40 for singles/doubles. The *Bottom Pub/ Kuranda Hotel* (tel 93 7206) at the corner of Coondoo and Arara Sts has a pool and 12 motel-type rooms at similar rates. There's a caravan and camping park (tel 93 7316) two km out of town – follow the signs from one km along the Mareeba road.

We've also heard great reports on *Mrs Miller's Hostel* which is set in tropical gardens and costs $9.50 a night. They also run tours to the Atherton Tablelands.

Places to Eat

The *Bottom Pub* has the Garden Bar &

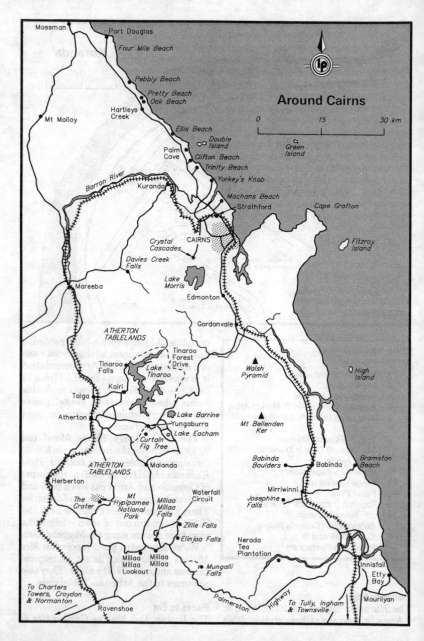

Grill, live bands on Sunday afternoons and a swimming pool. The *Top Pub* has lunch and dinner from $4 for burgers through to $10 for a fisherman's basket. At the hostel, the *Rainforest Restaurant* has excellent dinners for $6 and light lunches.

Up Coondoo St towards the highway, *Frogs Restaurant* is good value with full breakfasts from $4, felafels and souvlakis for around $4. Main meals start at $8. The *Mandomoni Cafe* in the Kuranda Village Centre on the top corner of Coondoo St has light lunches from $5 and sandwiches from $3. Nearby, *Down to Earth Foods* does cheap snacks, smoothies and juices.

Around the corner on Therwine St the excellent *Kuranda Village Bakery* has a large range of pastries. Where the road bends, *Monkey's Restaurant & Bar* has Asian and western meals from $8 plus light lunches. On Monday evenings, it has a pasta and games night, on Wednesday nights a 'feast' and live music. It's closed Tuesdays.

MAREEBA (Population 6614)

From Kuranda the Kennedy Highway runs west over the tableland to Mareeba, the centre of a tobacco and rice growing area, then continues south to Atherton in the centre of the tableland. From Mareeba the Peninsula Development Road heads 40 km north to Mt Molloy where it forks for Mossman and the coast one way, Cooktown and Cape York the other. This is the main road from Cairns to the north. Mareeba has a range of accommodation and in July hosts one of Australia's biggest rodeos.

CHILLAGOE (Population 250)

From Mareeba you can continue 140 km west to Chillagoe – after Dimbulah, 42 km along, the road is gravel and can be blocked in the wet but most of the year you can make this interesting trip in a conventional vehicle. At Chillagoe you can visit extensive and impressive limestone caves and rock pinnacles, Aboriginal rock art galleries, ruins of smelters from early this century, a working mine and a museum.

The caves are a national park and there's a ranger station (tel 94 7163) on Queen St in the town – ask there or at the Cairns national parks office about guided tours of some of the caves, usually given at 9 am and 1.30 pm. The rangers can also tell you about other caves with self guiding trails, for which you'll need a torch. Some of the caves are just outside the town, others are about four km south, and there are yet more at Mungana, about 15 km beyond Chillagoe. Some are important breeding places for bats and birds.

Places to Stay

There's a small national park camping site at Chillagoe and the *Chillagoe Caravan Park* (tel 94 7177) on Queen St has tent sites at $7 double. *Chillagoe Caves Lodge* (tel 94 7106) at 1 King St has hostel accommodation with cooking facilities at $10, or rooms at $15 to $26 single, $37 double. It also has an inexpensive restaurant.

Getting There & Away

The once weekly Cairns/Chillagoe train takes 12 hours and leaves Cairns on Wednesday, Chillagoe on Thursday. White Car Coaches has buses to Chillagoe twice a week – once from Cairns, once from Atherton, both through Mareeba. Cairns to Chillagoe takes about four hours and costs around $40 return. There are day tours from Cairns for about $85. The trip by Caving Capers (tel 31 1366 in Cairns) offers some actual caving with ropes and ladders. New Look Adventures (tel 51 7934 in Cairns) does an interesting $70 day-trip that also takes in Mt Mulligan and the Hodgkinson River gold field to the north of Chillagoe.

ATHERTON (population 4600)

Although it's a pleasant, prosperous town,

Atherton has little of interest in its own right. On the Herberton road nearer the centre is Atherton's old post office, now an art gallery, and the restored Chinese joss house.

Atherton Backpackers at 37 Alice St, not far from the centre of town, is run by the Caravella hostel family from Cairns. There's also accommodation in a few pubs and motels and *Millies Panorama Van Park* on the Kennedy Highway going south has good views. *Woodlands Tourist Park* on the Herberton road 1½ km from the town centre also has cabins and a bush setting.

LAKE TINAROO

From Atherton or nearby Tolga it's a short drive to this large lake created for the Barron River hydropower scheme. Tinaroo Falls, at the north-west corner of the lake where the waters flow out through a dam, has the *Tinaroo Lakes Motel* and *Lake Tinaroo Pines Caravan Park* which also offers tent sites, self-contained cabins and motel rooms. You can rent windsurfers over the road from the caravan park. A restaurant and kiosk overlook the dam.

The road continues over the dam as a gravel track which does a 31 km circuit of the lake, finally emerging on the Gillies Highway at Boar Pocket Rd four km east of Lake Barrine. This is called the Danbulla Forest Drive and it's a pleasant trip – though sometimes impassable for conventional vehicles after much rain. It passes several free lakeside camping grounds with showers and toilets, run by the Queensland forestry department. Lake Euramoo, about halfway along, is in a double volcanic crater beside which a 600 metre botanical walk has been laid out. Another 500 metre walk off the drive leads to another crater at Mobo Creek, then 25 km from the dam it's a short walk to the Cathedral Fig, a truly gigantic strangler fig tree.

YUNGABURRA

This pretty village is 13 km east of Atherton along the Gillies Highway. Three km out of Yungaburra on the Malanda road is the strangler fig known as the Curtain Fig for its aerial roots which form a 15 metre high hanging screen.

The *Lake Eacham Hotel* (tel 95 3515) is a fine old village centre pub with rooms at $30/38. Or there's the *Kookaburra Motel* at $38/44 and a couple of restaurants and take-aways. Four km north on the southern shores of Lake Tinaroo you can camp at the *Lakeside Motor Inn*.

LAKES EACHAM & BARRINE

These two lovely lakes in volcanic craters are off the Gillies Highway shortly east of Yungaburra, both reached by paved roads. Both are great swimming spots and have walking tracks through the rainforest round their perimeters – 6½ km round Lake Barrine, 4½ km round Lake Eacham. At Lake Barrine there's a restaurant and most of the year you can take twice daily 45 minute $4 cruises. Lake Eacham is quieter and more beautiful – but there's a kiosk open from 11.30 am to 5 pm from June to January, weekends and holidays only the rest of the year. Both lakes are national parks and you're not allowed to camp, but the *Lake Eacham Tourist Park* (tel 95 3730) with camping is two km down the Malanda road from Lake Eacham.

MALANDA

About 15 km south of Lake Eacham or 20 odd km south-east of Atherton, Malanda is one of the most pleasant spots to stay on the tableland – a small town with some old buildings in its centre, a couple of pubs and some good places to eat and stay. Malanda also has a huge dairy and claims to have the longest milk run in Australia since it supplies milk all the way to Darwin and the north of Western Australia.

Places to Stay

The *Gondwanaland Hostel* (tel (070) 96 5046) at 17 Mary St, behind the park in the middle of the town, is an excellent new place costing $11 in bright, spacious dorms with plenty of comfortable sitting space. You can have meals cooked for you or use the kitchen yourself. Bicycles are for hire and trips around the tableland may also be offered.

The slightly more basic but still pleasant small *Malanda Hostel* (tel 96 5933) at 20 James St, has a couple of dorms and the usual kitchen, bathroom and sitting room. Nightly cost is $8 including sheets.

Malanda Falls Caravan Park (tel 96 5314) is at 38 Park Ave, beside the Atherton road on the edge of town. It's spacious and next to a lovely swimming hole where the upper waters of the North Johnstone River tumble over Malanda Falls. Tent sites are $7 for two, or there are cabins and on-site vans for $17 to $30 double. There are motel rooms in the *Malanda Hotel-Motel* (tel 96 5101) on the corner of James and English Sts in the centre.

Places to Eat

The *Alcatraz Cafe*, on James St next to the Malanda Hostel, has meals from $6 or pizza from $7. It's open from Tuesday to Sunday. The *Malanda Hotel* has a licensed dining room and does counter lunches and teas daily except Sunday for $4 to $7. At the *Grapevine* cafe on James St you can get seemingly bottomless pots of tea for $2 plus home-made cakes.

MILLAA MILLAA (Population 343)

The 16 km 'waterfall circuit' road, mostly paved, near this small town 24 km south of Malanda passes some of the most picturesque falls on the tableland. You enter the circuit by taking Theresa Creek Rd one km east of Millaa Millaa on the Palmerston Highway. Millaa Millaa Falls, the first you reach, are the most spectacular and have the best swimming hole. On round the circuit you reach Zillie and then Ellinjaa Falls and return to the Palmerston Highway just 2½ km out of

Millaa Millaa. A further 5½ km down the Palmerston Highway there's a turning to Mungalli Falls, five km off the highway, with a teahouse/restaurant and a few self-contained units (tel 97 2358) at $8 a person. The Palmerston Highway continues through Palmerston National Park to Innisfail.

Millaa Millaa itself has a caravan park with tent sites at $7 double and cabins for $20 to $22, and the *Millaa Millaa Hotel* with accommodation and meals. The Eacham Historical Society Museum is on the main street.

A few km west of Millaa Millaa, the East Evelyn road passes the Millaa Millaa Lookout with its superb panoramic view.

THE CRATER

The Kennedy Highway between Atherton and Ravenshoe passes the eerie Mt Hypipamee crater. It's a scenic 400 metre walk from the picnic area, past the Dinner Falls, to this narrow, 138 metre deep crater with its spooky, evil looking lake far below. You can camp at the picnic area – permits from the Lake Eacham national parks ranger at 768 McLeish Rd (tel 95 3768).

HERBERTON (Population 1500)

On a slightly longer alternative route between Atherton and Ravenshoe this old tin mining town holds a colourful Tin Festival each September. On Holdcroft Drive is the Herberton Historical Village, with about 30 old buildings which have been transported here from around the tableland.

RAVENSHOE

At an altitude of 915 metres Ravenshoe is a forestry centre on the western edge of the tablelands. This was where the national environment minister was roughed up in 1987 when he came to talk about the proposed World Heritage listing for north Queensland rainforests. Ravenshoe has the usual caravan/camping park, a couple of pubs, two motels and *Millstream House* (tel 97 6217), a guest house on the Atherton road with accommodation from $12 a night per person and meals also available.

The Little Millstream Falls are a couple of km south of Ravenshoe on the Tully Gorge road. If you continue south the Tully Gorge and Eyrie lookouts are about 25 km out but the falls have lost their water flow to hydro projects.

The Kennedy Highway continues south-west from Ravenshoe for 114 km, from where you can head south to Charters Towers by paved road all the way, or west by the Gulf Developmental Road to Croydon and Normanton.

Six km past Ravenshoe and one km off the road are the Millstream Falls, the widest in Australia though only 13 metres high. You can camp here – permits from the Lake Eacham national park rangers. The small mining town of Mt Garnet –

which comes alive one weekend every May when it hosts one of Queensland's top outback race meetings – is 47 km west of Ravenshoe. About 60 km past Mt Garnet the road passes through Forty Mile Scrub National Park, where the semi-evergreen vine thicket is a descendant of the vegetation that covered much of the Gondwana super continent 300 million years ago – before Australia, South America, India, Africa and Antarctica drifted apart.

GULF DEVELOPMENTAL ROAD

From the Kennedy Highway to Normanton it's 460 km. The road is mostly paved, but some poor dirt stretches west of Georgetown make it a dry weather route only. The road goes through Mt Surprise, Georgetown and Croydon. There are hotels or motels and caravan/camping sites at Mt Surprise, Georgetown, Einasleigh and Forsayth. The region crossed by the road has many

Millstream Falls, Atherton Tableland

ruined gold mines and settlements and attracts some gem fossickers.

The Elizabeth Creek gem field, 42 km west of Mt Surprise and accessible by conventional vehicle in the dry, is Australia's best topaz field. You can get info on it at Mt Surprise service station (tel 62 3153). Between Mt Surprise and Georgetown, an unpaved road leads south to tiny Einasleigh, from where you could reach Kidston, Australia's richest gold mine. Einasleigh Gorge, good for swimming, is just over the road from Einasleigh pub. The former gold mining town of Forsayth is 40 km south of Georgetown, another old gold town.

North of Cairns

The Bruce Highway, which runs nearly 2000 km north from Brisbane, ends in Cairns but the surfaced coastal road continues another 110 km north to Mossman and Daintree. This final stretch, the Cook Highway, is a treat because it often runs right along the shore and there are some superb beaches. Shortly before Mossman there's a turn-off to fashionable Port Douglas, the departure point for the delightful Low Isles. Then just before Daintree village is the gravel turn-off to the Cape Tribulation rainforests. From Cape Tribulation, in a 4WD it's possible to continue up to historic Cooktown by the controversial Bloomfield Track. Alternatively there's the part surfaced inland road from Cairns but both roads to Cooktown can be cut after much rain.

Getting There & Away

Local Cairns buses run as far north as Ellis Beach. The Cooktown Bus Service runs three times a week each way between Cairns and Cooktown along the main (inland) road. You can book through Greyhound or Pioneer.

Coral Coaches is a Mossman based bus company which covers the Cairns to Cooktown coastal route via Port Douglas, Mossman, Daintree, Cape Tribulation and Bloomfield. Bookings and departures in Cairns are from Tropical Paradise Travel (tel 51 9533) at 25 Spence St. They run several buses daily between Cairns, Port Douglas (1¼ hours, $10) and Mossman ($11), and on to Daintree village. From Mossman you can get connections to Mossman Gorge ($4). Road conditions permitting, services from Cairns to Cape Tribulation go two or three times daily, and on to Cooktown via the Bloomfield Track three days a week.

Coral Coaches usually let you stop over as often as you like along the route, so they're as good as any tour. Owing to the ruggedness of some of the roads, the possibility of delays and the frequent hopping in and out of the variety of vehicles which cover different sections of the route, riding with Coral Coaches is about as close as Australia comes to travelling in the Third World – and it's fun.

There are some very good deals available from Cairns hostels combining transport to and from Cape Tribulation with accommodation there. Other options include hovercraft, fast catamarans and planes.

CAIRNS TO PORT DOUGLAS

It's beach after beach and great views along the Coral Sea-lapped coast all the way along the Cook Highway. Shortly after Hartleys Creek is Turtle Cove, a pleasant little beach with a motel/backpacker resort (tel 55 3666/55 3606) costing from $17. Further north there's Pebbly Beach before the superb sweep of Four Mile Beach up to the headland at Port Douglas.

PORT DOUGLAS (Population 1300)

In the early days of the far north's development Port Douglas was a rival for Cairns, but Cairns got the upper hand and Port Douglas became a sleepy little backwater. Recently people began to

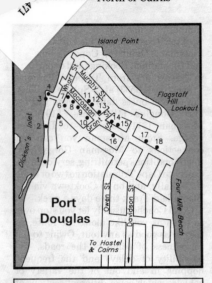

1	Marina
2	Fish Market
3	Public Wharf
4	Ben Cropp Museum
5	Gallery Bistro
6	Catalina Seafood Restaurant & Danny's Brasserie
7	Court House Hotel
8	Post Office
9	Central Hotel
10	Tourist Information Centre
11	Mocka's Pies
12	Bike Hire
13	Plaza Coffee Lounge & Restaurant
14	Bandito's
15	Bodensee Cafe
16	PJ's
17	Coconut Grove Motel
18	Travellers Palm Motel

realise what a delightful place it was but even the multi-million dollar Sheraton Mirage resort hasn't destroyed all Port Douglas' charm.

Along with the resort have come a golf course, a heliport, fast catamaran services from Cairns, a marina and an avenue of palms lining the road from the Cook Highway to Port Douglas. 'Port" is now a retreat of the rich and fashionable – but it

has managed to keep most of its relaxed feel, and there is still cheap accommodation.

The little town has a couple of good central pubs with outdoor sitting areas, and a string of interesting little shops and restaurants to wander round when the beach, the boats and the lookout get dull. You can make trips to the Low Isles, the Barrier Reef, Mossman and Cape Tribulation.

Information & Orientation
It's six km from the highway along a long, low spit of land to Port Douglas. The Sheraton resort occupies a long stretch of Four Mile Beach and Port Douglas proper is just a few streets on the western half of the end of the spit, beside and back from Dickson's Inlet. There's a fine view over the coastline and sea from the Flagstaff Hill lookout.

The helpful Port Douglas Tourist Information Centre (tel 99 3211) is at 27 Macrossan St. It's open from 7 am to 7 pm daily and can help you find accommodation.

Things to See
On the pier off Anzac Park Ben Cropp's Shipwreck Museum is quite interesting and open from 9 am to 5 pm daily, admission $2.50. Coral Sea Diving Services (tel 98 5254), with a shop down near the public wharf at the end of Anzac Park, runs $245 open water diving certificate courses. You get three days' pool and lecture tuition, then two days on the reef.

Places to Stay
Port Douglas Travellers Hostel (tel 98 5200) at 111 Davidson St, about 1½ km from the town centre, is one of the best hostels on the coast, well kept with pleasant open sided cooking and sitting areas, a small store, garden and pool. Accommodation is in bunk rooms for $10 a night and there are bicycles for hire. You can book various tours and diving courses here.

Most of the caravan and camping parks

along Davidson St have pools. Next to the hostel the *Pandanus Caravan Park* (tel 98 5255) is quite pleasant with tent sites at $4 per person and on-site vans for $27 double. Towards the town the *Kulau Caravan Park* (tel 98 5449) at 24 Davidson St is quite good with tent sites at $10 double and self-contained cabins for $36 to $40.

Most of the motels and holiday flats are expensive. The *Travellers Palm Motel* (tel 98 5198) and the *Coconut Grove Motel* (tel 98 5124), both on Macrossan St near the corner of Davidson St, have some singles/doubles for $39/44. You'll find a few rooms at $41 in the *Archipelago Motel* (tel 98 5387) at 72 Macrossan St. *Four Mile Beach* (tel 98 5281) on Reef St in Craiglie, about five km back towards the highway, has holiday units with cooking facilities at $35 and linen for hire. Check the notice board by the post office for longer term accommodation.

Places to Eat

There's nowhere near the hostel where you can get a cheap bite. But in the centre there are plenty of places including *Mocka's Pies* on Macrossan St.

Also on Macrossan St, not far from the Davidson St corner, the *Bodensee Cafe* does delicious pastries and meals at $8 to $11, including German and vegetarian specials. A couple of doors along, *Bandito's* has nachos for $6 and other snacks a bit cheaper. Over the road, *PJ's Charcoal Chicken & Gourmet Take-Away* serves up specials like satay prawns or Tahitian raw fish salad for $4, or you can get a quarter chicken for $2.50. Near the corner of Macrossan and Grant Sts you'll find more take-aways.

On Wharf St, to the left from the Court House pub, after the more expensive outdoor *Catalina Seafood Restaurant* and *Danny's Brasserie* you reach the *Galley Bistro* with seafood meals $8.

Entertainment

The *Central Hotel* on Macrossan St has live bands a couple of nights a week and on weekend afternoons.

Getting There & Away

Apart from the Coral Coaches buses, there's the Quicksilver fast catamaran service six days a week from Port Douglas to Cooktown and back. It's $50 one way, $85 return ($60 and $98 with a coach transfer between Cairns and Port Douglas). The Quicksilver booking office (tel 98 5373) in Port Douglas is beside the public wharf.

Getting Around

Car & Bicycle Hire Avis, National and Budget all have offices on Macrossan St. Smaller firms include Port Rent-A-Car at 4 Macrossan St, with small cars for $49 a day, 4WDs for $69 and bicycles for $10 a day. The Travellers Hostel has a few bikes for hire if you're staying there – or go to Tropic Life Pushbike Rentals at 26-30 Macrossan St which has good bikes for $10 a day.

Reef Trips Quicksilver fast cats do daily trips to Agincourt Reef on the outer reef. For $75 you get snorkelling gear, a semisub ride, underwater observatory viewing and lunch. For divers two 40 minute dives will cost an extra $45 with all gear provided.

For snorkellers the $49 day-trip in the *Wavelength* has received good reports. You get five hours on the reef, use of snorkel gear and lunch. The *Aquanaut* is said to be an excellent diving boat and it offers outer reef day-trips to snorkellers for $75, divers $105, including gear.

The MV *Reefer* is another fast vessel running fishing, snorkelling and dive charters from the public wharf. A day's fishing including tackle and snorkel gear is $70. The *Reefer* is connected with Port Douglas Dive Centre (tel 98 5327) which also organises dive trips.

Tours The $8 Mossman Gorge trip run by the Travellers Hostel – five to six hours including a swim and rainforest walk – is good value. With the regular operators a day-trip to Cape Tribulation is $45 to $55. A two day Cooktown loop – up via the inland road, back by the Bloomfield Track – is about $160. Bally Hooley Rail Tours (tel 98 5899) runs trips in a miniature steam train from its station off the Port Douglas approach road to Mossman sugar mill and Drumsara sugar plantation beyond Mossman. Half a day to the mill only is $15, the full day $45.

LOW ISLES

Offshore from Port Douglas is a fine little coral cay surrounded by a lagoon and topped by an old lighthouse. This is a very different sort of reef island from hyped up Green Island off Cairns. The sail catamaran *Hardy's Courier* makes daily trips to the Low Isles from Port Douglas and the $40 price includes lunch, snorkel gear and boom-netting. The Quicksilver fast catamarans from Port Douglas do Low Isles trips for the same price, including lunch, snorkel gear, a guided snorkel tour and a glass-bottomed boat ride.

MOSSMAN & DAINTREE

Mossman, the most northerly sugar town, has a big Italian population and is becoming a centre for tropical fruit growing. At beautiful Mossman Gorge, five km west, a three km circuit walking track leads through rainforest to swimming holes and rapids. Coral Coaches run buses up to the gorge ($4 one way, $8 return) from Mossman – it's advisable to book in advance.

There are several accommodation possibilities in Mossman, including a creekside caravan/camping park next to the swimming pool at the north end of town. You can get good cheap meals in the *Post Office Hotel* on Mill St and the *Royal Hotel*. Coral Coaches also runs buses between Mossman and Mareeba, two hours away on the Atherton Tableland, three days a week.

The highway continues 35 km beyond Mossman to the village of Daintree, with the gravel turn-off to the Daintree River

ferry and Cape Tribulation coming after 24 km. In Daintree village the Butterfly Farm at Barratt Creek is open from 10 am to 4 pm daily. Daintree Wildlife Safari does 2¾ hour river trips on the rainforest and mangrove lined Daintree River twice a day for $22 and usually runs one hour, $7 cruises too. Crocodile sightings are fairly common on the river in the cooler months.

CAPE TRIBULATION AREA

It's 39 km of gravel road, with a few hills and creek crossings, from the Mossman to Daintree road to Cape Tribulation. Unless there has been much rain or the tide is very high at Coopers Creek and the other crossings in the northern half of the journey, conventional vehicles can make it, with care, to Cape Trib.

Cape Tribulation was named by Captain Cook, since it was a little north of here that his troubles started when he ran his ship on to the Endeavour Reef. Mt Sorrow was also named by him.

In the '70s much of this coast was a hippie outpost with a number of settlements, particularly the infamous Cedar Bay, north of Cape Trib between Bloomfield and Cooktown. Today Cape Tribulation is becoming more and more popular with visitors. This stretch of coast is incredibly beautiful and is one of the few places in Australia where the rainforest runs right down to the water line. There are some excellent beaches.

Remember this is rainforest – take mosquito repellent with you. Approaching Cape Trib from the south, the last bank is at Mossman and the last public telephone is just north of the Daintree ferry. You can get petrol at two or three places between Mossman and Cooktown by this coastal route.

Rainforest

Nearly all of Australia was covered in rainforest 50 million years ago but when Europeans arrived only about 1% of the rainforest was left. Logging and clearing for farms have reduced

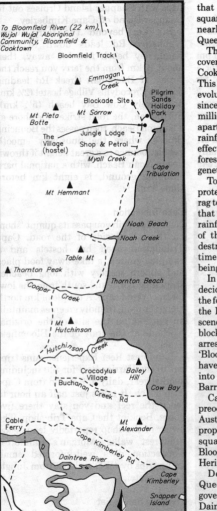

**Around Cape
Tribulation**

To Bloomfield River (22 km),
Wujal Wujal Aboriginal
Community, Bloomfield &
Cooktown

Bloomfield Track

Emmagan
Creek

Blockade Site

Mt Pieta
Botte

Mt Sorrow

Pilgrim
Sands
Holiday Park

Jungle Lodge
Shop & Petrol

The Village
(hostel)

Myall Creek

Cape
Tribulation

Mt Hemmant

Noah Beach

Noah Creek

Table Mt

Thornton Peak

Cooper Creek

Thornton Beach

Mt Hutchinson

Hutchinson Creek

Crocodylus
Village

Bailey
Hill

Buchanan Creek Rd

Cow Bay

Cable Ferry

Mt Alexander

Cape Kimberley Rd

Daintree River

Cape Kimberley

To Daintree

Snapper Island

TRINITY BAY

To Mossman

0   3   6 km

that to less than 0.3% today – about 20,000 square km. More than half of what's left, and nearly all the *tropical* rainforest, is in Queensland.

The biggest surviving virgin rainforest area covers the ranges from south of Mossman up to Cooktown. It's called the Greater Daintree. This is one of the few places on earth where evolution has gone on virtually uninterrupted since flowering plants first appeared about 130 million years ago. Conservationists argue that apart from the normal reasons for saving rainforests – such as combating the greenhouse effect and preserving species habitats – this forest is extra valuable as it's such a diverse genetic storehouse.

To the timber industry the idea of total protection of the Greater Daintree is like a red rag to a bull. Their case, aside from job losses, is that more than 90% of Queensland's remaining rainforest is on government land and only 19% of that is used for timber – and then not destructively, since cutting is selective and time is left for the forest to regenerate before being logged again.

In 1983 the local Douglas Shire Council decided to bulldoze a gravel road 22 km through the forest from just north of Cape Tribulation to the Bloomfield River. Cape Trib became the scene of a classic 'greenies versus bulldozers' blockade. Several months and numerous arrests later, the road builders won and the 'Bloomfield Track' was opened. The road works have caused large amounts of soil to wash out into the ocean, raising serious fears for the Barrier Reef.

Cape Trib was not the only Queensland issue preoccupying conservationists and in 1987 the Australian government was persuaded to propose the 'Queensland Wet Tropics' – 9000 square km of rainforest from north of Bloomfield down to near Townsville – for World Heritage listing.

Despite strenuous resistance by the Queensland timber industry and state government, it seems certain that the Greater Daintree and most of the rest of north Queensland's rainforest will be saved. It's an issue that has set not only timber workers against conservationists, but longer term residents against more recent arrivals, northern country people against 'southern city intellectuals', and independent minded Queenslanders against 'interfering Canberra'!

Daintree River to Cape Tribulation

Five km along the road to the cape from the Mossman to Daintree road you reach the Daintree River ferry, operating from 6 am to 6 pm daily, plus 6 to 7 pm and 11 pm to midnight on Fridays. It costs $2 for a car, $1.70 for a motor bike, plus 70c for each passenger.

You can take rainforest and mangrove river cruises from beside the ferry landing on the the *Spirit of Daintree* ($18.50 for 2½ hours) or the *Crocodile Express* (a bit more expensive). Departures are usually around 10 am and 1 pm. You can take $49

Cape Tribulation, Northern Queensland

trips with Snapper Island Cruises out to Snapper Island off Cape Kimberley.

Six km beyond the ferry, Cape Kimberley Rd leads down to Cape Kimberley beach five km away, then about 12 km from the ferry you reach the corner of Buchanan Creek Rd leading down to Crocodylus Village hostel (2½ km) and lovely Cow Bay beach (5½ km). Further on, the road strikes the shore at Thornton Beach, then passes the Bouncing Stones, where the unusually smooth pebbles bounce to a great height if thrown down. Noah Beach, with a national park camping ground, is eight km before Cape Trib.

Cape Tribulation

Near Cape Trib you pass its quaint 'shop' on the inland side of the road. Cape Tribulation itself has hostels and a camping ground, a take-away food place and superb scenery with long beaches stretching north and south from the low, forest covered cape. A couple of km north along the road, friendly greenies maintain an outpost on the site of the original blockade at the start of the Bloomfield Track.

Rainforest Reef Experience runs trips out to the Barrier Reef for $40 including snorkel gear, daily at 9.30 am from Cape Trib beach. It takes just half an hour to reach the reef and you stay there five hours. Book at the Cape Trib shop. The owner of the shop reportedly leads good rainforest walks. Morgan's Rainforest Connection does well-informed small group trips by 4WD and foot from Jungle Lodge hostel.

Places to Stay & Eat

At Cape Kimberley beach the *Daintree Rainforest Resort* (tel 98 7500) has 50 camping sites plus on-site tents for hire. You can rent windsurfers.

Crocodylus Village (tel Cairns 31 1366) is 2½ km off the main Cape Trib road, down Buchanan Creek Rd. It's one of Australia's best hostels – set in the rainforest with spacious, airy, off ground cabins. There's a pool, a small store and a bar. You can cook for yourself or buy good meals from the 'village kitchen'. Nightly costs are $10 in a dorm ($1 for a sleeping sheet) or $11 in a six berth cabin with its own shower and toilet. You can hire bikes and the hostel vehicle runs guests to and from Cow Bay beach, three km away. There are several fine forest walks round about, and the hostel organises popular and informative three hour guided walks every morning and night – they cost $11.

Thornton Beach has cheap council camping and a good little licensed cafe/shop. At Noah Beach there's a national parks camping ground with toilets and water – get permits from the ranger station at Cape Trib. Cape Tribulation itself has two hostels a few hundred metres apart. The established *Jungle Lodge* (tel Cairns 53 6500) is off the road just before the cape and is similar in style to Crocodylus Village but bigger. It's on cleared land and its 'Drysdale Arms' bar and restaurant (decent dinners for $7) is a convivial meeting spot, with a pool just outside. The guests' kitchen was appallingly equipped when we stayed. The range of sleeping accommodation ranges from cramped, hot double rooms with six beds squeezed in, to spacious airy six person cabins with bathroom and kitchen. It all costs $10 a night. You can do reef trips or guided bushwalks and the half day horse riding trips are popular at $20.

The Village (tel Cairns 31 2125) is newer and is right by the road near the cape. It's slightly more up-market with quite comfortable log cabins, pool, bar, a restaurant with à la carte menu and wine list, guests' kitchen and uniformed staff. Nightly cost is $10 and reef trips are available. The *Boardwalk Take-Away*, over the road from The Village, sells milk, bread and a few basics, and does good breakfasts, snacks and meals up to $6.

Just off the road 1½ km north of Cape Tribulation, *Pilgrim Sands Holiday Park* (tel Cairns 51 7366) has tent sites for $6/8,

or five person units with their own kitchen and bathroom at $38 double (bed linen for hire).

Getting There & Away

Road conditions permitting, Coral Coaches runs buses from Cairns to Cape Tribulation two or three times daily, and on to Bloomfield and Cooktown via the Bloomfield Track three days a week. They'll detour to the hostels at Cow Bay and Cape Trib. Fares from Cairns are $17.80 ($32 return) to Cape Trib (four hours), $25 ($46) to Bloomfield, and $35 ($64) to Cooktown.

Some excellent deals can be found in Cairns combining transport to Cape Tribulation with hostel accommodation – for instance $39 including two nights at Crocodylus Village, or $49 with one night at Crocodylus and one at Jungle Lodge, through Cairns Hostel Tours. The Ansett Trailways 'Jungle Express' bus will give you two nights at Jungle Lodge and return transport for $50, or $40 if you have an Aussiepass. The Village Hostel is involved in similar deals.

It's quite easy to hitch since beyond the Daintree ferry there's nowhere else to go. Matt Lock's service station on Buchanan Creek Rd has a few cars and 4WDs to rent.

CAPE TRIBULATION TO COOKTOWN

Just north of Cape Tribulation, the Bloomfield Track – 4WD only – heads through the forest as far as Wujal Wujal Aboriginal community 22 km north, on the far side of the Bloomfield River crossing. Even for 4WD vehicles the Bloomfield River and some of the 'track' are impassable after heavy rain. From Wujal Wujal another dirt road – rough but usually passable in a conventional vehicle – heads 46 km north through the tiny settlements of Bloomfield and Helenvale to meet the main Cairns to Cooktown road, also mostly dirt, 28 km before Cooktown.

At the 'roadhouse' at Bloomfield you can camp for $4 or sleep in very basic bunkrooms for $9 (bedding $2 extra). Bloomfield River cruises ($10) and trail rides are offered. Beyond Bloomfield you pass through Cedar Bay National Park and at Helenvale the *Lion's Den* is a good place to halt – it's a colourful 1875 bush pub. You can camp beside the river for $2 or the pub has a few rooms.

CAIRNS TO COOKTOWN – THE INLAND ROAD

The 'main' road up from Cairns loops through Kuranda, Mareeba, Mt Molloy, the wolfram mining town of Mt Carbine, Palmer River crossing and Lakeland, where the road up Cape York Peninsula splits off. Most of the second half of this 341 km road is unpaved and often corrugated.

In Mt Molloy the *National Hotel* (tel 94 1133) has singles/doubles for $11/16. James Venture Mulligan, the man who started both the Palmer River and Hodgkinson River gold rushes, is buried in the Mt Molloy cemetery. At the Palmer River crossing there's a cafe/petrol station and a camping ground. The 1873 to 1883 gold rush for which the Palmer River is famous happened in very remote country about 70 km west of here. Its main towns were Palmerville and Maytown, of which very little is left today.

Shortly before Cooktown the road passes Black Mountain, a pile of thousands of granite boulders. It's said there are ways between the huge rocks which will take you under the hill from one side to the other, but people have died trying to find them. Black Mountain is known to Aborigines as Kalcajagga – mountain of death. The colour comes not from the rocks themselves but from lichen which grow on them.

COOKTOWN (Population 913)

Cooktown can claim to have been Australia's first British settlement. From June to August 1770, Captain Cook beached his barque *Endeavour* here, and while they were here, Joseph Banks, the chief naturalist, took the chance to study Australian fauna and flora along the banks of the Endeavour River. Banks collected 186 plant species and wrote the first European description of a kangaroo. The north side of the river has scarcely changed since then.

The explorers had amicable contacts with the local Aborigines but race relations in the area turned a great deal worse a century later when Cooktown was founded as the unruly port for the 1873 to 1883 Palmer River gold rush 140 km south-west. Hell's Gate, a narrow pass on the track between Cooktown and the Palmer, was the scene of frequent ambushes as Aborigines tried to stop their lands being overrun, and Battle Camp, about 60 km inland from Cooktown, saw the only mass battle between whites and Cape York Aborigines.

In 1874, before Cairns was even thought of, Cooktown was the second biggest town in Queensland. At its peak there were no less than 94 pubs, almost as many brothels, and the population was over 30,000! As many as half of these were Chinese, whose industrious presence led to some wild race riots.

After the gold rush ended, cyclones and a WW II evacuation came close to killing Cooktown. The opening of the excellent James Cook Historical Museum in 1970 started to bring in some visitor dollars although Cooktown's population is still less than 1000 and just three pubs remain. The effort of getting here is rewarded not just by the atmosphere but by some fascinating reminders of the area's past. With a vehicle you could use Cooktown as a base for visiting the Quinkan rock art near Laura or even Lakefield National Park. Like everywhere else on the Queensland coast, Cooktown is today trying to attract more tourists: projects in the pipeline include a marina and a resort. However a planned large scale replica of the *Endeavour* and a recreation of the street where Captain Cook lived in England are looking less likely.

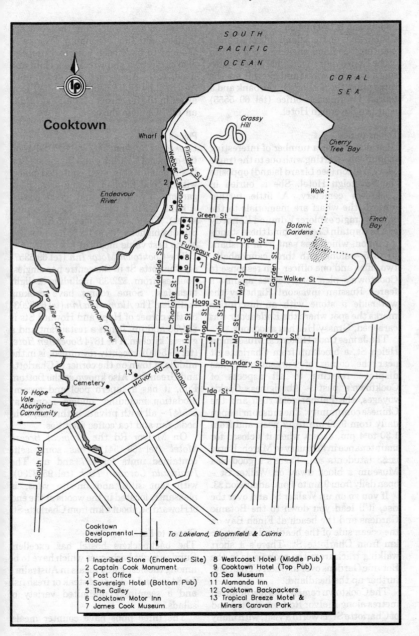

Cooktown

SOUTH PACIFIC OCEAN

CORAL SEA

Grassy Hill

Wharf

Cherry Tree Bay

Walk

Endeavour River

Finch Bay

Green St

Botanic Gardens

Pryde St

Furneaux St

Garden St

Walker St

Webber Esplanade

Flinders St

Adelaide St

Charlotte St

Helen St

Hope St

John St

May St

Hogg St

Howard St

Boundary St

Ida St

Annan St

McIvor Rd

Two Mile Creek

Chinaman Creek

Cemetery

To Hope Vale Aboriginal Community

South Rd

Cooktown Developmental Road

To Lakeland, Bloomfield & Cairns

1 Inscribed Stone (Endeavour Site)	8 Westcoast Hotel (Middle Pub)
2 Captain Cook Monument	9 Cooktown Hotel (Top Pub)
3 Post Office	10 Sea Museum
4 Sovereign Hotel (Bottom Pub)	11 Alamanda Inn
5 The Galley	12 Cooktown Backpackers
6 Cooktown Motor Inn	13 Tropical Breeze Motel &
7 James Cook Museum	Miners Caravan Park

Information & Orientation

Cooktown is on the inland side of a north-pointing headland sheltering the mouth of the Endeavour River. Charlotte St runs south from the wharf and along it are the three pubs, the post office, the bank and a tourist information office (tel 69 5555) near the Sovereign Hotel.

Things to See

Charlotte St has a number of interesting monuments starting with one to the tragic Mary Watson (see Lizard Island) opposite the Sovereign Hotel. She is buried in Cooktown cemetery. A little further towards the wharf are memorials to the equally tragic explorer Edmund Kennedy and to Captain Cook. Behind these stands a cannon, which was sent from Brisbane in 1885 – along with three cannonballs, two rifles and one officer – in response to Cooktown's plea for defences against a feared Russian invasion! Right by the waterside a stone with an inscription marks the spot where the *Endeavour* was careened. Grassy Hill has a lookout.

The James Cook Historical Museum on Helen St, a block up from Charlotte St near the corner of Furneaux St, has displays relating to all aspects of Cooktown's past – Aborigines, Cook's voyages, the Palmer gold rush and the Chinese community. The museum is open daily from 9.30 am to 12 noon and from 1.30 to 4 pm, except when it's closed for maintenance in February or March. Entry is $3 (students $2). There's a good Sea Museum a block away on Walker St – open daily from 9 am to 4 pm, admission $3.

If you go on up Walker St and over the rise, it'll lead you down to the Botanic Gardens and the beach at Finch Bay on the ocean side of the headland, about 1½ km from Charlotte St. There's a short walking track from the rock pools in the Botanic Gardens over to Cherry Tree Bay, further up the headland.

The Cooktown cemetery, a few hundred metres along McIvor Rd from the top end of Charlotte St, is worth a visit, with many interesting graves including those of Mary Watson and the 'Normanby Woman' – thought to have been a north European who survived a shipwreck as a child and lived with Aborigines for years until 'rescued' by white people. She died soon after. In the far corner of the graveyard is an 1887 Chinese shrine.

Places to Stay

Cooktown Backpackers (tel 69 5166) is on the corner of Charlotte and Boundary Sts. It's a comfortable, well equipped place, with a good kitchen, dining area, pool, garden, TV lounge and great views. A bunk is $10 a night ($1 for a sleeping sheet). There are bicycles for hire. The Sunday night barbecue for $5 has to be one of the best value meals in Australia.

The *Cooktown Motor Inn* (tel 69 5357) on Charlotte St in the centre has singles/doubles from $22/33 including a light breakfast. Some rooms have cooking facilities. The *Alamanda Inn* (tel 69 5203) on the corner of Hope and Howard Sts is $24/30 and up. It has a restaurant and a guests' kitchen. The 1874 *Sovereign Hotel* (tel 69 5400), recently revamped, is in the middle of town on the corner of Charlotte and Green Sts. Also known as the Bottom Pub, it has a superb pool and accommodation including 'budget rooms' at $35/47 – all with private bathroom, twin beds, fan and tea/coffee facilities.

On McIvor Rd the *Tropical Breeze Motel* (tel 69 5417) has some self-contained units for $27 and up. The *Peninsula Caravan Park* (tel 95 3730), with tent sites and on-site vans, is pleasantly located in the woods at the end of Howard St, about a km from Charlotte St.

Places to Eat

The backpackers hostel has excellent Sunday night barbecues which have to be among the best value meals in Australia – for $4 we had a choice of steak or fresh fish and a seemingly unlimited variety of salads.

The three pubs have counter meals.

The *Cooktown Hotel* (Top Pub) has lunches and dinners, Monday to Saturday, from \$3, plus the slightly more expensive Tavern Restaurant/Garden Lounge and a great beer garden. The *Westcoast Hotel* (Middle Pub) has counter meals from \$3. On Friday nights people descend on this pub from miles around for the area's only regular live band. The *Sovereign Hotel* (Bottom Pub) offers similar food and prices with a little more variety at the budget end. The pubs stop taking food orders about 7.30 pm.

The *Galley*, a take-away coffee shop/restaurant in Sovereign Square next to the hotel with pizzas, salads and curries, provides the best variety and value in town. A good large pizza is \$11. It's open daily to 8.30pm. There are a couple of fast food places on Charlotte St with the usual fare. *Endeavour Inn*, just beyond the Reef Cafe, is a more up-market licensed restaurant, open for breakfast, lunch and dinner. Some motels have good restaurants.

Getting There & Away
Air Sunbird (tel Cairns 53 4899) flights between Cairns and Cooktown operate six days a week and cost \$84 one way. Cooktown Backpackers and Hinterland Aviation in Cairns (tel 53 7323 or ask at Tropical Paradise) have organised Backpackers Charters which makes scenic flights between Cairns and Cooktown, with a drop off at Cow Bay possible. You need at least four people but the price per head is a worthwhile saving on the scheduled flights.

Bus Coral Coaches go to and from Bloomfield three days a week and you can get connections to/from Cape Trib and Cairns the same day. Cairns to Cooktown is \$35 one way, \$64 return, and takes about nine hours.

The Cooktown Bus Service (tel Cairns 51 1064) runs two or three times a week each way between Cairns and Cooktown along the main (inland) road. It's six or seven hours and normally \$35 one way,

\$55 return. Cooktown Backpackers was offering cheaper tickets on this service when we stayed there – contact the hostel or Tropical Paradise Travel at 25 Spence St in Cairns to ask about this discount. Greyhound Bus Pass holders pay \$9.50 one way, Aussiepass holders \$17.50. Tropical Paradise is the main departure point in Cairns.

Boat The Quicksilver 'wave piercer' catamaran runs daily except Tuesday from Port Douglas to Cooktown and back, taking 2½ hours one way. Fare is \$50 one way, \$85 return.

Getting Around
You can rent bicycles from Cooktown Backpackers hostel or the Sovereign Hotel. The Cooktown Motor Inn has Mokes at \$35 a day and 4WDs from \$60. Rates include insurance and 150 km but not petrol.

Tours Endeavour River Mangrove Cruises (tel 69 5377) do just what their name suggests twice daily and three nights a week in an eight person craft. Cost is around \$14 and you stand a good chance of catching your evening meal with the fishing lines and bait supplied. You can take horse-drawn wagon tours of the town for \$14. Cook's Landing Bus Tours (tel 69 5101) does morning tours to Black Mountain, the Lion's Den bush pub, and the prawn farm and gorges on the Annan River, for \$25 three days a week.

Strikie's Feral Safaris run a variety of good fun 4WD trips to places like Black Mountain, the Lion's Den and Cedar Bay National Park, Hope Vale Aboriginal community north of Cooktown, Aboriginal rock art sites, waterfalls and Normanby station. A day outing costs \$65 or more.

It's possible to join tour groups to Cape York in Cooktown – probably at a bit of saving on the price from Cairns. You can make diving and fishing trips from Cooktown.

Cape York Peninsula

The 'tip', Cape York, is the most northerly point on the mainland of Australia and between here and Papua New Guinea, just 150 km away, a scatter of islands dot the Torres Strait. The Cape York Peninsula is one of the wildest and least populated parts of Australia.

Getting up to the north along the rough and rugged Peninsula Development Road is still one of Australia's great road adventures. It's a trip for the tough and experienced since the roads are *all* dirt and even at the height of the dry there are several serious rivers to be forded. In the last few years several tour operators have sprung up to offer this adventure to those who can't or don't want to go it alone.

Ron and Viv Moon's book *Cape York, An Adventurer's Guide* provides all the necessary detail. It costs about $13 from many Queensland bookshops.

Getting There & Away

Air Australian Regional Airlines, owned by Australian Airlines, flies from Cairns to Weipa ($179), Thursday Island ($225), and Bamaga ($187) several days a week. Sunbird Airlines, based at Cairns airport (tel 53 4899), also has an extensive network around the peninsula and the Torres Strait Islands. Sunbird also flies from Cairns to Cooktown and Lockhart. Flight West (tel 53 5511) goes to Aurukun, on the coast south of Weipa, via Coen and back three times a week from Cairns.

Driving to the Top Every year growing numbers of hardy travellers equipped with their own 4WD vehicles or trail motorcycles, make the long haul up to the top of Cape York. Apart from being able to say you have been as far north as you can get in Australia, you also test yourself against some pretty hard going and see some wild and wonderful country into the bargain. It's no easy trip, and during the wet season nothing moves by road at all.

The travelling season is from mid-May to mid-November but the beginning and end of that period are borderline, depending on how late or early the wet season is. The best time is June to September. Conventional vehicles can usually reach Coen and even, with care and skill, get across to Weipa on the Gulf of Carpentaria but it's *very* rough going. If you want to continue north from the Weipa turn-off to Cape York, you'll need 4WD, a winch and plenty of strong steel wire.

The major problem is the many river crossings; even as late as June or July they will still be swift flowing and frequently alter their course. The rivers often have very steep banks. The Great Dividing Range runs right up the spine of the peninsula and rivers run east and west off it. Although the rivers in the south of the peninsula only flow in the wet season, those further north flow year round.

The ideal set up for a Cape York expedition is two 4WD vehicles travelling together – one can haul the other out where necessary. You can also make it to the top on motorcycles, floating the machines across the wider rivers. There are usually large truck inner tubes left at the river crossings for this purpose. Beware of crocodiles!

After the Archer River Roadhouse, 65 km beyond Coen, Weipa on the coast and usually Bamaga, just south of the tip, are the only places for a regular supply of petrol and mechanical repairs. Visits to the RACQ and the National Parks office in Cairns are well worthwhile before you head north.

You no longer need a permit to visit Aboriginal communities on the peninsula or traverse their land but it's advisable to make contact beforehand by letter or radio phone. The same applies to Torres Strait Islander communities. Apart from Bamaga, most of the mainland Aboriginal communities are well off the main track north, and do not have any facilities or accommodation for travellers.

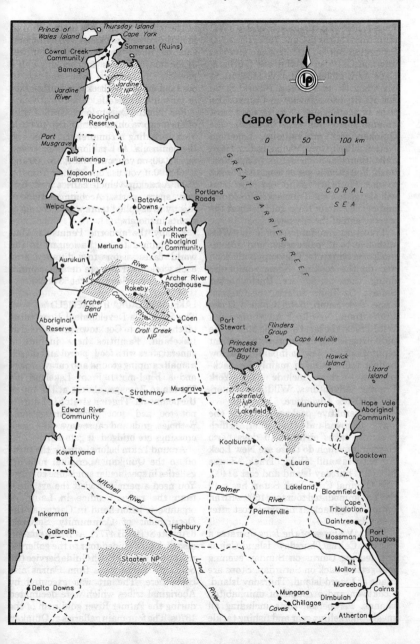

Cape York Peninsula

0   50   100 km

Tours A host of companies operates 4WD tours from Cairns to Cape York. The FNQ Promotion Bureau in Cairns can give you information. Also helpful are Cairns & Cape York Holidays (tel 52 1155) at 51 Sheridan St and Going Places at 26 Abbott St, two agencies in Cairns. The trips typically take 10 to 14 days, cost around $1400, and take in Laura, the Quinkan rock art galleries, Lakefield National Park, Coen, Weipa, Indian Head Falls, Bamaga, Somerset and Cape York itself. You usually get at least the chance to visit Thursday Island and most trips will also go to Cape Tribulation, Cooktown and/or the Palmer River gold fields at the start or end of the odyssey.

Travel on standard tours is in 4WDs with five to 12 passengers, and accommodation is in tents. They supply the food and do the cooking. Some companies doing these trips are Bushwhacker Safaris, Oz Tours Safaris, the Original Cape York Safari, John Crook's Down Under Tours, New Look Adventures and Wild Track, the last two being among the most experienced operators with excellent reputations. A few companies do low budget tours catering mainly for backpackers – these include Cape York Frontier Adventures, Wild Encounters and Outback Adventure.

An alternative package is to fly one way, go overland the other, which generally takes eight to 10 days. Two companies which do these are New Look Adventures and Wild Track. These include Thursday Island and cost $1400. The Original Cape York Safari has a 10 day accommodated tour for $1600 with an option to fly back at no extra cost after seven days.

The MV *Queen of the Isles* operates a weekly Cairns/Thursday Island/Cairns trip leaving Cairns on Sunday evening and getting back on Saturday. Stops are made at Lizard Island, Thursday Island, Cooktown and a couple of uninhabited islands. Per person costs including all meals, snorkelling gear and fishing tackle range from $550 in a six berth cabin to $1150 in a double with attached bathroom. Contact Royal Tropic Cruise Line (tel 31 1844) in Cairns for bookings. It's possible to sail one way and travel overland the other – check with Bushwacker or Oz tours for details.

Far North Queensland Trail Tours offers a two week motorbike trip to Cape York including a comprehensive look at the peninsula. As a pillion passenger you pay $1000: on your own bike it's $1300 and it's $2100 if you use one of their Yamaha 250s. A backup vehicle carries food, fuel and spare parts. Accommodation is mostly in supplied tents with a couple of nights in motels.

Finally the airborne Peninsula Mail Run, claimed to be the longest in the world, takes visitors to a different area each weekday. For more details, contact Cape York Air Services (tel 53 5858).

LAKELAND, LAURA & LAKEFIELD

The Peninsula Development Road turns off the Cairns to Cooktown inland road at Lakeland. Facilities here include a general store with food, petrol and diesel, a small camping ground and caravan park and a hotel-motel. From Lakeland it's 734 km to Bamaga, almost at the top of the peninsula. The first stretch to Laura is not too bad, just some corrugations, potholes, grids and causeways – the creek crossings are bridged. It gets worse.

Around 12 km before Laura is the turnoff to the Quinkan Aboriginal rock art galleries in spectacular sandstone country. You need a permit to visit the art site – from the ranger's office in Laura or organise it beforehand in Cairns at the Department of Community Services, 6 Abbott St (tel 51 4777). At Laura you can also pick up a guided tour to the galleries, run by the Trezise Bush Guide Service (tel 60 3236). Some tours from Cairns also come here. The art was executed by Aboriginal tribes which were decimated during the Palmer River gold rush of the 1870s. The four main galleries at Quinkan

– the only ones open to visitors – contain some superb examples of well preserved rock paintings dating back 13,000 to 14,000 years.

Laura has a general store with food and fuel, a place for minor mechanical repairs, a post office, a pleasant pub, an airstrip and a museum with Aboriginal art. The major annual event is the two day Cape York Aboriginal Dance Festival, normally held at the beginning of July. All the Cape York Aboriginal communities assemble for this festival which is a great opportunity for outsiders to witness living Aboriginal culture.

The main turn-off to Lakefield National Park is just past Laura and it's only about a 45 minute drive from Laura into the park. Conventional vehicles can get as far as the New Laura ranger station and possibly well into the northern section of the park during the dry season. Lakefield is the second largest Queensland national park and the most accessible of those on the Cape York Peninsula. It's best known for its wetlands and associated wildlife. Its extensive river system drains into Princess Charlotte Bay on its northern perimeter. This is the only national park on the peninsula where fishing is permitted and a canoe is a good way to investigate the park. Watch out for the crocs! You can bush camp at a number of sites – get permits from the ranger stations at New Laura or Lakefield further north in the park.

The wide sweep of Princess Charlotte Bay, which includes the coastal section of Lakefield National Park, is the site of some of Australia's biggest rock art galleries. Unfortunately it's extremely hard to reach except from the sea.

MUSGRAVE, COEN & ARCHER RIVER ROADHOUSE

It's 135 km from Laura to Musgrave with its historic fortress telegraph station, built in 1887. Before Musgrave, there's the Hann River crossing and a roadhouse at

the 75 km mark. Musgrave has petrol, diesel, food, beer and an airstrip.

Coen, 245 km north of Laura, is virtually the capital of the peninsula with a pub, a general store, a hospital, school and police station. You can get mechanical repairs done here. Coen has an airstrip and a racecourse where picnic races are held each August. The whole peninsula closes down for this event, even the mining town of Weipa. There are a few free camping sites both in and around town.

Apart from a few telegraph stations, the only habitation on the 402 km stretch from Coen to Bamaga is the Archer River Roadhouse, 65 km north of Coen. This is the final stop for regular petrol and mechanical repairs; you can also camp and get a hot shower and buy your last supplies before Bamaga.

NORTHERN NATIONAL PARKS

Four national parks can be reached from the main track north of Coen. You must be completely self-sufficient. Only a few km north of Coen, before Archer River Roadhouse, you can turn west to Rokeby and Archer Bend National Parks – the ranger station is in Rokeby, about 45 km off the main track. Access is for 4WD only. These little-visited parks cover a large area including the McIllwraith Range in Rokeby and, in the west of very remote Archer Bend, the junction of the Coen and Archer Rivers. There are no facilities but bush camping is permitted at a number of river sites in Rokeby. These parks are best explored by bushwalkers.

Around 21 km north of the Archer River Roadhouse is the turn-off to Portland Roads, the Lockhart River Aboriginal community and Iron Range National Park. The 150 km road into the tiny coastal settlement of Portland Roads passes through the national park. While still pretty rough, this track has been improved. If you visit the national park, register with the ranger on arrival. It has the rugged hills of the Janet and Tozer ranges, beautiful coastal scenery and

Australia's largest area of lowland rainforest, plus some animals which are also found in New Guinea but no further south in Australia.

The fourth of the northern national parks is the Jardine.

WEIPA (Population 2500)

Weipa is 135 km from the main track. The southern turn-off to it is about 20 km north of the Iron Range turn-off. You can also get to Weipa from Batavia Downs which is a little further up the main track and has a 19th century homestead. The two approaches converge about halfway along and are both pretty bad, but upgrading has started from the Weipa end.

Weipa is a modern mining town which works the world's largest deposits of bauxite – the ore from which aluminium is processed. The mining company, Comalco, runs regular tours of its operations from May to December. The town has a wide range of facilities including a motel and a camping site. Round about, there's interesting country to explore, good fishing and some pleasant camping sites. The Queensland government has plans for an international space launch station at Port Musgrave, north of Weipa.

NORTH TO THE JARDINE

Back on the main track, after Batavia Downs there are almost 200 km of rough road and numerous river crossings before you reach the Jardine River, formerly the most difficult Cape York crossing but now with a ferry. The Wenlock and the Dulhunty are the major crossings today. About 55 km past the Dulhunty is the turn-off to Indian Head Falls, also called Eliot Falls, a beautiful camping spot.

Jardine National Park stretches east to the coast from the main track. The Jardine River spills more fresh water into the sea than any other river in Australia. It's wild impenetrable country. There's a good camping spot on the banks of the Jardine at the crossing. There's a ranger station at Heathlands, 80 km south of the Jardine River.

BAMAGA, SOMERSET & CAPE YORK

Bamaga, the first settlement north of the Jardine River, is a mainly Torres Strait Islander community. There's a motel (advance bookings required) and camping grounds at nearby Seisa and Cowral Creek. The town has postal facilities, a hospital, Commonwealth Bank agency, STD phones, a supermarket and some petrol (availability not always guaranteed). It's only about 40 km from Bamaga to the very northern tip. Daily ferries run between Bamaga and Thursday Island.

Beyond Bamaga, off the Cape York track but only about 11 km south-east of the cape, is Somerset which was established in 1863 as a haven for shipwrecked sailors and a signal to the rest of the world that this was British territory. It was hoped at one time that it might become a major trading centre, a sort of Singapore of north Queensland, but it was closed in 1879 when its functions were moved to Thursday Island, which was also thought more suitable for a pearling industry. The story of Somerset is inextricably linked with the adventurous Jardine family, one of whom stayed on after Somerset was officially closed to run his own cattle stations, coconut plantation and pearling business. He married a Samoan princess and entertained passing British dignitaries. He and his wife are buried at Somerset. Apart from a few of Jardine's coconut trees, there's sadly nothing much left at Somerset now, but it has good fishing and lovely views.

At Cape York itself are two resorts. *Cape York Wilderness Lodge* 400 metres from the tip is a luxury resort costing $140-plus per night. It also has a small camping ground with a kiosk, toilets and showers. For further information, contact Cape York Wilderness Lodge (tel 50 4305), PO Box 1381, Cairns. *Punsand Bay Private Reserve* provides more modest accommodation on the western side of the cape.

There are permanent tents or you can pitch your own in the camping ground. You can book in Cairns at the Going Places agency. A ferry runs from Punsand Bay to Thursday Island daily at 7.30 am, costing $45 return.

TORRES STRAIT ISLANDS

The Torres Strait Islands have been a part of Queensland since 1879, the best known of them being Thursday Island. The 70 other islands are sprinkled from Cape York in the south almost to New Guinea in the north but only 17 of them are inhabited, and all but three are set aside for native islanders. Most visitors to Cape York take a look at Thursday Island or the nearby islands.

Torres Strait Islanders mainly came from Melanesia and Polynesia about 2000 years ago, with a more material culture than mainland Aborigines. The strait saw violence from early days right through to WW II, including head-hunters, marauding pirates, greedy men in pursuit of pearls, 'blackbirders' and Japanese bombs. Christianity, replacing warlike islander cults, has done well this century. Possession Island, close to Cape York, uninhabited and now a national park, was where Captain Cook 'claimed' all the east coast of Australia for England in 1770.

The islands' economy is based on fishing but it's hard to compete with the technology used by outfits on Australia's east coast. There is high islander unemployment and economic difficulties have led to cries for compensation, even independence. In the past the islanders have not been allowed to share in managing the area's few resources nor have they been provided with adequate education. The cries for secession will probably bring more self-government, but not independence.

Thursday Island is hilly, just over three square km in area and 39 km off Cape York. At one time it was a major pearling centre and the pearlers' cemeteries tell the hard tale of what a dangerous occupation it was. Some pearls are still produced here from seeded 'culture farms' which don't offer much employment to the locals. The island has also lost its importance as a halt for vessels but it's still a popular pause for passing yachties. It's an attractive and easy-going place and its main appeal is its cultural mix. It has a large Islander population but it has been a real cultural crossroads with Asian, European and Pacific Islander contributions to its history.

Accommodation and food are available in Thursday Island's four hotels and one motel. The airport is on nearby Horn Island and a ferry links the two islands. There's a camping ground near the wharf on Horn Island, but none on Thursday Island. You can hire boats for fishing trips and cruising around. You might be able to find accommodation on other islands by asking around.

Sunbird Airlines regularly flies to most of the inhabited islands. At least two ferry services operate from Bamaga and Punsand Bay to Thursday Island, both taking roughly an hour one way and costing about $45 return.

LIZARD ISLAND

The furthest north of the Barrier Reef resort islands, about 100 km from Cooktown, Lizard Island was named by Joseph Banks after Captain Cook spent a day there, trying to find a way out through the reef to the open sea. A Queensland tragedy took place here in 1881 when a settler's wife, Mary Watson, took to sea in a large metal pot with her son and a Chinese servant, after Aborigines killed her other servant while her husband was away fishing. The three eventually died on a barren island to the north. Their tragic story is told at the Cooktown museum.

The island has superb beaches, swimming and snorkelling, the remains of the Watsons' cottage, a pricey resort and a national parks camping ground. There

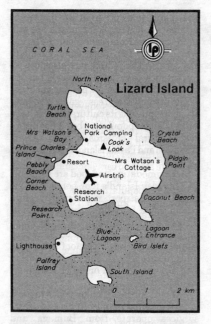

are plenty of bushwalks and bird life and great views from Cook's Look, the highest point on the island, from where Captain Cook surveyed the area in search of a passage through the reef. Australian Regional flies from Cairns for $117.

In the resort, accommodation including all meals and use of the facilities costs from $230 per day. As the island has no telephones or TV, it's been a favourite retreat of celebrities, and a popular stop for yachties, for many years. The small national park camping ground is at Mrs Watson's Bay. It has a fireplace, pit toilet, picnic table and a hand pumped water supply 250 metres away. If you want to camp you need a permit from the national parks office at 41 The Esplanade in Cairns, and you must take all supplies with you as the resort won't sell you any. You can't take stove fuel on the plane but there's enough driftwood on the beach for cooking.

Lizard Island Research Station may accept tertiary students interested in the Great Barrier Reef. Some have stayed there for $18 per day, supplying their own dive equipment and food. For details, write to Norman Quinn at Lizard Research Island Station, PMB 37, Cairns 4870.

The Gulf

North of Mt Isa and Cloncurry is the Gulf country, a sparsely populated region cut by a great number of rivers. During the 'big wet', the dirt roads turn to mud and even the surfaced roads can be flooded so June to September is the safest time to visit this area. Burke and Wills were the first Europeans to pass through the Gulf country but the coast of the Gulf of Carpentaria had been charted by Dutch explorers even before Captain Cook's visit to Australia. The actual coastline of the Gulf is mainly mangrove swamps which is why there is little habitation right on the coast.

Two of the settlements in the region, Burketown and Normanton, were founded in the 1860s, before better known places on the Pacific coast like Cairns and Cooktown came into existence. Europeans settled the area as sheep and cattle country, also in the hope of providing a western port for produce from further east and south in Queensland.

Today the Gulf country is mainly cattle country. It's a remote, hot, tough region. There are lodges set up for barramundi fishers at places like Escott, 20 km west of Burketown, and Dorunda, north of Normanton. Both places are also cattle stations. The Gulf area is also crocodile country. Mornington Island, in the Gulf itself 120 km north of Burketown, is an Aboriginal community.

Getting There & Away
The main road into the Gulf region is from Cloncurry to Normanton (378 km,

surfaced all the way) with a turn-off to Burketown at the Burke & Wills Roadhouse, where the road from Julia Creek (also all surfaced) meets it. Between Cloncurry and Normanton the flat plain is interrupted by a solitary hill beside the road – Bang Bang Jump-up. There's also an unpaved 332 km road from Camooweal, west of Mt Isa, to Burketown, with a turn-off at the Gregory Downs supply stop to Lawn Hill National Park. If you're driving any of these roads, make sure to ask about fuel stops and carry water with you.

From the Atherton Tableland the Gulf Developmental Road runs to Normanton through Georgetown and Croydon. The last stretch into Normanton on this route could be made on the famous Gulflander rail service which runs just once weekly in each direction between Croydon and Normanton. The four hour, 151 km trip, in a very vintage looking rail motor, is made from Croydon on Thursday and from Normanton on Wednesday.

Campbell's Coaches has a two or three times weekly bus service between Mt Isa, Normanton and Karumba. Two small airlines, Sunbird and Flight West, both fly a few times a week between Mt Isa and Cairns with stops at various places in the Gulf country on the way.

BURKETOWN

This tiny town is probably best known for its isolation. In the centre of a cattle raising area, Burketown is 65 km south of the Gulf and can be reached by road from Cloncurry, Julia Creek or Camooweal. You've got at least 150 km of unpaved road to cover to reach Burketown, whichever direction you come from.

Much of Nevil Shute's famous novel *A Town Like Alice* is set in Burketown. The town has a caravan park or you can get rooms in the *Albert Hotel* (tel 45 5104). The *Saltpan Store* is said to do good barramundi meals. You can also camp at the *Escott Barramundi Lodge* 20 km west.

NORMANTON (Population 926)

Normanton was set up as a port for the Cloncurry copper fields but then became Croydon's gold rush port, with a population of 3000 in 1891. The huge railway station on the edge of town, a monument to the gold era, still functions twice a week. The centre of town life today is the *Albion Hotel-Motel*, especially on Friday night when people crowd in from the surrounding area. You can get rooms in the Albion or the *Central* or *National* hotel-motels. There are also two caravan/camping parks.

KARUMBA (population 670)

Karumba, 69 km from Normanton by paved road and actually on the Gulf at the mangrove fringed mouth of the Norman River, is a prawn, barramundi and crab fishing centre. It's possible to charter boats for fishing trips from here and, in an effort to attract more tourism, the little town even has plans to start hovercraft trips along the coastline! Karumba has the *Karumba Lodge Hotel-Motel* (tel 45 9143) and the *Gulf Country Caravan Park* (tel 45 9148).

CROYDON

Connected to Normanton by that curious rail-motor service, this old gold mining town was once the biggest in the Gulf and has many interesting old buildings. It's reckoned there were once 50,000 gold mines in the area and remnants of them are scattered all around the country. There's a bit of a resurgence of gold mining there again today. The town has hotel rooms and a caravan park.

Townsville to Mt Isa

It's 887 km from Townsville inland to Mt Isa and they're mostly flat, dry and boring km although there are several points of interest along the way. The road's paved all the way across to the Northern Territory and is generally in better condition than much of the coastal Bruce Highway.

RAVENSWOOD

From Mingela, 83 km out of Townsville, a paved road leads 40 km south to Ravenswood, once a gold rush centre. Two pubs, a church, a school and a couple of hundred people linger on amid the old mines and near abandoned streets. Recently the place has come back to life a little as part of the reviving gold industry in the Charters Towers area. You can camp in the showgrounds, where there are cold showers.

Eighty km on down the road past Ravenswood, the big Burdekin Falls Dam, completed in 1987, holds back over 200 square km of water which will open up new areas for agriculture. Ansett Pioneer Express runs a $45 day-trip from Townsville to Ravenswood and the Burdekin Dam on Sundays.

CHARTERS TOWERS (Population 6823)

This busy town 130 km inland from Townsville was Queensland's fabulously rich second city in gold rush days 90 years ago. Many old houses, with classic verandahs and lace work, and imposing public buildings and mining structures remain. It's possible to day-trip here from Townsville and get a glimpse of outback Queensland on the way.

You're 336 metres above sea level at Charters Towers and the dry air is a welcome change from the humid coast. The gleam of gold was first spotted in 1871, in a creek bed at the foot of Towers Hill, by an Aboriginal boy called Jupiter Mosman. Within a few years the surrounding area was peppered with diggings and a large town had arisen. By its heyday around the turn of the century Charters Towers had a population of around 30,000, nearly 100 mines, and even its own stock exchange. It attracted wealth seekers from far and wide and came to be known as The World. Mosman

St, the main street in those days, had 25 pubs.

The gold ran out in the 1920s and Charters Towers shrank but survived as a centre for the beef industry. Since the mid-1980s it has seen a bit of a gold revival as modern processes have enabled companies to work deposits in the area that were previously uneconomical.

Information & Orientation

Central Charters Towers is basically two streets – Gill St and Mosman St which meet at right angles. Towers Hill stands over the town to the south. Buses arrive and depart at the central Goldfield Star service station on the corner of Gill and Church Sts. The railway station (tel 87 2239) is on Enterprise Rd, 2½ km east along Gill St from the centre.

There are two tourist offices – one, privately run, at 61 Gill St (tel 87 1280) which is open from Monday to Friday and Saturday mornings, and another in the Stock Exchange Arcade on Mosman St. Pick up the free *Guide to Charters Towers* booklet and a copy of the National Trust's walking tour leaflet.

Charters Towers has an Olympic size swimming pool on Plummer St, north of the centre, but it's closed in winter.

Things to See

On Mosman St a few metres up the hill from the corner of Gill St is the picturesque Stock Exchange Arcade, built in 1887 and restored in 1972. Here the wealthy and the hopeful of Charters Towers bought and sold shares in local mine concerns and other companies. Inside today there's the National Trust office, a tourist office, a couple of galleries and shops and a poorly displayed mining museum ($1).

Just up the hill from the stock exchange is the former Bank of Commerce (1891), now a private home, and just down the hill is the City Hall (also 1891) which is still performing its original function. A block further down at 62 Mosman St is the Zara

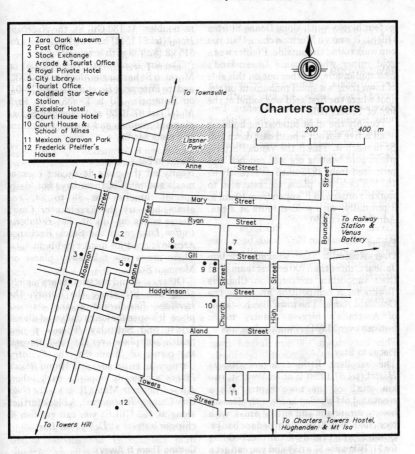

Charters Towers

1 Zara Clark Museum
2 Post Office
3 Stock Exchange
   Arcade & Tourist Office
4 Royal Private Hotel
5 City Library
6 Tourist Office
7 Goldfield Star Service
   Station
8 Excelsior Hotel
9 Court House Hotel
10 Court House &
    School of Mines
11 Mexican Caravan Park
12 Frederick Pfeiffer's
    House

To Townsville

Lissner Park

0   200   400 m

Anne   Street
Mary   Street
Ryan   Street
Gill   Street
Hodgkinson   Street
Aland   Street
Towers   Street

Mosman   Deane   Church   High   Boundary   Street

To Railway
Station &
Venus
Battery

To Towers Hill

To Charters Towers Hostel,
Hughenden & Mt Isa

Clark Museum, with an interesting collection focusing on transport and lifestyles in early Charters Towers. Admission is $3 and it's open daily from 10 am to 1 or 3 pm.

On Gill St Stan Pollard's Store (1906), near the Mosman St end, has an ancient 'flying fox' - a sort of aerial runway which transports cash from the counters to the central till. There's also a great selection of country hats. Impressive old buildings along Gill St include the former Bank of NSW building (1880) which is now the city library, the post office (1892) and the

police station (1900). The Court House Hotel and the Excelsior (1882) on the corner of Church St are two of the original pubs - notice their 'bat wing' saloon doors.

A block south along Church St from the Excelsior, on the corner of Hodgkinson St, you'll find the court house (1886) and the former school of mines (1900). Three blocks north along Church St from Gill St is Lissner Park, with the picturesque Boer War memorial kiosk.

Probably the finest of the town's old houses is Frederick Pfeiffer's, on Paull St –

go four blocks south along Deane St from Gill St. It's now a Mormon chapel but you can walk round the outside. Pfeiffer was a gold miner who became Queensland's first millionaire. Further out on this side of town there's a small monument on the spot where the first gold was found at the foot of Towers Hill.

Possibly the most interesting building of all is five km out – head east down Gill St to reach it. This is the Venus Battery, where gold-bearing ore was crushed and processed from 1872 until as recently as 1972. There are plans to restore it to working order and it's open from 10 am to 3 pm daily, with guided tours at 2 pm. Admission is $2.50.

Events

Over Australia Day weekend in late January, more than 100 cricket teams and their supporters converge on Charters Towers for a competition known as the Goldfield Ashes. The town also hosts one of Australia's biggest country music festivals over May Day weekend each year.

Places to Stay

The excellent little Charters Towers Hostel (tel 87 1028) is at 58 York St, two km south of the town centre. It's a renovated old wooden house with pleasant breezy verandahs and sitting areas, with room for about 30 people in beds or bunks. Cost is $9 a night and you can rent bedding for $1. Bikes are $7 a day and you can get a cheap combined ticket for some of the town's museums and the Venus Battery. In addition canoe trips are organised through cattle stations along the Burdekin River for $25 a day – when the river's flowing.

The Mexican Caravan Park (tel 87 1161) is fairly central, south of Gill St at 75 Church St. As well as tent sites at $7 for two people, it has on-site vans and units for $22 and up, plus a swimming pool and store. The next cheapest beds in town are in the old Court House Hotel (tel 87 1187) at 120 Gill St. Singles are $14 but there are

no doubles. At 130 Gill St, the Excelsior Hotel (tel 87 1544) has singles/doubles for $15/28 ($22/39 with breakfast).

The Rix Hotel-Motel (tel 87 1605) on Mosman St has singles/doubles for 26/32, and the Enterprise Hotel-Motel (tel 87 2404) on Enterprise Rd is $30/38. The Park Motel (tel 87 1022) at 1 Mosman St has pleasant grounds and a good restaurant and costs $44/50.

Places to Eat

Nearly all the pubs do decent counter meals and most of them have hot 'daily special' lunches for $3 to $4. For atmosphere try the Excelsior or Court House hotels on Gill St. The Billabong Coffee Lounge in the Stock Exchange Arcade is good for drinks and light eats. There are a few take-away places on Mosman St.

Other cafes and restaurants are mainly along Gill St: above the library, the Heritage Restaurant is the classiest place. It's open for lunch daily and dinner Friday and Saturday. There's a new health food place over the road. Beyond the corner of Deane St, the Country Carvery (in an arcade) and Mama Rosa's Pizzas are nearly opposite each other. A few doors from Mama Rosa's is the Gold City Chinese Restaurant. A block further along at 162 Gill St you can get fish & chips or burgers at Deb's Fish Bar.

Getting There & Away

Air Flight West Airlines has three departures a week to Townsville ($75) and Mt Isa ($184). You can make transport bookings and enquiries at the helpful Towers Travel (87 1546) at 114 Gill St.

Bus It's about 1¾ hours from Townsville to Charters Towers by bus and costs $15 to $21. From Charters Towers on to Mt Isa, it's nine hours and costs $57 to $70. Licence rules prevent some bus companies from dropping you off or picking you up in Charters Towers unless you're travelling interstate. Ansett Pioneer runs day tours from Townsville to Charters Towers for $27.50.

Train By train it's three hours to/from Townsville and costs $14.50, economy only. As well as the twice weekly Inlander running between Townsville and Mt Isa, there's a rail-motor service leaving Charters Towers for Townsville once weekly.

Getting Around
The hostel hires bikes and Gold Nugget Scenic Tours (tel 87 1568) runs $10 city tours most weekdays.

CHARTERS TOWERS TO HUGHENDEN
There are a few small towns, mostly with caravan/camping parks and a single motel, along this 243 km stretch. Around Hughenden, sheep begin to take over from cattle on the stations. Grass seed, which is abundant to the east, ruins sheep's wool.

The *Hughenden Rest Easi* caravan park, on the highway on the west side of town, has limited camping space but offers rooms for $35/44. The *Allan Terry Caravan Park* on Resolution St has a large swimming pool next door but can get noisy from the railway yard over the road. Tent sites are $7 double and on-site vans $22 for two.

Porcupine Gorge
If the weather has been dry and you're not in a hurry and have a vehicle, take a trip out to Porcupine Gorge National Park, an oasis in the dry country north of Hughenden off the mostly unpaved, often corrugated Kennedy Developmental Road. The best spot to drive to is the Pyramid lookout, about 80 km from Hughenden. You can camp here and it's an easy 30 minute walk down into the gorge, with some fine rock formations and a permanently running creek. Few people come here and there's a fair bit of wildlife. The Kennedy Developmental Road would eventually take you to the Atherton

Tableland but it would be a pretty rough trip.

HUGHENDEN TO CLONCURRY
Keep your eyes open for wild emus and brolgas on this stretch. Richmond, 112 km from Hughenden, and Julia Creek, 144 km further on, are small towns both with motels and caravan/camping parks. From Julia Creek a surfaced road turns off north to Normanton (420 km) and Karumba (494 km) near the Gulf. You can also reach Burketown (467 km) this way.

Cloncurry is 134 km west of Julia Creek. Fourteen km before Cloncurry the mostly surfaced Landsborough Highway turns off south-east to McKinlay (91 km), Kynuna (165 km), Winton (328 km) and Longreach (501 km). At McKinlay is the *Walkabout Creek Hotel*, where the pub scenes in *Crocodile Dundee* were shot. Greyhound buses between Mt Isa and Brisbane via Longreach make a meal stop here when they come through three times a week. The *Blue Heeler* at Kynuna is another renowned old outback pub.

CLONCURRY (Population 1961)
The centre for a copper boom in the last century, Cloncurry was the largest copper producer in the British empire in 1916. Today it's a pastoral centre and base for the Flying Doctor Service.

Cloncurry's museum, just off the highway on the east side of town, is partly housed in buildings transported from Mary Kathleen. The collection (admission $2) includes Burke & Wills relics and a big collection of local rocks and minerals. You can see steam engines outside free. A new museum being built at John Flynn Place will house mining, flying doctor and School of the Air stuff.

Cheapest motel in Cloncurry is the *Wagon Wheel Motel* (tel 42 1485) at 54 Ramsay St with singles/doubles at $27/41. You can camp in the *Cloncurry Caravan Park* opposite the museum, for $7 double, or take an on-site van for $22.

The Burke Developmental Road, north

from Cloncurry, is paved all the way to Normanton (375 km) and Karumba (449 km) near the Gulf of Carpentaria. Burketown is 443 km from Cloncurry.

CLONCURRY TO MT ISA

This stretch is 117 km. At Corella River, 41 km west of Cloncurry, there's a memorial cairn to the Burke & Wills expedition, which passed here in 1861. Ten km beyond this is the site of Mary Kathleen, a uranium mining town from the 1950s to 1982. It has been completely demolished.

The turning to Lake Julius, Mt Isa's reserve water supply, is 36 km beyond Mary Kathleen. There's a camping site at the lake and Battle Mountain, north of the Lake Julius dam wall, was the scene of the last stand of the Kalkadoon people, a rare pitched battle between Aborigines and Europeans in 1884.

Mt Isa

Population 23,679

Mt Isa is a one activity town – an immensely rich copper, silver, lead and zinc mine. It's a rough and ready but prosperous town, and the job opportunities have attracted people from about 60 different ethnic groups to make up a diverse population. There's plenty of low cost accommodation for travellers stopping over here, and you can tour the mines.

The first Mt Isa deposits were discovered in 1923 by a prospector called John Campbell Miles who gave Mt Isa its name – a corruption of Mt Ida, a gold field in Western Australia. Since the ore deposits were big and low grade, working them required the sort of investment only a company could make. Mt Isa Mines was founded in 1924 but it was during and after WW II that Mt Isa really took off and today it's the western world's biggest silver and lead producer. Virtually the

whole town is run by Mt Isa Mines and the ore is railed 900 km to Townsville on the coast.

Information & Orientation

There's a tourist office (tel 43 7966) on Marian St between Corbould and Mullan Sts. It's open Monday to Friday from 8 am to 5 pm, plus Saturdays and Sundays from April to September, 8.30 am to 1.30 pm.

The Crusade Bookshop at 11 Simpson St is the best between Townsville and Darwin. The town centre is a fairly compact area, immediately east of the Leichhardt River which separates it from the mining area. Greyhound and Pioneer buses stop right in the centre on Miles St.

Things to See

The mines are the major attraction and there are two tours available. Make bookings for both at the tourist office. The three hour underground tour, on which you don a hard hat and miner's suit, takes you down into some of the 380 km of tunnels. Since only nine people are allowed on each tour, it's advisable to book as far ahead as possible by phoning the tourist office. The trips leave the tourist office at 8.45 am and 12 noon Monday to Friday and cost $15. Two hour surface tours by bus go twice a day Monday to Friday year round, and once on Saturday and Sunday mornings April to September. This trip costs around $10 and picks up from both the tourist office and the Greyhound/Pioneer terminal.

The mine company also runs a mining display and visitor centre on Church St near the town centre, open from 9 am to 12 noon and from 1 to 4 pm Monday to Friday, from 10 am to 2 pm Saturday and Sunday. The $2 entry fee (students $1) includes a film. Also interesting is the Frank Aston Museum, a part underground complex on a hill close to the town centre at the corner of Shackleton and Marian Sts. This rambling place has a very diverse collection ranging from old mining

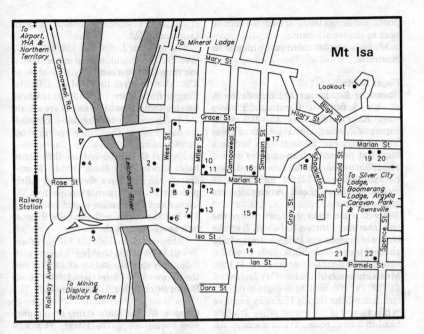

1	Billabong Inn Carvery
2	Civic Centre
3	Clicks Cafe
4	School of the Air & Flying Doctor
5	Swimming Pool
6	Argent Hotel
7	Australian Airlines
8	Hotel Boyd
9	Mt Isa Hotel
10	Greyhound & Pioneer Bus Terminal
11	Flamenco Cafe
12	Post Office
13	Ansett
14	The Tavern
15	Crusade Bookshop
16	Kentucky Fried
17	Golden Dragon Restaurant
18	Frank Aston Museum
19	Tourist Office
20	Kalkadoon Tribal Centre
21	Campbell's Coaches
22	Travellers Haven

gear to ageing flying doctor radios, and displays on the Lardil Aborigines of Mornington Island in the Gulf of Carpentaria and the Kalkadoons from the Mt Isa area. It's open daily from 10 am to 3 pm and admission is $4 (students $1).

You can visit the Royal Flying Doctor Service base at the corner of Grace St and Camooweal Rd, Monday to Saturday from 9 am to 4 pm. The $2 admission includes a film. Next door the School of the Air, which brings children in remote places, is open Monday to Friday from 9 am to 12 noon (admission free). The Kalkadoon Tribal Centre & Culture-Keeping Place, on Marian St next to the tourist office, is open most weekdays (admission $1). It's partly a museum and you can see some artefacts.

Mt Isa has a big, clean, open air swimming pool on Isa St and the 80c entrance fee includes use of showers. The pool's just across the river from the centre, next to the tennis courts.

Mt Isa's August rodeo is the biggest in Australia.

Places to Stay
Hostels & Backpacker Accommodation A short walk from the Greyhound/Pioneer stop, the *Hotel Boyd* (tel 43 3000) on the corner of Marian and West Sts charges backpackers just $7 each for a bed in a basic but perfectly clean single or double room. Showers and toilets are shared. Non backpackers pay $22/38 for the same rooms. Counter meals downstairs are good value too.

About a km from the town centre the new *Travellers Haven* (tel 43 3077) on the corner of Spence and Pamela Sts is a fully air-con place with bunk beds from $9, single and double rooms from $13/20. Meals are available. *Silver City Lodge* (tel 43 3297) at 105 East St is slightly further out, just off the Barkly Highway a couple of blocks east of the tourist office. It's $9 a head in a twin room, $11 in a single. All rooms are air-con and have fridge and TV. There's a pool table but the kitchen/sitting area is on the small side. Both these places will pick you up from the town centre if you call.

Mt Isa's 28 bed *Youth Hostel* (tel 43 5557) is pretty basic and in the shadow of the mines at Wellington Park Rd, about a two km walk from the town centre, but it's open all day and only charges $8 a night.

Motels & Lodges Opposite the tourist office at 28 Marian St *Budget Accommodation* (tel 43 4004) has a few air-con motel-type rooms, with TV and tea/coffee making facilities, for $17/22 including breakfast. The *Welcome Inn* (tel 43 2241) at 118 Camooweal St has rooms at $19/26 or shared accommodation for $13. Rooms are air-con and have fridge and tea making facilities. Bathrooms and toilets are communal. There's no guest kitchen but breakfast is available. Camooweal St runs through the town centre a block east

of Miles St - don't confuse it with Camooweal Rd.

The *Mineral Lodge* (tel 434322) at 107 West St is a straightforward motel about a km from the town centre, with doubles at $33. More central at 97 Marian St the *Copper Gate Motel* (tel 43 3233) is $29/37 for singles/doubles. The rooms are a little old-fashioned but they're self-contained, air-con, have a TV, fridge and in most cases cooking facilities. The *Boomerang Lodge* (tel 43 2019) is outside the centre, hidden away at 11 Boyd Parade. Rooms are air-con and have shower and toilet, plus there's a communal kitchen and TV lounge and a swimming pool. Doubles are $33 but the rooms will also take three or four people at $39/46.

Other motels include the *Inland Motel* (tel 43 3433) at 195 Barkly Highway, with room only singles/doubles at $30/37, and the *Copper City Motel* (tel 43 2033) at 105 Butler St charging $33/38 room only.

Camping Mt Isa has a string of camping sites, some along the Barkly Highway going east, others in the north of town and all about two km from the centre. At all of them tent sites cost $5 per person and on-site vans $22 to $27 double.

Two with nice big swimming pools on the highway are the *Mt Isa Caravan Park* (tel 43 3252) and the *Argylla Caravan Park* (tel 43 4733) which is the first one you reach coming from the east. Probably the best spot, however is four km out of town going west, at *Moondarra Caravan Park* (tel 43 9780).

Places to Eat
Excellent counter meals can be had lunch time and evening at the *Hotel Boyd (Boydie's)*, in the centre of town on the corner of Marian and West Sts, and *The Tavern* a couple of blocks away on Isa St. At Boydie's you pay $5 and up. The Tavern does very cheap 'workers' specials' for $3 - in its public bar, and more expensive fare in its bistro. There are also good but slightly more expensive bistro

meals in the Silver Bar of the *Argent Hotel* on Isa St near the corner of West St.

There are a number of centrally located pizzerias, cafes and so on including *Clicks* on West St, which offers no less than 16 varieties of burger! *Flamenco*, on Marian St near the corner of Miles St, has burgers, sandwiches and 20 flavours of ice cream. Round the corner on Miles St, in the arcade over the road from the Greyhound stop, the *Fountain Restaurant* is pleasantly cool and offers chicken & chips for $4 and fish & chips for $6. The *Golden Dragon*, a Chinese restaurant at 15 Simpson St just south of Grace St, does a Monday to Saturday lunch smorgasbord for $6 and on Thursday nights a bigger $9 smorgasbord with hot and cold dishes and salads.

For a substantial feed, locals recommend the *Billabong Inn Carvery* on the corner of West and Grace Sts. It's a glossy, American-style place. In the south of town, the *Irish Club* (tel 43 2577) on the corner of Buckley and Nineteenth Aves reportedly serves good value meals.

Entertainment
There are bands in the *Hotel Boyd* on weekend evenings. Also popular is the *Cave* nightclub in the *Mt Isa Hotel* on the corner of Marian and Miles Sts, the *Irish Club* (live rock and roll Friday and Saturday nights, disco on Saturday) and the *Buffalo Club* on Grace St.

Getting There & Away
Air Ansett and Australian Airlines both have nonstop flights two to four times weekly from Alice Springs at $175 ($140 standby), Brisbane $301, Cairns $196 and Darwin $266. Both lines also fly from Townsville for $193. There are many other flights to and from these and other centres, but fares vary. Ansett NT flies nonstop to Ayers Rock once a week ($248). Ansett and Ansett NT (tel 44 1767) and Australian (tel 44 1222) are all on Miles St, half a block south of Marian St.

Sunbird flies three times a week from Mt Isa to Doomadgee ($150), Mornington Island ($175) and Cairns ($286), also stopping once a week at Burketown ($155). Another small airline, Flight West (tel 44 1744, or 43 9333 at Mt Isa airport), links Mt Isa with Townsville, Normanton, Karumba and various places along the Flinders Highway every day. It also does a Brisbane / Longreach / Winton / Mt Isa route three times weekly and the Cairns / Mornington Island / Doomadgee / Mt Isa run three times weekly with some stops at Burketown, Normanton and Karumba.

Bus Greyhound, Pioneer, Deluxe and McCafferty's all run daily between Townsville and Three Ways, passing through Mt Isa. Deluxe and McCafferty's will give you a free stopover in Mt Isa. Between Townsville and Mt Isa takes 10 or 11 hours; on to Three Ways or Tennant Creek it's six or seven hours. All the companies have connections at Three Ways or Tennant Creek for Alice Springs and Darwin. Greyhound also goes five times a week to/from Brisbane (about 28 hours) by the inland route. Typical one-way fares from Mt Isa are Tennant Creek $70, Alice Springs $70, Darwin $100, Charters Towers $60, Townsville $75, Brisbane $137 (inland route $130), Longreach $52.

Campbell's Coaches goes to/from Normanton and Karumba two or three times a week. Greyhound Australia Pass holders can use this service on payment of a $14.50 supplement.

Pioneer (tel 43 4888) and Greyhound (tel 43 6655) are both at 24 Miles St in Mt Isa, near the corner of Marian St. McCafferty's operates from the Campbell's terminal (tel 43 2006) at the corner of Pamela and Stanley Sts; Deluxe stops at the Shell Roadhouse.

Train The air-con Inlander operates Townsville / Charters Towers / Hughenden / Cloncurry / Mt Isa. Departures from Townsville are on Sunday and Wednesday at 6 pm, arriving in the Isa 18 hours later. From Mt Isa departures are on Monday and Thursday at 3 pm. Townsville to Mt Isa costs $76.90 in economy, $144.40 in 1st.

Getting Around

A taxi to the airport costs around $8. Four car rental companies have airport desks.

A few tours are available in the town: in the winter season Copper City Tours (tel 43 7966, 43 2006) offers a full day outback trip including Aboriginal rock paintings, an old copper mine and Mary Kathleen; and a $250 three day camping trip to Riversleigh, the site of fossils up to 15 million years old which have revealed much about Australia's prehistoric animals and Lawn Hill gorge. They also do an $8, two hour surface tour of the mines.

Mt Isa to Three Ways

There's nothing much for the whole 650 km to the Three Ways junction in the Northern Territory. Camooweal is 188 km from Mt Isa, just before the Queensland-Northern Territory border and it's the only place of any size at all. West of Camooweal, the next petrol (and the most expensive anywhere between Townsville and Darwin) is 270 km along at *Barkly Homestead* (tel 64 4549). You can camp here for $3 per person. Motel rooms are $50/57.

Lawn Hill National Park

Amid arid country 400 km from Mt Isa and 100 km west of Gregory Downs on the Camooweal to Burketown road, this is an oasis of gorges, creeks, ponds and tropical vegetation that the Aborigines have enjoyed for maybe 30,000 years. Their paintings and old camping sites abound. Two rock art sites have been made accessible to visitors. There are freshwater crocodiles – the inoffensive variety – in the creek. Also in the park are extensive and virtually unexplored limestone formations.

Getting there is the problem – it's a beautiful, pristine place that's miles from

anywhere or anybody. The last 300 km or so from Mt Isa – after you leave the Barkly Highway – are unsealed and often impassable after much rain. Four wheel drive is recommended, though not always necessary in the dry season. There's a camping site with showers and toilets in the park, and 17 km of walking tracks. One tour runs to Lawn Hill. The nearest petrol to the park is at Gregory Downs. There's accommodation at the *Gregory Downs Hotel* and you can camp not far away beside the Gregory River.

Darling Downs

West of the Great Dividing Range, stretch the rolling plains of the Darling Downs, some of the most fertile and productive agricultural land in Australia. In the state's early history the Darling Downs were something of a back door into the region. Nobody was allowed within a 50 mile radius of the penal colony of Brisbane but settlers gradually pushed their way north from New South Wales through this area.

West of the Darling Downs the population becomes more scattered as you move out of the crop producing area into sheep and cattle country centred on towns like Roma, Charleville and Cunnamulla.

From Ipswich, just inland from Brisbane, there are two main routes west: a southern one through Warwick and Goondiwindi to Cunnamulla, and a northern one through Toowoomba and Roma to Charleville, from where you could continue west to the Channel Country or turn north for Longreach. The region is linked to New South Wales by three main trunk roads: the New England Highway from Warwick down to Tamworth, the Newell Highway from Goondiwindi to Dubbo, and the Mitchell Highway from Charleville and Cunnamulla down to Bourke and Dubbo.

Places to Stay

All sizeable towns have hotels and/or motels, and caravan/camping parks. There are youth hostels at Warwick, Jondaryan and Roma. It's also possible to stay on cattle stations or homesteads in some places.

Getting There & Away

Air Sunstate (tel 38 1199 in Toowoomba) and Sabair both fly between Brisbane and Toowoomba at least once daily. Flight West (tel Roma 22 1416, Charleville 54 1121) flies Brisbane to Charleville and back six days a week, with stops at Roma five days.

Bus Many long-distance buses between Brisbane and Sydney or Victoria go through the Darling Downs. Ipswich, Toowoomba and Warwick are on the New England Highway route. Similarly Ipswich, Toowoomba and Goondiwindi are on the Newell Highway route. Brisbane to Goondiwindi takes about five hours and costs $30 with Pioneer or Deluxe. You usually have to travel a minimum distance – sometimes even interstate – to use these trunk route buses.

Greyhound runs a variety of buses west into Queensland from Brisbane: to Mt Isa five days a week through Ipswich, Toowoomba (2½ hours, $12.60), Roma (7½ hours, $41), and Charleville (11 hours, $51.50); to Longreach daily through the same places; plus several other services daily to Toowoomba or Roma.

Skennars has daily buses from Brisbane to Ipswich, Toowoomba, Warwick, Goondiwindi, Roma and Charleville, also between Toowoomba and Warwick twice daily, and five days a week between Warwick and the Gold Coast. McCafferty's runs a bus service between Ipswich and Toowoomba several times a day to coordinate with the suburban trains between Brisbane and Ipswich. Other McCafferty's routes are Toowoomba/Gold Coast ($15) and Brisbane/Rockhampton through Ipswich, Toowoomba and Miles.

Train The air-con Westlander runs twice a week from Brisbane to Cunnamulla and Quilpie, through Ipswich, Toowoomba, Roma and Charleville. It's 777 km from Brisbane to Charleville and takes about 17 hours. Fares from Brisbane are Toowoomba $14 economy; Roma $43.20 economy, $97.70 1st class; Charleville $61.50 economy, $126.70 1st class; Cunnamulla and Quilpie $76.90 economy, $144.40 1st class.

Non air-con trains run twice weekly between Brisbane and Dirranbandi, through Ipswich, Toowoomba, Warwick and Goondiwindi. Going back to Brisbane you have to change to a coordinated bus service between Toowoomba and Ipswich and then get on a suburban train from Ipswich. Brisbane to Goondiwindi is 457 km and takes 12 hours. Fares from Brisbane are Warwick $25.80 economy, $41 1st class; Goondiwindi $39.90 economy, $63.30 1st class; Dirranbandi $54.90 economy, $87.30 1st class.

IPSWICH (Population 75,000)

Virtually an outer suburb of Brisbane now, Ipswich was a convict settlement as early as 1827 and one of the most important early Queensland towns. It's the main gateway to the Darling Downs. On the way from Brisbane to Ipswich, Wolston House at Wacol is an 1850s country house with a collection of early Australian furniture, open from 10 or 11 am to 4.30 pm Wednesday to Sunday.

Ipswich has many fine old houses and public buildings: if you're interested in Queensland's distinctive architecture, pick up the excellent *Ipswich City Heritage Trails* leaflet which will guide you round a great diversity of buildings. The kiosk in Queens Park, above the town centre, doubles as a tourist information office (tel 281 5167).

IPSWICH TO WARWICK

South-west of Ipswich, the Cunningham Highway to Warwick crosses the Great Dividing Range at Cunningham's Gap, with 1100 metre mountains rising either side of the road. Main Range National Park, which covers the Great Dividing Range for about 20 km north and south of Cunningham's Gap, is great walking country, with a variety of walks starting from the car park at the crest of Cunningham's Gap. Much of the range is covered in rainforest. The park HQ (tel (076) 66 1133) and a camping area are by the road on the west side of the gap. Spicer's Gap, in the range south of Cunningham's Gap, has excellent views and another camping area. To reach it you turn off the highway five km west of Aratula, back towards Ipswich.

WARWICK (Population 8853)

South-west of Brisbane, 162 km inland and near the New South Wales border, this is the oldest town in Queensland after Brisbane. It's a busy Darling Downs farming centre noted for roses and its rodeo on the last weekend in October. Pringle Cottage on Dragon St, dating from 1863, is a museum, open daily. There is a tourist office (tel 61 3686) on Palmerin St. The *Youth Hostel* (tel 61 2698), with 18 beds at $6 a night, is at 6 Palmerin St.

South-east of Warwick near the New South Wales border is Killarney, a pretty little town in an area of fine mountain scenery with a number of lovely waterfalls. Among them is the 40 metre Queen Mary Falls, tumbling into a rainforested gorge 10 km east of Killarney in the flanks of the Great Dividing Range. There's a caravan/camping park on the road near the falls.

South of Warwick on the New England Highway is Stanthorpe, near the New South Wales border. At 915 metres it's the coolest town in the state and a centre for fruit production and wine making, with over 20 vineyards, some of which you can tour. Stanthorpe tourist office (tel 81 1799) is at 61 Marsh St. There's a museum, open daily, on High St. Wildflowers bloom profusely in the area in July and August.

From the highway 26 km south of Stanthorpe, a paved road leads nine km east up to Girraween National Park, an area of steep hills over 1000 metres, valleys and big granite outcrops. In spring there are a lot of wildflowers and it's a good area for wildlife spotting. The park has an information centre, two camping grounds with hot showers, and several walking tracks of varying length. Girraween adjoins Bald Rock National Park over in New South Wales. It can fall below freezing on winter nights up here but summer days are warm. You can book camping sites in advance – phone (076) 84 5157.

GOONDIWINDI & FURTHER WEST

West of Warwick, Goondiwindi is on the New South Wales border and the Macintyre River. It's a popular stop on the Newell Highway between Melbourne and Brisbane. There's a small museum in the old customs house and a wildlife sanctuary at the Boobera Lagoon. If you continue inland from Goondiwindi you reach St George, where cotton is grown on irrigated land.

Much further west is Cunnamulla, 254 km north of Bourke in New South Wales and very definitely out in the outback. This is another sheep raising centre, noted for its wildflowers. The Yowah opal fields are about 150 km further west.

TOOWOOMBA (Population 80,000)

On the edge of the Great Dividing Range and the Darling Downs, 138 km inland from Brisbane, this is the largest city in the region. It's a gracious city with parks, tree lined streets, several art galleries and many early buildings. The old Bull's Head Inn on Brisbane St, Drayton, six km west, dates from 1847 and you can visit it from 10 am to 4 pm, Thursday to Monday, for $2. In Toowoomba itself there's the

Cobb & Co Museum on the corner of James and Water Sts, and botanical gardens in Queens Park on the corner of Margaret and Lindsay Sts. The tourist information centre (tel 32 1988) is at 541 Ruthven St.

The two cheapest hotels in town are the *Ruthven Hotel*, near the Information Centre, which is $10 for a bed, and *Law Courts Hotel*, on the corner of Margaret and Neil Streets, which is $14 a bed or $17 with breakfast. Both are pretty basic.

North of Toowoomba is Crows Nest which took its name from a local Aborigine, Jim Crow, who lived in a hollow tree. Follow the Valley of Diamonds signs to Crows Nest Falls National Park where there are good walking trails to a gorge and falls, also swimming holes and a camping site.

TOOWOOMBA TO ROMA

It's about 350 km west along the Warrego Highway from Toowoomba to Roma, across the Darling Downs. Three km south of Jondaryan, which is about 45 km out of Toowoomba, there's an associate youth hostel at the 1859 *Jondaryan Woolshed* (tel 92 2229) – which is also a wool pioneer complex with museums and daily shearing and blacksmithing demonstrations. Nightly cost in the hostel is $5 – there are only 10 beds so call ahead.

Dalby is a crossroads town in probably the richest grain growing area in Australia. There's a big rodeo here in mid-September. At Dalby you can turn north to the Bunya Mountains National Park. Chinchilla is another busy agricultural town with an interesting folk museum, open daily, on Villiers St, and a pioneer cottage. It holds its rodeo in October.

Miles has an historical village (open daily), a war museum and a wildflower festival in the first week of September. North from Miles the Leichhardt Highway leads to Taroom and Isla Gorge National Park, with sandstone gorges and ridges and, in spring and summer, lots of wildflowers. The park is good for bushwalking and has a camping site.

ROMA (Population 5706)

An early Queensland settlement and now the centre for a huge sheep and cattle raising area, Roma also has some curious small industries. There's enough oil around here to support a small refinery, producing just enough petroleum for local use. Gas deposits are rather larger; Roma supplies Brisbane through a 450 km pipeline. There's also the small Romavilla Winery which is open daily; a wine festival is held in November.

The Roma *Youth Hostel* (tel 22 1806) is on the corner of Station and Edwards Sts, near the railway station. It has room for 18 people at a cost of $6 a night.

Roma is a crossroads town for travellers. North from Roma, through Injune, you can reach Carnarvon National Park. Injune has an Aboriginal museum.

CHARLEVILLE (Population 3523)

About 800 km from the coast, Charleville is the end of the Warrego Highway and the centre of another huge cattle and sheep raising region. This was an important centre for early explorers and something of an oasis in the outback, on the Warrego River. It was a real frontier town around the turn of the century.

There are various reminders around town of the early explorers and an historical museum in the 1880 Queensland National Bank building on Albert St. The South-West Queensland Annual Show takes place here in May. West of Charleville you reach Quilpie on the edge of the Channel Country, while to the north the Mitchell then the Landsborough Highways take you up to Longreach.

The Channel Country

The remote and sparsely populated south-west corner of Queensland, bordering the Northern Territory, South Australia and New South Wales, takes its name from the myriad channels which crisscross the area. In this inhospitable region it hardly ever rains but water from the summer monsoon further north pours into the Channel Country along the Georgina, Hamilton and Diamantina rivers and Coopers Creek. Flooding towards the great depression of Lake Eyre in South Australia the mass of water arrives on this huge plain until it eventually dries up in waterholes or salt pans or simply sinking back into the ground.

Only on rare occasions (this century only in the early '70s and 1989) does the vast amount of water actually reach Lake Eyre and fill it. For a short period after each 'wet' season, however, the Channel Country does become fertile and cattle are grazed here.

Getting There & Around

Some roads from the east and north to the fringes of the Channel Country are paved but during the October to May wet season, even these are often cut – and the dirt roads become quagmires. In addition, the summer heat is unbearable so a visit is best made in the cool winter from May to September. Visiting this area requires a sturdy vehicle, 4WD if you want to get off the beaten track, and some experience of outback driving. Anywhere west of Cunnamulla or Quilpie, always carry plenty of petrol and drinking water and notify the police so that if you don't turn up at the next town the necessary steps can be taken.

The Greyhound bus service between Brisbane and Mt Isa through Charleville, Longreach and Winton, goes via Boulia twice weekly in each direction on its Winton to Mt Isa leg.

You can reach Quilpie on the Westlander train from Brisbane twice a week. Brisbane to Quilpie takes 22 hours and costs $73 in economy, $109 in 1st class.

Flight West Airlines (tel 252 1152 in Brisbane) goes once a week from Brisbane

to Birdsville and back, via Charleville, Quilpie and Windorah. Augusta Airways flies from Port Augusta in South Australia to Birdsville, Bedourie and Boulia on Saturdays, and back on Sundays.

DIAMANTINA DEVELOPMENTAL ROAD

The main road through the Channel Country is the Diamantina Developmental Road that runs south from Mt Isa through Boulia to Bedourie and then turns east through Windorah and Quilpie to Charleville. In all it's a long and lonely 1340 km, a little over half of which is surfaced.

Boulia is the 'capital' of the Channel Country. An 1888 stone house in the little town has been restored to its original condition and is a museum. Boulia has the *Australian Motel-Hotel* (tel 46 3144) with singles/doubles at $22/30, or $24/37 with private bathroom, a caravan park with tent sites at $7 double, and a couple of cafes. Burke and Wills passed through here on their long trek. Near Boulia the mysterious min min light, a sort of earthbound UFO, is sometimes seen. It's said to resemble the headlights of a car and can hover a metre or two above the ground before vanishing and reappearing in a different place.

Bedourie, about halfway between Boulia and Birdsville, is in the middle of a vast beef cattle area. It has a pub and a caravan/camping park and holds its horse races on the second weekend in September.

Windorah is either very dry or very wet and has a pub and a caravan/camping park. Quilpie is an opal mining town and the railhead from which cattle, grazed here during the fertile wet season, are railed to the coast. It has two pubs with rooms, a motel and a caravan/camping park. Charleville is a comparatively large town.

OTHER ROUTES

The Kennedy Developmental Road runs from Winton to Boulia and is mostly surfaced with a couple of fuel and accommodation stops, at Middleton and Hamilton, on the way.

From Quilpie to Birdsville you follow the Diamantina road through Windorah but then branch off south to Betoota. It's 394 dull km from Windorah to Birdsville. Betoota, with one store and one pub, is all there is along the way.

South of Quilpie and west of Cunnamulla is Thargomindah, with a couple of motels and a caravan/camping park. From here camel trains used to cross to Bourke in New South Wales. Noccundra, further west, was once a busy little community. It now has just a hotel (with fuel, food and accommodation) and a population of three!

BIRDSVILLE

This tiny settlement, with a population of about 30, is the most remote place in Queensland and possesses one of Australia's most famous pubs – the *Birdsville Hotel*, which dates from 1884. You can stay there for \$38/55 single/double. There's also a caravan/camping park.

Birdsville is only 12 km from the South Australian border and it's the northern end of the 481 km Birdsville Track which leads down to Marree in South Australia. In the late 19th century Birdsville was quite a busy place as cattle were driven south to South Australia and a customs charge was made on each head of cattle leaving Queensland. With federation the charge was abolished and now railways and roads carry the cattle, so Birdsville

has become almost ghost-like. Its big moment today is the annual Birdsville Races on the first weekend in September when as many as 3000 racing and boozing enthusiasts make the trip to Birdsville. Birdsville gets its water from a 1219 metre deep artesian well which delivers the water at 65°C.

To the south, the Birdsville Track passes between the Simpson Desert to the west and Sturt's Stony Desert to the east. The first stretch from Birdsville has two alternative routes. Ask local advice about which is better. The Inner Track – marked 'not recommended' on most maps – crosses the Goyder Lagoon (the 'end' of the Diamantina River) and a big wet will sometimes cut this route. The longer, more easterly Outside Track crosses sandy country at the edge of the desert where it is sometimes difficult to find the track. Travellers driving the Birdsville Track must fill in a 'destination' card with Birdsville police and then report to the police at the other end of the track, which is Marree in South Australia.

West of Birdsville the Simpson Desert National Park is Queensland's biggest at 5000 square km, and with no water. Conventional cars can tackle the Birdsville Track quite easily but the Simpson requires far more preparation. Official advice is that crossings should only be tackled by parties of at least three 4WD vehicles and that you should have a radio to call for help if necessary.

South Australia

Area	984,277 square km
Population	1,390,000

South Australia is the driest of the states, even Western Australia doesn't have such a large proportion of desert. It is also the most urbanised. Adelaide, the capital, once had a reputation as the 'wowser's' capital and is referred to as 'the city of churches'. The churches may still be there, but otherwise times have changed.

Today the city's cultural spirit is epitomised by the biennial Adelaide Arts Festival. The death of wowserism is nowhere better seen than in the Barossa Valley Wine Festival held every two years. An example of South Australia's relatively liberal attitude is Australia's first legal nudist beach just a short drive south of the city. The state also has the most progressive legislation for Aboriginal land rights, national parks, cannabis and homosexuality. Since 1985 Adelaide has hosted the Australian Formula One Grand Prix.

Outside Adelaide, the state is best known for its vineyards and wineries. The famous Barossa Valley, north of the city, is probably the best known wine-producing area in the country, even though the amount of 'Barossa wine' produced annually far exceeds the grape-growing capacity of the valley! South Australia also has the fine Clare and Coonawarra valleys and the southern vineyards are only a very short drive from the city. Wine festivals in South Australia are frequent and fun.

Further north, the rugged Flinders Ranges make an ideal area for all sorts of outdoor activities; this is another of my favourite Australian places. The far north and west of the state has some of the most barren, inhospitable land in Australia although several years of unexpectedly heavy rain turned some of the inland salt

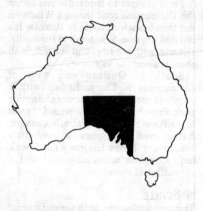

lakes temporarily into the real, water-filled thing in the '70s and in 1989.

The drive across the Nullarbor used to be one of the more accessible of Australia's outback driving adventures, but the new road opened in '76 (it was already surfaced westward from South Australia's border with Western Australia) has civilised even that long drive. The road runs close to the cliff tops along the Great Australian Bight. That still leaves you the Murray River, the interesting coast towards the Victorian border, fascinating Kangaroo Island, plus the Eyre, Yorke and Fleurieu peninsulas to explore.

William Light landed at Holdfast Bay (today Glenelg) in 1836, proclaimed the area a British colony and chose a site about 10 km inland for the capital which he named Adelaide after his wife. At first, progress was slow and only British government funds saved the independently managed colony from bankruptcy. The colony became self-supporting by the mid-1840s and, self-governing in 1856. Steamers on the Murray River linked the state with the east and agricultural and pastoral activity became the main industry.

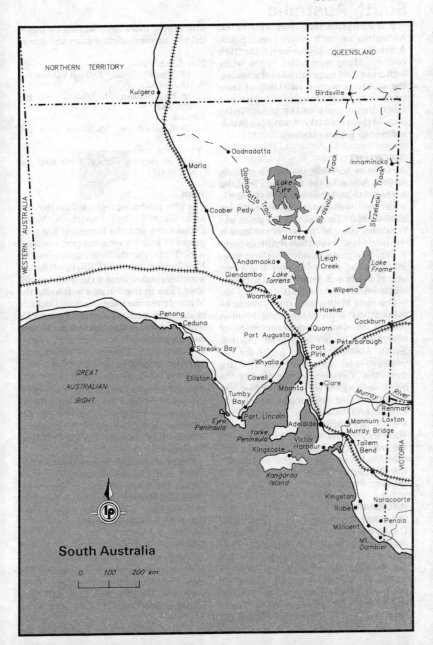

South Australia

0   100   200 km

It is estimated that there were 12,000 Aborigines leading nomadic lives in South Australia at the beginning of the 19th century. Many were killed by the white settlers or died from introduced diseases; the survivors were pushed out of their traditional lands to the more barren and inhospitable parts of the state. Today most of the state's 5000 Aborigines live on reserves or mission stations.

GEOGRAPHY

Apart from Adelaide, the state is sparsely settled. Adelaide, the Fleurieu Peninsula to the south and the country to the north, with the well-known wine-producing Barossa and Clare valleys, are green and fertile but most of the rest of the state is definitely not. As you travel further north it becomes progressively drier and more inhospitable; most of the north is a vast area of desert and dry salt-lakes with only scattered, tiny settlements.

One area of this dry land is not to be missed; that's the magnificent Flinders Ranges, a desert mountain range of exceptional beauty and great interest. South Australia is also noted for the coastline and its peninsulas. Starting from the Victorian border there's the south-east region with Mt Gambier, the wine-producing Coonawarra area and the long, coastal lake of the Coorong. Then there's the Fleurieu Peninsula and nearby Kangaroo Island, the Yorke Peninsula, the remote Eyre Peninsula merging into the Great Australian Bight, and finally the Nullarbor Plain which leads to Western Australia.

INFORMATION

The South Australian Government Travel Centre has offices in Melbourne, Sydney and Perth as well as in Adelaide. They have a series of regional brochures which are amongst the most useful literature produced by state tourist offices in Australia. These brochures have maps, sightseeing and accommodation details, even restaurants. The travel centres can also supply more basic leaflets on travel details, accommodation costs and so on.

New South Wales
    143 King St, Sydney 2000 (tel 232 8388)
South Australia
    18 King William St, Adelaide 5000 (tel 212 1644)
Victoria
    25 Elizabeth St, Melbourne 3000 (tel 614 6522)
Western Australia
    111 St Georges Terrace, Perth 6000 (tel 321 0141)

Work

The wine producing regions of the Barossa and Clare Valleys, Southern Vales, Coonawarra and the Riverland are good places to look for seasonal grape-picking work. Either visit the local Commonwealth Employment Service (CES) or phone the wineries yourself from a centrally located town. The fruit-growing towns along the Murray river like Berri, Loxton, Waikerie or Renmark can be even better places for seasonal work as they never seem to have enough pickers.

GETTING AROUND
Air

Kendell Airlines (book through Ansett) is the main regional operator with flights fanning out from Adelaide to Mt Gambier, Kangaroo Island, Port Lincoln, Streaky Bay, Ceduna, Coober Pedy and Broken Hill.

Other local operators include State Air, Lloyd and Lincoln Airlines. There are flights to Oodnadatta, Innamincka, Birdsville, Hawker and a host of operations to Kangaroo Island. The chart shows South Australian air fares.

Bus

As well as the major interstate bus companies there are services within the state by Stateliner, Premier, Yorke Peninsula Bus, Barossa Bus and King Island Connection.

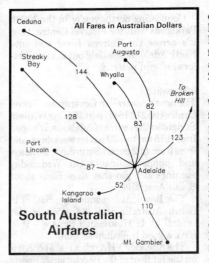

Ceduna

All Fares in Australian Dollars

Port Augusta

Streaky Bay

144

Whyalla

To Broken Hill

82

128

83

123

Port Lincoln

87

Adelaide

52

Kangaroo Island

110

South Australian Airfares

Mt Gambier

ACTIVITIES
Bushwalking

Close to Adelaide there are many good walks in the Mt Lofty Ranges including Belair Park, Cleland Park, Morialta Park, Deep Creek Park, Bridgewater-Aldgate, Barossa Reservoir and Parra Wirra Park.

In the Flinders Ranges, 400 km from Adelaide, there are excellent walks in the Wilpena Pound area as well as further south in the Mt Remarkable National Park or further north in the Arkaroola-Mt Painter Sanctuary area. Some of the walks in this area are for the more experienced walker since conditions can be extreme. Get a copy of *Flinders Ranges Walks*, produced by the Conservation Council of South Australia.

The Heysen Trail is a walking trail from Cape Jervis at the southern tip of the Fleurieu Peninsula up to the Barossa Valley. It's planned to link this up with a series of walking trails right up into the Flinders. You can walk north from Crystal Brook, but it's still easier to walk south from Wilpena Pound which is more accessible to those who don't have their own transport. There are several bushwalking clubs in the Adelaide area which

organise weekend walks in the Mt Lofty Ranges or longer weekend walks in the Flinders. Information can also be obtained from bushgear shops like Paddy Pallin and Thor Adventure Equipment (tel 232 3155), 228 Rundle St, Adelaide.

Water Sports

Swimming & Surfing There is no surf at popular city beaches like Glenelg, but as you travel further south there are plenty of good beaches with good surf. Seacliff, Brighton (sailing too), Somerton, Glenelg, West Beach, Henley Beach, Grange, West Lake, Semaphore, Glanville and Largs Bay are all popular. Skinny-dipping is permitted at Maslins Beach, 40 km south of the city. You have to get over to Pondalowie on the Yorke Peninsula for South Australia's best board riding.

Other good surf areas can be found along the Eyre Peninsula; close to Adelaide at Boomer and Chiton, between Victor Harbour and Port Elliott, and near Goolwa.

Scuba Diving There are lots of diving possibilities around Adelaide. If you have proof of diving experience, you can hire equipment in the city. Several of the shipwrecks off Kangaroo Island are easily accessible to scuba divers. Port Noarlunga Reef Marine Reserve (18 km south) and Aldinga (43 km south) are good centres for boat diving. The reefs around Schnapper Point are suitable places for snorkelling. At Rapid Bay (88 km south), there's abundant marine life; you can dive from the jetty. Wallaroo on the Yorke Peninsula, Port Lincoln on the Eyre Peninsula and Second Valley (65 km south of Adelaide) are other good areas.

Sailing & Canoeing There is good sailing all along the Adelaide shoreline of Gulf St Vincent and there are lots of sailing clubs. The Murray River and the Coorong are popular for canoeing trips and visitors can hire equipment and join in canoe trips organised by canoeing associations in South Australia.

Adelaide

Population 1,003,000

Adelaide is a solid, dare I say gracious, city. It cerainly looks that way; when the early colonists built they generally built with stone. The solidity goes further than architecture, for despite all the liberalism of the Dunstan years, Adelaide is still an inherently conservative city – an 'old money' place. In part that's due to Adelaide's role in Australia. It can't compete with Sydney or Melbourne in the big city stakes nor with Perth or Brisbane as a go-ahead centre for the resources boom, so it goes its own way; for the visitor that's one of the nicest things about it. Adelaide is civilised and calm in a way no other Australian city can match. What's more, it has a superb setting – the city centre is surrounded by green parkland. The whole metropolitan area is rimmed by a fine range of hills, the Mt Lofty Ranges, which crowd the city against the sea.

Orientation

Adelaide is laid out on a clear grid pattern, with several city squares. The main street is King William St, with Victoria Square at the heart of the city. The GPO is on King William St by Victoria Square. Continue north up King William St; the tourist bureau is on the other side of the road.

Across King William, the streets change name. The main shopping and restaurant street is Hindley St on the west side, changing to Rundle St on the east. Rundle St is a mall from King William through to Pulteney St. The next block up is North Terrace with the casino and local railway station just to the west and a string of major public buildings including the university and the museum to the east.

Continuing north, you're in the North Parklands with the Festival Centre; then it's across the Torrens River and into North Adelaide, also laid out in a straightforward grid pattern.

Information

The South Australian Government Travel Centre (tel 212 1644) is at 18 King William St right in the centre of Adelaide. It's open from 8.15 am to 5.30 pm on weekdays, and from 9 am to 2 pm on Saturdays, Sundays and public holidays. On Wednesday evenings at 8 pm they show films about South Australia.

The Royal Automobile Association of South Australia (tel 223 4555) is also central at 41 Hindmarsh Square – they have a good bookshop section.

The Adelaide YHA office (tel 51 5583) is on the 1st floor of the Recreation & Sports Centre at the corner of King William and Sturt Sts. It's open from 9.30 am to 4.30 pm on weekdays.

Standard Books at 136 Rundle Mall is a big bookshop of the old-fashioned school with a wide range of titles. Try the excellent Europa Bookshop at 16 Pultney St for its selection of foreign-language books. Both the University and the State Library on North Terrace have very good bookshops. The Third World Bookshop at 103 Hindley St is open until about 1 am, has a good range of radical literature and also sells secondhand books, tapes and records.

Around the City

Adelaide's most interesting streets are Rundle Mall and Hindley St. Rundle Mall was one of Australia's first city malls and is certainly one of the most successful. It's colourful, always a hive of activity and you'll find most of the big city shops here. Buskers add to the fun. Across King William St (the main drag of Adelaide), Rundle Mall becomes Hindley St. This is Adelaide's left-bank/sin centre, if a place like Adelaide can be imagined to have such a centre. Well, you'll find the odd

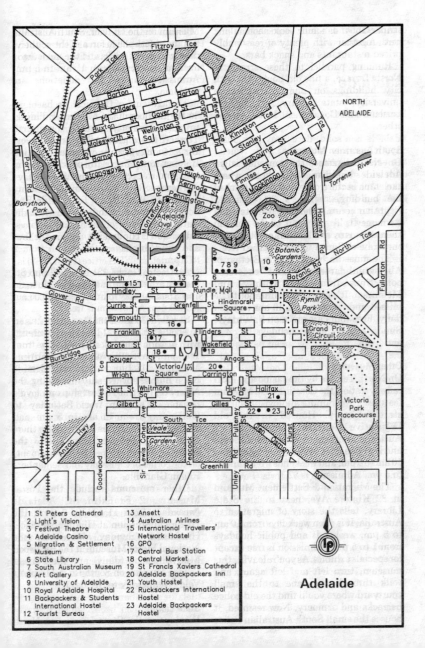

1 St Peters Cathedral
2 Light's Vision
3 Festival Theatre
4 Adelaide Casino
5 Migration & Settlement Museum
6 State Library
7 South Australian Museum
8 Art Gallery
9 University of Adelaide
10 Royal Adelaide Hospital
11 Backpackers & Students International Hostel
12 Tourist Bureau
13 Ansett
14 Australian Airlines
15 International Travellers' Network Hostel
16 GPO
17 Central Bus Station
18 Central Market
19 St Francis Xaviers Cathedral
20 Adelaide Backpackers Inn
21 Youth Hostel
22 Rucksackers International Hostel
23 Adelaide Backpackers Hostel

Adelaide

strip club and 'adult book shop' along here, together with plenty of reasonably priced restaurants and snack bars.

Running parallel to these streets is North Terrace, a fine old boulevard with city buildings on one side and the university, state library, art gallery, museum and Government House on the other.

South Australian Museum

On North Terrace, the museum is an Adelaide landmark with huge whale skeletons in the front window. In front of the building, there's a 3000-year-old Egyptian column thought to date from Rameses II. To the right of the column there are many small fossils embedded in the stone wall next to the petrified tree.

The museum has a huge collection of Aboriginal artefacts and excellent collections from New Guinea and Melanesia. It's a fine museum, not to be missed and is open from 10 am to 5 pm daily. Free tours are given on Saturdays, Sundays and public holidays at 2.15 and 3 pm.

Other Museums

On North Terrace by the casino and local railway station, the Constitutional Museum features a 100 minute audiovisual on the state's history. Housed in the old Legislative Council building this is Australia's only political history museum and it's open from Monday to Friday from 10 am to 5 pm, and weekends from 12 noon to 5 pm. Admission is $2.

The Migration & Settlement Museum at 82 Kintore Ave, next to the State Library, tells the story of migration to Australia. It is open weekdays from 10 am to 5 pm, weekends and public holidays from 1 to 5 pm. Admission is free except for specials exhibits. As you're leaving this museum, turn left and left again, and walk through the lane to the small courtyard where you'll find the old police barracks and armoury. Now restored, it houses the small South Australian Police

Museum on the 1st floor. South Australia has the oldest police force in the country, dating from the 1860s and the museum is open on weekends from 11 am to 5 pm. Admission is free but donations are welcome.

The Museum of Classical Archaeology on the 1st floor of the Mitchell Building, in the university grounds on North Terrace, has a good collection of Greek, Etruscan, Egyptian and other antiquities. It's open from 12 noon to 3 pm during term time and weekends; admission is free.

There's a Railway Museum on Railway Terrace off West Beach Rd at Mile End South. It tells the history of railways in the state and displays early locomotives. Admission is 60c and it's open on the first and third Sunday of the month from 2 to 5 pm.

At Electra House, 131 King William St, there's a Telecommunications Museum open from Sunday to Friday from 10.30 am to 3.30 pm. Admission is free.

St Kilda, 30 km from the centre, has an Australian Electrical Transport Museum with historic vehicles, open Sundays from 1 to 5 pm. The South Australian Maritime Museum, 117 Lipson St, Port Adelaide has a number of old ships including the *Nelcebee*, the third oldest ship on Lloyd's register. It's open from Saturday to Wednesday from 10 am to 5 pm and admission is $4. Buses 154 to 157 go there from North Terrace. There's also the Shipping Museum (open by appointment) on the corner of Causeway and Semaphore Rds in Glanville.

Other museums include the Postal Museum, 2 Franklin St, Adelaide (weekdays from 11 am to 2 pm); the Historical Museum at Hindmarsh Place, Hindmarsh (Sunday afternoons); the National Motor Museum at the Birdwood Mill, Birdwood (daily) and the Pioneer Village Museum on South Rd in Morphett Vale (Wednesday to Sunday).

State Library

Displays at the State Library on North

Terrace include Colonel Light's surveying equipment, an 1865 photographic panorama of Adelaide and, in the Historic Treasures Room, memorabilia of cricket star Sir Donald Bradman. The library is open weekdays from 9.30 am, until 9.30 pm on Thursdays, and until 5 pm on other days.

Art Galleries

On North Terrace, the Art Gallery of South Australia has a good selection from contemporary Australian and overseas artists, as well as some fine minor works from many periods. The South-East Asian ceramic collection is of particular note. The gallery has a pleasant little coffee shop with outside tables. It is open daily from 10 am to 5 pm, admission is free and there are tours at 11 am.

The Royal South Australian Society of Art's gallery on the 1st floor on the corner of North Terrace and Kintore Ave hosts frequent visiting exhibitions. It's open weekdays from 11 am to 5 pm, weekends from 2 to 5 pm and admission is free. Other galleries include the Union Gallery on the top floor of the Adelaide University Union Building (open weekdays) and the Festival Centre gallery near the Playhouse. There are also numerous private galleries.

Ayers House & Edmund Wright House

Ayers House is on North Terrace close to the city centre. This fine old mansion was originally constructed in 1846, but was added to over the next 30 years. Now completely restored, it houses two restaurants but is open for visitors from Tuesday to Friday between 10 am and 4 pm and on weekends between 2 and 4 pm. Admission is $2 and on weekdays there are tours on the hour. The elegant bluestone building serves as the headquarters of the South Australian National Trust.

At 59 King William St, Edmund Wright House was originally built in an elaborate Renaissance style with intricate decoration in 1876 for the Bishop of South Australia. It is now used as government offices and for official functions.

Other City Buildings

The imposing town hall, built in 1863-66 in 16th century Renaissance style, looks out on King William St. Faces of Queen Victoria and Prince Albert are carved into the facade. The post office across the road is almost as imposing. On North Terrace, Government House was built between 1838 and 1840 with a later addition in the centre in 1855. The earliest section is one of the oldest buildings in Adelaide. Parliament House on North Terrace has a facade with 10 Corinthian marble columns. Building commenced in 1883, but was not completed until 1939.

Holy Trinity Church, also on North Terrace, was commenced in 1838 and was the first Anglican church in South Australia. Other early churches are St Francis Xavier Cathedral on Wakefield St (commenced around 1856) and St Peter's Cathedral in Pennington Terrace, North Adelaide (built between 1869 and 1876). St Francis Xavier Cathedral is beside Victoria Square, where you will also find a number of other important early buildings: the 1847-50 Magistrate's Court House (originally used as the Supreme Court); the 1869 Supreme Court; and the Treasury Building.

Festival Centre

The Adelaide Festival Centre is close to the Torrens River. Looking uncannily like a squared-off version of the vastly more expensive Sydney Opera House, it performs a similar function with its variety of auditoriums and theatres. The complex was completed in 1977. There are tours from Monday to Friday at 10 and 11 am, 1, 2 and 3 pm, and on Saturdays at 10.30 and 11.30 am, 2 and 3 pm. The tours cost $2. Phone 216 8713 to check starting times.

One of the most pleasant aspects of the Festival Theatre is its riverside setting; people picnic on the grass in front of the theatre and there are several places to eat. You can also hire pedal paddle-boats nearby or enjoy often free concerts and exhibitions here. In the Piano Room, you can hear Adelaide's top pianists during happy hour on Fridays between 4.30 and 6 pm. Admission is free. On Saturday nights from 10.30 pm till late, you can catch a free band that plays anything from romantic jazz to contemporary, energetic pop.

Living Arts Centre

On the corner of Morphett St and North Terrace the Living Arts Centre is planned as a focus for a broad spectrum of arts-related actvities and when complete it will include galleries, stage areas, artists' studios, craft workshops and cinemas.

Adelaide Arts Festival

South Australia enjoys two of Australia's major festivals: the Barossa Valley Vintage Festival on odd-numbered years; and the Adelaide Arts Festival in February-March of the even-numbered years. The three week festival of the arts attracts culture-vultures from all over Australia to drama, dance, music and other live performances, plus a writers' week, art exhibitions, poetry readings and other activities with guest speakers and performers from all over the world. The Fringe Festival, which takes place at the same time as the main festival, is often even more interesting.

Adelaide Grand Prix

The Australian Formula One Grand Prix takes place in Adelaide in late October or early November each year and is the final race of the Grand Prix season. The track is along city streets immediately to the east of the city centre. The cars reach 300 kph down Dequetteville Terrace.

With practice sessions and supporting races, the event goes on for five days and all Adelaide gets into it. This must be one of the easiest Grands Prix in the world to get to since you can easily find a place to park (if you don't mind a 10 minute walk to the track) and there's plenty of public transport. Big improvements in the spectator embankments and viewing areas mean you can easily get a good view without having to meet the expense of a seat in the stands.

Botanic Gardens & Other Parks

On North Terrace, the botanic gardens have pleasant artificial lakes and are only a short stroll from the city centre. The glass Palm House was made in Germany in 1871. The central area of Adelaide is completely surrounded by green parkland, and the Torrens River, itself bordered by park, separates Adelaide from North Adelaide which is also surrounded by park. Every Tuesday and Friday at 10.30 am, free guided tours of the botanic gardens, taking about 1½ hours, leave from the kiosk. The gardens are opened weekdays from 7 am to sunset, and on the weekends and public holidays from 9 am to sunset.

Rymill Park in the East Parkland has a boating lake and a 600 metre jogging track. The South Parkland contains Veale Gardens with streams and flowerbeds. To the west are a number of sports grounds while the North Parkland borders the Torrens and surrounds North Adelaide. The Adelaide Oval, site for Test cricket matches, is north of the Torrens River in this part of the park. The North Parkland also contains Bonython Park, Pinky Flat and Elder Park which adjoins the university and Festival Centre.

Light's Vision

On Montefiore Hill, north of the city centre across the Torrens River, stands the statue of Light's Vision. Adelaide's founder is said to have stood here and mapped out his plan for the city. It is a good place to start your exploration of the city centre since you get a good bird's eye view of the modern city, with green parkland and the gleaming white Festival Centre at your feet. Another fine Adelaide view, particularly at night, can be enjoyed from Windy Point Lookout in Belair Rd, a continuation of Unley Rd.

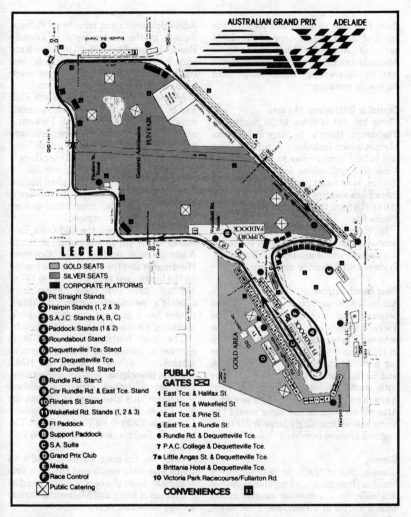

AUSTRALIAN GRAND PRIX   ADELAIDE

LEGEND

GOLD SEATS
SILVER SEATS
CORPORATE PLATFORMS

1 Pit Straight Stands
2 Hairpin Stands (1, 2 & 3)
3 S.A.J.C. Stands (A, B, C)
4 Paddock Stands (1 & 2)
5 Roundabout Stand
6 Dequetteville Tce. Stand
7 Cnr Dequetteville Tce. and Rundle Rd. Stand
8 Rundle Rd. Stand
9 Cnr Rundle Rd. & East Tce. Stand
10 Flinders St. Stand
11 Wakefield Rd. Stands (1, 2 & 3)
A F1 Paddock
B Support Paddock
C S.A. Suite
D Grand Prix Club
E Media
F Race Control
⊠ Public Catering

PUBLIC GATES ⊠

1 East Tce. & Halifax St.
2 East Tce. & Wakefield St.
3 East Tce. & Pirie St.
4 East Tce. & Rundle St.
5 Rundle Rd. & Dequetteville Tce.
7 P.A.C. College & Dequetteville Tce.
7a Little Angas St. & Dequetteville Tce.
8 Brittania Hotel & Dequetteville Tce.
10 Victoria Park Racecourse/Fullarton Rd.

CONVENIENCES 🚻

Adelaide Zoo

On Frome Rd, the zoo has a noted collection of Australian birds as well as other important exhibits including sloths, giant ant-eaters, spider monkeys and ring-tailed lemurs. The zoo is open every day from 9.30 am to 5 pm. Admission is $5.50. The best way of getting to the zoo is to take a cruise down-river on board the *Popeye*. The trip costs just $1.40 ($2.20 return) and departs from Elder Park in front of the Festival Centre. You can also catch bus No 272 or 273 from North Terrace.

North Adelaide

Interesting old bluestone buildings and pubs abound in North Adelaide, only a short bus ride through the park to the north of the centre. It's one of the oldest parts of Adelaide; Melbourne St is Adelaide's swankiest shopping street with lots of interesting little shops and expensive restaurants.

Central & Brickworks Markets

Three km out of town at 36 South Rd, Thebarton, there's the large Brickworks Market which includes a leisure complex and is held from Friday to Monday from 9 am to 5 pm selling food, arts, crafts, clothes, books and plain old junk. To get there from the city take bus No 112, 114, 116 or 118 from the corner of Grenfell and Currie Sts.

In town, the Central Market with produce, fish and crafts, is on Grote St. It's open on Tuesdays, Thursdays, Fridays and Saturday mornings.

West Beach Airport

Adelaide's airport is centrally located between the city and Glenelg. The Vicker's Vimy which made the first flight between England and Australia way back in 1919 is on display in a showroom in the car park. At the controls were Sir Keith and Sir Ross Smith; the flight took 27 days with numerous stops along the way. A similar aircraft made the first non-stop Atlantic crossing in the same year. (The Vimy was a surprisingly large WW I twin-engined biplane bomber.)

Glenelg

Glenelg, one of the most popular of the beaches stretching in a long chain south of Adelaide, is a suburban seaside resort with a couple of attractions. First of all, it's an excellent place to stay – there are many guest houses, hotels and holiday flats here if you can't find something suitable in the city. Secondly, it's one of the oldest parts of Adelaide – the first South Australian colonists actually landed in Glenelg – so there are a number of places of historic interest. As a bonus, Glenelg is exceptionally easy to get to.

Adelaide's only tram runs from Victoria Square in the centre right to Glenelg Beach. It costs $1.80 ($1.10 between 9 am and 3 pm) and is commendably fast (taking about 30 minutes) as its route keeps it separate from the road traffic.

At the jetty in front of the Town Hall and by the beach is Bay World; you can't miss the camel out the front. Pick up a map or walking or cycling tour brochure from the helpful information desk here. Aside from the souvenirs sold here there is a museum-aquarium with sea-life in tanks and apparently a shrunken human head amongst the curios. Admission is $2.50. You can also rent bicycles here before you set off to explore.

On Macfarlane St, the Old Gum Tree marks where the proclamation of South Australia was read in 1836. Governor Hindmarsh and the first colonists landed on the beach near here and bus No 167 or 168 will take you there. Apart from Glenelg's fine collection of early buildings, it also has a popular amusement park, including a waterslide, behind the beach.

The boat harbour shelters a large number of yachts and Glenelg's premier attraction: a reproduction of HMS *Buffalo*, the original settlers' conveyance. Used as a rather expensive seafood restaurant, it's also open to visitors for $2.50 from 10 am to 5 pm daily (closed 12 noon to 2.30 pm on Wednesdays). The original *Buffalo* was built in 1813 in India.

Jetty Rd, the main street, is lined with shops and restaurants and the tram line goes right down the centre. Shell Land at the corner of Mary and Melbourne Sts has a large collection of sea shells.

Marineland Park

Just north of Glenelg and adjoining Adelaide airport is the 'dolphins through the hoops' marine park on Military Rd, West Beach. The seals and dolphins go through their paces at 11 am, 12.30 and 3 pm daily. The park also has an aquarium with sharks and rays and a 360° audiovisual show. Admission is $6.

Other Suburbs

In Jetty St, Grange you can see Sturt's Cottage, the home of the famous early Australian explorer. Preserved as a museum, it's open from Wednesday to Sunday and public holidays from 1 to 5 pm. In Semaphore there's Fort Glanville, built in 1878 when Australia was having its phase of Russia-phobia as a result of the Crimean War. It's open during the summer.

In Port Adelaide you can make boat trips from North Parade Wharf except during July. Carrick Hill at 590 Fullarton Rd, Springfield is built in the style of an English Elizabethan manor house set in an English-style garden.

Places to Stay

Adelaide has several cheap backpackers hostels in the city area and a YHA. The city also has standard old hotels and moderately priced guest houses. Other than that you have to move out of the centre, particularly to the beach suburb of Glenelg which also has a hotel offering dorm beds and several camping sites.

Hostels Most of the hostels are clustered in the south-east corner of the city centre. You can get there on any bus No 191 to 198 from Pulteney St in the centre or take any bus going to the South Terrace area, although it's not really that far to walk.

Adelaide's *Youth Hostel* (tel 223 6007) is at 290 Gilles St and has recently been renovated and expanded. Now it has 50 beds, for $9 each. There's a book outside the door listing alternative places if the hostel is full when you arrive. The hostel is closed between 9.30 am and 1 pm.

Nearby is the very pleasant, low-key *Adelaide Backpackers Hostel* (tel 223 5680) at 263 Gilles St. Nightly cost is $9 in the section which closes from 11 am to 3 pm. There's another section that's open all day; nightly cost here is $10. The

office is open from 8 to 11 am and from 3 to 10 pm. The couple who run this hostel also run *Backpackers Inn* (tel 223 6635), two streets closer to the centre at 112 Carrington St. This hostel was formerly a pub and has dorm beds at $10.50 or double rooms for $20. There is a cheap coffee shop next door serving breakfast from 6.30 am. If both of these hostels are full they have a couple of annexes for overflow purposes. Next door to the Backpackers Hostel is the *Rucksackers International Hostel* (tel 232 0823) at 257 Gilles St. It is another pleasant little hostel with kitchen, lounge, colour TV and pool table for only $9 per bed.

The *International Travellers' Network Hostel* (tel 211 7335) at 57 North Terrace has a very friendly atmosphere and is very easy going. The dorms have four to five beds and cost $8 per person. Opposite the botanic gardens, the *Backpackers & Students International Hostel* (tel 232 0823), 307 North Terrace is another fully equipped hostel with kitchen, laundry, TV room, etc. A dorm bed costs $8.

The *YMCA* (tel 223 1611) at 76 Flinders St is very central and takes guests of either sex. Dorms are $8, share-twin rooms are $10, singles are $15 and doubles are $24. Weekly rates are six times the daily rates. Office hours are 9 am to 9 pm Monday to Friday, and 9 am to 12 noon and 4 to 8 pm on weekends and holidays. Dorms open at 4 pm.

Finally for emergencies women might try the Salvation Army's *Sutherland Lodge* (tel 223 3423) at 341 Angas St and for men there's the *Mens Hostel* (tel 51 4302) at 62 Whitmore Square.

Hotels – city The *Metropolitan Hotel* (tel 231 5471) at 46 Grote St is central and cheap at $15 single or $28 double. Around the corner and down the block from the youth hostel, the *Afton Private Hotel* (tel 223 3416) at 260 South Terrace has long term accommodation only for $60 a week with a full English breakfast. There are kitchen facilities but if you arrive after

8 pm phone ahead before turning up. It's a big place with 100 rooms but is apparently always full in winter.

Other central hotels include the *Plaza Private Hotel* (tel 231 6371) at 85 Hindley St. Rooms with washbasins cost from $23/34.

The Plaza is an old but well-kept place built around a very pleasant palm-filled central courtyard. At 205 Rundle St the *Austral Hotel* (tel 223 4660) has singles/doubles for $23/41.

The *Criterion Hotel* (tel 51 4301) at 137 King William St is conveniently close to the Central Bus Station and costs $25/38. At 437 Pultney St the *Hotel Hanson* (tel 223 2442) costs $31/46 including breakfast. This is a better place with air-con, colour TV and tea/coffee making facilities but there are only seven rooms.

Motels - city The centrally located *Clarice City Motel* (tel 223 3560) is at 220 Hutt St, just around the corner from the youth hostel. There are some cheaper rooms here in the old part of the building with doubles from $37 but the motel units are $50. At 262 Hindley St the *Princes Arcade Motel* (tel 51 9524) costs $39/55 including a light breakfast.

Motels - other Although you'll find motels all over Adelaide – some are also covered under Glenelg – there's a 'motel alley' along Glen Osmond Rd, which is the road that leads in to the city centre from the south-east. There's a good selection, but this is quite a busy road so some places can be a bit noisy.

Powell's Court (tel 271 7995) is only two km from the centre at 2 Glen Osmond Rd, Parkside. Rooms cost from $40/50, they all have kitchens and there are also rooms big enough for three or four for not much more than the price of a double.

The *Sunny South Motel* (tel 79 1621) is four km out at 190 Glen Osmond Rd, Fullarton and offers the usual sort of motel standards for $38/43 and up. Across the road is *Princes Highway* (tel 79 9253)

Pub, North Adelaide

at 199 Glen Osmond Rd, Frewville which costs $38/43 and up.

Alternatively, there's the *Sands* (tel 379 0066) at 198 Glen Osmond Rd, Fullarton which costs $38/43; or the *Motel 277* (tel 79 9911) at 277 Glen Osmond Rd, Glenunga, four km from the centre. It's excellent value at $38 for a standard room (there are also rooms with kitchens) but prices go up on holidays and long weekends. Weekly rates are five times the daily rate.

Glenelg Accommodation There's a lot of accommodation in Glenelg: a couple of old hotels, a number of good guest houses, a handful of reasonably priced motels and a lot of holiday flats. The main road down to the sea in Glenelg is Jetty Rd. The road along the seafront is South Esplanade, which becomes North Esplanade on the other side of the boat harbour entrance.

Down at the waterfront at 2 Jetty Rd is

the spacious old *Glenelg Pier Hotel* (tel 295 4116). This is a seaside hotel of the old school and rooms are $29/40, or $48/54 with private facilities. At 16 South Esplanade the old-fashioned *Oriental Private Hotel* (tel 295 2390) costs $25/29 including a substantial breakfast, and they have dorms for $10 per person. The *St Vincent Hotel* (tel 294 4377) at 28 Jetty Rd has rooms ranging from $32/48 for singles/doubles with breakfast.

Colley House (tel 295 7535), at 22 Colley Terrace opposite the reserve, offers serviced apartments all the way from $46 to $66. There are a lot of holiday flats and serviced apartments in Glenelg; most of them quote weekly rather than daily rates. At 7 North Esplanade the *Alkoomi Holiday Motel* (tel 294 6624) has double rooms from $42 to $46 all with private facilities, fridges and tea/coffee-making equipment. The adjoining *Wambini Lodge* (tel 295 4689) is the same price and is run by the same people.

The *Norfolk Motel* (tel 295 6354) is at 69-71 Broadway, a few blocks south of Jetty Rd. It's a fairly small motel with 20 units for $36/41 including breakfast. The *Bay Hotel Motel* (tel 294 4244) is $40/46 with air-con, colour TV and tea/coffee-making facilities. It's at 58 Broadway, about half a km from the beach. The hotel section does counter lunches. There are lots of restaurants and take-away places down Jetty Rd; Glenelg is noted for its Greek food.

The tourist office has a list of holiday flats here and in other beach suburbs. They average $32 to $46 depending on the time of year.

Other Beach Suburbs Glenelg isn't the only beach suburb with accommodation possibilities; you can also find plenty of places to stay at West Beach and Henley Beach, a little further north. West Beach in particular has a variety of holiday flats while at Henley Beach there are holiday flats and the reasonably priced *Del Monte Backpackers Hostel* (tel 353 5155) on the Esplanade at 209 with dorm beds at $9 and rooms at $31/42.

Colleges The usual vacation-only, students-preferred rules apply but the Adelaide universities are no longer such good places to try for a room. St Ann's College (tel 267 1478) is probably the cheapest at $10 per person, available in January only. You might try others like Lincoln College (tel 267 2588), St Mark's (tel 227 2211) or the Flinders University Halls of Residence.

Camping There are quite a few camping sites around Adelaide although some of the more convenient ones do not take tents, only caravans. The tourist bureau has a useful brochure on camping and caravan parks around the city. The following are within a 15 km radius; all camping charges are per site.

Recreation Caravan Park (tel 278 3540), National Park, Belair, 13 km south; camping sites $9 per day, on-site vans $22.

Sturt River Caravan Park (tel 296 7302), Brookside Rd, Darlington, 13 km south; camping $7.50 per day.

Adelaide Caravan Park (tel 42 1563), Bruton St, Hackney, only two km north-east and by the Torrens River; camping $13 per day but limited number of tent sites, on-site vans from $26 per day.

Glenbrook Caravan Park (tel 42 2965), Portrush Rd and River St, Marden, five km north-east; camping $8 per day, on-site vans from $23 per day.

Marion Caravan Park (tel 276 6695), 323 Sturt Rd, Bedford Park, 12 km south; camping $11 per day, on-site vans for up to five or six people $24 per day.

Brownhill Creek Caravan Park (tel 271 4814), Brownhill Creek in the foothills of the Mt Lofty Ranges at Mitcham, eight km south; camping $9 per day, air-con on-site vans $20.

Norwood Caravan Park (tel 31 5289), 290 Portrush Rd, Kensington, three km east; no camping but cabins for two from $26 per day and powered caravan sites for $9.

Levi Park Caravan Park (tel 44 2209), Lansdowne Terrace, Walkerville, five km north-east; camping $7 per day (for four), on-site vans from $28 per day.

West Beach Caravan Park (tel 356 7654), Military Rd, West Beach, eight km west; camping $8.50 to $10 per day depending on season.

Marineland Caravan Village (tel 353 2655), Military Rd, West Beach, eight km west; no camping, on-site vans $25 to $38 per day depending on season.

Windsor Gardens Caravan Park (tel 261 1091), 78 Windsor Grove, Windsor Gardens; six km north-east, camping $8 per day.

Places to Eat

Although Adelaide does not have the variety or quality of cuisine of Melbourne or Sydney, it certainly has quite enough to ensure survival with style! Furthermore, Adelaide has lots of places where you can eat outside. Licensing laws are more liberal in South Australia than in Sydney or Melbourne so a higher proportion of restaurants are licensed. Those which claim to be BYO are often just licensed restaurants which allow you to bring your own alcohol if you wish.

Open Air & Lunch Adelaide is one of the best cities in Australia for alfresco dining; the climate is dry so you're unlikely to get rained on, it's sunny so being outside is nice, and it's not so super-hot that for much of the year you're risking sunstroke.

Hindmarsh Square is a good place to start looking if you're after a lunch in the sun. On the north Pulteney St corner *Carrots* is a long-running health-food place. It's a nice, airy place to sit and look out over the square. It's open only from Monday to Friday from 10 am to 4 pm and they have magazines and books to flip through.

At No 37 on the west side of the square, the *Indonesian House of Food* has tables and umbrellas and a $6.50 lunch special. Next door is the *Jasmin Indian Restaurant* with good main courses for around $10. There's a second location just a few doors down but they're closed on Sundays. At the corner with Grenfell St, the *Phoenician Restaurant* serves Lebanese and vegetarian food; a three-course meal is $12.

Another outdoor place is the *Festival Bistro* in the Festival Centre overlooking the Torrens River. It has sandwiches and snacks, is open late into the evenings, but is closed on Sundays. The gardens around the Festival Centre are a good place for a picnic.

La Strada, on the corner of North Terrace and Austin St, is a cafeteria that also serves pizzas, pasta, etc for $3 to $6. Just around the corner in Austin St is *Off The Terrace* and they have quiche, chicken salads, bagel sandwiches, etc from $4 to $7.

The *Al Fresco Gelateria* at 260 Rundle St has tables out on the footpath; it is a good place for a gelati, cappuccino or a variety of sweets. They also operate *Al Fresco on the Terrace*, on the corner of North Terrace and Charles St.

Snacks, Fast Foods & Late at Night If you're after late-night eats, then look for the *Pie Carts* which appear every night from 6 pm till the early hours; they're an Adelaide institution. If a pie floater (the great Australian meat pie floating on a thick pea soup) is your thing then look for their vans at the corner by the GPO and on North Terrace near the railway station. If a floater does not sound like your thing (and I sincerely hope it doesn't for your stomach's sake!) then they also have other, more straightforward pies.

The *Pancake Kitchen* (see the Around the City section) and *Bertie's Pancake Factory* downstairs in the Southern Cross Arcade are open late. They have specials for $5 to $6.

Adelaide has *McDonalds* and other front runners in the fast food stakes including *Hungry Jacks* with a branch right in the centre on the corner of Pulteney and Rundle Sts. The railway station has a cafeteria and the YMCA's restaurant is very economical. Adelaide University's union building is also conveniently close to the city centre – try the *Bistro* there. It's open from Monday to Friday from 12 noon to 2.30 pm and from

5.30 to 8.30 pm, their main courses vary from $5 to $8.50. The Union Cafeteria on the ground floor is cheaper: a cup of coffee is bottomless.

Crossways at 79 Hindley St is a Hare Krishna place offering all-you-can-eat three course vegetarian meals for $3 from 12 noon to 3 pm on weekdays. There are lots of fast food and take-away places, good for a quick lunch, in the modern Southern Cross Arcade which runs through to St James Place from King William St, just down from Rundle Mall. *Hav-a-Chat* is the best lunch bar here, offering lots of salads, sandwiches and quiches.

The *Terrace Plaza* on North Terrace is a cafeteria with sandwiches, quiches and salads for $3 to $6. *Sidewalk Cafe*, next to the Botanic Hotel on the corner of North Terrace and East Terrace, has sandwiches and light snacks for $3 to $5. *Light Delights* at 108 Gawler Place is very popular for lunch Monday to Friday; it is wise to book for Thursdays and Fridays.

Despite its enormous size, the *Left Bank* at 165 Pulteney St still feels like a cafe. It has snacks, light meals and fairly inexpensive breakfasts but, as with most places in Adelaide, it's closed on Sundays.

The *Impian* is a good Malaysian restaurant at 204 Rundle St where a three course meal costs around $17. Further down at 236 Rundle St is *Cafe Michael* with lunch time seafood platters for $13. Close by at No 270 is *Rossini's Restaurant*, an Italian place offering a starter and main course at lunch time for $11 *including* a litre of wine at every table. Their main courses are reasonably priced at $8 to $11. *Cafe Boulevard* at 15 Hindley St is pleasantly old fashioned and reasonably priced; it's a good place to observe the passing parade on Hindley St.

Finally the *Halifax Lounge* at 65 Flinders St is run by one of the local churches and offers a place to go from 10 am to 4 pm. There's tea and coffee and you can hang around reading and writing if you like.

Food Centres As in other cities around Australia the Singapore-style food centres, where a group of kitchens share a communal eating area, are excellent places to eat.

The best and one of the cheapest would have to be *Hawker's Corner* on the corner of West Terrace and Wright St. It's open for lunch and dinner except on Mondays and has Chinese, Vietnamese, Thai and Indian food for $4 to $5. Next to the Central Market on Moonta St the *International Food Plaza* is open until 5.30 pm, seven days a week. It has good, cheap Thai, Indian, Chinese and Vietnamese food at $4 to $5.

The *City Cross Arcade* off Grenfell St has European and Australian as well as Asian food. The many snack stalls and kitchens serve seafood, gourmet salads, potatoes and Chinese or Italian dishes for $3 to $6. On the 1st floor of the Renaissance Tower Centre at Rundle Mall the *Gallerie of International Cuisine* also has Asian and European stalls with meals from $4 to $9. It's open for lunch or dinner.

The Gallerie Shopping Centre runs from North Terrace through to Gawler Place, on the basement level beside the John Martins Department Store. Here you'll find *The Food Affair* with booths offering Chinese, Greek, pizza, health foods, crepes and fish & chips. It's not a bad place to eat and it's very busy at lunch time. A plate of food is $5 to $6; a slice of pizza or various specials are about $4. It's open to 6 pm and until 9 pm on Fridays.

Counter Meals Adelaide is very well represented in this category, particularly at lunch time. Just look for those telltale blackboards standing outside. Meals don't come any cheaper than at the *Old Queen's Arms*, a few blocks from the centre at 88 Wright St. It's plain food at prices that are hard to beat; meals go for around $4.50.

The *Talbot Hotel* at 104 Gouger St has a nice deal with the Gouger Cafe next door.

Excellent seafood at $6 to $9 for main courses is served in the hotel's pleasant beer garden. This is a more up-market pub where some money has been spent on decor. Another block along brings you to Franklin St where you'll find the Central Bus Station and several places including the *Hotel Franklin* at 92 Franklin St which does counter meals for $4 to $5.

Hindley and Rundle Sts have a number of pubs with good food. On the corner of Rundle St and East Terrace, *The Stag* is an ordinary looking pub with a good reputation for its food; main courses are generally $7 to $11, counter lunches are as low as $6. On the corner of Grenfell St and Hindmarsh Square the *Park Tavern* is a ritzy pub with a bistro where you'll pay $5 to $8 but there's also a cheaper counter meal section where you can get an excellent dinner for $3.50 to $4.50 or have a lunch special for $3.15 including a schooner of beer. The *Somerset*, centrally located on the corner of Pulteney and Flinders Sts, has steaks and grills for about $7. The *Austral Hotel* on the corner of Bent and Rundle Sts has daily counter meal specials for $3.50 to $4.50. The *Brecknock Hotel* at 401 King William St has good counter meals for around $9 and they're well known for their 'green beer' on St Patrick's day.

Across in North Adelaide, *The British* at 58 Finniss St has a 'touch of the British' about it, plus a pleasant beer garden where you can grill the food yourself at the barbecue. Main courses are $9.50 to $10.50 ($1 less if you cook your own). Out at Glenelg on the beach end of Jetty Rd, the *Glenelg Pier Hotel* offers cheap, filling lunches.

Hindley St If Adelaide has a food centre, it has to be Hindley St where you'll find a whole series of Italian, Greek, Lebanese, Chinese and Eastern European restaurants, interspersed with Adelaide's small and seedy collection of strip clubs, and the Third World Bookshop which stays open until 1 or 2 am. The cheaper restaurants offer meals at $6 to $7; the more expensive ones are $8 to $9.

In the basement at 33 Hindley St you'll find *Chinatown*. It's an unpretentious place with most dishes in the $8 to $11 bracket but the food really is good. Lunches are cheaper at around $6 to $8. Across the road at 68 Hindley St, the *Feed Bag* is strictly American fast food in style. It's cheap, clean, open until late and is not bad at all, plastic though it may be. *Central Pizza* at 73 Hindley St has Italian fare, even on Sundays when most places are closed. It's open from midday to midnight. Dishes are from $6 to $8.

One of the nicest places on the street is the cheap and friendly Abdul & Jamil's *Quiet Waters*. Downstairs in this pleasant Lebanese coffee lounge they serve really good food; vegetarian dishes for around $3.50 to $5.25 and meat dishes, mainly lamb, about $6. It's tastefully decorated and has live music on Wednesday and Saturday. *Pagana's* at 101 Hindley St does pastas from $7 to $9 or main courses from $9 to $13.50. It's good authentic Italian food and there's wine at 65c a glass. Then there is a string of steak/charcoal-grill places. *Noah's Ark* at 116 Hindley St has felafels for $3 or at No 133 the *Jerusalem Shish Kebab House* is another Middle Eastern place.

At 117A *Nicks Down Under* has good Aussie tucker. The *Royal Admiral Hotel* at 125 has fresh fish with salad and chips for $8 and the usual counter meals. For Malaysian there's *Shah's* next door where main courses are $7 to $8. There are also numerous Greek places like *Hindley's Olympic Restaurant* at No 139 which serves souvlaki and spiced lamb.

The *Hickory Hollow* at 141 specialises in ribs for about $9. Further along at 179 is the *Deep South Restaurant* offering American soul food and a few Mexican items as well. It's open from 6 pm till late every day and has live soul or blues music on Thursday to Saturday nights. For Indian food, the *Madras Cafe* at No 142 has main courses from $7 to $10.

Just off Hindley St on Club House Lane, the *King Luc* is a low-price Chinese place with lunches from $4.20. Also close to Hindley St one of the best Indian restaurants would have to be *Taj Tandoor* at 76 Light Square; main courses are in the $8 to $11 range.

Around the City Lots more places can be found around the city. The east end of Rundle St, for example, has quite an Italian flavour. At 201 Rundle St, *Don Giovanni's* is a very popular Italian eatery with reasonable prices. Pizzas range from $5.50 to $7.50. *Mezes* is a small, casual Greek place at 285 Rundle St with an open-view kitchen. Main courses are $11 to $14.50 and it's open till late.

Right in the centre, *Chief's* at 12 Grenfell St is rather plastic and fast-food in flavour but seafood or mushroom and chicken crepes with salad cost just $6. At 69 Grote St, *Ellinis* a Greek restaurant which specialises in seafood serves excellent and reasonably priced food. Gilbert Place, a small lane across the corner of King William and Hindley Sts in the centre, has several places worth a look. The *Pancake Kitchen* is notable for being open 24 hours a day, seven days a week; it's also pretty good value, especially if you're after 'steak & pancakes'? Next door, the *Penang Coffee Shop* serves Malay-Chinese food. Round the corner is *D'Angelo's Restaurant* – a pleasant Italian place with main dishes in the $7 to $9 range with pastas a bit cheaper. The long established, but more expensive *Arkaba Steak Cellar* is also in this compact little group; their steaks are around $11.

To feel the sea-breeze, head across to Gouger St which is the fish and seafood centre of Adelaide. Some of the places here have been running for many years and recently, a lot of new places have joined them. There's *Paul's* at 79 and the *Gouger Cafe* at 98. Main courses in the latter are $8 to $10; it also handles the counter meals next door in the *Talbot Hotel*. There's also *George's* at 111 and *Stanley's* at 76.

Also on this street is *Star of Siam* at 83A which serves good Thai food; a three-course dinner costs about $16 and they have $5 lunch specials. The *Mamma Getta Restaurant* at 55 Gouger St is, if you haven't guessed, Italian. Most dishes are under $7 with most pastas just $5.80. At the corner of Morphett St, the *Tequila Sunrise* has moderately priced Mexican food

The *Central Market* between Gouger and Grote Sts near Victoria Square is very good value for food, fruit, vegetables and bread. It also has a good, cheap restaurant called *Malacca Corner* where the most expensive dish is $5. A bit further away at 131 Pirie St *Fasta Pasta* is a cheap, popular Italian restaurant. On the next street down, you can try the Russian restaurant *Volga* at 116 Flinders St where a three-course meal with live music is about $14. The *Pullman Adelaide Casino Restaurant* is surprisingly good value with a smorgasbord for $20.

Away from the Centre The cheapest restaurant in Adelaide, if not Australia, must be *The Abode of the Friendly Toad* at 85 Henley Beach Rd, Mile End. The main course is $3.75; dessert is 50c. These plain surroundings are frequented by a very interesting, unusual clientele. Definitely a place not to miss. Another good cheapie is the *Bengal Tiger* at 151 Marion Rd, Richmond. The food is very good, the garlic content is high, and the most expensive item on the menu costs $4.50; they do take-aways as well. There's a free feast on Sundays at the *Hare Krishna Temple*, 60 Belair Rd in Kingswood, at 4.30 pm.

For a splurge you can try the excellent Mexican restaurant *Cha-Chi's* at 205 Glen Osmond Rd in Frewville. The main courses are between $10 to $12 and you get large portions. Desserts and their frozen margaritas are worth trying.

There are quite a few eating places

along O'Connell St in North Adelaide including a fish & chips take-away, a Lebanese place and a couple of Italian ones; most of them are on the pricey side. *Rakuba* at 33 O'Connell St is unusual with its African (Sudanese) emphasis. A three-course meal with meat and vegetarian dishes using coconut, couscous and dates with good bread costs about $11 and the portions are large.

Scrumptious, at the corner of Ward and O'Connell Sts, is a small snack bar with milk shakes, filled croissants and espresso coffee. Nearby, the unusual *Das Cafe*, on Tynte St near the corner with O'Connell St, is an old house with a log fire in winter. They serve interesting teas (a pot for two is $3) plus milk, coffee and chocolate drinks, including potions with a difference like 'mint ice lemon'. It is opened Tuesday to Saturday from 6 pm until late plus Sunday afternoons.

There are numerous places along Jetty Rd in Glenelg which offer something for everyone. At 30 Jetty Rd you can try the *National Fish Cafe* that specialises in seafood and Greek food. Their fried fish is $5.50 and the fisherman's basket is $6.60. The *Pier Hotel* also serves counter meals.

Entertainment

There are lots of pubs with entertainment in Adelaide and a host of 'what's on' information, including a regular news-sheet put out by the SAGTC; also check Thursday's *Advertiser* newspaper; or you can ring radio stations like 5MMM (tel 42 7911) or SA FM (tel 272 1990).

Pubs & Music A number of pubs in Adelaide brew their own beer. The best of these is the *Port Dock Brewery Hotel* at 10 Todd Place in Port Adelaide. Their beer is sold in 13 other hotels around town. Black Diamond Bitter is their best. The *Earl of Aberdeen* on Light Square is a more up-market place which brews good beer.

The usual rock pub circuit operates around Adelaide. It includes places like the *Arkaba* at 150 Glen Osmond Rd or the *Highway Inn* on the Anzac Highway in Plympton. The *Findon Hotel* on Grange Rd, Findon also has rock bands.

Popular city pubs with regular rock music include the *Angas Hotel* on Angas St, *Exeter* at 246 Rundle St and the *Tivoli* at 261 Pirie St. The *New Century Hotel* on Hindley St is good for alternative music. Places like the *Austral* at 205 Rundle St or the *Saracen's Head Tavern* on Carrington St have free bands.

The *Old Lion Hotel* is a trendy place on trendy Melbourne St, North Adelaide. It brews its own beer, has bars, an expensive dining room, a disco and more rock music. Adelaide University often has big-name rock bands on at the union. Every Friday lunch time during term, there is a free band playing upstairs in the union bar.

Adelaide also has a string of places with folk and jazz, particularly on Friday and Saturday nights. You'll find them in the 'what's on' guides too. The Union Bistro in Adelaide University's Union each Friday night has free jazz bands playing until 10.30 pm; you can get a good cheap dinner until 8.30 pm.

On the third Sunday of each month, there's the Hills Folk Club Concert at the *Bridgewater Inn* in Bridgewater. It starts at 6.30 pm and costs $4.50. There's always something on at the *Adelaide Festival Centre*; the SAGTC's 'what's on' guide tells all. There are usually free concerts with good local bands in the amphitheatre at the Festival Centre on Sundays from 2 to 4 pm. Also check the *Piano Bar* here for free shows.

The Downtown Leisure Centre at 65 Hindley St has heaps of pinballs and roller-skating. The various hostels often have 'things to do' notices posted on the notice boards.

Cinemas There are a number of commercial cinemas around town, particularly on Hindley St. Alternative cinemas include the *Chelsea Cinema* at 275 Kensington Rd, Kensington; the *Piccadilly* at 181 O'Connell St or the *Capri* at 141

Goodwood Rd, Goodwood, which has an organist on weekend evenings.

There is a good selection of interesting film centres in Adelaide. The university film club often shows good films in the union or check out the *Chelsea* at 275 Kensington Rd, Kensington Park – good films and student discounts. There are free lunch time films at the *State Film & Video Library*.

Casino The *Adelaide Casino* is housed in the old railway station on North Terrace and, with the new Adelaide Convention Centre and the Hyatt Regency Adelaide Hotel, it's part of the Adelaide Plaza complex. Apart from gambling facilities (including a two-up game of course) there are five bars and a restaurant. It's open from 10 am to 4 am on weekdays, for 24 hours on weekends and 'smart casual dress' is required.

The Ice Arena Adelaide's ice skating rink also has an artificial indoor snow skiing centre. The 150 metre long slope is called Mt Thebarton. It's open seven days a week and costs from $6 for the first hour plus $4 for ski hire. The ice rink costs $5 for each session plus $1.20 for skate hire. The Ice Arena (tel 352 7977) is at 23 East Terrace, Thebarton. you can get there on any bus No 154 to 157 departing from in front of the railway station on North Terrace.

Things to Buy
For Aboriginal arts and crafts visit the New Gallery of Aboriginal Art at 28 Currie St. Quality Five is an excellent craft gallery and shop in the City Cross Arcade. The Jam Factory at 169 Payneham Rd in St Peters is a government established centre for the production and sale of crafts.

Getting There & Away
Air Adelaide is the major departure point from the southern states for Alice Springs and Darwin. Many flights from Melbourne and Sydney to the Northern Territory go via Adelaide. Fares to or from Adelaide include Brisbane $307 ($246 standby), Sydney $249 ($199), Melbourne $170 ($136), Perth $362 ($290), Alice Springs $269 ($215), Darwin $411 ($329). Australian Airlines (tel 217 3333) is at 144 North Terrace, Ansett (tel 212 1111) is at 150 North Terrace.

Bus Bus Australia, Pioneer, Greyhound and Deluxe all operate to Adelaide from Sydney, Melbourne, Perth, Alice Springs and other main centres. From Melbourne it's 9½ hours and around $42, Sydney is 21 hours and $87, Perth 34 hours and $131, and Alice Springs 21 hours and $112. There are various other bus operators, particularly on the Perth route, and frequent special deals on offer.

Bus Australia (tel 212 7999), Pioneer (tel 231 2076), Greyhound (tel 233 2777) and Deluxe (tel 212 2077) operate from the Central Bus Station at 101 to 111 Franklin St. You'll also find Stateliner, Premier and other South Australian operators here. Stateliner have services to Alice Springs, the Eyre Peninsula, Arkaroola and to Broken Hill in New South Wales. Premier go to Victor Harbor, Moonta and Murray Bridge. See the appropriate sections for details.

Train There are two stations in Adelaide: the big one on North Terrace, now only for suburban trains, and the new interstate terminal on Railway Terrace, Keswick, just out of the centre.

Adelaide is connected by rail with Sydney, Melbourne, Perth, Broken Hill, Alice Springs and other centres. To Melbourne the daily overnight Overland takes about 13 hours and costs $50 in economy or $70 in 1st ($107 with sleeper). There are *caper* advance purchase fares available more than seven days in advance for $35 in economy or $49 in 1st ($75 with sleeper). The standby economy fare is $25.

You can travel between Sydney and Adelaide either via Melbourne (daily) or via Broken Hill on the Indian-Pacific (four times a week). The economy fare via Melbourne is $121, via Broken Hill it's $127 or $196 with meals and a sleeper. In 1st class via Melbourne it's $170 ($244 with sleeper), via Broken Hill it's $178 ($259 with meals and sleeper). There's also the Speedlink – a bus-train connection which is not only cheaper but also five or six hours faster. Sydney to Albury is with the XPT train, Albury to Adelaide a V/Line bus. Travel time is about 20 hours, the fare $80 in economy, $85 in 1st.

Between Adelaide and Perth you can travel on the three-times-weekly Indian-Pacific or the two-times-weekly Trans-Australian. The Adelaide to Perth trip takes about 42 hours. Fares are $130 for an economy seat, $354 for an economy sleeping berth with meals or $481 in a 1st class sleeping berth with meals. With one week's advance purchase the *caper* discount fare prices are $105 economy, $284 economy sleeper and $385 1st class sleeper.

The Ghan between Adelaide and Alice Springs operates weekly (twice weekly from May to October) and takes 23 hours. The fare is $152 in economy, $208 in an economy sleeper with meals or $292 in a 1st class sleeper with meals. Caper fares are $240, $160 and $115 respectively.

You can also go by train to Broken Hill by taking the daily train to Peterborough to connect with the three-times-weekly Indian-Pacific. State rail services also operate to Port Pirie and Mt Gambier. Rail bookings in Adelaide are made by phoning 217 4455. It's wise to book ahead for interstate journeys, particularly on the Ghan which is very popular.

Boat MV *Island Seaway* runs a passenger service from Port Adelaide to Kingscote (Kangaroo Island) and Port Lincoln several times a week, the frequency depends on the time of the year. You can get more information from R W Miller & Co (tel 47 5577), Port Adelaide or Patrick Agencies (tel (086) 82 1011), Port Lincoln.

The fare from Adelaide to Kingscote (seven hours) and from Kingscote to Port Lincoln (11 hours) is $26; from Adelaide to Port Lincoln (18 hours) is $37.

Hitching For Melbourne take the bus No 161 or 164 to 166 from Pulteney St to Old Toll Gate on Mt Barker Rd and thumb from there. To Port Augusta and Perth take bus No 224 from King William St to Port Wakefield Rd in Gepps Cross, walk or get a lift to Carvans Petrol Station and start from there.

Hitching Across the Nullarbor from Adelaide to Perth

Many people start hitching in Port Augusta from the petrol station furthest away from Adelaide, on the Eyre Highway. While this hitching spot is popular, many people have waited up to 48 hours for a ride. The traffic here is *light*. Cars and trucks are accelerating as they leave town and are not inclined to stop. The petrol station closer to the town centre is certainly a better alternative.

The best time to hitch and get rides from truckies on the Adelaide end is on Friday evening/Saturday morning, and coming back from Perth on Tuesday evening and Wednesday morning.

Getting Around

Airport Transport Adelaide's modern international airport is conveniently located. There's an airport bus service (tel 381 5311) operating between hotels every half hour from 7 am to 10 pm for $2.60. From the airport to central Victoria Square takes about 25 minutes. A taxi costs about $9. You can travel between the city and the airport entrance on bus No 276 or 277.

Budget, Hertz, Avis and Thrifty have rent-a-car desks at the airport. There's a reasonably priced coffee bar/restaurant at the airport.

Local Transport Adelaide has an integrated local transport system operated by the STA (State Transport Authority). For information you can call 210 1000 until

10.30 pm daily. Adelaide is divided into three zones; travel within one or two sections costs $1, one or two zones $1.80, or three zones $2.40. The multitrip and cash tickets for all zones cover unlimited travel for up to two hours. You could, for example, come into Adelaide on the Glenelg tram, take a bus to the station and go out the other side by train, all on the same ticket. In fact, the ticket lasts from the start of the next hour so if you buy a ticket at 9.05 am your two hours isn't up until 12 noon.

Between 9 am and 3 pm on weekdays the $2.40 fare drops down to $1.60; $1.80 fare drops down to $1.10; the $1 to 80c. In the city centre there is also a free bus service: the Bee Line service basically runs down King William St from the Glenelg tram terminus at Victoria Square and round the corner to the railway station. It operates every five minutes from 8 am to 6 pm weekdays, to 9 pm on Fridays and 8 am to 12.15 pm on Saturdays.

Day Tripper tickets are available for unlimited use from 9 am daily throughout the Adelaide metropolitan area for $3.10. Another good deal is the Multitrip ticket where you buy 10 tickets for the price of seven.

Four buses a day operate between the Ansett Building on North Terrace and the interstate train station for $2.50 – phone 217 4444 for times. For two or more people, a taxi is just as cheap.

Apart from buses and trains there's also a solitary tram service to Glenelg, which will whisk you out to the seaside suburb from Victoria Square for $1.80 ($1.10 between 9 am and 3 pm).

The STA at 79 King William St has tickets, timetables and maps (30c) and is open from 8.30 am to 5.30 pm weekdays and 8 to 11.30 am on Saturdays. Buses are colour coded; red for radial bus routes (to & from the city), blue for rail feeder bus routes, purple for the circle line bus route and green for cross suburban bus routes.

Tours Several companies offer sightseeing trips; check at the tourist office. Daily 1½ hour Heritage Walks may no longer be operating. Check with the tourist office for latest details.

Half-day city tours cost about $16. You can go further afield, to Hahndorf in the Adelaide Hills, to Birdwood Mills and the Torrens Gorge, or to the Mt Lofty Ranges and the Cleland Reserve for about $17.

E&K Mini-Tours' (tel 268 3743, 337 8739) short tours are popular with travellers. They have a half-day trip to the Adelaide Hills for $10 or a two hour Adelaide by Night tour for $6. Transit Regency Coaches (tel 381 5311) also have cheap tours. Check with the tourist office or the YHA.

Day tours, such as those out to the Barossa Valley, to the valley and Kapunda, or to Goolwa and the Murray Mouth, cost around $23 to $38. Other tours include day excursions to Victor Harbor, flying day-trips to Kangaroo Island for about $130 and in summer there are historic steam-locomotive rail tours organised by the Australian Railway Historical Society. Further afield there are 4WD trips through the Flinders Ranges.

Car Rental The major rent-a-car firms are all represented in Adelaide. Cheaper companies include Rent-a-Bug (tel 234 0911) or Rent-A-Civic (tel 268 1879) where Honda Civics cost $22 a day plus 10c a km beyond the first 160 km. Adelaide has a selection of the Rent-a-Wreck, Hire-a-Hack folk; find them in the yellow pages.

Motorcycle Rental The SA Motorcycle Centre (tel 269 6811) at 126 Main North Rd in Prospect rent bikes from 80 cc up to 250 cc from $30 to $60 per day. Action Moped (tel 211 7060) at 269 Morphett St have mopeds for $25 a day, $18 a half day or $6 an hour, plus a $50 deposit.

Bicycle Rental Action Moped (tel 211 7060) rent bicycles for $10 per day. Bike Moves (tel 271 1854) at 1A White Ave in Fullarton rent mountain bikes for $15 per day and 10-speed bikes for $12 per day. Out at Glenelg there's a bike hire place right next door to the information centre at the seashore end of Jetty Rd. They cost $2.50 an hour and there are cheaper daily rates. They have tandems as well.

Around Adelaide

Adelaide is fortunate to have so much so easily accessible to the city; the Barossa is an easy day-trip, the wineries of the Southern Vales are a morning or afternoon visit, and the Adelaide Hills are less than half an hour from the city.

ADELAIDE HILLS

Adelaide is flanked by hills to the south and east. The highest point, Mt Lofty at 771 metres, is just a 30 minute drive from the city and offers spectacular views over Adelaide, particularly from Windy Point at night. The hills are scenic and varied, with tiny villages which look for all the world as though they have been transplanted straight from Europe. The Montacute Scenic Route is one of the best drives through the hills. Walking tracks, 1000 km of them altogether, also crisscross the hills.

Parks in the hills include the Cleland Conservation Park, just 19 km from the city on the slopes of Mt Lofty. There's a wide variety of wildlife and it's open from 9 am to 5 pm daily. There are walking tracks, barbecues, waterfalls and a rugged gorge at the Morialta Park near Rostrevor. Other parks include the Parra Wirra Park to the north of the city and the Belair Recreation Park to the south. The Warrawong Sanctuary (tel 388 5380) on Williams Rd, Mylor has a variety of indigenous wildlife including some rarely seen nocturnal animals.

Heading out of Adelaide, on the Princes Highway in Glen Osmond, you'll pass the Old Toll House at the foot of the hills. Tolls were collected here for just five years from 1841.

Places to Stay

The YHA operates five 'limited access' hostels in the Mt Lofty Ranges at Para Wirra, Norton Summit, Mt Lofty, Mylor and Kuitpo. You must book these hostels in advance and obtain the key from the YHA office in Adelaide.

Fuzzie's Farm (tel 390 1464) opposite Morialta Park at Norton Summit 15 km from the city in a bushland setting, provides visitors with the opportunity to join in farm activities. You can stay here for $16 a day including meals, but longer stays are encouraged by the residents. Volunteer workers pay $5 per night to stay in bunkhouse accommodation, to eat good meals (vegetarian or non-vegetarian) and to use the laundry service, the swimming pool and hot tub provided by the resident family. The farm has an organic garden, goats and a craft studio.

In Gumeracha the *Gumeracha Hotel* (tel 389 1001) on Albert St has rooms for $16 per person.

BIRDWOOD

Less than 50 km from Adelaide, Birdwood Hill Museum has the largest collection of old cars and motorcycles in Australia. The collection, which includes other pioneering exhibits, is housed in an 1852 flour mill and is open daily from 10 am to 5 pm. The town was once a gold-mining centre and has various other old buildings. You can get to Birdwood via Chain of Ponds and Gumeracha or via Lobethal, passing through the spectacular Torrens River Gorge en route.

Gumeracha has a toy factory with a 20-metre high rocking horse – yes, another of those Australian 'big' attractions. Lobethal has a fine little historical museum open on Tuesday and Sunday afternoons. The Gorge Wildlife Park at Cudlee Creek has one of the largest private wildlife collections in Australia in natural bushland surroundings.

To stay at the *Blumberg Hotel* (tel (085) 685243), opposite the Birdwood Mill, costs $20 per person with breakfast. Torrens Valley Coach Lines operate a regular service to Birdwood from the Central Bus Station for $2.40.

HAHNDORF (population 1300)

The oldest surviving German settlement in Australia, Hahndorf is 29 km southeast of Adelaide and is a popular day-trip. Settled in 1839 by Lutherans who left Prussia to escape religious persecution, the town took its name from the ship's captain Hahn; dorf is German for 'village'.

Various German festivals and celebrations are held in the town including the annual mid-January Scheutzenfest beer festival. The German Arms Hotel at 50 Main St dates from 1834. The Hahndorf Academy, established in 1857, houses an art gallery and museum. The Antique Clock Museum at 91 Main St has a fine collection of time pieces. Admission is $2.

Places to Stay & Eat

The *Hahndorf Holiday Village* caravan park (tel 388 7361) is 1.5 km out of town on Main St. Camping sites are $9.50 and onsite vans are $30 for two. The *Amular Lodge* (tel 388 5662) has rooms for $65. Hahndorf restaurants have good, solid, German food, of course; you can eat at the *German Arms* or at the *Cottage Kitchen* on Main St.

Getting There & Away

There is a daily bus service from Bowen St, Adelaide for $2.80 one way.

Fleurieu Peninsula

South of Adelaide is the Fleurieu Peninsula, so close that most places on it can be seen on easy day-trips from the city. Gulf St Vincent has a series of fine beaches down to Cape Jervis, looking across to Kangaroo Island. The southern coast of the peninsula, from Cape Jervis to the mouth of the Murray, is pounded by the high seas of the Southern Ocean.

There are some good surfing beaches along this rugged coastline. Inland there's rolling countryside and the fine vineyards of the McLaren Vale area. The peninsula was named by Frenchman Nicholas Baudin after Napoleon's Minister for the Navy who financed Baudin's expedition to Australia. In the early days settlers on the peninsula ran a busy smuggling business but in 1837 the first whaling station was established at Encounter Bay. This grew to become the colony's first successful industry.

Places to Stay

The Fleurieu Peninsula is a popular holiday area so there are plenty of places to stay whether you're looking for camping sites, motels, hotels or guest houses. There's a youth hostel in the Inman Valley, near Glacier Rock 20 km from Victor Harbor.

Getting There & Away

You can get down to the peninsula on buses which operate from the Central Bus Station in Adelaide. Premier (tel 217 0777) have up to three services daily on the Adelaide / McLaren Vale / Willunga / Port Elliot / Victor Harbor route. It takes about two hours and fares are McLaren Vale $4, Willunga $4.20, Port Elliot and Victor Harbor $7.60.

The Kangaroo Island Connection (tel 272 6680) run a service twice a day to Cape Jervis via various towns on the peninsula. The fares are Aldinga $3.60, Yankalilla $6.20, Cape Jervis $8.70; it's $6.65 to Goolwa with Johnsons (tel 339 2488).

The railway line has now been closed to normal passenger services and is run as a tourist attraction using steam trains. The Steamranger usually runs between Adelaide and Victor Harbor on Sundays

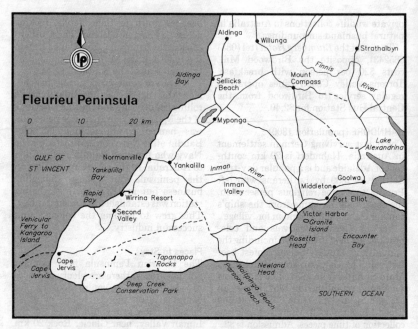

Fleurieu Peninsula

0   10   20 km

GULF OF ST VINCENT

Aldinga
Willunga
Strathalbyn
Aldinga Bay
Sellicks Beach
Mount Compass
Finnis River
Myponga
Lake Alexandrina
Normanville
Yankalilla
Yankalilla Bay
Inman River
Goolwa
Rapid Bay
Wirrina Resort
Inman Valley
Middleton
Port Elliot
Second Valley
Victor Harbor
Granite Island
Encounter Bay
Vehicular Ferry to Kangaroo Island
Rosetta Head
Tapanappa Rocks
Cape Jervis
Newland Head
Deep Creek Conservation Park
Waitpinga Beach
Parsons Beach
SOUTHERN OCEAN

and public holidays, but check with the tourist offices in either town. The fare is $25. During the summer months when fire danger is high, a diesel engine is used instead of the steam one. For steam engine buffs there is the *Cockle Train* which runs on Sundays all year round, between Victor Harbor and Goolwa. It departs Victor Harbor at 2 pm, returns at 3.45 pm and the fare is $8.

GULF ST VINCENT BEACHES

There is a string of fine beaches south of Adelaide along the Gulf St Vincent coast of the peninsula. The beaches extend from Christie's Beach (a good beach below red sandstone cliffs) to Port Noarlunga, Seaford Beach and Moana Beach before you reach the best-known beach on the peninsula – Maslins Beach, the southern end of which became the first legal nude bathing beach in Australia.

Further south, beyond Aldinga Beach and Sellicks Beach, the coastline is

rockier but there are still good swimming beaches at Myponga, Normanville and a number of other places. The coast road eventually runs through the small town of Delamere and ends at Cape Jervis at the tip of the peninsula. From here you can look across the narrow Backstairs Passage to Kangaroo Island, 13 km away. Ferries run across the straits from Cape Jervis most of the year. Near Cape Jervis there's a 12-hectare fauna park. The cape, with its high cliffs and strong sea breezes, is a popular spot for hang-gliding; you can often see enthusiasts swooping above the coastline.

Wilson's Cape Jervis Tavern, the only place to stay in Cape Jervis, has rooms for $35/40 and also serves food.

MORPHETT VALE

Adelaide has sprawled out so far that the small town of Morphett Vale has become an outer suburb. Amongst the historic buildings in the town is St Mary's, the first Roman Catholic church in South Australia, built in 1846. On the Main South Rd, at the Noarlunga turn-off, the Morphett Vale Pioneer Village recreates an early South Australian settlement from around 1860. There are a number of historic buildings with period furnishings and equipment. The village is open from 10 am to 5 pm from Wednesday to Sunday and on public holidays, but it isn't worth the $2.50 admission.

SOUTHERN VALES

There is a string of wineries on the Fleurieu Peninsula; McLaren Vale is the centre of the wine-growing area but you'll also find wine makers at Reynella, Willunga and Langhorne Creek. The area is particularly well suited to red wines. There are around two dozen wineries in the McLaren Vale area alone and about 40 in the whole region. Many of them have tastings and also sell their wines; you can make a pleasant tastings crawl around the various wineries.

The first winery in the area, in Reynella, was established in 1838 and some of the wineries date back to the last century and have fine old buildings. Most of them are open to the public Monday to Saturday; many of them on Sunday as well. A number have picnic or barbecue areas close to the cellar door sales. Some good small wineries are Wirra Wirra, Coriole and Hardy's Chateau Reynella.

The McLaren Vale Wine Bushing Festival takes place over a week in late October to early November each year. It's a busy time of wine tastings and tours and the whole thing is topped by a grand Elizabethan Feast. At McLaren Flat, near McLaren Vale, there's the Manning Fauna & Flora Reserve.

Places to Stay & Eat

Hotel McLaren in McLaren Vale has rooms for $19/36 including breakfast. The hotel does reasonable counter meals for $7 to $9. The wine tasters' lunches can be a good deal; the *Oliverhill Winery* (tel 323 8922) at Seaview Rd has Italian and Chinese main courses for $6 but *James Haselgrove Wines* (tel 323 8706) on the corner of Kangarilla and Foggo Rds has the best meals from $8.

WILLUNGA (population 500)

In the south of the Southern Vales winery area, this small town has a long history and a collection of fine buildings from the colonial era – several of them classified by the National Trust. Many of the old bluestone buildings and pug cottages have roofs made from locally quarried slate. Some of the quarries still operate today. Buildings include the old Court House with a National Trust display (visits are by appointment only, phone (085) 56 2195) and the fine old *Bush Inn* which now operates as a restaurant.

Willunga was once an important stopping point on the road from Adelaide to Victor Harbor. Today it's the centre for almond growing in Australia and the Almond Blossom Festival is held here each July. At the Mt Magnificent Conservation Park, 12 km east of Willunga, you can see grey kangaroos and take pleasant walks.

The *Willunga Hotel* has rooms for $29/40. The public bar of the *Alma Hotel* does good cheap counter meals.

PORT ELLIOT (population 800)

On Horseshoe Bay, a smaller part of Encounter Bay, Port Elliot was established in 1854 as the sea port for the Murray River trade and was the first town on Encounter Bay. At this time, nearby Victor Harbor was still just a whaling station. Port Elliot proved less than ideal as a port; in 1864, Victor Harbor took over its functions with Granite Island providing a safer, more sheltered anchorage.

Today the town is a popular holiday resort with fine views along the coast to the mouth of the Murray and the Coorong. Horseshoe Bay has a sheltered, safe swimming beach with a good cliff-top walk above it. This stretch of coast is particularly popular with surfers and Boomer Beach, on the edge of town to the west, is one of the best surfing beaches. Middleton Beach, to the east of town towards Goolwa, is another beach that attracts the board riders.

Places to Stay & Eat

The *Royal Family Hotel* (tel 54 2219) at 32 North Terrace has rooms for $17/29 and reasonable counter meals. You can camp at the *Port Elliot Caravan Park* in Horseshoe Bay for just $2.25 per person. The *Arnella Gallery Restaurant* and the *Chicken Run* take-away are both on the main street.

VICTOR HARBOR (population 4500)

The main town on the peninsula, 84 km south of Adelaide, Victor Harbor looks out on to Encounter Bay where Flinders and Baudin had their historic meeting in 1802. Up on the headland known as the Bluff, there's a memorial to the 'encounter' which took place on the bay below. It's a steep climb up to the Bluff for the fine views.

The port is protected from the high southern seas by Granite Island, a small island out in the bay which is connected to the mainland by a causeway. The old train to Granite Island has been stopped and replaced by a 19th century horse-drawn tram for $1 one way or $1.40 return. On the island there's a chair lift up to the top from where there are fine views across the bay. You may see fairy penguins and seals on the shores of the island.

Victor, as the town is often referred to, was established early in South Australia's history as a sealing and whaling centre. South of the town at Rosetta Bay, below the Bluff, is Whaler's Haven with many interesting reminders of those early whaling days. The first whaling station was established here in 1837 and another followed soon after on Granite Island; whaling ceased here in 1864, only 27 years later.

Other historic buildings in the town include St Augustine's Church of England

from 1869, the Telegraph Station built in 1869, the Fountain Inn built in 1840, the Museum of Historical Art (admission is $1) and the Cornhill Museum & Art Gallery.

There are also some interesting places to visit around the town. The Urimbirra fauna park, with a nocturnal house, is only five km out. You can take pleasant bushwalks around the Hindmarsh Valley Falls. Spring Mount Conservation Park is 14 km to the north-west. Also in this direction is the Myponga Conservation Park with many grey kangaroos and Glacier Rock 19 km out. Along the coast from Victor Harbor towards Cape Jervis, Waitpinga Beach is another popular surfing beach and updraughts from the cliffs attract hang-gliders; it's no good for swimming though.

The Victor Harbor Tourist Office is on Torrens St, next to the police station.

Places to Stay

Warringa Guest House (tel 52 1028) on Flinders Parade is an associate youth hostel. Originally built in 1910 as a guest house it has a prime seafront location and a warm and friendly atmosphere. A bed in the hostel is $9 while singles/doubles in the guest house are $28/50 and worth a splurge. They also have a pricier restaurant serving breakfast, lunch and dinner.

The *Grosvenor Hotel* (tel 52 1011) on Ocean St is reasonable at $23/35 or there's the slightly cheaper *Clifton* (tel 52 1062) at $22/29. The *Adare Caravan Park* (tel 52 1657) on Wattle Drive 1.5 km from the city centre has camping sites for $7 and on-site caravans for $25.

Places to Eat

The *Original Fish & Chip Shop* on Ocean St has good fish & chips for under $8. The *Hotel Victor* provides speedy service and the best counter meals in town for $6 to $11. The *Ocean Chinese Restaurant* on Ocean St has good and reasonably priced meals at around $8. A three-course dinner at the classier *Apollon Restaurant* on Torrens St will be about $23.

GOOLWA (population 1600)

On Lake Alexandrina near the mouth of the Murray, Goolwa initially rose to prominence with the growth of trade along the mighty Murray. The Murray mouth then silted up and large ships were unable to get up to Goolwa so a railway line, the first in South Australia, was built from Goolwa to nearby Port Elliot. In the 1880s a new railway line to Adelaide spelt the end for Goolwa as a port town.

Today Goolwa is a popular resort with a number of interesting old buildings including the National Trust museum in the 1852 house, the first built in the area. The old paddle steamer *Captain Sturt* can be seen in the town and on the main street there's a horse-drawn railway carriage from the early days of the railway line. Goolwa is an access point to the Coorong Park. This long stretch of beach to the mouth of the Murray can be driven along; there's a ferry crossing over to Hindmarsh Island. You can also take cruises on Lake Alexandrina on the MV *Aroona* or PS *Mundoo* from $11.

Goolwa is the departure point for up-river cruises on the *Murray River Queen*. Milang, on Lake Alexandrina was a centre for the river trade even before Goolwa. In the early days of the river-shipping business, bullock wagons carried goods overland between here and Adelaide.

There's a Goolwa Tourist Office on the corner of Cadell St and Single Point.

Places to Stay & Eat

The *Corio Hotel* (tel 55 2011) on Railway Terrace, has singles/doubles for $23/35 with breakfast. The *River Murray Caravan Park* (tel 55 2144) on Liverpool Rd has tent sites for $6 and on-site vans from $23 for two people.

Goolwa has pubs with counter meals, a variety of fast food places including *Charcoal Chickens*, a health food shop and the *Goolwa Chinese Restaurant*.

STRATHALBYN (population 1750)

Situated on the Angas River well inland from the coast, this picturesque town was settled back in 1839 by Scottish immigrants. St Andrew's Church, the original 'kirk', is one of the best known country churches in Australia. It was built in 1848 and its tower overlooks the river. There's also an attractive memorial gardens on the river banks with a large contingent of resident water birds.

The town has many old buildings with a distinctly Scottish flavour to them: there's a National Trust pioneer museum ($1 admission), an old police station and court house, a historical folk museum, the Angas flour mill of 1852; in all, enough reminders of the region's early history to qualify Strathalbyn as a 'heritage town'.

Places to Stay & Eat

The *Commercial Hotel* has rooms for $17 per person including breakfast. At the *Strathalbyn Caravan Park* (tel 36 2223) on Coronation Rd sites for two are $7.

The *Terminus* and the *Commercial Hotels* have reasonable counter meals or there's *Strath Eats*, a cafe and pizza bar. Eat early – on Mondays in winter you can find everything shut by 7 pm.

The Barossa Valley

South Australia's famous valley vies with the Hunter Valley in NSW as the best known wine-producing area in Australia. The gently sloping valley is about 40 km long and five to 11 km wide. The Barossa turns out a quarter of all the wine in Australia, and since it is only about 50 km from Adelaide, it's a very popular place to visit.

The Barossa still has some German flavour from its original settlement in 1842. Fleeing religious persecution in Prussia and Silesia, those first settlers weren't wine makers but fortunately someone soon came along and recognised the valley's potential. The name, curiously enough, is actually a misspelling of

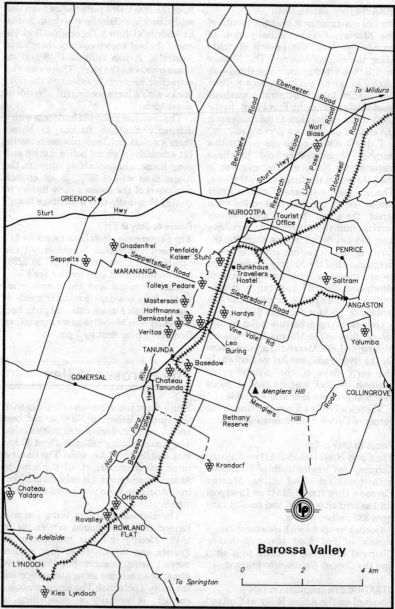

Barossa Valley

To Mildura

Ebeneezer Road

Belvidere Road

Wolf Blass

Sturt Hwy Road

Research Road

Light Pass Road

Stockwell Road

GREENOCK

Sturt Hwy

NURIOOTPA

Tourist Office

PENRICE

Gnadenfrei

Seppelts

Seppeltsfield Road

Penfolds/ Kaiser Stuhl

Bunkhaus Travellers Hostel

Saltram

MARANANGA

Tolleys Pedare

Masterson

Hoffmanns

Bernkastel

Siegersdorf Road

Hardys

ANGASTON

Veritas

Vine Vale Rd

Leo Buring

Yalumba

TANUNDA

Basedow

GOMERSAL

Chateau Tanunda

Menglers Hill

COLLINGROVE

Bethany Reserve

Menglers Hill Road

North Para River

Barossa Valley Hwy

Krondorf

Chateau Yaldara

Orlando

Rovalley

ROWLAND FLAT

Kies Lyndoch

LYNDOCH

To Adelaide

To Springton

0   2   4 km

Barrosa in Spain, close to where the Spanish sherry comes from. Prior to WW I the Barossa probably sounded even more Germanic because during the war many German place names were patriotically Anglicised. When the jingoistic fervour died down some were changed back.

There is a variety of places to stay in the Barossa and a leisurely tastings crawl around the various wineries is a popular activity for visitors. On first impressions, this area is a little disappointing since it's rather wide and flat; from the central road it doesn't really appear very valley-like at all. Furthermore, that main road through Lyndoch, Tanunda and Nuriootpa (the main towns) is rather busy and noisy – not at all like the peaceful valley you might expect. You must get off the main road to begin to appreciate the Barossa. Take the scenic drive between Angaston and Tanunda or the palm-fringed road to Seppeltsfield and Marananga; wander through the sleepy historic settlement of Bethany.

Information
There's a tourist information centre in Coulthard House at 66 Murray St, Nuriootpa.

Lyndoch (population 1500)
Coming up from Adelaide, Lyndoch (at the foot of the low Barossa Range) is the first valley town. The fine old Pewsey Vale Homestead is near Lyndoch.

Tanunda (population 3200)
In the centre of the valley is Tanunda, the most Germanic of the towns. You can still see some early cottages around Goat Square, the site of the original Ziegenmarkt. The Tanunda Hotel, originally built in 1845, was damaged by fire in 1895 and rebuilt 10 years later.

At 47 Murray St there's the Barossa Valley Historical Museum with exhibits on the valley's early settlement; it's open from Monday to Friday from 1 to 5 pm and on weekends from 2 to 5 pm. Storybook Cottage (admission $3) on Oak St is a park created for children.

The Kev Rohrlach Collection on the main road between Nuriootpa and Tanunda is a private museum of transport, aviation, history and technology. It's open daily from 9 am to 5 pm, admission is $3. There are also a number of art and craft galleries around the town.

There are fine old churches in all the valley towns but Tanunda has some of the most interesting. The Tabor church dates from 1849 and is Lutheran, as is the 1868 St John's Church with its life-size wooden statues of Christ, Moses, and the apostles Peter, Paul and John.

From Tanunda, turn off the main road and take the scenic drive through Bethany and via Mengler Hill to Angaston. It runs through beautiful, peaceful country; the view over the valley from Mengler Hill is especially good.

Nuriootpa (population 3200)
At the north end of the valley Nuriootpa, known locally as 'Nuri', is the commercial centre of the Barossa. Coulthard House, the home of a pioneer settler in the 1840s, is now used as the local tourist information centre. Nuriootpa also has several pleasant picnic grounds and a swimming pool in the park. The town was once a stopping place on the way to the copper mines at Burra.

Angaston (population 1900)
On the eastern side of the valley, this town was named after George Fife Angas, one of the area's pioneers. Collingrove is a fine old homestead built by his son in 1853 and now owned by the National Trust; it's open from Wednesday to Sunday from 10 am to 4.30 pm between 1 October and 31 May.

Other Places
Bethany, near Tanunda, was the first German settlement in the valley. There's an Art & Craft Gallery in a fine old restored cottage. Old cottages still stand

around the Bethany reserve and the Landhaus is claimed to be the smallest hotel in the world. Gomersal is near Tanunda and trained sheep dogs go through their paces here at Breezy Gully on Monday, Wednesday and Saturday at 2 pm.

Springton, in the south-east of the valley, has the Herbig tree – an enormous hollow gum tree where a pioneer settler lived with his family from 1855 to 1860.

Wineries

The Barossa has over 50 wineries; many of them are open to the public and offer guided tours or free wine tastings. Get a copy of the SAGTC's Barossa leaflet for full details of locations and opening hours.

Some of the most interesting wineries include:

Chateau Yaldara at Lyndoch. Established in 1947 in the ruins of a 19th-century winery and flour mill it has a notable art collection which can be seen on conducted tours.

Gramp's Orlando at Rowland Flat, between Lyndoch and Tanunda, was established in 1847 and is one of the oldest wineries in the valley.

Krondorf at Tanunda is currently one of the glamour wine makers with a high reputation for their wine.

Chateau Tanunda also in Tanunda, is a magnificent old bluestone building built in 1889 but it is not open to the public.

Leo Buring Chateau Leonay is also in Tanunda and is another winery fantasy with turrets and towers although it dates only from 1945.

Seppelts in Seppeltsfield was founded in 1852; the old bluestone buildings are surrounded by gardens and date palms. The extensive complex includes a picnic area with gas barbecues. There is also a family mausoleum.

Kaiser Stuhl and Penfolds in Nuriootpa have recently combined, becoming one of the largest wineries in the southern hemisphere. The imposing building fronts the main road. This is a very large, commercial winery but they have an excellent winery tour.

Yalumba in Angaston was founded way back in 1849; the blue marble winery topped by a clock tower and surrounded by gardens is the largest family owned winery in the valley.

Saltrams also in Angaston is another old winery. Established in 1859, it has friendly and informative staff.

Wolf Blass out beyond Nuriootpa was only founded in 1973, but by a combination of excellent wines and clever marketing they've quickly become one of the best known wine makers in Australia.

There are plenty of other wineries around the valley and often the smaller, less well-known places like the Rockfords Winery, Henschke or the Bethany Winery can be the most interesting to visit.

Barossa Events

The Vintage Festival is the Barossa's big event, taking place over seven days starting from Easter Monday in odd-numbered years (1991, 1993, etc). The colourful festival features processions, brass bands, games of tug-of-war between the wineries, maypole dancing and, of course, a lot of wine tasting. It's not the only Barossa occasion though: there is an Oom Pah Fest in January, Essenfest in March, Folk Festival in April, Hot Air Balloon Regatta in May, Classic Gourmet Weekend in August and Brass Band Competition in November.

Of course the main events in the Barossa move with the grape-growing seasons. It takes four to five years for grape vines to reach maturity after they are first planted in September to October. Their useful life is usually around 40 years. The vines are pruned back heavily during the winter months (July-August) and then grow and produce fruit over the summer. The busiest months in the valley are from March to early May when the grapes are harvested during the vintage season. The majority of the grapes are actually grown by small independent growers who sell them to the large wine-making firms.

After harvesting, the grapes are crushed and the fermentation process is started by the addition of yeast. Red wines get their colouring not from the use of red grapes but from leaving the grape skins in with the juice during fermentation. With white wines, the skins are separated and the juice is fermented alone. Wines are usually aged in wood casks, but white wines are not usually aged before they are bottled. Many of the wineries give free tours from which you can develop a better understanding of the wine-making process.

Places to Stay

Hostels The *Bunkhaus Travellers Hostel* (tel (085) 62 2260) is a km outside Nurioopta on the main highway between Nurioopta and Tanunda (look for the keg on the corner). It's a pleasant, well kept little place with room for 12 at $8.50 per night plus a double unit. You can even drink your Barossa wine with dinner. The helpful owners have bicycles for hire and the Adelaide/Barossa bus will stop at the door on request.

The *Kersbrook YHA Hostel* (tel (08) 389 3185) is at Roachdale Farm, 20 km south of Lyndoch and costs $4. Buses run to Chain of Ponds, eight km from the hostel, but not on weekends; you'll need your own transport to visit the valley.

Hotels & Motels There are some reasonably priced hotels. Starting from the northern end in Nurioopta, the *Vine Inn Hotel* (tel (085) 62 2133), right in the middle of town at 14 Murray St, has comfortable rooms at $65. Also in Nurioopta, the *Angas Park Hotel* (tel (085) 62 1050) at 22 Murray St is cheap at $17 per person including a light breakfast. The *Karawatha Guest House* (tel (085) 62 1746) on Greenock Rd costs $28 per person including breakfast. The *Barossa Gateway Motel* (tel (085) 62 1033) on Kalimna Rd is one of the cheaper motels in the valley at $32/49.

Angaston has the *Barossa Brauhaus* (tel (085) 64 2014) at 41 Murray St, a fine hotel with bed & breakfast rates of $22 per person. Just down the street at No 59 is the *Angaston Hotel* (tel (085) 64 2428) with bed & breakfast at $18 per person. Good for a splurge in Angaston is the National Trust's 1856 *Collingrove Homestead* (tel (085) 64 2061). The two rooms are part of the old servants' quarters and the rate of $54 for two people includes breakfast.

Tanunda has the reasonable *Tanunda Hotel* (tel (085) 63 2030) at 51 Murray St with singles/doubles from $23/34. In Lyndoch, the *Lyndoch Hotel* (tel (085) 24 4211) on Gilbert St is $17 per person. Five km north of Tanunda on Nuriap Rd, a family offers accommodation at $7 per person. They only have one room with a double and a single bed. Phone 62 2260 before 10 am or after 6 pm to get directions.

The tourist office has a list of 'alternative' accommodation in the valley, but most are a bit pricey ranging from $30 to $70 for two.

Camping There are camping sites in Lyndoch, Tanunda and Nurioopta. They've all got on-site vans and the Lyndoch site also has cabins. The pleasant campground in Nurioopta goes one better; they have possums who come down from the trees at night and monster you for their share of whatever's going down in the eats department.

Barossa Caravan Park (tel (085) 24 4262), Barossa Valley Highway, Lyndoch; camping $7.50, on-site vans from $25, cabins from $27.
Barossa Valley Tourist Park (tel (085) 62 1404), Penrice Rd, Nurioopta; camping $8.50 for two, on-site vans from $21, cabins from $28.
Langmeil Rd Caravan Park (no phone), two km from PO, Tanunda; camping $6.50 for two.
Tanunda Caravan & Tourist Park (tel (085) 63 2784), Barossa Valley Highway, Tanunda; camping $8.50 for two, on-site vans from $28, cabins $30.

Places to Eat

Nurioopta The *Zinfandel Tea Rooms* at 58 Murray St specialises in light lunches and continental cakes. The *Vine Inn Hotel* at 14 Murray St is good for reasonably priced counter meals. *Die Weinstube Restaurant*, south of Nuriootpa, is very pleasant with its outdoor eating area. The valley is famed for its fine bakeries and bread. Linke's *Nuriootpa Bakery* at 40 Murray St is one of the best and is also a good place for breakfast.

Tanunda The valley is renowned for its solid, German-style eating places but most of them tend to be decidedly expensive. One definite exception is the *Heinemann Park Restaurant*, just on the Adelaide side of Tanunda, directly opposite the caravan park. It's simple and reasonably priced with main courses from $7.50 to $10. *Die Gallerie Restaurant* in Tanunda is an atmospheric place with hewn beams, open fireplaces and an outdoor eating area. Meals range from $10 to $15.

At 51 Murray St the *Tanunda Hotel* has a nice lounge with counter meals in the $7 to $9 bracket. The *Apex Bakery* on Elizabeth St uses wood-fired ovens.

Lyndoch The valley's only true German-style bakery is the *Lyndoch Bakery & Restaurant* off the Barossa Valley Highway in Lyndoch. They have many varieties of rye, wheat and other breads and rolls. The restaurant's menu features traditional Bavarian dishes at $6 to $11 and huge cakes. It's open daily except Mondays, from breakfast until 6 pm.

Getting There & Away

There are several routes from Adelaide to the valley; the most direct one is via the Main North Rd through Elizabeth and Gawler. More picturesque routes go through the Torrens Gorge, Chain of Ponds and Williamstown or via Chain of Ponds and Birdwood.

There is a privately owned Adelaide/Barossa bus service which operates from the Franklin St bus terminal in Adelaide, takes 1½ hours and costs $6.40

Getting Around

Valley Tours (book at the tourist office in Nuriootpa) offer a good day-tour of the Barossa for $20, a three course lunch is included. A flight over the valley also costs $20 (tel (085) 22 5603 for bookings) or a hot air balloon flight costs $120 (contact the tourist office for details).

Keil's in Tanunda and the Nariootpa Caravan Park rent bicycles or the Golden Fleece petrol station in Tanunda rents mopeds. Otherwise a car is nice to have in the valley, but don't plan on very much wine tasting if you're driving.

North of Adelaide

Two main routes run north of Adelaide. The first runs to Gawler where you can turn east to the Barossa Valley and the Riverland area, or continue north through Burra to Peterborough where you have the option of turning north-west to the Flinders Ranges or continuing on the Barrier Highway to the north-east for the long, dull run to Broken Hill in New South Wales. The second route from Adelaide heads off slightly north-west through Wakefield, then to Port Pirie and Port Augusta on the Spencer Gulf. You can then travel to the Flinders or the Eyre Peninsula or simply head west towards Western Australia.

This area to the north of Adelaide includes some of the most fertile and pleasant land in the state. Sunshine, rainfall and excellent soil combine to make this a prosperous agricultural region with excellent wine-making areas like the Clare Valley. Apart from the two main routes north there is a network of smaller roads which crisscross this region.

ADELAIDE TO THE BAROSSA

On the way north to the Barossa or Clare valleys you pass through Elizabeth, an industrial satellite city of Adelaide with major automotive manufacturing plants.

Gawler, just after the turn-off from the Sturt Highway to the Barossa, is on the edge of the valley. Like Adelaide it was planned by Colonel Light and the old telegraph station, built in 1860, now houses a Folk Museum which is open from Tuesdays to Thursdays from 2 to 4 pm. There is also a National Trust Telecom Telecommunications Museum in the same building – open the same hours, plus on Sundays from 2 to 5 pm.

Getting There & Away
The Adelaide/Barossa bus service runs through Gawler and continues all the way to Kapunda for $5.90.

KAPUNDA (population 1350)
About 80 km north of Adelaide and a little north of the Barossa Valley, Kapunda is actually off the main roads which head north, but you can take a pleasant backroads route from the valley through the town and join the Barrier Highway a little further north. Copper was found here in 1842 and Kapunda became the first mining town in Australia and for a while was the biggest country town in South Australia. At its peak, it had a population of 10,000 with 22 hotels but the mines closed in 1888.

There's a lookout point in the town with views over the old open-cut mines and mine chimneys. Kapunda has a Historical Museum with old mining relics plus the old courthouse and jail tearooms – a good place for a country-style tea. An eight-metre high bronze statue of 'Map Kernow' (the Son of Cornwall in old Cornish) stands at the Adelaide end of town as a tribute to pioneer miners. It's a pleasant drive north-east of Kapunda to Eudunda.

CLARE (population 2400)
This pleasant little town, 135 km north of Adelaide, is another important wine producing centre although it is far less commercial than the Barossa. It was originally settled in 1842 and named after County Clare in Ireland. Over Easter, Clare has the Irish Affair Festival with art exhibitions, horse races, wine tastings and other events.

The first vines were planted here in 1848 by Jesuit priests and communion wines are produced to this day. The Jesuit's St Aloysius Church dates from 1875 and the associated Sevenhill Cellars still produce some fine wines. There are many other wineries in the valley including the well-known Stanley Wine Company, dating from 1894.

The town has a number of interesting buildings including, in what seems to be a South Australian norm, a police station/courthouse dating from 1850 which is preserved as a National Trust museum. The Bungaree Station is a working property with many historical exhibits and can be seen only on a half hour tour (minimum of eight people) which can be booked by phoning 42 2677. The Wolta Wolta Homestead dates from 1864, while Christison Park has a fauna and flora reserve and picnic grounds. At the Pioneer Memorial Park there are walking trails and barbecue facilities.

Clare has a Tourist Office in the town hall at 229 Main St.

Places to Stay & Eat
On Main St the *Taminga Hotel* (tel (088) 42 2808) and the *Clare Hotel* (tel (088) 42 2816) are basic country hotels with rooms from $13 to $34. There are several motels in town including a motel section at *Bentley's Hotel* (tel (088) 42 2815) on Main St at $40/52. The *Clare Central Motel* (tel (088) 42 2277) at 325 Main North Rd is more expensive. The *Christison Park Caravan Park* (tel (088) 42 2724) is the closest camping ground to town and has sites for $8 or on-site vans for $23.

On the main street the *Pantry Plus Coffee Shop* is good and the *Clare Valley Cafe* offers cheap basic food.

Getting There & Away
You can visit the Barossa on your way

north to the Clare Valley and in turn Clare can be visited en route to the Flinders Ranges. If you are driving from Adelaide turn off at Watervale for the scenic 22 km drive to Clare. It takes you through country little changed since before white settlement. There's a daily bus to Riverton which connects to trains to Adelaide. The daily Stateliner bus from Adelaide costs $10.

BURRA (population 1200)

This really pretty little town was a copper-mining centre from 1847 to 1877. The district Burra Burra takes it name from the Hindi word for 'great great' according to one account, from the name of the creek according to another.

Information

The Tourist Office in Market Square in the middle of town is open 10 am to 4 pm daily. They have an interesting *Burra Historic Tour* booklet and also hold the keys to the miners dugouts, the old jail and the powder magazine.

Around Town

The town has many solid, old stone buildings and tiny Cornish cottages and

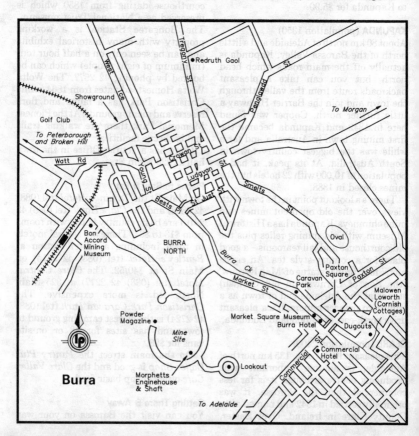

Burra

numerous reminders of the mining days. On Market St near the tourist office, there's the Jinker which was a 12 metre long, 4½ ton wooden vehicle built to carry the boiler for Morphetts Enginehouse from Port Adelaide to Burra. The Market Square Museum is also across from the tourist office.

The 33 cottages at Paxton Square were built for Cornish miners in the 1850s and have been restored by the National Trust. In Burra's early days nearly 1500 people lived in dugouts by the creek and a couple of these old miners' dugouts have been preserved. The historic tour booklet describes many other interesting old buildings including Redruth Gaol and more Cornish cottages on Truro St, north of the centre.

The Bon Accord Museum is on the site of an original mine. It's open from Thursday to Monday, admission is $2. There's a lookout over the town at the old mine site, near the powder magazine and Morphetts Enginehouse and mineshaft. Mining ceased in Burra back in 1877 and the town became an agricultural centre but in 1969 mining recommenced and continued until 1981 when it closed down again. The big open-cut site by the lookout is from that second short period of mining.

Beyond the Town

Burra Gorge and picnic area is 27 km from town on the Morgan road. North of Burra the country rapidly becomes drier and more barren. From the road you'll see plenty of galahs and possibly the odd emu. In the early morning or evening you may also see kangaroos although driving along the road to Broken Hill during the '82 drought the number of dead roos was phenomenal – they were almost continuous all the way to the New South Wales border. Over one five km stretch I counted 47 recently killed. The unfortunate animals are attracted by the roadside vegetation which grows because of water run-off from the road.

Places to Stay & Eat

The *Burra Hotel* (tel (088) 92 2389) has singles/doubles at $19/32 or you can camp at the *Burra Caravan Park* (tel (088) 92 2442) for $7 or rent an on-site van for $21. *Rooms with a View* (tel 92 2069) at 3 Mt Pleasant Rd has very pleasant rooms with open fireplaces and great views over the town for $75.

The *Burra Hotel* has very good counter meals and you can get a good cheap lunch at *Polly's Tea Rooms*.

Getting There & Away

Murtons AB Coaches will get you to Burra from Adelaide's Central Bus Station for $11.20, but there is no public transport between Clare and Burra only 43 km away.

PORT PIRIE (population 14,700)

Just 84 km south of Port Augusta at the northern end of the Spencer Gulf, this is a major port and industrial centre with huge lead smelters that handle the output sent down by rail from Broken Hill. There are tours of the smelters on weekday afternoons. It's also an important port for shipping of agricultural produce and just happens to be the home of country & western music in South Australia.

Port Pirie has lots of interesting old buildings including some fine hotels down the main street of the town. On Ellen St, the National Trust Museum includes the ornate old railway station, the old police station and the customs house. Carn Brae is an old house with turn of the century furniture, paintings and other memorabilia. Near Port Pirie there's an interesting museum on Weerona Island, 13 km out, and the Telowie Gorge park is also within easy reach.

Places to Stay & Eat

The *International Hotel* (tel (086) 32 2422) on Ellen St has rooms from $18/28. The *Port Pirie Caravan Park* (tel (086) 32 4275) has sites for $6 or on-site vans for $18. Port Pirie has plenty of fish & chip take-aways and other places like the *Cafe*

Lunch Inn or the *Port Pirie Chinese Restaurant*.

BALAKLAVA (population 1300)

This picturesque town on the northern edge of the Adelaide plains has a National Trust museum open on Sundays. It's a short trip from here to Wakefield at the northern end of Gulf St Vincent.

You can stay at the *Balaklava Hotel* or the *Balaklava Caravan Park* (tel (088) 62 1795). The *Family Affair Coffee Lounge* has good food. Premier have a bus on weekdays between Adelaide and Balaklava for $7.50.

OTHER MID-NORTH TOWNS

Jamestown, north of the Clare Valley, at the southern edge of the Flinders Ranges, is a country town with a Railway Station Museum open Sundays from 2 to 4 pm.

Peterborough is another gateway town to the Flinders. This is an important railway centre and also a place where the problems railway engineers in Australia have to cope with are clearly illustrated. The colonial bungling which led to Australia's mixed up railway system managed to run three different railway gauges through Peterborough! Steamtown is a working railway museum and on holiday weekends, narrow-gauge steam-train trips set out from Peterborough. The old town hall in Peterborough is now a museum and art gallery.

North from here into the Flinders, a land boom in the 1870s took place as settlers, encouraged by easy credit from the South Australian government, established farming towns. Sturdy farms and towns sprung up, but the wet seasons that had encouraged hopes of wheat farming soon gave way to the normal dry conditions and as the land dried out, the towns tumbled into ruins. Some of the most interesting reminders of those days can be seen in the southern Flinders.

Kangaroo Island

Population 4000

The third biggest island in Australia (after Tasmania and Melville Island off Darwin in the Northern Territory), Kangaroo Island is a popular holiday resort for Adelaide. It's about 110 km from Adelaide to Kingscote, the main town on the island, but the north-east corner of Kangaroo Island is actually only 13 km off the southern tip of the Fleurieu Peninsula. Kangaroo Island is about 150 km long by 30 km wide, but sparsely populated. It offers superb scenery; pleasant, sheltered beaches along the north coast; a rough, rugged and wave-swept south coast plus lots of native wildlife. The island also has excellent fishing.

Like other islands off the south coast of Australia, Kangaroo Island had a rough and ready early history with sealers, whalers and escaped convicts all playing their often-ruthless part. Many of the place names around the island have a distinctly French flavour since it was first charted by the French explorer Nicholas Baudin. He had just met Matthew Flinders, who was in the process of circumnavigating Australia, at nearby Encounter Bay off Victor Harbor. Flinders had already named the island after the many kangaroos he saw there, but Baudin went on to name many other prominent features. Apart from beaches, bushwalks and wildlife, the island also has more than its fair share of shipwrecks. A number of interest to scuba divers.

Kingscote (population 1250)

The main town on Kangaroo Island, Kingscote is also the arrival point for the ferries and flights to the island. This was actually the first settlement in South Australia, although it was soon superseded by Adelaide and other mainland centres. Although there were other Europeans on the island many years earlier, Kingscote

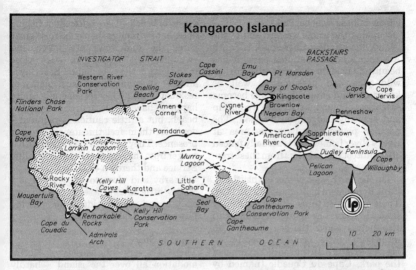

was formally settled in 1836 and all but abandoned a few years later.

There's a rock pool for swimming and Brownlow Beach is also a good swimming place. The old cottage 'Hope', built in 1858, is a National Trust museum and the headstones in Kingscote's cemetery make interesting reading. St Alban's Church, built in 1884 has beautiful stained-glass windows.

American River (population 120)

Between Kingscote and Penneshaw the small settlement of American River takes its name from the group of American sealers who built a boat here in 1803-4. The town is on a small peninsula and shelters an inner bay, named Pelican Lagoon by Flinders, which today is a bird sanctuary. American River is a popular tourist resort, good for sailing and fishing.

Penneshaw

Looking across the narrow Backstairs Passage to the Fleurieu Peninsula, Penneshaw is a quiet little resort town with a pleasant beach at Hog's Bay and

the tiny inlet of Christmas Cove as a boat harbour. You can sometimes see penguins on the rocks below the town. Frenchman's Rock is a monument housing a replica of the rock Baudin left here in 1803. The actual rock he marked to note his visit is now in the South Australian Art Gallery. The Old Penneshaw School houses a folk museum with exhibits showing the history of the district.

The Dudley Peninsula, the knob of land on the eastern end of the island on which Penneshaw is located, has several other points of interest. There's surf at Pennington Bay and the sheltered waters of Chapman River are very popular for canoeing. The Cape Willoughby lighthouse, the oldest in South Australia, first operated in 1852; it's open from 1 to 3.30 pm Monday to Friday.

North Coast

There are a series of fine sheltered beaches along the north coast of the island. Near Kingscote, Emu Bay has a beautiful, long sweep of sand. Other good beaches include Stokes Bay, Snelling Beach and the sheltered, sandy stretch of Snug Cove.

Flinders Chase National Park

Occupying the whole western end of the island, the Flinders Chase park is South Australia's largest national park. It has beautiful eucalyptus forests with koalas, wild pigs and possums as well as kangaroos and emus which have become so fearless of humans that they'll come up and brazenly badger you for food. The popular picnic and barbecue area at Rocky River homestead is actually fenced off to protect park visitors from these freeloaders.

On the north-west corner of the island, Cape Borda has a lighthouse built in 1858. There are guided tours Monday to Friday from 2 to 4 pm. The lighthouse is on a cliff 150 metres above the sea. There's an interesting little cemetery nearby at Harvey's Return. In the southern corner of the park, Cape du Couedic (named by Nicholas Baudin, of course) is wild, remote and rugged. An extremely picturesque lighthouse built in 1906 tops the cape; you can follow the path from the car park down to Admirals Arch – a natural archway pounded by towering seas. You can often see seals and penguins here.

At Kirkpatrick Point, only a couple of km east of Cape du Couedic, the Remarkable Rocks are a series of bizarre granite rocks on a huge dome stretching 75 metres down to the sea. You can camp at the Rocky River park headquarters, or elsewhere with a permit.

South Coast

The south coast of the island is rough and wave-swept compared with the north coast. At Hanson Bay, close to Cape du Couedic at the western end of the coast, there's a colony of fairy penguins. A little further east you come to Kelly Hill Caves, a series of limestone caves discovered in the 1880s when a horse – appropriately named Ned Kelly – fell through a hole in the ground. There are tours hourly to 3.30 pm.

Vivonne Bay has a long and beautiful

sweep of beach. There is excellent fishing here, but swimmers should exercise great care; the undertows are fierce and swimmers are advised to stick close to the jetty or the river mouth. Seal Bay is another sweeping beach with plenty of resident seals. They're generally quite happy to have two-legged visitors on the beach, but a little caution is required – don't let them feel threatened by your presence. They can only be visited with a ranger from the National Parks & Wildlife Service and there's a $2.50 fee.

Nearby and close to the south coast road is 'little Sahara', a series of enormous white sand dunes, ideal for playing Lawrence of Arabia.

Places to Stay

There is a very wide variety of accommodation all over the island – hardly surprising for such a popular holiday resort – including three associate youth hostels.

Hostels The *Penneshaw Youth Hostel* (tel (0848) 31 173) costs $8.50 and the same people also operate the *Flinders Chase Youth Hostel*, bookings are essential. The *Hill Farm Hostel* (tel (0848) 22 778) is at Brownlow Beach, four km from Kingscote, and costs $9.50. Transport from Kingscote can be arranged.

Hotels & Motels All the Penneshaw hotels and motels are closed in the mid-winter month of July. In American River the *Linnetts Island Club* (tel (0848) 33 053) has rooms for $22 per person. In Kingscote *Ellsons Seaview* (tel (0848) 22 030) on Chapman Terrace has rooms from $57. Penneshaw has the expensive *Sorrento Resort Motel* (tel (0848) 31 028).

Camping & Holiday Flats There are numerous camping sites and a wide selection of holiday flats, in some cases costing under $35 a night with room for four to six. On a weekly basis costs are even lower.

They include cabins at the *Ravine Wildlife Park* (tel (0848) 93 256) at Flinders Chase; *Beachfront Cottages* (tel Adelaide 332 1083) or the *Hoey House* (tel Adelaide 47 5837) in Penneshaw; *Eleanor River Holiday Cabins* (tel (0848) 94 250) in Vivonne Bay and *Cranmore Holiday Flats* (tel (0848) 33 020) in American River. All these places have rooms at $17 to $34.

Watch out for kangaroos if you are camping in the Flinders Chase National Park. They get into tents looking for food and can cause a lot of damage. A camping permit is required from the park ranger.

Getting There & Away
Air Air Transit (tel (08) 352 3128) have daily services to American River, Kingscote and Penneshaw from Adelaide. If you fly into American River you must arrange a transfer into town. Lloyd Aviation (tel (08) 224 7500) have a daily Adelaide/Kingscote service and can be booked through Australian Airlines. Albatross Airlines fly Adelaide/Kingscote twice daily. One way fares are $45 to $55, advance purchase return fares are available on certain off-peak flights.

Ferry The *Island Seaway* crosses to Kingscote from Port Adelaide from two to four times weekly, depending on the season. The crossing takes 6½ hours and costs $26. Accompanied bicycles cost $3.20, motorcycles $25 and cars $76.

Once weekly the ferry continues to Port Lincoln on the Eyre Peninsula and returns. From Port Lincoln the rates are the same as from Adelaide. There are some seasonal variations in summer, over school holidays and on public holidays. Shipping agents are R W Miller (tel 47 5577), 3 Todd St, Port Adelaide. In Kingscote you can find R W Miller (tel (0848) 22 273) on Commercial Rd.

You can also get to Kangaroo Island on the *Philanderer III* from Cape Jervis. The crossing takes about an hour and there are two or three services a day at $44 return;

YHA members get a discount. The King Island Connection (tel 272 6680 after 6 pm) bus service from Adelaide costs $8 one way and leaves twice daily from the Central Bus Station to connect with sailings to Kangaroo Island. For ferry bookings, phone Philanderer Ferries in Penneshaw on (0848) 31 122.

Getting Around
There's an airport bus running from the Kangaroo Island Airport to Kingscote for $3. Kingscote Taxi & Tours Service provides a daily service between American River, Kingscote (town and airport) and Penneshaw; advance booking is usually necessary (tel (0848) 22 640). The Penneshaw YH runs a link-up bus to their other hostel stopping along the way at Seal Bay, Kelly Hill Caves, Admirals Arch and the Remarkable Rocks.

There are a variety of rental cars and motorcycles; the SAGTC has a car hire leaflet for the island. The 'big three' have agencies and there are a number of independent operators with typical charges being a Laser for $49 with 200 free km per day plus 25c a km after that. Cheaper is Kangaroo Island Rental Cars (tel (0848) 22 390) in Kingscote with unlimited km rates of $40 per day plus $5 insurance.

It's possible, but often difficult, to hitch around the island. Hitching is especially difficult in the off-season. Bicycling is also hard work as the roads are mainly gravel and get very dusty. The distances are surprisingly large also; from Penneshaw to Cape Borda is 140 km. Bicycles can be hired from Kingscote Take-away (tel (0848) 22 585) in Kingscote, Linnet's Island Club (tel (0848) 33 053) in American River, and the Sorrento Motel (tel (0848) 31 028) in Penneshaw. Scooters can be hired from the Penneshaw YH (tel (0848) 31 173).

The South-East

The south-east of South Australia is the area through which most travellers between Melbourne and Adelaide pass. Between the two cities you can either take the Western-Dukes Highway or the Princes Highway through the south-east region.

The Western-Dukes is the most direct route between the two cities (729 km) but the Dukes Highway stretch in South Australia is not terribly exciting – it just runs through a lot of flat, dull, agricultural land. South of this route there is some rather more interesting country and you can take slightly longer detours, but the Princes Highway along the coast is of greater interest. Along this road from Victoria you pass through Mt Gambier with its impressive crater lakes and then along the extensive coastal lagoon system known as the Coorong.

Getting There & Away

Air Kendell fly Melbourne/Mt Gambier/Adelaide most days of the week. The fare is $110 Melbourne/Mt Gambier or Adelaide/Mt Gambier. There's also an $88 standby fare from Adelaide. O'Conners Air Services also fly between Adelaide and Mt Gambier.

Bus Mt Gambier Motor Service (tel 217 0777) operates from the Central Bus Station in Adelaide to Mt Gambier six days a week. The trip takes about six hours and fares are Kingston $22, Robe $23.80, Millicent or Mt Gambier $24. Greyhound operate Adelaide/Melbourne via the Princes Highway once a week. The fares to Mt Gambier are $42 from Melbourne, $33 from Adelaide.

Train Phone 217 4455 for rail bookings in Adelaide. There are services between Adelaide and Mt Gambier most days of the week. The trains follow the Melbourne line to just beyond Bordertown before turning south to Naracoorte and Mt Gambier. Adelaide/Mt Gambier takes about eight hours. Fares from Adelaide are Bordertown $19, Naracoorte or Mt Gambier $23.

MENINGIE (population 400)

On the southern edge of Lake Albert and at the north of the Coorong, this small town is a popular gateway to the Coorong. A wide variety of water sports is available on Lake Albert and there are also good bushwalks in the area. The bird life around Meningie is prolific – a wide range of water birds can be seen.

THE COORONG

The Coorong is a unique national park – a long, narrow strip curving along the coast for 145 km south of Adelaide. The northern end is marked by Lake Alexandrina where the Murray reaches the sea; the southern end is marked by the small town of Kingston SE. Consisting of a long, narrow, shallow lagoon and a complex series of salt pans – all separated from the sea by the huge sand dunes of the Younghusband Peninsula, more usually known as the Hummocks – the whole area is a superb natural bird sanctuary with vast numbers of water birds. Cormorants, ibis, swans, terns, shags, ducks and others can all be seen, but it is the pelicans for which the Coorong is best known. *Storm Boy*, the story about a young boy's friendship with a pelican, was filmed on the Coorong. At Salt Creek you can take the nature trail turn-off from the Princes Highway and follow the old road which runs along the shore of the Coorong for some distance.

KINGSTON SE (population 1300)

At the southern end of the Coorong, Kingston is a popular beach resort and a good base for visits to the Coorong. The town was originally named Maria Creek after a ship wrecked at Cape Jaffa in 1840. No lives were lost in the actual shipwreck, but as the 27 crew and

Top: Adelaide Festival Centre, SA (TW)
Bottom: Supermarket mural, Coober Pedy, SA (TW)

Top: Sign on the Eyre Highway, Nullarbor Plain, SA (RN)
Left: Ghost gum, Wilpena Pound, Flinders Ranges, SA (TW)
Right: Glenelg, Adelaide, SA (TW)

passengers made their way south towards Lake Albert they were all massacred by Aborigines. There's a memorial to the *Maria* in Kingston, but it's said that Policeman's Point was named as the place where white man's retribution caught up with the Aborigines.

Other attractions are the National Trust Pioneer Museum and the nearby Cape Jaffa Lighthouse which is open from 2 to 5 pm daily. Kingston is a centre for rock lobster fishing but Kingston's best known lobster – and a major landmark in its own right – is hardly edible. Towering by the roadside, it's 'The Big Lobster' – a superb piece of Australian kitsch; the amazingly realistic lobster is made of fibreglass and steel and marks a tourist centre with restaurants, souvenirs, information and other tourist needs. You can, however, buy crayfish freshly cooked at the jetty.

The Jip Jip National Park is 45 km north-east of Kingston and features huge granite outcrops in the bush. From Kingston conventional vehicles can drive 16 km along the beach to the Granites while with 4WD you can continue right along the beach to the Murray River mouth.

ROBE (population 600)

A small port steeped in history, Robe which dates from 1845 was one of South Australia's first settlements. Early buildings include the 1863 Customs House which is now a National Trust museum. It's open on Tuesdays and public holidays (daily in January) from 2 to 4 pm. Admission is 50c. There is also an old jail up on the cliffs and a small arts and crafts gallery.

The citizens of Robe made a colourful fortune in the late 1850s as a result of the Victorian gold rush. The Victorian government instituted a £10 head tax on Chinese gold miners in 1855 and 16,000 ingenious Chinese circumvented the tax by getting to Victoria via Robe in South Australia; 10,000 arrived in 1857 alone. The Chinamen's Wells in the region are a reminder of that time. There are fine views along the coast from the Obelisk at Cape Dombey.

BEACHPORT (population 400)

South of Robe this quiet little seaside town is, like other places along the coast, a busy lobster and crayfishing centre. There's a small National Trust museum in the old wood and grain store plus a couple of other old buildings. There's good surfing near Beachport at the 'blowhole'; the nearby salt lake is called the 'Pool of Siloam'.

The *Beachport YHA Hostel* (tel (087) 35 8197) has beds at $5.

MILLICENT (population 5250)

At Millicent the 'Alternative 1' route through Robe and Beachport rejoins the main road. The town has a central swimming lake; there's a National Trust museum and the Admella Gallery, both on George St. A narrow gauge steam engine is also on display nearby. There's also a Historical & Maritime Museum in the town.

The Canunda National Park with its enormous sand dunes is 13 km west of Millicent. Tantanoola, 21 km away, has the stuffed 'Tantanoola Tiger' on display at the Tantanoola Tiger Hotel. This beast, actually an Assyrian wolf, was shot in 1895 after a lot of local publicity. It was presumed to have escaped from a shipwreck, but quite why a ship would have a wolf on board is not clear! Tantanoola also has limestone caves which are open from 9 am to 5 pm daily.

MT GAMBIER (population 20,000)

The major town and commercial centre of the south-east, Mt Gambier is 486 km from Adelaide. The town is built on the slopes of the volcano which gives it its name. The volcano has three craters, each with its own lake. The beautiful and spectacular Blue Lake is the best known although from about March to November the lake is more grey than blue. In November it changes back to blue again, just in time for the holiday season! The lake is 70 metres deep and there's a five-km scenic drive around it.

Mt Gambier also has many parks including the Cave Park with its deep 'cave', actually more of a steep-sided hole, which is right in the city. Mt Gambier is in a rich agricultural area, but timber and limestone (cut in blocks for use as a building material) are the main products. The poet Adam Lindsay Gordon, who committed suicide in 1870, is also connected with Mt Gambier where he lived for some years.

Black's Museum, open daily, has displays of Aboriginal artefacts. On Sunday afternoons you can visit the museum in the old courthouse. There are also tours of the sawmills around Mt Gambier. Check with the Mt Gambier Tourist Information Centre on Casterton Rd.

PORT MACDONNELL (population 700)
South of Mt Gambier, this quiet little fishing port is a centre for rock lobster fishing. At one time it was a busy shipping port, hence the surprisingly big 1863 customs house, now used as a restaurant. Adam Lindsay Gordon's home Dingley Dell is now a museum.

There are some fine walks around Port MacDonnell including the path to the top of Mt Schank, an extinct volcano crater. On Wednesdays and Thursdays from 2 to 4 pm you can visit the Cape Northumberland Lighthouse on the superb coastline west of the port.

ALONG THE DUKES HIGHWAY
The Dukes Highway, the main Melbourne to Adelaide route, is not terribly exciting, particularly from Tailem Bend through to the South Australian border.

Bordertown (population 2150)
Just on the South Australian side of the border, Bordertown is in a prosperous agricultural area. There's a wildlife sanctuary by the roadside on the east side of the town with emus and kangaroos but

Bordertown has another claim to fame: Australian prime minister Bob Hawke was born in Bordertown and lived here for the first six years of his life. There's a bust of Bob outside the town hall.

Other Towns
Keith is another farming town; it also has a small museum and the Mt Rescue Conservation Park 16 km north. This area was once known as 90-mile Desert. Tintinara is the other town of any size; it's also an access point to the Mt Rescue Park. Coonalpyn, a tiny township, is a jumping-off point for the Mt Boothby Conservation Park.

NARACOORTE (population 4750)
Settled in the 1840s, Naracoorte is one of the oldest towns in South Australia and one of the largest country towns in the south east. It has the Old Mill Museum, a National Trust museum and the Naracoorte Art Gallery. On Jenkins Terrace, the Naracoorte Museum & Snake Pit (!) has gems, antiques and a reptile park. It's open from 10 am to 5 pm daily, except Sundays when it's open from 2 to 5 pm. Pioneer Park has restored locomotives and the town also has a swimming lake. The Naracoorte Tourist Information Centre is at 128 Smith St.

Naracoorte Caves are 11 km out of town – Fossil Cave has ice-age fossils; it's open daily. There are three other caves with stalactites and stalagmites. Bat Cave, with lots of bats that make a spectacular departure every evening, is 17 km out of the town. At a similar distance from the town, you can see numerous water birds at the Bool Lagoon Reserve. The types of birds vary during the year.

COONAWARRA
This fine wine-producing area is 10 km north of Penola; there are 10 wineries in the area. Wynn's Coonawarra Estate is the best known of the wineries here, although it is not open to the public like some of the smaller wineries. Most of

them are open from Monday to Friday, some also on Saturdays and Sundays. Penola is the main town in the area. Bushman's Inn in Penola North has displays of coins and Aboriginal artefacts.

Murray River

Australia's greatest river starts in the Snowy Mountains in the Australian Alps and for most of its length forms the boundary between New South Wales and Victoria. But it's in South Australia that the Murray comes into its prime. First, it flows west through the Riverland area where irrigation has turned unproductive land into an important wine and fruit growing region. Although names like the Barossa and Hunter are better known, the Riverland actually produces 40% of Australia's wine. Then at Morgan the river turns sharply south and flows through the Lower Murray region to the sea. In all, it is 650 km from the border of South Australia with New South Wales and Victoria to the sea.

The Murray has lots of water sport possibilities, plenty of wildlife (particularly water birds) and in the Riverlands section, a positive surfeit of wineries to visit. This is also a river with a history. Before the advent of the railways, the Murray was the Mississippi of Australia with paddle-steamers carrying trade from the interior down to the coast. Many of the river towns still have a strong flavour of those riverboat days. If you've the cash and inclination, you can still ride a paddle-steamer forging its leisurely way on a cruise down the mighty Murray.

Life on the River

The Murray River region has plenty of conventional accommodation including hostel accommodation in Loxton, but to really get to grips with the Murray the ideal way is, of course, out on the river. From Renmark, for example, you can

make short day trips on the MV *Barrangul* and the MV *Kookaburra* from Murray Bridge.

If you've got a family or a group of people, a very pleasant way to explore the Murray is to rent a houseboat and set off along the river by yourself. Houseboats can be hired in Morgan, Waikerie, Loxton, Berri, Renmark and other river centres, but they are very popular so it's wise to book well ahead. The SAGTC can advise you about prices and make bookings. The cost depends on what you hire, where you hire it and, more importantly, when you hire it. Typically prices are around $500 a week for a four-berth houseboat, around $950 for larger eight or 10-berth boats. These costs can drop in low season.

Finally, there are the trips on riverboats such as the huge paddle-wheeler PS *Murray River Queen* which makes five-day trips from Goolwa to Swan Reach and back (food and accommodation included, $720 per person) or the MV *Aroona* with regular day-cruises to the Murray mouth and the Coorong for $15 per person, also from Goolwa.

You could take the MV *Murray Princess* from Mammum to Waikerie or the PS *Murray Princess* from Renmark up to the New South Wales-Victoria stretch of the Murray, then back down to Loxton and finally up to Renmark again; these trips, however, are definitely not cheap!

Getting There & Away

Air Sunstate Airlines (tel 217 3333) flights can be booked through Australian Airlines, 144 North Terrace, Adelaide. They fly to Renmark from Adelaide twice daily Monday to Friday.

Bus Alternatively you can get there by bus. Stateliner (tel 212 1777) operates Adelaide / Blanche Town / Waikerie / Loxton with fares of $11.70 to Blanche Town, $14.70 to Waikerie and $18.40 to Loxton and Renmark. Stateliner is at the Central Bus Station, Franklin St, Adelaide.

Bus Australia, Greyhound, Pioneer and Deluxe pass through here on their Adelaide to Sydney journey.

RENMARK (population 3500)

In the centre of the Riverland irrigation area, 295 km from Adelaide, Renmark was not only a starting point for the great irrigation projects that revolutionised the area, but also the first of the river towns. Irrigation was started in 1887 by the Canadian Chaffey brothers; you can see one of their original wood-burning irrigation pumps on Renmark Ave. Olivewood, Charles Chaffey's home (built around 1890) is also on Renmark Ave. It's open daily except Wednesday from 2.30 to 4 pm. There's a tourist office on Murray Ave – call 86 6703.

Today the area earns its living from vineyards, orchards and other fruit growing. There are plenty of wineries which provide free tastings. In the town, you can inspect the 1911 paddle-steamer *Industry* which is now a museum. There are several art galleries in the town and Goat Island in the river is a wildlife sanctuary with many koalas, but bypass Bredl's depressing Reptile Park & Zoo five km out of town.

Places to Stay & Eat

Grays Caravan Park (tel 86 6522) has camping sites for $7 and on-site vans for $23. The *Renmark Hotel* (tel 86 6755) has rooms from $31/40 and counter meals from $6. *Sophies Restaurant* has good cheap Greek food and a take-away downstairs.

The *Berri*, *Renmark* and *Barmera Hotels* have a disco or bands playing from Wednesday to Saturday nights.

BERRI (population 3400)

At one time a refuelling stop for the wood-burning paddle-steamers, the town takes its name from the Aboriginal words 'berri berri' – 'big bend in the river'. It's the economic centre of the Riverland and there are a number of wineries nearby.

Berri Estates Winery, at Glossop, 13 km to the west, is one of the biggest wineries in Australia, if not in the whole southern hemisphere.

Berri also has a large fruit juice factory with tours four times a day on weekends. Lovers of Australian kitsch should visit the 'big orange', four km out of Berri on the road to Renmark. This 16-metre diameter, fibreglass 'orange' houses exhibits telling the economic story of the Riverland region. There's also a display of vintage cars and motorcycles in the adjacent Riverland Display Centre. It's open from 9 am to 5 pm daily and admission is $2. There's a tourist office (tel 82 1655) on Vaughan Terrace.

In the town you can climb up to the lookout on Fiedler St for views over the town and river. There's a koala sanctuary near the Martins Bend recreation area on the river. Near Berri the small town of Monash has a huge children's playground with no less than 180 different children's amusements.

The annual big event in Berri is the Berri Rodeo which takes place each Easter Monday. Punts still cross the river from the Berri Hotel on Riverside Ave to Loxton.

Places to Stay & Eat

The *Berri Riverside Caravan Park* (tel 82 1718) on Riverview Drive has sites for $7 and on-site vans for $23. The *Winkie Holiday Cottages* (tel 86 6703) on Lower Winkie Rd cost $29 for a double. At the *Berri Hotel* (tel 82 1411) on Riverview Drive singles/doubles are $46/52 and you can get cheap counter meals at the public bar. They have entertainment Wednesday to Saturday nights. *Pam's Coffee Shop* is good for lunch.

LOXTON (population 3100)

From Berri the Murray makes a large loop south of the Sturt Highway; Loxton is at the bottom of this loop which is an additional 38 km off the main road. The town is involved in the usual Riverland activities of fruit growing and wine making. The town has expanded dramatically since WW II due to a land settlement scheme instituted for returned servicemen.

Loxton's major attraction is the Historical Village on the riverside which includes a replica of the town's first house – a pine and pug hut built by William Charles Loxton in 1878. In all, over two dozen buildings recreate a working village of the Riverland district at the turn of the century. It's open daily from 10 am to 4 pm on weekdays, to 5 pm on weekends.

There's a tourist office – the Loxton Tourist & Travel Centre – in the Loxton Hotel on East Terrace. Riverland Canoeing Adventures (tel 84 1494) on Alamein Ave, rent out kayaks for $10 or $15 a day; they also have cycles to rent.

Places to Stay & Eat

The *Loxton Riverfront Caravan Park* (tel 84 7862) has a former hostel building which is still operated as an alternate hostel. The *Loxton Hotel-Motel* (tel 84 7266) on East Terrace has rooms from $18/29. You can eat at the *Colonial Coffee Lounge* or the *Loxton Pizza Bar*.

BARMERA (population 2000)

On the shores of Lake Bonney, where English record-holder Donald Campbell made an attempt on the world water-speed record in 1964, Barmera was once on the overland stock route along which cattle were driven from New South Wales. The ruins of Napper's Old Accommodation House, built in 1850 at the mouth of Chambers Creek, are a reminder of that era, as is the Overland Corner Hotel on the Morgan road, 19 km out of town. It takes its name from a bend in the Murray River where overlanders, travellers and explorers once halted. Later drovers paused here and the old hotel built in 1859 has some interesting exhibits from those pioneering days. It is now preserved as a National Trust museum and is open from Wednesday

to Sunday from 10 am to 5 pm and additional days during holiday periods.

There's also a National Trust Art Gallery & Museum in the town. Lake Bonney, which has sandy beaches, is popular for swimming and water sports. There's even a nude beach at Pelican Point. On the Sturt Highway five km west from Barmera, the Cobdogla Irrigation Museum has the world's only working Humphrey Pump – a sort of giant water cannon. Display and operating days are infrequent so phone 82 0211 first, admission is $3. There's a Barmera tourist office on Barwell Ave.

Places to Stay & Eat

Barmera Hotel Motor Inn (tel 882111) has rooms from $17/29 or at the *Lake Bonney Reserve Holiday Complex* (tel 88 2234) doubles are $29. The hotels have counter meals or *Jules Gourmet* has good food, but small portions.

WAIKERIE (population 1600)

The town takes its name from the Aboriginal word for 'anything that flies', after the teeming bird life on the lagoons and river around Waikerie. Curiously, anything that flies also includes gliders, for Waikerie has the most active gliding centre in in Australia. You can arrange to make a glider flight here, phone 41 2644.

Wine tasting, Pooginook Conservation Park (12 km north-east) which has echidnas and hairy-nosed wombats, the Kangaroo Park, Holder Bend Reserve and the Waikerie Producers Co-op, which is the largest citrus packing house in the southern hemisphere, are other attractions in and around the town. There is a tourist centre at 20 McCoy St.

MORGAN (population 400)

In its prime, this was the busiest river port in Australia and the massive wharves towering 12 metres high may be quiet today but they're certainly still there. Railway Terrace has lots of interesting old buildings; there's also a car ferry across the Murray at this point. Morgan is off the Sturt Highway to the north and from here a pipeline pumps water to Whyalla on Spencer Gulf.

Places to Stay

The *Commercial Hotel* (tel 40 2107) has rooms from $15/30 or there's *Morgan Riverside Caravan Park* (tel 40 2207) with camping sites for $9 and on-site vans for $20.

BLANCHE TOWN

This is the site of the first river lock on the Murray (built in 1922). Nearby is the small Brookfield Conservation Park, specifically intended for the hairy-nosed wombat.

SWAN REACH (population 200)

This sleepy little old town has very picturesque river scenery and, hardly surprisingly, lots of swans. Just downriver the river makes a long, gentle curve for 11 km in all. The bend is appropriately known as Big Bend; there's a picnic reserve here and many white cockatoos. The *Murray River Queen* ends its upriver cruise at Swan Reach.

MANNUM (population 2000)

The *Mary Ann*, Australia's first riverboat, was built here and made the first paddle-steamer trip up the Murray from Mannum in 1853. The river is very wide here and there are many relics of the pioneering days on the river, including the 1898 paddle-wheeler *Marion*, now a floating museum (open daily 10 am to 4 pm).

You can also see a replica of Sturt's whaleboat and relics of the *Mary Ann*. The Halidon Rd Bird Sanctuary has pelicans, ducks, swans and other water birds. The Cascade Waterfalls, 11 km from Mannum on Reedy Creek, are also worth visiting. Off Purnong Rd there's a lookout tower.

MURRAY BRIDGE (population 8700)

South Australia's largest river town is only 82 km from Adelaide. It's a popular area for fishing, swimming, water-skiing and barbecues. From here you can make day cruises on the MV *Kookaburra*.

If you're stuck in Murray Bridge, you can arrange to see antique doll collections, a pipe collection, chocolate manufacturing or pay a visit to Mary the Blacksmith at 41 Dotle Rd. This very entertaining and interesting woman forges iron over a 200 year old anvil. Admission is $2, Friday to Tuesday from 10 am to 4 pm. In the Sturt Reserve by the river, there's a 20c coin-in-the-slot bunyip and a very long children's slide, running down by the riverside.

Near Murray Bridge is Monarto – the town that never was. A grandiose plan was drawn up to build a second major city for South Australia by the turn of the century. This site was chosen and land purchased in the early 1970s, but nothing further happened and a few years ago the project was totally abandoned.

The Tourist Office is in Pine Park just off Swanport Rd.

Places to Stay & Eat

The Balcony Private Hotel (tel 32 3830) costs $17 per person and the friendly owner is very knowledgeable about the area. The centrally located *Oval Caravan Park* (tel 32 2267) has tent sites for $10 and on-site vans for $23. You can eat at the *Oriental Garden* or at the *Murray Bridge Hotel* where the best counter meals can be found.

Getting There & Away

Murray Bridge Passenger Service buses run four times a day weekdays, less frequently on weekends to and from Adelaide for $6. There's a local bus service on weekdays for 75c.

TAILEM BEND (population 1700)

At a sharp bend in the river, Tailem Bend is near the mouth of the Murray River. After Wellington the Murray opens into huge Lake Alexandrina; there are lots of water birds, but sometimes boating is tricky. The river mouth is near Goolwa –

see the Fleurieu Peninsula section. You can take a ferry across the river at Jervis from where it's 11 km to the interesting old town of Wellington.

Yorke Peninsula

The Yorke Peninsula is a popular holiday area within easy driving distance from Adelaide. There are some pleasant beaches along both sides, the Innes National Park on the tip of the peninsula and plenty of opportunities for fishing. The area's economy was originally based on the copper mines of 'little Cornwall'. As the mining declined, agriculture took its place and much of the land is now devoted to growing barley and other grains.

Places to Stay
There are camping sites, hotels, motels – a variety of holiday accommodation all over the peninsula. Port Vincent has a youth hostel.

Getting There & Away
Bus services between Adelaide and towns on the Yorke Peninsula depart from the Central Bus Station. Premier (tel 217 0777) operates daily Adelaide / Kadina / Wallaroo / Moonta / Port Hughes / Moonta Bay. It takes about three hours to Moonta and costs $10.

Yorke Peninsula Bus Service (tel 212 7999) have a daily service to Turton. The bus runs from Adelaide to Ardrossan ($10.60), Port Vincent ($14.50), Edithburgh and Yorketown ($15). The trip takes two hours to Ardrossan and four hours to Yorketown. Unfortunately these services to the west and east coast of the peninsula do not interconnect and so from Kadina you have to cross over to Port Wakefield to get further down the peninsula.

CORNWALL & COPPER MINES
In the early 1860s, copper was discovered in the Moonta-Kadina-Wallaroo area and

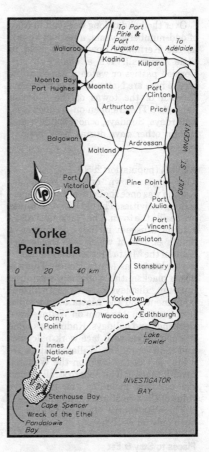

within a few years a full-scale copper rush was on. Most of the miners were from Cornwall in England and the area still has a strong Cornish influence. There are many old cottages and churches which look for all the world as if they have been transplanted straight from Cornwall. The mining boom continued right through into this century reaching its peak around the turn of the century, but in the early 1920s a slump in copper prices, rising labour costs and competition from mines abroad forced the closure of all the peninsula copper mines.

Over the holiday long weekend in May of odd-numbered years, a festival known as the Kernewek Lowender is held in little Cornwall. It's a chance to try Cornish pasties or watch a wheelbarrow race. There are National Trust museums in each of the towns of the 'Cornish Triangle'. They're open on Wednesdays, Saturdays, Sundays, school holidays and certain other days during peak holiday seasons.

KADINA (population 2950)

The largest town on the peninsula, Kadina was once the centre of the copper-mining activities. The old Wallaroo mines are beside the town. The National Trust's Kadina Museum includes a number of buildings, one of which was the former home of the Matta Matta mine manager – it was known as Matta House. There is also a blacksmith's workshop, a printing museum, displays of early agricultural equipment and the Matta Matta mine. It's open from 2 to 5 pm on Wednesdays, weekends and holidays. Kadina has some fine old hotels with lace-work balconies and wide verandahs. Wallaroo Mines are a km west of the town on the Wallaroo road. It takes half an hour to stroll around the complex including the impressive ruins of the two-storey engine building.

There's a tourist office on Graves St, open only on weekdays.

Places to Stay & Eat

Wombat Hotel (tel 21 1108) on Taylor St charges $19 per person. The *Kadina Caravan Park* (tel 21 2259) has camping sites for $7 or on-site vans for $23. Cornish pasties, a local specialty, are found in many shops; *Prices Bakery* has excellent ones. *Sarah's Place* is a good place for pancakes and Cornish cooking.

WALLAROO (population 2000)

The second part of the Yorke Peninsula's 'Cornish triangle', this port town was a major centre during the copper boom. 'The big stack', one of the great chimneys

from the copper smelters, built in 1861, still stands, but now the port's main function is exporting agricultural products. Situated in the original town post office, the National Trust Maritime Museum has many ship models and items from the town's early history as a port. There are other interesting buildings like the old railway station, now the Talyllyn restaurant, and also good beaches.

Places to Stay & Eat

Wallaroo Hotel has rooms for $18/28 or at the *Riley Holiday Village* (tel 23 2057) fully self-contained units are $46. Some of the hotels have counter meals, you can get snacks from *Prices Bakery* or there's interesting Celtic food at the *Talyllyn Restaurant*.

MOONTA (population 1900)

At Moonta, a little south of Wallaroo, the copper mine was once said to be the richest mine in Australia. The town grew so fast that its school once had over 1000 students; the building now houses the largest country museum in the state (admission $2). It's part of the collection of mine works ruins at the Moonta Heritage Site which you can explore with a self-guiding map from the museum or the tourist office. On weekends only, the tourist railway takes you on a 50 minute trip around the Moonta Mines Complex.

Other sights include numerous old Methodist churches (the town had 14 at one time, the most important being the Wesleyan), a National Trust restored Cornish miner's cottage and Freemasons Hall with a display of lodge regalia. Moonta Bay, the port for Moonta, is three km west of the town.

Places to Stay & Eat

Cornwall Hotel (tel 25 2304) has rooms for $18/30 or at the *Moonta Bay Caravan Park* (tel 67 3103) sites cost $8. Moonta has another *Prices Bakery*; you could try the *Cornish Kitchen* for local specialities or the *Moonta Pizza Cafe*.

MAITLAND (population 1100)

In the centre of the peninsula, this agricultural commercial centre has a National Trust museum, open on Sundays only. The *Maitland Hotel* which has rooms for $20/$31 is the only place to stay.

MINLATON (population 900)

Another agricultural commercial centre, Minlaton was the home town of pioneer aviator Harry Butler. His 1916 Bristol monoplane, nicknamed the 'Red Devil', is on display in the Harry Butler Museum. Nearby is the National Trust museum on Main St, while close to town there's an arts & crafts centre at the Gum Flat Homestead Gallery (two km out) and the Koolywurtie Museum with pioneer exhibits (11 km out). Minlaton was originally known as Gum Flat.

Places to Stay

The *Minlaton Hotel* has singles/doubles from $20/34 or there's the *Minlaton Caravan Park* with sites for $6.

INNES NATIONAL PARK

The southern tip of the peninsula, marked by Cape Spencer, is all part of the Innes National Park. Stenhouse Bay, just outside the park, and Pondalowie Bay, within the park, are the principal settlements. Pondalowie Bay is the base for a large crayfishing fleet and also has a fine surf beach. The park has fine coastal scenery; camping is allowed with permits from the park rangers who are stationed at Stenhouse Bay.

The main landmark in the park is the wreck of the barque *Ethel*, a 711 ton ship which ran ashore on the beach in 1904. An attempt to refloat her later that year was almost successful, but today all that remains are the ribs of the hull rising forlornly from the sands. The ship's anchor is mounted in a memorial on the clifftop above the beach.

Just past the Cape Spencer turn-off, watch for a historical marker which directs you to the six ruined buildings at the Inneston historic site.

Places to Stay

Stenhouse Bay has a caravan park with limited facilities. With a permit, you can camp in most places in the park, phone (088) 54 4040 for details.

Getting There & Away

There is no public transport to the end of the peninsula. Yorke Peninsula Bus Service will take you as far as Warooka and then you can try to hitchhike, but traffic is sparse.

WEST COAST

The west coast, looking out onto the Spencer Gulf, also has plenty of beaches, but the road generally runs some way inland. The main port towns are Port Broughton, with its pleasant harbour and jetty, Wallaroo and Moonta Bay in the little Cornwall area.

Mike's North Park (tel 35 2397) has camping sites for $8 and on-site vans for $25. The old stone *Port Broughton Hotel* (tel 35 2004) has rooms at $25/39 and the bar serves counter meals. Try the *Captains Way Restaurant* for seafood.

EAST COAST

The east coast road from the top of Gulf St Vincent right down to Stenhouse Bay near to Cape Spencer closely follows the coast. There are many pleasant sandy beaches and secluded coves. Port Clinton is the northernmost beach resort. A little south is Price, where salt is produced at salt-pans just outside town.

Ardrossan, 150 km from Adelaide, is the largest port on the east coast. There's the Ardrossan & District Historical Museum on Fifth St; ploughing enthusiasts will be delighted to hear that Ardrossan was the place where the 'stump-jump plough' was invented.

Continuing south, the road runs through Pine Point, Black Point, Port Julia and Port Vincent (each has a sandy beach) in the next 50 km. Port Vincent has the *Tuckerway YHA Hostel* (tel (088) 53 7285) which costs $5.50. The road continues to hug the coast through Stansbury, Wool Bay, Port Giles and Coobowie until Edithburgh.

Edithburgh has a rock swimming pool in a small cove; from the clifftops you can look across to the small islands of the Troubridge Shoals where there is good scuba diving. There's also a small Maritime Museum and nearby Sultana Bay is a good spot for swimming. The southern part of the peninsula is sparsely populated but the road from Edithburgh to Stenhouse Bay is very scenic.

The route known as Hillocks Drive is private property; there's a $2.50 entry charge and permission is required to camp. Phone (088) 54 4002 for details. There's superb scenery and lots of kangaroos, emus and native birds.

Eyre Peninsula

The wide Eyre Peninsula points south between Spencer Gulf and the Great Australian Bight. It's bordered on the north side by the Eyre Highway from Port Augusta to Ceduna. The coastal run along the peninsula is in two parts: first the Lincoln Highway south-west from Port Augusta to Port Lincoln and then the Flinders Highway north-west to Ceduna. It's 468 km from Port Augusta direct to Ceduna via the Eyre Highway while the loop south totals 763 km.

This is a popular beach resort area with many fine beaches, sheltered bays and pleasant little port towns. Further along the Port Lincoln-Streaky Bay-Ceduna stretch there are superb surf beaches and some of Australia's most spectacular coastal scenery. Offshore, further west, is home to the great white shark. This is a favourite locale for making shark films - some of the scenes from *Jaws* were filmed here. The Eyre Peninsula also has a flourishing agricultural sector while the iron ore deposits at Iron Knob and Iron Baron are processed and shipped from the busy port of Whyalla.

The stretch of coast from Port Lincoln to Streaky Bay had one of the earliest European contacts. In 1627 the Dutch explorer Peter Nuyts sailed right along the north and west coasts of Australia in his ship the *Gulden Zeepard*. He continued along the south coast, crossed the Great Australian Bight, but finally gave up at Streaky Bay and turned back to more hospitable climes. It was left to Abel Tasman, 15 years later, to complete the circumnavigation of the continent and it was more than a century later that Cook 'discovered' the fertile east coast.

In 1802 Matthew Flinders charted the peninsula and named many of its prominent features during his epic circumnavigation of Australia. The peninsula takes its name from Edward John Eyre, the hardy explorer who made the first east to west crossing of the continent.

Places to Stay

There are plenty of places to stay on the Eyre Peninsula since many of the coastal towns are popular resorts - lots of camping grounds, holiday flats, hotels and motels.

Getting There & Away

Air Kendell Airlines (tel 212 1111) are booked through Ansett in Adelaide. They fly to Port Lincoln ($87), Whyalla ($86), Streaky Bay ($128) and Ceduna ($153) on the Eyre Peninsula. The Port Lincoln flights operate several times daily. Lloyd Airlines (tel 224 7500) have flights every day to Port Lincoln ($76) and Whyalla ($68). State Air (tel 352 2877) and Lincoln Airlines (tel (086) 82 5688) fly to Port Lincoln for $65 and $60 respectively. Eyre Commuter (tel (086) 86 2329) has a daily service to Tumby Bay.

Bus Bus Australia, Greyhound, Deluxe

and Pioneer's Adelaide/Perth services operate through Port Augusta ($22) and Ceduna ($43). It takes 9½ hours from Adelaide to Ceduna. Stateliner (bookings and departures from the Greyhound terminal) have services from Port Wakefield to Streaky Bay ($40) and Ceduna ($45) along an inland route through Wudinna and to Port Lincoln ($38.20) and all points between.

Train A new rail service has been established between Adelaide and Whyalla ($22) on Mondays, Wednesdays and Fridays. It stops in Crystal Brook, Port Pirie, Port Germein and Port Augusta.

Boat The MV *Island Seaway* sails once weekly from Adelaide via Kangaroo Island to Port Lincoln. It takes seven hours Adelaide/Kangaroo Island and another 11 hours on to Port Lincoln. Fares are $37 from Adelaide, $25.50 from Kangaroo Island. Cars cost $76 from Kangaroo Island, motorcycles $25, bicycles $3.20.

Port Lincoln services stop between mid-December and early January when extra trips are made to Kangaroo Island from Adelaide. Agents for the ferry are R W Miller (tel 47 5577) at 3 Todd St, Port Adelaide. In Port Lincoln they are at Patrick Agencies (tel 82 1011), 33 Edinburgh St.

PORT AUGUSTA (population 15,300)

At the head of Spencer Gulf this busy port city is a crossroads for travellers and the gateway to the outback region of South Australia. Matthew Flinders was the first European to set foot in the area, but the town was not established until 1854. From here, roads head west across the Nullarbor to Western Australia, north to Alice Springs and Darwin in the Northern Territory, south to Adelaide and east to Broken Hill and Sydney in New South Wales. It is also on the main railway line between the east and west coasts and on the Adelaide/Alice Springs Ghan route.

Apart from its importance as a supply centre for goods going by rail or road into the outback it's also a major electricity generating centre, burning coal from the Leigh Creek open-cut mines. You can take a tour of the Thomas Playford Power Station or the Australian National Railways workshops, the latter at 2 pm from Monday to Friday.

Other city attractions include the Curdnatta Art & Pottery Gallery in what was Port Augusta's first railway station. The Homestead Park Pioneer Museum has the usual display of pioneer buildings and machinery. Old buildings include the Greenbush Gaol from 1869, the old town hall, the Grange from 1878 and Homestead Park pioneer museum which also includes a railway museum (on the corner of Elsie and Jaycee Sts).

Information

Tourist Information is at Homestead Pioneer Museum, Elsie St. Fullerton's Bus Service (tel 42 2707) organises tours or there are 4WD outback tours by companies like Butlers (tel 42 2188).

Places to Stay

The *Great Northern Hotel* has rooms for a dirt cheap $13/23 or there's the *Commonwealth Hotel* (tel 42 2844) at $17/30. There are a number of motels on the road into and out of town including the up-market *Augusta Westside* (tel 42 2555) at $48/52. *Fauna Caravan Park* (tel 42 2974) has sites for $7 and on-site vans for $20.

Places to Eat

Ridge-Didge Steak House in Commercial Rd has $6 lunch specials and also cheap dinners. Across the road you can try *Your Choice Coffee Lounge* or further down there's *Ozzie's Coffee Lounge*. *Price's Bakery* on Church St has good bread and take-aways.

The Four Ways Hotel has *The Vault* nightclub and other hotels have live bands or a disco on the weekends.

WHYALLA (population 30,000)

The largest city in South Australia after Adelaide, Whyalla is a major steel-producing centre and also a busy deep-water port for shipping steel and iron products. The town was originally known as Hummock Hill. Whyalla also had a major shipyard, but it was closed in the '70s. There are tours of the BHP steel works in Whyalla at 9.30 am on Mondays, Wednesdays and Saturdays. They start from the Tourist Centre and cost $4 for adults, $1.50 for children, and $10 for a family ticket.

Ore comes to Whyalla from Iron Knob, Iron Monarch and Iron Baron. Iron Knob was the first iron ore deposit in Australia to be exploited; there are also tours of its mining operation at 10 am and 2 pm on weekdays and at 2 pm on Saturdays. For safety reasons, visitors on either of the Whyalla area tours must not wear sandals, thongs or other open shoes.

Apart from its industrial aspect, Whyalla also has fine beaches and a fauna and reptile park on the Lincoln Highway near the airport. On Ekblom St, there are historical exhibits in the National Trust Mt Laura Homestead Museum which is only open on Sundays and public holidays (from 2 to 4 pm). The Historical & Maritime Museum is a diver's private collection. Studio 41, on the corner of Wood and Donaldson Terrace, includes an exhibition of local art.

The Whyalla Tourist Centre is on the Lincoln Highway, next to BHP. Whyalla has a local bus service on weekdays and Saturday mornings.

Places to Stay & Eat

The *Whyalla Hotel* (tel 45 7411) has singles/doubles at $17/32 or at the *Lord Gowrie Hotel* (tel 45 8955) they are $20/29. *Whyalla Foreshore Caravan Park* (tel 45 7474) has sites from $7 and on-site vans from $25.50. The *Oriental Inn* Chinese restaurant has good food – count on around $16 for a three-course meal.

WHYALLA TO PORT LINCOLN

It's 280 km from Whyalla to Port Lincoln at the tip of the peninsula and there are quite a few places of interest along the way.

Cowell (population 600)

Cowell is close to a very large jade deposit. The Cowell Jade Factory on Second St has a display of cutting and polishing operations.

The town also has a small National Trust museum in the old post office and an agricultural museum. Cowell has good beaches on Franklin Harbour, an expanse of water which is only open to the sea through a very narrow inlet.

Places to Stay & Eat

Franklin Harbour Hotel (tel 29 2015) has rooms for $17/23. The *Schultz Farm* (tel 29 2194) farmhouse overlooks the sea and has accommodation for $16 per person and home-cooked meals. *Cowell Foreshore Caravan Park* (tel 29 2307) has sites for $7 and on-site vans for $17.

Cleve & Arno Bay

Cleve is 43 km inland from Cowell and has an interesting fauna park with a nocturnal house. Continuing 47 km further south, Arno Bay is a popular little beach resort.

Places to Stay

The *Arno Hotel* (tel 28 0001) is only 100 metres from a good beach and has rooms at $23/38. Close by is the *Arno Bay Caravan Park* (tel 28 0085).

Further South

South again you reach Port Neill (another beach resort) and then Tumby Bay with its long, curving, white sand beach, the C L Alexander Museum and a number of interesting old buildings around the town. The Sir Joseph Banks group of islands are 15 km offshore from Tumby Bay; there are many attractive bays and reefs here plus a wide variety of sea birds which nest on the islands.

North Shields is a small settlement only 13 km north of Port Lincoln on the shore of Boston Bay. The Karlinda collection has over 10,000 shells, rocks and examples of marine life.

Places to Stay & Eat The historic *Wheatsheaf Hotel* (tel 84 3531) in North Shields has accommodation ($17 per person) and meals or there is the *Port Lincoln Caravan Park* (tel 84 3512), also in North Shields

PORT LINCOLN (population 10,700)

At the southern end of the Eyre Peninsula, 662 km from Adelaide by road but only 250 km as the crow flies, Port Lincoln was named by Matthew Flinders in 1801. The first settlers arrived in 1839 and the town has grown to become the tuna fishing capital of Australia; the annual Tunarama Festival in January of each year signals the start of the tuna fishing season with boisterous merriment over the Australia Day weekend.

Port Lincoln is pleasantly situated on Boston Bay with a variety of opportunities for water sports. There are a number of historic buildings in the town including the Old Mill on Dorset Place which houses a small pioneer museum. The Lincoln Hotel dates from 1840, making it the oldest hotel on the peninsula. On the Flinders Highway, Mill Cottage is another museum and it's open from 2 to 5 pm daily. The Axel Stenross Maritime Museum has a working blacksmith shop. There are also a number of islands off Boston Bay.

Fourteen km offshore from the town is Dangerous Reef, the world's largest breeding area for the white pointer shark. Believe it or not, a charter company runs trips out here for divers looking for that extra little bite. Even at over $400 per person they're always fully booked, bringing in gamblers from the USA, Europe and Japan.

At one time Port Lincoln was considered as an alternative to Adelaide as the state capital and it still operates as an important deep-water port.

Information

There is a tourist office (tel 82 3255) at the Eyre Travel Centre on Tasman Terrace, the main street.

Places to Stay

Boston Hotel (tel 82 1311) has older rooms for $16/32 or at the *Pier Hotel* (tel 82 1322) rooms with a shower are $20/32. *Kirton Caravan Park* (tel 82 2537) has sites from $7, on-site vans from $23 and camping at $5 per person.

Places to Eat

Dial-a-Curry in Tasman Mall is a good cheap Indian restaurant. *Bugs Pastificio* in Harwill Court and *Castle Family* restaurants have good cheap meals at around $7 a main course. The counter meals at the *Port Lincoln Hotel* are the best value in town and the *Tasman Gallery* in the Tasman Mall has the best hamburgers in town.

Entertainment

Several hotels have a disco or a live band. The most popular seems to be the *Port Lincoln Hotel* with a video screen in one bar until midnight and a band playing in the rear of the hotel until 3 am.

Getting There & Away

Daily Stateliner buses can get you here from Adelaide via Cummins or Tumby Bay for $39, but there is no public transport between here and Streaky Bay. You either have to go back to Port Augusta for the Adelaide/Streaky Bay/Ceduna bus or hitch.

Getting Around

Tunarama Coachlines (tel 82 3255) have tours of Port Lincoln and the surrounding area. For details see the tourist office. The local bus service operates weekdays and Saturday mornings. Lincoln Cycles at 60 Liverpool St rent out bicycles for $5 a day.

AROUND PORT LINCOLN

Cape Carnot, better known as Whalers'

Way, is 32 km south of Port Lincoln and a permit ($9) to enter the conservation reserve must be obtained from the tourist office in Port Lincoln before you travel down there. A 15-km drive around the reserve takes you past stupendous cliffs, pounded by huge surf. It has some of the most impressive coastal scenery in Australia and at Sleaford Bay there is the remains of an old whaling station.

Also south of Port Lincoln is the Lincoln National Park, again with a magnificent coastline. You can visit offshore islands like Boston Island, Wedge Island or Thistle Island; the tourist office will help you find a boat to get out to them. Just north of Port Lincoln, Poonindie has an unusual old church with a chimney.

PORT LINCOLN TO STREAKY BAY
Coffin Bay

Soon after leaving Port Lincoln the road passes by Coffin Bay, a sheltered stretch of water with some fine beaches. Coffin Bay itself is a tiny township and from here you can find spectacular coastal scenery at Point Avoid, Almonta Beach and Yangie Bay. There's a 25 km trail to Yangie Bay but you need 4WD from there to Point Sir Isaac. You can see emus, Cape Barren geese and other wildlife at the Kellidie Bay Conservation Park.

Places to Stay The *Coffin Bay Caravan Park* (tel 85 4170) has sites for $7 and on-site vans for $20 and is the only place you can camp. There are many units around town for rent.

Coffin Bay to Talia

Further north towards Elliston (turn-off past Coulta), there's good surfing at Greenly Beach. Near Coulta is *Wepowie Farm* (tel (086) 87 2063) where you can camp or stay in the farm cottage for $23/32.

From the beach resort of Elliston further along the coast, you can get out to a number of offshore islands. A return flight to Flinders Island, 30 km off Elliston in the Bight, costs $50. *Club 15 Holiday*

Homestead has self-contained units from $23 per person. There are good swimming beaches around Waterloo Bay while Blackfellows has fine surf. Talia, further up the coast, has impressive granite rock faces and the limestone Talia Caves.

Venus Bay & Point Labatt

At Port Kenny on Venus Bay, there are more beaches and whales are often seen off the coast when they come here to breed in October. Venus Bay has an active fleet of prawn trawlers.

Shortly before Streaky Bay, the turn-off to Point Labatt takes you to the conservation park where you can see the only permanent colony of sea lions on the Australian mainland. You look down on their rocks from the clifftop, 50 metres above. There's magnificent coastal scenery from here to Streaky Bay, 40 km north.

STREAKY BAY (population 1000)

This popular little resort town takes it name from the 'streaky' water, caused by seaweed in the bay. The town is surrounded by bays, caves and high cliffs. It was at Streaky Bay that the Dutch explorer Peter Nuyts gave up and turned back. The Kelsh Pioneer Museum has old farm machinery and an 1886 cottage with local historical exhibits. It's open on Fridays from 2 to 5 pm and at other times by prior arrangement.

Curious granite outcrops known as *inselbergs* are found at numerous places around the Eyre Peninsula. You can see a particularly good group in the wheat fields close to the highway about 20 km south-east of Streaky Bay. They've been nicknamed 'Murphy's Haystacks'. Perlubie Beach is north of Streaky Bay and is another good surfing beach.

Places to Stay

Streaky Bay Community Hotel (tel 26 1008) has rooms for $28/32 or there's the *Foreshore Tourist Park* (tel 26 1666) with sites for $6.50, on-site vans for $20 and cabins for $29.

SMOKEY BAY (population 100)

This small town is well known for its annual Rodeo at Easter which draws many competitors and spectators from all over the country. The only place to stay is a caravan park (tel (086) 78 7130) that also has on-site vans and cabins.

CEDUNA (population 2800)

Just past the junction of the Flinders and Eyre Highways, Ceduna marks the end of the Eyre Peninsula area and the start of the long, empty stretch of highway across the Nullarbor Plain into Western Australia. The town was founded in 1896 although a whaling station had existed on St Peter Island, off nearby Cape Thevenard, back in 1850.

There is an overseas telecommunications earth station 34 km north of Ceduna, from where microwave communications are bounced off satellites. Tours are made at 10 and 11 am, 2 and 3 pm from Monday to Friday. The Old Schoolhouse National Trust Museum has local pioneer exhibits and artefacts of the British atomic weapons programme from Maralinga.

There are many beaches and sheltered coves around Ceduna while 13 km out of town, you can see the old McKenzie Ruin at the earlier township site of Denial Bay. Near Point Sinclair, 95 km beyond Ceduna, turn off at Penong and after 20 km you'll reach Cactus Beach, with huge sand dunes and strong surf that draws enthusiasts to this remote surfing spot. The beach is private property, but the owner (tel (086) 25 1036) permits camping at $3.50 per person although there are no facilities. In summer there is a small general stall here that sells some food.

Places to Stay & Eat

Ceduna Community Hotel (tel 25 2008) has rooms from $18/25 and a good cheap bistro. *Ceduna Caravan Centre* (tel 25 2150) has sites from $7 and on-site vans from $23. *Country Kitchen* has health food or there's *Alano's Pizza* and a good coffee lounge opposite the tourist office.

OTHER PLACES

Cummins, inland and north of Port Lincoln, is a small town with the very good Koppio Museum showing early agricultural equipment. Admission is $1.50 and it's open every day except Mondays. Along the Eyre Highway the road passes through Kimba, Kyancutta and Wudinna, all important as agricultural centres but otherwise of little interest. Kimba is on the very edge of the outback and you can visit Lake Gilles and the Gawler Ranges from here.

Mt Wudinna, near Wudinna, is the second largest rock in the south of Australia. Tortoise Rock, which is also near Wudinna, looks much like a tortoise.

The Flinders Ranges

Rising from the northern end of Gulf St Vincent and running north for 800 km into the dry outback region, the Flinders Ranges are desert mountains offering some of the most spectacular scenery in Australia. It's a superb area for bushwalks, wildlife or simply taking in the ever-changing colours of the Australian outback. In the far north of the Flinders region, the mountains are hemmed in by barren salt lakes.

The ranges, like so much of Australia, are geologically ancient but, worn though the peaks may be, the colours are amazing – this area has always been a favourite of artists. Like other dry regions of Australia, the vegetation is surprisingly diverse and colourful; in the spring, when rain is most likely, the country is at its greenest and is carpeted with wildflowers. In summer the nights are cool, but the days can be searingly hot. Winter is probably the best time for a Flinders visit, although there are attractions at any time of year.

In 1802, when Flinders first set foot in the ranges that were to be named after him, there were a number of Aboriginal

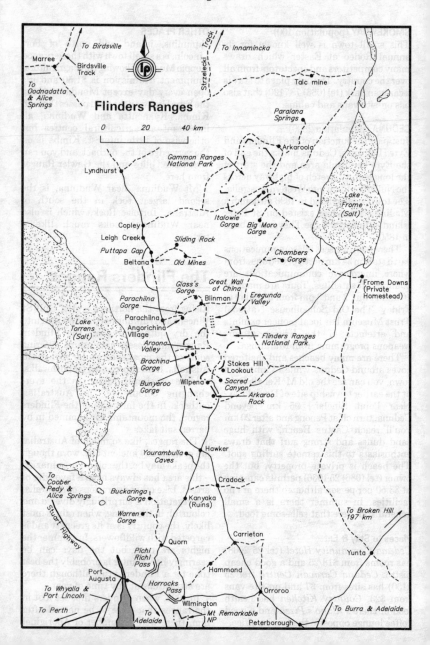

Flinders Ranges

0   20   40 km

To Birdsville

Marree

Birdsville Track

To Oodnadatta & Alice Springs

To Innamincka

Strzelecki Track

Talc mine

Paralana Springs

Arkaroola

Lake Frome (Salt)

Gammon Ranges National Park

Lyndhurst

Copley

Leigh Creek

Puttapa Gap

Beltana

Italowie Gorge

Big Moro Gorge

Sliding Rock

Old Mines

Chambers Gorge

Glass's Gorge

Great Wall of China

Frome Downs (Private Homestead)

Parachilna Gorge

Blinman

Eregunda Valley

Lake Torrens (Salt)

Parachilna

Angorichina Village

Aroona Valley

Flinders Ranges National Park

Brachina Gorge

Stokes Hill Lookout

Bunyeroo Gorge

Wilpena

Sacred Canyon

Arkaroo Rock

Yourambulla Caves

Hawker

To Coober Pedy & Alice Springs

Buckaringa Gorge

Cradock

Warren Gorge

Kanyaka (Ruins)

To Broken Hill 197 km

Stuart Highway

Carrieton

Yunta

Quorn

Hammond

Pichi Richi Pass

Port Augusta

To Whyalla & Port Lincoln

Horrocks Pass

Orroroo

To Burra & Adelaide

Wilmington

Mt Remarkable NP

Peterborough

To Perth

To Adelaide

tribes in the region. You can still see evidence of these people and can visit some of their sites: the rock paintings at Yourambulla (near Hawker) and Arkaroo (near Wilpena), and the rock-cut patterns at Sacred Canyon (near Wilpena) and Chambers Gorge. In the early mornings and evenings, you've got a good chance of spotting wildlife including emus, a variety of kangaroos and many different types of lizards. The bird life is especially prolific with colourful parrots, galahs, rosellas and many others – often in great numbers.

Bushwalking is one of the main attractions of the area. Campers can generally find water in rock pools during cooler months when the day time temperatures are pleasant. This is wild, rugged country and care should be taken before setting out. Wilpena Pound, the Arkaroola-Mt Painter Sanctuary and the Mt Remarkable National Park all have excellent walks, many of them along marked trails.

Information

It's definitely worth getting a good map of the Flinders Ranges since there are so many back roads and such a variety of road surfaces. The SAGTC's Flinders leaflet is quite good and the RAA, SAGTC and the National Parks office all put out maps of the whole ranges area and of Wilpena Pound. *Touring in the Flinders Ranges* is a good little book produced by the RAA and available from their offices. If you're planning on doing more than just the standard walks in the Flinders, look for a copy of *Flinders Ranges Walks* for more information.

Places to Stay

There are hotels and caravan parks as well as many cottages and farms offering all sorts of accommodation. Contact either Quornucopia (tel (086) 486 282) or the SAGTC (tel (08) 212 1644) for further details.

Getting There & Away

Bus Stateliner (tel 217 0777) have a bus service from Adelaide to Wilpena Pound on Fridays and the return trip is on Sunday. It costs $35. On Monday, Wednesday and Friday they have a service via Quorn ($25), Hawker and Parachilna to Arkaroola. The fare all the way to Arkaroola is $52. The bus service to Leigh Creek costs $43. The railway service from Adelaide to Quorn is no longer operating.

Road If you're driving to the Flinders it's good surfaced road all the way north to Wilpena Pound, but the dirt road begins as soon as you leave here. The Marree road skirting the western edge of the Flinders is surfaced up to Lyndhurst.

There are three routes to Arkaroola. The fastest is to continue up the Marree road beyond Parachilna and turn off at Copley, near Leigh Creek. An alternative is to travel up the Barrier Highway towards Broken Hill as far as Yunta and then turn north and follow the long (310 km) gravel road via Frome Downs, skirting the edge of Lake Frome and crossing the dingo-proof fence twice. There is no petrol or water available along this road and it's best to travel earlier in the day because the sun in your eyes can be unpleasant in the late afternoon.

Probably the most interesting route is to go via Wilpena Pound and take the road via Chambers Gorge, meeting the Frome Downs road south of Balcanoona. This road tends to be difficult after rain.

Getting Around

You can make a loop that takes you around an interesting section of the southern part of the Flinders. From Port Augusta you go through the Pichi Richi Pass to Quorn and Hawker and on up to Wilpena Pound. From the Pound, you continue north through the Flinders Ranges National Park to Blinman then down through the Parachilna Gorge to Parachilna, back on to the plains and south to Hawker – thus looping right round Wilpena Pound. From the Pound, you can also loop north into the Flinders Ranges National Park through Bunyeroo Gorge and the Aroona Valley.

Tours There are plenty of tours from Adelaide to the ranges and also tours out from Wilpena Pound and Arkaroola. Bus Australia, Greyhound and Pioneer have tours from Adelaide. Four-wheel drive tours are offered by companies like Butlers Outback Safaris (tel (086) 42 2188), Desert Trek (tel (08) 264 7200), Intrepid Tours (tel (086) 48 6277) and Gawler Outback Tours (tel (085) 22 2254). Horse riding treks are also available with Woodleigh Farm (tel (088) 23 2334) or Melrose Mountain Rides (tel (086) 66 2193). Transcontinental Safaris (tel (08) 489 3256) offer camel treks.

Air tours made from the Pound include day-trips to Arkaroola. Road tours go to the Aroona Valley, Blinman and Parachilna Gorge, Chambers Gorge or to Arkaroola.

MT REMARKABLE NATIONAL PARK

South-east of Port Augusta and in the southern stretch of the Flinders Ranges, the Mt Remarkable National Park is near Wilmington and Melrose. From Wilmington you can drive into the park and walk through narrow Alligator Gorge; in places the walls of this spectacularly beautiful gorge are only two metres apart. Hancocks Lookout, just north of the park near Horrocks Pass, offers excellent views of Spencer Gulf. There is a camping ground in the Mambray Creek section and bush camping is permitted in specified areas.

MELROSE

This tiny town is the oldest settlement in the Flinders Ranges. It's on the southern edge of the Mt Remarkable National Park, at the foot of Mt Remarkable itself. There's a walking trail to the top of the mountain. The old police station and court house now houses a National Trust

Mt Remarkable National Park, Flinders Ranges

museum while the North Star Hotel, built in 1854, is the oldest hotel in the Flinders.

Although it was licensed three years later, the Mt Remarkable Hotel is actually older – built in 1846 – and its exterior has scarcely changed over the past 140-plus years. There are a number of other interesting and picturesque old buildings in this enjoyable little town. Pleasant walks lead alongside the creek through the town and up to Mt Remarkable (956 metres). West of town along Mt Remarkable Creek is Cathedral Rock.

Places to Stay & Eat

The *Mt Remarkable Hotel* (tel 66 2119) and the *North Star Hotel* (tel 66 2110) both have rooms at $17/25. The Mt Remarkable Hotel probably has more character; the floors slope, the doors won't close and you expect to see a ghost round every corner! Both hotels serve counter meals. *Melrose Caravan Park* (tel 66 2060) is in a picturesque spot along the creek and has sites from $7 and on-site vans from $20.

OTHER TOWNS

Other towns in the south of the Flinders include Carrieton where a major rodeo is held each October. Bruce and Hammond, near Wilmington, were both railheads at one time but have now faded away to ghost towns. Orroroo is an agricultural centre and nearby Black Rock Peak has good bushwalks and terrific views over the surrounding countryside. You can see Aboriginal rock carvings at Pekina Creek and the ruins of the nearby Pekina Station Homestead are also worth visiting.

Between Melrose and Port Germein you pass through the scenic Germein Gorge, while Bangor has the ruin of the Gorge Hotel. Further down at Wirrabara there's a *YHA Hostel* (tel (086) 68 4158) with beds at $5.50. You can get there by Stateliner bus.

QUORN (population 1050)

The 'gateway to the Flinders' is about 330 km north of Adelaide and only 46 km from Port Augusta. This was once an important railway town after the completion of the Great Northern Railway in 1878; it still has a lot of the flavour of the old pioneering days. The line was closed down in 1957, but since 1974 parts of the line have been re-opened as a tourist attraction by railway enthusiasts. On winter weekends and public holidays, a vintage steam engine makes a 43-km round-trip from Quorn to the scenic Pichi Richi Pass at a cost of $12 for adults.

The town, picturesquely sited in a valley in the ranges, has a couple of art galleries. Quornucopia offers a range of unusual crafts and gifts and there's the small Quorn Mill Museum and restaurant in an old bakery and flour mill. From Quorn you can make 4WD trips into the Flinders and visit the nearby Warren Gorge (which has good rock climbing), the

Buckaringa Gorge (good for picnics) and the Waukarie Creek Trail which runs from Woolshed Flat to Waukarie Creek. Closer to the town, you can follow walking trails to the top of Devil's Peak and Dutchman's Stern.

Information is available at the District Council Office, Seventh St.

Places to Stay & Eat

The Pichi Richi Hotel has singles/doubles for $20/28, but the *Grand Junction Hotel* (tel 48 6025) is better at $20/30. Their counter meals are all right, otherwise there are a few take-away places. *Quorn Caravan Park* (tel 48 6066) has sites for $6, on-site vans for $20.

KANYAKA

North of Quorn, about halfway to Hawker, are the ruins of the old Kanyaka settlement. Founded in 1851, it supported 70 families at its peak before being abandoned in the 1870s. Only the ruins of the solid, stone-built houses remain to remind of the high hopes that early settlers had for this harsh area.

If you're coming from the north, don't be fooled by the signs for the Kanyaka settlement; all there is here is a solitary gravestone by the creek bed. The ruins, deserted except for kangaroos and galahs, are further south. There are two groups of ruins – the second group is a couple of hundred metres away along the dirt road, obscured from view by a rise. The first group also has an old graveyard – note the solid stone dunnies, clearly built to last.

It's about one km along the creek to the cookhouse and shearing shed. The track continues around 1½ km to a picturesque permanent water hole, overlooked by the Kanyaka Death Rock.

HAWKER (population 350)

In a sheep-raising area, the town of Hawker has a tiny museum of minerals in the Mobil station. There are a number of places of interest which can be conveniently visited from here, including the Kanyaka ruins to the south and Wilpena Pound, only a short drive north. Willow Waters is another old property abandoned in the 1890s when crops failed.

There are Aboriginal rock paintings south of Hawker at Yourambulla Cave, a hollow in the rocks, high up on the side of Yourambulla Peak, a half hour walk from the road.

Places to Stay & Eat

The *Hawker Hotel* (tel (086) 48 9195) costs $23/34 for old-fashioned but quite OK small rooms. In the new motel part, rooms are $46/57 for singles/doubles. The counter meals here are certainly filling. There's another motel or the *Flinders Ranges Holiday Centre* (tel (086) 489 1150) has sites from $6, on-site vans from $20.

Getting There & Away

Apart for the Stateliner bus service, you can also get to Wilpena Pound on the 7 am newspaper run from in front of the Hawker Shopping Centre. Just ask inside.

WILPENA POUND

The best known feature of the ranges is the huge natural basin known as Wilpena Pound. This vast basin covers about 80 square km, ringed by a circle of cliffs and accessible only by the narrow opening at Sliding Rock through which the Wilpena Creek sometimes flows. From outside the Pound the cliff face is almost sheer – soaring to 1000 metres – but inside, the basin floor slopes gently away from the peaks. There are many excellent walks here including the climb to 1190 metre high St Marys Peak with superb views of the Pound. There are day walks on marked trails including this climb. Other walks are those to Edeowie Gorge and Malloga Falls, and to Mt Ohlssen Bagge.

There is plenty of wildlife in the Pound, particularly bird life which includes everything from rosellas, galahs and

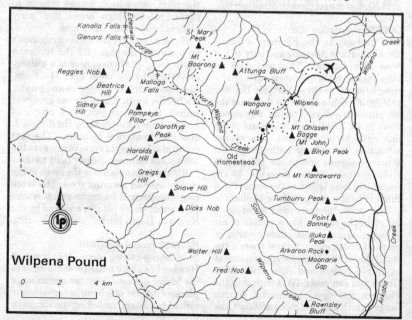

Wilpena Pound

0   2   4 km

Wilpena Pound, Flinders Ranges

budgerigars to wedge-tailed eagles. You can make scenic flights over the Pound (booking at the Wilpena Pound Motel – a 30 minute flight costs \$33) or make excursions to other places of interest in the vicinity. Sacred Canyon, with rock-cut patterns, is off to the east. North of Wilpena Pound is the Flinders Ranges National Park where scenic attractions include the Bunyeroo and Brachina gorges and the Aroona Valley.

Walks

You can take an excellent day-long walk from the camping site to St Marys Peak and back – either as an up-and-down or a round-trip expedition. Up and back, it's faster and more interesting to take the route outside the Pound and then up to the Tanderra Saddle since the scenery is much more spectacular. The final climb up to the saddle is fairly steep and the stretch to the top of the peak is a real

scramble. The views are superb from the saddle and the peak; the white glimmer of Lake Torrens is visible off to the west and the long Aroona Valley stretches north. Descending from the peak to the saddle you can then head back down on the same direct route or take the longer round-trip walk through the Pound via the homestead and Sliding Rock. This is the same track you take to get to Edeowie Gorge.

There is a series of bushwalks in the park, clearly marked by blue triangles along the tracks. Pick up a copy of the Wilpena leaflet issued by the National Parks & Wildlife Service, or the similar leaflet from the tourist office – both have maps which are quite OK for day walks on the marked trails. It is recommended that you do not walk solo and that you are adequately equipped – particularly with drinking water and sun protection in the summer. Most of the walks start from the camping ground and the walking times indicated are for a reasonably easy pace. The St Marys Peak walk is probably the most interesting, but there are plenty of others worth considering. They vary from short walks suitable for those with small children, to longer ones taking more than a day.

Places to Stay & Eat
Unless you've got a tent there is no cheap accommodation at the Pound. If you're equipped for camping there's a camping site at the Pound entrance with facilities including a well-stocked store. The cost for a site for two is $7. Otherwise the *Wilpena Pound Motel* has all mod cons including a restaurant and swimming pool but you can count on paying around $80 a night.

You can get pies and pasties in the shop, as well as food to prepare yourself, or counter lunches are available and there's the motel restaurant.

BLINMAN (population 100)
From the 1860s to the 1890s this was a busy copper town but today it's just a tiny country town on the circular route around Wilpena Pound. It's a useful starting point for visits to many of the scenic attractions in the area and the delightful *Hotel North Blinman* has the real outback pub flavour – bed & breakfast is $23 per person.

AROUND BLINMAN
The beautiful Aroona Valley and the ruins of the Aroona Homestead are to the south of Blinman. Further south is the Brachina Gorge, another typically spectacular gorge of the Flinders. Between Blinman and the Pound is the Great Wall of China, a long ridge capped with ironstone. Between Parachilna and Blinman it's a scenic drive on a rough dirt road through the Parachilna Gorge where there are good picnic areas.

Angorichina Tourist Village (tel (086) 4891 Angorichina 1) is about halfway between Blinman and Parachilna in the Parachilna Gorge and has camp sites ($6), units ($32) and chalets ($38). YHA members get a 10% discount. The owners are friendly and apart from providing good accommodation they can also advise on travel in this picturesque and rugged area.

North, on the Oodnadatta road, Beltana is almost a ghost town today but you can turn east here and visit the old copper mines at Sliding Rock. At one time Beltana was a major camel-breeding station and much of the town is now being restored. You can get a guide to the town from the old railway station which is now a museum. It's a long drive from anywhere to Chambers Gorge, well to the north-east towards Lake Frome. The deep gorge has rock carvings and from Mt Chambers you can see Lake Frome and the Flinders Ranges all the way from Mt Painter to Wilpena. There are camping facilities at Mt Chambers.

LEIGH CREEK (population 1000)
North again, along the Oodnadatta road, Leigh Creek's huge open-cut coal mine supplies the Port Augusta power station. Tree planting has transformed this once barren town; you can do a drive-yourself tour of the coal works by following the green arrow signs.

From Leigh Creek, you can visit the Aroona Dam; the Gammon Ranges National Park (64 km to the east) is also reached from here, but it's a remote and rugged area for experienced bushwalkers only. In 1982 the whole town was shifted south a few km because the site of the original town is now being mined.

ARKAROOLA
The tiny settlement of Arkaroola, in the northern part of the Flinders, was only established in 1968. It's a privately operated wildlife sanctuary in rugged and spectacular country. From the settlement you can take a 4WD trip along the 'ridge top' through rugged mountain country and there are also scenic flights and many

Arkaroola, Flinders Ranges

walking tracks. The ridge-top tour costs $35 ($31 for children under two) – expensive but it's a spectacular four hour trip through amazing scenery.

Arkaroola used to be a mining area and old tracks cut during the mining days lead to rock pools at the Barraranna Gorge and Echo Camp and to water holes at Arkaroola and Nooldoonooldoona. Further on is the Bolla Bollana Springs and some ruins of an old copper smelter.

Mt Painter is a well known and very scenic landmark in the region while there are fine views from Freeling Heights across Yudnamutana Gorge or from Siller's Lookout from where you can see the salt flats of Lake Frome. This is the real, red outback country and Mt Painter is a spectacular example of that outback landscape. The Arkaroola area is of geological significance since Paralana Hot Springs is believed to be the site of the last volcanic activity to have taken place in Australia.

There are many interesting walks in this area, but take water – and care. You get out of sight of civilisation surprisingly fast and you'll quickly realise what an inhospitable place the outback can be, particularly when it's hot. This is rough and rugged country.

Places to Stay & Eat

The resort camping site costs $9 ($15 with power) for two and there is a variety of other accommodation possibilities. In the bunkhouse, bunk beds are $16 but these are intended mainly for groups. It's the same price, however, in the 'Shearers' Quarters'.

Holiday-flat-style units cost $34 with shared facilities or the motel units are $57 for a double in the *Greenwood Lodge* and $70 in the *Mawson Lodge*.

There's a small shop where you can buy basic supplies or in the restaurant main courses are $11 to $17.

Getting There & Away

The Stateliner bus service from Adelaide cost $52 and comes up to Arkaroola on Saturdays and Wednesdays, returning on Sundays and Thursdays.

The Outback

North of the Eyre Peninsula and the Flinders area stretches the vast, empty area of South Australia's far north. It's sparsely populated and difficult to travel through yet has much of interest. Large parts of the far north are prohibited areas (either Aboriginal reserves or the Woomera military area) and without 4WD or camels it's not possible to stray far from the main roads as there is virtually no surfaced road in the far north.

THE ROUTES NORTH

The last stretch of the Stuart Highway to be sealed was opened in 1987 so you can now drive on a smooth bitumen road all the way from Adelaide to Alice Springs. The new road is not only smooth and straight, it also follows a much more direct route so you've got less distance to travel as well. It's still a long way, though – 931 km from Port Augusta to the Northern Territory border. The temptation to rush along that smooth road has resulted in more than a few high speed meetings between cars and cattle. Take care.

For those who want to travel to the Northern Territory the hard way, there is still the Oodnadatta Track. This old road runs from Port Augusta through the Flinders to Leigh Creek, Lyndhurst, Marree, Oodnadatta and eventually joins the Stuart Highway not far south of the Territory border. For most of the way it runs close to the old railway line route. The road is surfaced as far as Lyndhurst, after that it's a typical outback track. There are a number of routes across from Oodnadatta to the Stuart Highway. From Oodnadatta to Coober Pedy is 194 km.

The two other routes of interest in the far north are the famous Birdsville Track and the Strzelecki Track. These days the tracks have been so much improved that during the winter season it's quite feasible to do them in any regular car that's in good condition – 4WD is not necessary. Rain or summer heat can be quite a different story. For more information on these outback routes check with the state automobile associations. Algona Publications (16 Charles St, Northcote, Victoria 3070) do a good *Simpson Desert South – Lake Eyre* map which covers all three tracks.

The South Australian outback includes much of the Simpson Desert and the harsh, rocky land of Sturt's Stony Desert. There are also huge salt-lakes which every once in a long while fill with water. Lake Eyre, used by Donald Campbell for his attempt on the world's land-speed record in the '60s, filled up for a time in the '70s. It filled up again in 1989, only the third occasion since white men first reached this area. When the infrequent rains do reach this dry land the effect is amazing – flowers bloom and plants grow at a breakneck pace in order to complete their life cycle before the dry returns. There is even a species of frog that goes into a sort of suspended animation, remaining in the ground for years on end only to pop up with the first sign of rain. On a much more mundane level, roads can be washed out and the surface turned into a sticky glue. When this occurs, vehicles on the road are often stuck for days – or even weeks.

WOOMERA

During the '50s and '60s Woomera was used to launch experimental British rockets and conduct tests in an abortive European project to orbit a satellite. The projects were later abandoned, but Woomera is still a military base and there are also American military personnel based here. About 2000 people live here today, against 5000 at the town's peak.

A small 'heritage' museum in the centre

of town has various local oddments and a collection of old aircraft and missiles. The museum tells you something about the missile testing in the past but very little about what goes on today. The plutonium 'mistake' of the '50s doesn't get a mention, although along the highway you'll see the signs warning you that the country west of the road is off-limits.

Places to Stay
The *Eldo Complex* (tel (086) 73 7867) on Katana Place is a hotel with rooms at $29/40.

Getting There & Away
Air Kendell Airlines fly Adelaide/Woomera most days of the week for $131.

Bus The township of Woomera is six km off the Stuart Highway from the tiny and scruffy little settlement of Pimba, 173 km north of Port Augusta. Greyhound, Bus Australia, Deluxe and Pioneer Express all go through Woomera daily on their Adelaide/Alice Springs services. It's about $34 from Adelaide, $83 from Alice Springs. Stateliner also operate to Woomera.

ANDAMOOKA (population 400)
Off the Stuart Highway, north of Woomera and west of Lake Torrens, Andamooka is a rough & ready little town devoted to opal mining. Many of the residents live in dugout homes to give some relief from the temperature extremes. It's about 100 km from Pimba to Andamooka and although the road is fair it very quickly becomes impassable after rain. Uranium has been discovered at Roxby Downs near Andamooka. You can get to Andamooka and Roxby Downs by Stateliner bus.

GLENDAMBO
It's 367 km from the Pimba turn-off for Woomera to Coober Pedy. Glendambo is 113 km north of Pimba, 254 km south of Coober Pedy. It's a new store, pub/motel and caravan park, all developed since the

completion of the new Stuart Highway. The size and modernity of this establishment is indicative of the increased traffic up the road since it was sealed.

COOBER PEDY (population 2000)
On the Stuart Highway, 935 km north of Adelaide, Coober Pedy is one of the best known towns in the outback. The name is Aboriginal and means 'white fellow's hole in the ground', which aptly describes the place, as a large proportion of the population lives in dugouts to shelter from daytime temperatures that can soar to over 50°C and winter nights which can get uncomfortably cold.

Coober Pedy is in an extremely inhospitable area and the town looks it; even in the middle of winter it looks dried out and dusty with piles of junk everywhere. This is no attractive little settlement, in fact it's hardly surprising that much of the filming of *Mad Max III* took place in Coober Pedy – the town looks like the end of the world!

Information
The Underground Bookshop is pretty good for local information.

Opal Mining
The town survives from opals which were first discovered in 1911. Keen fossickers can have a go themselves after acquiring a prospecting permit from the Mines Department in Adelaide. Fossicking through the outcasts is known as noodling. There are literally hundreds of mines around Coober Pedy but surprisingly the mining is generally very small scale; there are no big operators. What seems to happen is somebody makes a find at a particular place and immediately dozens of others head off to the same area.

Around the town there are mine tours, opal cutting demonstrations and polished stones and jewellery on sale. Coober Pedy Tours have daily three hour tours at 10 am and 1.30 pm which cost $7 (children $4).

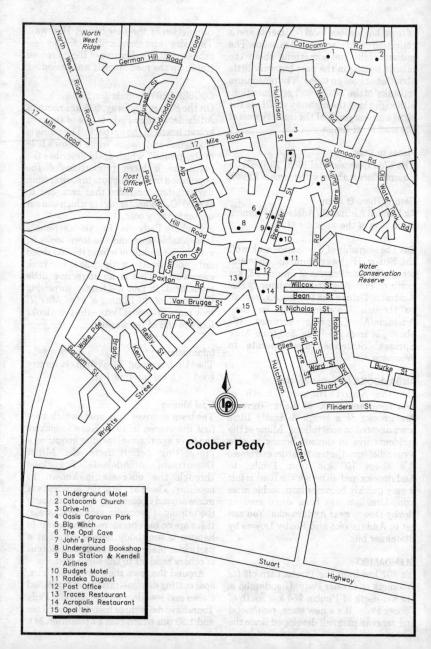

Coober Pedy

1 Underground Motel
2 Catacomb Church
3 Drive-In
4 Oasis Caravan Park
5 Big Winch
6 The Opal Cave
7 John's Pizza
8 Underground Bookshop
9 Bus Station & Kendell Airlines
10 Budget Motel
11 Radeka Dugout
12 Post Office
13 Traces Restaurant
14 Acropolis Restaurant
15 Opal Inn

Coober Pedy township

These cover the sights in the town and take you underground into an opal mine.

There are many migrant groups in Coober Pedy – Greeks, Yugoslavs and Italians are the biggest groups, but the gem buyers are mainly from Hong Kong. They stay in the Opal Inn while they're in town and when one heads back to base (often the Hong Kong travellers' centre Chungking Mansions in Kowloon) another Hong Konger takes the room over.

Opals

Australia is the opal producing centre of the world and South Australia is where most of Australia's opals come from. Opals are hardened from silica suspended in water and the colour is produced by light being split and reflected by the silica molecules. Valuable opals are cut in three different fashions: solid opals can be cut out of the rough into *cabochons* – domed-top stones; *triplets* consist of a layer of opal sandwiched between an opaque backing layer and a transparent cap; and *doublets* are simply an opal layer with an opaque backing. In addition, some opals from Queensland are found embedded in rock; these are sometimes polished while still incorporated in the surrounding rock.

An opal's value is determined by its colour and clarity – the brighter and clearer the colour the better. Brilliance of colour is more important than the colour itself. The type of opal is also a determinant of value – black and crystal opals are the most valuable, semi-black and semi-crystal are in the middle, milk opal at the bottom. The bigger the pattern the better, and visible flaws (like cracks) also have a bearing on the value.

Shape is also important inasmuch as a high dome is better than a flat opal. Finally, given equality of other aspects, the size is important. As with any sort of gemstone don't expect to find great bargains unless you clearly know and understand what you are buying.

Dugout Homes

Many of the early dugout homes were simply worked out mines but now they're often cut specifically as homes, using the same equipment as for mine shafts and drives. There are a number of 'display' homes around the town – all you have to do is create an eccentric enough abode and you can charge admission! Harry's Crocodile Nest is about five km out of town, charges $1 (children 50c) and is definitely one of the more eccentric. It makes an appearance towards the end of *Mad Max III*. Various other homes are open for $1 to $1.50 including the popular display home with an indoor swimming pool!

Other Attractions

Out of town towards Crocodile Harry's you pass Underground Potteries which has some nice pottery for sale. Right in the middle of town, the Big Winch is a lookout over the town. The Underground Catacomb Church is another local attraction.

Breakaways

Less than 30 km from Coober Pedy, the Breakaway Reserve is an area of low hills which have 'broken away' from the Stuart Range. You can drive to the Lookout in a conventional vehicle and see the natural formation known as the Castle, which featured in *Mad Max III*. With 4WD you can make a longer 65 km loop from Coober Pedy, following the Dog Proof Fence back to the road from Coober Pedy to Oodnadatta. The Underground Bookshop has a leaflet and map or Coober Pedy Tours run trips to the Breakaways

Places to Stay

Hostels The *Backpacker's Inn* at Radeka's Dugout Motel (tel (086) 72 5223) offers hostel-style underground dormitories at $9 overnight or $11 for 24 hours. The *Coober Pedy Oasis Caravan Park* (tel (086) 72 5169) also has accommodation.

Hotels & Motels There are a number of hotels and motels, some underground, some with big air-conditioners! The *Umoona Opal Mine* (tel (086) 72 5288) on the Main Rd has rooms for $14 per person.

Bathrooms are communal but there are kitchen facilities. The *Coober Pedy Budget Hotel* (tel (086) 72 5163) has rooms from $17 to $40 and the *Stable Inn* (tel (086) 72 5034) from $19 to $50.

Other motels generally cost from around $60 for two, they include the *Radeka Dugout* (tel (086) 72 5223), *The Underground* (tel (086) 72 5324) and the *Opal Inn* (tel (086) 72 5054) where the Chinese opal buyers stay.

Camping There are a number of caravan parks in the town with sites at around $7 to $10. The *Coober Pedy Opal Fields Park* (tel (086) 72 5551) has cabins from $17, on-site vans from $25. The *Coober Pedy Oasis Caravan Park* (tel (086) 72 5169) also has cabins and vans, but at slightly higher prices.

Places to Eat

The *Acropolis* is great value – their mixed meat plate ($9) or mixed fish plate ($16) gives you *lots* of solid food – not bad food either. Other places include *John's Pizza & Coffee Shop, Traces Restaurant* and the *Desert Cafe*. The *Opal Inn* does pretty good counter meals. *Lucas Supermarket* is the best of the supermarkets.

Getting There & Away

Air Kendell Airlines fly Adelaide/Coober Pedy most days of the week ($194), Coober Pedy/Ayers Rock once weekly ($152).

Bus It's 420 km from Coober Pedy to Kulgera, just across the border into the Northern Territory. Deluxe, Bus Australia, Pioneer Express and Greyhound all pass through on the Adelaide/Alice Springs route. It's about $60 from Adelaide and $51 from Alice Springs. Stateliner also operate Adelaide to Coober Pedy at least twice daily, arriving there at a God-awful middle-of-the-night hour.

MARLA

Not far south of the Northern Territory border, Marla is a new settlement where the Ghan railway line crosses the new Stuart Highway. The opal mining fields of Mintabie are 50 km west. Marla has motel rooms, camping facilities, supplies and so on.

MARREE (population 400)

On the rugged alternate road north through Oodnadatta, Marree is a tiny township once used as a staging post for the Afghani-led camel trains of the last century. There are still a few old date palms standing as reminders of those days. Marree is also the southern end of the Birdsville track. Just six km north is Frome Creek, a dry creek bed that, with rain, can cut the track for weeks on end.

Stateliner have a weekly bus service from Adelaide to Marree for $52.

OODNADATTA (population 200)

The tiny town of Oodnadatta (like Marree, it got even tinier with the old Ghan track's closure) is at the point where the road and the old railway lines diverged. It was an important staging post during the construction of the overland telegraph line and later was the railhead for the line from Adelaide, from its original extension to Oodnadatta in 1884 until it finally reached Alice Springs in 1929.

Places to Stay

The *Oodnadatta Caravan Park* (tel (086) 70 7822) has sites from just $3. Or there's the *Transcontinental Hotel* (tel (086) 70 7804) with rooms at $38 per person.

BIRDSVILLE TRACK

Years ago cattle from the south-west of Queensland were driven down the Birdsville Track to Marree where they were loaded aboard the train – these days they're trucked out on the 'beef roads'. It's 481 km between Marree and Birdsville, just across the Queensland border. Although even conventional vehicles can manage the Birdsville without difficulty, it's worth bearing in mind that it's a long way to push if you break down – and that

traffic along the road isn't exactly heavy. Petrol is, it appears, no longer available at Mungeranie, about 200 km north of Marree and 280 km south of Birdsville.

The track is more or less at the meeting point between the sand dunes of the Simpson Desert to the west and the desolate wastes of Sturt's Stony Desert to the east. There are ruins of a couple of old homesteads scattered along the track and artesian bores gush out boiling-hot salty water at many places. At Clifton Hill, about 150 km south of Birdsville, the track splits and one route or other may be better – seek local advice. The last travellers to die on the track took the wrong route, got lost, ran out of petrol and died before they were discovered.

STRZELECKI TRACK

The Strzelecki Track is longer than the Birdsville at 494 km, but these days it too can be handled by regular vehicles. The track starts from Lyndhurst, about 80 km south of Marree, and runs to the tiny outpost of Innamincka. The discovery of natural gas deposits near Moomba has brought a great deal of development and improvement to the track. The new Moomba-Strzelecki track is better kept but longer and less interesting than the old track which follows the Strzelecki Creek. Fuel is available at Moomba only in emergencies.

INNAMINCKA

At the northern end of the Strzelecki Track, Innamincka is near Cooper's Creek where the Burke and Wills expedition of 1860 came to its tragic conclusion. From here you can visit the Burke and Wills 'dig' tree, the memorials and markers where their bodies were found and the marker where King, the sole survivor, was found. He was cared for by Aborigines until his rescue. There is also a memorial where Howitt, who led the rescue party, set up his depot on the creek.

Although Cooper's Creek only flows

during floods, there are water holes along the creek which never dry up. For this reason the area was long a centre for local Aboriginal populations and was a popular base for the European explorers of the 1800s.

Algona Publications' *Innamincka – Coongie Lakes* map is a good source of information on the Innamincka area. For a moving account of the often bumbling and foolhardy, but ultimately tragic Burke and Wills expedition read Alan Moorehead's *Cooper's Creek*.

Places to Stay

The *Innamincka Hotel* (tel (086) 42 5555) has just four rooms at $25 per person. The *Innamincka Trading Post* (same number) has cabins at $46 double. There are plenty of places to camp along the creek.

THE GHAN

See the Northern Territory chapter for details of the famous train line from Adelaide to Alice Springs.

Tasmania

Area	68,000 square km
Population	448,700

Hobart, Tasmania's capital, was Australia's second European settlement, founded fairly soon after Sydney became established.

The first European to reach Tasmania was the Dutch navigator Abel Tasman, who arrived in 1642 and named it Antony van Diemens Land after the Governor of Batavia. In 1772 the island was visited by the French Captain Marion du Fresne. The first Englishman to see it, Captain Tobias Furneaux, came upon it accidentally, also in 1772. He was followed by Captains James Cook and William Bligh. All believed that Tasmania was part of the Australian mainland.

European contact with the Tasmanian coast became more frequent after the soldiers and convicts of the First Fleet settled at Sydney Cove in 1788, as ships heading to the colony of New South Wales from the west had to sail around the island.

In 1789 Captain John Henry Cox, en route to China, recognised the commercial potential of the huge colonies of seals in Tasmanian waters: skins and oils from these seals became Australia's first real exports.

It was not until 1798 that Lieutenant Matthew Flinders, on the sloop *Norfolk*, circumnavigated Van Diemens Land, proving that it was an island. He named the strait after his ship's surgeon, George Bass. Using Bass Strait shortened the journey to Sydney from India or the Cape of Good Hope by a week.

European rivalry over Tasmanian waters in the late 1700s prompted Governor King of New South Wales to establish a second settlement, south of Sydney Cove, before another country did so. After a cursory glance at Port Phillip Bay, in Victoria (no good, was the report), he decided on the Derwent River estuary.

Hobart Town was established in 1804 and quickly grew to rival Sydney. Other parts of the island were opened up for farming and mining.

Later, as the agricultural potential of the huge expanses of land in New South Wales was realised, Hobart became less important than Sydney. The preservation of many of Tasmania's historic buildings may be a result of its slower development.

In 1855 Van Diemens Land was officially renamed Tasmania. The following year the first Tasmanian two chamber parliament was elected and transportation abolished.

Reminders of the convict days are especially evident in Tasmania, as the worst of the convicts were shipped there: it was dubbed 'that isthmus between earth and hell'. There are a number of interesting penal settlement ruins – Port Arthur being the best known – and many convict built bridges and buildings. Early mining also left a mark; Tasmania has a number of fascinating ghost towns, not to mention some more modern mining sites.

For many visitors Tasmania's real fascination won't be charming old buildings or ruins but the wild, natural scenery and the smaller, almost un-

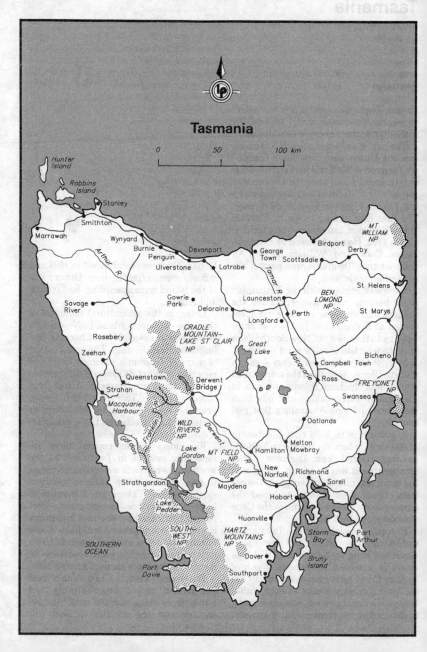

Tasmania

0   50   100 km

Top: Wrest Point Casino, Hobart, Tas (PS)
Left: Lobster fishing, Tas (PS)
Right: Eaglehawk Neck, Tasman Peninsula, Tas (TW)

Top: Pieman River, Tas (TT)
Left: Constitution Dock, Hobart, Tas (PS)
Right: Van Diemens Land Company Store, Stanley, Tas (PT)

Australian scale of the island. There is spectacular coastline, rugged mountains, magnificent rivers, beautiful lakes and forests, excellent bushwalking trails and some of the best parks in Australia.

TASMANIAN ABORIGINES

The story of Australia's Aborigines since European settlement has not been a happy one, but nowhere has the story been more tragic than in Tasmania.

Tasmania's Aborigines became separated from the Aborigines of the mainland over 10,000 years ago when rising ocean levels, caused by the thawing of the last ice age, cut Tasmania off from the rest of the country. From that time their culture diverged from that of the mainland population. They lived by hunting, fishing and gathering, sheltered in bark or leaf lean-tos and, despite Tasmania's cold weather, went naked apart from a coating of grease and charcoal. Their society was based on sharing and exchange – a concept the European invaders failed to come to terms with.

European settlers found Tasmania fertile and easily divided and fenced to make farms. As the Aborigines gradually lost their traditional hunting grounds they realised that the Europeans had come to steal their land, not share it, and they began to fight for what was theirs. By 1806 the killing on both sides was out of control. The Aborigines speared stock and shepherds and in turn were hunted and shot. Europeans abducted Aboriginal children to use as forced labour, raped and tortured Aboriginal women, gave poisoned flour to friendly tribes, and laid steel traps in the bush.

In 1828 martial law was proclaimed by Governor Arthur, giving soldiers the right to arrest or shoot on sight any Aborigine found in an area of European settlement. The Aboriginal people fought back with spears and fire and the settlers retaliated with the wholesale slaughter of men, women and children.

In 1830 the settlers launched a military operation known as the *Black Line* – a human chain, comprised of every able-bodied European male in the colony. For three weeks they moved east and south across the settled areas in an attempt to corner the Aborigines on the Tasman Peninsula. They only managed to capture an old man and a boy, but succeeded in clearing the rest out of the settled districts.

Finally, between 1829 and 1834, George Augustus Robinson, the Conciliator, travelled the island collecting the survivors of this once proud and peaceful race. The last 135 Aborigines from the Tasmanian mainland were resettled on a reserve (read 'prison') on Flinders Island – to be 'civilised' and Christianised. With nothing to do but exist, most of them died of despair, homesickness, poor food or respiratory diseases. During those first 35 years of European settlement 183 Europeans and nearly 4000 Aborigines were killed.

The 47 survivors of the Flinders Island group were transferred to Oyster Cove in 1847. Of those, all but Fanny Cochrane Smith, the daughter of an Aboriginal woman and a European sealer, were dead by 1876. The last full-blooded male died in Hobart in 1874 and Truganini, the last surviving full-blooded member of mainland Tasmania's Aboriginal population, died in 1876.

European sealers had been working in Bass Strait since 1798 and although they occasionally raided tribes along the coast for women, killing the men who tried to protect them, for the most part their contact with the indigenous people was based on trade. They exchanged flour, tobacco, tea and dogs for seal and kangaroo skins. Aboriginal women were also traded by Aboriginal men. Many of the sealers settled on the Bass Strait islands with their Aboriginal women and the families they had started. By 1847 the new Aboriginal community, centred on the Furneaux group of islands, had grown to about 50 people and had established a lifestyle based on both Aboriginal and European ways. It was this community that saved the Tasmanian Aboriginal society from total extinction, and it is descendants of these people who today wage a daily battle not only for their rights but for recognition of their very existence in a white society that is still taught that the last Tasmanian Aborigine died in 1876.

GEOGRAPHY

Tasmania is a varied, and in places, quite un-Australian island. It has a relatively dispersed population despite its compact size and there are still some areas that remain uninhabited. This is not, as in most other unpopulated Australian regions, due to a lack of water – Tasmania's south-west wilderness, for example, enjoys abundant rainfall. It was, however, distinct geographical features such as impenetrable rainforests and rugged mountains that governed the early regional development of the island and led to European settlements being established in the fertile stretches inland and on the north and east coasts. Many parts of Tasmania that were originally too wild for Europeans to attempt to settle are now protected.

Tasmania's population is mainly in the east and along the north coast where the land is rolling and fertile. The coast and its bays are accessible and inviting with many beautiful coves and beaches. The Midlands region is almost a re-creation of the green England so beloved of early settlers, and the highland lakes country in the centre of the state, though less populated, is accessible and beautiful.

By contrast the south-west and the west coast are amazingly wild and virtually untouched. Raging seas often batter the full length of the west coast, where Strahan is the only port of any size and its bay, difficult though it is to enter, the only safe harbour. Inland, the forests and mountains of the south-west form one of the world's last great wilderness areas; this is the region for which conservationists

in the early '80s fought the 'profits today, to hell with tomorrow' developers intent on flooding more and more of the most beautiful rivers in their quest for hydroelectric power.

INFORMATION

The Tasmanian Government Tourist Bureau (TGTB), also known as Tourism Tasmania, is in Hobart, Launceston, Devonport, Burnie and Queenstown. On the mainland it has branches in:

Australian Capital Territory
 5 Canberra Savings Centre, City Walk, Canberra 2600 (tel 47 0070)
New South Wales
 129 King St, Sydney 2000 (tel 233 2500)
Queensland
 217-219 Queen St, Brisbane 4000 (tel 221 2744)
South Australia
 32 King William St, Adelaide 5000 (tel 211 7411)
Victoria
 256 Collins St, Melbourne 3000 (tel 653 7999)
Western Australia
 100 William St, Perth 6000 (tel 321 2633)

The offices have information on the usual tourist sights, accommodation, restaurants and travel. Every two months the bureau produces *Tasmanian Travelways*, a free newspaper covering facilities, accommodation, public transport and current costs throughout the state.

The Wilderness Society, at 130 Davey St, Hobart, (and in other Australian capital cities) can tell you just about anything you want to know about the natural Tasmania and has a wonderful selection of books, brochures and leaflets ideal to use while exploring the wild side of this beautiful island.

The Tasmanian Tourist Council has information at its offices, a variety of shops and restaurants. It produces an annual *Visitors' Guide to Tasmania* ($1.85) which is available from Tasmanian Travel Centres. It's an excellent publication with information on most places in Tasmania and good maps in the back. The council also produces a whole series of *Let's Talk About* brochures, which provide more comprehensive local information on towns, areas around larger towns, wildlife, parks and so on.

The Royal Automobile Club of Tasmania produces a tourist map of the island for $2 (free to members and reciprocal members). It also puts out an accommodation guide and has offices in most larger towns.

Outside the larger towns there are not a great many bank branches, so don't let your money run low.

Despite the many YHA hostels in Tasmania it is advisable to book during peak holiday periods. *Tasmanian Travelways* has a good list of accommodation possibilities, but there are other places which are not listed. Accommodation in Tasmania is seasonal. In summer prices rise and it is wise to book, particularly for popular tourist centres. Strahan is one place that has been especially tight for summer accommodation.

Tasmanian Travelways and the automobile club's guide both list camping sites and caravan parks with on-site vans. You'll find sites at most towns, in the national parks, at some beaches and at more out-of-the-way places – like Bruny and Maria Islands. The Department of Lands, Parks & Wildlife's *Camping on Crown Land* pamphlet lists the camping areas it manages around the island. Facilities at these sites are pretty basic.

ACTIVITIES
Bushwalking

Not unexpectedly, Tasmania, with its rugged, mountainous country, much of it still barely touched by people, is ideal for bushwalking. It has some of the finest bushwalking in Australia and many walkers believe that the superb Cradle Mountain-Lake St Clair walk is the equal of any of the better known walks in New Zealand.

Good information sources on bushwalking include the Federation of Tasmanian Bushwalking Clubs in Hobart, and the Department of Lands, Parks & Wildlife, at 134 Macquarie St, Hobart, and 1 Civic Square, Launceston. The department's Tasmaps range in scale from 1:25,000 to 1:100,000. Lands, Parks & Wildlife also produces aerial photographs from 1:5000 to 1:45,000. Tasmaps are widely available at bush gear shops, Wilderness Society shops and newsagencies in Tasmania.

Good books include *100 Walks in Tasmania*, by Tyrone Thomas, and *South West Tasmania*, by John Chapman. John Chapman is also the co-author of Lonely Planet's *Bushwalking in Australia* which includes a large section detailing the pick of Tasmania's bushwalks. Other good sources of information are the excellent bush gear shops such as Paddy Pallin in Hobart and Launceston, and Allgoods in Launceston. The Wilderness Society, at 130 Davey St, Hobart, is dedicated to protecting wilderness areas and has people on hand who know what they're talking about. It has bookshops on Salamanca Place, Hobart, and in Devonport and Launceston.

Summer is the best time for Tasmanian bushwalks although even then the mountain country can spring some nasty surprises on the unwary. Be prepared for sometimes viciously changeable weather.

Cradle Mountain-Lake St Clair National Park, with its 80 km track, is one of the classic long bushwalks in Australia (see the separate section on this walk). Frenchmans Cap National Park is for the experienced bushwalker only – there are huts at Lake Vera and Lake Tahure. South-West National Park, with Lake Pedder and the peaks of the Arthur Range, is also mainly for the experienced walker, although there are shorter, easier paths. The Hydro-Electric Commission (HEC) has several lodges there. The South-West Track, from Port Davey to Cockle Creek, is a magnificent 10 day walk but again, only experienced walkers should tackle this one.

On the east coast, Freycinet National Park has good coastal walks which can be undertaken at any time of year, including a popular 27 km walking circuit. Ben Lomond National Park, south-east of Launceston, also has good walks and one hut.

Water Sports

Swimming There are good bayside beaches near Hobart including Bellerive, Long Beach, Kingston and Nutgrove. Good surf beaches are unpatrolled. On the west coast the surf is ferocious and there are very few access points to beaches.

Canoeing Canoeing is popular on several of the state's rivers.

Diving The often rugged Tasmanian coast also provides some fine scuba diving opportunities. Equipment can be rented in Hobart and Launceston and good diving can be found on the north-east and east coasts.

Skiing

Tasmania has two ski resorts, Ben Lomond and Mt Mawson, which offer cheaper, although less developed, ski facilities than the major resorts in Victoria and New South Wales. Despite its southerly latitude Tasmania's snowfalls tend to be fairly light and unreliable.

Ben Lomond is 60 km from Launceston and most mornings during the ski season (depending on snow cover) Redline and Mountain Stage Line buses travel to the slopes. Redline buses depart from the terminal at 112 George St, and Mountain Stage Line buses leave from the Paddy Pallin Outdoor Shop, 59 Brisbane St, and cost $15. Redline also operate a service from Hobart. You can catch a shuttle bus from Jacobs Ladder to the ski village car park for $6.

Mt Mawson is in Mt Field National Park, 75 km west of Hobart. It's smaller and lower key and the snow coverage is

often poor but the ski-touring can be exceptional.

Cross-country skiing is popular on the western field at Cradle Mountain and at Mt Rufus, in the Cradle Mountain-Lake St Clair National Park.

GETTING THERE & AWAY

Air

To Hobart With Ansett or Australian Airlines the fares from Melbourne are $166 one way, $133 standby and $216 Apex return; from Sydney it costs $270 one way, $351 return. East-West Airlines fly from Melbourne for $216 return with an advance purchase fare; from Sydney the same fare costs $307. East-West operate to the Gold Coast from Hobart for $415 return.

Hobart is also an international port of entry. Air New Zealand operate flights between Hobart and Christchurch and Qantas fly to Auckland from Hobart.

Copyright Tasmanian Department of Tourism 1985

Tasmanian devils and apples are the symbols of Tasmania

To Devonport & Wynyard The cheapest flights from the mainland are to Devonport or Wynyard. East-West fly from Melbourne to Devonport for $131 one way, $100 standby or $172 return with an advance purchase ticket; Ansett fly to Wynyard for the same price. More restrictive tickets cost as little as $140 return to either destination. From Sydney fares are $237 one way or $311 return.

Of the small airlines, Aus-Air will fly you from Melbourne's Moorabbin Airport to Wynyard or Devonport for $110. You can also fly to Wynyard from Phillip Island in Victoria with Phillip Island Air Service (tel (057) 56 7316) for $86 one way or $66 standby. Promair operates out of eastern Victoria with flights from Welshpool to Devonport for $120 one way or $200 return.

To Launceston Launceston is serviced by Ansett and Australian Airlines. From Melbourne it costs $142 one way, $114 standby, and $185 Apex return; from Sydney the fares are $213, $170 and $277 respectively. Ansett Flexi-Fares and Australian Airlines Excursion 45 fares cost $156 return from Melbourne.

Promair have flights from Traralgon in eastern Victoria to Launceston for $140 one way or $240 return.

Other Destinations Airlines of Tasmania fly from Melbourne's Essendon Airport to Flinders Island ($94), Queenstown ($128), Smithton ($89), Strahan ($128) and Launceston ($128). Aus-Air also fly to Smithton ($100) and King Island from Melbourne. Kendell Airlines fly from Melbourne to King Island and Promair fly to Flinders Island.

Boat

The Melbourne to Devonport shipping service is particularly popular with people who want to bring their vehicles to Tasmania. The *Abel Tasman* has a coffee shop, lounges, bar, a disco, restaurant, sauna, pool and gym and makes three crossings a week each way. The boat departs Station Pier, Melbourne, at 6 pm Monday, Wednesday and Friday, and arrives 14½ hours later at 8.30 the following morning. The returning boat departs Devonport at 6 pm Sunday, Tuesday and Thursday, and arrives at 8.30 the following morning. A free bus service running between the Melbourne city centre and the docks connects with departures and arrivals.

Fares vary: there is the holiday season (December to February), the shoulder seasons (February to May, September to December), and the bargain season (May to September). The cheapest fares are for a two, three or four berth cabin with shared facilities in the lower decks. These cost $78/97/120 a person one way. Then there is a variety of two, three and four berth cabins ranging in price to $155/195/228 for a suite on the top deck. Children and students under 18 get a 50% discount, and students up to 26 get a 25% discount if they have a student card.

The cost for accompanied vehicles also varies with the seasons, and with the size of the vehicle, but rates start from around $86/110/125. You can take a motorcycle across for $43/55/63; bicycles cost $10/12/14.

One important point to consider if you plan to take the ferry in the holiday or shoulder seasons is that it will be heavily booked; you must plan well ahead. For bookings and fare information contact the TT-Line Terminal in Melbourne (tel (03) 645 2766) or Devonport (tel (004) 27 9751).

There are plans to start a high speed catamaran service to Tasmania in late 1990 or early 1991. The service will operate between Port Welshpool, which is near Wilsons Promontory, about 200 km southeast of Melbourne, and George Town in Tasmania. The 275 km crossing of the Bass Strait will be made in just four hours. The catamaran will carry 350 passengers and 70 cars. It will be made in Hobart – two similar vessels have been sold to operators in Britain.

GETTING AROUND

Air

Airlines of Tasmania operate a fairly extensive network in Tasmania and also fly between Tasmania and Melbourne's Essendon Airport. You can fly from Melbourne to Tasmania via Flinders Island for little more than a regular fare from Melbourne directly to mainland Tasmania. The price chart shows the main routes and costs around the island with the smaller airlines. More information is given in the relevant Getting There & Away sections.

Bus

All the main towns are connected by bus services. Tasmanian Redline Coaches are the main operators and Greyhound and Pioneer passes are valid on their services.

Tasmanian Redline also offer a Tassie Pass at $75 for 14 days or $60 for seven days. If, however, you intend to make the east coast trip between Hobart and Launceston this pass won't get you right along the coast as a number of the connecting services are run by private operators.

Redline have terminals in Hobart,

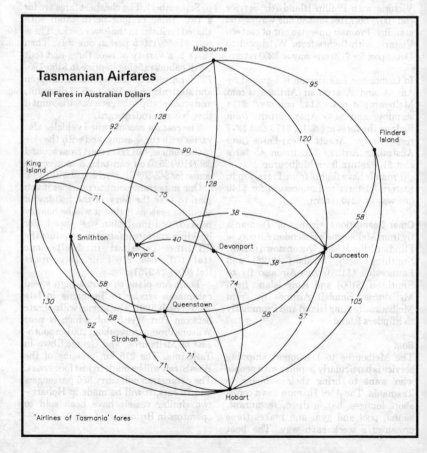

Tasmanian Airfares

All Fares in Australian Dollars

Melbourne

95

128

92

Flinders Island

90

120

King Island

128

75

71

38

58

Smithton

40

Devonport

Wynyard

Launceston

38

58

74

130

Queenstown

58

105

58

57

92

Strahan

71

71

Hobart

'Airlines of Tasmania' fares

Launceston, Devonport, Burnie, Smithton and Queenstown. Services operate between those towns via the Midland, Bass, Murchison and Lyell highways. Redline's West Coast Service also operates from Hobart via Derwent Bridge and Queenstown to Strahan or north to Burnie. Routes include Hobart to Launceston ($13.80), Hobart to Devonport ($23.40), Launceston to Burnie ($26.60), Launceston to Devonport ($9.60), Burnie to Queenstown ($21), Queenstown to Hobart ($24.20), Queenstown to Strahan ($4), and Derwent Bridge to Hobart ($16.50).

You can make the east coast Tasman Highway trip from Hobart to Launceston, using a number of connections, for $31.70. The main operators are Hobart Coaches, Peakes and Haley's. Hobart Coaches also have buses to the Huon Valley. For more information on individual connections refer to the Hobart and the East Coast Getting There & Away sections.

Tasmanian Motorways services the Derwent Valley and New Norfolk, and the run between Hobart and Port Arthur (weekdays only). There are also companies that provide transport to the main bushwalking destinations such as Lake St Clair, Cradle Mountain, Cockle Creek, etc. Tasmanian Travelways has details of timetables and fares around the country.

Train

There are no longer any passenger rail services in Tasmania – the Hobart to Launceston line stopped passenger services 'for economic reasons'. There are, however, a couple of tourist train jaunts. Although the Emu Bay run no longer takes passengers, you may be able to arrange to get on it privately, but only when it's not carrying explosives. It's run by mining companies and travels through some exciting mountain passes between Burnie and Roseberry. The Ida Bay Railway is a quaint little tourist train running from Ida Bay, near Hastings, to Deep Hole – a whole seven km!

Car & Motorcycle

Many people bring their own cars from the mainland to Tasmania on the ferry, but for a short visit it's not that economical. Tasmania has a comprehensive selection of rent-a-car operators, including a host of local firms. Rates are generally lower than on the mainland and even the big companies often have special lower rates for Tasmanian hire. The comparatively short distances travelled on the island also make car rental cheaper, and rental firms are generally quite happy about one-way hire. You can pick up a car in Launceston, Devonport, Burnie or Wynyard in the north and leave it in Hobart in the south without any additional 'repositioning' charges.

Tasmanian Travelways lists all the rental firms, but when comparing their rates remember to take into account mileage, insurance and any 'seasonal adjustments'. Some Tasmanian firms have late model cars at better rates than the big national operators. Advance Car Rentals have offices in Launceston (tel (003) 44 2164), Devonport (tel (004) 24 8885) and Hobart (tel (002) 31 1566) and are among the cheapest, with small cars (Corolla, Laser, Pulsar) from around $40 a day or $250 a week. They also deliver and pick up from the airports. Other companies include Curnow's (tel 23 7336), Annie's Auto Rent (tel 28 0252) and Drive-Away (tel 31 2222), all in Hobart.

Cheapest of all are the companies renting older cars like early '70s Kingswoods, Falcons, Valiants and Volkswagens, for around $25 a day, or less than $150 a week. However, many of them levy bonds, and windscreen and tyre damage may not be covered by insurance. In Hobart you could try Rent-A-Bug (tel 34 9435), Mercury Auto Rentals (tel 72 1755), and Bargain Car Rentals (tel 34 4122). Others include Economy (tel 31 2562), in Launceston; Alternative (tel 27 9222), in Devonport; and Axxon (tel 31 1860), in Burnie. Lo-Cost Auto Rent has offices in Hobart (tel 31 0550), Launceston (tel 31 2222) and

Devonport (tel 24 9922). Rental cars are also available on King and Flinders islands.

There are companies in Hobart, Launceston, Devonport and on Flinders Island that hire campervans. Costs range from about $400 to $700 a week. Motorcycles can be hired from Bargain Motor Bike Rentals (tel 34 4122) in Hobart, and from King Island Auto Rentals (tel 62 1297) on King Island. A 250cc bike costs around $25 a day or $150 a week.

Tasmania is just the right size for exploring on a small motorcycle. Or at least you'd think so. But an entry in the Launceston youth hostel log book warned, 'all you would-be travelling bikers: unless you're on a 650cc or bigger, have pannier bags, heavy wet weather gear, a pillion passenger to talk to, and you're slightly mad – don't consider riding around Tassie'. The note added that rental motorcycles were not worth it – you could rent a car for the same price and the condition of the bikes was not always good.

Not all Tasmanian roads have a good reputation. The highway from Hobart to Wynyard via Launceston, Devonport and Burnie is very good, but some other roads can be narrow and winding in places, while the back roads vary from reasonable to very rough. Fortunately the distances are usually fairly short and the traffic is not heavy by any standards.

Hitching

Travel by thumb is generally pretty good in Tasmania. Some people say it is better than in any other state of Australia. It can get a bit hard on both the east and west coasts though, especially during the off-season when there is very little traffic. The back roads, which often lead to the most interesting places, suffer from the same problem. And remember, it can get mighty cold in Tassie in winter – you don't want to get stuck somewhere on the Murchison Highway between Burnie and Queenstown when it starts to snow!

Tours

Many of the TGTB tours don't operate unless there are sufficient numbers or you pay extra to charter a taxi. This means that trips in the off-season are few, especially away from the major centres like Hobart and Launceston.

A number of small airlines operate scenic flights to or over places like Cradle Mountain, the South-West National Park, Maria Island, the Freycinet Peninsula or Flinders Island. Prices vary according to distances or time in the air, but if you can afford to splurge a bit this would be a great way to see some of Tassie's wilder parts.

Bicycle

Many people hire bicycles in Tasmania and a number of bike hire places are set up to cater for bicycle touring. Launceston Rent-A-Cycle has fully equipped 10 speed touring bikes for about $48 a week, including helmet and panniers; and in Hobart Graham McVilly Cycles has 10 speed tourers for $40 a week ($10 a week extra for helmet and panniers). Both have reducing rates for two or three week hire, but if you are planning an extended ride it is worth considering buying a bicycle and reselling it at the end. There are also bike renters in Devonport, Stanley and on Flinders Island, but some of these are more for the one day cyclist than the long distance tourer. *Tasmanian Travelways* has the latest information on bike hire companies.

If you want to bring your own bike with you on the *Abel Tasman* it's no problem as long as you've booked far enough ahead to ensure you get aboard. By air, Ansett and Australian Airlines will carry one item of baggage free and that one item can be your bike. If you travel light enough it's even possible to make that your only item of baggage. Pack it well – if possible wrap it so that the baggage loaders aren't tempted to lift it by the wheel spokes. It's probably easier to get your bike over to Tassie on the flights to Hobart or Launceston than on the Wynyard and Devonport flights, because larger jets are used on the former.

Count on 10 to 14 days for a trip halfway round – Launceston to Hobart by east or west coast for example. For a full circuit of the island allow 14 to 28 days. You're likely to encounter fewer headwinds if you travel anticlockwise. Many of the youth hostels are keen promoters of bicycle touring, the Launceston hostel in particular.

Hobart

Population 180,000

Australia's second oldest capital city is also the smallest state capital and the most southerly. In winter the temperatures in Hobart often drop close to freezing and even in summer, sunny though it is, temperatures rarely climb above 25°C. Straddling the mouth of the Derwent River and backed by mountains which provide a fine view over the city, Hobart is an engaging, colourful little place which has managed to combine the progress and benefits of a modern city with the rich heritage of its colonial past. The timeworn buildings, the busy and beautiful harbour and the easy-going atmosphere all make Hobart one of the most enjoyable Australian cities.

Hobart's life has centred on the magnificent Derwent River estuary, one of the world's finest deep water harbours, since the island's first little colony, led by Lieutenant John Bowman, set up camp at Risdon Cove in 1803. In February 1804 Lieutenant-Colonel David Collins, who was appointed governor of the new settlement in Van Diemens Land, sailed up the Derwent and decided a cove about 10 km below Risdon on the opposite shore was a better place to settle. Tasmania's future capital city began as a village of tents and wattle-and-daub huts with a population of 178 convicts, 25 marines, 15 women, 21 children, 13 free settlers and 10 civil officers.

Hobart Town, as it was known until 1881, was proclaimed a city in 1842. Its development was based on trade and commerce, and early exports included corn and merino wool. Many merchants made their fortunes from the whaling trade and ship building, and one of Australia's great industrial empires, the IXL jam and fruit company, was founded there by Henry Jones.

Orientation

Hobart is an easy city to find your way around. It's small enough to be manageable and very simply laid out. The central streets are in a straightforward grid pattern. Liverpool St is the main shopping street. Both Australian Airlines and Ansett have their city terminals along Liverpool St, while the tourist office and the GPO are on Elizabeth St, which runs across it. The Cat & Fiddle Arcade in the centre of town is one of Hobart's most popular shopping areas.

Salamanca Place, the old warehouse area, is along the waterfront, while south of this is Battery Point, the delightful early colonial area of Hobart that has been maintained, basically, in its original form. Follow the river around from Battery Point and you'll come to Sandy Bay, site of the University of Tasmania and the Wrest Point Casino – one of Hobart's major landmarks.

The north side of the centre is bounded by the Queens Domain and the Royal Botanical Gardens, then the Derwent River. From here the Tasman Bridge crosses the river to the northern suburbs and the airport.

Walking Tour One of the best ways to get a feel for Hobart's interesting history is to take the Saturday morning walking tour organised by the National Trust and the

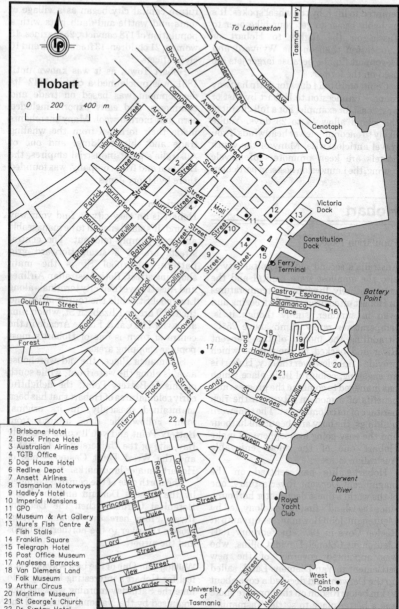

Hobart

0   200   400 m

To Launceston

Tasman Hwy

Cenotaph

Victoria Dock

Constitution Dock

Ferry Terminal

Battery Point

Castray Esplanade

Salamanca Place

Derwent River

Royal Yacht Club

Wrest Point Casino

University of Tasmania

1 Brisbane Hotel
2 Black Prince Hotel
3 Australian Airlines
4 TGTB Office
5 Dog House Hotel
6 Redline Depot
7 Ansett Airlines
8 Tasmanian Motorways
9 Hadley's Hotel
10 Imperial Mansions
11 GPO
12 Museum & Art Gallery
13 Mure's Fish Centre &
   Fish Stalls
14 Franklin Square
15 Telegraph Hotel
16 Post Office Museum
17 Anglesea Barracks
18 Van Diemens Land
   Folk Museum
19 Arthur Circus
20 Maritime Museum
21 St George's Church
22 Dr Syntax Hotel

TGTB. The 2½-hour tour starts at 9.30 am at Franklin Square and costs $3. The walk centres around historic Battery Point, includes the small Maritime Museum and ends at the colonial warehouses on Salamanca Place. You can make a similar do-it-yourself tour with the aid of a leaflet from the TGTB.

Information

The Tasmanian Government Tourist Bureau (TGTB) (tel 30 0211) is at 80 Elizabeth St and is open from 8.45 am to 5.30 pm Monday to Friday, and from 9 am to 12 noon on weekends and holidays. The Tasmanian Visitor Corporation (tel 31 0055), at 7 Franklin Wharf, also has a good range of tourist literature. The Royal Automobile Club of Tasmania (tel 38 2200) is on the corner of Murray and Patrick Sts.

The Tasmanian Youth Hostel Association office (tel 34 9617) is at 28 Criterion St and is open from 11 am to 5 pm Monday to Friday. Paddy Pallin (tel 31 0777) is next door at 32 Criterion St. The Wilderness Society (tel 34 9366) is at 130 Davey St and the Wilderness Shop is in the Galleria Arcade on Salamanca Place. The National Trust shop is in the same arcade.

The Department of Lands, Parks & Wildlife (tel 30 2620) has its head office at 134 Macquarie St, and their Tasmap Centre (tel 30 3382) is on the ground floor. They have lots of information on Tasmania's many parks and reserves and are an essential contact for would-be walkers.

Money Webster Travel (tel 38 0200), at 138 Collins St, is the agent for American Express. You can cash travellers' cheques outside banking hours at the Wrest Point Casino or the Sheraton, but the Sheraton charges $5 a transaction for non-guests.

Inner City

One of the things that sets Hobart apart from other Australian cities is its wealth of old buildings, built mostly from local sandstone or brick and remarkably well preserved. More than 90 buildings in Hobart have National Trust classification; you'll find 60 of these, featuring some of Hobart's best Georgian architecture, in Macquarie and Davey Sts. For architecture buffs, an excellent booklet to get is *Hobart – An Architectural Guide to the City* (Royal Australian Institute of Architects, Tasmanian Chapter) which has photographs and short descriptions of Hobart's more important Georgian buildings, and it also covers later styles. It's available from the National Trust shop for $2.95.

Close to the centre of the city is St David's Park – with its lovely old trees and pioneer cemetery with graves dating from the earliest days of the colony, it's a good place to pause and relax.

The old Parliament House, built by convicts between 1835 and 1841 and originally used as a customs house, is on Murray St, across from the park. The Theatre Royal, at 29 Campbell St, was built in 1837 and is the oldest theatre in Australia. The stage has played host to quite a few famous performers including Edmund Kean, Laurence Olivier, Vivien Leigh, Noel Coward and Dame Sybil Thorndyke.

On Davey St you can see one of the three royal tennis courts in the southern hemisphere. (The other two are 100 metres from my house in Richmond, Victoria.) You can look in at the courts on the walking tour. The National Trust also has tours of the historic Penitentiary Chapel and Criminal Courts, on the corner of Brisbane and Campbell Sts. Tours cost $2.50 and operate between 10 am and 2 pm daily.

Waterfront

Hobart's waterfront area around Franklin Wharf is very close to the centre of the city and still a colourful scene, although it's no longer the rough-house it was in the early whaling days. It has a fine row of Georgian warehouses on Hunter St that rivals Salamanca Place, but it hasn't been developed as a tourist attraction. The area is a seafood centre with floating fish stalls and more expensive seafood restaurants.

Constitution Dock really comes alive at the finish of the annual New Year Sydney to Hobart Yacht Race and during the Royal Hobart Regatta in February. The regatta, first held in 1838, is the largest aquatic carnival in the southern hemisphere.

Salamanca Place

The row of Georgian sandstone warehouses on the harbour front at Salamanca Place is a prime example of Australian colonial architecture. Dating back to the whaling days of the 1830s they were the centre of Hobart Town's trade and commerce. These days they're occupied by galleries, restaurants, offices and shops selling everything from vegetables to antiques and arts and crafts of all kinds. A popular open-air market is held on Salamanca Place every Saturday morning during the summer – it's well worth seeing; in winter it moves inside one of the old warehouses if the weather is poor. From Salamanca Place you can climb up the precipitous Kelly's Steps, wedged between two warehouses, into Battery Point.

Battery Point

Behind the city docks and north of Sandy Bay is the historic centre of Hobart, the old port area known as Battery Point. It takes its name from the gun battery that stood on the promontory by the 1818 guardhouse, the oldest building in the area. In Hobart's early days this was a colourful maritime village of pubs, churches, conjoined houses and narrow, winding streets. It was home to master mariners, shipwrights, sailors, fishermen, coopers and merchants, and the houses reflect their varying life styles. Battery Point has been lovingly preserved and is a real delight to wander around, highlighted by glimpses of the harbour between the many interesting buildings.

Places of special interest in Battery Point include Arthur Circus, a small circle of quaint little cottages built around the former village green; the National Trust house 'Narryna'; and old pubs like the Shipwright's Arms and the Lord Nelson.

Van Diemens Land Folk Museum

Australia's oldest folk museum is housed in Narryna, a fine old Georgian home at 103 Hampden Rd, Battery Point. Built in 1836 it stands in beautiful grounds and the museum re-creates the early pioneering days in Tasmania. It's open Monday to Friday from 10 am to 5 pm and on weekends from 2 to 5 pm. Admission is $1.50. You can easily walk to it from the centre or take a Sandy Bay bus.

St George's Anglican Church

The church is on Cromwell St, Battery Point, only a short stroll from Narryna. Construction started in 1836 but the tower was not completed until 1847. It was designed by two of the best known Tasmanian colonial architects – James Blackburn and John Lee Archer.

Maritime Museum

In historic Secheron House is the fascinating Tasmanian Maritime Museum which has an extensive collection of photos, paintings, models and relics depicting Tasmania's (and particularly Hobart's) colourful shipping history. At only 50c admission, it's excellent value. Secheron House was built in 1831 and has been classified by the National Trust and the National Heritage Commission.

Anglesea Barracks

Built in 1811 this is the oldest military establishment in Australia still used by the army. On weekdays between 9 am and 5 pm you can tour the grounds and inspect some of the restored buildings; admission is free.

Tasmanian Museum & Art Gallery

The excellent Tasmanian Museum & Art Gallery is itself a museum piece as it incorporates Hobart's oldest building, the Commissariat Store built in 1808. The museum features an Aboriginal display and exhibits on the state's colonial history; the Art Gallery has an excellent collection of colonial art. It's open daily and admission is free.

Other Museums

The Allport Museum & Library of Fine Arts has a collection of rare books on Australasia and the Pacific region. It's in the State Library in Murray St and is open weekdays from 9 am to 5 pm; admission is free.

The Post Office Museum at 19-21 Castray Esplanade has an interesting display on the development of the post and telegraphic services. It's open from 9 am to 5 pm weekdays and from 9 to 11 am Saturdays; again, admission is free.

Others include the John Elliott Classics Museum, at the University of Tasmania, in Sandy Bay; Beattie's Historic Photo Museum, in Cat & Fiddle Arcade; Godfrey's Dockside Store Museum, at 17-19 Old Wharf; and the first public museum in Australia, the Lady Franklin Museum, in Lenah Valley.

Other Attractions

Hobart is dominated by the 1270 metre high Mt Wellington, often dusted with snow in the winter. There are fine views over the city and the Derwent River from the summit and there are also many walking tracks in the area, but be warned – it can get very cold up there even in summer! There are also good views from the Old Signal Station on top of Mt Nelson, above Sandy Bay.

The city is on both sides of the Derwent. The river is spanned by the Tasman Bridge, which collapsed in 1975 after being rammed by a runaway cargo ship. Government House and the Botanical Gardens are at the base of the bridge on the city side.

If you head west from the centre along Sandy Bay Rd, past Battery Point, you soon come to the University of Tasmania and then the Wrest Point Casino in Sandy Bay. The casino, Australia's first (well, first legal anyway), and hotel quickly became a symbol of the city. Tasmania has very successfully capitalised on Australia's gambling mania.

Beyond Sandy Bay, on the way to Taroona, is the fascinating 'Tudor Court', in Lower Sandy Bay. John Palotta, a victim of poliomyelitis, spent most of his life creating a scale model of a Tudor village – his home town in Kent. It's on Sandy Bay Rd, open from 9 am to 5 pm daily and costs $3. Take a Taroona bus from Franklin Square.

North of the city is Runnymede, a gracious, finely restored National Trust house with good views over the surrounding country. It was built in 1844 for Robert Pitcairn, the first lawyer to qualify in Tasmania and a leading advocate for the abolition of transportation. It's open from 10 am to 4.30 pm daily. Admission is $2.50. It's at 61 Bay Rd, New Town.

Another popular short trip from the city is the guided tour of the Cadbury chocolate factory; it costs $10, including transport, if you go on a TGTB tour. At Kangaroo Bluff there are the ruins of an old fort, built to repel a feared Russian invasion; similar forts can be seen in Sydney and Newcastle, NSW. Near here, Lauderdale, Seven Mile Beach and Cremorne are popular Hobart beaches. Clifton is the place to go for surf.

Places to Stay

Apart from the youth hostels, most budget accommodation is in the city centre, within walking distance of most of Hobart's attractions. North Hobart and New Town also have some reasonably priced accommodation, but even though they are only a short bus ride from town, you're probably better off staying in the city centre.

The best area to stay is Battery Point, but you pay for the privilege. Sandy Bay, just to the south of Battery Point, towards the casino and the university, is one of Hobart's more prestigious suburbs and has a few moderately priced hotels.

Hostels Hobart has two youth hostels, one on either side of the Derwent River, and both cost $7 a night. *Woodlands* (tel 28 6720), the larger of the two, is at 7 Woodlands Avenue, New Town, just three km from the city centre. It's a superb building and one of New Town's original homes. To get there take a New Town bus from various places in the city, such as a 100 or 102 from outside the Tasmanian Travel Centre in Elizabeth St (get off at Stop 13).

The *Bellerive Hostel* (tel 44 2552), on the eastern shore of the Derwent, at 52 King St, Bellerive, is an old stone schoolhouse built in 1869. It's a good hostel but not so well positioned as the New Town one, especially on weekends when the ferry is not operating. To get there catch any of Bellerive bus Nos 83 to 87 from outside Fitzgerald's in Collins St, get off at Stop 19 and walk south along Scott St. The Dog House (see Hotels) also has dormitory accommodation.

Guest Houses & Private Hotels There are only a couple of reasonably priced guest houses in Hobart. Most of these are in the city or in Sandy Bay, towards the university and the casino. If you can afford to pay more, however, there are some wonderful places in Battery Point, mostly in old colonial houses.

For cheaper, longer-term accommodation scan the *Mercury* newspaper.

The *Imperial Private Hotel* (tel 23 7509) is in the centre of the city, at 138 Collins St. Enter from the alley next to Webster's Travel. It's a big, rambling old place but has recently had a face lift. It's clean, has good beds and costs $27.50/44 for singles/doubles and a good continental breakfast.

The *Astor Private Hotel* (tel 34 6384), at 157 Macquarie St, is very central and has a certain old-fashioned charm, but at $32/48 for singles/doubles with continental breakfast it's a bit overpriced.

Adelphi Court (tel 28 4829), at 17 Stoke St, New Town, is reasonable at $25/40 for singles/doubles with breakfast. It also has newer, more expensive rooms with baths. In Sandy Bay there's *Red Chapel House* (tel 25 2273), at 27 Red Chapel Avenue, past the casino. It costs $32/42 for bed & breakfast and is a warm, old-fashioned sort of place.

Old World Accommodation (tel 23 3743), at 27 Colville St, is the cheapest in Battery Point and for $35/45 you get a room with bath and colour TV, and continental breakfast. It's a well run place, very comfortable and worth the extra money. Battery Point has a number of other very good guest houses in old colonial cottages. They are lovely places to stay but cost around $45/60 a single/ double for bed & breakfast. In this range try *Barton Cottage* (tel 28 6808), at 72 Hampden Rd; *Colville Cottage* (tel 23 6968), at 32 Mona St; or *Cromwell Cottage* (tel 23 6734), at 6 Cromwell St.

Hotels The cheapest in town is the *Dog House* (tel 34 4090), at 41 Barrack St, just around the corner from the Redline depot. It has five bed 'bunkrooms' for $10 a head, and singles/doubles for $15/25. The rooms are fairly basic but the hotel is within walking distance of Hobart's attractions and is in a good area for cheap eats and entertainment. One drawback is that the Dog House has bands six nights a week, which is great if you like music but not if you want to sleep before midnight.

Just around the corner from the Dog House, at 281 Liverpool St, is the *Bavarian Tavern* (tel 34 7498), costing $30/40 a single/double for bed & breakfast. It's clean and comfortable but nothing special.

At the other end of Liverpool St, near the mall, is the *Brunswick Hotel* (tel 34 4981), at 67 Liverpool St. It's central but the rooms are dreary, depressing and over priced at $22/35. The *Alabama Hotel*, across the road, at 72 Liverpool St, is less drab and costs $25/40 for bed & breakfast.

Two blocks up from the mall, at 145 Elizabeth St, is the *Black Prince* (tel 34 3501), with large, modern singles/doubles with bath and colour TV for $30/40. The *Brisbane Hotel* (tel 34 4920), at 3 Brisbane St, on the corner of Campbell St, is also a good buy at $28/44 including breakfast. The rooms are comfortable, with bath and colour TV, but the hotel is in a dead area of town.

If you want to stay by the waterfront, the *Telegraph Hotel* (tel 34 6254), at 19 Morrison St, is down by Franklin Wharf and only a short stroll from the city centre and Salamanca Place. It has good rooms for $25/35 but it's worth paying an extra $3 for a room overlooking the docks. A few doors away, the *Customs House Hotel* (tel 34 6645), at 1 Murray St, has even better views of the waterfront and has heard many a sailor's yarn in days gone by. At $30/45 with continental breakfast, you're paying for the history rather than for the room.

There are also a couple of moderately priced hotels in Sandy Bay. *Dr Syntax Hotel* (tel 23 6258), at 139 Sandy Bay Rd, in the Sandy Bay shopping centre, is very close to Battery Point. It has small but comfortable motel-style rooms with colour TV and bath for $28/38. The *Beach House Hotel* (tel 25 1161), at 646 Sandy Bay Rd, is on the Derwent, two km past Wrest Point. It's a good hotel, with singles/doubles with bath for $30/35 and more expensive rooms with colour TV.

If none of the cheaper hotels appeal, there is a good choice of first-class accommodation. A room in the *Wrest Point* tower block will set you back $130/140 a night or $70/90 in the adjoining Motor Inn. The *Sheraton* (tel 25 0112) is

an ugly intrusion in the historic waterfront area, but considered by many to be superior to the Wrest Point. Rooms start at $145 a double.

Hadley's Orient Hotel (tel 23 4355), at 34 Murray St, is in the centre of the city. Last edition it was a budget hotel but it has undergone massive renovations to become one of Hobart's best hotels, while still retaining its character. It has a lot more charm than the international hotels and is considerably cheaper, at $88/105. Or there's the wonderful *Lennah of Hobart* (tel 23 2911), set in an old mansion at 20 Runnymede St, Battery Point, which costs $115/125.

Motels & Holiday Flats The *Shoreline Motel* (tel 47 9504) is the cheapest in Hobart, at $30/35 for singles/doubles. It's on the corner of Rokeby Rd and Shoreline Drive in Howrah, seven km from the city, past Bellerive. Closer to town, the *Marina* (tel 28 4748), at 153 Risdon Rd, Lutana, costs $37/43 for singles/doubles. It's just beyond New Town, past the Botanical Gardens, four km from the city centre. The *Hobart Tower Motel* (tel 28 0166), at 300 Park St, New Town, costs $46/50. The *Argyle Motor Lodge* (tel 34 2488), at 2 Lewis St, North Hobart, has units from $49/53. *Motel Mayfair* (tel 31 1188) is very central, at 17 Cavell St, West Hobart, and costs $55/63.

There are other reasonably priced motels around but they tend to be a long way out. *Highway Village Motor Inn* (tel 72 6721), at 897 Brooker Highway, Berriedale, is on the outskirts of Hobart as you enter from the north. It costs $38/42.

The *Blue Hills Motel*, in Battery Point, has been recommended. It costs $65 for a double room.

Hobart has a number of self-contained holiday flats with fully equipped kitchens. Close to town, the *Domain View Holiday Apartments* (tel 28 0690), at 352 Argyle St, North Hobart, costs $35 for two and $5 for each extra person. There is a one night surcharge. *Knopwood Holiday Flat* (tel

23 2290), at 6 Knopwood St, Battery Point, costs $41 a double and $9 for each extra person, with a one night surcharge. *Crelin Lodge Holiday Units* (tel 43 9895), at 1 Crelin St, Battery Point, costs $48 for two and $6 for each additional person.

Colleges During the December to February summer vacation and the May and August holidays you can stay at the residential halls at the University of Tasmania. *Christ College* (tel 23 5190), on College Rd, Sandy Bay, has room-only rates of $13 for students and $20.50 for others. *Jane Franklin Hall* (tel 23 2000), at 6 El Boden St, South Hobart, costs $18 a person.

Camping The handiest camping ground is the *Sandy Bay Caravan Park* (tel 25 1264), less than four km from the centre, at 1 Peel St, Sandy Bay. It's uphill from the casino intersection and a No 54 or 55 bus will get you there. Camping costs $7 for two. On-site vans are $27 for two and $6 for each extra person, with the usual extra charges for blankets and linen, but showers are also extra. Other, less convenient sites are in the northern suburbs of Glenorchy and Berriedale.

Places to Eat

Hobart has a surprising variety of restaurants for a city of its size so to ease restaurant hunting you can divide it into three main food areas. In the city itself and in the Sandy Bay area you'll find a variety of places, although you'll have to hunt around a bit. In Battery Point you'll find the smaller, more intimate places, most of the exotica, and prices to go with them. You can easily walk from the city to Battery Point, and even Sandy Bay if you're feeling mildly energetic. Don't expect to find anything much apart from greasy spoon stuff or expensive meals on Saturday or Sunday afternoons.

If it's plain, straightforward food you want then try the lunch time cafes such as the *Piccadilly*, at 136 Collins St; the *Domino*, at 55 Elizabeth St; and *Chequers*, at 53A Murray St. The *Plaza Coffee Lounge*, in the Elizabeth St Mall, has snacks and pancakes. The *Criterion Coffee Lounge*, at 10 Criterion St, has delicious crayfish sandwiches for $2.50. The *Blues Cafe*, at 253 Elizabeth St, has take-aways for breakfast and lunch. There are a couple of tables if you want to eat in.

There's the usual selection of pizzerias and Italian food specialists. *Etna Pizza House*, at 201 Elizabeth St, is a good eat-in or take-away place. You can get a good value lunch at the *Commonwealth Government Cafeteria* in the Commonwealth Centre, at 188 Collins St, or at the 2nd floor cafeteria in *Fitzgerald's* department store in Collins St.

For wholefoods and other dishes, the *Eumarra Cafe*, at 39 Barrack St, is good and open from 12 noon till late. It also has music. The *Carlton Restaurant*, at 50 Liverpool St (corner of Argyle St), is a no-nonsense sort of place for breakfast and grills. It is open till 8 pm every day and is one of the few places in the city where you can get breakfast on Sundays.

At Constitution Dock you can sit in the sun and watch the boats while munching on fish & chips. There are floating take-away stalls such as *Mako Quality Seafoods* and *Flippers* that have a good range of seafood. There are also stalls selling fresh fish.

Counter Meals There are lots of places serving counter meals. For around $6 you can get a hearty meal at the *Brunswick*, at 67 Liverpool St; the *Wheatsheaf Hotel*, at 314 Macquarie St; the *Telegraph Hotel*, at 19 Morrison St; the *Shamrock*, on the corner of Liverpool and Harrington Sts; and the *Brisbane Hotel*, at 3 Brisbane St.

Stoppy's Waterfront Inn, on Salamanca Place, also has reasonably priced counter meals, and nightly entertainment from Thursday to Saturday. Also in Salamanca Place is *Knopwoods*, with lunches and dinners for $5 to $7 in the wine bar on the ground floor. The wine bar is a place to be seen and gets crowded in the evenings. There is also a more expensive restaurant upstairs and the trendy Caribbean Room nightclub on the 2nd floor.

Restaurants The *Little Bali Restaurant* (tel 34 3246), at 84A Harrington St, near the Redline depot, is a BYO Indonesian restaurant and one of Hobart's best buys. The menu isn't extensive but you can get a tasty meal with rice for only $5. It is open Monday to Friday for lunch and dinner, and dinner only on Saturday and Sunday.

Across the road, *La Cuisine*, at 79 Harrington St (also 138 Collins St and 85 Bathurst St), is a better class of cafe and take-away for the lunch time crowds. It has excellent continental cakes, quiches, croissants, patés and other nouveau fast foods. You can get a good light meal for $5 or less.

Mr Wooby's is a trendy little eatery on Salamanca Place. It has a good atmosphere and good food, with prices in the $3 range for snacks and from $6 for main meals. It's licensed and stays open quite late. *Cafe Orient*, in Hadley's Hotel, at 34 Murray St, is open from breakfast till late and has snacks and light meals. It's moderately priced but the main reason to eat here is to savour the atmosphere under the three storey atrium.

The *Mandarin*, at 177 Liverpool St, is a Chinese restaurant of the bare tables and straightforward food variety. It's another place that's open every day, and the lunches are particularly good value. The *Kan Kwan Cafe*, at 404 Elizabeth St, North Hobart, is another Chinese cheapie.

La Suprema (tel 31 0770), at 255 Liverpool St, is a BYO restaurant and has good home-made pasta for $6 to $7. In the same price range, *Bertie's Pasta* (tel 23 3595), at 115 Collins St, is licensed and also has good pasta. *Riviera Pizza Ristorante*, at 15 Hunter St, is a bit more up-market but one of the cheapest around Constitution Dock. It has pizzas starting from $6 and à la carte dishes from $10.

There are a couple of good Italian restaurants in Sandy Bay. You can get a great Italian meal for around $12 at the licensed *Tarantella*, in Princes St. *Don Camillo's*, in the Sandy Bay shopping centre, has a good reputation in Hobart; main courses are around $10 – good veal dishes and saltimbocca. There's a cheaper coffee bar section in the front, as well as the pricier, licensed restaurant behind.

The *Beefeater* (tel 23 8700), at 37 Montpelier Retreat, Battery Point, is the place for meat eaters (try the excellent rack of lamb), with a good lunch menu of soup, main meal, salad and coffee for $8.95. At night it's a bit more expensive. The *Ball & Chain* (tel 23 2925), at 87 Salamanca Place, is good for charcoal-grilled steaks, and also serves some seafood dishes. It is licensed and moderately priced. *Beards* (tel 34 6905) is in an old brick cottage in town, at 101 Harrington St, and has an interesting blackboard menu. It has lunch time specials and you can get an excellent meal for $10.

Among the other ethnic restaurants in Hobart is the *Taj Indian Restaurant* (tel 23 4550), which has good curries for around $10. It is in a lovely old house, at 149 Davey St. The *Aegean Restaurant* (tel 31 1000), at 121 Collins St, is a very popular Greek restaurant with impressive decor. It has a good range of dips, and main meals from $12. The *Ali Akbar* (tel 31 1770), at 321 Elizabeth St, North Hobart, has Lebanese food – for a real pig-out try their $20 banquet. For Japanese food *Sakura*, at 85 Salamanca Place, has excellent food in pleasant surroundings. *Taco Bill* (tel 23 5297), at 41 Hampden Rd, Battery Point, is the texmex answer to Ronald McDonald. It is licensed and serves the usual Mexican fare for around $10 a main dish.

Top End Hobart has some very pleasant, more pricey restaurants. *Mure's Fish House* (tel 23 6917), at 5 Knopwood St, Battery Point, is an award winning seafood restaurant. *Mure's Fish Centre*, on Constitution Dock, is their annex. It is in fact three restaurants with an expensive Upper Deck, a cheaper, more casual Lower Deck, and a sushi bar.

The Paris (tel 23 5028), at 356 Macquarie St, is a good BYO French restaurant. If you want a good bottle of wine to go with your meal, check out Aberfeldy Cellars, at 124 Davey St, which has an excellent selection of Australian and imported wines.

If money is no object, *Dear Friends* (tel 23 2646), at 8 Brooke St, has a reputation as one of Hobart's best restaurants.

Entertainment

Check the *Mercury* for a guide to what's on and where. You still run into the 'no jeans, no running shoes' nonsense at some of Hobart's entertainment spots, especially discos.

For rock, blues and jazz bands, head to the *Dog House*. It has something on till 12 midnight every night except Sunday. There is no cover charge, no hassles and counter meals are available. The *Eumarrah Cafe*, next to the Dog House, has more laid back music on Thursday, Friday and Saturday nights. The *Red Lion Tavern*, at 129 Macquarie St, tries to be more up-market and has bands till the early hours of the morning on Saturdays and from 4 to 8 pm on Sundays. The cover charge is $5 and 'no jeans' rules apply. For jazz, try the *St Ives Hotel*, on Sandy Bay Rd. *Tattersalls*, at 112 Murray St, and the *Travellers Rest Hotel*, at 394 Sandy Bay Rd, are other regular venues.

From Tuesday to Saturday the Wrest Point casino has a number of rather insipid venues, including *Regines* disco, the *Ten O'clock Club* and a piano bar. For $6 you get entry to all their 'hot spots'. The casino also features the stars from the past at top prices.

Hobart doesn't have too many cinemas. Hoyts and Village, in the city, show the latest *Rambos* and *Crocodile Dundees*. The *State Cinema*, at 375 Elizabeth St, North Hobart, is Hobart's art house theatre and has interesting movies for $6.50 ($4 for students).

Getting There & Away

Air You can fly to Hobart from Melbourne, Sydney or Brisbane, and from other places in Tasmania. Airlines of Tasmania

PREMIUM LAGER

BREWED AND BOTTLED BY TASMANIAN BREWERIES   345 mL   156 COLLINS STREET HOBART 7000 AUSTRALIA

operate a number of services around the state. You can fly from Hobart to Launceston for $57, to Devonport for $73.50, to Queenstown for $71, to Smithton for $92, to Strahan for $71, to Wynyard for $73.50, to Flinders Island for $105, and to King Island for $130. Australian Airlines (tel 38 3333) are at 4 Liverpool St. Ansett and Airlines of Tasmania (tel 38 1111) are at 178 Liverpool St.

Bus The main bus lines in Hobart are Tasmanian Redline Coaches (tel 34 4577), at 96 Harrington St; Tasmanian Motorways (tel 23 8388), at Shop 3, Centreway Arcade, Collins St; and Hobart Coaches (tel 34 4077), who have their freight depot at 123 Murray St and another departure point at Fullers Bookshop, 27 Murray St.

Bushwalkers Transport (tel 34 2226), at 28 Criterion St, operate regular services throughout the year to Cockle Creek and Scotts Peak. They also have charter services to other popular bushwalking destinations such as Cradle Mountain, Lake St Clair, Collingwood River, etc. Redline also have buses to Ben Lomond in the ski season.

See the sections on other destinations around Tasmania for information about how to get to these places from Hobart.

Getting Around
Airport Transport Hobart's airport is across the river, 26 km from the city centre. Tasmanian Redline Coaches run an airport bus service for $4. It departs from their depot at 96 Harrington St an hour before flight departures. Alternatively, a taxi costs about $20.

Bus Local buses are run by the Metropolitan Transport Trust (MTT) and depart from various central city streets. For only $1.80 you can get an unlimited travel Dayrover bus ticket for use between 9 am and 4.45 pm and after 6.30 pm on weekdays, and all day on weekends. The tourist bureau has timetables for $1 and route maps for 50c.

To reach Mt Wellington, the alternative to taking a tour is to catch a No 48 Fern Tree bus from Franklin Square, Macquarie St, to the base of the mountain – after which it's a 12 to 13 km walk! You might be lucky enough to get a ride.

To get out of town to a point where you can start hitching north, take a Bridgewater or Glenorchy bus.

Boat The ferry from Hobart to Bellerive is a pleasant way to get to the youth hostel. There's even a bar on board. The ferry operates only on weekdays. Departures from Hobart are at 6.30, 7.10, 7.45 and 8.20 am and at 4.35, 5.15 and 5.55 pm. From Bellerive there are services at 6.55, 7.30, 8.05 and 8.40 am and at 4.50, 5.30 and 6.10 pm.

Car See the introductory Getting Around section for information on the many car rental firms in Hobart. *Tasmanian Travelways* gives you a comprehensive run down on the latest hire rates. Some of the cheaper car rental firms include Cheapa (tel 34 4512), Lo-cost (tel 341 0550), Economy (tel 31 2562), Mercury (tel 72 1755) and Rent-a-Bug (tel 34 9435).

Bicycle You can hire bikes in Hobart from Graham McVilly Cycles (tel 23 7284), at 63 King St, Sandy Bay. They have a variety of bikes for $3 an hour or $15 a day. The weekly rate for a 10 speed is $40, plus an extra $10 for helmet and panniers, with reducing rates for longer periods. They can have bicycles delivered to the airport, and you can arrange to return your bicycle by dropping it off at a bus depot.

Tours The TGTB operates a variety of day and half day tours in and around Hobart. Typical half day local tours include trips to Mt Wellington and Kingston ($14), Richmond and Risdon Cove ($16), New Norfolk ($16), and Mt Nelson and the city sights ($12). There are day-trips to Port Arthur ($30), Lake Pedder and Russell

Falls ($28), and the Huon Valley and Hastings Caves ($36).

There are also boat trips on the Derwent River and around Hobart's harbour, leaving from around the ferry terminal. The *Commodore I*, *Derwent Explorer*, *Emmalisa*, *Carmel D* and *Prudence* all offer cruises. On the *Emmalisa* it costs around $9 for a two hour afternoon or evening cruise around the harbour, and there are other cruises to Cadbury's, Bruny Island or New Norfolk. On Friday and Saturday nights you can take a five hour jazz and dinner cruise on the *Derwent Explorer* for $38.

Around Hobart

Roads fan out from Hobart in all directions and you can make a number of day-trips from the capital. Places of interest include Richmond, on the way to Port Arthur, and New Norfolk, on the way up the Derwent Valley towards the west coast. There are also a few good beaches within easy driving distance of the city.

TAROONA

Continue on beyond Wrest Point and you'll soon see Taroona's famous shot tower, completed in 1870. From the top of the 66 metre tower you can get a fine view over the Derwent River estuary. The small museum at the base was built in 1855 and the adjoining residence in 1835. The tower, museum, art gallery and beautiful grounds are open daily until dusk. Lead shot was once produced in high towers like this by dropping molten lead from the top. On the way down the globule of lead formed a perfect sphere, solidifying when it hit water at the bottom.

KINGSTON

Eleven km south of Hobart is Kingston, the headquarters of the Commonwealth Antarctic Research Division. It's open for inspection from 9 am to 4 pm on weekdays. There are good beaches around Kingston, including Blackmans Bay, Tinderbox and Howdon, and fine views across to Bruny Island from Piersons Point.

BRIDGEWATER (population 2800)

This market town, 19 km north of Hobart, is so named because it marks the main north-south crossing of the Derwent River. The causeway here was built in the 1830s by 200 convicts undergoing secondary punishment in chain gangs. Despite the chains, they managed to move two million tonnes of stone and clay. The old watch house at Granton, on the other side of the river, was built by convicts in 1838 to guard the causeway. It is now a petrol station.

PONTVILLE (population 910)

Further north, on the Midland Highway is the historic town of Pontville, which has a number of interesting buildings dating back to the 1830s. Pontville's quarries supplied much of the freestone used in Tasmania's early buildings and two of the quarries are still working today. In the adjoining town of Brighton there is a wildlife park on Briggs Rd featuring native Tasmanian animals. Admission is $2.50.

NEW NORFOLK (population 9750)

Set in the lush rolling countryside of the Derwent Valley, New Norfolk is one of the most historically interesting towns in Tasmania. First settled in 1803, it's the centre of hop growing in Australia and is dotted with old oast houses, the conical buildings used to dry hops.

Originally called Elizabeth Town, it was renamed after the arrival in 1807 of settlers from the abandoned Pacific Ocean colony on Norfolk Island. Early hop growing experiments proved successful and by the 1860s nearly all the farmers in the valley were in the same business. The hop field planted at Bushy Park in the

Styx Valley in 1864 became the largest and most successful in the southern hemisphere. Although hop growing is no longer the domain of the small farmer the oast houses, colonial buildings and the tall poplars planted to protect the crops from winds give New Norfolk its special charm, particularly in autumn.

Things to See

In 1864 the first rainbow and brown trout in the southern hemisphere were bred in the Salmon Ponds at Plenty, 11 km west of New Norfolk, making possible the stocking of streams and lakes in Australia and New Zealand. You can visit the ponds and museum and enjoy the restaurant's speciality – guess what! The Australian Newsprint Mills is the other major industry of the area. It produces 40% of the country's newsprint. The mill (tel 61 2222) can be inspected.

The Oast House Museum is devoted to the history of the hop industry and also serves Devonshire teas. Admission is $2. St Matthew's Church of England, built in 1823, is Tasmania's oldest existing church; and the Bush Inn is claimed to be the oldest continuously licensed hotel in Australia. The Old Colony Inn, a museum of colonial furnishings and artefacts, also serves colonial lunches.

A modern New Norfolk diversion is a ride through the Derwent River rapids on a white-water jet boat. If it takes your fancy it costs $25 for a 30 minute ride and you can book at the Bush Inn (tel 61 3460).

The Visitors Historical & Information Centre is next to the Council Chambers in High St. It has a photographic and memorabilia exhibit and provides good information.

Places to Stay

The New Norfolk *Youth Hostel* (tel 61 2591) is in the historic Bridge Toll House and costs $5 a night. There are camping sites at the *New Norfolk Camping Ground*. Bed & breakfast singles/doubles at the *Norfolk Lodge* (tel 61 3291), at 93 High St, are $15/25. At the *Bush Inn* (tel 61 2011) they cost from $22/35. The *Amaroo Motel* (tel 61 2000), on the Lyell Highway, has rooms from $40/50.

Getting There & Away

New Norfolk is 38 km from Hobart. Tasmanian Motorways (tel 23 8388) have regular buses leaving Hobart between 10 am and 10.15 pm Monday to Friday, and from 6.25 am on Saturday and Sunday. Their depot in New Norfolk is at 15 Stephen St. The fare is $3.20 and the trip takes 50 minutes. Redline Coaches heading to Queenstown along the Lyell Highway also stop in New Norfolk.

MT FIELD NATIONAL PARK

Spectacular mountain scenery, alpine moorland, dense rainforest, lakes, waterfalls and abundant wildlife are all just 73 km from Hobart. Mt Field is the state's oldest national park and features the magnificent 40 metre Russell Falls, fine bushwalks and Lake Dobson. The park also has ski fields for beginners and intermediate skiers, though the snow cover is often disappointing.

Places to Stay

The *National Park Youth Hostel* is in the township of National Park, on the Strathgordon to New Norfolk road. It is 200 metres past the turn-off to the national park and costs $7 a night. *Lake Dobson Cabins* (tel 88 1149) has six bunks and costs $10 a cabin. *Russell Falls Holiday Cottages* (tel 88 1198) are considerably more comfortable and cost $35 a double.

Getting There & Away

The Tasmanian Motorways bus to New Norfolk goes to Mt Field. They also have buses to the park during the week departing Hobart at 4 pm. The trip costs $6.80. It terminates at Maydena, but Bushwalkers Transport (tel 34 2226) have regular services continuing on to Scotts Peak in summer.

ROKEBY

Tasmania's first wheat crop and the first export apples were grown here, across the Derwent River from Hobart. Rokeby has a village green, and a few historic buildings remain, including the St Matthew's Church. There are good beaches south of Rokeby at South Arm and good surfing at Clifton Beach. Hobart MTT bus Nos 95 and 99 go to Opossum Bay via Rokeby and South Arm.

RICHMOND (population 590)

Richmond is Tasmania's premier historic town and a popular tourist destination. The famous and much photographed Richmond Bridge, built by convicts when the town was founded in 1823, is the oldest road bridge in Australia. Straddling the Coal River, Richmond developed as an important granary town and crossing place for travellers heading to the east coast. With the completion of the Sorell Causeway in 1872 the town was by-passed by traffic travelling between Hobart and Port Arthur.

Things to See

Richmond jail, which predates Port Arthur by five years, is the best-preserved convict jail in Australia. It's open daily, costs $2 and has records of the road gang convicts who were confined there. Other places of interest include St John's Church (1836), the oldest Catholic church in Australia; St Luke's Church of England (1834); the court house; the old post office; the Bridge Inn; the granary; and the Richmond Arms. Barnes' Museum of Photographica is in the restored Buscombe's General Store. Ashmore serves Devonshire teas in a building built in 1850. There is also a maze in Richmond but it may be some years before hedges replace the unlovely wooden planking divides.

Sorell, south of Richmond, at the junction of the Tasman and Arthur Highways, is the centre of an important agricultural area. In the early 1800s it was the granary for Tasmania and New South Wales. The Carlton and Dodges Ferry area has many good beaches.

The famous Richmond Bridge

Places to Stay

The *Richmond Caravan Park* has on-site vans from \$24 a double and camping space. The *Richmond Country Bed & Breakfast* (tel 62 4238), on Prosser Rd, has bed & breakfast for \$30/42.

Getting There & Away

If you have your own car, Richmond is an easy day-trip from Hobart or a detour en route to Port Arthur. The TGTB operates coach tours to Richmond via Risdon Cove for \$16. The Bicheno bus operated by Hobart Coaches (tel 34 4077) stops in Richmond but you have to stay overnight. The bus takes half an hour and leaves Hobart at 2.30 pm Monday to Thursday, and 3.45 pm Friday. Coming from Bicheno, the bus arrives in Richmond at around 9.30 am.

South-East Coast

South of Hobart are the scenic fruit growing and timber areas of the Huon Peninsula, D'Entrecasteaux Channel and Esperance, as well as beautiful Bruny Island and the Hartz Mountains National Park.

Although timber from the Huon and Channel areas was made into sleepers for the Trans-Siberian Railway and piers for the Melbourne docks, it was the fruit, especially the apples, from the Huon Valley that really put Tasmania on the international export map. Around January and February there's work picking apples and hops but competition for the jobs is stiff.

Getting There & Away

The Channel Highway runs out of Hobart past the Taroona Shot Tower, through Kingston and right around the Huon Peninsula. The Huon Highway runs south from Huonville through Franklin, Geeveston and Dover to Southport, 103 km from Hobart.

Hobart Coaches have buses from Monday to Friday at 9 am and 3, 5.15 and 6.15 pm to Geeveston via Huonville. The 5.15 pm bus continues on to Dover and arrives at 7 pm. The fare to Huonville is \$4.40 and to Dover it's \$9.90. There is also a connecting service from Huonville to Cygnet. Tag Along Tours (tel 34 2226) have buses to Cygnet via Oyster Cove. They leave from the Treasury Building, Lower Murray St, Hobart, at 5.15 pm from Monday to Friday and cost \$4. They also have a service to Dover on Sunday at 4.15 pm.

Bushwalkers Transport travel to Cockle Creek on Monday, Wednesday and Friday at 9.30 am, and they can drop you at Lune River if you want to visit the Ida Bay Railway there.

KETTERING (population 300)

This small port, on a sheltered bay 34 km south of Hobart, is the terminal for the Bruny Island car ferry. Eight km north of Kettering is the town of Snug which has good swimming at Coningham Beach, a walking track to Snug Falls, and the Channel Historical Museum which tells you all about the pioneer days. In Gordon, 29 km south of Kettering, there's a monument to the French navigator Bruny D'Entrecasteaux. There are camping grounds at Snug and Gordon.

BRUNY ISLAND (population 300)

The sparsely populated island of North and South Bruny, joined by a narrow isthmus, was visited by Furneaux, Cook, Bligh and Cox but was named after Rear Admiral Bruny d'Entrecasteaux who explored the area in 1792. It's believed that William (Mutiny on the Bounty) Bligh planted Tasmania's first apple tree on the island during a visit in 1788.

The island's history is recorded in the Bligh Museum, at Adventure Bay. It's open daily and also has a collection of antique celestial and terrestrial globes. The lighthouse on South Bruny was built in 1836 and is the second oldest lighthouse in Australia. A walking trail encircles Mt Bruny on the southern peninsula. There's good surf at Cloudy Bay, superb coastal scenery and fine swimming beaches.

Places to Stay

House Sofia (tel (002) 60 6277) is a hostel at Dennes Point. It costs $20 a person for a bed and three meals or $7 just for the bed. Also at Dennes Point is the *Channel View Guest House* (tel 60 6266), which has singles/doubles for $20/30 with breakfast.

In Adventure Bay, the *Lumeah Hostel* (tel 93 1265) is good and has dormitory beds for $12, and the *Captain James Cook Caravan Park* has on-site vans costing $27 for two people.

Getting There & Away

The ferry to Bruny Island departs from Kettering and takes 15 minutes to do the three km crossing to Roberts Point. There are regular departures daily, every 45 minutes or so from 7.15 am to 6.30 pm, however the weekend schedule can vary. The return fare for car and passengers is $8 weekdays and $14 on weekends and Friday afternoons.

CYGNET (population 700)

Port Cygnet, on which this small town stands, was named by d'Entrecasteaux for the many swans (*cygne* in French) seen on the bay. There are some good beaches in the area, a winery four km out of town and plenty of accommodation.

Places to Stay

Balfe's Tea House (tel 95 1551), a hostel on Sandhills Rd, about five km from town, costs $7 a night.

You can get bed & breakfast singles at the *Commercial Hotel* (tel 95 1368), on Mary St, for $17, and at the *Wilfred Lodge* (tel 95 1604), at 22 Channel Highway, for $20.

HUONVILLE & SOUTH

Named after D'Entrecasteaux's second in command, Huon D'Kermandec, this busy,

small town on the picturesque Huon River is a major apple growing centre. The valuable softwood Huon Pine was first discovered here, though large stands are now found only around the Gordon River.

A little further south is Franklin, also an apple growing town, although timber milling is the main activity. First settled in 1804, it's the oldest place in the Huon area. It has an interesting apple industry museum. The Huon River at Franklin is one of Australia's leading rowing courses.

Geeveston, 31 km south of Huonville, is another timber town. An administrative centre for Esperance, Australia's most southerly municipality, it is also the gateway to the wild Hartz Mountains National Park.

HARTZ MOUNTAINS NATIONAL PARK

This wild area of glacial lakes, snow capped mountains and dense rainforest is only 84 km from Hobart. The Arve Loop Rd, which runs north along the Arve River, is a dramatic rainforest drive. There's a fine view from Waratah Lookout (24 km from Geeveston); the jagged peaks of Mt Snowy, the Devils Backbone and Hartz Peak are something to see. Rugged mountains give way to deep gorges and alpine moorlands. There are good bushwalks in the park, including a track to Mt Picton and the Arthur Range near Federation Peak.

DOVER (population 400)

This very attractive little fishing port, another 20 km south on the Huon Highway, has curious old houses, fine beaches and excellent bushwalks. In the bay are three islands: Faith, Hope and Charity. The felling, processing and exporting of Huon pine was the major industry last century. Sleepers made here and in the nearby timber towns of Strathblane and Raminea were shipped to China, India and Germany, while street paving and wharf piles went to England. Casey's Living Steam Museum has working steam powered exhibits and is open daily except in July. There's also an apple industry museum.

Places to Stay

The *Dover Hotel* (tel 98 1210) has rooms at $20 a person for bed & breakfast. The *Dover Beachside Caravan Park* (tel 98 1301) has camping sites; on-site vans are $23 a double. The *Three Island Holiday Apartments* (tel 98 1396) has holiday flats for $35 a double. If you're heading towards the South East Cape, this is your last chance to get all provisions except petrol, which is also available at Southport.

There's a camping ground at Southport, which is 24 km beyond Dover. It's a pretty little town with a history going back to the whaling days. The Huon Highway ends here, but secondary roads lead further south.

HASTINGS

Today, three spectacular limestone caves are all that attract visitors to the once thriving logging and wharf town of Hastings. There are daily tours of the caves year round at 11.15 am and 1.15, 2.15 and 3.15 pm, with an extra tour at 4.15 pm between December and April. The tour costs $4 for adults and $2 for children. A spiral staircase takes you down into the well lit depths.

Hastings is about six km off the Huon Highway, north-west of Southport. There's a good walk through rainforest to Adamsons Falls and a thermal pool.

LUNE RIVER

A few km south-west of Hastings is Lune River, a haven for gem collectors and the site of Australia's most southerly post office. The quaint Ida Bay Railway, which once carried limestone, now carries passengers on a scenic trip from the township of Ida Bay to The Deep Hole, a beautiful beach on the bay opposite Southport.

The most southerly drive you can make in Australia is along the secondary road from Lune River to Cockle Creek and beautiful Recherche Bay. An area of

spectacular mountain peaks, endless beaches and secluded coves, it's ideal for camping and bushwalking.

Places to Stay

The Lune River *Youth Hostel*, also known as The Doing Place, is a good place to get information for exploring the surrounding area. It costs $7 a night. Bring plenty of food with you as the hostel only has basic supplies.

Tasman Peninsula

PORT ARTHUR

Port Arthur has been Tasmania's premier tourist attraction since it ceased operation as a penal settlement in 1877. Even in the 1920s there were many visitors fascinated by tales of desperate convicts and attracted by the superb scenery of the Tasman Peninsula.

In 1830 Governor Arthur chose the peninsula as the place to confine those prisoners convicted of crimes in the colony. The main feature of this 'natural penitentiary' was the unique garrison at Eaglehawk Neck, the narrow isthmus connecting the peninsula to the mainland. All but a few escape attempts were thwarted by a line of ferocious guard dogs chained up across the Neck and the rumour that the waters on either side were shark infested.

About 12,500 convicts served sentences here between 1830 and 1877. The township of Port Arthur became the centre of a network of penal stations on the peninsula and was itself much more than a prison town. It had fine buildings and thriving industries including timber milling, ship building, coal mining and brick, nail and shoe making. Australia's first railway ran the seven km between Norfolk Bay and Long Bay with power provided by convicts who pushed the carriages along the tracks. A semaphore

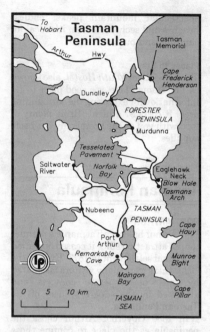

telegraph system allowed instant communication between Port Arthur, the scattered penal outstations and Hobart. Convict farms provided fresh vegetables; a boys prison was built at Point Puer to reform and educate juvenile convicts; and a church – today one of the most readily recognised tourist sights in Australia – was erected.

The Isle of the Dead, in the middle of the bay, was the cemetery for 1769 convicts and 180 free settlers and officers. Convicts were buried six or seven to a grave with no headstones, their bodies wrapped in sailcloth and covered with quicklime.

In 1979 the $9 million government funded Port Arthur Conservation & Development Project was launched. Many of the town's surviving buildings have been restored, and well researched information boards provide a fascinating insight into Port Arthur's gruesome history. You can explore the penitentiary, the model prison, the round tower guard house, several cottages and the church. The lunatic asylum is now a museum, with early records, photographs of the convicts with details of their crimes, and displays of their tools, leg irons and clothing. There's a model of Port Arthur as it was in 1860 and an audio-visual history of the settlement.

It is difficult to imagine that this picturesque, peaceful setting was once a living hell for thousands of convicts. Some of the most inhumane punishments were meted out in the model prison. Its system of solitary confinement and religious contemplation was seen as an advancement in prison reform. Instead of the brutal beatings and starvation that preceded it, this system had prisoners called by number instead of name and confined in total isolation. They wore head masks to prevent them seeing other prisoners; the chapel was designed with individual boxes so they could not see or talk to each other even in the presence of God.

The $5 fee for entry to Port Arthur is collected at a toll booth on the main road into the settlement. It is valid for 24 hours and covers the cost of admission to the museum and a guided tour. The tours are well worthwhile and leave hourly from 9.30 am to 2.30 pm.

In keeping with its status as Tasmania's number one tourist attraction, Port Arthur has a host of private operators offering bus, 4WD, and horse and carriage tours of the settlement and the Tasman Peninsula. There are also $5 scenic cruises to the Isle of the Dead and Point Puer.

Places to Stay

The Port Arthur *Youth Hostel* (tel 50 2311) has a prime location on the edge of the settlement, with excellent views of the ruins. It costs $7. If you are going to stay at the hostel don't enter the settlement via the main road but continue ½ km to the side road leading to the hostel and the

Four Seasons hotel. You can buy your entry ticket at the hostel, but hostellers do not have to pay the $5 if they merely walk through the ruins to the shop or the waterfront.

Camping sites at the spacious *Garden Point Caravan Park*, two km before Port Arthur, overlooking Stewarts Bay, cost $8 for two people. The park has cooking shelters and a laundry.

Motels and hotels in Port Arthur tend to be expensive, though some of the smaller holiday flats drop their prices dramatically in the off-season. A good place to stay is the *Seascape Guest House* (tel 50 2367), on the main highway a few km before the settlement. Bed & breakfast singles/doubles cost $25/40. The *Tanglewood Host Farm* (tel 50 2210) is a guest house on Nubeena Rd, three km from the settlement, with bed & breakfast doubles for $36.

If you have your own car you can stay in the pleasant seaside town of Nubeena, 11 km beyond Port Arthur. The *White Beach Caravan Park* (tel 50 2142) has on-site vans for $22 for two people, while *Parker's Holiday Cottages* (tel 50 2138) cost $30 for two and $5 for each additional person. There are also basic camping facilities at Lime Bay, Fortescue Bay and White Beach and bush camping is permitted along the walking trails.

Places to Eat

The *Black Arrow* is right in the settlement, next to the car park, and serves good cafeteria food at very reasonable prices. It opens for breakfast and closes at 6 pm (5 pm in the off-season). It is also a souvenir shop, and sells groceries and basic supplies. The shop next to the service station on the highway also sells groceries and some take-aways.

The only other places to eat in Port Arthur are the expensive hotels. The *Four Seasons* has very bland food on its aptly named 'convict menu'. It's not cheap, except for its filling lunch time 'paupers' mess', which is $5.

For a good, reasonably priced counter meal, go to the *Nubeena Tavern* in Nubeena.

Entertainment

Yes, tiny Port Arthur does have entertainment other than the occasional three piece band in the hotels. *For the Term of His Natural Life* is a classic 1926 silent film based on Marcus Clark's novel and filmed on location in Port Arthur. It screens nightly at the Black Arrow from October to March, and judging by its popularity it's set for a record breaking run. The cost is $5 including supper.

Getting There & Away

The only ways to visit Port Arthur for a single day are by private transport or on a $30 TGTB tour from Hobart. The coach leaves at 9 am on Wednesdays, Fridays and Sundays. The fare includes admission to the ruins.

The Tasmanian Motorways bus leaves Hobart at 3.45 pm from Monday to Friday, arriving in Port Arthur at 5.45 pm. It departs the ruins at 7.45 am, stopping in Nubeena and Eaglehawk Neck. The fare is $8.50 one way and $14 return.

AROUND THE PENINSULA

The Tasman Peninsula has many bushwalks, superb stretches of beach and beautiful bays. Near Eaglehawk Neck there are several incredible coastal formations: on Pirates Bay there's the Tessellated Pavement; further round, the Tasman Sea thunders in through the Devils Kitchen, the Blowhole and Tasmans Arch. South of Port Arthur is Remarkable Cave. When the tide is out you can walk through this amazing sea cave. You can also visit the remains of the penal outstations of Cascades (now Koonya), Saltwater River and Impression Bay (Premaydena), and the ruins of the Coal Mines Station, the most dreaded place of punishment.

Other places of interest include the Tasmanian Devil Park and the Port

Arthur Marine Park, at Taranna; the Bush Mill, on the Arthur Highway; and the Country Life Museum, at Koonya.

East Coast & North-East

The eastern seaboard, with its magnificent coastline, long sandy beaches, fine fishing and quiet backwater atmosphere, is probably the least visited of the accessible regions of Tasmania. It boasts 2250 hours of sunshine a year, and while the rest of Tasmania freezes in winter, the east coast can be surprisingly mild. For the budget traveller there is an excellent network of youth hostels along the coast.

Exploration and settlement of the area, which was found to be most suitable for grazing, proceeded rapidly after the establishment of Hobart in 1804. Offshore fishing and particularly whaling also became important, as did tin mining and timber cutting, but bushrangers, poor communication and isolation all contributed to the difficulties faced by the early settlers. The vital coastal traffic of the 19th century provided their only link with the outside world.

Many of the convicts who served out their terms in the area stayed on to help the settlers lay the foundations of the fishing, wool, beef and grain industries which are still important today. The largest town on the coast is St Helens, with a population of only 1000. Although it's quiet, a leisurely trip up the Tasman Highway is highly recommended. The spectacular scenery around Coles Bay is not to be missed and Bicheno and Swansea are pleasant seaside towns to spend a few restful days.

Getting There & Away

It's 358 km by the east coast route between Hobart and Launceston if you turn off the coast at St Marys and travel through Fingal and Avoca. If you continue up to St Helens and Scottsdale it's 434 km, and further still if you go north to Bridport and George Town or branch off to the Tasman Peninsula and Port Arthur in the south.

Bus Travelling by bus along this route involves a number of changes and it takes a couple of leisurely days – longer if the weekend intervenes. Check *Tasmanian Travelways* for the latest information on fares and schedules.

Hobart Coaches has two buses a day during the week between Hobart and Bicheno, and one bus a day between Launceston and Bicheno via Swansea and Campbell Town. Their office in Hobart (tel (002) 34 4077) is at 123 Murray St, and in Launceston (tel (003) 31 8677) at 168 Brisbane St. Hobart coaches stop at Sorell (or Richmond), Orford, Triabunna and Swansea. The fare is $12.50 to Swansea and $15.50 to Bicheno.

Hobart Coaches' service to Launceston travels via the Lake Leake Rd. From Swansea and Bicheno there are connecting services to St Marys, St Helens and the north-east.

Tasmanian Redline Coaches operate Launceston/Scottsdale/Derby in the north-east and Launceston/Conara/St Marys/St Helens. They also have a connecting bus between St Helens and Hobart from Monday to Saturday. It leaves St Helens at 8 am and goes via St Marys and the Midland Highway. The Hobart bus departs at 3.45 pm and takes four hours to St Helens.

There are also smaller operators with buses between St Helens and St Marys, Swansea and St Marys, St Helens and Derby, and Bicheno and Coles Bay. See under those towns for more information.

Bicycle Touring

The east coast is a popular route for bicycle touring; you can ride from Hobart to Launceston in about eight to 10 days. While it is generally considered to be easier riding than on the west coast, the hills of the north-east should not be underestimated.

This route is popular with youth hostellers as the hostels are conveniently spaced and provide good information for cyclists. The Launceston hostel is a good place to start as the warden has a vast array of bicycles for hire (for non-members also) and can fill you in on all the details. In Hobart try Graham McVilly Cycles in Sandy Bay.

Opinions vary as to whether it is best to ride from Hobart to Launceston or vice versa, though generally you will encounter fewer headwinds riding north from Hobart. In any case, it is best to do most of your cycling in the mornings, as the winds are worse in the afternoon. By taking a bicycle on the bus, you can avoid some of the more difficult stretches and make a shorter tour.

Apart from the youth hostels, there is a wide choice of other accommodation. Camping is good in camping grounds or, provided you carry your own water, on the beaches. There are some long stretches between towns so make sure you take some food and drink.

Hobart to Orford If you are heading straight to the east coast it is worth considering taking the bus to Orford or Triabunna. This stretch is hilly and relatively uninteresting, and there can be heavy traffic on the road between Hobart and Sorell. If you are heading down to Port Arthur, take the coastal road through Dodges Ferry to Dunalley.

Orford to Bicheno This can be done in two days, though it's worth taking an extra day or two to explore the coast, especially around Coles Bay. From Orford to Swansea you have to follow the highway, though the traffic is not usually heavy. The road tends inland until you hit the wonderful beaches 20 km before Swansea.

From Swansea, turn off the highway four km north of town and follow the Dolphin Sands Rd along Nine Mile Beach. At the end there is a boat across the inlet to Swanwick, just north of Coles Bay, but you have to arrange this in advance at the Swansea youth hostel, or by ringing Kirk Dalwood on (002) 57 0239 before you leave Swansea (or Bicheno if you come from the north). This is a special service for cyclists and walkers and costs $5; however, the boat usually only operates from October to mid May.

From Coles Bay it is 28 km north along a mostly dirt road back to the highway and then another 11 km to Bicheno.

Bicheno to St Helens From Bicheno the highway follows the coast for 20 km until it turns inland and starts the long hard climb up Elephant Pass and on to St Marys. From St Marys the road is narrow and makes a winding descent back to the coast. This route is only for the most hardened cyclists. Others should take the road through Four Mile Creek. The road is rough in parts, but it is a pleasant ride along the coast. Bicheno to St Helens is a long day's ride, but there are plenty of opportunities for camping if you carry your own water, or you can stay in Scamander, about 20 km before St Helens.

St Helens to Launceston The stretch between St Helens and Launceston takes you through pleasant dairy country interspersed with occasional fern glades and myrtle stands. The terrain is very hilly though, and some of the climbs can be as heartbreaking as anything on the west coast. It is a good three day ride, so if you dread hills or are running short of time, catch the bus to Launceston. If you are staying in hostels you can stop in Winnaleah, a short detour off the highway between St Helens and Scottsdale.

BUCKLAND (population 200)
This tiny township, 61 km from Hobart, was once a staging post for coaches. Ye Olde Buckland Inn, which welcomed coach drivers and travellers a century ago,

still provides refreshments and counter lunches.

The old stone church of St John the Baptist, dating from 1846, has a stained-glass window with an interesting history. Originally part of the 14th century Battle Abbey, built on the site of the Battle of Hastings in England, it was rescued from the abbey before Cromwell sacked it in the 17th century. The Marquis of Salisbury presented the window to Reverend Fox who was the first rector of the Buckland Church.

ORFORD (population 350)

Surrounded by tall hills, Orford is a popular little seaside resort on the Prosser River. There's good fishing and swimming, and charter boats are available for fishing and trips to Maria Island. Sandstone quarried from the nearby cliffs was used in many of Melbourne's early buildings.

There's a camping and caravan park by the bay, with sites for $6 a person. *Blue Waters Motor Hotel* (tel 57 1102) has singles/doubles for $35/42, and the *Island View Motel* (tel 57 1114) costs $35/45.

TRIABUNNA (population 924)

The larger town of Triabunna, a little further north, was a whaling station and garrison town when nearby Maria Island was a penal settlement. The tall timbers of the east coast are processed at a woodchip plant south of the town. Triabunna is still a busy fishing port and is also the departure point for charter boats to the Maria Island National Park. For good surfing try Boltons Beach, about a 20 minute drive north of Triabunna.

Places to Stay & Eat

The Triabunna *Youth Hostel* (tel 57 3439) in Spencer St has had good reviews and costs $6 a night. They can also arrange transport to the Maria Island ferry for hostellers. The *Triabunna Caravan Park* (tel 57 3248) has camping sites and their on-site vans cost $22 a double. The *Sandy Bay Hotel* has cheap counter meals.

MARIA ISLAND

Named by Dutch explorer Abel Tasman after the wife of Governor Van Diemen of the Dutch East India Company in Batavia, Maria Island is now a wildlife sanctuary. In 1825 it became the site for Tasmania's second penal settlement (the first was Sarah Island near Strahan) but was abandoned in 1832. The remains of the penal village at Darlington are remarkably well preserved but the peace and beauty of the island today belies its convict past. In later years there was a successful but short lived cement industry. Attempts were also made to establish a winery and a grazing industry, but both proved uneconomic.

The isolation that was such a barrier to settlement now helps preserve its natural and historical heritage. It's very quiet (the only car on the island is used by the park rangers) and has plenty of wildlife and magnificent scenery, particularly the cliffs on the north and east coasts. The open forests, scrublands, paddocks and fern gullies are now home to Cape Barren geese, emus, Forester kangaroos, wallabies and other native animals. It's a great, out of the way place for anyone into swimming, scuba diving, bushwalking or fishing.

Places to Stay

Many of the old buildings at Darlington and the rooms in the penitentiary have been converted into bunkhouses for visitors. It costs $4 a person, but it's wise to ring the warden in advance (tel (002) 57 1420) as the bunkhouses can be full with school groups. There are extensive camping grounds with toilets and fresh water but all other supplies must be brought with you from the mainland.

Getting There & Away

The ferry MV *James McCabe* travels from Louisville (a resort between Orford and Triabunna) across the Mercury Passage to Darlington. It departs daily at 10.30 am and arrives at 11.15 am. The return fare is $10 for day visitors ($5 for children) and $11 for campers. The ferry leaves the island at 2 pm, which doesn't really leave enough time to explore it on a day-trip. Bad weather occasionally delays the ferry so you must be prepared for a longer stay. You can ring the ferry office on (002) 57 1362.

SWANSEA (population 428)

On the shores of beautiful Great Oyster Bay, with superb views across to the Freycinet Peninsula and a good beach, Swansea is a popular place for camping, boating, fishing and surfing. It was settled in the 1820s and is the administrative centre for Glamorgan, Australia's oldest rural municipality. The original council chambers are still in use. Other interesting historic buildings include Morris' General Store and the 1860 Community Centre. The latter now houses a museum of local history and a full size billiard table.

The Swansea Bark Mill & East Coast Museum is worth a visit. Last century the mill processed black wattle bark, a basic ingredient used in the tanning of heavy leathers, then one of the main local industries. The adjoining museum features whaling implements, farming equipment and photographs. It is open daily from 9 am to 5 pm and admission is $3.50.

You can get tourist information at Morris' General Store and you can hire bicycles and windsurfers at the youth hostel.

Places to Stay & Eat

Swansea has a wide choice of accommodation for such a small town. The Swansea *Youth Hostel* (tel 57 8367) is at 5 Franklin St, right near the beach, and costs $6 a night. The *Kenmore Caravan Park* and *Swansea Caravan Park* have camping areas, on-site vans for $28 a double and cabins for $30 a double. *Oyster Bay Guest House* (tel 57 8110), on Franklin St, opposite the youth hostel, is a wonderful old place with bed & breakfast singles/doubles for $30/45.

Just Maggies, at 26 Franklin St, is a good place for coffee, cakes and light lunches. The *Swan Motor Inn* has counter meals. For something special, try the *Shy Albatross*, the licensed restaurant attached to the Oyster Bay Guest House.

Getting There & Away

Hobart Coaches buses from Hobart pass through Swansea around 11 am and 5 pm Monday to Friday and continue on to Bicheno, 45 minutes away. Buses south to Triabunna, Orford, Richmond and Hobart leave around 7.30 am and 3 pm. Hobart Coaches also have one bus a day during the week between Swansea and Launceston.

Peakes Coach Service also has a service to Bicheno that continues on to St Marys. It departs Swansea at 1.30 pm from Monday to Friday and arrives in Bicheno at 2.50 pm and St Marys at 4 pm. There is also a 10.50 am departure on Saturday. It costs $3 to Bicheno and $5.80 to St Marys. Buses leave from Morris' General Store.

COLES BAY & FREYCINET NATIONAL PARK

The tiny township of Coles Bay is sheltered by the spectacular 300 metre high red granite mountains known as the Hazards. It serves as the gateway to the many good beaches, secluded coves, rocky cliffs and excellent bushwalks of the Freycinet National Park. The park incorporates Freycinet Peninsula and beautiful Schouten Island and is noted for its coastal heaths, orchids, wildflowers and wildlife, which includes black cockatoos, yellow wattlebirds, Bennetts wallabies and possums. Moulting Lagoon is a breeding ground for black swans. There is a 27 km walking circuit of the park plus many other shorter tracks; the walk to Wineglass Bay is well worth the effort.

Jolly Jill Cruises (tel 75 1444) have cruises from Coles Bay to the Hazards Beach and the islands of the Freycinet National Park. The 2½ hour cruises leave at 10 am and 1.30 pm and cost $22.

The only general store in Coles Bay sells groceries, basic supplies and petrol. If you arrive after dark, especially in winter, you'll be hard pressed to find anywhere to eat.

Places to Stay & Eat

Sites at the *National Park Caravan Park* (tel 57 0107) should be booked at the ranger's office. If you're planning to camp in the National Park you should also inform the ranger. There is a family hostel but it caters only for groups, and advance bookings are essential. The *Iluka Holiday Centre* (tel 57 0115) has on-site vans and cabins from $25 for two people. *Pine Lodge Cabins* (tel 57 0113) cost $35 each, but there is a surcharge for one night stays. *The Chateau* (tel 57 0101), on the other side of the inlet from the town, consists of groups of quite luxurious cabins leading down to the water's edge. Bed & breakfast starts at $28 a person.

Julies is a BYO restaurant and has take-aways. You can get a good meal for $7 but it is closed in winter. Apart from that, *The Chateau* has fairly pricey set meals.

Getting There & Away

The school bus takes passengers from Bicheno to Coles Bay at 7 am and 2.45 pm, and there is an additional service at 9.45 am on Saturday. The fare is $3.35. The schedule can vary so enquire at the newsagent in Bicheno.

BICHENO (population 680)

This old coal mining port on a grassy cape overlooking the Gulch, a tiny picturesque harbour, was first used by sealers and whalers in the early 1800s. The lookouts on the hills over the town, were used to keep watch for passing whales. In the 1850s coal was hauled into the port by horse-drawn carts from the Denison River mines. Crayfish, abalone and oysters are the main produce of the town today. (In Tasmania the term crayfish usually means lobsters.) Bicheno is one of the best places on the east coast to rest for a few days. It has more charm and a better beach than St Helens, and it has a few more attractions and better facilities than Swansea.

The Bicheno Sea Life Centre on the foreshore features many species of marine life, and you can hire diving equipment at the Bicheno Dive Centre over the road. At nightfall you may be lucky enough to see the fairy penguins at the northern end of Redbill Beach. At low tide you can walk out to Diamond Island. The 35 hectare East Coast Bird & Wildlife Park is seven km north of the town.

There is a good foreshore walkway that runs for three km from Redbill Point to the Blowhole, and from there you can continue south around the beach to Cape Lodi and Courlands Bay. From Cape Lodi a track heads back inland towards Bicheno. You can also walk up to the two lookouts in town.

About 30 km north of Bicheno the Tasman Highway climbs up over the spectacular Elephant Pass. If you're thirsty when you get to the top try the *French Tea House* which serves coffee and pancakes and has a great view of the coast.

Places to Stay

The Bicheno *Youth Hostel* (tel 75 1293) is three km north of the town, on the beach opposite Diamond Island, and costs $6.50 a night. It can be full in summer. The *Bicheno Diving Centre* (tel 75 1138), on the highway, opposite the Sea Life Centre, caters mainly for divers but anyone can stay there. It has three self-contained cabins, with six bunks in each. At $12 a person or $15 with linen it is good value, especially if you get your own cabin. If no one is around ring 75 1143.

On-site vans are $25 at the *Bicheno Campervan Park* (tel 75 1280) and $28 at the *Treasure Island Caravan Park*; both have camping sites. On the northern outskirts of town, at 35 Gordon St, is the *Wintersun Lodge* (tel 75 1225), a good value motel at $35/45.

Places to Eat

The *Silver Sands* and *Beachfront* hotels have good, cheap counter meals, including a seafood selection. The *Galleon Coffee Shop* is not the most hospitable of establishments but it has reasonable lunches. Check the prices first. *Cyrano's*, at 77 Burgess St, is good for a splurge. It's a French restaurant and one of the few places in town serving crayfish.

For a fishing town, Bicheno is one place where it's surprisingly hard to buy fresh fish, though you can try the boats around the jetty where you can sometimes get crayfish. At the Chain of Lagoons, 40 km north of Bicheno, a roadside stand sells small, cooked crays for around $15 – one of the highlights of the east coast!

Getting There & Away

Hobart Coaches have two buses a day to Hobart and one to Launceston from Monday to Friday. They leave at 7 am (6.25 am on Mondays) and 2.30 pm (Hobart only) from the Shell service station. Peakes Coach Service (tel 72 2390) operates a service to Swansea and St Marys from Monday to Saturday. For buses to Coles Bay see under that section.

ST MARYS (population 650)

This charming little town, in the shadow of the Mt Nicholas Range, is 10 km inland, at the headwaters of the South Esk River which meets the sea at Launceston.

Fifteen km north, through St Marys Pass and four km off the Tasman Highway, is the tiny coastal township of Falmouth which has some early convict built buildings and good beaches.

At St Marys the Tasman Highway meets the Esk Main Rd which heads west through Fingal and Avoca to Conara Junction where it joins the Midland Highway. Fingal, 21 km from St Marys, is the headquarters of Tasmania's coal industry and has a number of historic buildings. Avoca serves the mining areas of Rossarden and Storys Creek, in the

foothills of Ben Lomond National Park. You can arrange to inspect the historic home 'Bona Vista' by contacting the caretaker.

Places to Stay

The superbly situated St Marys *Youth Hostel* (tel 72 2341), on 'Seaview Farm', has magnificent views of the coast, ocean and mountains. It's on German Town Rd, eight km from St Marys up a dirt road. The warden picks up hostellers from the post office between 10 and 11 am every day except Sunday. If you come on the Peakes bus it can take you to the hostel. The hostel costs $6 a night. St Marys also has a hotel and camping area.

Getting There & Away

Peakes has a bus to Bicheno and Swansea at 9.15 am Monday to Friday and at 8.30 am on Saturdays. The Redline coach to Launceston leaves at 8.40 am during the week. On the way to St Helens it passes through St Marys, at 7.20 pm Monday to Thursday and 8.20 pm Fridays.

SCAMANDER

North of St Marys is the popular resort town of Scamander, with excellent beaches for swimming and surfing, and good fishing in the sea and river.

The *Youth Hostel* (tel 72 5170), one km north of the bridge, costs $4 a night but bookings are essential. The *Home for Tea* tearooms has a couple of rooms at $15 a person, and the *Kookaburra Caravan Park* has on-site vans at $18 for two people.

ST HELENS (population 1000)

The largest town on the east coast is a popular resort on George Bay. Once again, fishing, particularly for crayfish, is a major business. St Helens was first settled in 1830 and 40 years later became the outlet for the Lottah and Blue Tier tin mining fields. The town has a museum and small history room, and good fishing (including offshore game fishing on charter boats). The bay, estuaries and lagoons are good for bird watching.

While the beaches in town are not very good for swimming, there are excellent scenic beaches around town at Binalong Bay, Sloop Reef and Stieglitz, as well as at St Helens and Humbug Points. You can also visit the St Columba Falls, near Pyengana.

Places to Stay & Eat

St Helens has plenty of accommodation and lots of places to eat. The *Youth Hostel* is in Cameron St, towards the bay, behind the main road, and costs $7. *St Helens Caravan Park* (tel 76 1290) has plenty of camping space as well as on-site vans at $26 for two, as does the *Hillcrest Caravan Inn* (tel 76 1298) at Stieglitz.

St Helens Guest House (tel 76 1234) is a fairly basic guest house but cheap enough at $20/30 for singles/doubles. It is at 71 Cecelia St, just beyond the library. *St Helens Motor Hotel* (tel 76 1131), at 49 Cecilia St, has singles/doubles from $26/36. They have good counter meals, as does the Bayside Inn.

Getting There & Away

Cashboult's Newsagency (tel 76 1182) is the agent for Redline, which has a service from St Helens to Launceston at 8 am seven days a week, with an additional bus at 4.30 pm on Sundays. Haley's Coaches (tel 76 1807) depart from the post office and travel to St Marys as well as to Derby in the north-east Monday to Friday. Redline have a service from Derby to Launceston.

WELDBOROUGH

The eastern approach to the Weldborough Pass, with its mountain scenery and dense rainforests, is quite spectacular. Hundreds of Chinese migrated to Tasmania during the tin mining boom last century and many made Weldborough their base.

GLADSTONE

About 25 km off the main Tasman Highway between St Helens and Scottsdale, the tiny town of Gladstone is one of the few tin mining centres still operating in the north-east of Tasmania. At one time there were a number of mining communities in the area and a large Chinese population. Today most are ghost towns. An unsurfaced road leads from Gladstone to the Eddystone Light, built in 1887. There are camping facilities at Eddystone Point, the most eastern point of the Tasmanian mainland, but campers need to take their own water supplies.

DERBY

Picturesquely set on the Ringarooma River, Derby is an historic town where tin was discovered in 1874 and worked at the Briseis mine. The museum has old photographs and mining implements and there is a re-creation of an old mining shanty town.

Places to Stay & Eat

The *Dorset Hotel* costs $22 a person for bed & breakfast. It also has counter meals. The tea shop in the museum has good meals and cakes. About 10 km from Derby is the peaceful *Merlinkei Farm Hostel* (tel (003) 54 2152), near Winnaleah, which costs $6 for YHA members. Visitors are welcome to participate in life on a dairy farm, and you can even earn your 'milk certificate'.

Getting There & Away

Redline have two buses a day during the week from Launceston via Scottsdale. The morning bus arrives in Derby at 12 noon and continues on to Winnaleah. There is only one bus on Saturdays and Sundays. The Haley's bus to St Helens departs from the Derby post office at 12.30 pm Monday to Friday.

SCOTTSDALE (population 1800)

The major town in the north-east is a quiet place in a beautiful setting. It serves some of the richest agricultural and forestry country in the state. There are two hotels and a good caravan park with camping sites in the town. Bridport is a beach resort on Bass Strait, 21 km north of Scottsdale. There's a fine old 1839 homestead there. You can also get to the pine forests en route to Branxholm and the beaches of Tomahawk.

BEN LOMOND NATIONAL PARK

This 165 square km park 50 km south-east of Launceston includes the entire Ben Lomond Range, and its magnificent scenery, dense rainforests and alpine slopes make it an ideal place for skiing, walking, climbing and photography.

The highest point is Legges Tor (1573 metres). At the southern end of the plateau is Stacks Bluff, which overlooks the Midlands and the Fingal Valley.

The ski slopes and snow cover are better here than at Mt Field and fine for beginners and intermediate skiers. The snow is not always good, however, so ring Ben Lomond Ski Rentals (tel (003) 31 1312) for snow reports. Skis, poles and boots can be rented for $18 a day, and lift tickets cost $16 a day or $75 a week.

Places to Stay & Eat

Ben Lomond is more of a day resort, but there is accommodation, meals and booze at the *Creek Inn* (tel (003) 72 2444), starting from $26 a person.

Getting There & Away

The park is reached by back roads, via White Hills or Evandale, and the Blessington Rd. The final climb up Jacobs Ladder is very narrow, steep and winding. Access during the season is easy as the Mountain Stage Line runs daily bus services from Paddy Pallin, 59 Brisbane St, Launceston. The fare is $18 return. From Hobart, Burnie and Queenstown Redline have a service when the snow cover is good. There are also shuttle buses from the Jacobs Ladder car park to the ski village for $6.

The Midlands

The tranquil, rolling midlands of Tasmania have a definite English feel about them due to the diligent efforts of early settlers who planted English trees and hedgerows. It was the fertility and agricultural potential of the area along the cart track and stock route between the two major towns of Hobart and Launceston that promoted Tasmania's rapid settlement and contributed to its early prosperity.

Coach stations, garrison towns, stone villages and pastoral properties soon sprang up along the route as convict gangs constructed the main road between Tasmania's northern and southern settlements. Fine wool, beef cattle and timber milling put the Midlands on the map. They are still the main industries of the area.

The course of the Midland Highway has changed slightly from its original route and many of the historic towns are now by-passed, but it is definitely worth making a few detours. Using this road it's just 199 km from Hobart to Launceston. Melton Mowbray (54 km from Hobart) is the junction for the alternative Lake Highway to Bothwell and Tasmania's highland lake country. The Midlands are best explored by car, but the regular Redline buses between Launceston and Hobart stop at all the towns mentioned in this section.

OATLANDS (population 545)

Eighty-four km north of Hobart is Oatlands, one of four military posts along the historic main road. The town has the largest collection of Georgian architectural styles in Australia. The oldest building is the convict built court house (1829), and most of the houses, hotels, schools and churches were constructed in the boom days of the 1830s. Life then revolved around military operations and the local industries of milling and brewing. The town is on the shores of Lake Dulverton, a wildlife sanctuary and popular fishing area. St Peters Pass, just north of the town, features hawthorn hedges cut in the shapes of animals.

Places to Stay

The Oatlands *Youth Hostel* (tel 54 1320), at 9 Wellington St, costs $6 a night. The *Oatlands Lodge* (tel 54 1444), at 92 High St, is a charming guest house with bed & breakfast singles/doubles for $53/65. There are also more expensive holiday flats in town.

TUNBRIDGE

First settled in 1809 and formerly called Tunbridge Wells, this town became the central stopover for coaches between Hobart and Launceston. Historical buildings of interest include the Tunbridge Wells Inn and adjoining stables, the Victoria Inn with its sandstone coaching steps, the Blind Chapel and Rosemere, former home of the local blacksmith. A sandstone bridge built in 1848 by convicts spans the Blackman River on the northern side of the town. Tunbridge is in the centre of the area of the state in which superfine wool is grown, and stages a huge district sheep sale annually, during the third week of January.

ROSS (population 500)

This charming ex-garrison town, 120 km from Hobart, was established in 1812 to protect travellers on the main north-south road and was also an important coach staging post and stock market. The convict built Ross Bridge is the third oldest bridge in Australia and historically the most important. A convict sculptor, Daniel Herbert, was granted a pardon for his work on the 184 panels which decorate the arches. He also carved the memorial which marks his grave in the old military burial ground – an interesting place to visit. Ross is famous for two of Australia's earliest and most highly regarded educational establishments, Ellenthorpe Hall and Horton College.

Things to See

The Four Corners, in the traditional heart of the town, represent Temptation (Man O' Ross Hotel), Salvation (Catholic church), Recreation (town hall) and Damnation (old jail). Other interesting historic buildings include the Scotch Thistle Inn, first licensed in 1830 as a coaching inn and now fully restored as a licensed restaurant; the Old Barracks, restored by the National Trust and now used as a wool and craft centre; the Uniting Church and St John's Church of England; and the Ross Memorial Library. The former rectory of St John's is now the Village Tea Rooms.

Ross has a military museum (entry $3). The Tasmanian Wool Centre is a museum and craft centre dedicated to the wool industry (entry $4). The town's major annual event is on the first Saturday in November, when horse riders come from all over Australia and overseas to take part in the annual Ross Rodeo.

Places to Stay

The *Man O'Ross Hotel* has bed & breakfast for $15 a person. There is also a caravan park and camping ground adjacent to the Ross bridge.

CAMPBELL TOWN (population 900)

Another former garrison post is Campbell Town, 12 km from Ross and 66 km south of Launceston. The most interesting examples of its early colonial architecture include the large brick and stone house known as The Grange, St Luke's Church of England, the Campbell Town Inn, Balmoral Cottage, the building known as the 'Fox Hunters Return' and the old brewery (now the Masonic Temple).

There's a secondary road from Campbell Town through the excellent fishing and bushwalking area around Lake Leake (32 km), to Swansea on the east coast. From Conara Junction, 11 km north of Campbell Town, the Esk Main Rd heads east from the Midland Highway to St Marys.

Launceston

Population 86,000

Launceston is renowned for its quiet charm, beautiful old homes and grand public buildings. Nestled in the wide, rich agricultural valleys formed by the Tamar and Esk River systems, it has long been the geographic and commercial hub of northern and midland Tasmania. It is Australia's third oldest city and the state's second largest.

The discovery of the Tamar River estuary in 1798 by Bass and Flinders, who were actually trying to find out if Van Diemens Land was joined to the rest of Australia, led to early settlement attempts in the area closer to the coast.

It wasn't until 1805 that the city of Launceston, on the upper reaches of the Tamar River at the confluence of the North and South Esk rivers, was officially founded by Lieutenant-Colonel William Paterson. The settlement was originally called Patersonia, but the city's first commandant later changed the name in honour of Governor King, who was born in Launceston, a town settled 1000 years before on the Tamar River in Cornwall, England.

Orientation

The central section of Brisbane St, between Charles and St John Sts, is a pedestrian mall around which the town is centred. The Quadrant is another mall, and Yorktown Square is an interesting open area of restored buildings turned into shops and restaurants. The main attractions of Launceston are all within walking distance of the centre.

Information

The Tasmanian Travel Centre (tel 32 2488) is on the corner of St John and Paterson Sts. Compared to most Travel Centres, the Launceston office isn't particularly informative, but they can give you a map of Launceston and a copy of *Launceston This Week*. You can buy flowers at their booth in the mall, but forget about travel information.

The post office is on the corner of Cameron and St John Sts. All the major Australian banks are represented in Launceston. You may want to visit one if you're heading to the east coast, where banks are few and far between. For camping gear Paddy Pallin, at 59 Brisbane St, and Allgoods, at 60 Elizabeth St, are both excellent.

Cataract Gorge

The magnificent Cataract Gorge, where almost vertical cliffs line the banks of the South Esk River as it enters the Tamar, is Launceston's best known attraction. The 1½ square km reserve is rich in native flora and fauna.

Only 10 minutes' walk from the centre of the city, a 1½ km path winds up the gorge to the Cliff Grounds and the First Basin recreation area on the other side of the river. A flock of peacocks lord over the beautiful gardens and there's a swimming pool, kiosk and restaurant – a popular place for picnics and Devonshire teas. A visitor information centre in the old bandstand features a changing information display.

A chair lift links the two sections of the reserve and the breathtaking six minute ride covers a distance of 457 metres across the river. It costs $2.50. A good walking trail leads further up the gorge to the deserted ruins of the old Duck Reach turbine driven power station which provided electricity for the city from 1895 to 1955.

Penny Royal World

The Penny Royal entertainment and accommodation complex began with the relocation of an 1825 corn mill, moved stone by stone from Barton, 60 km away. Penny Royal World now features working 19th century water mills and windmills. The corn mill building includes the shops

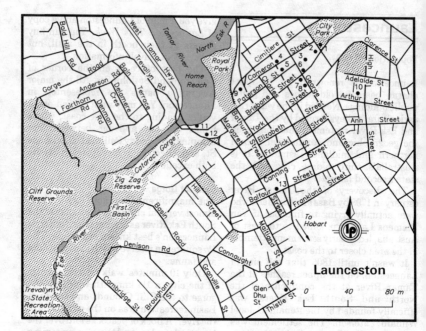

Launceston

0   40   80 m

1	Tasmanian Design Centre
2	Royal Oak Hotel
3	Yorktown Square
4	GPO
5	Tasmanian Travel Centre
6	Ansett Airlines
7	Australian Airlines
8	Redline Depot
9	Queen Victoria Museum & Art Gallery
10	Ashton Gate Guest House
11	Ritchies Flourmill & Lady Stelfox River Cruises
12	Penny Royal World
13	Centennial Hotel
14	Youth Hostel

of the millwright, blacksmith and wheelwright as well as a gift shop and museum. The nearby water mill, also originally located in Barton, is now part of the luxury Penny Royal motel.

A farmhouse, jail, gunners' quarters, underground armoury magazine, a 10 gun sloop, a cutter, waterfalls and a restaurant are other attractions of the complex. A restored Edwardian tram takes visitors to the gunpowder mill at the old Cataract quarry where there's also a foundry for casting cannons, and a model steam railway. Penny Royal World is interesting but not worth the $12 fee.

Museum

The Queen Victoria Museum & Art Gallery in Royal Park was built late last century and displays the splendour of the period both inside and out. It has a unique collection of Tasmanian fauna, Aboriginal artefacts, penal settlement relics, colonial paintings and a planetarium. A major attraction of the museum is the splendid Chinese Joss House donated by the descendants of Chinese settlers. The museum, in Wellington St, is open daily (afternoon only on Sunday) and admission is free.

Historic Buildings

Macquarie House, in the City Square, was built in 1830 as a warehouse but was later used as a military barracks and office building. It now houses a section of the Queen Victoria Museum & Art Gallery and a restaurant. It is open daily but only afternoons on weekends.

The Old Umbrella Shop, built in the 1860s, is the last genuine period shop in the state. Tasmanian blackwood lines the interior of this unique shop, which has been classified by the National Trust and houses a selection of umbrellas. The Trust uses the building, at 60 George St, as an information centre and gift store and it's open from 9 am to 5 pm on weekdays and from 9 am to 12 noon on Saturdays.

Franklin House, one of Launceston's most attractive early homes, has been beautifully restored and furnished by the National Trust. An outstanding feature of the interior of this Georgian house is the woodwork, which is all New South Wales cedar. Built in 1838 for Mr Britton James, a Launceston brewer and innkeeper, the house became the W K Hawkes School for Boys in 1842. Franklin House is six km from the city centre, on the main Hobart Rd (Midland Highway). It is open daily and entry is $2.50.

Parks & Gardens

Launceston's beautiful public squares, parks and private gardens have earned it the well deserved reputation of being Tasmania's garden city.

The 13 hectare City Park is a fine example of a Victorian garden and features an elegant fountain, Victorian bandstand, a monkey park, a wallaby enclosure and a conservatory. Albert Hall, built in 1891 for the Tasmanian International Exhibition, features a magnificent water organ.

Princes Square, between Charles and St John Sts, features a bronze fountain bought at the 1858 Paris Exhibition.

Other public gardens include Royal Park, on the North Esk River, by the junction of the Tamar River; the Trevallyn Dam recreation area; and Punchbowl Reserve, with its wildlife sanctuary and magnificent rhododendron garden.

Other Attractions

The Design Centre of Tasmania, on the corner of Brisbane and Tamar Sts, has displays of work by the state's top artists and craftspeople. Ritchie's Flour Mill, on Bridge Rd (near Penny Royal), has been transformed into an art gallery. Built in 1845, the four level complex includes a quaint Georgian miller's cottage which is now a tearoom.

The Waverley Woollen Mills, established in 1874, are the oldest operating woollen mills in Australia. They are open daily till 4 pm and you can watch the process. The mills are five km from the city centre, on Waverley Rd.

The paddle steamer *Lady Stelfox* can take you on a leisurely 45 minute cruise up Cataract Gorge and around the harbour. The boat leaves Ritchie's Landing Stage (near the Penny Royal) and costs $3.

There's a good view over the city from the Talbot Rd lookout, south-east of the centre, and from Freelands Lookout Reserve, off Bald Hill Rd.

Places to Stay

Hostels The Launceston *Youth Hostel* (tel 44 9779) is two km from the GPO, at 36 Thistle St. Housed in the former woollen mills canteen, it has dorm beds and family rooms and costs $7 a night. There are also 10 speed bicycles and bushwalking gear for hire.

Guest Houses The *Ashton Gate* (tel 31 6180), at 32 High St, near Arthur St, is good value at $18.50 a person for bed and a delicious breakfast. A few doors away, the *Windmill Hill Tourist Lodge* (tel 31 9337), at 22 High St, costs $22/30 for singles/doubles. They also have self-contained holiday flats for around $40.

If you can afford extra there are some lovely guest houses in old colonial buildings, such as *Airlie House* (tel 34 0304), at 163 George St, where singles/doubles with colour TV and attached bath are $47/60 including breakfast. *Hillview House* (tel 31 7388), at 193 George St, is similar and cheaper at $40/50.

Or you can rent your own fully furnished two bedroom cottage classified by the National Trust. The wonderful *Ivy Cottage*, at 17 York St, and *Alice's Place*, next door, are only a short stroll from the city centre and have their own small gardens. They cost $68 for two people and $10 for each additional person. Contact the owner on 31 8431 or 31 7481.

Hotels Launceston has a large selection of hotels for a town of its size. Two cheapies, both fairly basic, are the *Crown Hotel* (tel 31 4137), at 152 Elizabeth St, which costs $16/25 including breakfast, and the *Enfield* (tel 31 4040), at 169 Charles St, which is $16.50/32 but for room only. Slightly better than these two is the *Sportsman Hall Hotel* (tel 31 3968) which costs $16/30 including breakfast. It is at 252 Charles St, just south of the city centre, past Princes Square.

O'Keefes Hotel (tel 31 4015), at 124 George St, near the Redline depot, has reasonable rooms for $20 a person including a light breakfast. The *Royal Hotel* (tel 31 2526), at 90 George St, costs $18/35, including breakfast.

The *Star Hotel* (tel 31 9659), at 113 Charles St, has good rooms with bath for $22/40, including breakfast. The *Centennial Hotel* (tel 31 4957), at 11 Balfour St, on the corner of Bathurst St, has bed & breakfast singles/doubles for $25/40 with bath and colour TV. It is comfortable but can get a lot of traffic noise.

Motels & Holiday Flats The *Mews Mini-Motel* (tel 31 2861) is at 89 Margaret St,

quite close to the centre. Rooms are $38/49, including an excellent breakfast. The *Motel Maldon* (tel 31 3979), at 32 Brisbane St, is right in the city and costs $40/50 for bed and continental breakfast.

Launceston also has some holiday flats and other self-contained accommodation. *Clarke Holiday Flat* (tel 31 7712) is at 19 Nieka Ave, near the corner of Basin Rd and Brougham St on the way to the gorge. It is good value at $30 for two, and the management is friendly and sympathetic to travellers.

Camping The most convenient caravan park is *Treasure Island* (tel 44 2600), past the youth hostel, at Glen Dhu St, Glen Dhu. Phone first to check if they'll let you camp there as they don't seem to be too enthusiastic about tent campers. The park gets crowded and is right next to the freeway but it is well equipped and has on-site vans for $28 a double.

The other two caravan parks are both 12 km out of town but worth the trouble to get to. The *Legana Tourist & Caravan Park* (tel 30 1714, after hours 30 1462) is on the West Tamar Highway near Westlands nursery; and the *Launceston Caravan Park* (93 6391) is on the Bass Highway, near Hadspen. Both have on-site vans and holiday flats.

Places to Eat

Banjo's, in Yorktown Square, is good for pastries, cakes and coffee (the refills are free). It is open weekdays from 7.30 am to 5.30 pm, Saturdays till 6 pm and Sundays till 2 pm. Yorktown Square also has a few more up-market cafes, such as *Molly York's* where you can dine alfresco. It's hard to get anything cheaper than the cafeteria on the 6th floor of the *Myer* department store on the corner of the Mall. You can get lunch for $3 and the view across Launceston is a winner.

Hollow Legs, on Charles St, is a popular take-away delicatessen. They have excellent sandwiches and light meals such as lasagna for $2.50. *The Eatery*, at

91 George St, near the Redline depot, is a pleasant BYO cafe for breakfast or lunch. It is open from 9 am to 5 pm Monday to Friday and from 10 am to 2 pm on the weekend.

Counter Meals Almost all of Launceston's many hotels have filling, reasonably priced counter meals. The *Royal Oak*, on the corner of Brisbane and Tamar Sts, is a convivial place and serves good counter meals for around $5 in their Flynn's Bistro, dedicated to Tasmania's number one son, Errol Flynn.

Other hotels with counter meals in the $5 to $7 range include *Lloyd's Hotel*, on the corner of Cimitiere and George Sts; *St Georges Hotel*, on the corner of York and St John Sts; the *Tasmania Hotel*, at 191 Charles St; and *O'Keefes Hotel*, on the corner of York and George Sts. The *Centennial Hotel*, on the corner of Balfour and Bathurst Sts, is close to the youth hostel and also has good, cheap counter meals.

Restaurants There are a few good restaurants in Launceston charging $7 to $10 for a main meal. *Calabrisella* (tel 31 1958), at 51 Wellington St, has good Italian food and is open till 2 am on Fridays and Saturdays. Their pasta costs around $7, their veal dishes around $10. They serve pizzas in the take-away section at the front. The *Capri Pizza Restaurant*, at 76 St John St, also serves pizzas. The *Pasta House*, in Yorktown Square, is a licensed restaurant with pasta dishes for around $7.

The *Canton* (tel 31 9448), at 203 Charles St, is one of the best Chinese restaurants in town and moderately priced. The *New York* (tel 31 2782), at 61 Brisbane St, is another good Chinese restaurant. For Mexican food, *Montezuma's* (tel 23 4770), at 63 Brisbane St, has main meals for $9 to $10.

For $10 or more, there's the *Akbar* (tel 34 0024), at 63 Cimitiere St, which has an Asian menu: Indian, Indonesian, and

Chinese. The *Satay House* (tel 44 5955), out at the Kingscourt Shopping Centre, in Kings Meadows, has excellent Indonesian food. *Shrimps* (tel 34 0584), at 72 George St, is a good choice for seafood, and *Dicky White's* (tel 31 9211), at 107 Brisbane St, is the place for steaks. *The Gorge Restaurant* (tel 31 3330), at Cataract Gorge, has good food and undoubtedly the best setting in town.

Entertainment

Most of the hotels in Launceston have some sort of entertainment, either bands or discos. Check the *Examiner* or *Launceston This Week*, which has a good gig guide. The *Victoria Hotel*, on the corner of Bathurst and Brisbane Sts, and the *Royal Hotel*, on George St, have rock bands on Friday and Saturday nights.

Other regular venues include *Night Moves*, at 30 The Kingsway, and *Rosie's Tavern*, on the corner of George and Elizabeth Sts. In the disco department, there's the terribly pretentious *Hot Gossip*, in the Launceston Hotel, Brisbane St, which is open Wednesday to Saturday. *Regines* is an expensive disco at the casino.

The publican at the *Royal Oak Hotel*, Brisbane and Tamar Sts, has plans to put on bands but all he has to do is turn up the stereo and the place is packed. It's an easy-going pick-up place for the young set, particularly on Friday and Saturday nights.

If you want to risk a few dollars or just observe how the rich people play, check out Tasmania's second casino, the *Launceston Federal Country Club Casino*, at Prospect, 10 km out of the city centre. Entry is free, but if you wear anything that looks like jeans, it is assumed you are a mass murderer, and you won't be allowed in. The drinks are expensive but the gambling is not – as long as you don't get carried away!

Most Launceston venues are annoyingly fussy about dress, so if you didn't bring your best clothes at least make sure you're neat or you could spend your evening just looking for a place that will let you in.

Getting There & Away
Air Ansett (tel 31 7711) and Australian Airlines (tel 31 4411) are both on corners of George and Brisbane Sts. Melbourne ($142, standby $114) is only an hour away, and there are now direct flights to Sydney and Brisbane.

You can fly Ansett between Hobart and Launceston for $83 or with Airlines of Tasmania for $57, but Australian Airlines' 'Skyway' fare costs just $25.

Airlines of Tasmania also have flights between Launceston and Devonport ($38.50); Flinders Island ($58); Wynyard ($38.50); King Island ($90); Queenstown ($58); and Strahan ($58).

Bus Tasmanian Redline Coaches (tel 31 9177), at 112 George St, have a number of services to and from Launceston. The Midland Highway trip to Hobart takes about 2½ hours. The fare is $13.80 ($17.20 express) and there are six buses a day from Monday to Friday, two on Saturday and three on Sunday. Express buses leave Hobart for Launceston at 7 am and 2.15 and 3.45 pm during the week, and at 12.30 pm on Sunday. There are five daily buses to Devonport ($9.60) and the 3.30 pm buses on Tuesday, Thursday and Sunday meet the *Abel Tasman*. Some buses continue on to Burnie ($10.60), Wynyard and Smithton ($20.20).

Redline has one afternoon bus every day to St Helens, via Conara and the Midland Highway. They also have two buses a day to Derby and Winnaleah in the north-east (one only on weekends) via Scottsdale with connections to Lilydale and Bridport. From Derby there are buses to St Helens.

Redline also have three services daily to George Town and buses to Bell Bay. At 4.15 pm Monday to Friday there is a bus to Mole Creek via Deloraine.

Hobart Coaches (tel 31 8677) have an afternoon bus Monday to Friday to Swansea and Bicheno on the east coast. Buses depart from 168 Brisbane St, travelling via the Tasmanian Travel Centre.

Mountain Stage Line (tel 34 0427), at 59 Brisbane St, has charter buses for bushwalkers and operates on demand. During the peak season you should have no problems getting a bus to either Cradle Mountain ($24 one way) or Lake St Clair ($30) to do the Overland Track. They also travel to Mienna and Great Lake, and to Ben Lomond in the ski season.

Car Launceston is 199 km from Hobart by the direct route, 434 km by the east coast route. It's 89 km to Devonport and another 54 km to Burnie.

Getting Around
Airport Transport The Tasmanian Redline bus to Launceston Airport costs $4; by taxi it's about $12.

Bus The MTT run the local buses and offer a $1.80 all-route all-day Dayrover bus ticket. Most routes do not operate in the evening and Sunday services can be few and far between. The Punch Bowl bus leaves from Brisbane St opposite Kingsway but there's no evening service and next to no service at all on Sunday. There is a free map with a route map on the back.

If you're hitching to Devonport and the north-west, catch a Prospect bus from outside the Launceston Bank for Savings, on St John St. For Hobart and the east coast, catch a Franklin Village bus near the HEC on St John St. The Tasman Highway route to the east coast is longer and more scenic but also harder. For this route catch a Waverley bus from opposite Quadrant Mall, on St John St. There is no bus service north of George Town on the Tasman Highway apart from the twice daily service to Bridport. There's no traffic either, especially to Tomahawk.

Car See the Tasmania introductory Getting Around section for information on renting cars. The major car rental firms all have offices either in Launceston or at Launceston Airport.

Tours The Tasmanian Travel Centre offers half day coach tours of the city for $16 and of the Tamar Valley for $19. They also have full day tours to the Mole Creek caves and Deloraine for $29, and a Tasmanian highland tour for $19.

Bicycle The youth hostel, at 36 Thistle St (tel 44 9779), has a huge range of bicycles including 10 speed tourers. They cost $7 a day or $48 a week, including helmet and panniers. There is a reducing rate for each additional week. You can leave your luggage, or send the bicycle back by bus.

Around Launceston

Early in the 19th century Launceston was a gateway for the settlers and farmers who were opening up the north of Tasmania. They headed inland and along the north-west coast to exploit the region's fertile soils and grazing lands and south to develop one of the wealthiest farming areas in the state. The number of towns and fine early houses around Launceston is indicative of the prosperity the new colony quickly developed from this rich agricultural potential.

HADSPEN (population 950)
Tasmania's best known historic home is the beautiful Entally House, at Hadspen, built in 1819 by Thomas Haydock Reibey. As a historic showpiece it creates a vivid picture of what life must have been like for the well-to-do on an early farming property.

The Reibeys didn't always have it so good though; in 1790 Mary Haydock, the matriarch of this prosperous family, was convicted of horse stealing and transported to New South Wales. She was then 13 years old. On the voyage from England she met and later married Thomas Reibey, a sub-lieutenant in the service of the East India Company. The young couple prospered and Mary, being a very astute businesswoman, made quite a name for herself in the early days of the colony. It was the Reibey family shipping enterprises that brought Mary's sons to Tasmania, where Thomas built Entally House on the 10½ square km property and his son Thomas became one of the state's first premiers.

Entally House, 13 km from Launceston and just west of Hadspen, has been faithfully restored. Entry is $2.50 and well worth it.

In Hadspen itself you'll find the Red Feather Inn, built in 1843. Tearooms and a craft shop now operate in an adjoining building and the village has a caravan park and camping ground.

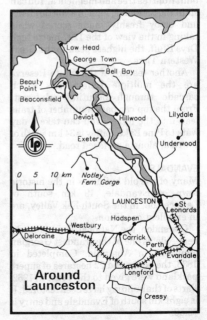

Around Launceston

Nearby Rutherglen Village, on the banks of the South Esk River, is primarily a convention and entertainment centre but as well as accommodation and leisure facilities it features an art gallery, working pottery, a museum and an animal and bird sanctuary. Entry is $2.50.

The wonderful ivy covered bluestone Carrick Mill, two km west of Hadspen, is now a restaurant specialising in Devonshire teas and traditional English fare. The roadside flour mill by the Liffey River began work in 1810 but lay derelict for many years before its restoration.

LIFFEY VALLEY

This valley, at the foot of the Great Western Tiers, on the Liffey River, is a very popular destination for bushwalkers and fishermen. Day visitors are attracted by an amazing fernery which has the largest variety of ferns for sale in the state. The fernery and nearby tearooms were built from tea tree and melaleuca. You can sit in the tearooms, high in a wattle glade, and enjoy freshly made scones while taking in the view of the 1297 metre high Drys Bluff, the highest peak in the Great Western Tiers.

Another feature of this State Reserve are the multiple Liffey Falls which cascade through beautiful rainforest. From the top car park a number of trails lead into the forest. You can take a day walk to Pine Lake. Liffey is 34 km south of Carrick, along a surfaced road.

EVANDALE

Many of the old buildings in the historic town of Evandale, 19 km south of Launceston, in the South Esk Valley, are in excellent condition.

Clarendon, the National Trust property near Nile, is one of the grandest Georgian mansions in Australia. Completed in 1838, the house and 22 hectares of superb parkland were given to the Trust in 1962. Parts of the building have been restored. It is eight km south of Evandale and entry is $2.50.

In Evandale, there is accommodation at the *Prince of Wales Hotel* (tel 91 8381), on Nile St, at $20 a single for bed & breakfast.

PERTH (population 1230)

This is yet another historic town by the South Esk River, 19 km from Launceston. The site for the town was chosen by Governor Macquarie in 1821. Noteworthy buildings in the town are the Eskleigh Home, the Methodist and Baptist churches and the Leather Bottle, Old Crown and Jolly Farmer Inns.

LONGFORD (population 2030)

Longford, also a National Trust classified town, is set in the midst of a rich pastoral area watered by the South Esk and Lake rivers. Its many colonial buildings, mostly built by convicts, include Christ Church, Jessen Lodge, the Queen's Arms Hotel and Brickendon Mansion. It's an easy day-trip from Launceston (only 27 km), but you can stay overnight at the caravan park, which has tent sites on the bank of the Lake River.

The annual Tasmanian Folk Festival, which has an international reputation, is held in Longford on the Australia Day weekend in January.

The Longford Wildlife Park, on Pateena Rd, about 14 km from the town, was created to provide a permanent conservation area for native Tasmanian flora and fauna. The 70 hectare bush and pasture park has kangaroos, wallabies, echidnas, Cape Barren geese, wild ducks and native birds.

CRESSY

A little further south-west, in Cressy, you can visit historic Palmerston House. Cressy was once the richest wheat growing district in Tasmania but today earns its living from oats, barley, peas, beans and poppies – the latter for use in the (legal) production of drugs. The town, 36 km from Launceston, is also a good base for trout fishing in nearby Brumbys Creek and the Macquarie Lake and Liffey River.

At the *Ringwood Hotel* (tel 97 6161) bed & breakfast costs $20/30 a single/double.

The Tamar Valley

The Tamar River separates the East and West Tamar districts and links Launceston with its ocean port of Bell Bay. The river is tidal to Launceston and wends its way through orchards, pastures, forests and the vineyards which are an important part of Tasmania's developing wine industry. The black swan is just one of the many species of wildlife that makes its home along the waterway and the river has become a popular recreation area.

European history in the valley dates from 1798 when Bass and Flinders discovered the estuary. The district developed slowly and was a port of call for the sailors and sealers from the Bass Strait islands and a sanctuary for some of the desperate characters who took to the bush during the convict days.

With the discovery of gold in the Cabbage Tree Hill (now Beaconsfield) area in the late 1870s the fortunes of the valley took a new turn. The region boomed and for a time Beaconsfield was the third largest town in Tasmania, with over $6 million worth of gold being extracted before water seepage forced the mines to close.

NOTLEY FERN GORGE

Notley Fern Gorge is the only remnant of the dense rainforest that once blanketed the West Tamar. Originally saved from the settler's axe because of its inaccessibility, the 10 hectare reserve of ferns, trees and shrubs is also a wildlife sanctuary. Early last century the notorious bushranger Matthew Brady and his gang eluded capture for some time by hiding in the Notley forests. The gorge is 23 km from Launceston, off the West Tamar Highway, via Legana.

EXETER

Near Exeter, base for the West Tamar farming and orchard industries, are the river resorts of Paper Beach, Blackwall and Gravelly Beach.

Five km south of Exeter, Bradys Lookout is a high rocky outcrop used by the bushranger to check on troop movements and potential 'clients'. Brady was eventually captured in 1826 by a party led by John Batman (one of the founders of Melbourne) and was hanged in Hobart at the age of 27.

DEVIOT

The Tamar Valley Vineyards, at Deviot (north of Exeter), are open to the public. Other vineyards and wineries are at Legana, Rosevears, Blackwall, Rowella, Glengarry and Lalla. The Tasmanian Rock Oyster Company also has its headquarters at Deviot.

BEACONSFIELD (population 900)

The once thriving gold mining town of Beaconsfield is still dominated by the ruins of the three mine buildings. One of these buildings has been restored and houses the Grubb Shaft Museum with a good display of local memorabilia including mining, orchard and farming equipment. It's open Tuesday to Sunday from 10 am to 4 pm. You can also visit a restored miner's hut and the original Flowery Gully School.

There is a camping ground at picturesque Beauty Point, four km downstream from Beaconsfield. At the mouth of the Tamar River the holiday and fishing resorts of Greens Beach and Kelso have good beaches and caravan and camping grounds.

LOW HEAD

The East Tamar district on the other side of the river is also worth a visit. The pilot station at Low Head on the north coast is one of the oldest in Australia and now houses a maritime museum. The original lighthouse overlooking the mouth of the Tamar was built in the 1830s and the present structure dates from 1888. East Beach, on Bass Strait, is good for surfing and the quieter Lagoon Bay, on the river, is safe for swimming.

GEORGE TOWN (population 5600)

George Town, site of the original though accidental landing by Colonel Paterson in 1804 (his ship HMS *Buffalo* ran aground during a storm), was first settled in 1811 and is now a commercial and residential town for the Bell Bay industrial area. The old watch house, built in 1843, has been restored as a folk museum and is open daily from 8 am to 5 pm.

The Grove, formerly the port officer's residence, has been classified by the National Trust and is open from 10 am to 5.30 pm. In this fine Georgian home on the corner of Elizabeth and Cimitiere Sts, the staff dress in period costume; refreshments and lunches are available and handicrafts are on sale. Also of interest is the St Mary Magdalen Anglican Church, on Anne St, and the cemetery, on the northern outskirts of town, which has some interesting headstones dating from 1833.

There is a caravan and camping ground and the *George Town Hotel* (tel 82 1219) has bed & breakfast singles from $17.50.

HILLWOOD

Keep heading south to the attractive rural area of Hillwood where you can pick your own strawberries and buy other berries and apples in season. Hillwood is also noted for its fishing and river views. Further south is the pretty town of Windermere and historic St Matthius church.

UNDERWOOD

In about 1940 the Alexander Patent Racquet Company planted more than 100,000 English ash trees near Underwood for the production of tennis racquets.

Unfortunately – for them at least – the demand diminished considerably before the trees reached maturity so the magnificent stands of ash trees are now part of the 70 hectare Hollybank Reserve.

The Hollybank Apiary nearby is a commercial bee keeping enterprise where visitors can watch the bees going about their business in glass hives. You can buy honey (good) and honey mead (terrible).

LILYDALE

The small town of Lilydale, 27 km from Launceston, stands at the foot of 1187 metre Mt Arthur and is a convenient base for bushwalkers heading to the mountain and along a variety of other tracks and scenic trails in the area. Three km from the town the Lilydale Falls Reserve has camping facilities and two picturesque waterfalls. On the weekend a good produce and craft market is held at Lalla, three km west of Lilydale.

North Central

Behind the northern coastal strip the Great Western Tiers rise up into Tasmania's central mountains and the Cradle Mountain-Lake St Clair National Park. There are some interesting and scenic spots in this area. The Bass Highway continues west from Launceston to Deloraine and the start of the north-west route.

WESTBURY (population 1200)

Westbury, 18 km west of Hadspen, is another classified historic town. The traditional village green is still used for fêtes. Colonial furnishings are a feature of the White House built in the 1840s. Its outhouses display vintage vehicles, 'fashions of the day', and a collection of 19th century toys. St Andrew's Church features some superb examples of the work of Mrs Nellie Payne, one of Tasmania's most famous wood carvers.

The beautiful St Mary's Church is the focal point of the little township of Hagley, five km from Westbury. The foundation stone was laid in 1861 by Sir Richard Dry, Australia's first knight who, in 1866, became Tasmania's first native born premier.

For accommodation try the *Westbury Hotel* (tel 93 1151) where bed & breakfast is $25/40 a single/double.

DELORAINE (population 1930)

This picturesque town, surrounded by lush countryside, is the centre of an important agricultural district, noted for its oats since the 1840s. The Deloraine flour mills were established in 1859 and by 1870 there were 125 square km under cultivation.

Many of the town's Georgian and Victorian buildings have been restored, some for commercial purposes and others as historic showpieces. The Bowerbank Mill Gallery, two km east of town, carries the National Trust's highest rating. Built in 1853, the old corn mill ceased production in 1929 and was re-opened in 1973 as an art and craft gallery.

Other places of interest include the Folk Museum & Cider Bar, the Deloraine Antiques and Old Sewing Box Museum, St Mark's Church of England, Bonney's Inn – which serves lunches and Devonshire teas – and a wildlife park. At Lemana Junction, seven km from the town, on the Mole Creek Rd, there's a small smokehouse where eels, trout, abalone and scallops are smoked or processed.

There are also a number of waterfalls in the Deloraine area including Montana, Meander and Liffey Falls (the latter is described in the Around Launceston section).

Places to Stay

The Deloraine *Youth Hostel* (tel 62 2996) is in a spacious house at 8 Blake St. It offers a superb view of the Great Western Tiers and is open all day. There are bicycles for hire and snacks available. A bed costs $6. The warden takes bushwalks and provides very reasonably priced transport to the trails of Cradle Mountain ($25), and Great Lakes and Liffey Falls ($20). The hostel is closed during July, August and September. Deloraine also has a caravan park and camping area.

Of the town's three hotels, the *Bush Inn* (tel 62 2365) is probably the most comfortable and good value at $20/30 for singles/doubles including breakfast. However, it can't match the charm of the *Deloraine Hotel* (tel 62 2022), on the main street, near the river. The hotel has seen better days and the beds are more like hammocks, but it's a grand old place with big lacework verandahs and furnishings that recall its former opulence. Singles/doubles, some with bath, are $20/35, including a huge cooked breakfast.

Getting There & Away

Deloraine is on the main highway between Devonport and Launceston and most of the Redline buses between these two cities stop at the Golden Fleece service station. Redline also has an afternoon bus during the week from Launceston to Mole Creek via Deloraine.

MOLE CREEK (population 300)

Limestone caverns, leatherwood honey and a wildlife park are the main attractions of the Mole Creek area west of Deloraine. Marakoopa Cave, 11 km from the township of Mole Creek in the foothills of Western Bluff, consists of a large complex of caverns, two underground streams, gypsum formations and glow-worms. Tours of the caves leave every 1½ hours between 10 am and 4 pm and cost $4. About 16 km from the town is King Solomon Cave, a more spacious, dry cavern with many passages.

Mole Creek is a centre for the production of Tasmania's famous leatherwood honey which is produced from the blossoms of the leatherwood tree.

Two km beyond Chudleigh, on the way to Mole Creek, is the Tasmanian Wildlife Park with a noctarium for viewing nocturnal animals. There are a surprising number of animals found only in Tasmania and this park has one of the best collections anywhere. Admission is $4.

PARRAMATTA CREEK

If you leave the main Bass Highway at Elizabeth Town (north of Deloraine) and head for Railton you'll find an extraordinary teahouse just off the road at Parramatta Creek. Built by a local guy who had 'money to spare', the Conservatory Teahouse looks like it's been transplanted from an English country estate. The high arched windows on all sides look out on the bushland, there are plants and classical music inside and Devonshire teas and light lunches.

SHEFFIELD (population 950)

Dominated by the impressive Mt Roland (1234 metres), the scenery around Sheffield in the Mersey Valley is superb. Set in the foothills of the Great Western Tiers, the town is surrounded by peaceful farmlands, virgin forests, quiet streams, rugged mountain gorges and rivers brimming with fish. Nearby Lake Barrington, formed by the Devils Gate Dam which is part of the Mersey-Forth hydroelectricity scheme, is a major rowing venue and state recreation reserve. Apples are still an important crop in the Mersey Valley and mushrooms are also grown. Sheffield also has a number of good murals painted on the walls around town.

There is a caravan park and camping ground, and the *Sheffield Hotel* costs $19/31 for bed & breakfast singles/ doubles.

Devonport

Population 21,500

The city of Devonport straddles the mouth of the Mersey River almost in the centre of Tasmania's north coast. Nestled behind the dramatic lighthouse-topped Mersey Bluff, it is the terminus for the vehicular ferry from Melbourne and a base for exploring the north-west coast.

Bluff Lighthouse was built in 1889 to direct the colony's rapidly growing sea traffic and its light can be seen up to 27 km out to sea. A year later, as the area became a vital port, the towns of Torquay and Formby joined to become Devonport.

Nearby Spreyton, where Tasmania's apple growing industry had its beginnings in 1898, is still one of the state's main orchard districts. Devonport is the focal point for one of Australia's richest and most beautiful farming areas and has been exporting local products, including apples, vegetables, berries and fine wool, for nearly 100 years.

Devonport doesn't have a great deal that is of interest in its own right except for a couple of museums and the Aboriginal Cultural & Art Centre, but it tries hard to attract visitors and there's enough to occupy a bit of time either on arrival in Tasmania or prior to departure.

Information

The government run Tasmanian Travel Centre (tel 24 1526) has its office at 18 Rooke St on the corner of King St. There is also an office at the ferry terminal in East Devonport. It has good information on Devonport and Tasmania in general. The Devonport Showcase, at 5 Best St, also has a complete range of tourist information and brochures on the Devonport area and across the north-west. There are also displays and workshop demonstrations of arts and crafts and a coffee shop.

There's a Wilderness Information Centre at 31 Stewart St where you can buy good maps. You'll find a laundrette at 157 Rooke St (the Victoria Parade end).

Tiagarra

The Tasmanian Aboriginal Cultural & Art Centre, known as Tiagarra, is on Mersey Bluff, at the north side of Devonport. It's open daily and admission is $2. The word means 'keep' in the Tasmanian Aboriginal language and the centre is intended to preserve their art and culture. Tiagarra also has a rare collection of more than 250 Aboriginal rock engravings.

Museums

Transport of one form or another seems to be the theme of most of Devonport's museums. The Maritime Museum on Gloucester Ave has a good model collection of the sailing ships that visited Tasmania in the early days as well as other interesting nautical items. It's open Tuesday to Sunday from 2 to 4 pm in winter and from 1 to 4.30 pm in summer (October to March); admission is $1.

Bramich's Early Motoring & Folk Museum (tel 24 4575) takes you back to the age of 'genteel motoring'. It's at 3 Don Rd and is open only by appointment.

The Don River Railway, out of town on the Bass Highway to Ulverstone, has Tasmania's only full sized passenger railway still in operation. Vintage steam locomotives haul carriages on a 30 minute trip along the banks of the picturesque Don River. During summer the train runs every day, except Saturday, between 11 am and 4 pm but in winter it only operates on Sundays and public holidays. At Don Village the Van Diemen Light Railway Society has a collection of restored locomotives, rolling stock and steam driven machines. Admission is $4.

Other Attractions

The Devonport Gallery & Arts Centre, at

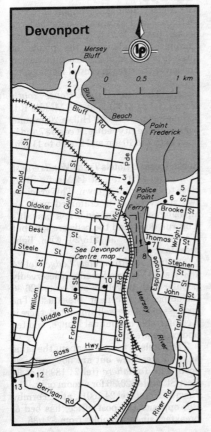

1	Tiagarra
2	Bluff Caravan Park
3	River View Lodge
4	Elimatta Hotel
5	Terminal Caravan Park
6	Shoreline Caravan Park
7	Mersey Ferry
8	Bass Strait Ferry Terminal
9	Sports Centre Lodge
10	Trade Winds Guest House
11	Argosy Motor Inn
12	Home Hill
13	Youth Hostel

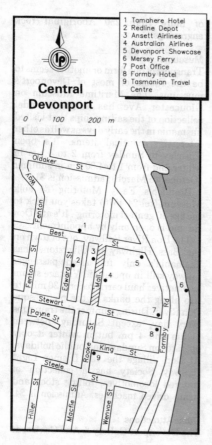

Central Devonport

0   100   200 m

1 Tamahere Hotel
2 Redline Depot
3 Ansett Airlines
4 Australian Airlines
5 Devonport Showcase
6 Mersey Ferry
7 Post Office
8 Formby Hotel
9 Tasmanian Travel Centre

weekends from 2 to 4 pm. Admission is $2.50 for adults and $1 for children.

Taswegia, at 56-57 Formby Rd, is a working design house with a printing museum and craft shop. It displays old printing presses and has interesting explanations of the printing processes of the past and not-so-distant past.

The Serendipity Fun Park, at 2 Main Rd, has lots of rides and other attractions to shut the kids up. It's open every day and costs $12 for adults and $10 for children under 12.

Places to Stay

The Mersey divides Devonport into two sections. East Devonport, where the ferry docks, has a few hotels, motels and camping grounds, but the points of interest and most of the accommodation are across the river in central Devonport.

Hostels The *Mac Wright House Youth Hostel* (tel 24 6133) is at 115 Middle Rd, 400 metres past Home Hill, a 20 minute walk from the city centre. It costs $7 and is open from 7 to 10 am and from 5 to 11 pm.

Guest Houses & Hotels *Trade Winds Guest House* (tel 24 1719), at 44 Macfie St, is close to the centre of town. This gracious two storey house is crammed with an amazing collection of old bric-a-brac. It's a bit run down and the beds are soft, but it's good value at $15/20 with light breakfast.

The friendly *River View Lodge* (tel 24 7537), at 18 Victoria Parade, is deservedly popular with travellers and costs $26/36 including an excellent breakfast. The spotless rooms are well appointed, there is a comfortable communal lounge, and tea and coffee are free.

The hotels in town cost about the same as the River View but are not nearly as good. The *Tamahere* (tel 24 1898), at 34 Best St, costs $20/36 for a room only. The *Formby Hotel* (tel 24 1601), at 82 Formby Rd, opposite the post office, has bed & breakfast singles/doubles from $24/36.

43 Stewart St, is open Tuesday to Friday from 10 am to 4.30 pm and Sundays from 2 to 4.30 pm.

Home Hill, built in 1916 and now administered by the National Trust, was the home of Joseph and Dame Enid Lyons. Joseph Lyons is the only Australian to have been both the premier of his state and prime minister of Australia. In 1943 Dame Enid Lyons became the first woman member of the House of Representatives. Home Hill, 77 Middle Rd, is open Tuesday to Thursday and on

Motels The *Sports Centre Lodge* (tel 24 4109), at 34 Forbes St, is more like a basic holiday flat with parking space than a motel. It's nothing special but cheap enough at $16/24 for singles/doubles with bath. The *Edgewater Motor Inn* (tel 27 8441), at 2 Thomas St, East Devonport, is right near the ferry terminal and costs $34/39. It's not very attractive but it's relatively cheap and the attached hotel has good counter meals.

The *Elimatta Motor Inn* (tel 24 6555), at 15 Victoria Pde, is a notch up in quality at $42/47. It is probably worth spending a bit extra to stay at the first class *Argosy Motor Inn* (tel 27 8872), on Tarleton St, East Devonport, which costs $50/57.

Camping The *Mersey Bluff Caravan Park* (tel 24 8655) is out at the Bluff by Tiagarra and camping costs $7 for two. The park is 2½ km from town but it's in a pleasant setting and there are good beaches nearby.

East Devonport has three caravan parks just north of the ferry terminal at the head of the Mersey River. The *Abel Tasman Caravan Park* (tel 27 8794), at 6 Wright St, East Devonport, has camping sites and on-site vans for $26 a double. *Devonport Caravan Park* (tel 27 8886), on Caroline St, East Devonport, costs $6 for two to camp, $32 for an on-site van for two. *Shoreline Caravan Park* (tel 27 8185), at 3 Brooke St, East Devonport, has on-site vans at $20 for two.

Places to Eat

Apart from counter meals in the pubs, for cheap eats try the coffee lounges and take-aways in the Mall. They usually close around 5 pm but are open for breakfast and lunch. The *Coffee Shoppe*, in the Devonport Showcase, is open every day and has reasonably priced meals and good breakfasts.

The *Tamahere*, at 34 Best St, the *Elimatta*, at 12 Victoria Parade, and the *Formby*, at 82 Formby Rd, all have counter meals for around $6 or $7. If you are staying in East Devonport, the *Edgewater Hotel*, at 2 Thomas St, has good counter meals – nothing is over $5.

Devonport has a good selection of moderately priced restaurants. *Greex* (tel 24 6793), at 159 Rooke St, is mainly Greek, with a few Lebanese selections. It's around $10 to $12 a main dish. It has a good light lunch special for $5. The *Silky Apple* (tel 24 4148) is a Chinese restaurant in the Plaza Arcade, at 3 Rooke St. It has meals for $8 to $12. *Taco Bill* (tel 23 5297), on the corner of Oldaker and Kempling Sts, has Mexican food for around $10 a main meal. For Italian food, try *Il Mondo Antico* (tel 24 7157), at 142A William St.

Entertainment

The *Elimatta* has a disco and occasional bands from Thursday to Saturday. The *Tamahere* also has a disco. *City Limits* is a nightclub at 18 King St.

Getting There & Away

Air Together, Ansett and East-West have half a dozen flights a day between Melbourne and Devonport. See the Tasmania Getting There & Away section for details.

Airlines of Tasmania operate between Devonport and Hobart ($73.50), Launceston ($38.50), Wynyard ($39.50) and King Island ($74.50).

Bus Tasmanian Redline Coaches (tel 31 2660) have five services a day to Launceston and the fare is $9.60 ($11.20 express); the fare to Hobart is $23.40 ($28.40 express). The regular buses going south stop at the towns on the main highway, including Deloraine. There are regular buses throughout the day to Burnie, and during the week two buses a day continue on to Smithton with a connecting service to Stanley. For Wynyard, you have to change buses in Burnie.

Staffords Coaches (tel 24 3628) provide a charter service to Cradle Valley for $25, which operates daily from December to

May and on Monday, Wednesday and Friday in the off-season. Other services include Lake St Clair, at $35; Walls of Jerusalem at $25; and Frenchmans Cap and the walking tracks from the Franklin, Jane and Collingwood Rivers at $40.

Boat See the introductory Tasmania Getting There & Away section for full details on the ferry service between Melbourne and Devonport. From Devonport the ferry departs at 6 pm on Tuesday, Thursday and Sunday, arriving at Station Pier, Melbourne, the following day at 8.30 am. If you have a car it must be there between 4 and 5 pm. If you're on foot, embarkation is between 4.30 and 5.45 pm, although the terminal is open earlier if you have nothing else to do. The cheapest passenger fares, in a four berth cabin, range from $74 in the off-season (April to September) to $114.

Getting Around

Morse's Motors run a local bus service but it's so limited you might as well forget it. The buses run from the corner of Rooke and Stewart Sts to East Devonport, North Devonport via Mersey Bluff and to West Devonport. Fortunately most places are within walking distance anyway; it's a pleasant stroll along the waterfront to most of Devonport's attractions.

There's a ferry across the Mersey (remember the song?) which operates every 20 or 30 minutes Monday to Thursday from 7 am to 6.30 pm, Friday from 7 am to 9.30 pm, Saturday from 8 am to 12 pm and Sunday from 10 am to 6 pm. The one way fare is 50c for adults, 30c for kids and 20c for bicycles.

All the major car rental firms have offices in Devonport. Hire-a-Bike operates at the Bluff near the Maritime Museum on weekends in summer; ring 24 3889.

AROUND DEVONPORT

From Braddons Lookout, near Forth, seven km from Devonport, you have a fine view along the coast. The coastal resorts of Turners Beach and Leith are also west of the city. Turners Beach has two caravan parks and camping areas and there's good mullet and salmon fishing in the Forth River.

On the Rubicon River estuary, just 19 km east of Devonport, is Port Sorell, a popular seaside resort with a wildlife reserve, the picturesque Squeaking Point and the wide sands of Hawley Beach. Port Sorell is actually the oldest settlement on the north-west coast. In its early days it was visited by sealers and fishermen and before Devonport became more important as a port, it was doing a thriving trade in wattle bark. There's a caravan park and camping ground at Port Sorell and the *Moomba Holiday Park Cabins* (tel 28 6140), in Kermode St, cost $22 a double.

Only a few km south of Devonport, at Latrobe, there is a scenic path and extensive picnic area which follows the winding Mersey River along Bell's Parade. In the 1870s, when Latrobe was the terminus for trains during the construction of the north-western railway, Bell's Parade was lined with warehouses handling goods from the railway and cargo from the small ketches and barges which came up the Mersey inlet.

The North-West

Tasmania's magnificent north-west coast is a land as rich in history as it is diverse in scenery. Its story goes back 37,000 years to a time when marsupial rhinoceroses and giant kangaroos and wombats roamed the area. Aboriginal tribes once took shelter in the caves along the coast, leaving a legacy of rock engravings and middens.

Europeans also quickly realised the potential of the region. As settlers moved further and further west, building towns along the coast and inland on the many rivers, the area soon became a vital part of the young colony's developing economy.

Goods exported in the early days included timber, limestone, wool, potatoes, chaff and thousands of tonnes of grey peas (the latter went to England for pigeon feed); the many river and sea ports bristled with activity.

For the visitor, the north-west has beach resorts and lush pastoral scenery of patchwork fields and plains rolling inland towards impressive mountain ranges.

ULVERSTONE (population 9500)

Ulverstone, at the mouth of the Leven River, is the business centre for a rich agricultural district that stretches almost 50 km from the coast south to the mountains. Ulverstone's major industry is International Canners, Australia's largest frozen vegetable processor. The fine beaches in the area make it a popular holiday resort and a good base for exploring the surrounding countryside.

You can make an interesting round trip (105 km) from Ulverstone out through Sprent, Castra and Nietta to Leven Canyon near Black Bluff (1339 metres) and back via Preston, Gunns Plains and North Motton. Leven Canyon is a spectacular gorge with a number of walking tracks, one of which leads to a lookout over the canyon – not for the faint-hearted! There's also a lower cliff walk to the Jean Brook Waterfall. At Gunns Plains you can take a 30 minute tour of the limestone caves which are open daily between 10 am and 4 pm. Tours run on the hour and cost $3.

Places to Stay

Ulverstone has camping areas, as well as two caravan parks, one in Water St and the other in Queen St, with on-site vans for $22 a double. *Furner's Hotel*, in the centre of town, at 42 Reibey St, costs $22/

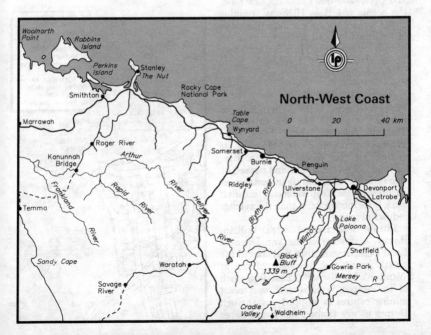

North-West Coast

0   20   40 km

Woolnorth Point, Rabbins Island, Perkins Island, Stanley, The Nut, Smithton, Rocky Cape National Park, Marrawah, Roger River, Table Cape, Wynyard, Somerset, Arthur, Burnie, Penguin, Kanunnah Bridge, Ridgley, Ulverstone, Devonport, Latrobe, Temma, Frankland, Rapid River, River, Helliner River, Blythe River, Wilmot R., Lake Paloona, Sandy Cape, Waratah, Black Bluff 1339 m, Sheffield, Gowrie Park, Mersey R., Savage River, Cradle Valley, Waldheim

32 for singles/doubles. For something better, the best value in town is the *Ocean View Guest House* (tel 25 5401) at 1 Victoria St, only 100 metres from the beach. It's a lovely old refurbished house and doubles cost \$37 including full breakfast.

PENGUIN (population 2600)

Located on three bays with good swimming beaches, the township of Penguin took its name from the many fairy penguins found in rookeries along the coast. The penguins can be seen from November to March around Johnson Beach near the caravan park. Penguin also has a couple of National Trust classified churches.

There are excellent views from the 471 metre summit of Mt Montgomery, in the Dial Range State Forest (five km from town), as well as some interesting walking trails.

If you're driving between Devonport and Ulverstone don't take the new road; the scenic old Bass Highway, running closer to the coast, offers some fine views of the coastline and across to the small islands known as the Three Sisters. There is an abundance of birdlife on these islands and also along the coast.

BURNIE (population 20,400)

Paper production is the main industry of Burnie, which makes the drive into Tasmania's fourth largest city a trifle unpleasant on a windy day. However, its setting on the shores of Emu Bay, surrounded by green hills and backed by rich farming land, and its importance as an international deep water port, means it has a little more to offer than the average industrial town.

Burnie was named after William Burnie, a director of the Van Diemens Land Company, in 1828 and started life quietly until the discovery of tin at Waratah's Mt Bischoff. These days much of the output from several west coast mining centres is shipped out through Burnie as are timber, dairy and paper

products and vegetables. Port facilities have also improved considerably since the 1870s when visitors were brought close to shore in rowboats, then climbed into a basket and were hauled aloft by a crane.

The Tasmanian Travel Centre (tel 31 8111), at 48 Cattley St, is very helpful and a mine of information on the north-west and Tasmania in general.

Things to See

The Pioneer Village Museum, on High St, behind the Law Courts, re-creates Burnie's turn of the century commercial centre. It features a blacksmith's shop, general store, printery, livery stable, boot shop, wheelwright's shop and dental surgery. It's open Monday to Friday from 10 am to 5 pm and admission is \$2.

Burnie Park incorporates an animal sanctuary which has wallabies, ducks, peacocks and Burnie's original 'settlers' –

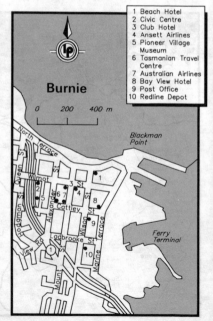

1	Beach Hotel
2	Civic Centre
3	Club Hotel
4	Ansett Airlines
5	Pioneer Village Museum
6	Tasmanian Travel Centre
7	Australian Airlines
8	Bay View Hotel
9	Post Office
10	Redline Depot

Burnie

0   200   400 m

Blackman Point

Ferry Terminal

emus. It also features Burnie Inn, the town's oldest building, which was restored and moved to the park from its original site and is open during the summer.

The Burnie Art Gallery and the Civic Centre, in Wilmot St, are worth a visit. Railway enthusiasts should visit the 'Loco Bar', in the Burnie Town House, in Wilson St, which features early Emu Bay Railway history. You can see cheese being made at the Lactos factory and make a tour of the Associated Pulp & Paper Manufacturers (APPM) factory.

There are a number of waterfalls and viewpoints in the Burnie area including Roundhill Lookout and Fern Glade, just three km from the centre, and Guide Falls, 16 km out.

Places to Stay

Burnie suffers from a lack of good budget accommodation. The nearest youth hostel is 19 km away, in Wynyard.

The *Bay View Hotel* (tel 31 2711), at 14 Marine Terrace, the *Club Hotel* (tel 31 2244), at 14 Mount St, and the *Regent* (tel 31 1933), at 25 North Terrace, are all basic and cost around $20/35 for singles/doubles. The *Beach Hotel* (tel 31 2333), at 1 Wilson St, is better. It has been refurbished but is a little expensive at $35/50.

Three km west on the Bass Highway, at Cooee, there's a *Treasure Island* campsite where camping costs $5 for two. It has on-site vans for $26.

Places to Eat

Cheap breakfasts and lunches can be found in cafes around the main shopping block bounded by Mount, Wilmot, Wilson and Cattley Sts. The *Zodiac*, in Cattley St, has cheap lunches, or try the *Napoli* cafe, above Fitzgerald's department store on the corner of Wilson and Cattley Sts.

The hotels have counter lunches and meals from Monday to Saturday and the *Beach Hotel* puts on a good spread, with meals for around $7.

Burnie has a reasonable selection of restaurants. There are three on Ladbroke St, between Mount and Wilson Sts. *Amourette's* has a changing menu with meals for around $10, and next door is *Kasbah Pizza*. Across the road is the *Li Yin*, which has good Chinese food and is open for lunch and dinner from Monday to Saturday and dinner on Sundays.

Mama Rosa's, at 63 Mount St, has pizzas, but for other Italian food go to the *Rialto*, at 46 Wilmot St. It's another of those rare Burnie creatures – a restaurant that is open for dinner on Sundays.

Entertainment

See the *Advocate* for entertainment listings. There's a disco from Thursday to Saturday at the *Menai Hotel*, on the corner of Menai and Edwards Sts. The *Beach Hotel* is a popular watering hole on Friday nights, and the *Regent* sometimes has bands on a Friday or Saturday night. The *Civic Centre* occasionally has bands, plays, dance groups, etc.

Getting There & Away

Air The nearest airport is at Wynyard, 20 km from Burnie. Ansett Airlines (tel 31 5677) are on the corner of Wilmot and Mount Sts.

Bus Tasmanian Redline Coaches (tel 31 2660), at 177 Wilson St, have frequent services to Devonport and Launceston, and during the week there are two direct buses to Hobart. From Monday to Saturday there are regular buses to Wynyard, Smithton and Stanley, and an 8.30 am bus to Queenstown.

The MTT (tel 31 3822) also have buses to Ulverstone, Penguin and Wynyard from Monday to Friday. They depart from outside Fitzgerald's department store.

Train The Emu Bay Railway is a privately owned railway that operates to the west coast but it only carries freight. It has been known to take passengers when the train is not carrying explosives but it's not encouraged. Nonetheless, dedicated train enthusiasts can give it a try. Ring 31 2822 for information on the train.

Getting Around

Local buses are run by the MTT and, as in Launceston, you can get an unlimited travel, all day ticket. There are no bus services in the evenings or on weekends.

WYNYARD (population 4600)

Sheltered by the impressive Table Cape and unique Fossil Bluff, the township of Wynyard is built along the seafront and the banks of the Inglis River. Flying into Wynyard on one of the regular flights from the mainland is perhaps the best way to appreciate the beauty of the patchwork farmlands that extend west along the coast from Table Cape to Stanley. Wynyard is a good base for exploring some of the neighbouring attractions but the town itself has little to offer the visitor.

You can get tourist information from the Council Chambers, on Saunders St, from the Golden Fleece service stations on the Bass Highway in Wynyard and Somerset, and from the Seaway Motel, at Boat Harbour Beach.

Places to Stay & Eat

The Wynyard *Youth Hostel* (tel 42 2013), at 36 Dodgin St, is one block south of the main shopping centre and costs $6 a night. It is a five minute walk from the airport – take the road out of the airport and turn right into Dodgin St. The *Federal Hotel* (tel 42 2056), in the centre of town, at 82 Goldie St, is the pick of the pubs for cheap accommodation. Bed & breakfast doubles cost $25/45 and have good counter meals seven days a week.

Leisure Ville (tel 42 2291) is a caravan park four km east of town on the scenic road to Penguin. They have motel units and cabins, and on-site vans cost $24 a double. There is a surcharge for one night stays. The *Municipal Caravan Park* is closer to town and camping sites cost $4.50.

Getting There & Away

Air One of the two major airports of the north-west is only a few minutes' walk from the centre of Wynyard. Ansett Airlines fly from Melbourne. See the Tasmania Getting There & Away section for full details.

Airlines of Tasmania operate between Wynyard and Hobart ($74), Devonport ($40), Launceston ($39), Queenstown ($45), Strahan ($45) and King Island ($71).

Western Aviation (tel 42 3838) offer scenic flights from Wynyard over Cradle Mountain and the north-west coast for about $55.

Bus Redline have regular connections to Burnie, Smithton and Stanley. MTT also have buses to Burnie. The Redline agent is the BP service station next to the post office on the main street.

AROUND WYNYARD

At Fossil Bluff, the oldest marsupial fossil found in Australia was unearthed. The soft sandstone of the area has many fossils of shells deposited when the level of Bass Strait was much higher. The Bluff is beyond the Wynyard Golf Course and the scenery alone is worth the seven km trip. Table Cape has a lighthouse and spectacular, unforgettable views along the coast.

Attractions in the immediate area include the superb stretches of sandy beach at Boat Harbour Beach and Sisters Beach, nearby Detention Falls (just south of Myalla), the excellent walking area of the Rocky Cape National Park and the forests of Hellyer and other inland gorges. There is also splendid trout, fly and sea fishing in the Flowerdale, Inglis, Cam and Calder rivers and estuaries and some of Tasmania's best diving waters can be explored with the help of the Scuba Centre in East Wynyard.

Boat Harbour Beach

Fourteen km west of Wynyard, this small township is noted for its beautiful bay, white sand, rock and coral formations and crystal clear water. There is no public transport but the Redline bus will drop you at Boat Harbour on the highway and you can hitch the three km to the beach.

Places to Stay & Eat There is a camping area, and a caravan park (tel 45 1253) with on-site vans for $24 and cabins for $21. The *Kalinda Crags Lodge* (tel 45 1111) is a motel right near the beach and costs $35/40 for singles/doubles with continental breakfast. There are other motels and flats but it is wise to book over summer. During the winter you'll have the beach to yourself.

The caravan park has a general store and serves take-aways and snacks. *The Harbour* is an up-market seafood restaurant. They also rent windsurfers and surfboards but are closed in winter.

Sisters Beach

At nearby Sisters Beach, in a valley within the Rocky Cape National Park, you can enjoy a five km expanse of glistening white sand, safe swimming and good fishing. There are more than 60 species of birds in the area and you may be lucky enough to see a rare sight – the eyrie of the sea eagle. Well marked nature trails reveal an amazing variety of unique coastal flora and there's a 10 hectare Birdland Nature Park open daily from 9 am to 5 pm. Admission is $1.50.

The area of the Rocky Cape National Park was a favourite hunting ground of the Tasmanian Aborigines and evidence of their occupation has been found in a number of caves and middens.

Dip Falls

The popular scenic and picnic area of Dip Falls, near Mawbanna, is reached by turning off the Bass Highway at Black River, an easy drive from Stanley or Smithton. There are short walks around the falls and you can visit the 'big tree'.

The turn-off to the falls is five km west of Port Latta, an ugly iron ore port.

STANLEY (population 600)

Trading ships and whalers have been calling at this idyllic little town since the Van Diemens Land Company established its headquarters here in 1826. Nestled at the foot of Circular Head – the extraordinary rock formation known commonly as The Nut – Stanley is the oldest town on the north-west coast and has changed little since its early days.

The Van Diemens Land Company, formed in London, was granted a charter in 1825 to settle and cultivate the Circular Head region to rear well-bred sheep with fine wool. The area boomed when large quantities of mutton, beef and potatoes were shipped to the Victorian gold fields and its prosperity continued when settlers discovered the rich dairying land behind Sisters Hills and a 'Mountain of Tin' at Mt Bischoff.

The boom is over but modern fishing boats, seeking crays and sharks, still operate from Stanley. It is the spectacular seascape, historic buildings and Cornish fishing village atmosphere that attracts visitors these days.

Pick up a walking tour map from De Jonge's Souvenirs or the Discovery Centre, both on Church St. The Plough Inn is also good for tourist information and they rent bicycles.

The Nut

The striking basalt formation of The Nut can be seen for many km around Stanley. A walking trail starting from opposite the post office rises the 120 metres from sea level to the plateau and offers expansive views of the coast. The charming old cemetery, at the foot of The Nut and overlooking the sea, has many interesting historical headstones. It is a hard 10 minute climb to the top of The Nut, but you can always take the chair lift, which operates from 10 am to 6 pm and costs $3 one way or $5 return.

Historic Buildings

The Plough Inn, built in 1840, has been fully restored and is lived in by the present owners, who have furnished it with period furniture. It's on Church St, is open daily for inspection ($2 to see the main part of the house) and features a craft shop.

The Discovery Centre is an amusing little folk museum with marine and pioneering relics, shell and mineral collections, old photographs and paintings by local artists. Admission to the museum is $1.

There's a particularly fine old bluestone building near the wharf which served as a grain store. It was built in 1843 of stones brought to Stanley as ship's ballast. Another seafront building – the VDL store – was designed by Tasmania's famous colonial architect John Lee Archer who was then a magistrate in Stanley. His home, which is now a private residence, is known as Poet's Cottage.

The Union Hotel, on Church St, is now the only licensed hotel in Stanley. The original bluestone school is more than 100 years old and is owned by the National Trust. The Presbyterian Church, which was probably the first prefabricated building in Australia, was bought in England, transported and re-erected in Stanley in 1853 for the all-inclusive cost of £800. Lyons Cottage was the birthplace of former Australian Prime Minister Joseph Lyons; and Highfield, built in 1835 just out of the town centre, was the original headquarters of the Van Diemens Land Company.

Places to Stay

Stanley has a wide selection of accommodation. The *Stanley Caravan Park* costs $6.50 to camp, or $22 in an on-site van. There's also a *Youth Hostel* at the caravan park. It costs $6 a night. The *Union Hotel* (tel 58 1161), on Church St, has bed & breakfast singles/doubles for $25/35. *Pol & Pen* (tel 58 1344), on Cripps St, is very good value for couples and groups. These two self-contained cottages each have two bedrooms, a fully equipped

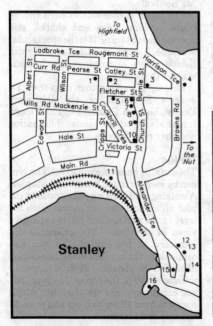

1	The Rectory
2	Pen & Pol Holiday Flats
3	Commercial Hotel (1842)
4	Old Stanley Cemetery
5	St James Presbyterian Church (1855)
6	St Paul's Church of England (1880)
7	Stanley Discovery Centre
8	Plough Inn (1842)
9	Sullivan's Restaurant
10	Union Hotel (1849)
11	Caravan Park
12	Bay View Hotel (1849)
13	PM J A Lyons' birthplace
14	Poet's Cottage
15	Customs House
16	Old Wharf

kitchen and colour TV. They cost $35 a double and $6 for each additional person.

There are a few bed & breakfast guest houses in historic cottages such as *Touchwood Cottage* (tel 58 1348), which costs $30/50, and *Laughton House* (tel 58 1301) at $45/60. Both are on Church St.

Places to Eat

The *Union Hotel* has counter meals, and *Sullivans* is a licensed restaurant open for lunch and dinner from Wednesday to Sunday. The *Galleon Tea Rooms*, at The Nut reserve, has Devonshire teas and snacks. The *Craypot* is a take-away shop on the main street with good fish & chips, pizzas, etc, and there is another good fish shop down near the dock.

Getting There & Away

From Monday to Friday the 9.30 am, and 3.30 and 7.30 pm Redline buses from Burnie to Smithton make the detour to Stanley. In the other direction, the 7.10 am, and 12.15 and 4 pm buses from Smithton go via Stanley.

SMITHTON (population 3400)

The town of Smithton is the administrative centre of Circular Head and serves the agricultural and forestry areas of the far north-west.

Early settlers were quick to discover the value of the rich alluvial flats of the Duck River and the town soon overshadowed Stanley in economic importance. Smithton's economic growth began in the early 1900s with the building of a butter factory and several large sawmills. Although Stanley maintained its importance as the major port in the region, owing to the tidal limitations of Duck Bay, the municipal government of Circular Head was transferred to Smithton in the 1920s.

These days the town is the centre of one of Tasmania's greatest forestry areas. Other major products include dolomite,

dairy produce, vegetables, oysters and fish.

While there's good fishing and boating on the river and Duck Bay, Smithton doesn't have Stanley's charm and the cost of Smithton's accommodation makes Stanley a better base for exploring the surrounding countryside.

Places to Stay & Eat

The *Bridge Hotel* (tel 52 1398) is warm and friendly and has a relatively inexpensive bistro, but it is overpriced at $48/55 for singles/doubles. There are adjoining motel units for $60/70. *Macvilla Holiday Units* (tel 52 1278) on Nelson St costs $50/60.

Barb's Kitchen, at 54 Emmett St, has cheap lunches and great coffee.

Getting There & Away

Air Airlines of Tasmania fly between Smithton and Melbourne ($89), Hobart ($92), Queenstown ($58) and Strahan ($58).

Bus Circular Head Motors (tel 52 1262), at 13 Smith St, is the Redline agent. From Monday to Friday there are regular buses to Burnie, Devonport, Launceston and Hobart, and three buses a day go via Stanley. There is only one bus on Saturdays and none on Sundays.

AROUND SMITHTON

Woolnorth, a 220 square km property on the very north-western tip of Tasmania, is the only remaining holding of the Van Diemens Land Company. Fully escorted day coach tours of this historic property and its magnificent coastline operate from Smithton and Burnie. For more information ring (004) 52 1252 or book through the Tasmanian Travel Centre.

Massive manferns, myrtles, fungi and lichens are features of the Milkshake Forest Reserve, 45 km south of Smithton. A little further west of the reserve, set in beautiful virgin rainforest, is tranquil Lake Chisholm.

MARRAWAH

Marrawah, the most western town in Tasmania, is at the end of the Bass Highway where the wild Southern Ocean occasionally throws up the remains of ships wrecked on the rugged coast.

This part of the coast was once a favourite home of the Tasmanian Aborigines and particular areas have been proclaimed reserves to protect the environment and remaining relics, which include rock carvings, middens and hut depressions. The main Aboriginal sites are at Mt Cameron West, near Green Point, and at West and Sundown Points.

The township of Marrawah consists only of a hotel and a general store for petrol and supplies. The hotel has meals but no accommodation; however camping is permitted on Crown Land and there is a very basic camping area at Green Point, two km from the township. The area is good for fishing, camping and bushwalking, or just for getting away from it all, but the main attraction is Marrawah's surf beach. It has Tasmania's best surf and the state titles are held here every year, usually in January over the Australia Day long weekend.

Getting There & Away

It is really only feasible to visit Marrawah if you have your own vehicle, but hardened campers or surfers without wheels can catch the bus from Smithton. Star Taxi Service (tel 52 1348) does the freight run and takes passengers. It's in Gibson St, directly behind the Redline depot, and departs at 10.30 am from Monday to Friday.

ARTHUR RIVER

The sleepy town of Arthur River, 14 km south of Marrawah, is just a collection of holiday houses for people who come here to fish. There are no shops, public transport or accommodation but there is a basic camping area. The only reason to visit is to explore the Arthur Pieman

Protected Area, or to take a cruise on the Arthur River.

The attractions of the Arthur Pieman Protected Area include magnificent ocean beaches, waterfalls on the Nelson River, Rebecca Lagoon, Temma Harbour, the old mining town of Balfour, the Pieman River and the Norfolk Ranges.

Some roads are suitable only for 4WDs, others are off limits to all vehicles and permits are needed in some areas. It is possible to drive back to Smithton along a graded road from Arthur River across to Lake Chisholm and the Milkshake Hills. Before setting out it is best to contact the ranger or the Crown Lands warden in Smithton, or ask for directions in Arthur River. A good map is essential for further exploration.

Arthur River Cruise

Turk Porteous has cruises departing at 10 am and returning at 3 pm. He took almost five years to clear a landing through the dense rainforest at the confluence of the Arthur and Frankland rivers, where his boat, the *George Robinson* stops for lunch and a one hour walk. George's boat cannot match the high-tech turbos on the more popular Gordon River, but he is an excellent source of information on the local flora and fauna. The cruises run most days in summer and cost $24 including lunch. A minimum of eight people is required. For bookings ring (004) 57 1158 or book through a Tasmanian Travel Centre.

SOUTH TO QUEENSTOWN

From Somerset, on the north coast (between Burnie and Wynyard), to the historic mining town of Queenstown, 170 km to the south, the Waratah/Murchison Highway passes through some pretty impressive scenery.

Hellyer Gorge is a serene myrtle forest reserve on the banks of the Hellyer River, 40 km from the coast. Further south is the turn-off to the mining towns of Waratah and Savage River, and Corinna on the

Pieman River. The Mt Bischoff mine, near Waratah, was once the world's richest tin mine, but these days it is the iron ore of Savage River that keeps mining alive in the region. The ore is crushed, mixed with water to form a slurry and then pumped down a pipeline to Port Latta.

Corinna

Corinna, 28 km south-west of Savage River, was once a thriving gold mining settlement but is now little more than a ghost town. These days it's the scenery and a popular cruise on the Pieman River that attracts the visitors. The launch *Arcadia II* makes a regular four hour trip from Corinna to Pieman Heads through forests of eucalypts, ferns and Huon pine. Bookings should be made at a Tasmanian Travel Centre or the Savage River Motor Inn.

Roseberry (population 2700)

Mining began in Roseberry in 1900 with the completion of the Emu Bay Railway between Burnie and Zeehan, but with the closure of the Zeehan lead smelters in 1913 operations here also shut down. The Electrolytic Zinc Company then bought the mine and with new mining processes it was re-opened in 1936 and has operated successfully ever since. There's a spectacular series of aerial buckets which transport ore down the mountainside from Williamsford, seven km away. Roseberry is 55 km from Queenstown, in the Pieman River Valley at the base of Mt Murchison. The *Roseberry* and *Kirkpatrick* hotels have accommodation and there's a caravan park.

Just north of Roseberry is Tullah, where the HEC have works. They have a tourist information office, which explains the hydroelectricity projects in the area. They'll give an ear bashing on what a great job the HEC has done in opening up the south-west.

The West Coast

Nature at its most awe inspiring is the attraction of Tasmania's rugged and magnificent west coast. Formidable mountains, lonely valleys, unique buttongrass plains, deep and ancient rivers, tranquil lakes, dense rainforests and a treacherous coast – all contribute to the compelling beauty of this area.

Were it not for its vast mineral and timber wealth, the region would probably still be uninhabited. In fact, until the completion of the road from Hobart to Queenstown in 1932 the only way into the area was through the port of Strahan, and even then the difficulty of access into Macquarie Harbour meant that only small boats could use it. The sparse population of the west coast today is a strong reminder of the pioneering spirit that tried to tame and exploit this inhospitable and often impenetrable land.

However, centuries before the white man arrived to extract the minerals and harvest the Huon pine, the west and south-west was home to Aboriginal tribes. Australia's richest archaeological material has been found just above the Franklin River in an area abandoned by its original inhabitants some 20,000 years ago.

European settlement of the region has been turbulent, brutal, courageous, profitable and heartbreaking. The west coast has seen explorers, convicts, soldiers, loggers, prospectors, railway gangs, road builders, fisherfolk, settlers, outdoor adventurers, environmentalists and blockaders.

The area has seen the flooding of Lake Pedder and the creation of a huge system of lakes on the upper reaches of the Pieman River to establish massive hydroelectricity schemes. It is also home to the Franklin River – Australia's most controversial river and scene of the greatest environmental debate in the nation's history.

The surviving mining towns such as Zeehan and Queenstown still thrive on their rich mineral resources and tourism is booming in the historic coastal town of Strahan where thousands of people come to experience the natural beauty of the Gordon River.

While the environmentalists and big business continue to battle over the issues of wilderness versus electricity and world heritage area versus wood chip, nature herself has begun to reclaim what is hers. The rusting relics, disused railways,

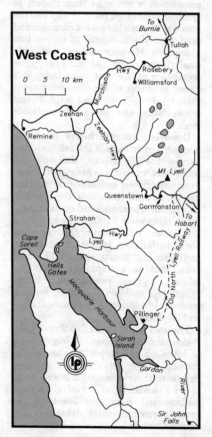

abandoned mines and deserted towns of the early west coast mining days remain as mere spectres in the bush.

ZEEHAN (population 2000)

The discovery of rich deposits of silver and lead in Zeehan in 1882 changed the face of this quiet little town 38 km north of Queenstown. By the turn of the century it had a population of 5000 (it peaked at nearly 10,000), its 26 hotels were doing a roaring trade and the stage of the Gaiety Theatre, then the largest in Australia, was being graced by the likes of Nellie Melba and Caruso. More than £8 million worth of ore was produced at the Zeehan mines before they began to fail, and the town declined just after 1908. Zeehan is now experiencing a revival, however, with the re-opening of the Renison Tin Mine at Renison Bell.

From Zeehan, rough roads lead to Trial Harbour, 23 km away on the coast, and Dundas, a mining town which has now all but disappeared. The road south-west from Zeehan has been upgraded for the 47 km to Strahan.

Things to See

There are a few buildings remaining from those early boom days including the once famous Grand Hotel (now flats), the Gaiety Theatre, the post office, the bank and St Luke's Church.

The excellent West Coast Pioneers' Memorial Museum is housed in what was the School of Mines, built in 1894. It features a working model of the Mt Bischoff Mill at Waratah, a mine diorama of underground workings, an excellent mineral collection, and displays of Tasmanian birds, animals and Aboriginal artefacts. Outside there's an exhibit of steam locomotives and carriages used on the early west-coast railways.

Places to Stay

You can see the sights of Zeehan in an hour or two but if you want to stay overnight the Cecil Hotel (tel 71 6221) in Main St has bed & breakfast for $18 a person. The *Heemskirk Motor Hotel* costs $57/62 for singles/doubles. You can camp at the primitive *Crocoite Caravan Park*, on Hurst St.

Getting There & Away

The Redline bus from Burnie to Queenstown stops in Zeehan, arriving at 12.15 pm. Going the other way, it leaves at 9.45 am for Burnie. There is no service on Sundays. The school bus to Queenstown also takes passengers and departs at 7.30 am, leaving Queenstown at 3.10 pm.

QUEENSTOWN (population 4300)

The view during the final winding descent into Queenstown from Hobart is dramatic, strangely beautiful and totally unforgettable. There is no escaping the fact that this is a mining town and that the destruction of the surrounding hills is a direct result of the region's major industry. It is a stunning sight. Queenstown sits, almost defiantly, in a valley surrounded by deep eroded gullies and naked, multi-coloured hills.

It was the discovery of alluvial gold in the Queen River valley in 1881 that first brought prospectors to the area. Two years later mining began on the rich Mt Lyell deposits around an outcrop known as the Iron Blow. For nearly a decade miners toiled on the Mt Lyell ore, extracting a few ounces of gold a day and ignoring the millions of pounds of copper. Finally in 1891 the Mt Lyell Mining Company transported 100 tonnes of ore to Strahan for smelting and copper became the most profitable mineral on the west coast. American metallurgist Robert Sticht produced the first copper on-site in 1896 and later became manager of the Mt Lyell Mining Company.

The first major link with the outside world was the company's Queenstown to Strahan railway built in 1899 to transport copper and passengers to the coast. It covered 35 km of spectacular terrain and required 48 bridges. Some sections were so steep that the rack and pinion system had to be used to assist the two steam engines hauling the train.

The North Lyell Copper Company, which had been set up in competition with the Mt Lyell mine, built a second railway line from Linda, via Crotty, to Pillinger, also on Macquarie Harbour. However, after the failure of the furnaces at Crotty the company merged with Mt Lyell and the tracks were pulled up.

At the turn of the century Queenstown, with a population of 5051, was the third largest town in Tasmania. It had 14 hotels, there were 28 mining companies working the Mt Lyell deposits, and 11 furnaces were involved in the smelting process. The Mt Lyell Mining & Railway Company eventually acquired most of the mines or leases and since 1933 it has worked the area without a rival.

Within 20 years of the start of mining, the area around Queenstown, which had been thick rainforest, was denuded of vegetation. In that short space of time hundreds of timber cutters managed to cut down some three million tonnes of timber to feed the furnaces. By 1900, uncontrolled pollution from the copper smelters had killed all the vegetation that had not already been cut down. Because of the sulphur impregnated soils and dead stumps, bush fires raged through the hills every summer till there was no regrowth left at all and then the area's heavy rainfall (the highest in the state) completed the total destruction of the surrounding hills since, with no growth to hold it, the original soil was simply washed into the Queen River.

Information

The Tasmanian Travel Centre (tel 71 1099) is at 39-41 Orr St. You can also get information from the local hotels and there's a guide map in Driffield St near Orr St.

Galley Museum

The Galley Museum, on the corner of

Sticht and Driffield Sts, began life as the Imperial Hotel and was the first brick hotel in Queenstown. It has since served as a hospital (during the 1919 flu epidemic), a guest house, and a single men's quarters for the Mt Lyell Company. The museum features an excellent photographic history of Queenstown and the west coast as well as mining equipment, personal effects and household goods from the early days of the town.

Mt Lyell Mine

There are guided tours of the Mt Lyell Mine and the new Mining Museum from September to May on weekdays at 9.15 am and 4.30 pm, and weekends and public holidays at 9.15 am and 4 pm. During the rest of the year tours depend on numbers but there is usually one tour a day. The tours leave from Farmer's Store in Driffield St and cost $4 for adults and $2 for kids. Apart from the millions of tonnes of copper being mined, the present-day mining operations also produce significant quantities of gold, silver and pyrite.

Other Attractions

The Miner's Siding, on Driffield St, is a public park area featuring a restored ABT steam locomotive and a display detailing the history of the Queenstown to Strahan railway.

Even though the tracks have been torn up, if you have a trail bike or 4WD you can take a trip down part of the old Linda to Pillinger line, built by the North Lyell Company, to the magnificent railway bridge that crosses the fast flowing King River.

The Western Arts & Crafts Centre, on Orr St, has local wood crafts, pottery, paintings and leatherwood honey. It's open daily.

Places to Stay

Mountain View Holiday Lodge (tel 71 1163), just over the bridge on the road to Strahan, has rooms for only $7 a person. The lodge is the old single men's quarters

so it's very basic, but you get your own room and there are cooking facilities. Some rooms have been renovated as motel style units and cost $40 a double. They also run the caravan park, on Grafton St, where on-site vans cost $25.

Hunter's Hotel, on Orr St, has singles for $14, or $18 with breakfast. It's nothing special but good value at that price. The *Empire Hotel* (tel 71 1699), at 2 Orr St, is only slightly better than Hunter's but costs $35/45 for singles/doubles. On Driffield St is the *Commercial Hotel* (tel 71 1511), with clean but small and windowless rooms. It costs $22/34 including breakfast.

The *Pine Lodge* (tel 71 1852) is a small guest house at 1 Gaffney St with bed & breakfast for $28/38. There are more expensive rooms with shower and toilet. The *Mount Lyell Motor Hotel* (tel 71 1888), at 1 Orr St, has motel suites for $36/48. The management is friendly and they have good counter meals in the hotel section.

Places to Eat

JJ's, on Orr St, has good cakes and light snacks for about $3 and light lunches for around $5. There is also a chicken shop and pizza place, but apart from these, for the budget traveller it's back to the staple diet of counter meals.

Getting There & Away

Airlines of Tasmania fly to Queenstown from Melbourne ($128), Hobart ($71), Smithton ($58), Wynyard ($45) and Launceston ($58).

By road Queenstown is 254 km north-west of Hobart and 175 km south-west of Burnie. Redline Coaches has a bus from Queenstown to Hobart at 9 am from Monday to Saturday. The fare is $25. The bus to Burnie also leaves at 9 am and costs $21. The bus to Strahan leaves at 3.10 pm Monday to Friday, and 2.30 pm on Saturday. The Queenstown depot of Tasmanian Redline Coaches (tel 71 1011) is behind the shops in Orr St, down the alley near the Tasmanian Travel Centre.

Hitching into Queenstown along the Lyell Highway from Hobart is quite easy as there's a fair bit of traffic. The Waratah/Murchison Highway from the north coast may be a little harder though. Remember that it gets pretty cold here in winter and snowfalls along these two highways are not uncommon.

STRAHAN (population 400)

Strahan today may retain but a shadow of its former glory but the town and its harbour are rich in the history of its convict, logging and mining days.

On Macquarie Harbour, 40 km from Queenstown, this is the only town actually on the rugged and treacherous west coast. Rough seas, the lack of natural harbours and the high rainfall discouraged settlement of the region until Macquarie Harbour was discovered by explorers searching for the source of the Huon pine that frequently washed up on the southern beaches. The harbour's main disadvantage was its narrow entrance – the formidable sand bar and rushing tides of Hells Gates allowed access only to shallow-draught boats.

In 1821, in order to isolate the worst of the colony's convicts and use their muscle to harvest the huge stands of Huon pine, a penal settlement was established on Sarah Island. This barbaric institution in Macquarie Harbour became one of the most notorious places of punishment in Australia's history. The convicts worked upriver 12 hours a day, often in leg irons, felling the pines and rafting them back to the island's saw-pits where they were used to build ships and furniture.

Punishment for the slightest infringements of settlement law was brutal. A total of 33,723 lashes was inflicted on an average of 167 prisoners a year from 1822 to 1826. The most dreaded punishment was confinement on tiny Grummet Island, where up to 40 convicts at a time were held in appalling conditions on what

was little more than a windswept rock – for some, death was a welcome release. There were many escape attempts during the 12 year history of the prison on Sarah Island, but once at large, there was really nowhere for the escapees to go. Of the 112 convicts who made a bid for freedom 15 were recaptured and executed for further crimes while at large, 68 perished in the bush and six were murdered and eaten by their desperate comrades. Sarah Island, which was abandoned in 1834 following the establishment of the 'escape proof' penal settlement at Port Arthur, is the setting for Marcus Clark's graphic novel of convict life, *For the Term Of His Natural Life*.

As the port for Queenstown, Strahan reached its peak of prosperity with the west-coast mining boom and the completion of the Mt Lyell Company's railway line in the 1890s. At the turn of the century it was a bustling centre with a population of more than 2000. Steamers operated regularly between Strahan and Hobart, Launceston and Melbourne carrying copper, gold, silver, lead, timber and passengers. The closure of many of the west coast mines and the opening of the Emu Bay railway from Zeehan to Burnie led to the decline of Strahan as a port. These days it's a charming seaside village making a living from fishing and tourism.

Things to See

Strahan's main attractions are the Gordon River cruises – otherwise it is just a sleepy little fishing village. Nonetheless, the imposing post office and Union Steam Ship Company building, probably the finest buildings on the west coast, hint at the town's former importance, while the lighthouse on Cape Sorell on the south head of the harbour is the third largest in Tasmania. There's an interesting little gemstone and mineral museum by the caravan park. Strahan's botanical gardens are worth visiting and it's just a short walk to the delightful Hogarth Falls.

Six km from the town is the impressive

40 km Ocean Beach where huge seas crash on to enormous sand dunes. The beach is also a mutton bird rookery in October when the birds return from their winter migration.

Strahan also has another unique, if rather odd, attraction. It is home to Tasmania's own self-styled eccentric aristocrat – Prince John, the Duke of Avram, who lives in historic Ormiston Mansion, deals in his own currency and runs the 'Royal Bank of Avram' in the centre of town near the wharf, which sells souvenirs.

Gordon River Cruises

The Gordon River rises in Lake Richmond, high in the King William Range, and crosses the unique buttongrass plains known as the Vale of Rasseleas before it turns westward. It then plunges through rugged mountains to the magnificent calm of its lower reaches, finally making its way to the ocean through Macquarie Harbour.

If you don't have time to explore the spectacular gorges, white water rapids, waterfalls, quiet reaches, rainforests and rugged mountains of the Franklin and Gordon Rivers from your own canoe or raft, then one of the excellent cruises that operate out of Strahan is the best way to appreciate the indescribable beauty of the Gordon River.

Three modern, comfortable launches make half day and day long trips up the Lower Gordon River, taking in Marble Cliffs, St John Falls and Warners Landing – site of the 11 week blockade to save the river. The boats return across Macquarie Harbour via Sarah Island and Hells Gates.

The *Gordon Explorer* and *James Kelly II* half day tours cost $35 (children $14), leave at 9 am and return at 1.30 pm. The *Wilderness Seeker* tour (from 9 am to 3.30pm) includes lunch and costs $35 (children $17). Services are reduced in winter but there is always at least one boat

a day. You can book at the wharf, or ring (004) 71 7187 in advance.

Places to Stay

The *Christian Drop-in Centre* (tel 71 7255) is the associate youth hostel in Harvey St and costs $7 a night. It's the cheapest place in town but it gets this edition's award for the most unpopular youth hostel in Tasmania. Tread carefully here and watch the curfew! There are two basic camping grounds, at Ocean Beach and Macquarie Beach, and a caravan park.

Happy Hamer's Hotel (71 7191) has the prime position in town opposite the wharf but the rooms are tiny and not particularly good value at $25 a person including continental breakfast.

Much better is the *Strahan Lodge* (tel 71 7142) at $20/30 with breakfast. The historic lodge was once the Mt Lyell mines manager's house until it was transported to Strahan. The only drawback is that it is three km from town on the road to the airport and Ocean Beach – two km past the youth hostel.

Royal lovers can stay at the Duke's place, *Strahanberry Cottage* (tel 71 7141) at Ormiston, on Innes St, about a km around the harbour from the wharf. Bed & breakfast cost $36/48 in rooms with bath and colour TV.

There are plenty of 'chateaus', 'villas' and 'lodges' in Strahan, most of which have motel style accommodation, but for something special try the *Franklin Lodge*, an old mansion being restored and due to open in 1989.

Places to Eat

The *Harbour Cafe* has take-aways and tables with views across the wharf, and *Happy Hamer's* has good counter meals. For something better, the motels such as the *Regatta Point Tavern* also have food.

Getting There & Away

Airlines of Tasmania fly into Strahan from Hobart ($71), Launceston ($58), Wynyard ($45) and Smithton ($58).

There is one bus a day to Queenstown at 7.20 am Monday to Saturday.

FRANKLIN - LOWER GORDON WILD RIVERS NATIONAL PARK

This park includes the catchment areas of the Franklin and Olga rivers and part of the Lower Gordon, and Frenchmans Cap. Along with the South-West and the Cradle Mountain-Lake St Clair national parks it forms Tasmania's World Heritage Area, proclaimed in 1982 after prolonged conservationists' battles to protect this wilderness area. The park contains a number of unique plant species, and there's a major Aboriginal archaeological site at Kutikina Caves.

Much of the park is wild rainforest and impenetrable, but the park is cut by the Lyell Highway which provides access to a few short walks. These include the walk to Donaghys Hill, from which you can see the Franklin River and the magnificent white quartzite dome of Frenchmans Cap. There are short walks to Nelson Falls and at Collingwood River. You can take the four day walk to Frenchmans Cap, or spend a few days walking right into the Cap over buttongrass fields and through rainforests. However, the best way to see this magnificent country is to raft down the Franklin River.

Rafting the Franklin

The Franklin is indeed a wild river and this can be a hazardous journey. Experienced rafters can tackle it if they are fully equipped and prepared, or tour companies offer complete packages. All expeditions should register with the ranger at the Collingwood River Ranger Station (tel (004) 71 1446), who can provide details on river levels.

The Wilderness Society puts out a good booklet on rafting the Franklin, and Wilderness Guides (tel (08) 296 7093) in South Australia has a comprehensive rafting map series.

Camp sites are positioned along the river and an eight to 14 day expedition starts at Collingwood River and ends at the St John Falls jetty, where the Gordon River cruise boats can pick you up. Tour companies that arrange complete packages include Open Spaces (tel (002) 31 0977), at 28 Criterion St, Hobart; Peregrine Expeditions (tel (03) 602 3066), on the 9th Floor of 343 Collins St, Melbourne; World Expeditions (tel (02) 264 3366), on the 3rd Floor of 377 Sussex St, Sydney; and Wilderness Expeditions, at 2 Sharp St, Cooma, NSW. The going rate including food and all transport from Hobart is around $100 a day.

SOUTH-WEST NATIONAL PARK

There are few places left in the world as isolated and untouched as Tasmania's south-west wilderness. It is the home of some of the world's last tracts of virgin temperate rainforest, which contribute so much to the unique grandeur and extraordinary diversity of this ancient area. It is the habitat of the endemic Huon pine, which lives for more than 3000 years, and of the swamp gum, the world's tallest hardwood and flowering plant. About 300 species of lichens, mosses and ferns (some rare and endangered) festoon the dense rainforest; superb glacial tarns decorate the jagged mountains and in summer the delicate alpine meadows are ablaze with wildflowers and flowering shrubs. And through it all, wild rivers race down rapids, along deep gorges and by caves, countless waterfalls and cliffs. Each year more and more people are venturing into the heart of this incredible part of Tasmania's World Heritage Area, seeking the peace, isolation and challenge of a region as old as the last ice age and unspoilt by human development.

The traditional walk in the South-West National Park is between Cox Bight or Port Davey and Cockle Creek, near Recherche Bay, and takes about 10 days. This should only be tackled by experienced, well prepared hikers. Light planes are used to airlift bushwalkers into the south-west (and for scenic flights) and there is vehicle access to Cockle Creek. There is also a variety of escorted wilderness treks that offer flying, hiking, rafting, canoeing, mountaineering, caving and camping. More information can be obtained from a Tasmanian Travel Centre or the Wilderness Society.

At the edge of the wilderness lies Lake Pedder, once the crown jewel of the region, but now part of the Gordon River Power Development. Lake Pedder was flooded in the early 1970s to help feed the giant underground power station at the Gordon Dam. Together with nearby Lake Gordon it covers over 500 square km and contains 27 times the volume of water in Sydney Harbour. It is the largest inland freshwater storage in Australia – constructed by the HEC.

The HEC township of Strathgordon is the base from which to visit Lake Pedder and the Gordon Dam and power station. There is a walking track between Port Davey on the south-west coast and Scotts Peak Dam at the southern edge of Lake Pedder. You can also make day or overnight walks off the Scotts Peak road to Mt Eliza or Mt Anne.

Vehicle access to Strathgordon is along the 85 km Gordon Rd from Maydena, reached via the Derwent Valley.

Strathgordon has camping and caravan facilities and the *Lake Pedder Motor Inn* (tel 80 1166) has singles/doubles for $40/45.

Cradle Mountain-Lake St Clair

The best known feature of Tasmania's superb central highland lake country is the 1262 square km Cradle Mountain-Lake St Clair National Park. It is one of the most glaciated areas in Australia and includes Tasmania's highest mountain, Mt Ossa (1617 metres). The rugged mountain peaks, tarns, lakes, streams, alpine moorlands, and the reserve's incredible variety of flora and fauna extend from the Great Western Tiers in the north to the Lyell Highway at Derwent Bridge in the south.

The spectacular 85 km Overland Track between Cradle Mountain, which dominates the northern end of the park, and beautiful Lake St Clair, Australia's deepest natural freshwater lake, is one of the finest bushwalks in the country. The walk takes five or six days at an easy pace but there is so much to see and do along the way that it's a great temptation to spend more time here. The only limitation is the amount of supplies that can be carried.

Despite its magnificence and easy accessibility it is not an area to be taken lightly as it is notorious for vicious changes in weather. Even in summer there can be heavy snowfalls and sudden blizzards so adequate clothing, equipment and supplies are essential. The best time to walk the Overland Track is during summer when the flowering plants are most prolific and the weather is at least a little more predictable. Spring and autumn also have their attractions and you can even walk the track in winter if you're well prepared and experienced.

The park's pamphlet gives general information and is necessary reading if you're preparing for any walk in the area. There are no roads through the park but motorists have access to both ends – Lake St Clair and Cradle Valley. A third access route to the park is along the Arm River walking track coming in to the park from the east.

The park owes much to an Austrian, Gustav Weindorfer, who fell in love with the area and in 1912 built a chalet out of King Billy pine at the northern end of what was later to become the national park. Waldheim (which means 'forest home' in German) Lodge is fitted with bunks and is at the northern end of the trail.

Walking the Track

The Overland Track is easy to follow for

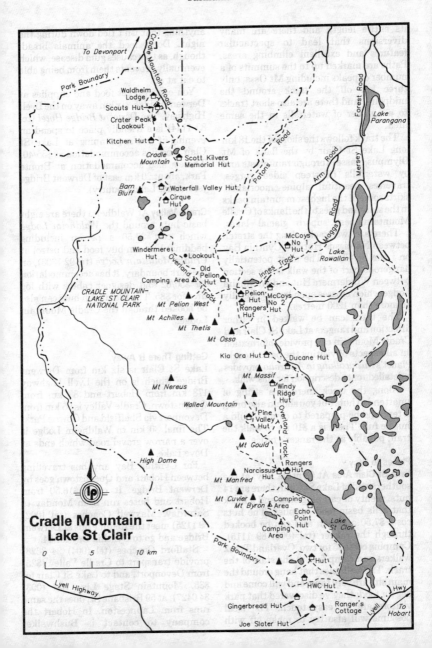

Cradle Mountain – Lake St Clair

0   5   10 km

To Devonport

Park Boundary

Waldheim Lodge
Scouts Hut
Crater Peak Lookout
Kitchen Hut

Cradle Mountain Road

Cradle Mountain
Scott Kilvers Memorial Hut

Barn Bluff
Waterfall Valley Hut
Cirque Hut

Windermere Hut
Lookout
Old Pelion Hut
Camping Area

CRADLE MOUNTAIN-
LAKE ST CLAIR
NATIONAL PARK

Overland Track

Mt Pelion West
Mt Achilles
Mt Thetis
Mt Ossa

Mt Nereus

Walled Mountain

High Dome

Mt Gould

Mt Manfred
Mt Cuvier
Mt Byron

Kia Ora Hut
Ducane Hut

Mt Massif
Windy Ridge Hut
Pine Valley Hut

Rangers Hut

Narcissus Hut
Rangers Hut

Camping Area
Echo Point Hut
Camping Area

Lake St Clair

Hut

Gingerbread Hut
Joe Slater Hut

HWC Hut

Ranger's Cottage

Park Boundary

Lyell Highway

Lyell Hwy

To Hobart

Forest Road
Lake Parangana

Patons Road
Arm Road
Moggs Road
Mersey

McCoys No 1 Hut
Lake Rowallan

Innes Track

Pelion Hut
McCoys No 2 Hut
Rangers Hut

its entire length and there are many diversions that lead to spectacular features and excellent climbing areas. Paths are marked up to the summits of a number of peaks including Mt Ossa, only three km off the track around the midpoint, and there are also short tracks to a number of waterfalls in the same area.

The track follows the shore of the 18 km long Lake St Clair by the flank of Mt Olympus, passes through rainforests and by waterfalls in steep sided gorges, traverses beautiful alpine moorlands, skirts some of the highest mountain peaks in the state and rises to the flanks of Cradle Mountain past superb glacial lakes.

There are two tracks along the stretch between Narcissus Hut and Cynthia Bay on Lake St Clair. The most potentially dangerous part of the walk is the section between Windermere Hut and Waldheim Lodge which crosses open land, generally at more than 1200 metres.

The track can be walked in either direction and rangers at Lake St Clair and Cradle Mountain can provide information on all aspects of visiting the park. Lonely Planet's *Bushwalking in Australia* provides a detailed route description for this walk.

Along the track there is a string of unattended huts but you should also bring a tent and be prepared to camp should a hut be full. There is a $10 fee to walk the trail, payable at the ranger's office.

Places to Stay

Lake St Clair Area At Cynthia Bay, at the southern end of Lake St Clair, there are 14 huts, plenty of camping sites and a kiosk that sells basic food supplies. The huts costs $7.50 a person and can be booked through the ranger (tel (002) 89 1115). Camping costs $5 for two. Overland Track walkers can camp free at the start of the track. The wallabies that hang around the main site are very tame and will come and beg for food; they've discovered that park visitors are an easy touch. The local possums will also try to make off with anything that isn't tied down during the night. Don't feed the animals bread, though, as this causes gum disease, which eventually prevents them from being able to eat at all.

You can also get food and supplies at Derwent Bridge, six km away on the Lyell Highway. The *Derwent Bridge Hotel* (tel 89 1144) is a friendly place to spend an evening if you're camping at Lake St Clair, and has accommodation at $35/40. There's also accommodation at Bronte Park, about 20 km east of Derwent Bridge (see under Lake Country).

Cradle Valley At Waldheim there are eight basic huts around the *Waldheim Lodge* which cost $7.50 a person including bedding. You can buy food and petrol at *Cradle Mountain Lodge* (tel 92 1303), on the park boundary. It has accommodation for $50/62 and designer cabins with log fires for $85. The Waldheim huts can also be booked through the Cradle Mountain Lodge.

Getting There & Away

Lake St Clair is six km from Derwent Bridge which is on the Lyell Highway 178 km from Hobart and 83 km from Queenstown. Cradle Valley is 95 km from Devonport via Sheffield and Gowrie Park. The final 30 km to Waldheim Lodge is over a narrow gravel road which ends at Dove Lake.

For Cynthia Bay any bus travelling between Hobart and Queenstown goes by Derwent Bridge. It costs $16.50 from Hobart and buses run from Monday to Saturday. Maxwell Coaches (tel (002) 89 1125) meet the Redline bus at Derwent Bridge and go to Cynthia Bay for $4.

Stafford Coaches (tel (004) 24 3628) provide transport to Cradle Valley ($25) from Devonport, and to Lake St Clair for $35. Mountain Stage Line (tel (003) 34 0427), at 59 Brisbane St, does the same runs from Launceston. In Hobart the company to contact is Bushwalker

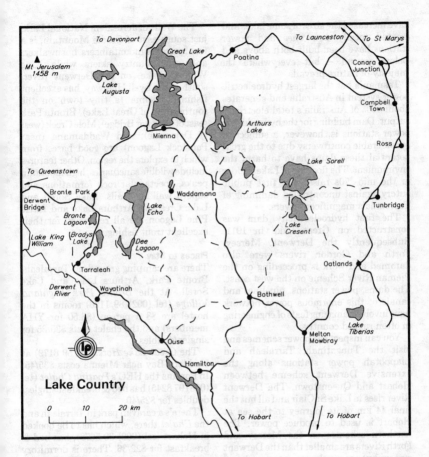

Lake Country

0   10   20 km

To Devonport
To Launceston
To St Marys
Mt Jerusalem 1458 m
Great Lake
Poatina
Conara Junction
Lake Augusta
Campbell Town
Arthurs Lake
Mienna
Ross
Lake Sorell
To Queenstown
Lake Echo
Waddamana
Lake Cresent
Bronte Park
Derwent Bridge
Bronte Lagoon
Tunbridge
Lake King William
Bradys Lake
Dee Lagoon
Oatlands
Tarraleah
Bothwell
Derwent River
Wayatinah
Lake Tiberias
Ouse
Melton Mowbray
Hamilton
To Hobart
To Hobart

Transport (tel (002) 34 2226), at 28 Criterion St.

Lake Country

The highland lake country of Tasmania's central plateau is a region of breathtaking scenery, fine trout fishing and ambitious hydroelectricity schemes. There are steep mountains, hundreds of glacial lakes, crystal clear streams, waterfalls and an amazing variety of flora and fauna.

Until the development of the central highlands for hydroelectricity production, the region was the domain of hardy bushwalkers and adventurers and it remains one of the most sparsely populated of Tasmania's settled areas. However, the access roads for the power schemes have opened up large recreational areas for all to enjoy.

Rivers have been harnessed, HEC dams

have increased the sizes of some lakes and created totally new ones and power stations have been built both above and below ground – but everywhere the majesty of nature prevails.

Tasmania has the largest hydroelectric power system in Australia and generates about 10% of Australia's total electricity output. Dam building for the hydroelectric power stations is, however, a subject of considerable controversy due to the great potential these dams have to harm the environment. The flooding of Lake Pedder in the mid '70s raised the first public outcry against uncontrolled damming of Tasmania's magnificent rivers.

The first hydroelectricity dam was constructed on Great Lake in 1911. Subsequently the Derwent, Mersey, Forth and Gordon rivers were also dammed and work is proceeding on the Pieman River Scheme on the west coast. The dams, power stations, pipelines and canals of this enormous power network have involved amazing feats of engineering in often rugged country.

You can inspect the power schemes and visit the Tungatinah, Tarraleah and Liapootah power stations along the extensive Derwent scheme between Hobart and Queenstown. The Derwent River rises in Lake St Clair and all but the final 44 km of its journey to the sea at Hobart is used to produce power. The northern schemes on the Mersey and Forth Rivers are smaller than the Derwent system but are much more spectacular as they lie in a short length of very steep river valley.

Although the conservationists won the battle over the proposed damming of the Franklin and Lower Gordon rivers there are still on-going disputes over other projects. Public opinion in Tasmania is split and many Tasmanians support the dams and see them as a source of employment in a shrinking Tasmanian economy. The Wilderness Society is the major focus for the conservation movement in Tasmania and welcomes support.

The Walls of Jerusalem National Park, just south-east of Cradle Mountain, is a focal point for mountaineers, bushwalkers and cross-country skiers while King William Lake, on the Derwent River, south of the Lyell Highway, has excellent fishing. Mienna (a tiny town on the southern tip of Great Lake), Bronte Park (east of Derwent Bridge), Mole Creek (west of Deloraine), and Waddamana (near Penstock Lagoon) are good bases from which to explore the region. Other features include wildlife sanctuaries, high mountain peaks, spectacular rock formations and superb walking trails. Lake Sorell and Lake Crescent, Arthurs Lake and Little Pine Lagoon are all renowned for their excellent trout fishing.

Places to Stay

There are camping grounds at Tarraleah, Bronte Park, Arthurs Lake and Lake Sorell. At the *Bronte Park Highland Village* (tel (002) 89 1126) rooms in the hostel are $8 a person ($6.50 for YHA members) and the chalet costs $30/35 for singles/doubles.

The *Great Lake Hotel* (tel 59 6179) at Haddens Bay near Mienna costs $35/45. In Poatina the HEC's *Poatina Chalet* (tel (003) 97 8245) has bed & breakfast singles/doubles for $25/40.

There's a caravan park in Tarraleah and the *Chalet* there, which has to be booked in Hobart (tel (002) 30 5678), has bed & breakfast for $22/36. There is dormitory style accommodation in Waddamana through the Division of Recreation (tel (002) 30 3745). The *Lachlan Hotel* (tel 87 1215), in Ouse, has singles/doubles for $17/30.

Getting There & Away

The highland lakes area is easily accessible by the Lyell Highway in the south, via the Marlborough Highway (B11), through Bronte Park; by the Lake Highway (A5), north from Hobart via Melton Mowbray and Bothwell or south from Deloraine; by the Poatina Highway

(B51) from Launceston; or by the B53 from the Midland Highway. Public transport is virtually non-existent and the hitching is not good.

BOTHWELL (population 400)

Bothwell, in the beautiful Clyde River Valley, is the southern gateway to the Central Highlands. This charming town has the usual Tasmanian quota of historic buildings including 18 classified by the National Trust. There is a variety of old homesteads and mills in the vicinity and in the town there's a colonial museum in the 'Coffee Palace' in Dalrymple St, the delightful 1831 St Luke's Church and the restored Georgian 'Slate Cottage' of 1835.

Bothwell, on the Lake Highway (A5), 72 km north of Hobart, is a popular base for fishing on the lakes and has a camping site.

HAMILTON

On the Lyell Highway, 30 km south-west of Bothwell, is Hamilton, an historic town with a number of sandstone buildings dating from convict days. Glen Clyde House is a National Trust classified tea room and souvenir shop, and worth the stop for a snack or their Devonshire teas.

Bass Strait Islands

Tasmania has two islands which guard the eastern and western entrances to Bass Strait. Once the temporary and sometimes notorious home of sealers, sailors and prospectors and a refuge from the treacherous waters of the Strait, King and Flinders islands are now retreats of unspoiled beauty, rich in bird and marine life. Though their early history of white contact is marred by bloody and tragic periods, it is the isolation and natural beauty of these islands that attracts visitors today. They're rough and rugged places, great if you really want to get away from it all, and both have excellent fishing, bushwalking and scuba diving opportunities.

KING ISLAND

At the western end of Bass Strait this rugged island is 64 km across at its widest point and has over 145 km of unspoilt coastline with beautiful beaches and quiet lagoons.

Named after Governor King of New South Wales, the island was discovered in 1798. In the early days of the century it gained a worldwide reputation as a home and breeding ground for huge colonies of sea elephants and seals – which were forthwith hunted almost to extinction. The violent 'Straitsmen' – sealers and sailors with a reputation similar to the pirates of the Spanish Main – decimated vast populations of seals for their valuable skins and oil.

The stormy seas of Bass Strait claimed many ships over the years and at least 57 wrecks have been charted in the coastal waters around King Island, including that of the *Cataraque*, an immigrant ship which went down in 1845 taking 399 lives.

The first permanent settlement of King Island was in 1855 and gold and tin were being mined in 1905. Today the island is one of the world's major producers of scheelite, used in the manufacture of armaments. Other industries include abalone and crayfish harvesting, kelp drying and farming.

The main towns are the administrative centre of Currie, on the west coast, and the deep water port town of Grassy, in the south-east. About half the island is still undisturbed native bush with an amazing variety of wildlife including wallabies, pheasant, platypuses, ducks, quail and penguins.

There is excellent bushwalking, especially along the unpopulated north coast. You can wander through a calcified forest, take a pony ride over rolling sand dunes or go fishing and swimming at the lagoons, lakes and beaches. The crystal clear waters and many shipwrecks also make

King Island a fascinating place for scuba diving. For cholesterol lovers, King Island is famous for its dairy products – the butter and cheese factory is just north of the airport; the double brie is superb.

Places to Stay

Most of the accommodation is in and around Currie and there are holiday flats and a hostel in Naracoopa, on the east coast. A good way to see the island is to take a tent and spend a week walking around the coast.

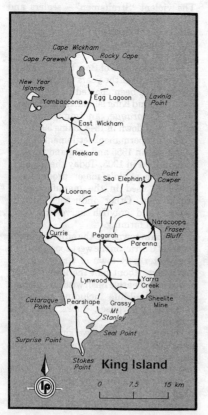

Currie *King Island A-line Units* (tel 62 1563), on North Rd, have A-frame holiday flats costing $26/39 for singles/doubles. *Daisy Flats* (tel 62 1173), on South Rd, have bed & breakfast singles/doubles for $35/45. *Top Tours* (tel 62 1245), at 13 Main St, in the centre of Currie, have bed & breakfast for $30/41; and the *Boomerang Motel* (tel 62 1288) costs $53/60, including breakfast.

On-site vans in the *Bass Caravan Park* (tel 62 1260) cost $20 a double and $3 for each extra person.

Naracoopa *Naracoopa Lodge* (tel 62 1124) on the east coast, has hostel style accommodation at $10 a night for room only. *Naracoopa Holiday Units* (tel 61 132), on Beach Rd, cost $30 for two and $5 for each extra person.

Getting There & Away

You can fly to King Island from Melbourne with Kendell Airlines for $93 or $74 standby. Advance purchase return fares are $140. Phone (004) 62 1322, or (03) 670 2677 in Melbourne, for bookings and further information. Kendell also offer accommodation and airfare packages. Aus-Air have flights from Melbourne for $84. To book, phone (03) 580 6166, or (008) 33 1256 toll free.

Airlines of Tasmania service King Island from Hobart ($130), Launceston ($90), Devonport ($75) and Wynyard ($71).

Getting Around

In Currie you can rent cars from King Island Auto Rentals (tel 62 1272) or Bourke's Car Rentals (tel 62 1297) for about $50 a day.

Some King Island roads are two wheel ruts in deep sand, and either 4WD or lots of digging gear is recommended.

FLINDERS ISLAND

Flinders is the largest of the Furneaux group of islands which cover an area of 1968 square km off the north-east tip of Tasmania. The 50 islands in the group feature an incredible variety of scenery and wildlife.

The area was charted by the young navigator Matthew Flinders who first visited the islands as part of an expedition sent from Sydney in 1797 to search for survivors of the *Sydney Cove*, wrecked on tiny Preservation Island.

Like King Island, the Furneaux Group was used intermittently by sealers until the first permanent settlement.

The early sealers were a notoriously cruel and rough lot, thinking nothing of leaving helpless seal pups to die after slaughtering the mothers. Nor were they able to resist the temptation of a little piracy from time to time, and apparently even lured ships on to the rocks by displaying false lights. It's likely that quite a few of the 120 odd ships wrecked around the Furneaux Group got there with a little outside help.

The most tragic saga in the history of Flinders Island was the part it played in the history of the Tasmanian Aborigines. In 1830 the first permanent settlement of Flinders Island was established with the last of mainland Tasmania's Aborigines – those who had not been killed when martial law gave soldiers the right to arrest or shoot any Aborigine found in settled areas. The 135 survivors transported to Flinders Island were to be Christianised and 'civilised' by the Europeans who had all but wiped them out. They were settled at Wybalenna, an Aboriginal word meaning 'black man's house', but this last ditch attempt to save the original Tasmanians was doomed. Most died, and in 1847 the remaining 47 were taken on their last journey, to Oyster Cove on the mainland; of these, all but one were dead by 1876.

It was not until 1888 that the island was finally and permanently settled though it remained sparsely populated till well after WW II when its agricultural potential was finally realised. It is the unspoilt scenery and unique wildlife of Flinders Island and others in the

Furneaux Group that attracts visitors these days.

You can dive among the many shipwrecks dotted around the islands, a couple of which are clearly visible above water. In 1877 the *City of Foochow* went down off the east coast with a load of coal, while the *Farsund* went aground near Vansittart in 1912. You can go walking in Mt Strzelecki National Park and climb the 800 metre granite peak, fish or swim in the many beautiful lagoons and secluded beaches,

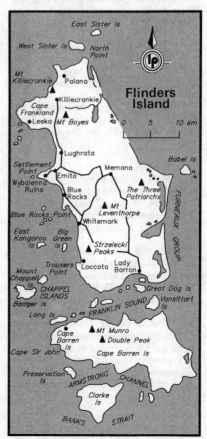

fossick for Killiecrankie 'diamonds' (actually white topaz) in Killiecrankie Bay, wander through wildlife sanctuaries or take a trip to Cape Barren Island to see the unique Cape Barren geese. And if you're there in spring or summer you can see the amazing mutton birds – or *youla*, as the Aborigines called them. These migratory birds give Flinders its nickname – 'Island of the Moonbirds'.

The inscriptions in the cemetery at Wybalenna (now known as Settlement Point), tell the tragic story of Tasmania's mainland Aborigines who couldn't survive White domination long enough to die on their own land. The small settlement's church has been restored by the National Trust. There's a good museum at Emita, near Wybalenna, with items from the sealing and whaling days and the Aboriginal settlement, and relics salvaged from shipwrecks.

Whitemark is the main town on the island and is close to the airport but Lady Barron, in the south, has the deep water port.

Places to Stay

There are a number of hotels and motels on Flinders Island. At Whitemark is *Bluff House* (tel 59 2084), costing $21.50 a person for bed & breakfast; the *Interstate* (tel 59 2144) is $16 a person for room only.

The slightly more luxurious *Furneaux* (tel 59 3521), at Lady Barron, is also rather more expensive, at $45/60 for room only, but this includes colour TV and other mod cons.

Greenglades Host Farm (tel 59 8506), in Emita, costs $25 a person for full board. The *Flinders Island Cabin Park* (tel 59 2188), in Whitemark, has self-contained cabins for $25 a double and $8 for each extra person. You can also find private accommodation and holiday flats on the island, and there are many camping sites.

Getting There & Away

Promair fly from Melbourne's Moorabbin Airport to Flinders Island from Monday to Friday for $110 one way or $190 return. You can book through any Tasmanian Travel Centre or Promair agent. They also fly from Welshpool in eastern Victoria. Airlines of Tasmania operate services between Flinders Island and Melbourne ($94), Hobart ($105) and Launceston ($58).

Getting Around

Cars can be hired in Whitemark from Flinders Island Transport Services (tel 59 2060) for around $60 a day; Flinders Island Car Hire (tel 59 2188) has old Holdens for $40 a day; Bowman Flinders Island Hire (tel 59 2008) charges $60 a day.

Flinders Island Bike Hire (tel 59 6432) rents mountain bikes.

Mutton Birds

Each September the mutton birds (also known as stormy petrels or shearwaters) return to Flinders, King and other Bass Strait islands. They arrive from their northern summer haunts along the Japanese, Siberian and Alaskan coasts to clean out and repair their burrows from the previous year. They then head out to sea again before returning in November for the breeding season which lasts till April.

All the millions of eggs are laid in one three day period and the parents then take turns, two weeks at a time, to incubate their charge. Once they have hatched their single chick, both parents feed the fluffy little fledgling until mid-April when all the adult birds depart, leaving the young to fend for themselves and hopefully to follow their parents north. Unfortunately for the well fed little mutton birds, they are tasty and once the adult birds leave the nests the 'birders' or mutton bird hunters move in.

The Furneaux Group is also home to the Cape Barren goose. At one time it was feared that it would be hunted to extinction but the completely protected bird is no longer at risk.

Victoria

Area	228,000 square km
Population	4,100,000

When Australia's founders up in Sydney decided it was time to get a foothold on some other part of the continent they had a go at establishing a settlement on Port Phillip Bay in 1803. Through a combination of bad luck and bad management they soon decided it was a lousy place to live and moved down to Tasmania. So it is not surprising that when Melbourne did become established, a long lasting rivalry with Sydney began.

In 1835 the first permanent European settlement was made at the present site of Melbourne, although whalers and sealers had used the Victorian coast for a number of years. The earliest settlers, John Batman and John Pascoe Fawkner, came to Melbourne in search of the land they had been unable to obtain in Tasmania. Not until 1837, by which time several hundred settlers had moved in, was the town named Melbourne and given an official seal of approval.

Their free enterprise spirit naturally led to clashes with the staid powers of Sydney. The settlers were not interested in the convict system for example, and on a number of occasions turned convict ships away. They wanted to form a breakaway colony, and their PR efforts included naming it after the Queen and the capital city after her Prime Minister, Lord Melbourne.

Finally, in 1851, the colony of Victoria was formed and separated from New South Wales. At about the same time, gold was discovered and the population doubled in little more than a year. Few people made fortunes but many stayed on to establish new settlements and work the land. Some of the most interesting historical areas in Victoria are associated with those gold rush days.

Melbourne, as Australia's second city, is naturally the state's prime attraction. Although it is not as intrinsically appealing as Sydney, it does lay claim to being the fashion, food and cultural centre of Australia and also the financial focus. Victoria is the most densely populated of the Australian states and also the most industrialised.

Of course Victoria is much more than its capital city. The Great Ocean Rd runs south-west towards South Australia and has some of the most spectacular coastal scenery in the world, and evocative reminders of the whaling days in some of the small port towns that predate Melbourne. To the south-east of the capital is Phillip Island with its nightly penguin parade. Further south is Wilsons Promontory – the southernmost point on the Australian mainland and also one of the best loved national parks, with excellent scenery and bushwalks. Continuing east towards the New South Wales border there's more great coast in the Gippsland region.

Victoria's stretch of the Great Dividing Range includes the Victorian Alps, which have some of the best ski fields in Australia and are much closer to

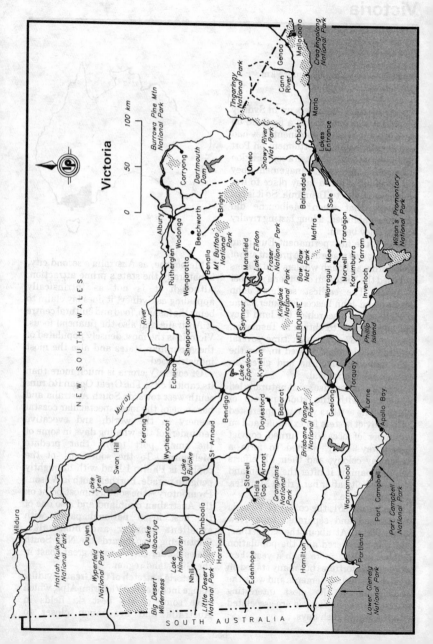

Melbourne than New South Wales' fields are to Sydney. Skiing on weekends is easy for Melbournians while in summer the mountains are popular for camping, walking and a whole host of outdoor activities. Of course you don't have to go all the way to the Alps to get into the hills; the ever popular Dandenongs are less than an hour from the centre of Melbourne while the spectacular Grampians, another popular mountain area, are further to the west.

Finally, there's the Murray River region in the north, which has many historic river towns, such as Swan Hill and Echuca. Victoria also has its wine growing areas, particularly in the north on the slopes of the Great Dividing Range. And the gold country certainly shouldn't be forgotten – towns like Bendigo and Ballarat still have a strong flavour of those heady gold rush days and lucky prospectors are still finding gold today.

GEOGRAPHY

Victoria's geography is probably more diverse than that of any other Australian state as it includes both the final stretch of the Great Dividing Range and associated outcrops plus a swath of the flatter country to the west. The Great Dividing Range reaches its greatest altitude across the Victoria-New South Wales border and the Victorian alpine region is a popular area for skiing in winter and bushwalking in summer. The mountains run south-west from the New South Wales border, then bend around to run more directly west as the range crosses north of Melbourne and finally fades out before the South Australian border.

The Victorian coast is particularly varied. On the eastern side is the mountain-backed Gippsland region while to the west is spectacular coastline running to South Australia.

The north-west of the state, beyond the Great Divide, is flat plains. It is especially dry and empty in the extreme north-west of the state, where you'll find the eerie

Sunset Country. For most of the length of the border between New South Wales and Victoria, the mighty Murray River forms the actual boundary.

CLIMATE

Victoria, and Melbourne in particular, has a single major drawback – the bloody climate. Statistically it's not that bad; the average temperature summer or winter is only a few degrees less than Sydney's and it's certainly far less humid than Sydney or Brisbane. The annual rainfall is also less than either of those damp cities. The trouble with Melbourne's climate is that it's totally unpredictable; you can boil one day and shiver the next. What the hell am I talking about – it's the next minute, not the next day! In Melbourne if you don't like the weather, so they say, just wait a minute. It's not that Melbourne has four distinct seasons, it's just that they often all come on the same day. You simply can't trust the sun to shine in summer or, for that matter, the winter to be cold; it's totally fickle. Although the weather is basically somewhat cooler in Melbourne than elsewhere in continental Australia, you'll still never need more than a light overcoat or jacket even in the depths of winter.

INFORMATION

The Victorian Tourism Commission operates the following offices around Australia:

Australian Capital Territory
    Jolimont Centre, corner of Northbourne Ave and Rudd St, Canberra 2601 (tel 47 6355)
New South Wales
    192 Pitt St, Sydney 2000 (tel 233 5499)
Queensland
    221 Queen St, Brisbane 4000 (tel 221 4300)
South Australia
    16 Grenfell St, Adelaide 5000 (tel 51 4129)
Tasmania
    126 Collins Sts, Hobart 7000 (tel 31 0499)
Victoria
    230 Collins St, Melbourne, Melbourne 3000 (tel 619 9444)

Western Australia
56 William St, Perth 6000 (tel 481 1484)

ACTIVITIES
Bushwalking
Victoria has some great bushwalking areas and a number of very active clubs. Check the bushgear shops around Hardware and Little Bourke Sts in Melbourne for local club news and magazines. For more information about bushwalking in Victoria look for the handy walking guides *50 Bush Walks in Victoria* and *50 Day Walks Near Melbourne* both by Sandra Bardswell and published by Anne O'Donovan.

Walking areas close to the city include the You Yangs, 56 km to the west, with a wide variety of bird life; and the Dandenongs right on the eastern edge of the metropolitan area. Wilsons Promontory is to the south-east in Gippsland. 'The Prom' has many marked trails from Tidal River and from Telegraph Bay – walks that can take a few hours to a couple of days. If you are overnighting in the park a permit must be obtained from the park office at Tidal River.

The Alpine Walking Track starts at Mt Erica, 144 km east of Melbourne, and ends at Tom Groggin on the New South Wales border. This is a very long trail for the experienced walker. There are other popular marked trails in the Bright and Mt Buffalo areas of the Alps.

The Grampians are 250 km west where Victoria's only remaining red roos hang out. Mallacoota Inlet in east Gippsland is equally rugged inland but the coastal walks are easier.

Rock Climbing
Again the Hardware St bushgear shops are good info sources. If you just want to scramble around in rather crowded conditions there is Hanging Rock (of *Picnic* fame) 72 km north-west. Sugarloaf and Jawbones are 112 km out in the Cathedral Range State Park, a popular weekend spot. The Grampians, 250 km from Melbourne, have a wide variety of climbs as does Mt Arapiles, 330 km out near Natimuk. At Mt Buffalo, 369 km north in the alpine area, the hardest climb is Buffalo Gorge.

Water Sports
Swimming & Surfing Although there is reasonably good swimming on the eastern side of Port Phillip Bay you have to get outside the bay to find surf. Some of the bay beaches close to the city are not too special but as you get further round the bay they get a lot better. Along the Mornington Peninsula you have the choice between sheltered bay beaches on one side and the open ocean beaches, only a short distance away on the other side of the peninsula.

Further out there are excellent beaches at Phillip Island and right along the Gippsland coast. Similarly, on the western side of the state the coast from Point Lonsdale to Apollo Bay is particularly popular for surfing.

Skin Diving Flinders, Portland, Kilcunda, Torquay, Anglesea, Lorne, Apollo Bay, Mallacoota, Portsea, Sorrento and Wilsons Prom are all popular diving areas. In Melbourne there are clubs, and organisations renting equipment.

Boats & Sailing There are many sailing clubs all around the bay in Melbourne and on Albert Park Lake. Elsewhere around the state there are many lakes popular for sailing. On the large Gippsland Lakes system you can hire yachts and launches, which work out to be quite economical among a few people.

At Studley Park, in the Melbourne suburb of Kew, you can hire a whole selection of rowing boats, canoes and kayaks by the hour. Good fun although a fair few people seem to find themselves upside down in the muddy Yarra!

Further upstream at Fairfield Park, there is another boathouse, restored to its original Edwardian elegance, offering Devonshire teas and other snacks, and boats and canoes for hire. You might catch a performance in the outdoor amphitheatre on a bend in the river in the natural bushland.

Canoes can also be rented by Como Park, further down the Yarra towards the city. At Albert Park Lake you can hire rowing boats and sailing boats.

Running & Cycling

The four km jogging track (popularly known as 'the Tan') around the Kings Domain and the Royal Botanic Gardens in central Melbourne is one of the most popular running circuits in Australia. Albert Park Lake is also busy. With its relatively flat terrain Melbourne is very popular with bike riders – quite a few of us at Lonely Planet ride bicycles to work.

It's easy to hire bicycles on the popular Yarra-side bicycle track but not so easy to find them for longer-term hire in Melbourne. Contact Bicycle Victoria (tel 670 9911) for information on tours and organised rides in Victoria. They also run the Great Victorian Bike Ride, held annually around November, in which thousands of cyclists take part. They may be able to tell you where you can hire a touring bike.

GETTING AROUND

V/Line has a fairly comprehensive rail network of InterUrban and InterCity services. The rail services are supplemented by connecting V/Line buses. Phone 619 3333 for information. The principal rail routes radiating from Melbourne are:

1 west through Geelong to Warrnambool in the south-west.
2 north-west through Ballarat and on through the central west to South Australia.
3 also through Ballarat, then up to Mildura on the Murray River in the north-west.
4 north through Bendigo and the central highlands up to Swan Hill on the Murray.
5 north up to Shepparton and Numurkah in the Goulburn Valley.
6 north up the Hume Highway route to Albury/Wodonga on the route to Sydney.
7 east through Traralgon and Sale to Bairnsdale in Gippsland.

V/Line have a timetable of all their services, available from station bookstalls. *Transport in Victoria* is a map showing all the country bus and rail routes.

Tours

There are many tours available in Victoria, ranging from day-tours to extended hikes. Check at the tourist office, and also on notice boards at hostels and backpacker places as they often run their own tours.

Melbourne

Population 2,900,000

Melbourne has always had a fierce rivalry with Sydney. It goes right back to their founding; Sydney had nearly 50 years head start on its southern sister and even then the foundation of Melbourne was a rather haphazard affair. Not until 1835, following exploratory trips from Tasmania, was Melbourne eventually founded by a group of Tasmanian entrepreneurs.

In 1851 the colony of Victoria became independent of New South Wales and almost immediately the small town of Melbourne became the centre for Australia's biggest and most prolonged gold rush. In just a few years Melbourne suddenly became a real place on the map and the city's solid, substantial appearance essentially dates from those heady days. For a while last century Melbourne was the larger and more exciting city, known as 'Marvellous Melbourne', but Sydney gradually pulled ahead and Melbourne

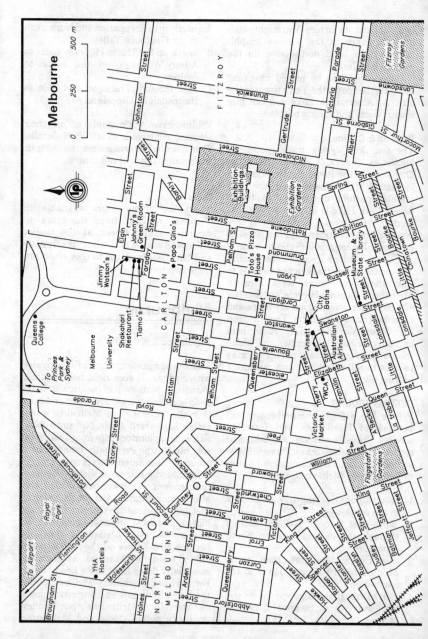

Melbourne

0   250   500 m

To Airport

Royal Park

YHA Hostels

NORTH MELBOURNE

To Princes Park & Sydney

Queens College

Melbourne University

Shakahari Restaurant

Tiamo's

Jimmy Watson's

Johnny's Green Room

Papa Gino's

Toto's Pizza House

CARLTON

Exhibition Buildings

Exhibition Gardens

FITZROY

Fitzroy Gardens

Museum & State Library

City Baths

Ansett
Australian Airlines

YWCA

Victoria Market

Flagstaff Gardens

Chinatown

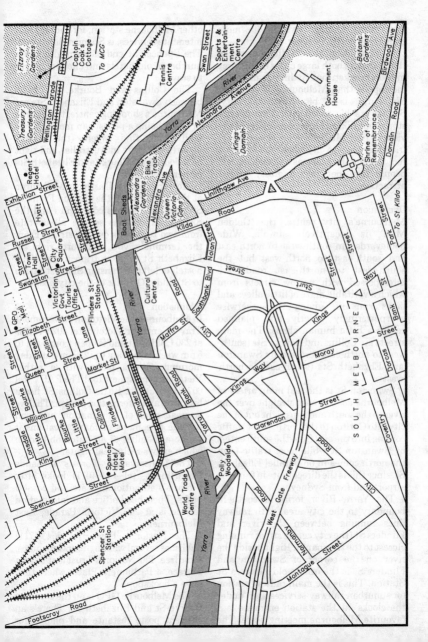

now ranks number two to its more glamorous northern sister.

In population there's little between them; they're both large cities in the three million bracket, but Sydney is more the metropolis than Melbourne. These days Melbourne is a big Australian city, Sydney's a big world one. This doesn't stop people liking Melbourne more. Many visitors find Melbourne an easier going, friendlier place, a city where you can get a real feel for the place as somewhere real people live, not just a glossy tourist attraction.

Orientation

Melbourne's city centre, the 'Golden Mile', is deceptively simple. Wide boulevards run south-west to north-east and south-east to north-west but the south-west to north-east roads are interspersed with narrow streets from which a veritable maze of little alleys and lanes run off, giving the otherwise overpoweringly orderly and planned centre a little human chaos. The main streets are Collins and Bourke Sts (south-west to north-east) crossed by Swanston and Elizabeth Sts (south-east to north-west).

Swanston St is the real main artery of Melbourne as it crosses straight over the river to the south and runs right out of the city into Carlton to the north. Most traffic coming into the city from the south enters by Swanston St while most traffic from the north comes in on parallel Elizabeth St, since this is the direct route in from the airport and from Sydney.

The Yarra River forms a southern boundary to the city area, with railway lines running between the river and Flinders St (the city centre street running closest to the riverbank). Right beside the river on the corner of Swanston and Flinders St is the ornate old Flinders St Station. This is the main railway station for suburban railway services and 'under the clocks' at the station entrance is a favourite Melbourne meeting place. The

other Melbourne station, for country and interstate services, is Spencer St Station. The Spencer St end of town also has a number of old hotels and cheaper places to stay.

The Collins and Bourke St blocks between Swanston and Elizabeth Sts are Melbourne's shopping centre, the Bourke St block being a pedestrian mall. On the mall you'll find Myers (the biggest department store in Australia) and right next door on the Bourke and Elizabeth Sts corner is the GPO.

Most travellers will arrive in Melbourne at the north side of the city, on Franklin St. The big four bus companies and the Skybus airport bus service all operate from two terminals on this street. From the terminals you can turn right to Elizabeth St to get a tram to the YHA hostels or left to Swanston St to get a tram to St Kilda. Or walk to the city hostels.

Information

In Melbourne, the Victorian Government Travel Centre or Victour (tel 602 9444) is at 230 Collins St and is open from 9 am to 5 pm weekdays, 9 am to 12 noon Saturday mornings. It's a place with a rather Victorian atmosphere too! The RACV (tel 607 2137) at 422 Little Collins St has a bookshop and information section. They've a great deal of information and can provide free maps of many locations if you're a member of an automobile club which enjoys reciprocal rights.

The Conservation, Forests & Lands Department (tel 412 4011) looks after Victoria's 40 national, state and coastal parks. Their head office and information service is at 240 Victoria Parade, East Melbourne.

The National Trust (tel 654 4711) publishes several walking-tours brochures, some free. The National Trust is at Tasma Terrace, 4 Parliament Place, where they have a bookshop.

The Melbourne GPO is on the corner of Bourke St and Elizabeth St. There's an efficient poste restante and phones for interstate and international calls. Phone centres can also be found right behind the GPO on Little Bourke St and right across the road on Elizabeth St.

The YHA (tel 670 7991) has its helpful Melbourne office at 205 King St, on the corner with Little Bourke St. It's quite close to Spencer St Station. They handle membership enquires and travel bookings.

If you're after bushgear or information on bushwalking the centre for bushgear shops is around the junction of Hardware St and Little Bourke St, close to the GPO. You can have backpacks and camping equipment repaired by Aiking Repairs at 377 Little Bourke St, above the Mountain Designs shop.

The Environment Centre (tel 654 4833) at 247 Flinders Lane has a wide variety of books, calendars, posters and magazines and is a good place for information about activities in the environment and conservation movements.

Recently opened, a Travellers' Medical & Vaccination Centre (tel 650 7600) is at 6/165 Flinders Lane in the city. They're open weekdays from 8.30 am to 5.30 pm, and later by appointment.

Melbourne has a lot of excellent bookshops including a big Angus & Robertson on Elizabeth St, several Collins Bookshops around the city, and the agreeably chaotic McGills on Elizabeth St opposite the GPO (good for interstate and overseas newspapers). Whole Earth at 83 Bourke St is more 'alternative' and is open late; Readings on Lygon St in Carlton is more literary and has an excellent window notice board where you'll find all sorts of offers to share accommodation or rides.

The Yarra River

Melbourne's prime natural feature, the 'muddy' Yarra, is the butt of countless jokes but is actually a surprisingly attractive river and is slowly but surely becoming more and more of an attraction as new parks, walks and buildings are built along its banks. Despite the cracks about it 'running upside down' it's just muddy, not dirty.

Mongolian barbecue on the Yarra River

When the racing rowing boats are gliding down the river on a sunny day, or you're driving along Alexandra Ave towards the city on a clear night the Yarra can really look quite magical. Best of all there's a bicycle track along the riverbank so you can bike it for kms along the riverside or ride to work without risking being wiped out by some nut in a Holden. The bike track has been gradually extended further upstream and hopefully will eventually start to move further downstream as well. On weekends you can hire bicycles – see Getting Around.

There are also barbecues beside the river and near Como Park in South Yarra and you can hire canoes and rowing boats further upstream. Studley Park in Kew is the most popular place for boating. Canoes for two cost $10 for the first hour and canoes for three cost $12; subsequent hours cost $5 or $6. You can also hire kayaks and rowing boats.

A more leisurely way to boat down the river is on one of the tour boats which operate on the river from Princes Walk beside Princes Bridge (across from Flinders St Station). 'Bar-b-boats' (tel 696 1241) at 1 South Wharf Rd, opposite the World Trade Centre, offer cruising barbecues for up to 12 people. You supply the snags and they charge $72 an hour (minimum two hours).

There are some really beautiful old bridges across the Yarra; and Alexandra Parade, the riverside boulevard on the south side, provides delightful views of Melbourne by day or night.

Polly Woodside Maritime Museum

Close to Spencer St Bridge, immediately south of the city centre, is the *Polly Woodside*. Built in Belfast, Northern Ireland, in 1885 she's an old iron-hulled sailing ship which carried freight in the dying years of the sailing era. The *Polly Woodside* and the adjacent nautical museum will eventually form the centre for a major redevelopment project on this run-down riverside docks area. The ship

and museum are open from 10 am to 4 pm weekdays, 10 am to 5 pm on weekends; admission is $5 (children $2, family ticket $10). Across the river stands the World Trade Centre.

City Square

Across Collins St from the Town Hall, at the intersection of Collins and Swanston Sts, is Melbourne's city square, something of an architectural disaster despite much advance planning and architectural competitions

The only interest the city square has ever really had for the people of Melbourne was due to the 'yellow peril' when it was first completed. This big chunk of modern sculpture was intended to give the square a central focus but, unfortunately, it was the sort of thing that makes the you-call-that-art brigade foam at the mouth. Doubly unfortunately Melbourne's city council at that time had absolutely nothing better to do than foam at the mouth and after endless arguments and veritable zeppelins full of hot air the council got the sack and the yellow peril was spirited away to a new (and obscure) home in a riverside park down towards Spencer St.

With the sculpture gone Melbournians appeared to lose interest completly in the square, the adjacent shops went broke and now plans are being formulated to tear it down and start again. Beside the square there's a derelict old theatre which has been a political football for many years and nobody dares to get rid of it. Still standing in the square in late '88 was a statue of the luckless explorers Burke and Wills, looking suitably heroic and unlucky. This statue has had quite an interesting history of moving from place to place around the city and now looks set to move again.

Around the City

Continuing up Collins St beside the City Square you come to the 'Paris End' where graceful trees shade the street and do give it something of a Parisian look although many of the fine old buildings that used to line the street have now disappeared. Two big hotels on Collins St are popular meeting and eating places – see the Hyatt and Regent hotels under Places to Eat.

Up Collins St the other way you come to the Melbourne Stock Exchange at 351. You can visit the 3rd floor visitors' gallery from 9 am to 12 noon and 2 to 5 pm, Monday to Friday. Those interested in the forces of capitalism at work can also have a free tour of the exchange.

Bourke St has more shops but less style than Collins St although it too can boast a Melbourne fiasco: when, in the '70s, every Australian city had to have a pedestrian mall Melbourne got one too but the Bourke St Mall has been a non-starter from the very beginning. Melbourne has one big difference to any other Australian city – trams. It soon became very clear that there's no way a pedestrian mall can work if you've got 30 tonne trams barrelling through the middle of it every few minutes. Or at least it soon became very clear to the likes of you and me; it's still not at all clear to the powers that be and several multi-million dollar re-arrangements of the potted plants and the benches still haven't made it any clearer.

Half a block up from Bourke St is something that's much more of a Melbourne success story – Chinatown on Little Bourke St. This narrow lane was a thronging Chinese quarter even back in the gold rush days and it's now a busy, crowded couple of blocks of often excellent Chinese restaurants, Asian supermarkets and shops. The successful touch here was the addition of decorative street lamps and Chinese tiled arches over the lane. Yes, I know they're artificial and garish but they look great. Another half block up to Lonsdale St brings you to the central city's Greek quarter.

City Buildings

Melbourne's an intriguing blend of the soaring new and the stately old. Carrying the 'new' banner are buildings like the Rialto on Collins St. Its semi-reflective glass looks stunningly different under varying light – it's something of a city Ayer's Rock! The Rialto is the tallest office building in Australia and beside it is the imaginative Menzies at the Rialto Hotel which uses the facades of two old buildings and cleverly incorporates an old stone paved alleyway which used to run between them.

Or there's Nauru House on Exhibition St; Nauru is a tiny Pacific island whose entire population could comfortably be housed in this big office block. It is an extremely wealthy island since it's basically solid phosphate, hence the building's nickname of 'birdshit house'. Only a sparrow hop away is the equally soaring Regent Hotel with its central atrium, starting on the 35th floor. A great place to stay if you can stretch to $200 a night.

On Spring St is a hotel of quite another era: the gracious old Windsor Hotel. Across the road from this is the imposing State Parliament House, a relic of Melbourne's gold rush wealth. It served as the national parliament while Canberra was under construction.

Other old buildings in the centre include the 1853 Treasury Building in the Treasury Gardens, the 1872 Old Royal Mint and the 1842 St James Cathedral, both beside Flagstaff Gardens. Victoriana enthusiasts may find some very small Melbourne buildings of interest – scattered around the city are a number of very fine cast-iron men's urinals (like French *pissoirs*). They mainly date from 1903 to WW I and one on the corner of Exhibition and Lonsdale St is classified by the National Trust. Other good examples include one outside the North Melbourne Town Hall where there is also a very fine drinking fountain.

On the corner of Swanston and Flinders Sts is the main railway station for local trains in Melbourne, the grand old Flinders St Station. Across the road from the station is one of Melbourne's best known pubs, Young & Jacksons, which is famed mainly for the painting of Chloe hanging in the upstairs bar. Judged indecent at the Melbourne Exhibition of 1880 she has gone on to become a much loved symbol of Melbourne. The pub has been carefully restored.

The Melbourne Club, pillar of the Melbourne establishment, is off Spring St up at the Treasury Gardens end of town. This end block of Bourke St is popular and has some good restaurants, bookshops and record shops. St Patrick's Cathedral, one of the city's most imposing churches, is also at this end of town.

Over the other side of the city is the Victoria Market, on the corner of Peel and Victoria Sts. It's the city's main retail produce centre, a colourful and popular scene on Tuesdays, Thursdays, Fridays and Saturday mornings when the stall operators shout, yell and generally go all out to move the goods. On Sundays the fruit and vegies give way to general goods – everything from cut price jeans to second-hand records.

Museum & Library

Extending for a block between Swanston St and Russell St beside La Trobe St is the interconnected collection of the National Museum and the Science Museum, plus the State Library and La Trobe Library. The State Library is a gracious old library with a large, octagonal, domed reading room and any book lover will enjoy its atmosphere. Its collection of more than a million books and other reference material is particularly notable for its collection in humanities and social sciences, as well as art, music, performing arts, Australiana and rare books, dating back to a 4000 year old Mesopotamian tablet.

The main entrance to the National Museum is on Russell St, the Science Museum on Swanston St, but you can actually get to either collection from either end. Exhibitions range from the first car and aircraft in Australia to the stuffed remains of Phar Lap, the legendary racehorse which nearly disrupted Australian-American relations when it died a suspicious death in the US. The complex also includes a planetarium.

The museum is open from 10 am to 5 pm every day and admission is free except to special exhibits. In 1992 the museum is scheduled to move to a new home across the river, near the *Polly Woodside*.

Old Melbourne Gaol

A block further up Russell St is this gruesome old jail and penal museum. It was built of bluestone in 1841 and was used right up to 1929. In all, over 100 prisoners were hanged in the jail. It's a dark, dank, spooky place which often terrifies young children. The museum displays include death masks of noted bushrangers and convicts, Ned Kelly's armour, the very scaffold from which Ned took his fatal plunge and some fascinating records of early 'transported' convicts, indicating just what flimsy excuses could be used to pack people off to Australia's unwelcoming shores. It's an unpleasant reminder of the brutality of Australia's early convict days. It is open from 10 am to 5 pm daily, and admission is $3.50 (children $2, family $9).

Melbourne Zoo

Just north of the city centre in Parkville is Melbourne's excellent zoo. There are numerous walk-through enclosures in this well planned zoo. You walk through the aviary, around the monkey enclosures and even over the lions' park on a bridge. This is the oldest zoo in Australia and one of the oldest in the world.

The zoo is open from 9 am to 5 pm every day of the week and admission is $5.60 (children $2.80). You can get to it on a No 55 or 56 tram from William St (not Sundays). The zoo is in Royal Park; a marker in the park indicates where the Burke and Wills expedition set off on its ill fated journey in 1860.

Handicrafts

Melbourne has many shops and galleries displaying crafts by local artists, as well as goods from almost every region of the world. The local craft scene is especially strong in the fields of ceramics, jewellery, stained glass and leathercraft.

Go to the Meat Market Craft Centre (tel 329 9966) in North Melbourne to see the state craft collection and other exhibitions. It's at the corner of Courtney and Blackwood Sts, North Melbourne.

Other craft galleries worth a visit are Distelfink (tel 818 2555), 432 Burwood Rd, Hawthorn, and Devise Gallery (tel 690 6991), 263 Park St, South Melbourne. Or just take a walk along the St Kilda Esplanade any Sunday where there is a street market of varying styles and quality.

There are a number of good craft shops in the inner suburbs, usually with an eclectic mix of local and imported crafts. One of the longest running is Ishka Handcrafts at 409 Chapel St, South Yarra, and also at South Melbourne, Kew, Camberwell and elsewhere.

In many suburbs there are weekend craft markets, and further out there are craft places in Warrandyte and the small towns in the Dandenongs. Several country cities and towns have interesting craft outlets, notably Geelong and Lorne to the south-west, and Castlemaine, Maldon and Beechworth to the north.

For more details, pick up a copy of the Victorian Craft Association's *Craft Outlets in Victoria*, available at the Meat Market, Ishka or other craft places.

The Melbourne Cup

If you happen to be in Melbourne in November you can catch the greatest horse race in Australia, the prestigious Melbourne Cup. Although its position as the bearer of the largest prize for an Australian horse race is constantly under challenge, no other race can bring the country to a standstill.

For about an hour during the lead-up to the race on the first Tuesday in November, a public holiday in Victoria, people all over the country get touched by Melbourne's spring racing fever.

Serious punters and fashion-conscious racegoers pack the grandstand and lawns of the Victoria Racing Club's beautiful Flemington Racecourse, once-a-year betters make their choice or organise Cup syndicates with friends, and the race is watched or listened to on televisions and radios in hotels, clubs and houses across the land. Australia virtually comes to a halt for the three-or-so minutes during which the race is actually run.

The two mile flat race, a true test of stamina, has in recent years attracted horses and owners from Europe and the Middle East, breaking the stranglehold that New Zealand horses and trainers had on the coveted gold cup for many years.

Many people say that to be in Melbourne in November and not go to the Cup is like going to Paris and skipping the Louvre, or turning your back on the bulls in Pamplona!

Melbourne Cricket Ground

The MCG is one of Australia's biggest sporting stadiums and was the central stadium for the 1956 Melbourne Olympics. In Yarra Park, which stretches from the city and East Melbourne to Richmond, the huge stadium can accommodate over 100,000 spectators, and does so at least once a year. The big occasion is the annual Australian Rules football Grand Final in September. This is Australia's biggest sporting event and brings Melbourne, which engages in a winter of Aussie Rules football mania each year, to a fever pitch. The only other sporting event which generates the same sort of national interest in Australia is the Melbourne Cup horse race each November.

Cricket is, of course, the other major sport played in the MCG; international test and one-day matches as well as interstate Sheffield Shield and other local district games take place here over the summer months.

On the city side of the stadium there's the Australian Gallery of Sport, a museum dedicated to Australia's sporting passions. It's open from 10 am to 4 pm every day except Monday and admission is $3 (children $1).

Cultural Centre Complex

As you cross the river to the south of the city, Swanston St becomes St Kilda Rd, a very fine boulevard which runs straight out of the city towards the war memorial, takes a kink around the shrine and then continues to St Kilda. Beyond the memorial it's ad agency alley, with many office blocks lining the road.

Right by the river is Melbourne's large arts centre. The National Gallery was the first part of the complex to be completed, back in 1968, and although it's a rather dull cubic building and the 'fish shop' front window has been the butt of local jokes, it houses a very fine collection of art. The gallery has local and overseas collections, with some outstanding works from a variety of periods, an excellent photography collection and many fascinating temporary exhibits from all over the world. The stained-glass ceiling in the Great Hall is a high point of the gallery. The gallery is open from 10 am to 5 pm except Mondays and the admission is $1.20 (students and children 60c). There are additional charges for some special exhibits.

Beside the gallery is the Concert Hall complex. It may look rather like a grounded prison ship from Star Wars but it houses (mostly underground) an excellent concert hall, the state theatre, playhouse, studio and a performing arts museum, all topped by that tall pointy spire; well it does look nice at night. Inside it looks nice at any time and there's something on virtually every night. The Performing Arts Museum in the centre has changing exhibits on all aspects of the performing arts: it might be a display of rock musicians' outfits or an exhibit on horror in the theatre! Opening hours are weekdays 11 am to 5 pm and weekends 12 noon to 5 pm, admission is $2.40 ($1.20 for children).

Parks & Gardens

Victoria has dubbed itself 'the garden state' and it's certainly true in Melbourne; the city has many swaths of green all around the central area. They're varied and delightful – formal central gardens like the Treasury and Flagstaff Gardens, wide empty parklands like Royal Park, a particularly fine Botanic Gardens and many others.

Royal Botanic Gardens Certainly the finest gardens in Australia and arguably one of the finest in the world, this is one of my favourite spots in Melbourne. There's nothing more genteel to do in Melbourne than to have scones and cream by the lake on a Sunday afternoon. The beautifully laid out gardens are right beside the Yarra River; indeed the river once actually ran through the gardens and the lakes are the remains of curves of the river, cut off when the river was straightened out to lessen the annual flood damage. The garden site was chosen in 1845 but the real development took place when Baron Sir Ferdinand von Mueller took charge in 1852.

There's a surprising amount of fauna as well as flora in the gardens. Apart from the ever present water fowl and the frequent visits from cockatoos you may also see rabbits and possums if you're lucky. In all more than 50 varieties of birds can be seen in the gardens. In '82 a large contingent of fruit bats, usually found in the warmer climes of north Queensland, took residence for the summer and seem to have been back every summer since.

You can pick up guide-yourself leaflets at the park entrances; these are changed with the seasons and tell you what to look out for at the different times of year.

Kings Domain The Botanic Gardens form a

corner of the Kings Domain, a park which also contains the Shrine of Remembrance, Governor La Trobe's Cottage and the Sidney Myer Music Bowl. It's flanked by St Kilda Rd. The whole park is encircled by the 'tan track', a four km running track which is probably Melbourne's favourite venue for joggers. It's another of my Melbourne regulars, I do a couple of laps every Sunday morning. The track has an amusing variety of exercise points – a mixture of the stations of the cross and miniature golf, someone once said.

Beside St Kilda Rd stands the massive Shrine of Remembrance, a WW I war memorial which took so long to build that WW II was well underway when it eventually opened. The shrine is another example of the Melbourne architectural jinx – huge though it is and imposing though it was intended to be the shrine somehow manages to look completely anonymous; you could almost forget it was there. It's worth climbing up to the top as there are fine views to the city along St Kilda Rd and you can clearly see how St Kilda Rd runs so straight out of the city and on to St Kilda, but makes a distinct detour around the memorial. The shrine's big day of the year is Anzac Day. Back during the Vietnam era some commendably enterprising individuals managed to sneak up to the well guarded shrine on the night before Anzac Day and paint 'PEACE' across the front in large letters. The shrine is open to visitors daily from 10 am to 5 pm.

Across from the shrine is Governor La Trobe's Cottage, the original Victorian government house sent out from the mother country in prefabricated form in 1840. It was originally sited in Jolimont, near the MCG, and was moved here when the decision was made to preserve this interesting piece of Melbourne's early history. The simple little cottage is open daily except Friday from 11 am to 4.30 pm and admission is $2.50 (children $1.50, family $6).

The cottage is flanked by the Old Observatory and the National Herbarium. On some nights the observatory is open to the public for a free view of the heavens between 8 and 10 pm. You have to book, phone the Museum of Victoria on 669 9942 for details. Amongst other things the herbarium tests suspected marijuana samples to decide if they really are the dreaded weed.

The imposing building overlooking the Botanic Gardens is Government House where Victoria's governor resides. It's a copy of Queen Victoria's palace on England's Isle of Wight.

Across the road from the herbarium on Dallas Brooks Drive is the Australian Centre for Contemporary Art which is open Tuesday to Friday from 10.30 am to 5 pm, Saturdays and Sundays from 2 to 5 pm. Up at the city end of the park is the Sidney Myer Music Bowl, a functional outdoor performance area in a natural bowl. It's used for all manner of concerts in the summer months although of late not rock concerts, due to too much trouble afterwards from some younger idiots!

Treasury & Fitzroy Gardens These two popular formal parks lie immediately to the east of the city centre, overshadowed by the Hilton Hotel. The Fitzroy Gardens, with its stately avenues lined with English elms, is a popular spot for wedding photographs; on virtually every Saturday afternoon there's a continuous procession of wedding cars pulling up for the participants to be snapped. The pathways in the park are actually laid out in the form of a Union Jack!

The gardens contain several points of interest including Captain Cook's cottage. It was uprooted from its native Yorkshire and reassembled in the park in 1934. Actually it's not certain that the good captain ever did live in this house but never mind, it looks very picturesque. The house is furnished in period style and has an interesting Captain Cook exhibit. It's open from 9 am to 5 pm daily and admission is $1.10 (children 40c).

In the centre of the gardens, by the refreshment kiosk, is a small miniature Tudor village and a fairy-tale-carved tree. Off in the north-west corner of the park is the people's pathway – a circular brick paved path made with individually engraved bricks. Anybody who dropped by here on 5 February 1978 got to produce their own little bit of art for posterity and it's quite intriguing to wander around.

The two gardens have a large resident population of possums, you may see them in the early evening or at night. You might see me too, I regularly jog round the Fitzroy Gardens in the morning!

Other Parks The central Flagstaff Gardens were the first public gardens in Melbourne. From a lookout point here, ships arriving at the city were sighted in the early colonial days. A plaque in the gardens describes how the site was used for this purpose. Closer to the seafront is Albert Park Lake, a shallow lake created from a swamp area. The lake is popular for boating and there's another popular jogging track around the perimeter. You can hire boats on the lake, the Jolly Roger Boathouse is at the city end of the lake and rents rowing boats for $7 or $10 an hour, sailing boats at $15 or $20 an hour. On Saturday the two sailing clubs here have races on the lake – I'm usually bringing up the rear in the Mirror class with *Tangkuban Prahu* ('upside down boat' in Indonesian).

On the north side of the city the Exhibition Gardens are the site of the Exhibition Buildings, a wonder of the southern hemisphere when they were built for the Great Exhibition of 1880. Later they served as the Victorian parliament building for 27 years while the Victorian parliament was used by the national legislature until Canberra's parliament building was finally completed. They're still a major exhibition centre today and a new extension is one of the few successful uses of the 'mirror building' architectural craze which gripped

Melbourne for a spell. There are some fine old fountains around the building, one of them well reflected in the mirror building.

In the Melbourne suburb of Heidelburg, Heide Park & Gallery was formerly the home of two prominent Australian artists, John and Sunday Reed, and houses an impressive collection of 20th-century Australian art. The sprawling park is an informal combination of deciduous and native trees, with a carefully tended kitchen garden and scattered sculpture gardens running right down to the banks of the Yarra. Heide is open from Tuesday to Friday between 10 am and 5 pm, and on Saturdays and Sundays between 12 noon and 5 pm.

Other Old Buildings

Como Overlooking the Yarra River from Como Park in South Yarra, Como was built between 1840 and 1859. The home with its extensive grounds has been authentically restored and furnished and is operated by the National Trust. Aboriginal rites and feasts were still being held on the banks of the Yarra when the house was first built and an early occupant writes of seeing a cannibal rite from her bedroom window.

Como is open from 10 am to 5 pm every day and admission is $4.50 (students $3, children $2.20) and you can get there on a No 8 tram from the city.

Ripponlea Ripponlea is at 192 Hotham St, Elsternwick, close to St Kilda. It's another fine old mansion with elegant gardens inhabited by peacocks. Ripponlea is open 10 am to 5 pm daily and admission is $4 (children $2, family $9).

Montsalvat In Eltham, the mud-brick and alternative lifestylers suburb, Montsalvat on Hillcrest Ave (26 km out) is Justus Jorgensen's eclectic re-creation of a European artists' colony which today houses all manner of artists and artisans and is often the venue for smaller concerts, open dawn to dusk daily.

Other Museums

There are a number of smaller museums around Melbourne. In Chinatown in the city centre the Museum of Chinese Australian History is on Cohen Place, close to the corner of Lonsdale and Exhibition Sts. Housed in an 1890s Victorian warehouse the museum traces the history of the Chinese in Australia. It's open weekdays except Fridays from 10 am to 5 pm, weekends from 12 noon to 5 pm and admission is $3 (children $1).

Close to Flinders St Station, Leone Ryan's Hall of Australian Bush Life is in the Banana Alley Vaults by the riverside at the corner of Flinders and Queen Sts. It has an extensive collection of Australian bush life scenes recreated in clay models. It's open from Tuesday to Friday from 10 am to around 4 pm and Saturday to Sunday, 12 noon to 5 pm and entry is $5 (children $2.50; maximum for a family group $15) – this includes a 'cuppa' (cup of tea).

The Melbourne Fire Brigade Museum is at 8 Gisborne St, East Melbourne, and is open Fridays from 10 am to 2 pm and Sundays from 10 am to 4 pm; admission is $2 (children $1). It's ideal for fire fighting enthusiasts.

Out at Moorabbin Airport, Cheltenham, the Moorabbin Air Museum has a collection of old aircraft including a number from WW II. It's open weekdays from 9.30 am to 5 pm, weekends from 11 am to sunset; admission is $3 (children $1.50, family $6.50). There's a second aviation museum on the other side of the city at Point Cook.

Trams

If Melbourne has a symbol then it's a movable one – trams. Not those horrible, plastic-looking modern ones either; real Melbourne trams are green and yellow, ancient looking and half the weight of an ocean liner. Trams are the standard means of public transport and they work remarkably well. More than a few cities which once had trams wish they still did today.

The old trams are gradually being replaced by new ones and some of the older trams have been turned into mobile works of art, painted from front to back by local artists. I liked the one covered in sheep. If you like old trams then watch out for them on weekends when some delightful vintage examples are rolled out on summer Sundays and used in place of the modern ones on the Hawthorn run from Princes Gate.

To come to grips with Melbourne and its trams try a ride on a No 8. It starts off along Swanston St in the city, rolls down St Kilda Rd beside the Kings Domain, turns round by the war memorial and on to Toorak Rd through South Yarra and Toorak. Another popular tram ride is No 15 or 16 which cruises right down St Kilda Rd to St Kilda.

Trams are such a part of Melbourne life they've even been used for a play – act one of *Storming Mont Albert by Tram* took

Melbourne tram

place from Mont Albert to the city, act two on the way back. The passengers were the audience, the actors got on and off along the way. It wasn't a bad play! There's even a tram restaurant: the *Colonial Tramcar Restaurant* cruises Melbourne every night and you can have dinner on the move for $40 to $75 including drinks, depending on the time and the night. Phone 596 6500 for reservations.

Melbourne trams should be treated with some caution by car drivers. You can only overtake a tram on the left and must always stop behind one when it halts to drop or collect passengers (except where there are central 'islands' for passengers). In the city centre at most junctions a peculiar path must be followed to make right hand turns, in order to accommodate the trams. Note that in rainy weather tram tracks are extremely slippery, motorcyclists should take special care. Cyclists must beware of tram tracks at all times, if you get a wheel into the track you're on your face immediately. I've done that twice in Melbourne, smashing a pair of glasses on one occasion.

Melbourne Suburbs

Melbourne's inner city suburbs have gone through the same 'trendification' process that has hit Sydney suburbs like Paddington and Balmain. Carlton is the most obvious example of this activity but Parkville, Fitzroy, South Melbourne, Albert Park, Richmond and Hawthorn are other popular inner city suburbs with a strong Victorian flavour.

Carlton This is one of Melbourne's most interesting inner city suburbs – partly because here you'll find probably the most attractive collection of Victoriana, partly because the university is here and partly because Carlton is also the Italian quarter of Melbourne with the biggest collection of Italian restaurants in Australia.

Lygon St is the backbone of Carlton and along here you'll find enough Italian restaurants, coffee houses, pizzerias and gelaterias to satisfy the most rabid pasta and cappuccino freak. The Lygon St Festa is held annually in November and always gets a good turn-out. Carlton is flanked by gracious Parkville and the seedy/trendy mixture of Fitzroy.

South Yarra & Toorak South of the Yarra River (as the name indicates) South Yarra is one of the more frenetic Melbourne suburbs, Toorak one of the most exclusive. The two roads to remember here are Toorak Rd and Chapel St. Toorak Rd is one of Australia's classiest shopping streets, frequented by those well known Toorak matrons in their Porsches and Benzes. Apart from expensive shops and some of Australia's best (and most expensive) restaurants, Toorak Rd also has a number of very reasonably priced places to eat. Toorak Rd forms the main artery through both South Yarra and Toorak.

Running across Toorak Rd is Chapel St in South Yarra; if the word for Toorak Rd is 'exclusive' then for Chapel St it's 'trendy'. The street is virtually wall-to-wall boutiques ranging from punk to Indian bangles and beads, op-shop to antique, plus restaurants, the imaginative Jam Factory shopping centre and the delightful Prahran Market. The market is a great place for fruit and vegetables and you'll find me shopping here early most Friday mornings. Chapel St fades away into Prahran but take a right turn by the Prahran Town Hall and wander along Greville St, at one time Melbourne's freak street, which still has some curious shops.

South Yarra also has one of Australia's finest colonial mansions, Como House, and the Royal Botanic Gardens flank the suburb.

Richmond As Carlton is to Italy so Richmond is to Greece; this suburb, just to the east of the city centre, is the Greek centre for the third largest Greek city in the world. That's right, after Athens and

Thessaloniki, Melbourne is the next largest city in terms of Greek population. Richmond is, of course, the best place for a souvlaki in Melbourne! More recently Richmond became the centre for a huge influx of Vietnamese and colourful Victoria St is known as 'Little Saigon'. Richmond's also where I live!

The suburb is another centre for Victorian architecture, much of it restored or currently in the process of restoration. Bridge Rd is something of a Melbourne fashion centre with shops where many Australian fashion designers sell their seconds and rejects.

St Kilda This seaside suburb is Melbourne's most cosmopolitan and is very lively on weekends, particularly on Sundays. It's also the somewhat feeble excuse for a Melbourne sin centre; if you're after seedy nightlife you'll do better in Sydney's Kings Cross but if you want a meal late at night or some activity on the weekends then St Kilda is the place to be. Fitzroy and Acland Sts, with their numerous restaurants, snack bars and take-aways, are the main streets in St Kilda.

Sunday morning along the Esplanade in St Kilda features an interesting amateur art show, while along Acland St gluttons will have their minds blown by the amazing selection of cakes in the coffee shop windows. St Kilda has lots of local Jewish and ethnic colour. The huge old Palais Theatre and the raucous Luna Park amusement centre, with roller-coasters and the like, can also be found here.

The St Kilda Festival is held on the second weekend in February. Acland St is usually turned into a mall with foodstalls and entertainment and in Fitzroy St all the restaurants bring their tables out onto the footpath. Stages are set up in a number of places and there is music and dancing, with rock bands and ethnic groups performing. The finale of the festival and the weekend is a fireworks display over the beach.

Williamstown At the mouth of the Yarra this is one of the oldest parts of Melbourne and has many interesting old buildings and lots of waterside activity. Williamstown remained relatively isolated from developments in the rest of Melbourne until the completion of the West Gate Bridge suddenly brought it to within a short drive of the centre.

Moored in Williamstown, HMAS *Castlemaine*, a WW II minesweeper, is now preserved as a Maritime Museum and is open on weekends from 12 noon to 5 pm; admission is \$2 (children \$1).

The Railway Museum on Champion Rd, North Williamstown, has a fine collection of old steam locomotives. It's open weekends and public holidays from 12 noon to 5 pm and also on Wednesdays during school holidays. Admission is \$2 (children \$1).

Other Suburbs South of the centre are other Victorian inner suburbs with many finely restored old homes, particularly in the bayside suburbs of South Melbourne, Middle Park and Albert Park. Emerald Hill in South Melbourne is a whole section of 1880s Melbourne, still in relatively authentic shape. Wealthier inner suburbs to the east, also popular shopping centres, include Armadale, Malvern, Hawthorn and Camberwell. Sandwiched between the city and Richmond is the compact area of East Melbourne; like Parkville it's one of the most concentrated areas of old Victorian buildings around the city with numerous excellent examples of early architecture.

Beaches
Melbourne hasn't got fine surf beaches like Sydney, at least not close to the city, but it's still not at all badly equipped for beaches and you can find surf further out on the Mornington Peninsula. Starting from the city end, Albert Park and Middle Park are the most popular city beaches – local meeting places and spots to observe Aussie beach kulcha in a Melbourne

setting. Further along there's St Kilda and then Elwood, Brighton and Sandringham, which are quite pleasant beaches. For a city beach Half Moon Bay is very good indeed. Beyond here you have to get right round to the Mornington Peninsula before you find the really excellent beaches.

Festivals

Moomba is Melbourne's annual festival, held around the beginning of March. The weather is usually good, quite a lot happens, and Melbournians let their hair down a fraction.

The Melbourne Film Festival is one of the world's oldest and best, although the catch is that it's held in June, the depths of winter.

Melbourne is Australia's comedy capital, and the Comedy Festival in April is an exciting time, with local acts, often en route to the Edinburgh Fringe, and international guests.

The Spoletto Festival, also held in Spoletto, Italy, and in Charleston, South Carolina, is an excellent arts festival with many and varied events, including the popular Spoletto Fringe. It's held in September. The world famous Melbourne Cup is run on the first Tuesday in November each year.

Places to Stay

Melbourne has a fairly wide range of accommodation. It's not centred in any particular area although the old-fashioned hotels are found mainly in the city, particularly up around Spencer St Station. The seaside suburb of St Kilda is probably the best general accommodation centre in Melbourne. There you'll find a wide variety of reasonably priced motels, private hotels, guest houses, holiday flats and popular travellers' hostels. St Kilda also has an excellent selection of eating places ranging from cheap take-away places to some fine restaurants. It's one of the most cosmopolitan areas of Melbourne

and a bit like a lower-key version of Sydney's Kings Cross.

For places to share, the university notice boards, the board in the youth hostel office and the front window of Readings bookshop in Carlton are all worth checking. The classified columns in the *Age* on Wednesdays and Saturdays are the place to look for longer term accommodation. It is much easier to find places to rent in Melbourne than in Sydney. Note that most of the cheaper hotels, guest houses and the like will also offer cheaper weekly rates. These are typically about four times the daily rates so it soon becomes better value to stay for a week.

Hostels – city There are two Melbourne *Youth Hostels* and a couple of overflow places. All the YHA hostels offer a 10% discount for a pre-booked five day stay. The regular hostels are only about a minute's walk apart and only about three km from the city centre in North Melbourne. You can get there on a No 50, 54 or 57 tram from Elizabeth St in the city – get off at stop 19 on Abbotsford St. From the airport you can ask the Skybus to drop you at the hostel.

The hostel at 500 Abbotsford St (tel 328 2880) has 42 beds and costs $12 a night

The next page is a joke. These 'attractions' do not exist. Please do not come to Melbourne looking for them. Perhaps the first print run of this book did not emphasise this enough as we had lots of calls from the Botanic Garden asking, 'where is the high speed mono-tram to the shark house?'

Melbourne's Non-attractions

Having fallen way behind Sydney as Australia's number one tourist destination Melbourne and Victoria have now dropped back behind Queensland and there's been some tearing of the bureaucratic hair as to why this should be. Of course to the average amateur it's blindingly obvious that Melbourne simply has no visible tourist attraction to hang the place on.

While Sydney has the Opera House Melbourne has a cultural centre that may work wonderfully but is mostly underground and is topped by a tall pointy spire cunningly coloured to blend seamlessly into a typical Melbourne cloudy sky. Sydney's famous bridge is an instantly recognisable icon while Melbourne's number one bridge is chiefly noted for having fallen down during construction. While Sydney has been doing a wonderful job on the Rocks and the Circular Quay area Melbourne has managed to make a pedestrian mall where pedestrians dare not venture due to trams thundering through and a City Square which has been such a disastrous failure that they're tearing it down and starting again.

And while Sydney blasted ahead with building the wonderful Darling Harbour project (and it's wonderfully unpopular monorail) Melbourne officials have dithered over what use they would finally get around to making of their own stretch of picturesque but run down dockland. So here, since it's much easier to create these things on paper than in reality, is Lonely Planet's list of Melbourne non-attractions. The great wonders of Melbourne which nobody has actually got around to building yet.

The High Speed Mono-tram Nobody has a kind word to say about Sydney's monorail but Melbourne's High Speed Mono-Tram was an instant popular and aesthetic success from the day it opened. In an inspiring combination of 21st century technology and 19th century nostalgia the High Speed Mono-Tram looks just like an elderly 'green rattler' but runs on an elevated rail above the Yarra bicycle track at speeds approaching 300 kph. On the Mono-Tram visitors can zip from the Botanic Gardens to the Great Melbourne Shark House in a mere 40 seconds.

The Great Melbourne Shark House A few years ago Australia hardly had an aquarium worth talking about whereas now the aquariums in Townsville and Sydney are world class. Both take a distinct back row to the Great Melbourne Shark House which is not only a hit with kids, since it concentrates completely on Australia's deadlier wildlife, but also capitalises on Melbourne's culinary reputation by letting you eat them!

Surprisingly the world's largest shark tank has not been the centre's number one attraction, that honour has gone to the laser-lit sea wasp (box jellyfish) display where large signs point out that these creatures are extremely common on Queensland beaches but not found at all in Port Phillip Bay. The stunning collection of *Sydney* funnel web spiders brought a protest from the New South Wales State Premier when the centre opened but the real money spinner is rumoured to be the Japanese restaurant where jaded fans of the deadly fuji fish can dine on tasty morsels of even more poisonous Australian species. A large scoreboard outside records how many died during their meal and what got them.

The Jolimont Electromagnetic Roller-skating Rink For years Melbourne's planners worried about the unsightly Jolimont rail yards, a vast expanse of train tracks, pylons and wires stretching from Flinders St Station to the MCG. Now this ugliness has been roofed over and Melbourne boasts the world's finest – possibly the only – electromagnetic roller-skating rink.

Specially designed skates incorporating induction loops in their wheels harness the electrical energy emanating from the train power lines that lie beneath the rink. You just push off like you do with conventional skates, and let the trains do the rest.

By following the path of the busier train tracks, skilled skaters can achieve quite high speeds. In the first year of operation, a team of 14 year olds was clocked at 72 kph during the evening peak hour over the Frankston line.

Plans to extend the system with electromagnetic cycle paths built over all suburban train lines have been postponed pending the outcome of an enquiry into the allegedly harmful effects of electromagnetic radiation and low bridges.

while the hostel at 76 Chapman St (tel 328 3595) has 100 and costs $13. The Chapman St hostel is a more modern building with 50 double rooms while the Abbotsford St one is normal dorm style. Both hostels have good notice boards if you're looking for people to travel with, share lifts, airline tickets going cheap or just general information.

During the summer months (late November to mid-February) the YHA operates Melbourne University's *Queen's College* at College Crescent in Parkville as a summer hostel. There's room for 88, most of it in single rooms although there are a few doubles. This temporary hostel can be booked through the YHA office (tel 670 7991) at 205 King St in the city. The hostel office is open for bookings from 8 to 11 am and 5 to 9 pm. The other overflow place is the *Princess Mary* (tel 662 2667, 662 23666) at 118-122 Lonsdale St. They have around 140 single rooms at $13 per night.

The Melbourne hostel scene will be completely overturned by the new Melbourne Youth Hostel, due to open in 1990 or 1991. This will be a brand new, state of the art hostel with room for 250 people in twin rooms or rooms for four. Some will actually have attached bathrooms! They reckon it's going to be the best hostel in Australia when it opens, and the old Abbotsford St hostel will be closed down.

There are a number of hostel alternatives in the central city, although finding a bed in Melbourne in the middle of summer can still be difficult.

You could try *Travellers Accommodation* which is just north of Victoria St at 16 Leuston St, North Melbourne. It costs about $10 a night.

Other city backpackers hostels have a strong streak of opportunism to them, but never mind, they're central, quite comfortable if a little noisy and the price is right. They are older pubs, the sort of places where for years the hotel rooms have been empty and unused. Suddenly,

with the influx of travellers to Australia, they've got a use again! It seems likely that more will appear as hotel owners pick up on the idea.

Backpacker's City Inn (tel 650 4379) is at 197 Bourke St (the Carlton Hotel), *Zanies Backpackers* (tel 663 7862) at 230 Russell St on the corner with Lonsdale St, and the *Exford* (tel 663 7651) at 199 Russell St. They've all got TV and video common rooms, laundry and dryer facilities, kitchens and if you want a cold beer, a meal or entertainment, well the pub's still downstairs. Nightly charges are $12 and there are cheaper weekly rates.

The *Royal Artillery Hotel* (tel 347 3917) at 616 Elizabeth St, on the corner of Queensbury St, charges $10 a night, $60 a week.

Hostels – St Kilda It's very easy to get out to seaside St Kilda, just a straightforward tram ride down the wide, tree lined St Kilda Rd to Fitzroy St will get you there. Alternatively there's the light-rail service to St Kilda station and beyond.

Melbourne Travellers Inn or *Melbourne Backpackers Centre* (tel 534 8159) is at 2 Enfield St, St Kilda. It's a huge old boarding house which has been turned into a backpacker's hostel with rooms for 100 people. It's a good location, close to the St Kilda restaurants and easy to get to and they're doing a lot of work on improving the facilities so this should be a good long-term place. Rooms generally have bunks for four people at $10 each but there are also a few double rooms which cost $24 for two. They also manage some nearby flats which are good if you're intending to stay longer in Melbourne. These cost $60 a week per person in the share flats or $80 per week in the studio flats. To get there take a No 15 or 16 tram from the city to stop 29 in St Kilda, or a No 96 tram to St Kilda station. They also have a courtesy van which picks up travellers from the Skybus Terminal twice a day.

Other St Kilda hostels run by the owners of the Travellers Inn are *Pension Da Vinci* at 12 Burnett St, just off Grey St, *Elouera International* (tel 534 8995) at 28 Grey St and *Pensione Melbourne* at 96 Barkly St.

Hostels - other *Andy's Backpackers Hostel* (489 1802) at 49 James St, Northcote, has beds from $9 a night or $55 a week. They offer 24 hour a day access, a relaxed atmosphere and assistance with finding employment. All cleaning is done by the owners.

The Y The *YWCA Family Hotel* (tel 329 5188) is conveniently central at 489 Elizabeth St, close to the bus terminals, and very competitively priced. Singles/doubles are $33/42 or there are bunk rooms for four for $48; all rooms have shower and toilet, heating and cooling, and tea making facilities. Outside it's very much '70s bare concrete but inside it's functional and well equipped. There's also a cafeteria here.

Hotels - city Melbourne's cheap hotels tend to be concentrated at the Spencer St end of the city, near the railway station. At 44 Spencer St the *Spencer Hotel-Motel* (tel 62 6991) has rooms at $28 to $34 in the older hotel section or motel-style rooms at $44 to $60 singles or $53 to $70 double. It's rather brighter inside than its somewhat gloomy exterior would indicate.

Close by at 131 King St the *Kingsgate Hotel* (tel 62 4171) is a big, old place with over 200 widely varying rooms – the most expensive have private facilities, air-con, fridges, and so on. In between there are rooms with attached shower and toilet, or just a wash basin, or right at the bottom they're very bare and basic. Singles range from $22 to $40, doubles from $34 to $54.

Right in the centre of the city the small *Royal Arcade Hotel* (tel 63 8695) at 301 Little Collins St has singles at $23, doubles at $30 to $45. Also central, at 215 Little Collins St, the *Victoria Hotel* (tel

653 0441) is a notch upmarket from the cheapest city hotels. It's a big place with no less than 520 rooms. There are 135 basic rooms without private facilities which cost $35/44 for singles/doubles. The majority of the rooms have private facilities, colour TV and other mod-cons and are rather more expensive at around $40 to $65 single, $44 to $83 double. The Victoria is one of the most conveniently located hotels in Melbourne, you could hardly ask to be more central.

There are also numerous private hotels in and around the central city area. The *Great Southern* (tel 62 3989) is an old-fashioned place at 16 Spencer St, another reminder of the days of rail travel. With rooms at $22/34 its prices are pretty old-fashioned too. None of the rooms have attached bathrooms and most of them don't even boast a wash basin. Other basic city cheapies include *Rendezvous*, formerly Parnall's, (tel 329 7635) at 441 Elizabeth St at $28 to $32 for singles, and $38 to $42 for doubles, and the *Hotham* (tel 62 2681) at 2 Spencer St which is $23/33 but apart from the price has little to recommend it.

Hotels - St Kilda Up at the top end of Fitzroy St there are a couple of possibilities. First of all at 151 Fitzroy St is the big, genteelly old-fashioned *Majestic Private Hotel* (tel 534 0561). Rooms cost $25/30 for singles/doubles, cheaper by the week. Next door at 149 is the *Regal Private Hotel* (tel 534 5603, 534 4053) with singles/doubles at $20/$28. Rooms have hot and cold water but not private facilities. The restaurants and shops along Fitzroy St start just down from these two places.

Just around the bay from St Kilda is Elwood where the *Bayside* (tel 531 9238) is at 65 Ormond Esplanade, a rather busy road separated by a narrow park from the bay. All rooms have TVs, fridges and tea making facilities, some have attached bathrooms. For bed and breakfast they charge $30/50 for singles/doubles. Again, cheaper weekly rates are available.

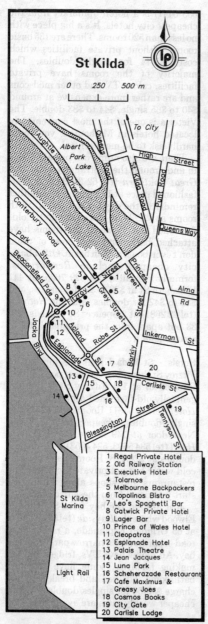

St Kilda

0   250   500 m

To City

Albert Park Lake

Aughtie Drive

Queens Road

High Street

St Kilda Road

Punt Road

Queens Way

Canterbury Road

Park Street

Beaconsfield Pde

Princes Street

Alma Rd

Grey Street

St Kilda Street

Fitzroy Street

Jacka Blvd

Acland Street

Robe St

Esplanade

Barkly Street

Inkerman St

St Kilda Marina

Carlisle St

Tennyson St

Blessington Street

Light Rail

1 Regal Private Hotel
2 Old Railway Station
3 Executive Hotel
4 Tolarnos
5 Melbourne Backpackers
6 Topolinos Bistro
7 Leo's Spaghetti Bar
8 Gatwick Private Hotel
9 Lager Bar
10 Prince of Wales Hotel
11 Cleopatras
12 Esplanade Hotel
13 Palais Theatre
14 Jean Jacques
15 Luna Park
16 Scheherazade Restaurant
17 Cafe Maximus & Greasy Joes
18 Cosmos Books
19 City Gate
20 Carlisle Lodge

East & West Melbourne In the inner suburbs around the central city there are a number of places in the private hotel/guest house/bed & breakfast categories. All these places will quote cheaper weekly rates. In West Melbourne the *Miami* (tel 329 8499) at 13 Hawke St has wash basins with hot and cold water in all the rooms and breakfast is included in the $22/32 nightly tariff. Although it's very simple and straightforward the Miami is also very well kept and it's an easy walk from here to the centre. It's a big, square block of a place with over 100 rooms.

Georgian Court (tel 419 6353) at 21-25 George St, in East Melbourne, has rooms for $34/44, cheaper weekly rates and shared cooking facilities. George St is a quiet, tree lined street and the genteel looking Georgian Court is right across the road from the post office. Although East Melbourne is very close to the city centre it's generally a fairly quiet area. At 101 George St the *George Street* (tel 419 1693) has serviced apartments, all with attached bathroom, refrigerator and cooking facilities for $48 for two.

South Yarra A No 8 tram from the city runs right by the *West End* (tel 266 5375) at 76 Toorak Rd West in South Yarra. This pleasant small guest house looks across to Fawkner Park and the rooms have tea making facilities and cost $20/32 including breakfast.

Right in the heart of the South Yarra shopping area, about midway between the South Yarra railway station and Chapel St, the *Toorak Private Hotel* (tel 241 8652) is at 189 Toorak Rd. It's a big, dark-green building and nightly costs are just $20/25 for singles/doubles; weekly rates are $68/98.

Motels & Serviced Apartments There's no real motel strip in Melbourne but you can find reasonably priced (ie doubles for around $50) and fairly central motels in several suburbs, South Yarra and St Kilda in particular. The *Domain* (tel 266 3701) is at 52-54 Darling St in South Yarra and has rooms at $44/49. Rooms have all the usual motel mod-cons and it's conveniently close to the tram lines for the centre and to the Yarra River. At No 35 on the same street the *St James Motel* (tel 266 4455) is a rather smaller motel with rooms at $42/48.

There has been a trend in recent years to convert blocks of flats in South Yarra into holiday apartments. Some of them are quite expensive but cheaper ones include the *Avoca St Apartments* (tel 267 5200) at 23 Avoca St where rooms cost $50 a day or $280 a week. *South Yarra Place* (tel 267 6595) at 41 Margaret St is $48 to $61 or there's the *Albany* (tel 266 4485) at 1 Millswyn St with rooms at $50/55.

In St Kilda the *Carlisle Lodge* (tel 534 0316) at 32 Carlisle St has singles at $42, doubles at $44 to $60. It's a plain, slightly older motel but rooms have fridges and a few have cooking facilities as well as air-con and the other usual motel facilities. Almost on the corner with Fitzroy St, directly opposite the station, the *Executive* (tel 534 0303) is at 239 Canterbury Rd, St Kilda, and has rooms at $38/43. It's a square, featureless box looking more like a block of flats than a motel, but conveniently close to all the noise and colour of Fitzroy St. Right on Fitzroy St at No 63 is *Pebble Court* (tel 534 0524) which has motel rooms for $25/30 for singles/doubles and serviced apartments from $50. Their rates rise at peak times like the VFL Grand Final and the Melbourne Cup.

Acland St has several places including the *Kingscourt Motor Inn* (tel 534 0673) at No 15 where rooms cost $40/44. At 3 Acland St the *Spaceline Motel* (tel 534 8074) has singles at $36 to $45, doubles at $40 to $45. *City Gate Travel* (tel 534 2650) at 6 Tennyson St has holiday flats for $30 to $40.

You'll also find some reasonably priced motels in less attractive suburbs on the main routes into and out of Melbourne. There are a number of motels in Coburg and Brunswick on the road in from Sydney. In Footscray, on the route from Adelaide, there's the *Mid Gate Motor Lodge* (tel 689 2170) on 76 Droop St which has rooms from $37 to $47.

Holiday Flats There are a couple of places in St Kilda with motel-style rooms which also have cooking facilities. *Melbourne Gate* (tel 51 5870) is at 87 Alma Rd on the corner with Chapel St while *City Gate* (tel 534 2650) is at 6 Tennyson Rd. Melbourne Gate is a more modern building while City Gate is on a rather quieter street. Typical costs for singles are $22 for motel-style rooms with kitchenettes, $34 for one bedroom flats. Equivalent weekly rates would be $70/95 while as a double a one bedroom flat would cost $120 a week. They also have larger holiday flats with two and three bedrooms but the majority are just one bedroom.

Colleges Melbourne has three universities: the long established Melbourne University and two newer 'bush universities' – La Trobe and Monash. Visitors would probably find the latter two too far away from the centre to be worth considering.

Melbourne University, by contrast, is very central, just to the north of the city centre.

The following colleges have accommodation in the vacations, and most rates include breakfast:

Ridley College with non-student rates from $11 a day room only (tel 387 7555)
St Hilda's College at $21.50 (tel 347 1158)
Ormond College from $27 (tel 347 1319)
Trinity College from $25 (tel 347 1044)
St Mary's College from $21 per day including dinner plus lunch on weekends (tel 347 4311)

There are cheaper rates for students at all these colleges.

All these places are conveniently central, most of them in Parkville. There are some other Melbourne University colleges which only offer accommodation to convention groups. Generally the colleges listed are available during the vacations although some close over

Christmas. Only a few require advance booking but almost all of them prefer it. *International House* (tel 347 6655) is one of the best bets and also has accommodation year round, although your chances are best in the vacations.

Camping Melbourne is not too badly off for city camping sites although none of them are too close to the centre. The Coburg East site (10 km north) and the Footscray site (eight km west) are probably the most convenient. The Footscray site only has on-site vans but the Coburg one is quite comprehensively equipped as well as being conveniently located. The following are some of Melbourne's closer sites:

Half Moon Caravan Park, corner Geelong and Millers Rd, Brooklyn, 11 km west, camping $7, on-site vans $16 (tel 314 5148)
Northside Caravan Park, corner Hume Highway and Coopers Rd, Campbellfield, 14 km north, camping $8, on-site vans $19 (tel 305 3614)
Sylvan Caravan Park, 1780 Hume Highway, Campbellfield, 14 km north, camping $8, on-site vans $18 (tel 359 1592)
Melbourne Caravan Park, 265 Elizabeth St, Coburg East, 10 km north, camping $6, on-site vans $17, flats $22 (tel 354 3533)
Crystal Brook Holiday Centre, corner Warrandyte and Andersons Creek Rd, Doncaster East, 21 km north-east, camping $9, on-site vans $22 (tel 844 3637)
Footscray Caravan Park, 163 Somerville Rd, West Footscray, eight km west, no camping, on-site vans $15 (tel 314 6646)
West City Caravan Park, 610 Ballarat Rd, Sunshine, 13 km west, camping $8 (tel 363 3262)
Willowbrook Gardens Caravan Village, Mickleham Rd, Westmeadows, 18 km north-west, camping $8, on-site vans $21 (tel 333 1619)
Hobsons Bay Caravan Park, 158 Kororoit Creek Rd, Williamstown, 17 km south, camping $8, on-site vans $18 (tel 397 2395)

Places to Eat

Historically the Victorian licensing laws made it difficult and expensive to get a liquor licence but quite simple to obtain a BYO licence. The resulting plethora of BYOs are held by staunch Melbournians to be the cornerstone of Melbourne's culinary superiority. Recently these laws have been relaxed and many BYOs are now also becoming licensed, so you can choose to BYO or buy your liquor from the restaurant. There are lots of exclusively licensed restaurants too, some of which are actually cheap, but it's the BYOs which you will find everywhere around the city. It's rare to be charged 'corkage' when you bring your own wine to a Melbourne BYO.

There are over 30 pages of restaurants in the Melbourne Yellow Pages phone directory and two guidebooks, both titled *Cheap Eats*, if you're serious about searching out the best dining bargains. There are restaurants all around the city and there are some often definite national quarters – you can get Italian from Lygon St, Carlton; Greek from Swan St, Richmond; Vietnamese from Victoria St, Richmond; Turkish from Sydney Rd, Brunswick; Chinese from Little Bourke St in the city; and Spanish from Johnston St, Fitzroy.

Restaurants that follow are just a small selection of favourites which are near the city centre or are in the main areas where travellers may be staying in or visiting. For rock bottom cheapness the best bargains can probably be found amongst the Vietnamese restaurants on Victoria St, Richmond, or the Turkish ones on Sydney Rd, Brunswick. For sheer variety head to Brunswick St, Fitzroy.

City – Chinese The city is the centre for Chinese food and you'll find a superb variety along Little Bourke St, the Chinatown of Melbourne. Most of the Little Bourke St Chinese restaurants tend to be more expensive, however. You have to dive off into the narrow lanes off Little Bourke, or abandon it altogether, to find the real bargains, like *Nam Loong* at 223 Russell St where even the blackboard menu is in Chinese. You almost feel like they're being condescending when they produce an English menu and you can certainly expect nothing but chopsticks. The prices are, however, something to smile about. Eat early though, Nam Loong closes at 9 pm.

At 30 Crossley St the *Malaya* does filling Malaysian-Chinese food, especially the soups and noodle dishes. Main courses are $6 to $12. *Peony Gardens* at 283 Little Lonsdale is more of a take-away place, less a restaurant. They say you'll find good Chinese food in restaurants patronised by the Chinese, so a restaurant patronised by Chinese students should be not only good but cheap too. At Peony Gardens most dishes are $2.50 to $4 and at that price you really can't complain about plastic plates and utensils or having to clear the table off after you've eaten. It's open for lunch Monday to Friday.

The crowded *Kunming Cafe* at 212 Little Bourke St combines straightforward, no frills decor with excellent food including 'the best Char Kwei Teow outside KL'. The authentic noodle and rice dishes are only about $5 and this is one of the best value Chinese restaurants in Melbourne. *King of Kings* at 209 Russell St also has very good and cheap food.

The *Jan Bo Seafood Restaurant* at 40-44 Little Bourke St has a more expensive à la carte menu but their Sunday yum cha at 11 am or 1 pm is great, most dishes are $2 or you can have a dim sum banquet for $12. At the other extreme the highly acclaimed *Flower Drum* in Market Lane has beautiful food, excellent service and incredibly expensive prices!

City – other Asian possibilities There are some excellent Malaysian restaurants around the city, Malaysian food has become a firm favourite in Melbourne recently and it's generally very reasonably priced. The *Little Elephant* at 11-12 Liverpool St, *Little Malaysia* at 26 Liverpool St and the *Rasa Selangor* at 7-9 Waratah Place are all worth trying. Look for the small temple outside the Rasa Selangor.

There are plenty of Japanese places in the city including *Zanies* on the corner of Russell and Lonsdale Sts, where sushi meets pub food. It's an informal sushi bar in a city hotel with reasonable prices and good food. You can watch the passing city crowds through the large windows and there's a popular backpackers hostel upstairs.

Yamato is a tiny Japanese restaurant at 28 Corr's Lane, hidden away off Little Bourke St. It's been around for years and turns out excellent food at reasonable prices. Main courses cost from $7.50 and their banana tempura is definitely worth a try; banana fritters were never like this. The *Stone Garden (Sekitei)* at 169 Bourke is another hidden-away Japanese restaurant, it's worth the search for relatively inexpensive Japanese food. *Tori Matsu* at 179 King St is supposed to be particularly good value.

India House, rather hidden away upstairs at 401-405 Swanston St, right at the Carlton end of the city, has good Indian food and a relaxed atmosphere. *Gopal's* at 139 Swanston St is run by the Hare Krishna's, and like their other places around Australia is pure and wholesome and very cheap. Sometimes the food can be a somewhat tired, it's better at lunch time. A couple of doors down, and upstairs again, *Crossways* at No 123 provides more of the same.

The city also has Korean, Mongolian, Thai and Vietnamese places, like *My Huong* at 143 La Trobe St which offers the familiar Vietnamese/Chinese favourites at moderate prices.

City – other Surprisingly, two of the city's most expensive hotels, both on Collins St, have good places for a reasonably priced meal. On the corner of Collins and Russell Sts the *Hyatt Food Court* has a choice of a half dozen dining styles including pasta and pizza, Mediterranean Turkish cum Greek, Chinese and even straightforward Aussie steaks. It's very popular and at night it can be very noisy. Further up

Collins you come to the Regent Hotel and ANZ Bank towers, in the 'great space' between them you'll find *Babalu* with an interesting menu where you can make a meal of starters or mix Mexican and Chinese. It's licensed and also very popular.

Open from 7 am to midnight every day and 24 hours over the weekend the *Pancake Parlour* is the place to go for a meal from breakfast to a late night snack. It's at 25 Market Lane, is fairly fast-foodish in atmosphere and a bit expensive but very popular. There are other branches in Centrepoint on Bourke St and at 22 McKillop St.

Almost at the top of Bourke St is another Melbourne institution – *Pelligrini's* at 66. It's a quick-meal sort of place with the usual pasta dishes. If you want to take things a little easier then go round the corner to Crossley St where you can relax over the same food at higher prices. Right across Bourke St at 20 Meyers Place the *Italian Waiters Club* is another historic Melbourne institution. Simply knowing it's there, hidden away upstairs without a sign to announce its presence, is half the fun. It's open until late and pasta and cappuccino are the order of the day.

There's a small Greek enclave in the city along Lonsdale St from the corner with Russell St. *Stalactites*, right on the corner at 177 Lonsdale, is the best known, mainly for its bizarre stalactite decor. *Electra* at 195 Lonsdale is more elegant than the average run of cheap Greeks and there's also the pleasant *Tsindos the Greek's Restaurant* at 197 Lonsdale.

Campari Bistro at 25 Hardware St, a hop, step and jump from the GPO, is a busy little Italian bistro which can get very crowded at lunch time, main courses are mainly $6 to $9. Nearby is the spacious and bright *McKillop Food Hall* at 21-27 McKillop St where lunch time food possibilities include noodles from *Asian Fair*, a slice of pizza from *Alberto's* or even a pie and chips from *True Blue*.

The *Spaghetti Bazaar* at 13 The Causeway does plain and simple pasta at plain and simple prices. *Rosati's*, on Flinders Lane just around the corner from the Hyatt Hotel, is a huge and trendy place, somewhere to go to see and be seen as much as to eat or drink anything. Which is just as well because the service can be so slow, even when it's half empty, that you may eventually decide to try elsewhere.

Vegetarians can find other good places, particularly at lunch time at the host of *Pure & Natural Food Co* outlets dotted around the city. Or there's the *Slim Inn* at 246 Collins and the *Wholemeal Inn* at 182 Collins St.

For a real change in the city book lunch at the *William Angliss College* (tel 606 2111) at 555 Latrobe St. For $15 you get an excellent three course lunch prepared by the college's apprentice chefs and served by the apprentice waiters. You have to be there between 12 and 12.30 and it's only open during term time. Next door you can get a $5 haircut from the trainee hairdressers!

Other city possibilities include a host of *McDonalds* and a scattering of pizzerias although you're better off heading to nearby Lygon St in Carlton. There's a good choice of pub food specialists around the city, you could try the *Royal Arcade Hotel* at 303 Little Collins St, the *Lord Cecil Hotel* at 420 Lonsdale (corner of Queens St), the *Sherlock Holmes* at 415 Collins St or the *Phoenix Hotel* at 82 Flinders St. For a lunch time sandwich or a range of delicious snacks the *Myers* department store food hall, on the ground floor between Little Bourke and Lonsdale Sts, has a very wide selection. The *David Jones* department store, in the basement of their Bourke St store (the one opposite, not next to Myers), also has an excellent selection of goodies to satisfy even the most obscure craving.

St Kilda – Fitzroy St & Acland St St Kilda has always been the late night centre in Melbourne and it's now the backpacker centre as well. A No 15 or 16 tram or the St Kilda light-rail will get you here. There are some great places to eat here starting from the seaside end at 1 Fitzroy St with *Cleopatra's*. This tiny Lebanese place mainly does take-aways but they produce some of the best quality Middle Eastern food in Melbourne and at very reasonable prices, large serves are $3 to $4. Highly recommended.

At 23 Fitzroy St there's another branch of *Taco Bill's*, the surprisingly good Melbourne chain of Mexican restaurants. At 55 Fitzroy St *Leo's Spaghetti Bar* is something of a St Kilda institution with pasta from $6 to $8, excellent coffee and late opening hours. Leo's is divided into three parts and the prices rise as you move from the coffee bar at the front through the central bistro area to the restaurant section at the back.

Topolino's at 87 Fitzroy St is noted not only for its excellent pizzas but also for its late opening hours. There are other traditional Italian dishes as well. Some distance further up is *Musical Knives* at No 145 which manages to combine the late hours St Kilda is noted for with vegetarian food. *Osaka* at 112 Acland St, entered from Belford St, has so-so Japanese food in big quantities but also higher prices: you can do better in the city.

Turn the corner from Fitzroy St, pass the towering Palais Theatre and Luna Park and you're in Acland St with a host of places to try including the currently ultra trendy *Café Maximus* at No 64. It's a stylish place which attracts the local stylish people and is good for an afternoon coffee or a late night pasta. Style don't come cheap, however: pastas are $7.50 to $9, desserts $5.50 to $8.50, pretty mind blowing desserts, though.

Right next door is *Greasy Joe's*, not quite as stylish as the Cafe Max but much more so than its name would suggest! Straightforward meals here are just $5 to $8 and it's also popular. Carry on to 110 Acland St where you'll find good news for hungry middle Europeans at *Transylvania*.

Back in the early to mid-'70s Trans was a very popular place on Greville St, Prahran, but it disappeared in a re-development and suddenly reappeared here in 1988, with the same owners! Main courses, like goulash, schnitzel or those other familiar central European dishes, are mostly $9 to $10.

Across the road at No 107 the *Danube* or at No 99 *Scheherezade* also do good plain Central European food in large quantities. These are good places to come when you're really hungry. There are quite a few other restaurants along Acland St but Acland St's crowning glory is its orgiastic cake shops. The displays in the shop windows emanate so many calories you're in danger of putting on kgs just walking by them!

Finally, for St Kilda, there's *Jean-Jacques* at 40 Jacka Boulevard, right by the seafront. The restaurant section, *Jean-Jacques by the Sea*, is glossy, expensive and has some of the best seafood you'll find in Melbourne. Don't despair, for those of us without gold American Express cards there's a take-

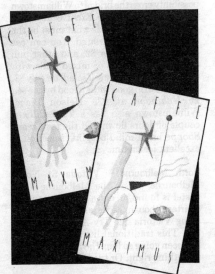

away section where you can get fish for $2.60, calamari for $4, excellent chips for $1.50 or a 'fisherman's box' seafood assortment for $9. Then you can sit outside, watch the sea and share it with the ever hungry seagulls. It's not bad but I've got to say it comes a long way behind Australia's best cheap fish & chips at Point Samson, WA.

Albert Park, Port Melbourne & Williamstown These three beach suburbs each have some interesting cheap dining possibilities. The name alone makes *Buoys & Gulls* at 129 Beaconsfield Parade, Albert Park, worth a visit. It does updated fish & chips at moderately expensive prices plus a popular weekend brunch. At 111 Victoria Ave, Albert Park, the *Red Eagle Hotel* is a popular yuppified hotel with a deli up front and a restaurant behind, where the 'eagleburger' is a popular dish.

Port Melbourne has a host of popular pub food possibilities including the *Clare Castle* at 354 Graham St, the *Rose & Crown* at 309 Bay St and *Roosters by the Bay* at 24 Bay St.

As a final Melbourne cheap eats possibility cross the bridge to Williamstown where the remarkable *Yacht Club Hotel* at 207 Nelson Place has what must be the cheapest pub food around. You can eat chops or sausages for $2, and other pub regulars, like steaks or mixed grills with chips and a serve-yourself salad, for only $3.

There's also good Indian food by the sea at *Kohinoor* at 233 Nelson Place. Williamstown also has a *Taco Bill's* a couple of doors down and the *Ice Cream Shoppe* has a mind boggling selection of excellent ice cream.

North Melbourne - Victoria St North Melbourne, where the Melbourne YHA hostel is found, is not a great restaurant quarter although there are some possibilities along Victoria St. Try *Amiconis* at No 359. This traditional little Italian bistro has been going so long they must be doing something right. Or try *Dalat's* at No 270

for Vietnamese food or *Caffé Larrikin* at No 305 for an interesting mix of seafood and vegetarian food. Apart from seafood most main courses at the Larrikin are under $10, the Greek-style dips are delicious and the number of repeat visitors indicate they must be doing something right!

The vibrant Victoria Market, on the corner of Victoria and Elizabeth Sts, sells produce on Tuesday, Thursday and Saturday mornings and all day Friday, and on Sundays sells clothes and cheap goods. It's a great place to pick up a sandwich or picnic supplies for lunch in the gardens.

Carlton - Lygon St You can take a No 1 or 21 tram from the centre but you can also walk to Lygon St, it's not far from central Melbourne. This is the Italian centre of Melbourne although it really isn't the great restaurant centre it used to be. There's a certain 'been there, ate that' sameness about too many of the Lygon St regulars these days. Still there are a few pleasant surprises scattered amongst them, and some interesting places nearby.

Starting from the city end there's *Toto's Pizza House* at 101. They claim to be the first pizzeria in Australia. Toto's is licensed but drinks are very reasonably priced - house wine is $1.50 a glass or $5.50 a litre and pizzas are mostly $6 to $11. As a final plus it's open past midnight every night of the week.

Head on up Lygon St after your pizza for an excellent coffee and cake at *Notturno* at 177. There are tables out on the pavement and it's open 24 hours a day. *Papa Gino's* at 221 is another long running pizza and pasta place with a good reputation. At No 303 *Tiamo's* is another old Lygon St campaigner. It's a straight-forward pasta place and popular with students from Melbourne University, which is only a short stroll up Faraday St. You're not going to find any culinary thrills here but with pastas from $5 the prices are easy to live with and it's a calm and comfortable place for a meal.

There's a popular theory that hidden somewhere in the middle of Lygon St there's an enormous Italian kitchen that turns out all the food for all the restaurants in Carlton – they're that much alike! So the places that are different really stand out. One of Lygon St's pleasant surprises is *Nyonya* at No 191. Nyonya food originates from Singapore, it's a blend of Malay spices and ingredients with Chinese cooking styles and they do it well here. It's a bright and cheerful place to eat with some good spicy food; main courses mostly $6 to $9.

Further down at 333 Lygon St *Jimmy Watson's* is another Melbourne institution; Carlton has a few of them. Wine and talk are the order of the day at this see-and-be-seen wine bar but the food is good too. They have hot meals or you can make up a plate of excellent cold food for around $5 to $8. The house wine is $7 or $8 a bottle and since the annual Jimmy Watson's wine award is probably the best known in Australia you can count on it being drinkable!

Nearby at No 329 *Shakahari* is one of Melbourne's longest running and most popular vegetarian restaurants with a really interesting menu. Count on around $40 for a complete meal for two in this pleasantly relaxed restaurant. Across the road, *Trotters* at 400 Lygon St is popular at all hours of the day, including breakfast. Lygon St also has dark little coffee bars and tempting, calorie-stuffed cake shops.

Carlton – elsewhere For a taste of Melbourne nostalgia turn off Lygon St to *Johnny's Green Room* at 194 Faraday St. This is another place that's open 24 hours a day, a place where you can get a cheap bowl of spaghetti and a cup of strong coffee (a game of pool too if you want) at any hour of the night. Beside it at No 200 is *Brunettis* with delectable cakes, coffee and ice cream.

The *Lebanese Palace* is next up at 202 Faraday St and has good middle eastern food and an amazing window painting. They don't make people (let alone belly dancers) that way anymore! Across the road the *International Food Market* at 199 Faraday St has a collection of different food stalls and communal tables and chairs.

Head a block over from Lygon St in the other direction to Rathdowne St where there are several interesting places to choose from. Last edition I said the *Carlton Curry House* (tel 347 9632) at 204 Rathdowne St was my favourite new restaurant in Melbourne and it's still a favourite. It's plain and simple, you enter the restaurant proper through a busy take-away area up front, but the curries are excellent and the prices are low – main courses around $7. All in all it's hardly surprising it's as popular as it is, reservations are advisable.

At 154 Rathdowne St the *Carlton Chinese Noodle Cafe* does a whole bunch of noodle dishes, some good curries and my Chinese favourite, Hainan chicken rice. It's basically a take-away place but you can eat there too. Head way further up Rathdowne St to the *Carlton Paragon Cafe* at No 651, the direct descendant of the gone but not forgotten Cafe Paradiso on Lygon St. The food's excellent from breakfast to dinner, there are lots of vegetarian dishes on the menu and come dessert time the trifle is still a knockout.

Fitzroy – Brunswick St Brunswick St seemed suddenly to zoom from nowhere to somewhere in the restaurant business and for sheer variety this strip can't be beat. Not only does Brunswick St have several of the best Thai restaurants in Melbourne it also has the only Ethiopian and Afghan restaurants!

Working our way up Brunswick St from the city end interesting places to try include *Nyala* at 113 Brunswick St. I learnt to love Ethiopian food in California and this place does a pretty good go at it.

The $12 combination plate gives you an interesting variety of dishes to try, you scoop them up with the spongy bread known as *injera*.

Annick's at 153 Brunswick St is one of my Melbourne favourites. A straightforward but comfortable little restaurant with very reasonable prices for such excellent French food. Starters are mostly around $6, main courses around $11, desserts $4.50. It's deservedly popular so you have to phone 419 3007 to book a table.

Further up towards Johnston St the popular *Thai Thani* at No 293 and, just beyond Johnston St, *Patee's* at No 371 are both excellent restaurants for lovers of hot and spicy Thai food. Patee's probably started the Melbourne Thai restaurant practice of taking your shoes off at the door and sitting cross legged on the floor.

Afghanistan is not a place noted for it's cuisine but if you want to give it a go (steaks, kebabs, curries basically) then head for the *Afghan Gallery Restaurant* at 327 Brunswick St. Also not noted for the intricacies of it's cuisine is the famous *Black Cat* at No 252, still an arty-trendy coffee bar, ideal for coffee and cake at late hours. Better for food, however, is *Mario's* at 303 Brunswick St. It's a vaguely old-fashioned cafe with straightforward food, vaguely Italian in flavour! Mario's opens early for breakfast but it isn't even BYO, no alcohol at all!

Round the corner on Johnston St you'll find Melbourne's Spanish quarter with restaurants like the very Spanish *Costa Brava* at No 36. Seafood is the speciality; try their terrific paella for two or more. At No 60 the *Colmao Flamenco* (tel 417 4131) also does wonders with the garlic and the seafood. It's not all that cheap, but there's a flamenco guitarist on Friday and Saturday nights.

At 15 Johnston St, near the corner of Nicholson St, *Chishti's* is well known for its excellent Indian food, some of the best Indian food in Melbourne according to curry fanatics. Main courses are around

$9 and the service is friendly and efficient. It's open seven nights a week. Go a block over to *Shiva* at 265 Smith St, Fitzroy, for more good Indian food. There's an extensive range of tandoori and vegetarian dishes at $9 to $12 and live Indian music on Friday and Saturday nights.

North across Alexandra Parade, at 477 Brunswick St, is the wonderfully quirky *Bohemia Cafe* (tel 489 9739), with some amazing interior design – something like a cross between a museum and a junkyard. It's open every day from 6 pm to 1 am for snacks and until 11 pm for mainly Thai meals, with main dishes costing around $8. It's popular, so book.

Brunswick – Sydney Rd Head directly north of the city centre along that majestic avenue Royal Parade and you suddenly find yourself in the narrow, congested shopping street of Sydney Rd, Brunswick. This is indeed the road to Sydney but it's also one of the worst bottlenecks in Melbourne, at least in the rush hours. In the evenings it's no problem at all and this is one of Melbourne's Turkish restaurant areas. You can get there from Elizabeth St in the city centre on a No 18, 19 or 20 tram. The Turkish restaurants along Sydney Rd often bake their own delicious bread (*pide*) on the premises.

Alasya at 555 Sydney Rd is so popular that it's engulfed the places next door and spawned an identical offshoot, *Alasya 2*, closer to the city at 163 Sydney Rd. Here, as at most of the other Turkish places, you can choose from the menu or opt for a fixed price meal which gets you 10 (yes!) starters, a mixture of main courses, a selection of desserts, heaps of freshly baked bread and coffee all for a fixed $16. It's terrific value and you'd better bring a healthy appetite with you.

Quite a bit further up Sydney Rd, the *Golden Teras* (or Terrace) has moved across the road from it's old location to a new home at 803-805. It's also got a bit more spacious and a bit classier looking but the food is still cheap and delicious.

Big and busy and with a belly dancer on Friday and Saturday nights the spacious *Sultan Ahmet* at 835 is more of the same with a fixed price menu for just $12 or you can choose items.

Sydney Rd isn't all Turkish however, at 217 you can head for Spain at *La Paella* and yes, their paella is superb. Opposite La Paella is a large, popular Italian restaurant called *La Nostalgia*. Pizzas start at $6, and pasta dishes range from entrees for $5.50 to main courses for $10.

Richmond – Swan St, Bridge Rd & Victoria St

Richmond is Melbourne's Greek and Vietnamese centre. Take a No 70 tram from Batman Ave, by the river in the city, and get off on Swan St at the Church St junction in Richmond. The 100 metres or so along Swan St away from the city past Church St is virtually wall to wall Greek restaurants.

For years the *Laikon* at 272 was one of the best Greek food bargains in Melbourne. Inside, the Laikon is still plain and simple and the food straightforward and tasty but it's no longer top of the list. There's no menu so just go to the counter and order zatsiki and taramasalata (both dips), pitta bread to dip in it, and souvlaki (kebabs) which comes with salad. With a sticky sweet dessert and coffee you'll pay about $15 a head. While you're at the counter you'd better grab the wine bottle opener to uncork your wine too – the bottle shop on the corner of Swan and Church Sts sells retsina. The *Laikon* does good take-aways too.

Some of the other Swan St Greek restaurants provide food at virtually rock bottom prices but with somewhat brighter surroundings. Try *Elatos* at 213 where the seafood is particularly good or *Agapi* at 262 with the standard assortment of dips and starters plus sardines, stuffed peppers, moussaka, souvlaki and all the other Greek favourites. At 256 *Kaliva* looks a bit smarter and also has live music on Thursday to Sunday nights. Again seafood is a speciality here. And there's

Salona at 260A, with more of the standard Greek menu.

Greek food may have been Richmond's original claim to cheap eats popularity but these days it's just as well known for its bargain priced Vietnamese restaurants. Richmond has a large Vietnamese population and Victoria St has become Melbourne's 'Little Saigon', packed with Vietnamese shops, businesses and some superb restaurants. At some of these places you may find you're the only non-Vietnamese diner in the house. No problem, they always have an English menu and you always get a friendly reception. A No 23 (peak hours only) or 42 tram will get your there from Victoria Parade, north of the city centre.

The two Thy Thys are possibly Victoria St's best known Vietnamese restaurants. *Thy Thy 1* at 142 Victoria St is hidden away upstairs and is popular, basic and dirt cheap. *Thy Thy 2* at No 116 is equally straightforward, crowded and noisy and equally good value.

My Victoria St favourite is the bare, basic but very friendly *Sanh Sanh* at 270 Victoria St. There's no pretensions about this place at all but the food is excellent, rock bottom in price and served with a smile. *Vao Doi* at 120 Victoria St is not the cheapest along here but the decor is definitely somewhat flashier, not quite so cafe like. Main courses are generally between $5 and $7 for the regular dishes so a couple can eat well here for less than $15.

Greek and Vietnamese food is not all Richmond has to offer. If you continued a km or so further along Swan St beyond the Greek enclave you come to *Rumah Makan* at No 506. The prices here are slightly higher but the Malay food is really excellent. It's open Wednesday to Saturday nights only. At 103 Swan St, back towards the city, *Mexicali Rose* is Mexican with a difference. They do indeed have all the usual tacos and tostadas but also a number of dishes which don't appear in every other Melbourne Mexican.

Right in the middle of little Saigon you

can also find one of Melbourne's better Turkish restaurants, *Pamukkale* at 375 Victoria St. Great dips, kebabs and Turkish pizzas. Or at No 385 there's one of the better Mexican restaurants, *El Rincon*. Apart from the Mexican regulars they also offer a changing variety of South American dishes and there's Latin American music some nights.

Bridge Rd, the road out from the city midway between Swan St and Victoria St also has some great food possibilities. Take a No 48 or 75 tram (or a 24 during rush hours) from Flinders St in the city to these restaurants. Starting at the city end of Bridge Rd there's the *Uptown Deli* at 14-16 Bridge Rd. With pastas at around $8 to $10 it's not the cheapest eating around but the food is good and it's a bright, cheerful, convenient place to eat. At 78 Bridge Rd the *Tofu Shop* is definitely one for those on a vegetarian/health kick. It can be a squeeze finding a stool at the counter at lunch time but never mind, the salads, vegetables, filled filo pastries and soyalaki (great invention) are tasty and filling for around $5 to $6.

Sweet Jamaique at 127 Bridge Rd has a deli section downstairs and a more expensive restaurant area upstairs. Downstairs the food is reasonably priced and does indeed have some Caribbean curry with a creole touch. Nearby is *Rajdoot* at 142 Bridge Rd, if you've travelled in India you'll remember that as a popular Indian motorcycle brand! It's a small place with excellent Indian food including some great tandoori dishes.

The *London Tavern* at 238 Lennox St (midway between Swan St and Bridge Rd) used to be Lonely Planet's local pub, until we moved office. It rose to local pub food fame under a chef who liked India and curries and despite his departure the menu still has some interesting dishes plus there's a bright and sunny courtyard where you can eat outside.

Richmond has several other pubs noted for their good food.

South Yarra – Toorak Rd & Chapel St Take a No 8 tram from Swanston St in the city to South Yarra. Along Toorak Rd you'll find some of Melbourne's most expensive restaurants – places where a couple would have no trouble paying over $100 for a meal. Fortunately there are some more relevant places in between – like *Pinocchio's* at 152 Toorak Rd. This remains my number one Melbourne pizzeria and it also has a blackboard menu of other standard Italian favourites. It's a pleasant and convenient place to eat and the pizzas are excellent; the take-away prices are lower.

Only a couple of doors away at 156 is *Tamani's*, Italian once again and something of a Melbourne institution. It's a popular restaurant with good pasta dishes and salads. Just across the railway tracks at 164, *Alfio's* is almost too smoothly trendy-looking for its own good but the prices aren't bad, there's a nice sunny courtyard out back and their pasta can be superb. Backtrack down Toorak Rd to number 74 where you'll find a similar ambience and similar food at the *Barola Bistro* – a pleasant little espresso bar with a blackboard menu, snappy service and a small courtyard out back. Or cross the road to the pleasantly relaxed and old-fashioned looking *Yarra's* at 97 Toorak Rd, directly opposite the post office. It's open from breakfast time right through to reasonably late at night.

South Yarra's not all Italian; there are also a number of the currently trendy deli places, in particular *The Deli* at 26 Toorak Rd. This large, airy place has good food, excellent salads and is fine for a late night coffee or a not-too-early breakfast. Tables are also set out on the footpath and it's very much a place to be seen. Upstairs at 177 Toorak Rd the *Mt Lebanon* has excellent Lebanese food (and a belly dancer) but it's more expensive than the regular string of Middle East eateries.

Backtrack towards the city on Toorak Rd and just a short distance from St Kilda Rd you'll find the *Fawkner Club*, which isn't a club at all. The straightforward pub food is in the $9 to $14 bracket and it's a gathering place for local yuppies. The Fawkner is convenient for the Toorak Rd guest houses, the Botanic Gardens and, most important, it has a big sunny courtyard with a sliding glass roof.

An eclectic blend of deli food, open air eating and expensive restaurants can also be found along Chapel St. Turn right from Toorak Rd and there are places to try all the way. At 571 there's *Spaghetti Graffiti* where the people are friendly, the pasta is quite good and, most important, it's open round the clock. Right next door at 569 is *Kanpai*, a neat little Japanese restaurant with surprisingly modestly priced dishes. Further along at 517 there's *The Tandoor* which has excellent Indian food but is definitely not cheap.

Across the road at 478 Chapel St *Amigo's* offers standard Mexican fare from tacos to enchiladas. Cross back to *African Tukul* at No 425; Melbourne doesn't have many African restaurants and this is an interesting place to try. Continue down Chapel St almost to Commercial Rd and you'll find *Soda Sisters Drugstore* at 382. It's a facsimile of a '50s American soda fountain with ice cream sodas, sundaes, hamburgers and other representatives of American kulcha.

Patra at 359 Chapel St is a popular Greek restaurant with a pleasant courtyard. The immensely popular Prahran market is back from the Chapel St-Commercial Rd junction – go here for some of the best fresh vegetables, fruit and fish in Melbourne.

Prahran - Chapel St & Greville St If you continue across Commercial Rd you enter Prahran where at 310 Chapel St the *Ankara Restaurant* does Turkish regulars, with a good fixed price complete meal. Further down at 68 Chapel St in Windsor the *Marmara* is even better with great marinated kebabs and delicious thick Turkish bread.

At 270 Chapel St the *Court Jester*

serves slightly upmarket pub food and some adventurous dishes amongst the counter regulars, a truly artistic blackboard menu and reasonable prices. At 188 Chapel St *Himalaya* does Indian curries with some South-East Asian influence.

Turn into Greville St beside the town hall and down beside the railway tracks at No 95 and you'll find the ever popular *Feedwell Cafe*. This long running vegetarian restaurant is open from 7.30 am for breakfast through to 5 pm and does great cakes and baked goodies. Soups, sandwiches, vegetarian pizza slices and the like cost around $3.50 to $5. On the way down Greville St check the curious collection of recycled clothes and furniture shops, and the train emerging from the wall opposite Feedwell.

South Melbourne At 266 Clarendon St the *Old Paper Shop Deli* was one of the originators of the Melbourne deli craze and although it's no longer at the forefront of the trend it's still popular with good food at reasonable prices. It's another place where you can eat outside on the pavement.

A bit further along at 331 is the *Chinese Noodle Shop* - excellent authentic noodles dishes at around $6.50 to $9, pleasant surroundings and fast, friendly service. Further again to *Taco Bill's* at 375 - strictly mass market Mexican food but good value for all that. There's a whole string of Taco Bills around Melbourne, all very similar; check the addresses in the phone directory. To any Americans out there: Taco Bill's is about 100 times better than Taco Bells!

If you're feeling financially flush and ready for a good night out check out *The Last Aussie Fishcaf* just off Clarendon St at 256 Park St. It's a sort of movie musical vision of a '50s fish & chips cafe with prices already in the '90s! Never mind, the food's good (how many '50s fishcafs had sushi on the menu?), and there's music and entertainment. Book well ahead as it's very popular.

Entertainment

The best source of 'what's on' info in Melbourne is the *Entertainment Guide* which comes out every Friday with the *Age* newspaper.

During the summer months watch out for the FEIPP (Fantastic Entertainment In Public Places) programme with activities put on in city parks and public places on weekday lunch times and on the weekends. There's also often something going on in the City Square.

Melbourne has a number of concert halls and other venues. Right by the river the Arts Centre concert hall is the focus for opera and concert music. There's also the Dallas Brooks Hall and the outdoor Sidney Myer Music Bowl. Big rock concerts are usually held at the old and barn-like Festival Hall, the ex-swimming-pool Sports & Entertainment Centre with its quirky acoustics, or the new National Tennis Centre.

Rock Music A lot of Melbourne's night time scene is tied up with rock pubs – some of the big crowded places can afford the top Australian bands and it's for this reason that Melbourne is very much Australia's rock music centre. It's on the sweaty grind around the Melbourne rock pubs that Australia's best bands really prove themselves. The *Entertainment Guide* and FM stations like MMM (commercial) or RRR (public) will tell you who's on and where. Cover charges at the pubs vary widely – some nights it's free, generally it's from around $6, big names on weekend nights can cost $10 or more. Music generally starts around 9.30 pm, although the bigger the name the later the show. Those that follow are just a few of the places offering a variety of music.

Although it's not what it once was the small *Station Hotel* on Greville St, Prahran still attracts the crowds. It's one of the longest running of the rock pubs, a place with a bit of a Melbourne rock history. The Saturday arvo sessions are popular. Also in Greville St, upstairs from

the Barcelona restaurant, is *ID's* which has bands and the occasional comedy act. It's about $8 to get in.

In St Kilda the *Palace*, next door to the Palais on the Lower Esplanade, is another big place which has popular bands. In Fitzroy St, St Kilda there is the *Prince of Wales Hotel* which also starts late. You can hear some good jazz and blues here as well as rock, punk, etc. Also in St Kilda is the well-known *Esplanade Hotel*, on the Esplanade of course, which has live music every night and Sunday afternoons, free of charge. It's also a great place just to sit with a beer and watch the sun set over the pier, with Williamstown and the West Gate Bridge in the background.

Between these extremes are places like the *Armadale Hotel* in Armadale, not a bad place with upstairs and downstairs rooms. The *London Tavern* in Caulfield caters mainly for students with middle of the road to bland music. Ditto for the *Prospect Hill* in Kew which attracts fairly big bands. The *Central Club* in Richmond is a student type of pub which mainly caters for small bands.

The *Club* in Collingwood is similar, attracting interesting fringe bands. The big *Club Chevron* on St Kilda Rd, Prahran, is free some nights and has a good atmosphere.

Folk & Acoustic Music Yes there are also folk pubs. In the *Entertainment Guide* check the acoustic music listings as well as folk. One of the most popular is the *Dan O'Connell Hotel*, (the 'Dan') on the corner of Princes and Canning Sts in Carlton. For those interested in Irish music they claim 'we sell more Irish whiskey than Scotch' as proof of their Irish authenticity. Usually it's folk music on Wednesday and Thursday, Irish music on Friday and sometimes Saturday.

At 1221 High St, Malvern the long running *Green Man Music Club* is still a popular folk venue with shows over dinner or supper. On trendy Brunswick St the *Troubadour* puts on some of the best acoustic music in Melbourne, usually on Thursday to Saturday nights. A meal and the show costs around $15 to $25.

Jazz Just like there are pubs that specialise in rock or folk there are also pubs that specialise in jazz. Popular ones include the *Tankerville Arms* on the corner of Nicholson and Johnston Sts in Fitzroy, *Bell's Hotel* on the corner of Moray and Coventry Sts in South Melbourne, the *Eureka Hotel* at 1 Church St in Richmond and the *Museum Hotel* at 293 La Trobe St in the city. Or there's the *Victoria Hotel* in Albert Park, the *Limerick Arms* in South Melbourne and the *Beaconsfield Hotel* in St Kilda.

Nightclubs & Discos Melbourne has Australia's biggest and most fiercely competitive selection of nightclubs and discos. In fact, and many a bet has been won on this fact, Melbourne has more discos than New York. There seems to be a continuous competition to create the next 'biggest, brashest, most exclusive' club. There will be some sort of dress standards at all of them and the more 'exclusive' spots are likely to be selective about who they let in. Door charges are generally from $6 to $12.

Popular places include the sophisticated *Metro* disco at 20 Bourke St with no less than eight bars, in what used to be the Metro Theatre. The place was given a high-tech multi-million dollar renovation in '87 to become the biggest disco in the Southern Hemisphere. Long running places include the three level *Inflation* at 60 King St and the big and more middle of the road *Underground* at 22 King St. In King St you will also find the *Hippodrome*, *X* and the *Grainstore*, making this *the* nightclub street of Melbourne.

Latest arrival on the Melbourne places-to-be-seen-scene is *Checkpoint Charlie's* with post-holocaust decor at Commercial Rd, Prahran. Around the corner at 386 Chapel St is *Chasers*, another disco/

nightclub with a flashy interior, which also has bands occasionally.

For something a little different (no disco music here) try *Madigan's* at 402 Sydney Rd, Brunswick. Here you can lounge on a couch to listen to jazz, acoustic guitar or blues/rock while large wooden fans spin overhead. It's open Thursday to Sunday, 10 pm till late and costs about $8.

Pubs & Wine Bars Apart from the music pubs there are quite a few other popular pubs and wine bars. Top of the wine bar list would have to be *Jimmy Watson's* on Lygon St, Carlton – very much a place to see and be seen, especially at around lunch time Saturday, but a good place for a glass of wine anytime. It has a delightful (when the sun is shining) open courtyard out back.

Also in Carlton the *Lemon Tree Hotel* at 10 Grattan St, by the Exhibition Gardens, is another popular gathering place with a pleasant courtyard and good food. In nearby Fitzroy the *Lord Newry Hotel* at 543 Brunswick St is a pub which puts effort into its wine list so it straddles the pub/wine bar category.

Other popular pubs, often with open courtyards for those occasional sunny days, include the *The Fawkner Club* at 52 Toorak Rd West and the *New Argo Inn* at 64 Argo St, both in South Yarra. The *Capitol Wine Bar* at 257 Toorak Rd in South Yarra is a comfortable modern place.

Or there's the *Cricketer's Arms Hotel* at 69 Cruickshank St in Port Melbourne. There's another *Cricketer's Arms* at 327 Punt Rd in Richmond, popular after a game at the MCG.

Other popular pubs include *Lord Jim's* (very much a place for pick-ups) at 36 St George's Rd, North Fitzroy, or the *Council Club* in South Melbourne. The *Moonee Valley* (known as the Punters' Club) in Brunswick St, Fitzroy, is a good sleazy place to hang out if you like wearing black.

Theatre Restaurants No mention of Melbourne's eating/entertainment possibilities would be complete without a section on theatre restaurants. They've always been a popular idea but Melbourne's particular inspiration is combining eating out with fringe theatre. The peak days of the theatre/restaurant revolution have passed and they're even a mite establishment these days, but never mind, they're still good fun.

Granddaddy of these places is the *Last Laugh* on the corner of Smith and Gertrude Sts in Collingwood. It's an old cinema/dole office, done up in a dazzling mish-mash of styles from high kitsch up and down. Inside there's room for 200 people to have a good time. The food is reasonably good and there's a bar. Like other fringe places vegetarians are well catered for. You have time to get through the appetisers, soup and main course before part one of the show and dessert comes up before part two. The shows can be almost anything; years ago at a Circus Oz performance I remember considering the possibility of a tightrope walker landing in my lap half way through the meal. It costs, depending on the night and the show, \$29 to \$38 for dinner and show, and \$16 to \$22 for show only.

Upstairs there's *Le Joke*, where smaller acts appear. It costs \$25 to \$29 for dinner and show, \$8 to \$15 for show only.

Cinema Melbourne's best alternative cinemas include the *Valhalla* at 89 High St, Northcote, which shows different films every night. They produce a superb six month film calendar detailing all their shows. On Friday nights, the midnight showing of *Blues Brothers* has a cult following. The *Carlton Moviehouse* at 235 Faraday St has a similar programme. It's locally known as the 'bughouse'. Various other cinemas around Melbourne specialise in non-mainstream films. They include the *Longford Cinema* at 59 Toorak Rd, South Yarra; the *Astor Theatre* at 1 Chapel St on the corner of Dandenong Rd,

St Kilda, and the glossy new *Kino* at Collins Place, 45 Collins St in the city. At the universities you can try the *Agora* at La Trobe, way out in Bundoora, or the *Union Theatre* at Melbourne University. Finally there's the *State Film Theatre* at 1 Macarthur St, East Melbourne.

Theatre There's lots of theatre in Melbourne too, ranging from the commercial places up the east end of the central city area to the many and varied smaller and experimental theatres.

La Mama at 205 Faraday St in Carlton has not only been brave it's also been a long term survivor where many of the big names of Australian theatre made their debut. Readings Bookshop in Lygon St handles tickets. The *Melbourne Writers Theatre* is in the Carlton Courthouse at 329 Drummond St in Carlton.

The *Universal Theatre* at 13 Victoria St in Fitzroy manages to pack them in with productions which may only appeal to a minority but are always adventurous and interesting. The *Anthill Theatre* at 199 Napier St, South Melbourne, and the *Australian Contemporary Theatre* in the church at 500 Burwood Rd, Hawthorn, are other theatres noted for their experimental productions.

The *Melbourne Theatre Company* puts on big plays at the Playhouse at the Arts Centre, smaller productions at the Russell St Theatre at 19 Russell St, Melbourne. The *Playbox Theatre Company* also appears at the Arts Centre.

Commercial theatres, the places you go to see *Cats* or the *Rocky Horror Show*, are *The Athenaeum* at 188 Collins St, the *Comedy Theatre* at 240 Exhibition St, *Her Majesty's Theatre* at 219 Exhibition St and the *Princess Theatre* at 163 Spring St.

The Footy Despite the heretical moves to a national competition, Melbourne is still very much the stronghold of Aussie Rules football. If you're here between April and

September you won't be able to avoid The Footy. Although it's no longer a daring innovation for a TV station not to show match replays on Saturday nights, there's still an awful lot of media coverage of topics such as Johnno's knee, Dermie's thigh or Brian's groin.

You should try to see a match, as much for the crowds as the game. Footy is one of those satisfying games in which the umpire's interpretation of some pretty convoluted rules plays a big part. This gives the fans something to agree on – the umpire is blind or biased. Other than this, the fans don't agree on much at all, and the sheer energy of the barracking at a big game is exhilarating. Despite the fervour of the fans, crowd violence is almost unknown.

Big matches are often scheduled at the MCG. Collingwood, a mighty club that has somehow remained mighty despite failing to win a Premiership since 1958, always provides excited crowds. Their home ground, Victoria Park, is in Johnston St, Collingwood. Carlton and Hawthorn are other teams worth seeing, and their shared ground at Princes Park, on Sydney Rd north of Melbourne University, is also close to the city. You can book seats through BASS, although you often won't need to.

Things to Buy

Although Melbourne is far from the main centres for Aboriginal crafts there are some interesting places to look. Aboriginal Handcrafts is on the 9th floor of Century House at 125 Swanston St and is open weekdays from 10 am to 4.30 pm. The Gallery Gabrielle Pizzi at 141 Flinders Lane, just round the corner from the Hyatt Hotel, specialises in Aboriginal art; expensive but interesting to see.

There are a number of other Aboriginal craft shops and countless junk souvenir places. Melbourne also has a number of delightful Australiana shops selling amusing (and intentional) examples of Australian kitsch. Art galleries and craft

centres can be found all over Melbourne, check the weekly *Entertainment Guide* in *The Age* for what's on. The Meat Market Craft Centre at 42 Courtney St, North Melbourne, near the YHA hostels, is a big centre with workshops and exhibitions.

For general shopping in the city there are a number of intimate and elegant little shopping arcades apart from the glossier modern affairs. The Royal Arcade off Bourke St Mall is noted for its figures of Gog and Magog which strike the hours. Head to Lygon St, Carlton, or Toorak Rd and Chapel St, South Yarra for up-market shopping. For interesting local designs, curio and antique shops, try Brunswick St, Fitzroy and Chapel and Greville Sts, Prahran.

Getting There & Away

Air Melbourne is the second arrival and departure gateway in Australia. Melbourne's international airport is rather more spacious than Sydney's and also gets rather fewer flights so if you make this your Australian arrival point you're likely to get through immigration and customs a little more speedily, although it can still get very crowded.

There are frequent connections between Melbourne and other state capitals – Melbourne/Sydney flights depart hourly during the airport operating hours. Fares include Adelaide $170 (standby $136), Brisbane $277 ($222), Canberra $141 ($113), Perth $419 ($335) or Sydney $181 ($145). Connections to Alice Springs are mostly via Adelaide when it costs $345, direct flights are $335.

Melbourne is the main departure point from the mainland to Tasmania. Hobart flights cost $166 (standby $133), Launceston $142 ($114) with Ansett or Australian Airlines. Flights to Devonport and Burnie both cost $131 (standby $100) and are operated by Ansett. East-West Airlines also fly to Devonport.

The Australian Airlines office (tel 665 3333) is at 50 Franklin St while Ansett (tel 668 2222) is at 501 Swanston St. Both have smaller offices dotted around the city. East-West (tel 63 7713) are on the 2nd floor at 230 Collins St.

Bus The major bus companies – Bus Australia, Deluxe, Greyhound and Pioneer Express – all operate through Melbourne. There is some variance in fares from company to company but they're all pretty much the same.

Adelaide connections are made at least once daily by each company; the trip takes 10 or 11 hours but the fares can vary from around $31 (or less) to $47 depending on the company, the service and what special deal is available at the time. Most services start out by dipping down from Melbourne to Geelong then back up to Ballarat but some bypass Geelong or offer a feeder service connection. Greyhound have a weekly service that follows the coast through Geelong, Port Fairy and Mt Gambier.

Services connect through to Perth via Adelaide and the fare is $150 to $160. Canberra takes eight or nine hours for $37 to $42.

Melbourne to Sydney services go direct (Hume Highway, usually via Canberra), via Wagga Wagga or up the coast (Princes Highway). The trip takes anything from 13 hours (Hume Highway skipping Canberra) to over 17 hours (Princes Highway). The fare varies from around $40 to $50 but like Adelaide there are often special deals available.

There are also direct services between Melbourne and Brisbane, either via Sydney and the Gold Coast or via Dubbo and Toowoomba, continuing from Brisbane to the Gold Coast. The trip takes about 24 to 30 hours and typically costs about $85 to $90 to either Brisbane or the Gold Coast.

There are also a variety of other services from Melbourne apart from all the towns along the main routes. Greyhound have a Melbourne/Mildura/Broken Hill service for example. V/Line also operate a

number of bus services around the state. See the introductory Getting Around section for Victoria.

Two smaller companies are Sunliner Express who operate up the east coast from Melbourne as far as Cairns. Their fares are generally a few dollars less than the big four. Ditto for Inter-Capital Express who operate the same route.

The bus companies all operate from up at the top end of the city centre area, most of them on Franklin St where you also find the Ansett and Australian Airlines offices. Bus Australia (tel 662 2788) and Deluxe (tel 663 6144) are at 58 Franklin St, from where the airport Skybus service also operates. Greyhound (tel 668 2666) and Pioneer Express (tel 668 3144) are at the corner of Franklin and Swanston Sts, in the Ansett building. Sunliner Express (tel 663 4900) and Inter-Capital Express (same number) are both at 260 La Trobe St.

Train Rail tickets for interstate services can be booked by phoning 620 0771, at most suburban stations, and at the Spencer St Railway Station in Melbourne from where the interstate services depart. Phone 619 1500 for V/Line information.

Vintage train enthusiasts should enquire about the Steamrail Victoria (tel 629 4086) excursions in old steam locomotives.

Train – interstate Melbourne/Sydney takes 12½ to 13 hours by train. The Intercapital Daylight operates every day except Sunday while the overnight Sydney Express from Melbourne or Melbourne Express from Sydney operates every night. The fare is $71 economy, $100 in 1st class. A 1st class sleeper costs $137, there are no economy sleepers. You can take a car on the Melbourne/Sydney services for $95.

To get to Canberra by rail you take the Intercapital Daylight as far as Yass Junction from where a bus connects for the one-hour trip into Canberra – total fare $50 ($70 in 1st) and it takes 9½ hours from Melbourne. There's also the daily

Canberra Link which involves a train to Wodonga on the Victoria-New South Wales border and then a bus from there. This takes about an hour less and is also cheaper at $39 ($49 1st class).

To or from Adelaide the Overland operates overnight every day of the week. The trip takes 12 hours and costs $50 in economy, $70 in 1st or $107 for a 1st class sleeper. The Daylink involves a train to Dimboola near the border and a bus from there. This trip is about an hour faster than the through train and costs $50 in economy, $62 in 1st. You can transport a car to or from Adelaide for $59.

To get to Perth by rail from Melbourne you take the Overland to Adelaide and then the Trans Australian (which originates in Adelaide) or the Indian-Pacific (which comes through Adelaide from Sydney). The Melbourne to Perth fare is $180 for a seat in economy. Including meals a sleeping berth costs $404 in economy, $588 in 1st. It's a two days and three nights trip all the way from Melbourne to Perth. People have driven to Perth from the east coast in not much more than 24 hours (way over the speed limit all the way) so you can see trains are not too fast!

Services to Alice Springs are also operated via Adelaide connecting with the Ghan which goes twice weekly from May to October, once weekly the rest of the year. The trip takes a day and two nights and costs $199 for an economy seat or $399 in 1st class, which includes meals and a sleeping berth. For some reason they do not quote a sleeping berth fare in economy – there are no economy sleepers Melbourne/Adelaide but there are Adelaide/Alice Springs.

If you're travelling to or from any of the major cities and can book at least seven days in advance, you can save up to 30% with the 'Caper' fares (Customer Advance Purchase Excursion Rail – would you believe). Standby fares are available Melbourne/Sydney ($30) and Melbourne/Adelaide ($25).

Train – within Victoria For V/Line services within Victoria there are a number of special fares available. Super Saver fares give you a 40% discount for travelling at off-peak times. Basically this means arriving in Melbourne after 9.30 am and leaving Melbourne at any time except between 4 and 6 pm if you're travelling within the Melbourne 'Commuter Zone'. Going further afield it means travelling on Tuesdays, Wednesdays or Thursdays. A Victoria Pass gives you two weeks unlimited travel within the state for $99.

See the relevant country towns for information on V/Line train, bus or bus-train travel from Melbourne.

Getting Around

Airport Transport Although Melbourne Airport (Tullamarine) is 22 km from the city it's quite easy to get to since the Tullamarine Freeway runs almost into the centre. A taxi between the airport and city centre will cost about $20 but there's the regular Skybus service which costs $7 (children $3.50). In the city the Skybus departs from 58 Franklin St near the Ansett and Australian Airlines offices. There are buses about every half hour, sometimes even more frequently. Phone 663 1400 for details of city pick-up points for city to airport services.

There is also a fairly frequent bus by Gull Airport Service between the airport and Geelong. It costs $16 one way, $30 return. The Geelong terminus is at 45 McKillop St. You can get timetables for these services from the information counter in the international section at the airport.

Tullamarine is a modern airport with a single terminal; Australian Airlines at one end, Ansett at the other, international in the middle. There's an information desk upstairs in the international departure area. It's the most spacious airport in Australia and doesn't suffer the night flight restrictions which apply to some other Australian airports. The snack bar and cafeteria sections are if anything somewhat worse than the airport norm for quality and price but if you're stuck at the airport for any reason you can stroll over to the customs agents building – turn right out of the terminal and it's about a 200 metre walk – where there's a cheap snack bar. There's another in the small centre beyond the car park by the Travelodge Motel.

If you're flying out with Qantas they have a city check in facility at the Hyatt Hotel in the centre. This means you can check in hours early, get your seat assigned and not have to bother about turning up at the airport so early, or carrying all your bags out there.

Public Transport Melbourne's public transport system, The Met, is based on buses, suburban railways and the famous trams. The trams are the real cornerstone of the system; in all there are about 750 of them and they operate as far as 20 km out from the centre. They're frequent and fun.

Buses are the secondary form of public transport, supporting the trams where tram lines do not go, even replacing them at quiet weekend periods. There are also a host of private bus services as well as the public ones. The train services provide a third link for Melbourne's outer suburbs. There is even an underground city loop which was completed in 1985.

For information on Melbourne transport phone the Transport Information Centre (tel 617 0900). It operates 7.30 am to 8.30 pm Monday to Saturday, 9.15 am to 8.30 pm on Sunday. The Met Shop at 103 Elizabeth St in the city also has transport information and sells souvenirs and some tickets. They also have a 'Discover Melbourne' kit. If you're in the city they're probably a better bet for information than the telephone service, which is always engaged. Railway stations also have some information.

In 1990 The Met was trying, some years behind the rest of the first world, to replace tram conductors but hadn't really decided what with. Meanwhile you can buy tickets from Met Shops (in the city and several remote suburbs), 7 Elevens, certain newsagents, Amcal chemists, train stations if there's anybody at them and certain other outlets. Eventually they will probably have to install some sort of automatic ticketing machines.

Before boarding the tram, train or bus you must scratch out the date and time (on three hour tickets) or just the date (on day tickets). You can then travel on any form of Met transport within your chosen zone for the next three hours or for all of that day. Melbourne is divided up into three zones but the inner zone, Zone 1, covers the inner city and quite a distance out through the inner suburbs. A three hour Zone 1 ticket costs $1.40, all day is $2.50.

The problem with this new, and hopefully temporary, system is finding someplace to buy a ticket. If you simply cannot find a place to get a ticket you can buy a three hour ticket on the tram or bus for $2.

If you're making short trips (up to two 'sections') by bus or tram (not by train) and completely within Zone 1 you can buy a Short Trip ticket which lets you make 10 such voyages for $8. The Short Trip ticket is punched as you board the bus or tram. Other options include weekly, monthly and family tickets.

Car Rental All the big car rental firms operate in Melbourne. Avis, Budget, Hertz and Thrifty have desks at the airport and you find plenty of others in the city. The city offices tend to be at the north end of the city or in Carlton or North Melbourne.

Melbourne also has a number of rent-a-wreck style operators, renting older vehicles at lower rates. Their costs and conditions vary widely so it's worth making a few enquiries before going for one firm over another. You can take the 'from $15 a day' line with a pinch of salt because the rates soon start to rise with insurance, km charges and so on. Beware of distance from the city restrictions, within a certain distance of the city, typically 100 km.

Typical are Rent-a-Bomb (tel 429 4003) at 507 Bridge Rd, Richmond. Their weekly rate works out at around $18 a day for older Holdens, plus $5 for insurance. It includes unlimited km but you're limited to the Melbourne metropolitan area. The telephone yellow pages list lots of other firms including some reputable local operators who rent newer cars but don't have the nationwide operations (and overheads) of the big operators.

Bicycle Melbourne's not a bad city for cycling – there are several lengthy riverside bicycle tracks and other bicycle tracks and lanes around the city, plus it's reasonably flat so you're not pushing and panting up hills too often. Look for a copy of *Weekend Bicycle Rides* for a pleasant introduction to bike rides around Melbourne. There are also bicycle route maps available from newsagents which detail the ever expanding network of bike paths and roads with bicycle lanes. There are quite a few rides you can make in the surrounding country by taking one train out of Melbourne then riding across to a different line to get the train back. An example is to take the train out to Gisborne and ride the ridge down to Bacchus Marsh from where you can get another train back in to the city.

Unfortunately, if you don't already have a bike, Melbourne's not a great place to try and hire one – at least not if you want to do more than just dawdle along the pleasant cycle path by the river, a popular pastime on weekends. There are hire places by the boat sheds at Princes Gate, opposite the Botanic Gardens, beside Como Park in Burnley and at the Kevin Bartlett Reserve in Richmond. Hire-a-Bicycle (tel 288 5177), one of the riverside operators, also hires out bikes at other times. The rates are: $4 per hour and $2 each hour after that; $12 per day and $20 per week, all with a small deposit.

Hillman Cycles (tel 380 9685), at 44 Grantham St in West Brunswick, hire mountain bikes for around $15 per day, although they want a deposit larger than you'd need to hire a car. I haven't seen their hire bikes, but Hillman make top professional track bikes so they're probably very good. Watch the fine print though. Get there on tram 55 or 56 from William St.

Phone Bicycle Victoria (tel 670 9911) for more information or drop into their shop at 31 Somerset Place, off Little Bourke St in the city. They'll be able to put you onto local clubs and tours.

Tours Melbourne's latest tourist attraction is the *Spirit of Victoria* (tel 62 6997), a high speed ferry which takes visitors on trips around Port Phillip Bay. It departs from Station Pier in Port Melbourne at 10 am and 2 pm on Fridays and Saturdays, going to Mornington, Sorrento and Portarlington and takes about 3½ hours for the round trip. On Sundays it departs at 11 am for a six hour trip to Queenscliff and Sorrento. The fare is $24 and tickets are available on the boat.

The Age 'City Explorer' double-decker bus operates hourly from 10 am to 4 pm from Flinders St Station and calls at six major attractions around town. Tickets cost $5 and you can get on or off when and where you like.

The usual variety of tours is available in and around Melbourne. Typical costs include half day city tours from around $22 or full days tours to Healesville, Phillip Island, the Great Ocean Rd or Ballarat for around $40.

The old steam tug *Wattle* makes two-hour trips on weekends around the Port of Melbourne and Williamstown, leaving from 20 Victoria Dock at 10 am, 1 pm and 3.30 pm for $8.

Heritage Walks leave the Victour office in Collins St at 10 am on Mondays, Wednesdays and Fridays for 1½ hour tours of Collins St and South Melbourne for $10.

Around Melbourne

You don't have to travel far from Melbourne to find places worth visiting. There are the beaches and towns around Port Phillip Bay, the old gold towns to the north and west, and the hills to the east which give a good introduction to the bush at its best.

THE DANDENONGS

The Dandenong Ranges to the east of Melbourne are one of the most popular day-trips. In fact they're so popular with Melbournians that the city now laps at their edge. The Dandenongs are cool due to the altitude (Mt Dandenong is all of 633 metres tall) and lushly green due to the heavy rainfall. The area is dotted with fine old houses, classy restaurants, beautiful gardens and some fine short bushwalks. You can clearly see the Dandenongs from central Melbourne (on a smog free day) and they're only about an hour's drive away.

The small Ferntree Gully National Park has pleasant strolls and lots of bird life including, if you're extremely lucky, the lyrebirds for which the Dandenongs are famous but which are now very rare. The Sherbrooke Forest Park is similarly pleasant for walks and you'll see lots of rosellas.

The William Ricketts sanctuary (tel 751 1300), Olinda Rd, Mt Dandenong, is named after its delightfully eccentric resident sculptor. The forest sanctuary is filled with his artwork and you can see more of his work far away in Alice Springs. It's open every day from 10 am to 4.30 pm and admission is $3.

Puffing Billy

One of the major attractions of the Dandenongs is Puffing Billy – a restored miniature steam train which makes runs along the 13 km track from Belgrave to Lakeside at the Emerald Lake Park. Puffing Billy was originally built in 1900 to bring farm produce to market. Emerald is a pretty little town with many craft galleries and shops. At Lakeside there's a whole string of attractions from barbecues and waterslides to a huge model railway with over two km of track! It's hard to drag kids away. At Menzies Creek beside the station there's a Steam Museum open every Sunday and public holiday from 11 am to 5 pm. It houses a collection of early steam locomotives.

Phone 870 8411 for recorded Puffing Billy timetable details; it runs every day except Christmas day but more frequently on weekends and holidays. The round trip takes about 2½ hours and costs $9.70 for adults, $6.50 for children aged four to 14. Family concessions are only available on Saturdays. Note that Puffing Billy does not run on days of total fire ban. You can get out to Puffing Billy on the regular suburban rail service to Belgrave, and the one-way fare is $3.10, return is $5.

WEST TO BALLARAT

The trip out to the old gold town of Ballarat is a favourite excursion from Melbourne and there are several points of interest along the way. Bacchus Marsh is just 49 km from Melbourne and accessible by train and bus. It has some fine old National Trust classified buildings as well as a noteworthy 'Avenue of Honour' and is a good base for walks and picnics in the vicinity. Good spots include the Werribee Gorge, Lerderderg Gorge, Wombat State Forest (a little to the south in the Brisbane Ranges National Park) and the Anakie Gorge, which is particularly scenic and a popular barbecue spot.

SOUTH-WEST TO GEELONG

It's a quick trip down the Princes Highway to Geelong – it's freeway all the way. You can leave Melbourne quickly over the soaring West Gate Bridge and enjoy the fine views of the city on the way.

Werribee Park

Not far out of Melbourne is Werribee Park with its free range zoological park and the huge Italianate Chirnside Mansion, built between 1874 and '77. The flamboyant building is surrounded by formal gardens but there are also picnic and barbecue areas.

Entrance to the park is free, but admission to the mansion costs $3.20 (children $1.60) and the safari bus tours cost $5 (children $2.50). Werribee Park is open weekdays from 10 am to 3.45 pm, weekends from 10 am to 4.45 pm. The Werribee railway station is part of the Melbourne suburban rail network.

National Aviation Museum
Near Werribee is the National Aviation Museum at the RAAF Base at Point Cook. Displays include one on WW I German ace Baron von Richtofen. It's open Sundays to Thursdays from 10 am to 4 pm and admission is free.

You Yangs
You can also detour to the You Yangs, a picturesque range of volcanic hills just off the freeway. Walks in the You Yangs include the climb up Flinders Peak, the highest point in the park with a plaque commemorating Matthew Flinder's scramble to the top in 1802. There are fine views from the top, down to Geelong and the coast.

Wineries
There are also a number of wineries in the Geelong area. The Idyll Vineyard at 265 Ballan Rd, Moorabool, is credited with re-establishing the area's name for wines after a lapse of many years. Other Geelong area wineries are the Rebenberg Vineyard at Feehans Rd in Mt Duneed and the Tarcoola Vineyards at Spiller Rd in Lethbridge.

Brisbane Ranges
You can make an interesting loop from Melbourne out to the You Yangs and back through the Brisbane Ranges park and Bacchus Marsh. The scenic Anakie Gorge in the Brisbane Ranges is a popular short

bushwalk and a good spot for barbecues. You may see koalas in the trees near the car park/picnic area.

Fairy Park, on the side of Mt Anakie at the southern edge of the Brisbane Ranges, has 100 clay fairy-tale figures.

Meredith
On the Midland Highway, just the other side of the Brisbane Ranges park, is Meredith, one of Victoria's oldest towns and once a popular stop on the way to the gold fields around Ballarat.

NORTH-WEST TO BENDIGO
It's about 150 km north-west of Melbourne along the Calder Highway to the old mining town of Bendigo and there are some interesting walks along the way.

Organ Pipes National Park
You've hardly left the outskirts of Melbourne, with the Tullamarine Airport control tower visible off to the east of the road, when you pass by the small but surprisingly pretty Organ Pipes National Park on the right and Calder motor racing circuit on the left. A little further north is the turn-off to Sunbury, the site for a number of large Australian Woodstock-style rock festivals in the early '70s.

Gisborne & Macedon
Gisborne is a pleasant little town, at one time a coaching stop on the route to the Bendigo and Castlemaine gold fields. Soon after Gisborne you come to Macedon and the turn-off to Mt Macedon, a 1013 metre high extinct volcano with fine views from the top. This area was devastated by the 1983 Ash Wednesday bushfires and the process of rebuilding is still continuing. Despite this, it is still a popular weekend outing for Melbournians and there are a number of good walks in the country around here, and some of the area's elegant old houses with beautifully kept gardens managed to survive the bushfires.

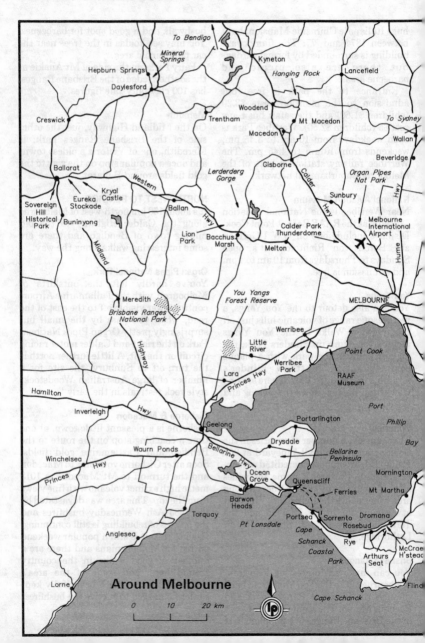

Around Melbourne

0   10   20 km

Hanging Rock

Just north of Mt Macedon is Hanging Rock, a popular picnic spot which became famous from the book and later the film *Picnic at Hanging Rock*. At that mysterious picnic, three schoolgirls on a school trip to the rock disappeared without trace; in an equally mysterious way one of the girls reappeared a few days later. The rocks are great fun to clamber over and there are superb views from higher up. While it is highly unlikely that you'll find the missing girls, if you look carefully you may well see koalas lazing in the trees, high above the jumble of rocks.

Just south of the rocks, on Straws Lane, the back road from Mt Macedon, there's a stretch of road where a stationary car will appear to roll uphill. This sort of optical illusion is not uncommon but on this particular piece of road it's very convincing. Back on the Calder Highway, Woodend is another pleasant old town. This is the closest you can get to Hanging Rock by public transport; the one-way train fare is $4.90/6.90 for economy/first.

Kyneton & Malmsbury

The road continues through Kyneton with its fine bluestone buildings. The Historical Centre building was originally a two storey bank, dating from 1855. Kyneton also has an eight hectare botanic gardens. Although Kyneton did not directly participate in the Victorian gold rush it prospered by supplying food and produce to the booming towns on the gold fields. A further 11 km brings you to Malmsbury with an historic bluestone railway viaduct and a magnificent ruined grain mill, part of which has been converted into a delightful, if a little upmarket, restaurant.

HEALESVILLE & THE HILLS

You don't have to travel far to the east of Melbourne before you start getting into the foothills of the Great Dividing Range. In winter you can find snow within 100 km of the city centre.

Healesville is on the regular Melbourne

suburban transport network; trains operate to Lilydale from where connecting buses run to Healesville. A Met Anywhere Ticket will get you there. MacKenzies Bus Lines (book through Whites Tours, tel 654 5311, 134 Flinders St) has a daily bus to Healesville which continues on to Eildon on weekdays but only as far as Marysville on weekends. The bus leaves from White's Tours and the one-way fare to Eildon is $13.80.

Yarra Valley Wineries

On the Melbourne side of Healesville there are wineries from Yarra Glen along the Yarra Valley. These places make a good day-trip from Melbourne and include the Chateau Yarrinya Winery on Main Yea Rd, Dixon's Creek; St Hubert's Wines on St Hubert's Rd, Coldstream, and Yarra Burn Vineyards on Settlement Rd, Yarra Junction.

Healesville (population 4500)

Healesville is on the outskirts of Melbourne, just where you start to climb up into the hills. There are some pleasant drives from Healesville, particularly the scenic route to Marysville, but the Sir Colin MacKenzie

Wildlife Sanctuary is a prime attraction. This is one of the best places to see Australian wildlife in the whole country. Most of the enclosures are very natural, some of the birds seem to just pop in for the day.

Some enclosures are only open for a few hours each day so you may want to plan your visit accordingly. The platypus, for example, is only on show in it's glass sided tank from 11.30 am to 1 pm and 1.30 to 3.30 pm. The nocturnal house, where you can see many of the smaller bush dwellers which only come out at night, is open from 10 am to 4 pm while the reptile house is open from 10.30 am to 4.30 pm. The whole park is open from 9 am to 5 pm and admission is $5.30 (children and students $2.80). There are barbecue and picnic facilities in the pleasantly wooded park.

Warburton

Beyond Healesville is Warburton, another pretty little hill town in the Great Dividing Range foothills. There are good views of the mountains from the Acheron Way nearby and you'll sometimes get snow on Mt Donna Buang, seven km from town. Warburton, in the Upper Yarra

Rock formation, Fraser National Park

Valley, is one of a number of picturesque spots along the upper reaches of the Yarra River.

Marysville (population 600)

This delightful little town is a very popular weekend escape from Melbourne. There are lots of bush tracks to walk, especially to Nicholl's Lookout, Keppel's Lookout, Mt Gordon and Steavenson Falls. Cumberland Scenic Reserve, with numerous walks and the Cumberland Falls, is 16 km east of Marysville. The cross-country skiing trails of Lake Mountain Reserve are only 10 km beyond Marysville.

Lake Eildon

Continuing beyond the hill towns of Healesville and Marysville you come to Lake Eildon, a large lake created for hydro power and irrigation purposes. It's a popular resort area with lots of boats and houseboats to hire. Trout breeding is carried out at Snob's Creek Fish Hatchery and there's a fauna sanctuary nearby. The Snob's Creek Falls drop 107 metres. On the shores of the lake the Fraser National Park has some good short walks including an excellent guide-yourself nature walk. On the south side of the lake is the old mining town of Jamieson. Alexandra and Eildon are the main centres near the lake.

The Goulburn Valley Highway starts from Eildon and runs to Seymour and Shepparton. North of Yarra Glen is Yea, a good centre for the Kinglake National Park with waterfalls, fern gullies and other attractions including abundant wildlife. Gulf Station, a couple of km from Yarra Glen, is part of an old grazing run dating from the 1850s. Operated by the National Trust it's open Wednesdays to Sundays and on public holidays from 10 am to 4 pm. There is an interesting collection of rough old timber buildings plus the associated pastures and a homestead garden typical of the period.

Mornington Peninsula

The Mornington Peninsula is the spit of land down the east side of Port Phillip Bay, bordered on its eastern side by the waters of Westernport Bay. The peninsula really starts at Frankston, 40 km from the centre of Melbourne, and from there it's almost a continuous beach strip, all the way to Portsea at the end of the peninsula, nearly 100 km from Melbourne. At the tip of the peninsula is a park recently opened on the site of a military base. From here you can look out across 'The Rip', the narrow entrance to Port Phillip Bay.

This is a very popular Melbourne resort area with many holiday homes; in summer the accommodation and camping sites along the peninsula can be packed right out and traffic can be very heavy. In part this popularity is due to the peninsula's excellent beaches and the great variety they offer. On the north side of the peninsula you've got calm water on the bay beaches (the front beaches) looking out on to Port Phillip Bay, while on the south side there's crashing surf on the rugged and beautiful ocean beaches (the back beaches) which face Bass Strait.

Town development tends to be concentrated along the Port Phillip side; the Westernport Bay and Bass Strait coasts are much less developed and you'll find pleasant bushwalking trails along the Cape Schank Coastal Park, a narrow coastal strip right along the Bass Strait coast from Portsea to Cape Schank. Frankston is the start of the peninsula, linked by rail to Melbourne.

There's a Tourist Information Centre in Dromana on the coast road down the peninsula and the National Park Service's *Discovering the Peninsula* brochure tells you all you'll want to know about the peninsula's history, early architecture and walking tours.

Places to Stay & Eat

There is a string of camping sites along the

bay front but over Christmas finding a place to set up tent can be very difficult. There are a number of hotels and motels along the peninsula but no travellers' bargains. Counter meals are available at the Sorrento hotels – the *Lady Nelson Bistro* in the Sorrento, the *Tavern Bar* in the Continental, the bistro in the *Koonya*. You can also get counter meals in the *Portsea Hotel* where there's a pleasant beer garden overlooking the beach, and excellent fish & chips at the *Hungry Eye* in Rye.

Getting There & Away

There's a regular bus service from Frankston through to Portsea (tel 602 9444 for details) and suburban trains run from Melbourne to Frankston.

During the summer a passenger ferry makes the crossing from Sorrento and Portsea to Queenscliff on the other side of the heads; by road it's a couple of hundred km right round the bay. From late December to the end of January it operates 10 times daily, then to Easter five times daily. In November and December it operates three times daily on weekends and it also operates in the May and August school holidays. The adult fare is $4 one way, $6 return, and for the first couple of morning departures there's a connecting bus into Geelong.

A car ferry runs all year, departing Queenscliff every two hours from 7 am to 5 pm with a 7 pm service during the peak periods. A car and passengers cost $32, or its $6 for pedestrians.

FRANKSTON TO BLAIRGOWRIE

Beyond Frankston you reach Mornington and Mt Martha, early settlements with some old buildings along the Mornington Esplanade and fine, secluded beaches in between. Dromana is the real start of the resort development and just inland a winding road leads up to Arthur's Seat lookout at 305 metres; you can also reach it by a scenic chairlift (weekends and holidays in summer only). On the slopes of Arthur's Seat, in McCrae, the McCrae Homestead is a National Trust property, dating from 1843 and open daily from 10 am to 5 pm from December to Easter and weekends the rest of the year. Coolart on Sandy Point Rd, Balnarring, is another historic homestead on the peninsula. Coolart is also noted for the wide variety of bird life which can be seen on the reserve. Balnarring is on the other side of the peninsula.

After McCrae there's Rosebud, Rye and Blairgowrie before you reach Sorrento. Rosebud has a Marine & Reptile Park and there's the Peninsula Gardens Tourist & Fauna Park (sounds like a great combination).

SORRENTO

Just as you enter Sorrento there's a small memorial and pioneer cemetery from the first Victorian settlement at pretty Sullivan Bay. The settlement party arrived from England in October 1803, intending to forestall a feared French settlement on the bay. Less than a year later, in May 1804, the project was abandoned and transferred to Hobart, Tasmania. The main reason for the settlement's short life was a lack of water; they had simply chosen the wrong place as there was an adequate supply further round the bay. The settlement's numbers included an 11 year old boy, John Pascoe Fawkner, who 25 years later would be one of the founders of Melbourne. It also included William Buckley, a convict who escaped soon after the arrival in 1803 and lived with Aborigines for the next 30 years as the 'wild white man'.

Sorrento has a rather damp and cold little aquarium and an interesting small historical museum in the old Mechanic's Institute building on the Old Melbourne Rd. From the 1870s paddle-steamers used to run between Melbourne and Sorrento. The largest, entering service in 1910, carried 2000 passengers. From 1890 through to 1921 there was a steam-powered tram operating from the Sorrento pier to the back beach. The magnificent hotels built of local limestone in this period still stand – the Sorrento (1871), Continental (1875) and Koonya (1878).

PORTSEA

Portsea, at the end of the Nepean Highway, offers another choice between front and back beaches. At the Portsea back beach there's the impressive natural rock formation known as London Bridge, plus a cliff where hang-gliders make their leap into the void. There are fine views across Portsea and back to Melbourne from Mt Levy Lookout by the back beach. Portsea is a popular diving centre and scuba diving trips on the bay operate regularly from Portsea Pier.

At the entrance to the recently opened government zone at the end of the peninsula are two historic gun barrels which fired the first shots in WW I and WW II. In 1914 a German ship was on its way out from Melbourne to the heads when news of the declaration of war came through on the telegraph. A shot across its bows at Portsea resulted in its capture. The first shot in WW II turned out to be at an Australian ship!

Cheviot Beach, at the end of the peninsula, featured more recently in Australian history. In 1967, then Prime Minister Harold Holt went for a swim here and was never seen again. The area was closed to the public for many years but has recently been reopened.

THE OCEAN COAST

The southern (or eastern) coast of the peninsula faces Bass Strait and Westernport Bay. A connected series of walking tracks is being developed all the way from London Bridge to Cape Schank and Bushrangers Bay. Some stretches of the Peninsula Coastal Walk are along the beach, some are actually cut by high tide, but in all the walk extends for over 30 km and takes over 12 hours to walk from end to end. The walks are best done in stages

because the park is narrow and is easily reached at various points.

Cape Schank is marked by the 1859 lighthouse and there are good walking possibilities around the cape. The rugged coast further east towards Flinders and West Head has natural features like the Blowhole. Towns like Flinders and Hastings on this coast are not quite as popular and crowded in the summer as those on Port Phillip Bay. Point Leo, near Shoreham, has a good surf beach. Off the coast in Westernport Bay is French Island, once a prison farm, which is virtually undeveloped, although there are a few camping sites and a lodge. Koalas were introduced some years ago, and the thriving colony now provides top-ups for depleted areas elsewhere in Victoria. A ferry operates between Stony Point and Cowes on Phillip Island, stopping at French Island on the way.

Phillip Island

At the entrance to Westernport Bay, 128 km south-east of Melbourne, Phillip Island is a very popular holiday resort for the Melbourne area. There are plenty of beaches, both sheltered and with surf, and a fascinating collection of wildlife including the island's famous fairy penguin colony. The island is joined to the mainland by a bridge from San Remo to Newhaven.

Information & Orientation

There is an excellent information centre in Newhaven just after you cross the bridge to the island. Cowes is the main town on the island. It's on the north side of the island and has a pleasant, sheltered beach. The south side of the island has the surf beaches like Woolamai, Cat Bay and Summerland, which in the evenings is the site of the famous penguin parade. Rhyll is a small fishing village on the east of the

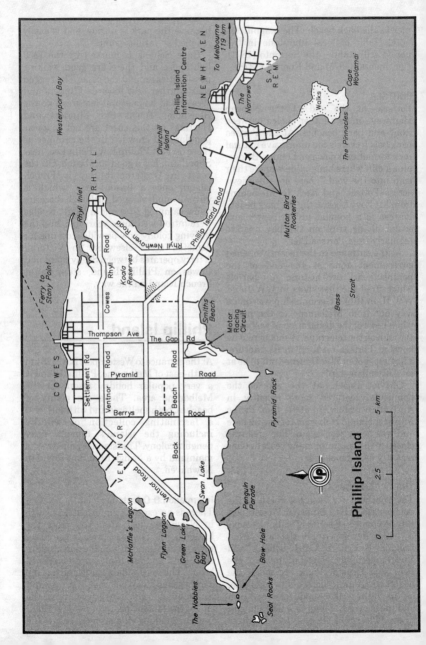

Phillip Island

island, while Ventnor is on the western coast.

Hotels, motels, camping grounds, restaurants, snack bars and other amenities can all be found in Cowes, which also has a Tourist Information Centre at 71 Thompson Ave.

Penguins, Koalas & Seals

Every evening at Summerland Beach in the south-west of the island, the tiny fairy penguins which nest there perform their 'parade', emerging from the sea and waddling resolutely up the beach to their nests – totally oblivious of the sightseers. The penguins are there year round but they arrive in far larger numbers in the summer when they are rearing their young. It's no easy life being the smallest type of penguin – after a few hours of shut-eye, it's down to the beach again at dawn to start another hard day's fishing.

The parade, which takes place like clockwork a few minutes after sunset each day, is a major tourist attraction so there are big crowds in summer. To protect the penguins you're strictly regimented – keep to the viewing areas, don't get in the penguins' way and no camera flashes. The admission charge is $3.50 but it's money well spent to see this unique sight. Or at least most of the time it is, occasionally the penguins seem to take a day off from fishing and the spectators far outnumber the handful of performers!

Off Grant Point, the extreme south-west tip of the island, a group of rocks rise from the sea. They're known as The Nobbies and are inhabited by a colony of about 5000 fur seals. You can view them through coin-in-the-slot binoculars from the food kiosk in the carpark on the headland, as long as it's open. There is also a ferry which makes the trip out to The Nobbies so you can view the seals at close proximity.

Koalas are the third wildlife attraction on the island. There are a number of koala sanctuaries around the island where you can see the lazy little creatures close up.

Phillip Island also has mutton-bird rookeries, particularly in the sand dunes around Cape Woolamai. The birds arrive in November each year from their migration flight from Japan and Alaska. You'll also find a wide variety of water birds including pelicans, ibis and swans in the swampland at the Nits at Rhyll. On Thompson Rd, Kingston Gardens Zoo is open daily and has a variety of native Australian wildlife as well as domesticated animals.

Other Attractions

Swimming and surfing are popular island activities and the old motor racing circuit was revamped to stage the Australian Motorcycle Grand Prix for the first time in 1989. At the circuit the Len Lukey Museum has a fine collection of veteran and vintage cars and racing cars. It's on Back Beach Rd and is open Sundays to Fridays from 10 am to 5 pm and Saturdays from 12 noon to 5 pm.

There's a blowhole, spectacular when the seas are high, at Grant Point. Rugged

Cape Woolamai with its walking track is particularly impressive. There's a real contrast between the high seas on this side of the island and the sheltered waters of the northern (Cowes) side.

Churchill Island is a small island with a restored house and beautiful gardens. It's connected to Phillip Island by footbridge and the turn-off is well signposted about one km out of Newhaven. It's open on weekends from 10 am to 5 pm, and from 1 to 5 pm on Mondays, Wednesdays and Fridays.

Places to Stay & Eat

Phillip Island is a very popular weekend (or longer) escape from Melbourne so there are all sorts of guest houses, motels, holiday flats and camping sites in Cowes, Newhaven, Rhyll and San Remo.

Phillip Island Backpackers (tel (059) 52 2167), also known as the *Penguin Inn*, is at 1-3 McKenzie Rd in Cowes and has accommodation from $9. At the *Anchor Belle Holiday Park* (tel (059) 52 2258) at 272 Church St, Cowes, YHA members can get a bed for $8.50. There are only 15 of them so it's advisable to book.

All the usual eating possibilities can be found in Cowes including some good fish & chip places. *The Jetty*, right by the jetty in Cowes, has excellent pub meals particularly the seafood. It's a bit expensive but the service is snappy and the surroundings pleasant.

Getting There & Around

Monday to Friday you can take a train from Spencer St to Dandenong from where a connecting V/Line bus continues around Westernport Bay to Cowes. The trip takes about three hours and costs $11.60.

The usual route to Phillip Island by public transport is in three parts: first a train from Flinders St to Frankston, then a bus (once on Saturdays, twice daily the rest of the week) to Stony Point, followed by the twice daily ferry service across to

Cowes via Tankerton on French Island. The one-way ferry fare is $5.

Phillip Island is also a cheap departure point for flights to Tasmania so you could continue on from one island to another. There are flights to Wynyard in Tasmania on Fridays and Sundays, and also on Wednesdays in January and February. They cost $90 each way, or there's a $70 standby fare. It's possible to combine these flights with a fly/drive package if you book through a travel agent. Contact Phillip Island Air Services (tel (059) 56 7316) for more information.

Tours There are many tours of Phillip Island available, mostly day-trips from Melbourne. One tour that's been recommended by backpackers is run by Autopia Tours, which operate from the YHA hostel (tel 328 3595) in Chapman St, North Melbourne. Their Phillip Island tour departs from the hostel on Sundays and Wednesdays at 1 pm and returns there at 10.30 pm. The cost is $30, which includes entrance to the penguin parade.

Geelong

Population 150,000

Geelong began as a sheep grazing area when the first settlers arrived in 1836 and it initially served as a port for the dispatch of wool and wheat from the area. This function was overshadowed during the gold rush era when it became important as a landing place for immigrants and for the export of gold. Around 1900 Geelong started to become industrialised and that's very much what it is today – an industrial city near Melbourne and Victoria's second largest city. In general there are no real 'not to be missed' attractions in Geelong and it is basically a place people transit on their way to greater attractions like the Great Ocean Road or the Otways.

Information

There's a tourist office (tel 97 220) at 83 Ryrie St. They have lots of information and are very useful if you're going down along the coast to the Otways or other areas around Geelong.

Historic Houses

The city has more than 100 National Trust classified buildings. Barwon Grange on Fernleigh St, Newtown, is a National Trust property built in 1856. It's open Saturday, Sunday and public holidays from 2 to 5 pm and admission is $3. That admission will also get you into a second National Trust property: The Heights at 140 Aphrasia St, which is open the same hours. This 14 room timber mansion is an example of a prefabricated building brought out to the colony in pieces. It has an unusual watchtower.

Another prefabricated building is Corio Villa, made from iron sheets in 1856. The bits and pieces were shipped out from Glasgow but nobody claimed them on arrival! Osborne House and Armytage House are other fine old buildings. These three are private houses and not open for inspection.

Museums & Art Gallery

The impressive National Wool Centre, corner of Brougham and Moorabool Sts, is housed in an historic bluestone woolstore and has a museum, a number of wool craft and clothing shops and a restaurant. It is open every day from 10 am to 5 pm and admission to the museum section is $4. The Port of Geelong Maritime Museum in Brougham St (near Yarra St) is open Wednesdays as well as Sundays in summer. There is also a small War Museum near the pier at the end of Moorabool St.

The Art Gallery on Little Malop St is open daily except Mondays and has lots of Australiana and some interesting modern art. Admission is $1.

Other Attractions

Geelong has a Botanic Gardens which contains the Customs House, Victoria's oldest wooden building, displaying telegraph equipment and memorabilia. Eastern Beach is Geelong's popular swimming spot and promenade where boats and bicycles can be hired on weekends in summer. There is also a signposted scenic drive route along the beach front. 'Bill the Boatman' has boat trips around the bay. They leave from Yarra Pier on weekends; phone 78 1697 for details.

Places to Stay

The small Geelong *Youth Hostel* (tel 21 6583) is at 1 Lonsdale St and costs $6. The colleges at Deakin University, on the outskirts of Geelong towards Colac, also have cheap accommodation in the summer holidays. Two cheap central hotels are the *Wool Exchange Hotel* (tel 9 5577) at 59 Moorabool St which has bed & breakfast rooms for $15 per person while the *Corio Hotel* (tel 9 2922) at 69 Yarra St has singles/doubles costing $12/20 without breakfast.

There are plenty of motels in Geelong. The *Colonial Lodge* (tel 21 3521) at 57 Fyans St is $29/35 for singles/doubles. Only one km from the centre the *Kangaroo* (tel 21 4022) is at 16 The Esplanade South and costs $26 to $35 single, $32 to $35 double.

Geelong has plenty of camping grounds. The closest to the city are in Belmont near the Barwon River. *Billabong*, *Riverglen* and *Southside* caravan parks are all on Barrabool Rd and camping sites cost around $9 and on-site vans $22.

Places to Eat

There are lots of cafes, take-aways, pubs with counter meals and a whole host of restaurants. You can get a cheap lunch at the food stalls in the Bay City Plaza on Moorabool St. The *Wholefoods Kitchen* in McLarty Place has good food and is

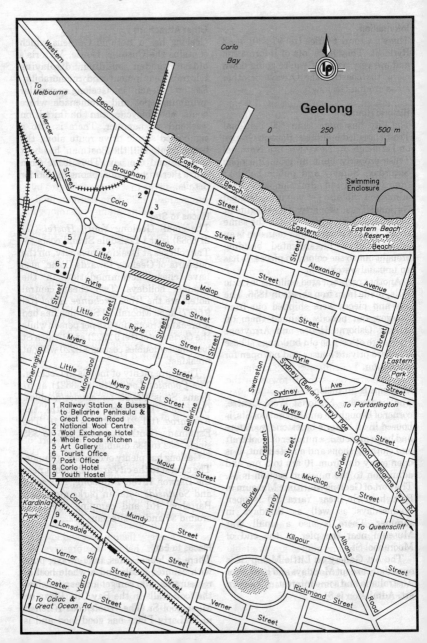

Geelong

Corio Bay

Swimming Enclosure

Eastern Beach Reserve

0   250   500 m

1 Railway Station & Buses
  to Bellarine Peninsula &
  Great Ocean Road
2 National Wool Centre
3 Wool Exchange Hotel
4 Whole Foods Kitchen
5 Art Gallery
6 Tourist Office
7 Post Office
8 Corio Hotel
9 Youth Hostel

To Melbourne

Western Beach

Mercer Street

Brougham

Corio Street

Malop Street

Eastern Beach

Alexandra Avenue

Little

Ryrie Street

Little Street

Ryrie Street

Swanston Street

Myers Street

Little

Myers Street

Yarra Street

Cheringhap

Moorabool Street

Bellerine Street

Sydney (Bellarine Hwy) Pde

Sydney

Myers

Ryrie

Ave

Street

Eastern Park

To Portarlington

Ormond (Bellarine Hwy) Rd

Garden Street

Street

McKillop Street

Bourke Street

Fitzroy Street

Crescent

St Albans Road

To Queenscliff

Kilgour Street

Maud Street

Carr Street

Kardinia Park

Lonsdale

Mundy Street

Verner St

Foster Street

Yarra St

Verner Street

Richmond Street

Verner Street

To Colac &
Great Ocean Rd

open during the day from Monday to Friday, and Friday evenings from 6.30 pm.

Getting There & Away

Trains between Melbourne and Geelong run at least hourly on weekdays starting before 6 am and continuing until 9 pm (from Geelong) or until 11.30 pm (from Melbourne). On Saturdays there's also an hourly service but over more restricted hours.

On Sundays there are only eight or nine trains, from 8 am to 8.20 pm ex-Geelong, 9.35 am to 10.45 pm ex-Melbourne. The fare is $5.50 economy, $7.30 1st. Trains run on from Geelong to Warrnambool via Colac and Winchelsea.

There's a twice daily railways bus between Geelong and Ballarat railway stations. The fare is $6.50 and the trip takes just under two hours. It's a pretty route with a number of small towns along the way; the bus stops to deliver things to little bluestone railway stations. There's a regular bus service between Geelong and Melbourne's Tullamarine Airport – see the Melbourne Getting Around section for details.

Bellarine Transit (tel 9 1173 or ring V/line) operates buses to all towns on the Bellarine Peninsula, as well as Torquay and Jan Juc. Buses leave from the railway station or you can catch them in Moorabool St near the Mall. There are frequent buses during the week, around four on Saturdays but only two on Sundays.

To Queenscliff costs $3.40, Torquay $2.90. For buses further down the coast see the Great Ocean Road section.

Getting Around

Geelong has an extensive city bus network and timetables and routes are available from the tourist office. On weekends you can hire bikes at the Barwon Valley Fun Park, near the Barwon River, and at Eastern Beach.

Bellarine Peninsula

Beyond Geelong the Bellarine Peninsula is a twin to the Mornington Peninsula, forming the other side of the entrance to Port Phillip Bay. Like the Mornington Peninsula this is a popular holiday resort and boating venue.

AROUND THE PENINSULA

Round the peninsula in Port Phillip Bay is Indented Head where Flinders landed in 1802, one of the first visits to the area by a European. In 1835 John Batman landed at this same point, on his way to buy up Melbourne.

At Portarlington there's a fine example of an early steam-powered flour mill. Built around 1856, the massive, solid building is owned by the National Trust and is open from 2 to 5 pm on Sundays from September to May and on weekends and Wednesdays during January. Portarlington has an associate *Youth Hostel* at 12 Grassy Point Rd and costs $5 a bed. St Leonards is a popular little resort just south of Indented Head.

QUEENSCLIFF (population 3200)

Queenscliff was established around 1838 as a pilot station to guide ships through The Rip at the entrance to Port Phillip Bay. Its heyday came in the 1880s when Queenscliff was the favourite resort of Melbourne's gentry and most of the town's fine buildings date from this period. Fort Queenscliff was built in 1882 to protect Melbourne from the perceived Russian threat and at the time it was the most heavily defended fort in the colony.

Queenscliff later fell from favour to become a sleepy fishing port and low-key resort, which helped to preserve its delightful Victorian character. Over the past few years it has been sand-blasted, paint-stripped and rediscovered by Melbourne's new gentry. Along the waterfront the Ozone and the Queenscliff are two hotels in the Victorian seaside 'grand' manner, very popular (and expensive) for leisurely weekend lunches.

Things to See

Queenscliff has a fascinating little Historical Centre beside the post office on Hesse St. It's open daily from 2 to 4.30 pm and over the main school holiday seasons it's also open from 10 am to 12 noon. You can get an interesting *Visitor's Guide to Queenscliff* here and explore the town with the walking-tour guide.

Queenscliff's Fort now houses the Australian Military College. The 'Black Lighthouse', dating from 1862, is within the fort; tours take place every day at 2 or 3 pm and cost $4. There's a fine ocean lookout below the fort.

Railway enthusiasts will enjoy the Bellarine Peninsula Railway (tel 52 2069), which operates from the old Queenscliff station with a fine collection of old steam trains. On Sundays, public holidays and most school holidays steam trains make the 16 km return trip to Drysdale ($6 adults, $3 children) or shorter runs to Laker's Siding ($3, $1.50).

Queenscliff also has a Maritime Centre down near the pier. It is open weekends and summer holidays; entry is $1. Queenscliff Historic Tours has one hour bus tours of Queenscliff and Point Lonsdale every day except Sundays from Christmas to Easter. Buses leave every hour and meet the passenger ferry at the pier. The cost is $7. They also operate day tours from Melbourne for $28 including all fares and lunch. Ring Keith Davidson on (052) 52 3403 for details.

Places to Stay

Seaview House (tel 52 1763), 86 Hesse St, is a guest house which costs $25 per person for bed & breakfast during the week, rising to $35 on weekends. The *Esplanade Hotel* (tel 52 1919) overlooks the foreshore and costs $30/45 for singles/doubles with breakfast. There are also four camping grounds and three have on-site vans for around $20. Nothing would be finer than

to stay in one of the restored grand hotels. With rooms starting from $50 and going way up, you can stay at the *Royal*, *Ozone*, *Belle Vue* or *Queenscliff* hotels.

Getting There & Away

A passenger ferry and a car ferry operate between Queenscliff and Sorrento on the Mornington Peninsula. See the Mornington Peninsula Getting There & Away section for details.

POINT LONSDALE

Point Lonsdale and Queenscliff are practically joined. The lighthouse guides ships through the narrow and often turbulent Rip into the bay. You can view The Rip from a lookout and walk to the lighthouse. Below the lighthouse is Buckley's Cave where the 'wild white man', William Buckley, lived with Aborigines for 32 years after escaping from the settlement at Sorrento on the Mornington Peninsula. Actually this area is dotted with 'Buckley Caves'!

OCEAN GROVE (population 6800)

This resort on the ocean side of the peninsula has good scuba diving on the rocky ledges of the Bluff and further out there are wrecks of ships which failed to make the tricky entrance to Port Phillip Bay. Some of the wrecks are accessible to divers. The beach at the surf life saving club is very popular with surfers. Ocean Grove is a real estate agent's paradise and has grown to become the biggest town on the peninsula.

Places to Stay & Eat

Ocean Grove has motels and holidays flats but there is no budget accommodation. There are plenty of caravan parks but even an on-site van will cost around $30. The *Ocean Grove Foreshore Caravan Park*, on the highway opposite the main beach, has sites for $12 and in December and January some of the foreshore is open for camping.

There are plenty of take-aways and

cafes in the shopping centre. The Terrace, the main shopping street, has four restaurants: *Ocean Grove Pizzas*, the *Ming Terrace* or the *Mexican Wave* have main courses for $10 or less, while the *Bay Leaf* is a bit more upmarket and has an interesting menu.

BARWON HEADS

Barwon Heads is a small resort just along from Ocean Grove. It has sheltered river beaches and surf beaches around the headland. The *Barwon Heads* hotel, overlooking the river, is a popular place for a drink or a meal, but the accommodation is overpriced at $50 a single. Barwon Heads also has caravan parks and a motel, and the *Moonlight* is a cheap Chinese restaurant on Hitchcock St.

The Great Ocean Road

For over 300 km, from Torquay (a short distance south of Geelong) almost to Warrnambool where the road joins the Princes Highway, the Great Ocean Road provides some of the most spectacular coastal scenery in Australia. For most of the distance the road hugs the coastline, passing some excellent surfing beaches, fine diving centres and even some hills from which hang-gliding enthusiasts launch themselves to catch the strong uplifts coming in from the sea in the evenings. If anything the scenery is even more impressive west of Lorne as the road climbs around steep cliffs, then drops to cross the numerous small creeks that flow down from the hills.

The coast is well equipped with camping sites and other accommodation possibilities and if the seaside activities pall, you can always turn inland to the bushwalks, wildlife, scenery, waterfalls and lookouts of the Otway Ranges which back the coast. The Great Ocean Road was only completed in 1932 as a works project during the depression, and stretches of the country through which it runs are still relatively untouched. The area was devastated by the firestorms of Ash Wednesday in 1983 and away from

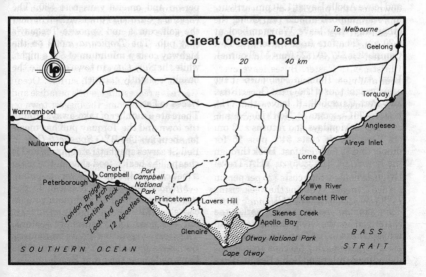

the road pockets of pine plantations nibble at the edges, but it's still magnificent.

Places to Stay

The whole coastal stretch is often heavily booked during the peak summer season and at Easter, when prices also jump dramatically. Accommodation is generally expensive, which only leaves camping or on-site vans for budget travellers, though there are associate youth hostels at Port Campbell and near Cape Otway.

Getting There & Away

V/Line have a bus service from Geelong railway station along the Great Ocean Road to Apollo Bay three times daily Monday to Friday, twice on Saturday and on Sunday. Fares from Geelong are Torquay $2.90, Anglesea $5.20, Lorne $9 and Apollo Bay $13.70. Bellarine Transit buses run more frequently from Geelong to Torquay and Jan Juc (see under Geelong).

V/line also has a new extended service to Port Campbell and Warrnambool on Fridays. Buses depart Geelong at 9.55 am and leave Apollo Bay at 1.40 pm, arriving in Port Campbell at 3.25 pm. Going the other way they leave Warrnambool at 9.20 am. The fare from Geelong to Port Campbell is $17.40 ($23 from Melbourne).

Tours Autopia Tours in Melbourne have an overnight tour of the Great Ocean Road and Port Campbell. It leaves the YHA hostel at 76 Chapman St, North Melbourne, at 9 am on Mondays and returns at 3 pm on Tuesdays. It costs $45, plus $5 for dinner and $2 for breakfast. Book through the hostel (tel 328 3595) or YHA Travel (tel 670 9611).

TORQUAY (population 5000)

This popular resort town marks the eastern end of the Great Ocean Road and is just 22 km south of Geelong. Some of the most popular surfing beaches are nearby, including Jan Juc and Bell's Beach. Bell's hosts an international surfing championship every Easter and waves can reach six metres or more. Around the town, Fisherman's Beach is the least crowded but often windy; the Front Beach and Back Beach are the most popular and best for swimming. In the new shopping complex on the Great Ocean Road are huge surf shops such as Rip Curl and Quicksilver.

There are tennis courts and a golf course at the western end of town. Past the golf course and just out of Torquay along Duffields Rd is Ocean Country Park which has a grass ski slope and waterslide.

The Surf Coast Walk follows the coastline from Jan Juc to Airey's Inlet. The full distance takes about 11 hours, but can be done in stages.

Places to Stay

There are three caravan/camping sites. *Zeally Bay* is right on Fisherman's Beach on the corner of the Esplanade and Darian Rd. *Bernell's* is on the Ocean Road near the new shopping complex. In peak periods they provide a free bus service to the beaches. A powered site costs $9 per person and on-site vans cost $30. The *Foreshore Caravan Park* is on Bell St near the golf course and opposite Torquay's only pub. The *Tropicana* motel on the highway costs a minimum of $50 a night, while the *Surf City*, in town opposite the beach, is slightly cheaper.

Places to Eat

There are a number of take-aways around the town and the Torquay pub has meals for about $9. The BYO *Spaghetti Cafe* in Bell St serves spaghetti and pizzas and is cheap. The health food shop in the main street close to the beach is very popular.

Micha's serves good Mexican food – starters are around $5 and main courses cost about $10. *Ida's* is slightly up-market but has good food, especially seafood. They serve vegetarian dishes on request. Both restaurants are BYOs and are on the Esplanade near the Front Beach.

The *Southern Rose Garden* is on the Great Ocean Road just out of Torquay on the way to Jan Juc. It has an à la carte ($25) and Mauritian banquet ($20) menu. It's licensed and there's a pleasant beer garden.

ANGLESEA (population 1500)

Another popular seaside resort, Anglesea is 44 km from Geelong and apart from beach activities it also offers the nearby Angahook Forest Park with many bushwalking trails, Iron Bark Grove, Treefern Grove, Melaleuca Swamp and the Currawong Falls. From Anglesea there is a 45 minute cliff walk – the local tourist organisation puts out a leaflet. The golf course at Anglesea is well known for the frequent visits by kangaroos which can be seen grazing the fairways. Another 10 km along the Great Ocean Road is Aireys Inlet, a pleasant smaller resort.

Places to Stay

Anglesea has a number of caravan parks, with on-site vans for around $25, as well as motels and a hotel. The *Debonair* (tel 63 1440) is a guest house and motel, with guest house rooms from $34/42 for singles/doubles (including breakfast) in the low season.

LORNE (population 1000)

The small town of Lorne, 73 km from Geelong, was a popular seaside resort even before the Great Ocean Road was built. The mountains behind the town not only provide a spectacular backdrop but also give the town a mild, sheltered climate year round. Lorne has good beaches, surfing and bushwalks in the vicinity. It's also losing its low-key, low rise beach resort feeling as flashier summer houses are appearing, BMWs become increasingly the car of choice and the high rise Cumberland Resort towers over the town centre.

Climb up to Teddy's Lookout behind the town for the fine views along the coast. The beautiful Erskine Falls are also close

behind Lorne; you can drive there or follow the walking trail beside the river, passing Splitter's Falls and Straw Falls on the way. There are numerous other short and long walks around Lorne. Pick up a copy of the useful Lorne tourist leaflet from the shops or the BP service station.

When you tire of walking or the beach you can always poke around in the rock pools at low tide or catch a film at Lorne's little cinema. In the season there's music most nights at the Lorne hotels.

In between Lorne and Apollo Bay are a number of small settlements that are rapidly becoming resorts in their own right, such as Wye River, Kennett River and Skeynes Creek.

Places to Stay

Prices soar and the no-vacancy signs go out during the summer school holiday season when half of Melbourne seems to move down. Even pitching a tent in one of the camping sites could prove difficult at peak periods.

The *Lorne Hotel* (tel (052) 89 1409) on the Great Ocean Road has rooms at $40 in the low season, all with attached bathroom. You need to book ahead for weekends all year. Further along by the pier the *Pacific Hotel* (tel (052) 89 1609) has similar rooms at similar prices. *Torrens Motel* (tel (052) 89 1307) at 124 Mountjoy Parade in the centre of town has rooms at $45 to $65 in the low season, up towards $100 in the high. Motel and holiday flat prices are very variable with season.

Lorne has a number of old-fashioned guest houses, best known of which is *Erskine House* (tel (052) 89 1209) on Mountjoy Parade. Rooms range from $70 per person including all meals. Past guests include Rudyard Kipling who stayed here in 1891. The *Chalet Lorne* (tel (052) 89 1241) at 4 Smith St is a cheaper alternative.

The Lorne Foreshore Committee has four camping sites at Lorne; the *Erskine River Section* is pleasantly sited by the river and right in the thick of things. The *Queens Park Section* is above it all, on the headland overlooking the pier. Site prices are in the $11 to $15 range and there are minimum booking requirements at peak periods.

Places to Eat

There's no chance of boredom when it comes to eating out in Lorne although at the fancier restaurants you should make sure you have a table booked during the season.

At the economical end of the scale there are counter meals at the *Lorne Hotel* and the *Pacific Hotel*; a collection of fast-food, pizza and take-away places; or great pita bread and other health-food at the *Beach Bite* on the beach by the swimming pool. Plus there's a *Pancake Parlour* by the cinema with a pleasant open air deck and the famous *Arab* which has been a Lorne institution since the mid-'50s. Main courses at the Arab are typically $8 to $12.

Moving up the scale there's *Kosta's Tavern* which is much more international

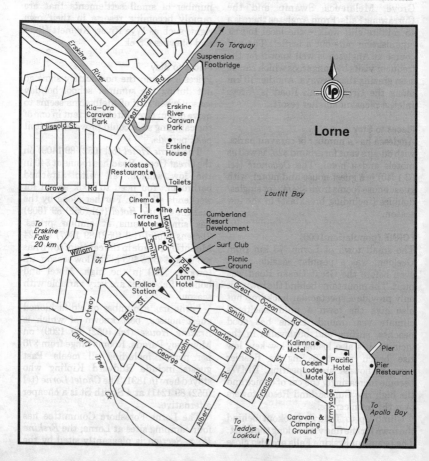

than its Greek name would indicate; while down at the pier, the *Pier Gallery* serves seafood (and vegetarian food and steaks) in a very Californian ambience. Coffee or a snack sitting outside watching the fishing boats is very pleasant.

Just past the pier on the Apollo Bay side of town *Point Grey Country Kitchen* is famed for its scones.

APOLLO BAY (population 920)

The pretty port of Apollo Bay, 118 km from Geelong, is a fishing town and popular resort (but more relaxed than Lorne). There is a small historical museum, open Sundays and holidays, and a shell museum, but the real attraction is the beaches and Apollo Bay is a good base from which to explore the Otway Ranges. Mariners Lookout a few km from town provides excellent views along the coast. The town has a good tourist information centre.

Places to Stay

The *Bay Hotel* (tel 37 6240) is good value and has off season singles/doubles for $18/28 in the hotel section. The *Koonjeree Guest House* (tel 37 6290), a few streets behind the Bay on the corner of Nelson and Diana Sts, is a drab prefab place but cheap enough with singles/doubles for $18/28 in the guest house or $22/34 in the motel section. You can probably negotiate the price when things are quiet. For a cheap motel the *Bay Pine* (tel 37 6732), 1 Murray St, is very pleasant and costs $28/40 for singles/doubles. There are also plenty of caravan parks such as the *Waratah* near the golf course where a site costs $10 and on-site vans are $26.

Places to Eat

The *Bay Hotel* and the *Apollo Bay Hotel* are in competition for the best bistro meals, and they both have very good food at high prices. The Bay's bistro charges around $14 a meal, but you can get less fancy fare for half that price in the bar. *Flipz* offers a variety of pancake meals,

including breakfast, or for fancier dining there's the *Beacon Point Restaurant*.

CAPE OTWAY

From Apollo Bay the road temporarily leaves the coast to climb up and over Cape Otway. The coast is particularly beautiful and rugged on this stretch and there have been many shipwrecks. Cape Otway is covered in rainforest, much of it still relatively untouched, and although many of the roads through the cape are unsurfaced and very winding, they present no problems for the average car.

There are a number of scenic lookouts and nature reserves along here but Melba Gully is probably the best, with the beautiful ferns for which the cape is noted. In this reserve is one of the area's last remaining giant gums – it's over 25 metres in circumfrence. Just beyond this small park is Lavers Hill, a tiny township which once had a thriving timber business. Waterfalls, such as Hopetoun Falls and Beachamps Falls, and gemstones found at Moonlight Head are other Otway attractions.

The 1848 convict-built Cape Otway Lighthouse is nearly 100 metres high and is 15 km off the main road. The lighthouse is open Monday to Friday from 10 am to 4 pm; at other times you can't get to the end of the cape but there is a path beside the fence which leads to the cliff and good views back along the coast.

The Great Ocean Road continues from Lavers Hill past the turn-off to Johanna, which has camping and good surfing, to Princetown where there is camping, and camel rides in December and January. At Princetown the road rejoins the coast and runs right along it again, through the spectacular Port Campbell National Park.

Places to Stay

The Department of Conservation leaflet shows camping sites in the national park. Pick one up at the tourist information centre in Apollo Bay or the general store in Lavers Hill. *Bimbi Park* (tel 37 9246) is an adventure camp and caravan park offering horse riding. For youth hostel members, accommodation in tents costs $3 or $7 in a caravan if available – for others it is $5 and $22 respectively. Take the Cape Otway road from the main highway and the Bimbi Park turn-off is about three km before the lighthouse. It is then about a km to the park.

PORT CAMPBELL NATIONAL PARK

If the Great Ocean Road offers some of the most dramatic coastal scenery in Australia, then the stretch through Port Campbell is the most exciting part. The views are fantastic with beautiful scenes like the rock formations known as the Twelve Apostles where 12 huge stone pillars soar out of the pounding surf. Or there's London Bridge, a bridge-like promontory arching across a furious sea.

Loch Ard Gorge has a sadder tale to tell: in 1878 the iron-hulled clipper *Loch Ard* was driven onto the rocks offshore at this point. Of the 50 or so on board only two were to survive: an apprentice officer and an immigrant girl, both aged 18. They were swept into the narrow gorge now named after their ship. Although the papers of the time tried to inspire a romance between the two survivors, the girl, the sole survivor of a family of eight, soon headed back to Ireland's safer climes. This was the last immigrant sailing ship to founder en route to Australia.

A little further along the coast is Port Campbell itself, the main centre in the National Park and again sited on a spectacular gorge with some fine walks in the hills behind the town. Port Campbell has a pleasant beach and calm waters.

Soon after Port Campbell the Great Ocean Road veers away from the coast at Peterborough to join the Princes Highway just before Warrnambool. The spectacular, eroded sandstone coastline continues and there are turn-offs to places like the Bay of Islands.

Places to Stay & Eat

In Port Campbell township, the associate YHA *Tregea Hostel* (tel (055) 98 6379) is a pleasant, easy-going place overlooking the gorge. A dorm bed costs $8 and enquiries should be made at Elson's

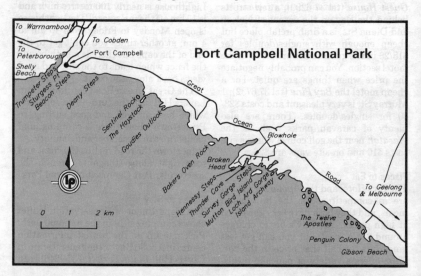

general store. Port Campbell has three motels and the *Port Campbell Hotel* has overpriced rooms at $30 a single with breakfast. The caravan park faces the gorge and has camping sites for $6. The hotel has counter meals and the *Gallery* has take-aways and sit-down meals.

The South-West Coast

At Warrnambool the Great Ocean Road ends and you're on the final south-west coast stretch to South Australia on the Princes Highway. This stretch includes some of the earliest settlements in the state.

V/Line operate between Melbourne and Warrnambool via Geelong and Colac, with connecting buses on to Port Fairy and Portland. Economy fares from Melbourne (1st class in brackets) are: Colac $13 ($18.30), Warrnambool $21.70 ($30.30), Port Fairy $23 ($32) and Portland $29 ($38). Buses also run from Warrnambool to Hamilton and Casterton. V/line also has buses along the Great Ocean Road from Apollo Bay via Port Campbell.

There are buses and flights to Hamilton from Melbourne with connections to

Portland, Warrnambool and Mt Gambier in South Australia. Greyhound operate along the coast route between Melbourne and Adelaide once a week. From Melbourne fares include Warrnambool $25, Port Fairy $27 and Portland $34.

WARRNAMBOOL (population 22,900)
Warrnambool is 264 km from Melbourne and has sheltered beaches as well as surf beaches. Gun emplacements intended to repel the Russian invasion which Australia feared in the 1880s can be seen near the lighthouse. This is now the site of the Flagstaff Hill Maritime Village with a museum, restored sailing ships and port buildings of the era. It's open daily from 9.30 am to 4.30 pm. Warrnambool also has a History House and a Time & Tide Museum. At Logan's Beach there is a whale viewing area. Southern right whales visit the beach every year and every third year they amass in large numbers to give birth.

The Heritage Trail walk starts from the tourist office, while 12 km west of the town is Tower Hill with its huge crater lake and a game reserve with many emus.

The tourist information centre (tel 64 7837) at 600 Raglan Parade produces

Cliffs, Port Campbell National Park

the excellent *Warrnambool Handbook* with detailed information on sights, accommodation, transport, etc.

Places to Stay & Eat

There are over 50 motels, hotels, holiday flats and caravan parks in Warrnambool. There are a number of cheap hotels in Liebig St, including the *Commercial*, which has singles/doubles for \$15/25 with a light breakfast, and *Tattersalls* with single/double rooms for \$12/18.

There are many restaurants, both BYO and fully licensed, cafes and take-aways. Warrnambool must have a sweet tooth – you can buy ice-creams and chocolates at *Flaherty's* on Kepler St every day until midnight.

PORT FAIRY (population 2400)

This small fishing port 27 km west of Warrnambool was one of the first European settlements in the state, dating back to 1835, although there were temporary visitors right back in 1826. These first arrivals were whalers and sealers seeking shelter along the coast; Port Fairy is still the home port for one of Victoria's largest fishing fleets.

Port Fairy was originally known as Belfast and although the name was later changed there's still a Northern Irish flavour about the place and a Belfast Bakery on the main street.

There are many fine old buildings dating back to the town's early days and 50 are classified by the National Trust. One of the finest is the bluestone home originally built for Captain Mills, a whaling boat skipper. Parts of Mott's Cottage date from 1845 and it's now owned by the National Trust and is open from 2 to 4 pm on Saturdays, Sundays too during the summer. The early ANZ Bank, the old Caledonian Inn and Seacombe House are other interesting buildings. Built in 1844 the Caledonian is the oldest licensed pub in Victoria.

Also worth a look is the historical centre on Bank St, the old fort and signal station at the mouth of the river, and Griffiths Island which is reached by a causeway from the town and has a lighthouse and a mutton bird rookery.

On the Labour Day long weekend in early March the Port Fairy Folk Festival is held. It's a major festival, with the emphasis on Irish-Australian music, and it attracts top performers. The town's population swells by around 500% during the festival and except for camping accommodation is non-existent.

Places to Stay & Eat

There are several camping sites and a number of guest houses, hotels and motels. The *Emoh Youth Hostel* (tel (055) 68 2468) is at 6 Cox St and costs \$7.50.

There is a surprisingly wide variety of places to eat for such a small town, and the emphasis is naturally on fresh seafood.

PORTLAND (population 9300)

Continuing west 72 km from Port Fairy you reach Portland, just 75 km from the South Australian border. This is the oldest settlement in Victoria. Established in 1834 it predates Port Fairy by one year. It's an indication of the piecemeal development of Victoria that the first 'official' visitor, Major Thomas Mitchell, turned up here on an overland expedition from Sydney in 1836 and was surprised to find it had been settled two years earlier. Whalers knew this stretch of coast long before the first permanent settlement and there were even earlier short-term visitors.

Portland has numerous classified buildings including the old Steam Packet Inn at 33 Bentinck St which is owned by the National Trust. Dating from 1842, this early inn was prefabricated in Tasmania and is now open from 2 to 4 pm on Wednesdays and weekends. Other early buildings include Mac's Hotel and the Customs House and Court House on Cliff St. The lighthouse at the tip of Cape Nelson, south of Portland, is also classified by the National Trust.

From Cape Bridgewater you can make pleasant walks to Cape Duquesne and Discovery Bay. From Portland the Princes Highway turns inland through Heywood and Dartmoor before crossing the border to Mt Gambier in South Australia but there is also a smaller road which runs closer to the coast, fringed by the Discovery Bay Coastal Park. It meets the coast just before the border at the delightful little town (village even) of Nelson, a popular resort for Mt Gambier. This is also a good access point to the Lower Glenelg National Park with its deep gorges and brilliant wildflowers.

Places to Stay

Portland has numerous camping sites, guest houses and motels. The *Nioka Farm Home Hostel* (tel (055) 20 2233) is 40 km west of Portland at Mt Richmond. Book ahead since there's only room for five at $14 per day for YHA members including breakfast and dinner. This is a good opportunity to stay on a working sheep farm. They will arrange to pick you up from Portland.

Western District

The south-west of the state, inland from the coast and stretching to the South Australian border, is particularly affluent sheep raising and pastoral country. Malcolm Fraser was just one of the wealthy prime ministers to come from the Western District. Early explorer Thomas Mitchell dubbed this fertile region 'Australia Felix'.

V/Line will get you to Hamilton via Ballarat by bus or via Ballarat and Ararat by train and then bus. They also have a combination train and bus service via Terang or Warrnambool to Hamilton and Casterton and on to Mt Gambier in South Australia. From Melbourne the 1st/economy fare is $32/24.70 to Hamilton, from Hamilton it's $11.60 to Mt Gambier.

Hamilton is quite a centre for local buses; you can travel to Mt Gambier, Portland, Horsham, Warrnambool or Ballarat. Hamilton is also connected to Melbourne by air – Flinders Island Air (tel (03) 580 3777) charges $190 return.

MELBOURNE TO HAMILTON

You can reach Hamilton, the 'capital' of the Western District, via Ballarat along the Glenelg Highway or via Geelong along the Hamilton Highway. On the Glenelg Highway the Mooramong homestead at Skipton is owned by the National Trust and open by appointment. Further along the highway the small town of Lake Bolac is beside a large freshwater lake, popular for watersports. Inverleigh is an attractive little town along the Hamilton Highway.

The Princes Highway runs further south, reaching the coast at Warrnambool. Winchelsea is on the Princes Highway and has a museum in the 1842 Barwon Hotel and there's also the Barwon Park Homestead. The stone Barwon Bridge dates from 1867. You can reach the Grampians on a scenic route from Dunkeld on the Glenelg Highway.

COLAC (population 10,500)

On the eastern edge of the Western District there are many volcanic lakes in the vicinity of the town. Alvie and Red Rock Lookouts give good views over the area. Colac has a botanic garden on the shore of Lake Colac. Provan's Mechanical Museum displays old cars and other mechanical antiques and is open Monday to Friday and on Saturday mornings.

South of the town are the Otway Ranges and scenic routes run through the ranges to the Great Ocean Road. Around Beech Forest there are still traces of the railway which was built to serve the timber industry, when it was on a much larger scale. Weeaproinah, near Beech Forest, is one of the wettest places in Victoria.

Places to Stay

Colac has a number of motels; the

Commercial Hotel (tel (052) 31 5777) on the main street has motel-style rooms from $35/45 for singles/doubles.

CAMPERDOWN (population 3500)

There are many volcanic crater lakes around this pleasant town; you can see nearly 40 of them from the lookout on top of Mt Leura, itself an extinct volcano. Lake Gnotuk and Lake Bullen Merri, two crater lakes close to the town, are notable because although they are very close together their water levels are about 50 metres different! Also close to Camperdown is Victoria's largest lake: the salt Lake Corangamite. From Camperdown roads lead south through Cobden to Port Campbell and the Great Ocean Road.

Places to Stay

On the main street is the *Commercial Hotel* (tel (055) 93 1187) which has singles/doubles from $20/40 with breakfast, and the *Leura Hotel* (tel (055) 93 1062) with singles/doubles for $14/24. There are also motels, camping sites and a *Youth Hostel* (tel (055) 93 1864) at 15 Church St which charges just $6 a night.

HAMILTON (population 9700)

The major town of the area, Hamilton is particularly known for its superb art gallery on Brown St; it's one of the best in any Australian country town. Lake Hamilton is right in the centre of town and there's a zoo in the botanic gardens. The South-West Regional Authority tourist office is on Lonsdale St. The Hamilton & Western District Museum (tel (055) 73 0444), on Gray St, houses an Aboriginal 'keeping place' – the works of craft and art of the local tribes preserved by them as a means of maintaining their history and culture. It's open Wednesday to Friday 11 am to 1 pm and 2 to 4 pm and admission is $1.

Wannon Falls (15 km from Hamilton) and Nigretta Falls (seven km) are two local attractions. Mt Eccles National Park is 33 km out and has the crater Lake Surprise. There are two other extinct volcanoes close to town. These reminders of volcanic origins are evident all through the south-west region.

There are great views from the summit of Mt Napier.

Beyond Hamilton is Casterton with an historical museum in the old railway building and the very fine National Trust classified homestead Warrock, open daily.

Coleraine, another very early Victorian settlement, is between Hamilton and Casterton.

LAKE CONDAH

At Lake Condah Aboriginal Mission (tel (055) 78 4242) about 25 km south of Hamilton on the Portland road there is an important project tracing the history and culture of local tribes.

Most of Victoria's Aborigines suffered early and rapid detribalisation, especially in the Western District where the squatters (land-grabbers who became wealthy pastoralists – today's 'squattocracy') quickly cleared the land of its people in their hurry to begin intensive sheep farming.

Part of the legalistic argument against granting Aboriginal land claims in the '70s was that as they were a nomadic people who didn't work the land they couldn't be said to have ever 'owned' Australia. That argument was eventually thrown out of court, and the recent discovery of permanent stone dwellings and a complex system of stone canals and fish traps at Lake Condah should be enough to convince the most materialistic Aussie that by any criteria the Aborigines did indeed own Australia.

The mission is now run by the Kerrup-jmara community – there are four-bed cabins which cost $30 a night and also a couple of family units and larger units for groups.

Central West & the Wimmera

Several roads run west from the Victorian gold country to the South Australian border. The main road is the Western Highway which is also the busiest route between Melbourne and Adelaide. From Ballarat the road runs north of the Little Desert while to the north and south is the Wimmera – the seemingly endless Victorian wheatfields.

From Horsham the Wimmera Highway splits off the Western Highway and runs through this area which also extends north-east to Warracknabeal and Donald. In the south of the region is one of the area's major attractions, indeed one of the most spectacularly scenic areas of Victoria – the mountains of the Grampians.

The Western Highway is the main route between Melbourne and Adelaide and the Melbourne/Adelaide railway line takes the same route so there is no shortage of transport along this way. The nightly Overland runs right through to Adelaide while Monday to Saturday V/Line have a Daylink train service which runs as far as Dimboola with a connecting bus through to Adelaide. There's also a Monday to Saturday night train to Dimboola and a Sunday day train.

First/economy fares from Melbourne include Ararat $24.30/17.30, Horsham $31.60/24.70, Stawell $28.70/20.50, Dimboola $41.30/29.30, Nhill $41.30/29.30, Kaniva $43.30/31.

The interstate bus lines all operate Melbourne/Adelaide along this route with fares of Ararat $29, Stawell $32, Horsham $32, Dimboola $39, Nhill $40 and Kaniva $42. Buses head north from Horsham to Ouyen and Mildura or south to Hamilton in the Western District.

BEAUFORT

After leaving Ballarat by its long, tree-lined memorial drive you reach Beaufort about halfway to Ararat. For a brief period in its gold rush heyday this small town had an enormous population chasing the elusive metal at Fiery Creek. Today it's a quiet farming centre with good bushwalking areas in the Mt Cole State Forest, 16 km to the north-west. The *Beaufort Motel* (tel (053) 49 2297) has singles/doubles from $34/42, or you can camp at the *Beaufort Lake Caravan Park* (tel (053) 49 2196) for $8.

ARARAT (population 9000)

After a brief flirtation with gold in 1857, Ararat settled down as a farming centre. It has a folk museum with an Aboriginal collection, an art gallery and some fine old bluestone buildings. The tourist information centre is on the corner of Barkly and Vincent Sts.

Only 16 km north-west of Ararat on the Western Highway, Great Western is one of Australia's best known champagne regions. Seppelt's Great Western vineyards were established in 1865. The unique Sisters Rocks are between here and Stawell. There are walks and barbecue sites in the Langi Ghiran State Forest, 14 km east. On the Melbourne side of Ararat there are some historic buildings in Buangor. Old gold towns in the area include Cathcart and Mafeking, which once had a population of 10,000. In nearby Moyston on Boxing Day they host the world rabbit-skinning championships!

Places to Stay

There are two caravan parks with on-site vans and camping facilities, and a range of motel and hotel accommodation. The *Ararat Hotel* (tel (053) 52 2477) and the *Turf Hotel* (tel (053) 52 2393) are on Barkly St and both have rooms from $15/26 for singles/doubles, with breakfast.

STAWELL (population 6800)

A centre for visits to the Grampians and another early Victorian gold town, Big Hill was the site of the town's first gold discovery. There is a tourist information office (tel (053) 58 2314) on London Rd.

The attractive little town has a number of National Trust classified buildings, an illuminated fountain, an animated clock in the town hall and a whole collection of war and other memorials. Mini-World has models of everything from the Eiffel Tower to a Dutch windmill; you can safely bypass it. Every Easter the Stawell Gift, a foot-race carnival with big prize-money and a big betting ring, is held in Central Park.

Bunjil's Cave, with Aboriginal rock paintings, is 11 km south and other attractions include Sisters Rocks, Roses Gap Wildlife Reserve 17 km south, and the National Trust Tottington Woolshed, 55 km north-east.

Places to Stay & Eat

There are a number of pubs in Stawell with good counter meals – try the *Albion Hotel* on Gold Reef Mall in the centre.

Accommodation choices are varied – there are farms where you can stay from around $55 a double; cabins; on-site vans and camping sites at two caravan parks; and various motels and hotels.

THE GRAMPIANS

Named after the mountains of the same name in Scotland, the Grampians are the south-west tail end of the Great Dividing Range. The area is a large national park renowned for fine bushwalks, superb mountain lookouts, excellent rock climbing opportunities, prolific wildlife and, in the spring, countless wildflowers. The Grampians are at their best from August to November when the flowers are most colourful. On a weekend in early spring there's a wildflower exhibition in the Halls Gap Hall. There are also many Aboriginal rock paintings in the Grampians. Waterfalls, such as the spectacular McKenzie Falls, are another Grampians attraction.

There are many fine bushwalks around the Grampians, some of them short strolls you can make right from the middle of Halls Gap. Keep an eye out for koalas and kangaroos; you sometimes see koalas right in the middle of Halls Gap.

There is talk of returning the Grampians to their traditional Aboriginal owners, although they would be leased back to the government in the same way that Ayers Rock/Uluru is. Whether or not this happens the government seems set on changing the name back to the Aboriginal name of Guriward.

Information & Orientation

The Grampians lie immediately west of Ararat and south of the Western Highway between Stawell and Horsham. Stawell, 25 km away, has the closest railway station to the tiny town of Halls Gap. Halls Gap, about 250 km from Melbourne, is also right in the middle of the region and has camping and motel facilities. The Grampians Tourist Information Centre in Halls Gap (tel (053) 56 4247) has a good selection of maps and information sheets.

Things to See

To the west, the rugged Victoria Range is known for its redgums, and there are many Aboriginal rock paintings in the area, including those at the Glenisla Shelter near Glenisla on the Henty Highway. Victoria Valley, in the centre of the Grampians, is a secluded wildlife sanctuary with beautiful bush tracks to drive down.

To the north at Zumsteins, 22 km from Halls Gap, kangaroos gather in a paddock late every afternoon for the free feed they've grown to expect.

Be warned that these are wild animals and should not be treated like domestic pets.

Activities

The many walks in the Grampians range from well-marked (although often quite arduous) trails to some very rugged walking in the large areas which have been kept free of trails. The best known established trails are in the Wonderland

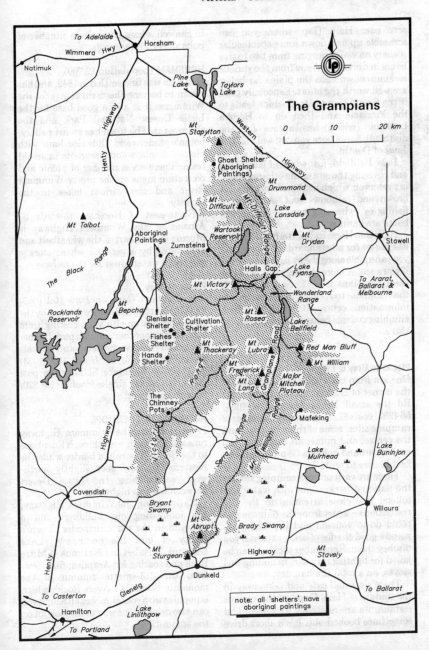

The Grampians

0   10   20 km

To Adelaide

Wimmera Hwy

Horsham

Natimuk

Pine Lake

Taylors Lake

Mt Stapylton

Ghost Shelter (Aboriginal Paintings)

Mt Drummond

Mt Difficult

Lake Lonsdale

Mt Talbot

Aboriginal Paintings

Zumsteins

Wartook Reservoir

Mt Dryden

Halls Gap

Lake Fyans

The Black Range

Mt Bepcha

Mt Victory

Wonderland Range

To Ararat, Ballarat & Melbourne

Rocklands Reservoir

Glenisla Shelter

Cultivation Shelter

Mt Rosea

Lake Bellfield

Fishes Shelter

Mt Thackeray

Hands Shelter

Mt Lubra

Red Man Bluff

Mt William

The Chimney Pots

Mt Frederick

Major Mitchell Plateau

Mt Lang

Grampians Road

Mafeking

Lake Muirhead

Lake Buninjon

Cavendish

Bryant Swamp

Mt Abrupt

Brady Swamp

Willaura

Mt Sturgeon

Dunkeld

Lake Stavely

To Casterton

Glenelg Highway

To Ballarat

Hamilton

Lake Linlithgow

To Portland

Western Highway

Stawell

Henty Highway

Victoria Range

Serra Range

Mt Difficult Range

note: all 'shelters' have aboriginal paintings

area near Halls Gap, where you can scramble up and down some spectacular scenery on walks ranging from two to five hours in duration. Views from the various lookouts down onto the plains far below are well worth the effort. Especially good is the Grand Canyon trail which leads to the Pinnacle and then on to Boroka Lookout (which has access for the disabled). From here you can walk to The Jaws of Death!

Lake Bellfield, just south of Halls Gap and covering the site of the original town, is a reservoir which has been stocked with brown and rainbow trout. A bonus of fishing or swimming here is that power boats are banned.

Halls Gap Horse Riding (tel (053) 56 4327) has horses for all standards of riders, and you can amble along the trails unsupervised if you want. A more leisurely way of seeing the Grampians is by hot-air balloon. If that sounds too easy, ask the tourist information centre if there are rock climbing courses being held while you are there.

Places to Stay & Eat

One km from the centre of Halls Gap on the corner of Buckler St and Grampians Rd the small *Youth Hostel* (tel (053) 56 4262) costs $7.50. There are a number of camping sites, some of them right around the centre, and numerous motels. If you enquire around in Halls Gap you can also find houses to rent.

There are various bush camping sites in the national park, some with water and toilets. Pay close attention to the fire restrictions – apart from the damage you could do to yourself and the bush, you stand a good chance of being caught if you disobey them. Remember that you can be jailed for lighting *any* fire, including fuel stoves, on a total fire ban day.

There's a small cafe and take-away in the middle of Halls Gap but the various restaurants are relatively expensive and sometimes booked out. It's a short drive to Stawell where there are a number of pubs with counter meals.

HORSHAM (population 12,700)

Horsham was first settled in 1842, and has grown to become the main centre for the Wimmera. It is also a good base for the Little Desert National Park and the Grampians. The town has an art gallery, botanic gardens and 'Olde Horsham' with historic displays and a tearoom in an old tram. There are a number of picnic and recreation areas on the pretty Wimmera River and the various lakes in the vicinity.

North-east of Horsham towards St Arnaud on the Wimmera Highway is Murtoa in the heart of the wheatbelt and dominated by a gigantic wheat storage silo and a water tower for the railway.

Places to Stay

The *Horsham Caravan Park* (tel (053) 82 3476) is at the end of Firebrace St by the river and has on-site vans costing from $20. There's another caravan park further out, and many motels and hotels including the *Royal Hotel* (tel (053) 82 1255) on Firebrace St near the post office, which has singles/doubles for $20/35 with breakfast.

HORSHAM TO EDENHOPE

From Horsham the Wimmera Highway runs slightly south-west through Edenhope to the South Australian border while the Western Highway goes slightly north-west, sandwiching the Little Desert between the two highways.

Natimuk, on the Wimmera Highway, has interesting old buildings and a museum in the old courthouse. There's plenty of bird life on nearby Lake Natimuk. Just beyond Natimuk is Mitre Rock and soaring Mt Arapiles; fine views from the 213 metre summit of the monolith, 'Victoria's Ayers Rock', which is popular with rockclimbers although you can also drive all the way to the lookout on the summit.

There are a number of lakes around Edenhope including Lake Wallace with its many water birds. The tiny town of Harrow, 32 km south-east, is a very early Victorian country settlement with old buildings including the 1851 Hermitage Hotel and an 1862 log jail.

DIMBOOLA (population 1700)

The name of this quiet, typical Australian country town on the Wimmera River is a Sinhalese word meaning 'land of the figs'. The Pink Lake, just south of the highway, is a little beyond Dimboola. Beside the Wimmera River nearby you can see Aboriginal canoe trees where canoes have been cut out in one piece from the bark of the redgums. The Ebenezer Mission Station was established in Antwerp, north of Dimboola, to tend to local Aborigines in 1859.

Places to Stay

The *Dimboola Caravan Park* (tel (053) 89 1416) is in Wimmera St by the river and has on-site vans costing from $15. There's also a motel and a couple of hotels.

NHILL (population 2300)

The excellent film *Wrong World* used Nhill as a metaphor for Australian spiritual emptiness, but that was a little unfair. Nhill is a pleasant little town midway between Melbourne and Adelaide and is another Wimmera wheat farming centre, also acting as a centre for the Mallee region to the north. The 1881 post office is classified by the National Trust and in the town centre is a memorial to the Clydesdale horses which were used extensively in the development of the Wimmera. The grassy park strip right in the centre of town is a good place for an impromptu picnic.

Places to Stay

The *Nhill Caravan Park* on the Western Highway has on-site vans from $12. There are several motels and hotels, including the *Farmers Arms* and the *Union* which are near the post office and have singles/doubles for around $16/26, with breakfast.

KANIVA (population 1000)

Further west and just before the South Australian border, Kaniva is also on the edge of the Little Desert. There's an interesting three km walking track, the Billy-Ho Bush Walk, about 10 km from the town with numbered examples of desert flora.

Kaniva has an historical museum and a wildlife reserve with emus on the South Australian side of town.

Serviceton, almost on the South Australian border, has a National Trust classified railway station with an enormously long platform and basement dungeons.

Places to Stay

You can camp at the *Kaniva Caravan Park* (tel (053) 92 2515) or try the motel or one of the hotels.

LITTLE DESERT

Just south of the Western Highway and reached from Dimboola or Nhill, the Little Desert National Park is noted for its brilliant display of wildflowers in the spring. The name is a bit of a misnomer because it isn't really a desert at all nor is it that little – in fact it's Victoria's second largest national park, and the 'desert' extends well beyond the national park boundaries.

If you intend really to explore the bushland of the park you'll need 4WD. The desert is at its finest in the spring when it is carpeted with wildflowers. A little beyond Dimboola the Kiata Lowan Sanctuary is an easily accessible area in the north of the park with walks and a resident ranger.

You can camp in the park at sites 10 km south of Kiata, just east of Nhill. There is tank water and no showers. Phone the park ranger on (053) 91 1275 for information. The *Little Desert Lodge* (tel (053) 91 5232, 91 1714), in the park and

16 km south of Nhill, caters to groups of 12 or more and includes an environmental study centre and the world's only aviary with the fascinating Mallee Fowl. They have a lot of information on the area and run 4WD tours for groups of five or more. You can camp here and use the facilities – contact the lodge for more information or Little Desert Tours at 26 Brougham St, Nhill.

WARRACKNABEAL (population 3100)
A major Wimmera wheat town, there's an historical centre on Scott St and the town also has a number of interesting old buildings, some of them National Trust classified. The North-Western Agricultural Machinery Museum is just outside town. North of Warracknabeal towards the Wyperfeld National Park, Hopetoun has the National Trust classified Hopetoun House, built for Edward Lascelles who was responsible for much development in the Mallee area.

The tourist information centre (tel (053) 98 1632) is next to the post office – pick up a leaflet detailing a 90 minute self-drive tour.

Places to Stay
There's a caravan park with on-site vans and several hotels and motels.

NORTHERN WIMMERA
Jeparit is on the shores of Lake Hindmarsh, the largest natural freshwater lake in the state.

Jeparit has the Wimmera/Mallee Pioneer Museum, a collection of colonial buildings and old farming equipment. Australia's longest serving prime minister, Sir Robert Menzies, was born here.

North again from Jeparit towards the Wyperfeld National Park is Rainbow with the National Trust classified Yuranga homestead and a tourist information centre on Federal St. It's open only on Sundays.

The Mallee

North of the Wimmera is the least populated part of Australia's most densely populated state. Forming a wedge between South Australia and New South Wales this area even includes the one genuinely empty part of Victoria. The contrast between the wide, flat Mallee, with its sand dunes and dry lakes, and the lush alpine forests of East Gippsland is striking – despite being the smallest mainland state, Victoria really does manage to cram in a lot.

The Mallee takes its name from the mallee scrub which once covered the area. Mallee roots are hard, gnarled and slow-burning. Some great Aussie kitsch such as mallee-root ashtrays and egg-cups can still be found, although I suspect that they may have crossed that thin line from being kitsch to being 'collectables'.

The Mallee region extends from around the Wyperfeld National Park in the south, all the way up to the irrigated oasis surrounding Mildura. Most of it is crown (public) land, except for a couple of strips of hard-won wheatland along the Murray River to the north and straddling the Ouyen highway which bisects the region. The main town in the Mallee is Ouyen, on the Sunraysia highway which runs north-south along the eastern edge. Mildura to the north and Nhill to the south are other major centres nearby. The north-west corner of the Mallee is known as 'sunset country' – a fine name for the edge of the arid wilderness that stretches right across the continent.

In summer it can get very hot here, and the flies can be a real nuisance.

Mallee Wildlife Parks
Pink Lakes State Park Reached from Linga, a tiny town 60 km west of Ouyen on the Ouyen Highway, the Pink Lakes park has camping sites but only limited water supplies. The lakes are pink because of

their high salt and algae content, and are pinkest in the spring.

Wyperfeld National Park Best reached from Albacutya, north of Rainbow, this large park contains a chain of often-dry lakes, including Lake Albacutya. A combination of river gums on the flood-plains, sandy mallee scrubland and treed plains supports a wide variety of wildlife, including emus and kangaroos. There are walking tracks from six km in length up to overnight walks. The park information centre has details of these and on the area's flora and fauna, which includes the mallee fowl. There are tent sites but only limited water.

Big Desert Wilderness This large wilderness area contains no roads, tracks or any other facilities, which makes it difficult and dangerous to travel in except for those with considerable wilderness experience. It consists of sand dunes and mallee scrub, and wildlife abounds. If you aren't equipped to venture into the wilderness you can get a glimpse of the Big Desert along the dry-weather road which runs from Nhill north to Murrayville on the Ouyen Highway. There are camping sites and bore water at Broken Bucket Reserve about 55 km north of Nhill.

Hattah-Kulkyne National Park With the near-desert of the mallee country, woodlands and the gum-lined edges of lakes and the Murray River, Hattah-Kulkyne is a diverse and beautiful park. The Hattah Lakes system fills when the Murray floods and supports many species of water birds. There is a good information centre at Lake Hattah, a few km into the park from the small town of Hattah, on the Sunraysia Highway 35 km north of Ouyen. Check at the centre on the condition of tracks in the park – they are often unsuitable for vehicles after rain. There are camping facilities at Lake Hattah and Lake Mournpall, but note

that there is limited water and the lake water, when there is any, is muddy.

OUYEN (population 1500)
At the junction of the Sunraysia and Ouyen Highways, Ouyen is a good example of a small country town and you could make it a base for visits to the area's parks. There is a tourist information office (tel (050) 92 1550) at 22 Rowe St.

Places to Stay
There are a few motels, and the *Victoria Hotel* (tel (050) 92 1550) at 22 Rowe St has singles/doubles from $22/35, with breakfast. The *Ouyen Caravan Park* (tel (050) 92 1426) has tent sites from $4 and on-site vans from $15.

Ballarat

Population 78,300

The area around present day Ballarat, which is the largest inland city in Victoria, was first settled in 1838. When gold was discovered at the small township of Bunninyong in 1851 the rush was on and within a couple of years the town that grew out of the Ballarat diggings had a population of 40,000.

Ballarat's fabulously rich quartz reefs were worked by the larger mining companies until 1918. About 28% of the gold unearthed in Victoria came from Ballarat.

Today there are still many reminders of this gold-mining past although Ballarat doesn't have quite the historical flavour of Bendigo. Ballarat is 112 km from Melbourne on the main Western Highway to Adelaide.

The Gold Rush
In May 1851 E H Hargraves discovered gold near Bathurst in New South Wales. It was not the first time the mineral had been found in Australia but the sensational accounts of the

potential wealth of the find caused an unprecedented rush as thousands of people dropped everything to try their luck.

The news of the discovery reached Melbourne at the same time as the accounts of its influence on the people of New South Wales. Sydney had been virtually denuded of workers and the same misfortune soon threatened Melbourne. Victoria was still in the process of being established as a separate colony so the loss of its workforce to the northern gold fields would have been disastrous.

A public meeting was called by the young city's businessmen and a reward was offered to anyone who could find gold within 300 km of Melbourne. In less than a week gold was rediscovered in the Yarra but the find was soon eclipsed by a more significant discovery at Clunes. Prospectors began heading to central Victoria and over the next few months the rush north across the Murray was reversed as fresh gold finds and new rushes became an almost weekly occurrence in Victoria.

Gold was found in the Pyrenees, the Lodden and Avoca rivers, at Warrandyte and Bunninyong. Then in September 1851 the greatest gold discovery ever known was made at Ballarat, followed by others at Bendigo, Mt Alexander, Beechworth, Walhalla, Omeo and in the hills and creeks of the Great Dividing Ranges.

By the end of 1851 about 250,000 ounces of gold had already been claimed. Farms and businesses lost their workforce and in many cases were abandoned altogether as employers had no choice left but to follow their workers. Hopeful miners began arriving from England, Ireland, Europe, China and the failing gold fields of California. During 1852 about 1800 people a week arrived in Melbourne.

The government introduced a licence fee of 30 shillings a month for all prospectors, whether they found gold or not. This entitled the miners to a claim, limited to eight feet square, in which to dig for gold and provided the means to govern and enforce the laws that were improvised for the gold fields.

The administration of each field was headed by a chief commissioner whose deputies, the state troopers, were empowered to organise licence hunts and to fine or imprison any miner who failed to produce the permit.

Though this was later to cause serious unrest on the diggings, for the most part it successfully averted the complete lawlessness that had characterised the California rush.

There were, however, the classic features that seem to accompany gold fever, like the back-breaking work, the unwholesome food and hard drinking, and the primitive dwellings. There was the amazing wealth that was to be the luck of some, the elusive dream of others; and for every story of success there were hundreds more of hardship, despair and death.

In his book *Australia Illustrated*, published in 1873, Edwin Carton Booth wrote of the gold fields in the early 1850s:

' . . . it may be fairly questioned whether in any community in the world there ever existed more of intense suffering, unbridled wickedness and positive want, than in Victoria at (that) time . . . To look at the thousands of people who in those years crowded Melbourne, and that most miserable adjunct of Melbourne, Canvas Town, induced the belief that sheer and absolute unfitness for a useful life in the colonies . . . had been deemed the only qualification requisite to make a fortunate digger.'

While the gold rush certainly had its tragic side and its share of rogues, including the notorious bushrangers who regularly attacked the gold shipments being escorted to Melbourne, it also had its heroes who eventually forced a change in the political fabric of the colony. (See the Rebellion section, under Ballarat.)

Above all, perhaps, the gold rush ushered in a fantastic era of growth and material prosperity for Victoria and opened up vast areas of previously unexplored country.

In the first 12 years of the rush Australia's population increased from 400,000 to well over a million, and in Victoria alone it rose from 77,000 to 540,000. To cope with the moving population and the tonnes of gold and supplies the development of roads and railways was accelerated.

The mining companies which followed the independent diggers poured incredible wealth back into the region over the next couple of decades. The huge shanty towns of tents, bark huts, raucous bars and police camps were eventually replaced by the timber and stone buildings that were the foundation of many of Victoria's modern provincial cities, most notably Ballarat, Bendigo, Maldon and Castlemaine.

It was in the 1880s that the gold towns reached their heights of splendour but although gold production was gradually to lose its importance after that time, the towns of the region by then had stable populations, and agriculture and other activities steadily supplanted gold as the economic mainstay of the area.

Gold also made Melbourne Australia's largest city and financial centre, a position it held for nearly half a century.

Information

The Gold Centre Regional Tourist Office (tel (053) 32 2694) is just over the railway line on Lydiard St and is open Monday to Friday from 9 am to 5 pm and on weekends from 10 am to 3 pm. It's well stocked with lots of printed information and the staff are very helpful. The RACV (tel 32 1946) has an office on Doveton St.

In early March Ballarat holds its annual Begonia Festival which is 17 days of fun, flowers and the arts.

Sovereign Hill

Ballarat's major tourist attraction is Sovereign Hill, a fascinating re-creation of a gold mining township of the 1860s. The main street features shops, a hotel, a post office, blacksmith's shop, printing shop, bowling saloon, a bakery and a Chinese joss house. It is a living history museum with people performing their chores dressed in costumes of the time.

The site was actually mined back in the gold era so much of the equipment is original, as is the mineshaft, and there's a variety of above-ground and underground mining works.

Next to the entrance there is an orientation centre which houses exhibitions and film presentations on the gold rush.

On the top of the hill, overlooking the other buildings, is a reconstruction of the original 1857 Government Camp which then serviced and policed the gold fields and now also provides accommodation. Buildings include the military barracks, court house and superintendent's office of the gold era, as well as the excellent youth hostel.

Sovereign Hill is open daily from 9.30 am to 5 pm and admission is $9.50 for adults ($7.50 for students) – expensive but well worth it. There is also a combination ticket for Sovereign Hill and the nearby Gold Museum for $11 ($8 for students), which is not a big saving but the museum is one 'attraction' that is definitely worth seeing.

Gold Museum

Over the road from Sovereign Hill and built on the mullock heap from an old mine, this museum has imaginative displays and samples from all the old mining areas in the Ballarat region. There's also a large section devoted to the history of gold coins around the world. It's open 9.30 am to 5.20 pm daily and is well worth the $2 admission.

Rebellion

Life on the gold fields was a great leveller, erasing all pre-existing social classes as doctors, merchants, ex-convicts and labourers toiled side by side in the mud. But as the easily won gold began to run out the diggers came to recognise the inequality that existed between them and the privileged few who held the land and government power.

The limited size of the claims, the inconvenience of the licence hunts coupled with the police brutality that often accompanied the searches, the very fact that while they were in effect paying taxes they were allowed no political representation, and the realisation that they could not get good farming land, fired the unrest that led to the Eureka Rebellion at Ballarat.

In September 1854 Governor Hotham ordered that the hated licence hunts be carried out twice a week. A month later a miner was murdered near a Ballarat hotel after an argument with the owner, James Bentley.

When Bentley was found not guilty, by a magistrate who just happened to be his business associate, a group of miners rioted over the injustice and burned his hotel down. Though Bentley was retried and found guilty, the rioting miners were also jailed, which fueled the mounting distrust of the authorities.

Creating the Ballarat Reform League, the diggers called for the abolition of the licence fees, the introduction of the miners' right to vote and increased opportunities to purchase land.

On 29 November about 800 miners tossed their licences into a bonfire during a mass meeting and then set about building a stockade at Eureka where, led by an Irishman called Peter Lalor, they prepared to fight for their rights.

On 3 December, having already organised brutal licence hunts, the government ordered the troopers to attack the stockade. There were only 150 diggers within the makeshift barricades at the time and the fight lasted only 20 minutes, leaving 30 miners and five troopers dead.

Though the rebellion was short-lived the miners were ultimately successful in their protest. They had won the sympathy of most Victorians and with the full support of the gold fields' population behind them the government deemed it wise to acquit the leaders of the charge of high treason.

The licence fee was abolished and replaced by a Miners' Right, which cost one pound a year. This gave them the right to search for gold; the right to fence in, cultivate and build a dwelling on a moderate-sized piece of land; and the right to vote for members of the Legislative Assembly. The rebel miner Peter Lalor actually

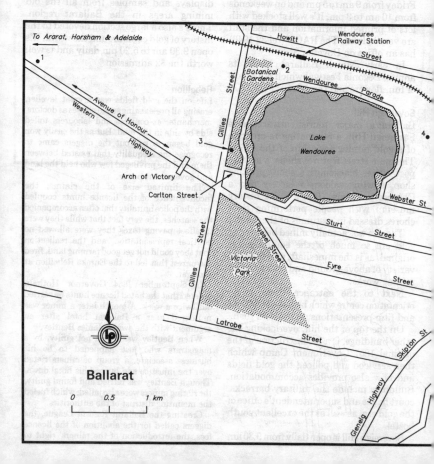

To Ararat, Horsham & Adelaide

Howitt Street

Wendouree Railway Station

Botanical Gardens

Wendouree Parade

Western Highway

Avenue of Honour

Gillies Street

Lake Wendouree

Arch of Victory

Carlton Street

Webster St

Russel Street

Sturt Street

Eyre Street

Gillies Street

Victoria Park

Latrobe Street

Skipton St

Glenelg Highway

Ballarat

0   0.5   1 km

became a member of parliament himself some years later.

Eureka Stockade

The site of the Eureka Stockade is now a park on Stawell St South. There's a monument to the miners and a coin-in-the-slot diorama gives you an action replay of the events and causes of this revolt against British rule.

Eureka Exhibition

On Eureka St opposite the Eureka Memorial is this much-vaunted but disappointing museum. It's a series of walk-through, 'computer-controlled' scenes depicting various facets of the rebellion. It's open daily from 9 am to 5 pm but is overpriced at $3 (students $1.50) especially when the diorama across the road gives you much the same thing for 20c.

Botanic Gardens

Ballarat's excellent 40 hectare Botanic Gardens are beside Lake Wendouree

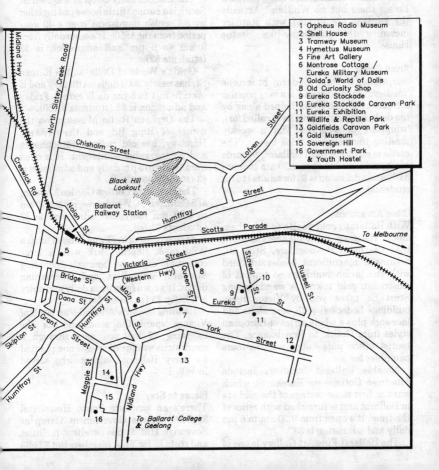

1 Orpheus Radio Museum
2 Shell House
3 Tramway Museum
4 Hymettus Museum
5 Fine Art Gallery
6 Montrose Cottage /
  Eureka Military Museum
7 Golda's World of Dolls
8 Old Curiosity Shop
9 Eureka Stockade
10 Eureka Stockade Caravan Park
11 Eureka Exhibition
12 Wildlife & Reptile Park
13 Goldfields Caravan Park
14 Gold Museum
15 Sovereign Hill
16 Government Park
   & Youth Hostel

Midland Hwy
North Slatey Creek Road
Creswick Rd
Chisholm Street
Black Hill Lookout
Nolan St
Ballarat Railway Station
Humffray Street
Scotts Parade
Street
To Melbourne
Victoria Street
(Western Hwy)
Bridge St
Main St
Queen St
Stawell St
Russell St
Dana St
Eureka St
Grant Street
Humffray St
Skipton St
York Street
Magpie St
Midland Hwy
To Ballarat College & Geelong
Lofven Street

which was used as the rowing course in the 1956 Olympics. A paddle-steamer makes $2 tours of the lake, the cottage of poet Adam Lindsay Gordon stands in the gardens and there's also a Shell House.

On weekends and holidays a tourist tramway operates around the gardens from a depot at the southern end. Tram fares are 80c and there is also a free museum and photographic display at the depot. A little Ballarat joke is the Avenue of Past Prime Ministers, a pathway lined with busts of Australian PMs – there's a Fraser there but no Whitlam! Actually the gardens are littered with statuary including the glasshouse-like 'Statue House'.

Kryall Castle

Surprisingly this modern bluestone 'medieval English castle' is a very popular attraction. It's no doubt helped along by the daily hangings (volunteers called for), 'whipping of wenches' and a weekly jousting tournament – kids love it. The castle is eight km from Ballarat, towards Melbourne, and is open 9.30 am to 5 pm daily and admission is $8 for adults ($6 for students).

Other Attractions

With Ballarat's gold wealth to help them along, the early town planners ensured that the main thoroughfare, Sturt St, became a magnificent boulevard lined with the lavish buildings so typical of Australian gold towns. A wander along Sturt St takes you by Victorian-era buildings bedecked with verandahs and lacework plus a whole series of European styles from Gothic to Renaissance. The tourist office puts out a walking-tours pamphlet for 50c.

Notable Ballarat buildings include Montrose Cottage on Eureka St which was the first stone cottage of the gold era in Ballarat and is furnished with relics of the time. It's open from 9.30 am to 5 pm daily and admission is $3.

The Ballarat Fine Art Gallery is one of Australia's best provincial galleries and is particularly strong in its Australiana collection. A feature is the original Eureka Flag, or at least what's left of it after souvenir hunters have chopped bits off over the last 100 years. The gallery, at 40 Lydiard St North, is open Tuesday to Friday from 10.30 am to 4.30 pm, and on weekends from 12.30 to 4.30 pm. Admission is $2 (students $1) and there are free tours at 2 pm Tuesday to Friday and 2.30 pm on the weekends.

The Old Curiosity Shop at 7 Queen St South is a curious little house put together by a Cornish immigrant over a 40 year period from the 1850s. It's open daily from 9 am to 6 pm and admission is $3 (students $2).

Golda's World of Dolls, at 148 Eureka St, has nearly 2000 dolls on display and is open from 1 to 5 pm daily except Friday and admission is $2 (students $1.50).

The Orpheus Radio Museum, on the corner of Ring Rd and the Western Highway, has old radios, gramophones and photographic equipment. It is open from 10 am to 5 pm daily and admission is $2 (students $1).

The Hymettus Cottage Garden Museum at 8 Cardigan St, Wendouree, is open 10 am to 6.30 pm daily and admission is $2 (students $1.50).

At the corner of York and Russell Sts is a Wildlife & Reptile Park with a large collection of native animals including saltwater crocodiles and Tasmanian devils. It's open from 9 am daily and entry is a hefty $5 (students $4).

Heading towards Adelaide, an Arch of Victory spans the road and for the following 22 km you pass through a continuous avenue of trees – one planted for every Ballarat resident who served in WW I.

Places to Stay

There's an associate *Youth Hostel* (tel 33 3409) in the Government Camp at Sovereign Hill. It has excellent facilities and costs $9 for YHA members but $28/35 for others and it's wise to book in advance. If you stay there you get a 10% discount on entry to Sovereign Hill. The entrance to the hostel is on Magpie St.

During the summer months the college of advanced education students' residence on the campus at Mt Helen and Gilles Sts has beds for $13 a night for YHA members. Phone the campus amenities manager (tel 33 9000 ext 388, or 33 9480 after hours).

Hotels *The Provincial Hotel* (tel 32 1845), 121 Lydiard St, opposite the Ballarat railway station, has rooms for $20/35 including breakfast. Right outside the station is the recently renovated *Tawana Lodge* (tel 31 3461) which costs $15 per person in a nice basic single and $38 in a luxurious double, including breakfast. It also houses a theatre restaurant and a museum.

A short stroll down the street to No 27 brings you to the *George Hotel* (tel 31 1031) with singles/doubles from $15/30. There are also four modern motel units.

Other hotels include the *Criterion Hotel* (tel 31 1451), 18 Doveton St South, with rooms for $15 per person and the *Western Hotel* (tel 32 2218), 1221 Sturt St, which charges $20/32 for singles/doubles including breakfast.

Craigs' Royal Hotel (tel 31 1377), 10 Lydiard St South, is an old place with singles/doubles at $45/55 for bed & breakfast. This is the town's first hotel, full of history, and is being restored to its original grandeur, hence the upmarket prices.

Motels Ballarat has plenty of motels too, most of which are on the Western Highway on either side of the centre. The *Ballarat* (tel 34 7234), seven km east, has

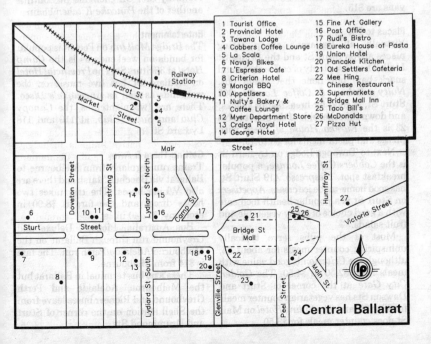

1 Tourist Office	15 Fine Art Gallery
2 Provincial Hotel	16 Post Office
3 Tawana Lodge	17 Rudi's Bistro
4 Cobbers Coffee Lounge	18 Eureka House of Pasta
5 La Scala	19 Union Hotel
6 Navajo Bikes	20 Pancake Kitchen
7 L'Espresso Cafe	21 Old Settlers Cafeteria
8 Criterion Hotel	22 Mee Hing
9 Mongol BBQ	Chinese Restaurant
10 Appetisers	23 Supermarkets
11 Nulty's Bakery &	24 Bridge Mall Inn
Coffee Lounge	25 Taco Bill's
12 Myer Department Store	26 McDonalds
13 Craigs' Royal Hotel	27 Pizza Hut
14 George Hotel	

Central Ballarat

rooms from $30 to $36 a single, and $37 to $43 a double. Just a bit further out is the *Brewery Tap Hotel-Motel* (tel 34 7201) which costs $25/32 for singles/doubles with a continental breakfast. Another reasonably priced motel is the *Eureka Lodge* (tel 31 1900), 119 Stawell St South, with singles/doubles for $34/42 including a light breakfast. The *Red Lion Hotel-Motel* (tel 31 3955), 221 Main Rd, is close to Sovereign Hill and has singles/doubles with a light breakfast for $34/44.

Camping There are plenty of camping grounds in and around Ballarat with the most convenient being the *Goldfield Caravan Park* (tel 32 7888) at 108 Clayton St, 200 metres north of Sovereign Hill. Tent sites are $9 for two and on-site vans cost $22. Also handy is the *Eureka Stockade Caravan Park* (tel 31 2281), right next to the Eureka Stockade Memorial. Tent sites are $7.50 and on-site vans are $15.

Places to Eat

Virtually all Ballarat's cheap eating places are on Sturt St and the Bridge St Mall. There are plenty of coffee shops and snack bars but none that stand out. *Nulty's Bakery & Coffee Lounge*, 306 Sturt St, is good for breakfast or snacks; and down the other side of the street at No 23 is the *Eureka House of Pasta* with pizzas and pasta meals for $5 to $9.

Next to Tawonga Lodge on Lydiard St is the *Cobbers Coffee Lounge*, a popular breakfast spot. *L'espresso*, 419 Sturt St, has good home-made ice cream. *Appetisers* on Sturt St is a popular health food cafe with a good choice of many vegetable and fruit salads.

Most of the pubs serve typically uninspiring counter meals for about $6, although the *Criterion* is good value with meals from $2.50 to $4.50. The *Golden City Gate* at the corner of Sturt and Dawson Sts has vegetarian counter meals for $6 to $8, and *The Siding Hotel* on Mair St does counter meals for $3.50.

In the Bridge St Mall the *Old Settlers Cafeteria* offers fish from $8 and pasta dishes from $7; and the *Mee Hing* Chinese restaurant opposite has a banquet for two people at $14 a head. The *Mongolian Barbecue* upstairs at 315 Sturt St has a good lunch special where you serve yourself and try to squash as much meat and vegetables in a large bowl as you can for $5.40. Myers on Sturt St have a cafeteria on a lower ground floor.

Rudi's Bistro on Sturt St is the fully licensed but recommended for a splurge as is the very up-market *La Scala* at 120 Lydiard St, where you're looking at $65 for two, plus drinks. It's in a restored bluestone warehouse with the *Winery* wine bar and has become Ballarat's trendy hangout.

If fast food is what you're after, there's *McDonalds, Taco Bills* and the *Pizza Hut*, all near the corner of Victoria and Humfray Sts. On Glenville St South is another of the *Pancake Kitchen* chain.

Entertainment

The *Bridge Mall Inn* on Peel St is popular for bands on weekends as is the *Camp Hotel* at 36 Sturt St. The *Provincial Hotel* on Lydiard St has live music on the weekends as well as *Angelique's Disco*. There are two nightclubs, the *Canopy Club* and *Super Club*, at 116 and 118 Lydiard St.

Getting There & Away

Trains run regularly from Melbourne to Ballarat via Bacchus Marsh and there are also V/Line buses. The trip takes two hours direct and the fare is $8.90 in economy, $12.40 in 1st.

Bus Australia, Pioneer, Deluxe and Greyhound run through Ballarat on the Melbourne/Adelaide/Perth run. The fare is $14 from Melbourne.

There's no bus terminal in Ballarat but the Melbourne, Adelaide and Perth Greyhound and Pioneer buses leave from the Shell station on the corner of Sturt and Drummond Sts.

Bus Australia stops opposite Myers on Sturt St and Deluxe stops on Curtis St, adjacent to the car park.

On weekdays V/Line buses go to Warrnambool at 2.15 pm for $15.75; to Hamilton at 9.40 am for $15.75; to Maryborough at 7.15 am for $4.60; and to Geelong at 6.35 and 9.15 am and 3.15 pm for $6.20. There are also buses to Donald from Monday to Thursday at 2.30 pm for $15. Tickets are available at the railway station.

Getting Around
There's a tourist bus service, the Explorer Shuttlebus, which makes daily one hour trips around the major sights with a running commentary. The bus leaves from the railway station, but also picks up people at Sovereign Hill, and bookings can be made at the office of Ballarat Promotions, 209 Sturt St, or you can pay the driver. The cost is $8 for adults, $6 for students.

Navajo Bikes 'n' Gear at 408 Sturt St hire bikes for $15 per 24 hours.

Ballarat Transit is the local bus service operated by Davis and Clark Bus Lines. You can get a timetable from the railway station or the tourist office.

An 80c ticket lasts an hour and the service can take you to all the major tourist attractions.

BUNINYONG
The township of Buninyong, founded on the site of one of Victoria's earliest gold finds, is just south of Ballarat. The impressive, tree lined main street boasts several fine Victorian buildings from the gold days including the old Crown Hotel, first licensed in 1842.

There's an interesting signposted historic walk, the nearby Leigh River Animal Farm which provides Devonshire Teas and every February is the Gold King Festival.

Central Victoria

CRESWICK (population 4480)
Creswick is a pleasant small town 18 km north of Ballarat on the Midland Highway. There are many visible signs of the diggings during the gold rush days when, at its peak, there were 60,000 people living there.

Of interest is the little Creswick Historical Museum, the Battery built in 1918 to extract gold from the local basalt, a graveyard with some early memorial stones from the gold era as well as a Chinese section, an ornate town hall, the St Helena Vineyard and many excellent bushwalks.

Four km north-west of town is the site of the Australasia No 2 Mine, a deep shaft mine sunk in 1877 and worked till the country's worst mining disaster closed it in 1882.

About 15,000 people attended the funeral service of the 22 men who drowned when the shaft flooded.

Places to Stay
The *Calembeen Caravan Park* (tel (053) 45 2411) has tent sites for $8 and on-site vans and cabins for $22 and $28 a double. The *Hill View Holiday Farm* (tel 45 2690) costs $30 per person in a cottage with cooking facilities.

CLUNES (population 760)
Clunes was the site of one of Victoria's very first gold discoveries in June 1851. Although other finds soon diverted interest, there are still many fine buildings as reminders of the former wealth of this charming little town.

The small hills around Clunes are extinct volcanoes, nearby Mt Beckworth is noted for its orchids and bird life, you can visit the old gold diggings of Jerusalem and Ullina, and at Smeaton, between Clunes and Daylesford, an impressive bluestone water-driven mill is being restored.

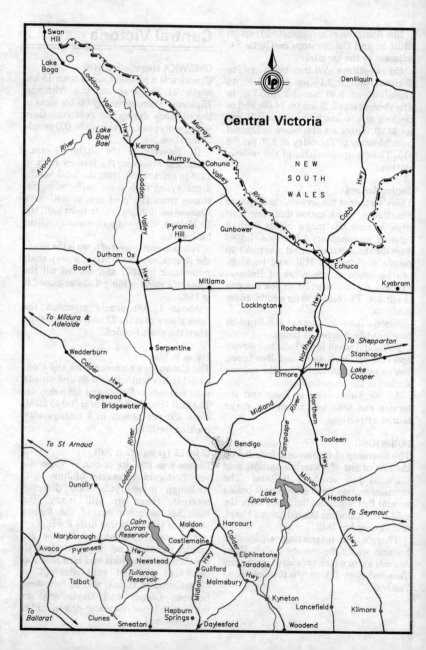

Central Victoria

NEW SOUTH WALES

Places to Stay & Eat

The *Clunes Caravan Park*, Purcell St, has tent sites for $5 and on-site vans for $15 to $20 a day. Clunes also has a guest house and a motel. The *Club* and *National* hotels are OK for counter meals.

MARYBOROUGH (population 7800)

The district around Charlotte Plains was already an established sheep run, owned by the Simson brothers, when gold was discovered at White Hills and Four Mile Flat in 1854. A police camp established at the diggings was named Maryborough and by 1854 the population had swelled to over 40,000. Gold mining ceased to be economical in 1918 but Maryborough by then had a strong manufacturing base in the town's secondary industries and is still a busy town today.

Its Victorian buildings include a magnificent railway station. In fact a century ago Mark Twain described Maryborough as 'a railway station with town attached'.

Maryborough's Highland Gathering has been held every year on New Year's Day since 1857 and the annual 16 day Golden Wattle Festival is celebrated in September with all sorts of entertainment, exhibitions, contests and processions.

Maryborough, north of Ballarat, is on the Pyrenees Highway between Castle-maine and Avoca. Bowenvale-Timor, six km north of Maryborough, was a busy mining town at the height of the rush; Majorca 11 km south-east is an old ghost town; and the fine old township of Carisbrook, seven km east, was originally part of the extensive sheep run established by the Simson brothers before the gold rush.

Places to Stay & Eat

Apart from several motels, hotels and guest houses there's the *Princes Park Caravan Park*, Holyrood St, which has tent sites for $6, on-site vans for $17 a day; and the *Golden Country Caratel*, Park Rd, which has self-contained sites for $12 and on-site vans for $17 a day. There are

cafes and restaurants in town, a couple of Chinese food places and the *Bull & Mouth Hotel* has a good bistro.

There's also a motel in Carisbrook which costs $28/34 a single/double and a restaurant called *Carolines* built in the town's original grocery store.

DUNOLLY (population 600)

The sheep run taken up and named Dunolly by a Scotsman in 1845 was completely overrun by diggers following the discovery of gold in 1852. The actual siting of present-day Dunolly, which is about 23 km north of Maryborough, followed another gold find in 1856 which saw more than 30,000 people flood into the area to try their luck.

The largest gold nugget ever found, the 65 kg *Welcome Stranger*, was unearthed at Moliagul 13 km north-west of Dunolly, and the district's gold fields produced more nuggets than any other in Australia.

It's not surprising then that there are some interesting buildings along Dunolly's main street and it's worth taking a stroll around town. The Goldfields Historical Museum (open Sundays and public holidays) displays replicas of some of the more notable finds, including the *Welcome Stranger*. The Dunolly Gold Winery, established in the 1850s, is on Broadway and is open weekdays from 9 am to 5 pm and Saturdays from 9 am to noon.

In the district you can visit Moliagul and the site of the *Welcome Stranger*; the quaint little town of Bealiba, 21 km north-west; the bushwalking area of the Bealiba Ranges; and 13 km north-east, the ghost town of Tarnagulla.

Places to Stay

The *Progress Caravan Park* on the corner of Thompson and Desmond Sts has tent sites for $4 and on-site vans for $11 a double. The *Golden Triangle Motel* (tel (054) 681166) costs $30/38 a single/ double.

DAYLESFORD (population 4900)

Originally called Wombat, after the pastoral run where gold was first discovered, Daylesford is a picturesque town set amongst lakes, hills and forests. It boasts more of that sturdy Victorian and Edwardian architecture and, along with nearby Hepburn Springs, is having a revival as the 'spa centre of Victoria'.

There is much evidence, in the well-preserved and restored buildings, of the prosperity that visited this town during the gold rush as well as the lasting influence of the many Swiss-Italian miners who expertly worked the tunnel mines in the surrounding hills.

The health-giving properties of the town's mineral springs were known of before gold was discovered in the area. By the 1870s Daylesford was a popular health resort, attracting droves of fashionable Melbournians. It was claimed that the waters, which were bottled and sold, could cure any complaint and the spas and relaxed scenic environment of the town could rejuvenate even the most stressed turn-of-the-century city dweller.

The current trend towards healthy lifestyles has prompted a revival of interest in Daylesford as a health resort and the elaborate bath houses and charming guest houses are again being used.

The excellent Historical Society Museum is worth visiting as are the lovely Wombat Hill Botanic Gardens. The volcanic crater of Mt Franklin, 10 km north, is visible from the lookout point in the gardens.

Daylesford is on the Midland Highway, about 45 km north-east of Ballarat and 80 km south of Castlemaine. You can also get there and to Hepburn Springs easily from the Calder Highway by heading west at Woodend.

Places to Stay & Eat

Victoria Park Caravan Park, Ballan Rd, has tent sites for $6, and on-site vans and cabins for $25 to $30 a double. The *Jubilee Caravan Park*, on Lake Rd, has tent sites for $6, on-site vans for $20 a double and

cabins for $30 a double. The *Wentworth Hotel* (tel (053) 48 2648) on King St offers bed & breakfast singles/doubles for $25/40.

The *Royal Hotel* on Vincent St serves Asian food; the *Swiss Mountain Hotel*, out of town on the Midland Highway, serves good evening meals; *Sweet Decadence*, in the centre of town, serves light meals, afternoon teas and home-made chocolates; and *Argus Terrace* is a cafe and BYO restaurant.

HEPBURN SPRINGS (population 500)

Renowned for over a century for its medicinal spas and bottled mineral water, Hepburn Springs is a delightful little town nine km from Daylesford. During the gold rush when, amongst many other miners, there were at least 20,000 Italians working the diggings here, the townspeople had to form an organisation to protect the valuable mineral waters from the disturbances caused by mining.

They began collecting the waters in iron bottles for sale throughout the colony and when the gold began to run out they successfully promoted the town as a resort for therapeutic rest and rejuvenation.

Hepburn's Mineral Springs Reserve has four main springs, of magnesium, iron, lime and sulphur, and the bubbling waters contain at least 10 different minerals.

These days the Hepburn Spa Complex, in the town's historic spa building, is offering the same services and Hepburn Springs is again attracting visitors who just want to relax in the natural spas.

Places to Stay

The *Spring Park Caravan Park* on Forest Ave has only limited facilities but tent sites cost $6. The *Spring Park Holiday Farm*, Forest Ave, has one and two bedroom flats for $30 to $40 a day. *Liberty House Guest House* (tel (053) 48 2809), Mineral Springs Crescent, has bed & breakfasts for around $35/55 for singles/doubles. For a touch of old-world elegance you could try the delightful *Bellinzona*

Country House (tel (053) 48 2271) where bed & breakfast will set you back $75/125.

CASTLEMAINE (population 7600)

Settlement of this district dates back to the 1830s when most of the land was taken up for farming. The discovery of gold at Specimen Gully in 1851, however, radically altered the pastoral landscape as 30,000 diggers worked a number of gold fields known, collectively, as the Mt Alexander diggings.

The township that grew up around the Government Camp, at the junction of Barkers and Forest creeks, was named Castlemaine in 1853 and soon became the thriving market place for all the gold fields of central Victoria.

Castlemaine's importance was not to last, however, as the district did not have the rich quartz reefs that were common to Bendigo and Ballarat. The centre of the town has been virtually unaltered since the 1860s when the population began to decline as the surface gold was exhausted.

These days Castlemaine is a charming town where the legacy of its rapid rise to prosperity lies in the splendid architecture of its public buildings and private residences and in the design of its streets and many gardens.

The Castlemaine State Festival, one of Victoria's leading celebrations of the arts, is held every second October and features a host of home-grown and international music, theatre and art.

The town is also famous for its Castlemaine Rock – a unique taste treat that is definitely worth trying. First made in 1853 it was the traditional confection of the Victorian gold fields, and the recipe is still a well-kept family secret.

Information

There is a well-stocked tourist office in a rotunda on Duke St (near the Castle Motel on the Pyrenees Highway). Castlemaine is at the junction of the Midland and Calder highways, not far off the Calder Highway about 38 km from Bendigo.

Market Museum

Castlemaine's original market building, on Mostyn St, is now a museum with audiovisual displays and artefacts depicting the colourful history of the gold fields. Built in 1862, along classical Roman lines, the market building is classified by the National Trust and is considered to be the region's finest gold-era buildings. The museum is open daily from 10 am to 5 pm.

Buda

Originally built by a retired Indian Army officer in 1857 this is a superb example of Victorian-era colonial architecture. The house and magnificent gardens were extended in the 1890s by a Hungarian gold and silversmith, Ernest Leviny. Before her death in 1981, Miss Hilda Leviny arranged that Buda would be purchased by the Castlemaine Art Gallery. The house and gardens are now open to the public and provide an insight into the town's refined and gracious past. Buda, on the corner of Urquhart and Hunter Sts, is open from 10 am to 5 pm daily except Friday.

Art Galleries

The Castlemaine Art Gallery, Lyttleton St, was established in 1913 and has an excellent collection of colonial and contemporary art, as well as an historical museum featuring photographs, relics and documents.

The Goldfields Gallery, Fryers St, Guildford, is an original 1850s miner's cottage and store housing antiques, paintings, pottery and crafts.

The Wallace Brothers Gallery, 50 Hargraves St, represents contemporary artists and craftspeople; and the Hargraves St Gallery nearby specialises in works by established Australian artists.

Cannie Ridge Pottery, set amongst the apple orchards of Harcourt (on the Calder

Highway, nine km from Castlemaine) is renowned for its hand thrown stoneware pottery. It's open from 8 am to 5 pm on weekdays and from 10 am to 5 pm on weekends.

Castlemaine Botanic Gardens

These beautiful gardens, designed in the 1860s by Baron von Mueller, the government botanist and director of the Melbourne Botanic Gardens, are amongst the oldest in the state. It's worth taking the time for a picnic by the lake or just a stroll amongst the 'Significant Trees' registered by the National Trust.

Other Attractions

Other places of interest include the Theatre Royal (now a cabaret, bistro and disco as well as a theatre and cinema); Camp Reserve, the site of the original Government Camp of the gold rush; the Burke & Wills Monument, if you're into statues; and a host of gold rush buildings, such as the town hall, the sandstone jail, several hotels and the court house.

Places to Stay

The *Botanic Gardens Caravan Park*, on Walker St, next to the gardens, has tent sites for $7.50 and on-site vans for $18 a double; and the *Carracourt Caravan Park*, 101 Barker St, has the same for a little more.

The *Cumberland Hotel* (tel (054) 72 1052), on Barker St, has singles for $15 and doubles for $24. Breakfast, served in the dining room, is extra. The *Midland Hotel* (tel 72 1805), 2 Templeton St, has bed & breakfast for $35 a single. The *Campbell St Lodge* (tel 72 3477) at 33 Campbell St, has doubles from $45 to $52.

Elimatta (tel 72 4454), 233 Barker St, is a guest house, with a cafe-restaurant, that has singles and doubles from $65 to $75, including a light breakfast. The *Castle Motel* (tel 72 2433), 1 Duke St, has rooms for around $38/45.

Places to Eat

The *Bridge Hotel*, 21 Walker St, has great and inexpensive counter meals; and the *Cumberland Hotel*, Barker St, has a good bistro.

Bing's Cafe, 71 Mostyn St, has a good selection of home-made food and is a good place for breakfast, lunch or afternoon tea. The *Stables Tearooms*, Main Rd, Campbells Creek, (three km south of Castlemaine) is a great setting for lunch and Devonshire Teas.

Elimatta offers morning and afternoon tea, bistro lunches and up-market dining in the evening. For a splurge, the *Parsley 'N' Sage Restaurant*, 56 Lyttleton St, is worth the average $17 for main courses.

AROUND CASTLEMAINE

The surrounding district is another good reason to spend a couple of days in Castlemaine. You can visit the Wattle Gully Gold Mine and the Garfield Waterwheel in Chewton, four km south of Castlemaine.

Around the 1860s Guildford (11 km south) had one of the largest Chinese communities in Victoria. At Guildford, Vaughn and Campbells Creek there are interesting Chinese cemeteries.

At Fryerstown (formerly Fryers Creek) there are more gold field buildings. The 'Mosquito' mine worked here by the Rowe brothers yielded more than 100,000 ounces of gold.

Barkers Creek (four km north) features the renovated 1860s *Old England Hotel*, and at Vaughn (12 km south-east) there are mineral springs.

MALDON (population 1000)

The current population of Maldon is a scant reminder of the 20,000 who used to work the local gold fields but the whole town is a well-preserved relic of the era with many fine buildings constructed from the local stone.

In 1966 the National Trust named Maldon as the country's first 'notable town', an honour bestowed only on towns where the historic architecture was intact and valuable. In fact Maldon was considered so important in the history of Victoria that special planning regulations, the first of their kind in the state, were implemented to preserve the town for posterity.

There's a tourist information centre on High St and an historical museum which is open on weekends and public holidays from 1.30 to 4 pm.

The interesting buildings around town and along the verandahed main street include Dabb's General Store (now the supermarket) with its authentic shopfront; several restored public houses, including the Maldon, Kangaroo and Grand hotels; the Eaglehawk Gully Restaurant; the 24 metre high Beehive Chimney; and the Union Mine Kilns.

There are some good bushwalks around the town and amateur gold hunters still scour the area with some success.

Places to Stay & Eat

The *Maldon Caravan Park*, Hospital St, has tent sites for $8 and on-site vans for $25 a double.

The *Derby Hill Lodge* (tel (054) 75 2033), Phoenix St, has singles for $20; and the *Eaglehawk Gully Motel* (tel 75 2911), Reef St, has doubles for $60. It's much cheaper to stay in Castlemaine and visit Maldon from there.

The *Cumquat Tea Rooms* are good for lunch or afternoon tea; the freshly made fare from the *Maldon Bakery* is great; and apart from that there are the hotel counter meals.

Bendigo

Population 63,000

The solid, imposing and at times extravagant Victorian-era architecture of Bendigo is a testimony to the fact that this was one of Australia's richest gold mining towns.

In the 1850s thousands upon thousands of diggers converged on the fantastically rich Bendigo Diggings, which actually covered more than 300 square km, to claim the easily obtained surface gold. As this began to run out and diggers were no longer tripping over nuggets they turned their pans and cradles to Bendigo Creek and other waterways around Sandhurst (as Bendigo was then known) in their quest for alluvial gold.

The arrival of thousands of Chinese miners, while causing a great deal of racial tension at the time, had a rather exotic and lasting effect on the town.

By the 1860s the easily won ore was running out and the scene changed again as reef mining began in earnest. Independent miners were soon outclassed by the large and powerful mining companies, with their heavy machinery for digging and crushing, who poured money into the town as they extracted enormous wealth from their network of deep mine shafts. The last of these was worked until the 1950s.

Bendigo today is the third largest city in country Victoria, a busy market town with a number of local industries that makes the most of its gold mining past to promote tourism.

Information

The regional tourist office (tel (054) 47 7161), on the Calder Highway four km south of the centre, is open from 9 am to 5 pm on weekdays and 10 am to 3 pm on weekends. The Bendigo Trust Tourist Office (tel 42 1205) is in Charing Cross, and is open daily from 10 am to 4 pm. The RACV (tel 43 9622) has an office at 72 Pall Mall. The La Trobe Bookshop, 271 Lyttleton Terrace, has a good selection of books and there's a book exchange on High St.

Central Deborah Mine

This 500 metre deep mine, worked on 17

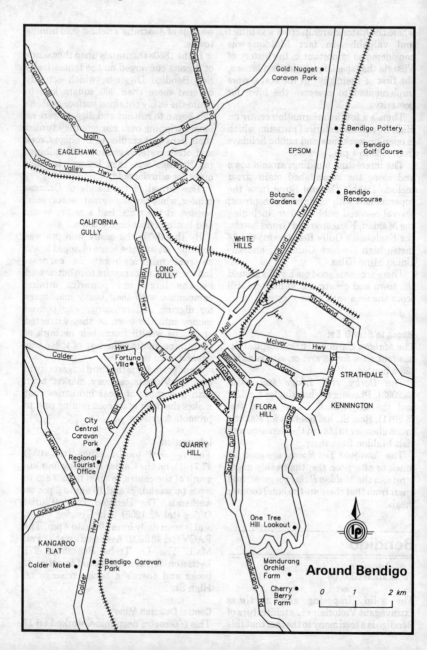

Gold Nugget
Caravan Park

Bendigo Pottery

EPSOM

Bendigo
Golf Course

EAGLEHAWK

Main

Simpsons

Avery's

Jobs Gully

Eaglehawk Nellborough Rd

Fosmia Rd – Bendigo – Eaglehawk Rd

Loddon Valley Hwy

CALIFORNIA
GULLY

LONG
GULLY

Loddon Valley Hwy

WHITE
HILLS

Botanic
Gardens

Bendigo
Racecourse

Midland Hwy

Calder Hwy

Fortuna
Villa

View St

Pall Mall

McIvor Hwy

Strickland Rd

STRATHDALE

St Aidans

High St

Williamson St

Mitchell St

Russel St

Hargreaves St

Specimen Hill

KENNINGTON

FLORA
HILL

St

Edwards Rd

Reservoir Rd

City
Central Caravan
Park

Regional
Tourist
Office

Olympic Pde

QUARRY
HILL

King St

Sandy

Lockwood Rd

KANGAROO
FLAT

One Tree
Hill Lookout

Calder Hwy

Calder Motel

Bendigo Caravan Park

Mandurang
Orchid
Farm

Cherry
Berry
Farm

Mandurang Rd

Around Bendigo

0   1   2 km

levels, became operational in the 1940s and was connected to the two other earlier Deborah shafts which date back to the early days of the gold fields. A great deal of gold was removed before it closed in 1954 and it has now been restored and developed as a museum. It's well worth a visit as there are lots of interesting exhibits and many photographs taken from the mid-1800s onwards. The mine is on Violet St – you can't miss it – and is open from 9 am to 5 pm daily. Admission is $8 ($7 for students) for a complete tour and $2.50 ($2 for students) for a surface tour only.

The Joss House

The Chinese joss house on Finn St, the only one remaining of four which existed during the gold rush, is built of timber and hand-made bricks. The building is painted red, the traditional Chinese colour denoting strength and good luck, and is a small place with a central temple, flanked by an ancestral temple and a caretaker's residence. Exhibits include embroidered and stone-rub banners, figures representing the 12 years of the Chinese solar cycle, commemorative tablets to the deceased, paintings and Chinese lanterns. The caretaker is a very friendly man who may give you an informative private tour if he's not busy. The house is open from 10 am to 5 pm daily and admission is $2 ($1.50 for students).

There's a Chinese section in the White Hills Cemetery on Killian St and also a prayer oven where paper money, and other goodies which you can't take with you, are burnt. Bendigo has an annual Chinese parade at Easter, featuring a 30 metre long ceremonial dragon.

Bendigo Tram

A vintage tram makes a regular tourist run from the Central Deborah Mine, through the centre of the city and out to the tramways museum (which is free if you have a tram ticket) and the joss house, with a commentary along the way. On weekdays it departs at 9.30 am and 1 and 2 pm from the Central Deborah Mine, or five minutes later from the fountain. On weekends and school holidays it operates hourly from 9.30 am. For more info phone 43 8070; the fare is $4 ($3 for students).

Sacred Heart Cathedral

Construction of the massive Sacred Heart Cathedral, the largest Gothic-style building outside Melbourne, was begun last century and completed in 1977. Angels poke out of some of the nice wooden arches, there's a beautifully carved bishop's chair, some good stained-glass windows, the pews are magnificent Australian blackwood and the marble is Italian.

Bendigo Art Gallery

The Bendigo Art Gallery, 42 View St, was built in the 1880s and has an outstanding collection of Australian colonial and contemporary paintings. It's open Monday to Friday from 10 am to 5 pm and on weekends from 2 to 5 pm; admission is $1.

The Shamrock Hotel

The third hotel of the name on the same site, this magnificent incarnation was built in 1897. It's a fully restored and very fine example of the hotel architecture of the period. Its size gives some indication of how prosperous the town was in the gold mining era when, so the story goes, the floors were regularly washed down to collect the gold dust brought in on miners' boots.

The Shamrock is on the corner of Pall Mall and Williamson St and is a good place for a drink in the bar or on the upstairs balcony.

Dai Gum San

Dai Gum San, on View St, is a small museum of life-size wax statues depicting scenes from Imperial China. The figures, made by a Chinese woman, formed part of a larger collection in Hong Kong until they were donated to the Bendigo Trust. The figures include a concubine with bound feet, a fortune teller and Dr Sun Yat-Sen while other displays, some distinctly on the gory side, include a beheading and finger nail removal. It's open daily from 10 am to 4 pm and admission is $2 ($1.40 for students).

Other Attractions

There are some fine old buildings around Pall Mall/McCrae St including the extremely elaborate post office, the Alexandra Fountain at Charing Cross, the war memorial and the town hall at the end of Bull St.

The jail, old police barracks, St Paul's Church and the Goldmines Hotel were all built around the late 1850s. Wesley Church on Forest St is worth a glance; but Victoria Hill, the site of some of the richest mines, is now just some big holes and a few rusting hulks of machinery.

Dudley House, classified by the National Trust, is a fine old residence with beautiful gardens, open weekends and daily during school holidays from 2 to 5 pm. Fortuna Villa is a stately mansion with a lake and Italian fountain, once owned by George Lansell, the 'Quartz King'. It's now the Army Survey Regiment Headquarters and is only open to the public on Sundays for a $3 tour at 1 pm.

The Militaria Museum on View St has a collection of military paraphernalia. Entrance is $1.50 ($1 for students) and it's open on Mondays and Wednesdays from 12.30 to 4.30 pm and Saturdays from 10 am to 4.30 pm.

Rosalind Park is a pretty little place with a lookout tower that was once the mine shaft head of the Garden Gully United Gold Mining Company. There are good views across the town from the top.

Places to Stay

The Youth Hostel (tel 43 6937) at 362 High St, which is a privately owned establishment (part of the Central City Caravan Park outside town), is open all day and beds cost $8 per person. You can get there on the city bus.

The only other reasonably cheap possibility is the college of advanced education (tel 40 3458) which has cheap accommodation during the vacation periods for $10 per bed. Phone the Residential Secretary for details.

Hotels & Motels The Albert-On-McCrae Hotel (tel 43 7588), 131 McCrae St, is a very central place and good value with bed & breakfast for $18 per person. Close to the railway station at 150 Williamson St the Brougham Arms Hotel (tel 43 8144) costs $30/38 for singles/doubles.

Some other places to consider include the Captain Cook Motel-Hotel (tel 43 4168) at 358 Napier St which costs $36/47; the Oval Motel (tel 43 7211) at 194 Barnard St for $30/39; or the Calder Motel (tel 47 7411) out on the Calder Highway, 7½ km south of town, which has rooms for $29/36.

The famous Shamrock Hotel (tel 43 0333) where the rooms still retain some of their gold rush character, is a nice place for a splurge. Ordinary singles/doubles cost from $54/65, while the suites are in the $95 to $135 range. It's on the corner of Pall Mall & Williamson St, opposite the GPO.

Camping There are lots of camping grounds in and around Bendigo, and out at Lake Eppalock. The closest to the centre is the Central City Caravan Park (tel 43 6937), three km south on the Calder Highway, where tent sites are $7 for two and on-site vans are $24. Most other grounds also permit camping and nightly costs are in the $5 to $8 range.

Places to Eat

Most of the city's 54 pubs do counter meals in the $3 to $7 range. The Golden Gate Hotel, on the corner of High and Wattle Sts, has bar lunch specials for $3; and the Hopetoun Hotel, on the corner of Mitchell and Wills Sts, has them for $2.50.

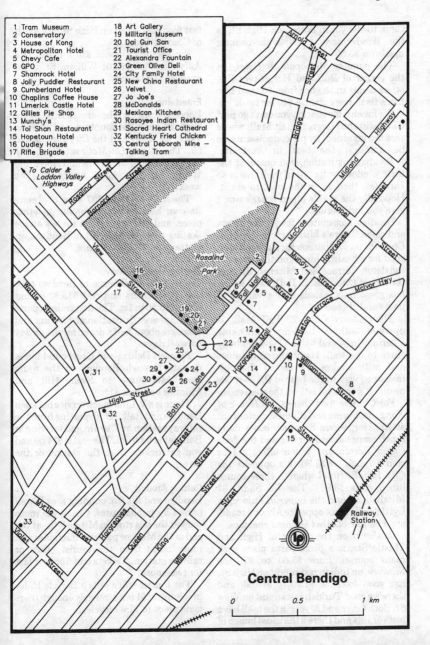

1 Tram Museum
2 Conservatory
3 House of Kong
4 Metropolitan Hotel
5 Chevy Cafe
6 GPO
7 Shamrock Hotel
8 Jolly Puddler Restaurant
9 Cumberland Hotel
10 Chaplins Coffee House
11 Limerick Castle Hotel
12 Gillies Pie Shop
13 Munchy's
14 Toi Shan Restaurant
15 Hopetoun Hotel
16 Dudley House
17 Rifle Brigade

18 Art Gallery
19 Militaria Museum
20 Dai Gun San
21 Tourist Office
22 Alexandra Fountain
23 Green Olive Deli
24 City Family Hotel
25 New China Restaurant
26 Velvet
27 Jo Joe's
28 McDonalds
29 Mexican Kitchen
30 Rasoyee Indian Restaurant
31 Sacred Heart Cathedral
32 Kentucky Fried Chicken
33 Central Deborah Mine –
   Talking Tram

To Calder &
Loddon Valley
Highways

Rosalind Park

Railway
Station

Central Bendigo

0   0.5   1 km

Close to the youth hostel, on High St, is the *Windermere Hotel* with counter meals for $3.50

The popular *Metropolitan Hotel*, on the corner of Bull and Hargreaves Sts, offers meals in the bar from $6 (and also has a flash restaurant – $40 for two).

For lunch time snacks, you can't go past *Gillies*, in the Hargreaves St Mall, whose pies are regarded, by pie connoisseurs, to be amongst the best in Australia. A Bendigo institution, you queue at the little window, order one of their five or so varieties, then sit in the mall to eat it. Hopefully the mall's piped muzak won't give you indigestion.

Bendigo has quite a few coffee shops and cafes. There's *Munchy's* in the mall; *Chaplins* on Williamson St; *Cafe Naturel*, good for a healthy lunch, on the corner of Lyttleton Terrace and Mitchell St; and the *Green Olive Deli* in Bath Lane which has great rolls, salads and a variety of pates and cheeses.

Then *Chevy Cafe*, 22 Pall Mall, is upstairs with a balcony overlooking Charing Cross and half a Chevrolet body stuck to the wall. Hamburgers, hot dogs and milk shakes are served the old-fashioned way to the beat of the best 50s music. It's open till late on the weekends.

For Chinese food there's the *House of Kong*, a Chinese and Siamese restaurant at 200 Hargreaves St which has a daily lunch smogasboard for $7; and the *New China Restaurant* which offers a four course lunch for $7.80 (it's opposite the *City Family Hotel* where a three course lunch costs $8.90). The *Toi Shan*, 67 Mitchell St, and the *Imperial Palace*, in Lyttleton Terrace opposite Abbot Arcade, are a couple of other Chinese cheapies.

Jo Joe's, on the corner of High and Thistle Sts, is a pizza-pasta place with main courses from $5.60 to $7; the *Rasoyee*, an Indian restaurant on High St, has good food for $7.50 to $10.50; and there's a good Turkish restaurant on View St. Both *Coles* and *Myers* in the mall have restaurants and there's the usual bunch of fast food places, all on High St just south of Charing Cross.

For a splurge, about $30 a meal, *The Jolly Puddler*, at 101 William St, is an excellent restaurant.

Entertainment

Bendigo's nightclubs are mostly along High St near the fountain and include *Velvet* at No 87 and the *City Club* at No 55. The *Albert-On-McCrae Hotel*, 131 McCrae St, and the *Brougham Hotel*, 150 Williamson St, have bands on the weekends.

The *Rifle Brigade*, 137 View St, brews its own beer and is a popular meeting place, and believe it or not there's an ice skating rink (tel 41 3000) in Bendigo, on Hattam St, Golden Square.

Getting There & Away

Trains from Melbourne to Bendigo take about two hours and cost $13.90 in 2nd class, $19.50 in 1st. The first train departs from Spencer St Station at 8.35 am and there are about half a dozen services a day on weekdays.

Pioneer, Deluxe and Greyhound buses operate through Bendigo on the route from Melbourne to Swan Hill and Mildura and cost $15.

There is a V/Line coach service between Bendigo and Ballarat, departing from the railway station at 7.10 am and arriving in Ballarat at 9.05 am. The cost is $14.50 and you get tickets from the station or the driver.

Getting Around

Bendigo and it's surrounding area is well served by public buses. Check the route map at the bus stop on Mitchell St, at the end of the Mall, or pick up timetables and route maps from the tourist office or railway station. Tickets cost 75c and last for two hours.

The tourist office sells a Bicycle Rides brochure for $1 but strangely enough there is no place to hire bicycles.

Tours There are daily tours of Bendigo run by Bendigo Tours (tel 41 2390); the routes change daily so ring first. Barry Maggs runs Goldseeker Tours (tel 47 9559), taking people gold hunting with metal detectors.

AROUND BENDIGO

Sandhurst Town is a re-created gold town at Myers Flats, 10 km from Bendigo. It includes a working 24-inch-gauge railway line, a eucalyptus distillery, colonial stores, and the chance to pan for gold. The town (tel 46 9033 for info) is open daily except Friday.

The Eaglehawk Mechanics Institute has a Gold Mining Museum with historical and gold mining exhibits.

Bendigo Pottery, the oldest pottery works in Australia, is on the Calder Highway at Epsom. As well as roofing tiles and the like, which keep the works financial, the historic kilns are still used to produce fine pottery. There are guided tours of the works and you can buy finished pieces.

Also at Epsom, which is seven km north of Bendigo, is a large undercover Sunday market. Hartland's Eucalyptus Oil Factory in the Whipstick Forest was established in 1890 and the production process can be inspected.

Other things of interest in the area include the Mohair Farm on the Maryborough road, the Native Plant Arboretum on Vahland Rd in Strathfieldsaye, and the Cherry Berry Farm Water Adventure Land and the Mandurang Orchid Nursery on Tannery Lane in Mandurang.

There are also several good wineries in the district which are open for tastings, including Chateau Le Amon, Balgownie and Chateau Dore.

Lake Eppalock & Heathcote

The large Lake Eppalock reservoir, about 30 km from Bendigo, provides the town's water supply and is popular for all sorts of water sports.

There are some fine lookouts in the vicinity of Heathcote a quiet little highway town, with a gold mining past and a wine making present. The town, 47 km from Bendigo, is surrounded by vineyards where tasters are made very welcome.

Central Highlands to North Central Victoria

The gold country of central Victoria, extending from Ballarat to Bendigo and beyond, is part of the Central Highlands. Continuing north you drop down onto the rich agricultural land of the northern plains which extend to the Murray River. Heading towards the north-west of the state you enter the sparsely populated and dry Mallee region. Farming is difficult in this area, though the stunted Mallee gum tree manages to survive the extremely low rainfall.

AVOCA (population 1000)

Already an established town when gold made its impact on the area, Avoca is now a major pastoral and agricultual region and the centre of an expanding wine district.

The foothills of the nearby Pyrenees Ranges offer plenty of opportunity for bushwalking; there are good walking tracks, waterfalls and Mt Avoca which, at 760 metres, is the highest peak in the ranges. There are several wineries, including Taltarni and Mount Avoca, scattered around the district which are good for relaxed wine tasting. Avoca, which is at the junction of the Sunraysia and Pyrenees highways 185 km north-west of Melbourne, holds an annual Wool & Wine Festival in October.

Places to Stay

The *Avoca Caravan Park* on Liebig St has tent sites and on-site vans for $5 and $17 a double; and the *Avoca Motel* costs $35 a double for bed and a light breakfast.

THE SUNRAYSIA HIGHWAY

From Avoca the Sunraysia Highway runs north-west to Mildura, merging with the Calder Highway just before Ouyen, the last major town before the Murray.

Before the road heads into the dry Mallee region it passes through Redbank, and the nearby Redbank Valley Vineyard (18 km north-west of Avoca); St Arnaud; Donald, a busy wheat-growing and sheep-raising centre with an agricultural museum; and Birchip, one of the last areas of Victoria to be settled.

Between the tiny townships of Lascelles and Speed, the highway is about 30 km east of the excellent Wyperfeld National Park (see the section on the Mallee).

St Arnaud

Another charming old gold town, St Arnaud is set in pleasant hill country about 62 km from Avoca. The main street has been classified by the National Trust and the town has many fine old buildings adorned with lacework, and excellent botanic gardens. An Historical Society Museum is open on weekends.

Other old towns you can visit in the St Arnaud district include Logan, where the *Avoca Forest Hotel* is a good place to eat and drink.

Places to Stay The *St Arnaud Caravan Park* on Dundas St has tent sites and on-site vans for $6 and $15 a double. The *Botanical* and the *St Arnaud* hotels on Napier St cost about $18/30 a single/double for bed & breakfast, $25/45 including dinner.

THE CALDER HIGHWAY

The Calder Highway also runs north-east from the Central Highlands right up to the Mallee, more or less parallel to the Sunraysia, finally turning sharply east to meet that highway just before Ouyen.

Inglewood

From Bendigo it's 45 km to Inglewood, another town with its roots firmly planted in the gold fields. The local brick kilns provided sturdy material for Inglewood's charming buildings. Eucalyptus oil has been distilled in the area for over 100 years. There's an old distillery in town and many eucalyptus farms in the area.

West of the town, towards St Arnaud in the Kooyoora State Park, are the Melville Caves named after the gentleman bushranger Captain Melville who used to hide out there. In 1980 the 27 kg *Hand of Faith* gold nugget was unearthed in Kingower, 10 km west of Inglewood.

Wedderburn

Small gold nuggets are still being found around Wedderburn, where you can get prospecting maps and other equipment (including metal detectors), so this may be a good place to try your luck! The town's museum and general store are typical of buildings of the gold rush era and there are a number of other interesting buildings including the government battery, a boomerang factory and eucalyptus distilleries.

Wycheproof

The Calder continues north from Wedderburn through Charlton, located on both sides of the Avoca River (check out the Golden Grain Museum), to Wycheproof on the edge of the Mallee.

Huge wheat trains actually pass right along the main street of Wycheproof, though the town is best known for the annual King of the Mountain footrace. Competitors have to carry a 63.5 kg sack of wheat to the summit of the 43 metre high Mt Wycheproof which, at just 8805 metres lower than Mt Everest, is registered as the lowest mountain in the world!

THE LODDEN VALLEY HIGHWAY

The Loddon Valley Highway follows the Loddon River to Kerang where it meets the Murray Valley Highway heading west to Swan Hill and Mildura and east to Echuca.

The town of Pyramid Hill is about 19 km north-east of the highway from Durham Ox (45 km south of Kerang). Named by the early explorer Major Mitchell after the strange 187 metre pyramid-shaped hill nearby, the town has a good historical museum which is open on Sundays between 2 and 4 pm. To the east near Terrick Terrick there's a picnic ground and some good walks in the vicinity of Mt Hope Creek.

Kerang

About 26 km south of the Murray River, Kerang is best known for its huge flocks of ibis. During spring the area's lakes and swamps, north-west of the town, form one of the world's largest breeding rookeries with at least 150,000 white, straw-knecked and glossy ibis. There are more than 50 lakes, some of which are also popular for sailing, on either side of the Murray Valley Highway between Kerang and Lake Boga. To get a closer look at the ibis, visit the bird hide at the ibis rookery on Middle Lake.

In the town itself there is also plenty of birdlife, as well as other native wildlife, in Korina Park which is open daily from 9 am to 5 pm. Strathclyde Cottage is a local arts and crafts centre and the Kerang Museum, opposite the Water Tower, has an extensive exhibit of the region's history since settlers first took up land in the 1850s.

Places to Stay The *Ibis Caravan Park* at the junction of the Loddon and Murray Valley highways has tent sites for $7 a double and on-site vans for $20 to $26 a double. *Macropus Park* (tel (054) 57 6222) is a holiday farm 18 km from town which has bunk rooms for $28 per person including all meals, and units for $24 a double or $32 per person for dinner, bed & breakfast. Kerang also has a couple of hotels and motels.

THE MIDLAND & NORTHERN HIGHWAYS

The Midland Highway heads north from Bendigo to Elmore where it meets, or becomes, the Northern Highway which follows the Campaspe River to Echuca on the Murray.

Rochester

Rochester, on the Northern Highway, was first settled in the 1840s and has been a rich agricultural area since irrigation was introduced in the 1880s. These days nearly 800 square km of land in the Rochester region is serviced by irrigation canals from the Campaspe Weir and the Waranga Reservoir.

Wheat, oats, barley and tomatoes are grown in the district and local dairy farms supply the Rochester Murray Goulburn complex, part of the Murrary Goulburn Co-operative which is the largest manufacturer of dairy products in Australia.

Places to Stay & Eat *Rochester Caravan Park* in Church St has tent sites for $4 and on-site vans for $17 a double. The *Kimbob Recreation Farm* (tel (054) 86 5252), at nearby Bamawm, has tent sites for $4 and a bunk room for $8 per person. *Random House* (tel (054) 84 1792), a homestead built last century by the Campaspe River, provides accommodation, by booking only, for its dinner guests. Rochester's *Shamrock Hotel* does good counter meals.

For something a little different Rich River Horsedrawn Caravans (tel 86 5274) hire out fully equipped caravans, drawn by Clydesdale horses. Minimum bookings are $240 for four days per one caravan.

The Murray River

The Murray River is Australia's most important inland waterway flowing from the mountains of the Great Dividing Range in north-east Victoria to Encounter

Bay in South Australia, a distance of some 2500 km. The river actually has its source in New South Wales, close to Mt Kosciusko, but soon after forms the border between the two states though most of the places of interest are on the Victorian side.

The mighty Murray is also a river with a history. It was travelled along by some of Australia's earliest explorers, including Mitchell, Sturt and Eyre, and later became a great trade artery and a means of opening up the interior.

Long before roads and railways crossed the land the Murray was an antipodean Mississippi with paddle-steamers carrying supplies and carting wool to and from remote sheep stations and homesteads. The north-eastern township of Echuca became Australia's leading inland port as boats traded for hundreds of km along the Murray's winding waterways, to other thriving river towns like Swan Hill and Mildura, as well as up and down the Murrumbidgee, Goulburn and Darling rivers.

Many of the river towns have good museums, old buildings from the riverboat era or well-preserved paddle-steamers that recall that colourful era.

The Murray is also of great economic importance as it supplies the vital water for the irrigation schemes of northern Victoria that have made huge areas of previously barren land agriculturally viable.

As early as the 1890s Victorian MP Alfred Deakin (later prime minister) recognised the agricultural potential of developing irrigation projects in the state's north. He encouraged the Chafey brothers of California to design and install pumps and irrigation facilities using the Murray water. The brothers also planned the township of Mildura which, together with the new farming possibilities, soon attracted settlers from all over the country and overseas.

The Murray and its irrigation projects now support prosperous dairy farms, vineyards, vegetables and the citrus orchards which provide fresh fruit and supply the thriving dried fruit industry.

The river is also famous for its magnificent forests of red gums, its plentiful bird and animal life and as a great place for adventurous canoe trips, relaxing riverboat cruises or leisurely riverbank camping.

Getting There & Away

The following information covers transport by bus and train to the main Murray River towns of Mildura, Swan Hill and Echuca. See the Mildura section for details of air services, and the North-East Victoria section for more details of transport to Wodonga and other Murray towns in that area.

Bus & Train The interstate bus companies go through Mildura, Greyhound as usual having the best connections. Greyhound have a Melbourne/Mildura/Broken Hill route which runs along the Murray twice a week. Fares from Melbourne include Echuca $21, Swan Hill $23, Robinvale or Mildura $33. Other fares to or from Mildura include Adelaide $25, Broken Hill $24 and Sydney $77.

V/Line have bus, train or combination bus and train services which connect Melbourne with Bendigo, Ballarat and other centres with the Murray River towns, as well as bus services along the Murray between Albury and Swan Hill. Fares include: Bendigo to Swan Hill $15; Bendigo to Mildura $31; Echuca to Swan Hill $14.50; Swan Hill to Mildura $13.40; Ballarat to Mildura $31; and Albury to Swan Hill $26.80.

Boat Of course the most appropriate way to travel on the Murray would have to be by boat. The paddle-steamers of Echuca and Swan Hill provide day or overnight trips, and there are numerous places that rent houseboats. The latter combine accommodation with a leisurely few days along the river. Check the tourist information offices in Mildura, Swan Hill and Echuca for details on the houseboats. The average cost, in the peak season, is around $1100 per week for up to 10 people.

THE MURRAY VALLEY HIGHWAY

In the north-west of Victoria the Murray Valley Highway begins where it meets the Sunraysia Highway at a T-junction 67 km south of Mildura. From there it follows, for the most part, the course of the Murray River eastwards as far as Corryong, which is almost back to the river's source near Mt Kosciusko in New South Wales.

The following covers the smaller towns on the highway between Mildura and Wodonga (basically Robinvale to Yarrawonga) and a few towns right on the river, north of the highway. The main Murray towns of Mildura, Swan Hill and Echuca follow this section, while info on Wodonga and other river towns in that part of the state are covered in the section on north-east Victoria.

The western end (or beginning) of the Murray Valley Highway runs beside and through the Hattah-Kulkyne National Park, which partly borders the Sunraysia Highway, then follows a loop in the Murray through Bannerton, 14 km south of Robinvale. This park (see the Mallee section) is one of the few fragments of virgin Mallee scrub still remaining in the region. It's a valuable reminder that in this part of the country the Murray is really running through a desert and only the great irrigation projects have made the desert bloom.

Robinvale

Robinvale on the river, though a little off the Murray Valley Highway, is almost ringed in by a loop of the river. The first major town east of Mildura, Robinvale is a centre for grape and citrus growing. It has a busy wine industry with local wineries open for visits and tastings. Just downstream from the town is a weir and one of the largest windmills in Australia.

The most direct route from Mildura to Robinvale is to cross the river into New South Wales and take the Sturt Highway. North of the Murray is very empty country, stretching across the great

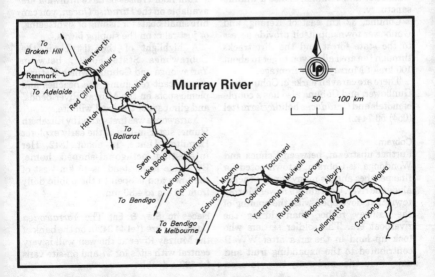

expanse of outback New South Wales to Broken Hill.

A little north of the highway, near Narrung, is the junction of the Murray and Murrumbidgee rivers. From Robinvale to Swan Hill the Murray Valley Highway runs close to the river.

Murrabit

The small river town of Murrabit, 26 km north of Kerang, has a local market on the first Saturday of each month. Further along the river you can explore the forest tracks around Koondrook to get a better view of the Murray's mighty red gums, or follow the Murray River Track from there to Gunbower. Koondrook and Barham, just over the river in New South Wales, are 24 km north-east of Kerang.

Gunbower State Forest

The superb Gunbower State Forest, which is actually on a long 'island' enclosed by the Murray and Gunbower Creek, features magnificent river red gums, abundant animal and bird life and plenty of walking tracks. Kow Swamp, between Gunbower and Cohuna, is also a wildlife sanctuary.

Cohuna, 32 km east of Kerang, and Gunbower township itself provide access to the state forest and the dirt tracks through the area allow you to get to about 100 km of Murray River frontage.

There are caravan parks in Cohuna and Gunbower, and Cohuna also has a couple of motels and *Craddocks* holiday farm (tel (054) 56 7442).

Cobram

Further upstream, between Echuca and Wondonga, is Cobram, a town noted for fine peaches and its many sandy beaches along the river. Cobram is a newer Murray town that developed with the coming of the railway rather than during the riverboat era. The soldier settlers who took up land in the area after WW II contributed to the expanding fruit and dairy industries and every two years, on the Australia Day weekend, the town celebrates its heritage with a Peaches & Cream festival.

Yarrawonga

About 40 km east of Cobram on the banks of Lake Mulwala, Yarrawonga is known for its fine and sunny weather, for a host of aquatic activities including windsurfing, swimming, power boating and water skiing, and as a retirement centre.

Lake Mulwala was formed by the completion, in 1939, of the Yarrawonga Wier which in turn was part of the massive Hume Dam project (near Albury) to harness the waters of the Murray for irrigation purposes.

Yarrawonga has a tourist information centre on the corner of Belmore St and Irvine Parade.

The Tudor House Clock Museum, 21 Lynch St, features hundreds of clocks from all over the world and is open daily except Friday from 10 am to 4.30 pm. Hallworth House Gallery, Oaten St, which houses paintings, glassware and pottery, is open daily from 10 am to 5 pm.

Half hour cruises of Lake Mulwala are available on the *Paradise Queen*, you can hire small boats for fishing or sightseeing, or just relax on the sloping lawns.

A highlight of the district is the Cobrawonga State Forest, between Yarrawonga and Cobram, which features magnificent red gums, the beaches and picnic spots on the Murray River bends, and glimpses of the local wildlife.

Yarrawonga was first settled by Elizabeth Hume, sister-in-law of the early explorer Hamilton Hume, in about 1842. Her interesting octagonal-shaped home, Byramine Homestead, is 15 km west of the town and is open to the public daily from 10 am to 4.30 pm.

Places to Stay & Eat The *Yarrawonga Caravan Park* (tel 44 3420) on the bank of the Murray River at the weir wall is very central with sites for $7 and on-site vans for $20 a double.

The *Terminus* (tel 44 3025) and *Criterion* (tel 44 3839), both on Belmore St, are the cheapest hotels in town. Bed & breakfast singles/doubles cost around $19/34.

The *Victoria Hotel* (tel 44 3009), also on Belmore St, has singles/doubles, with breakfast, for $22/32 and their counter meals are the best and cheapest food in town.

Pinkies at 25 Belmore St, tucked away in the corner of a shopping mall, is a good cafe for a light lunch or a snack.

MILDURA (population 15,700)

Noted for its exceptional amount of sunshine, Mildura was the site of the first Murray River irrigation projects. In the 1850s Alfred Deakin, the Commissioner for Public Works (who later became prime minister), was a great believer in the possibilities of irrigation. He persuaded the Chaffey brothers of California to come out to Australia to develop irrigation projects along the Murray. Deakin's vision proved to be correct and the extensive irrigated land around Mildura and down through South Australia all stems from the Chaffey brothers' early work.

The brothers also designed the town which became an irrigation farming colony, attracting settlers from all over. W B Chaffey, who actually settled in Mildura and became its first mayor, was also one of the region's first winemakers. You can see his statue on Deakin Ave and his original home, Rio Vista (opposite the Chaffey Improved Pumping System) is now a museum and part of the Mildura Arts Centre.

Information

The Murray Tourist Office is in a booth in Langtree Mall and Ron's Tourist Centre at 41 Deakin Ave is good for tour information and bookings.

Fruit Picking For fruit-picking work, write to or phone the Commonwealth Employment Service around the first week of February and there's a good chance of getting a job as a grape picker or cart operator. After a few days, you'll get used to the back-breaking 10 hour a day labour. Picking usually starts around February and lasts for a month. It's hard work but if you've done it before, it can mean big bucks, like about $350 a week. Some farmers provide accommodation, but take a tent if you're not sure.

Things to See

Mildura has an Aboriginal Arts Centre at the Ninth St end of the mall. The Pioneer Cottage at 3 Hunter St has a small museum on the history of the Mallee. The Wesley Methodist Church on the corner of Deakin Ave and 10th St has an unusual rounded shape while the Mildura Workingman's Club boasts one of the longest bars in the world – visitors can inspect the bar from 9.30 to 11 am.

Amongst Mildura's other attractions one of the most interesting is the Orange World citrus plantation tour (one hour, $3). It's a fascinating introduction to how citrus fruit is produced.

Lest you forget that this is riverboat country you can take paddle-steamer trips from the Mildura Wharf. On weekday afternoons and Sundays the PS *Melbourne* does a two hour trip for $10, while other paddle-steamers like the *Coonawarra* or *Rothbury* have different deals.

Mildura is also wine country with a number of popular wineries around the district.

Places to Stay

Mildura's backpackers motel is the *Archway Lodge* (tel 23 0047) at 183 Deakin Ave (part of the Archway Motel). The two bed rooms are nice and clean and cost from $10 per person. There's a lounge with colour TV, kitchen, laundry and air conditioning.

Rosemont Holiday House (tel 23 1535), 154 Madden Ave, is an associate YHA hostel with bed & breakfast for $15 per person. The rooms are clean with all the usual facilities and the owners are very helpful and hospitable. The *Mildura Travel Lodge*, 102 Madden Ave, costs $10 per person a night or $40 per week. The place is for men only and is slightly run down. The *Wintersun Hotel* (tel 23 0365), 124 Eighth St, has bed & breakfast singles/doubles from $22/30.

Mildura, especially along Deakin Ave, is overrun with motels which has created lot of competition to lure in customers, so prices are quite low with special deals being offered all the time. Try the *Vineleaf Motel* (tel 23 1377) on the corner of Tenth St and Pine Ave which has singles/doubles for $25/31 including a light breakfast; or the *Riviera Motel* (tel 23 3696), 157 Seventh St, where singles/doubles cost from $28/36. One of the best motels for a splurge is the *Chaffey International Motor Inn* (tel 23 5833), 244 Deakin Ave, with singles/doubles from $48/58.

There are also many caravan parks in the area but the most central is *Cross Roads Caravan Park* (tel 23 3239) on the corner of Deakin Ave and Fifteenth St. Tent sites cost $9.50 for two and on-site vans are $22.

Places to Eat

The Chinese restaurant *The Boat* on Langtree Ave is a good and popular place where meals cost between $6 and $10 (avoid the beef satay though). Good fish & chips, for around $5, can be found at the *Busy Bee Cafe* on Langtree Ave. *Good Friday* is a vegetarian restaurant on Chaffey Ave with meals starting at $5 for mainly Indian, Japanese and Middle Eastern type food.

For an early breakfast or lunch try *The Early Bird* on Deakin St opposite Ron's Tourist Centre. You can try the *Grand Hotel* on the corner of Deakin Ave and Seventh St or the *Hotel Wintersun* in Eighth St for cheap counter meals. The gambling clubs on the New South Wales side of the Murray River provide good, cheap lunches and free transport.

Getting There & Away

Air Sunstate Airlines (tel 22 2444) fly to Melbourne ($131) and Broken Hill ($85). Kendell Airlines (tel toll free (008) 33 8894) fly to Mildura from Melbourne for $130.

Bus & Train Sunday to Friday there is a rail service that connects Melbourne with Mildura and on Saturday there is a bus service; the fare is $36.50.

V/Line has a daily bus service connecting all the towns along the Murray River between Mildura and Albury; the fare all the way to Albury is $36.50. Greyhound have a twice weekly service between Melbourne and Broken Hill for $62; the fare from Melbourne to Mildura is $36 and from Broken Hill to Mildura is $26. Greyhound and Deluxe have a daily Adelaide to Sydney service stopping in Mildura; from Sydney the fare is $85 and from Adelaide it's $29. Pioneer's Adelaide to Canberra service also stops in Mildura.

Getting Around

Mildura Bus Lines provide a regular bus service around town from Monday to Saturday. You can get a timetable from the tourist office. Ron's Tourist Centre provides many tours of the town and the surrounding area. Free coaches to the New South Wales gambling clubs also leave from in front of their office at 41 Deakin St.

AROUND MILDURA

Leaving Mildura you don't have to travel very far before you realise just how desolate the country around here can be. Continuing west, now on the Sturt Highway, the road runs arrow-straight and deadly dull to South Australia, about 130 km away.

Crossing into New South Wales you follow the Murray another 32 km to Wentworth, one of the oldest river towns, where you can visit the Old Wentworth

Gaol with the Nanya Exhibit and the Morrison Collection, then strike off north for 266 km along the Silver City Highway to remote Broken Hill.

A popular excursion from Mildura is to Mungo Station in New South Wales to see the strange natural formation known as the Wall of China.

SWAN HILL (population 8400)

One of the most interesting and popular towns along the entire length of the Murray, Swan Hill was named by the early explorer Major Thomas Mitchell, who spent a sleepless night here due to a large contingent of noisy black swans.

Swan Hill is 340 km from Melbourne and has a tourist information centre (tel 32 3033) at 306 Campbell St.

The town's major attraction today is the extensive riverside Swan Hill Pioneer Settlement. The feature exhibit of this working re-creation of a river town of the paddle-steamer era is the *Gem*, one of the largest riverboats on the Murray.

The settlement has everything from an old locomotive to a working blacksmith's shop, an old newspaper office and the most amazing collection of old bits and pieces. The settlement is definitely worth a visit and is open daily. Admission is $8.25 including a free ride on one of the horse-drawn vehicles that act as transport around the old buildings.

Each night there is a 45 minute world class Sound & Light Show for $5.50, during which you are driven around the settlement in a transporter while enjoying the sights and sounds of the past. The paddle-steamer *Pyap* makes short trips from the pioneer settlement for $5.50.

The Swan Hill Regional Art Gallery at Horseshoe Bend, just outside the settlement, features the works of many Australian artists as well as many temporary exhibitions.

The Military Museum and the Dowling House Arts & Crafts Centre are worth looking into. There's also Olsen's Pheasant Farm, 32 km north of Swan Hill, and the Amboc Mohair Farm at Mystic Park 30 km south-east.

The historic Murray Downs sheep station and the old Tyntynder Homestead, are fine examples of working properties from the earliest days of European settlement along the Murray. Murray Downs, which is about two km east of Swan Hill, is open on weekends and school holidays from 9 am to 5 pm. A great way to visit the homestead is aboard the PS *Pyap* on a return trip from the Pioneer Settlement down the Murray. Tyntynder, 17 km north of the town, also has a small museum of pioneering and Aboriginal relics and many reminders of the hardships of colonial life, like the wine cellar! Admission is $4.50, which includes a rather rushed tour, and the homestead is open daily from 9 am to 4.30 pm.

The Swan Hill area also has a few wineries worth visiting, such as Buller's at Beverford (14 km north) and Best's at Lake Boga (17 km south).

Places to Stay

The *Swan Hill Riverside Caravan Park* (tel 32 1494), Monash Drive, has sites at $6 and on-site vans for $24. The *Pioneer City Park* (tel 32 4372), on the Murray Valley Highway just north of town, has tent sites for $8, on-site vans for around $21 a double, and cabins for $33 a double.

The *Federal Hotel* (tel 32 1238) in Murray Downs, just across the McCallum bridge over the Murray River, is quite central, and has basic rooms for $12 per person. The *Commercial Hotel* (tel 32 1214), 91 Campbell St, has nice and clean singles/doubles from $15/30.

The cheapest of the many motels in town is the *Murray River Motel* (tel 32 2067), 481 Campbell St, with singles/doubles for $24/30; and the best motel for a splurge is the *Lady Augusta Motor Inn* (tel 32 9677) where singles/doubles are $46/53.

Places to Eat

A good, cheap pasta place is the *Mediterranean Pizza House* on Campbell St. There are some good coffee lounges on the same street; try *Banjo's* or *Melody's* for lunch.

Murray Downs Homestead put on lunch and afternoon tea during school holidays, and *Puck's Room*, near Mystic Park, has good light lunches and Devonshire teas.

Captain Beattie's Riverboat Restaurant, in the paddle steamer *Gem* at the Pioneer Settlement, is a great place for a splurge and a chance to try local specialities like witchetty grub or kangaroo tail soup, damper and yabbies.

Getting There & Around

Air Flinders Island Airlines fly between Melbourne and Swan Hill for $92.50.

Bus & Train V/Line has a rail and bus service to and from Melbourne ($27.40), Mildura ($13.40) and Echuca ($14.50). The Greyhound, Pioneer and Deluxe services from Adelaide to Sydney (via Canberra) all stop in Swan Hill once a day. The fare from Adelaide is $55 and Sydney is $84. Greyhound also has a Melbourne to Broken Hill service, on Fridays and Saturdays, that stops here and in Echuca and Mildura.

Swan Hill has an hourly local bus service on weekdays and Saturday mornings for 50c.

ECHUCA (population 8000)

Strategically sited where the Goulburn and Campaspe rivers join the Murray, Echuca, which is an aboriginal word meaning 'the meeting of the waters', was founded in 1853 by the enterprising ex-convict Henry Hopwood.

In the riverboat days this was the busiest inland port in Australia and the centre of the thriving river trade as paddle-steamers journeyed up and down the mighty Murray transporting wool and supplies. In the 1880s the famous red gum wharf was more than a km long and there were stores and hotels all along the waterfront.

Echuca's romantic pioneering days are thriving again, this time for the tourists, around the old Port of Echuca area and the restored red gum wharf. The paddle-steamers *Adelaide*, the second oldest riverboat in the world, and *Pevensey* are moored at the wharf and the original port Bond Store is now a wax museum.

The Star Hotel, built in 1867, is now the Port Visitors Centre and the the the Bridge Hotel, built by Henry Hopwood, is a fine example of pioneering architecture and also has a good restaurant.

Other places of interest around the town include the Echuca Historical Society Museum, an Auto & Folk Museum, the 1880s Pump House which now houses a gem collection, the Red Gum Works which is a working museum demonstrating the milling industry that kept the steam-powered boats on the water, and the Joalah Game Birds & Fauna Park.

In late October Echuca hosts its annual Rich River Festival which is 12 days of entertainment and games.

You can take a Murray River cruise on one of the many paddle-steamers that are still operating. You can phone ahead (area code 054) for more info or bookings. The PS *Canberra* does short tours as does the PS *Tisdall Princess* (tel 82 2141), the PS *Pride of the Murray* and the *Echuca Princess* (tel 82 5244), and the PS *Mary Ann* (tel 82 3044). For overnight trips there's the PS *Emmylou* (tel 82 3801).

You can hire bicycles at the Park Gate General Store at the corner of Dickson and Crofton Sts for $2 per hour, $6 per half a day and $10 per day.

Jack and Elaine O'Mullane run 'campanoeing' trips on the Murray River. Each canoe can fit two people plus camping gear and supplies and costs $30 for the first day and $10 for each successive day. Their address is PO Box 62, Echuca (tel 82 4063).

If you want to try your luck at the pokies then Echuca's smaller sister town, Moama, is right across the river in New South Wales.

Places to Stay

The *Echuca City Council Caravan Park* (tel 82 2157) in Crofton St has sites for $6 for two people and on-site vans for $20.

The cheapest place in town is the *Echuca Hotel* (tel 82 1087) in High St which has bed & breakfast for $17, as well as cheap counter meals. The *Palace Hotel* (tel 82 1031), 37 Heygarth St, has singles/doubles for $17/35; and the *American Hotel* (tel 82 5044), 239 Hare St, has singles/doubles with a good continental breakfast for $20/35.

For something different you could spend the night on the Murray aboard the PS *Emmylou*; or contact Magic Murray Houseboats (tel 82 2177) or Dinki-Di Houseboats (tel 82 5223) for details about hiring your own houseboat to tie where you please for a night on the Murray.

Places to Eat

The *Shamrock Hotel*, 583 High St, has good cheap counter meals. The historic *Bridge Hotel* by the port has a fine restaurant and the *Steam Packet Hotel*, 610 High St, does good lunches and dinners. For a light lunch there's *The Tangled Garden* at 433 High St, and if you're after a vegetarian fix the *Mexican Gallery* has an extensive menu.

Getting There & Away

V/Line has a combination train and bus service between Melbourne and Echuca ($19) and also a service from Echuca to Albury-Wodonga for $19.40 and Swan Hill for $14.50.

Goulburn Valley

The Goulburn Valley region runs in a wide band from Lake Eildon north-west across the Hume Highway and up to the New South Wales border. The Goulburn River joins the Murray upstream of Echuca. You'll also find Goulburn Valley centres mentioned in the Around Melbourne, Hume Highway and Murray River sections of this chapter, but a description of the stretch from Seymour on the Hume Highway up to the Murray River follows.

Getting There & Away

V/Line have trains or buses from Melbourne to Shepparton and on to Cobram and Tocumwal which is across the Murray. (From Tocumwal you can connect to Sydney.) There's also a connection from Cobram to Yarrawonga, Shepparton to Benalla or to Kyabram and Echuca. Economy fares from Melbourne are Shepparton $14.30, Numurkah $16.50 and Cobram $19.50.

Pioneer Express and Greyhound have some services which operate up the Goulburn Valley with fares to Shepparton of $20 and to Echuca $21.

NAGAMBIE (population 1100)

On the shores of Lake Nagambie (created by the construction of the Goulburn Weir), Nagambie has some interesting old buildings, an historical society display and many good picnic spots.

Two of the best known wineries in Victoria are close by: Chateau Tahbilk is a beautiful old building with notable cellars, while just a few km away the Mitchelton Winery is ultra-modern with a strange 'control tower' looming unexpectedly from the surrounding countryside. Mitchelton Winery is part of a complex which includes restaurant and barbecue facilities and a swimming pool. Boat tours operate from Nagambie on the lake and up the river to the winery which is built on the riverbanks.

The *Old Lake Kitchen* serves tasty snacks and picnic food and you can stay at the *Nagambie Motor Inn* (tel (057) 94 2388) on High Street.

SHEPPARTON (population 28,000)

In a prosperous irrigated fruit and vegetable growing area, Shepparton and its adjoining centre of Mooroopna have a number of points of interest including a modern civic centre which has an art gallery and other facilities. There's the International Village, the Shepparton & Goulburn Valley Historical Society Museum (open on Sunday afternoons), the green lawns around Lake Victoria, the lakeside Raymond West swimming pool, and the Redbyrne Potteries a few km out of town to the east. Good views of the Goulburn Valley and the city surrounded by orchards can be seen from the Shepparton Lookout Tower (near the post office). You can tour the Shepparton Preserving Company cannery (the largest in the southern hemisphere) during the canning season from January to April. Tours operate between 8.30 and 11 am and between 12 and 3.30 pm on weekdays.

From January to April it's the fruit picking season – a good time to get some casual work. It's best to start looking in December as demand for jobs is high when the apricots, then peaches and pears, ripen.

There are places to eat and many good motels along the Goulburn Valley Highway (Wyndham St) to the north and south of the main shopping centre. For a special occasion, you could dine at *Abbey's* restaurant (tel (058) 31 1058), 27 Fryers St, or have a lunch of fresh local produce in their bistro. The tourist information centre is on Wyndham St opposite Lake Victoria.

RUSHWORTH (population 1000)

This historic town, about 20 km west of the Goulburn Highway, was a mining centre in the gold days and now has a National Trust classification. You can visit the local history museum on weekends or the Cheong Homestead a few km south of town at Whroo. The Whroo Historic Centre has a visitor centre, walking tracks and picnic areas. Lake Waranga is popular for water sports.

NUMURKAH (population 2700)

North of Shepparton and not far from the Murray River, Numurkah is another irrigation-area town. It has a Steam & Vintage Machinery Display, and Devonshire teas are served at the historic Brookfield Homestead nearby.

KYABRAM (population 5400)

Kyabram is a little south of Echuca and has a fauna and waterfowl park at the southern end of the town. Morning and afternoon teas as well as light lunches are available at the park where there's a restored pioneer's hut, an old shearing shed and an old farmhouse (tel (058) 62 2353) where visitors can stay. Kyabram promotes itself as a garden town and was the centre for a prosperous fruit growing district.

North-East Victoria

The Hume Highway

The Hume Highway is the direct route between Melbourne and Sydney. It's not Australia's most exciting road: in fact it's downright dull in stretches and the heavy traffic can make life a little tedious. En route to the New South Wales border you pass through the interesting 'Kelly Country', where Australia's most famous outlaw, Ned Kelly, had some of his most exciting brushes with the law. Kelly and his gang of bushrangers shot three police officers at Stringybark Creek in 1878, and robbed banks at Euroa and Jerilderie before their lives of crime ended in the siege at Glenrowan. Not far east of the Hume are the Victorian Alps – in winter you'll catch glimpses of the snow-capped peaks from the highway.

Getting There & Away

As the Hume Highway is the main artery between Australia's two biggest cities it's not surprising that there are plenty of transport alternatives.

If you're driving north along the Hume take extra care at night when the big trucks come out to play – it can be horrendous. During the day the traffic is usually no problem, but watch out for police radar speed-traps, they make a lot of money on this road.

Air East-West Airlines connect Albury-Wodonga with Melbourne ($100, standby $80) and Sydney ($138, standby $110). Kendell also fly from Melbourne to Albury ($94, standby $75).

Bus The various bus companies operate up and down the Hume. Fares from Melbourne include Benalla $22, Wangaratta or Albury-Wodonga $30. Fares vary a few dollars from company to company. Bus services fan out from Wangaratta and Wodonga to Beechworth, Bright, Corryong and other towns in the foothills and to the snow resorts.

Train Apart from the Melbourne to Sydney through trains there are several trains running from Melbourne to Albury or from Sydney to Albury. From Melbourne, economy fares include Seymour $6.70, Benalla $15.10, Wangaratta $18, Wodonga $23.50, Albury $24.60.

Victorian Wineries
Some of Australia's best wines are made in Victoria. Grape growing and wine production started with the gold rush of the 1850s and Victorian fortified wines had established a fine reputation in Europe before the turn of the century. Then phylloxera, a disease of grapevines, devastated the Victorian vineyards and changing tastes in alcohol completed the destruction. From the 1960s, the Victorian wine industry started to recapture its former glory and to produce fine table wines as well as the fortified ones.

Victoria's oldest established wine producing region is in the north-east, particularly around Rutherglen, but also extending to Milawa, Glenrowan and beyond. Other fine wine growing areas include the Goulburn Valley river flats south of Shepparton, Great Western

between Stawell and Ararat on the Adelaide highway, around the Geelong area, and in the Yarra Valley near Melbourne. In the far north-west, the irrigation areas along the Murray at Robinvale and Mildura also produce wine.

MELBOURNE TO EUROA
The new Hume Freeway bypasses Kilmore, Broadford near Mt Disappointment and the Murchison Falls, and Seymour which is near several interesting vineyards including the very old Chateau Tahbilk and the very modern Mitchelton Winery – see the Goulburn Valley section. From Seymour you can take the Shepparton turn-off to Highway 39 – the Goulburn Valley Highway which becomes the Newell Highway, the alternative route to Sydney or Brisbane.

EUROA (population 2800)
From Euroa you can take a scenic drive to Gooram Falls near where Kelly performed one of his more amazing robberies at Faithfull Station – it's re-enacted every December. The importance of sheep and wool in the Australian economy is evident at Seven Creeks Run (open daily from 9 am). You can watch shearing demonstrations or sheep dog trials here just north of the town.

BENALLA (population 8800)
Bypassed by the freeway, Benalla has a small pioneer museum with some interesting old costumes and Ned Kelly exhibits. There are picnic areas along the Broken River through town and an excellent waterside art gallery. The town is also a very popular gliding centre and holds its annual Rose Festival from late October to early November. *Georgina's*, a long-established restaurant in the main street, is highly recommended.

GLENROWAN (population 200)
In 1880, the Kelly gang's exploits finally came to an end in a bloody shoot-out here, 230 km from Melbourne and 24 km up the highway from Benalla. Kelly was captured

alive and eventually hanged in Melbourne. Glenrowan has everything from a giant statue of Ned with his armoured helmet to a life-size working replica of the shoot-out. There's also a 'computerised hanging room'. It all tells you as much about the modern Australian tourist industry as about 19th century cops and robbers. The ruins of the Kelly family homestead can be seen a few km off the highway at Greta, though little remains of the slab bush hut.

WANGARATTA (population 16,200)

'Wang', as it is commonly known, is at the junction of the King and Ovens rivers; it's also the turn-off point for the Ovens Highway to Mt Buffalo and the north of the Victorian Alps. The town has some pleasant parks and bushranger Mad Dog Morgan is buried there in the local cemetery. At Wangaratta Airport, four km off the Hume and south of town, Air World has a vintage aircraft and Holden car collection (admission $5) and offers joy rides in Tiger Moth biplanes. Some buses stop here for meals so you might be able to fit in a quick flight while you're waiting!

There's lots of interest in the surrounding area: the Warby Range State Park with its ancient grass trees; old gold towns like Eldorado which has picnic spots by the creek; the old dredge; a pottery and Verita's Galleria – an art gallery; the Alps; the King Valley; and the wineries at Glenrowan, Milawa, Oxley and Rutherglen. You can taste mustard at Milawa Mustards or wine at Brown Brothers Milawa Vineyard. Wang has a tourist office on the Hume Highway south of the town.

Places to Stay & Eat

You can stay in motels in town; the *Central Wangaratta Motel* (tel (057) 21 4469) on Ely St, is one of these. The *Gateway* (tel 21 8399) and the *Hermitage* (tel 21 7444) are new and more expensive. *Painters Island Caravan Park* (tel 21 3380) by the river on Pinkerton

Crescent has on-site vans and is very close to the main shopping area.

Places to eat include the *Sydney Hotel* on Templeton St near the stockbridge across the river – the $2 counter meals are recommended. The *Pinsent* and the *North Eastern* hotels are popular, pleasant places for a meal or a drink. For a light lunch try *Margaret's Lunch Inn* in the main street or *Indulge* on Victoria Pde (the lane off Reid St near the Co store).

CHILTERN (population 870)

Close to Beechworth and only one km off the Hume Highway between Wang and Wodonga, Chiltern once swarmed with miners in search of their fortunes. This is another gold town with many reminders of its boom era. Author Henry Handel Richardson's home, Lake View, is preserved by the National Trust and is open from 10 am to 4 pm on weekends and school and public holidays. In the old Grape Vine Hotel (now delicensed) a courtyard is sheltered by the largest grape vine in Australia. You can visit and see the antiques on display too.

RUTHERGLEN (population 1500)

Close to the the Murray River and north of the Hume, Rutherglen is the centre of Victoria's major wine growing area and has long been famous for its fortified wines. You can cycle from winery to winery – contact Bogong Jack's Adventures (tel 27 3382) in Wangaratta or Bicycle Victoria (see the Getting Around section for Melbourne).

Among the several wineries you can visit in the area is All Saints, with a wine museum and a National Trust classified winery building, eight km from Rutherglen at Wahgunyah on the Murray. Wahgunyah was once a busy port for the Ovens Valley gold towns. Its customs house is a relic of that era.

Mrs Mouse's Teahouse at 12 Foord St is a good place to eat. It's open for teas and lunch daily from 10 am to 5 pm; you can also order a picnic basket for $11 a person.

There are several motels which provide good accommodation on the Murray Valley Highway (Main and Moodemere Sts).

WODONGA (population 25,300)

The Victorian half of Albury-Wodonga is on the Murray River, the border between Victoria and New South Wales. The combined cities form the main economic and industrial centre of this region. The Albury-Wodonga Development Corporation (tel (060) 24 0322) organises free half day tours of the area which has new housing estates, parks and industries – part of a government plan to decentralise the population and limit the urban sprawl of Sydney and Melbourne.

A famous group of young people, The Flying Fruit Fly Circus, live here when they're not touring the world.

There are motels and places to eat on Melbourne Rd and High St if you're staying overnight in the area.

CORRYONG (population 1400)

Corryong, the Victorian gateway to the Snowy Mountains and the Kosciusko National Park, is close to the source of the Murray River which, at this point, is merely an alpine stream.

Corryong's main claim to fame, however, is as the last resting place of Jack Riley, 'The Man from Snowy River'. Though some people dispute that Banjo Patterson based his stockman hero on Riley, a tailor turned mountain man who worked this district, the 'man' is nevertheless well-remembered in Corryong.

Jack Riley's grave is in the town cemetery and there's a 'Man from Snowy River' museum in the town, which is open daily, but only in the mornings.

TALLANGATTA (population 950)

In the 1950s, following the construction of the Hume Weir at Albury-Wodonga, the original site of Tallangatta was flooded by the rising waters of Lake Hume. Most of the actual township had already been relocated, however, on what became the shoreline of the new lake.

Just east of the town, especially if the waters of Lake Hume are low, you can see the streetscape of Old Tallangatta. There's also a few remaining buildings across the bridge.

The Tallangatta Arts Festival held annually in October attracts people from all over the district for nine days of arts, theatre, concerts, cultural exchanges and street parades.

The town, on the Murray Valley Highway east of Wodonga, is popular as a water sports centre and as a convenient base for the alpine region. The Kiewa Valley Rd takes you to the Bogong National Park, or across to the Ovens Valley Highway and the Mt Buffalo National Park. The Omeo Highway heads south over the Bogong and Dargo High Plains, through Omeo and on to Bairnsdale on the Gippsland coast.

Places to Stay

The *Lakelands Caravan Park*, Queen Elizabeth Drive, has tent sites for $6, and on-site vans for $23 a double. The *Victoria Hotel* (tel (060) 71 2672), on the corner of Banool Rd and Akuna Ave, has bed & breakfast singles for $18.

MITTA MITTA

Mitta Mitta, in a picturesque valley, is a popular destination for canoeing and trout-fishing enthusiasts. You can also try your luck fossicking for gold or enjoy a drive along the Tawonga Summer Track.

YACKANDANDAH (population 500)

There's a saying, around these parts, that 'all roads lead to Yackandandah'. If you *were* to get mislaid in the beautiful hills and valleys of this district you would find that most of the signposts do indeed point to this charming little town.

The pretty little 'strawberry capital', 32 km south of Wodonga, 23 km from

Beechworth and always on the way to somewhere, has been classified by the National Trust; not just the odd building but the entire town.

Yackandandah was a prosperous gold town and, back then, a welcome stopover for travellers on the old main road between Melbourne and Sydney. It has many fine old buildings, including the 1850 Bank of Victoria which is now a museum. The well-preserved buildings along the main street now house a variety of local craft shops, antique stores, cafes and tearooms.

You can still pan for gold in the creek and so many strawberries are grown here they even make them into strawberry wine. In the district there are other picturesque country settlements, like Dederang, Kiewa and Tangambalanga.

The *Yackandandah Camping Park*, on the Dederang Rd close to some good bushwalks, has tent sites for $4 and on-site vans for $20 a double.

BEECHWORTH (population 3200)

This picturesque town set amid the rolling countryside of the Ovens Valley, at the foothills of the Victorian Alps, has been attracting tourists for a good many years. In fact way back in 1927 it won the Melbourne *Sun News Pictorial's* 'ideal tourist town' competition.

It is still a pleasure to visit Beechworth and spend a few days enjoying its wide tree-lined streets, with their fine and dignified gold rush architecture, or exploring the surrounding forested valleys, waterfalls and rocky gorges. It's a perfect place for walking or cycling.

The town is 35 km east of Wangaratta, and if you're travelling between Wang and Wodonga the detour through Beechworth makes a worthwhile alternative to the frenetic pace of the boring Hume Highway.

There's a visitors information centre in the Rock Cavern, which is a gemstone and mineral museum on the corner of Ford and Camp streets.

In the 1850s Beechworth was the very prosperous hub of the Ovens River gold mining region. Signs of the gold wealth are still very much in evidence, reflected in the fact that 32 buildings are classified by the National Trust. They include Tanswell's Hotel with its magnificent old lacework, the post office with its clocktower, and the training prison where Ned Kelly and his mother were imprisoned for a while.

Beechworth actually has a quite few links with the notorious Kelly Gang. There's a a dank little cell, under the Town Hall, where young Ned once spent a night, and it was in the court house here that Ned's final trial began.

The old 1859 powder magazine is now a National Trust museum which is open 10 am to 4.30 pm daily from 26 December to 31 May and on Sundays and public holidays the rest of the year. The Trust's Carriage Museum, behind Tanswell's Hotel, is open the same hours and has a collection of old carriages including a Cobb & Co coach.

The Burke Museum, in Lock St, has relics from the gold rush and a replica of the main street a century ago, complete with 16 shop fronts. The hapless explorer Robert O'Hara Burke was a police officer in Beechworth during the early days of the gold rush before he set off on his historic trek north with William Wills. According to local stories it wasn't all that surprising that the expedition ended in tragedy as the townspeople of Beechworth were forever organising search parties for Officer Burke who kept getting himself lost.

Other things of interest in and around Beechworth include the historic Murray Brewey Cellars established in 1872 on the corner of William and Last Sts; the Chinese Burning Towers and Beechworth Cemetery, where the towers, altar and many graves are all that remain of the town's huge Chinese population during the gold rush; and the Golden Horseshoe Monument to a local pioneer who made gold horseshoes for his friend who had won a seat in parliament to represent miners.

Woolshed Falls, just out of town on the road to Chiltern, is a popular picnic area and the site of a major alluvial gold field which yielded over 85,000 kg of gold in 14 years. Further west at Eldorado a gigantic gold dredge still floats on the lake where it was installed in 1936. At the time it was the largest dredge in the southern hemisphere.

Heading south from Beechworth along the Myrtleford road, you come to the Golden Hills Trout Farm at Hurdle Flat where there are fresh catch-your-own trout for sale. The small village of Stanley, 10 km out along this road, is the centre of a thriving little apple-growing industry and there are great alpine views from Mt Stanley (1064 metres).

Places to Stay & Eat

The *Youth Hostel* (tel (057) 28 1426) in the National Trust classified old Star Hotel on the main street charges $8 a night.

Tanswell's Hotel (tel 28 1480), 30 Ford St, has bed & breakfast singles from $18 to $28, and doubles for $33 to $45. The *Nicholas Hotel* (tel 28 1051), on the corner of Camp and High streets, has room-only singles/doubles for $15/20; and the *Hibernian Hotel* (tel 28 1070), Camp St, has bed & breakfast singles/doubles for $25/45.

The Old Priory (tel 28 1024), on Loch St, is a guest house in an historic convent. A dorm bed costs $15, singles are $20, and doubles are $35, all for bed & breakfast.

Tanswell's Hotel does good counter meals, the *Hibernian* has an excellent bistro and the *Bakery* on Camp St has an irresistible selection of hot bread and cakes.

AROUND BEECHWORTH

On the road to Wodonga is the old cemetery with its Chinese section, a reminder of the Chinese presence on the gold fields. Further out along the same road is the turn-off to Chiltern and to Woolshed Falls – a popular picnic area and the site of a major alluvial gold field which yielded over 85,000 kg of gold in 14 years. Further west at Eldorado a gigantic gold dredge still floats on the lade where it was installed in 1936. At the time it was the largest dredge in the southern hemisphere.

East along the Myrtleford road, you come to the trout farm at Hurdle Flat where fresh trout are for sale, and I mean *fresh*; or you can hire a fishing pole and catch your own. The small village of Stanley is 10 km out along this road and is the centre of a thriving little apple growing industry.

The Victorian Alps

These mountains lie in the north-east part of the state. They begin just east of Melbourne in the Dandenongs, which are a spur of the Great Dividing Range that spreads north and north-east to the New South Wales border. The Victorian Alps are just as popular and good for winter and summer activities as New South Wales' Snowy Mountains. The Victorian ski fields are at lower altitudes than those in New South Wales, but they receive as much snow and have similar conditions above and below the snow line. Falls Creek, Mt Hotham and Mt Buller are Victoria's largest skifields with good skiing and all facilities. Mt Buffalo and Mt Baw Baw are smaller in size and offer fewer facilities. Lake Mountain, Mt Stirling, Mt Donna Buang and Mt St Gwinear are small with mainly cross-country skiing and no overnight facilities.

The roads are fully sealed to Falls Creek and Mt Buller; to all other ski resorts roads are unsealed or partially unsealed. In winter, snow chains must be carried (unless you want to pay a hefty fine) to all ski resorts. Other roads that crisscross the Great Dividing Range are unsealed for at least part of their way and only traversable in summer.

The skiing season officially commences

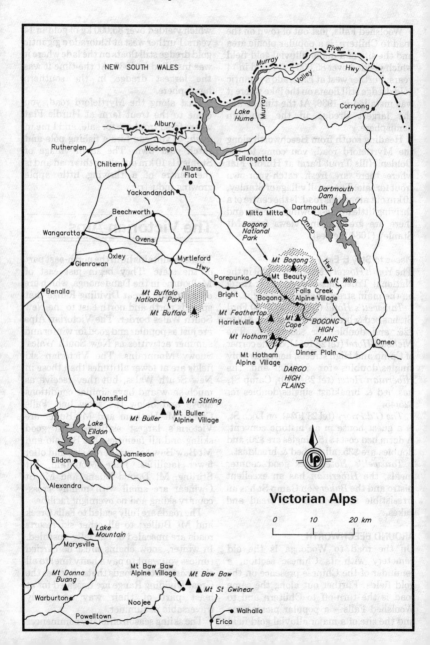

Victorian Alps

0   10   20 km

the first weekend of June and closes on the last weekend of September. On the opening weekend there is rarely any skiable snow and most people go there for the party atmosphere. The closing weekend usually has some skiable snow and is action packed with a fancy dress competition and many other events. The season basically lasts three months from July to September, August being the best month. Spring skiing can be good as it is sunny and warm with no crowds, and usually enough snow until the end of September.

In the summer months, especially from December to February, the area is ideal for bushwalking, climbing, fishing, camping and observing the native flora and fauna.

Places to Stay

There are many places to stay, especially in the ski resorts, which are basically full of accommodation for the skiers in winter. Overall, these are very expensive in winter and many people prefer to stay in towns below the snow line and drive the short distance up to skifields. In August it is advisable to book your accommodation, especially for weekends. In July or September it is usually possible to find something if you just turn up. Hotels, motels, chalets, self-contained flats and units, and caravan parks abound in the region. There are also youth hostels at Beechworth, Mt Hotham, Mt Buller and Mt Baw Baw.

The cheapest accommodation in the ski resorts is a bed in one of the club lodges or it is possible to cut costs by cramming in many people as possible into a flat. Telephone the Victorian Ski Association accommodation and booking line on (03) 699 4413 and they should be able to assist you in finding a place. If you are really keen to stay up on the mountain and cannot afford it, but have your own vehicle you can sleep in your car, like a few desperates do each year. Make sure you have a warm sleeping bag as it gets very cold. Below the snow line caravans are cheap to stay in and all right in winter as they are supplied with electric heaters.

Getting There & Away

Albury-Wodonga is the closest town with regular flights from Melbourne, Sydney and Mildura with East-West Airlines. Trains and buses also run from Melbourne and Sydney to Albury-Wodonga. See the Hume Highway section and each respective resort for more details. Regular buses connect Mt Buller, Falls Creek and Mt Hotham with Melbourne, Wangaratta and Wodonga and their respective access towns. On the other side of the range Omeo is connected by a bus service from Bairnsdale in Gippsland.

MYRTLEFORD (population 2815)

Another Ovens Valley centre, Myrtleford is handy for old towns like Beechworth and Bright, the various wineries of the Rutherglen region and the popular Mt Buffalo National Park. In the town itself there's an historic park with a collection of antique steam engines.

Places to Stay

The *Myrtleford Hotel* (tel 52 1078) at the corner of Standish and Smith Sts has singles/doubles from $16/27. The two caravan parks *Arderns* (tel 52 1394) and *Myrtleford* (tel 52 1598) are close to town and similarly priced at around $6 for sites for two and $20 for caravans.

MT BUFFALO NATIONAL PARK

Apart from Mt Buffalo itself, the park is noted for its many pleasant streams and fine walks. The mountain was named back in 1824 by explorers Hume and Hovell on their trek from Sydney to Port Phillip Bay. The mountain is surrounded by huge granite tors – great blocks of granite broken off from the massif by the expansion and contraction of ice in winter and other weathering effects. There is abundant plant and animal life around the park as well as over 140 km of walking tracks. Leaflets are available for the Gorge

Nature Walk, View Point Nature Walk and the Dicksons Falls Nature Walk. A road leads up almost to the summit of 1720 metre Mt Buffalo. In summer Mt Buffalo is a hang gliders' paradise (definitely not for beginners) and the near-vertical walls of the Gorge provide one of the most challenging rock climbs in Australia. Lake Catani is good for swimming and canoeing, while in winter Mt Buffalo turns into a ski resort with downhill and cross-country skiing being the most popular activities. For accommodation and other details see the Mt Buffalo section.

BRIGHT (population 1545)
Deep in the Ovens Valley, Bright today is a focal point of the winter sports region, a summer bushwalking centre and is renowned for its beautiful golden shades in autumn. In 1857 this was near where the notorious Buckland Valley riots took place, when the diligent Chinese gold miners were forced off their claims and given much less than a fair go. It is an easy drive from town to the snowfields of Mt Hotham, Falls Creek and Mt Buffalo.

Bright has a museum in the railway station while around the town are a number of excellent walking trails. You'll also enjoy excellent views if driving from Bright along the Alpine Way. Places of interest in the vicinity include the Stoney Creek Trout Farm, the pioneer park open-air museum and Buckland Gold which has demonstrations and lectures about gold panning.

Mt Bogong, to the east of Bright, is the highest mountain in Victoria at 1985 metres.

Places to Stay
There are plenty of motels and units, but they are not in the budget range. The Bright Alps Guest House (tel 55 1197), at 83 Delaney Ave, has bed & breakfast from $21 per person. The Alpine Hotel (tel 55 1366), at 7 Anderson St, has singles/doubles for $25/42. The motels are all

similarly priced with Ovens Valley Motor Inn (tel 55 2022) on the corner of Ovens Highway and Ashwood Ave, being the best value with singles/doubles starting from $35/43. Alpine Caravan Park (tel 55 1064) on Mountbatten Ave is the most central with sites from $6 for two and on-site vans from $18.

HARRIETVILLE (population 100)
This pretty little town sits in the valley at the fork of the east and west branches of the Ovens River, and is surrounded by the high Alps. Harrietville is well known for its beautiful natural surroundings and its proximity to the ski resort of Mt Hotham. The Dargo Plains spread from Mt Hotham and in spring wildflowers on the plains make a colourful spectacle. A gold dredge continued operating in Harrietville right up to 1956 when it was sold and shipped off to Malaysia.

Places to Stay
Harrietville is an access town to the ski resort of Mt Hotham and is used by skiers as an alternative place to stay as accommodation is cheaper. The Snowline Hotel (tel 59 2524) has singles/doubles with breakfast from $20/35. One of the few other places you can try is the Harrietville Alpine Lodge (tel 59 2532) where bed & breakfast is from $25 per person. As usual the Harrietville Caravan Park (tel 59 2523) is the cheapest alternative with sites from $7.50 for two and on-site caravans for $24.

OMEO (population 272)
This small town is on the Omeo Highway, the southern access route to the snow country. In summer it's a popular departure point for the Bogong High Plains. The road from here to Corryong, near the New South Wales border, is scenic but rough. Omeo still has a handful of interesting old buildings despite two earthquakes and one disastrous bushfire since 1885. Omeo's log jail and courthouse are two buildings that are worth searching

out. The town also had its own little gold rush.

Places to Stay

The *Golden Age Hotel* (tel 59 1344) in Day Ave has bed & breakfast from $18 per person. Apart from a couple of other hotels there is the *Holston Tourist Park* (tel 59 1351) with tent sites from $5.50 for two and on-site vans from $20.

Getting There & Away

There are trains from Melbourne to Bairnsdale from Monday to Friday, but only the 7.44 am train (which arrives in Bairnsdale at 11.55 am) has a connecting bus service to Omeo. The train fare is $20 ($28.80 in 1st class). The bus leaves at various times in the afternoon between 1.30 and 3.45 pm; the travelling time to Omeo is two hours and the fare is $14.

MANSFIELD (population 1920)

High in the foothills of the Victorian Alps, Mansfield was established as a mining town in the gold rush days and later became a farming town. It is close to Mt Buller, Mt Stirling and Lake Eildon. Ned Kelly's monument stands here recalling one of his clashes with the law. The graves of three police officers he shot at Tolmie in 1878 are in the Mansfield cemetery. There is good canoeing and kayaking as well as bushwalking in the area. There are also a few wineries.

Places to Stay

The *Mansfield Hotel* (tel 75 2101) at 86 High St, and *Commercial Hotel* (tel 75 2046) at 83 High St, have bed & breakfast for $20 per person. There are a few motels the cheapest being the *Mansfield Motel* (tel 75 2377) at 3 Highett St, with singles/doubles from $38/40. *Mansfield Caravan Park* (tel 75 2705) on Ultimo St is the most convenient on the edge of town with tent sites at $6.50 for two and on-site vans for $18.

MERRIJIG (population 150)

This is a small, quiet town which is good for off-mountain accommodation as it is only 28 km from Mt Buller skiing village. In summer the town is a popular base for bushwalks, fishing and horse riding.

Places to Stay

The *Merrijig Hunt Club Hotel* (tel 77 5508) has only six rooms at $16 per person. The *Merrijig Lodge* (tel 77 5590) has dinner, bed & breakfast from $23 to $35 per person. *Brumby's Run Homestead* not only offers accommodation, but also horse rides at $25 for half a day, $40 for a full day (including lunch). The lodge accommodates up to 14 people for $1200 per week in August; other months are much cheaper. They also have special deals that include horse riding, accommodation and meals. For further information and bookings call (03) 486 2525 or (057) 77 5665.

SKI RESORTS

Skiing in Victoria goes back to the 1860s when Norwegian gold miners introduced it in Harrietville. It was not until the 1920s that the Buffalo Chalet, the first commercial accommodation, was built and the Norwegian manageress imported some skis from her native land for the chalet's customers to use. From then it has grown into a multi-million dollar industry with three major ski resorts and six minor ski areas. None of these resorts is connected to another by a lift system, but it is possible to cross-country ski from Mt Hotham to Falls Creek across the Bogong High Plains. There is an annual race that covers this route.

The Victorian resorts are closer to Melbourne than the Snowy resorts are to Sydney, so they're even more popular on the weekends. See the New South Wales Snowy Mountains section for general information on skiing. The following are the Victorian ski resorts, with the elevation of the village in metres.

Falls Creek (1780 metres)

It sits at the edge of the Bogong High Plains overlooking the Kiewa Valley, 375 km and a five hour drive from Melbourne. Falls Creek is one of the best resorts in Victoria and in the last few years has received the heaviest snow falls. It is the only ski village in Australia where everyone can ski from their lodge and back again in normal conditions.

The skiing is spread over two bowls with 30 km of trails, and a vertical drop of 267 metres. It has plenty of runs for intermediate skiers but only a handful of difficult runs for the experienced skiers. The village bowl has a nursery slope, some intermediate skiing and the summit which is one of the most challenging mogul runs in Australia. The Summit Masters, the most prestigious mogul skiing competition in Australia, is held here annually. The Sun Valley area is a large intermediate and beginners area with plenty of lifts, but in peak season it is still too crowded, with long lift-queues.

Around the resort is good cross-country skiing, but it is a fair hike up the mountain out of the village, unless you take a ski lift. The Bogong High Plains offer some excellent ski touring with tracks leading to Mt Hotham. Falls Creek has plenty of places to stay and eat, with the nightlife also being very good. A day ticket costs $36, a seven day ticket costs $230 and a five day lift and lesson package costs $229.50.

In summer there are plenty of opportunities for alpine walking to places like Ruined Castle, Ropers Lookout, Wallaces Hut and Mt Nelse which is part of the Alpine Walking Track.

Places to Stay There is very little cheap accommodation in Falls Creek. Even the club lodges that offer cheaper lodging in Mt Hotham and Mt Buller are more expensive and fewer in number here. Ski club lodges are difficult to find room in during the high season, but otherwise it is possible to find a bed from $40 a night.

Normally a room is shared between four people and kitchen facilities are available. The Falls Creek accommodation service (tel (057) 58 3325) can help to find beds on the mountain.

The *Viking Lodge* (tel 58 3247) has bed & breakfast for $380 per person a week, and kitchen facilities are available. A number of ski lodges offer bed, breakfast & dinner packages per week or weekend. One of the best and cheapest is the *Silver Ski Lodge* (tel 58 3375), normally fully booked during peak season, and costing $570 per person weekly. *Diana Lodge* (tel 58 3214) costs from $470 per person weekly.

Places to Eat As with accommodation, there are no food bargains in Falls Creek. One of the best value restaurants is the *Silver Ski* where you can have a daily special set menu (and if you are still hungry, return for seconds). *Kokie* is another good place for lunch and dinner – their speciality is fondue. *Coonies*, in the Hub shopping complex, is a good, cheap restaurant with a varied menu. *The Man* pizzeria and *Cynthia's* Chinese restaurant both have reasonable food at affordable prices.

Entertainment The *Frying Pan* and the *Falls Creek Motel* are popular at après-ski time. *The Man* has live bands and a disco downstairs and there's usually a free light rock band in the upstairs bar. The *Frying Pan* also has live bands and is not normally very crowded. The *Sundance Inn* is good for late night drinks between 11 pm and 3 am, but it can become very crowded after 1 am when all other bars close.

Getting There & Around Pyles Coaches (tel (03) 654 5311) have buses to and from Melbourne on Fridays to Sundays for $38 ($58 return). A daily service to and from Albury is $19 ($35 return), and Mt Beauty is $9.50 ($18 return). These buses do meet selected East-West Airlines, Kendell

Top: Melbourne city at night, Vic (RN)
Left: Puffing Billy steam train, Dandenongs, near Melbourne (TW)
Right: Collins St, Melbourne (PS)

Top: London Bridge, Port Campbell, Vic (TW)
Bottom: The Pinnacle, Halls Gap in the Grampians, Vic (TW)

Airlines and V/Line rail services in Albury. These services operate from June to September. If you are driving up the mountain, chains must be carried.

There is oversnow transport available from the car park to the lodges and back again.

Mt Baw Baw (1480 metres)

This is a small resort with eight lifts on the edge of the Baw Baw plateau. It is 173 km and an easy three hour drive from Melbourne. It's popular on the weekends, but generally is not overcrowded as the snow cover tends to be thin. There are intermediate and beginner runs with a vertical drop of 140 metres. This is an ideal mountain on which to learn to ski, and is a cross-country skiers' paradise with many trails extending across the Baw Baw plateau. It is also possible to ski to Mt St Gwinear, which has an extensive trail network from its car park area that is approachable from the town of Erica. In summer it's ideal for bushwalking.

Places to Stay & Eat There is a *Youth Hostel* (phone the YHA office (tel (03) 670 7991) in Melbourne for information and bookings) in the village, and close to all the facilities. It is open during the ski season, but sometimes takes groups in summer. Advance bookings are essential; it costs $33 for the weekend in peak season and less at other times. The hostel has all the usual facilities, but you need to bring your own food as there are no shops in the village.

Apart from the youth hostel there is no other cheap place to stay. *Watzmann Haus Ski Lodge* (tel 65 1124) is an expensive guest house or you can stay in *Cascade Ski Apartments*. Mt Baw Baw Information & Booking Service (tel (03) 763 7101) can make bookings for you in most of these establishments and even get you into one of the small club lodges which are the cheapest after the youth hostel.

Watzmann Haus has a fully licensed expensive restaurant and disco. Apart from this there is only *Rusty's* and *Skiosk* which provide take-away food at lunch time.

Getting There & Away No public transport is available but there is a road from Melbourne via the access town of Noojee. There is a twice daily bus service from Warragul (railway station) to Noojee, and the mail contractor at Tanjil Bren is licensed to carry passengers in his car. Chains must be carried.

Mt Buffalo (1400 metres)

This is a national park and apart from the two guest houses there are no private lodges on the mountain. From Melbourne it is 333 km by road and takes about five hours.

It is another small place more suited to intermediate and beginner skiers, but again has more challenging cross-country skiing. The lifts and thus downhill skiing are in two separate areas: Cresta has five lifts and more advanced skiing, while Dingo Dell has only three lifts for beginners. The vertical drop in Victoria's oldest ski resort is only 157 metres. It is a picturesque and not overly expensive village, but the skiing is not very good and the snow does not last as long as in some of the other resorts.

Places to Stay & Eat *Lake Catani Campground* (tel 55 1466) next to the lake has sites from $3.40, but is only open from November to May. *Mt Buffalo Chalet* (tel 55 1500) was the first place built on the mountain and still has the charm of the 1920s. The rooms are from $60 per person. The *Tatra Inn* (tel 55 1322) has accommodation in motel-type units where bed & breakfast is from $63 per person. Both of these places have a restaurant and ski hire.

Getting There & Away There is no public transport to the village; access is from Melbourne via Myrtleford. Alternatively

V/Line offer a train and bus trip to the Chalet. Chains must be carried.

Mt Buller (1600 metres)

Less then a three hour drive from Melbourne and only 246 km away, Mt Buller is the most crowded resort in Victoria, especially on the weekends. It has a large lift network with 23 lifts, including the only gondola/chairlift in Australia which begins in the car park and ends in the middle of the ski runs. A feature is that skiers can ski the northern, southern and eastern parts of the mountain, giving them a larger variety of skiing over 80 km of ski trails and a vertical drop of 400 metres. When there is enough snow it offers good skiing for beginners, intermediates and advance skiers, but in the last few years the snow has been rather unreliable. The snow cover has always been light and, with Buller being so popular, it is normally skied out much sooner than at Falls Creek or Mt Hotham. A day ticket costs $38, a seven day ticket costs $238 and a five day lift and lesson package costs $232. Cross-country skiing is possible around Buller and there is access to Mt Stirling which has some good trails.

In summer, there are plenty of opportunities for bushwalking to the summit of Mt Buller, Mt Stirling and down to the Howqua River Valley.

Places to Stay There is plenty of accommodation. The *Youth Hostel* (03) 670 7991) is of course the cheapest on the mountain. In winter it is necessary to book via the YHA office in Melbourne. The Monday to Friday rate is $125 per person and the weekend rate is $50 per person. In summer the rate is $7.50 per person per day.

Club lodges are again the best value starting at about $30 per person per night, with mostly bunk accommodation and kitchen facilities. If there is a larger group of people, self-contained apartments can also be good value. It is best to contact the Mt Buller Accommodation Centre on (03) 598 3011 or (057) 77 6280 for details.

Lantern Ski Lodge (tel (057) 77 6326) has one of the best deals on bed, breakfast & dinner for a week at $495 per person in a twin room. Another ski lodge is the *Avalanche* (tel (03) 874 7990) which costs $550 per person, per week for bed, breakfast & dinner.

Places to Eat The cheapest way to eat is to cook your own food. If you have to eat out, one of the cheapest and best places is the popular *Abomb Restaurant*. The *Alpine Retreat* is a good mid-range restaurant and the *Kooroora* and *Arlberg* hotels have reasonably good, cheap bar meals. One of the best, but more expensive, restaurants is *Pension Grimus* which has good European food served in an Austrian atmosphere – definitely worth it for a splurge.

Entertainment Both the *Arlberg* and *Kooroora* hotels have a disco and live bands playing on certain nights. They are also frequented at après-ski time. The *Abomb* and *Pension Grimus* are popular with the après-ski crowd – the latter especially for a glühwein.

Getting There & Around During winter only, there is a daily V/Line bus from Melbourne to Mt Buller, via Mansfield with extra services on the weekend. The fare is $31.50. There are also taxis and other local bus services operating from Mansfield – call Mansfield-Mt Buller Bus Lines on (057) 75 2606 – and Merrijig.

Around the village and to and from the car park, there is an oversnow transport shuttle service that operates daily in winter from 7 am to 5 pm. If you are coming just for a day-trip you can take the gondola/quad chairlift from the car park into the skiing area and save time and money by bypassing the village. There are rental facilities in the car park.

Mt Hotham (1750 metres)

Known as Australia's powder capital, it does get the lightest snow in the country, but don't expect anything like Europe or North America. It is 373 km from Melbourne and a five and a half hour drive, the last part being on an unsealed road.

It used to have the most consistent snow cover, but in the last few years it has been receiving less snow than Falls Creek. The lift system is not well integrated and some walking is necessary, even though the zoo cart along the main road offers some relief. The skiing here is good: a quarter of the runs are for beginners, a third for intermediates and almost half are for experienced skiers. This is a skiers mountain with a vertical drop of 428 metres and the nightlife mainly happening in ski lodges. There is some good off-piste skiing in steep and narrow valleys. A day ticket costs $36; a seven day pass, $182; and a lift and lesson five day package costs $195.

Cross-country skiing is good around Hotham and ski-touring is very good on the Bogong High Plains which you can cross to Falls Creek. These trails can be reached from Bright as well as Omeo. There is an annual cross-country race that begins in Hotham and ends in Falls Creek. Another cross-country area is the Dinner Plain, which is also an accommodation centre. There are trails around the village, as well as a link up to Mt Hotham.

In summer there are many walking tracks on the Bogong and Dargo high plains. The Bogong National Park surrounds most of Mt Hotham and one of the best hikes is the ascent of Mt Feathertop (1922 metres) via the Razorback. The Alpine Waking Track also passes through the village.

Places to Stay Most of the accommodation is in club lodges. These have bunk type accommodation with kitchen facilities. It is possible to find beds in these or apartments through the Mt Hotham Accommodation Service on (057) 59 3636, or phone them direct.

Some of the cheapest apartments are in the *Arlberg Hotel* (tel 59 3618) for $580 in a twin room with dinner, bed & breakfast. The *Snowbird Inn* (tel 59 3503) is similarly priced. There are also *Henkell Apartments* (tel 59 3522) for $750 in a twin room or *Jack Frost Apartments* (tel 59 3586) for $1650 in a twin.

It is also possible to stay at Dinner Plain, eight km from Mt Hotham Village. There are several places to stay including the *Foard Apartments* (tel (051) 59 6455) where a twin room is $540 per person.

Places to Eat *Jack Frost* would have to be the best eating place on the mountain, definitely not in the budget range but worthwhile for a splurge. Best value is the *Dinner Plain Hotel* in Dinner Plain, where you get good portions for a reasonable price. Otherwise there is the *Snowbird Inn* and *Zirky's* for lunch or dinner, but both are rather expensive.

Entertainment Most of the entertainment happens in lodges in the form of parties, but both *Zirky's* and the *Arlberg* have a nightly disco. The *Snowbird* has bands and videos, and is more of a locals' place. The *General Store* has videos and, if it's not crowded, it is good for a quiet drink. The *Snowbird* and *Zirky's* are popular at après-ski time.

Getting There & Around In winter, Hoys (tel (03) 59 2622) have a bus service to and from Melbourne from Friday to Monday for $41 ($58 return). There is a daily connection to and from Harrietville for $12 ($19 return) and to and from Bright for $15 ($21 return). Hoys also connect with some East-West Airline flights and V/Line rail services in Albury, and fares are $28 ($43 return).

The village was built on a ridge almost at the top of the mountain and is strung out along the road. Luckily, there are shuttle buses that run frequently all the way to Dinner Plain, and the 'zoo cart' takes skiers from their lodges to the lifts between 8 am and 5 pm. If you plan to party late into the night you better have a car to return to your lodge in or be prepared for a long walk, as the shuttle bus stops running at 12.30 am.

Other Resorts

There are three other ski areas that are mainly good for beginners and cross-country skiing or sightseeing and have no accommodation. Mt Donna Buang is the closest to Melbourne (95 km) via Warburton, and Lake Mountain is 109 km via Marysville. Mt St Gwinear is 171 km from Melbourne via Moe and has connecting cross-country ski trails with Mt Baw Baw. Mt Stirling is a few km from Mt Buller and so far it is only developed as a cross-country ski area.

Gippsland

The Gippsland region is the south-east slice of Victoria. It stretches from Western Port, near Melbourne, to the New South Wales border on the east coast, with more coast to the south and the Great Dividing Range to the north.

Named in 1839 by the Polish explorer Count Paul Strzelecki after Sir George Gipps, the former governor of New South Wales, Gippsland was first settled by prospectors in the 1850s, then by farmers after the completion of the railway from Melbourne in 1887. Extremely fertile and well-watered, Gippsland is now the focus of the state's dairy industry.

While thousands of people were attracted to the region's scattered gold fields last century it is now the huge brown coal deposits which keep the miners employed. The mines and power stations of the Latrobe Valley supply most of Victoria's electricity, while the offshore wells in Bass Strait provide most of Australia's petroleum and natural gas.

Gippsland is an area of often breathtaking beauty with a multitude of attractions. There are lush rainforests, countless waterfalls, quiet streams, raging rapids, deserted beaches, tranquil lakes, coastal waterways, rolling pastures and high and rugged forested mountains.

The Latrobe Valley

In 1939 Richard Llewellyn wrote a novel about life in a mining village in Wales. The title, *How Green Was My Valley*, is probably the most perfect description of Gippsland's Latrobe Valley.

While the mine, the huge power plants and the briquette factories provide employment, electricity and a certain amount of tourism they are nonetheless an ugly great scar on a once beautiful landscape.

The region between Moe and Traralgon is the site of one of the world's largest deposits of brown coal. Electricity generated in the power stations built on the coal fields at Yallourn, Morwell and Loy Yang provide 85% of Victoria's power requirements.

The massive Morwell open-cut mine, which has a surface area of about three square km, produces about 14 million tonnes of brown coal every year. The coal is transported on conveyors to the power stations at Hazelwood and Yallourn.

The Hazelwood Pondage, a huge artificial lake (quite popular for water sports), was created to provide the nearly 200 million litres of water needed every hour by Hazelwood Power Station's steam condensers.

The Yallourn Power Station and the briquette works at Morwell are fed by the coal extracted by the huge 12 storey bucket dredges at the Yallourn open-cut.

The immense new Loy Yang Power Station near Traralgon will be the largest in the southern hemisphere when it's finished.

The SEC offers conducted tours of the Morwell open-cut and Hazelwood Power Station daily between 8 am and 3 pm, from the Morwell Visitors Centre (tel (051) 35 3415).

The other blots on the valley's landscape are the smoking chimney stacks of the Australian Paper Manufacturers' mill at Maryland near Morwell. The factory is the largest pulp and paper mill in Australia.

This is, thankfully, just a part of the Latrobe Valley which overall provides an interesting

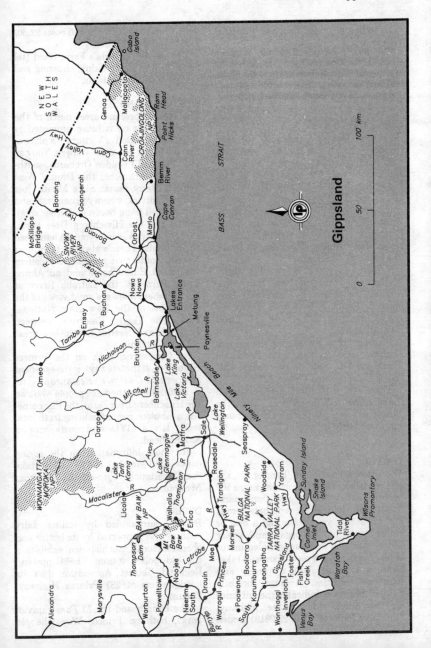

cross section of urban, rural and industrial activity.

The region extends from the southern reaches of the Victorian Alps in the north to the spectacular Wilsons Promontory in the south, and from Yarragon in the west to the Gippsland Lakes and the vast Ninety Mile Beach in the east.

Getting There & Away

Soon after leaving Dandenong the road divides – the Princes Highway continues east through the Latrobe Valley to Bairnsdale, near the coast, then on into New South Wales, and the South Gippsland Highway heads off to the south-east to Phillip Island and Wilsons Promontory. You can follow the South Gippsland Highway, go via the Prom and rejoin the Princes Highway at Sale, 214 km from Melbourne.

V/Line operates a regular daily Melbourne / Traralgon / Sale / Bairnsdale service, sometimes by bus from Sale onwards. Economy fares from Melbourne are Traralgon $12, Sale $17 and Bairnsdale $21.

Buses going to Sydney via the Princes Highway also go this way. Fares are Traralgon $20, Sale or Bairnsdale $24, Lakes Entrance and Orbost $27.

There's no public transport service all the way down to Wilsons Prom – about the closest you can get is Fish Creek (buses run there fairly regularly).

TYNONG

The main attraction of Tynong, 74 km east of Melbourne, is Gumbuya Park, a 100 hectare native fauna and flora park. Apart from kangaroos, wombats, emus and pheasants you'll also find a host of amusements like toboggan and water slides, mini golf and four-wheeled motor bikes. There's also a restaurant and take-away, a souvenir shop, a nursery and barbecue facilities. A huge, brightly painted pheasant indicates the entrance on the north side of the highway. Gumbuya Park (tel (056) 29 2613) is open

daily from 10 am to 5 pm and costs $2.50/1.50 for adults/children.

The nearby Victoria's Farm Shed (tel 29 2840) provides milking, shearing and sheepdog demonstrations.

WEST GIPPSLAND

The West Gippsland area, north of the Princes Highway, is being promoted as 'The Gourmet Deli of Victoria' – a place of fine foods and beautiful scenery. You can visit Witchell's Golden Orchards, south-east of Labertouche; the Drouin West Fruit & Berry Farm; Sid's Meats, just before Jindivick, where you can taste and buy smoked ham, bacon and other small goods; and the Hirschberg Deer Farm, east of Jindivick, where you can hand feed the animals. There's also the farm near Neerim South that makes the excellent Gippsland Blue Cheese and an Alpine Trout Farm by the Latrobe River at Noojee where there are great views of the mountains of the Baw Baw National Park. The Tarago Reservoir, between Jindivick and Neerim South, is a great place for a picnic.

At Longwarry, back on the Princes Highway (off the freeway), is the excellent *Pimpernel Gourmet Restaurant* (tel 29 9496). Run by the same people who own the Hirschberg Deer Farm, the Pimpernel has a fabulous menu featuring fresh local food. It's a BYO and costs around $25 per head.

For more information on the region contact Sid Marchek (tel 28 5217) or take the Labertouche turn-off, 85 km from Melbourne.

DROUIN

Drouin, surrounded by rolling dairy country and supported by its butter and cheese factories, has historical exhibits in the old police staion. The Gippsland Regional Tourist Association has its headquarters at 231 Princes Highway, Drouin.

The *Drouin* and the *El Paso* caravan parks, both on Princes Way (the old highway), have tent sites for around $5 and on-site vans for $20 a double.

WARRAGUL

A regional centre for the district's dairy farms which provide most of Melbourne's milk, Warragul is the first major town east of Dandenong. The excellent West Gippsland Arts Centre, part of Warragul's Civic Centre, caters for all local and visiting art forms, both performance and visual. Just outside of Warragul there's a maze and slippery slide.

The *Warragul Caravan Park*, in Burke St, has tent sites for $4 and on-site vans for $20 and the *Club Hotel* (tel (056) 23 1636), 51 Queens St, has singles for $17, doubles for $27.

MOE

The main attraction of this Latrobe Valley coal mining centre is the Gippsland Folk Museum on the Princes Highway where a 19th century community has been re-created on four hectares of parkland. The 30 or so buildings are authentic, having been collected from all over Gippsland and then reassembled here. Old Gippstown is open Thursdays to Mondays from 10 am to 5 pm. Devonshire teas are served in the historic Bushy Park Homestead on Sundays.

You can visit the Yallourn Power Station from Moe, and the site of the township of Yallourn, which was relocated or simply torn down to provide access to the brown coal deposits underneath. From the hill behind the town site there is a lookout with some information for visitors and views of the vast 'open cut'.

There's a scenic road from Moe north to Walhalla, the Baw Baw National Park, and Mt Erica from where a secondary road continues north across the Victorian Alps. You can get onto the panoramic Grand Ridge Rd across the Strzelecki Ranges easily from either Trafalgar or Moe via the lovely little townships of Narracan or Thorpdale.

The *Moe Caravan Park* on Mitchells Rd has tent sites for $5 and the *Baw Baw Motor Inn* (tel (051) 27 1000)on Lloyd St has bed & breakfast singles/doubles for $30/38.

MORWELL

Morwell was founded in the 1880s, and before the turn of the century, it became the supply centre for diggers and traders heading for the gold fields at Walhalla.

These days Morwell is basically an industrial town servicing the massive open-cut mine, the Hazelwood Power Station, the APM pulp mills and the local briquette works.

The SEC's Visitors Centre (tel (051) 35 3415), signposted off Commercial Rd, houses models and displays of the Latrobe Valley's coal mining and power generating activities. There are also guided tours of the Morwell Open Cut and the Hazelwood Power Station.

Places to Stay & Eat

The *Morwell Caravan Park*, Maryvale Cresent, has tent sites for $5 a double and on-site vans for $17 a double. The *Merton Rush Hotel* (tel 34 2633) on the corner of Princes Highway and Collins St has bed & breakfast singles/doubles for $25/36 and the *Morwell Hotel*, on the corner of the Princes Highway and Vincent Rd, has good counter meals.

TRARALGON

The original township was a rest stop and supply base for miners and drovers heading further into the gold and farming country of Gippsland. Traralgon, which is Aboriginal for 'river of little fish', grew in size and importance following the completion of the railway from Melbourne in 1877.

It is now the centre of the state's paper and pulp industry and a major Latrobe Valley electricity centre. Its future is assured by the colossal Loy Yang Power Station, six km to the south. The SEC is apparently so proud of this incredible construction that there is a tourist road right through the middle of the structure so you can view it from the inside.

Traralgon has a number of historic buildings including the post office and court house; the surrounding countryside, especially to the south, is worth exploring if you have time.

Places to Stay & Eat

The *Park Lane Caravan Park* on Park Lane has tent sites for $8 and on-site vans for $18 a double. The *Grand Junction Hotel* (tel (051) 74 6011), Franklin St, has singles/doubles for $22/30. The *Royal Exchange* (74 1281), 64 Princes Highway, has bed & breakfast singles for $20.

There are a few coffee shops and good pie shops in town. *Cafe Giovanni* serves good Italian food, the *Grand Junction Hotel* has a good bistro for lunch and dinner, the *Royal Exchange* has counter meals and some of the many motels around town have restaurants.

WALHALLA

At the end of 1862 Edward Stringer, one of a small party of prospectors who had made it over the mountains, found gold in a creek running through a deep wooded valley north of Moe. The payable gold in Stringer's Creek attracted about 200 miners but it was the later discovery of Cohen's Reef, the outcrop of a reef almost two miles long, that put the growing township of Walhalla on the map.

The extraction of this hard-to-get underground gold could only be managed by mining companies with the necessary capital and equipment. As a result of the money going into mining and building in the valley, Walhalla had an air of permanence that was lacking in the early canvas-town atmospheres of other gold fields.

Work began on the Long Tunnel Mine, the single most profitable mine in Victoria, in 1865 and continued for 49 years. Walhalla reached its peak betwen 1885 and 1890 when there were over 4000 people living in and around the town. It

had six suburbs, a brewery (which won international awards for its ales), a cordial factory, two funeral parlours and several hotels.

The railway line from Moe, incorporating a truly amazing section of tunnels and trestle bridges between Erica and Walhalla, was finally completed in 1910 just as the town's fortunes began to decline.

Though the population is far smaller these days, there's plenty of history to see in Walhalla and the area in general is quite beautiful. There are a number of old buildings (some of which are classified by the National Trust) including the fire station, Spetts Cottage, Windsor House and the gold vault. There's a museum, a very interesting cemetery, and the Long Tunnel Extended Gold Mine, which is open on weekends and public holidays from noon to 4 pm.

South of Walhalla, there is a carpark and marked trail to the summit of Mt Erica which offers a good taste of Victoria's alpine bushland.

There are several good camping spots around the town or you could try the *Rawson Holiday Resort* (tel (051) 65 3200) about 12 km north of Walhalla.

HEYFIELD

Though nothing special in itself Heyfield, about 43 km north-east of Traralgon (or north of the Princes Highway from Rosedale), provides access to Victoria's largest alpine national park, a couple of artificial lakes and a number of other stunning natural attractions. The forest road to Licola is particularly beautiful.

LAKE GLENMAGGIE

The lake is open to the public for recreational use. The town of Glenmaggie has a camping site and a general store and provides boat access to the lake.

LICOLA

Licola, 45 km north-west along the Macalister River valley, is a departure point for Wonnangatta-Moroka National

Park. There's a general store. *Licola Caravan Park* has tent sites for $6 a double, powered sites for $9 and on-site vans at $20 to $24 a double.

LAKE TARLI KARNG

This is the only natural lake in the Victorian Alps. The walk to it, which begins 15 km north of Licola on the Mt Tamboritha road, is popular with bushwalkers.

WONNANGATTA-MOROKA NATIONAL PARK

This park, 200 km north-east of Melbourne, is the largest alpine national park in Victoria and is a great area for bushwalkers and ski-tourers. The mountains are spectacular.

SALE (population 13,000)

At the junction of the Princes and Gippsland Highways, Sale is a supply centre for the Bass Strait oil fields. There's an Oil & Gas Display Centre on Princes Highway on the western side of town. The Port of Sale, also on this side of town, was a busy centre in the paddle-steamer days and you can still take cruises from Sale into the Gippsland Lakes.

In the city centre, Lake Guthridge has picnic and barbecue spots and the city also has some fine old buildings like the Criterion Hotel with its intricate lace-work. On the Princes Highway there is an historical museum.

There are many popular excursions and local attractions around Sale like Seaspray beach with good surfing south of the city. Lake Wellington is very popular for sailing and boating. Just beyond Sale at Stratford, you can turn north on the unsurfaced road across the spectacular Dargo High Plains to Mt Hotham.

Tourist information is available from the Oil & Gas Display Centre.

BAIRNSDALE (population 9500)

Bairnsdale, at the junction of the Princes and Omeo Highways, is a popular base both for the mountains to the north and the lakes immediately to the south. For parents travelling with children, there is one of the most interesting playgrounds in Victoria – Howitt Park, complete with flying foxes, on the Princes Highway on the east side of town.

West of Bairnsdale is Lindenow and the small Glenaladale National Park which has good bushwalking tracks and the Den of Nargun, an Aboriginal ceremonial ground in a gorge of the Mitchell River. Mitchell River National Park is north-west of Bairnsdale.

There are a number of hotels, motels and camping/caravan parks. The *Riversleigh Hotel* (tel (051) 52 6996) is claimed by epicureans to be worth the drive from Melbourne. It's not a cheap place to eat, but worth it for special occasions.

The Omeo Highway leads north from Bairnsdale through several historic townships onto the Bogong High Plains. Buchan, the main trading centre of earlier days is where you'll find the famous Buchan Caves. Horse tours ranging from weekend to week long riding adventures are taken on the High Plains. Tourist info can be obtained from the Victorian Eastern Development Association at 63 Main St, Bairnsdale (tel (051) 52 6444).

BUCHAN (population 220)

There are a number of limestone caves around the tiny town of Buchan. Tours take place three times daily at the Royal and Fairy caves.

Buchan has a delightful camping ground with a swimming pool continuously fed by an icy underground stream flowing from a cave in the hillside. Very refreshing!

SNOWY RIVER

The road north from Buchan runs roughly parallel to the Snowy River, passing through superb bush and mountain scenery, descending to the riverside near the New South Wales border at Willis – a place with a name and nothing else. The road, a bit rough but never dull, continues up to Jindabyne in the Snowy Mountains of New South Wales. If you take a side road (about 82 km north of Buchan) to McKillops Bridge you can have a dip in the river or camp on its sandy banks. The view from the lookout over Little River Gorge is spectacular.

The classic canoe or raft trip down the Snowy River from Willis or McKillops Bridge to a pull-out point near Buchan takes at least four days and offers superb scenery: rugged gorges, raging rapids, tranquil sections and excellent camping spots on broad sand bars. A number of commercial operators including World Expeditions (tel (03) 670 8400) and Peregrine (tel (03) 602 3066) organise raft trips on the Snowy; the cost is about $480.

THE GIPPSLAND LAKES

The Lakes area is where three major rivers, the Mitchell, Nicholson and Tambo, flow into an extensive lake system separated by a coastal strip from 90 miles of beach. It's an area popular for its surf, fishing, boating and spectacular scenery.

Wine lovers can spend a day doing the vineyards of the area. Start at Bairnsdale and visit Golvinda winery. Drive east from there along the Princes Highway to the Nicholson River Winery (signposted) and then, if you can, on to Lakes Entrance and the Wyanga selection.

Paynesville is a resort on the lakes; you can cross to nearby Raymond Island by punt or to 90 Mile Beach by boat. the island has a koala population which outnumbers its human population – 300 to 250. You can camp there or stay at Swan Cove Units (tel (051) 56 6716) or at the Anglican Conference Centre which has cabins for rent (tel 56 6513).

Bring your own food or you can get something at Rick Edney's Tea House (tel 56 6180) where you can have your hair cut or hire a bicycle. It's at 12 Seventh Ave. If you like sailing you can visit Captain Clarke's historic ketch the *Jaeger* at the Raymond Island Jetty or charter a dingy, motor cruiser or yacht from Adventure Yacht Charters & Cruises on Fourth Ave (tel 56 6188).

For naturalists interested in seeing East Gippsland an essential book to buy is the Australian Conservation Foundation's *Car Tours & Bushwalks in East Gippsland*. This book has photos and a grading system rating the ease or difficulty of each tour and/or walk, and gives an excellent idea of the spectacular beauty of the area.

Metung (population 350)

This interesting little fishing village between Bairnsdale and Lakes Entrance is built on a land spit between Lake King and Bancroft Bay. The town offers hot sulphur springs in two outdoor pools, a museum, gallery and houseboats which can be hired from Bull's Cruises (tel 56 2208) to tour the lakes. The small Angus McMillan cottage museum is nearby at Chinaman's Creek.

There is plenty of accommodation to choose from, including the pub (tel (051) 56 2446) right on the water.

Lakes Entrance (population 4500)

At the eastern end of the lakes is Lakes Entrance where there's a walking bridge across Cunningham's Arm to 90 Mile Beach. This is also the largest fishing port in Victoria and lots of cruise boats operate from here to tour the rivers and lakes. The *Thunderbird* (tel 55 1246/527) is the largest boat touring the lakes and does two hour cruises twice daily.

The Lakes Entrance Fishing Co-operative, just off the Princes Highway, provides a viewing platform which puts you in the middle of the boats unloading their fish. Sunday morning is the best time to go. The co-op fish shop is guaranteed to sell the freshest fish in town.

There's a shell museum on Marine Rd, an antique car museum on the Princes Highway, and an Aboriginal art museum also on the Princes Highway. You can visit the Buchan Caves from here.

Places to Eat A novel place to eat at is the

sloop *John D* (tel 55 1400). This glassed-in restaurant is moored, and so floats surrounded by the local fishing fleet.

Places to Stay There's an associate youth hostel in Willis St at the *Lakes Main Caravan Park* (tel 55 2365) for $8 a night.

TO THE NEW SOUTH WALES BORDER

From Orbost the Bonang Highway leads up through beautiful hill country into New South Wales. The route to Buchan and beyond is equally scenic so you can make a fine loop from Orbost around the Snowy River National Park by taking one road north and the other south. Most of this route is on unsurfaced road.

From Orbost you can also take the road down to the coast at Marlo and on to Cape Conran. Beyond Orbost is Cann River and a series of coastal national parks stretching all the way to the New South Wales border.

Croajingolong National Park

Stretching along the north-east coast of Victoria, approximately 560 km from Melbourne via the Princes Highway, Croajingolong National Park extends for about 100 km from Sydenham Inlet to Cape Howe on the New South Wales border and is undoubtedly among the finest of coastal national parks in Victoria. Magnificent unspoiled beaches, inlets, estuaries and nearby forests make this park the ideal place for walking, swimming, surfing or just lazing around. The four inlets – Sydenham, Tamboon, Wingan and Mallacoota are very popular for canoeing and fishing. There are several roads leading from the highway to different parts of the park. The more suitable for conventional vehicles are the Old Coast Rd west of Cann River, Tamboon Rd (about 15 km) from Cann River to the coast at Thurra River. The West Wingan Rd (about 19 km east of Cann River) to Wingan Inlet is no good for caravans, while the East Wingan Rd is not recommended. Driving to Wingan Inlet

(34 km) takes about an hour – the road is unsealed and is a bit slippery in places. The National Parks Service Office at Cann River will give you more information about vehicular access.

There are numerous camping sites within Croajingolong National Park as well as a couple of caravan parks at Cann River. If you decide to camp at any of the camping areas within the park, it is best to make a site reservation (especially at Wingan Inlet) during school or public holidays. Contact the ranger at Cann River National Parks Service Office (tel (051) 58 6251) for information. The cost for overnight camping is $5.10 for a site.

Mallacoota (population 720)

The Mallacoota National Park around the Mallacoota inlet is the best known and most popular. The town is the main centre for this area.

Places to Stay There's a great deal of holiday accommodation here including the *Adobe* mud-brick flats (tel 58 0329) which cost $25 to $50 a day or $120 to $300 a week. They've been built using recycled materials where possible and have been designed with the environment and ecology in mind. Mallacoota also has a number of camping grounds and the associate hostel the *All Nations Hostel* (tel 58 0362) at the Shady Gully Caravan Park for $7 a night.

SOUTH GIPPSLAND

Way back at Dandenong you can opt to take the route south into the south Gippsland area rather than continue east on the Princes Highway to Sale. This route takes you down to Phillip Island and Wilsons Promontory.

On the way south to Wilsons Prom you pass Koo-wee-rup with the nearby Bayles Flora & Fauna Park. Wonthaggi, close to the coast, was once a major coal mining centre and from here there are good beaches at the small resorts of Inverloch, Tarwin Lower and Walkerville. Waratah

Bay has good beaches from Walkerville right round to Sandy Point toward Wilsons Promontary.

Korumburra (population 2800)
Near Korumburra is the Coal Creek Historical Park, a very popular recreation of a coal mining town of the 19th century. Coal was first discovered here in 1872 and the Coal Creek mine operated from the 1890s right up to 1958.

The Strzelecki Ranges
Between the Latrobe Valley and the South Gippsland coastal areas are the beautiful 'blue' rounded hills of the Strzelecki Ranges. The winding Grand Ridge Rd traverses the top of these ranges, from behind Trafalgar to the back of Traralgon, providing a fabulous excursion through fertile farmland that was once covered with forests of mountain ash.

The Guinness Book of Records lists the 114.3 metre Cornthwaithe Tree in Thorpdale as the tallest tree ever found. It was measured by a qualified surveyor in 1880, then chopped down!

Many of the largest specimens of mountain ash were lost in the 1939 'Black Friday' bushfires or to the timber industry, though some large trees can still be seen at Noojee, the Mt Worth National Park and in far eastern Victoria at Erinundra.

A good base for this area is the township of Mirboo North which straddles the Grand Ridge Rd south of Trafalgar. There are some excellent bushwalking opportunities within half an hour of the town, including Turtons Creek and the Mt Worth State Park. There's also the Lyrebird Forest Walk which takes you nearly five km through the Strzelecki State Forest.

Mirboo North itself boasts the Strzelecki Brewery in the historic old Butter Factory building. The complex not only produces quality beers but also features a cosy bar, a restaurant, an Italian coffee shop, a Sunday craft market and an art gallery.

There's a caravan park in Mirboo North, opposite the Shire Hall, which has tent sites for $5.

Leongatha (population 4100)
A little to the south is Leongatha with some beautiful countryside around it. The turn-offs to the Prom are at Meeniyan or at Foster.

Welshpool (population 2800)
Welshpool is a dairying town which is also involved in fishing at nearby Port Welshpool while the Bass Strait oil rigs are supplied from nearby Barry Beach. There's a maritime museum in Port Welshpool while the Agnes Falls, just north of the highway, are the highest in Victoria.

Port Albert (population 200)
Further along the coast, Port Albert was the first port in the state and an entry point for Chinese miners in the Gippsland gold-rush days. Until a railway was constructed between Melbourne and Sale most of the region's trade was carried on through this port. The tiny town has a number of historic buildings along the main street while the Port Albert Hotel (first licensed in 1842) near the waterfront, could well be the oldest pub in the state.

Yarram (population 2100)
Yarram is an access point to the western end of 90 Mile Beach. Woodside and Seaspray are two particularly popular patrolled beaches. North of the town is beautiful hill country with dense woods, fern glades and plenty of rosellas and lyrebirds. Here you will find the Tarra Valley and Bulga national parks, on the scenic Grand Ridge Rd. At Hiawatha, north-west of Yarram, are the Minnie Ha Ha Falls.

WILSONS PROMONTORY
'The Prom' is one of the most popular national parks in Australia. It covers the peninsula that forms the southernmost

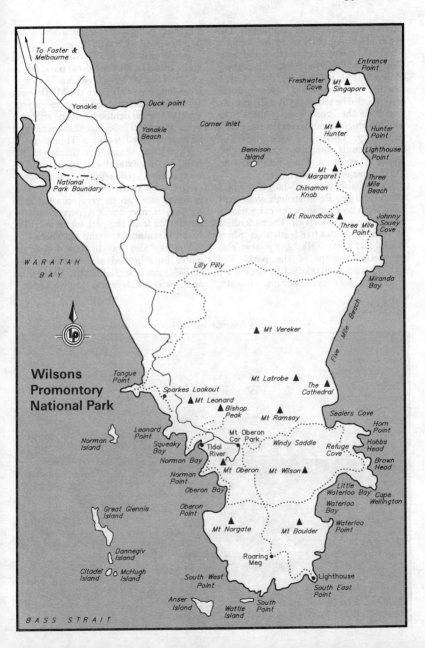

part of the Australian mainland. The Prom offers superb variety including a wonderful selection of beaches and more than 80 km of walking tracks. The variety of beaches is another big attraction – whether you want surfing, safe swimming or a secluded beach all to yourself, you can find it on the Prom. Finally there's the wildlife which abounds despite the park's popularity. There is a wide variety of bird life, emus, kangaroos and, at night, plenty of wombats. The wildlife around Tidal River is very tame.

It's probably walkers who get the best value from the Prom though, you don't have to go very far from the car parks to really get away from it all. The park office at Tidal River has free leaflets on 'Short Walks' and 'Long Walks' and you can also get detailed maps of the park. The walking tracks will take you through ever-changing scenery: swamps, forests, marshes, valleys of tree ferns and long beaches lined with sand dunes.

Don't miss the Mt Oberon walk – it starts from the Mt Oberon car park, takes one hour and is about three kms each way. It's a long day-walk from the Mt Oberon car park to the tip of the Prom and if you want to see the lighthouse at the end you must phone (tel (056) 80 8529) ahead and arrange it for a Tuesday or Thursday.

Tidal River, the main settlement in the park, has an extensive camping area, a general store, a park office and information centre. At peak holiday times the camping site can be very crowded and booking is necessary. A permit, easily obtainable from the park office at Tidal River, is required to camp elsewhere.

You can also stay in flats, lodges or motor huts but advance bookings (tel 80 8538) are essential for the Christmas and Easter holidays and long weekends.

View from Little Waterloo Bay, Wilsons Promontory

Western Australia

Area	2,525,500 square km
Population	1,556,000

The first European to land on the Western Australian coast was Dutchman Dirk Hartog, in 1616. The first Englishman to sight the coast was William Dampier, who landed somewhere near Broome in 1688. Their reports of a dry, barren land discouraged attempts at settlement. It was not until 1829, three years after Britain had formally claimed the land, that the first European settlers arrived in Perth. Their presence was intended to forestall settlement by other European nations.

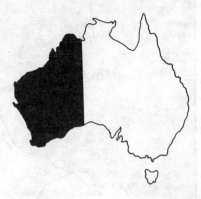

The arrival of the Europeans had disastrous consequences for the local Aborigines. During the 40,000 year history of Aboriginal occupation of Western Australia these people, hunting and gathering in small nomadic groups, had managed to live in harmony with nature, despite the harshness of the environment. Now they were pushed off their traditional lands. Of those who were not killed by the colonisers, many died of European diseases, against which they had no immunity.

Western Australia's development as a British colony was painfully slow – hardly surprising, given its distance from the main Australian settlements. It was not until the gold rushes of the 1890s that the colony really began to progress. Today a larger and far more technologically advanced mineral boom forms the basis of the state's prosperity.

There's a lot to see in Western Australia. Reasonably close to the capital, Perth, is the wine producing Swan Valley. In the north there's the harshly beautiful Pilbara gorge country, site of the state's immense mineral wealth, and the old pearling town of Broome, now enjoying a tourist boom all its own. In the top corner is the wild Kimberley area, one of Australia's last frontiers, while in the east there are gold field ghost towns and in the south, rugged coast and giant karri forests.

GEOGRAPHY

Western Australia's geography is a little like a distorted reflection of that of the eastern side of Australia except, of course, that the west is far drier than the east. The equivalent of the long fertile coastal strip on the east coast is the small south-western corner of WA. As in the east, hills rise behind the coast, but in WA they're much smaller than those of the Great Dividing Range. Further north it's dry and relatively barren. Along the north-west coast is the Great Sandy Desert, a very inhospitable region running right to the sea.

There are a couple of interesting variations, such as the Kimberley, in the extreme north of the state – a wild and rugged area with a convoluted coast and spectacular inland gorges. It gets good annual rainfall, but all in the 'green' season. Taming the Kimberley has been a long held dream which has still only been partially realised. It's a spectacular area well worth a visit.

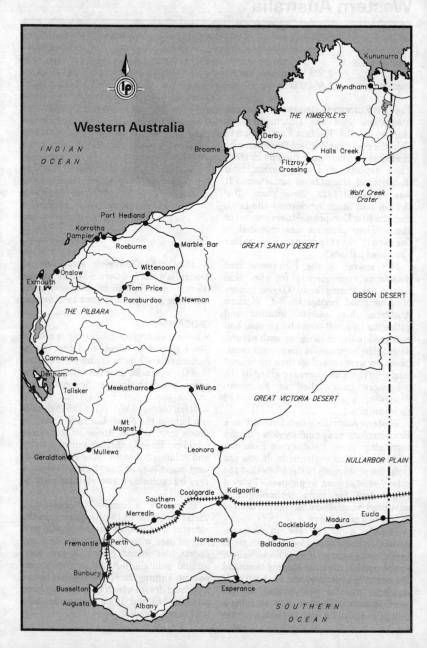

Western Australia

INDIAN OCEAN

THE KIMBERLEYS

Kununurra

Wyndham

Derby

Broome

Halls Creek

Fitzroy Crossing

Wolf Creek Crater

Port Hedland

Karratha

Dampier

Roeburne

Marble Bar

GREAT SANDY DESERT

Onslow

Wittenoom

Exmouth

Tom Price

GIBSON DESERT

Paraburdoo

Newman

THE PILBARA

Carnarvon

Denham

Talisker

Meekatharra

Wiluna

GREAT VICTORIA DESERT

Mt Magnet

Geraldton

Mullewa

Leonora

NULLARBOR PLAIN

Coolgardie

Kalgoorlie

Southern Cross

Merredin

Cocklebiddy

Madura

Eucla

Fremantle

Perth

Norseman

Balladonia

Bunbury

Busselton

Esperance

Augusta

Albany

SOUTHERN OCEAN

Further south is the Pilbara, an area with more magnificent gorge country and the treasure house from which the state derives its vast mineral wealth. Away from the coast however, most of Western Australia is simply a vast empty stretch of outback: the Nullarbor Plain in the south, the Great Sandy Desert in the north, and the Gibson and Great Victoria Deserts in between.

WILDFLOWERS

Western Australia is famed for its wildflowers, which bloom from August to October. Even some of the driest deserts will put on a technicolour display after just a little rainfall.

The south-west alone has over 3000 species, many of which, because of the state's isolation, are unique. They're known as everlastings because the petals stay attached even after the flowers have died. The flowers seem to spring up almost overnight and transform vast areas within days.

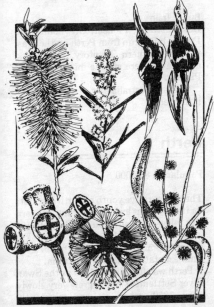

You can find the flowers almost everywhere in the state, but the jarrah forests in the south-west are particularly rich. The coastal parks also put on brilliant displays. Near the capital, the John Forrest National Park, in the Darling Range, and the Yanchep National Park are both excellent prospects. But you don't even have to leave Perth to see the flowers, as there's a section of Kings Park where they are cultivated.

INFORMATION

Western Australia is well represented in the eastern states with tourist offices in the major cities.

New South Wales
    92 Pitt St, Sydney 2000 (tel 233 4400)
Queensland
    243 Edward St, Brisbane 4000 (tel 221 9732)
South Australia
    108 King William St, Adelaide 5000 (tel 212 1344)
Victoria
    35 Elizabeth St, Melbourne 3000 (tel 614 1346)

ACTIVITIES
Bushwalking

There are a number of bushwalking clubs in Perth. Popular areas for walking include the Stirling Range National Park and Porongurup National Park, both near Albany. There are also a number of coastal parks in the south and south-west with good tracks.

There are good walks in the hills around Perth at places like Piesse Brook, Mundaring Weir, the Serpentine, Kalamunda and Bickley. They're particularly pleasant during the August to September wildflower season. If you're a really enthusiastic walker there is 640 km of marked walking track all the way from Perth to Albany, along old forest tracks.

Water Sports

People in Perth often claim that their city has the best beaches and surf of any

Australian city. Particularly popular surfing areas elsewhere in the state include Denmark near Albany, Bunbury south of Perth, and Geraldton to the north.

Good diving areas can be found along the large stretch of coast from Esperance to Geraldton, and between Carnarvon and Exmouth. You can get to the islands and reefs off the coast in small boats. Good areas include Esperance, Bremer Bay, Albany, Denmark, Windy Harbour, Margaret River, Bunbury, Rottnest Island, Lancelin, Abrolhos Island (near Geraldton), Carnarvon and all around the North West Cape (Exmouth, Coral Bay).

ACCOMMODATION

An interesting alternative to the usual hostels and hotels is available through Homestay of WA. They offer home and farm accommodation and will meet people at Perth airport. Costs are typically $25 a person for bed & breakfast. You can contact them at Lot 40 Union Rd, Carmel 6076, or phone them on 293 5347. Another organisation that has fully self-contained flats is the Country Women's Association (CWA) (tel 321 6081), at 1174 Hay St, West Perth. Their flats usually work out to be cheap if two or more people share. They can be found in most country areas.

GETTING THERE & AWAY

Western Australia is the largest, most lightly populated and most isolated state in the country. Yet in spite of the vast distances that must be travelled, you can now drive across the desert of the Nullarbor Plain from the eastern states to Perth and then all the way up the Indian Ocean coast and through the Kimberley to Darwin on sealed roads.

Even so, there's absolutely no way of covering all those km cheaply. Sydney to Perth is 3284 km as the Airbus flies, and more like 4000 km by road: a one-way economy rail ticket on the route is $251, a standby air ticket costs $374, while a seat on one of the cheaper bus lines costs around $185.

Hitching across the Nullarbor is not all that easy; waits of three or four days are not uncommon in some places.

Driving yourself is probably the cheapest way of getting to Perth. You'd probably spend around $350 to $400 on fuel, travelling coast to coast; between four people that's about $85 to $100 a head.

GETTING AROUND

Air

Ansett WA have a comprehensive network of flights connecting the northern towns with Perth. The frequency of flights seems ridiculous, given the small population of the north, until you realise that the area is the site of many mining and oil drilling projects, and companies often find it easier to fly their workers back and forth than have them live up there.

On some routes Skywest are in spirited competition with Ansett WA. The chart details the main WA routes and flight costs.

Bus & Train

Bus Australia, Pioneer, Greyhound and Deluxe buses run from Perth up the coast to the Northern Territory. Greyhound also travel there via the interior and the Pilbara.

Western Australia's internal rail network is limited.

Perth

Population 809,000

The comparative youth of Perth accounts for its clean-cut look. It is a shiny, modern city, pleasantly sited on the Swan River, with the port of Fremantle a few km downstream. It's claimed to be the sunniest state capital in Australia.

Perth was founded in 1829 as the Swan River Settlement but it grew very slowly until 1850, when it was reluctantly

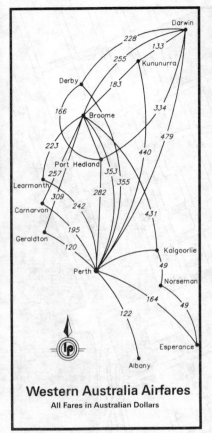

Western Australia Airfares

All Fares in Australian Dollars

city. Many of the residents, however, protested at the time that their life style and the character of their community were damaged by the development.

Orientation

The city centre is fairly compact, situated on a sweep of the Swan River. Murray St and parallel Hay St are the main shopping streets, and the centre section of Hay St is a mall, at its busiest on Thursday nights. Forrest Place, in front of the GPO, is also a small mall and a quiet place in the centre of the city. The railway line bounds the central city area on the northern side. Immediately across the line, in North Perth, there's a restaurant enclave, and a number of popular hostels and other cheap accommodation. This busy section of town is sometimes referred to as Northbridge.

The west end of Perth slopes up to the pleasant Kings Park, which overlooks the city and the Swan River. The river links the city to its port, Fremantle, but there are suburbs all the way along. Suburbs also extend as far as Perth's superb Indian Ocean beaches.

Information

The Western Australian Government Travel Centre (tel 322 2999), also called Holiday WA, is at 772 Hay St, just down from Hay St Mall. The centre is open from 8.30 am to 5.30 pm Monday to Friday and from 8.30 am to 1 pm Saturday. It has an excellent series of town brochures with good maps, a *What's On This Week* brochure and a *Perth-Fremantle Visitor's Guide* with a good map of both cities. There's a Perth City Tourist Booth in the Hay St Mall and travellers' information centres in the domestic (tel 277 9799) and international (tel 477 1151) airport terminals.

The Royal Automobile Club of WA (RACWA) (tel 421 4444) is at 228 Adelaide Terrace. Their bookshop has an excellent travel section. Other good city bookshops are Angus & Robertsons, at 196 Murray

decided to bring in convicts. Even then Perth's development lagged behind that of the eastern cities, until the discovery of gold in the 1890s sparked interest in the region.

In 1987 the city was the site of the unsuccessful defence of what was, for a brief period, one of Australia's prize possessions – the America's Cup yachting trophy. Preparations for the influx of tourists associated with the competition certainly transformed Fremantle into a more modern, colourful and expensive

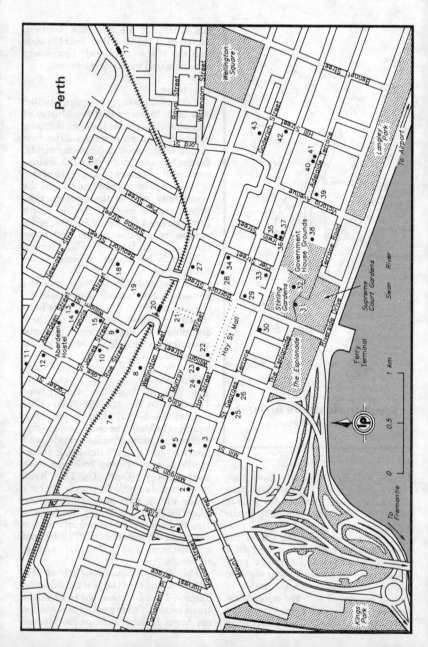

Perth

1	Barrack's Arch
2	Aboriginal Arts
3	The Cloisters
4	Citipac Food Centre
5	Down To Earth Books
6	Shafto Lane Tavern
7	Entertainment Center
8	Central Bus Terminal
9	Sylvana Pastry
10	Plaka Shish Kebab
11	Top Notch Hostel
12	Mamma Maria's
13	Brittania Hotel
14	Francis Street Youth Hostel
15	Great Western Hotel
16	Newcastle Street Youth Hostel
17	East Perth Railway Station (Country & Interstate)
18	Museum of Western Australia
19	Art Gallery of Western Australia
20	Central Perth Railway Station
21	GPO
22	Ansett Travel Centre
23	Qantas
24	Western Australian Travel Centre
25	Old Perth Boys School
26	Transperth Bus Information
27	Grand Central
28	YMCA
29	Perth Town Hall
30	Australian Airlines
31	Supreme Court House
32	Government House
33	Deanery
34	Miss Maud's
35	Ansett Airlines
36	Ansett WA
37	Pioneer Bus Lines
38	Concert Hall
39	YHA Office
40	Girls Friendly Society
41	RAC of Western Australia
42	Downtowner Lodge
43	Jewell House YMCA
44	Aberdeen Lodge

St, and Down to Earth Books, downstairs at 874-876 Hay St. In Fremantle the Market St Book Arcade, at 50 Market St, is good.

The Youth Hostel Association has its office (not the hostel) at 257 Adelaide Terrace. At the Perth Environmental Office, on Hay St, there's a notice board with information on cheap tickets, rides and accommodation.

Perth's daily newspapers are the *West Australian* and the *Daily News*.

Kings Park

Unfortunately, in early 1989 about half of Kings Park was burnt out in bushfires believed to be the work of arsonists.

There are superb views across Perth and the river from the lookout tower in this four square km park. The park includes a 12 hectare botanical garden and a section of natural bushland. In spring there's a cultivated display of WA's famed wildflowers.

From the top of Kings Park the steep steps of Jacobs Ladder will take you down to Mounts Bay Rd by the river. Look for the huge karri trunk on display in the park, and the crosscut section of a California redwood showing just how old a tree can be.

Beside the park is the Legacy Lookout, on top of Dumas House, on Kings Park Rd. It's open from Monday to Friday from 9.30 am to 4.30 pm. Free guided tours, available from April to October, should be booked one month in advance by phoning 321 4801, but it's worth trying to get in even if you can only give a couple of days' notice – you might be lucky. Get to the park on bus Nos 25, 27 or 28 from St Georges Terrace (alight at the War Memorial); or walk up Mount St to the park from the city centre. The park has a restaurant with a coffee shop and a good view of Perth.

City Buildings

The Cloisters, towards the park end of St Georges Terrace, dates from 1858 and is noted for its beautiful brickwork. It was originally a school and has now been integrated into a modern office development. On the corner of St Georges Terrace and Pier St is the Deanery, built in 1850 and one of the few houses in WA surviving from that period. Close by, on St Georges Terrace, is Government House, a Gothic-looking fantasy built between 1859 and 1864. At the corner of St Georges Terrace and William St is the Palace Hotel, dating back to 1895. It's now a renovated banking chamber.

There are tours of the modern Council House, at 27 St Georges Terrace, four times daily. Behind it, in Stirling Gardens, is the old court house, one of the oldest buildings in Perth, built in Georgian style in 1836. Other old buildings include the town hall, on the corner of Hay and Barrack Sts (1867-70); the Treasury Building, on Barrack St and St Georges Terrace, opposite King St (built in 1854 and now used by the National Trust); and the recently restored His Majesty's Theatre, on the corner of King and Hay Sts.

The memorial plaque in the pavement near the old town hall on the corner of Hay and Barrack Sts marks the founding of Perth in 1829. The hall was built by convicts. On Mounts Bay Rd, at the foot of Mt Eliza, is Governor Kennedy's Fountain, fed by a spring which was Perth's first public water supply.

Other Buildings

You can tour the parliament buildings at 11.15 am and 3.15 pm Monday to Friday when parliament is not in session. When it is in session there are still brief tours from Monday to Friday. Take a No 2, 3, 4 or 6 Subiaco bus to Parliament House, on Harvest Terrace. In front of the building is the old Barracks Archway, the remains of an 1860 barracks.

On the corner of Pier and Murray Sts is the Post & Telecom Museum – a fine example of early colonial architecture. On an artificial island en route to the airport, off the Great Western Highway, Victoria Park, is Perth's Burswood Casino, open all day every day.

Museums

On Francis St, across the railway lines from the city centre, is the Museum of Western Australia, which includes a gallery of Aboriginal art, a 25 metre whale skeleton and a good collection of meteorites, the largest of which weighs 11 tonnes. (The Australian outback is a particularly good area for finding meteorites as they are unlikely to have been disturbed.) The museum complex also includes Perth's original prison, built in 1856 and used until 1888. Admission to the museum is free and it is open from 10.30 am to 5 pm Monday to Thursday and from 1 to 5 pm Friday, Saturday and Sunday.

The Small World Museum, at 12 Parliament Place, has the largest collection of miniatures in the country. The cars, kitchens, jigsaw puzzles and books are all one-twelfth life size. It's open every day from 10 am to 5 pm. To get there catch a Green Clipper bus.

The Army Museum of WA, on the corner of Bulwer and Lord Sts has a display of army memorabilia. It is open Sundays from 1 to 4.30 pm and admission is free. Bus Nos 41 to 44 and 47, 48 and 55 will get you there from Perth. The Fire Safety Education Centre & Museum is on the corner of Murray and Pier Sts.

Perth Zoo

Perth's popular zoo is across the river from the city, at 20 Labouchere Rd, South Perth. It has an interesting collection including a nocturnal house which is open from 12 noon to 3 pm daily. The zoo itself is open from 10 am to 5 pm daily and admission is $3. You can reach the zoo on a No 36 or 38 bus from St Georges Terrace or by taking the ferry across the river and then just strolling up the road from the Mends St Jetty.

Art Galleries

The Art Gallery of Western Australia is housed in a modern building which runs from James St through to Roe St, behind the railway station. It has a very fine permanent exhibition of European, Australian and Asian-Pacific art. The gallery is open from 10 am to 5 pm daily.

Gallery Australia, at 96 Fitzgerald St, has a collection of Australian art, and is open from 10.30 am to 6 pm Tuesday to Friday and on Sunday from 2 to 5 pm. Over at Northbridge the Alexander Gallery, at 12 Aberdeen St, is open Tuesday from 10 am to 3 pm and Sunday from 3 to 6 pm.

Other Parks

On the Esplanade, between the city and the river, is the Alan Green Conservatory. It houses a controlled-environment display and is open from 10 am to 5 pm Monday to Saturday and from 2 to 6 pm Sunday. Also close to the city are the Supreme Court Gardens, a popular place to eat lunch. In the summer there are often outdoor concerts in the music shell in the park.

Queens Gardens, at the eastern end of Hay St, form a pleasant little park with lakes; get there on a Red Clipper bus. The lake in Hyde Park, Highgate, is popular for the water birds it attracts. Lake Monger in Wembley is another hangout for local feathered friends, particularly Perth's famous black swans. Get there on a No 90 or 91 bus from the Central Bus Station.

Beaches

Perth residents claim that it has the best beaches and surf of any Australian city. There are calm bay beaches on the Swan River at Crawley, Peppermint Grove and Como, or you can try a whole string of patrolled surf beaches on the Indian Ocean coast including Perth's very popular nude beach at Swanbourne. Some of the other surf beaches are Cottesloe, Port, City, Scarborough and Trigg Island. Most can be reached by public transport. There's also Rottnest Island, just off the coast of Fremantle.

Old Mill

Across Narrows Bridge is one of Perth's landmarks: the finely restored Flour Mill, built in 1835. It's open from 1 to 5 pm Sunday, Monday, Wednesday and Thursday and from 1 to 4 pm Saturday. On display in the mill are relics of the pioneering era. Ride to the mill on a No 4 bus from St Georges Terrace or walk there along the river from the Mends St Jetty.

Other Attractions

Between Hay St and St Georges Terrace is the narrow London Court, a photographer's delight. It looks very Tudor English but in fact dates from just 1937. At one end of this shopping court St George and his dragon appear above the clock each quarter of an hour, while at the other ends knights joust on horseback. The Hay St Mall clock face is a miniature replica of Big Ben. The mall is usually full of activity.

Perth has a modern Concert Hall on St Georges Terrace (sometimes providing free concerts) and an even more modern Entertainment Centre on Wellington St, just down from the bus depot.

Over in West Perth there are excellent views of the city from the 14th floor of the PWD Building, on the corner of Kings Park Rd and Havelock St. The building is open on weekdays from 9.30 am to 4.30 pm, and Devonshire teas are available.

Perth Suburbs

Armadale The Pioneer Village at Armadale, 27 km south-east of the city, is the suburb's major attraction. It's a working model of a 19th century village, with shops, public buildings, goldfield operations and craftsmen working at now out-dated skills. It's open from 10 am to 5 pm Monday to Friday, 1 to 9.30 pm Saturday and 10 am to 6 pm Sunday. Admission is $8.50. You can get to Armadale on a No 219 bus or a local train.

Just beyond Armadale is Elizabethan Village. It's open from 10 am to 5 pm daily and admission is $3. It's a half hour walk from the bus stop in Armadale. At Kelmscott, just before Armadale, the

Museum of WA has its Historical Shanty Town, open from 10 am to 5 pm on weekends and full of relics of the colonial era.

History House Museum, on Jull St, is a free museum in a 19th century pioneer's house, with exhibits about Armadale's early settlers.

You can ride a miniature railway through the Cohunu Wildlife Park, where there are many animals, some of which can be fed by hand. There are also plenty of water birds and a walk-in aviary. It's about a 35 minute drive from Perth, on Mill Rd, Gosnells, and it's open from 10 am to 5 pm Wednesday to Sunday (daily during the school holidays). Boulder Rock is a pleasant picnic spot off the Brookton Highway near Armadale.

Up the Swan River There are a number of attractions up the Swan River, particularly in Guildford. On Maylands Peninsula, enclosed by a loop of the Swan River, is the beautifully restored Tranby House of 1839. It's open daily from 2 to 5 pm. Gallop House is another well restored historic home from the 1870s. It's open on Sundays from 11 am to 6 pm.

The Rail Transport Museum, on Railway Parade, Bassendean has all sorts of railway memorabilia and is open from 1 to 5 pm on Sundays and public holidays. The Halls Museum, at 105 Swan St, Guildford, has an enormous collection of Australiana and other items, housed in a building behind the 1840 Rose & Crown Hotel. It's open from 10 am to 4.30 pm daily except Monday and admission is $2.50; get there on a No 306 bus.

Nearby, on Meadow St, is Mechanics Hall, now a small folk museum open from 2 to 5 pm from March to mid-December. Guildford Goal, in Meadow St, includes a loft and four brick, vaulted cells. It is open Sunday from 2 to 5 pm. Woodbridge is a restored and furnished colonial mansion overlooking the river. It's open from 1 to 4 pm Monday to Saturday and from 11 am to 5 pm Sunday but closed Wednesday. This is one of the few pioneer

homes in Perth which you can visit; get there on a No 306 bus. In West Swan is the Caversham Wildlife Park, which has a collection of Australian animals and birds. It's open from 10 am to 5.30 pm daily except Friday.

In Midland is the unusual Crescent Moon Gallery, at 51 The Crescent; it has an eclectic collection of arts and crafts. The Gomboc Gallery, at James Rd, Middle Swan, claims to be the largest private gallery in the state and is open Wednesday to Sunday from 10 am to 5 pm.

The Swan Valley vineyards are dotted along the river, from around Guildford right up to Upper Swan. Many of them are open for tastings, except on Sundays. Olive Farm Winery is the oldest in the region and named after the olive trees that were also planted on the property. Houghton Winery was established later but produced the first commercial vintage in 1842. The river cuts a narrow gorge through the Darling Range at Walyunga National Park in Upper Swan, off the Great Northern Highway. There are walking tracks along the river and it's a popular picnic spot.

Other Suburbs In Subiaco there's a Museum of Childhood, at 160 Hamersley Rd. Across the Canning River, towards Jandakot Airport, there is the excellent Aviation Museum, on Bull Creek Drive, Bull Creek. It's open from 11 am to 4 pm weekdays except Wednesdays; admission is $3. Take bus No 105 from St Georges Terrace to Booragoon and transfer to bus No 168 to the museum.

In Melville, just off the Canning Highway, on the way to Fremantle, is Wireless Hill Park & Telecommunications Museum. It has a variety of exhibits, ranging from early pedal-operated radio equipment used in the outback to modern NASA communications equipment. It's open weekends from 2 to 5 pm.

Further down the Canning Highway towards Fremantle, near the corner of Stock Rd, is Miller Bakehouse Museum, at 7 Baal St, Palmyra, which has a rare old wood-fired baking oven. It's open from 2 to 5 pm on Sundays and admission is 50c. The Claremont Museum, in the Freshwater Bay School, at 66 Victoria Ave, Claremont, concentrates on local history and is open Wednesday, Saturday and Sunday from 2 to 5 pm.

In Cannington, on the road to Armadale, is Woodloes, a restored colonial home of 1874. It's open Sundays from 2 to 4.30 pm. The small Liddelow Homestead, in Kenwick, is another restored homestead. It's open Thursday from 10 am to 2 pm and Sunday from 11 am to 3 pm. Yet another early home is the mud-brick and shingle Stirk's Cottage, in Kalamunda. Built in 1881, it's open from March to November on Sundays from 2 to 4.30 pm.

Adventureworld is at 179 Progress Drive, Bibra Lake, south of the centre and accessible by Transperth bus No 600. It's a large amusement park with rides, a zoo, the country's largest swimming pool and various other diversions. It's open daily in summer, and weekends only in winter. The $13 admission covers all the attractions.

On the way to Yanchep is the Underwater World, at Boat Harbour, West Coast Highway, Hillarys. It's an underwater tunnel aquarium displaying 5000 sea creatures and open daily from 9 am to 9 pm.

Places to Stay

If you have trouble finding a place to stay in Perth try ringing the Westralian Accommodation Centre (tel 277 9199): they claim to be able to find you just what you're after and at no cost to you. They have desks at both the domestic (tel 277 0799) and international (tel 477 1151) airport terminals.

Hostels Perth's hostels, particularly the two youth hostels, are all reasonably central. The main *YHA Hostel* (tel 328 1135), at 60-62 Newcastle St, was at one time the busiest youth hostel in Australia.

The hostel is about a 15 minute walk from the city centre; just go straight up Barrack or William St, crossing the railway line, until you hit Newcastle St, then turn right. The cost is $11 a night and office hours are 8 to 10 am and 5 to 10.30 pm.

The second *YHA Hostel* (tel 328 7794), at 46 Francis St, is in an old house on the corner of William St, a little closer to the city. It has small dorms and has the same office hours and cost as the Newcastle St hostel. Both hostels have bicycles for hire.

Backpackers Perth Inn (tel 328 9958), at 194 Brisbane St, is further north of the centre than other hostels but the nicely renovated colonial house is very clean and has a pleasant garden and a barbecue. Bus Nos 18 to 20 travel there from stand 6 on Barrack St – ask for the Northbridge Hotel, which is next door to the hostel. Dorms cost from $7 a night.

A good alternative is the *North Lodge* (tel 227 7588) at 225 Beaufort St. It's clean, friendly, has all the usual facilities and comfortable beds for $10 a person. The Blue Clipper free bus from Barrack St will get you there on weekdays and many other buses, like the No 59 or 60, also go that way.

The *Top Notch Hostel* (tel 328 6667), at 194 Aberdeen St, is a 20 minute walk from the mall. Follow the directions for the Newcastle St YHA hostel but turn left at Aberdeen St. Five bed dorms are $7.50 a person, twin shares $9.50 each. Weekly rates are six times the daily rates. It's reasonable value but somewhat neglected, although there is a good kitchen, billiard table and bicycle hire. Some travellers have reported that it is often overcrowded and rowdy.

Aberdeen Hostel (tel 227 6137), at 79 Aberdeen St, is the most central but the least appealing since it's crowded and also somewhat neglected. Dorms are $9 a day or $55 a week and twin shares are $11 a day or $65 a week.

Finally, there's *Travel Mates* (tel 328 6685), at 496 Newcastle St. A No 15 bus from Barrack St will take you some of the way. Dorm beds are $9.50 ($63 by the week) and bedding costs $4; Rooms for couples can be arranged. There's also a late arrivals room. The hostel is open all the time, the office hours are irregular and the place more or less runs itself.

YMCAs & Guest Houses Perth's very central YMCAs take both men and women. There are also a couple of modern 'lodges' a few km from the centre. The main *YMCA* building (tel 325 2744) is in the centre at 119 Murray St and is not that bad. Residents include pensioners and semi-permanents but a fair number of travellers pass through. Singles are $17 a night. Twin rooms are $26 and weekly rates are five times the daily rates. Office hours are 8 am to midnight and the facilities are minimal.

The other *YMCA*, known as Jewel House (tel 325 8488), is only a couple of blocks further along Murray St, at 180 Goderich St (as Murray St becomes after Victoria Square). It offers 200 comfortable, clean, modern rooms. Singles are $24, doubles $34, and family rooms $55; weekly rates are six times the daily rate. Morning and evening meals are available and there are sandwiches at lunch time. The office is open 24 hours a day and there's free baggage storage.

Centrally located and good value is the *Downtowner Lodge* (tel 325 6973), at 63 Hill St, opposite the Perth Mint. The 12 rooms are clean and pleasant and it's a very quiet, non-smoking place with a TV room and car park. It's $17 for one night in twin rooms, $11 a night for more than one night, and $65 a week. The *Girls Friendly Society Lodge* (tel 325 4143), at 240 Adelaide Terrace, takes women only at $27 a night; full board is available.

Hotels There are quite a number of old-fashioned hotels around the centre of Perth. The *Grand Central* (tel 325 5638), at 379 Wellington St, is rather basic (no sinks in the room) but quite OK. Rooms are $20/30. In the mall is the *Savoy Plaza*

Hotel (tel 325 9588), at 636 Hay St. It has a wide range of rooms – singles are around $32 depending on facilities and doubles from $53. All rates include a cooked breakfast.

Other cheaper hotels include the *Grosvenor* (tel 325 3799) at 339 Hay St, at $19/35 and the *Court* (tel 328 5292), at 50 Beaufort St, at $20 a single (there are no doubles). Across the railway lines, at 253 William St, is the *Britannia* (tel 328 6121), with dorms at $10 a person and basic rooms from $15/28. The better rooms are at the back on the verandah – the others are lit by a skylight. There is even a laundry.

Perth has a number of luxury hotels, including the *Burswood Hotel* (tel 362 7777), off the Great Eastern Highway, Victoria Park, in the casino complex. Rooms (and that great view over the soaring central atrium) start from $160.

Motels & Holiday Flats *City Waters Lodge* (tel 325 5020), at 118 Terrace Rd, down by the river, is conveniently central and good value with cooking facilities, attached bathroom, colour TV and so on. There's also a laundrette in the block. Daily costs are $40/55 for singles/doubles. Triples and family rooms are also available.

Ladybird Lodge (tel 444 7359) is a little further out, at 193 Oxford St, Leederville and costs $18/26 including breakfast. North-east of Perth is the *Pacific Motel* (tel 328 5599), at 111 Harold St, Highgate, which has singles/doubles for $32/40. The *Adelphi Centre* (tel 322 4666), at 130A Mounts Bay Rd, has rooms for $45/51. Like those in the City Waters Lodge, the rooms here are very well equipped and even have kitchen facilities, although they are a step up in price. Here again it's wise to book.

Across the bridge, on the South Perth side, is the *Canning Bridge Auto Lodge* (tel 364 2511), at 891 Canning Highway, Applecross, which costs $50 for doubles. The *Como Beach Motel* (tel 367 7955), at 2 Preston St, Como, costs $39/42.

In Scarborough, *Scarborough Beach Holiday Accommodation* (tel 341 6655), on the corner of Brighton and West Coast Highways, has dorms for $10 a person or $56 a week; doubles in fully self-contained units are $35 a night. A full breakfast is $3.50 and dinner costs from $7. Bus Nos 268 and 269 travel there from the Perth Central Bus Station. The tourist office has a list of other holiday flats in and around Perth.

Colleges College accommodation may be available during the vacations at the University of Western Australia and at Murdoch University. UWA colleges are St Columba's (tel 386 7177), Kingswood College (tel 389 0389), Currie Hall (tel 380 2771), St Thomas More College (tel 386 8712), St George's College (tel 382 5555), and St Catherine's (tel 386 5847), which takes women. At Murdoch University (tel 332 2211) there are flats at Yarallda Court, where one week is the minimum-stay period.

Camping Perth is not well endowed with camping sites at a convenient distance from the centre, although there are many about 20 km out. The list below covers the sites within a 20 km radius of the city centre. Central Caravan Park, Kenlorn Caravan Park and Como Beach Caravan Park are the most central; all within 10 km of the centre although the Como Beach site does not permit camping.

Forrestfield Caravan Park, 18 km east, Hawtin Rd, Forrestfield, camping $10 for two, on-site vans $24 (tel 453 6378)
Perth Tourist Caravan Park, 15 km east, 319 Hale Rd, Forrestfield, camping $10 for two, on-site vans $27 (tel 453 6677)
Orange Grove Caravan Park, 19 km south-east Kelvin Rd, Orange Grove, camping $8 for two, on-site vans $22 (tel 453 6226)
Guildford Caravan Park, 19 km north-east, 372 Swan Rd, Guildford, camping $10 for two, on-site vans $28 (tel 274 2828)
Central Caravan Park, seven km east, 34 Central Ave, Redcliffe, camping $10 for two, on-site vans $115 a week (tel 277 5696)
Kenlorn Caravan Park, nine km south-east, 229 Welshpool Rd, Queens Park, camping $11 for two, on-site vans $80 a week (tel 458 2604)
Como Beach Caravan Park, six km south, 4 Ednah St, Como, camping not permitted, on-site vans from $88 to $130 a week (tel 367 1286)
Careniup Caravan Park, 14 km north, 467 Beach Rd, Gwelup, camping $9 for two, on-site vans for $25 (tel 447 6665)
Starhaven Caravan Park, 14 km north-west, 14-18 Pearl Parade, Scarborough, camping $10 for two, on-site vans from $25 to $30 (tel 341 1770)
Kingsway Caravan Park, 15 km north, Wanneroo Rd, Greenwood, camping $8.50 for two, on-site vans for $28 (tel 409 9267)
Caversham Caravan Park, 12 km north-east, Benara Rd, Caversham, camping $9 for two, on-site vans from $110 to $145 a week (tel 279 6700)
Springvale Caravan Park, Maida Vale Rd, Maida Vale, camping $10 for two, on-site vans around $25 (tel 454 6829)

Places to Eat

City The city centre is especially good for lunches and light meals. The busy *Bernadis*, at 528 Hay St, has good sandwiches, quiches and salads. Further along, at 570 Hay St, is *Cini Coffee Lounge*, which is cheap. Back on Hay St Mall, in the Carillon Centre, *Pancakes at Carillon* is a good place for breakfast, lunch or dinner.

The *Granary* is downstairs at 37 Barrack St, south of Hay St. It offers a wide range of vegetarian dishes for $6 at lunch time and $15 at dinner. Further down, at 137, is the good and cheap *Anne Malaysian Restaurant* where you can get a three course meal for $18. On the other side, at 138, is the very popular *Magic Apple*, a health food place with all sorts of salads and smoothies. Across the street, at 129, is the Hare Krishna *Crossways* restaurant, which has excellent value vegetarian meals. Back on Hay St, other health food places include *Tastes Galore* and the *Wholemeal Health Food Restaurant*.

Ruby's Restaurant, at 37 Pier St, has a good three course lunch special for $25. Toward the other end of Hay St, near Kings Park, there's a string of places, including *Fast Eddy's*, which is on the corner of Milligan St, has a wide variety of burgers from $5 and is open 24 hours a day. The *Hayashi Japanese BBQ*, at 107 Pier St, has excellent value set lunches for $6 to $10.

For a flashier lunch there's *Broodjeswinkel* beside the AMP building, on the corner of William St and St Georges Terrace. At 117 Murray St, beside the YMCA, is the pleasant and very reasonably priced little Japanese restaurant called *Jun & Tommy's* where main courses are $6 to $10.

Near the Oxford Cinema, *Uncle Vinces* has great mussels in chilli sauce – between four you can have mussels, spaghetti and a carafe of house red for $8 each. *Cariban's*, at 623 Wellington St, has something for everyone – steaks, seafood, Italian and vegetarian dishes in the $6 to $10 range.

The Kings Park restaurant is good for a splurge, with great views over the city and the river. A complete dinner will come to $30 (plus drinks) and there's live music as well. Lunch and morning and afternoon teas are also served.

Perth has the usual selection of counter meals in the city centre area. The *Railway Hotel*, at 130 Barrack St, has cheap meals from $3 for a burger to more expensive meals at the $7.50 mark. *Sassella's Tavern*, in the City Arcade, off Hay St, does reasonably priced bistro meals for $7 and has entertainment. Over the railway line north of the city, at 198 Brisbane St, the *Northbridge Hotel*, next to the Backpackers Hostel, has good, cheap counter meals for $6 to $10.

Food Centres Perth pioneered food centres in Australia and they're great places to eat. Essentially they're a group of kitchens which share a dining room. You can get your meal from one place, your partner can eat from another, you can have drinks from a third and select dessert from a fourth. This terrific Singaporean idea has really taken off and nightly crowds prove that it's a popular alternative to fast food.

The *City Centre Market*, in the Hay St Mall, downstairs near William St, has stalls offering Chinese, Mexican, Indonesian, Indian and many other types of food. At the Singapore booth a tasty meal sets you back just $4 or so. The centre is open for lunch and dinner and is very busy in the evenings when there is live entertainment from Thursdays to Saturdays until 9 pm. There are other centres in the city area but none match the City Centre.

William St Area North of the city the area bounded by William St on the east and Lake St on the west is full of ethnic restaurants. They come in all price ranges too, from cheap cappuccino bars to posh seafood restaurants.

Kim Anh, at 178 William St, is a Vietnamese BYO place where two can eat well for $22 to $30. Across the street, at 175, is *Cafe La Quan*, a cheaper Vietnamese. Nearby, at 188, is the moderately priced and popular *Romanys*, one of the city's really long-running Italian places. *Stefan's*, at 195, is a Mediterranean restaurant with live music and main courses from $13.

At 197 William St is *Sylvana Pastry*, a comfortable Lebanese coffee bar with an amazing selection of those sticky Middle Eastern pastries which look, and usually taste, delicious. On the corner of Aberdeen and William Sts is *Bar Italia*, open from breakfast until 1 am.

Off William St, *Mamma Maria's*, at 105 Aberdeen St, on the corner of Lake St, has a pleasant ambience and a reputation as one of Perth's best Italian eateries. It's main courses are priced from $10.

A good, cheap vegetarian place is *Phuoc Thani*, at 73 James St. *Plaka Shish*

Kebab, also on James St, has dishes from $4.50 to $6. *Leo's*, at 103, has mixed seafood special for $13.50. The *Garlic Clove*, at 16 Milligan St, has great three course lunches Wednesday to Friday for $15.50. Further away, at 193 Brisbane St, is *Ly Tao*, a Vietnamese Restaurant opposite the Backpackers Inn. It has excellent food and main courses are $7 to $9.

In Subiaco is *Little Lebanon*, at 357 Rokeby Rd, which has good Lebanese food; especially good is the two course special, which includes a soft drink, for $5.

Entertainment

Perth has plenty of pubs, discos and nightclubs. The Friday *Daily News* has a fairly comprehensive nightlife guide. In the centre is *Mango's*, at 100 Murray St, a piano bar with music and exotic cocktails. *F-Scotts* is at 237 Hay St, and further down, at 397, on the corner of Shafto Lane, there's the *Shafto Lane Tavern* which is usually crowded and noisy later on with bands or a disco.

Next door is *Pinocchio's*, which has a cover charge of $5 to $10, depending on the night and who is on. The *Old Melbourne Hotel*, on the corner of Milligan and Hay Sts, has everything from a jungle bar to a piano bar and striptease. It is open 24 hours a day and has good bands on weekends. There's dancing to the latest music at *Jules*, at 104 Murray St.

Popular clubs for interesting live music are *Rockwells*, at 156 James St, and the *Great Western Hotel*, on the corner of William and James Sts. The graffiti covered *Limbo's*, at 232 William St, is popular with backpackers.

For folk music you could try *Jenny's Place*, in the back room of 24 Hedley St, Bentley, on Sundays from 8 to 11.30 pm. Several pubs in and around town feature jazz on Saturday afternoons – check the listings in the daily papers.

Away from the centre there's the usual rock pub circuit with varying cover charges depending on the night of the week and who is playing. Popular venues

include the *Leederville Stockade*, Vincent St, Leederville; the *Subiaco Hotel*, Hay and Rokeby Sts, Subiaco; *Hotel Cottesloe (The Cott)*, John St, Cottesloe; the *Boomerang Hotel*, 1120 Albany Highway, Bentley; and the *Broadway Tavern*, Broadway Shopping Centre, Nedlands, near the university.

The *Kimberley Cinema*, on central Barrack St, shows some quality films, as does the *New Oxford*, on the corner of Vincent and Oxford Sts.

Things to Buy

At 251 St Georges Terrace, right up at the Kings Park end of town, is Aboriginal Arts, a friendly place with a good collection of Aboriginal arts and crafts.

Getting There & Away

Air Australian Airlines (tel 323 3333) and Ansett (tel 325 0201) have flights to and from Sydney, Melbourne, Brisbane and Adelaide. Some Sydney and Melbourne flights go direct, some via Adelaide or, in the case of Sydney, via Melbourne. Lowest fares (standby in brackets) to Perth are Adelaide $362 ($290), Melbourne $419 ($335), Sydney $467 ($374), Brisbane $493 ($394).

There are flights to and from North Queensland via Alice Springs. Fares are $348 ($278) from Alice Springs, $483 from Cairns and $479 from Townsville. Darwin to Perth flights go via Alice Springs or Port Hedland – Ansett WA fly from Darwin to Perth along the coast daily. Fares are between $467 and $501.

Skywest (tel 478 9898), at 140 St Georges Terrace, are an associate of Australian Airlines and fly to places like Albany, Esperance, Kalgoorlie, Geraldton and Port Hedland. Mid-State Air (tel 277 4022) have regular flights to Kalgoorlie.

Bus Bus Australia, Pioneer, Greyhound and Deluxe have daily bus services from Adelaide to Perth. Fares are $131 with Bus Australia and the trip takes about 34 hours. Bus Australia not only charge slightly less but also have more stopover options. Other typical prices are Melbourne $165, Sydney $185 and Brisbane $219.

Bus Australia (tel 277 1077) are at 30 Pier St and Deluxe (tel 322 7877) are at 141 Adelaide Terrace. Pioneer (tel 479 1600) and Greyhound (tel 478 1122) operate from the Ansett Terminal at 26 St Georges Terrace – see the relevant sections for travel up the coast from Perth. The journey from Perth to Darwin takes 60 hours by bus and costs $229. Greyhound also operate to Port Hedland via the more direct, inland route through Newman.

Westrail operate bus services to a number of WA centres including Bunbury and Collie ($12), Hyden (Wave Rock) ($16, twice weekly), Esperance ($38, twice weekly), Geraldton ($30, almost daily) and Mullewa ($30, twice weekly).

Train Along with the Ghan to Alice Springs, the long Indian-Pacific run is one of Australia's great railway journeys – a 65 hour trip between the Pacific Ocean on one side of the continent and the Indian Ocean on the other. Travelling this way you see Australia at ground level and at the end of the journey you really appreciate the immensity of this country.

From Sydney you cross New South Wales in the late afternoon and overnight, arriving in Broken Hill around breakfast time. Then it's on to Port Pirie in South Australia and across the Nullarbor. From Port Pirie to Kalgoorlie the seemingly endless crossing of the virtually uninhabited centre takes nearly 30 hours, including the 'long straight' on the Nullarbor – at 478 km this is the longest straight stretch of railway line in the world. Unlike the trans-Nullarbor road, which runs south of the Nullarbor along the coast of the Great Australian Bight, the railway line actually crosses the Plain. From Kalgoorlie it's a straightforward run into Perth.

To or from Perth fares with sleeper are Adelaide $354 economy, $481 1st or $130 in an economy seat with no meals; Melbourne $404 economy, $588 1st, or $180 seat only ; Sydney $547 economy, $736 1st or $257 seat only. 'Caper' fares offer good reductions if you book at least seven days in advance. Melbourne and Adelaide passengers connect with the Indian-Pacific at Port Pirie. Cars can be transported between Adelaide and Perth ($250) and most other major cities.

The full distance from Sydney to Perth is 3961 km. You can break your journey at any stop along the way and continue on later as long as you complete the one-way trip within two months; return tickets are valid for up to six months. West bound departures are made on Sunday, Thursday and Saturday (arriving in Perth on Wednesday, Sunday and Tuesday). Heading east the train departs on Sunday, Monday and Thursday (arriving in Sydney on Wednesday, Thursday and Sunday). Try to book at least a month in advance.

The main difference between economy and 1st class sleepers is that 1st class compartments are available as singles or twins, economy as twins only. First class twins have showers and toilets; 1st class singles have toilets only, with showers at the end of the carriage. In the economy seating compartments the showers and toilets are at the end of the carriage. Meals are included in the fare for 1st class and economy berth passengers but not for economy seat passengers. First class passengers also have a lounge compartment complete with piano.

Between Adelaide and Perth you can also travel on the twice weekly Trans-Australian. Fares are as for the Indian-Pacific and the trip takes 38 hours.

The only rail services within WA are the Prospector to Kalgoorlie and the Australind to Bunbury – see the relevant sections for details. The trains from the east coast and the WA services all run to or from the terminal in East Perth, as do the Westrail Buses. For Westrail bookings ring 326 2222 or visit the WA Government Travel Centre in Hay St.

Hitching The hostel notice boards are worth checking for lifts and share trips to points around the country. Also check the alternative life style notice board at the Perth Environment Centre, in Hay St.

If you're hitching out of Perth to the north or east take a train to Midland. For travel south take a train to Armadale. Some sexist noted in the youth hostel visitors book that you shouldn't try hitching across the Nullarbor 'unless you've got big tits and nice legs'. Trans-Nullarbor hitching is not that easy and the fierce competition between bus companies has made bus travel much more attractive.

Getting Around

Perth has a central public transport organisation, the Transperth. There are Transperth Information Offices at 125 St Georges Terrace and at the Perth Central Bus Station, in Wellington St. Both are open from 7 am to 6 pm Monday to Friday and from 7.30 am to 2.45 pm on weekends. Transperth operate buses, trains and ferries. They can give you information and advice about getting around Perth and supply route maps and timetables. Phone 221 1211 for information.

Airport Transport Perth's airport is busy night and day. It has to operate at night, since Perth's isolation from the east coast and the airport's function as an international arrival point mean planes arrive and depart at all hours.

A taxi to the airport is around $12 with an 80c surcharge at night. The Skybus costs $4 to the domestic terminal and $5 to the international terminal. It runs frequently but irregularly from 4.45 am to 11.30 pm. Phone 328 6223 for pick-ups. They'll usually collect from the hostels.

Alternatively you can get into the city for just $1.15 on a 338 Transperth bus to William St. It departs the northern end of the terminal every 30 minutes from 5.30 am to 11 pm on weekdays and for nearly as long on Saturdays. Sunday services are less frequent.

The domestic and international terminals are 10 km apart. The international terminal has money changing facilities. Budget, Avis, Thrifty and Hertz have desks at both terminals and there's also a desk for the Westralian Accommodation Centre, who claim to be able to book accommodation at any price level and at no cost.

Bus There are four free City Clipper services, which operate Monday to Friday. The Yellow Clipper and a bus following a shortened Red Clipper route also operate on Saturday mornings.

Red Clipper
These make a loop up and down St Georges Terrace-Adelaide Terrace and Wellington St.
Yellow Clipper
These operate around the very central area of the city.
Blue Clipper
These run between Northbridge and the Esplanade along Barrack and William Sts then down Beaufort St. They go past the Central Bus Station, the WA Museum and very close to the youth hostel.
Green Clipper
These travel between the Central Bus Station and West Perth.

On regular buses a short ride of two sections costs 65c but anything longer is a zone ticket which allows you unlimited travel within the zone for two hours from the time of issue and can be used on Transperth buses, trains and ferries. One zone costs 95c, two zones $1.15, and three zones $1.40. You can get an all day, three zone ticket for $4.80. Zone 2 extends as far as Fremantle, 20 km from the centre, so you have quite an area of action. Using your two hour ticket, you could, for example, go down to the jetty in Perth, take the ferry from there to the zoo, then an hour or so later take the bus back, all for $1.15. The ticket also covers all suburban train services. See the Tours section for the Transperth Sunday bus tours.

A Multirider ticket gives you 10 journeys for the price of nine. A Transperth Sightseers Ticket covers bus, train and ferry services at $4 for one day or $17 for five. It takes you as far as Atlantis Marine Park and Madurah and also offers discounts on some tourist attractions.

Some useful bus services include the No 106 and the longer No 105 to Fremantle. The No 103 also goes to Fremantle after heading around Kings Park. Bus Nos 3 and 6 operate to Subiaco and bus Nos 71 and 72 go to the university.

The Perth Tram doesn't run on rails. It takes you around some of Perth's main attractions in 1½ hours for $6.50, and there's a commentary to explain the sights, such as the city, Kings Park, Barrack St Jetty and the Casino. The tram also makes a regular trip from the city to the Casino and back, for $2 one way.

The *Transperth Route Map* has all the bus routes and numbers on it as well as the train lines; pick one up at the tourist office or Transperth Information Office, along with timetables. The *What's On This Week* guide lists bus routes to many local attractions.

Train Suburban trains all go from the city station on Wellington St. Your rail ticket can also be used on Transperth buses and ferries within the ticket's area of validity.

Boat Ferries all depart from the Barrack St Jetty in Perth. Services cross the river to Mends St in South Perth every half hour for 65c. Take this ferry to get to the zoo. See the Rottnest Island section for details on the ferries from Perth and Fremantle to Rottnest.

Between September and May the Transperth MV *Countess II* departs daily except Saturday on a three hour cruise towards the Upper Swan River. Departures are at 2 pm from the Barrack St Jetty and the price is $10. There are also special school holiday trips and other more expensive river cruises – see the Tours section.

Rental Cars Hertz, Budget, Avis and Thrifty are all represented in Perth, along with a string of local organisations. You could try Bateman Car Rental (tel 322 2592), at 789 Wellington St, with cars from as low as $28 including 100 km (excess at 13c a km). Econo-Car (tel 328 6888), at 133 Pier St, has Mokes at $35 a day with 150 km free. Bigger cars and even vans for eight are available at higher but still reasonable rates. Bayswater Hire Cars (tel 325 1000), at 160 Adelaide Terrace, rent small cars from $24 a day with 100 km free (excess at 10c a km).

Tours See the Government Travel Centre about the many Perth tours. City tours are about $15. For a similar price you could go up to Swan Valley. Tours to places like Yanchep, El Caballo Blanco and other attractions in the Perth vicinity range from $25 to $40, with the average being $32. There are full day and half day trips and some night trips, which include drinks and dining or dancing.

There are also tours to the Darling Ranges, Wave Rock ($43), Yanchep and Atlantis Marine Parks and Caves ($40) and other natural sites. There's also a women only 4WD trip.

A three hour Swan River Cruise costs $10 with Transperth or $14 with the Captain Cook Cruise. Others include lunch and wine. For $37 a vineyard tour takes you to wineries up the river – 'good value' wrote some travelling wine enthusiasts.

Another favourite of imbibers is the free tour of the Swan Brewery. The tour takes two hours (followed by a couple of complimentary beers) and departs 10 am and 2.30 pm Mondays to Wednesdays and 10 am Thursdays. The brewery is at 25 Baile Rd, Canning Vale, but you must phone 350 0650 to make reservations.

Top: Perth City, WA (PS)
Left: London Court, Perth (RN)
Right: Old minehead, Kalgoorlie, WA (TW)

Top: The Pinnacles, Cervantes National Park, WA (RN)
Left: Wave Rock, Hyden, WA (RN)
Right: Japanese pearl diver's grave, Broome, WA (TW)

Bicycle The youth hostel in Francis St rents bicycles for $8 a day and mountain bikes for $10 a day. Ride-a-away (tel 354 2393) also rent cycles. There's a bicycle route around the river area, all the way to Armadale, down to Fremantle and out to the northern suburbs.

Around Perth

The are plenty of places around Perth that can be visited in a day, including resorts and parks along the coast to the north and south and inland along the Avon River. The Darling Range runs parallel to the coast close to Perth and there are many places in the ranges for walks, picnics and barbecues. Many can be reached on Transperth city buses.

FREMANTLE (Population 21,000)
Fremantle ('Freo' to enthusiastic name shorteners), Perth's port, is at the mouth of the Swan River, 19 km south-west of the city centre. Over the years Perth has sprawled to engulf Fremantle, which is now more a suburb of the city than a town in its own right. Despite the America's Cup races in 1987 Fremantle has a wholly different feeling than gleaming, sky-scrapered Perth. It's a place with a very real sense of history and a very pleasant atmosphere.

Like Perth, Fremantle was founded in 1829 but, also like Perth, the settlement made little progress until it was reluctantly decided to take in convicts. This cheap and hard worked labour constructed most of the town's earliest buildings, some of them amongst the oldest in WA. As a port, Fremantle was abysmal until the brilliant engineer C Y O'Connor (see the WA Gold Fields section for more of his tragic story) built an artificial harbour in the 1890s. The town has numerous interesting old buildings and a couple of really excellent museums. The National Trust produces two walking tour leaflets on Fremantle.

Information
The Information Centre is on the corner of William St and the mall in a souvenir shop.

Fremantle Museum & Arts Centre
The museum, originally constructed by convict labourers as a lunatic asylum in the 1860s, is on Finnerty St. It houses a great collection including exhibits on Fremantle's early history, the colonisation of WA and the early whaling industry. It also tells the intriguing story of the Dutch East India ships which first discovered the western coast of Australia and in several instances were wrecked on its inhospitable coast. It really is an excellent museum. The arts centre occupies one wing, and it's a living centre where various crafts are practised. The museum is open from 10.30 am to 5 pm Monday to Thursday and from 1 to 5 pm Friday to Sunday; admission is free.

The Maritime Museum
On Cliff St, near the waterfront, is the Maritime Museum, which occupies a building constructed in 1852 as a commissariat. The museum has a display on WA's maritime history with particular emphasis on the famous wreck of the *Batavia*. One gallery is used as a working centre where you can see timbers from the *Batavia* actually being preserved. At one end of this gallery is the huge stone facade intended for an entrance to Batavia Castle in modern day Jakarta, Indonesia. It was being carried by the *Batavia* as ballast when she went down. The museum is open Friday to Sunday and on Wednesday from 1 to 5 pm; admission is free. The museum is well worth a visit.

Sails of the Century
In B-Shed, Victoria Quay, is a collection of historical and sailing boats, including the America's Cup winning 12 metre yacht *Australia II*. It's open daily from 1 to 5 pm and admission is free.

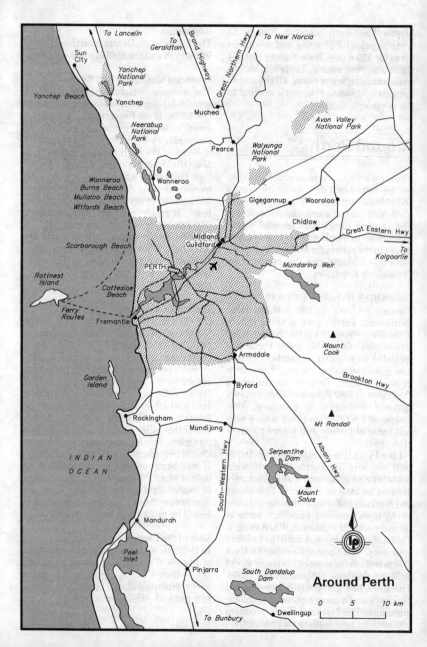

Around Perth

0   5   10 km

The Round House

On Arthur Head, near the Maritime Museum, is the Round House. Built in 1831, it's the oldest public building in WA. It actually has 12 sides and was originally a local prison (in the days before convicts were brought into WA). It was the site of the colony's first hanging. Later the building was used to hold Aborigines before they were taken to Rottnest Island. Admission is free and it's open from 10 am to 5 pm daily.

Convict Era Buildings

Other buildings date from the period after 1850, when convict labour was introduced. They include Fremantle jail, the unlucky convicts' first building task. It's still used as a prison today. The entrance on Fairbairn St is particularly picturesque. Beside the prison gates, at 16 The Terrace, is a small museum on the convict era in WA. It's open from 9.30 am to 1.30 pm Monday to Friday, from 1 to 4 pm on Saturdays, and from 11 am to 5 pm on Sundays; admission is free. Warders from the jail still live in the 1850s stone cottages on Henderson St.

Later Landmarks

Fremantle boomed during the WA gold rush and many buildings were constructed during, or shortly before, this period. They include Samson House, a colonial home of 1880 in Ellen St; the fine St John's Church of 1882; Fremantle Town Hall of 1887, in St John's Square; the former German consulate building, at 5 Mouat St, built in 1902; the Fremantle Railway Station of 1907; and the Georgian-style Old Customs House, on Cliff St. The water trough in the park in front of the station is a memorial to two men who died of thirst on an outback expedition. Proclamation Tree, near the corner of Adelaide and Edwards Sts, is a Moreton Bay fig tree planted in 1890.

Other Attractions

Fremantle is well endowed with parks, including the popular Esplanade Reserve, beside the picturesque fishing boat harbour off Marine Terrace. There are several art galleries, including the Fremantle Art Gallery, which is at 43 High St. It has a good exhibition of contemporary Western Australian art and is open daily from 12 noon to 5 pm. Praxis Gallery, at 33 Pakenham St, exhibits paintings, sculptures and other work of local and international artists. It's open from 10 am to 5 pm Tuesday to Saturday and from 2 to 5 pm Sunday. The Gallery of Original Arts & Artefacts, in Crook Lane, has boomerangs, didgeridoos, bark paintings and baskets. It is open from 10 am to 5 pm Tuesday to Friday and from 2 to 5 pm weekends.

The city is a popular centre for craft workers of all kinds and one of the best places to find them is at the imaginative Bannister St Workshops. It's open from 10 am to 5 pm Tuesday to Friday, and 12.30 to 5.30 pm weekends. There's a potters' workshop beside the Round House.

From the viewing platform on top of the Port Authority Building you can enjoy a panoramic view of Fremantle harbour. A statue of C Y O'Connor stands in front of the building. It's necessary to book for a trip to the Port Authority Building as you are required to have an escort and they're not always available at short notice.

A prime attraction is the Fremantle Markets, on South Terrace, on the corner of Henderson St. Originally opened in 1892, the market was re-opened in 1975 and attracts crowds looking for anything from craft work to vegetables, jewellery and antiques. There is a great tavern bar where buskers often perform, open from 9 am to 9 pm on Fridays, from 9 am to 5 pm on Saturdays, and from 11 am to 5 pm on Sundays.

Places to Stay

The *Bundi Kudja YHA Hostel* (tel 335 3467), at 96 Hampton St costs $10 per person. The *Freo 100* and *Freo 200 YHA Hostels* (tel 335 3537), at 81 Solomon St,

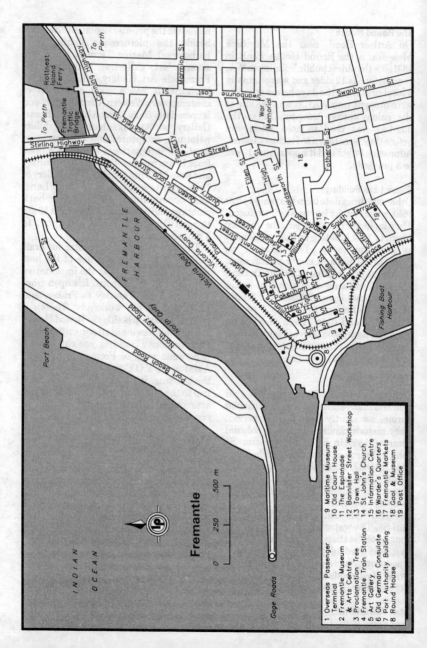

Fremantle

0   250   500 m

1 Overseas Passenger Terminal
2 Fremantle Museum & Arts Centre
3 Proclamation Tree
4 Fremantle Train Station
5 Art Gallery
6 Old German Consulate
7 Port Authority Building
8 Round House
9 Maritime Museum
10 Old Court House
11 The Esplanade
12 Bannister Street Workshop
13 Town Hall
14 St John's Church
15 Information Centre
16 Warder's Quarters
17 Fremantle Markets
18 Gaol & Museum
19 Post Office

operate as summer and long-term accommodation only. YHA members can only stay from 1 December to 31 March at $10 a night.

Both the *Federal* (tel 335 1645), at 23 William St, and the *Orient* (tel 336 2455), at 39 High St, have singles/doubles from $18/22, but the former is better value. The *Lordship*, on the corner of Moat and Phillimore Sts, is a nicely renovated hotel with rooms for $27/33. A good place for a splurge is the *Esplanade Plaza* (tel 430 4000), on the corner of Marine Terrace and Collie Sts; it has rooms from $90 to $220.

Places to Eat

There are plenty of places to eat and plenty of picturesque old pubs for a beer. Along South Terrace there's a string of places, like the popular *Papa Luigis*, at 17, which has coffee and gelati. It's packed on Sunday afternoons. Next door is the *Mexican Kitchen* and across the road is *Pizza Bella Roma*.

Upmarkets Food Centre, opposite the market, has stalls where you can get cheap Thai, Vietnamese, Japanese, Chinese and Italian food for $5 to $7 and it's excellent value. In High street *Glifada of Athens* has good souvlaki. *Roma*, at 13 High St, serves good food at good prices but not with the world's friendliest service.

The nearby *Round House* is good for a cheap breakfast or a quick snack. For Vietnamese food try the *Vung Tau*, at 19 High St, with a vegetarian menu and meals from $9 to $15.

Perth's *Fast Eddy's* has a similar place at 13 Essex St. At 31 Market St, behind the GPO, is the *Princess Coffee Lounge* – excellent value. Fish & chips on the Esplanade by the Fishing Boat Harbour is something of a Fremantle tradition. There are good, cheap counter meals at the *Newcastle Club Tavern*, on Market St. The *Federal Hotel*, on William St, and the *Lordships Hotel*, on the corner of Moat and Phillimore Sts, brew their own beer.

Entertainment

There are a number of places that have bands or a disco, the majority concentrated in the High St area. The *New Orleans Bourbon* has jazz bands (and a steak house). The *Exchange*, at 810, has a disco (and a restaurant). The *Auld Mug Tavern*, also on High St, and the *Newport Arms*, on South Terrace, also have entertainment. *Tarantella*, on Mouat St, between High and Phillimore Sts, is an exclusive nightclub.

Getting There & Away

The train between Perth and Fremantle runs every half hour or so throughout the day. Bus Nos 106 and 111 go from St Georges Terrace (north side) to Fremantle via the Canning Highway; or take the 105, which takes a longer route south of the river. Bus Nos 103 and 104 also depart from St Georges Terrace (south side) but go to Fremantle via the north side of the river. Some of the Rottnest Island ferries from Perth stop at Fremantle.

Getting Around

The Fremantle Tram is very much like the Perth Tram and does a tour of Fremantle with full commentary for $3. You can combine this tour with a tour up the Swan River to Burswood Casino for $28.

ROTTNEST ISLAND

Rotto, as it's known by the locals, is a sandy island about 19 km off the coast of Fremantle. It's 11 km long and five km wide and is very popular with Perth residents. The island was discovered by the Dutch explorer Vlaming in 1696. He named it 'Rats' Nest' because of the numerous king size rats he saw there. Actually they weren't rats at all but quokkas – marsupials that are even more prolific today.

What do you do on Rotto? Well, you cycle around, laze in the sun on the many superb beaches (the Basin is the most popular, while Parakeet Bay is the place for skinny-dipping), climb the low hills, go fishing or boating, ride a glass-bottomed boat (Rotto has some of the southernmost coral in the world and a number of shipwrecks), swim in the crystal clear water or even go quokka spotting (they're most active early in the morning).

The Rottnest settlement was originally established in 1838 as a prison for Aborigines from the mainland – the early colonists had lots of trouble imposing their ideas of private ownership on the nomadic Aborigines. The prison was abandoned in 1903 and the island soon became an escape for Perth society. It's only in the last 20 years, however, that it has really developed as a popular day-trip. The original prison settlement is of great interest as the buildings are among the oldest in WA apart. The '87 America's Cup races were held in the waters close to Rottnest.

Information

The Rottnest Island Board has an information centre just to the left of the wharf as you arrive. Here, and at the museum, you can get useful publications, such as one describing a walking tour of the old settlement buildings and another about the various shipwrecks around the island. Rottnest is very popular in the summer when the ferries and the accommodation are both heavily booked – plan ahead.

Things to See

There's an excellent little museum with exhibits about the island, its history, wildlife and shipwrecks. You can pick up the walking tour leaflet here and wander around the interesting old convict built buildings including the octagonal 1864 'Quad' where the prison cells are now hotel rooms. Vlamings Lookout, on View Hill, not far from Thomsons Bay, offers a panoramic view of the island. The island's main lighthouse was built in 1895 and is visible 60km out to sea.

The island has a number of low lying salt lakes and it's around them that you are most likely to spot quokkas, although the bus tours have regular quokka feeding points where the small marsupials seem to appear on demand.

Some of Rottnest's shipwrecks are

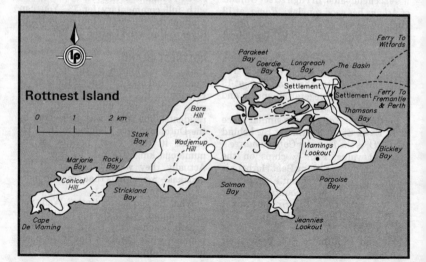

accessible to snorkellers but to get to most of them requires a boat. There are marker plaques around the island telling the sad tales of how and when the ships came to grief. Snorkelling equipment, fishing gear and boats can be hired.

Places to Stay & Eat

Most visitors to Rotto come only for the day but it's equally interesting to stay on the island. You can camp for $7 for two in hired tents at *Tent-Land* (tel 292 5033) or there are safari cabins from $12 to $22 a night. You should book hired tents and cabins in advance, although you can usually just turn up if you have your own tent.

The *Hotel Rottnest* (tel 292 5011) costs $40/65 including breakfast, and was originally built in 1864 as the residence of the governor of Western Australia. The *Rottnest Lodge Resort* (tel 292 5026) has units ranging from $30 to $90 for two.

The island has a general store, and a bakery that is famed for its fresh bread and pies. There's also a fast food centre, the licensed *Rottnest Restaurant*, and the *Hotel Rottnest*, affectionately known as the Quokka Arms.

Getting There & Away

You can fly or take the ferry to Rotto. The MV *Rottnest Explorer* plies between the Barrack St Jetty and Thompsons Bay on Rottnest once a day; there's a second service on Monday, Wednesday, Friday and Saturday. The fare is $25 return from Perth and $20 from Fremantle. There's also the faster and more expensive *Sea Spirit* motor launch. Both are operated by Boat Torque Cruises (tel 325 6033). *Golden Swan* is run by Golden Swan Cruises (tel 325 9916) at similar times, for the same prices and from the same jetty. Check at the Barrack St Jetty and in the newspapers for cheaper return tickets.

You can also get across by air in just 11 minutes from Perth Airport with WA Air Charter. The flight costs $40 return. It's even cheaper if there are two or more of you, and there are slight reductions for students. The flights leave from the new Perth Flight Centre, at the airport. There's a connecting bus between the Rottnest Airport and the wharf area.

Getting Around

Bicycles are the time-honoured way of getting around Rottnest. The number of motor vehicles is strictly limited, which makes cycling a real pleasure. Furthermore, the island is just big enough to make a day's ride fine exercise. You can bring your own bike over on the ferry ($5 return) or rent one of the 1200 available on the island for $6 a day or $36 a week. Choose carefully. If you really can't hack cycling, there's a two hour bus tour round the island. *Underwater Explorer* is a boat with windows below the waterline for viewing shipwrecks and marine life. An interesting 45 minute trip costs $8.

NORTH COAST

The coast north of Perth often has spectacular scenery with long sand dunes but it quickly becomes the inhospitable land that deterred early visitors.

Quokka

Yanchep

The Yanchep National Park is 51 km north of Perth – there's bush, caves (including the limestone Crystal and Yondemp Caves), Loch McNess, bush-walking trails and a wildlife sanctuary. Yanchep Sun City is a major marina and was the base for several unsuccessful Australian America's Cup challenges. The Atlantis Marine Park, on Two Rocks Rd, has the usual dolphins, seals and sharks.

There are a handful of places to stay, including the *Yanchep Inn* (tel (095) 61 1033), which has rooms from $28/38, and a guest house and holiday units. Bus No 356 goes to Yanchep from Perth Central Bus Station but only once daily on weekdays.

Near Yanchep is Wanneroo, an outer suburb of Perth and a popular wine producing area. Wanneroo has a lion park and the Underwater World walk-through aquarium. On Prindiville Drive, Wangara Centre, there's a miniature model village at the Gumnut Factory. On weekends the Wanneroo Markets are a worthwhile outing from Perth.

North of Yanchep is Guilderton, a popular holiday resort. The *Vergulde Draek* (Gilt Dragon), a Dutch East Indiaman, ran aground near here in 1656. The coast road ends at Lancelin, a small fishing port 130 km north of Perth, but coastal tracks continue north and may be passable with 4WD.

The Pinnacles

The small seaport of Cervantes, 257 km north of Perth by road, is the entry point for the unusual Pinnacles Desert. Here, in the coastal Nambung National Park, the flat sandy desert is punctured with peculiar limestone pillars, some only cms high, some towering up to five metres.

Check in Cervantes before attempting to drive into the park – 4WD may be necessary, but the road is normally in good condition for normal vehicles. The Pinnacles are a very popular excursion from Perth – day tours from Perth cost $40. It's possible to pick up the tour in Cervantes for $12 and save your car's suspension.

A coastal track, again 4WD, runs north to Jurien, a crayfishing centre, and south to Lancelin. The sand dunes along the coast are spectacular.

Inland

The small town of New Norcia has a curiously Spanish flavour; it was established as a Spanish Benedictine mission in 1846 and has changed little since. The monastery and abbey have some interesting paintings. The museum and art gallery is worth seeing for its old paintings, manuscripts and religious artefacts. Moora, further north, is a farming community. In the nearby Berkshire Valley an old cottage and flour mill have been restored and are now operated as a museum.

SOUTH COAST

The coast south of Perth has a softer appearance than the often harsh landscape to the north. This is another very popular beach resort area for Perth residents and many have holiday houses along the coast.

Rockingham (population 25,000)

Rockingham, just 45 minutes south of Perth, was founded in 1872 as a port, but that function, in time, was taken by Fremantle. Today Rockingham is a popular seaside resort. Close by is Penguin Island (yes, it does have penguins); boats travel there regularly in the summer, or you can walk across at low tide. The navel base of Garden Island, also close by, is not open to the public.

From Rockingham you can also head inland to the Serpentine Dam and the Serpentine Falls National Park, where there are wildflowers and pleasant bushland. You can get to Rockingham on a No 120 bus from Fremantle or a No 116 from Perth.

Places to Stay & Eat The *CWA Rockingham* (tel 527 9560), at 108 Parkin St, is operated by a friendly couple and is good value, with two units, each sleeping six, at $15 a person for members, $20 for non-members. The *Palm Beach Caravan Park* is at 37 Fisher St. The *Ocean Clipper Inn* (tel 527 8000), on Patterson Rd, has singles/doubles for 50/67.

For meals try the hotels. Otherwise, there is *El Roccos*, at 84 Parkin St, for good Mexican food or the *Silver Dragon*, on Rockingham Rd.

Mandurah (population 11,000)

At the mouth of the huge estuary of the Serpentine River, Mandurah is yet another popular beach resort, 80 km south of Perth. Dolphins are often seen in the estuary. The town also has Hall's Cottage (open Sunday afternoon), built in the 1830s, and a geological museum. Prolific bird life can be seen on the narrow coastal salt lakes Clifton and Preston, 20 km south. A No 116 bus from Perth or a No 117 from Fremantle will get you to Mandurah.

Places to Stay & Eat The *Brighton Hotel* (tel 535 1242), on Mandurah Terrace, is the best deal in town, with singles/doubles starting at $20/40; they also have good, cheap counter meals. The similarly priced *Oll 'Roy Lodge* (tel 535 1265) is at 52 Pinjarra Rd. One of the most convenient of the many caravan parks is *Baxter Court* (tel 535 1363) with sites for $8 for two and on-site vans from $90 a week.

The *Madora Bay Tavern*, on Madora Bay Rd, is a good cheap place to eat, and has live music. The *Mei Jing* Chinese restaurant is reportedly excellent.

Inland

Head inland from the coast to Pinjarra, a town with a number of old buildings picturesquely sited on the banks of the Murray River. About two km from the town is the Old Blythewood Homestead, an 1859 colonial farm. Hotham Valley Railway steam trains run from here in winter only (May to October) to Dwellingup. This quiet little town has fine

views over Peel Inlet, behind Mandurah, and out across the Indian Ocean. This is an area of jarrah forests, as is Boddington, further inland.

Places to Stay & Eat In Pinjarra the *Premier Hotel* costs $16 a person. The *Exchange Hotel* (tel 31 1209) has singles/doubles for $20/30. The *Heritage Tea Rooms* has sandwiches, quiche or even a ploughman's lunch for $5.

AVON VALLEY

The green and lush Avon Valley looks very English and was a delight to homesick early settlers. In the spring this area is particularly rich in wildflowers. The valley was first settled in 1830, only a year after Perth was founded, so there are many early buildings to be seen.

Getting There & Away

The Avon Valley towns all have bus connections to Perth; contact Westrail on 326 2222. Fares from Perth are $7.40 to Toodyay, Northam and York; $3.50 to Mundaring Weir; $6.10 to Wooroloo, and $10 to Beverley. It is also possible to take the *Prospector* rail service to Toodyay ($7.40) and Northam ($8.70).

Toodyay (population 600)

There are numerous old buildings in this historic town, many of them built by convicts. The local tourist centre is housed in the 1850s Connor's Mill, on Stirling Terrace.

The old Memorial Hall is now a public toilet. Don't miss the Old Newcastle Goal Museum on Clinton St, or the 1862 St Stephen's Church. The Moondyne Gallery is interesting for the story it tells of bushranger Joseph Bolitho Johns. Close to town there's a winery which began operating in the 1870s, while in the town itself there's a pleasant, old country pub with a shady beer garden. Downriver from Toodyay is the Avon Valley National Park.

Places to Stay & Eat The centrally located

Old Toodyay Club YHA Hostel (tel 574 2435), on Stirling St, costs $8. Opposite is the *Freemasons Hotel* (tel 574 2201) with basic rooms for $16 a person and reasonably priced counter meals. On the same street is the *Victoria Hotel/Motel* (tel 574 2206), with rooms for $12 a person and units for $28/48. *Toodyay Caravan Park* (tel 574 2612), on Marshalling Yard Rd, has sites from around $5 for two.

Northam (population 6800)

Northam, the major town of the Avon Valley, is a busy farming centre on the railway line to Kalgoorlie. At one time the line from Perth ended abruptly here and miners had to make the rest of the weary trek to the gold fields by road.

The tourist office is at 3 Beavis Place. The 1836 Morby Cottage houses a museum, open Sunday only. The old railway station is being restored and turned into a museum also.

At Wooroloo, about midway between Northam and Midland, is El Cabello Blanco. This is a major Perth tourist attraction with performing Andalusian horses, plenty to amuse the kids, sport facilities, a restaurant and a motel. Performances are at 2.15 pm from Tuesday to Sunday and cost $9. For further details call (008) 095 525 toll free.

Places to Stay & Eat The *Northam YHA Hostel* (tel 22 3323), on Fitzgerald St, is in the old railway station and has some dorms in railway carriages for $7. On the same street, at 426, is the *Grand Hotel* (tel 22 1024) with basic rooms for $12 a person. The *Avon Bridge Hotel* (tel 22 1023) has singles/doubles for $18/30 and $2 lunch specials. Every second Sunday the Music Club has a music evening from 4 to 8 pm at the *Commercial Hotel* (tel 22 1049), which also has singles/doubles for $20/35. *O'Harah's at the Shamrock* has good counter meals from $5 to $10; the *Colonial Kitchen* is much pricier.

York (population 1100)

The oldest inland town in Western Australia, York was first settled in 1830. It has a tourist office at 105 Avon St. A stroll down the main street, with its many old buildings, is a real step back in time. The excellent Residency Museum from the 1840s, the old town hall, Castle Hotel dating from the coaching days, Faversham House, the Motor Museum, the old police station and court house, the Sandalwood Press printing museum and Settlers' Hall are all of interest. Near York is the Balladong Farm Museum - a working farm of the pioneering era.

Places to Stay & Eat The *YHA Hostel* (tel 41 1372) is on South St, not far from the old railway station, and has dorm beds for $7. The *Castle Hotel* (tel 41 1007), on Avon Terrace, is good value with rooms from $28/45. The only caravan park is *Mt Bakewell* (tel 41 1421) with sites for two for $8.

The *Castle* and *York* hotels have good counter meals. The *Whispers Restaurant* has good home-made bread, meals in the $5 to $10 range and a Friday night smorgasbord.

Beverley (population 750)

South of York is Beverley, noted for its fine aeronautical museum. Exhibits include a locally constructed biplane, built between 1928 and 1930. The Avondale Research Station is five km west of Beverley and has a large collection of agricultural machines as well as stables and barns. Further upriver are Brookton and Pigelly, in an area well known for its wildflowers.

Places to Stay The ordinary *Beverley Hotel* (tel 46 1190), on Vincent St, has singles/doubles with breakfast for $26/45. The *Beverley Caravan Park* (tel 46 1200), on the same street, has camping sites for $8.

THE DARLING RANGE

The hills that fence Perth in against the coast are popular for picnics, barbecues and bushwalks. There are also some excellent lookouts from which you can see over Perth and down to the coast. Araleun with its waterfalls, the fire lookout at Mt Dale and Churchman's Brook are all off the Brookton Highway. Other places of interest include the Zig Zag at Gooseberry Hill and Lake Leschenaultia.

From Kalamunda there are fine views over Perth. The *Kalamunda YHA Hostel* (tel 293 3869), on the Mundaring Weir Rd, costs $7. Get there on a No 298, 300 or 302 bus via Maida Vale and Forrestfield; or No 292, 299 or 305 via Wattle Grove and Lesmurdie. Taking one route out and the other back makes an interesting circular tour of the hill suburbs. There's a good walking track at Sullivan Rock, 69 km south-east, on the Albany Highway.

Mundaring Weir

Mundaring, in the ranges only 40 km from Perth, is the site of the Mundaring Weir – the dam built at the turn of the century to supply water to the gold fields over 500 km to the east. The reservoir has an attractive setting and is a popular excursion for Perth residents. The C Y O'Connor Museum has models and exhibits about the water pipeline, in its time one of the most amazing engineering feats in the world. It's open Monday, Friday and Saturday from 2 to 4 pm, Wednesday from 10 am to 12 noon and Sunday from 1 to 4 pm.

Near Mundaring is the Old Mahogany Inn. Built in 1837 as an outpost for travellers it now houses a museum and tearoom. It's open from Wednesday to Sunday from 11 am to 6 pm. The John Forrest National Park in the Darling Range is also near Mundaring.

Places to Stay The *YHA Hostel* (tel 295 1809), on Mundaring Weir Rd, is eight km from the town and costs $7. In town, the *Mundaring Hotel* (tel 295 1006), on the corner of Nicholl and Jacoby Sts, has singles/doubles for $18/28. The *Mundaring Caravan Park* (tel 205 1125) is a km west

of town, on the Great Eastern Highway, and has sites for $6.50.

The Nullarbor

It's a little over 2700 km between Perth in Western Australia and Adelaide in South Australia - not much less than the distance from London to Moscow. The long, lonely Eyre Highway crosses the edge of the vast Nullarbor Plain - bad Latin for 'no trees' and an accurate description of this flat, treeless wasteland. (Along the road there actually are trees, because this coastal fringe receives regular rain, especially in winter.)

The road across the Nullarbor takes its name from John Eyre, the explorer who made the first east-west crossing, in 1841. It was a superhuman effort that took five months of nightmare hardship and resulted in the death of Eyre's companion John Baxter. In 1877 a telegraph line was laid across the Nullarbor, roughly delineating the route the first road would take. Later in the century miners en route to the gold fields of WA followed the same telegraph line route across the empty plains. In 1896 the first bicycle crossing was made and in 1912 the first car was driven across, but in the next 12 years only three more cars managed to traverse the continent.

In 1941 the war inspired the building of a trans-continental highway, just as it had the Alice Springs to Darwin route. It was a rough-and-ready track when completed, and in the '50s only a few vehicles a day made the crossing. In the '60s the traffic flow increased to more than 30 vehicles a day and in 1969 the WA government surfaced the road as far as the South Australian border. Finally, in 1976, the last stretch from the South Australian border was surfaced and now the Nullarbor crossing is a much easier drive, but still a hell of a long one.

There are actually three routes across

the Nullarbor. The new, surfaced road runs close to the coast on the South Australian side. The Nullarbor region ends dramatically on the coast of the Great Australian Bight, at cliffs that drop sheerly into the roaring sea. It's easy to see why this was a seafarer's nightmare, for a ship driven on to the coast would quickly be pounded to pieces against the cliffs, and climbing them would be a near impossibility. On the South Australian side, the old Eyre Highway is a little distance north of the coast while the third route, the Indian-Pacific Railway, is about 150 km north of the coast and actually on the Nullarbor Plain – unlike the road, which only runs on the fringes of the great plain. One stretch of the railway runs dead straight for 478 km – the longest piece of straight railway line in the world.

THE EYRE HIGHWAY

Ceduna is really the end of the line on the South Australian side of the Eyre Highway. You might travel this far to see places in South Australia, but if you went any further west, it would only be for one reason – to leave South Australia and go to Western Australia. Ceduna is still 520 km from Eucla, which is on the South Australia/Western Australia border. From Ceduna it's another 729 km to Norseman, where the Eyre Highway ends. By anyone's standards, that's a long way. Ceduna's name comes from an Aboriginal word meaning 'a place to sit down and rest' – perhaps it's aptly named.

Penong (South Australia)

Westbound from Ceduna there are several places with petrol and other facilities along the road. Penong sees the end of all traces of cultivation and the start of the real treeless plain. You can make a short detour south of the town to see the Pink Lake, Point Sinclair and Cactus Beach – a little known surf beach that is a 'must' for any serious surfer making the east-west journey. Between Penong and Nundroo is Fowlers Bay, a ghost town. There is good fishing in the waters around the bay. Nearby is Mexican Hat Beach, named after a rock island that of course looks like a mexican hat.

The *Penong Hotel* (tel (086) 25 1050) has basic rooms for $16 a person. It also

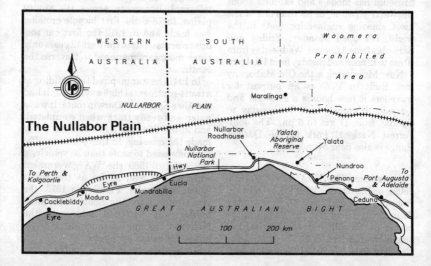

serves counter meals. The Golden Fleece service station across the road has a restaurant and a take-away.

Nundroo (South Australia)

Nundroo is the real edge of the Nullarbor. Colona Homestead is the start of the last section of the highway to have been surfaced. The road passes through the Yalata Aboriginal Reserve and you'll often see Aborigines selling boomerangs and other souvenirs by the side of the road. You can also buy these in the roadhouse.

The *Nundroo Hotel-Motel* (tel (086) 25 6120) has singles/doubles for $43/48 and camping sites from $5. There is a licensed restaurant, take-away food and a swimming pool. The *Yalata Aboriginal Community Roadhouse* (tel (086) 25 6990) has rooms from $38/42 and tent sites from $3.50. There's a restaurant and take-away and many locally made Aboriginal artefacts on sale.

Nullarbor Roadhouse (South Australia)

For most of the way across, the highway runs to the south of the Nullarbor Plain on the sloping stretch closer to the coast. Around Nullarbor Roadhouse are many caves that should be explored only with extreme care and are recommended to experienced cave explorers only. If you're walking around watch out for the numerous wombat holes and poisonous snakes. A dirt road leads to a nice beach 30 km away – ask directions at the roadhouse. From the tiny settlement of Nullarbor Station, where you can actually see the plain, to the WA border 184 km to the west, the new road has been built right along the coast, with scenic lookouts offering superb views over the Great Australian Bight.

The *Nullarbor Hotel-Motel* (tel (086) 25 6271) has rooms from $40/50, camping sites from $5 and on-site vans from $23.

The Border & Eucla

At the border a sign tells you to put your watch back 45 minutes. From here to Caiguna you're in an intermediate time zone, halfway between South Australian and Western Australian time. There's a Travellers' Village at the border with camping facilities, a motel, cabins and a restaurant. Many people have their photo taken with the international sign pinpointing distances to many parts of the world. Behind it is a tasteless five metre high fibreglass kangaroo.

Just across the border is Eucla, which has picturesque ruins of an old telegraph repeater and weather station, first opened in 1877. The telegraph line now runs along the railway line, far to the north. The station, five km from the roadhouse, is gradually being engulfed by the sand dunes. You can also inspect the historic jetty, which is visible from the top of the dunes. The dunes are a spectacular sight as you leave Eucla and drop down into the Eucla Pass. The Eucla area also has many caves, including the well-known Koonalda Cave with its 45 metre high chamber. You enter by ladder. Like other Nullarbor Caves, it's really for experienced cave explorers only.

The *WA-SA Border Village* (tel (090) 39 3474) has rooms from $30/35 and tent sites from $5. The *Eucla Amber Hotel-Motel* (tel (090) 39 3468) has rooms from $17/26 and tent sites from $1 a person. Both places have a restaurant, take-away food and a bar; the Eucla Hotel also has a swimming pool.

Mundrabilla & Madura

After Eucla the next sign of life is the tiny settlement of Mundrabilla, which has a bird sanctuary behind the motel. Next up is Madura, close to the hills of the Hampton Tablelands. At one time horses were bred here for the Indian army. You get good views over the plains as the road climbs. The ruins of the Old Madura Homestead, several km west of the new homestead by a dirt track, have some old machinery and other equipment. Caves in the area include the large Mullamullang

Caves, north-west of Madura, with three lakes and many side passages.

The *Mundrabilla Motor Hotel* (tel (090) 39 3465) has rooms from $10 a person and tent sites from $5. The *Madura Hospitality Inns* (tel (090) 39 3464) has rooms from $44/55 and tent sites from $5.

Cocklebiddy

At Cocklebiddy are the stone ruins of an Aboriginal mission. The Cocklebiddy Cave is the largest of the Nullarbor caves – in 1983 a team of French explorers set a record there for the deepest cave dive in the world. With 4WD you can travel south of Cocklebiddy to Twilight Cove, where there are 75 metre high limestone cliffs. The Eyre Bird Observatory, established in 1977, is housed in the Eyre Telegraph Station, an 1897 stone building in the Nuytsland Nature Reserve, surrounded by mallee scubland. Other fauna and flora are studied there as well as birds. A small museum at the rear of the station has exhibits from the days of the telegraph line and of the legendary stationmaster, William Graham.

At Caiguna turn your watch back another 45 minutes to Western Australian time. The roadhouse Telegraph Museum depicts the history of communications.

Places to Stay & Eat The *Cocklebiddy Hotel/Motel* (tel (090) 39 3462) has rooms for $60/70 and tent sites from $3. The *Eyre Bird Observatory* (tel (090) 39 3450) provides accommodation by prior arrangement only. Full board and return transport from Cocklebiddy or Microwave Tower is included in the price of $48 for the first night and $33 for subsequent nights. Guests staying only one night pay an extra $10 and YHA card holders get a $5 discount. The observatory is 42 km southeast of Cocklebiddy and 4WD is needed to get there. Guests are expected to help out with washing and cooking.

At Caiguna the *John Eyre Motel* (tel (090) 39 3459) has rooms for $50/58, tent sites from $5 and on-site vans from $10.

Balladonia

It's one of the loneliest stretches of the Nullarbor from Cocklebiddy to Balladonia, including a straight stretch of road 144 km long! Shortly before Balladonia, three km north of the road, are a number of natural rock waterholes known as Afghan Rocks. They often hold water far into the summer and were named after an Afghani camel driver who was shot when he was found washing his feet in the water. Balladonia and Newmanns Rocks are also worthwhile seeing. The Crocker family have a fine art gallery with paintings of the Eyre Highway. Visits can be arranged by phoning (090) 39 3456 between 9 am and 4.30 pm, admission is $1.50.

After Balladonia you may see the remains of old stone fences built to enclose stock. Clay saltpans are also visible in the area. The mine shafts and mullock heaps around Norseman signal the end of the Eyre Highway and the point where you either turn north to the gold fields or south to the coastal area.

Places to Stay & Eat The *Balladonia Hotel/Motel* (tel (090) 39 3453) has rooms from $33/44 and tent sites from $3 for two.

The *Fraser Range Station* (tel (090) 39 3457) is a km from the Eyre Highway, about 102 km east of Norseman and 88 km west of Balladonia. This family run sheep station is set in picturesque countryside with kangaroos, emus, wild camels and many birds. The station is an associate *YHA Hostel* with basic but adequate facilities. Rooms in the restored stone shearing quarters have bunk beds for $11 ($8 for YHA members) or there are camping sites for $6. There's a kitchen with a wood burning stove and a refrigerator but bring your own supplies. If you are travelling by bus phone from the closest town for a pick up from the Eyre Highway turn-off.

Crossing the Nullarbor

See the Perth Getting There & Away section for air, rail, hitching and bus information across the Nullarbor. Although the Nullarbor is no longer a torture trail where cars get shaken to bits by potholes and corrugations or where you're going to die of thirst waiting for another vehicle if you break down, it's still wise to avoid difficulties whenever possible.

The longest distance between fuel stops is about 200 km, so if you're foolish enough to run out of petrol midway, you'll have a nice long round trip to get more. Getting help for a mechanical breakdown could be equally time consuming and very expensive, so make sure your vehicle is in good shape and that you've got plenty of petrol, good tyres and at least a basic kit of simple spare parts. Carry some drinking water just in case you do have to sit it out by the roadside on a hot summer day. Take it easy on the Nullarbor – plenty of people try to set speed records and plenty more have made a real mess of their cars when they've run into big roos, particularly at night.

Gold Country

Fifty years after its establishment in 1829 the WA colony was still going nowhere, so the government in Perth was delighted when gold was discovered at Southern Cross in 1887. That first strike petered out pretty quickly but more discoveries followed and WA profited from the gold boom for the rest of the century. It was gold that put WA on the map and finally gave it the population to make it viable in its own right, rather than just a distant offshoot of the east coast colonies.

The major strikes were made in 1892 in Coolgardie and nearby Kalgoorlie, but in the whole gold fields area, Kalgoorlie is the only large town left. Coolgardie's period of prosperity lasted until 1905 and many other gold towns went from nothing to populations of as much as 10,000 then back to nothing in just 10 years. Nevertheless, the towns made the

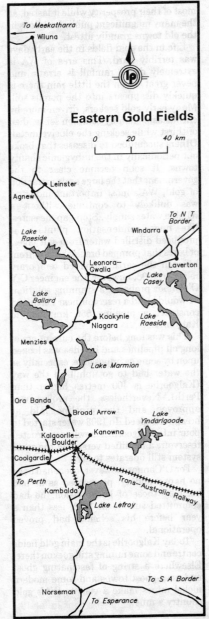

most of their prosperity while it lasted, as the many magnificent public buildings in the old towns grandly attest.

Life in the gold fields in the early days was terribly hard. This area of WA is extremely dry – rainfall is erratic and never great. Even the little rain there is quickly disappears into the porous soil. Many early gold seekers, driven more by enthusiasm than by common sense, died of thirst while seeking the elusive metal. Others succumbed to diseases that broke out periodically in the unhygienic shanty towns. It soon became clear to the government that the large scale extraction of gold, WA's most important industry, was unlikely to continue without a reliable water supply. Stop-gap measures, like huge condensation plants that produced distilled water from salt lakes, or bores that pumped brackish water from beneath the earth, provided temporary relief. In 1898, however, the engineer C Y O'Connor proposed a stunning solution: he would build a reservoir near Perth and construct a pipeline 556 km long to Kalgoorlie.

This was long before the current era of long oil pipelines and his idea was looked upon by some as impossible, especially as the water had to go uphill all the way (Kalgoorlie is 400 metres higher than Perth). Nevertheless, the project was approved and the pipeline laid at breakneck speed. In 1903 water started to pour into Kalgoorlie's newly constructed reservoir; a modified version of the same system still operates today.

For O'Connor, however, there had been no happy ending: persecuted as he had been by those of lesser vision, he had committed suicide in 1902, less than a year before his scheme had proved operational.

Today Kalgoorlie is the main gold fields centre and some mining still goes on there. Elsewhere a string of fascinating ghost and near-ghost towns and some modern nickel mines make a visit to WA's gold country a must.

KALGOORLIE (population 20,000)

Kalgoorlie, the longest lasting and most successful of the WA gold towns, rose to prominence later than Coolgardie. In 1893 Paddy Hannan, a prospector from way back, set out from Coolgardie for another gold strike but stopped at the site of Kalgoorlie and found, just lying around on the surface, enough gold to spark another rush. As in so many places, the surface gold soon petered out but at Kalgoorlie the miners went deeper and more and more gold was found. There weren't the storybook chunky nuggets of solid gold – Kalgoorlie's gold had to be extracted from the rocks by costly and complex processes of grinding, roasting and chemical action – but there was plenty of it.

Kalgoorlie quickly reached fabled heights of prosperity and the enormous and magnificent public buildings of the turn of the century are evidence of its fabulous wealth. After WW I, however, increasing production costs and static gold prices led to Kalgoorlie's slow but steady decline. Today the 'golden mile' of Kalgoorlie's heyday is a shadow of its once hectic self and the only major operation is the huge Mt Charlotte Mine, close to Paddy Hannan's original find. This limited gold mining, the opening of nickel mines in the area and a busy tourist trade ensure Kalgoorlie's continuing importance as an outback centre.

Orientation

Although Kalgoorlie sprang up close to Paddy Hannan's original find, the mining emphasis soon shifted a few km away to the golden mile, a square mile which was probably the wealthiest gold mining area for its size in the world. The satellite town of Boulder developed to service this town. There's a direct road between the two towns, as well as a longer route via by the airport.

Kalgoorlie itself is a grid of broad, tree lined streets. The main street, Hannan St, is flanked by imposing public buildings and is, of course, wide enough to turn a camel train in – a popular outback measure. You'll find most of the hotels, restaurants and offices on or close to Hannan St.

Information

There's an informative tourist bureau on Hannan St where you can get a good map of Kalgoorlie and buy the excellent and information packed *Gold Rush Country* map, for 50c. The office is open from 8.30 am to 5 pm Monday to Friday and from 9 am to 5 pm weekends. For an excellent account of the fascinating Kalgoorlie story read *The Glittering Years*, by Arthur Bennet (St George Books). There's a daily paper in Kal (as it's known to its friends), the *Kalgoorlie Miner*.

Kal can get very hot in December and January, and overall the cool winter months are the best time to visit. From late August to the end of September, however, the town is packed and accommodation of any type can be difficult to find. The RACWA (tel 21 1900) has an office on the corner of Porter and Hannan Sts.

Hainault Tourist Mine

Kalgoorlie's biggest attraction is the Hainault Mine, right in the golden mile, near Boulder. Opened in 1898, the mine ceased operation in the 1960s. Today you can take the lift cage 60 metres down into the bowels of the earth and make an enthralling tour around the drives and crosscuts of the mine, guided by an ex-

1	Inland City Hotel
2	Railway Hotel
3	Town Hall
4	Kalgoorlie Hotel
5	Pizza Cantina
6	Geological Museum
7	Victora Tavern
8	Tourist Office
9	Post Office
10	Airlines of WA
11	Palace Hotel
12	Exchange Hotel
13	Surrey House
14	RAC of WA
15	Golden Mile Museum
16	Hannan Tree

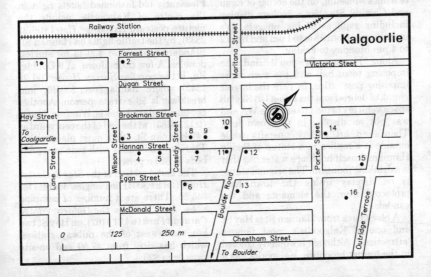

miner. There's also a tour of the surface workings and an audio-visual show on mining and Kalgoorlie itself. It costs $7.20 for an underground tour, and $8.30 for a surface tour as well. You can wander around the surface workings yourself for free. Underground tours are made at 10.30 am, and 1, 2.30 and 3.15 pm daily.

Near the mine is Lions Lookout, which provides a good view over the golden mile, Boulder and Kalgoorlie. You can make an interesting loop around the golden mile by catching the 'Rattler', a tourist train complete with commentary which makes an hour long trip Monday to Friday at 11 am and on Sunday at 1.30 and 3 pm. It leaves from Boulder railway station, passing the old mining works and the huge mountains of 'slime' – the cast-offs from the mining process.

Other Attractions

Just off the end of Hannan St you can climb the road (ignore the 'private' sign) to Mt Charlotte and the town's reservoir. The view over the town is good but there's little to see of the reservoir, which is covered to limit evaporation. The School of Mines Museum, on the corner of Egan and Cassidy Sts, has a geology display including replicas of big nuggets. It's usually open from 9 am to 1 pm and from 2 to 4 pm Monday to Friday.

Along Hannan St you'll find the imposing town hall and the even more imposing post office. In 1979 the largest chunk of debris from the fallen US Skylab space vehicle crashed to earth in WA and was put on display in the town hall. There's an art gallery upstairs while outside is a replica of a statue of Paddy Hannan himself holding a water bag that is a drinking fountain. The original statue is on display inside the town hall, protected from the elements and the vandals.

A block back from Hannan St is Hay St and one of Kalgoorlie's most famous 'attractions'. Although it's quietly ignored in the tourist brochure, Kalgoorlie has a block long strip of brothels where the ladies of the night beckon passing men to their true-blue Aussie galvanised iron doorways. Nelson's eye has been turned to this activity for so long that it has become an accepted and historical part of the town. Usually Kalgoorlie's famous (and illegal) two-up schools are also ignored but in late '82 a Perth gaming squad raid caused outrage amongst local citizens, including the mayor.

On Outridge Terrace the tiny British Arms Hotel (the narrowest hotel in Australia) now houses the interesting Golden Mile Museum, which has many relics from Kalgoorlie's pioneering days. It's open from 10.30 am to 4.30 pm daily, and admission is $1.50. A little further along Outridge Terrace is Paddy Hannan's tree, marking the spot where the first gold strike was made. The Royal Flying Doctor Base can be visited from Monday to Friday at 2.30 pm. Hammond Park is a small fauna reserve with a miniature German castle. It is open seven days a week from 9 am to 5.30 pm.

Places to Stay

Pleasantly old-fashioned hotels right in the centre of Kalgoorlie include the picture-postcard *Exchange Hotel* (tel 21 2833), by the traffic lights on Hannan St. Standard rooms cost $30/45 for singles/doubles. A few doors down, at 9 Boulder Rd, is the popular *Surrey House* (tel 21 1340) where rooms cost $30/40, and breakfast is $6 extra a person. Another popular budget hotel is *Windsor House* (tel 21 5483), at the end of the courtyard at 147 Hannan St. It's a quiet place with a TV room and rooms with twin or double beds at $20 a person.

The motel section of the *Star & Garter Hotel* (tel 21 3004) has singles/doubles for $45/55. There are a number of camping sites. The closest is the *Golden Village Caravan Park* (tel 21 4162), on Hay St two km south-west of the railway station, which has sites from $7.50 and on-site vans from $23.

Places to Eat

There are plenty of counter meal pubs and cafes, particularly along Hannan St. The *Victoria Tavern* does good counter food at lunch times and in the evenings. The *Exchange Hotel*, on the corner of Hannan and Boulder Sts, has the Winter Lounge with main courses $8. In the front bar there are cheaper meals in the $4 to $6.50 range. The *Hotel York* also does counter meals in the Steak Bar.

At 275 Hannan St is the *Kalgoorlie Cafe*, which has burgers and other fast food. *Matteo's*, at 113, does the best pizzas. Try the *Victoria Cafe*, at 246 Hannan St, for an early breakfast. The *Union Club Bistro*, in the Midas Motel, 409 Hannan St, is a good restaurant for a splurge.

Kalgoorlie brews its own beer, called Hannan's.

Getting There & Away

Air Ansett WA fly from Perth to Kalgoorlie several times daily for $147. The Ansett WA office (tel 21 2277) is at 70 Maritana St.

Skywest have two direct flights a day for $139; for reservations call Ansett WA. Mid-State Air (tel (09) 277 4022) fly from Perth via Southern Cross for $105. Goldfields Air Services fly several times a week from Esperance to Kalgoorlie, via Norseman for $98.

Bus Pioneer, Deluxe and Greyhound buses operate through Kalgoorlie on their Sydney ($190), Melbourne ($170) and Adelaide ($135) to Perth services. The fare to Perth is $51 but most of the buses pull into Kalgoorlie at an ungodly hour of the night when everything is closed up and finding a place to stay can be difficult. The distance from Kalgoorlie to Perth is 595 km.

There's a bus three times a week to Esperance – once via Kambalda and Norseman and twice via Coolgardie and Norseman; the trip takes 5½ hours and costs $43.

Train The daily Prospector railcar service from Perth takes eight hours and costs $48 including a meal. It's modern, comfortable and provides good views of the generally monotonous scenery. From Perth you can book seats at the WAGTC office in Hay St or at the Westrail terminal (tel 326 2222). It's wise to book as this service is fairly popular, particularly in the tourist season.

Most days of the week the Prospector, like the bus services, arrives in Kalgoorlie at an uncomfortably late hour.

The Indian-Pacific and Trans-Australian also go through Kalgoorlie. Fares are $130 to Adelaide, $174 to Melbourne and $236 to Sydney for economy class seats without meals. There are also economy and 1st class berths.

Getting Around

You can rent cars from Hertz, Budget, Avis or Letz (at the airport). If you want to explore very far you'll either have to have wheels, hitch or take a tour since public transport is limited. A taxi to the airport costs $7. You can hire bicycles at Johnston Cycles (tel 21 1157), at 76 Boulder St, for $3 an hour or $11 a day.

Between Kal and Boulder there's a regular bus service (timetable from the tourist office) costing 95c. You'll have to walk about two km from the Boulder junction to the Hainault Mine but hitching shouldn't be too difficult. In the morning you can take the school bus to Coolgardie; the return bus leaves in the afternoon.

Goldrush Tours are the main tour operators in Kalgoorlie. Book through the tourist office or direct from their office at Palace Chambers, Maritana St. They have town tours ($14, not including admission charges) and tours to Coolgardie ($21), Kambalda ($17.50) and ghost towns ($26). There's also a gold detector tour for avid fossickers ($17.50), and in August and September there are wildflower tours for $31.

Around Kalgoorlie

Kalgoorlie is the hub of the gold fields but there are other towns of great interest, although many are mere ghost towns today. Coolgardie, only 40 km from Kalgoorlie, is the best known while others vary from odd heaps of rubble to tiny outposts with superb town halls and equally magnificent hotels, kept alive only by the tourist trade.

Before setting out to explore this area get a copy of the excellent and highly informative *Gold Rush Country* map. Remember that this is a remote, sparsely populated, rugged and very dry area – carry plenty of water and be prepared if you intend to wander off the beaten track. There is still quite a bit of local private mining going on – the lure continues!

BOULDER

The tourist office is at 106 Bart St, sharing the Goldfields War Museum building. The office is open from 9 am to 1 pm and from 1.30 to 4 pm Monday to Friday, and from 9 to 11.30 am Saturday.

There is a fine old town hall in Boulder. The Goldfields War Museum is open from 9 am to 1 pm and from 1.30 to 4.30 pm daily, and admission is $1. The Boulder Station is an 1897 building and the home to the Eastern Goldfields Historical Society Museum. It is open from 10 am to 12.30 pm Monday to Saturday and from 10 am to 4 pm Sunday; admission is 50c.

In the heyday of the golden mile the rip-roaring hotels of the Boulder Block never closed and thirsty miners off the shifts poured into them night and day. There's nothing much to see now, but there are plans to redevelop the Boulder Block area. On the other side of the golden mile loop, on the corner of Contention and Beal Sts, Fimiston, is the 1896 Boulder Block Tavern with a mine shaft right in the lounge bar. Miners used to sneak nuggets to the bartender via this shaft.

In Boulder you can get counter meals at

Tattersalls. *Lindrum's*, on the corner of Bart and Lane Sts, is a good bar and restaurant, with main meals from $10 to $15. You can try the *Wah On* Chinese restaurant, next to the Goldfields War Museum.

COOLGARDIE (population 900)

A popular pause for people crossing the Nullarbor and also the turn-off for Kalgoorlie, Coolgardie really is a ghost of its former self. You only have to glance at the huge town hall and post office building to appreciate the size that Coolgardie once was. Gold was discovered here in 1892 and by the turn of the century the population had boomed to 15,000. The gold then petered out and the town withered away just as quickly. There's still plenty to interest the visitor though.

For a start there are 150 informative historical markers scattered in and around the town. They tell of what was once there or what the buildings were formerly used for. The Goldfields Exhibition is open from 8 am to 4.30 pm daily and has a fascinating display of gold fields memorabilia. You can even find out about American President Herbert Hoover's days on the WA gold fields. It's the largest museum in the gold fields and worth the $3.50 admission, which includes a film, shown at the Coolgardie Tourist Bureau (in the same building as the museum). The railway station is also operated as a museum and here you can learn the incredible story of the miner who was trapped 300 metres underground by floodwater in 1907 and rescued by divers 10 days later.

Just out of town, on the Perth side, is the town cemetery, which includes many old graves such as that of pioneer explorer Edward Giles. During Coolgardie's unhealthiest period it's said that 'one half of the population buried the other half'. Coolgardie's most amazing sight, however, is Prior's Museum. Right by the road, it's a large empty lot, cluttered with every kind of antique junk you can imagine, from old mining equipment to half a dozen rusting old cars. It's open 24 hours a day, 365 days a year and admission is free!

Other attractions are Swn-Y-Gwynt Wildlife Park (admission $1, feeding time 3.30 pm); Warden Finnerty's National Trust restored house (admission $2); the Bottle Collection & Aboriginal Artifacts (above the tourist bureau) and the Prison Tree and jail. At the Camel Farm (tel 26 6159), four km west of town on the Great Eastern Highway, you can take camel rides or organise longer camel treks. Tom Neacy's Tours have town tours departing from the Coolgardie Tourist Bureau for $12 – see the bureau for more details.

Places to Stay & Eat

Coolgardie's fine old *Youth Hostel* (tel 26 6051), at 56-60 Gnarlbine Rd, costs $7.50. Singles/doubles are $20/30 in the *Railway Lodge* (tel 26 6166) or $15/30 in the *Denver City Hotel* (tel 26 6031), both on Bayley St. The fine old Denver City has long shady verandahs and is one of Coolgardie's original hotels.

At the *Safari Village Holiday Centre* (tel 26 6037), at 2 Renou St, singles/doubles cost $30/38. The *Coolgardie Caravan Park* (tel 26 6009) has sites for $6 and on-site vans for $25.

The *Denver Hotel* does counter lunches and teas. Surprisingly the *Golden Fleece Roadhouse* has good grilled fish with salad for $9. *Pinkys Cafe* does good breakfasts and light meals for $8.

Getting There & Away

Greyhound, Pioneer and Deluxe all pass through Coolgardie, as well as through Kalgoorlie. Bus Australia stop in Coolgardie only. The Kalgoorlie trains also stop at the Bonnie Vale Station, 12 km away.

NORSEMAN (population 1900)

To most people Norseman is just a crossroad where you turn east for the trans-Nullarbor Eyre Highway journey, south to Esperance along the Leeuwin Way or north to Coolgardie and Perth.

The town also has gold mines, some still in operation, and the Historical & Geological Museum which has household items and mining tools from the gold rush days. It's open weekdays from 10 am to 4 pm and admission is $2. At the State Battery it is possible to see the ore from local mines being crushed weekdays between 10 am and 4 pm.

The graffiti covered Dundas Rocks are huge boulders in picturesque countryside 28 km south of Norseman. There's a tourist bureau on Roberts St.

Places to Stay

The *Norseman Backpackers Hostel*, at the junction of the highways to Kalgoorlie, Esperance and the Nullarbor, has beds from $6 a person. Otherwise there's the *Norseman Hotel* (tel 39 1115), the *Norseman Eyre Motel* (tel 39 1130) and the *Norseman Caravan Park* (tel 39 1262).

Getting There & Away

Skywest fly to Norseman from Perth via Kalgoorlie for $89. Goldfields Air Services (tel 21 2116) fly from Kalgoorlie to Esperance via Norseman, the Kalgoorlie to Norseman sector costs $49. For bus information see under Kalgoorlie.

KAMBALDA (population 4500)

Kambalda died as a gold mining town in 1906 but nickel was discovered there in 1966 and today this is the major mining centre in the gold fields region. The town is on the shores of the salt Lake LeFroy and land yachting is a popular activity.

NORTH OF KALGOORLIE

The road is surfaced from Kalgoorlie all the way to Leonora-Gwalia, 240 km north, and from there to Laverton (130 km north-east) and Leinster (160 km north). Off the main road, however, traffic is virtually non-existent and rain can quickly cut the dirt roads.

Towns of interest include Kanowna, just 22 km from Kal along a dirt road. In 1905 this town had a population of 12,000,

16 hotels, many churches and an hourly train service to Kalgoorlie. Today, apart from the station and the odd pile of rubble, absolutely nothing remains!

Broad Arrow now has a population of 20, compared with 2400 at the turn of the century, but one of the town's original eight hotels operates in virtually unchanged condition. Ora Banda has gone from 2000 to less than 50. Menzies, 130 km north of Kal, has about 90 people today, compared with 5000 in 1900. Many early buildings remain, including the railway station with its 120 metre long platform and the town hall with its clockless clocktower. The ship bringing the clock from England sank en route.

With a population of 500, Leonora serves as the railhead for the nickel from Windarra and Leinster. In adjoining Gwalia, the Sons of Gwalia Goldmine, closed in 1964, was the largest in WA outside Kalgoorlie. At one time the mine was managed by Herbert Hoover, later to become president of the USA. The Gwalia Historical Society is housed in the 1898 mine office – it's a fascinating local museum, open daily. Off the main road is Koolkynie, an interesting little place with a population of just 10. In 1905 it was 1500. Nearby Niagara is a ghost town.

From Leonora you can turn north-east to Laverton, where the surfaced road ends. The population here declined from 1000 in 1910 to 200 in 1970 when the Poseidon nickel discovery (beloved of stockmarket speculators in the late '60s and early '70s) revived mining operations in nearby Windarra. The town now has a population of 900. From here it is just 1710 km north-west to Alice Springs, but you'll need 4WD or good ground clearance, permission to enter the Aboriginal reserves along the way, and enough fuel for at least 650 km. Don't even consider doing it from November to March due to the extreme heat.

North of Leonora the road is now surfaced to Leinster, another modern nickel town. Nearby Agnew is another old gold town that has all but disappeared. It's 170 km north to Wiluna, which is another 170 km from Meekatharra, on the surfaced Great Northern Highway that continues 860 km to Port Hedland. Through the '30s, when arsenic was mined there, Wiluna had a population of 8000 and was a modern, prosperous town. The ore ran out in 1948 and the town quickly declined. Today the minute population is mainly Aboriginal.

The South & South-West

Many travellers on the road between the east and west coasts take the direct route through WA – across the Nullarbor then north from Norseman to Coolgardie and directly west to Perth. It's certainly worth getting up into the gold fields around Kalgoorlie and Coolgardie but turning south from Norseman to Esperance and then travelling along the Leeuwin Way, around the south-west corner of Australia, is an equally interesting trip. This is a varied area, which in places contrasts greatly with the dry and barren country found in so many other parts of the state.

The southern stretch, 'The Great Southern', has some magnificent coastline pounded by huge seas but there is also the spectacular and rugged Stirling Range and Porongorups inland, as well as Albany, the oldest settlement in Western Australia. The south-west corner is one of the greenest and most fertile areas of WA. Here you will find the great karri and jarrah forests, prosperous farming land and more of the state's beautiful wildflowers.

Places to Stay

The towns in the region are popular holiday resorts with plenty of accommodation, including youth hostels at Esperance, Albany, Denmark, Tingledale,

Pemberton, Augusta, Bridgetown, Borden, Noggerup, Yallingup and Quindalup. Enough hostels, in fact, to make a really interesting hostelling circuit possible.

Getting There & Away
Air Skywest (tel (09) 323 1188 in Perth) have flights to Albany ($122) and Esperance ($104). Goldfields Air Services have flights between Kalgoorlie and Esperance via Norseman for $98 ($120 Apex return).

Bus & Train Westrail have a number of bus and rail services including bus services from Kalgoorlie and from Perth to Esperance. There are also Westrail bus services from Perth to Hyden ($26), Manjimup ($22), and Albany and Denmark ($28). A bus ($14) and the 'Australind' train service ($12) travel to Bunbury. The Westrail bus continues to Busselton ($17), Yallingup ($19), Margaret River ($20) and Augusta ($23).

Deluxe is the only interstate bus carrier that has a regular bus service through the south-west, stopping at places like Manjimup, Denmark, Albany and Esperance. Due to bus regulations passengers from Perth cannot alight between Perth and Albany unless they are on an interstate trip. Greyhound bus passes can be used on South-West Coachlines bus between Perth and Margaret River (via Bunbury and Busselton).

Esperance is 720 km from Perth via Lake Grace and 894 km via Albany. To do a complete road loop from Perth out to Kalgoorlie, down to Esperance and back around by the coast would involve more than 2000 km.

ESPERANCE (population 6400)
Esperance, on the coast 200 km south of Norseman, has become a popular coastal resort for the region. Although the first settlers came to the area in 1863, it was during the gold rush in the 1890s that the town really became established as a port.

When the gold fever subsided Esperance went into a state of suspended animation until after WW II. In the 1950s it was discovered that adding missing trace elements to the soil around Esperance would restore it to fertility and since then the town has grown rapidly as an agricultural centre.

Information
The Esperance Tourist Bureau, on Dempster St, next to the museum, is open daily from 9 am to 5 pm and books tours along the coast and islands and into the national parks.

Things to See
Esperance has some excellent beaches and the seas offshore are studded with the many islands of the Recherche Archipelago. The Esperance Museum Park includes the tourist bureau and various old buildings and a major Skylab display. (When the USA's Skylab crashed to earth in 1979, it made its fiery re-entry right over Esperance.) The museum park is between The Esplanade and Dempster Sts and the best time to visit is between 10.30 am and 4 pm daily; the museum itself is on the corner of James and Dempster Sts and is open daily from 1.30 to 4.30 pm. George's Oceanarium has a marine life display and you can also see the town's original homestead on Dempster St, although it's not open to the public.

Only three km from the town is the Pink Lake, which has prolific bird life and which really is pink (the colouring is caused by an algae called Dunalella Salina); as much as half a million tonnes of salt are dredged from the lake annually. Twilight Bay and Picnic Cove are popular local swimming spots. You can look out over the bay and islands from nearby Observatory Point or from the Rotary Lookout on Wireless Hill.

There are about 100 small islands in the Recherche Archipelago. On them are colonies of seals, penguins and a wide variety of water birds. Woody Island is a wildlife sanctuary and there are regular trips to this and other islands in January and February. At the top of Six Mile Hill, eight km from Esperance, is Baker's Born Free Wildlife & Wildflower Park. Fossicker's Finds has a collection of 2000 old bottles. Close by is the Australian Parrot Farm, with parrots and other native birds. To get there go east on Fisheries Rd and five km past Cape Le Grand turn-off on Merivale Rd. Both are open from 9 am to 5 pm daily.

Cape Le Grand National Park is a coastal park extending from about 20 to 60 km east of Esperance. The park has spectacular coastal scenery, some good beaches and excellent walking tracks. There are fine views from Frenchmans Peak, at the western end of the park. Further east is the coastal Cape Arid National Park, at the start of the Great Australian Bight and on the fringes of the Nullarbor Plain.

Places to Stay

The large and popular *Youth Hostel* (tel 71 1040) is on Goldfields Rd, two km north of the town centre, and costs $9.

The *Esperance Motor Hotel* (tel 71 1555), in Andrew St, is well located and costs from $20/35. The less central *Pink Lake* (tel 71 2075), at 85 Pink Lake Rd, is $18/30.

The most central camping site is the *Esperance Bay Caravan Park* (tel 71 2237), on the corner of the Esplanade and Harbour Rd, near the wharf. Camping sites are $7 for two and on-site vans are from $25. Limited-facility camping sites are $7.50 at Cape Le Grand (tel (090) 75 9022) and $5 at Cape Arid (tel (090) 75 0055). Apply for permits with the ranger at the park entrance.

Getting There & Away

Skywest fly daily from Perth to Esperance for $164 and Goldfields Air Services fly from Kalgoorlie via Norseman for $104. Westrail has a bus three times a week from Kalgoorlie to Esperance and an 11 hour Perth to Esperance service that runs on Mondays via Jerramungup, and on Tuesday and Friday via Lake Grace, for $43. The daily Deluxe Perth to Adelaide bus stops in Esperance.

ESPERANCE TO ALBANY (476 km)

From Esperance the road runs inland, skirting the Fitzgerald River National Park before turning back to the coast at Albany.

Stokes Inlet National Park

Just west of Young River, 70 km west of Esperance, is the turn off to the Stokes Inlet National Park. This is a new park with limited facilities (bring your own water and food) and an interesting walk around the estuary to the beach.

Ravensthorpe (population 300)

The tiny town of Ravensthorpe was once the centre of the Phillips River gold field; Later copper was also mined there. The historic 1868 homestead Cocanarup has a display of farm machinery. The ruins of a disused government smelter and the Catlin (copper) Mine near the town can also be explored. The Ravensthorpe Historical Society is housed in Dance Cottage and holds a wildflower show each year in September.

Places to Stay The *Palace Hotel* (tel 38 1005) is classified by the National Trust, and singles/doubles are $27/45 with breakfast more in the motel section. *Ravensthorpe Caravan Park* (tel 38 1050) has sites at $7 for two.

Further West

The fine beaches and bays around Hopetoun are immediately to the south while to the north is the Frank Hann National Park, which has a cross section of typical sand plain region flora. The Fitzgerald River National Park can be reached from here or from Jerramungup further west. This park has a very scenic coastline, sand plains, mountains and deep, wide river valleys.

In Jerramangup you can visit the Military Museum. Ongerup, a small wheatbelt town, has an annual wildflower show in mid-September with hundreds of local species on show. The town also has the biggest sheep shearing competition in WA, during the Queen's Birthday weekend in September.

ALBANY (population 15,000)

The commercial centre of the southern region, the pretty town of Albany, is the oldest settlement in the state, established in 1826, shortly before Perth. Its excellent harbour, on King George Sound, led to Albany becoming a thriving whaling port. Later, when steamships started travelling between the UK and Australia, Albany was a coaling station for ships bound for the east coast.

Information

The Albany Tourist Bureau (tel 41 1088) is on the corner of Peels Place and York St.

Old Buildings

Albany has some fine old colonial buildings – Stirling Terrace is particularly noted for its Victorian shopfronts. The 1851 Old Gaol & Museum is now a folk museum, open daily from 1.30 to 4.15 pm. There's a full-scale replica of the brig *Amity*, the ship that brought Albany's founding party to the area. The museum is open daily from 9 am to 5 pm.

The Albany Residency Museum, originally built in the 1850s as the home of the resident magistrate, is open Monday to Friday from 10 am to 5 pm and Saturday from 2 to 5 pm. The 1870 old post office was recently restored and has a Postal History Museum (open daily from 10 am to 5 pm) and a restaurant. Apart from the post office the building also housed a customs and bond store and a court with cells and magistrate's and jury rooms.

The 1832 Patrick Taylor Cottage houses a collection of period costumes and furniture and is open daily from 2 to 4.30 pm.

The old farm at Strawberry Hill is one of the oldest in the state, having been established in 1872 as the government farm for Albany. It's open daily from 2 to 5 pm except during July when it's closed. From September to April it is also open from 10 am to 12 noon.

Views & Beaches

There are fine views over the coast and inland from the Twin Peaks, which overlook the town. On top of Mt Clarence is the Desert Mounted Corps Memorial, originally erected in Port Said as a memorial to the events of Gallipoli. It was brought here when the Suez crisis in 1956 made colonial reminders less than popular in Egypt. Mt Clarence can be climbed from the west along a new, as yet unmarked trail. The Blowhole and Gorge and Dog Rock are beside the road to Middleton, a long sweep of sand.

Places to Stay

The Albany *Youth Hostel* (tel 41 3949) is at 49 Duke St, only 400 metres from the town centre, and costs $9 a night. The hostel is often full in season.

Some of the more central hotels include the *Albany Hotel* (tel 41 1031), on York St, with rooms including breakfast from $24/40 and the *London Hotel* (tel 41 1048), on Stirling Terrace, from $20/38, again including breakfast.

The *Parkville Colonial Guest House* (tel 41 3704), at 136 Brunswick St, has 14 clean rooms and charges $20/36. The *Camberlea Guest House* (tel 41 1669), at 158 York St, has singles/doubles for $20/33 including a light breakfast. The *CWA Albany Seaside Flats* (tel 41 1591), at 37 Flinders Parade, are self-contained flats from $28 for two.

The *Mt Melville Caravan Park* (tel 41 4616) is a km north of the centre, on the corner of Lion and Wellington Sts. There are camping sites at $6 for two and on-site vans for $25.

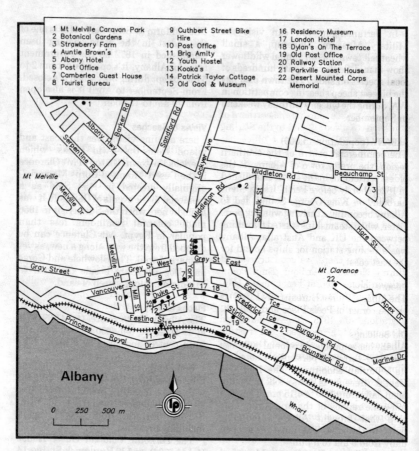

1 Mt Melville Caravan Park
2 Botanical Gardens
3 Strawberry Farm
4 Auntie Brown's
5 Albany Hotel
6 Post Office
7 Camberlea Guest House
8 Tourist Bureau
9 Cuthbert Street Bike Hire
10 Post Office
11 Brig Amity
12 Youth Hostel
13 Kooka's
14 Patrick Taylor Cottage
15 Old Gaol & Museum
16 Residency Museum
17 London Hotel
18 Dylan's On The Terrace
19 Old Post Office
20 Railway Station
21 Parkville Guest House
22 Desert Mounted Corps Memorial

Albany

0   250   500 m

Places to Eat

Breakfasts at the *Wildflower Cafe* have been recommended. Counter meals in the *Premier Hotel*, York St, the *London Hotel*, Stirling Terrace, or the *Esplanade*, Middleton Beach, are good value. *Dylan's on the Terrace*, at 82 Stirling Terrace, has good take-aways and light meals; try their hamburgers or pancakes. *Auntie Brown's*, at 280 York St, has a very good smorgasbord Monday to Saturday. *Kooka's*, at 205 Stirling Terrace, is a good up-market restaurant in a restored old house; count on $30 for an excellent three course meal.

Getting There & Away

Skywest fly daily from Perth to Albany for $122. Westrail have daily buses from Perth via different Wheatbelt towns for $28, and through Denmark once a week. Deluxe's daily Perth to Adelaide service comes through Esperance, Albany and Denmark.

Getting Around

Love's Bus Service run a regular service around town week days and Saturday mornings. The main bus will take you along Albany Highway from Peel St to the Roundabout; others go to Spencer Park, Middleton Beach and Emu Point. The YHA Albany has tours up the northern or southern coast for $10 and to the Stirling Ranges for $20. The tourist office has many local tours for $15 to $30.

Rent bicycles from 38 Cuthbert St (tel 41 8176), very close to the Duke St YHA Hostel, or at King Sound Vehicle Hire (tel 41 8466) in the service station at 145 Albany Highway. They both have 10 speed and other bikes for $5 a day.

AROUND ALBANY

Near Albany there are good beaches at Jimmy Newhill's Harbour, Emu Point, Salmon Holes, and at Frenchmans Bay, 21 km from Albany, where the Cheynes Beach Whaling Station only ceased operations in 1978. The Whaleworld Museum has a restored and rusting 'Cheynes 4' whale chaser and you can inspect the station after seeing a short film on whaling operations. A fast talking retired whaler gives free guided tours. It's open daily from 9 am to 5 pm and admission is $3.50.

Impressive rock formations and blow-holes along the coast include The Gap and Natural Bridge, 16 km south of town. Two Peoples Bay is a nature reserve east of Albany with a nice little scenic beach and coastline.

MT BARKER (population 1500)

Directly north of Albany is Mt Barker, which is south of the Stirling Range and west of the Porongorups. It is overlooked by the enormous TV tower on top of Mt Barker. The town has been settled since the 1830s and the old police station and jail of 1868 is preserved as a museum. The area is developing a reputation for wine producing.

Kendenup, 16 km north of Mt Barker,

was the actual site of WA's first gold discovery, though this was considerably overshadowed by the later and much larger finds in the Kalgoorlie area. North of Mt Barker is Cranbrook, an access point to the Stirling Range National Park. Mt Barker has a tourist office at 47 Lowood St, a couple of hotels and a caravan park.

THE STIRLING RANGE & PORONGORUPS

The beautiful Porongorup range has panoramic views, beautiful scenery and excellent bushwalks. Castle Rock (570 metres) and Nancys Peak (652 metres) are easy climbs. The Devils Slide (670 metres) is another popular Porongorups walk.

In the Stirling Range, Toolbrunup (for views and a good climb), Bluff Knoll (for the height – at 1037 metres it's the highest peak in the range) and Toll Peak (for the wildflowers) are popular half day walks. The 96 km range is noted for its spectacular colour changes through blues, reds and purples. The mountains rise abruptly from the surrounding flat and sandy plains.

Places to Stay

You can camp in the Stirling Range park on Chester Rd, near the Toolbrunup turn-off; see the ranger (tel (098) 27 9278) for details. There are very limited facilities and sites are $4. The *Stirling Range Caravan Park* (tel (098) 27 9229) is off the main road to Borden, on the north boundary of the park, and is an associate YHA hostel with beds for $8 in self-contained units.

DENMARK (population 1000)

Denmark is 55 km west of Albany. It has fine beaches (William Bay for swimming, Ocean Beach for surfing) and is a good base for trips into the karri forests. The town is picturesquely sited on the Denmark River and first became established supplying timber for gold field developments. In the town, the Goundreey's

Winery, in the Old Butter Factory, is open for inspection and wine tasting daily from 10 am to 4 pm except Sunday. Copenhagen House, opposite the Denmark Tourist Bureau on Strickland St, shows local crafts.

There are fine views from Mt Shadforth Lookout while the William Bay National Park, 15 km west of Denmark, has fine costal scenery of rocks and reefs.

Places to Stay

There is an associate *Youth Hostel* (tel 48 1267) at the Wilson Inlet Holiday Park, three km south of Denmark. Phone in advance during the summer months. *Denmark Hotel* (tel 48 1690), on the Esplanade, has basic rooms from $18 a person. *Norton's* (tel 48 1690), at 12 Inlet Drive, has bed & breakfast for $22 a person. *Rivermouth Caravan Park* (tel 48 1262), at Inlet Drive, has sites for $7 for two and on-site vans for $23.

Places to Eat

Denmark Coffee Shop, on Holling Rd, has very good German food – no meal is over $9. For a quick meal or take-away *Kettle's Deli*, on the corner of High St and Holling Rd, is good. Across from the deli and upstairs is the *Bridge Restaurant*, with probably the best reasonably priced food in town. They have set menus on Friday and Saturday nights for $23.

Getting There & Away

Westrail's Perth to Albany service comes through Denmark once a week and costs $28 from Perth. The daily Deluxe Perth to Adelaide bus also comes through Denmark.

Getting Around

Contact the tourist bureau about local tours which are priced from $8. Denmark Bike Hire (tel 48 1548) has bikes for $5 a day.

NORNALUP-WALPOLE

The road continues close to the coast to Nornalup, a small town on the banks of the tranquil Frankland River. The heavily forested Walpole-Nornalup National Park stretches between Nornalup and Walpole and contains the 'Valley of the Giants', a stand of giant karri and tingle trees including one that soars 46 metres high. Pleasant, shady and ferny paths lead through the forest. The Frankland River is popular with canoeing enthusiasts.

From Walpole the road turns away from the coast to Manjimup, 120 km north. You can explore this area by car or with a Denmark Tourist Bureau tour. There is an associate *Youth Hostel* (tel 40 8073) off the Valley of the Giants Rd – booking is strongly recommended. You need a car to get to this hostel, where beds are $5.

MANJIMUP (population 4100)

Manjimup is the commercial centre of the south-west, a major agricultural centre noted for apple growing and wood-chipping. In the town is the Timber Park complex, which includes various museums, old buildings and the Manjimup Tourist Bureau.

One Tree Bridge, or what's left of it, is 22 km down the Graphite Rd. Most of the tree was swept away during floods in 1966. The four superb karri trees, known as the Four Aces, are believed to be over 300 years old and are just 1½ km from One Tree Bridge. Fonty's Pool, a great spot to cool off during those hot summer days, is seven km out of town along Seven Day Rd. Nine km south of town, along the South-West Highway, is the Diamond Tree Lookout, which provides spectacular views of the surrounding countryside.

The Manjimup Tourist Bureau is on the corner of Rose and Edwards Sts and is open daily from 9 am to 5 pm.

Places to Stay & Eat

The *Manjimup Caravan Park* (tel 71 2093) has a *Youth Hostel* with beds for $7.50 a person, as well as sites at the same price and on-site vans from $20. Two other caravan parks also have sites and on-site vans. The *Manjimup Hotel* (tel 71 1322) has rooms from $23 a person, and there are several motels.

At meal time try *Uncle Eddy's*, at 30 Rose St. At the *Country Cafe*, at 78 Giblet St, meals are $12.

Getting There & Away

Westrail have a Perth to Manjimup bus service via Bunbury, Bridgetown and on to Pemberton four times a week for $22.

PEMBERTON (population 900)

Deep in the karri forests, the delightful little town of Pemberton has a very good local Pioneer Museum displaying old forestry equipment, an art gallery housed in a restored squatter's cottage, the Pemberton Sawmill where you can observe timber being sawn, and a trout hatchery that supplies fish for the state's dams and rivers. The restored Brockman Sawpit shows timber cutting activities of the 1860s.

If you're feeling fit you can make the scary 60 metre climb to the top of the Gloucester Tree, the highest fire lookout tree in the world. The view makes the climb well worthwhile. It's just south of Pemberton, on the Northcliffe road. You can camp in the Warren National Park on the scenic Warren River.

There's a tourist office on Brockman St and farm labouring work is often available in the area.

Places to Stay & Eat

The *Youth Hostel* (tel 76 1153) at Pimelea costs $8 a night and is in a beautiful forest location but it's 10 km out of town and hitching there can be difficult. In town the centrally located *Warren Lodge* (tel 76 1105), on Brockman St, has single rooms from $8. *Pemberton Hotel* (tel 76 1017), also on Brockman St, has bed & breakfast singles/doubles for $28/45. It serves counter meals. The *Pemberton Caravan Park* (tel 76 1300) has on-site vans for $23 for two in addition to camping sites for $8.

The town, for its size, has many places

to eat. *Munchies*, on Brockman St, has good, basic, cheap food like hamburgers, Lebanese rolls and seafood platters. The *Shamrock*, on the same street, is a good a-la-carte steak and seafood restaurant where a three course meal costs around $24.

Getting There & Away

Westrail Perth to Pemberton buses operate four times a week, travel via Bunbury, Donnybrook and Manjimup and cost $24. The Pemberton Tramway Company runs a 1907 era tram from Pemberton to Northcliffe, on a four hour journey through the karri and marri forests.

NORTHCLIFFE (population 200)

Northcliffe, 32 km south of Pemberton, has a pioneer museum (open daily from 11 am to 2 pm except in July and August when it's closed), a forest park that has good walks and is in walking distance of the town, and the popular and picturesque Lane Poole Falls. Windy Harbour, on the coast south of Northcliffe, is something of a hippie hangout, and true to its name, is very windy. The cliffs around here are popular with rockclimbers and there's a great lighthouse at Point D'Entrecasteaux.

Places to Stay & Eat

Northcliffe Hotel (tel 76 7089), with basic singles/doubles for $20/35, is the only hotel in town. The *Pine Tree Caravan Park* (tel 76 7193) has sites at $6.50 for two and cabins at $30.

At Windy Harbour the only place to stay is the *Windy Harbour Camping Area* (tel 76 7056) where sites are $3.50.

Getting There & Away

The Perth to Pemberton Westrail bus goes through Northcliffe three times a week and costs $25 but you need your own transport to get to Windy Harbour.

BRIDGETOWN (population 1500)

A quiet country town in an area of karri forests and farmland, Bridgetown has some old buildings, including Blechynden House. Built of mud and clay by the area's first settler in 1862, it has been restored by the National Trust. Boyup Brook has a number of points of interest, including a fauna reserve and a large butterfly and beetle collection. Interesting features of the river valley are the 'blackboys' and large granite boulders. Nearby is Norlup Pool with glacial rock formations, and Wilga which is an old timber mill with vintage engines.

Places to Stay

Bridgetown has an associate *Youth Hostel* (tel (097) 61 1934) housed in an historic mud brick hotel built in 1870. It's on the corner of Steere and Roe Sts and costs $7.50 a night. Deep in the karri forest is the *Donnelly River Holiday Village* (tel 72 1292) with hostel type accommodation in cottages for $7 a night. It is 28 km south-west of Bridgetown along the Bibbulmun Track.

NANNUP (population 550)

Continuing west from Bridgetown you reach Nannup, which has the largest jarrah sawmill in WA and the fine old Colonial House, dating from 1895. The tourist information centre is in the 1922 police station. There are also several interesting and scenic drives you can do from here: Nunnup to Balingup along the Blackwood River; Nunnup to Pemberton; and Nunnup to Augusta via Sue's Bridge, along an unsealed road that might not be safe in winter but is passable in summer.

AUGUSTA

A popular holiday resort, Augusta is only a little north of Cape Leeuwin with its lighthouse (admission $2) and salt encrusted 1895 waterwheel. The Augusta Historical Museum has local exhibits. Between here and Margaret River, to the north, there are a number of limestone caves. These include the Jewel Cave (the most picturesque), Lake Cave and Mammoth Cave, where fossilised skeletons

of Tasmanian tigers have been found. In all, 120 caves have been discovered between Cape Leeuwin and Cape Naturaliste but only these three, and Yallingup Cave, which is near Busselton, are open to the public.

Places to Stay & Eat

There's a small associate *Youth Hostel* (tel 58 1433) costing $7 a night. It's on the corner of Bussell Highway and Blackwood Ave, opposite the Doonbanks Caravan Park and adjacent to the Blackwood River estuary. *Doonbanks* is the most central caravan park. It has sites for $9 and on-sight vans for $23. Some of the holiday flats have reasonable rates but mostly on a weekly basis; an exception is the *Calypso Flats* (tel 58 1514), which costs $23 for two.

The *Augusta Hotel* does counter meals; or head for *Squirrels*, where you can find wholemeal bread, Lebanese pitta bread and other city delicacies!

MARGARET RIVER

There are some fine beaches and good surfing spots between Augusta and the town of Margaret River, which is prettily situated on – you guessed it – the Margaret River. The Augusta-Margaret River Tourist Bureau is on the corner of the Bussell Highway and Tunbridge Rd.

Old Settlement Craft Village conjures up images of 1920s farm living and has a blacksmith who gives demonstrations. Bellview Shell Museum is at Witchlife, six km south down the Bussell Highway. The historic 1865 Wallcliffe House, on Wallcliffe Rd, towards Prevelly Park, is open to the public.

The old coast road between Augusta, Margaret River and Busselton is a good alternative to the direct road which runs slightly inland. The coast here has real variety – cliff faces, long beaches pounded by rolling surf, and calm, sheltered bays. The area also has many good wineries.

Places to Stay

The *Margaret River Lodge* (tel 57 2532)

backpackers hostel is not far from the town centre at 220 Railway Terrace. It's clean, friendly and modern with all the facilities including a good swimming pool and an open fireplace. There are double bedrooms, bunkrooms and dormitories from $9 a person.

Other possibilities include the *Margaret River Caravan Park* (tel 57 2180), on Station Rd, which has sites for $8 and on-site vans for $23, and the *Captain Freycinet* (tel 57 2033) motel, on the Bussell Highway, at $65/70.

Places to Eat

Among the many places to eat is *Settler's Tavern*, on Bussell Highway, which has good, basic pub food for $8 to $10 – Margaret River Lodge guests get a 10% discount. On the same road you can try Mexican food at the *Bandaleros Cantina* or gourmet hamburgers from $7.50 at *Hot 'n' Hunky*.

BUSSELTON (population 6500)

Like Bunbury further north, Busselton is a popular holiday resort. The town has a cinema museum with a collection of early cinematic equipment, the National Trust Wonnerup House of 1859, and what was (until it was shortened by a cyclone in 1978) the longest timber jetty in Australia. The old court house has also been restored and is now an arts centre. The old butter factory on the banks of the Vassa River past the historic and picturesque St Mary's Church, is a small museum of butter making! Near the jetty there is an Oceanarium run by Apex. *Ballarat*, the state's first locomotive, stands in the park at the outskirts of the town. The Whistle Stop is a miniature railway 11 km from Busselton on the Nunnup Highway.

Yallingup, to the south-west, is a Mecca for surfers. Nearby is Yallingup Cave and some fine coastal lookouts such as Cape Naturaliste, which has a lighthouse. South of Yallingup, at Millbrook Farm, is the Old Waterwheel, an historic property with about half a dozen restored buildings

and a mill. Dunsborough, just to the west of Busselton, is a pleasant little town with fine beaches such as Meelup, Eagle Bay and Bunker Bay. The Bannamah Wild Life Park is two km from the town. Other attractions include Greenacres Shell Museum and Hutchings Antique Shop & Museum.

Busselton has a tourist bureau in the civic centre, on Southern Drive.

Places to Stay

There is a great deal of accommodation along this stretch of coast. *Villa Carlotta Guest House* (tel 52 1034), on Adelaide St, is good and friendly and has bed & breakfast singles/doubles for $19/28, and organises tours. *Geographe Guest House* (tel 52 1451), on West St, is similarly priced and very clean. The most central caravan park is *Kookaburra No 1* (tel 52 1516) with sites for $8 for two and on-site vans for $18.

Near Dunsborough, in Quindalup, is the refurbished *Youth Hostel* (tel 55 3107), at 258 Geographe Bay Rd, which costs $8.50 and hires bicycles, windsurfers and canoes. *Greenacres Caravan Park* (tel 55 3087) is on the seafront with sites for $8 for two and on-site vans from $27.

Yallingup's summer *Youth Hostel* (book through the Dunsborough hostel) can be used any time of the year with prior arrangement and costs $5. The hostel is on Wildwood Rd, at the turn-off to the Old Waterwheel, only two km from the beach.

Places to Eat

The numerous places to eat include *Albertini's*, on Queen St; the *Golden Fleece Roadhouse*, at 259 Bussell Highway, and the carvery at *The Geographe*, on Bussell Highway.

BUNBURY (population 22,000)

As well as being a port, industrial town and holiday resort, Bunbury is also where the blue manna crabs – a gourmet's delight – are found. The town's old buildings include King's Cottage, which now houses a museum, and St Mark's Church. The Arts Complex, on Wittenoom St, is in a restored 1897 convent building. There's a 25 metre high lighthouse on Apex Drive and an 800 metre miniature railway track at Forrest Park. Two old steam trains, the *Leschenault Lady* and the *Koombana Queen*, are now in the Transport Museum, in Boyanup. The South-West Museum, on the Bussell Highway in Gelorup, has displays of minerals, seashells, fossils and petrified wood.

The tourist bureau, in the old railway station on Carmody Place, organises bushwalking tours from $10.

Places to Stay & Eat

There is now a backpackers hostel – *Bunbury Backpackers* – at 22 Wittenoom St, one block from the Tourist Information Centre and the Indian Ocean. It cost $11 a night. The *Captain Bunbury Hotel* (tel 21 2021), at 8 Victoria St, has basic rooms including breakfast for $14.50. The *Prince of Wales* (tel 21 2016), on Stephen St, and *Parade Hotel* (tel 21 2093), at 100 Stirling St, also offer bed & breakfast but at slightly higher prices. *Koombana Park* (tel 21 2516) is the most central caravan park, with sites for $10 for two and on-site vans for $28.

Rose Hotel, on Wellington St, has good counter meals; or try *Our Pancake Place*, on Victoria St, or the *Friendship Chinese Restaurant*, on the same street.

AUSTRALIND (population 800)

Australind, yet another holiday resort, is a pleasant 11 km drive from Bunbury. The town takes its name from an 1840s plan to make it a port for trade with India. The plan never worked but the strange name (Australia-India) remains. Australind has the tiny St Nicholas Church, just four by seven metres and said to be the smallest in Australia. There's also Henton Cottage, built in 1843, and a gemstone and rock museum in the town. The scenic drive between Australind and Binningup is along Leschenault Inlet.

The town's *Caravan Park* (tel 97 1095) has sites for $10 and on-site vans for $28.

INLAND

Inland from the south-west coast, interesting centres include Harvey, in a popular bushwalking area of rolling green hills to the north of Bunbury. This is the home of WA's Big Orange, on the South-West Highway. There are dam systems and some beautiful waterfalls nearby. The Yalgorup National Park is north of town. There's a tourist office on Young St.

Further south of Bunbury is Donnybrook, in the centre of an apple growing area. Collie is WA's only coal town and has a historical museum and a steam locomotive museum. There is some pleasant bushwalking country around the town and plenty of wildflowers in season. The tourist bureau is on Throssell St.

Places to Stay

In Donnybrook the *Brook Lodge* (tel 31 1520), on Bridge St, is a private lodge that welcomes YHA members and costs $8.50 a person.

Wheatlands

Stretching north from the Albany coastal region to the areas beyond the Great Eastern Highway (the Perth to Coolgardie road) are the WA wheatlands. The area is noted for its unusual rock formations, best known of which is Wave Rock, near Hyden, and for its many Aboriginal rock carvings.

CUNDERDIN & MECKERING

Meckering was badly damaged by an earthquake in 1968 and the Agricultural Museum in Cunderdin has exhibits relating to that event. The museum is housed in an old pumping station used on the gold fields water pipeline. Further east is Kellerberrin, which has an historical museum in the old courthouse of 1897 and is overlooked by a hill named Killabin by Aborigines.

MERREDIN (population 3500)

On the Perth to Kalgoorlie railway line and the Great Eastern Highway is Merredin. It has a National Trust restored homestead and an old railway station that has been preserved as a museum. North of Merredin there are some interesting rock formations around Koorda.

The *Merredin Olympic Motel* (tel 41 1588) has hostel type accommodation for $9.

SOUTHERN CROSS (population 800)

Although the gold quickly gave out, Southern Cross was the first gold rush town on the WA gold fields. The big rush soon moved further east to Coolgardie and Kalgoorlie. Like the town itself, Southern Cross's streets are named after the stars and constellations. The Yilgarn History Museum, in the old court house, has local displays. Situated 378 km east of Perth, this is really the end of the wheatlands area and the start of the desert; when travelling by train the change is very noticeable. In the spring the sandy plains around Southern Cross are carpeted with wildflowers.

HYDEN & WAVE ROCK

Just three km from the tiny town of Hyden is the unusual rock formation known as Wave Rock. It's a real surfer's delight – the perfect wave, 15 metres high and frozen in solid rock. Wave Rock is 350 km from Perth and is one of WA's major tourist attractions. The curling rock is marked with different colour bands. Other interesting rock formations in the area bear names like Hippo's Yawn and The Humps. Bates Caves have Aboriginal rock paintings and there's a wildlife sanctuary by Wave Rock itself.

Diep's Guest House (tel 80 5089), on Clayton St, in Hyden, has bed & breakfast for around $33 a person, or there is the *Hyden Hotel* (tel 80 5052), on Lynch St, with singles/doubles for $35/45. At Wave Rock itself the *Wave Rock Caravan Park* (tel 80 5022 has sites for $6, on-site vans for $22 and chalets for $33.

A Westrail bus leaves Perth on Tuesday and returns the following day; it costs $26 one way.

OTHER TOWNS

There is a fine rock formation known as Kokerbin, an Aboriginal word for 'high place', near Bruce Rock. Corrigin has a folk museum. Jilakin Rock is 18 km from Kulin, while further south-east there's Lake Grace, near the lake of the same name.

Narrogin is an agricultural centre with a courthouse museum, historic village, the Albert Facey Homestead and a giant ram in the town, and a couple of unusual rock formations nearby. Dumbleyung also has an historical museum. Wagin has an art gallery and some fine old buildings. There is good bushwalking around Mt Latham, six km to the west. Katanning (population 5300) has a large Muslim community, complete with a mosque built in 1980. Other attractions include the old mill that houses the tourist information centre, an historic museum, winery ruins and the King George Hotel.

Up the Coast

Highway 1, which encircles Australia, is now sealed all the way round. The last unsealed section was between Fitzroy Crossing and Halls Creek, in the Kimberley area in the north of WA. The long, dull stretch between Port Hedland and Broome was sealed in the early 1980s.

The route from Perth to Darwin may still be a hell of a long way but it's no longer an endurance test. There's a fair bit to see if you want to break the journey. Don't underestimate it – from Perth to

Port Hedland is 1770 km by the coast and in summer they can be very hot km.

Getting There & Away
Air Ansett WA fly from Perth to Geraldton ($120), Carnarvon ($195) and Learmonth (for Exmouth) ($242) as well as to centres in the north-west Kimberley region.

Bus Westrail have bus services to Geraldton, Kalbarri and Meekatharra. Greyhound have a daily bus up the coast to Port Hedland and beyond to Darwin. Deluxe have a daily service to Darwin. They also have a service to Broome, and another to Port Hedland. Bus Australia have daily services up the coast to Broome, continuing to Darwin three days a week.

From Perth it is $58 to Geraldton, $74 to Overlander Roadhouse (turn-off for Shark Bay), $76 to Carnarvon, $79 to Minilya Roadhouse (turn-off for Exmouth) and $79 to Nanutarra (turn-off for Wittenoom).

PERTH TO GERALDTON (421 km)
From Perth you follow the Brand Highway past the turn-off to Jurien and the Pinnacles Desert, which is a major tourist attraction. It's a wide sandy plain studded with weird looking limestone pillars of varying sizes, ranging from stony 'twigs' to columns more than two metres tall. Half day tours to the Pinnacles cost $12 (children $6) and depart the Cervantes Shell service station at 1 pm. Phone Pinnacles Travel (tel (09) 325 9455) for details.

The main road comes back to the coast at Dongara – a pleasant little port with fine beaches and lots of crayfish. Russ Cottage, open Sundays and public holidays from 2 to 5 pm, is a local attraction.

Further north, only about 20 km south of Geraldton, is Greenough, once a busy little mining town but now just a quiet farming centre. The Pioneer Museum,

which is open daily from 10 am to 4 pm, dates from 1860.

INLAND
The area inland of Dongara and Geraldton is noted for its spring wildflowers. Mingenew, Morawa and Mullewa all have brilliant wildflower displays in the spring. Tallering Peak and Gorges, 58 km north of Mullewa, are particularly splendid.

Mingenew has a small museum. Carnamah, near the Yarra Yarra Lake, is noted for its bird life. This area is also a gateway to the Murchison gold fields; there are old gold mining centres and ghost towns around Perenjori.

GERALDTON (population 21,000)
Geraldton, the major town in the midwest region, is situated on a spectacular stretch of coast. It's 421 km north of Perth and has a fine climate, particularly in the winter.

Dutch Shipwrecks
During the 17th century ships of the Dutch East India Company, sailing from Europe to Batavia in Java, would head due east from the horn of Africa then beat up the Western Australian coast to Indonesia. It only took a small miscalculation for a ship to run aground on the coast and a few did just that, usually with disasterous results. The west coast of Australia is often decidedly inhospitable and the chances of rescue at that time were remote.

Four wrecks of Dutch East Indiamen have been located, including the *Batavia* – the earliest and, in many ways, the most interesting. In 1629 the *Batavia* went aground on the Abrolhos Islands, off the coast of Geraldton. The survivors set up camp, sent off a rescue party to Batavia (now Jakarta) in the ship's boat and waited. It took three months for a rescue party to arrive and in that time a mutiny had taken place and more than 120 of the survivors had been murdered. The ringleaders were hanged, but two of the mutineers were unceremoniously dumped on the coast.

In 1656 the *Vergulde Draeck* (Gilt Dragon) struck a reef about 100 km north of Perth and although a party of survivors made its way to

Batavia, no trace, other than a few scattered coins, was found of the other survivors who had straggled ashore. The *Zuytdorp* ran aground beneath the towering cliffs north of Kalbarri in 1712. Wine bottles, other relics and the remains of fires have been found on the cliff top but again no trace of survivors.

In 1727 the *Zeewijk* followed the ill-fated *Batavia* to destruction on the Abrolhos Islands. Again a small party of survivors made its way to Batavia but many of the remaining sailors died before they could be rescued. Many relics from these shipwrecks, particularly the *Batavia*, can be seen today in the museums in Fremantle and Geraldton.

Information

The Geraldton Tourist Bureau (tel 21 3999) is in the Bill Sewell Recreation Centre, on Chapman Rd, across from the railway station and beside the Northgate Shopping Centre. It's open from 9 am to 5 pm Monday to Saturday and from 10 am to 2 pm Sundays and public holidays.

Geraldton's annual Sunshine Festival, with windsurfing contests and other activities, takes place in June, July or August each year. In March there's a Wind Festival with kite-flying contests – Geraldton is a very windy city.

Geraldton Museum

The town's museum is in two separate, but nearby, buildings. The Maritime Museum tells the story of the early wrecks and has assorted relics from the Dutch ships, including items from the *Batavia* and the *Zeewijk* and the carved wooden sternpiece from the *Zuytdorp* found in 1927, by a local stockman, on top of the cliffs above the point at which the ship had run ashore. It was not until the 1950s that the wreckage was positively identified as that of the *Zuytdorp*.

The miniature submarine displayed outside was intended to be used for fishing green crayfish but proved unworkable. The Old Railway Building has displays on the flora and fauna of the region and on its settlement by Aborigines and later by Europeans. The museums are open Monday to Saturday from 10 am to 5 pm and Sundays and holidays from 1 to 5 pm.

Cathedral

Geraldton's St Francis Xavier Cathedral is just one of a number of buildings in Geraldton and the WA midwest designed by Monsignor John Hawes, a strange priest-cum-architect who left WA in 1939 and spent the rest of his life (he died in 1956) a hermit on an island in the Carribbean. Construction of the cathedral commenced in 1916, the year after Hawes arrived in Geraldton, but his plans were too grandiose and the partially built cathedral was not completed until 1938.

Other Attractions

The Geraldton Art Gallery, on the corner of Chapman Rd and Durlacher St, is open daily. The Lighthouse Keeper's Cottage, on Chapman Rd, is the Geraldton Historical Society's headquarters and is open Thursdays from 10 am to 4 pm. You can look out over Geraldton from the Waverley Heights Lookout, on Brede St, or watch the lobster boats at Fisherman's Wharf, at the end of Marine Terrace. Point Moore Lighthouse, in operation since 1878, is also worth a visit.

Places to Stay

Hostels The Geraldton *Youth Hostel* (tel 21 2549) is at 80 Francis St and costs $8.50 a night.

Guest Houses & Hotels Geraldton has some old-fashioned seaside guest houses, particularly along Marine Terrace. The *Grantown* (tel 21 3275) is at 172 and has rooms at $16 a person ($4 more with breakfast). At 184 is the *Sun City* (tel 21 2205), offering bed and a light breakfast for $18 a single or $28 to $30 a double. The *Bethel Guest House* (tel 21 4770) is at 311 and bed and light breakfast there is $16.

Cheap rooms are also available at some of the older-style hotels. The *Freemason's* (tel 21 1688), on Marine Terrace, is $27 a single or $46 to $50 a double, including breakfast. The *Geraldton* (tel 21 3700), just off Marine Terrace, at 19 Gregory St, is cheaper at $22/30.

Motels The *Hacienda* (tel 21 2155), on Durlacher St, has rooms at $40/50. The *Mariner Motor* (tel 21 2544), at 298 Chapman Rd, is cheaper at $30/40. A number of places also have family units.

Point Moore Cottages (tel 21 1047), at 24 Captain's Crescent, has cottages at $33 to $55 a double. *Geraldton's Ocean West*, on the corner of Haddaway and Willcock Drive, at Mahomets Beach, is similar.

Camping Geraldton has half a dozen camping sites with sites for $9 to $11. Most have on-site vans, for $25 a night. A couple are only two km from the centre of town.

Places to Eat

There are a number of small snack bars and cafes along Marine Terrace, like *Thuy's Cake Shop*, at 202, which is open from early in the morning. *Maria's Cafe*, at 174 Marine Terrace, does straightforward cafe food at down to earth prices. The *Sail Inn Snack Bar* is by the museum, on Marine Terrace.

Anita's Pizzas is at 205 Marine Terrace. The *Victoria Hotel*, at 183-187 Marine Terrace, does counter meals.

Chinese restaurants include the *Golden Coin* and the *Jade House*, both on Marine Terrace. At 105 Durlacher St, just back from the centre, is *Los Amigos*, a good, straightforward, licensed Mexican place. It's popular, and deservedly so. Fancier restaurants include *Reflections*, on Foreshore Drive.

Getting There & Away

Air Skywest and Ansett WA fly from Perth to Geraldton ($120). Skywest fly further north to Meekatharra and other points. Ansett WA have direct flights to Carnarvon.

Bus Westrail, Greyhound, Bus Australia and Deluxe all operate regular services from Perth to Geraldton. The trip costs

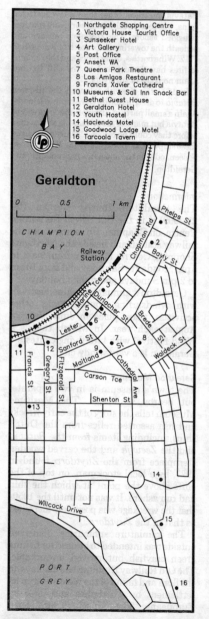

1	Northgate Shopping Centre
2	Victoria House Tourist Office
3	Sunseeker Hotel
4	Art Gallery
5	Post Office
6	Ansett WA
7	Queens Park Theatre
8	Los Amigos Restaurant
9	Francis Xavier Cathedral
10	Museums & Sail Inn Snack Bar
11	Bethel Guest House
12	Geraldton Hotel
13	Youth Hostel
14	Hacienda Motel
15	Goodwood Lodge Motel
16	Tarcoola Tavern

Geraldton

$58. Westrail continues north to Meekatharra or to Kalbarri. The other operators follow Highway 1 through Port Hedland and Broome to Darwin. Westrail and Bus Australia stop at the railway station, Greyhound and Deluxe at the tourist office.

NORTH OF GERALDTON

Northampton is near the Hutt River Province, where a local farmer, deciding that tourism must be an easier game than farming, appointed himself 'Prince Leonard of Hutt' and seceded from Australia. Today 60,000 people visit his 'independent principality' annually, although it's actually nothing much more than a bare outback station. The turn-off is north of Northampton, towards Kalbarri.

The area inland of Northampton is noted for its wildflowers. Northampton was founded to exploit lead and copper, discovered in 1848; lead is still produced here. An early mine manager's home, Chiverton House, is now a fine Municipal Museum. The stone building was constructed between 1868 and 1875 using local materials. Horrocks Beach, 21 km away, is a popular holiday resort. The nearby Gwalia Church cemetery also tells its tales of the early days. Lynton, near Port Gregory, has the ruins of a convict hiring station.

KALBARRI (population 800)

On the coast at the mouth of the Murchison River is Kalbarri, a pleasant holiday resort 66 km off the main highway. The area is intimately associated with the west coast's Dutch shipwrecks. The *Zuytdorp* was wrecked about 65 km north of Kalbarri in 1712 but earlier, in 1629, two *Batavia* mutineers were marooned at Wittecarra Gully, an inlet just south of the town. Diving on the *Zuytdorp* is very difficult as a heavy swell and unpredictable currents batter the shoreline but in 1986 divers from the Geraldton Museum did manage to raise a quantity of material.

The Kalbarri Travel Service (tel 37 1104) is on Grey St.

Around Town

There are some superb cliff faces south of town. Red Bluff, by Wittecarra Gully, is spectacular. There are some fine surfing breaks along the coast – Jakes Corner, 3½ km south of town, is reputed to be one of the best in the state.

Rainbow Jungle is a stretch of rainforest and a bird park four km from town towards Red Bluff. Fantasyland is a doll collection on Grey St. Pelicans, which can often be seen on the river estuary in front of the town, are fed in front of Fantasyland at 8.30 am most mornings. Boats can be hired on the river and river tours are made on the lower reaches of the river on the *Kalbarri River Queen*.

Kalbarri National Park

Kalbarri National Park, on the Murchison River, has many spectacular gorges. From Kalbarri it's only 35 km to the Loop and Z-Bend, two particularly impressive gorges. Short walking trails lead down into the gorges from the road access points but there are also longer walking trails through the park. It takes about two days to walk between Z-Bend and the Loop. The park puts on a particularly gorgeous display of wildflowers in the spring.

Places to Stay & Eat

Kalbarri is a popular resort and there's a wide selection of caravan parks, holiday units, hotels and motels. *Averest Duplexes* (tel 37 1101), on Mortimer St, have a special deal for YHA members, with units at $20 for two and $2 for each extra person.

In Kalbarri Arcade there's a good health food shop with sandwiches and delicious cakes. Next door is a bakery and there are several snack bars. The *Gulgai Tavern* does counter meals. The *Zuytdorp* is the town's fancy restaurant.

Getting There & Away

Westrail buses come into Kalbarri twice a week, Deluxe three times a week. Kalbarri Coach Tours (tel (099) 37 1104) have a service from Geraldton to Kalbarri. They also have tours to the Loop, Z-Bend and the Hutt River Province.

SHARK BAY

Shark Bay has some spectacular beaches and the famous dolphins of Monkey Mia. The first recorded landing on Australian soil by a European took place at Shark Bay in 1616 when the Dutch explorer Dirk Hartog landed on the island that now bears his name. He nailed an inscribed plate to a post on the beach but a later Dutch visitor collected it and it's now in a museum in Amsterdam although there's a reproduction in the Geraldton Museum.

Denham, the main population centre of Shark Bay, is 135 km off the main highway from the Overlander Roadhouse. Denham is the most westerly town in Australia and was once a pearling port. Today prawns are the local money maker.

Around Town

On the way in from the highway look for the signs of stromatolites, a rare form of 'living rock'. The long stretch of Shell Beach, just beyond Nanga Station, is solid shells nearly 10 metres deep! In places in Shark Bay the shells are so tightly packed that they can be cut into blocks and used for building construction. Freshwater Camp is a pioneer homestead museum at Nanga. At Eagle Bluff there are superb views from the cliff. Hamelin Pool, at the southern end of the bay, is a marine reserve.

Monkey Mia Dolphins

Monkey Mia is 26 km from Denham, on the other side of the peninsula. It's believed that dolphins have been visiting there since the early '60s, although it's only in the last 10 years that it's become world famous. Monkey Mia's dolphins simply drop by to visit humans; they swim

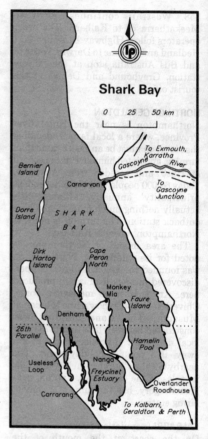

Shark Bay

0   25   50 km

right into knee-deep water and will nudge up against you, even take a fish if it's offered, although they seem to do it almost out of courtesy rather than with any thought of a free feed.

The dolphins generally come in every day during the winter months, less frequently during the summer. They may arrive singly or in groups of five or more, but as many as 13 were recorded on one occasion. They seem to come in more often in the mornings.

Monkey Mia reserve has an interesting dolphin information centre; the entry fee to the reserve is $5 a car. There are some rules of good behaviour for visitors:

1. Let them come to you – if you stand in the shallows they'll swim up to you. Don't chase them or try to swim with them.
2. Stroke them along their sides with the back of your hand. Don't touch their fins or their blowhole.
3. If you offer them fish it should be whole, not gutted or filleted. They will take defrosted fish but only if it has completely thawed.

Places to Stay

Accommodation in Shark Bay can be very tight during school vacations. You can camp at Monkey Mia, Denham or 50 km south of Denham at Nanga Station. The *Monkey Mia Caravan Park* (tel 48 1320) has sites at $9 and on-site vans. The *Denham Seaside Park* (tel 48 1242), *Tradewinds* (tel 48 1222) and *Shark Bay Park* (tel 48 1387) are similarly priced. Tradewinds also has chalets from $33 a night.

The large and well equipped *Nanga Bay Caravan Park*, at Nanga Station, has sites at $11, bunkhouses at $17 a person, cabins from $33 to $44, fishermen's huts from $38 to $44 and two bedroom home units at $66.

The *Shark Bay Hotel* (tel 48 1203) has rooms from $44 to $66. There are a number of holiday cottages, villas and the like. *Shark Bay Holiday Cottages* (tel 48 1200) and *Tradewinds Chalets* are good value.

The Shark Bay shire produces a useful leaflet with a rundown on all the accommodation possibilities. The Shark Bay Accommodation Service (tel 48 1323) has a number of houses available, usually by the week.

Bay Lodge (tel (099) 48 1278) has been recommended for its good value and great atmosphere.

Places to Eat

In Denham *Hungry Jim's* does fish & chips and other fast food. The *Shark Bay Hotel* has counter meals, or there's the more expensive *Old Pearler* restaurant. At Nanga Station there's the *Nanga Barn Restaurant*.

Getting There & Away

North from Kalbarri it's a fairly dull, boring and often very hot run to Carnarvon. The Overlander Roadhouse, 290 km north of Geraldton, is the turn-off to Shark Bay.

Deluxe have a bus service into Denham three times a week. Northland Coaches (tel 41 1475) have a Saturday afternoon service from Carnarvon to Denham. It then continues to Monkey Mia on the Sunday morning and spends two hours there before returning to Denham and Carnarvon on the Sunday afternoon. Three days a week there's a Denham / Overland Roadhouse / Denham / Monkey Mia bus service. The return fare from Denham to Monkey Mia is $10 – phone 48 1253 for details.

CARNARVON (population 5100)

Carnarvon, at the mouth of the Gascoyne River, is noted for its tropical fruit, particularly its bananas. Subsurface water, which flows even when the river is dry, is tapped to irrigate the riverside plantations. Salt is produced near Carnarvon and prawns and scallops are harvested. On the nearby Browns Range is the 'big dish', a 26½ metre reflector of the Overseas Telecommunications Commission earthstation. The main street of Carnarvon is 40 metres wide, a reminder of the days when camel trains used to pass through.

Information

The Carnarvon District Tourist Bureau (tel 41 1146) is on Robinson St. It operates day tours of the area.

Things to See

Carnarvon was once a NASA station and there's a museum beside the tourist office relating the town's role in NASA space shots.

If you're lucky you might actually see dolphins in the river right in the middle of town. Carnarvon's long jetty is a popular fishing spot. There's a little railway line out to the end and you can trundle along it in a toy train for 50c (children 25c) each way. The small Lighthouse Keeper's Cottage Museum is beside the jetty and is open from 10 am to 12 noon and from 2 to 4 pm daily.

Pelican Point, only five km from town, is a good swimming and picnic spot, but you'll need 4WD to get to Bush Bay (turn-off 20 km) or New Beach (40 km).

Other attractions in the vicinity are the spectacular blowholes 70 km north; there's a fine beach about one km south of the blowhole. Cape Couvier, where salt is loaded for Japan, is 100 km north. Rocky Pool is a superb swimming hole 55 km inland along the Gascoyne River. Remote Gascoyne Junction is 164 km inland from Carnarvon in the gemstone-rich Kennedy Range.

Places to Stay

Hostels The *Accommodation Centre* (tel 41 2511) costs $11 a night a person; there's a 10% discount for YHA members. It's at 23 Wheelock Way – look for the sign as you come into Carnarvon from the main highway.

Hotels & Motels Carnarvon has some old-fashioned hotels with old-fashioned prices. The *Gascoyne* (tel 41 1412), on Foss St, has rooms at $20/22. Or there's the *Port Hotel* (tel 41 1704), on Robinson St, which has rooms from $22 to $44. The *Carnarvon* (tel 41 1181), on Olivia Terrace, is $17/33 in the older hotel section, $33/55 in the newer motel part.

The *Carnarvon Motor Inn* (tel 41 1532), on the North-West Coastal Highway, is more expensive at $44/55. Or there are holiday units at the *Carnarvon Beach Holiday Resort* (tel 41 2226), at Pelican Point, for $50 for two. The *Fascine Lodge* and *Hospitality Inn* motels are more expensive, with rooms from $60 to $100.

Camping There is a series of caravan parks along the North-West Coastal Highway as it comes into town. Sites are typically $9, on-site vans from $25.

Places to Eat

There are plenty of places to eat in Carnarvon. Try *Carnarvon Fresh Seafoods* or *San-n-Tone*, both on Robinson St, for fish & chips; pizzas are sold by the latter. On the same street are *Mamies* and the *Outlet*, both standard coffee lounges. You can get counter meals at the *Gascoyne Hotel* or the *Carnarvon Hotel*, straightforward food at $10 to $12. The *Port Hotel's* Garden Restaurant is a bit fancier but with the same familiar pub food dishes at very similar prices – good food but somewhat slow service.

There is the *Dragon Pearl* Chinese restaurant or, if you're looking for a night out, you could try the *Cordon Nurk*, on Robinson St, which specialises in French-Gaelic cuisine! Main courses are $15 to

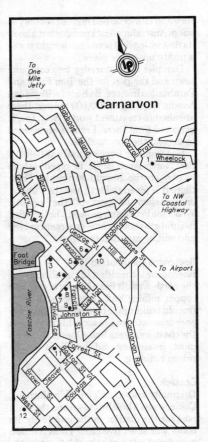

Carnarvon

To One Mile Jetty

To NW Coastal Highway

To Airport

Foot Bridge

Fascine River

1. Accommodation Centre Hostel
2. Fascine Lodge Motel
3. Gascoyne Hotel
4. Tourist Bureau
5. Port Hotel
6. Fresh Seafoods Fish & Chips
7. Ansett WA, Outlet Snack Bar & Post Office
8. Cordon Nurk Restaurant & Bikeland Bicycle Hire
9. Dragon Pearl Chinese Restaurant
10. San-n-Tone Pizza & Fish & Chips
11. Carnarvon Hotel
12. Hospitality Inn

\$20 and sound delicious but this is still WA: a sign in the window announces, 'No thongs, singlets or footy shorts – No Exceptions'!

Getting There & Away

Air Ansett WA fly to Carnarvon from Perth (\$195), Geraldton (\$133), Learmonth (\$105) and other centres.

Bus Greyhound, Deluxe and Bus Australia all pass through Carnarvon on their way north or south. It's \$76 from Perth.

Getting Around

You can hire bicycles from Bikeland, next to Fitz's Newsagency, on Robinson St.

EXMOUTH (population 2600)

The road to Exmouth forks away from the main coast road and runs up to the US navy base at the top of the North-West Cape. Here a very hush-hush communications base is marked by 13 very low-frequency transmitter stations. Twelve of them are higher than the Eiffel Tower, and all to support the 13th, which is 396 metres high, the tallest structure in the southern hemisphere. The base cost almost \$100 million to build and tours can be arranged with the tourist bureau.

Exmouth is a new town, built to service the navy base. It's a long haul off the main coast road but I've got a soft spot for the town as it was the first place I set foot in Australia. Some years back Maureen and I hitched a ride from Bali on a yacht and ended up there.

The Exmouth Tourist Bureau (tel 49 1176) is on Thew St.

Around Town

There's a shell museum on Pellew St. The area is chiefly noted for its commercial prawning and excellent fishing. There are some fine beaches on the Exmouth Gulf and natural features like the Yardie Creek Gorge.

The Ningaloo Reef

Running along the western side of the North-West Cape for 260 km is the Ningaloo Reef, rapidly becoming much better known. This miniature version of the Great Barrier Reef is actually much more accessible since in places it is only a few km offshore. Coral Bay, just eight km off the main road up the cape, is the main access point for the reef and glass-bottomed boat trips are made from there. Greenback turtles lay their eggs along the cape beach and placid whale sharks, the world's largest fish, can also be seen in the reef's waters.

Getting There & Away

Bus Australia has services to Exmouth from Perth twice weekly. Ansett WA fly regularly to Learmonth from Perth ($242) and have less frequent connections with other centres.

ROEBOURNE AREA

The Roebourne area is a busy little enclave of historic towns and modern port facilities. The area serves as the port for the ore produced at Tom Price and Pannawonica and is also the onshore base for the North-West Shelf natural gas fields. Enquire locally before venturing into the sea in this area, particularly during the summer months.

Karratha, the dormitory town for the area, is a modern, rapidly growing and rather expensive place.

Information

North-West Explorer Tours, in the shopping centre in Karratha, acts as an information centre. The Roebourne District Tourist Association (tel 82 1060), at 173 Roe St, Roebourne, is particularly helpful.

Dampier (population 2500)

Dampier, on King Bay, faces the islands of the Dampier Archipelago. They were named after the English pirate-explorer William Dampier who visited the area in 1699 and immortalised himself not only as one of Australia's first knockers but also as its first whingeing pom – he thought it was a pretty miserable place.

Dampier is a Hamersley Iron company town and the port for the Tom Price and Paraburdoo iron ore. Its huge facilities can handle ships up to 230,000 tonnes; there are also ore treatment works. Salt, too, is exported from there. Permits are needed to inspect the port facilities.

Gas from the huge natural gas fields of the North-West Shelf is piped ashore nearby on the Burrup Peninsula. From there it is piped to Perth and the Pilbara, or liquefied as part of the gigantic Woodside Petroleum project; The liquefied natural gas should come on stream in 1989 and will be exported to Japan.

Roebourne (population 1700)

Roebourne is the oldest town still active in the north-west. It has a history of gold and copper mining and there are still some fine old buildings to be seen. The town was once connected to Cossack, 13 km away on the coast, by a tram line. One of the town's most interesting old buildings is the prison building.

Cossack

Originally known as Tien Tsin Harbour, Cossack was a bustling town and the main port for the district in the late 1800s. Its boom was short lived and Point Samson soon supplanted it as the chief port for the area. The sturdy old buildings date from 1870 to 1890 and much of the now deserted ghost town was restored as a Bicentennial project in 1988. Beyond the town there's a pioneer cemetery with a small Japanese section dating from the old pearl diving days. There are excellent beaches in the area and the cooler, drier months are best for a visit.

Wickham (population 2400)

Wickham is the Cliffs Robe River Iron company town, handling their ore exporting facilities 10 km away at Cape

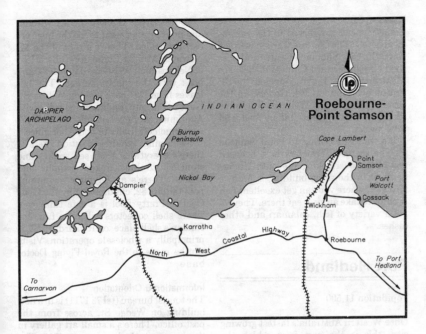

Roebourne-
Point Samson

INDIAN OCEAN

DAMPIER
ARCHIPELAGO

Burrup
Peninsula

Cape Lambert

Point
Samson

Port
Walcott

Nickol Bay

Dampier

Cossack

Wickham

Karratha

Coastal   Highway

Roebourne

North   –   West

To Port
Hedland

To
Carnarvon

Lambert, where the jetty is three km long. Ore is railed there from the mining operations inland at Pannawonica.

Point Samson

This port, beyond Wickham, supplanted Cossack when the old port silted up. In turn it has been replaced by the modern port facilities of Dampier and Cape Lambert. Today the rickety old jetty is popular for fishing and there are also good beaches at Point Samson itself and at nearby Honeymoon Cove. This is a popular local resort area.

Other Places of Interest

Python Pool, on the Wittenoom road, was once an oasis for Afghani camel drivers and still makes a good place for a pause today. Millstream is another pleasant oasis, further south of Python Pool and Mt Herbert. Whim Creek, 80 km east of

Roebourne, was the site of the first significant Pilbara mineral find and once had a large copper mine.

Places to Stay

There are camping sites in Roebourne and Karratha and hotel or motel facilities in Dampier, Karratha, Roebourne and Wickham. Karratha is very expensive – a couple of motels have rooms at well in excess of $100 a night. The *Victoria Hotel* (tel 82 1001), on Roe St, Roebourne, is the cheapest regular motel around, with rooms at $33/44.

Omars Village (tel 85 2868), on Mooligunn Rd, Karratha, is essentially single men's quarters, with simple little bed-in-a-box rooms at $32/55 for singles/ doubles including meals. The other local bargain is *Samson Accommodation* (tel 87 1052), at Point Samson, with units with a share kitchen from $20/33.

Places to Eat

Counter meals are served in the various local hotels. The *Chinese Garden* is in the Karratha City Shopping Centre and does good straightforward Chinese dishes. For Mexican try *Los Amigos*, opposite the BP station on Balmoral Rd. *Oodles*, on the corner of Sharpe and Welcome Rd, in the shopping centre, does Italian food and take-aways.

It's worth detouring to Point Samson for the seafood. *Trawlers* is a licensed restaurant overlooking the pier. Underneath it in the same building is *Moby's Kitchen*, where you can get excellent fish & chips to take away or eat there. They've got a variety of fish, calamari and other dishes.

Port Hedland

Population 11,500

Once Western Australia's fastest growing city, this is the port from which the Pilbara's iron ore is shipped to Japan. The town is built on an island connected to the mainland by causeways. The main highway into Port Hedland enters along a causeway three km long. The port handles the largest annual tonnage of any Australian port. Like other towns along the coast it's also a centre for salt production; huge 'dunes' of salt can be seen six km from the town.

Even before the Marble Bar gold rush, the town had been important: it had been a grazing centre since 1864, while during the 1870s a fleet of 150 pearling luggers had been based there. By 1946, however, the population had dwindled to a mere 150.

The port is on a mangrove fringed inlet – there are plenty of fish, crabs and oysters and birds around. As Port Hedland has grown, satellite towns have sprung up, both to handle the mining output of the area and also to accommodate the area's workers.

You can visit the wharf area without any prior arrangement to see the huge ore carriers loaded. There's a tour of the Mt Newman Mining Company's operations at Nelsons Point every weekday at 10.30 am; book with the tourist bureau. The bus leaves from the main gate on Wilson St. Next to the gate is a limestone ridge with Aboriginal carvings but unfortunately it's very much off limits to non-Aborigines.

Swimming requires caution here – there's everything from sea snakes and stonefish to blue ringed octopus and sharks. There's an Olympic swimming pool (adults $2, children $1) by the Civic Centre. Pretty Pool is a safe tidal pool where shell collectors will have fun. Joe Rinken's shell place, on Richardson St, is principally a wholesale operation. Visits can be made to the Royal Flying Doctor base.

Information & Orientation

The tourist bureau (tel 73 1711) is in a new building on Wedge St, across from the post office. There's a small art gallery in the bureau and also showers ($1). The bureau is open 8.30 am to 5.30 pm and 8.15 to 10.15 pm daily. It has an excellent map of the town and a Port Hedland heritage walk brochure.

Port Hedland really sprawls. The main part of town is basically a long, narrow island. It's several km south to the airport and several km south again to the dormitory town of South Hedland. October to March is the cyclone season in Port Hedland.

Places to Stay

Hostels The *Backpacker's Hostel* (tel 73 2198), at 20 Richardson St, between Edgar and McKay, is run by Geoff Schafer who is something of a Port Hedland institution. It's a bit rough and ready but friendly. It costs $7 a night and has kitchen and laundry facilities. Although Port Hedland is not a great tourist attraction some travellers pause here for short-term work.

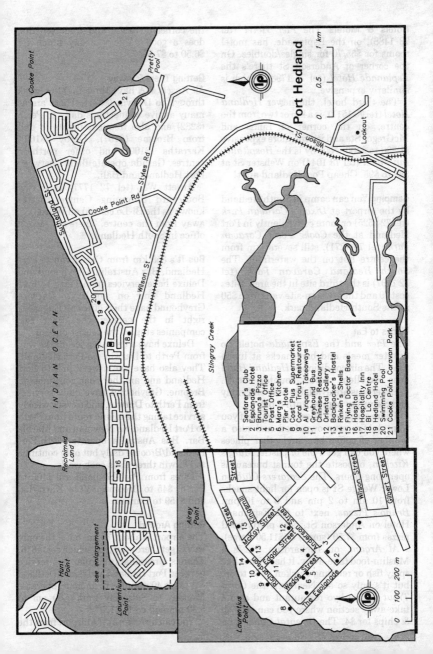

Port Hedland

1 km
0.5
0

1 Seafarer's Club
2 Esplanade Hotel
3 Brunni's Pizza
4 Tourist Office
5 Post Office
6 Marg's Kitchen
7 Pier Hotel
8 Cost Plus Supermarket
9 Al Argam Takeaways
10 Chinese Restaurant
11 Greyhound Bus
12 Oriental Gallery
13 Backpacker's Hostel
14 Rinken's Shells
15 Flying Doctor Base
16 Hospital
17 Hospitality Inn
18 Bi Lo Centre
19 Hedland Hotel
20 Swimming Pool
21 Cooke Point Caravan Park

200 m
100
0

Hotels & Motels The *Pier Hotel* (tel 73 1488), on the Esplanade, has motel rooms for \$55/70 for singles/doubles. On the corner of Anderson St there's the *Esplanade Hotel* (tel 73 1798), which is similarly expensive.

The third hotel, the newer *Hedland Hotel* (tel 73 1511), is a km or two from the centre, on the corner of Lukis and McGregor Sts and is even more expensive at \$80 to \$100. Nearby is the *Hospitality Inn Motel* (tel 73 1044) on Webster St at \$85 to \$95. Cheap Port Hedland ain't!

Camping You can camp in South Hedland by the airport at *Dixon's Caravan Park* (tel 72 2525) or more conveniently in Port Hedland at the *Cooke Point Caravan Park* (tel 73 1271), still several km from the centre but on the waterfront. The *South Hedland Caravan Park* (tel 72 1197) is the third site in the area. Sites cost \$9 and there are on-site vans from \$50 at the South Hedland park.

Places to Eat

The *Pier* and the *Esplanade* hotels do counter meals and bar snacks at lunch time. The air-conditioned *Hedland Hotel* does excellent value counter meals. Counter teas are available only on Friday and Saturday nights, until 8 pm.

There are plenty of supermarkets if you want to fix your own food and also a number of coffee bars and other places where you can get a pie or pastie. *Marg's Kitchen*, opposite the tourist bureau, is open long hours. The *Seafarers Club* on Lower Wedge St is open for light snacks from 10 am to 2 pm and 6 to 10 pm. *Bruno's Pizzas*, next to the Esplanade Hotel on Anderson St, does pretty good pizzas from \$7.50 (small) or \$11.50 (large).

Al Arqam, on Richardson St, is a Muslim-food take-away. It has dishes like spicy fish or rendang chicken at \$5 to \$6, but it's only so so. Nearby is the *Coral Trout* with a byo restaurant and also a take-away section where you can get fish & chips for \$4. The *Oriental Gallery*, on the corner of Edgar and Anderson Sts, does a good value weekday lunch for \$6.50 to \$7.50.

Getting There & Away

Air Ansett WA have three flights a week through to Darwin (\$334). There are as many as five connections daily to Perth (\$282) and also frequent flights to and from Broome (\$137), Derby (\$166), Karratha (\$100) and other northern centres. Garuda operate flights between Port Hedland and Bali.

Ansett WA (tel 72 1777) is in the Boulevard Shopping Centre (better known as the Bi-Lo centre) on Wilson St, away from the centre. There's a second office in South Hedland.

Bus It's 855 km from Carnarvon to Port Hedland. Bus Australia, Greyhound and Deluxe have services from Perth to Port Hedland and on north to Darwin. Greyhound have their office on Edgar St, right in the centre; the other two companies stop at the tourist bureau.

Deluxe have a daily service all the way from Perth to Darwin via Port Hedland. They also have one a week just to Port Hedland and another that continues to Broome. Greyhound have daily services from Perth to Darwin, and a twice weekly service taking the inland route from Perth to Port Hedland via Newman and Marble Bar. Bus Australia operate Perth/Port Hedland/Broome daily but only continue to Darwin three days each week.

Fares from Port Hedland are \$106 to Perth, \$45 to Broome, \$30 to Karratha, and \$159 to Darwin.

Getting Around

The airport is about 10 km out - the only way to get there is by taxi, which costs \$16. There's a reasonably regular bus service between Port Hedland and South Hedland - it takes 40 minutes to an hour, operates Monday to Saturday from 7.50 am to 5.30 pm and costs \$1.70.

You can hire cars at the airport from the

usual operators. WK Motors, at the BP station at 36 Anderson St, has older cars for around town use only from $17 a day plus 10c a km. They rent motorscooters too. The Backpacker's Hostel has bikes at a mere $3 a day or $2 a half day.

The Great Northern Highway

Although most people heading for the north-west and the Kimberley travel up the coast, the Great Northern Highway is much more direct. The highway extends from Perth to Newman and then skirts the eastern edge of the Pilbara on its way to Port Hedland via Marble Bar. The total distance is 1692 km, of which about 350 km has still to be sealed.

The Great Northern Highway is not the most interesting road in Australia – for most of the way it passes through country that is flat, dull and dreary in the extreme. Once you've passed through the old gold towns of the Murchison River gold fields – Mt Magnet, Cue and Meekatharra – there's really nothing until you reach Newman, 400 km further on.

There are still some interesting old buildings of solid stone in Cue, while Meekatharra is still a mining centre. At one time it was a railhead for cattle brought down from the Northern Territory and the east Kimberley. There are various old gold towns in both areas. From Meekatharra you can travel south to the gold fields around Kalgoorlie. It's a bit over 700 km to Kalgoorlie, more than half of it on unsealed road.

Getting There & Away
Air Skywest (booked through Australian Airlines) fly from Perth to Meekatharra, Mt Magnet and Wiluna, and also from Meekatharra to Marble Bar and Port Hedland.

Bus Greyhound have three buses a week from Perth to Newman ($79) via Meekatharra ($56). Twice a week the bus continues on to Port Hedland.

The Pilbara

The Pilbara is the iron ore producing area accounting for much of WA's prosperity – from some of the hottest country on earth. Gigantic machines are used to tear the dusty red ranges apart. It's isolated, harsh and fabulously wealthy. The Pilbara towns are almost all company towns: either mining centres where the ore is wrenched from the earth or ports from which it's shipped abroad. Exceptions are the beautiful gorges of Wittenoom and earlier historic mining centres like Marble Bar.

Getting There & Away
Air Ansett WA fly from Perth to Newman and Paraburdoo with connections from there to other northern centres. Skywest have services to and from Marble Bar.

Bus Greyhound have three buses a week from Perth to Newman ($79). Two of them continue to Port Hedland. Greyhound also have a once weekly service from the Nanutarra turn-off to Tom Price.

There is no bus service to Wittenoom although it is sometimes possible to get on a tour bus from Port Hedland; otherwise, you really need your own transport. Most of the roads in the Pilbara are dirt. The Great Northern Highway is surfaced from Perth to Newman but much of the rest is still unsealed.

You can reach Wittenoom directly from Port Hedland (284 km off the Great Northern Highway), from near Roebourne (262 km off the North-West Coastal Highway) or from the Nanutarra turn-off (377 km off the North-West Coastal Highway). It's 181 km from Wittenoom to the Great Northern Highway at Roy Hill,

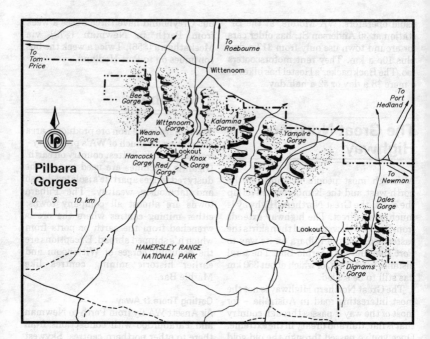

Pilbara Gorges

To Tom Price

To Roebourne

Wittenoom

To Port Hedland

Bee Gorge

Wittenoom Gorge

Kalamina Gorge

Yampire Gorge

Weano Gorge

Lookout

To Newman

Hancock Gorge

Knox Gorge

Red Gorge

Dales Gorge

HAMERSLEY RANGE NATIONAL PARK

Lookout

Dignams Gorge

0 5 10 km

---

north of Newman. Whichever route you take there's a lot of unsealed road to cover.

INLAND TO WITTENOOM

A little beyond Roebourne a road turns inland to Wittenoom. The road passes through the Chichester Range National Park, where Python Pool is a pleasant swimming hole and picnic spot. The small Millstream National Park is a little distance off the road – a pleasant oasis with pools, trees, ferns and lilies. Water from the natural spring there is piped to Dampier, Karratha, Wickham and Cape Lambert.

WITTENOOM (population 250)

Wittenoom is the Pilbara's tourist centre. It had an earlier history as an asbestos mining town but mining finally halted in 1966 and it is the magnificent gorges of the Hamersley Range which now draws people to the town. Wittenoom is at the northern end of the Hamersley Range National Park and the most famous gorge, Wittenoom Gorge, is immediately south of the town. A surfaced road runs the 13 km to this gorge, passing old asbestos mines and a number of smaller gorges and pretty pools.

Like other gorges in central Australia, those of the Hamersley Range are spectacular both in their sheer rocky faces and their varied colours. In the early spring the park is often carpeted with colourful wildflowers. Travel down the Newman road 24 km and there's a turn-off to the Yampire Gorge where blue veins of asbestos can be seen in the rock. Fig Tree Well, in the gorge, was once used by

Afghani camel drivers as a watering point. The road continues through Yampire Gorge to Dales Gorge but only the first couple of km of its 45 km length can be reached. On this same route you can get to Circular Pool and a nearby lookout, and by a footpath to the bottom of the Fortescue Falls.

The Joffre Falls road will take you to Oxers Lookout at the junction of the Red, Weano and Hancock gorges. Following the main road to Tom Price you pass through the small Rio Tinto Gorge, 43 km from Wittenoom, and just beyond this is the Hamersley Range, only four km from the road. Mt Meharry (1245 metres), the highest mountain in Western Australia, is in the south-east of the Hamersley Range National Park.

If you're on foot, be sure you can find your way back as all the bush looks the same and there are no people or waterholes. Notify somebody that you're going. For the more energetic there's a walk starting at the asbestos mine about 13 km from Wittenoom on the surfaced road. Walk up Wittenoom Gorge, then up Red Gorge (some swimming may be required) until you come out at the pool below Oscars Lookout. Then proceed up Hancock Gorge, cross the road and follow the footpath into Weano Gorge, which can be followed back to the junction pool – it involves two quite scary climbs, so be warned! The circuit is a good day's walk – get detailed directions from the Wittenoom Tourist Bureau on Second Ave. Weano Gorge, the most spectacular one, can be easily approached from near Oscars Lookout and can be followed down almost to the junction pool with no difficulty.

Places to Stay

The *Wittenoom Bungarra Bivouac* (tel 89 7026) is at 74 Fifth Ave and has beds at $7. Wittenoom also has a caravan park with on-site vans, a motel and a hotel with regular rooms and motel units. *Wittenoom Holiday Homes* (tel 89 7096), on Fifth

Ave, have houses with kitchen, bathroom and laundry from $20 a person.

Getting There & Away

Wittenoom Bus Lines (tel 89 7055) do a day-trip that makes a 250 km circuit of the area's gorges and other attractions. It costs $33 (children $16.50). Westate Air have connecting flights from Port Hedland, at $162 for the day. Bush Bus, based in Marble Bar, do week long circuits of the region from Newman or weekend trips to Wittenoom from Port Hedland. The tourist bureau in Port Hedland will arrange bookings.

NEWMAN (population 5500)

At Newman, a town which only came into existence in the 1970s, Mt Whaleback is being systematically taken apart and railed down to the coast. It's a solid mountain of iron ore and every day up to 120,000 tonnes of ore are produced, a task that requires moving nearly 300,000 tonnes of material. After crushing, the ore is loaded into 144 car, two km long trains which are sent down the 426 km railway line, Australia's longest private railway, to Port Hedland from where it is shipped overseas. Guided tours of the operations are available from the Mt Newman Company office several times daily in winter and once a day at 1 pm in the summer. The town of Newman is a modern, green company town built solely to service the mine.

TOM PRICE & PARABURDOO

Similar mining activities are also carried on in these two towns. The ore is railed to the coast at Dampier. Check with the Hamersley Iron office about inspecting the mine works.

GOLDSWORTHY & SHAY GAP

Goldsworthy was the first Pilbara iron town and, like Newman, its production is shipped to Port Hedland and loaded on to bulk carriers at Finucane Island. At one time Mt Goldsworthy was 132 metres high but it's now a big hole in the ground. Since mining operations shifted 70 km east to Shay Gap, the mine at Goldsworthy is starting to fill with water and there are only a few workers living there now, maintaining the electricity generators that run the massive shovels and provide town power at Shay Gap. Both these towns were badly damaged in 1980 by Cyclone Enid.

MARBLE BAR (population 350)

Reputed to be the hottest place in Australia, Marble Bar had a period in the 1920s when for 160 consecutive days the temperature topped 37°C (100°F). On one occasion, in 1905, the mercury soared to 49.1°C. From October to March days over 40°C are common – it's uncomfortable. The town is 193 km south-east of Port Hedland and takes its name from a bar of red jasper across the Coongan River, five km from the town.

The town came into existence when gold was found there in 1891. At its peak the population was 5000; today minerals other than gold are also mined there. In the town the 1895 government buildings are still in use. In late winter, as the spring flowers begin to bloom, Marble Bar is actually quite a pretty place.

The Comet Gold Mine, 10 km from Marble Bar, is still in operation and is open daily. The yearly race meeting attracts a large, noisy crowd from all over the Pilbara and is quite a spectacle.

Broome

Population 6000

The delightful old pearling port of Broome is a small, dusty place noted for its Chinatown, which looks for all the world like a set from a western movie. Although still isolated, Broome has certainly been discovered. During the 1980s the generally dull 624 km of road from Port Hedland

across the fringes of the Great Sandy Desert was sealed, sparking a tourist boom. Today the town is also something of a travellers' centre.

Pearling in the sea off Broome started in the 1880s and peaked in the early 1900s when the town's 400 pearling luggers, worked by 3000 men, supplied 80% of the world's mother-of-pearl. Today only a handful of boats operate.

Pearl diving was a very unsafe occupation, as Broome's Japanese cemetery attests. The divers were from various Asian countries. Rivalry between the different nationalities was always intense and sometimes took an ugly turn. Although those days are long over, the town still has a very cosmopolitan feel about it. In August the Shinju Matsuri or 'Festival of the Pearl' commemorates the early pearling years.

Orientation

The centre of Broome's new development and growth is in the southern portion of town, in the area surrounding the corner of Dampier Terrace and Saville St. The museum is there, as is the modern but semi-Chinese looking Seaview Shopping Plaza opposite.

Information

Broome's shiny new tourist office (tel 92 1176) is just across the sports field from Chinatown. It's open Monday to Friday from 8 am to 5 pm, Saturday from 9 am to 1 pm, and Sunday from 9 am to 5 pm. There's a useful notice board in the Seaview Shopping Centre.

Chinatown

The term 'Chinatown' is used to refer to the old part of town, although there is really only one block or so that is both Chinese and historic. Some of the plain and simple wooden buildings that line Carnarvon St still house Chinese merchants, but most are now restaurants and tourist shops. The bars on the

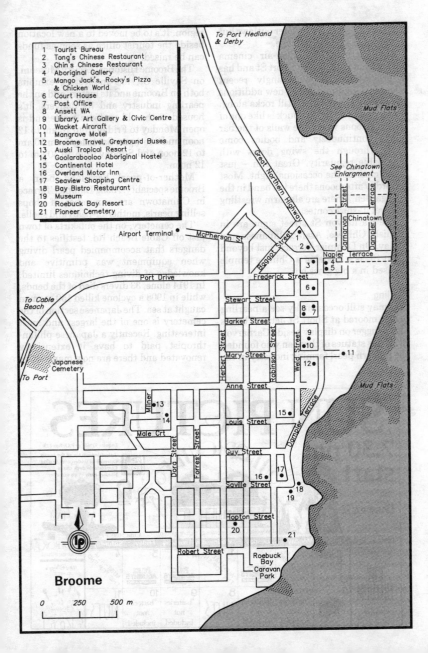

1 Tourist Bureau
2 Tong's Chinese Restaurant
3 Chin's Chinese Restaurant
4 Aboriginal Gallery
5 Mango Jack's, Rocky's Pizza
& Chicken World
6 Court House
7 Post Office
8 Ansett WA
9 Library, Art Gallery & Civic Centre
10 Wacket Aircraft
11 Mangrove Motel
12 Broome Travel, Greyhound Buses
13 Auski Tropical Resort
14 Goolarabooloo Aboriginal Hostel
15 Continental Hotel
16 Overland Motor Inn
17 Seaview Shopping Centre
18 Bay Bistro Restaurant
19 Museum
20 Roebuck Bay Resort
21 Pioneer Cemetery

To Port Hedland
& Derby

Great Northern Highway

Mud Flats

See Chinatown
Enlargement

Carnarvon Street

Dampier Terrace

Chinatown

Napier Terrace

Airport Terminal

McPherson St

Boogol Street

Frederick Street

Port Drive

Stewart Street

Barker Street

Mary Street

Anne Street

Louis Street

Guy Street

Saville Street

Hopton Street

Robert Street

Herbert Street

Robinson Street

Weld Street

Dampier Terrace

Mud Flats

To Cable
Beach

Japanese
Cemetery

To Port

Milner Street

Male Crt

Dora Street

Forrest Street

Roebuck
Bay
Caravan
Park

Broome

0   250   500 m

windows aren't there to deter outlaws but to minimise cyclone damage.

Sun Pictures, the open-air cinema dating from 1916, is near Short St and has a programme of surprisingly recent releases. Despite its fancy new appearance the Roebuck Bay Hotel still rocks along. A noisy night at the Roebuck is like one of those cartoons where the walls of the bar quake continuously and bodies come flying through the swing doors with reasonable regularity. Great fun – just stand clear of the occasional fight. Most Saturday afternoons there is a band in the beer garden. There are also arm wrestling and wet T-shirt contests.

The Carnarvon St street signs are in English, Chinese, Arabic, Japanese and Malay. On Dampier Terrace, just beyond Short St, is a model of a Chinese temple encased in a big glass box.

Pearling

You may still occasionally see a pearling lugger moored at Short St Jetty. There's also a lugger on display beside Carnarvon St. It has statues of the men who founded the modern pearl farming industry in the region. It's to be moved to a new location beside the tourist office as soon as funds can be raised.

The Broome Historical Society Museum, on Saville St, has interesting exhibits both on Broome and its history and on the pearling industry and its dangers. It's housed in the old customs house and is open Monday to Friday from 10 am to 12 noon and 2 to 4 pm, Saturday from 10 am to 12 noon and Sunday from 10.30 am to 12 noon.

Mother-of-pearl has long been a Broome speciality. Along Dampier Terrace in Chinatown are a number of shops selling pearls, mother-of-pearl and shells.

The cemetery, on the outskirts of town just off Cable Beach Rd, testifies to the dangers that accompanied pearl diving when equipment was primitive and knowledge of diving techniques limited. In 1914 alone, 33 divers died of the bends, while in 1908 a cyclone killed 150 seamen caught at sea. The Japanese section of the cemetery is one of the largest and most interesting. Recently a Japanese philanthropist paid to have it extensively renovated and there are now many shiny

new black tombstones scattered amongst the beautiful old sandstone ones.

Behind the neat Japanese section is the interesting but run-down section containing European and Aboriginal graves. The largest contingent of divers was Japanese, but Filipinos, Malays, Torres Strait Islanders, and 'Koepangers' from what is now Indonesian West Timor also collected the pearls.

Japanese Air Raid Relics

Broome's dramatic moment in history came with the Japanese air raid of March 1942. Broome was then a clearing station for refugees from the Dutch East Indies (now Indonesia) and on the morning of the raid the harbour was crowded with flying boats that had just arrived from Indonesia. A force of Japanese Zero fighters surprised the town with a daring raid that wiped out 15 flying boats in Roebuck Bay and

another seven aircraft at the airstrip. About 70 people were killed, many of them Dutch women and children who were still aboard the aircraft when the raid took place.

Remains of the flying boats can still be seen out in muddy Roebuck Bay. *WA's Pearl Harbour – The Japanese Raid on Broome* is a small booklet by Mervyn W Prime, available in Broome.

Other Attractions

Across Napier Terrace from Chinatown is Wing's Restaurant with a magnificent boab tree beside it. There's another boab tree behind, outside what used to be the old police lock-up, with a rather sad little tale on a plaque at its base. The tree was planted by a police officer when his son, who was killed in France in WW1, was born in 1898. The boab tree is still doing fine.

The Goolarabooloo Aboriginal Arts &

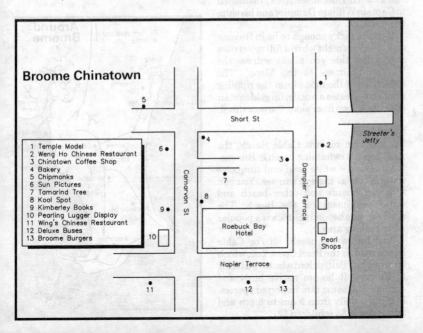

Broome Chinatown

1 Temple Model
2 Weng Ho Chinese Restaurant
3 Chinatown Coffee Shop
4 Bakery
5 Chipmonks
6 Sun Pictures
7 Tamarind Tree
8 Kool Spot
9 Kimberley Books
10 Pearling Lugger Display
11 Wing's Chinese Restaurant
12 Deluxe Buses
13 Broome Burgers

Short St

Streeter's Jetty

Carnarvon St

Dampier Terrace

Roebuck Bay Hotel

Pearl Shops

Napier Terrace

Crafts Gallery, on Hamersley St, has a collection of boomerangs, gourds and other artefacts. The 1888 court house, also at that end of town, was once used to house the transmitting equipment for the old cable station. The cable ran to Banyuwangi in Java, the ferry port across from Bali.

Further along Weld St, by the library and civic centre, is a Wackett aircraft that used to belong to Horrie Miller, founder of MacRobertson Miller Airlines, now Ansett WA. The plane is hidden away in a modern but absurdly designed building that most people pass without a second glance. Bedford Park has a handful of relics, including a decompression chamber.

There's a pioneer cemetery by the old jetty site at the end of Robinson St. Nearby there's a park and small beach. (The beach doesn't have much sand, but people do swim there.) In the bay, at the entrance to Dampier Creek, there's a landmark called Buccaneer Rock, dedicated to Captain William Dampier and his ship, the *Roebuck*.

If you're lucky enough to be in Broome on a cloudless night when a full moon rises over a low tide you might witness the 'Golden Staircase to the Moon'. The reflections of the moon from the rippling mud flats creates a wonderful golden stair effect, best seen from along the waterfront.

Out of Town

Six km from town is Cable Beach, the most popular swimming beach in Broome. It's a classic – white sand and turquoise water as far as the eye can see. You can hire surf boards and other beach and water equipment on the beach. The northern side beyond the rock is a popular nude bathing area.

Just before the beach, off the Cable Beach road, is the Pearl Coast Zoo, which is owned by a British lord who took a liking to Broome. It houses native birds and animals and some rare imported species. It is open daily from 9 am to 5 pm and admission is $5 (children $2).

Tucked in beside the zoo is a small crocodile park. It's open Monday to Saturday from 10 am to 12 noon and 2.30 to 3 pm. On Sunday it only opens for the 3 pm feeding session. Admission is $5 (children $3).

The long sweep of Cable Beach eventually ends at Gantheaume Point, seven km south of Broome. The cliffs there have been eroded into curious shapes. At extremely low tides dinosaur tracks 130 million years old are sometimes exposed. At other times you can inspect casts of the footprints on the cliff top. Anastasia's Pool is an artificial rock pool on the north side of the point; it fills at high tide.

At Entrance Point, at the end of Port Drive, eight km from town, the port is deep enough for ocean-going vessels. Broome can have enormous tides – up to 10 metres in the spring. Just before the point there's the Pearl Coast Aquarium,

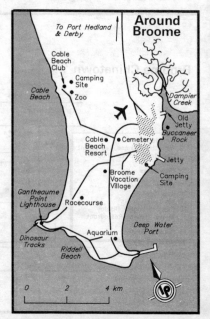

open from 9 am to 4 pm daily. Admission is $3 (children $1). It has tropical marine life and a pearling display.

There are several good fishing, swimming and camping spots outside Broome, including Crab Creek, Willies Creek, Barred Creek, Quondon Beach and Manari.

Places to Stay

Ever since Broome became a tourist hot spot accommodation has been hard to find. They've been building motels and camping sites like crazy but there still aren't enough of them and they all charge like wounded rhinos. Broome residents happily report that they have the most expensive camping sites in Australia. At certain times of year you really have to book if you want to be sure of a bed. Winter school holidays, when families flock north from Perth, are particularly bad. If you're really stuck ask at the tourist office; they'll know exactly what's available and where.

Hostels Broome does, at last, have a hostel but it's probably the most expensive in Australia. The *Broome Bunkhouse* is part of the expansive Roebuck Bay Hotel operation and a bed will cost you $18 a night in bunkrooms for four. There are no kitchen facilities but you're right in the centre of Broome's entertainment area.

Officially, the *Goolarabooloo Hostel* (tel 92 1747) is only for Aborigines but other people have been known to stay there. The hostel is off Dora St, at the end of Louis St, and the daily cost is $15 including meals.

Hotels & Motels The legendary *Roebuck Bay Hotel* (tel 92 1221), on the corner of Carnarvon St and Napier Terrace, Chinatown, has a bunkhouse (see above), as well as motel units that cost $65/80 in season.

The *Continental Hotel* (tel 92 1002) is a modern place on Weld St, on the corner of Louis St, with rooms at $80/90. The

Mangrove Motel (tel 92 1303), between the Continental and Chinatown, down near the water, costs $65/75, or there's the *Overland Motor Inn* (tel 92 1204) at $80 to $95.

There are several holiday units that are popular with families. The *Kimberley Holiday Home* (tel 921134), on Herbert St, has just a couple of rooms, at $44 to $66.

Typical of the new developments is *Auski Tropical Resort* (tel 93 1183), at 1298 Milner St. It has a swimming pool and all mod cons. Units with one or two bedrooms cost from $55 to $100. *Roebuck Bay Resort* (tel 92 1898), on Hopton St, has one, two or three bedroom units. *Cable Beach Resort* (tel 92 1824) is right at the start of Cable Beach Rd and costs from $75 to $100. Out at Cable Beach itself is the *Cable Beach Club*, Broome's most expensive establishment catering primarily for package tour visitors.

Beija Flor (tel 92 1476) has self-contained doubles at $60 a night. It's at Coconut Well, a tidal lagoon 23 km north of the town. It also has space for just a couple of caravans and tents at $8 a night. The tourist office can tell you how to get there. Write to PO Box 644 for details.

Camping Even camping can become impossible in Broome. At peak periods they turn the grounds of the local high school into a temporary camping site.

The *Roebuck Caravan Park* (tel 92 1366) is conveniently central and has sites from $12 without power and erected Campus Tents that cost $33 to $55 a night. The *Cable Beach Caravan Park* (tel 92 2066) is at the beach and has sites at $14 to $18. *Broome Caravan Park* (tel 92 1776) is on the Great Northern Highway four km from town and has sites from $12 and on-site vans from $45. Finally, the *Broome Vacation Village* (tel 92 1057) is on the road out to the port, just beyond the Cable Beach turn-off. It's a new place with sites from $10 without power and from $14 with power. It also has air-con cabins at $50 to $65.

Places to Eat

Light Meals & Fast Food Finding a place to stay in Broome may be a hassle but eating out is no sweat at all. *Kool Spot* is a sure sign of Broome's trendification: their food (breakfast and lunch time only) would have been pretty odd in Broome not so long ago – rolls, sandwiches, various fancy foods, exotic cakes, fruit juice and smoothies.

Mango Jacks, on Hamersley St, and *Chipmonks*, on Short St, dispense the usual sandwiches, burgers, chips and the like. In the same little shopping centre as Mango Jack's there's a *Chicken World* fried chicken place, and *Rocky's Pizza* which turns out distinctly average pizzas for $8 to $15.

There's a good bakery in Chinatown, on the corner of Carnarvon and Short Sts. The Seaview Shopping Centre also has a bakery, as well as an ice cream parlour and Broome's biggest supermarket.

Pubs & Restaurants The *Roebuck Hotel* has counter meals in the pleasantly rowdy old saloon bar on Dampier Terrace from 12 noon to 2 pm and from 6 to 8 pm. Prices range from $5 for sausage and chips to $10 or more for steaks. There are also several rather more expensive (and definitely less rowdy) dining places at the Roebuck. Their *Black Pearl Restaurant* does breakfasts from $5 to $12 – the 'Backpackers Special' is $5.

Chin's Chinese restaurant is on Hamersley St, opposite Mango Jacks, and has a variety of dishes from all over Asia. Prices range from $7 for an Indonesian *nasi goreng* or a fried rice to $12. There's a popular take-away section.

Other Chinese specialists are *Wing's*, on Napier Terrace, *Tong's*, just around the corner, and the recently opened *Weng Ho*, upstairs on Dampier Terrace.

The *Bay Bistro*, at 384 Dampier Terrace, has tables out on the lawn and sea views. The food is rather bland and a little expensive – fish & chips from $8.50, fancier seafood meals from $14 to $20.

Getting There & Away

Air Ansett WA fly to Broome regularly on their Perth to Darwin route. From Perth the fare is $353, from Darwin $255, from Derby $81, from Port Hedland $137. The Ansett WA office (tel 92 1101) is on the corner of Barker and Weld Sts.

Bus Greyhound, Deluxe and Bus Australia operate through Broome on their Perth to Darwin route. They all operate the Perth to Broome route daily but while Greyhound and Deluxe make the Broome to Darwin run daily, Bus Australia only cover that part three times a week. Typical fares from Broome include $130 to Perth, $45 to Port Hedland, $17 to Derby and $121 to Darwin. Greyhound also operate on the Great Northern Highway from Perth to Port Hedland through Newman.

All the buses will stop at the tourist office in Broome but Greyhound also have an office at Broome Travel and Deluxe have one on Napier Terrace, opposite the Roebuck Hotel.

Getting Around

Airport Transport There are taxis to take you from the airport to your hotel but the airport is so close to the centre that backpackers staying at the Broome Bunkhouse or elsewhere close by may well decide to walk.

Local Transport Three times daily there's a bus between the town and Cable Beach. The one-way fare is $2 and the return $3. Phone 92 1068 for details.

Cycling is the best way to see the area. There are a number of places that hire bicycles for $5 to $10 a day. Try Trendy Rollers, under the boab tree beside Wing's Restaurant, or Chinatown Bike Hire, at the Checkpoint Service Station, on the corner of Hamersley St and Napier Terrace. Some of the accommodation places also have bikes for hire. Broome is an easy area to ride around; it's flat and you'll usually have no problem riding out to Cable Beach (about seven km) as long as it's not too windy. Stay on the roads, though, or your tyres might be punctured by thorns.

Hertz, Budget, Avis and Thrifty have rent-a-car desks at the airport but there are better deals available if you just want something for bopping around town or out to the beach. Mokes and Suzuki jeeps are popular. Auski Resort, for example, has Suzukis for $35 a day plus 18c a km after the first 35 km. Topless Rentals, opposite the Seaview Centre, have VW Beetle convertibles for $40 a day, including insurance and unlimited km around Broome.

Motorscooters can be hired for $15.50 a day from Auski and for $18 a day from Thrifty. Buccaneer Boats have boats for $20 for the first hour, and jet skis can be hired at Cable Beach.

Tours Yes, there are lots of tours from Broome. You can even fly all the way to the Bungle Bungle Range in the east Kimberley for $400. Closer to home are town tours which go to Gantheaume Point for $22; other tours cost up to $60. A 4WD safari to Cape Leveque, including lunch and dinner, costs $80. You can even explore the northern coastal area along Cable Beach by camel for $35 or view Broome from a helicopter.

CAPE LEVEQUE ROAD

It's about 200 km from the turn-off nine km out of Broome to the Cape Leveque Lighthouse. About halfway is a diversion to the Beagle Bay Aboriginal Community which has a beautiful church in the middle of a green. Inside is an altar stunningly decorated with mother-of-pearl. Just before Cape Leveque is Lombadina Aboriginal Community which has a church built from mangrove wood.

Cape Leveque itself has a lighthouse and two wonderful beaches. Beyond it is One Arm Point – yet another Aboriginal community. Take note that the communities won't want you to stay on their land, but if you want to see their churches

or buy something from their shops they will be helpful. Check with the tourist office in Broome about road conditions before setting out.

BROOME TO DERBY

There's a free camping site beside the Fitzroy River, 155 km along the Great Northern Highway from Broome. Just over the all-weather bridge is the Willara Bridge Roadhouse and shortly after that is the turn-off to Derby, 43 km to the north. The main road continues into the heart of the Kimberley and on to Darwin.

The Kimberley

The rugged Kimberley, at the northern end of WA, is one of Australia's last frontiers. Despite enormous advances in the past decade this is still a little-travelled and very remote area of great rivers and magnificent scenery. The Kimberley suffers from climatic extremes – heavy rains in the wet followed by searing heat in the dry – but the irrigation projects in the north-east have made great changes to the region.

Nevertheless rivers and creeks can rise rapidly following heavy rainfall and become impassable torrents within 15 minutes. Unless it's a very brief storm, it's quite likely that the watercourses will remain impassable for three to four days. The Fitzroy River can become so swollen at times that after two or three days' rain it grows from its normal 100 metre width to a spectacular 11 km. River and creek crossings on the Great Northern Highway on both sides of Halls Creek become impassable every wet season. Since the last edition of this book the final stretch of Highway 1 through the Kimberley has been sealed, but several notorious crossings are still only fords, not all-weather bridges.

The best time to visit is between April and September. By October it's already getting hot (35°C), and later in the year daily temperatures of more than 40°C are common. On the other hand, from May to July nights can be piercingly cold, especially in Halls Creek.

Kimberley attractions include the spectacular gorges on the Fitzroy River, the huge Wolf Creek meteorite crater and the Bungle Bungle Range, only recently proclaimed a national park.

DERBY (population 3000)

Derby, only 221 km from Broome, is a major administrative centre for the west Kimberley and a good point from which to travel to the spectacular gorges in the region. The road beyond Derby continues to Fitzroy Crossing (256 km) and Halls Creek (288 km). Alternatively, there's the much wilder Gibb River Rd.

Derby is on King Sound, north of the mouth of the Fitzroy, the mighty river that drains the west Kimberley region. From Derby you can make trips right up into the north of the region as the roads have been much improved of late.

Information

The tourist bureau at the end of Clarendon St is open from 8.30 am to 4.30 pm Monday to Friday. The annual Boab Festival takes place over two weeks in late June/early July.

Things to See

There's a small museum and art gallery in the Derby Cultural Centre and a botanic garden. The old open-air Derby Pictures present a regular programme of movies, although they reserve the right to cancel if less than 40 people show up; heavy rain after 5 pm will also stop the show.

Wharfinger's House, at the end of Loch St, is being restored as an example of early housing in the area. You can visit the School of the Air and the Royal Flying Doctor base.

Derby's lofty wharf has not been used since 1983 for shipping but provides a handy fishing perch for the locals. The whole town is surrounded by huge

expanses of mud flats, baked hard in the dry season. They're occasionally flooded by king tides.

The Prison Tree, near the airport, seven km south of town, is a huge boab tree with a hollow trunk 14 metres around. It is said to have been used as a temporary lock-up years ago.

From Derby there are flights over King Sound to Koolan and Cockatoo Islands, both owned by the Dampier Mining Company. You can't go there unless invited by a resident, but scenic flights are available to the adjoining islands of the Buccaneer Archipelago.

Boabs

Boab trees are a common sight in the Kimberley and also in the Victoria and Fitzmaurice river basins of the Northern Territory. The boab or *Adansonia gregorii* is closely related to the baobab of Africa and the eight varieties of *Adansonia* found on the island of Madagascar. It's probable that baobab seeds floated to Australia from Africa, then developed unique characteristics.

The boab is a curious looking trees with branches rising like witches' fingers from a wide trunk that is sometimes elegantly bottle shaped, sometimes short, squat and powerful looking. Boabs shed all their leaves during dry periods, further accentuating their unusual appearance. Evidently it's a successful policy, for boabs are noted for their rapid growth, hardiness and extreme longevity. Derby has some fine boabs around the town, including a line of them transplanted along the centre of Loch St.

Places to Stay

Hostels The *Aboriginal Hostel* (tel 91 1867), at 233-235 Villiers St, may take non-Aborigines. The nightly cost is $15, which includes all meals.

Hotels & Motels *Coronway Lodge* (tel 91 1327) is at the edge of town, on the corner of Sutherland and Stanwell Sts, and has rooms with shared bathrooms and a shared kitchen for $28 to $45. There are also self-contained family units for $38 to $65.

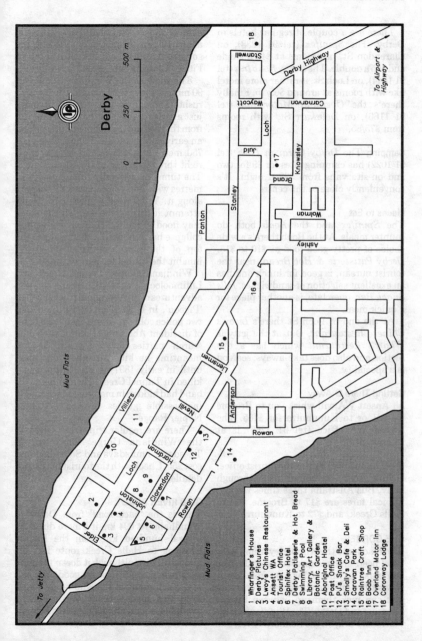

Derby

500 m

0   250   500 m

Mud Flats

Mud Flats

To Jetty

To Airport & Highway

Derby Highway

Stanwell
Waycott
Carnarvon
Loch
Juid
Stanley
Brand
Knowsley
Wolman
Ashley
Panton
Lhensen
Anderson
Nevill
Rowan
Villiers
Loch
Hardman
Johnston
Clarendon
Elder
Rowan

1 Wharfinger's House
2 Derby Pictures
3 Lwoy's Chinese Restaurant
4 Ansett WA
5 Tourist Office
6 Spinifex Hotel
7 Derby Patisserie & Hot Bread
8 Swimming Pool
9 Library, Art Gallery &
   Botanic Garden
10 Aboriginal Hostel
11 Post Office
12 PJ's Snack Bar
13 Smally's Cafe & Deli
14 Caravan Park
15 Raintree Craft Shop
16 Boab Inn
17 Overland Motor Inn
18 Coronway Lodge

There are a couple of regular hotels in Derby. The *Spinifex* (tel 91 1233), on Clarendon St, has rooms at $45 a single and $55 a double. The *Derby Boab Inn* (tel 91 1044), on Loch St, is rather more motel like with rooms at around $65/75. Finally there's the *Overland Motor Inn* (tel 91 1166), on Delewarr St, with rooms from $75/85.

Camping The *Derby Caravan Park* (tel 91 1022) has camping sites for $9 for two and on-site vans from $38 a night. It's conveniently close to the centre.

Places to Eat
The *Spinifex* and the *Boab* both do counter meals. At the Boab there's a wide choice of pretty good food at $10 to $15. *Derby Patisserie & Hot Bread*, near the tourist bureau, is good for lunch and has an excellent selection of sandwiches. *PJ's Snack Bar*, open late, is another place for a quick meal.

At the end of Loch St there's *Lwoy's Chinese Restaurant*. Out at the jetty is *Wharf's Restaurant* which has a byo section and also does take-aways; seafood is a speciality.

Getting There & Away
Air Ansett WA will whisk you to Broome for $81 or to Kununurra for $155. The Ansett WA office (tel 91 1266) is at 14 Loch St.

Bus The buses all stop at the tourist office. Deluxe and Greyhound pass through daily, Bus Australia three times weekly. Typical fares are $17 to Broome, $44 to Halls Creek, and $72 to Kununurra.

THE GORGES
The roads into the Kimberley from Derby have been much improved recently. You can make an interesting loop from Derby to visit the spectacular gorge country, or you can pick them up between Fitzroy Crossing and Derby. The Windjana Gorge National Park, on the Lennard River, and Tunnel Creek National Park are only about 100 km from Derby. Visiting the gorges only adds about 40 km to the trip to Fitzroy Crossing but the road is mostly dirt.

The walls at the Windjana Gorge soar 90 metres above the Lennard River which rushes through in the wet but becomes just a series of pools in the dry. Three km from the river are the ruins of Lillimooloora, an early police station. Tunnel Creek is a 750 metre long tunnel cut by the creek right through a spur of the Oscar Range. The tunnel is generally from three to 15 metres wide and you can walk all the way along it. You'll need a good light. Don't attempt it during the wet, as the creek may flood suddenly. Halfway through, a collapse has produced a shaft right to the top of the range. Flying foxes (bats) inhabit the tunnel for part of the year.

Windjana Gorge, Tunnel Creek and Lillimooloora were the scene of the adventures of an Aboriginal tracker called 'Pigeon'. In November 1894 Pigeon shot two police colleagues and then led a band of dissident Aborigines, skilfully evading search parties for 2¼ years. In the meantime he killed another four men, until in early 1897 he was trapped and killed in Tunnel Creek. He and his small band had hidden in many of the seemingly inaccessible gullies of the adjoining Napier Range.

There are regular trips from Derby to the Windjana Gorge. They go on Tuesdays, Thursdays and Saturdays and cost $55. Check with the tourist bureau for details.

GIBB RIVER ROAD
This is the 'back road' from Derby to Wyndham. At 694 km it's more direct by several hundred km than the Fitzroy Crossing to Halls Creek route but it's almost all dirt, although it doesn't require 4WD when conditions are good. You can also reach many of the Kimberley gorges from this road without 4WD. Fuel is available about halfway, at Mt Barnett station, near Manning Gorge.

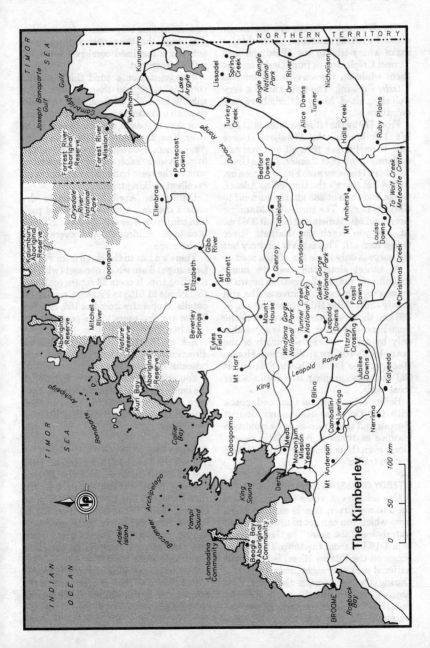

The Kimberley

NORTHERN TERRITORY

TIMOR SEA

Joseph Bonaparte Gulf

Cambridge Gulf

Kununurra

Lake Argyle

Wyndham

Lissadel

Spring Creek

Bungle Bungle National Park

Ord River

Turkey Creek

Nicholison

Turner

Alice Downs

Halls Creek

Ruby Plains

Forrest River Aboriginal Reserve

Forrest River Mission

Pentecost Downs

Durack Range

Bedford Downs

To Wolf Creek Meteorite Crater

Drysdale River National Park

Ellenbrae

Tableland

Mt Amherst

Louisa Downs

Kalumburu Aboriginal Reserve

Doongan

Gibb River

Glenroy

Lansdowne

Fossil Downs

Christmas Creek

Mt Elizabeth

Mt Barnett

Geikie Gorge National Park

Mitchell River

Nature Reserve

Aboriginal Reserve

Beverley Springs

Mount House

Windjana Gorge National Park

Tunnel Creek National Park

Leopold Downs

Fitzroy Crossing

Eyles Field

Mt Hart

Leopold Range

Blina

Jubilee Downs

Kalyeeda

Kuri Bay

Collier Bay

King

Cambalin

Liveringa

Nerrima

Bonaparte Archipelago

Oobagooma

Meda

Mowanjum Mission

Yeeda

Mt Anderson

TIMOR SEA

King Sound

Derby

Buccaneer Archipelago

Yampi Sound

Adele Island

INDIAN OCEAN

Lombadina Community

Beagle Bay Aboriginal Community

BROOME

Roebuck Bay

0 50 100 km

The Kimberley gorges are the major reason for taking this route. You could also make a day-trip to the Windjana and Tunnel Creek Gorges from Derby or visit them while on the way from Derby to Fitzroy Crossing. The gorges are not very well signposted. Many of them have rock paintings.

From Derby the bitumen extends 62 km. It's 118 km to the Windjana Gorge and Tunnel Creek turn-off and you can continue down that turn-off to the Great Northern Highway near Fitzroy Crossing. At 268 km there's the turn-off to Adcock Gorge and then at 285 km the turn-off to Galvans Gorge. The turn-off to Manning Gorge and Mt Barnett Station is at 306 km. At 328 you reach the Barnett River Gorge turn-off; This is 4WD territory but the gorge is only three km off the road.

At sunset along the road the many magnificent ranges change from brown to orange to crimson to mauve as the sun slowly sinks. After Gibb River Station, at 366 km, the road deteriorates as far as the huge Pentecost River, which is negotiable only by 4WD vehicles for much of the year. Jack's (or Joe's) Waterhole Homestead, on the Durack River Station, at 523 km, has camping and a number of local tours.

Before setting out on this road, check with the Derby or Kununurra Tourist Bureau and the police as to its condition because at times it is officially closed. Don't even think about hitching – there's just no traffic.

FITZROY CROSSING (population 430)

A tiny settlement where the road crosses the Fitzroy River, this is another place from which you can get to the gorges and waterholes of the area. The Geikie Gorge is just 19 km from the town. Part of the gorge, on the Fitzroy River, is in a small national park only eight km by three km. During the wet season the river rises nearly 17 metres, and the camping site by the river is seven metres below the waterline. In the dry the river stops

flowing, leaving only a series of waterholes. The ranges that the gorge cuts through are actually a fossilised coral reef some 350 million years old.

The vegetation around this beautiful gorge is dense and there is also much wildlife, including the freshwater crocodile. Sawfish and stingrays, usually only found in or close to the sea, can also be seen in the river. Kangaroos and wallabies live in the gorge sanctuary. Visitors are not permitted to go anywhere except along the prescribed part of the west bank, where there is an excellent walking track.

During the April to November dry season there's a two hour national park boat trip up the river at 9.30 am and 2.30 pm. It costs $6 (children $2) and covers 16 km of the gorge.

There's a bus to the gorge from Fitzroy Crossing at 8 am which connects with the morning trip. It costs $8 return (children $5). Phone 91 5163 in Fitzroy Crossing for details. It operates from Lot 185, Bell Rd. There are also tours to the gorge for $30 (children $16).

Ask at Brooking Springs Station for directions to the very pleasant and peaceful Brooking Gorge.

You must get permission to go through the land – some cattle stations lately have been restricting access to gorges on their land in response to thoughtless littering by visitors.

Places to Stay

There's the *Tarunda Park Caravan Park* (tel 91 5004) in town and the *Fitzroy Crossing Hotel & Caravan Park* by the river crossing. The Crossing Hotel is an historic place. It has cabins from $33 as well as more expensive motel rooms. It can get pretty noisy. There's a new motel and caravan park complex on the Halls Creek side of the town.

The small camping site at the *Geikie Gorge National Park* is open only in the dry season. It has limited facilities and sites are $9.

HALLS CREEK (population 1000)

Halls Creek, in the centre of the Kimberley and on the edge of the Great Sandy Desert, was the site of a the 1885 gold rush, the first in WA. The gold soon petered out and today the town is a cattle centre, 14 km from the original site where some crumbling remains can still be seen. Halls Creek Old Town is a fascinating place for poking around creeks and gullies in a 4WD searching for that elusive gold nugget. If you're really interested in doing a bit of fossicking, it's best to go with a local. 'Old Town' is in fact the general term for the hilly area behind Halls Creek and gold might be found anywhere there. You can swim in Caroline Pool, Sawpit Gorge and Palm Springs.

Five km east of Halls Creek and then about 1½ km off the road there's a natural China wall – Australia has a few of them. This one is short but very picturesquely situated. There's an Aboriginal art shop in the town where you can often see carvers at work making some high quality artefacts.

Although Halls Creek is a comfortable enough little place it's as well to remember that it sits on the edge of a distinctly inhospitable stretch of country. In late '86 two 16 year old jackaroos set out from a station near there. They took a wrong turn, got bogged and couldn't get out. In mid-1987 their truck and their skeletal remains were found. It caused a national scandal about working conditions for inexperienced young station hands but the message is clear – this can be rough land.

Wolf Creek Meteorite Crater

The 835 metre wide and 50 metre deep Wolf Creek Meteorite Crater is the second largest in the world. The turn-off to the crater is 16 km out of Halls Creek towards Fitzroy Crossing and from there it's 112 km by unsealed road to the south. It's easily accessible without 4WD and you can camp and get some limited supplies at the nearby Carranya Station homestead. If you can't handle one more outback road

you can fly over the crater from Halls Creek for $55 with the local operators.

Places to Stay

Halls Creek Caravan Park (tel 68 6169) is on Roberta Ave, towards the airport, and has sites at $9 or dusty on-site vans from $33. Opposite is the *Kimberley Hotel* (tel 68 6101), which has a variety of rooms from $33 to $75.

Swagman Halls Creek (tel 68 6060), on McDonald St, has basic cabins with air-con for $38. The *Halls Creek Motel* (tel 68 6001), on the Great Northern Highway, costs from $60 to $80. The *Shell Roadhouse* has rooms from about $38.

Places to Eat

The *Kimberley Hotel* has a pleasantly casual bar with standard counter meals at $8. You can eat out at the tables on the grass – very pleasant. Inside there's a surprisingly swish restaurant with meals at $15 to $18.

Getting There & Away

It's 359 km north-east to Kununurra, 460 km south-west to Derby. Bus Australia, Greyhound and Deluxe pass through Halls Creek.

The stretch of road between Fitzroy Crossing and Halls Creek was the last part of Highway 1 to be sealed. It's now a very good road, much better than other stretches of Highway 1 – in particular the very narrow road from Kununurra to Katherine in the Northern Territory.

The road to Wyndham and Kununurra, 360 km away, passes through the Carboyd Ranges – catch them at their best at sunset. You can swim in the river at the Dunham River bridge.

THE BUNGLE BUNGLE RANGE

Bungle Bungle National Park, proclaimed in 1987, is noted for its spectacular rounded rock towers, striped like tigers in alternate bands of orange (silica) and black (lichen). The only catch is that the range is hard to get to and because of the fragile nature of the rock formations you are not allowed to climb them. For these reasons scenic flights over the range are very popular. Even people who travel into the park by land often take helicopter flights, either to see the ranges better or to shorten the long walks required for access.

Echidna Chasm in the north or Cathedral Gorge in the south are only about a one hour walk from the car parks at the road's end but the soaring Piccaninny Gorge is an 18 km round trip that takes eight to 10 hours to walk. Access to the park costs $20 a car.

Places to Stay

From Three Ways it's five km north to *Kurrajong Camp* and 15 km south to *Bellburn Creek Camp*. At Bellburn Creek Camp there's a ranger station, and you can take a helicopter flight into Piccaninny Gorge.

Getting There & Away

Although it's only 55 km to Three Ways from the Halls Creek to Kununurra road turn-off, that stretch requires 4WD and takes three to four hours. From Three Ways it's another 20 km north to Echidna Chasm and 30 km south to Piccaninny Creek. And then you have to walk! All in all it's not surprising that flights over the range are so popular. There are regular scenic flights from Kununurra for $100 to $110 or from Halls Creek for $65 with operators like Slingair or Kingfisher. The Halls Creek flight is cheaper because it's so much shorter, but from either direction it's a wonderful flight and well worth the expense.

From Halls Creek three day tours to Bungle Bungle by 4WD cost $295 a person. You can make similar tours from Turkey Creek or by plane and 4WD from Kununurra.

WYNDHAM (population 1500)

Wyndham, a sprawling town, is suffering from Kununurra's boom in popularity but its Five Rivers Lookout on top of Mt Bastion is still a must. From there you can see the King, Pentecost, Durack, Forest and Ord Rivers. It's particularly good at sunrise and sunset. During the dry season saltwater crocodiles (extremely dangerous) congregate near the jetty and during the day one or two might be seen at the end of the outlet drain behind the meatworks. Signs warn swimmers of the crocs, and they mean it!

The Moochylabra Dam is a popular fishing and picnic spot about 25 km away. Near the town there's a rather desolate and decrepit little cemetery where Afghan camel drivers were buried last century. Near the Moochylabra Dam, south of Wyndham, there are some Aboriginal paintings and another prison boab tree. Grotto is a good swimming hole just off the Wyndham to Kununurra road. Crocodile Hole is further off the road and has a small population of freshwater crocs.

Places to Stay

The *Three Mile Caravan Park* (tel 61 1064) charges $8 for camping sites. Rooms in the *Wyndham Town Hotel* (tel 61 1003), on O'Donnell St, are from $65 to $85.

Try the *Wyndham Community Club* or the *Hungry Croc Restaurant* for cheaper but more basic rooms. Outback homestead accommodation and activities can be arranged at the *Home Valley Station* (tel 61 4322).

Getting There & Away

Ansett WA operate a bus service between Wyndham and Kununurra to connect with their flights to and from Kununurra. Greyhound operate a service to Wyndham from the Wyndham turn-off on the main Halls Creek to Kununurra road. The additional fare is $10.

KUNUNURRA (population 2100)

Founded in the 1960s, Kununurra is in the centre of the Ord River irrigation scheme and is quite a modern and bustling little town.

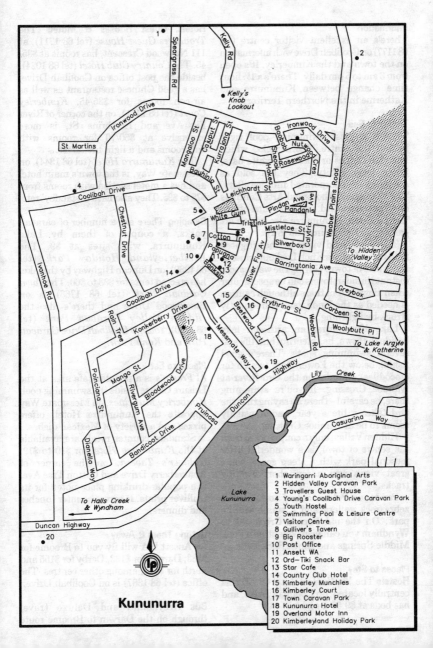

Kununurra

1 Waringarri Aboriginal Arts
2 Hidden Valley Caravan Park
3 Travellers Guest House
4 Young's Coolibah Drive Caravan Park
5 Youth Hostel
6 Swimming Pool & Leisure Centre
7 Visitor Centre
8 Gulliver's Tavern
9 Big Rooster
10 Post Office
11 Ansett WA
12 Ord–Tiki Snack Bar
13 Star Cafe
14 Country Club Hotel
15 Kimberley Munchies
16 Kimberley Court
17 Town Caravan Park
18 Kununurra Hotel
19 Overland Motor Inn
20 Kimberleyland Holiday Park

Lake Kununurra

Kelly Rd
Speargrass Rd
Kelly's Knob Lookout
Ironwood Drive
St Martins
Mangaloo St
Calytrix St
Kurrajong St
Nutwood
Baobab
Sheoak
Rosewood Cres
Hakea
Ironwood Drive
Coolibah Drive
Bauhinia St
Leichhardt St
Chestnut Drive
White Gum
Cotton Tree
Papuana
Banksia
Tristinia
Pindan Ave
Pandanis
Mistletoe St
Calytrix Ave
Silverbox
Weaber Plains Road
To Hidden Valley
Ivanhoe Rd
Coolibah Drive
River Fig Ave
Barringtonia Ave
Greybox
Konkerberry Drive
Beefwood Crt
Erythrina St
Carbeen St
Woolybutt Pl
Rain Tree
Messmate Way
Weaber Rd
To Lake Argyle & Katherine
Poinciana St
Mango St
Rivergum Drive
Bloodwood Drive
Pruinosa
Duncan Highway
Lily Creek
Casuarina Way
Dianella Way
Bandicoot Drive
To Halls Creek & Wyndham
Duncan Highway

Information

There's an excellent visitor centre (tel 68 1177) on Coolibah Drive with information on the town and the Kimberley. It's open from 8 am to 5 pm daily. There's a 1½ hour time change between Kununurra and Katherine in the Northern Territory.

Things to See

There's a great swimming pool right behind the centre. Zebra rocks, which have red stripes or dots on a white base, are a local oddity. They are sold as souvenirs or incorporated into jewellery. The Waringarri Aboriginal Arts Centre is on Speargrass Rd, at the turn-off to Kelly's Knob. Kununurra also has an art gallery, at 1560 Poinsettia Way.

There are good views of the irrigated fields from Kelly's Knob Lookout, close to the centre of town. During the wet season, distant thunderstorms can be spectacular when viewed from there although caution is needed as the Knob itself is frequently struck by lightning.

Lake Kununurra, an artificial lake beside the town, has plentiful bird life and several swimming spots. There's good fishing below the Lower Dam (watch for crocodiles) and also on the Ord River at Ivanhoe Crossing. If you're swimming there, be careful – there's a saying that the Ord takes a life a year, and it usually seems to be at Ivanhoe Crossing.

Hidden Valley, only a couple of km from the centre of town, is a wonderful little national park with a steep gorge, some great views and a few short walking tracks.

Pandanus Palms, out of town, has a zebra rock gallery and a small wildlife park. On the old Parry's Creek Rd to Wyndham you can visit Valentine's Pool, Middle Springs and Black Rock Falls.

Places to Stay

Hostels The *Youth Hostel* (tel 68 1372) is centrally located, on Coolibah Drive, and has beds at $9.50 a night.

Hotels, Guest Houses & Motels The *Travellers Guest House* (tel 68 1711), at 111 Nutwood Crescent, has rooms at $35/45. The *Country Club Hotel* (tel 68 1024), beside the post office on Coolibah Drive, has a good Chinese restaurant as well as air-con rooms for $35/45. *Kimberley Court* (tel 68 1411), on the corner of River Fig Ave and Erythrina St, is more expensive at $60/70 for rooms with bathrooms and a light breakfast.

The *Kununurra Hotel* (tel 68 1344), on Messmate Way, is the town's main hotel and has a motel section with rooms from $75 to $95. They also have a 'standby' rate.

Camping There are a number of caravan parks, a couple of them by Lake Kununurra, with sites at $9. The *Kimberleyland Holiday Park* (tel 68 1280), on Duncan Highway by the lake, has erected tents for $38 to $60. The *Town Caravan Park* (tel 68 1763) is on Bloodwood Drive and there's also the *Hidden Valley Caravan Park* (tel 68 1280), *Young's Coolibah Drive Caravan Park* and *Kona Park*.

Places to Eat

Al Fresco's is a popular cafe area at the Leisure Centre beside the swimming pool. *Kimberley Munchies*, on Messmate Way opposite the Kununurra Hotel, offers pizzas and a variety of Mexican dishes.

Standard counter meals are available at the *Kununurra Hotel* for $10 to $12. *Gulliver's Tavern*, on the corner of Konkerberry Drive and Cotton Tree Ave, is a popular drinking place noted for its Gulliver prints. It serves counter lunches and dinners.

Getting There & Away

Air Ansett WA will fly you to Broome for $183, Darwin for $133, Derby for $155 and Perth for $440, among other centres. The office (tel 68 1387) is on Coolibah Drive.

Bus Greyhound and Deluxe travel through on the Darwin to Broome route daily, Bus Australia three times weekly. Typical fares are $72 to Derby, $36 to Halls Creek, $33 to Katherine, and $65 to Darwin

Getting Around
You usually need 4WD to get off the main road. These and regular cars can be rented in Kununurra.

Tours & Flights There are a number of tours around town or to Lake Argyle with prices from $25 to $60. You can take a cruise on Lake Kununurra and the Ord River for $15 to $20.

Flights to Bungle Bungle are particularly popular and cost $90 to $110 a person. They take about two hours and also fly over the Argyle Diamond Mine project and the irrigation area north of the town.

LAKE ARGYLE
Created by the Ord River Dam, Lake Argyle is the second biggest storage reservoir in Australia, holding 12 times as much water as Sydney Harbour. Prior to its construction, there was too much water in the wet season and not enough in the dry. By providing a regular water supply the dam has made agriculture on a massive scale possible in the area.

At the lake there's a pioneer museum in the old Argyle Homestead, moved here when its original site was flooded. The *Lake Argyle Tourist Village* has expensive rooms and a camping site. Boats depart there for the huge lake each morning and afternoon. All around the lake there is now green farmland; rice is a principal crop. Encircling these flat lands are the small reddish mountains typical of the region. The wet or 'green' season is from early December to late March, the dry from early April to late September.

Just off the Lake Argyle Highway are some Aboriginal rock paintings. South of Kununurra is the huge Argyle Diamond Mine which has a visitor centre.

Index

NATIONAL PARKS, STATE FORESTS & RESERVES

MAPS

MAPS cont

from page 4

hostels and restaurants. Most importantly, we'd all really enjoyed ourselves. We'd climbed Ayers Rock, seen the dolphins at Monkey Mia, walked over the Sydney Harbour Bridge, spotted crocodiles in the Northern Territory, dived on the Barrier Reef; we'd been round Australia.

'Wait a minute,' I hear somebody saying. 'You missed a state out. What about Tasmania?' No, Peter Turner did that. Peter flew down there and completed a circuit of the apple island. Peter also covered Broken Hill in NSW and Geelong in Victoria. There were many other contributors – Richard covered Ballarat and Bendigo and, as resident LP powder-snow maniac, updated the skiing sections. Everybody at LP pitched in to cover their favourite places in our home state, Victoria.

Of course what we updated this time has gone through refinements and additions with each previous edition and we don't forget the people who worked on those earlier versions, including Lindy Cameron, Hugh Finlay, Simon Hayman, Mark Lightbody and Alan Samagalski. For help and assistance along the way John and Susan would like to thank Doss, Perry, Murph, Manfred, Kathy, Lloyd and Mr Technology, Barry (Cairns), Adrian and Sue, Lesley, Lizzie and Angie and John's parents. A thank you from Tony and Maureen to Mike and Burkie in Fremantle. Nor can we forget the many travellers who took the time to write and tell us where we'd gone wrong or what we'd missed out. Thanks to all the following people:

Jane Adams (Aus), M Agelasto (Chi), Tom Agoston (USA), Pam Alderson (Aus), Joyce Allan (Aus), Thomas Alles (Aus), K Almond (Aus), John Ambler (Aus), Stephen Anstey (Aus), Helen Apouchtine (C), Bridget Appleby (UK), Lee Arasu (Aus), Jenny Aurerena (UK), Karen Bailey, Steven Bainborough (C), S Barrett (Aus), Julie Barrie (UK), Thomas Barry (USA), Byron & Chris Bartlett (NZ), Chris Beatty (UK), Jeraen Bechers, Andy Beer (UK), Ian & Margaret Bell (Aus), Craig Bellamy (Aus), Gordon Benjamim (Aus), L Benny (C), Chris Berkly (UK), Beverley Bind (Aus), Linda Bispham (Aus), Garry Blanchard (Aus), Rupert Blunt (UK), Pernille Boegh, Henrik Bolding (Dk), Philip Booth (UK), Brendon Bourke (Aus), Phil & Robyn Bouveng (Aus), D Bradley (Aus), Glen Brandenburg (USA), Horst Braune (Aus), Erica Brauns (D), Ann & Mike Briggs (Aus), Jan Briggs (Aus), M J Brisco (UK), Michael Brisco (Aus), Helen Brooks (Aus), Craig Brown (Aus), Pete Brown (Aus), Jackie Bruce (UK), Jan Buck (Aus), Ken Buckland, Gordon Bunting (UK), Kathy Burgi (Aus), David Burrows (Aus), Mark Cameron (UK), Allan Campion (Aus), Monica Canova (CH), Berry Carter (Aus), Jerry Caruana (Aus), Jocelyn Cash (USA), Diana Cassidy (Aus), John Chappell (USA), Bothavry Chun (Fr), Mike Ciglic (C), Mark Clack (UK), Gabriela Clarke (Aus), Graham Clarke (Aus), Elizabeth Clay (UK), Deluxe Coachlines (Aus), Mike Cohen (USA), Doug & Noreen Colley (Aus), Sarah Collie (Aus), Wayne Condon (Aus), K Conroy (Aus), J L Coombes (Aus), Peter Copp (UK), Robert Cordie, Michael Coren (UK), Val Cother (Aus), Dahrl Court (Aus), Tracey Cowen (UK), Denis Crampton (UK), Adrienne Crawford (C), Shane Crilly (Aus), Belinda Cubitt (UK), Paul Cummings (Aus), Richard Curtis (J), Neil Da Costa (Aus), Lori Dalecki (C), Susan Danger (UK), Paul Daniel (UK), Lyn Dawson (NZ), Bill Day (Aus), Irene De Jongh (Aus), S Denny (UK), Peter Denton (Aus), A Devora (USA), Graham Diffey (Aus), Tom Dillenbeck (USA), Lyn Dimet (USA), Mike & Mary Dixon (Aus), H W Dohnu (D), Haub Donkers (Nl), Mark Donohue (Aus), Dave Dorst (Aus), Nick Dowson (NZ), Ian Duff (Aus), Alison Duncan (Aus), Alison Duncan (Aus), Paula Dunn (Aus), C Dymond (UK), Marjorie Eckman, Cathy Eggert (Aus), Caroline Eggington (Aus), Marion Eiken, Eran Elizur (I), Max Engers (UK), Lena Erikson (Sw), Bridget Evans (UK), Christine Evans, Emma Evans (Aus), Jan Evans (Aus), Ken Everett (NZ), Neil Everett (Aus), Dagmar Faekte (D), Richard Fahey (USA), Farm Koorana Croc, Vloos Fasel (USA), Barry Fenn (UK), Hugh Finlay, John Fioretta (USA), Bridgitte Fisher, George Fogel (Aus), John C Foitzik (Aus), Ian Fordham, Simon Fowler (NZ), Di Francis (Aus), Stephen Fynmore (Aus), Paul Gallagher (Aus), Christian Gapp (D), Larry A Gardner (USA), Isabella

Gassman (CH), Sander Gerrilsen (Nl), James Giles, Susan & Frank Gilliland (USA), Lesley Godwin (Aus), William Goldsmith (Aus), Zozi Goodman (Aus), Celina Grandchamp (USA), Allan Gray (Aus), Amanda Gray (UK), Richard Gray (Aus), Sandra Gray (Aus), Matthew Grey (Aus), Sharon Grimberg (Aus), Walter Grull (D), Joanne Gulf (Aus), Michelle Haft (UK), Patty Hagen (USA), Lloyd Hancock (Aus), Simon Hangwood (Aus), Catherine Hankery (Aus), M R Hanlon (Aus), Jacquie Hannam (Aus), John Hannan (Aus), Stan Haoust (Aus), Kerry Harley (Aus), Jolien Harmsen (Nl), Norman Haser (Aus), Louise Heinnemann (UK), Susan Heisler (CH), Andrew Hemming (UK), Drew Henderson, Corainne Herkir (Ire), Richard Herlick (C), Chris Hinchcliff (Aus), Donna Hislop (USA), Sean Hocking (Aus), Ruth Hodgson (Aus), Belinda Holliday (Aus), Peter Hollings, Mary Holman (Aus), Home Rule (Aus), Colin Howman (UK), Terry Hruby (C), Lousie Humberstone (UK), M Hunt (NZ), Andy Hunter (Aus), Janet & Roger Jeffrey (Aus), D Jelbart (Aus), Jewell House (Aus), Donald Jocz (USA), Johnan (Aus), Drew Johnson (Aus), Valerie Jon (Aus), Clare Jones (Aus), S Jordan (C), Richard Jordan (UK), Eva M Kalbheim (D), Phyllis Keenan (USA), Cynthia Kienzle (USA), M Kilmurray (Aus), Polly Kim (Aus), Rachel King-Underwood (UK), Carole Knight (Aus), Ray Kompe (Aus), Petlef Koster (D), Liccione Kothuber (Aus), Kirby Kourns (I), Barry & Vernon Kowen (C), Sandra Krause (USA), Bob & Mary Laird (Aus), Dean Lambert (Aus), Catherine Landraud (Fr), Graham Latemore (Aus), Alex Law (Aus), Mr J & Dr A Leask (C), Frankie Lim (Sw), Marion Limb (UK), Jenny Limond (UK), M Lloyd (Aus), Robin Loan, Tak Wan Loong (HK), Ralph Lowenstein (C), David Lowry, Susan Luedee (Aus), Justin Lynch (Aus), Peter Lynch (Aus), Maureen Magee, Eveleen Mandikos (Aus), Catriona Mann (UK), Julian Marie (Aus), Chris Markert (Nl), Lee Marling (Aus), Ms M Martin (Aus), Jan Matthew (Aus), Jan & Barry Matthew (Aus), Jan Matthews (Aus), Pierre Matthey (CH), Marlene McBrien (Aus), Maureen McDermott (Aus), Simon McDonald (Aus), Paul McKay (Aus), Sue McKichan (UK), Andrew McNeil (Aus), Tim McOnough (USA), Trish McPherson (Aus), Meredith Mercer (USA), Doug & Lorna Mettam (C), Alison Miller, Peter Millios (Aus), Sara Minkoff (USA), Roberta Moore (UK), Karen Morrison (Aus), John Morrow (Aus), Stephen Mortimer (UK), Wendy Mozenauer, Susan Murray (Aus), Keith Myers (UK), Rebecca Nash (Aus), Claire Neilson (Aus), Andrew Neverley (Aus), Elizabeth Nicholson (Aus), Claire Nielsen (Aus), David Nighy (UK), Mrs Gai Nimbkar (Ire), John Noble (Aus), Julie Nock (UK), Linda Norman (Aus), Pam Nowak (Aus), P Nyman (Sw), Christina Nystrom (Sw), Paul O'Brien (Aus), Merv O'Neil (Aus), M O'Neill (Aus), Padraig O'Neill (Ire), Megan O'Donnell (USA), Pam Olink (Aus), Sue Oliver (UK), Alan Osborne (Aus), Mark Ozzard (Aus), Hotel Paddington Bar (Aus), Karen Padolchak (C), Paul Page (Aus), M T Pates (Aus), Lee Patterson, Scott & Coleen Paul (C), Johan Pauline (C), R Pearson (UK), Bay Pearson (Aus), Hilda Perrin (Aus), C Perry (Aus), Shane Petroff (C), Mia Pettersson (Sw), Danny Pieta Derek Pinchbeck (UK), Diedre Pini (Ire), Marcel Ponti (Aus), Nora Pope (C), Mogens Poppe (D), C Porter (USA), Anna Potter (Aus), E Price (Aus), Alan Quartly (Aus), Julie Quincey (UK), Sue Rance (UK), Tim Reed (UK), Cris Reid (UK), Francis & Lily Reid (Aus), Rent-a-car Half Price, Phil Richards (Aus), Derek Richards (Aus), Ernest Romero (USA), Christopher Ross (UK), Christian Rudbeck (Dk), P J Rumbelow (UK), Karin Saemann, T Sahey (Aus), Susan Sanders (USA), Andy Saunders (USA), R Schubert (Aus), James M Scott (Aus), Hugh Scott (Aus), Keven Seaver (USA), Adam Serle (Aus), G Shaw (Aus), Cath Sherlock (UK), Alistair Shields (Aus), Jon Shipley (Aus), Mark Siccoks (Aus), Daniel Simon (UK), Terry Simpson (Aus), Charles Skele (Aus), Barb Smith (Aus), Patrick Smith (Aus), Arthur Sofiandis (Aus), Rochelle Sokoll, Ted & Jennifer Sommer (Aus), Ruth Stanley (Aus), Jill Statton (Aus), S & W Stephen (Aus), Ruth Stevenson (UK), Jan Stewart (C), Nancy Stewart (C), Graeme Stielow (Aus), Risto Suomio (Aus), Ralph Suters (Aus), Morten Ryhl Svendsen (Aus), Karen Swift (Aus), Penny Syddall (UK), Hotel Sydney Tourist, Patricia Sykes (Aus), Sarah Tattersall (UK), Tawana Lodge, Joan Taylor (Aus), Myron Tetreault, Fransoise Thilliez (Fr), T Thomas (Aus), Mrs Frances Thomas (Aus), Penny Thomas (UK), Bridget Thomas (UK), S Thomson (C), Richard Toni (Aus), Western Australian Tourism Commission (Aus), Tree Tops Youth Hostel (Aus), Al Trujillo (USA), Ruth Tugwell (Aus), Paula Turley (Ire), Alexander Twist (UK), Andriej Urbanik (Pol), Krister Valtonen (Sw), Jill van Os, V Vedik

(Aus), Miss M Vickers (UK), Mrs C Vidor (Aus), Katrina Von Pantzer (UK), Wm Wakeland (USA), Steven Walden (UK), J Walder (Aus), Sarah Wall (Aus), Glenn Wallace (Aus), Simon Wallis (UK), Ted Walsh (Aus), Ian Walter (Aus), Kathy Ward (USA), Peter Ward (Aus), Betty Ware (Aus), Graeme Warring (Aus), Paul Welsh (UK), Paula Welshman (Aus), Erika Werner (Sw), Sharon Wertheim (Aus), Martin Weyell (UK), Alison Wheeler (Aus), Brad Wheeler (USA), T B G Whitehead (C), Marie Whitley (Aus), Phil Wigglesworth (UK), Lisa Will (Aus), Caroline Williams (UK), Tim Williams (Aus), Russell Willis (Aus), Donald Wilson (Aus), Katie Wilson (Aus), Lucia Wilson (UK), David Wong (Aus), Jerry Wood (UK), Nick Woolfield (Aus), Alison Wright (UK), Adrian Wylde (UK), H Wynen (Aus), Kevin Ziv-El (Isr).

Aus – Australia, C – Canada, CH – Switzerland, Chi – China, D – West Germany, Dk – Denmark, Fr – France, HK – Hong Kong, I – Italy, Ire – Ireland, Isr – Israel, J – Japan, Nl – Netherlands, Pol – Poland, Sw – Sweden, UK – United Kingdom, USA – United States of America.

	In	*cm*

Temperature

To convert °C to °F multiply by 1.8 and add 32

To convert °F to °C subtract 32 and multiply by ·55

Length, Distance & Area

	multiply by
inches to centimetres	2.54
centimetres to inches	0.39
feet to metres	0.30
metres to feet	3.28
yards to metres	0.91
metres to yards	1.09
miles to kilometres	1.61
kilometres to miles	0.62
acres to hectares	0.40
hectares to acres	2.47

°C	°F
50	122
45	113
40	104
35	95
30	86
25	75
20	68
15	59
10	50
5	41
0	32

Weight

	multiply by
ounces to grams	28.35
grams to ounces	0.035
pounds to kilograms	0.45
kilograms to pounds	2.21
British tons to kilograms	1016
US tons to kilograms	907

A British ton is 2240 lbs, a US ton is 2000 lbs

Volume

	multiply by
Imperial gallons to litres	4.55
litres to imperial gallons	0.22
US gallons to litres	3.79
litres to US gallons	0.26

5 imperial gallons equals 6 US gallons
a litre is slightly more than a US quart, slightly less
than a British one

Dear traveller

Prices go up, good places go bad, bad places go bankrupt ... and every guide book is inevitably outdated in places. Fortunately, many travellers write to us about their experiences, telling us when things have changed. If we reprint a book between editions, we try to include as much of this information as possible in a Stop Press section. Most of this information has not been verified by our own writers.

We really enjoy hearing from people out on the road, and apart from guaranteeing that others will benefit from your good and bad experiences, we're prepared to bribe you with the offer of a free book for sending us substantial useful information.

Thank you to everyone who has written, and to those who haven't, I hope you do find this book useful – and that you let us know when it isn't.

Tony Wheeler

The city of Melbourne is still hoping to win the bid for the 1996 Summer Olympics. The federal government has promised the city a large sum of spending money should Melbourne be selected by the international judging panel.

This is the second stop press section we have published in this edition of *Australia – a travel survival kit*. There are no major changes. Thanks to the following travellers for contributing to this section: Richard Herlick (C), Daniel Simon (UK), Claudia Schmidt (D), Sarah Tattersall (UK), and Greg Watson (Aus).

Places to Stay
One of the most noticeable changes in accommodation throughout the country is the increasing number of cheap hostels for backpackers. There are now hostels in many coastal towns and in all of the major tourist areas. Many pubs have converted their accommodation into dormitory rooms where beds cost from A$10 to A$15 per night.

Since this book was published dozens of new places have opened. We haven't managed to inspect them all, but many travellers have sent us favourable reports. In Victoria, *The Bells* (tel (059) 84 4323), a YHA hostel at 3 Miranda St, Sorrento, on the

Mornington Peninsula, has been recommended. In Newcastle, NSW, *Backpackers Newcastle* (tel (049) 693 436) at 42 Denison St, Hamilton, seems to be popular. Both hostels charge A$10 per night in dormitories. Another place which has been recommended is *Somewhere to Stay* (tel 846 2858) at 47 Brighton Rd, Highgate Hill, Brisbane. It's two km from the town centre and has double rooms for A$21.

If you don't want to stay at hostels but can't afford tourist hotels, at Home Down Under (tel (02) 960 4481) is an organisation which provides inexpensive homestay accommodation throughout Australia.

Getting Around
The most important news is that all domestic air fares published in this book have been increased by 10%.

If you intend to travel by bus, student bus passes are available from the major bus lines if you have an ISIC card. The best deal for the passes on the east coast is the Three Ways Pass which allows you to travel Sydney/Townsville/Alice Springs/Adelaide/Melbourne/Canberra/Sydney for A$345. You can stop anywhere in between as long as you continue in the same direction. Passes are valid for six months.

Deluxe Coachlines has two new travel passes for use in Western Australia. The Dolphin Pass, at A$209, offers express travel for six months from Perth to Darwin or vice versa. Stopovers are limited to five, and passengers must make at least one. The pass gives people the opportunity to visit popular destinations on the coast such as Geraldton, Kalbarri, Denham, Monkey Mia, Carnarvon, Port Hedland, Broome, Derby, Kununurra and the Kimberley Region.

The South-West Wanderer, at A$99, offers 30 days of express travel on a circular itinerary of south-west Western Australia. Travel is via Perth, the south-west coast, returning via the goldfields (Kalgoorlie) or vice versa. Passengers are able to stop at intermediate points along the route provided travel is in the one direction. You must stop at least twice.

Deluxe also has a new bus service from Sydney to Cairns. It operates every five days in each direction. The one way fare is A$169 direct or A$199 with unlimited stopovers. Tickets are valid for six months. You can book individual sectors along the way.

If you want to purchase a car, it's best to buy one through the *Trading Post* newspaper, which comes out weekly in the capital cities. You can get a better deal than you can through car dealers.

Outback Safaris

The fairly recent growth of tourism in Australia has resulted in a flood of overland budget tours for travellers.

One company that has been recommended is Independent Safaris (tel toll free 008 89 6124), PO Box 1732, Cairns, QLD 4870, which arranges one way, three day trips between Cairns and Alice Springs (either direction) for A$199 per person.

You travel with a guide and a small group of people in an air-conditioned 4WD. You need to bring your own food, sleeping bag and insect repellent. They take you through lush tropical rainforest, dairy farming areas, isolated sheep and cattle stations, and the wilderness of outback desert country.

Russell Willis runs trips through Kakadu

National Park that have been recommended as the 'best off-the-beaten-track experiences available to travellers within Australia'. Russell (tel (089) 85 2134) can be contacted at 12 Carrington St, Millner. What makes Russell's trips unique is that you get to see parts of Kakadu that can't be reached by four-wheel drive or helicopter. It's also a great achievement carrying 15 days' food yourself! It costs A$450 for 15 days and this includes all transport from Darwin, insurance, evening meals, and Russell's expert and extensive knowledge of the national park.

Travellers' Tips & Comments

I made a recent trip to north Queensland and, there were some interesting changes. In Airlie Beach, the dormitory town for the Whitsunday Islands, there were two popular new backpackers' hostels both closer to the centre of town than the ones we currently list. *Habitat* is on Shute Harbour Rd, opposite the Airlie Beach Hotel while *Whitsunday Backpackers* is at 13 Begley St, south of the post office.

On Magnetic Island the Hideaway Hostel has become the *Backpackers' Headquarters* and sports a paint job which it would be hard to miss. There have been some restaurant openings and closings on this popular travellers' island.

Up in Cairns the hostel scene is unchanged but on the waterfront there's a new five star hotel called the *Radisson Plaza* with an entrance lobby which is a not-to-be-missed. Disneyland couldn't have done a better job than this superb multi-storey plastic rainforest complete with everything from crocodiles and cockatoos to cassowaries.

While I was up in the north I finally got a chance to dive that most popular of Cairns dive sites the Cod Hole, near Lizard Island. It's a wonderful experience, worth every word of breathless praise it's had.

Tony Wheeler – Australia

The beautiful Grampians are north-west of Melbourne. The V-line train goes to Stawell for A$29 return and from there you can catch the mail truck (A$65) on its morning newspaper run to Halls Gap. The mail truck waits for the train to arrive. You can also take the truck to meet the morning train back to Melbourne.

Phyllis Keenan – USA

Guides to the Pacific

Australia - a travel survival kit
The complete low-down on Down Under – home of
Ayers Rock, the Great Barrier Reef, extraordinary
animals, cosmopolitan cities, rain forests, beaches. . .
and Lonely Planet!

New Zealand - a travel survival kit
Magnificent scenery, fresh open air and outdoor
activities are New Zealand's feature attractions. It's
not a big country, but for sheer variety it's hard to
beat.

Fiji - a travel survival kit
Whether you prefer to stay in camping grounds,
international hotels, or something in-between, this
comprehensive guide will help you to enjoy the
beautiful Fijian archipelago.

Solomon Islands - a travel survival kit
The Solomon Islands are the best-kept secret of the
Pacific. Discover remote tropical islands, jungle
covered volcanoes and traditional Melanesian villages
with this detailed guide.

Tahiti & French Polynesia - a travel survival kit
Tahiti's reputation as an idyllic island paradise
continues to enchant travellers. . . and after you have
explored Tahiti, more than 100 other islands await you
across the crystal clear water.

Rarotonga & the Cook Islands - a travel survival kit
Rarotonga and the Cook Islands have history, beauty
and magic to rival the better-known islands of Hawaii
and Tahiti, but the world has virtually passed them by.

Micronesia - a travel survival kit
The glorious beaches, lagoons and reefs of these 2100
islands would dazzle even the most jaded traveller.
This guide has all the details on island-hopping across
the north Pacific.

Papua New Guinea - a travel survival kit
With its coastal cities, villages perched beside mighty
rivers, palm-fringed beaches and rushing mountain
streams, Papua New Guinea promises memorable
travel.

Bushwalking in Australia
John & Monica Chapman

Australia's huge wilderness areas offer some of the world's best walking – and some of its most diverse. There are the rugged, pristine Tasmanian forests, the spectacular mountains of the Great Divide, the eerie outback beauty of the Flinders Ranges, Queensland rainforests, and much more.

John and Monica Chapman, respected bushwalkers and authors, have written descriptions of 23 of Australia's best walks, in all states. The walks are rated from easy to hard, with most suitable for those with only a little experience.

With 29 detailed maps and full information on essentials such as climate, equipment and useful organisations to contact, *Bushwalking in Australia* opens up a side of Australia often missed by visitors – and locals.

Lonely Planet Guidebooks

Lonely Planet guidebooks cover virtually every accessible part of Asia as well as Australia, the Pacific, Central and South America, Africa, the Middle East and parts of North America. There are four main series: 'travel survival kits', covering a single country for a range of budgets; 'shoestring' guides with compact information for low-budget travel in a major region; trekking guides; and 'phrasebooks'.

Australia & the Pacific
Australia
Bushwalking in Australia
Papua New Guinea
Papua New Guinea phrasebook
New Zealand
Tramping in New Zealand
Rarotonga & the Cook Islands
Solomon Islands
Tahiti & French Polynesia
Fiji
Micronesia
Tonga
Samoa
New Caledonia

South-East Asia
South-East Asia on a shoestring
Malaysia, Singapore & Brunei
Indonesia
Bali & Lombok
Indonesia phrasebook
Burma
Burmese phrasebook
Thailand
Thai phrasebook
Philippines
Pilipino phrasebook

North-East Asia
North-East Asia on a shoestring
China
China phrasebook
Tibet
Tibet phrasebook
Japan
Japanese phrasebook
Korea
Korean phrasebook
Hong Kong, Macau & Canton
Taiwan

West Asia
West Asia on a shoestring
Trekking in Turkey
Turkey
Turkish phrasebook

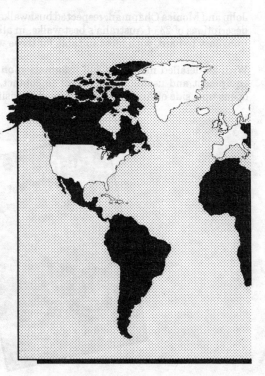

Indian Ocean
Madagascar & Comoros
Maldives & Islands of the East Indian Ocean
Mauritius, Réunion & Seychelles

Mail Order

Lonely Planet guidebooks are distributed worldwide and are sold by good bookshops everywhere. They are also available by mail order from Lonely Planet, so if you have difficulty finding a title please write to us. US and Canadian residents should write to Embarcadero West, 112 Linden St, Oakland CA 94607, USA and residents of other countries to PO Box 617, Hawthorn, Victoria 3122, Australia.

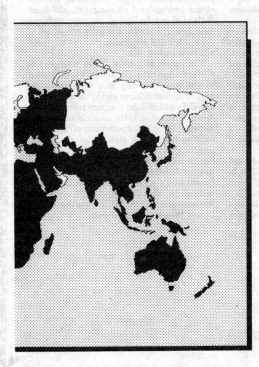

Lonely Planet

Lonely Planet published its first book in 1973. Tony and Maureen Wheeler had made a lengthy overland trip from England to Australia and, in response to numerous 'how do you do it?' questions, Tony wrote and they published *Across Asia on the Cheap*. It became an instant local best-seller and inspired thoughts of a second travel guide. A year and a half in South-East Asia resulted in their second book, *South-East Asia on a Shoestring*, which they put together in a backstreet Chinese hotel in Singapore in 1975. The 'yellow book', as it quickly became known, soon became *the* guide to the region and has gone through five editions, always with its familiar yellow cover.

Soon other writers came to them with ideas for similar books – books that went off the beaten track with an adventurous approach to travel, books that 'assumed you knew how to get your luggage off the carousel,' as one reviewer put it. Lonely Planet grew from a kitchen table operation to a spare room and then to its own office. Its international reputation began to grow as the Lonely Planet logo began to appear in more and more countries. In 1982 *India – a travel survival kit* won the Thomas Cook award for the best guidebook of the year.

These days there are over 70 Lonely Planet titles. Over 40 people work at our office in Melbourne, Australia and another half dozen at our US office in Oakland, California.

At first Lonely Planet specialised in the Asia region but these days we are also developing major ranges of guidebooks to the Pacific region, to South America and to Africa. The list of walking guides is growing and Lonely Planet now has a unique series of phrasebooks to 'unusual' languages. The emphasis continues to be on travel for travellers and Tony and Maureen still manage to fit in a number of trips each year and play a very active part in the writing and updating of Lonely Planet's guides.

Keeping guidebooks up to date is a constant battle which requires an ear to the ground and lots of walking, but technology also plays its part. All Lonely Planet guidebooks are now stored and updated on computer, and some authors even take lap-top computers into the field. Lonely Planet is also using computers to draw maps and eventually many of the maps will be stored on disk.

The people at Lonely Planet strongly feel that travellers can make a positive contribution to the countries they visit both by better appreciation of cultures and by the money they spend. In addition the company tries to make a direct contribution to the countries and regions it covers. Since 1986 a percentage of the income from each book has gone to aid groups and associations. This has included donations to famine relief in Africa, to aid projects in India, to agricultural projects in Central America, to Greenpeace's efforts to halt French nuclear testing in the Pacific and to Amnesty International. In 1989 $41,000 was donated by Lonely Planet to these projects.